The Management of Strategy

Concepts & Cases

8th Edition

R. Duane Ireland
Texas A&M University

Robert E. Hoskisson
Arizona State University

Michael A. Hitt
Texas A&M University

SOUTH-WESTERN
CENGAGE Learning™

Australia • Brazil • Canada • Mexico • Singapore • Spain • United Kingdom • United States

SOUTH-WESTERN
CENGAGE Learning

The Management of Strategy (Concepts and Cases) 8th Edition

R. Duane Ireland, Robert E. Hoskisson, and Michael A. Hitt

VP/Editorial Director: Jack W. Calhoun

VP/Editor-in-Chief: Melissa Acuña

Senior Acquisitions Editor: Michele Rhoades

Developmental Editor: Rebecca Von Gillern—Bookworm Editorial Services

Executive Marketing Manager: Kimberly Kanakes

Marketing Manager: Clint Kernen

Marketing Coordinator: Sara Rose

Senior Content Project Manager: Colleen A. Farmer

Technology Project Editor: Kristen Meere

Manufacturing Coordinator: Doug Wilke

Production Service: LEAP Publishing Services, Inc.

Compositor: ICC Macmillan, Inc.

Senior Art Director: Tippy McIntosh

Photo Manager: Sheri I. Blaney

Photo Researcher: Marcy Lunetta

Internal Designer: Craig Ramsdell, Ramsdell Design

Cengage Learning—Australia/New Zealand
www.cengage.com.au
tel: (61) 3 9685 4111

Cengage Learning—UK/Europe/Middle East/Africa
www.cengage.co.uk
tel: (44) 207 067 2500

Cengage Learning—Asia
www.cengageasia.com
tel: (65) 6410 1200

Cengage Learning—India
www.cengage.co.in
tel: (91) 11 30484837/38

Cengage Learning—Latin America
www.cengage.com.mx
tel: +52 (55) 1500 6000

Cengage Learning—Brazil
www.cengage.com.br
tel: (011) 3665-9900

Represented in Canada by Nelson Education, Ltd.
www.nelson.com
tel: (416) 752 9100 / (800) 668 0671

For product information and technology assistance, contact us at
Cengage Learning Academic Resource Center, 1-800-423-0563

For permission to use material from this text or product, submit all requests online at **www.cengage.com/permissions**
Further permissions questions can be emailed to
permissionrequest@cengage.com

Library of Congress Control Number: 2007940878
Student Edition ISBN 13: 978-0-324-58127-0
Student Edition ISBN 10: 0-324-58127-0

Concepts ISBN 13: 978-0-324-58130-0
Concepts ISBN 10: 0-324-58130-0

South-Western Cengage Learning
5191 Natorp Boulevard
Mason, OH 45040
USA

Cengage Learning products are represented in Canada by Nelson Education, Ltd.

Printed in Canada
1 2 3 4 5 6 7 11 10 09 08

To my beloved Grandmother, Rowena Steele Wheeler Hodge (1905–2007). You have been such a strong beacon of guiding light for me for so long. You are a treasured blessing. Rest in peace. I love you, Grandma.
—**R. DUANE IRELAND**

To my dear wife, Kathy, who has been my greatest friend and support through life, and I hope will remain so into the eternities.
—**ROBERT E. HOSKISSON**

To Shawn and Angie. I have been blessed to have two wonderful children. You have always been highly important to me; I love you very much and I am proud of your accomplishments.
—**MICHAEL A. HITT**

Brief Contents

Preface xviii

About the Authors xxiv

Part 1: Strategic Management Inputs   1

1. What is Strategic Management? 2

2. Exploring the External Environment: Competition and Opportunities, 32

3. Examining the Internal Organization: Activities, Resources, and
    Capabilities, 68

Part 2: Strategic Actions: Strategy Formulation   95

4. Building and Sustaining Competitive Advantage, 96

5. Strategy at the Business Level, 122

6. Corporate-Level Strategy, 152

7. Acquisition and Restructuring Strategies, 180

8. International Strategy, 210

9. Cooperative Strategy, 244

Part 3: Strategic Actions: Strategy Implementation   273

10. Corporate Governance, 274

11. Organizational Structure and Controls, 306

12. Strategic Leadership, 338

13. Strategic Entrepreneurship, 366

Part 4: Cases

Name Index, I-1

Company Index, I-13

Subject Index, I-17

Contents

Preface xviii

About the Authors xxiv

Part 1: Strategic Management Inputs 1

1: What is Strategic Management? 2

Opening Case: Boeing and Airbus: A Global Competitive Battle over Supremacy in Producing Commercial Aircraft 3

The Competitive Landscape 6

    The Global Economy 7

    Technology and Technological Changes 10

    Strategic Focus: *Apple: Using Innovation to Create Technology Trends and Maintain Competitive Advantage 11*

The I/O Model of Above-Average Returns 13

    Strategic Focus: *Netflix Confronts a Turbulent Competitive Environment 14*

The Resource-Based Model of Above-Average Returns 16

Vision and Mission 18

    Vision 18

    Mission 19

Stakeholders 20

    Classifications of Stakeholders 20

Strategic Leaders 22

    The Work of Effective Strategic Leaders 23

    Predicting Outcomes of Strategic Decisions: Profit Pools 24

The Strategic Management Process 24

Summary 26 • Review Questions 26 • Notes 27

2: Exploring the External Environment: Competition and Opportunities 32

Opening Case: Environmental Pressures on Wal-Mart 33

The General, Industry, and Competitor Environments 35

External Environmental Analysis 37

  Scanning 38

  Monitoring 38

  Forecasting 39

  Assessing 39

Segments of the General Environment 39

  The Demographic Segment 40

  The Economic Segment 42

  The Political/Legal Segment 42

  The Sociocultural Segment 43

  The Technological Segment 44

  The Global Segment 45

  Strategic Focus: *Does Google Have the Market Power to Ignore External Pressures? 46*

Industry Environment Analysis 48

  Threat of New Entrants 49

  Bargaining Power of Suppliers 52

  Bargaining Power of Buyers 52

  Threat of Substitute Products 52

  Intensity of Rivalry Among Competitors 53

Interpreting Industry Analyses 55

Strategic Groups 55

  Strategic Focus: *IBM Closely Watches Its Competitors to Stay at the Top of Its Game 57*

Competitor Analysis 58

Ethical Considerations 60

Summary 61 • Review Questions 61 • Notes 62

3: Examining the Internal Organization: Activities, Resources, and Capabilities 68

Opening Case: Managing the Tension Between Innovation and Efficiency 69

Analyzing the Internal Organization 71

  The Context of Internal Analysis 71

  Creating Value 72

  The Challenge of Analyzing the Internal Organization 73

  Strategic Focus: *Hyundai Cars: The Quality Is There, So Why Aren't the Cars Selling? 75*

Resources, Capabilities, and Core Competencies 76

  Resources 76

  Strategic Focus: *Seeking to Repair a Tarnished Brand Name 79*

  Capabilities 80

  Core Competencies 81

Building Core Competencies 81

  Four Criteria of Sustainable Competitive Advantage 81

  Value Chain Analysis 84

Outsourcing 87

Competencies, Strengths, Weaknesses, and Strategic Decisions 88

Summary 90 • Review Questions 91 • Notes 91

Part 2: Strategic Actions: Strategy Formulation 95

4: Building and Sustaining Competitive Advantage 96

Opening Case: Competition Between Hewlett-Packard and Dell: The Battle Rages On 97

A Model of Competitive Rivalry 99

Competitor Analysis 100

    Market Commonality 101

    Resource Similarity 102

Drivers of Competitive Actions and Responses 103

    Strategic Focus: *Who Will Win the Competitive Battles Between Netflix and Blockbuster? 105*

Competitive Rivalry 105

    Strategic and Tactical Actions 106

Likelihood of Attack 106

    Strategic Focus: *Using Aggressive Pricing as a Tactical Action at Wal-Mart 107*

    First-Mover Incentives 107

    Organizational Size 109

    Quality 110

Likelihood of Response 111

    Type of Competitive Action 112

    Actor's Reputation 112

    Dependence on the Market 113

Competitive Dynamics 113

    Slow-Cycle Markets 113

    Fast-Cycle Markets 114

    Standard-Cycle Markets 115

Summary 117 • Review Questions 118 • Notes 118

5: Strategy at the Business Level 122

Opening Case: From Pet Food to PetSmart 123

Customers: Their Relationship with Business-Level Strategies 125

    Effectively Managing Relationships with Customers 126

    Reach, Richness, and Affiliation 126

    Who: Determining the Customers to Serve 127

    What: Determining Which Customer Needs to Satisfy 128

    How: Determining Core Competencies Necessary to Satisfy Customer Needs 129

The Purpose of a Business-Level Strategy 129

Types of Business-Level Strategies 131

    Cost Leadership Strategy 132

    Differentiation Strategy 136

    Focus Strategies 139

Strategic Focus: *Caribou Coffee: When You Are Number Two, You Try Harder 140*

Integrated Cost Leadership/Differentiation Strategy 143

Strategic Focus: *Zara: Integrating Both Sides of the Coin 144*

Summary 147 • Review Questions 148 • Notes 148

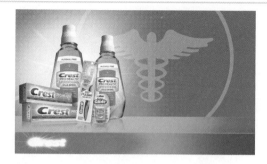

6: Corporate-Level Strategy 152

Opening Case: Procter and Gamble's Diversification Strategy 153

Levels of Diversification 155

Low Levels of Diversification 155

Moderate and High Levels of Diversification 156

Reasons for Diversification 157

Value-Creating Diversification: Related Constrained and Related Linked Diversification 158

Operational Relatedness: Sharing Activities 159

Corporate Relatedness: Transferring of Core Competencies 160

Market Power 161

Simultaneous Operational Relatedness and Corporate Relatedness 163

Unrelated Diversification 163

Strategic Focus: *Operational and Corporate Relatedness: Smith & Wesson and Luxottica 164*

Efficient Internal Capital Market Allocation 165

Restructuring of Assets 166

Value-Neutral Diversification: Incentives and Resources 166

Strategic Focus: *Revival of the Unrelated Strategy (Conglomerate): Small Firms Acquire Castoffs from Large Firms and Seek to Improve Their Value 167*

Incentives to Diversify 168

Resources and Diversification 171

Value-Reducing Diversification: Managerial Motives to Diversify 172

Summary 174 • Review Questions 174 • Notes 175

7: Acquisition and Restructuring Strategies 180

Opening Case: The Increased Trend Toward Cross-Border Acquisitions 181

The Popularity of Merger and Acquisition Strategies 183

Mergers, Acquisitions, and Takeovers: What Are the Differences? 184

Reasons for Acquisitions 184

Increased Market Power 184

Strategic Focus: *Oracle Makes a Series of Horizontal Acquisitions While CVS Makes a Vertical Acquisition 185*

Overcoming Entry Barriers 187

Cost of New Product Development and Increased Speed to Market 188

Lower Risk Compared to Developing New Products 189

Increased Diversification 189

Reshaping the Firm's Competitive Scope 190

Learning and Developing New Capabilities 190

Problems in Achieving Acquisition Success 191

Integration Difficulties 192

Inadequate Evaluation of Target 192

Large or Extraordinary Debt 193

Inability to Achieve Synergy 193

Too Much Diversification 194

Managers Overly Focused on Acquisitions 195

Too Large 196

Effective Acquisitions 196

Restructuring 198

Strategic Focus: *DaimlerChrysler Is Now Daimler AG: The Failed Merger with Chrysler Corporation 199*

Downsizing 200

Downscoping 200

Leveraged Buyouts 201

Restructuring Outcomes 202

Summary 203 • Review Questions 204 • Notes 204

8: International Strategy 210

Opening Case: Shanghai Automotive Industry Corporation: Reaching for Global Markets 211

Identifying International Opportunities: Incentives to Use an International Strategy 213

Increased Market Size 214

Return on Investment 215

Economies of Scale and Learning 215

Strategic Focus: *Does General Motors' Survival Depend on International Markets? 216*

Location Advantages 217

International Strategies 217

International Business-Level Strategy 218

International Corporate-Level Strategy 220

Environmental Trends 222

Liability of Foreignness 223

Regionalization 223

Choice of International Entry Mode 224

Exporting 225

Licensing 225

Strategic Alliances 226

Acquisitions 227

New Wholly Owned Subsidiary 228

Strategic Focus: *Has the Largest Automaker in the World Made Mistakes with Its International Strategy? 229*

Dynamics of Mode of Entry 230

Strategic Competitive Outcomes 231

International Diversification and Returns 231

International Diversification and Innovation 232

Complexity of Managing Multinational Firms 232

Risks in an International Environment 233

Political Risks 234

Economic Risks 234

Limits to International Expansion: Management Problems 235

Summary 235 • Review Questions 236 • Notes 237

9: Cooperative Strategy 244

Opening Case: Using Cooperative Strategies at IBM 245

Strategic Alliances as a Primary Type of Cooperative Strategy 247

Three Types of Strategic Alliances 247

Strategic Focus: *Partnering for Success at Kodak 248*

Reasons Firms Develop Strategic Alliances 250

Business-Level Cooperative Strategy 252

Complementary Strategic Alliances 252

Competition Response Strategy 253

Strategic Focus: *Using Complementary Resources and Capabilities to Succeed in the Global Automobile Industry 255*

Uncertainty-Reducing Strategy 256

Competition-Reducing Strategy 256

Assessment of Business-Level Cooperative Strategies 257

Corporate-Level Cooperative Strategy 258

Diversifying Strategic Alliance 258

Synergistic Strategic Alliance 259

Franchising 259

Assessment of Corporate-Level Cooperative Strategies 260

International Cooperative Strategy 261

Network Cooperative Strategy 262

Alliance Network Types 263

Competitive Risks with Cooperative Strategies 263

Managing Cooperative Strategies 265

Summary 266 • Review Questions 267 • Notes 267

Part 3: Strategic Actions: Strategy Implementation 273

10: Corporate Governance 274

Opening Case: How Has Increasingly Intensive Corporate Governance Affected the Lives of CEOs? 275

Separation of Ownership and Managerial Control 278

Agency Relationships 279

Product Diversification as an Example of an Agency Problem 280

Agency Costs and Governance Mechanisms 281

Ownership Concentration 283

The Growing Influence of Institutional Owners 283

Board of Directors 284

Enhancing the Effectiveness of the Board of Directors 286

Executive Compensation 287

Strategic Focus: *Executive Compensation Is Increasingly Becoming a Target for Media, Activist Shareholders, and Government Regulators 288*

The Effectiveness of Executive Compensation 289

Market for Corporate Control 290

Managerial Defense Tactics 292

International Corporate Governance 293

Corporate Governance in Germany 294

Corporate Governance in Japan 295

Strategic Focus: Shareholder Activists Invade Japan's Large Firms Traditionally Focused on "Stakeholder" Capitalism 296

Global Corporate Governance 297

Governance Mechanisms and Ethical Behavior 298

Summary 299 • Review Questions 300 • Notes 300

11: Organizational Structure and Controls 306

Opening Case: Are Strategy and Structural Changes in the Cards for GE? 307

Organizational Structure and Controls 308

Organizational Structure 309

Strategic Focus: Increased Job Autonomy: A Structural Approach to Increased Performance and Job Satisfaction? 310

Organizational Controls 311

Relationships between Strategy and Structure 312

Evolutionary Patterns of Strategy and Organizational Structure 313

Simple Structure 314

Functional Structure 314

Multidivisional Structure 314

Matches between Business-Level Strategies and the Functional Structure 315

Matches between Corporate-Level Strategies and the Multidivisional Structure 318

Matches between International Strategies and Worldwide Structure 324

Strategic Focus: Using the Worldwide Geographic Area Structure at Xerox Corporation 325

Matches between Cooperative Strategies and Network Structures 329

Implementing Business-Level Cooperative Strategies 330

Implementing Corporate-Level Cooperative Strategies 331

Implementing International Cooperative Strategies 331

Summary 332 • Review Questions 333 • Notes 333

12: Strategic Leadership 338

Opening Case: How Long Can I Have the Job? The Short Lives of CEOs and Top-Level Strategic Leaders 339

Strategic Leadership and Style 340

Strategic Focus: Doug Conant: Providing Effective Strategic Leadership at Campbell Soup Co. 343

The Role of Top-Level Managers 343

Top Management Teams 344

Managerial Succession 347

Key Strategic Leadership Actions 350

Determining Strategic Direction 350

Effectively Managing the Firm's Resource Portfolio 351

Sustaining an Effective Organizational Culture 354

Emphasizing Ethical Practices 355

Establishing Balanced Organizational Controls 356

Strategic Focus: What's Next? Strategic Leadership in the Future 359

Summary 360 • Review Questions 361 • Notes 361

13: Strategic Entrepreneurship 366

Opening Case: Googling Innovation! 367

Entrepreneurship and Entrepreneurial Opportunities 369

Innovation 370

Entrepreneurs 371

International Entrepreneurship 372

Internal Innovation 373

    Incremental and Radical Innovation 373

    Strategic Focus: *The Razr's Edge: R&D and Innovation at Motorola 374*

    Autonomous Strategic Behavior 376

    Induced Strategic Behavior 376

Implementing Internal Innovations 377

    Cross-Functional Product Development Teams 377

    Facilitating Integration and Innovation 378

    Creating Value from Internal Innovation 378

Innovation Through Cooperative Strategies 379

    Strategic Focus: *Does Whole Foods Really Obtain Innovation in Unnatural Ways? 381*

Innovation Through Acquisitions 382

Creating Value Through Strategic Entrepreneurship 382

Summary 384 • Review Questions 384 • Notes 385

Part 4: Cases

Preparing an Effective Case Analysis iii

Case 1: 3M: Cultivating Core Competency, 1

Case 2: A-1 Lanes and the Currency Crisis of the East Asian Tigers, 13

Case 3: AMD vs. Intel: Competitive Challenges, 25

Case 4: Boeing: Redefining Strategies to Manage the Competitive Market, 33

Case 5: Carrefour in Asia, 49

Case 6: Dell: From a Low-Cost PC Maker to an Innovative Company, 61

Case 7: Ford Motor Company, 75

Case 8: Jack Welch and Jeffrey Immelt: Continuity and Change
in Strategy, Style, and Culture at GE, 91

Case 9: The Home Depot, 105

Case 10: China's Home Improvement Market: Should Home Depot Enter
or Will it Have a Late-Mover (Dis)advantage? 117

Case 11: Huawei: Cisco's Chinese Challenger, 133

Case 12: ING DIRECT: Rebel in the Banking Industry, 145

Case 13: JetBlue Airways: Challenges Ahead, 157

Case 14: Lufthansa: Going Global, but How to Manage Complexity? 175

Case 15: Microsoft's Diversification Strategy, 185

Case 16: Nestlé: Sustaining Growth in Mature Markets, 203

Case 17: An Entrepreneur Seeks the Holy Grail of Retailing, 217

Case 18: PSA Peugeot Citroën: Strategic Alliances for Competitive Advantage? 221

Case 19: Sun Microsystems, 233

Case 20: Teleflex Canada: A Culture of Innovation, 241

Case 21: Tyco International: A Case of Corporate Malfeasance, 249

Case 22: Vodafone: Out of Many, One, 263

Case 23: Wal-Mart Stores, Inc. (WMT), 281

Case 24: WD-40 Company: The Squeak, Smell, and Dirt Business (A), 309

Name Index I-1

Company Index I-13

Subject Index I-17

Case Title	Manu-facturing	Service	Consumer Goods	Food/Retail	High Tech-nology	Transportation/Communication	International Perspective	Social/Ethical Issues	Industry Perspective
3M Cultivating Core Comp.	●		●		●		●		
A-1 Lanes	●						●		●
AMD vs Intel	●				●				●
Boeing	●						●		●
Carrefour in Asia				●			●		
Dell	●		●		●				●
Ford	●		●						●
GE Welch & Immelt	●	●			●			●	
Home Depot		●		●			●		
China's Home Improvement				●			●		
Huawei	●				●		●		
ING Direct		●		●					
JetBlue		●				●	●		●
Lufthansa		●				●	●		
Microsoft		●			●				
Nestlé	●		●	●				●	
PenAgain	●		●						
PSA Peugeot Citroën	●		●				●		
Sun Microsystems		●			●		●		
Teleflex Canada	●				●				
Tyco International	●							●	
Vodafone		●			●	●	●		
Wal-Mart Stores				●			●	●	
WD-40	●		●				●		

Case Matrix

Case Title	Chapter												
	1	2	3	4	5	6	7	8	9	10	11	12	13
3M Cultivating Core Comp.			●				●						●
A-1 Lanes								●					●
AMD vs Intel					●								●
Boeing				●	●			●	●				
Carrefour in Asia		●						●					
Dell		●		●		●							
Ford				●	●							●	
GE Welch & Immelt							●					●	●
Home Depot				●	●							●	
China's Home Improvement	●				●			●					
Huawei					●			●					
ING Direct				●								●	●
JetBlue		●		●	●								
Lufthansa								●	●		●		
Microsoft					●	●							
Nestlé	●							●			●		●
PenAgain									●				●
PSA Peugeot Citroën			●						●				
Sun Microsystems	●			●				●					
Teleflex Canada						●						●	●
Tyco International						●				●	●	●	
Vodafone	●		●				●	●					
Wal-Mart Stores	●	●	●	●									
WD-40			●	●				●					●

Our goal in writing each edition of this book is to present a new, up-to-date standard for explaining the strategic management process. To reach this goal with the 8th edition of our market-leading text, we again present you with an intellectually rich yet thoroughly practical analysis of strategic management.

With each new edition, we are challenged and invigorated by the goal of establishing a new standard for presenting strategic management knowledge in a readable style. To prepare for each new edition, we carefully study the most recent academic research to ensure that the strategic management content we present to you is highly current and relevant for organizations. In addition, we continuously read articles appearing in many different business publications (e.g., *Wall Street Journal, BusinessWeek, Fortune, Financial Times,* and *Forbes,* to name just a few); we do this to identify valuable examples of how companies use the strategic management process. Though many of the hundreds of companies we discuss in the book will be quite familiar to you, some companies will likely be new to you as well. One reason for this is that we use examples of companies from around the world to demonstrate how globalized business has become. To maximize your opportunities to learn as you read and think about how actual companies use strategic management tools, techniques, and concepts (based on the most current research), we emphasize a lively and user-friendly writing style.

Several *characteristics* of this 8th edition of our book will enhance your learning opportunities:

- This book presents you with the most comprehensive and thorough coverage of strategic management that is available in the market.
- The research used in this book is drawn from the "classics" as well as the most recent contributions to the strategic management literature. The historically significant "classic" research provides the foundation for much of what is known about strategic management; the most recent contributions reveal insights about how to effectively use strategic management in the complex, global business environment in which most firms operate while trying to outperform their competitors. Our book also presents you with many examples of how firms use the strategic management tools, techniques, and concepts developed by leading researchers. Indeed, this book is strongly application oriented and presents you, our readers, with a vast number of examples and applications of strategic management concepts, techniques, and tools. In this edition, for example, we examine more than 600 companies to describe the use of strategic management. Collectively, no other strategic management book presents you with the *combination* of useful and insightful *research* and *applications* in a wide variety of organizations as does this text. Company examples range from the large U.S.-based firms such as Wal-Mart, IBM, Kodak, Whole Foods, and Google to major foreign-based firms such as Toyota, Nokia, Hyundai, and Shanghai Automotive Industry

Corporation (SAIC). We also include examples of successful younger and newer firms such as Caribou Coffee and Mustang Engineering.

- We carefully *integrate* two of the most popular and well-known theoretical concepts in the strategic management field: industrial-organization economics and the resource-based view of the firm. Other texts usually emphasize one of these two theories (at the cost of explaining the other one to describe strategic management). However, such an approach is incomplete; research and practical experience indicate that both theories play a major role in understanding the linkage between strategic management and organizational success. No other book integrates these two theoretical perspectives effectively to explain the strategic management process and its application in all types of organizations.

- We use the ideas of prominent scholars (e.g., Raphael [Raffi] Amit, Kathy Eisenhardt, Don Hambrick, Constance Helfat, Ming Jer-Chen, Rita McGrath, Michael Porter, C. K. Prahalad, Richard Rumelt, Ken Smith, David Teece, Michael Tushman, Oliver Williamson, and numerous others) to shape the discussion of *what* strategic management is. We describe the practices of prominent executives and practitioners (e.g., Bill Gates, Jeffrey Immelt, Steven Jobs, Anne Mulcahy, Indra Nooyi, Howard Schultz, Meg Whitman, and many others) to help us describe *how* strategic management is used in many types of organizations.

- We, the authors of this book, are also active scholars. We conduct research on different strategic management topics. Our interest in doing so is to contribute to the strategic management literature and to better understand how to effectively apply strategic management tools, techniques, and concepts to increase organizational performance. Thus, our own research is integrated in the appropriate chapters along with the research of numerous other scholars.

In addition to our book's *characteristics,* there are some specific *features* of this 8th edition that we want to highlight for you:

- **New Opening Cases and Strategic Focus Segments.** We continue our tradition of providing all-new Opening Cases and Strategic Focus segments. In addition, new company-specific examples are included in each chapter. Through all of these venues, we present you with a wealth of examples of how actual organizations, most of which compete internationally as well as in their home markets, use the strategic management process to outperform rivals and increase their performance.

- **Strategy Right Now.** A new feature for this edition, Strategy Right Now is used in each chapter to highlight companies that are effectively using a strategic management concept examined in the chapter. In Chapter 3, for example, Volkswagen AG's effective use of a global mindset is described as the foundation for the success the firm is achieving today as a result of its decision to establish manufacturing facilities in Slovakia before competitors chose to do so. In Chapter 5, both Cemex and Target are signaled as firms that effectively use the strategic management process to create excellent business-level strategies. This feature is a valuable tool for readers to quickly identify how a firm is effectively using a strategic management tool, technique, or concept. We follow up with the most current research and information about these firms by using Cengage Learning's Business Company and Resource Center (BCRC). Links to specific current news articles related to these companies can be found on our Web site (international .cengage.com). Whenever you see the Strategy Right Now icon in the text, you will know that current research is available from the BCRC links posted to our Web site.

STRATEGY RIGHT NOW

- **An Exceptional Balance** between current research and applications of it in actual organizations. The content has not only the best research documentation but also the largest amount of effective real-world examples to help active learners understand the different types of strategies that organizations use to achieve their vision and mission.

- **24 All-New Cases** with an effective mix of organizations headquartered or based in the United States and a number of other countries. Many of the cases have full financial data (the analyses of which are in the Case Notes that are available to Instructors). These timely cases present active learners with opportunities to apply the strategic management process and understand organizational conditions and contexts and to make appropriate recommendations to deal with critical concerns.

- **All-New Enhanced Experiential Exercises** to support individuals' efforts to understand the use of the strategic management process. These exercises place active learners in a variety of situations requiring application of some part of the strategic management process. The exercises in this edition are creative and enriched relative to previous editions.

- **All-New Access to Harvard Business School (HBS) Cases.** We have developed a set of assignment sheets and assessment rubrics to accompany 10 of the best selling HBS cases. Instructors can use these cases and the accompanying set of teaching notes and assessment rubrics to formalize assurance of learning efforts in the capstone Strategic Management/ Business Policy course. The cases are Adolph Coors in the Brewing Industry, Cola Wars Continue: Coke vs. Pepsi in the 1990s, Nucor at a Crossroads, Marks & Spencer: The Phoenix Rises, Crown Cork & Seal in 1989, Bitter Competition: The Holland Sweetener Company vs. NutraSweet, The Brita Products Company, Wal-Mart Stores in 2003, Callaway Golf Company, and Sampa Video, Inc.

- **Lively, Concise Writing Style** to hold readers' attention and to increase their interest in strategic management.

- **Continuing, Updated Coverage** of vital strategic management topics such as competitive rivalry and dynamics, strategic alliances, mergers and acquisitions, international strategies, corporate governance, and ethics. Also, we continue to be the only book in the market with a separate chapter devoted to strategic entrepreneurship.

- **Full four-color** format to enhance readability by attracting and maintaining readers' interests.

To maintain current and up-to-date content, new concepts are explored in the 8th edition.

Chapter 6 illustrates an interesting trend towards small unrelated diversified firms that are buying "castoffs" from large diversified firms that are restructuring their operations. For instance, Jarden Corporation has acquired Coleman Camping Goods, Ball Canning Jars, Bicycle Playing Cards, and Crock-Pot Cookers. Jarden was able to acquire these firms at relatively low prices. The larger firms felt pressure to divest assets unrelated to their core operations as a path to improving their performance.

One of the interesting ideas introduced in Chapter 8, the International Strategy chapter, concerns the effect of country institutional environments on multinational firm strategies. Factors such as country laws and regulations, political systems, economic growth, and physical infrastructure (e.g., roads, airline flights, telephone lines) can have a major impact on how multinational firms operate in a country as well as the results of their competitive efforts in those countries. One example regards intellectual property rights laws and enforcement mechanisms. Multinational firms with operations in China and India have called for stronger laws to protect their intellectual property in those countries. Interestingly, many of India and China's companies are beginning to emphasize innovation instead of imitating other multinationals' products; therefore, these companies are emphasizing stronger patent protections for intellectual property because they provide more basic innovation that leads to first-mover advantages.

We expanded our discussion of international entrepreneurship in Chapter 13. We did this because of the increasing importance of international entrepreneurship on a global scale for the success of individual firms and different nations' economies. For example, 40 percent of the adult population in Peru is involved in entrepreneurial activity (the largest percentage of any country globally). The lowest percentage of the population involved in entrepreneurship is in Belgium (3 percent). Slightly more than

10 percent of the U.S. adult population engages in entrepreneurship. Entrepreneurship also is becoming quite important in former centrally planned economies such as China and Russia.

Supplements

Instructors

Instructor Case Notes   All new expanded case notes provide details about the 24 cases found in the second part of the main text. These new expanded case notes include directed assignments, financial analysis, thorough discussion and exposition of issues in the case and an assessment rubric tied to AACSB assurance of learning standards that can be used for grading each case. The case notes provide consistent and thorough support for instructors, following the method espoused by the author team for preparing an effective case analysis. The case notes for the 8th edition have been written in great detail and include questions and answers throughout along with industry and company background and resolutions wherever possible. The Instructor Case Note files can be found at international.cengage.com.

Instructor's Resource Manual   The Instructor's Resource Manual, organized around each chapter's knowledge objectives, includes teaching ideas for each chapter and how to reinforce essential principles with extra examples. The support product includes lecture outlines, detailed answers to end-of-chapter review questions, instructions for using each chapter's experiential exercises, and additional assignments. The Instructor Resource Manual files can be found at international.cengage.com.

Certified Test Bank   Thoroughly revised and enhanced, test bank questions are linked to each chapter's knowledge objectives and are ranked by difficulty and question type. We provide an ample number of application questions throughout and we have also retained scenario-based questions as a means of adding in-depth problem-solving questions. With this edition, we introduce the concept of certification, whereby another qualified academic has proofread and verified the accuracy of the test bank questions and answers. The test bank material is also available in computerized ExamView™ format for creating custom tests in both Windows and Macintosh formats. The Test Bank files can be found at international.cengage.com.

ExamView™   Computerized testing software contains all of the questions in the certified printed test bank. This program is an easy-to-use test creation software compatible with Microsoft Windows. Instructors can add or edit questions, instructions, and answers, and select questions by previewing them on the screen, selecting them randomly, or selecting them by number. Instructors can also create and administer quizzes online, whether over the Internet, a local area network (LAN), or a wide area network (WAN). The ExamView files can be found at international.cengage.com.

All-New Video Program (0-324-58129-7)   You spoke and we listened! For our 8th edition we have a selection of 13 brand-new videos that relate directly to chapter concepts. Provided by Fifty Lessons, these new videos are a comprehensive and compelling resource of management and leadership lessons from some of the world's most successful business leaders. In the form of short and powerful videos, these videos capture leaders' most important learning experiences. They share their real-world business acumen and outline the guiding principles behind their most important business decisions and their career progression.

PowerPoint®   An all-new PowerPoint presentation, created for the 8th edition, provides support for lectures emphasizing key concepts, key terms, and instructive graphics. Slides can also be used by students as an aid to note-taking. The PowerPoint files can be found at international.cengage.com.

WebTutor™   WebTutor is used by an entire class under the direction of the instructor and is particularly convenient for distance learning courses. It provides Web-based learning resources to students as well as powerful communication and other course management tools, including course calendar, chat, and e-mail for instructors. See international.cengage.com for more informaiton.

Product Support Web Site (international.cengage.com)   Our product support Web site contains all ancillary products for instructors as well as the financial analysis exercises for both students and instructors.

The Business & Company Resource Center (BCRC)   Put a complete business library at your students' fingertips! This premier online business research tool allows you and your students to search thousands of periodicals, journals, references, financial information, industry reports, and more. This powerful research tool saves time for students—whether they are preparing for a presentation or writing a reaction paper. You can use the BCRC to quickly and easily assign readings or research projects. Visit international.cengage.com to learn more about this indispensable tool. For this text in particular, BCRC will be especially useful in further researching the companies featured in the text's 24 cases. We've also included BCRC links for the Strategy Right Now feature on our Web site, as well as in the Cengage NOW product. Finally, we have incorporated data from BCRC into the exercises for financial analysis to facilitate students' research and help them focus their attention on honing their skills in financial analysis (see Web site).

Resource Integration Guide (RIG)   When you start with a new—or even familiar—text, the amount of supplemental material can seem overwhelming. Identifying each element of a supplement package and piecing together the parts that fit your particular needs can be time-consuming. After all, you may use only a small fraction of the resources available to help you plan, deliver, and evaluate your class. We have created a resource guide to help you and your students extract the full value from the text and its wide range of exceptional supplements. This resource guide is available on the product support Web site. The RIG organizes the book's resources and provides planning suggestions to help you conduct your class, create assignments, and evaluate your students' mastery of the subject. Whatever your teaching style or circumstance, there are planning suggestions to meet your needs. The broad range of techniques provided in the guide helps you increase your repertoire as a teaching expert and enrich your students' learning and understanding. We hope this map and its suggestions enable you to discover new and exciting ways to teach your course.

Students

Financial analyses of some of the cases are provided on our product support Web site (international.cengage.com) for both students and instructors. Researching financial data, company data, and industry data is made easy through the use of our proprietary database, the Business & Company Resource Center. Students are sent to this database to be able to quickly gather data needed for financial analysis.

Acknowledgments

We express our appreciation for the excellent support received from our editorial and production team at South-Western. We especially wish to thank Michele Rhoades, our Senior Acquisitions Editor; Rebecca von Gillern, our Development Editor; Kimberly Kanakes and Clinton Kernan, our Marketing Managers; and Colleen Farmer, our Content

Project Manager. We are grateful for their dedication, commitment, and outstanding contributions to the development and publication of this book and its package of support materials.

We are highly indebted to the reviewers of the seventh edition in preparation for this current edition:

Brent Allred,
The College of William and Mary

Jame Bronson,
University of Wisconsin, Whitewater

Daniel DeGravel,
California State University, Los Angeles

Steve Gove,
University of Dayton

Peggy Griffin,
New Jersey City University

Franz Kellermans,
Mississippi State University

Frank Novakowski,
Davenport University

Finally, we are very appreciative of the following people for the time and care that went into the preparation of the supplements to accompany this edition:

Brian Boyd,
Arizona State University

Judith Gebhardt,
Catholic University

Steve Gove,
University of Dayton

Dana Gray,
Rogers State University

R. Duane Ireland
Robert E. Hoskisson
Michael A. Hitt

R. Duane Ireland

R. Duane Ireland holds the Foreman R. and Ruby S. Bennett Chair in Business from the Mays Business School, Texas A&M University where he previously served as head of the management department. He teaches strategic management courses at all levels (undergraduate, masters, doctoral, and executive). His research, which focuses on diversification, innovation, corporate entrepreneurship, and strategic entrepreneurship, has been published in a number of journals, including *Academy of Management Journal, Academy of Management Review, Academy of Management Executive, Administrative Science Quarterly, Strategic Management Journal, Journal of Management, Strategic Entrepreneurship Journal, Human Relations, Entrepreneurship Theory and Practice, Journal of Business Venturing,* and *Journal of Management Studies,* among others. His recently published books include *Understanding Business Strategy, Concepts and Cases* (South-Western College Publishing, 2006), *Entrepreneurship: Successfully Launching New Ventures* (Prentice-Hall, Second Edition, 2008), and *Competing for Advantage* (South-Western College Publishing, 2008). He is serving or has served as a member of the editorial review boards for a number of journals, including *Academy of Management Journal, Academy of Management Review, Academy of Management Executive, Journal of Management, Journal of Business Venturing, Entrepreneurship Theory and Practice, Journal of Business Strategy,* and *European Management Journal,* and more. He has completed terms as an associate editor for *Academy of Management Journal,* as an associate editor for *Academy of Management Executive,* and as a consulting editor for *Entrepreneurship Theory and Practice.* He is the current editor of *Academy of Management Journal.* He has co-edited special issues of *Academy of Management Review, Academy of Management Executive, Journal of Business Venturing, Strategic Management Journal, Journal of High Technology and Engineering Management,* and *Organizational Research Methods* (forthcoming). He received awards for the best article published in *Academy of Management Executive* (1999) and *Academy of Management Journal* (2000). In 2001, his co-authored article published in *Academy of Management Executive* won the Best Journal Article in Corporate Entrepreneurship Award from the U.S. Association for Small Business & Entrepreneurship (USASBE). He is a Fellow of the Academy of Management. He served a three-year term as a Representative-at-Large member of the Academy of Management's Board of Governors. He is a Research Fellow in the National Entrepreneurship Consortium. He received the 1999 Award for Outstanding Intellectual Contributions to Competitiveness Research from the American Society for Competitiveness and the USASBE Scholar in Corporate Entrepreneurship Award (2004) from USASBE.

Robert E. Hoskisson

Robert E. Hoskisson is a Professor and W. P. Carey Chair in the Department of Management at Arizona State University. He received his Ph.D. from the University of California-Irvine. Professor Hoskisson's research topics focus on corporate governance, acquisitions and divestitures, corporate and international diversification, corporate entrepreneurship, privatization, and cooperative strategy. He teaches courses in corporate and international strategic management, cooperative strategy, and strategy consulting, among others. Professor Hoskisson's research has appeared in over 90 publications, including the *Academy of Management Journal, Academy of Management Review, Strategic Management Journal, Organization Science, Journal of Management, Journal of International Business Studies, Journal of Management Studies, Academy of Management Executive* and *California Management Review.* He is currently an Associate Editor of the *Strategic Management Journal* and a Consulting Editor for the *Journal of International Business Studies,* as well as serving on the Editorial Review board of the *Academy of Management Journal.* Professor Hoskisson has served on several editorial boards for such publications as the *Academy of Management Journal* (including Consulting Editor and Guest Editor of a special issue), *Journal of Management* (including Associate Editor), *Organization Science, Journal of International Business Studies* (Consulting Editor), *Journal of Management Studies* (Guest Editor of a special issue) and *Entrepreneurship Theory and Practice.* He has co-authored several books including *Understanding Business Strategy* (South-Western/Thomson), *Competing for Advantage,* 2nd edition (South-Western College Publishing, 2008), and *Downscoping: How to Tame the Diversified Firm* (Oxford University Press).

He has an appointment as a Special Professor at the University of Nottingham and as an Honorary Professor at Xi'an Jiao Tong University. He is a Fellow of the Academy of Management and a charter member of the Academy of Management Journals Hall of Fame. He is also a Fellow of the Strategic Management Society. In 1998, he received an award for Outstanding Academic Contributions to Competitiveness, American Society for Competitiveness. He also received the William G. Dyer Distinguished Alumni Award given at the Marriott School of Management, Brigham Young University. He completed three years of service as a representative at large on the Board of Governors of the Academy of Management and currently is on the Board of Directors of the Strategic Management Society.

Michael A. Hitt

Michael A. Hitt is a Distinguished Professor and holds the Joe B. Foster Chair in Business Leadership at Texas A&M University. He received his Ph.D. from the University of Colorado. He has co-authored or co-edited 26 books and 150 journal articles.

Some of his books are *Downscoping: How to Tame the Diversified Firm* (Oxford University Press, 1994); *Mergers and Acquisitions: A Guide to Creating Value for Stakeholders* (Oxford University Press, 2001); *Competing for Advantage* 2nd edition (South-Western College Publishing, 2008); and *Understanding Business Strategy* (South-Western College Publishing, 2006). He is co-editor of several books including the following: *Managing Strategically in an Interconnected World* (1998); *New Managerial Mindsets: Organizational Transformation and Strategy Implementation* (1998); *Dynamic Strategic Resources: Development, Diffusion, and Integration* (1999); *Winning Strategies in a Deconstructing World* (John Wiley & Sons, 2000); *Handbook of Strategic Management* (2001); *Strategic Entrepreneurship: Creating a New Integrated Mindset* (2002); *Creating Value: Winners in the New Business Environment* (Blackwell Publishers, 2002); *Managing Knowledge for Sustained Competitive Advantage* (Jossey-Bass, 2003); *Great Minds in Management: The Process of Theory Development* (Oxford University Press, 2005), and *The Global Mindset* (Elsevier, 2007). He has served on the editorial review boards of multiple journals, including the *Academy of Management*

Journal, Academy of Management Executive, Journal of Applied Psychology, Journal of Management, Journal of World Business, and *Journal of Applied Behavioral Sciences.* Furthermore, he has served as Consulting Editor and Editor of the *Academy of Management Journal.* He is currently a co-editor of the *Strategic Entrepreneurship Journal.* He is president of the Strategic Management Society and is a past president of the Academy of Management.

He is a Fellow in the Academy of Management and in the Strategic Management Society. He received an honorary doctorate from the Universidad Carlos III de Madrid and is an Honorary Professor and Honorary Dean at Xi'an Jiao Tong University. He has been ackowledged with several awards for his scholarly research and he received the Irwin Outstanding Educator Award and the Distinguished Service Award from the Academy of Management. He has received best paper awards for articles published in the *Academy of Management Journal, Academy of Management Executive,* and *Journal of Management.*

Part 1
Strategic Management Inputs

Chapter 1

What is Strategic Management?, 2

Chapter 2

Exploring the External Environment: Competition and Opportunities, 32

Chapter 3

Examining the Internal Organization: Activities, Resources, and Capabilities, 68

What is Strategic Management?

Studying this chapter should provide you with the strategic management knowledge needed to:

1. Define strategic competitiveness, strategy, competitive advantage, above-average returns, and the strategic management process.

2. Describe the competitive landscape and explain how globalization and technological changes shape it.

3. Use the industrial organization (I/O) model to explain how firms can earn above-average returns.

4. Use the resource-based model to explain how firms can earn above-average returns.

5. Describe vision and mission and discuss their value.

6. Define stakeholders and describe their ability to influence organizations.

7. Describe the work of strategic leaders.

8. Explain the strategic management process.

Boeing and Airbus: A Global Competitive Battle over Supremacy in Producing Commercial Aircraft

Boeing has historically been a global leader in manufacturing commercial airplanes. However, in 2001, Airbus had more orders than Boeing for the first time in their competitive history. But, in 2006, Boeing regained its supremacy with 1,044 versus 790 orders for commercial aircraft. The main turnaround in this battle for competitor orders has been most visible in the super jumbo category with Airbus's A-380 versus Boeing's 787.

Apparently in 1992, Boeing and Airbus's parent EADS agreed to a joint study on prospects for a super jumbo aircraft. The impetus for the study was the growing traffic in China and India. However, Airbus and Boeing reached different conclusions concerning the market trends, and the joint effort was disbanded.

Boeing's 787 Dreamliner design focused on long-range efficient flight, capable of transporting 250 passengers, whereas Airbus's strategy focused on long-haul flights with the A-380 offering 550-plus seats. In their diverging strategies, Airbus focused on flying to larger airports that use the hub-and-spoke system, whereas Boeing concentrated more on a point-to-point system in which smaller airports are more abundant. In reality, the Airbus A-380 aircraft, because of its size and weight, is currently able to land at approximately only 35 airports. The Boeing aircraft, on the other hand, can land at many more airports around the world and the number is growing in emerging economies, such as throughout Eastern Europe where smaller airports desire international connections.

Airbus won the competitor battle that occurred between 2001 and 2005 because it focused on the midsized market as well, using the A-320 strategy, which competes with Boeing's 737 and 757 aircraft. The A-320 was more efficient than the aircraft used by Boeing, and Boeing did not respond to customer demands to create new, efficient aircraft. In fact, it had slowed its innovation process in regard to new models. Besides the lack of new models, the commercial aircraft business was sluggish; new orders significantly ebbed due to the complications of the terrorist attacks and the subsequent recession. It was a bleak time for Boeing relative to Airbus.

More recently, Boeing's strategy in regard to overall design with the 787 Dreamliner is winning the day, as far as the order battle goes. It has also realized success by implementing a different strategy in regard to the production process. It has been able to speed up the process by creating an efficient global supply chain that involves many potential customers around the world, including Japan, China, and others. Moreover, Airbus is behind in its schedule to produce the A-380 and its midsized plane, the A-350, has also had redesign issues. The midsized A-350, comparable to the Boeing 787, is behind schedule and Airbus has had to provide significant incentive discounts to increase future orders.

Also, Airbus has been forced to produce more of its plane parts in European countries because governments have significant ownership and provide subsidies to Airbus. Accordingly, these governments—Spain, France, Germany, and the United Kingdom—want to maintain employment levels in these countries, and thus Airbus must continue to produce primarily in European countries. "Boeing outsources 85 percent of the work for its 787 'Dreamliner' aircraft. The corresponding figure for Airbus's A380 is 15 percent." As a result of the design and development delays, Airbus's development costs for the A-380 have risen to $14 billion versus the $8 billion invested by Boeing for the 787.

In making its decision to move ahead with the 787 Dreamliner versus a more jumbo aircraft comparable to the A-380, Boeing made a more concerted effort in connecting and getting input from its airline customers, as well as the ultimate customers, the passengers. Overwhelmingly the passengers in particular, and thereby the airlines, preferred smaller aircraft which would enable them to get to smaller airports quickly, without as many transfers on a point-to-point system. Additionally, Boeing followed up with the ultimate creditors, the leasing agents, and asked what they would prefer as far as risks were concerned. Again, the leasing agents preferred a smaller aircraft which would reduce their risks in financing versus the large super jumbo A-380. These business-level strategies have created an obvious advantage in the near-term for Boeing.

Interestingly, Boeing only receives 50 percent of its revenue from the commercial aircraft division as a result of its diversification strategy. The other 50 percent of its revenue comes from military contracts, as well as business from space satellite launching. Some crossover takes place in the technology used between military aircraft and commercial aircraft, which indirectly contributes to lower commercial aircraft development costs. This argument is used by Airbus when Boeing confronts it regarding the subsidies from local European governments. The ultimate battle will continue between these two firms, but currently Boeing has the winning edge and it looks like that will continue. Boeing's orders are now so plentiful, it will not be able to deliver all that are ordered in 2007 until the 2012–2013 range.

Sources: J. Bruner & G. Maidment, 2007, Breaking up Airbus, *Forbes*, http://www.forbes.com, March 20; N. Clark & L. Wayne, 2007, Airbus hopes its planes, not its setbacks, will stand out, *New York Times*, http://www.nytimes.com, June 18; G. Colvin, 2007, Boeing prepares for takeoff, *Fortune*, June 11, 133; C. Matlac & S. Holmes, 2007, Airbus revs up the engines, *BusinessWeek*, March 5, 41; D. Michaels, J. L. Lunsford, & M. Trottman, 2007, Airbus seals US Airways order in big boost for A350 jetliner, *Wall Street Journal Online*, http://www.wsj.com. June 18; D Michaels & J. L. Lunsford, 2007, Airbus faces wide game in A-350 orders, *Wall Street Journal*, June 13, A3; J. Newhouse, 2007, Boeing versus Airbus: The inside story of the greatest international competition in business, Toronto, Canada: Alfred A. Knoph; L. Wayne, 2007, A U.S. star turn for the jumbo of jets, *New York Times*, March 20, C1; D. Q. Wilber, 2007, Boeing's 2006 Jet orders surpass Airbus, *Washington Post*, January 18, D03; 2007, Boeing vs. Airbus: battle of the skies, *CNN*, http://www.cnn.com, May 7; D. Michaels, R. Stone, & J. L. Lunsford, 2006, Airbus superjumbo jet could be delayed further, *Wall Street Journal*, September 13, A3.

STRATEGY RIGHT NOW

Strategic competitiveness is achieved when a firm successfully formulates and implements a value-creating strategy.

A **strategy** is an integrated and coordinated set of commitments and actions designed to exploit core competencies and gain a competitive advantage.

As we see from the Opening Case, Boeing began outperforming Airbus in 2006, whereas Airbus was winning the competitive battle between 2001 and 2006. The basic reasons for this turn of events is the strategic decisions both firms have made. Both firms analyzed their similar competitive environments and made decisions that fit with their view of the facts. We can be confident in believing that both firms want to be highly competitive (something we call a condition of *strategic competitiveness*) and want it to earn profits in the form of *above-average/returns*. Firms seek to accomplish these important outcomes when using the strategic management process (see Figure 1.1). The strategic management process is fully explained in this book. We introduce you to this process in the next few paragraphs.

Strategic competitiveness is achieved when a firm successfully formulates and implements a value-creating strategy. A **strategy** is an integrated and coordinated set of commitments and actions designed to exploit core competencies and gain a competitive advantage. When choosing a strategy, firms make choices among competing alternatives. In this sense, the chosen strategy indicates what the firm intends to do, as well as what it does not intend to do. As the opening case indicates, Airbus chose to focus on super jumbo jets (550-plus person capacity) as the preeminent strategy in betting on its future, while Boeing focused on medium capacity (250 people) but with longer range and better

Figure 1.1 The Strategic Management Process

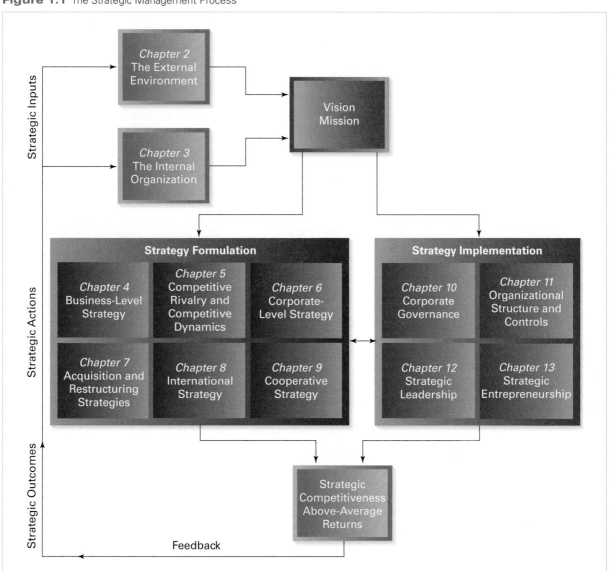

efficiency than current versions. While the battle continues, Boeing's decisions and associated strategy seem to be winning.

A firm has a **competitive advantage** when it implements a strategy competitors are unable to duplicate or find too costly to try to imitate.[1] An organization can be confident that its strategy has resulted in one or more useful competitive advantages only after competitors' efforts to duplicate its strategy have ceased or failed. In addition, firms must understand that no competitive advantage is permanent.[2] The speed with which competitors are able to acquire the skills needed to duplicate the benefits of a firm's value-creating strategy determines how long the competitive advantage will last.[3]

Above-average returns are returns in excess of what an investor expects to earn from other investments with a similar amount of risk. **Risk** is an investor's uncertainty about the economic gains or losses that will result from a particular investment.[4] Returns are often measured in terms of accounting figures, such as return on assets, return on equity, or return on sales. Alternatively, returns can be measured on the basis of stock market returns, such as monthly returns (the end-of-the-period stock price minus the beginning stock price, divided by the beginning stock price, yielding a percentage return).

A firm has a **competitive advantage** when it implements a strategy competitors are unable to duplicate or find too costly to try to imitate.

Above-average returns are returns in excess of what an investor expects to earn from other investments with a similar amount of risk.

Risk is an investor's uncertainty about the economic gains or losses that will result from a particular investment.

In smaller, new venture firms, performance is sometimes measured in terms of the amount and speed of growth (e.g., in annual sales) rather than more traditional profitability measures,[5] because new ventures require time to earn acceptable returns on investors' investments.[6] Understanding how to exploit a competitive advantage is important for firms that seek to earn above-average returns.[7] Firms without a competitive advantage or that are not competing in an attractive industry earn, at best, average returns. **Average returns** are returns equal to those an investor expects to earn from other investments with a similar amount of risk. In the long run, an inability to earn at least average returns results in failure. Failure occurs because investors withdraw their investments from those firms earning less-than-average returns.

The **strategic management process** (see Figure 1.1) is the full set of commitments, decisions, and actions required for a firm to achieve strategic competitiveness and earn above-average returns. The firm's first step in the process is to analyze its external and internal environments to determine its resources, capabilities, and core competencies— the sources of its "strategic inputs." With this information, the firm develops its vision and mission and formulates its strategy. To implement this strategy, the firm takes actions toward achieving strategic competitiveness and above-average returns. Effective strategic actions that take place in the context of carefully integrated strategy formulation and implementation actions result in desired strategic outcomes. It is a dynamic process, as ever-changing markets and competitive structures are coordinated with a firm's continuously evolving strategic inputs.[8]

In the remaining chapters of this book, we use the strategic management process to explain what firms should do to achieve strategic competitiveness and earn above-average returns. These explanations demonstrate why some firms consistently achieve competitive success while others fail to do so.[9] As you will see, the reality of global competition is a critical part of the strategic management process and significantly influences firms' performances.[10] Indeed, learning how to successfully compete in the globalized world is one of the most significant challenges for firms competing in the current century.[11]

Several topics are discussed in this chapter. First, we describe the current competitive landscape. This challenging landscape is being created primarily by the emergence of a global economy, globalization resulting from that economy, and rapid technological changes. Next, we examine two models that firms use to gather the information and knowledge required to choose their strategies and decide how to implement them. The insights gained from these models also serve as the foundation for forming the firm's vision and mission. The first model (industrial organization, or I/O) suggests that the external environment is the primary determinant of a firm's strategic actions. The key to this model is identifying and competing successfully in an attractive (i.e., profitable) industry.[12] The second model (resource-based) suggests that a firm's unique resources and capabilities are the critical link to strategic competitiveness.[13] Thus, the first model is concerned with the firm's external environment while the second model focuses on the firm's internal environment. After discussing vision and mission, direction-setting statements that influence the choice and use of organizational strategies, we describe the stakeholders that organizations serve. The degree to which stakeholders' needs can be met directly increases when firms achieve strategic competitiveness and earn above-average returns. Closing the chapter are introductions to strategic leaders and the elements of the strategic management process.

The Competitive Landscape

The fundamental nature of competition in many of the world's industries is changing.[14] The pace of this change is relentless and is increasing. Even determining the boundaries of an industry has become challenging. Consider, for example, how advances in interactive computer networks and telecommunications have blurred the boundaries of the entertainment industry. Today, not only do cable companies and satellite networks compete for entertainment revenue from television, but also telecommunication companies are moving into the entertainment business through significant improvements in fiber-optic lines with speeds "up to 50 times faster" than traditional broadband cable and DSL download speeds.[15] Partnerships among firms in different segments of the entertainment industry further blur industry boundaries. For example, MSNBC is co-owned by NBC Universal (which itself is owned by General Electric) and Microsoft.[16] Many firms are looking for the most profitable and interesting way to deliver video on demand (VOD) online besides cable and satellite companies. Raketu, a voice over the Internet protocol (VoIP) phone service in the United Kingdom, is seeking to provide a social experience while watching the same entertainment on a VOD using a chat feature on its phone service.[17] As the strategic focus later in the chapter suggests, Apple iPod has the current lead in offering VOD content; but others such as Netflix are vying to compete in this space because it would mean the probable death of their online DVD rental service. Blockbuster and Amazon are among others seeking a piece of this competitive pie.[18]

Other characteristics of the current competitive landscape are noteworthy. Conventional sources of competitive advantage such as economies of scale and huge advertising budgets are not as effective as they once were. Moreover, the traditional managerial mind-set is unlikely to lead a firm to strategic competitiveness. Managers must adopt a new mind-set that values flexibility, speed, innovation, integration, and the challenges that evolve from constantly changing conditions. The conditions of the competitive landscape result in a perilous business world, one where the investments required to compete on a global scale are enormous and the consequences of failure are severe.[19] Developing and implementing strategy remains an important element of success in this environment. It allows for strategic actions to be planned and to emerge when the environmental conditions are appropriate. It also helps to coordinate the strategies developed by business units in which the responsibility to compete in specific markets is decentralized.[20]

Hypercompetition is a term often used to capture the realities of the competitive landscape. Under conditions of hypercompetition, assumptions of market stability are replaced by notions of inherent instability and change.[21] Hypercompetition results from the dynamics of strategic maneuvering among global and innovative combatants. It is a condition of rapidly escalating competition based on price-quality positioning, competition to create new know-how and establish first-mover advantage, and competition to protect or invade established product or geographic markets.[22] In a hypercompetitive market, firms often aggressively challenge their competitors in the hopes of improving their competitive position and ultimately their performance.[23]

Several factors create hypercompetitive environments and influence the nature of the current competitive landscape. The two primary drivers are the emergence of a global economy and technology, specifically rapid technological change.

Lenovo, a Chinese company, recently purchased the PC assets of IBM. While IBM once held a competitive advantage in the area of personal computers, no competitive advantage is permanent.

The Global Economy

A **global economy** is one in which goods, services, people, skills, and ideas move freely across geographic borders. Relatively unfettered by artificial constraints, such as tariffs, the global economy significantly expands and complicates a firm's competitive environment.[24]

Interesting opportunities and challenges are associated with the emergence of the global economy.[25] For example, Europe, instead of the United States, is now the world's largest single market, with 700 million potential customers. The European Union and the other Western European countries also have a gross domestic product that is more than

A **global economy** is one in which goods, services, people, skills, and ideas move freely across geographic borders.

35 percent higher than the GDP of the United States.[26] "In the past, China was generally seen as a low-competition market and a low-cost land. Today, China is an extremely competitive market in which local market-seeking MNCs [multinational corporations] must fiercely compete against other MNCs and against those local companies that are more cost effective and faster in product development. While it is true that China has been viewed as a country from which to source low-cost goods, lately, many MNCs, such as P&G [Proctor and Gamble], are actually net exporters of local management talent; they have been dispatching more Chinese abroad than bringing foreign expatriates to China."[27] India, the world's largest democracy, has an economy that also is growing rapidly and now ranks as the world's fourth largest.[28] Many large multinational companies are also emerging as significant global competitors from these emerging economies.[29]

The statistics detailing the nature of the global economy reflect the realities of a hyper-competitive business environment, and challenge individual firms to think seriously about the markets in which they will compete. Consider the case of General Electric (GE). Although headquartered in the United States, GE expects that as much as 60 percent of its revenue growth between 2005 and 2015 will be generated by competing in rapidly developing economies (e.g., China and India). The decision to count on revenue growth in developing countries instead of in developed countries such as the United States and European nations, seems quite reasonable in the global economy. In fact, according to an analyst, what GE is doing is not by choice but by necessity: "Developing countries are where the fastest growth is occurring and more sustainable growth."[30] Based on its analyses of world markets and their potential, GE estimates that by 2024, China will be the world's largest consumer of electricity and will be the world's largest consumer and consumer-finance market (business areas in which GE competes). GE is making strategic decisions today, such as investing significantly in China and India, in order to improve its competitive position in what the firm believes are becoming vital sources of revenue and profitability.

The March of Globalization

Globalization is the increasing economic interdependence among countries and their organizations as reflected in the flow of goods and services, financial capital, and knowledge across country borders.[31] Globalization is a product of a large number of firms competing against one another in an increasing number of global economies.

In globalized markets and industries, financial capital might be obtained in one national market and used to buy raw materials in another one. Manufacturing equipment bought from a third national market can then be used to produce products that are sold in yet a fourth market. Thus, globalization increases the range of opportunities for companies competing in the current competitive landscape.[32]

Wal-Mart, for instance, is trying to achieve boundary-less retailing with global pricing, sourcing, and logistics. Through boundary-less retailing, the firm seeks to make the movement of goods and the use of pricing strategies as seamless among all of its international operations as has historically been the case among its domestic stores. The firm is pursuing this type of retailing on an evolutionary basis. For example, most of Wal-Mart's original international investments were in Canada and Mexico, because it was easier for the firm to rehearse or apply its global practices in countries that are geographically close to its home base, the United States. Based on what it has learned, the firm has now expanded into Europe, South America, and Asia. In 2007, Wal-Mart was the world's largest retailer (with 3,443 units in and 2,760 units outside of the United States). Globalization makes it increasingly difficult to think of firms headquartered

The globalization of business has led Wal-Mart to open stores all over the world.

in various economies throughout the world as domestic-only companies. Consider the following facts about two U.S.-based organizations: On an annual basis, Wal-Mart continues to increase the percent of its total revenue that is coming from its international operations. GE expects more than 60 percent of its growth in sales revenue in the foreseeable future to come from operations in emerging markets. The challenge to companies experiencing globalization to the degree of these three firms is to understand the need for culturally sensitive decisions when using the strategic management process, and to anticipate ever-increasing complexity in their operations as goods, services, people, and so forth move freely across geographic borders and throughout different economic markets.

Globalization also affects the design, production, distribution, and servicing of goods and services. In many instances, for example, globalization results in higher-quality goods and services. Global competitor Toyota Motor Company provides an example of how this happens. Because Toyota initially emphasized product reliability and superior customer service, the company's products are in high demand across the globe. Because of the demand for its products, Toyota's competitive actions have forced its global competitors to make reliability and service improvements in their operations. Toyota has done this also by building plants in foreign markets in the United States, Brazil, and Mexico, while maintaining quality.[33] Indeed, almost any car or truck purchased today from virtually any manufacturer is of higher quality and is supported by better service than was the case before Toyota began successfully competing throughout the global economy. In particular, Ford, GM, and Chrysler are "trying to hammer home the message that consumers' perception of Detroit-built vehicles as bland and unreliable has not kept pace with significant improvements in recent years."[34]

Overall, it is important for firms to understand that globalization has led to higher levels of performance standards in many competitive dimensions, including those of quality, cost, productivity, product introduction time, and operational efficiency. In addition to firms competing in the global economy, these standards affect firms competing on a domestic-only basis. The reason is that customers will purchase from a global competitor rather than a domestic firm when the global company's good or service is superior. Because workers now flow rather freely among global economies, and because employees are a key source of competitive advantage, firms must understand that increasingly, "the best people will come from . . . anywhere."[35] Overall, firms must learn how to deal with the reality that in the competitive landscape of the twenty-first century, only companies capable of meeting, if not exceeding, global standards typically have the capability to earn above-average returns.[36]

As we have explained, globalization creates opportunities (such as those being pursued by Toyota and Wal-Mart, among many other firms). However, globalization is not risk free. Collectively, the risks of participating outside of a firm's domestic country in the global economy are labeled a "liability of foreignness."[37]

One risk of entering the global market is the amount of time typically required for firms to learn how to compete in markets that are new to them. A firm's performance can suffer until this knowledge is either developed locally or transferred from the home market to the newly established global location.[38] Additionally, a firm's performance may suffer with substantial amounts of globalization. In this instance, firms may overdiversify internationally beyond their ability to manage these extended operations.[39] The result of overdiversification can have strong negative effects on a firm's overall performance.[40]

Thus, entry into international markets, even for firms with substantial experience in the global economy, such as Toyota and GE, requires proper use of the strategic management process. It is also important to note that even though global markets are an attractive strategic option for some companies, they are not the only source of strategic competitiveness. In fact, for most companies, even for those capable of competing successfully in global markets, it is critical to remain committed to and strategically competitive in the both domestic and international markets through staying attuned to technological opportunities and potential competitive disruptions due to innovation.[41]

Technology and Technological Changes

Trends and conditions can be placed into three categories: technology diffusion and disruptive technologies, the information age, and increasing knowledge intensity. Through these categories, technology is significantly altering the nature of competition and contributing to unstable competitive environments as a result of doing so.

Technology Diffusion and Disruptive Technologies

The rate of technology diffusion—the speed at which new technologies become available and are used—has increased substantially over the past 15 to 20 years. Consider the following rates of technology diffusion:

It took the telephone 35 years to get into 25 percent of all homes in the United States. It took TV 26 years. It took radio 22 years. It took PCs 16 years. It took the Internet 7 years.[42]

Perpetual innovation is a term used to describe how rapidly and consistently new, information-intensive technologies replace older ones. The shorter product life cycles resulting from these rapid diffusions of new technologies place a competitive premium on being able to quickly introduce new, innovative goods and services into the marketplace.[43] For example, "In the computer industry during the early 1980s, hard disk drives would typically ship for four to six years, after which a new and better product became available. By the late 1980s, the expected shipping life had fallen to two to three years. By the 1990s, it was just six to nine months."[44]

In fact, when products become somewhat indistinguishable because of the widespread and rapid diffusion of technologies, speed to market with innovative products may be the primary source of competitive advantage (see Chapter 5).[45] Indeed, some argue that increasingly, the global economy is driven by or revolves around constant innovations. Not surprisingly, such innovations must be derived from an understanding of global standards and global expectations in terms of product functionality.[46]

Another indicator of rapid technology diffusion is that it now may take only 12 to 18 months for firms to gather information about their competitors' research and development and product decisions.[47] In the global economy, competitors can sometimes imitate a firm's successful competitive actions within a few days. Once a source of competitive advantage, the protection firms previously possessed through their patents has been stifled by the current rate of technological diffusion. Today, patents may be an effective way of protecting proprietary technology in a small number of industries such as pharmaceuticals. Indeed, many firms competing in the electronics industry often do not apply for patents to prevent competitors from gaining access to the technological knowledge included in the patent application.

Disruptive technologies—technologies that destroy the value of an existing technology and create new markets[48]—surface frequently in today's competitive markets. Think of the new markets created by the technologies underlying the development of products such as iPods, PDAs, WiFi, and the browser.[49] These types of products are thought by some to represent radical or breakthrough innovations.[50] (We talk more about radical innovations in Chapter 13.) A disruptive or radical technology can create what is essentially a new industry or can harm industry incumbents. Some incumbents, though, are able to adapt based on their superior resources, experience, and ability to gain access to the new technology through multiple sources (e.g., alliances, acquisitions, and ongoing internal research).[51] When a disruptive technology creates a new industry, competitors follow. As explained in the Strategic Focus, Apple has sought to create disruptive trends in the industry through its new products strategy.

In addition to making innovative use of new product designs, Steve Jobs, CEO of Apple, developed a great sense of timing that has allowed for great marketing of its innovative designs. As such, Apple shows a strong competency in studying information about its customers as well as potential consumers of the new product. These efforts result in opportunities to understand individual customers' needs and then target goods and services to satisfy those needs. Clearly, Apple understands the importance of information

STRATEGY RIGHT NOW

Apple: Using Innovation to Create Technology Trends and Maintain Competitive Advantage

In partnership with *BusinessWeek*, the Boston Consulting Group conducts an annual survey of top executives of the "1,500 largest global corporations." In May of 2007 as a result of this survey, Apple was named by *BusinessWeek* as the most innovative company—for the third year in a row.

Apple started its regeneration in 2001 with its unveiling of the iPod, a portable digital music device; and then followed up with its complementary iTunes online music store, a service for downloading songs and other digital music and video clips. Even before iPod and iTunes, Apple had a strong foundation of innovation. Apple intends to continue its success in the future with the iPhone and Apple TV devices. Not only has it done well in producing simply designed products, such as the iPod and its other recent devices, but it also excels in marketing its aesthetic or elegant designs, which seem to please the customer and create a "market buzz" for Apple products.

While Apple focused on new product innovation, many other firms in the industry focused on cost control. Dell was successful with this strategy by being first to offer direct PC purchasing over the Internet. Through its efficient supply chain operations, Dell was able to manage powerful supplier firms such as Microsoft and Intel. However, more recently because of Apple's prowess in technology design and marketing, as well as excellent timing, it seems to surpass most other consumer electronics companies, including Dell and other traditionally strong manufacturers such as Sony.

Even at its stores, Apple has outpaced Sony and others who have failed, such as Gateway, and has forced Dell to enter into a recent alliance with Wal-Mart in order to have direct retail sales. Although HP has been able to manage the retail and direct sales approach, and has gained a lead over Dell in regard to PCs, it does not seem to have the same elegance and appeal for its products as Apple does.

In 2007, with more than 100 million products sold, the closest competitor to Apple's iPod has only 8 percent of the market share, leaving Apple with the vast majority. Although others are seeking to simply duplicate the complementary and innovative relationships between iPod and iTunes, Apple continues to innovate with products such as the iPhone and Apple TV. Apple's focus on innovation has helped it maintain a competitive advantage and marketing prowess over other industry players, who have historically been much stronger than Apple.

Apple uses innovative product design and ease of use for its products as a competitive advantage.

Apple seeks to "change the way people behave" versus just competing in the marketplace for traditional products. In doing so, it has been able to establish first mover advantages through radical concepts using elegant design, and relatively perfect market timing recently to establish its advantage. Others seem to compete in commodity businesses with incremental innovations, while Apple creates a new concept in the consumer's mind. It is most likely for this reason that other executives see Apple as a strong innovator in consumer electronics.

Sources: D. C. Chmielewski & M. Quinn, 2007, Movie studios fear the sequel to iPod: They see risk that new Apple TV signals effort to control distribution, *Los Angeles Times*, June 11, C1; J. McGregor, 2007, The world's most innovative companies: The leaders in nurturing cultures of creativity, *BusinessWeek*, http://www.businessweek.com, May 4; B. Schlender, 2007, The trouble with Apple TV, *Fortune*, June 11, 56; R. Stross, 2007, Apple's lesson for Sony's stores: Just connect, *New York Times*, http://www.nytimes.com, May 27; N. Wingfield, 2007, A new wireless player hopes to challenge iPod, *Wall Street Journal*, April 9, B1; 2007, Apple's "magical" iPhone unveiled, *BBC*, http://www.bbc.co.uk, January 9; R. Furchgott, 2006, Cell phones for the music fan, *The New York Times*, http://www.nytimes.com, December 28.

and knowledge (topics we discuss next) as competitive weapons for use in the current competitive landscape.

The Information Age

Dramatic changes in information technology occurred in recent years. Personal computers, cellular phones, artificial intelligence, virtual reality, and massive databases (e.g., LexisNexis) are a few examples of how information is used differently as a result of technological developments. An important outcome of these changes is that the ability to effectively and efficiently access and use information has become an important source of competitive advantage in virtually all industries. Information technology advances have given small firms more flexibility in competing with large firms, if that technology can be used with efficiency.[52]

Both the pace of change in information technology and its diffusion will continue to increase. For instance, the number of personal computers in use in the United States is expected to reach 278 million by 2010. The declining costs of information technologies and the increased accessibility to them are also evident in the current competitive landscape. The global proliferation of relatively inexpensive computing power and its linkage on a global scale via computer networks combine to increase the speed and diffusion of information technologies. Thus, the competitive potential of information technologies is now available to companies of all sizes throughout the world, not only to large firms in Europe, Japan, and North America.

The Internet is another technological innovation contributing to hypercompetition. Available to an increasing number of people throughout the world, the Internet provides an infrastructure that allows the delivery of information to computers in any location. Virtually all retailers, such as Abercrombie & Fitch, The Gap, and Benetton, use the Internet to provide abundant shopping privileges to customers in multiple locations. However, access to the Internet on smaller devices such as cell phones is having an ever-growing impact on competition in a number of industries. For example, Internet radio is projected to compete with satellite radio firms SIRIUS and XM, as small receiver devices are developed to receive radio transmissions over the Internet but on devices other than the personal computer. SanDisk's new Sansa Connect digital music player allows users to listen to online radio stations from Yahoo! Inc. when within range of WiFi connections.[53]

Increasing Knowledge Intensity

Knowledge (information, intelligence, and expertise) is the basis of technology and its application. In the competitive landscape of the twenty-first century, knowledge is a critical organizational resource and an increasingly valuable source of competitive advantage.[54] Indeed, starting in the 1980s, the basis of competition shifted from hard assets to intangible resources. For example, "Wal-Mart transformed retailing through its proprietary approach to supply chain management and its information-rich relationships with customers and suppliers."[55] Relationships, for instance with suppliers, are an example of an intangible resource.

Knowledge is gained through experience, observation, and inference and is an intangible resource (tangible and intangible resources are fully described in Chapter 3). The value of intangible resources, including knowledge, is growing as a proportion of total shareholder value.[56] The probability of achieving strategic competitiveness in the competitive landscape is enhanced for the firm that realizes that its survival depends on the ability to capture intelligence, transform it into usable knowledge, and diffuse it rapidly throughout the company.[57] Therefore, firms must develop (e.g., through training programs) and acquire (e.g., by hiring educated and experienced employees) knowledge, integrate it into the organization to create capabilities, and then apply it to gain a competitive advantage.[58] In addition, firms must build routines that facilitate the diffusion of local knowledge throughout the organization for use everywhere that it has value.[59] Firms are better able to do these things when they have strategic flexibility.

Strategic flexibility is a set of capabilities used to respond to various demands and opportunities existing in a dynamic and uncertain competitive environment. Thus, strategic

Strategic flexibility is a set of capabilities used to respond to various demands and opportunities existing in a dynamic and uncertain competitive environment.

flexibility involves coping with uncertainty and its accompanying risks.[60] Firms should try to develop strategic flexibility in all areas of their operations. However, those working within firms to develop strategic flexibility should understand that the task is not an easy one, largely because of inertia that can build up over time. A firm's focus and past core competencies may actually slow change and strategic flexibility.[61]

To be strategically flexible on a continuing basis and to gain the competitive benefits of such flexibility, a firm has to develop the capacity to learn. In the words of John Browne, CEO of British Petroleum: "In order to generate extraordinary value for shareholders, a company has to learn better than its competitors and apply that knowledge throughout its businesses faster and more widely than they do."[62] Continuous learning provides the firm with new and up-to-date sets of skills, which allow it to adapt to its environment as it encounters changes.[63] Firms capable of rapidly and broadly applying what they have learned exhibit the strategic flexibility and the capacity to change in ways that will increase the probability of successfully dealing with uncertain, hypercompetitive environments. Often having a strong ability to manage information systems is associated with better strategic flexibility[64] because such systems create an advantage over competitors, as is illustrated in the Strategic Focus on Netflix.

The I/O Model of Above-Average Returns

From the 1960s through the 1980s, the external environment was thought to be the primary determinant of strategies that firms selected to be successful.[65] The industrial organization (I/O) model of above-average returns explains the external environment's dominant influence on a firm's strategic actions. The model specifies that the industry in which a company chooses to compete has a stronger influence on performance than do the choices managers make inside their organizations.[66] The firm's performance is believed to be determined primarily by a range of industry properties, including economies of scale, barriers to market entry, diversification, product differentiation, and the degree of concentration of firms in the industry.[67] These industry characteristics are examined in Chapter 2.

Grounded in economics, the I/O model has four underlying assumptions. First, the external environment is assumed to impose pressures and constraints that determine the strategies that would result in above-average returns. Second, most firms competing within an industry or within a certain segment of that industry are assumed to control similar strategically relevant resources and to pursue similar strategies in light of those resources. Third, resources used to implement strategies are assumed to be highly mobile across firms, so any resource differences that might develop between firms will be short-lived. Fourth, organizational decision makers are assumed to be rational and committed to acting in the firm's best interests, as shown by their profit-maximizing behaviors.[68] The I/O model challenges firms to locate the most attractive industry in which to compete. Because most firms are assumed to have similar valuable resources that are mobile across companies, their performance generally can be increased only when they operate in the industry with the highest profit potential and learn how to use their resources to implement the strategy required by the industry's structural characteristics.[69]

The five forces model of competition is an analytical tool used to help firms with this task. The model (explained in Chapter 2) encompasses several variables and tries to capture the complexity of competition. The five forces model suggests that an industry's profitability (i.e., its rate of return on invested capital relative to its cost of capital) is a function of interactions among five forces: suppliers, buyers, competitive rivalry among firms currently in the industry, product substitutes, and potential entrants to the industry.[70] The Strategic Focus on Netflix provides an illustration of how some of these threats have affected competition in the online DVD (movie) rental business with many new entrants, powerful suppliers (movie makers), substitute products (e.g., video on demand [VOD]), and intense rivalry.

Founded by CEO Reed Hastings in 1998, Netflix revolutionized the movie rental business through its online service. In its brief history, Netflix has gained close to 7 million subscribers with a library of more than 80,000 movies, television, and other entertainment shows available on DVD. Hastings indicated in a recent interview that his only regret was that he went public too soon and, therefore, revealed to competitors that the online model used by Netflix was profitable.

Reed Hastings, founder of Netflix, used an information technology innovation to start his company. Now that Netflix operates in a very competitive environment, its commitment to technological innovation and tracking customer preferences allows it to remain competitive.

This move, from his point of view, made Blockbuster aware of the threat that the online rental business presented relative to its brick-and-mortar business. Subsequently in 2004, Blockbuster entered into the online rental business through its introduction of Blockbuster Online. In late 2006, Blockbuster renamed its service Blockbuster Total Access and gave its customers the option of returning videos through the mail or dropping them off at the local Blockbuster store. In mid 2007, Blockbuster introduced a new plan named "Blockbuster by Mail." With this mail-only option, the rates start as low $4.99, and three-at-a-time limited rental plans cost $16.99 per month. These packages undercut Netflix's comparable plans by $1. Interestingly, Blockbuster introduced these plans even as it continued to lose money on its Total Access plan. Although Netflix cut its fee for its one-movie-at-home-at-a-time plan by $1 to $4.99 in January 2007 to counter the initial introduction of Total Access, Netflix does not have free in-store video exchange, and subscribers cannot return online rentals by dropping them off at a store. Netflix customers have to wait for Netflix to receive the movie in the mail before the next DVD shipment is initiated. Accordingly, customers can save time by utilizing Blockbuster's service.

A number of other small and large competitors such as Amazon.com are in the online rental service, in addition to Blockbuster and other brick-and-mortar stores. However, thwarting competitors is not the only threat on the horizon for Netflix. Netflix's current service is based on DVD rental and shipping. The biggest threat on the horizon is Video on Demand (VOD). In this market, a number of competitors are racing to be the dominant player to deliver videos directly to the computer, or ultimately the television. In August of 2007, Blockbuster completed an acquisition of Movielink, LLC, which provides streaming video over the Internet and has access to large movie producers' content, in an effort to capture some of the VOD market. Of course, this service has been available from cable and satellite companies but not over the Internet. Among others, Apple, Amazon.com, CinemaNow, Wal-Mart, and Hewlett-Packard are seeking to establish a download business in this market. In 2007, Apple's iTunes accounted for about "76 percent of the market" of the current available video content, albeit small at this point. Also, Apple TV—a device that gets movies from the Internet to the television and works primarily with video purchased through Apple's iTunes store—could potentially increase iTunes lead. Although the market is relatively small, it has the potential to be a $35 billion market as more content is digitized. Besides the significant number of potential strong competitors seeking VOD, Netflix must also deal with powerful suppliers in the movie industry.

Because many of the traditional movie industry players, such as Warner Brothers and Disney, experienced a loss of a significant amount of revenues and other difficult circumstances in regard to online audio piracy, as they work to digitize the content in their vast vaults of movies and television they want to make sure that they can take advantage of this potential with as little piracy as possible. Accordingly, they are cautious with whom they will contract for selling their digitized content. Coming up with the right solution to use these digitized videos will be a key issue in getting contracts with the movie industry. For instance, one Wall Street analyst observed that these suppliers fear Apple "will come to dominate on-line distribution of movies as it now controls more than 70 percent of the digital-music market in the United States."

Reed Hastings recognizes that VOD will ultimately create a total substitute for current Netflix video rental service. Whether this transition happens right away, within the next 2–3 years, or in 5–10 years will determine whether Netflix's current business model will continue to be successful. Although Netflix has a significant amount of turbulence in its environment, it also has some strong, well-developed competencies that allowed it to be successful thus far. These competencies include a cost structure that helped it make money relative to its brick-and-mortar competitors, a well-developed technology base, and an internal infrastructure for creating new technology with which it can develop its supply chain, for distributing DVDs, and manage customer satisfaction in a way that creates customer loyalty. Netflix hopes to be able to use this customer loyalty and technological base to launch a successful service in the VOD market as movie producers digitize their content.

Sources: 2007, Blockbuster acquires Movielink, *New York Times*, http://www.nyt, August 8; M. Boyle, 2007, Reed Hastings, *Fortune*, May 28, 30–32; T. Calburn & A. Gonsalves, 2007, Big dreams for online video rentals, *Information Week*, January 22, 22; J. Fortt, 2007, HP reels in Hollywood, *Business 2.0*, May, 42; P. Gogoi, 2007, Wal-Mart enters the movie download wars, *BusinessWeek*, http://www.businessweek.com, February 6; M. Kirdahy, 2007, Blockbuster takes on Netflix, *Forbes*, http://www.forbes.com, January 3; A. Pruitt, 2007, Blockbuster's online plan undercuts Netflix's rates, *Wall Street Journal*, June 13, B4; J. Rose, 2007, Amazon, Netflix volume rise on takeover rumor, *Wall Street Journal*, June 7, C4; J Schuman, 2007, The morning brief: Apple rental ambitions target pay-per-view; *Wall Street Journal Online*, http://www.wsj.com, June 11; N. Wingfield, 2007, Boss Talk: Netflix versus naysayers: CEO Hastings keeps growth strong: Plans for the future after the death of DVDs, *Wall Street Journal*, March 28, B1; 2006, What's next for Netflix, *Financial Times*, http://www.ft.com, November 2.

© Don Hammond/Design Pics/Corbis

Firms can use this tool to understand an industry's profit potential and the strategy necessary to establish a defensible competitive position, given the industry's structural characteristics.[71] Typically, the model suggests that firms can earn above-average returns by manufacturing standardized products, or producing standardized services at costs below those of competitors (a cost leadership strategy), or by manufacturing differentiated products for which customers are willing to pay a price premium (a differentiation strategy). (The cost leadership and product differentiation strategies are fully described in Chapter 4.) Although Netflix is in a rather unattractive industry, given the industry forces that threaten its dominant business, the cost leadership strategy has helped to sustain Netflix performance in the face of these threats.

As shown in Figure 1.2, the I/O model suggests that above-average returns are earned when firms implement the strategy dictated by the characteristics of the general, industry, and competitor environments (environments that are discussed in Chapter 2). Companies that develop or acquire the internal skills needed to implement strategies required by the external environment are likely to succeed, while those that do not are likely to fail. Hence, this model suggests that returns are determined primarily by external characteristics rather than by the firm's unique internal resources and capabilities.

Research findings support the I/O model, in that approximately 20 percent of a firm's profitability can be explained by the industry in which it chooses to compete. This research also shows, however, that 36 percent of the variance in profitability could be attributed to the firm's characteristics and actions.[72] These findings suggest that both the environment and the firm's characteristics play a role in determining the firm's specific level of profitability. Thus, a reciprocal relationship is likely between the environment and the firm's strategy, thereby affecting the firm's performance.[73]

Figure 1.2 The I/O Model of Above-Average Returns

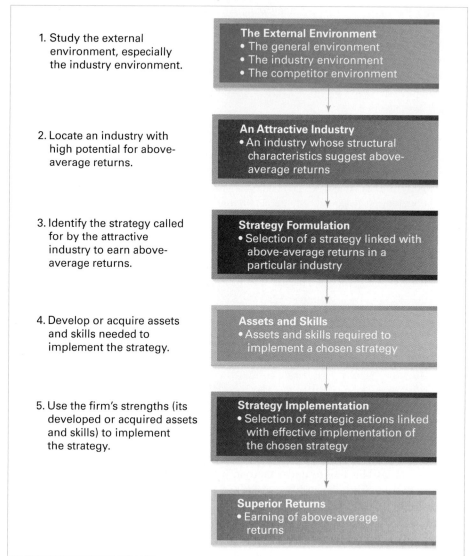

1. Study the external environment, especially the industry environment.

The External Environment
- The general environment
- The industry environment
- The competitor environment

2. Locate an industry with high potential for above-average returns.

An Attractive Industry
- An industry whose structural characteristics suggest above-average returns

3. Identify the strategy called for by the attractive industry to earn above-average returns.

Strategy Formulation
- Selection of a strategy linked with above-average returns in a particular industry

4. Develop or acquire assets and skills needed to implement the strategy.

Assets and Skills
- Assets and skills required to implement a chosen strategy

5. Use the firm's strengths (its developed or acquired assets and skills) to implement the strategy.

Strategy Implementation
- Selection of strategic actions linked with effective implementation of the chosen strategy

Superior Returns
- Earning of above-average returns

As you can see, the I/O model considers a firm's strategy to be a set of commitments, actions, and decisions that are formed in response to the characteristics of the industry in which the firm has decided to compete. The resource-based model, discussed next, takes a different view of the major influences on strategy formulation and implementation.

The Resource-Based Model of Above-Average Returns

The resource-based model assumes that each organization is a collection of unique resources and capabilities. The *uniqueness* of its resources and capabilities is the basis for a firm's strategy and its ability to earn above-average returns.[74]

Resources are inputs into a firm's production process, such as capital equipment, the skills of individual employees, patents, finances, and talented managers. In general, a firm's resources are classified into three categories: physical, human, and organizational capital. Described fully in Chapter 3, resources are either tangible or intangible in nature.

Individual resources alone may not yield a competitive advantage.[75] In fact, resources have a greater likelihood of being a source of competitive advantage when they are formed into a capability. A **capability** is the capacity for a set of resources to perform

Resources are inputs into a firm's production process, such as capital equipment, the skills of individual employees, patents, finances, and talented managers.

A **capability** is the capacity for a set of resources to perform a task or an activity in an integrative manner.

a task or an activity in an integrative manner. Capabilities evolve over time and must be managed dynamically in pursuit of above-average returns.[76] **Core competencies** are resources and capabilities that serve as a source of competitive advantage for a firm over its rivals. Core competencies are often visible in the form of organizational functions. For example, the preceding Strategic Focus suggests that even though Netflix operates in a turbulent competitive environment, its strong capabilities in technology and tracking customer preferences for movies allow it to remain competitive, while others such as Blockbuster continue to lose money in the online movie rental business—even though they are gaining market share.

According to the resource-based model, differences in firms' performances across time are due primarily to their unique resources and capabilities rather than to the industry's structural characteristics. This model also assumes that firms acquire different resources and develop unique capabilities based on how they combine and use the resources; that resources and certainly capabilities are not highly mobile across firms; and that the differences in resources and capabilities are the basis of competitive advantage.[77] Through continued use, capabilities become stronger and more difficult for competitors to understand and imitate. As a source of competitive advantage, a capability "should be neither so simple that it is highly imitable, nor so complex that it defies internal steering and control."[78]

The resource-based model of superior returns is shown in Figure 1.3. As you will see, the resource-based model suggests that the strategy the firm chooses should allow it to

> **Core competencies** are capabilities that serve as a source of competitive advantage for a firm over its rivals.

Figure 1.3 The Resource-Based Model of Above-Average Returns

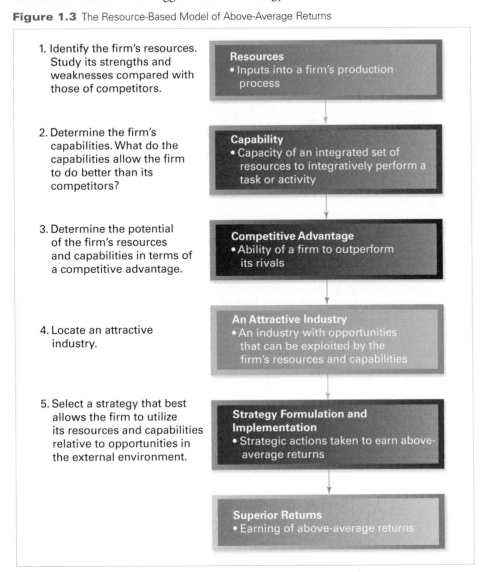

use its competitive advantages in an attractive industry (the I/O model is used to identify an attractive industry).

Not all of a firm's resources and capabilities have the potential to be the basis for competitive advantage. This potential is realized when resources and capabilities are valuable, rare, costly to imitate, and nonsubstitutable.[79] Resources are *valuable* when they allow a firm to take advantage of opportunities or neutralize threats in its external environment. They are *rare* when possessed by few, if any, current and potential competitors. Resources are *costly to imitate* when other firms either cannot obtain them or are at a cost disadvantage in obtaining them compared with the firm that already possesses them. And they are *nonsubstitutable* when they have no structural equivalents. Many resources can either be imitated or substituted over time. Therefore, it is difficult to achieve and sustain a competitive advantage based on resources alone.[80] When these four criteria are met, however, resources and capabilities become core competencies.

As noted previously, research shows that both the industry environment and a firm's internal assets affect that firm's performance over time.[81] Thus, to form a vision and mission, and subsequently to select one or more strategies and to determine how to implement them, firms use both the I/O and the resource-based models.[82] In fact, these models complement each other in that one (I/O) focuses outside the firm while the other (resource-based) focuses inside the firm. Next, we discuss the forming of the firm's vision and mission—actions taken after the firm understands the realities of its external (Chapter 2) and internal (Chapter 3) environments.

Vision and Mission

After studying the external environment and the internal environment, the firm has the information it needs to form a vision and a mission (see Figure 1.1). Stakeholders (those who affect or are affected by a firm's performance, as discussed later in the chapter) learn a great deal about a firm by studying its vision and mission. Indeed, a key purpose of vision and mission statements is to inform stakeholders of what the firm is, what it seeks to accomplish, and who it seeks to serve.

Vision

Vision is a picture of what the firm wants to be and, in broad terms, what it wants to ultimately achieve.

Vision is a picture of what the firm wants to be and, in broad terms, what it wants to ultimately achieve.[83] Thus, a vision statement articulates the ideal description of an organization and gives shape to its intended future. In other words, a vision statement points the firm in the direction of where it would eventually like to be in the years to come.[84] For example, in Disney's new vision focused on multimedia, hit movies and associated music would be available for download onto iPods. Cell phones would be provided with ringtones from movie lines or tunes. Online video on Disney.com would include cast interviews and interpretation of scenes. Portable multimedia players would have games developed to let fans, for instance, outwit a crew of rogues from a familiar seen of *Pirates of the Caribbean* to find buried treasure.[85] Vision is "big picture" thinking with passion that helps people *feel* what they are supposed to be doing in the organization.[86] People feel what they are to do when their firm's vision is simple, positive, and emotional, but a good vision stretches and challenges people as well.

It is also important to note that vision statements reflect a firm's values and aspirations and are intended to capture the heart and mind of each employee and, hopefully, many of its other stakeholders. A firm's vision tends to be enduring while its mission can change in light of changing environmental conditions. A vision statement tends to be relatively short and concise, making it easily remembered. Examples of vision statements include the following:

Our vision is to be the world's best quick service restaurant. (McDonald's)

To make the automobile accessible to every American. (Ford Motor Company's vision when established by Henry Ford)

As a firm's most important and prominent strategic leader, the CEO is responsible for working with others to form the firm's vision. Experience shows that the most effective vision statement results when the CEO involves a host of people (e.g., other top-level managers, employees working in different parts of the organization, suppliers, and customers) to develop it. In addition, to help the firm reach its desired future state, a vision statement should be clearly tied to the conditions in the firm's external and internal environments as is evidenced in the multimedia vision already mentioned for Disney. Moreover, the decisions and actions of those involved with developing the vision, especially the CEO and the other top-level managers, must be consistent with that vision. At McDonald's, for example, a failure to openly provide employees with what they need to quickly and effectively serve customers would be a recipe for disaster.

Mission

The vision is the foundation for the firm's mission. A **mission** specifies the business or businesses in which the firm intends to compete and the customers it intends to serve.[87] The firm's mission is more concrete than its vision. However, like the vision, a mission should establish a firm's individuality and should be inspiring and relevant to all stakeholders.[88] Together, vision and mission provide the foundation the firm needs to choose and implement one or more strategies. The probability of forming an effective mission increases when employees have a strong sense of the ethical standards that will guide their behaviors as they work to help the firm reach its vision.[89] Thus, business ethics are a vital part of the firm's discussions to decide what it wants to become (its vision) as well as who it intends to serve and how it desires to serve those individuals and groups (its mission).[90]

Even though the final responsibility for forming the firm's mission rests with the CEO, the CEO and other top-level managers tend to involve a larger number of people in forming the mission. The main reason is that mission deals more directly with product markets and customers, and middle- and first-level managers and other employees have more direct contact with customers and the markets in which they are served. Examples of mission statements include the following:

Be the best employer for our people in each community around the world and deliver operational excellence to our customers in each of our restaurants. (McDonald's)

Our mission is to be recognized by our customers as the leader in applications engineering. We always focus on the activities customers desire; we are highly motivated and strive to advance our technical knowledge in the areas of material, part design and fabrication technology. (LNP, a GE Plastics Company)

Notice how the McDonald's mission statement flows from its vision of being the world's best quick service restaurant. LNP's mission statement describes the business areas (material, part design, and fabrication technology) in which the firm intends to compete.

While reading the vision and mission statements presented here, you likely recognized that the earning of above-average returns (sometimes called profit maximization) was not mentioned in any of them. All firms want to earn above-average returns (meaning that this intention does not differentiate the firm from its rivals), and that desired financial outcome results from properly serving certain customers while trying to achieving the firm's intended future. In other words, above-average returns are the fruits of the firm's efforts to achieve its vision and mission. In fact, research has shown that having an effectively formed vision and mission has a positive effect on performance as measured by growth in sales, profits, employment, and

A **mission** specifies the business or businesses in which the firm intends to compete and the customers it intends to serve.

net worth.[91] In turn, positive firm performance increases the firm's ability to satisfy the interests of its stakeholders (whom we discuss next). The flip side of the coin also seems to be true—namely, the firm without an appropriately formed vision and mission is more likely to fail than the firm that has properly formed vision and mission statements.[92]

Stakeholders

Every organization involves a system of primary stakeholder groups with whom it establishes and manages relationships.[93] **Stakeholders** are the individuals and groups who can affect the vision and mission of the firm, are affected by the strategic outcomes achieved, and have enforceable claims on a firm's performance.[94] Claims on a firm's performance are enforced through the stakeholders' ability to withhold participation essential to the organization's survival, competitiveness, and profitability.[95] Stakeholders continue to support an organization when its performance meets or exceeds their expectations.[96] Also, recent research suggests that firms that effectively manage stakeholder relationships outperform those that do not. Stakeholder relationships can therefore be managed to be a source of competitive advantage.[97]

Although organizations have dependency relationships with their stakeholders, they are not equally dependent on all stakeholders at all times;[98] as a consequence, not every stakeholder has the same level of influence.[99] The more critical and valued a stakeholder's participation, the greater a firm's dependency on it. Greater dependence, in turn, gives the stakeholder more potential influence over a firm's commitments, decisions, and actions. Managers must find ways to either accommodate or insulate the organization from the demands of stakeholders controlling critical resources.[100]

Classifications of Stakeholders

The parties involved with a firm's operations can be separated into at least three groups.[101] As shown in Figure 1.4, these groups are the capital market stakeholders (shareholders and the major suppliers of a firm's capital), the product market stakeholders (the firm's primary customers, suppliers, host communities, and unions representing the workforce), and the organizational stakeholders (all of a firm's employees, including both nonmanagerial and managerial personnel).

Each stakeholder group expects those making strategic decisions in a firm to provide the leadership through which its valued objectives will be reached.[102] The objectives of the various stakeholder groups often differ from one another, sometimes placing those involved with the strategic management process in situations where trade-offs have to be made. The most obvious stakeholders, at least in United State's organizations, are *shareholders*—individuals and groups who have invested capital in a firm in the expectation of earning a positive return on their investments. These stakeholders' rights are grounded in laws governing private property and private enterprise.

In contrast to shareholders, another group of stakeholders—the firm's customers—prefers that investors receive a minimum return on their investments. Customers could have their interests maximized when the quality and reliability of a firm's products are improved, but without a price increase. High returns to customers might come at the expense of lower returns negotiated with capital market shareholders.

Because of potential conflicts, each firm is challenged to manage its stakeholders. First, a firm must carefully identify all important stakeholders. Second, it must prioritize them, in case it cannot satisfy all of them. Power is the most critical criterion in prioritizing stakeholders. Other criteria might include the urgency of satisfying each particular stakeholder group and the degree of importance of each to the firm.[103]

Stakeholders are the individuals and groups who can affect, and are affected by, the strategic outcomes achieved and who have enforceable claims on a firm's performance.

Figure 1.4 The Three Stakeholder Groups

When the firm earns above-average returns, the challenge of effectively managing stakeholder relationships is lessened substantially. With the capability and flexibility provided by above-average returns, a firm can more easily satisfy multiple stakeholders simultaneously. When the firm is earning only average returns, it is unable to maximize the interests of all stakeholders. The objective then becomes one of at least minimally satisfying each stakeholder. Trade-off decisions are made in light of how important the support of each stakeholder group is to the firm. For example, environmental groups may be very important to firms in the energy industry but less important to professional service firms.[104] A firm earning below-average returns does not have the capacity to minimally satisfy all stakeholders. The managerial challenge in this case is to make trade-offs that minimize the amount of support lost from stakeholders. Societal values also influence the general weightings allocated among the three stakeholder groups shown in Figure 1.4. Although all three groups are served by firms in the major industrialized nations, the priorities in their service vary because of cultural differences. Next, we provide more details about each of the three major stakeholder groups.

Capital Market Stakeholders

Shareholders and lenders both expect a firm to preserve and enhance the wealth they have entrusted to it. The returns they expect are commensurate with the degree of risk accepted with those investments (i.e., lower returns are expected with low-risk investments, and higher returns are expected with high-risk investments). Dissatisfied lenders may impose stricter covenants on subsequent borrowing of capital. Dissatisfied shareholders may reflect their concerns through several means, including selling their stock.

When a firm is aware of potential or actual dissatisfactions among capital market stakeholders, it may respond to their concerns. The firm's response to stakeholders who are dissatisfied is affected by the nature of its dependency relationship with them (which, as noted earlier, is also influenced by a society's values). The greater and more significant the dependency relationship is, the more direct and significant the firm's response becomes. Given Airbus's situation, as explained in the Opening Case, it is reasonable to expect that Airbus's CEO and top-level managers are thinking seriously about what should be done to improve the firm's performance in order to satisfy its capital market stakeholders. In fact, Airbus attempted to lay off a number of employees as well as outsource some operations to lower its costs and to make itself more competitive relative to Boeing given Airbus's cost overruns for key planes such as the super jumbo A-380. However, in Europe where Airbus is headquartered, a strong public emphasis on employee stakeholders provides support to union protests over the cuts.[105]

Product Market Stakeholders

Some might think that product market stakeholders (customers, suppliers, host communities, and unions) share few common interests. However, all four groups can benefit as firms engage in competitive battles. For example, depending on product and industry characteristics, marketplace competition may result in lower product prices being charged to a firm's customers and higher prices being paid to its suppliers (the firm might be willing to pay higher supplier prices to ensure delivery of the types of goods and services that are linked with its competitive success).[106]

As is noted in Chapter 4, customers, as stakeholders, demand reliable products at the lowest possible prices. Suppliers seek loyal customers who are willing to pay the highest sustainable prices for the goods and services they receive. Host communities want companies willing to be long-term employers and providers of tax revenue without placing excessive demands on public support services. Union officials are interested in secure jobs, under highly desirable working conditions, for employees they represent. Thus, product market stakeholders are generally satisfied when a firm's profit margin reflects at least a balance between the returns to capital market stakeholders (i.e., the returns lenders and shareholders will accept and still retain their interests in the firm) and the returns in which they share.

Organizational Stakeholders

Employees—the firm's organizational stakeholders—expect the firm to provide a dynamic, stimulating, and rewarding work environment. As employees, we are usually satisfied working for a company that is growing and actively developing our skills, especially those skills required to be effective team members and to meet or exceed global work standards. Workers who learn how to use new knowledge productively are critical to organizational success. In a collective sense, the education and skills of a firm's workforce are competitive weapons affecting strategy implementation and firm performance.[107] As suggested by the following statement, strategic leaders are ultimately responsible for serving the needs of organizational stakeholders on a day-to-day basis: "[T]he job of [strategic] leadership is to fully utilize human potential, to create organizations in which people can grow and learn while still achieving a common objective, to nurture the human spirit."[108] Interestingly, research suggests that outside directors are more likely to propose layoffs compared to inside strategic leaders, while such insiders are likely to use preventative cost-cutting measures and seek to protect incumbent employees.[109]

Strategic Leaders

Strategic leaders are people located in different parts of the firm using the strategic management process to help the firm reach its vision and mission. Regardless of their location in the firm, successful strategic leaders are decisive and committed to nurturing those around them[110] and are committed to helping the firm create value for customers and returns for shareholders and other stakeholders.[111]

When identifying strategic leaders, most of us tend to think of chief executive officers (CEOs) and other top-level managers. Clearly, these people are strategic leaders. And, in the final analysis, CEOs are responsible for making certain their firm effectively uses the strategic management process. Indeed, the pressure on CEOs to manage strategically is

Strategic leaders are people located in different parts of the firm using the strategic management process to help the firm reach its vision and mission.

stronger than ever.[112] However, many other people in today's organizations help choose a firm's strategy and then determine the actions for successfully implementing them.[113] The main reason is that the realities of twenty-first-century competition that we discussed earlier in this chapter (e.g., the global economy, globalization, rapid technological change, and the increasing importance of knowledge and people as sources of competitive advantage) are creating a need for those "closest to the action" to be the ones making decisions and determining the actions to be taken.[114] In fact, the most effective CEOs and top-level managers understand how to delegate strategic responsibilities to people throughout the firm who influence the use of organizational resources.[115]

Organizational culture also affects strategic leaders and their work. In turn, strategic leaders' decisions and actions shape a firm's culture. **Organizational culture** refers to the complex set of ideologies, symbols, and core values that are shared throughout the firm and that influence how the firm conducts business. It is the social energy that drives—or fails to drive—the organization.[116] For example, highly successful Southwest Airlines is known for having a unique and valuable culture. Its culture encourages employees to work hard but also to have fun while doing so. Moreover, its culture entails respect for others—employees and customers alike. The firm also places a premium on service, as suggested by its commitment to provide POS (Positively Outrageous Service) to each customer. Wal-Mart claims that its continuing success is largely attributable to its culture.[117]

Some organizational cultures are a source of disadvantage. It is important for strategic leaders to understand, however, that whether the firm's culture is functional or dysfunctional, their work takes place within the context of that culture. The relationship between organizational culture and strategic leaders' work continues to be reciprocal in that the culture shapes how they work while their work helps shape an ever-evolving organizational culture.

> **Organizational culture** refers to the complex set of ideologies, symbols, and core values that are shared throughout the firm and that influence how the firm conducts business.

The Work of Effective Strategic Leaders

Perhaps not surprisingly, hard work, thorough analyses, a willingness to be brutally honest, a penchant for wanting the firm and its people to accomplish more, and common sense are prerequisites to an individual's success as a strategic leader.[118] In addition, strategic leaders must be able to "think seriously and deeply . . . about the purposes of the organizations they head or functions they perform, about the strategies, tactics, technologies, systems, and people necessary to attain these purposes and about the important questions that always need to be asked."[119] Additionally, effective strategic leaders work to set an ethical tone in their firms. For example, Kevin Thompson, IBM's Manager of Corporate Citizenship suggests, "We don't think you can survive without integrating business and societal values." This approach to ethical behavior helped to place IBM at the sixth place on the 2007 list of 100 Best Corporate Citizens published by *CRO Magazine*.[120]

Strategic leaders, regardless of their location in the organization, often work long hours, and the work is filled with ambiguous decision situations for which effective solutions are not easily determined.[121] However, the opportunities afforded by this work are appealing and offer exciting chances to dream and to act.[122] The following words, given as advice to the late Time Warner chair and co-CEO Steven J. Ross by his father, describe the opportunities in a strategic leader's work:

There are three categories of people—the person who goes into the office, puts his feet up on his desk, and dreams for 12 hours; the person who arrives at 5 A.M. and works for 16 hours, never once stopping to dream; and the person who puts his feet up, dreams for one hour, then does something about those dreams.[123]

IBM's organizational culture holds that there is indeed a corporate responsibility to bettering society at large.

The organizational term used for a dream that challenges and energizes a company is vision (discussed earlier in this chapter). Strategic leaders have opportunities to dream and to act, and the most effective ones provide a vision as the foundation for the firm's mission and subsequent choice and use of one or more strategies.

Predicting Outcomes of Strategic Decisions: Profit Pools

Strategic leaders attempt to predict the outcomes of their decisions before taking efforts to implement them, which is difficult to do. Many decisions that are a part of the strategic management process are concerned with an uncertain future and the firm's place in that future.[124]

Mapping an industry's profit pool is something strategic leaders can do to anticipate the possible outcomes of different decisions and to focus on growth in profits rather than strictly growth in revenues. A **profit pool** entails the total profits earned in an industry at all points along the value chain.[125] (Value chain is explained in Chapter 3 and further discussed in Chapter 4.) Analyzing the profit pool in the industry may help a firm see something others are unable to see by helping it understand the primary sources of profits in an industry. There are four steps to identifying profit pools: (1) define the pool's boundaries, (2) estimate the pool's overall size, (3) estimate the size of the value-chain activity in the pool, and (4) reconcile the calculations.[126]

Let's think about how Airbus might map the commercial aerospace industry's profit pools. First, Airbus would need to define the industry's boundaries and, second, estimate its size. As discussed in the Opening Case, these boundaries would include markets across the globe, and the size of many of these markets, especially markets in emerging economies, continues to expand rapidly. Airbus would then be prepared to estimate the amount of profit potential in each part of the value chain (step 3). In this industry, product design and product features are likely more important sources of potential profits than marketing campaigns to sell the new designs. These types of issues are to be considered with the third step of actions used to map an industry's profit pool. Airbus would then have the information and insights needed to identify the strategies to use to be successful where the largest profit pools are located in the value chain.[127] As this brief discussion shows, profit pools are a tool the firm's strategic leaders can use to help recognize the actions to take to increase the likelihood of increasing profits.

A **profit pool** entails the total profits earned in an industry at all points along the value chain.

The Strategic Management Process

As suggested by Figure 1.1, the strategic management process is a rational approach firms use to achieve strategic competitiveness and earn above-average returns. Figure 1.1 also outlines the topics we examine in this book to present the strategic management process to you.

This book is divided into three parts. In Part 1, we describe what firms do to analyze their external environment (Chapter 2) and internal organization (Chapter 3). These analyses are completed to identify marketplace opportunities and threats in the external environment (Chapter 2) and to decide how to use the resources, capabilities, and core competencies in the firm's internal organization to pursue opportunities and overcome threats (Chapter 3). With knowledge about its external environment and internal organization, the firm forms its vision and mission.

The firm's strategic inputs (see Figure 1.1) provide the foundation for choosing one or more strategies and deciding how to implement them. As suggested in Figure 1.1 by the horizontal arrow linking the two types of strategic actions, formulation and implementation must be simultaneously integrated if the firm is to successfully use the strategic management process. Integration happens as decision makers think about implementation issues when choosing strategies and as they think about possible changes to the firm's strategies while implementing a currently chosen strategy.

In Part 2 of this book, we discuss the different strategies firms may choose to use. First, we examine business-level strategies (Chapter 4). A business-level strategy describes a firm's actions designed to exploit its competitive advantage over rivals. A company competing in a single product market (e.g., a locally owned grocery store operating in only one location) has but one business-level strategy. As you will learn though, a diversified firm competing in multiple product markets (e.g., General Electric) forms a business-level strategy for each of its businesses. In Chapter 5, we describe the actions and reactions that occur among firms while using their strategies in marketplace competitions. As we will see, competitors respond to and try to anticipate each other's actions. The dynamics of competition affect the strategies firms choose to use as well as how they try to implement the chosen strategies.[128]

For the diversified firm, corporate-level strategy (Chapter 6) is concerned with determining the businesses in which the company intends to compete as well as how resources, capabilities, and core competencies are to be allocated among the different businesses. Other topics vital to strategy formulation, particularly in the diversified corporation, include acquiring other companies and, as appropriate, restructuring the firm's portfolio of businesses (Chapter 7) and selecting an international strategy (Chapter 8). With cooperative strategies (Chapter 9), firms form a partnership to share their resources and capabilities in order to develop a competitive advantage. Cooperative strategies are becoming increasingly important as firms try to find ways to compete in the global economy's array of different markets.[129] For example, Marriott International Inc. and Ian Schrager Company, which focuses on designing luxury boutique hotels, are teaming to jointly produce hotels to compete with successful brands such as the W offered by Starwood Hotels and Resorts Worldwide.[130]

To examine actions taken to implement strategies, we consider several topics in Part 3 of the book. First, we examine the different mechanisms used to govern firms (Chapter 10). With demands for improved corporate governance being voiced today by many stakeholders,[131] organizations are challenged to learn how to simultaneously satisfy their stakeholders' different interests.[132] Finally, the organizational structure and actions needed to control a firm's operations (Chapter 11), the patterns of strategic leadership appropriate for today's firms and competitive environments (Chapter 12), and strategic entrepreneurship (Chapter 13) as a path to continuous innovation are addressed.

Before closing this introductory chapter, it is important to emphasize that primarily because they are related to how a firm interacts with its stakeholders, almost all strategic management process decisions have ethical dimensions.[133] Organizational ethics are revealed by an organization's culture; that is to say, a firm's decisions are a product of the core values that are shared by most or all of a company's managers and employees. Especially in the turbulent and often ambiguous competitive landscape of the twenty-first century, those making decisions that are part of the strategic management process are challenged to recognize that their decisions affect capital market, product market, and organizational stakeholders differently and to evaluate the ethical implications of their decisions on a daily basis.[134] Decision makers failing to recognize these realities accept the risk of putting their firm at a competitive disadvantage when it comes to consistently engaging in ethical business practices.[135]

As you will discover, the strategic management process examined in this book calls for disciplined approaches to the development of competitive advantage. These approaches provide the pathway through which firms will be able to achieve strategic competitiveness and earn above-average returns. Mastery of this strategic management process will effectively serve you, our readers, and the organizations for which you will choose to work.

- Firms use the strategic management process to achieve strategic competitiveness and earn above-average returns. Strategic competitiveness is achieved when a firm has developed and learned how to implement a value-creating strategy. Above-average returns (in excess of what investors expect to earn from other investments with similar levels of risk) provide the foundation a firm needs to simultaneously satisfy all of its stakeholders.

- The fundamental nature of competition is different in the current competitive landscape. As a result, those making strategic decisions must adopt a different mind-set, one that allows them to learn how to compete in highly turbulent and chaotic environments that produce disorder and a great deal of uncertainty. The globalization of industries and their markets and rapid and significant technological changes are the two primary factors contributing to the turbulence of the competitive landscape.

- Firms use two major models to help them form their vision and mission and then choose one or more strategies to use in the pursuit of strategic competitiveness and above-average returns. The core assumption of the I/O model is that the firm's external environment has more of an influence on the choice of strategies than do the firm's internal resources, capabilities, and core competencies. Thus, the I/O model is used to understand the effects an industry's characteristics can have on a firm when deciding what strategy or strategies to use to compete against rivals. The logic supporting the I/O model suggests that above-average returns are earned when the firm locates an attractive industry and successfully implements the strategy dictated by that industry's characteristics. The core assumption of the resource-based model is that the firm's unique resources, capabilities, and core competencies have more of an influence on selecting and using strategies than does the firm's external environment. Above-average returns are earned when the firm uses its valuable, rare, costly-to-imitate, and nonsubstitutable resources and capabilities to compete against its rivals in one or more industries. Evidence indicates that both models yield insights that are linked to successfully selecting and using strategies. Thus, firms want to use their unique resources, capabilities, and core competencies as the foundation for one or more strategies that will allow them to compete in industries they understand.

- Vision and mission are formed in light of the information and insights gained from studying a firm's internal and external environments. Vision is a picture of what the firm wants to be and, in broad terms, what it wants to ultimately achieve. Flowing from the vision, the mission specifies the business or businesses in which the firm intends to compete and the customers it intends to serve. Vision and mission provide direction to the firm and signal important descriptive information to stakeholders.

- Stakeholders are those who can affect, and are affected by, a firm's strategic outcomes. Because a firm is dependent on the continuing support of stakeholders (shareholders, customers, suppliers, employees, host communities, etc.), they have enforceable claims on the company's performance. When earning above-average returns, a firm has the resources it needs to at minimum simultaneously satisfy the interests of all stakeholders. However, when the firm earns only average returns, different stakeholder groups must be carefully managed in order to retain their support. A firm earning below-average returns must minimize the amount of support it loses from dissatisfied stakeholders.

- Strategic leaders are people located in different parts of the firm using the strategic management process to help the firm reach its vision and mission. In the final analysis, though, CEOs are responsible for making certain that their firms properly use the strategic management process. Today, the effectiveness of the strategic management process increases when it is grounded in ethical intentions and behaviors. The strategic leader's work demands decision trade-offs, often among attractive alternatives. It is important for all strategic leaders, and especially the CEO and other members of the top-management team, to work hard, conduct thorough analyses of situations, be brutally and consistently honest, and ask the right questions of the right people at the right time.

- Strategic leaders must predict the potential outcomes of their strategic decisions. To do so, they must first calculate profit pools in their industry that are linked to value chain activities. In so doing, they are less likely to formulate and implement ineffective strategies.

1. What are strategic competitiveness, strategy, competitive advantage, above-average returns, and the strategic management process?

2. What are the characteristics of the current competitive landscape? What two factors are the primary drivers of this landscape?

3. According to the I/O model, what should a firm do to earn above-average returns?

4. What does the resource-based model suggest a firm should do to earn above-average returns?

5. What are vision and mission? What is their value for the strategic management process?

6. What are stakeholders? How do the three primary stakeholder groups influence organizations?

7. How would you describe the work of strategic leaders?

8. What are the elements of the strategic management process? How are they interrelated?

Notes

1. J. B. Barney & D. N. Clark, 2007, Resource-based theory: Creating and sustaining competitive advantage, New York: Oxford University Press; D. G. Sirmon, M. A. Hitt & R. D. Ireland, 2007, Managing firm resources in dynamic environments to create value: Looking inside the black box, *Academy of Management Review*, 32: 273–292.

2. D. Lei & J. W. Slocum, 2005, Strategic and organizational requirements for competitive advantage, *Academy of Management Executive*, 19(1): 31–45.

3. G. Pacheco-de-Almeida & P. Zemsky, 2007, The timing of resource development and sustainable competitive advantage, *Management Science*, 53: 651–666; D. J. Teece, G. Pisano & A. Shuen, 1997, Dynamic capabilities and strategic management, *Strategic Management Journal*, 18: 509–533.

4. P. Shrivastava, 1995, Ecocentric management for a risk society, *Academy of Management Review*, 20: 119.

5. F. Delmar, P. Davidsson & W. B. Gartner, 2003, Arriving at a high-growth firm, *Journal of Business Venturing*, 18: 189–216.

6. T. Bates, 2005, Analysis of young, small firms that have closed: Delineating successful from unsuccessful closures, *Journal of Business Venturing*, 20: 343–358.

7. A. M. McGahan & M. E. Porter, 2003, The emergence and sustainability of abnormal profits, *Strategic Organization*, 1: 79–108; T. C. Powell, 2001, Competitive advantage: Logical and philosophical considerations, *Strategic Management Journal*, 22: 875–888.

8. J. T. Mahoney & A. M. McGahan, 2007, The field of strategic management within the evolving science of strategic organization, *Strategic Organization*, 5: 79–99; R. D. Ireland & C. C. Miller, 2004, Decision-making and firm success, *Academy of Management Executive*, 18(4): 8–12.

9. P. Nutt, 2004, Expanding the search for alternatives during strategic decision-making, *Academy of Management Executive*, 18(4): 13–28; S. Dutta, M. J. Zbaracki & M. Bergen, 2003, Pricing process as a capability: A resource-based perspective, *Strategic Management Journal*, 24: 615–630.

10. S. Tallman & K. Fladmoe-Lindquist, 2002, Internationalization, globalization, and capability-based strategy, *California Management Review*, 45(1): 116–135; M. A. Hitt, R. D. Ireland, S. M. Camp & D. L. Sexton, 2001, Strategic entrepreneurship: Entrepreneurial strategies for wealth creation, *Strategic Management Journal*, 22 (Special Issue): 479–491; S. A. Zahra, R. D. Ireland & M. A. Hitt, 2000, International expansion by new venture firms: International diversity, mode of market entry, technological learning and performance, *Academy of Management Journal*, 43: 925–950.

11. R. Kirkland, 2005, Will the U.S. be flattened by a flatter world? *Fortune*, June 27, 47–48.

12. A. Nair & S. Kotha, 2001, Does group membership matter? Evidence from the Japanese steel industry, *Strategic Management Journal*, 22: 221–235; A. M. McGahan & M. E. Porter, 1997, How much does industry matter, really? *Strategic Management Journal*, 18 (Special Issue): 15–30.

13. F. J. Acedo, C. Barroso & J. L. Galan, 2006, The resource-based theory: Dissemination and main trends, *Strategic Management Journal*, 27: 621–636; D. G. Sirmon & M. A. Hitt, 2003, Managing resources: Linking unique resources, management and wealth creation in family firms, *Entrepreneurship Theory and Practice*, 27(4): 339–358; J. B. Barney, 2001, Is the resource-based "view" a useful perspective for strategic management research? Yes, *Academy of Management Review*, 26: 41–56.

14. T. Friedman, 2005, *The World Is Flat: A Brief History of the 21st Century*, New York, NY: Farrar, Strauss and Giroux; M. A. Hitt, B. W. Keats & S. M. DeMarie, 1998, Navigating in the new competitive landscape: Building competitive advantage and strategic flexibility in the 21st century, *Academy of Management Executive*, 12(4): 22–42; R. A. Bettis & M. A. Hitt, 1995, The new competitive landscape, *Strategic Management Journal*, 16 (Special Issue): 7–19.

15. D. Searcey, 2006, Beyond cable. Beyond DSL. *Wall Street Journal*, July 24, R9.

16. 2005, NBC could combine network and cable news-NY Post, http://www.reuters.com, June 30.

17. P. Taylor, 2007, Tools to bridge the divide: Raketu aims to outperform Skype in Internet telephony while throwing in a range of information and entertainment services, *Financial Times*, May 11, 16.

18. W. Swarts, 2006, Get reel (Netflix, Blockbuster, Apple Computer, Amazon.com), *SmartMoney.com*, http://www.smartmoney.com, October 24.

19. G. Probst & S. Raisch, 2005, Organizational crisis: The logic of failure, *Academy of Management Executive*, 19(1): 90–105; M. A. Hitt & V. Pisano, 2003, The cross-border merger and acquisition strategy, *Management Research*, 1: 133–144.

20. R. M. Grant, 2003, Strategic planning in a turbulent environment: Evidence from the oil majors, *Strategic Management Journal*, 24: 491–517.

21. J. W. Selsky, J. Goes & O. N. Babüroglu, 2007, Contrasting perspectives of strategy making: Applications in "Hyper" environments, *Organization Studies*, 28(1): 71–94; G. McNamara, P. M. Vaaler & C. Devers, 2003, Same as it ever was: The search for evidence of increasing hypercompetition, *Strategic Management Journal*, 24: 261–278.

22. R. A. D'Aveni, 1995, Coping with hypercompetition: Utilizing the new 7S's framework, *Academy of Management Executive*, 9(3): 46.

23. D. J. Bryce & J. H. Dyer, 2007, Strategies to crack well-guarded markets, *Harvard Business Review* 85(5): 84–92; R. A. D'Aveni, 2004, Corporate spheres of influence, *MIT Sloan Management Review*, 45(4): 38–46; W. J. Ferrier, 2001, Navigating the competitive landscape: The drivers and consequences of competitive aggressiveness, *Academy of Management Journal*, 44: 858-877.

24. S.-J. Chang & S. Park, 2005, Types of firms generating network externalities and MNCs' co-location decisions, *Strategic Management Journal*, 26: 595–615; S. C. Voelpel, M. Dous & T. H. Davenport, 2005, Five steps to creating a global knowledge-sharing systems: Siemens/ShareNet, *Academy of Management Executive*, 19(2): 9–23.

25. R. Belderbos & L. Sleuwaegen, 2005, Competitive drivers and international plant configuration strategies: A product-level test, *Strategic Management Journal*, 26: 577–593.

26. 2005, Organisation for Economic Co-operation and Development, OCED Statistical Profile of the United States—2005, http://www.oced.org; S. Koudsi & L. A. Costa, 1998, America vs. the new Europe: By the numbers, *Fortune*, December 21, 149–156.

27. Y. Luo, 2007, From foreign investors to strategic insiders: Shifting parameters, prescriptions and paradigms for MNCs in China, *Journal of World Business*, 42(1): 14–34.

28. A. Virmani, 2005, India a giant economy? Yes, by 2035! *Rediff.com*, http://www.rediff.com, January 21.

29. T. Khanna & K. G. Palepu, 2006, Emerging giants: Building world-class companies in developing countries, *Harvard Business Review*, 84(10): 60–69.

30. K. Kranhold, 2005, GE pins hopes on emerging markets, *Wall Street Journal Online*, http://www.wsj.com, March 2.

31. G. D. Bruton, G. G. Dess & J. J. Janney, 2007, Knowledge management in technology-focused firms in emerging economies: Caveats on capabilities, networks, and real options, *Asia Pacific Journal of Management*, 24(2): 115–130; P. Williamson & M. Zeng, 2004, Strategies for competing in a changed China, *MIT Sloan Management Review*, 45(4): 85–91; V. Govindarajan & A. K. Gupta,

2001, *The Quest for Global Dominance*, San Francisco: Jossey-Bass.

32. T. Khanna, K. G. Palepu & J. Sinha, 2005, Strategies that fit emerging markets, *Harvard Business Review*, 83(6): 63–76.

33. N. Shirouzu, 2007, Toyota's new U.S. plan: Stop building factories, *Wall Street Journal*, June 20, A1, A14.

34. B. Simon, 2007, Ford brands improve on vehicle quality, *Financial Times*, June 7, 20.

35. M. A. Prospero, 2005, The march of war, *Fast Company*, May, 14.

36. G. Fink & N. Holden, 2005, The global transfer of management knowledge, *Academy of Management Executive*, 19(2): 5–8; M. Subramaniam & N. Venkataraman, 2001, Determinants of transnational new product development capability: Testing the influence of transferring and deploying tacit overseas knowledge, *Strategic Management Journal*, 22: 359–378.

37. S. Zaheer & E. Mosakowski, 1997, The dynamics of the liability of foreignness: A global study of survival in financial services, *Strategic Management Journal*, 18: 439–464.

38. Bruton, Dess & Janney, Knowledge management in technology-focused firms in emerging economies; R. C. May, S. M. Puffer, & D. J. McCarthy, 2005, Transferring management knowledge to Russia: A culturally based approach, *Academy of Management Executive*, 19(2): 24–35.

39. M. A. Hitt, R. E. Hoskisson & H. Kim, 1997, International diversification: Effects on innovation and firm performance in product-diversified firms, *Academy of Management Journal*, 40: 767–798.

40. D'Aveni, Coping with hypercompetition, 46.

41. R. D. Ireland & J. W. Webb, 2007, Strategic entrepreneurship: Creating competitive advantage through streams of innovation, *Business Horizons*, 50(1): 49–59; G. Hamel, 2001, Revolution vs. evolution: You need both, *Harvard Business Review*, 79(5): 150–156.

42. K. H. Hammonds, 2001, What is the state of the new economy? *Fast Company*, September, 101–104.

43. L. Yu, 2005, Does knowledge sharing pay off? *MIT Sloan Management Review*, 46(3): 5.

44. H. W. Chesbrough, 2007, Why companies should have open business models, *MIT Sloan Management Review*, 48(2): 22–28.

45. T. Talaulicar, J. Grundei1 & A. V. Werder, 2005, Strategic decision making in start-ups: The effect of top management team organization and processes on speed and comprehensiveness, *Journal of Business Venturing*, 20: 519–541; K. M. Eisenhardt, 1999, Strategy as strategic decision making, *Sloan Management Review*, 40(3): 65–72.

46. J. Santos, Y. Doz & P. Williamson, 2004, Is your innovation process global? *MIT Sloan Management Review*, 45(4): 31–37.

47. C. W. L. Hill, 1997, Establishing a standard: Competitive strategy and technological standards in winner-take-all industries, *Academy of Management Executive*, 11(2): 7–25.

48. C. Gilbert, 2003, The disruptive opportunity, *MIT Sloan Management Review*, 44(4): 27–32; C. M. Christensen, 1997, *The Innovator's Dilemma*, Boston: Harvard Business School Press.

49. P. Magnusson, 2005, Globalization is great—sort of, *BusinessWeek*, April 25, 25.

50. C. M. Christensen, 2006. The ongoing process of building a theory of disruption, *Journal of Product Innovation Management*, 23(1): 39–55; R. Adner, 2002, When are technologies disruptive? A demand-based view of the emergence of competition, *Strategic Management Journal*, 23: 667–688; G. Ahuja & C. M. Lampert, 2001, Entrepreneurship in the large corporation: A longitudinal study of how established firms create breakthrough inventions, *Strategic Management Journal*, 22 (Special Issue): 521–543.

51. C. L. Nichols-Nixon & C. Y. Woo, 2003, Technology sourcing and output of established firms in a regime of encompassing technological change, *Strategic Management Journal*, 24: 651–666; C. W. L. Hill & F. T. Rothaermel, 2003, The performance of incumbent firms in the face of radical technological innovation, *Academy of Management Review*, 28: 257–274.

52. K. Celuch, G. B. Murphy & S. K. Callaway, 2007, More bang for your buck: Small firms and the importance of aligned information technology capabilities and strategic flexibility, *Journal of High Technology Management Research*, 17: 187–197; G. Ferguson, S. Mathur & B. Shah, 2005, Evolving from information to insight, *MIT Sloan Management Review*, 46(2): 51–58.

53. S. McBride, 2007, Internet radio races to break free of the PC, *Wall Street Journal*, June 18, A1, A11.

54. A. C. Inkpen & E. W. K. Tsang, 2005, Social capital, networks, and knowledge transfer, *Academy of Management Review*, 30: 146–165; A. S. DeNisi, M. A. Hitt & S. E. Jackson, 2003, The knowledge-based approach to sustainable competitive advantage, in S. E. Jackson, M. A. Hitt & A. S. DeNisi (eds.), *Managing Knowledge for Sustained Competitive Advantage*, San Francisco: Jossey-Bass, 3–33.

55. M. Gottfredson, R. Puryear & S. Phillips, 2005, Strategic sourcing: From periphery to the core, *Harvard Business Review*, 83(2): 132–139.

56. K. G. Smith, C. J. Collins & K. D. Clark, 2005, Existing knowledge, knowledge creation capability, and the rate of new product introduction in high-technology firms, *Academy of Management Journal*, 48: 346–357; S. K. McEvily & B. Chakravarthy, 2002, The persistence of knowledge-based advantage: An empirical test for product performance and technological knowledge, *Strategic Management Journal*, 23: 285–305.

57. A. Capaldo, 2007, Network structure and innovation: The leveraging of a dual network as a distinctive relational capability, *Strategic Management Journal*, 28: 585–608; S. K. Ethiraj, P. Kale, M. S. Krishnan & J. V. Singh, 2005, Where do capabilities come from and how do they matter? *Strategic Management Journal*, 26: 25–45; L. Rosenkopf & A. Nerkar, 2001, Beyond local search: Boundary-spanning, exploration, and impact on the optical disk industry, *Strategic Management Journal*, 22: 287–306.

58. Sirmon, Hitt & Ireland, Managing firm resources.

59. P. L. Robertson & P. R. Patel, 2007, New wine in old bottles: Technological diffusion in developed economies, *Research Policy*, 36(5): 708–721; K. Asakawa & M. Lehrer, 2003, Managing local knowledge assets globally: The role of regional innovation relays, *Journal of World Business*, 38: 31–42.

60. R. E. Hoskisson, M. A. Hitt & R. D. Ireland, 2008, *Competing for Advantage*, 2nd ed., Cincinnati: Thomson South-Western; K. R. Harrigan, 2001, Strategic flexibility in old and new economies, in M. A. Hitt, R. E. Freeman & J. S. Harrison (eds.), *Handbook of Strategic Management*, Oxford, UK: Blackwell Publishers, 97–123.

61. S. Nadkarni & V. K. Narayanan, 2007, Strategic schemas, strategic flexibility, and firm performance: The moderating role of industry clockspeed, *Strategic Management Journal*, 28: 243–270.

62. L. Gratton & S. Ghoshal, 2005, Beyond best practice, *MIT Sloan Management Review*, 46(3): 49–55.

63. K. Shimizu & M. A. Hitt, 2004, Strategic flexibility: Organizational preparedness to reverse ineffective strategic decisions, *Academy of Management Executive*, 18(4): 44–59; K. Uhlenbruck, K. E. Meyer & M. A. Hitt, 2003, Organizational transformation in transition economies: Resource-based and organizational learning perspectives, *Journal of Management Studies*, 40: 257–282.

64. M. J. Zhang, 2006, IS support for strategic flexibility, environmental dynamism, and firm performance, *Journal of Managerial Issues*, 18: 84–103; Celuch, Murphy & Callaway, More bang for your buck.

65. R. E. Hoskisson, M. A. Hitt, W. P. Wan & D. Yiu, 1999, Swings of a pendulum: Theory and research in strategic management, *Journal of Management*, 25: 417–456.

66. E. H. Bowman & C. E. Helfat, 2001, Does corporate strategy matter? *Strategic Management Journal*, 22: 1–23.

67. J. Shamsie, 2003, The context of dominance: An industry-driven framework for exploiting reputation, *Strategic Management Journal*, 24: 199–215; A. Seth & H. Thomas, 1994, Theories of the firm: Implications for strategy research, *Journal of Management Studies*, 31: 165–191.

68. Seth & Thomas, 169–173.

69. M. B. Lieberman & S. Asaba, 2006, Why do firms imitate each other? *Academy of Management Journal*, 31: 366–385; L. F. Feldman, C. G. Brush & T. Manolova, 2005, Co-alignment in the resource-performance relationship: Strategy as mediator, *Journal of Business Venturing*, 20: 359–383.

70. M. E. Porter, 1985, *Competitive Advantage*, New York: Free Press; M. E. Porter, 1980, *Competitive Strategy*, New York: Free Press.

71. J. C. Short, D. J. Ketchen, Jr., T. B. Palmer & G. T. M. Hult, 2007, Firm, strategic group, and industry influences on performance, *Strategic Management Journal*, 28: 147–167.

72. A. M. McGahan, 1999, Competition, strategy and business performance, *California Management Review*, 41(3): 74–101; McGahan & Porter, How much does industry matter, really?

73. R. Henderson & W. Mitchell, 1997, The interactions of organizational and competitive influences on strategy and performance, *Strategic Management Journal 18* (Special Issue): 5–14; C. Oliver, 1997, Sustainable competitive advantage: Combining institutional and resource-based views, *Strategic Management Journal*, 18: 697–713; J. L. Stimpert & I. M. Duhaime, 1997, Seeing the big picture: The influence of industry, diversification, and business strategy on performance, *Academy of Management Journal*, 40: 560–583.

74. F. J. Acedo, C. Barroso & J. L. Galan, 2006, The resource-based theory: Dissemination and main trends, *Strategic Management Journal*, 27: 621–636.

75. B.-S. Teng & J. L. Cummings, 2002, Trade-offs in managing resources and capabilities, *Academy of Management Executive*, 16(2): 81–91; R. L. Priem & J. E. Butler, 2001, Is the resource-based "view" a useful perspective for strategic management research? *Academy of Management Review*, 26: 22–40.

76. S. A. Zahra, H. Sapienza & P. Davidsson, 2006, Entrepreneurship and dynamic capabilities: A review, model and research agenda, *Journal of Management studies*, 43(4): 927–955; M. Blyler & R. W. Coff, 2003, Dynamic capabilities, social capital, and rent appropriation: Ties that split pies, *Strategic Management Journal*, 24: 677–686.

77. S. L. Newbert, 2007, Empirical research on the resource-based view of the firm: An assessment and suggestions for future research, *Strategic Management Journal*, 28: 121–146; P. Bansal, 2005, Evolving sustainability: A longitudinal study of corporate sustainable development, *Strategic Management Journal*, 26: 197–218.

78. P. J. H. Schoemaker & R. Amit, 1994, Investment in strategic assets: Industry and firm-level perspectives, in P. Shrivastava, A. Huff, & J. Dutton (eds.), *Advances in Strategic Management*, Greenwich, CT: JAI Press, 9.

79. A. A. Lado, N. G. Boyd, P. Wright & M. Kroll, 2006, Paradox and theorizing within the resource-based view, *Academy of Management Review*, 31: 115–131; D. M. DeCarolis, 2003, Competencies and imitability in the pharmaceutical industry: An analysis of their relationship with firm performance, *Journal of Management*, 29: 27–50; Barney, Is the resource-based "view" a useful perspective for strategic management research? Yes.

80. C. Zott, 2003, Dynamic capabilities and the emergence of intraindustry differential firm performance: Insights from a simulation study, *Strategic Management Journal*, 24: 97–125.

81. E. Levitas & H. A. Ndofor, 2006, What to do with the resource-based view: A few suggestions for what ails the RBV that supporters and opponents might accept, *Journal of Management Inquiry*, 15(2): 135–144; G. Hawawini, V. Subramanian & P. Verdin, 2003, Is performance driven by industry- or firm-specific factors? A new look at the evidence, *Strategic Management Journal*, 24: 1–16.

82. M. Makhija, 2003, Comparing the resource-based and market-based views of the firm: Empirical evidence from Czech privatization, *Strategic Management Journal*, 24: 433–451; T. J. Douglas & J. A. Ryman, 2003, Understanding competitive advantage in the general hospital industry: Evaluating strategic competencies, *Strategic Management Journal*, 24: 333–347.

83. R. D. Ireland, R. E. Hoskisson & M. A. Hitt. 2006, *Understanding Business Strategy*, Cincinnati: Thomson South-Western, 32–34.

84. R. Zolli, 2006, Recognizing tomorrow's hot ideas today, *BusinessWeek*, September 25: 12.

85. S. Steptoe, 2007, Building a better mouse, *Time*, June 25, 1.

86. 2005, The CEO's secret handbook, *Business 2.0*, July, 69–76.

87. R. D. Ireland & M. A. Hitt, 1992, Mission statements: Importance, challenge, and recommendations for development, *Business Horizons*, 35(3): 34–42.

88. W. J. Duncan, 1999, *Management: Ideas and Actions*, New York: Oxford University Press, 122–125.

89. J. H. Davis, J. A. Ruhe, M. Lee & U. Rajadhyaksha, 2007, Mission possible: Do school mission statements work? *Journal of Business Ethics*, 70: 99–110.

90. A. J. Ward, M. J. Lankau, A. C. Amason, J. A. Sonnenfeld & B. A. Agle, 2007, Improving the performance of top management teams, *MIT Sloan Management Review*, 48(3): 85–90; J. A. Pearce & J. P. Doh, 2005, The high impact of collaborative social initiatives, *MIT Sloan Management Review*, 46(3): 30–39.

91. J. R. Baum, E. A. Locke & S. A. Kirkpatrick, 1998, A longitudinal study of the relation of vision and vision communication to venture growth in entrepreneurial firms, *Journal of Applied Psychology*, 83: 43–54.

92. R. Kaufman, 2006, *Change, Choices, and Consequences: A Guide to Mega Thinking and Planning*, Amherst, MA: HRD Press; J. Humphreys, 2004, The vision thing, *MIT Sloan Management Review*, 45(4): 96.

93. P. A. Argenti, R. A. Howell & K. A. Beck, 2005, The strategic communication imperative, *MIT Sloan Management Review*, 46(3): 83–89; J. Frooman, 1999, Stakeholder influence strategies, *Academy of Management Review*, 24: 191–205.

94. J. P. Walsh & W. R. Nord, 2005, Taking stock of stakeholder management, *Academy of Management Review*, 30: 426–438; T. M. Jones & A. C. Wicks, 1999, Convergent stakeholder theory, *Academy of Management Review*, 24: 206–221; R. E. Freeman, 1984, Strategic Management: A Stakeholder Approach, Boston: Pitman, 53–54.

95. G. Donaldson & J. W. Lorsch, 1983, *Decision Making at the Top: The Shaping of Strategic Direction*, New York: Basic Books, 37–40.

96. S. Sharma & I. Henriques, 2005, Stakeholder influences on sustainability practices in the Canadian Forest products industry, *Strategic Management Journal*, 26: 159–180.

97. A. Mackey, T. B. Mackey & J. B. Barney, 2007, Corporate social responsibility and firm performance: Investor preferences and corporate strategies, *Academy of Management Review*, 32: 817–835; A. J. Hillman & G. D. Keim, 2001, Shareholder value, stakeholder management, and social issues: What's the bottom line? *Strategic Management Journal*, 22: 125–139.

98. J. M. Stevens, H. K. Steensma, D. A. Harrison & P. L. Cochran, 2005, Symbolic or substantive document? The influence of ethics codes on financial executives' decisions, *Strategic Management Journal*, 26: 181–195.

99. M. L. Barnett & R. M. Salomon, 2006, Beyond dichotomy: The curvilinear relationship between social responsibility and financial performance, *Strategic Management Journal*, 27: 1101–1122.

100. L.Vilanova, 2007, Neither shareholder nor stakeholder management: What happens when firms are run for their short-term salient stakeholder? *European Management Journal*, 25(2): 146–162.

101. R. E. Freeman & J. McVea, 2001, A stakeholder approach to strategic management, in M. A. Hitt, R. E. Freeman & J. S. Harrison (eds.), *Handbook of Strategic Management*, Oxford, UK: Blackwell Publishers, 189–207.

102. C. Caldwell & R. Karri, 2005, Organizational governance and ethical systems: A convenantal approach to building trust, *Journal of Business Ethics*, 58: 249–267; A. McWilliams & D. Siegel, 2001, Corporate social responsibility: A theory of the firm perspective, *Academy of Management Review*, 26: 117–127.

103. C. Hardy, T. B. Lawrence & D. Grant, 2005, Discourse and collaboration: The role of conversations and collective identity, *Academy of Management Review*, 30: 58–77; R. K. Mitchell, B. R. Agle & D. J. Wood, 1997, Toward a theory of stakeholder identification and salience: Defining the principle of who and what really count, *Academy of Management Review*, 22: 853–886.

104. S. Maitlis, 2005, The social process of organizational sensemaking, *Academy of Management Journal*, 48: 21–49.

105. D. Michaels, 2007, Airbus seeks union support; justifying job cuts may prove critical to allaying anger, *Wall Street Journal*, March 1, A11.

106. B. A. Neville & B. Menguc, 2006, Stakeholder multiplicity: Toward an understanding of the interactions between

stakeholders, *Journal of Business Ethics,* 66: 377–391.

107. T. M. Gardner, 2005, Interfirm competition for human resources: Evidence from the software industry, *Academy of Management Journal,* 48: 237–256.

108. J. A. Byrne, 2005, Working for the boss from hell, *Fast Company,* July, 14.

109. N. Abe & S. Shimizutani, 2007, Employment policy and corporate governance—An empirical comparison of the stakeholder and the profit-maximization model, *Journal of Comparative Economics,* 35: 346–368.

110. D. Brady & D. Kiley, 2005, Short on sizzle, and losing steam, *BusinessWeek,* April 25, 44.

111. E. T. Prince, 2005, The fiscal behavior of CEOs, *MIT Sloan Management Review,* 46(3): 23–26.

112. D. C. Hambrick, 2007, Upper echelons theory: An update, *Academy of Management Review,* 32: 334–339.

113. A. Priestland & T. R. Hanig, 2005, Developing first-level managers, *Harvard Business Review,* 83(6): 113–120.

114. R. T. Pascale & J. Sternin, 2005, Your company's secret change agent, *Harvard Business Review,* 83(5): 72–81.

115. Y. L. Doz, M. Kosonen, 2007, The new deal at the top, *Harvard Business Review,* 85(6): 98–104.

116. D. Lavie, 2006, The competitive advantage of interconnected firms: An extension of the resource-based view, *Academy of Management Review,* 31: 638–658.

117. 2005, About Wal-Mart, www.walmart .com, July 3.

118. D. Rooke & W. R. Tolbert, 2005, Seven transformations of leadership, *Harvard Business Review,* 83(4): 66–76.

119. T. Leavitt, 1991, *Thinking about Management,* New York: Free Press, 9.

120. 2007, 100 Best Corporate citizens for 2007, *CRO Magazine,* www.thecro.com, June 19.

121. D. C. Hambrick, S. Finkelstein & A. C. Mooney, 2005, Executive job demands: New insights for explaining strategic decisions and leader behaviors, *Academy of Management Review,* 30: 472–491; J. Brett & L. K. Stroh, 2003, Working 61 plus hours a week: Why do managers do it? *Journal of Applied Psychology,* 88: 67–78.

122. J. A. Byrne, 2005, Great work if you can get it, *Fast Company,* April, 14.

123. M. Loeb, 1993, Steven J. Ross, 1927–1992, *Fortune,* January 25, 4.

124. Collins, Jim Collins on tough calls.

125. O. Gadiesh & J. L. Gilbert, 1998, Profit pools: A fresh look at strategy, *Harvard Business Review,* 76(3): 139–147.

126. O. Gadiesh & J. L. Gilbert, 1998, How to map your industry's profit pool, *Harvard Business Review,* 76(3): 149–162.

127. C. Zook, 2007, Finding your next CORE business, *Harvard Business Review,* 85(4): 66–75; M. J. Epstein & R. A. Westbrook, 2001, Linking actions to profits in strategic decision making, *Sloan Management Review,* 42(3): 39–49.

128. D. J. Ketchen, C. C. Snow & V. L. Street, 2004, Improving firm performance by matching strategic decision-making

processes to competitive dynamics, *Academy of Management Executive,* 18(4): 29–43.

129. P. Evans & B. Wolf, 2005, Collaboration rules, *Harvard Business Review,* 83(7): 96–104.

130. P. Sanders, 2007, Strange bedfellows: Marriott, Schrager, *Wall Street Journal,* June 14: B1, B5.

131. M. Useem, 2006, How well-run board make decisions, *Harvard Business Review,* 84(11): 130–138; I. Le Breton-Miller & D. Miller, 2006, Why do some family businesses out-compete? Governance, long-term orientations, and sustainable capability, *Entrepreneurship Theory and Practice,* 30: 731–746.

132. C. Eesley & M. J. Lenox, 2006, Firm responses to secondary stakeholder action, *Strategic Management Journal,* 27: 765–781.

133. S. J. Reynolds, F. C. Schultz & D. R. Hekman, 2006, Stakeholder theory and managerial decision-making: Constraints and implications of balancing stakeholder interests, *Journal of Business Ethics,* 64: 285–301; L. K. Trevino & G. R. Weaver, 2003, *Managing Ethics in Business Organizations,* Stanford, CA: Stanford University Press.

134. J. R. Ehrenfeld, 2005, The roots of sustainability, *MIT Sloan Management Review,* 46(2): 23–25.

135. B. W. Heineman Jr., 2007, Avoiding integrity land minds, *Harvard Business Review,* 85(4): 100–108; 2005, Corporate citizenship on the rise, *BusinessWeek,* May 9, S1–S7.

Exploring the External Environment: Competition and Opportunities

Studying this chapter should provide you with the strategic management knowledge needed to:

1. Explain the importance of analyzing and understanding the firm's external environment.

2. Define and describe the general environment and the industry environment.

3. Discuss the four activities of the external environmental analysis process.

4. Name and describe the general environment's six segments.

5. Identify the five competitive forces and explain how they determine an industry's profit potential.

6. Define strategic groups and describe their influence on the firm.

7. Describe what firms need to know about their competitors and different methods (including ethical standards) used to collect intelligence about them.

Environmental Pressures on Wal-Mart

Are key rivals outrunning Wal-Mart? Is the company receiving pressure because of its poor public image, environmental concerns, and accusations regarding the treatment of its associates? A recent article in *BusinessWeek* reported that Wal-Mart had the smallest percentage increase in sales for new stores opening in 2006, compared to competitors such as CVS, Target, and Kroger. In fact, same-store sales growth turned negative in November 2006 before rebounding to increase 1.6 percent in December. In the same time period, Costco and Target sales were up 9 percent and 4.1 percent, respectively. Additionally, Wal-Mart's stock (about $48 a share in the middle of 2007) was flat in an otherwise strong year for stocks. Because Wal-Mart is the nation's largest employer and the second-largest company by revenue, its every move is scrutinized. And, 2006 and 2007 proved to be tough years for the retail giant. Between legal troubles, public relations problems, and labor issues, Wal-Mart is beginning to experience problems with rivals' competitive actions.

Wal-Mart emerged from a small town in Arkansas to dominate the retail business market for nearly five decades. Its signature of "everyday low prices" is based on its cost leadership strategy on which its business model is built. But over the past two years, its growth formula has not worked as effectively as in the past, allowing opportunities for competitors. In 2006, its U.S. division only produced a 1.9 percent gain in same-store sales, which was its worst performance ever. By this key measure, competitors such as Target, Costco, Kroger, Safeway, Walgreens, CVS, and Best Buy now are all growing two-to-five times faster than Wal-Mart. Wal-Mart's growth in recent years has come primarily from opening new stores rather than from existing stores. For example, in 2005 Wal-Mart achieved an increase in U.S. revenues of 7.2 percent by opening new stores at the rate of nearly one a day. However, Wall Street is concerned about market saturation and Wal-Mart's stock price has stagnated. Many analysts also feel that Wal-Mart is relying too heavily on building new stores to compensate for sagging same-store sales.

Wal-Mart has been plagued by many other problems that likely are affecting its ability to attract new customers and increase sales. Some of the problems are political. For example, several cities erected legal obstacles to the location of Wal-Mart stores in specific areas. Wal-Mart has been criticized for the low pay and poor benefit packages provided to many of its associates. In response and to improve its image in communities, Lee Scott, Wal-Mart's CEO, pledged to raise wages 6 percent in a third of its stores. Critics are still not satisfied with his response because most of those funds will be offset by pay caps for longtime employees. Wal-Mart has also promised to reduce the cost of health care benefits to associates to as little as $23 a month.

Environmentalists are also applying pressure on Wal-Mart. Because of its position as one of the world's largest companies, with more than 3,000 stores in the United States, the firm's efforts to go "green" could have a major impact. To address this pressure, Wal-Mart is revamping its overall environmental strategy with the assistance of Conservation International, a nonprofit environmental group that works closely with companies in creating environmental policies and initiatives. Lee Scott told associates in a recent speech that Wal-Mart was establishing ambitious goals such as increasing the efficiency of its vehicle fleet by 25 percent within three years and doubling the efficiency in ten years. The firm has targeted reducing energy use in stores by 30 percent and reducing solid wastes in the stores by 25 percent over a three-year period. Wal-Mart has agreed to invest $500 million annually in environmental technologies to be used in its stores. The new green initiatives include working toward a goal of producing no waste, providing fuel from renewable resources, and working closely with its suppliers to promote good environmental practices.

Wal-Mart committed to issue an initial environmental sustainability report in 2007, and provide data on its Web site that can be used to track its reduction of waste and greenhouse gas production. Even with the $500 million pledge for greening the stories, it is still less than one-fifth of one percentage point of Wal-Mart's total sales in 2006.

The entities with which Wal-Mart must deal have grown in number and complexity as it has entered additional international markets over the last decade. For example, Wal-Mart has significant operations in 15 foreign countries, including China, several Latin American countries, and the United Kingdom. Wal-Mart obtains many products sold in its stores from Chinese manufacturers, but it also has 73 stores in China to serve Chinese customers. It recently signed an agreement to enter the Indian market in a joint venture (JV) with the Indian company, Bharti Enterprises. This JV allows it to avoid Indian laws prohibiting foreign retailers. Still, the Indian government is receiving pressure to investigate from those who dislike Wal-Mart because of its market power and reputation.

Sources: A. Bianco, 2007, Wal-Mart's Midlife Crisis, *BusinessWeek*, http://www.businessweek.com, April 30; 2007, Key rivals outrun Wal-Mart, *BusinessWeek*, http://www.businessweek.com, April 30; G. Weiss, 2007, Wal-Mart comes to India, *Forbes*, http://www.forbes.com, March 26; J. Carey, 2007, Wal-Mart: Big strides to become the Jolly Green Giant, *BusinessWeek*, http://www.businessweek.com, January 29; M. Guenther, 2006, Wal-Mart sees green, CNNMoney, http://www.cnnmoney.com, July 27; J. Birchall, 2006, Wal-Mart picks a shade of green, *Financial Times*, http://www.ft.com, February 6; J. Birchall, 2005, Wal-Mart sets out stall for a greener future, *Financial Times*, http://www.ft.com, October 25; J. Birger, 2007, The unending woes of Lee Scott, *CNN Money*, http://www.money.cnn.com, January 9; F. Harvey and E. Rigby, 2006, Supermarkets' green credentials attacked, *Financial Times*, http://www.ft.com, September 14.

As described in the Opening Case and suggested by research, the external environment affects firm growth and profitability.[1] Wal-Mart's growth has been slowed and its profitability affected most directly by its competitors. In addition, Wal-Mart must deal with other important external parties such as local, state, and national government bodies (foreign governments as well); unions; and even special-purpose organizations including groups interested in promoting green environmental practices. Major political events such as the war in Iraq, the strength of separate nations' economies at different times, and the emergence of new technologies are a few examples of conditions in the external environment that affect firms throughout the world. These and other external environmental conditions create threats to and opportunities for firms that, in turn, have major effects on their strategic actions.[2]

Regardless of the industry, the external environment is critical to a firm's survival and success. This chapter focuses on how firms analyze and understand the external environment. The firm's understanding of the external environment is matched with knowledge about its internal environment (discussed in the next chapter) to form its vision, to develop its mission, and to identify and implement actions that result in strategic competitiveness and above-average returns (see Figure 1.1, on page 5).

As noted in Chapter 1, the environmental conditions in the current global economy differ from those previously faced by firms. Technological changes and the continuing growth of information gathering and processing capabilities demand more timely and effective competitive actions and responses.[3] The rapid sociological changes occurring in many countries affect labor practices and the nature of products demanded by increasingly diverse consumers. Governmental policies and laws also affect where and how firms may choose to compete.[4] For example, deregulation of utility firms in the United States has had a major effect on the strategies employed by utility firms in recent years.[5] To achieve strategic competitiveness and thrive, firms must be aware of and understand the different dimensions of the external environment.

Firms understand the external environment by acquiring information about competitors, customers, and other stakeholders to build their own base of knowledge and capabilities.[6] On the basis of the new information, firms may take actions to build new capabilities and buffer themselves against environmental effects or to build relationships with stakeholders in their environment.[7] In order to take successful action, they must effectively analyze the external environment.

The General, Industry, and Competitor Environments

An integrated understanding of the external and internal environments is essential for firms to understand the present and predict the future.[8] As shown in Figure 2.1, a firm's external environment is divided into three major areas: the general, industry, and competitor environments.

The **general environment** is composed of dimensions in the broader society that influence an industry and the firms within it.[9] We group these dimensions into six environmental *segments:* demographic, economic, political/legal, sociocultural, technological, and global. Examples of *elements* analyzed in each of these segments are shown in Table 2.1.

Firms cannot directly control the general environment's segments and elements. Accordingly, successful companies gather the information required to understand each segment and its implications for the selection and implementation of the appropriate

The **general environment** is composed of dimensions in the broader society that influence an industry and the firms within it.

Figure 2.1 The External Environment

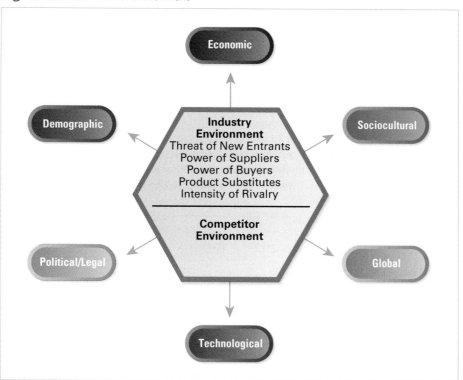

Table 2.1 The General Environment: Segments and Elements

Demographic Segment	• Population size • Age structure • Geographic distribution	• Ethnic mix • Income distribution
Economic Segment	• Inflation rates • Interest rates • Trade deficits or surpluses • Budget deficits or surpluses	• Personal savings rate • Business savings rates • Gross domestic product
Political/Legal Segment	• Antitrust laws • Taxation laws • Deregulation philosophies	• Labor training laws • Educational philosophies and policies
Sociocultural Segment	• Women in the workforce • Workforce diversity • Attitudes about the quality of work life	• Concerns about the environment • Shifts in work and career preferences • Shifts in preferences regarding product and service characteristics
Technological Segment	• Product innovations • Applications of knowledge	• Focus of private and government-supported R&D expenditures • New communication technologies
Global Segment	• Important political events • Critical global markets	• Newly industrialized countries • Different cultural and institutional attributes

strategies. For example, most firms have little individual effect on the economy or economies in which they compete, although each economy has a major effect on each firm's ability to operate and even survive. Thus, companies around the globe are challenged to understand the effects of individual economies' decline on their current and future strategies when it occurs.

The **industry environment** is the set of factors that directly influences a firm and its competitive actions and competitive responses[10]: the threat of new entrants, the power of suppliers, the power of buyers, the threat of product substitutes, and the intensity of rivalry among competitors. In total, the interactions among these five factors determine an industry's profit potential. The challenge is to locate a position within an industry where a firm can favorably influence those factors or where it can successfully defend against their influence. In fact, positioning is a major issue for retailers, as is suggested in the Opening Case. Even though it is exceptionally large and powerful in the market, Wal-Mart faces substantial competitive rivalry as Target, Costco, Kroger, Safeway, Walgreens, CVS, and Best Buy are beginning to increase their sales and market shares. However, Wal-Mart's market power cannot be ignored. The greater a firm's capacity to favorably influence its industry environment, the greater the likelihood that the firm will earn above-average returns.

How companies gather and interpret information about their competitors is called *competitor analysis*. Understanding the firm's competitor environment complements the insights provided by studying the general and industry environments. Understanding its competitor environment will continue to affect the outcomes Wal-Mart and its competitors achieve as they engage in marketplace competition.

Analysis of the general environment is focused on the future; analysis of the industry environment is focused on the factors and conditions influencing a firm's profitability within its industry; and analysis of competitors is focused on predicting the dynamics of competitors' actions, responses, and intentions. In combination, the results of the three

> The **industry environment** is the set of factors that directly influences a firm and its competitive actions and competitive responses: the threat of new entrants, the power of suppliers, the power of buyers, the threat of product substitutes, and the intensity of rivalry among competitors.

analyses the firm uses to understand its external environment influence its vision, mission, and strategic actions. Although we discuss each analysis separately, performance improves when the firm integrates the insights provided by analyses of the general environment, the industry environment, and the competitor environment.

External Environmental Analysis

Most firms face external environments that are highly turbulent, complex, and global—conditions that make interpreting those environments increasingly difficult.[11] To cope with often ambiguous and incomplete environmental data and to increase understanding of the general environment, firms engage in external environmental analysis. The continuous process includes four activities: scanning, monitoring, forecasting, and assessing (see Table 2.2). Analyzing the external environment is a difficult, yet significant, activity.[12]

An important objective of studying the general environment is identifying opportunities and threats. An **opportunity** is a condition in the general environment that, if exploited, helps a company achieve strategic competitiveness. For example, the number of people 65 and older is predicted to be slightly less than 20 million in 2014. This number represents a growth of almost 35 percent from the number 65 and older in 2004.[13] Retailers can target this market with goods and services designed to meet the needs of people in the age group and stage of their lives (e.g., leisure activities, medical supplies). In so doing, they can take advantage of the significant growth in the number of people in this market segment.

A **threat** is a condition in the general environment that may hinder a company's efforts to achieve strategic competitiveness.[14] The once-revered firm Polaroid can attest to the seriousness of external threats. Polaroid was a leader in its industry and considered one of the top 50 firms in the United States. When its competitors developed photographic equipment using digital technology, Polaroid was unprepared and never responded effectively. It filed for bankruptcy in 2001. In 2002, the former Polaroid Corp. was sold to Bank One's OEP Imaging unit, which promptly changed its own name to Polaroid Corp. Jacques Nasser, a former CEO at Ford, took over as CEO at Polaroid and found that the brand had continued life. Nasser used the brand in a partnership with Petters Group to put the Polaroid name on "TVs and DVDs made in Asian factories and sell them through Wal-Mart and Target."[15] Even though Polaroid went public again and was later sold to Petters Group in 2005, it was still a much smaller version of its original business. As these examples indicate, opportunities suggest competitive *possibilities,* while threats are potential *constraints.*

Several sources can be used to analyze the general environment, including a wide variety of printed materials (such as trade publications, newspapers, business publications, and the results of academic research and public polls), trade shows and suppliers, customers, and employees of public-sector organizations. People in *boundary-spanning*

An **opportunity** is a condition in the general environment that, if exploited, helps a company achieve strategic competitiveness.

A **threat** is a condition in the general environment that may hinder a company's efforts to achieve strategic competitiveness.

Table 2.2 Components of the External Environmental Analysis

Scanning	• Identifying early signals of environmental changes and trends
Monitoring	• Detecting meaning through ongoing observations of environmental changes and trends
Forecasting	• Developing projections of anticipated outcomes based on monitored changes and trends
Assessing	• Determining the timing and importance of environmental changes and trends for firms' strategies and their management

positions can obtain much information. Salespersons, purchasing managers, public relations directors, and customer service representatives, each of whom interacts with external constituents, are examples of boundary-spanning positions.

Scanning

Scanning entails the study of all segments in the general environment. Through scanning, firms identify early signals of potential changes in the general environment and detect changes that are already underway.[16] Scanning often reveals ambiguous, incomplete, or unconnected data and information. Thus, environmental scanning is challenging but critically important for firms competing in highly volatile environments.[17] In addition, scanning activities must be aligned with the organizational context; a scanning system designed for a volatile environment is inappropriate for a firm in a stable environment.[18]

Amazon.com uses special software to help with organizational scanning of its customers.

Many firms use special software to help them identify events that are taking place in the environment and that are announced in public sources. For example, news event detection uses information-based systems to categorize text and reduce the trade-off between an important missed event and false alarm rates.[19] The Internet provides significant opportunities for scanning. For example, Amazon.com, similar to many Internet companies, records significant information about individuals visiting its Web site, particularly if a purchase is made. Amazon then welcomes these customers by name when they visit the Web site again. The firm even sends messages to them about specials and new products similar to those purchased in previous visits.

Additionally, many Web sites and advertisers on the Internet use "cookies" to obtain information from those who visit their sites. These files are saved to the visitors' hard drives, allowing customers to connect more quickly to a firm's Web site, but also allowing the firm to solicit a variety of information about them. Because cookies are often placed without customers' knowledge, their use can be a questionable practice. Although computer cookies have been a boon to online advertisers, they have brought a significant threat of computer viruses, hacking ability, spyware, spam, and other difficulties to computer users. The U.S. government and several states have passed legislation regarding spyware. In fact, the Federal Trade Commission (FTC) has recently taken action against major spyware organizations levying fines as large as $1.5 million. However, the FTC believes that stronger legislation is needed and has asked the U.S. Congress for a larger budget to pursue spyware organizations.[20]

Monitoring

When *monitoring,* analysts observe environmental changes to see if an important trend is emerging from among those spotted by scanning.[21] Critical to successful monitoring is the firm's ability to detect meaning in different environmental events and trends. For example, the size of the middle class of African Americans continues to grow in the United States. With increasing wealth, this group of citizens is more aggressively pursuing investment options.[22] Companies in the financial planning sector could monitor this change in the economic segment to determine the degree to which a competitively important trend is emerging. By monitoring trends, firms can be prepared to introduce new goods and services at the appropriate time to take advantage of the opportunities identified trends provide.[23]

Effective monitoring requires the firm to identify important stakeholders. Because the importance of different stakeholders can vary over a firm's life cycle, careful attention must be given to the firm's needs and its stakeholder groups across time.[24] Scanning and monitoring are particularly important when a firm competes in an industry with high technological uncertainty.[25] Scanning and monitoring not only can provide the firm with information, they also serve as a means of importing new knowledge about markets and about how to successfully commercialize new technologies that the firm has developed.[26]

Forecasting

Scanning and monitoring are concerned with events and trends in the general environment at a point in time. When *forecasting,* analysts develop feasible projections of what might happen, and how quickly, as a result of the changes and trends detected through scanning and monitoring.[27] For example, analysts might forecast the time that will be required for a new technology to reach the marketplace, the length of time before different corporate training procedures are required to deal with anticipated changes in the composition of the workforce, or how much time will elapse before changes in governmental taxation policies affect consumers' purchasing patterns.

Forecasting events and outcomes accurately is challenging. Alcas Corporation is a direct marketing company that features Cutco Cutlery, a well-known brand that produces an assortment of knives and cutting utensils. Cutco Cutlery has an alliance with Vector Marketing, which is also closely held by Alcas, and one of its specialties is sales forecasting. However, it recently experienced a difficult forecasting problem. The company had forecasted a 25 percent increase in sales, but sales actually increased 47 percent. Although generally positive, this increase created a shortage, and Cutco Cutlery did not have the capacity to fill orders in its usual timely fashion. Normal delivery of two to three weeks eventually was pushed to five or six weeks. This problem was critical because the company had built its reputation on quick delivery as a way to differentiate the value it provides to consumers.[28] Forecasting is important in order to adjust sales appropriately to meet demand.

Assessing

The objective of *assessing* is to determine the timing and significance of the effects of environmental changes and trends on the strategic management of the firm.[29] Through scanning, monitoring, and forecasting, analysts are able to understand the general environment. Going a step further, the intent of assessment is to specify the implications of that understanding for the organization. Without assessment, the firm is left with data that may be interesting but are of unknown competitive relevance. Even if formal assessment is inadequate, the appropriate interpretation of that information is important: "Research found that how accurate senior executives are about their competitive environments is indeed less important for strategy and corresponding organizational changes than the way in which they interpret information about their environments."[30] Thus, although gathering and organizing information is important, investing resources in the appropriate interpretation of that intelligence may be equally important. Accordingly, after information has been gathered, assessing whether a trend in the environment represents an opportunity or a threat is extremely important.

Segments of the General Environment

The general environment is composed of segments that are external to the firm (see Table 2.1, on page 36). Although the degree of impact varies, these environmental segments affect each industry and its firms. The challenge to the firm is to scan, monitor, forecast, and assess those elements in each segment that are of the greatest importance. These efforts should result in recognition of environmental changes, trends, opportunities, and threats. Opportunities are then matched with a firm's core competencies (the matching process is discussed further in Chapter 3).

The **demographic segment** is concerned with a population's size, age structure, geographic distribution, ethnic mix, and income distribution.

Despite a declining birth rate, China is expected to remain one of the most populous countries in the world for years to come.

The Demographic Segment

The **demographic segment** is concerned with a population's size, age structure, geographic distribution, ethnic mix, and income distribution.[31] Often demographic segments are analyzed on a global basis because of their potential effects across countries' borders and because many firms compete in global markets.

Population Size

By the end of 2007, the world's population was slightly over 6.6 billion, up from 6.1 billion in 2000. Combined, China and India accounted for one-third of the 6.6 billion. Given the declining birth rate, experts speculate that the world population will reach about 9.2 billion by 2050. India (with more than 1.65 billion people projected) and China (with about 1.4 billion people projected) are expected to remain the most populous countries.[32] Interestingly, only slightly over 1 billion people live in developed countries whereas more than 5 billion live in developing countries.

Observing demographic changes in populations highlights the importance of this environmental segment. For example, in 2006, 20 percent of Japan's citizens were 65 or older, while the United States and China will not reach this level until 2036.[33] Aging populations are a significant problem for countries because of the need for workers and the burden of funding retirement programs. In Japan and other countries, employees are urged to work longer to overcome these problems. Interestingly, the United States has a higher birthrate and significant immigration, placing it in a better position than Japan and other European nations.

Age Structure

As noted earlier, in Japan and other countries, the world's population is rapidly aging. In North America and Europe, millions of baby boomers are approaching retirement. However, even in developing countries with large numbers of people under the age of 35, birth rates have been declining sharply. In China, for example, by 2040 there will be more than 400 million people over the age of 60. The 90 million baby boomers in North America are fueling the current economy because they seem to continue to spend as they age. They are also thus expected to fuel growth in the financial planning sector as they inherit $1 trillion over the next 15 years and rush to save more before retirement. However, the future surrounding baby boomers is clouded in at least two areas. One problem is the significant increase in health care costs. For instance, Canadian health care, which has strong government subsidies, is predicted to consume 40 percent of all government tax revenues by 2040. The other problem is that as the number of retired baby boomers swells, the number of workers paying Social Security and other taxes will decrease significantly, leaving governments in North America and Europe to face significant choices. It seems that governments will have to increase the retirement age, cut benefits, raise taxes, and/or run significant budget deficits.[34]

Although emerging economy populations are aging as well, they still have a significantly younger large labor force. The consumer products being produced so cheaply in China and exported to the United States are helping North American consumers to contain inflation. However, the basic prices of commodities such as copper, oil, and gas have been rising as China increases its productivity and seeks to maintain employment levels of its large population. As the workforce in the West ages and education levels rise in emerging economies, the United States and Canada will likely have to accept larger numbers of immigrant workers. At the same time, Western firms are outsourcing work to such countries as India, which has a growing high-tech sector. As can be seen, changes in the age structure have significant effects on firms in an economy.

Geographic Distribution

For decades, the U.S. population has been shifting from the north and east to the west and south. Similarly, the trend of relocating from metropolitan to nonmetropolitan areas continues. These trends are changing local and state governments' tax bases. In turn, business firms' decisions regarding location are influenced by the degree of support that different taxing agencies offer as well as the rates at which these agencies tax businesses.

The geographic distribution of populations throughout the world is also affected by the capabilities resulting from advances in communications technology. Through computer technologies, for example, people can remain in their homes, communicating with others in remote locations to complete their work.

Ethnic Mix

The ethnic mix of countries' populations continues to change. Within the United States, the ethnicity of states and their cities varies significantly. For firms, the Hispanic market in the United States has been changing significantly. CSI TV, the 24-hour cable channel for young Latinos, was launched in February 2004 and now has 10 million viewers. Its motto is "Speak English. Live Latin." Firms need to focus on marketing not only to the broader Hispanic market but also to those who want to be integrated and "don't want to be segregated."[35] This latter market segment wants to see their own lives being portrayed on television, rather than those of Anglos. They want to shop at the same stores and have a similar lifestyle. Men's Wearhouse learned this by the failure of its Eddie Rodriguez clothing stores, which targeted Latino men; all six stores were closed in 2005. Consumers simply said "no" to the concept because they wanted to be integrated. Hispanic Americans between the ages of 14 and 34 want to be spoken to in English but stay true to their Latino identity. The Latino spending power is important for large consumer sectors such as grocery stores, movie studios, financial services, and clothing stores among others. Overall, the Hispanic market is approximately $1 trillion in size.[36] Through careful study, companies can develop and market products that satisfy the unique needs of different ethnic groups.

Changes in the ethnic mix also affect a workforce's composition and cooperation.[37] In the United States, for example, the population and labor force will continue to diversify, as immigration accounts for a sizable part of growth. Projections are that the combined Latino and Asian population shares will increase to more than 20 percent of the total U.S. population by 2014.[38] Interestingly, much of this immigrant workforce is bypassing high-cost coastal cities and settling in smaller rural towns. Many of these workers are in low-wage, labor-intensive industries such as construction, food service, lodging, and landscaping.[39] For this reason, if border security is tightened, these industries will likely face labor shortages.

Income Distribution

Understanding how income is distributed within and across populations informs firms of different groups' purchasing power and discretionary income. Studies of income distributions suggest that although living standards have improved over time, variations exist within and between nations.[40] Of interest to firms are the average incomes of households and individuals. For instance, the increase in dual-career couples has had a notable effect on average incomes. Although real income has been declining in general, the household income of dual-career couples has increased. These figures yield strategically relevant information for firms. For instance, research indicates that whether an employee is part of a dual-career couple can strongly influence the willingness of the employee to accept an international assignment.[41]

The Economic Segment

The health of a nation's economy affects individual firms and industries. For this reason, companies study the economic environment to identify changes, trends, and their strategic implications.

The **economic environment** refers to the nature and direction of the economy in which a firm competes or may compete.[42] Because nations are interconnected as a result of the global economy, firms must scan, monitor, forecast, and assess the health of economies outside their host nation. For example, many nations throughout the world are affected by the U.S. economy.

The U.S. economy declined into a recession in 2001 that extended into 2002. In order to stimulate the economy, interest rates in the United States were cut to near record lows in 2003, equaling the rates in 1958.[43] Largely due to the low interest rates, the economy grew substantially in 2004 and 2005. Global trade was likewise stimulated. However, high oil prices have dampened global economic growth. Additionally, economic growth slowed in 2006 with the U.S. GDP growth slowing from more than 4 percent in 2005 to approximately 3.2 percent in 2006. This slowing growth is predicted to continue with a projected GDP growth of 2.3 percent in 2007.[44] Although bilateral trade can enrich the economies of the countries involved, it also makes each country more vulnerable to negative events in any one country. As our discussion of the economic segment suggests, economic issues are intertwined closely with the realities of the external environment's political/legal segment.

> The **economic environment** refers to the nature and direction of the economy in which a firm competes or may compete.

The Political/Legal Segment

The **political/legal segment** is the arena in which organizations and interest groups compete for attention, resources, and a voice in overseeing the body of laws and regulations guiding the interactions among nations.[45] Essentially, this segment represents how organizations try to influence government and how governments influence them. As the politics of regulations change, this segment influences the nature of competition through changing the rules (for other examples of political/legal elements, see Table 2.1, on page 36).

For example, when new regulations are adopted based on new laws (e.g., the Sarbanes-Oxley Act dealing with corporate governance—see Chapter 10 for more information), they often affect the competitive actions taken by firms (their actions are regulated). An example is the recent global trend toward privatization of government-owned or -regulated firms. The transformation from state-owned to private firms has substantial implications for the competitive landscapes in countries and industries.[46]

Firms must carefully analyze a new political administration's business-related policies and philosophies. Antitrust laws, taxation laws, industries chosen for deregulation, labor training laws, and the degree of commitment to educational institutions are areas in which an administration's policies can affect the operations and profitability of industries and individual firms. Often, firms develop a political strategy to influence governmental policies and actions that might affect them. The effects of global governmental policies on a firm's competitive position increase the importance of forming an effective political strategy.[47]

Business firms across the globe today confront an interesting array of political/legal questions and issues. For example, the debate continues over trade policies. Some believe that a nation should erect trade barriers to protect its companies' products. However, as countries continue to join the World Trade Organization (WTO), more countries seem to believe that free trade across nations serves the best interests of individual countries and their citizens. A Geneva-based organization, the WTO establishes rules for global trade. For instance, after joining the World Trade Organization, China ended a 40-year-old global textile-quota system regulating its exports. Earlier, to ease the problems created for other countries China had voluntarily enacted transition tariffs. When the quota system expired in early 2005, Chinese textiles flooded global markets, threatening domestic

> The **political/legal segment** is the arena in which organizations and interest groups compete for attention, resources, and a voice in overseeing the body of laws and regulations guiding the interactions among nations.

textile industries. Several countries responded by imposing even higher tariffs to level the playing field.[48]

The regulations related to pharmaceuticals and telecommunications, along with the approval or disapproval of major acquisitions, shows the power of government entities. This power also suggests how important it is for firms to have a political strategy. Countries tend to take different approaches to similar problems. For example, different policies have been applied by the United States' government and the leadership of the European Union (EU) with regard to genetically modified foods and on climate change. The U.S. government has taken a looser approach to genetically modified foods while the EU has been much more restrictive. As such, U.S. firms involved in genetically modified foods have experienced problems with their goods in the EU.[49] The regulations are too few for some and too many for others. Regardless, regulations tend to vary across countries and across central government administrations, and firms must cope with these variances.

The Sociocultural Segment

The **sociocultural segment** is concerned with a society's attitudes and cultural values. Because attitudes and values form the cornerstone of a society, they often drive demographic, economic, political/legal, and technological conditions and changes.

> The **sociocultural segment** is concerned with a society's attitudes and cultural values.

Sociocultural segments differ across countries. For example, in the United States, the per capita amount spent on health care is $5,711, almost 50 percent more than the second highest per capita health care expenditures in Norway. The per capita health care expenditures are $3,809 in Norway, $3,776 in Switzerland, $3,110 in Iceland, and $3,001 in Germany. Interestingly, the U.S. rate of citizens' access to health care is below that of these and other countries.[50]

The reverse is true for retirement planning. A study in 15 countries indicated that retirement planning in the United States starts earlier than in other countries. "Americans are involved in retirement issues to a greater extent than other countries, particularly in western Europe where the Social Security and pensions systems provide a much higher percentage of income in retirement."[51] U.S. residents start planning for retirement in their 30s, while those in Portugal, Spain, Italy, and Japan start in their 40s and 50s. Attitudes regarding saving for retirement also affect a nation's economic and political/legal segments.

As the labor force has increased, it has also become more diverse as significantly more women and minorities from a variety of cultures entered the labor force. In 1993, the total U.S. workforce was slightly less than 130 million, but in 2005, it was slightly greater than 148 million. It is predicted to grow to more than 162 million by 2014. In 2014, the workforce is forecasted to be composed of 47 percent female workers, 5 percent Asian American workers, 12 percent African American workers and 16 percent Hispanic workers.[52] The growing gender, ethnic, and cultural diversity in the workforce creates challenges and opportunities, including combining the best of both men's and women's traditional leadership styles. Although diversity in the workforce has the potential to add improved performance, research indicates that important conditions require management of diversity initiatives in order to reap these organizational benefits. Human resource practitioners are trained to successfully manage diversity issues to enhance positive outcomes.[53]

Another manifestation of changing attitudes toward work is the continuing growth of contingency workers (part-time, temporary, and contract employees) throughout the global economy. This trend is significant in several parts of the world, including Canada, Japan, Latin America, Western Europe, and the United States. The fastest growing group of contingency workers is in the technical and professional area. Contributing to this growth are corporate restructurings and downsizings that occur in poor economic conditions along with a breakdown of lifetime employment practices (e.g., in Japan).

The continued growth of suburban communities in the United States and abroad is another major sociocultural trend. The increasing number of people living in the suburbs has a number of effects. For example, longer commute times to urban businesses increase pressure for better transportation systems and superhighway systems (e.g., outer beltways to serve the suburban communities). Suburban growth also has an effect on the number of electronic telecommuters, which is expected to increase rapidly in the twenty-first century. Beyond suburbs lie what the U.S. Census Bureau calls "micropolitan" areas. These areas are often 100 or more miles from a large city and have 10,000 to 49,999 people. They offer rural-like living with many of the larger city amenities such as strip malls and chain restaurants like Starbucks, Chili's, Long John Silver's, and Arby's, but housing and labor costs are much cheaper.[54] Following this growth, some businesses are locating in the suburbs closer to their employees. This work-style option is feasible because of changes in the technological segment, including the Internet's rapid growth and evolution.[55]

Although the lifestyle and workforce changes referenced previously reflect the values of the U.S. population, each country and culture has unique values and trends. As suggested earlier, national cultural values affect behavior in organizations and thus also influence organizational outcomes.[56] For example, the importance of collectivism and social relations in Chinese and Russian cultures lead to the open sharing of information and knowledge among members of an organization.[57] Knowledge sharing is important for defusing new knowledge in organizations increasing the speed in implementing innovations. Personal relationships are especially important in China as guanxi (personal connections) has become a way of doing business within the country.[58] Understanding the importance of guanxi is critical for foreign firms doing business in China.

The Technological Segment

The **technological segment** includes the institutions and activities involved with creating new knowledge and translating that knowledge into new outputs, products, processes, and materials.

Pervasive and diversified in scope, technological changes affect many parts of societies. These effects occur primarily through new products, processes, and materials. The **technological segment** includes the institutions and activities involved with creating new knowledge and translating that knowledge into new outputs, products, processes, and materials.

Given the rapid pace of technological change, it is vital for firms to thoroughly study the technological segment.[59] The importance of these efforts is suggested by the finding that early adopters of new technology often achieve higher market shares and earn higher returns. Thus, firms should continuously scan the external environment to identify potential substitutes for technologies that are in current use, as well as to identify newly emerging technologies from which their firm could derive competitive advantage.[60]

However, not only is forecasting more difficult today, but a company that misses its forecast is often disciplined by the market with a reduction in stock price. For example, DreamWorks Animation, a division of DreamWorks SKG, based its forecast of *Shrek 2* DVD sales in part on the historically long sales life of animated DVDs. But because of increased competition (more firms are releasing an increasing number of DVDs) and limited shelf space, DVD titles now have a much shorter retail life. When retailers started returning millions of unsold copies, DreamWorks' earnings fell short of analysts' forecasts by 25 percent and its stock price tumbled. Misjudging how much a title will sell can have a substantial effect on the bottom line of small studios such as DreamWorks Animation, which releases only two films a year.[61] In contrast, studios that produce many films each year are shielded from the effects of a short life in one film.

Even though the Internet was a significant technological advance and provided substantial power to companies utilizing its potential, wireless communication technology is predicted to be the next critical technological opportunity. Handheld devices and other wireless communications equipment are used to access a variety of network-based services. The use of handheld computers with wireless network connectivity, Web-enabled mobile phone handsets, and other emerging platforms (e.g., consumer Internet-access devices) is expected to increase substantially, soon becoming the dominant form of communication and commerce.[62]

Clearly, the Internet and wireless forms of communications are important technological developments for many reasons. One reason for their importance, however, is that they facilitate the diffusion of other technology and knowledge critical for achieving and maintaining a competitive advantage.[63] Companies must stay current with technologies as they evolve, but also must be prepared to act quickly to embrace important new disruptive technologies shortly after they are introduced.[64] Certainly on a global scale, the technological opportunities and threats in the general environment have an effect on whether firms obtain new technology from external sources (such as by licensing and acquisition) or develop it internally.

The Global Segment

The **global segment** includes relevant new global markets, existing markets that are changing, important international political events, and critical cultural and institutional characteristics of global markets.[65] Globalization of business markets creates both opportunities and challenges for firms.[66] For example, firms can identify and enter valuable new global markets.[67] In addition to contemplating opportunities, firms should recognize potential competitive threats in these markets. China presents many opportunities and some threats for international firms.[68] China's 2001 admission to the World Trade Organization creates additional opportunities. As mentioned earlier, the low cost of Chinese products threatens many firms in the textile industry. For instance, buyers of textile products such as Marks & Spencer in the United Kingdom and others throughout the world cannot ignore China's comparative advantages, even with tariffs in place. China's average labor costs are 90 percent lower than those in the United States and Italy. Furthermore, Chinese manufacturers are more efficient than garment manufacturers in other low-cost countries such as India or Vietnam. The WTO member countries can restrict Chinese imports until 2008 if they can show that local markets are disrupted. However, even with quotas a number of firms such as Wal-Mart and hotel chains such as Hilton and Radisson are increasing their sourcing from Chinese firms because of the significant cost advantage.[69]

Exemplifying the globalization trend is the increasing amount of global outsourcing. However, recent research suggests that organizations incur a trade-off between flexibility and efficiency if all work in a particular function or product is outsourced. Custom work to fill special orders, for example, is more efficiently done through domestic manufacturing; outsourcing standard products to an offshore facility needs to save at least 15 percent to be justified. Even in the textile industry, where much outsourcing is done for efficiency reasons, many order adjustments or special orders require flexibility and cannot be readily handled by low-cost offshore producers.[70] Thus, the research shows that the most effective approach is to integrate some outsourcing with other tasks done internally. In this way, only specialized tasks rather than a complete function are outsourced and the outsourcing alliance is more effectively managed.[71]

Moving into international markets extends a firm's reach and potential. Toyota receives almost 50 percent of its total sales revenue from outside Japan, its home country. More than 60 percent of McDonald's sales revenues and almost 98 percent of Nokia's sales revenues are from outside their home countries.[72] Firms can also increase the opportunity to sell innovations by entering international markets. The larger total market increases the probability that the firm will earn a return on its innovations. Certainly, firms entering new markets can diffuse new knowledge they have created and learn from the new markets as well.[73]

Firms should recognize the different sociocultural and institutional attributes of global markets. Companies competing in South Korea, for example, must understand the value placed on hierarchical order, formality, and self-control, as well as on duty rather than rights. Furthermore, Korean ideology emphasizes communitarianism, a characteristic of many Asian countries. Korea's approach differs from those of Japan and China, however,

The **global segment** includes relevant new global markets, existing markets that are changing, important international political events, and critical cultural and institutional characteristics of global markets.

Does Google Have the Market Power to Ignore External Pressures?

Google's continued growth and expansion of its services puts fear in the hearts of its rivals. Currently, Google is the most widely used Internet search engine and as such, it dominates online advertising. In 2004 Google was worth $23 billion. By mid-2007, the firm's market capitalization hit $169 billion, making Google worth more than IBM. The company is known for its loose corporate culture, with informal principles, and appears to have the goodwill of its customers. But as Google's fortunes continue to extend its reach, it is also experiencing more pressures from the external environment.

Google's strategy of bringing to the market 'search with content' by acquiring YouTube, upset the global media industry. The industry felt that a search engine that can show films and other copyrighted content for free is the act of piracy. Viacom filed a $1 billion lawsuit against Google and YouTube alleging that they are airing clips of its hit programs without permission. The lawsuit cited "massive intentional copyright infringement." Viacom accused YouTube of violating copyright law. In February 2007, Viacom demanded that YouTube remove more than 100,000 clips, and YouTube agreed. Viacom stated that more than 160,000 clips available on YouTube are being used without Viacom's permission.

Google's continued growth and domination–including its acquisition of YouTube– have caused more pressure from the external environment.

In addition, Google is involved in other lawsuits focused around copyright violations and trademark infringements. In 2006, a Belgium court ruled that Google should refrain from posting news articles from French and German language newspapers on the Google News services. In the United States, the Authors Guild and some additional publishers, supported by the Association of American Publishers, sued Google for making digital copies of copyrighted books from libraries. Microsoft has also accused Google of "systematically violating copyright" by scanning millions of books and journals from libraries around the world and making them available online. Google disputes these accusations, suggesting that all of their products comply with copyright law. Google argues that because only a small extract of a copyrighted work is shown in its search process, it is not in violation of the copyright law. For books that have been digitized in U.S. libraries and under copyright, Google only reports that the book exists.

Google's acquisition of DoubleClick represents another critical building block in its strategy. But this move is being scrutinized by companies such as Microsoft and AT&T, in this case suggesting that Google is violating antitrust laws. Basically they argue that Google's share of the search advertisements placed on third-party Web sites, combined with the recent purchase of DoubleClick (online advertising company), will create a dominant position in the overall online advertising business. Central to this complaint is the question of whether the search and display advertising businesses, until now separate, should be treated as a single market for regulatory purposes. According to AT&T, this acquisition would make any Web company that depends on online advertising dependent on a single supplier and, in effect, Google would be able to influence the revenue lifeline of other rival Internet companies.

A combination of these external pressures has affected Google's standing on Wall Street. Google is no longer considered the hot company. In fact, its stock price has underperformed the broader market index in recent times because investors fear that retaliation from competitors could limit the company's growth (recent statistics show Google's growth is slowing). As a result, Google's stock price has fallen. Google is now facing a number of rivals and drawing more attention of government officials as well. Still the market power of Google draws advertisers to guide traffic to their sites.

Sources: R. Waters, 2007, All eyes on Google advertising, *Financial Times*, http://www.ft.com, April 16; R. Wachman, 2007, Google's expansion is coming at a price: It's losing its popularity, *The Observer*, http://www.observer.co.uk, March 25; R. Hof, 2006, Ganging up on Google, *BusinessWeek*, http://www.businessweek.com, April 24; M. Devichand, 2007, Is Google really flouting copyright law? *BBC Law in Action*, http://www.news.bbc.co.uk, March 9; 2007, Viacom sues Google and YouTube, *International Herald Tribune*, http://www.IHT.com, March 13.

in that it focuses on *inhwa,* or harmony. Inhwa is based on a respect of hierarchical relationships and obedience to authority. Alternatively, the approach in China stresses *guanxi*—personal relationships or good connections—while in Japan, the focus is on *wa,* or group harmony and social cohesion.[74] The institutional context of China suggests a major emphasis on centralized planning by the government. The Chinese government provides incentives to firms to develop alliances with foreign firms having sophisticated technology in hopes of building knowledge and introducing new technologies to the Chinese markets over time.[75]

Firms based in other countries, particularly from some emerging markets have become quite active in global markets. Global markets offer firms more opportunities to obtain the resources needed for success. For example, the "dragon" (multinational firms from Asia Pacific countries) are growing in market power. Examples of dragon multinationals include Acer, Ispat International, Li & Fung, and the Hong Leong Group. These firms are entering international markets at a rapid pace, using new strategic approaches, and developing innovation. They are becoming a force in global markets with which firms from developed markets such as the United States and Western Europe must learn how to compete effectively.[76]

Additionally, global markets involve risk. As such some firms take a more reasoned approach to competing in international markets. These firms participate in what some refer to as *globalfocusing.* Globalfocusing often is used by firms with moderate levels of international operations who increase their internationalization by focusing on global niche markets.[77] In this way, they build on and use their special competencies and resources while limiting their risks with the niche market. Another way in which firms limit their risks in international markets is to focus their operations and sales in one region of the world.[78] In this way, they can build stronger relationships in and knowledge of their markets. As they build these strengths, rivals find it more difficult to enter their markets and compete successfully.

As explained in the Strategic Focus, Google's charmed life is being challenged with pressure from its external environment. These pressures have come from the global segment with court rulings in Europe and in the political-legal segment of the general environment with arguments that it is violating copyright laws in the United States. Its size provides market power and slack financial resources, but it also makes it more visible and vulnerable to attacks by rivals. Google has entered related industries (e.g., with the acquisition of YouTube) and faces such rivals as Viacom, Microsoft, and AT&T. Thus, it must deal with competitors' actions and responses in the industries in which it operates. Although the Strategic Focus discussion makes clear that the general environment is important to it (e.g., political legal—potential antitrust actions; global—Belgium court disallowing the posting of French and German news articles), most of the actions are the result of rivals' complaints or lawsuits. Thus, industry rivalry has a significant influence on Google.

A key objective of analyzing the general environment is identifying anticipated changes and trends among external elements. With a focus on the future, the analysis of the general environment allows firms to identify opportunities and threats. As a result, it is necessary to have a top management team with the experience, knowledge, and sensitivity required to effectively analyze this segment of the environment.[79] Also critical to a firm's future operations is an understanding of its industry environment and its competitors; these issues are considered next.

Industry Environment Analysis

An **industry** is a group of firms producing products that are close substitutes.

An **industry** is a group of firms producing products that are close substitutes. In the course of competition, these firms influence one another. Typically, industries include a rich mixture of competitive strategies that companies use in pursuing above-average returns. In part, these strategies are chosen because of the influence of an industry's characteristics.[80] The Strategic Focus on Google illustrates how the competitive forces in an industry can affect firms' behaviors.

Compared with the general environment, the industry environment often has a more direct effect on the firm's strategic competitiveness and above-average returns.[81] The intensity of industry competition and an industry's profit potential are functions of five forces of competition: the threats posed by new entrants, the power of suppliers, the power of buyers, product substitutes, and the intensity of rivalry among competitors (see Figure 2.2).

The five forces model of competition expands the arena for competitive analysis. Historically, when studying the competitive environment, firms concentrated on companies with which they competed directly. However, firms must search more broadly to recognize current and potential competitors by identifying potential customers as well as the firms serving them. Competing for the same customers and thus being influenced by how customers value location and firm capabilities in their decisions is referred to as the market microstructure.[82] Understanding this area is particularly important, because in recent years industry boundaries have become blurred. For example, telecommunications companies now compete with cable broadcasters, software manufacturers provide personal financial services, airlines sell mutual funds, and automakers sell insurance and provide financing.[83] In addition to the focus on customers rather than on specific

Figure 2.2 The Five Forces of Competition Model

industry boundaries to define markets, geographic boundaries are also relevant. Research suggests that different geographic markets for the same product can have considerably different competitive conditions.[84]

Firms must also recognize that suppliers can become a firm's competitors (by integrating forward), as can buyers (by integrating backward). Several firms have integrated forward in the pharmaceutical industry by acquiring distributors or wholesalers. In addition, firms choosing to enter a new market and those producing products that are adequate substitutes for existing products can become a company's competitors.

Threat of New Entrants

Identifying new entrants is important because they can threaten the market share of existing competitors.[85] One reason new entrants pose such a threat is that they bring additional production capacity. Unless the demand for a good or service is increasing, additional capacity holds consumers' costs down, resulting in less revenue and lower returns for competing firms. Often, new entrants have a keen interest in gaining a large market share. As a result, new competitors may force existing firms to be more efficient and to learn how to compete on new dimensions (e.g., using an Internet-based distribution channel).

The likelihood that firms will enter an industry is a function of two factors: barriers to entry and the retaliation expected from current industry participants. Entry barriers make it difficult for new firms to enter an industry and often place them at a competitive disadvantage even when they are able to enter. As such, high entry barriers increase the returns for existing firms in the industry and may allow some firms to dominate the industry.[86] Interestingly, though the airline industry has high entry barriers (e.g., substantial capital costs), new firms entered the industry in the late 1990s, among them AirTran Airways (ATA) and JetBlue. Both entrants created competitive challenges for the major airlines, especially with the economic problems in the early twenty-first century. Both firms compete in the low-cost segments, where consumer demand has increased, making the major high-cost legacy airlines less competitive. In fact, they, along with Southwest Airlines, were partly responsible for the bankruptcy of several large legacy airlines such as Delta. In September 2005, Delta announced it was going into bankruptcy, and in May 2007, it announced coming out of bankruptcy after completing a $3 billion restructuring program. The Delta CEO stated that his airline will be a fierce competitor but acknowledged it is a tough industry.[87]

Gerald Grinstein, Delta Air Lines CEO, announces Delta's emergence from bankruptcy on May 3, 2007.

Barriers to Entry

Existing competitors try to develop barriers to entry. For example, cable firms are entering the phone service business. Accordingly, local firm services such as AT&T are bundling services (e.g., high-speed Internet services, satellite television, and wireless services) in a single package and low price to prevent customer turnover. Potential entrants such as the cable firms seek markets in which the entry barriers are relatively insignificant. An absence of entry barriers increases the probability that a new entrant can operate profitably. Several kinds of potentially significant entry barriers may discourage competitors.

Economies of Scale *Economies of scale* are derived from incremental efficiency improvements through experience as a firm grows larger. Therefore, as the quantity of a product produced during a given period increases, the cost of manufacturing each unit declines. Economies of scale can be developed in most business functions, such as marketing, manufacturing, research and development, and purchasing.[88] Increasing economies of scale enhances a firm's flexibility. For example, a firm may choose to reduce its price and capture a greater share of the market. Alternatively, it may keep its price constant to increase profits. In so doing, it likely will increase its free cash flow, which is helpful in times of recession.

New entrants face a dilemma when confronting current competitors' scale economies. Small-scale entry places them at a cost disadvantage. Alternatively, large-scale entry, in which the new entrant manufactures large volumes of a product to gain economies of scale, risks strong competitive retaliation.

Some competitive conditions reduce the ability of economies of scale to create an entry barrier. Many companies now customize their products for large numbers of small customer groups. Customized products are not manufactured in the volumes necessary to achieve economies of scale. Customization is made possible by new flexible manufacturing systems (this point is discussed further in Chapter 4). In fact, the new manufacturing technology facilitated by advanced information systems has allowed the development of mass customization in an increasing number of industries. Although customization is not appropriate for all products, mass customization has become increasingly common in manufacturing products.[89] In fact, online ordering has enhanced the ability of customers to obtain customized products. They are often referred to as "markets of one."[90] Companies manufacturing customized products learn how to respond quickly to customers' desires rather than develop scale economies.

Product Differentiation

Over time, customers may come to believe that a firm's product is unique. This belief can result from the firm's service to the customer, effective advertising campaigns, or being the first to market a good or service. Companies such as Coca-Cola, PepsiCo, and the world's automobile manufacturers spend a great deal of money on advertising to convince potential customers of their products' distinctiveness. Customers valuing a product's uniqueness tend to become loyal to both the product and the company producing it. Companies may also offer a series of different but highly related products to serve as an entry barrier (e.g., offering customers a variety of products from which to choose such as a series of different automobiles).[91] Typically, new entrants must allocate many resources over time to overcome existing customer loyalties. To combat the perception of uniqueness, new entrants frequently offer products at lower prices. This decision, however, may result in lower profits or even losses.

Capital Requirements

Competing in a new industry requires a firm to have resources to invest. In addition to physical facilities, capital is needed for inventories, marketing activities, and other critical business functions. Even when a new industry is attractive, the capital required for successful market entry may not be available to pursue the market opportunity. For example, defense industries are difficult to enter because of the substantial resource investments required to be competitive. In addition, because of the high knowledge requirements of the defense industry, a firm might enter the defense industry through the acquisition of an existing firm. But it must have access to the capital necessary to do it.

Switching Costs

Switching costs are the one-time costs customers incur when they buy from a different supplier. The costs of buying new ancillary equipment and of retraining employees, and even the psychic costs of ending a relationship, may be incurred in switching to a new supplier. In some cases, switching costs are low, such as when the consumer switches to a different soft drink. Switching costs can vary as a function of time. For example, in terms of credit hours toward graduation, the cost to a student to transfer from one university to another as a freshman is much lower than it is when the student is entering the senior year. Occasionally, a decision made by manufacturers to produce a new, innovative product creates high switching costs for the final consumer. Customer loyalty programs, such as airlines' frequent flyer miles, are intended to increase the customer's switching costs.

If switching costs are high, a new entrant must offer either a substantially lower price or a much better product to attract buyers. Usually, the more established the relationship between parties, the greater is the cost incurred to switch to an alternative offering.

Access to Distribution Channels   Over time, industry participants typically develop effective means of distributing products. Once a relationship with its distributors has been built, a firm will nurture it thus creating switching costs for the distributors. Access to distribution channels can be a strong entry barrier for new entrants, particularly in consumer nondurable goods industries (e.g., in grocery stores where shelf space is limited) and in international markets. New entrants have to persuade distributors to carry their products, either in addition to or in place of those currently distributed. Price breaks and cooperative advertising allowances may be used for this purpose; however, those practices reduce the new entrant's profit potential.

Cost Disadvantages Independent of Scale   Sometimes, established competitors have cost advantages that new entrants cannot duplicate. Proprietary product technology, favorable access to raw materials, desirable locations, and government subsidies are examples. Successful competition requires new entrants to reduce the strategic relevance of these factors. Delivering purchases directly to the buyer can counter the advantage of a desirable location; new food establishments in an undesirable location often follow this practice. Similarly, automobile dealerships located in unattractive areas (perhaps in a city's downtown area) can provide superior service (such as picking up the car to be serviced and delivering it to the customer thereafter) to overcome a competitor's location advantage.

Government Policy   Through licensing and permit requirements, governments can also control entry into an industry. Liquor retailing, radio and TV broadcasting, banking, and trucking are examples of industries in which government decisions and actions affect entry possibilities. Also, governments often restrict entry into some industries because of the need to provide quality service or the need to protect jobs. Alternatively, deregulation of industries, exemplified by the airline industry and utilities in the United States, allows more firms to enter.[92] Some of the most publicized government actions are those involving antitrust. For example, the U.S. and European Union governments pursued an antitrust case against Microsoft. The final settlement in the United States involved a relatively small penalty for the company. However, the EU judgments were more severe.[93] As noted in the earlier Strategic Focus, Google has been accused of violating antitrust laws but the government has not shown significant concern as yet.

Expected Retaliation

Firms seeking to enter an industry also anticipate the reactions of firms in the industry. An expectation of swift and vigorous competitive responses reduces the likelihood of entry. Vigorous retaliation can be expected when the existing firm has a major stake in the industry (e.g., it has fixed assets with few, if any, alternative uses), when it has substantial resources, and when industry growth is slow or constrained. For example, any firm attempting to enter the airline industry at the current time can expect significant retaliation from existing competitors due to overcapacity.

Locating market niches not being served by incumbents allows the new entrant to avoid entry barriers. Small entrepreneurial firms are generally best suited for identifying and serving neglected market segments. When Honda first entered the U.S. motorcycle market, it concentrated on small-engine motorcycles, a market that firms such as Harley-Davidson ignored. By targeting this neglected niche, Honda avoided competition. After consolidating its position, Honda used its strength to attack rivals by introducing larger motorcycles and competing in the broader market. Competitive actions and competitive responses between firms such as Honda and Harley-Davidson are discussed more fully in Chapter 5.

Bargaining Power of Suppliers

Increasing prices and reducing the quality of their products are potential means used by suppliers to exert power over firms competing within an industry. If a firm is unable to recover cost increases by its suppliers through its own pricing structure, its profitability is reduced by its suppliers' actions. A supplier group is powerful when

- It is dominated by a few large companies and is more concentrated than the industry to which it sells.
- Satisfactory substitute products are not available to industry firms.
- Industry firms are not a significant customer for the supplier group.
- Suppliers' goods are critical to buyers' marketplace success.
- The effectiveness of suppliers' products has created high switching costs for industry firms.
- It poses a credible threat to integrate forward into the buyers' industry. Credibility is enhanced when suppliers have substantial resources and provide a highly differentiated product.

The airline industry is one in which suppliers' bargaining power is changing. Though the number of suppliers is low, the demand for major aircraft is also relatively low. Boeing and Airbus strongly compete for most orders of major aircraft. However, China recently announced plans to build a large commercial aircraft that will compete with the aircraft sold by Boeing and Airbus. This competitive action could be highly significant because China is projected to buy 2,230 new commercial aircraft between 2007 and 2025.[94]

Bargaining Power of Buyers

Firms seek to maximize the return on their invested capital. Alternatively, buyers (customers of an industry or a firm) want to buy products at the lowest possible price—the point at which the industry earns the lowest acceptable rate of return on its invested capital. To reduce their costs, buyers bargain for higher quality, greater levels of service, and lower prices. These outcomes are achieved by encouraging competitive battles among the industry's firms. Customers (buyer groups) are powerful when

- They purchase a large portion of an industry's total output.
- The sales of the product being purchased account for a significant portion of the seller's annual revenues.
- They could switch to another product at little, if any, cost.
- The industry's products are undifferentiated or standardized, and the buyers pose a credible threat if they were to integrate backward into the sellers' industry.

Armed with greater amounts of information about the manufacturer's costs and the power of the Internet as a shopping and distribution alternative have increased consumers' bargaining power in many industries. One reason for this shift is that individual buyers incur virtually zero switching costs when they decide to purchase from one manufacturer rather than another or from one dealer as opposed to a second or third one.

Threat of Substitute Products

Substitute products are goods or services from outside a given industry that perform similar or the same functions as a product that the industry produces. For example, as a sugar substitute, NutraSweet (and other sugar substitutes) places an upper limit on sugar manufacturers' prices—NutraSweet and sugar perform the same function, though with different characteristics. Other product substitutes include e-mail and fax machines instead of overnight deliveries, plastic containers rather than glass jars, and tea instead of coffee. Newspaper firms have experienced significant circulation declines over the past 10 years. The declines are due to substitute outlets for news including Internet sources, cable television news channels, and e-mail and cell phone alerts. These products are increasingly popular, especially among younger people, and as product substitutes they have significant potential to continue to reduce overall newspaper circulation sales.

In general, product substitutes present a strong threat to a firm when customers face few, if any, switching costs and when the substitute product's price is lower or its quality and performance capabilities are equal to or greater than those of the competing product. Differentiating a product along dimensions that customers value (such as price, quality, service after the sale, and location) reduces a substitute's attractiveness. As the Strategic Focus illustrates, Google has market power because it is the largest and most often used search engine. As a result, advertisers clearly prefer Google over most of its competitors because it gives them access to the largest possible audience.

Intensity of Rivalry Among Competitors

Because an industry's firms are mutually dependent, actions taken by one company usually invite competitive responses. In many industries, firms actively compete against one another. Competitive rivalry intensifies when a firm is challenged by a competitor's actions or when a company recognizes an opportunity to improve its market position.

Firms within industries are rarely homogeneous; they differ in resources and capabilities and seek to differentiate themselves from competitors.[95] Typically, firms seek to differentiate their products from competitors' offerings in ways that customers value and in which the firms have a competitive advantage. Common dimensions on which rivalry is based include price, service after the sale, and innovation. As explained in the Opening Case, the rivalry between Wal-Mart and many of its competitors is intense. In fact, competitors have been making inroads into Wal-Mart's market share. Same-store sales by many of its competitors—Target, Costco, Kroger, Safeway, Walgreen's, CVS, and Best Buy—are growing two to five times faster than sales at existing Wal-Mart stores.

Next, we discuss the most prominent factors that experience shows to affect the intensity of firms' rivalries.

Numerous or Equally Balanced Competitors

Intense rivalries are common in industries with many companies. With multiple competitors, it is common for a few firms to believe that they can act without eliciting a response. However, evidence suggests that other firms generally are aware of competitors' actions, often choosing to respond to them. At the other extreme, industries with only a few firms of equivalent size and power also tend to have strong rivalries. The large and often similar-sized resource bases of these firms permit vigorous actions and responses. The competitive battles between Airbus and Boeing exemplify intense rivalry between relatively equivalent competitors, although Boeing's position relative to Airbus grew stronger in 2007.

Slow Industry Growth

When a market is growing, firms try to effectively use resources to serve an expanding customer base. Growing markets reduce the pressure to take customers from competitors. However, rivalry in no-growth or slow-growth markets (slow change) becomes more intense as firms battle to increase their market shares by attracting competitors' customers.[96]

Typically, battles to protect market share are fierce. Certainly, this has been the case in the airline industry. The instability in the market that results from these competitive engagements reduces profitability for all airlines throughout the industry.

High Fixed Costs or High Storage Costs

When fixed costs account for a large part of total costs, companies try to maximize the use of their productive capacity. Doing so allows the firm to spread costs across a larger volume of output. However, when many firms attempt to maximize their productive capacity, excess capacity is created on an industry-wide basis. To then reduce inventories, individual companies typically cut the price of their product and offer rebates and other special discounts to customers. However, these practices, common in the automobile manufacturing industry, often intensify competition. The pattern of excess capacity at the industry level followed by intense rivalry at the firm level is observed frequently in industries with high storage costs. Perishable products, for example, lose their value rapidly with the passage of time. As their inventories grow, producers of perishable goods often use pricing strategies to sell products quickly.

Lack of Differentiation or Low Switching Costs

When buyers find a differentiated product that satisfies their needs, they frequently purchase the product loyally over time. Industries with many companies that have successfully differentiated their products have less rivalry, resulting in lower competition for individual firms. Firms that develop and sustain a differentiated product that cannot be easily imitated by competitors often earn higher returns.[97] However, when buyers view products as commodities (i.e., as products with few differentiated features or capabilities), rivalry intensifies. In these instances, buyers' purchasing decisions are based primarily on price and, to a lesser degree, service. Personal computers have become a commodity product. Thus, the rivalry among Dell, HP, and other computer manufacturers is strong.

The effect of switching costs is similar to the effect of differentiated products. The lower the buyers' switching costs, the easier it is for competitors to attract buyers through pricing and service offerings. High switching costs partially insulate the firm from rivals' efforts to attract customers. Even though the switching costs—such as pilot and mechanic training—are high in aircraft purchases, the rivalry between Boeing and Airbus remains intense because the stakes for both are extremely high.

High Strategic Stakes

Competitive rivalry is likely to be high when it is important for several of the competitors to perform well in the market. For example, although it is diversified and is a market leader in other businesses, Samsung has targeted market leadership in the consumer electronics market and is doing quite well. This market is quite important to Sony and other major competitors, such as Hitachi, Matsushita, NEC, and Mitsubishi. The substantial rivalry in this market is likely to continue over the next few years.

High strategic stakes can also exist in terms of geographic locations. For example, Japanese automobile manufacturers are committed to a significant presence in the U.S. marketplace because it is the world's largest single market for automobiles and trucks. Because of the stakes involved in this country for Japanese and U.S. manufacturers, rivalry among firms in the U.S. and the global automobile industry is intense. It should be noted that while proximity tends to promote greater rivalry, physically proximate competition has potentially positive benefits as well. For example, when competitors are located near each other, it is easier for suppliers to serve them, and competitors can develop economies of scale that lead to lower production costs. Additionally, communications with key industry stakeholders such as suppliers are more efficient when they are close to the firm.[98]

High Exit Barriers

Sometimes companies continue competing in an industry even though the returns on their invested capital are low or negative. Firms making this choice likely face high exit barriers, which include economic, strategic, and emotional factors causing them to remain in an industry when the profitability of doing so is questionable. Exit barriers are especially high in the airline industry. Common exit barriers include the following:

- Specialized assets (assets with values linked to a particular business or location)
- Fixed costs of exit (such as labor agreements)
- Strategic interrelationships (relationships of mutual dependence, such as those between one business and other parts of a company's operations, including shared facilities and access to financial markets)
- Emotional barriers (aversion to economically justified business decisions because of fear for one's own career, loyalty to employees, and so forth)
- Government and social restrictions (often based on government concerns for job losses and regional economic effects; are more common outside the United States)

Interpreting Industry Analyses

Effective industry analyses are products of careful study and interpretation of data and information from multiple sources. A wealth of industry-specific data is available to be analyzed. Because of globalization, international markets and rivalries must be included in the firm's analyses. In fact, research shows that in some industries, international variables are more important than domestic ones as determinants of strategic competitiveness. Furthermore, because of the development of global markets, a country's borders no longer restrict industry structures. In fact, movement into international markets enhances the chances of success for new ventures as well as more established firms.[99]

Analysis of the five forces in the industry allows the firm to determine the industry's attractiveness in terms of the potential to earn adequate or superior returns. In general, the stronger competitive forces are, the lower the profit potential for an industry's firms. An unattractive industry has low entry barriers, suppliers and buyers with strong bargaining positions, strong competitive threats from product substitutes, and intense rivalry among competitors. These industry characteristics make it difficult for firms to achieve strategic competitiveness and earn above-average returns. Alternatively, an attractive industry has high entry barriers, suppliers and buyers with little bargaining power, few competitive threats from product substitutes, and relatively moderate rivalry.[100] Next, we turn to strategic groups operating within industries.

Strategic Groups

A set of firms that emphasize similar strategic dimensions and use a similar strategy is called a **strategic group**.[101] The competition between firms within a strategic group is greater than the competition between a member of a strategic group and companies outside that strategic group. Therefore, intrastrategic group competition is more intense than is interstrategic group competition. In fact, more heterogeneity is evident in the performance of firms within strategic groups than across the groups. The performance leaders within groups are able to follow strategies similar to those of other firms in the group and yet maintain strategic distinctiveness to gain and sustain a competitive advantage.[102]

A **strategic group** is a set of firms emphasizing similar strategic dimensions to use a similar strategy.

The extent of technological leadership, product quality, pricing policies, distribution channels, and customer service are examples of strategic dimensions that firms in a strategic group may treat similarly. Thus, membership in a particular strategic group defines the essential characteristics of the firm's strategy.[103]

The notion of strategic groups can be useful for analyzing an industry's competitive structure. Such analyses can be helpful in diagnosing competition, positioning, and the profitability of firms within an industry.[104] High mobility barriers, high rivalry, and low resources among the firms within an industry will limit the formation of strategic groups.[105] However, research suggests that after strategic groups are formed, their membership remains relatively stable over time, making analysis easier and more useful.[106]

Using strategic groups to understand an industry's competitive structure requires the firm to plot companies' competitive actions and competitive responses along strategic dimensions such as pricing decisions, product quality, distribution channels, and so forth. This type of analysis shows the firm how certain companies are competing similarly in terms of how they use similar strategic dimensions. For example, companies may use unique radio markets because consumers prefer different music formats and programming (news radio, talk radio, etc.). Typically, a radio format is created through choices made regarding music or nonmusic style, scheduling, and announcer style. It is estimated that approximately 30 different radio formats exist, suggesting the presence of many strategic groups in this industry. The strategies within each of the 30 groups are similar, while the strategies across the total set of strategic groups are dissimilar. As a result, Clear Channel Communications often owns several stations in a large city, but each uses a different format. Therefore, Clear Channel likely has stations operating in most or all of the 30 strategic groups in this industry. Additionally, a new strategic group has been added as the satellite radio companies XM and SIRIUS have formed an intense rivalry in trying to attract corporate customers such as auto manufacturers and rental car companies as well as individual subscribers.[107] Satellite radio could be considered a substitute because it is technologically different from terrestrial radio, but the satellite companies, each with more than 100 different channels, offer the same types of music formats and programming that traditional stations do. Although satellite companies obtain most of their revenue from subscriptions, they are similar to terrestrial radio in that some advertising is done on talk, news, and sports channels. Firms can increase their understanding of competition in the commercial radio industry by plotting companies' actions and responses in terms of important strategic dimensions mentioned previously. With the addition of satellite radio, the competition among different strategic groups has increased.

Strategic groups have several implications. First, because firms within a group offer similar products to the same customers, the competitive rivalry among them can be intense. The more intense the rivalry, the greater the threat to each firm's profitability. Second, the strengths of the five industry forces (the threats posed by new entrants, the power of suppliers, the power of buyers, product substitutes, and the intensity of rivalry among competitors) differ across strategic groups. Third, the closer the strategic groups are in terms of their strategies, the greater is the likelihood of rivalry between the groups.

Having a thorough understanding of primary competitors helps a firm formulate and implement an appropriate strategy. Clearly XM and SIRIUS are in a strategic group and compete directly against each other. XM has been successful in its focus on new technology, while SIRIUS has focused on signing innovative and exclusive content. Volkswagen tried to break out of its strategic group of companies selling mid-priced autos. But it was unsuccessful in entering the strategic group of firms with similar strategies selling premium autos (e.g., Mercedes-Benz, BMW). Because of these efforts, VW lost market share in its primary markets.[108]

IBM has been a pioneer in the introduction of new technology but also more recently in analyzing its industry and major competitors. As explained in the Strategic Focus, IBM carefully analyzes its major competitors and formulates a new strategy or adjusts its existing strategy to maintain is competitive advantage. The knowledge gained from its team's analysis of Hewlett-Packard and Sun Microsystems helped it

IBM Closely Watches Its Competitors to Stay at the Top of Its Game

It is critical for companies to study their major rivals to help them shape and implement their strategies to counter competitors' strengths and to exploit their weaknesses. Armed with effective analyses of competitors, companies can enhance their market position and increase returns on their investments. International Business Machines (IBM) is the world's top provider of computer products and services. IBM makes mainframes and servers, storage systems, and peripherals, but also has the largest computer service unit in the world; it accounts for more than half of IBM's total revenue. To remain competitive in its various markets, IBM established a competitive analysis team with the sole purpose of observing and analyzing competitors such as Hewlett-Packard (HP) and Sun Microsystems. IBM uses the data from these analyses to adjust its strategies and business plans accordingly to ensure that the firm effectively competes with its major rivals.

IBM's competitive analysis team found that Sun's direct sales team focuses on the top 1,500 accounts in its installed base, and that its remaining customers are being serviced by business partners. The IBM team also found that Sun's sales reps primarily emphasize selling hardware instead of solutions, a definitive weakness that provided opportunities for IBM to take away customers from Sun. In addition, IBM's team carefully analyzed a large number of HP announcements for its e-business weak points in its high availability campaign. IBM said that the 5Minutes campaign is only a vision that has little business value for its customers, but the campaign has strong marketing value for HP. The analysis showed that HP has low software and services revenues and thus is primarily a hardware company. HP lost approximately 15 percent of its potential customers because it lacked its own support and consulting services and is too reliant on EDS, Accenture, Cisco, and HP resellers.

IBM's competitive analysis teams observe and analyze competitors such as Hewlett-Packard and Sun Microsystems.

IBM was a pioneer of the multinational business model. It created mini-IBMs in each country each with its own administration, manufacturing, and service operations. Based on the analyses of rival Indian technology companies, IBM identified that a flatter structure and leaner organization was needed to compete effectively. Likewise the competitor analyses discovered that Chinese competitors provided high-quality goods and services for a much lower price. These competitor analyses led IBM to develop global integrated operations. IBM's global shift makes it possible to use lower-cost talent in India to manage machines and software in data centers. In addition, the data centers are interchangeable, so if India has problems, IBM can reroute computing jobs and calls to other locations. Eventually, international competitors will build global delivery hubs, but they will be unlikely to compete with IBM's scientific research capabilities. IBM's integrated global services and research organizations enable it to design innovative services. The cost savings achieved through its global integration efforts lead to a higher earnings growth. The overall goal of this global integration plan is to lower costs while simultaneously providing superior services to customers. In doing so, IBM can enhance its competitiveness, increase its market share, and drive revenue and profit growth.

Based on the information obtained from recent competitor analyses, IBM decided only a few adjustments were needed. For example, IBM decided to emphasize its higher-margin business consulting services, which help companies change the way they operate,

and to focus less on technology integration. IBM also changed the strategy of its software division. Because software is the fastest-growing and most profitable segment of the company, IBM has made several acquisitions of software companies, including FileNet, MRO Software, and Webify Solutions. These acquisitions fill holes in IBM's product portfolio and increase its ability to compete effectively with Sun Microsystems and similar rivals.

IBM's strategic actions are creating positive results. Total revenues for the first quarter of 2007 reached $22.0 billion, an increase of 7 percent from the first quarter of 2006. First-quarter 2007 income increased 8 percent over 2006 to $1.8 billion. And, its first-quarter 2007 earnings of $1.21 per share represented an increase of 12 percent over the first quarter of 2006.

Sources: S. Hamm, 2006, Big Blue shift, *BusinessWeek*, http://www.businessweek.com, June 6; T. P. Morgan, 1999, IBM's competitive analysis on Sun, HP, *Computergram International*, http://www.findarticles.com, Oct. 4; LEX: IBM, 2005, *Financial Times*, http://www.ft.com, May 5; S. Hamm, 2006, IBM's revved-up software engine, *BusinessWeek*, http://www.businessweek.com, Aug. 15; J. Krippel, 2007, International Business Machines Corporation, *Hoovers*, http://www.hoovers.com; 2007, http://www.ibm.com/news, May 5.

adjust its strategy and particularly remain at the forefront of its industry in computer and support services. To maintain that competitive advantage, IBM not only continues to improve its internal service capabilities but also adds to its portfolio by acquiring other high-quality, special-purpose service firms. It could not effectively design a strategy to maintain its competitive advantage without the knowledge gained from the analysis of its competitors.

Competitor Analysis

The competitor environment is the final part of the external environment requiring study. Competitor analysis focuses on each company against which a firm directly competes. For example, XM and SIRIUS satellite radio, Home Depot and Lowe's, and Boeing and Airbus should be keenly interested in understanding each other's objectives, strategies, assumptions, and capabilities. Furthermore, intense rivalry creates a strong need to understand competitors.[109] In a competitor analysis, the firm seeks to understand the following:

- What drives the competitor, as shown by its *future objectives*
- What the competitor is doing and can do, as revealed by its *current strategy*
- What the competitor believes about the industry, as shown by its *assumptions*
- What the competitor's capabilities are, as shown by its *strengths* and *weaknesses*[110]

Information about these four dimensions helps the firm prepare an anticipated response profile for each competitor (see Figure 2.3). The results of an effective competitor analysis help a firm understand, interpret, and predict its competitors' actions and responses. Understanding the actions of competitors clearly contributes to the firm's ability to compete successfully within the industry.[111] Interestingly, research suggests that analyzing possible reactions to competitive moves is not often carried out by executives.[112] This evidence suggests that those firms conducting such analyses can obtain a competitive advantage over firms that do not.

Critical to an effective competitor analysis is gathering data and information that can help the firm understand its competitors' intentions and the strategic implications resulting from them.[113] Useful data and information combine to form **competitor intelligence:** the set of data and information the firm gathers to better understand and better

Competitor intelligence is the set of data and information the firm gathers to better understand and better anticipate competitors' objectives, strategies, assumptions, and capabilities.

Figure 2.3 Competitor Analysis Components

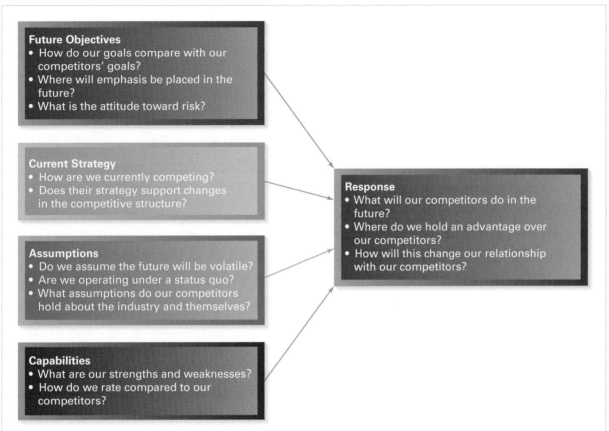

anticipate competitors' objectives, strategies, assumptions, and capabilities. In competitor analysis, the firm should gather intelligence not only about its competitors, but also regarding public policies in countries around the world. Such intelligence facilitates an understanding of the strategic posture of foreign competitors.

Through effective competitive and public policy intelligence, the firm gains the insights needed to make effective strategic decisions about how to compete against its rivals. Microsoft continues to analyze its competitor Google for ways to overcome and dominate the search engine business as it did in the browser contest with Netscape. *Fortune* magazine reported that Bill Gates, Microsoft's founder, was doing his own competitive intelligence on Google by browsing Google's Web site when he came across a help-wanted page: "Why, he wondered, were the qualifications for so many of them identical to Microsoft job specs? Google was a Web search business, yet here on the screen were postings for engineers with backgrounds that had nothing to do with search and everything to do with Microsoft's core businesspeople trained in things like operating-system design, compiler optimization, and distributed-systems architecture. Gates wondered whether Microsoft might be facing much more than a war in search. An e-mail he sent to a handful of execs that day said, in effect, 'We have to watch these guys. It looks like they are building something to compete with us.'"[114]

Microsoft has found Google to be a formidable competitor. As such, Microsoft has again explored a merger with Yahoo! Inc. in an effort to compete more effectively with Google. However, this announcement had no notable effect on Google's stock, suggesting that investors do not see such a merger as a competitive threat to Google. In 2007,

STRATEGY RIGHT NOW

Google has approximately 54 percent of the market for Internet searches, whereas Yahoo! has 22 percent of the market and MSN (Microsoft) has 10 percent. For 2007, it is projected that Google will garner almost 76 percent of the paid search advertising with Yahoo! garnering slightly over 16 percent and all others slightly over 8 percent combined. Some believe that a merger of Microsoft and Yahoo! would add value by integrating their respective strengths. Yet, most analysts do not agree. One Internet analyst suggested that "Instead of getting bigger, these companies need to think about getting smarter. I don't think that a partnership is necessarily going to achieve that goal."[115]

As the preceding analysis of Google suggests, one must also pay attention to the complementors of a firm's products and strategy.[116] **Complementors** are the network of companies that sell complementary goods or services or are compatible with the focal firm's own product or service. These firms might also include suppliers and buyers who have a strong "network" relationship with the focal firm. A strong network of complementors can solidify a competitive advantage, as it has in Google's case because of the number of Internet access products with which it functions smoothly. If a complementor's good or service adds value to the sale of the focal firm's good or service it is likely to create value for the focal firm. For example, a range of complements are necessary to sell automobiles, including financial services to arrange credit, luxury options including stereo equipment, and extended warranties. For this reason, analyzing competitors requires that its alliance network also be analyzed (see Chapter 9 for a complete examination of firm network and alliance strategies).[117] For example, a strength of Lufthansa and United is their participation in the STAR Alliance, an international network of commercial airlines. Firms must also be careful to identify the actions of firms that are performing poorly. Research suggests that some of these firms may find ways to create value and regain a competitive advantage or at least achieve competitive parity with specially designed strategic actions to turn around their performance.[118] Overlooking such firms in competitor analyses could be an error.

Ethical Considerations

Firms should follow generally accepted ethical practices in gathering competitor intelligence. Industry associations often develop lists of these practices that firms can adopt. Practices considered both legal and ethical include (1) obtaining publicly available information (e.g., court records, competitors' help-wanted advertisements, annual reports, financial reports of publicly held corporations, and Uniform Commercial Code filings), and (2) attending trade fairs and shows to obtain competitors' brochures, view their exhibits, and listen to discussions about their products.

In contrast, certain practices (including blackmail, trespassing, eavesdropping, and stealing drawings, samples, or documents) are widely viewed as unethical and often are illegal. To protect themselves from digital fraud or theft by competitors that break into their employees' PCs, some companies buy insurance to protect against PC hacking.[119]

Some competitor intelligence practices may be legal, but a firm must decide whether they are also ethical, given the image it desires as a corporate citizen. Especially with electronic transmissions, the line between legal and ethical practices can be difficult to determine. For example, a firm may develop Web site addresses that are similar to those of its competitors and thus occasionally receive e-mail transmissions that were intended for those competitors. The practice is an example of the challenges companies face in deciding how to gather intelligence about competitors while simultaneously determining how to prevent competitors from learning too much about them.

Open discussions of intelligence-gathering techniques can help a firm ensure that employees, customers, suppliers, and even potential competitors understand its convictions to follow ethical practices for gathering competitor intelligence. An appropriate guideline for competitor intelligence practices is to respect the principles of common morality and the right of competitors not to reveal certain information about their products, operations, and strategic intentions.[120]

Summary

- The firm's external environment is challenging and complex. Because of the external environment's effect on performance, the firm must develop the skills required to identify opportunities and threats existing in that environment.

- The external environment has three major parts: (1) the general environment (elements in the broader society that affect industries and their firms), (2) the industry environment (factors that influence a firm, its competitive actions and responses, and the industry's profit potential), and (3) the competitor environment (in which the firm analyzes each major competitor's future objectives, current strategies, assumptions, and capabilities).

- The external environmental analysis process has four steps: scanning, monitoring, forecasting, and assessing. Through environmental analyses, the firm identifies opportunities and threats.

- The general environment has six segments: demographic, economic, political/legal, sociocultural, technological, and global. For each segment, the firm wants to determine the strategic relevance of environmental changes and trends.

- Compared with the general environment, the industry environment has a more direct effect on the firm's strategic actions. The five forces model of competition includes the threat of entry, the power of suppliers, the power of buyers, product

substitutes, and the intensity of rivalry among competitors. By studying these forces, the firm finds a position in an industry where it can influence the forces in its favor or where it can buffer itself from the power of the forces in order to earn above-average returns.

- Industries are populated with different strategic groups. A strategic group is a collection of firms that follow similar strategies along similar dimensions. Competitive rivalry is greater within a strategic group than it is between strategic groups.

- Competitor analysis informs the firm about the future objectives, current strategies, assumptions, and capabilities of the companies with which it competes directly. A thorough analysis examines complementors that sustain a competitor's strategy and major networks or alliances in which competitors participate. They should also attempt to identify and carefully monitor major actions taken by firms with performance below the industry norm.

- Different techniques are used to create competitor intelligence: the set of data, information, and knowledge that allows the firm to better understand its competitors and thereby predict their likely strategic and tactical actions. Firms should use only legal and ethical practices to gather intelligence. The Internet enhances firms' capabilities to gather insights about competitors and their strategic intentions.

Review Questions

1. Why is it important for a firm to study and understand the external environment?

2. What are the differences between the general environment and the industry environment? Why are these differences important?

3. What is the external environmental analysis process (four steps)? What does the firm want to learn when using this process?

4. What are the six segments of the general environment? Explain the differences among them.

5. How do the five forces of competition in an industry affect its profit potential? Explain.

6. What is a strategic group? Of what value is knowledge of the firm's strategic group in formulating that firm's strategy?

7. What is the importance of collecting and interpreting data and information about competitors? What practices should a firm use to gather competitor intelligence and why?

1. S. R. Miller & L. Eden, 2006, Local density and foreign subsidiary performance, *Academy of Management Journal,* 49: 341–355; C. Williams & W. Mitchell, 2004, Focusing firm evolution: The impact of information infrastructure on market entry by U.S. telecommunications companies, 1984–1998, *Management Science,* 5: 1561–1575;.

2. J. Weiser, 2007, Untapped: Strategies for success in underserved markets, *Journal of Business Strategy,* 28(2): 30–37; J. Tan, 2005, Venturing in turbulent water: A historical perspective of economic reform and entrepreneurial transformation, *Journal of Business Venturing,* 20: 689–704; P. Chattopadhyay, W. H. Glick, & G. P. Huber, 2001, Organizational actions in response to threats and opportunities, *Academy of Management Journal,* 44: 937–955.

3. J. Gimeno, R. E. Hoskisson, B. D. Beal, & W. P. Wan, 2005, Explaining the clustering of international expansion moves: A critical test in the U.S. telecommunications industry, *Academy of Management Journal,* 48: 297–319; C. M. Grimm, H. Lee, & K. G. Smith, 2005, *Strategy as Action: Competitive Dynamics and Competitive Advantages,* New York: Oxford University Press.

4. J.-P. Bonardi, G. I. F. Holburn, & R. G. Vanden Bergh, 2006, Nonmarket strategy performance: Evidence from U.S. electric utilities, *Academy of Management Journal,* 49: 1209–1228; S. Rangan & A. Drummond, 2004, Explaining outcomes in competition among foreign multinationals in a focal host market, *Strategic Management Journal,* 25: 285–293;

5. M. Delmas, M.V. Russo, & M. J. Montes-Sancho, 2007, Deregulation and environmental differentiation in the electric utility industry, *Strategic Management Journal,* 28: 189–209.

6. G. Szulanski & R. J. Jensen, 2006, Presumptive adaptation and the effectiveness of knowledge transfer, *Strategic Management Journal,* 27: 937–957; K. G. Smith, C. J. Collins, & K. D. Clark, 2005, Existing knowledge, knowledge creation capability, and the rate of new product introduction in high-technology firms, *Academy of Management Journal,* 48: 346–357.

7. C. Eesley & M. J. Lenox, 2006, Firm responses to secondary stakeholder action, *Strategic Management Journal,* 27: 765–781; R. M. Grant, 2003, Strategic planning in a turbulent environment: Evidence from the oil majors, *Strategic Management Journal,* 24: 491–517.

8. M. T. Dacin, C. Oliver, & J.-P. Roy, 2007, The legitimacy of strategic alliances: An institutional perspective, *Strategic Management Journal,*

28: 169–187; M. Song, C. Droge, S. Hanvanich, & R. Calantone, 2005, Marketing and technology resource complementarity: An analysis of their interaction effect in two environmental contexts, *Strategic Management Journal,* 26: 259–276;

9. L. Fahey, 1999, *Competitors,* New York: John Wiley & Sons; B. A. Walters & R. L. Priem, 1999, Business strategy and CEO intelligence acquisition, *Competitive Intelligence Review,* 10(2): 15–22.

10. J. C. Short, D. J. Ketchen, Jr., T. B. Palmer, & G. T. Hult, 2007, Firm, strategic group, and industry influences on performance, *Strategic Management Journal,* 28: 147–167.

11. R. D. Ireland & M. A. Hitt, 1999, Achieving and maintaining strategic competitiveness in the 21st century: The role of strategic leadership, *Academy of Management Executive,* 13(1): 43–57; M. A. Hitt, B. W. Keats, & S. M. DeMarie, 1998, Navigating in the new competitive landscape: Building strategic flexibility and competitive advantage in the 21st century, *Academy of Management Executive,* 12(4): 22–42.

12. L. Välikangas & M. Gibbert, 2005, Boundary-setting strategies for escaping innovation traps, *MIT Sloan Management Review,* 46(3): 58–65.

13. Characteristics of the civilian labor force, 2004 and 2014, 2007. *Infoplease,* http://www.infoplease.com, May 2.

14. G. Panagiotou, 2003, Bring SWOT into focus, *Business Strategy Review,* 14(2): 8–10.

15. P. Lattman, 2005, Rebound, *Forbes,* March 28, 58.

16. K. M. Patton & T. M. McKenna, 2005, Scanning for competitive intelligence, *Competitive Intelligence Magazine,* 8(2): 24–26; D. F. Kuratko, R. D. Ireland, & J. S. Hornsby, 2001, Improving firm performance through entrepreneurial actions: Acordia's corporate entrepreneurship strategy, *Academy of Management Executive,* 15(4): 60–71.

17. K. M. Eisenhardt, 2002, Has strategy changed? *MIT Sloan Management Review,* 43(2): 88–91; I. Goll & A. M. A. Rasheed, 1997, Rational decision-making and firm performance: The moderating role of environment, *Strategic Management Journal,* 18: 583–591.

18. J. R. Hough & M. A. White, 2004, Scanning actions and environmental dynamism: Gathering information for strategic decision making, *Management Decision,* 42: 781–793; V. K. Garg, B. A. Walters, & R. L. Priem, 2003, Chief executive scanning emphases, environmental dynamism, and manufacturing firm performance, *Strategic Management Journal,* 24: 725–744.

19. C.-P. Wei & Y.-H. Lee, 2004, Event detection from online news documents for supporting environmental scanning, *Decision Support Systems,* 36: 385–401.

20. N. Anderson, 2007, FTC to Congress: Spyware purveyors need to do hard time, *Ars Technica,* http://www.arstechnica.com, April 11.

21. Fahey, *Competitors,* 71–73.

22. Characteristics of the civilian labor force, 2004 and 2014, *Infoplease;* P. Yip, 1999, The road to wealth, *Dallas Morning News,* August 2, D1, D3.

23. F. Dahlsten, 2003, Avoiding the customer satisfaction rut, *MIT Sloan Management Review,* 44(4): 73–77; Y. Luo & S. H. Park, 2001, Strategic alignment and performance of market-seeking MNCs in China, *Strategic Management Journal,* 22: 141–155.

24. K. Buysse & A. Verbke, 2003, Proactive strategies: A stakeholder management perspective, *Strategic Management Journal,* 24: 453–470; I. M. Jawahar & G. L. McLaughlin, 2001, Toward a prescriptive stakeholder theory: An organizational life cycle approach, *Academy of Management Review,* 26: 397–414.

25. M. L. Perry, S. Sengupta, & R. Krapfel, 2004, Effectiveness of horizontal strategic alliances in technologically uncertain environments: Are trust and commitment enough, *Journal of Business Research,* 9: 951–956; M. Song & M. M. Montoya-Weiss, 2001, The effect of perceived technological uncertainty on Japanese new product development, *Academy of Management Journal,* 44: 61–80.

26. F. Sanna-Randaccio & R. Veugelers, 2007, Multinational knowledge spillovers with decentralized R&D: A game theoretic approach, *Journal of International Business Studies,* 38: 47–63.

27. Fahey, *Competitors.*

28. Alcas corporation, 2007, http://www.alcas.com, May 5; K. Schelfhaudt & V. Crittenden, 2005, Growing pains for Alcas Corporation, *Journal of Business Research,* 58: 999–1002.

29. Fahey, *Competitors,* 75–77.

30. K. M. Sutcliffe & K. Weber, 2003, The high cost of accurate knowledge, *Harvard Business Review,* 81(5): 74–82.

31. J. M. Pappas & B. Wooldridge, 2007, Middle managers' divergent strategic activity: an investigation of multiple measures of network centrality, *Journal of Management Studies,* 44: 323–341; L. Fahey & V. K. Narayanan, 1986, *Macroenvironmental Analysis for Strategic Management,* St. Paul, MN: West Publishing Company, 58.

32. 2006, World Population Prospects: 2006, http://www.esa.un.org. May 5, 2007.

33. Ibid.; S. Moffett, 2005, Fast-aging Japan keeps its elders on the job longer, *Wall Street Journal,* June 15, A1, A8.

34. Ibid.; 2006, Per capita health expenditures, by country, *Infoplease*, http://www.infoplease.com, May 4, 2007; T. Fennell, 2005, The next 50 years, http://www.camagazine.com, April.

35. J. Ordonez, 2005, 'Speak English. Live Latin,' *Newsweek*, May 30, 30.

36. The growing Hispanic market in the United States, 2007, *Strictly Spanish Communications*, http://www.strictlyspanish.com, May 5.

37. J. A. Chatman & S. E. Spataro, 2005, Using self-categorization theory to understand relational demography-based variations in people's responsiveness to organizational culture, *Academy of Management Journal*, 48: 321–331.

38. Characteristics of the civilian labor force, 2004 and 2014, *Infoplease*.

39. J. Millman, 2005, Low-wage U.S. jobs get "Mexicanized," but there's a price, *Wall Street Journal*, May 2, A2.

40. A. McKeown, 2007, Periodizing globalization, *History Workshop Journal*, 63(1): 218–230.

41. R. Konopaske, C. Robie, & J. M. Ivancevich, 2005, A preliminary model of spouse influence on managerial global assignment willingness, *International Journal of Human Resource Management*, 16: 405–426.

42. A. Jones & N. Ennis, 2007, Bringing the environment into economic development, *Local Economy*, 22(1): 1–5; Fahey & Narayanan, *Macroenvironmental Analysis*, 105.

43. G. Ip, 2003, Federal Reserve maintains interest-rate target at 1%, *Wall Street Journal Online*, http://www.wsj.com, August 13.

44. GDP Picture, 2007, Economic Policy Institute, http://www.epi.org, April 27; Economists cut GDP forecast for 2007, 2007, Yahoo! News, news.yahoo.com, April 10.

45. J.-P. Bonardi, A. J. Hillman, & G. D. Keim, 2005, The attractiveness of political markets: Implications for firm strategy, *Academy of Management Review*, 30: 397–413; G. Keim, 2001, Business and public policy: Competing in the political marketplace, in M. A. Hitt, R. E. Freeman, and J. S. Harrison (eds.), *Handbook of Strategic Management*, Oxford, UK: Blackwell Publishers, 583–601.

46. W. Chen, 2007, Does the colour of the cat matter? The red hat strategy in China's private enterprises, *Management and Organizational Review*, 3: 55–80; I. P. Mahmood & C. Rufin, 2005, Governments' dilemma: The role of government in imitation and innovation, *Academy of Management Review*, 30: 338–360

47. M. A. Hitt, L. Bierman, K. Uhlenbruck, & K. Shimizu, 2006, The importance of resources in the internationalization of professional service firms: The good, the bad, and the ugly, *Academy of Management Journal*, 49: 1137–1157; D. A. Schuler, K. Rehbein, & R. D. Cramer, 2003, Pursuing strategic advantage through political means: A multivariate approach, *Academy of Management Journal*, 45: 659–672.

48. C. Hutzler, 2005, Beijing rescinds textile duties, slams U.S., EU on import limits, *Wall Street Journal*, May 31, A3.

49. J. P. Doh & T. R. Guay, 2006, Corporate social responsibility, public policy and NGO activism in Europe and the United States: An institutional-stakeholder perspective, *Journal of Management Studies*, 43: 48–73.

50. Per capita health expenditures, by country, 2006. *Infoplease*, http://www.infoplease.com, May 6, 2007; 2003, U.S. spends the most on healthcare but dollars do not equal health, *Medica Portal*, http://www.medica.de.

51. C. Debaise, 2005, U. S. workers start early on retirement savings, *Wall Street Journal*, January 20, D2.

52. Characteristics of the civilian labor force, 2004 and 2014, *Infoplease*; 2005, U.S. Department of Labor, Bureau of Labor Statistics data, http://www.bls.gov, April.

53. M. E. A. Jayne & R. L. Dipboye, 2004, Leveraging diversity to improve business performance: Research findings and recommendations for organizations, *Human Resource Management*, 43: 409–425.

54. M. J. McCarthy, 2004, New outposts: Granbury, Texas, isn't a rural town: It's a 'micropolis'; Census Bureau adopts term for main street America, and marketers take note; beans, ribs and Starbucks, *Wall Street Journal*, June 3, A1.

55. T. Fleming, 2003, Benefits of taking the superhighway to work, *Canadian HR Reporter*, 16(11): G7.

56. B. L. Kirkman, K. B. Lowe, & C. B. Gibson, 2006, A quarter of a century of culture's consequences: A review old empirical research incorporating Hofstede's cultural values framework, *Journal of International Business Studies*, 37: 285–320.

57. S. Michailova & K. Hutchings, 2006, National cultural influences on knowledge sharing: A comparison of China and Russia, *Journal of Management Studies*, 43: 384–405.

58. P. J. Buckley, J. Clegg, & H. Tan, 2006, Cultural awareness in knowledge transfer to China—The role of guanxi and mianzi, *Journal of World Business*, 41: 275–288.

59. A. L. Porter & S. W. Cunningham, 2004, Tech mining: Exploiting new technologies for competitive advantage, Hoboken, NJ: Wiley.

60. D. Lavie, 2006, Capability reconfiguration: An analysis of incumbent responses to technological change, *Academy of Management Review*, 31: 153–174; C. W. L. Hill & F. T. Rothaermel, 2003, The performance of incumbent firms in the face of radical technological innovation, *Academy of Management Review*, 28: 257–274;

61. M. Marr, 2005, How DreamWorks misjudged DVD sales of its monster hit, *Wall Street Journal*, May 31, A1, A9.

62. N. Wingfield, 2003, Anytime, anywhere: The number of Wi-Fi spots is set to explode, bringing the wireless technology to the rest of us, *Wall Street Journal*, March 31, R6, R12.

63. R. Sampson, 2007, R&D alliances and firm performance: The impact of technological diversity and alliance organization on innovation, *Academy of Management Journal*, 50: 364–386; A. Andal-Ancion, P. A. Cartwright, & G. S. Yip, 2003, The digital transformation of traditional businesses, *MIT Sloan Management Review*, 44(4): 34–41.

64. Y. Y. Kor & J. T. Mahoney, 2005, How dynamics, management, and governance of resource deployments influence firm-level performance, *Strategic Management Journal*, 26: 489–497; C. Nichols-Nixon & C. Y. Woo, 2003, Technology sourcing and output of established firms in a regime of encompassing technological change, *Strategic Management Journal*, 24: 651–666.

65. W. P. Wan, 2005, Country resource environments, firm capabilities, and corporate diversification strategies, *Journal of Management Studies*, 42: 161–182; M. Wright, I. Filatotchev, R. E. Hoskisson, & M. W. Peng, 2005, Strategy research in emerging economies: Challenging the conventional wisdom, *Journal of Management Studies*, 42: 1–30.

66. F. Vermeulen & H. Barkema, 2002, Pace, rhythm, and scope: Process dependence in building a multinational corporation, *Strategic Management Journal*, 23: 637–653.

67. M. A. Hitt, L. Tihanyi, T. Miller, & B. Connelly, 2006, International diversification: Antecedents, outcomes, and moderators, *Journal of Management*, 32: 831–867; F. T. Rothaermel, S. Kotha, & H. K. Steensma, 2006, International market entry by U.S. Internet firms: An empirical analysis of country risk, national culture, and market size, *Journal of Management*, 32: 56–82;

68. V. Nee, S. Opper, & S. Wong, 2007, Developmental state and corporate governance in China, *Managemement and Organization Review*, 3: 19–53; G. D. Bruton & D. Ahlstrom, 2002, An institutional view of China's venture capital industry: Explaining the differences between China and the West, *Journal of Business Venturing*, 18: 233–259.

69. M. Fong, 2005, Unphased by barriers, retailers flock to China for clothes, *Wall Street Journal*, May 27, B1, B2.

70. K. Cattani, E. Dahan, & G. Schmidt, 2005, Offshoring versus "Spackling," *MIT Sloan Management Review*, 46(3): 6–7.

71. F. T. Rothaermel, M. A. Hitt, & L. Jobe, 2006, Balancing vertical integration and strategic outsourcing: Effects on product portfolio, product success, and firm performance, *Journal of Management*, 27: 1033–1056.

72. R. D. Ireland, M. A. Hitt, S. M. Camp, & D. L. Sexton, 2001, Integrating entrepreneurship and strategic management actions to create firm wealth, *Academy of Management Executive*, 15(1): 49–63.

73. S. Li & H. Scullion, 2006, Bridging the distance: Managing cross-border knowledge holders, *Asia Pacific Journal of Management*, 23: 71–92; Z. Emden, A. Yaprak, & S. T. Cavusgil, 2005, Learning from experience in international alliances: Antecedents and firm performance implications, *Journal of Business Research*, 58: 883–892.

74. G. D. Bruton, D. Ahlstrom, & J. C. Wan, 2003, Turnaround in East Asian firms: Evidence from ethnic overseas Chinese communities, *Strategic Management Journal*, 24: 519–540; S. H. Park & Y. Luo, 2001, Guanxi and organizational dynamics: Organizational networking in Chinese firms, *Strategic Management Journal*, 22: 455–477; M. A. Hitt, M. T. Dacin, B. B. Tyler, & D. Park, 1997, Understanding the differences in Korean and U.S. executives' strategic orientations, *Strategic Management Journal*, 18: 159–167.

75. M. A. Hitt, D. Ahlstrom, M. T. Dacin, E. Levitas, & L. Svobodina, 2004, The institutional effects on strategic alliance partner selection: China versus Russia, *Organization Science*, 15: 173–185.

76. J. A. Mathews, 2006, Dragon multinationals: New players in 21st century globalization, *Asia Pacific Journal of Management*, 23: 5–27.

77. K. E. Meyer, 2006, Globalfocusing: From domestic conglomerates to global specialists, *Journal of Management Studies*, 43: 1110–1144.

78. C. H. Oh & A.M. Rugman, 2007, Regional multinationals and the Korean cosmetics industry, *Asia Pacific Journal of Management*, 24: 27–42.

79. C. A. Bartlett & S. Ghoshal, 2003, What is a global manager? *Harvard Business Review*, 81(8): 101–108; M. A. Carpenter & J. W. Fredrickson, 2001, Top management teams, global strategic posture and the moderating role of uncertainty, *Academy of Management Journal*, 44: 533–545.

80. V. K. Narayanan & L. Fahey, 2005, The relevance of the institutional underpinnings of Porter's five forces framework to emerging economies: An epistemological analysis, *Journal of Management Studies*, 42: 207–223; N. Argyres & A. M. McGahan, 2002, An interview with Michael Porter, *Academy of Management Executive*, 16(2): 43–52.

81. V. F. Misangyi, H. Elms, T. Greckhamer, & J. A. Lepine, 2006, A new perspective on a fundamental debate: A multilevel approach to industry, corporate, and business unit effects, *Strategic Management Journal*, 27: 571–590; G. Hawawini, V. Subramanian, & P. Verdin, 2003, Is performance driven by industry or firm-specific factors? A new look at the evidence, *Strategic Management Journal*, 24: 1–16.

82. S. Zaheer & A. Zaheer, 2001, Market microstructure in a global b2b network, *Strategic Management Journal*, 22: 859–873.

83. M. A. Hitt, J. E. Ricart, & R. D. Nixon, 1998, The new frontier, in M. A. Hitt, J. E. Ricart, & R. D. Nixon (eds.), *Managing Strategically in an Interconnected World*, Chichester: John Wiley & Sons, 3–12.

84. Gimeno, Hoskisson, Beal, & Wan, Explaining the clustering of international expansion moves; C. Garcia-Pont & N. Nohria, 2002, Local versus global mimetism: The dynamics of alliance formation in the automobile industry, *Strategic Management Journal*, 23: 307–321.

85. E. D. Jaffe, I. D. Nebenzahl, & I. Schorr, 2005, Strategic options of home country firms faced with MNC entry, *Long Range Planning*, 38(2): 183–196.

86. A. V. Mainkar, M. Lubatkin, & W. S. Schulze, 2006, Toward a product-proliferation theory of entry barriers, *Academy of management Review*, 31: 1062–1075; J. Shamsie, 2003, The context of dominance: An industry-driven framework for exploiting reputation, *Strategic Management Journal*, 24: 199–215.

87. Delta Airlines exits bankruptcy, 2007, *USA Today*, http://www.usatoday.com, May 1.

88. R. Makadok, 1999, Interfirm differences in scale economies and the evolution of market shares, *Strategic Management Journal*, 20: 935–952.

89. F. Salvador & C. Forza, 2007, Principles for efficient and effective sales configuration design, *International Journal of Mass Customisation*, 2(1,2): 114–127; B. J. Pine II, 2004, Mass customization: The new imperative, *Strategic Direction*, January, 2–3.

90. F. Keenan, S. Holmes, J. Greene, & R. O. Crockett, 2002, A mass market of one, *BusinessWeek*, December 2, 68–72.

91. Mainkar, Lubatkin, & Schulze, Toward a product-proliferation theory of entry barriers.

92. M. A. Hitt, R. M. Holmes, T. Miller, and M. P. Salmador, 2006, Modeling country institutional profiles: The dimensions and dynamics of institutional environments, presented at the Strategic Management Society Conference, October; G. Walker, T. L. Madsen, & G. Carini, 2002, How does institutional change affect heterogeneity among firms? *Strategic Management Journal*, 23: 89–104.

93. A. Reinhardt, 2005, The man who said no to Microsoft, *BusinessWeek*, May 31, 49; 2002, The long shadow of big blue, *The Economist*, November 9, 63–64.

94. China approves plan to build large commercial aircraft, 2007, Associated Press, http://www.ocregister.com, May 7.

95. S. Dutta, O. Narasimhan, & S. Rajiv, 2005, Conceptualizing and measuring capabilities: Methodology and empirical application, *Strategic Management Journal*, 26: 277–285; A. M. Knott, 2003, Persistent heterogeneity and sustainable innovation, *Strategic Management Journal*, 24: 687–705;.

96. S. Nadkarni & V. K. Narayanan, 2007, Strategic schemas, strategic flexibility, and firm performance: The moderating role of industry clockspeed, *Strategic Management Journal*, 28: 243–270.

97. D. M. De Carolis, 2003, Competencies and imitability in the pharmaceutical industry: An analysis of their relationship with firm performance, *Journal of Management*, 29: 27–50; D. L. Deephouse, 1999, To be different, or to be the same? It's a question (and theory) of strategic balance, *Strategic Management Journal*, 20: 147–166.

98. L. Canina, C. A. Enz, & J. S. Harrison, 2005, Agglomeration effects and strategic orientations: Evidence from the U.S. lodging industry, *Academy of Management Journal*, 48: 565–581; W. Chung & A. Kalnins, 2001, Agglomeration effects and performance: Test of the Texas lodging industry, *Strategic Management Journal*, 22: 969–988.

99. A. S. Cui, D. A. Griffith, S. T. Cavusgil, & M. Dabic, 2006, The influence of market and cultural environmental factors on technology transfer between foreign MNCs and local subsidiaries: A Croatian illustration, *Journal of World Business*, 41: 100–111; K. D. Brouthers, L. E. Brouthers, & S. Werner, 2003, Transaction cost-enhanced entry mode choices and firm performance, *Strategic Management Journal*, 24: 1239–1248.

100. M. E. Porter, 1980, *Competitive Strategy*, New York: Free Press.

101. M. S. Hunt, 1972, Competition in the major home appliance industry, 1960–1970 (doctoral dissertation, Harvard University); Porter, *Competitive Strategy*, 129.

102. G. McNamara, D. L. Deephouse, & R. A. Luce, 2003, Competitive positioning within and across a strategic group structure: The performance of core, secondary, and solitary firms, *Strategic Management Journal*, 24: 161–181.

103. M. W. Peng, J. Tan, & T. W. Tong, 2004, Ownership types and strategic groups in an emerging economy, *Journal of Management Studies*, 41: 1105–1129; R. K. Reger & A. S. Huff, 1993, Strategic groups: A cognitive perspective, *Strategic Management Journal*, 14: 103–123.

104. M. Peteraf & M. Shanley, 1997, Getting to know you: A theory of strategic group identity, *Strategic Management Journal*, 18 (Special Issue): 165–186.

105. J. Lee, K. Lee, & S. Rho, 2002, An evolutionary perspective on strategic group emergence: A genetic algorithm-based model, *Strategic Management Journal*, 23: 727–746.

106. J. A. Zuniga-Vicente, J. M. de la Fuente Sabate, & I. S. Gonzalez. 2004, Dynamics of the strategic group membership-performance linkage in rapidly changing environments, *Journal of Business Research*, 57: 1378–1390.

107. S. McBride, 2005, Battle stations: Two upstarts vie for dominance in satellite radio, *Wall Street Journal*, March 30, A1, A9.

108. V. J. Racanelli, 2005, Turnaround ahead at VW, *Barron's*, May 16, 26–27.

109. Gimeno, Hoskisson, Beal, & Wan, Explaining the clustering of international expansion moves.

110. Porter, *Competitive Strategy*, 49.

111. M. B. Lieberman & S. Asaba, 2006, Why do firms imitate each other? *Academy of Management Journal,* 31: 366–385; G. McNamara, R. A. Luce, & G. H. Tompson, 2002, Examining the effect of complexity in strategic group knowledge structures on firm performance, *Strategic Management Journal,* 23: 153–170.

112. D. B. Montgomery, M. C. Moore, & J. E. Urbany, 2005, Reasoning about competitive reactions: Evidence from executives, *Marketing Science,* 24: 138–149.

113. P. M. Norman, R. D. Ireland, K. W. Artz, & M. A. Hitt, 2000, Acquiring and using competitive intelligence in entrepreneurial teams, paper presented at the Academy of Management, Toronto, Canada.

114. F. Vogelstein & P. Lewis, 2005, Search and destroy, *Fortune,* May 2, 73–79.

115. J. Menn, 2007, Google shrugs at possible rival deal, *Los Angeles Times,* http://www.latimes.com, May 5; R. A. Guth & K. J. Delaney, 2007, Microsoft, Yahoo! discussed deal, *Wall Street Journal,* online.wsj.com, May 5.

116. A. Afuah, 2000, How much do your co-opetitors' capabilities matter in the face of technological change? *Strategic Management Journal,* 21: 387A; Brandenburger & B. Nalebuff, 1996, *Co-opetition,* New York: Currency Doubleday.

117. S. G. Lazzarini, 2007, The impact of membership in competing alliance constellations: Evidence on the operational performance of global airlines, *Strategic Management Journal,* 28: 345–367.

118. J. L. Morrow, D. G. Sirmon, M. A. Hitt & T. R. Holcomb, 2007, Creating value in the face of declining performance: Firm strategies and organizational recovery, *Strategic Management Journal,* 28: 271–283.

119. R. D'Ovidio, 2007, The evolution of computers and crime: Complicating security practice, *Security Journal,* 20: 45-49.

120. A. Crane, 2005, In the company of spies: When competitive intelligence gathering becomes industrial espionage, *Business Horizons,* 48(3): 233–240.

Examining the Internal Organization: Activities, Resources, and Capabilities

Studying this chapter should provide you with the strategic management knowledge needed to:

1. Explain why firms need to study and understand their internal organization.

2. Define value and discuss its importance.

3. Describe the differences between tangible and intangible resources.

4. Define capabilities and discuss their development.

5. Describe four criteria used to determine whether resources and capabilities are core competencies.

6. Explain how value chain analysis is used to identify and evaluate resources and capabilities.

7. Define outsourcing and discuss reasons for its use.

8. Discuss the importance of identifying internal strengths and weaknesses.

Managing the Tension Between Innovation and Efficiency

As we discussed in Chapter 1, being able to wisely use a firm's assets to continuously innovate in ways that create value for customers is an important source of competitive advantage. For decades, 3M, the widely diversified technology company with six business segments, was a model of successful corporate innovation. The firm's commitment to innovation, and the importance innovation had to its competitive actions, is suggested by its slogan: "The Spirit of Innovation. That's 3M." In a practical, everyday sense, innovation's importance is signaled by 3M's famous intention of generating at least one-third of its annual sales from products introduced to the marketplace in the most recent five years.

For decades, 3M was indeed recognized for its innovation-related abilities and resulting product successes. Relying on the skills of its scientists and engineers, the firm developed 30-plus core technologies that were the basis for more than 55,000 products it produced and sold to customers throughout the world. But times have changed. In mid-2007, only 25 percent of 3M's sales were earned from products introduced over the previous five-year period. Less money was being allocated to research and development (R&D), which typically is the wellspring of product innovations. A number of financial analysts criticized the reduction in R&D spending. Full-year (2006) profits were below expectations, an outcome that did little to convince investors and potentially other stakeholders (e.g., suppliers, customers, and perhaps even employees) that new CEO George Buckley was putting a strategy into place that would return 3M to its glory years.

What contributed to the change in 3M's outputs of innovations? Some believe that the introduction of a Six Sigma program under the tutelage of former CEO James McNerney (who served immediately prior to Buckley) helped to shape the recent form of 3M. Six Sigma is a widely used "series of management techniques designed to decrease production defects and increase efficiency." Focusing on work processes, Six Sigma techniques are used to spot problems and use rigorous measurements to reduce production variations and eliminate defects. McNerney became intimately familiar with Six Sigma as an upper-level executive at General Electric (GE) where the techniques were used extensively during Jack Welch's tenure as that firm's CEO.

Using techniques such as Six Sigma is completely appropriate in that reducing waste and increasing efficiency contribute to a firm's profitability. The issue is that innovation-generating and efficiency-generating actions can sometimes be at odds with each other. In an analyst's words: "When (Six Sigma) types of initiatives become ingrained in a company's culture, as they did at 3M, creativity (and innovation that result from it) can easily get squelched." Indeed,

Six Sigma focuses on actions to define, measure, analyze, improve, and control. Some argue that focusing on these actions creates *sameness* rather than *innovation*. One 3M employee internalized the tension between efficiency and innovation as "Six Sigma Control" versus "Innovative Freedom." Because 3M had been about innovation for so long, other employees concluded that what they believed was an overemphasis on the discipline generated by Six Sigma caused 3M to lose its *soul*.

Recently, CEO Buckley said that 3M's stakeholders can expect a reenergization of R&D. Buckley believes it is the way to refocus 3M on growth and innovation. However, the necessity of using highly efficient work processes will remain a priority at 3M.

Sources: D. DePass, 2007, 3M earnings disappoint Wall Street, *The Star Tribune,* January 31, D1, D3; B. Hindo, 2007, At 3M, a struggle between efficiency and creativity, *BusinessWeek,* June 3, 8–14; J. Rae, 2007, Have it both ways, *BusinessWeek,* June 3, 16; Scrutinize Six Sigma, 2007, *BusinessWeek,* July 2, 90–91.

STRATEGY RIGHT NOW

As discussed in the first two chapters, several factors in the global economy, including the rapid development of the Internet's capabilities[1] and of globalization in general have made it increasingly difficult for firms to find ways to develop a competitive advantage that can be sustained for any period of time.[2] As is suggested by 3M's experiences, innovation may be a vital path to efforts to develop sustainable competitive advantages.[3] Sometimes, product innovation serves simultaneously as the foundation on which a firm is started as well as the source of its competitive advantages. Artemis Pet Food Co., for example, emphasizes quality as it manufactures pet food. Using natural ingredients that are suitable for humans, the firm has grown rapidly and has a cadre of loyal customers even though some of its products are more than twice the price of competitors' offerings.[4] (In the Opening Case for Chapter 4, you will learn about the innovations of another firm—PetSmart—competing in the pet industry.)

Competitive advantages and the differences they create in firm performance are often strongly related to the resources firms hold and how they are managed.[5] "Resources are the foundation for strategy, and unique bundles of resources generate competitive advantages that lead to wealth creation."[6] As 3M's experience shows, resources must be managed to simultaneously allow production efficiency and an ability to form competitive advantages such as the consistent development of innovative products.

To identify and successfully use resources over time, those leading firms need to think constantly about how to manage them to increase the value for customers who "are arbiters of value"[7] as they compare firms' goods and services against each other before making a purchase decision. As this chapter shows, firms achieve strategic competitiveness and earn above-average returns when their unique core competencies are effectively acquired, bundled, and leveraged to take advantage of opportunities in the external environment in ways that create value for customers.[8]

People are an especially critical resource for helping organizations learn how to continuously innovate as a means of achieving successful growth.[9] In other words, "smart growth" happens when the firm manages its need to grow with its ability to successfully manage growth.[10] People are a critical resource to efforts to grow successfully at 3M, where the director of global compensation says that harnessing the innovative powers of the firm's employees is the means for rekindling growth.[11] And, people at 3M as well as virtually all other firms who know how to effectively manage resources to help organizations learn how to continuously innovate are themselves a source of competitive advantage.[12] In fact, a global labor market now exists as firms seek talented individuals to add to their fold. As Richard Florida argues, "[W]herever talent goes, innovation, creativity, and economic growth are sure to follow."[13]

The fact that over time the benefits of any firm's value-creating strategy can be duplicated by its competitors is a key reason for having employees who know how to manage resources. These employees are critical to firms' efforts to perform well. Because all competitive advantages have a limited life,[14] the question of duplication is not *if* it will happen, but *when*. In general, the sustainability of a competitive advantage is a function of three factors: (1) the rate of core competence obsolescence because of environmental changes, (2) the availability of substitutes for the core competence, and (3) the imitability of the core competence.[15] The challenge for all firms, then, is to effectively manage current core competencies while simultaneously developing new ones.[16] Only when firms develop a continuous stream of capabilities that contribute to competitive advantages do they achieve strategic competitiveness, earn above-average returns, and remain ahead of competitors (see Chapter 5).

In Chapter 2, we examined general, industry, and competitor environments. Armed with this knowledge about the realities and conditions of their external environment, firms have a better understanding of marketplace opportunities and the characteristics of the competitive environment in which those opportunities exist. In this chapter, we focus on the firm itself. By analyzing its internal organization, a firm determines what it *can do*. Matching what a firm *can do* (a function of its resources, capabilities, core competencies, and competitive advantages) with what it *might do* (a function of opportunities and threats in the external environment) allows the firm to develop vision, pursue its mission, and select and implement its strategies.

We begin this chapter by briefly discussing conditions associated with analyzing the firm's internal organization. We then discuss the roles of resources and capabilities in developing core competencies, which are the sources of the firm's competitive advantages. Included in this discussion are the techniques firms use to identify and evaluate resources and capabilities and the criteria for selecting core competencies from among them. Resources and capabilities are not inherently valuable, but they create value when the firm can use them to perform certain activities that result in a competitive advantage. Accordingly, we also discuss the value chain concept and examine four criteria to evaluate core competencies that establish competitive advantage.[17] The chapter closes with cautionary comments about the need for firms to prevent their core competencies from becoming core rigidities. The existence of core rigidities indicates that the firm is too anchored to its past, which prevents it from continuously developing new competitive advantages.

Using a global mind-set, Volkswagen's leaders decided that the firm should open facilities in Slovakia. Opening these facilities long before their competitors has led to a distinct competitive advantage for VW in Slovakia and surrounding countries.

Analyzing the Internal Organization

The Context of Internal Analysis

In the global economy, traditional factors such as labor costs, access to financial resources and raw materials, and protected or regulated markets remain sources of competitive advantage, but to a lesser degree.[18] One important reason is that competitors can apply their resources to successfully use an international strategy (discussed in Chapter 8) as a means of overcoming the advantages created by these more traditional sources. For example, Volkswagen began establishing production facilities in Slovakia "shortly after the Russians moved out" as part of its international strategy. With a total investment exceeding $1.6 billion, Volkswagen is thought to have a competitive advantage over rivals such as France's Peugeot Citroen and South Korea's Kia Motors, firms that are now investing in Slovakia in an effort to duplicate the competitive advantage that has accrued to Volkswagen.[19]

Increasingly, those who analyze their firm's internal organization should use a global mind-set to do so. A **global mind-set** is the ability to study an internal organization in ways that are not dependent on the assumptions of a single country, culture,

© AP Photo/CTK, Jan Koller

A **global mind-set** is the ability to study an internal organization in ways that are not dependent on the assumptions of a single country, culture, or context.

Value is measured by a product's performance characteristics and by its attributes for which customers are willing to pay.

or context.[20] Because they are able to span artificial boundaries,[21] those with a global mind-set recognize that their firms must possess resources and capabilities that allow understanding of and appropriate responses to competitive situations that are influenced by country-specific factors and unique societal cultures. Firms populated with people having a global mind-set have a "key source of long-term competitive advantage in the global marketplace."[22]

Finally, analysis of the firm's internal organization requires that evaluators examine the firm's portfolio of resources and the *bundles* of heterogeneous resources and capabilities managers have created.[23] This perspective suggests that individual firms possess at least some resources and capabilities that other companies do not—at least not in the same combination. Resources are the source of capabilities, some of which lead to the development of a firm's core competencies or its competitive advantages.[24] Understanding how to *leverage* the firm's unique bundle of resources and capabilities is a key outcome decision makers seek when analyzing the internal organization.[25] Figure 3.1 illustrates the relationships among resources, capabilities, and core competencies and shows how firms use them to create strategic competitiveness. Before examining these topics in depth, we describe value and its creation.

Creating Value

By exploiting their core competencies or competitive advantages to at least meet if not exceed the demanding standards of global competition, firms create value for customers.[26] **Value** is measured by a product's performance characteristics and by its attributes for which customers are willing to pay. Customers of Luby Cafeterias, for example, pay for meals that are value-priced, generally healthy, and served quickly in a causal setting.[27]

Firms with a competitive advantage offer value to customers that is superior to the value competitors provide.[28] Firms create value by innovatively bundling and leveraging their resources and capabilities.[29] Firms unable to creatively bundle and leverage their

Figure 3.1 Components of Internal Analysis Leading to Competitive Advantage and Strategic Competitiveness

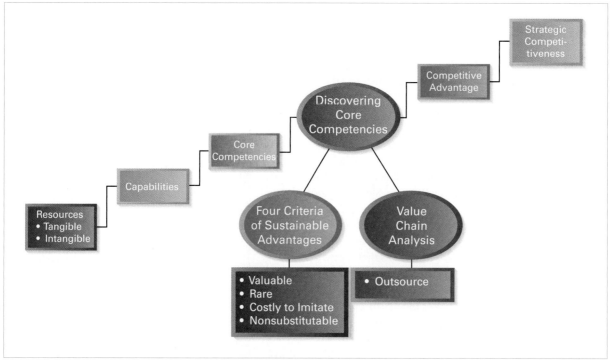

resources and capabilities in ways that create value for customers suffer performance declines. Sometimes, it seems that these declines may happen because firms fail to understand what customers value. For example, after learning that General Motors (GM) intended to focus on visual design to create value for buyers, one former GM customer said that in his view, people buying cars and trucks valued durability, reliability, good fuel economy, and a low cost of operation more than visual design.[30]

Ultimately, creating value for customers is the source of above-average returns for a firm. What the firm intends regarding value creation affects its choice of business-level strategy (see Chapter 4) and its organizational structure (see Chapter 11).[31] In Chapter 4's discussion of business-level strategies, we note that value is created by a product's low cost, by its highly differentiated features, or by a combination of low cost and high differentiation, compared with competitors' offerings. A business-level strategy is effective only when it is grounded in exploiting the firm's core competencies and competitive advantages. Thus, successful firms continuously examine the effectiveness of current and future core competencies and advantages.[32]

At one time, the strategic management process was concerned largely with understanding the characteristics of the industry in which the firm competed and, in light of those characteristics, determining how the firm should position itself relative to competitors. This emphasis on industry characteristics and competitive strategy underestimated the role of the firm's resources and capabilities in developing competitive advantage. In fact, core competencies, in combination with product-market positions, are the firm's most important sources of competitive advantage.[33] The core competencies of a firm, in addition to results of analyses of its general, industry, and competitor environments, should drive its selection of strategies. The resources held by the firm and their context are important when formulating strategy.[34] As Clayton Christensen noted, "Successful strategists need to cultivate a deep understanding of the processes of competition and progress and of the factors that undergird each advantage. Only thus will they be able to see when old advantages are poised to disappear and how new advantages can be built in their stead."[35] By emphasizing core competencies when formulating strategies, companies learn to compete primarily on the basis of firm-specific differences, but they must be very aware of how things are changing in the external environment as well.[36]

The Challenge of Analyzing the Internal Organization

The strategic decisions managers make about the components of their firm's internal organization are nonroutine,[37] have ethical implications,[38] and significantly influence the firm's ability to earn above-average returns.[39] These decisions involve choices about the assets the firm needs to collect and how to best use those assets. "Managers make choices precisely because they believe these contribute substantially to the performance and survival of their organizations."[40]

Making decisions involving the firm's assets—identifying, developing, deploying, and protecting resources, capabilities, and core competencies—may appear to be relatively easy. However, this task is as challenging and difficult as any other with which managers are involved; moreover, it is increasingly internationalized.[41] Some believe that the pressure on managers to pursue only decisions that help the firm meet the quarterly earnings expected by market analysts makes it difficult to accurately examine the firm's internal organization.[42]

The challenge and difficulty of making effective decisions are implied by preliminary evidence suggesting that one-half of organizational decisions fail.[43] Sometimes, mistakes are made as the firm analyzes conditions in its internal organization.[44] Managers might, for example, identify capabilities as core competencies that do not create a competitive advantage. This misidentification may have been the case at Polaroid Corporation as decision makers continued to believe that the skills it used to build its instant film cameras were highly relevant at the time its competitors were developing and using the skills required to introduce digital cameras.[45] When a mistake occurs, such as was the case at Polaroid, decision makers must have the confidence to admit it and take corrective actions.[46] A firm can still grow through well-intended errors; the learning generated by making and correcting mistakes can be important to the creation of new competitive advantages.[47] Moreover, firms and those managing them can learn from the failure resulting from a mistake—that is, what *not* to do when seeking competitive advantage.[48]

To facilitate developing and using core competencies, managers must have courage, self-confidence, integrity, the capacity to deal with uncertainty and complexity, and a willingness to hold people accountable for their work and to be held accountable themselves.[49] Thus, difficult managerial decisions concerning resources, capabilities, and core competencies are characterized by three conditions: uncertainty, complexity, and intraorganizational conflicts (see Figure 3.2).[50]

Managers face *uncertainty* in terms of new proprietary technologies, rapidly changing economic and political trends, transformations in societal values, and shifts in customer demands.[51] Environmental uncertainty increases the *complexity* and range of issues to examine when studying the internal environment.[52] Consider the complexity associated with the decisions Gregory H. Boyce is encountering as CEO of Peabody Energy Corp. Peabody is the world's largest coal company. But coal is thought of as a "dirty fuel," meaning that some think its future prospects are dim in light of global warming issues. What decisions should Boyce make given global warming and the nature of his company's core product? Obviously, the complexity of these decisions is quite significant.[53] Biases about how to cope with uncertainty affect decisions about the resources and capabilities that will become the foundation of the firm's competitive advantage.[54] For example, Boyce strongly believes in coal's future, suggesting that automobiles capable of burning coal should be built. Finally, *intraorganizational conflict* surfaces when decisions are made about the core competencies to nurture as well as how to nurture them.

In making decisions affected by these three conditions, judgment is required. *Judgment* is the capability of making successful decisions when no obviously correct model or rule is available or when relevant data are unreliable or incomplete. In this type of situation, decision makers must be aware of possible cognitive biases. Overconfidence, for example, can often lower value when a correct decision is not obvious, such as making a judgment as to whether an internal resource is a strength or a weakness.[55]

Figure 3.2 Conditions Affecting Managerial Decisions About Resources, Capabilities, and Core Competencies

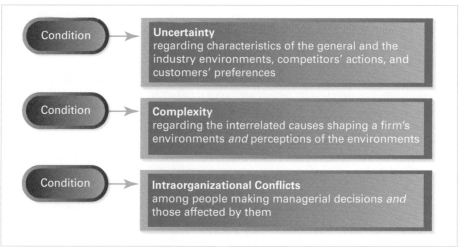

Hyundai Cars: The Quality Is There, So Why Aren't the Cars Selling?

Once known as a producer of cheap, entry-level cars that suffered from multiple manufacturing defects, Hyundai Motor Company has reversed its performance from the perspective of product quality. In fact, according to Strategic Vision, a well-known market research company and consultant to automakers, Hyundai had leadership positions in five categories (including large car, minivan, and small sport utility vehicle) in the firm's 2007 vehicle quality study. This performance caused one analyst to suggest that "when it comes to car quality, (consumers should) think Korean." This recommendation is consistent with the perspective of the firm's CEO who says that "At present, the Hyundai brand stands for high quality." Evidence from J.D. Power's Initial Quality Study appears to support these views in that Hyundai's quality is actually rated ahead of Toyota, trailing only Lexus and Porsche.

Surprisingly, at least to Hyundai officials, the significant improvements in product quality are not translating into sales growth in the key European and U.S. markets. In Europe, the firm's new car registrations in 2006 declined 5.7 percent from its registrations in 2005, resulting in a total European market share of 1.9 percent. (Leader Volkswagen had 20.3 percent of the European market in 2006.) In the United States, the firm's unsold inventory was swelling in 2007. As the fastest-growing carmaker in the U.S. market during 2000–2005, this inventory increase was unexpected. Based on its success in the early twenty-first century, Hyundai established a target of selling 1 million units in the United States in 2010. That goal has now been reduced to 700,000 units with a desire to sell 900,000 units in this particular market by 2012. In turn, sales declines, as represented by swelling inventories, had a significantly negative effect on the firm's earnings.

Hyundai's sales-related problems meant that the firm faced an uncertain and complex future and that judgment had to be used to make decisions. As a first step, executives needed to identify the cause of the firm's problems. According to Hyundai's vice president for sales, the firm needs a new story. In his words: "When we don't have a price story, we have no story." In consultation with others, the firm's new chief operating officer (COO) decided that Hyundai "needed a new 'big idea' to redefine its brand and move it away from an association with cheap, tin-pot vehicles." What is the new big idea? Essentially, the firm is being repositioned as an "overachieving, underappreciated brand that smart people are discovering." Decisions made to support this repositioning include those of allocating additional resources to R&D to focus the design image of its cars and establishing production facilities in Europe (Czech Republic) and India with the intention of better understanding local consumers needs while reducing manufacturing costs and making additional gains with product quality.

Sources: Hyundai Motor Company, 2007, *Hyundai Motor World*, 15(55): 1–15; D. Goodman, 2007, Hyundai takes lead in 2007 auto quality study, *The Salt Lake Tribune Online*, June 4, http://www.sltrib.com; D. Kiley, Hyundai still gets no respect; Marketing guru Steve Wilhite has to sell drivers a new story, *BusinessWeek Online*, May 21, http://businessweek.com; L. Rousek, 2007, Hyundai Motor breaks ground on its first European car plant, *Wall Street Journal Online*, http://wsj.com; C. A. Sawyer, 2007, Joe Piaskowski & Hyundai's exploratory approach, *Automotive Design & Production*, 119(4): 22.

© Don Hammond/Design Pics/Corbis

When exercising judgment, decision makers often take intelligent risks. In the current competitive landscape, executive judgment can be a particularly important source of competitive advantage. One reason is that, over time, effective judgment allows a firm to build a strong reputation and retain the loyalty of stakeholders whose support is linked to above-average returns.[56]

As explained in the Strategic Focus, Hyundai's executives use their judgment to make decisions as their firm faces an uncertain and complex future. Of course, the firm's

Some business analysts feel that Hermes's cautious entry into new international markets is too slow and ineffective.

executives hope that their decisions are the product of effective judgment. Decision makers at Hermes hope the same thing is true for them. This luxury retailer has been slow to enter international markets, opening its first store in India in 2008 "several years after competitors such as Louis Vuitton and Chanel."[57] Some believe that entering international markets slowly and cautiously is proving to be an ineffective decision for Hermes. A comprehensive decision-making process (a process in which a great deal of information is collected and analyzed)[58] may be what Hyundai and Hermes executives should use given the uncertainty and complexity of the conditions facing their firms.

Resources, Capabilities, and Core Competencies

Resources, capabilities, and core competencies are the foundation of competitive advantage. Resources are bundled to create organizational capabilities. In turn, capabilities are the source of a firm's core competencies, which are the basis of competitive advantages.[59] Figure 3.1, on page 72, depicts these relationships. Here, we define and provide examples of these building blocks of competitive advantage.

Resources

Broad in scope, resources cover a spectrum of individual, social, and organizational phenomena.[60] Typically, resources alone do not yield a competitive advantage.[61] In fact, a competitive advantage is generally based on the *unique bundling of several resources*.[62] For example, Amazon.com combined service and distribution resources to develop its competitive advantages. The firm started as an online bookseller, directly shipping orders to customers. It quickly grew large and established a distribution network through which it could ship "millions of different items to millions of different customers." Lacking Amazon's combination of resources, traditional bricks-and-mortar companies, such as Borders, found it difficult to establish an effective online presence. These difficulties led some of them to develop partnerships with Amazon. Through these arrangements, Amazon now handles the online presence and the shipping of goods for several firms, including Borders—which now can focus on sales in its stores.[63] These types of arrangements are useful to the bricks-and-mortar companies because they are not accustomed to shipping so much diverse merchandise directly to individuals.

Some of a firm's resources (defined in Chapter 1 as inputs to the firm's production process) are tangible while others are intangible. **Tangible resources** are assets that can be seen and quantified. Production equipment, manufacturing facilities, distribution centers, and formal reporting structures are examples of tangible resources. **Intangible resources** are assets that are rooted deeply in the firm's history and have accumulated over time. Because they are embedded in unique patterns of routines, intangible resources are relatively difficult for competitors to analyze and imitate. Knowledge, trust between managers and employees, managerial capabilities, organizational routines (the unique ways people work together), scientific capabilities, the capacity for innovation, brand name, and the firm's reputation for its goods or services and how it interacts with people (such as employees, customers, and suppliers) are intangible resources.[64]

The four types of tangible resources are financial, organizational, physical, and technological (see Table 3.1). The three types of intangible resources are human, innovation, and reputational (see Table 3.2).

Tangible resources are assets that can be seen and quantified.

Intangible resources include assets that are rooted deeply in the firm's history and have accumulated over time.

Table 3.1 Tangible Resources

Financial Resources	• The firm's borrowing capacity • The firm's ability to generate internal funds
Organizational Resources	• The firm's formal reporting structure and its formal planning, controlling, and coordinating systems
Physical Resources	• Sophistication and location of a firm's plant and equipment • Access to raw materials
Technological Resources	• Stock of technology, such as patents, trademarks, copyrights, and trade secrets

Sources: Adapted from J. B. Barney, 1991, Firm resources and sustained competitive advantage, *Journal of Management,* 17: 101; R. M. Grant, 1991, *Contemporary Strategy Analysis,* Cambridge, U.K.: Blackwell Business, 100–102.

Table 3.2 Intangible Resources

Human Resources	• Knowledge • Trust • Managerial capabilities • Organizational routines
Innovation Resources	• Ideas • Scientific capabilities • Capacity to innovate
Reputational Resources	• Reputation with customers • Brand name • Perceptions of product quality, durability, and reliability • Reputation with suppliers • For efficient, effective, supportive, and mutually beneficial interactions and relationships

Sources: Adapted from R. Hall, 1992, The strategic analysis of intangible resources, *Strategic Management Journal,* 13: 136–139; R. M. Grant, 1991, *Contemporary Strategy Analysis,* Cambridge, U.K.: Blackwell Business, 101–104.

Tangible Resources

As tangible resources, a firm's borrowing capacity and the status of its physical facilities are visible. The value of many tangible resources can be established through financial statements; but these statements do not account for the value of all the firm's assets, because they disregard some intangible resources.[65] The value of tangible resources is also constrained because they are hard to leverage—it is difficult to derive additional business or value from a tangible resource. For example, an airplane is a tangible resource or asset, but "You can't use the same airplane on five different routes at the same time. You can't put the same crew on five different routes at the same time. And the same goes for the financial investment you've made in the airplane."[66]

Although production assets are tangible, many of the processes to use these assets are intangible. Thus, the learning and potential proprietary processes associated with a tangible resource, such as manufacturing facilities, can have unique intangible attributes, such as quality control processes, unique manufacturing processes, and technology that develop over time and create competitive advantage.[67]

Intangible Resources

Compared to tangible resources, intangible resources are a superior source of core competencies.[68] In fact, in the global economy, "the success of a corporation lies more in its intellectual and systems capabilities than in its physical assets. [Moreover], the capacity to manage human intellect—and to convert it into useful products and services—is fast becoming the critical executive skill of the age."[69]

Because intangible resources are less visible and more difficult for competitors to understand, purchase, imitate, or substitute for, firms prefer to rely on them rather than on tangible resources as the foundation for their capabilities and core competencies. In fact, the more unobservable (i.e., intangible) a resource is, the more sustainable will be the competitive advantage that is based on it.[70] Another benefit of intangible resources is that, unlike most tangible resources, their use can be leveraged. For instance, sharing knowledge among employees does not diminish its value for any one person. To the contrary, two people sharing their individualized knowledge sets often can be leveraged to create additional knowledge that, although new to each of them, contributes to performance improvements for the firm.[71] With intangible resources, the larger is the network of users, the greater the benefit to each party.

Harley-Davidson's reputation, an intangible resource, has led to associations with other companies and an expansion of its own product lines.

As shown in Table 3.2, the intangible resource of reputation is an important source of competitive advantage. Indeed, some argue that "a firm's reputation is widely considered to be a valuable resource associated with sustained competitive advantage."[72] Earned through the firm's actions as well as its words, a value-creating reputation is a product of years of superior marketplace competence as perceived by stakeholders.[73] A reputation indicates the level of awareness a firm has been able to develop among stakeholders and the degree to which they hold the firm in high esteem.[74]

A well-known and highly valued brand name is an application of reputation as a source of competitive advantage.[75] A continuing commitment to innovation and aggressive advertising facilitate firms' efforts to take advantage of the reputation associated with their brands.[76] Because of the desirability of its reputation, the Harley-Davidson brand name, for example, has such status that it adorns a limited edition Barbie doll, a popular restaurant in New York City, and a line of L'Oréal cologne. Additionally, the firm offers a broad range of clothing items, from black leather jackets to fashions for tots through Harley-Davidson MotorClothes.[77] Other firms are trying to build their reputations. For example, Li-Ning, a manufacturer and marketer of athletic shoes, competes in the Chinese market against Nike and Adidas, firms with well-known brands. To prepare for the 2008 Olympic Games in Beijing, Li-Ning hired a veteran with experience at Procter & Gamble as vice president of marketing to build its image. The hired executive's first initiative was to partner with the National Basketball Association to use its logo on Li-Ning shoes.[78]

Because of their ability to influence performance, companies do everything possible to nurture and protect their brand name. When something happens to tarnish a brand, firms respond aggressively. For example, PepsiCo's brand name and reputation have been tarnished in India as explained in the Strategic Focus. But the firm is dealing directly with the matter. The interest, of course, is to restore the luster of the brand name in a market the firm considers "strategic" to its future success. While doing so, it seems that PepsiCo also seeks to contribute to the welfare of India's citizenry.

Seeking to Repair a Tarnished Brand Name

"For somebody to think that Pepsi would jeopardize its brand—its global brand—by doing something stupid in one country is crazy." These words, spoken by PepsiCo's CEO Indra K. Nooyi, demonstrate the intensity of the situation the firm (as well as its main rival, Coca-Cola Company) faces in India. A native of India, Nooyi believes that her home country is a top "strategic priority" for the growth of the firm she heads. (The fact that PepsiCo has 35 plants in India is one indication of the market's importance to the firm.) Taking actions that are consistent with the concept of "performance with purpose," Nooyi seeks to "make PepsiCo a groundbreaker in areas like selling healthy food and diversifying its workforce." Perhaps these intentions, and the underlying values they suggest, account for some of Nooyi's disappointment and surprise about the allegations being leveled against PepsiCo in India.

The foundation for the situation concerning Nooyi and her firm was laid in 2003 when tests conducted by the India-based Center for Science and Environment (CSE) suggested that the amount of pesticide residues in 12 soft drinks (including Pepsi products) ranged from 11 to 70 times the European-established limit. Because CSE is a private research and advocacy group, its announcement caused quite an uproar among consumers. Almost immediately, consumer rage was felt by Pepsi and other soft drink manufacturers in the form of a sales decline in the range of 30–40 percent for their products. Pepsi officials responded by saying that the water used in their soft drinks met local norms as well as those established in Europe and the United States. Also affecting the controversy were the results of tests conducted by a government agency. Seeking to verify CSE's assertions, the agency's results actually showed "pesticide residues in [the companies'] soft drinks to be far lower" than CSE contended. Pepsi officials also took action to contextualize the allegations, saying that drinking a single cup of tea made with the water available to many Indian citizens yields as much pesticide as 394 cups of soda.

Spring forward to 2007. PepsiCo (along with Coca-Cola again) is also being charged with consuming an excessive amount of Indian groundwater (water that is purified in the process of making soft drinks). Part of the issue here is the "meaning water holds for Indians." In response, Nooyi says that she is aware of the delicacy of issues related to water in her native land, but she also "points out that soft drinks and bottled water account for less than .04 percent of industrial water usage in India."

Wanting to be a good corporate citizen and desiring for its brand name to be respected and valued, Pepsi is taking various actions in India including digging wells in villages for local residents, harvesting rainwater, and teaching better techniques for growing rice and tomatoes. Nooyi and others throughout PepsiCo are committed to recapturing the value of its brand name in India and helping the citizenry while doing so. In Nooyi's words: "We have to invest in educating communities in how to farm better, collect water, and then work with industry to retrofit plants and recycle."

Sources: D. Brady, 2007, Pepsi: Repairing a poisoned reputation in India, *BusinessWeek,* June 11, 46–54; B. Bremner & N. Lakshman, 2006, India: Behind the scare over pesticides in Pepsi and Coke, *BusinessWeek Online,* September 4, http://www.businessweek.com; F. Hills, 2006, Coca-Cola: Lab tests prove Cokes sold in India are safe, *Financial Wire,* August 14, http://www.financialwire.com; J. Johnson, 2006, Giving the goliaths a good kicking, *Financial Times,* August 12, http://www.financialtimes.com.

Capabilities

Capabilities exist when resources have been purposely integrated to achieve a specific task or set of tasks. These tasks range from human resource selection to product marketing and research and development activities.[79] Critical to the building of competitive advantages, capabilities are often based on developing, carrying, and exchanging information and knowledge through the firm's human capital.[80] Client-specific capabilities often develop from repeated interactions with clients and the learning about their needs that occurs.[81] As a result, capabilities often evolve and develop over time.[82] The foundation of many capabilities lies in the unique skills and knowledge of a firm's employees[83] and, often, their functional expertise. Hence, the value of human capital in developing and using capabilities and, ultimately, core competencies cannot be overstated.[84]

While global business leaders increasingly support the view that the knowledge possessed by human capital is among the most significant of an organization's capabilities and may ultimately be at the root of all competitive advantages,[85] firms must also be able to utilize the knowledge they have and transfer it among their business units.[86] Given this reality, the firm's challenge is to create an environment that allows people to integrate their individual knowledge with that held by others in the firm so that, collectively, the firm has significant organizational knowledge.[87]

As illustrated in Table 3.3, capabilities are often developed in specific functional areas (such as manufacturing, R&D, and marketing) or in a part of a functional area (e.g., advertising). Table 3.3 shows a grouping of organizational functions and the capabilities that some companies are thought to possess in terms of all or parts of those functions.

Table 3.3 Examples of Firms' Capabilities

Functional Areas	Capabilities	Examples of Firms
Distribution	Effective use of logistics management techniques	Wal-Mart
Human resources	Motivating, empowering, and retaining employees	Microsoft
Management information systems	Effective and efficient control of inventories through point-of-purchase data collection methods	Wal-Mart
Marketing	Effective promotion of brand-name products	Procter & Gamble Polo Ralph Lauren Corp. McKinsey & Co.
	Effective customer service	Nordstrom Inc. Norrell Corporation
	Innovative merchandising	Crate & Barrel
Management	Ability to envision the future of clothing	Hugo Boss
	Effective organizational structure	PepsiCo
Manufacturing	Design and production skills yielding reliable products	Komatsu
	Product and design quality	Witt Gas Technology
	Miniaturization of components and products	Sony
Research & development	Innovative technology	Caterpillar
	Development of sophisticated elevator control solutions	Otis Elevator Co.
	Rapid transformation of technology into new products and processes	Chaparral Steel
	Digital technology	Thomson Consumer Electronics

Core Competencies

Defined in Chapter 1, *core competencies* are capabilities that serve as a source of competitive advantage for a firm over its rivals. Core competencies distinguish a company competitively and reflect its personality. Core competencies emerge over time through an organizational process of accumulating and learning how to deploy different resources and capabilities.[88] As the capacity to take action, core competencies are "crown jewels of a company," the activities the company performs especially well compared with competitors and through which the firm adds unique value to its goods or services over a long period of time.[89]

Innovation is thought to be a core competence at Xerox today. In ways, it is not surprising because this firm was built on a world-changing innovation—xerography. And even though Xerox was the first firm to integrate the mouse with the graphical user interface of a PC, it was Apple Computer that initially recognized the incredible value of this innovation and derived value from it. In 2000, then CEO Paul Allaire admitted that Xerox's business model no longer worked and that the firm had lost its innovative ability. Some seven-plus years later, things have changed for the better at Xerox. Using the capabilities of its scientists, engineers, and researchers, Xerox has reconstituted innovation as a core competence. In the main, these innovations are oriented to helping customers deal with their document-intensive processes. For example, the firm now produces new technologies that read, understand, route, and protect documents. Reconstituting innovation as a core competence has yielded financial payoffs as is shown by the three-fold increase in Xerox's profit margins since 2003.[90]

How many core competencies are required for the firm to have a sustained competitive advantage? Responses to this question vary. McKinsey & Co. recommends that its clients identify no more than three or four competencies around which their strategic actions can be framed. Supporting and nurturing more than four core competencies may prevent a firm from developing the focus it needs to fully exploit its competencies in the marketplace. At Xerox, services expertise, employee talent, and technological skills are thought to be core competencies along with innovation.[91]

Building Core Competencies

Two tools help firms identify and build their core competencies. The first consists of four specific criteria of sustainable competitive advantage that firms can use to determine those capabilities that are core competencies. Because the capabilities shown in Table 3.3 have satisfied these four criteria, they are core competencies. The second tool is the value chain analysis. Firms use this tool to select the value-creating competencies that should be maintained, upgraded, or developed and those that should be outsourced.

Four Criteria of Sustainable Competitive Advantage

As shown in Table 3.4, capabilities that are valuable, rare, costly to imitate, and nonsubstitutable are core competencies. In turn, core competencies are sources of competitive advantage for the firm over its rivals. Capabilities failing to satisfy the four criteria of sustainable competitive advantage are not core competencies, meaning that although every core competence is a capability, not every capability is a core competence. In slightly different words, for a capability to be a core competence, it must be valuable and unique from a customer's point of view. For a competitive advantage to be sustainable, the core competence must be inimitable and nonsubstitutable from a competitor's point of view.

A sustained competitive advantage is achieved only when competitors cannot duplicate the benefits of a firm's strategy or when they lack the resources to attempt imitation. For some period of time, the firm may earn a competitive advantage by using capabilities that are, for example, valuable and rare, but imitable. Take, for example, Artemis Pet

Table 3.4 The Four Criteria of Sustainable Competitive Advantage

Valuable Capabilities	• Help a firm neutralize threats or exploit opportunities
Rare Capabilities	• Are not possessed by many others
Costly-to-Imitate Capabilities	• Historical: A unique and a valuable organizational culture or brand name • Ambiguous cause: The causes and uses of a competence are unclear • Social complexity: Interpersonal relationships, trust, and friendship among managers, suppliers, and customers
Nonsubstitutable Capabilities	• No strategic equivalent

Food Co., the firm mentioned earlier in this chapter. Recall that Artemis uses natural ingredients in its foods for pets. However, competitors such as Natural Balance can and do use the same or similar ingredients,[92] suggesting that Artemis's competitive advantage is likely imitable. The length of time a firm can expect to retain its competitive advantage is a function of how quickly competitors can successfully imitate a good, service, or process. Sustainable competitive advantage results only when all four criteria are satisfied.

Valuable

Valuable capabilities allow the firm to exploit opportunities or neutralize threats in its external environment. By effectively using capabilities to exploit opportunities, a firm creates value for customers. Under former CEO Jack Welch's leadership, GE built a valuable competence in financial services. It built this powerful competence largely through acquisitions and its core competence in integrating newly acquired businesses. In addition, making such competencies as financial services highly successful required placing the right people in the right jobs. As Welch emphasized, human capital is important in creating value for customers.[93]

Rare

Rare capabilities are capabilities that few, if any, competitors possess. A key question to be answered when evaluating this criterion is, "How many rival firms possess these valuable capabilities?" Capabilities possessed by many rivals are unlikely to be sources of competitive advantage for any one of them. Instead, valuable but common (i.e., not rare) resources and capabilities are sources of competitive parity.[94] Competitive advantage results only when firms develop and exploit valuable capabilities that differ from those shared with competitors.

Costly to Imitate

Costly-to-imitate capabilities are capabilities that other firms cannot easily develop. Capabilities that are costly to imitate are created because of one reason or a combination of three reasons (see Table 3.4). First, a firm sometimes is able to develop capabilities because of *unique historical conditions*. "As firms evolve, they pick up skills, abilities and resources that are unique to them, reflecting their particular path through history."[95]

A firm with a unique and valuable *organizational culture* that emerged in the early stages of the company's history "may have an imperfectly imitable advantage over firms founded in another historical period"[96]—one in which less valuable or less competitively useful values and beliefs strongly influenced the development of the firm's culture. Briefly discussed in Chapter 1, *organizational culture* is a set of values that are shared by members in the organization, as we explain in Chapter 12. An organizational culture is a source of advantage when employees are held together tightly by their belief in it.[97]

Valuable capabilities allow the firm to exploit opportunities or neutralize threats in its external environment.

Rare capabilities are capabilities that few, if any, competitors possess.

Costly-to-imitate capabilities are capabilities that other firms cannot easily develop.

UPS has been the prototype in many areas of the parcel delivery business because of its excellence in products, systems, marketing, and other operational business capabilities. "Its fundamental competitive strength, however, derives from the organization's unique culture, which has spanned almost a century, growing deeper all along. This culture provides solid, consistent roots for everything the company does, from skills training to technological innovation."[98] Culture may also be a competitive advantage at Mustang Engineering (an engineering and project management firm based in Houston, Texas). Established as a place where people are expected to take care of people, Mustang offers "a company culture that we believe is unique in the industry. Mustang is a work place

Mustang Engineering's culture makes it a business that is costly to imitate.

with a family feel. A client once described Mustang as a world-class company with a mom-and-pop culture."[99]

A second condition of being costly to imitate occurs when the link between the firm's capabilities and its competitive advantage is *causally ambiguous*.[100] In these instances, competitors can't clearly understand how a firm uses its capabilities as the foundation for competitive advantage. As a result, firms are uncertain about the capabilities they should develop to duplicate the benefits of a competitor's value-creating strategy. For years, firms tried to imitate Southwest Airlines' low-cost strategy but most have been unable to do so, primarily because they can't duplicate Southwest's unique culture. Of all Southwest imitators, Ryanair, an Irish airline headquartered in Dublin, is the most successful. However, "Ryanair is also one of Europe's most controversial companies, praised by some, criticized by others."[101] As such, the firm's long-term future does not appear to be as certain as Southwest's.

Social complexity is the third reason that capabilities can be costly to imitate. Social complexity means that at least some, and frequently many, of the firm's capabilities are the product of complex social phenomena. Interpersonal relationships, trust, friendships among managers and between managers and employees, and a firm's reputation with suppliers and customers are examples of socially complex capabilities. Southwest Airlines is careful to hire people that fit with its culture. This complex interrelationship between the culture and human capital adds value in ways that other airlines cannot such as jokes by the flight attendants or the cooperation between gate personnel and pilots.

Nonsubstitutable

Nonsubstitutable capabilities are capabilities that do not have strategic equivalents. This final criterion for a capability to be a source of competitive advantage "is that there must be no strategically equivalent valuable resources that are themselves either not rare or imitable. Two valuable firm resources (or two bundles of firm resources) are strategically equivalent when they each can be separately exploited to implement the same strategies."[102] In general, the strategic value of capabilities increases as they become more difficult to substitute. The more invisible capabilities are, the more difficult it is for firms to find substitutes and the greater the challenge is to competitors trying to imitate a firm's value-creating strategy. Firm-specific knowledge and trust-based working relationships between managers and nonmanagerial personnel, such as existed for years at Southwest Airlines, are examples of capabilities that are difficult to identify and for which finding a substitute is challenging. However, causal ambiguity may make it difficult for the firm to learn as well and may stifle progress, because the firm may not know how to improve processes that are not easily codified and thus are ambiguous.[103]

Nonsubstitutable capabilities are capabilities that do not have strategic equivalents.

Table 3.5 Outcomes from Combinations of the Criteria for Sustainable Competitive Advantage

Is the Resource or Capability Valuable?	Is the Resource or Capability Rare?	Is the Resource or Capability Costly to Imitate?	Is the Resource or Capability Nonsubstitutable?	Competitive Consequences	Performance Implications
No	No	No	No	Competitive disadvantage	Below-average returns
Yes	No	No	Yes/no	Competitive parity	Average returns
Yes	Yes	No	Yes/no	Temporary competitive advantage	Average returns to above-average returns
Yes	Yes	Yes	Yes	Sustainable competitive advantage	Above-average returns

In summary, only using valuable, rare, costly-to-imitate, and nonsubstitutable capabilities creates sustainable competitive advantage. Table 3.5 shows the competitive consequences and performance implications resulting from combinations of the four criteria of sustainability. The analysis suggested by the table helps managers determine the strategic value of a firm's capabilities. The firm should not emphasize capabilities that fit the criteria described in the first row in the table (i.e., resources and capabilities that are neither valuable nor rare and that are imitable and for which strategic substitutes exist). Capabilities yielding competitive parity and either temporary or sustainable competitive advantage, however, will be supported. Some competitors such as Coca-Cola and PepsiCo may have capabilities that result in competitive parity. In such cases, the firms will nurture these capabilities while simultaneously trying to develop capabilities that can yield either a temporary or sustainable competitive advantage.

Value Chain Analysis

Value chain analysis allows the firm to understand the parts of its operations that create value and those that do not.[104] Understanding these issues is important because the firm earns above-average returns only when the value it creates is greater than the costs incurred to create that value.[105]

The value chain is a template that firms use to understand their cost position and to identify the multiple means that might be used to facilitate implementation of a chosen business-level strategy.[106] Today's competitive landscape demands that firms examine their value chains in a global, rather than a domestic-only context.[107] In particular, activities associated with supply chains should be studied within a global context.[108]

As shown in Figure 3.3, a firm's value chain is segmented into primary and support activities. **Primary activities** are involved with a product's physical creation, its sale and distribution to buyers, and its service after the sale. **Support activities** provide the assistance necessary for the primary activities to take place.

The value chain shows how a product moves from the raw-material stage to the final customer. For individual firms, the essential idea of the value chain is to create additional value without incurring significant costs while doing so and to capture the value that has been created. In a globally competitive economy, the most valuable links on the chain are people who have knowledge about customers. This locus of value-creating possibilities applies just as strongly to retail and service firms as to manufacturers. Moreover, for organizations in all sectors, the effects of e-commerce make it increasingly necessary for companies to develop value-adding knowledge processes to compensate for the value and margin that the Internet strips from physical processes.[109]

Primary activities are involved with a product's physical creation, its sale and distribution to buyers, and its service after the sale.

Support activities provide the assistance necessary for the primary activities to take place.

Figure 3.3 The Basic Value Chain

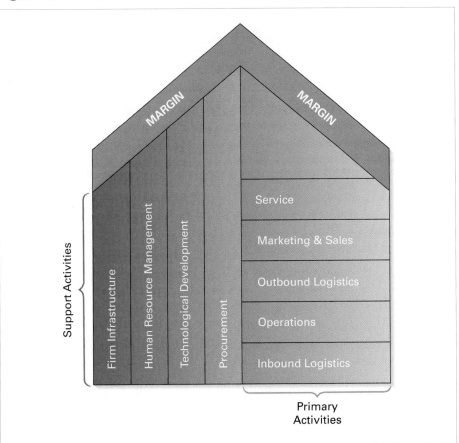

Table 3.6 lists the items that can be evaluated to determine the value-creating potential of primary activities. In Table 3.7, the items for evaluating support activities are shown. All items in both tables should be evaluated relative to competitors' capabilities. To be a source of competitive advantage, a resource or capability must allow the firm (1) to perform an activity in a manner that provides value superior to that provided by competitors, or (2) to perform a value-creating activity that competitors cannot perform. Only under these conditions does a firm create value for customers and have opportunities to capture that value.

Sometimes start-up firms create value by uniquely reconfiguring or recombining parts of the value chain. FedEx changed the nature of the delivery business by reconfiguring outbound logistics (a primary activity) and human resource management (a support activity) to provide overnight deliveries, creating value in the process. As shown in Figure 3.4, on page 87, the Internet has changed many aspects of the value chain for a broad range of firms. A key reason is because the Internet affects how people communicate, locate information, and buy goods and services.

Rating a firm's capability to execute its primary and support activities is challenging. Earlier in the chapter, we noted that identifying and assessing the value of a firm's resources and capabilities requires judgment. Judgment is equally necessary when using value chain analysis, because no obviously correct model or rule is universally available to help in the process.

What should a firm do about primary and support activities in which its resources and capabilities are not a source of core competence and, hence, of competitive advantage? Outsourcing is one solution to consider.

Table 3.6 Examining the Value-Creating Potential of Primary Activities

Inbound Logistics

Activities, such as materials handling, warehousing, and inventory control, used to receive, store, and disseminate inputs to a product.

Operations

Activities necessary to convert the inputs provided by inbound logistics into final product form. Machining, packaging, assembly, and equipment maintenance are examples of operations activities.

Outbound Logistics

Activities involved with collecting, storing, and physically distributing the final product to customers. Examples of these activities include finished-goods warehousing, materials handling, and order processing.

Marketing and Sales

Activities completed to provide means through which customers can purchase products and to induce them to do so. To effectively market and sell products, firms develop advertising and promotional campaigns, select appropriate distribution channels, and select, develop, and support their sales force.

Service

Activities designed to enhance or maintain a product's value. Firms engage in a range of service-related activities, including installation, repair, training, and adjustment.

Each activity should be examined relative to competitors' abilities. Accordingly, firms rate each activity as *superior, equivalent,* or *inferior.*

Source: Adapted with the permission of The Free Press, an imprint of Simon & Schuster Adult Publishing Group, from *Competitive Advantage: Creating and Sustaining Superior Performance,* by Michael E. Porter, pp. 39–40, Copyright © 1985, 1998 by Michael E. Porter.

Table 3.7 Examining the Value-Creating Potential of Support Activities

Procurement

Activities completed to purchase the inputs needed to produce a firm's products. Purchased inputs include items fully consumed during the manufacture of products (e.g., raw materials and supplies, as well as fixed assets—machinery, laboratory equipment, office equipment, and buildings).

Technological Development

Activities completed to improve a firm's product and the processes used to manufacture it. Technological development takes many forms, such as process equipment, basic research and product design, and servicing procedures.

Human Resource Management

Activities involved with recruiting, hiring, training, developing, and compensating all personnel.

Firm Infrastructure

Firm infrastructure includes activities such as general management, planning, finance, accounting, legal support, and governmental relations that are required to support the work of the entire value chain. Through its infrastructure, the firm strives to effectively and consistently identify external opportunities and threats, identify resources and capabilities, and support core competencies.

Each activity should be examined relative to competitors' abilities. Accordingly, firms rate each activity as *superior, equivalent,* or *inferior.*

Source: Adapted with the permission of The Free Press, an imprint of Simon & Schuster Adult Publishing Group, from *Competitive Advantage: Creating and Sustaining Superior Performance,* by Michael E. Porter, pp. 40–43, Copyright © 1985, 1998 by Michael E. Porter.

Figure 3.4 Prominent Applications of the Internet in the Value Chain

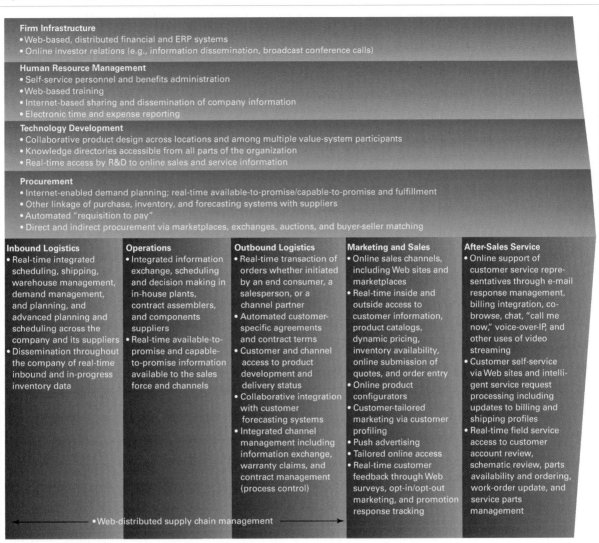

Firm Infrastructure
- Web-based, distributed financial and ERP systems
- Online investor relations (e.g., information dissemination, broadcast conference calls)

Human Resource Management
- Self-service personnel and benefits administration
- Web-based training
- Internet-based sharing and dissemination of company information
- Electronic time and expense reporting

Technology Development
- Collaborative product design across locations and among multiple value-system participants
- Knowledge directories accessible from all parts of the organization
- Real-time access by R&D to online sales and service information

Procurement
- Internet-enabled demand planning; real-time available-to-promise/capable-to-promise and fulfillment
- Other linkage of purchase, inventory, and forecasting systems with suppliers
- Automated "requisition to pay"
- Direct and indirect procurement via marketplaces, exchanges, auctions, and buyer-seller matching

Inbound Logistics	Operations	Outbound Logistics	Marketing and Sales	After-Sales Service
• Real-time integrated scheduling, shipping, warehouse management, demand management, and planning, and advanced planning and scheduling across the company and its suppliers • Dissemination throughout the company of real-time inbound and in-progress inventory data	• Integrated information exchange, scheduling and decision making in in-house plants, contract assemblers, and components suppliers • Real-time available-to-promise and capable-to-promise information available to the sales force and channels	• Real-time transaction of orders whether initiated by an end consumer, a salesperson, or a channel partner • Automated customer-specific agreements and contract terms • Customer and channel access to product development and delivery status • Collaborative integration with customer forecasting systems • Integrated channel management including information exchange, warranty claims, and contract management (process control)	• Online sales channels, including Web sites and marketplaces • Real-time inside and outside access to customer information, product catalogs, dynamic pricing, inventory availability, online submission of quotes, and order entry • Online product configurators • Customer-tailored marketing via customer profiling • Push advertising • Tailored online access • Real-time customer feedback through Web surveys, opt-in/opt-out marketing, and promotion response tracking	• Online support of customer service representatives through e-mail response management, billing integration, co-browse, chat, "call me now," voice-over-IP, and other uses of video streaming • Customer self-service via Web sites and intelligent service request processing including updates to billing and shipping profiles • Real-time field service access to customer account review, schematic review, parts availability and ordering, work-order update, and service parts management

• Web-distributed supply chain management ⟷

Outsourcing

Concerned with how components, finished goods, or services will be obtained, **outsourcing** is the purchase of a value-creating activity from an external supplier.[110] Not-for-profit agencies as well as for-profit organizations actively engage in outsourcing.[111] Firms engaging in effective outsourcing increase their flexibility, mitigate risks, and reduce their capital investments.[112] In multiple global industries, the trend toward outsourcing continues at a rapid pace.[113] Moreover, in some industries virtually all firms seek the value that can be captured through effective outsourcing. The auto manufacturing industry and, more recently, the electronics industry are two such examples. As with other strategic management process decisions, careful analysis is required before the firm decides to engage in outsourcing.[114]

Outsourcing can be effective because few, if any, organizations possess the resources and capabilities required to achieve competitive superiority in all primary and support activities. For example, research suggests that few companies can afford to develop internally all the technologies that might lead to competitive advantage.[115] By nurturing a smaller number of capabilities, a firm increases the probability of developing a competitive advantage because

Outsourcing is the purchase of a value-creating activity from an external supplier.

it does not become overextended. Too, by outsourcing activities in which it lacks competence, the firm can fully concentrate on those areas in which it can create value.

Firms must outsource only activities where they cannot create value or where they are at a substantial disadvantage compared to competitors.[116] To verify that the appropriate primary and support activities are outsourced, managers should have four skills: strategic thinking, deal making, partnership governance, and change management.[117] Managers need to understand whether and how outsourcing creates competitive advantage within their company—they need to be able to think strategically.[118] To complete effective outsourcing transactions, these managers must also be deal makers, able to secure rights from external providers that can be fully used by internal managers. They must be able to oversee and govern appropriately the relationship with the company to which the services were outsourced. Because outsourcing can significantly change how an organization operates, managers administering these programs must also be able to manage that change, including resolving employee resistance that accompanies any significant change effort.[119]

The consequences of outsourcing cause additional concerns.[120] For the most part, these concerns revolve around the potential loss in firms' innovative ability and the loss of jobs within companies that decide to outsource some of their work activities to others. Thus, innovation and technological uncertainty are two important issues to consider in making outsourcing decisions.[121] Companies must be aware of these issues and be prepared to fully consider the concerns about outsourcing when different stakeholders (e.g., employees) express them.

As is true with all strategic management tools and techniques, criteria should be established to guide outsourcing decisions. Outsourcing is big business (U.S. firms spent more than $68 billion on outsourcing in 2006 alone), but not every outsourcing decision is successful. For example, amid delays and cost overruns, Electronic Data Systems abandoned a $1 billion opportunity to run Dow Chemical Co.'s phone-and-computer networks. Stemming from customer complaints, Dell and Lehman Brothers Holdings decided not to move some of the customer call center operations to locations outside the United States.[122] These less-than-desirable outcomes indicate that firms should carefully study outsourcing possibilities to verify that engaging in them will indeed create value that exceeds the cost incurred to generate that value.

Competencies, Strengths, Weaknesses, and Strategic Decisions

At the conclusion of the internal analysis, firms must identify their strengths and weaknesses in resources, capabilities, and core competencies. For example, if they have weak capabilities or do not have core competencies in areas required to achieve a competitive advantage, they must acquire those resources and build the capabilities and competencies needed. Alternatively, they could decide to outsource a function or activity where they are weak in order to improve the value that they provide to customers.[123]

Therefore, firms need to have the appropriate resources and capabilities to develop the desired strategy and create value for customers and other stakeholders such as shareholders.[124] Managers should understand that having a significant quantity of resources is not the same as having the "right" resources. Moreover, decision makers sometimes become more focused and productive when their organization's resources are constrained.[125] In the final analysis, those with decision-making responsibilities must help the firm obtain and use resources, capabilities, and core competencies in ways that will generate value-creating competitive advantages. Top-level managers are responsible for verifying that these tasks happen.[126]

Tools such as outsourcing help the firm focus on its core competencies as the source of its competitive advantages. However, evidence shows that the value-creating ability of core competencies should never be taken for granted. Moreover, the ability of a core competence to be a permanent competitive advantage can't be assumed. The reason for these cautions is that all core competencies have the potential to become *core rigidities*. Leslie Wexner, CEO of Limited Brands, describes this possibility: "Success doesn't beget success. Success begets failure because the more that you know a thing works, the less likely you are to think that it won't work. When you've had a long string of victories, it's harder to foresee your own vulnerabilities."[127] Thus, a core competence is usually a strength because it is the source of competitive advantage. If emphasized when it is no longer competitively relevant, it can become a weakness, a seed of organizational inertia.

Inertia around organizational culture may be a problem at Ford Motor Company where some argue that in essence, the firm's culture has become a core rigidity that is constraining efforts to improve performance. In one writer's words: "One way or another, the company will have to figure out how to produce more vehicles that consumers actually want. And doing that will require addressing the most fundamental problem of all: Ford's dysfunctional, often defeatist culture."[128] In contrast, Toyota, which earned record profits of

What is the "Toyota Code of Conduct"?

Our daily business operations are built on and supported by the corporate philosophy and its values and methods that have developed through years of diligent effort and passed down from generation to generation throughout TOYOTA MOTOR CORPORATION and its subsidiaries ("**TOYOTA**").

The "Guiding Principles at Toyota" (originally issued in 1992, revised in 1997) summarize the corporate philosophy and reflects TOYOTA's vision of what kind of company TOYOTA would like to be. The "Guiding Principles at Toyota" were created with the expectation that we would understand and share our fundamental management principles, and that we would contribute to society by referring to these principles.

The "Toyota Way" and the "Toyota Code of Conduct" serve as important guiding tools when implementing our daily business operations to realize the "Guiding Principles at Toyota". "Toyota Way" (issued in 2001) describes the values and methods to be shared for the people of the global TOYOTA organization.

The present "Toyota Code of Conduct" (originally issued in 1998, revised in 2006) seeks to provide a basic code of conduct and to serve as a model and compass. It also provides detailed explanations and examples of the actions and issues that we must be aware of when carrying out actual business activities (including in our jobs and daily business operations) and living in our global society.

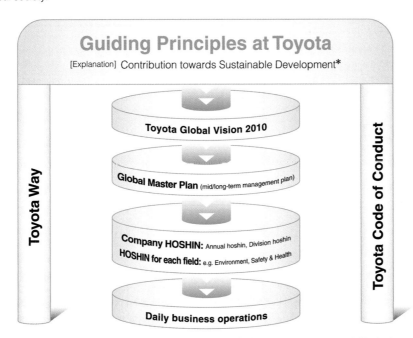

Guiding Principles at Toyota

[Explanation] Contribution towards Sustainable Development*

Toyota Way

Toyota Code of Conduct

Toyota Global Vision 2010

Global Master Plan (mid/long-term management plan)

Company HOSHIN: Annual hoshin, Division hoshin
HOSHIN for each field: e.g. Environment, Safety & Health

Daily business operations

*Interprets the "Guiding Principles at Toyota" from the standpoint of how TOYOTA can work towards sustainable development in its interactions with its stakeholders (Issued in January 2005).

Toyota's Code of Conduct clearly outlines, for its employees, the firm's competencies and methods for continuous improvement. This code has been revised twice and is based on Toyota's Guiding Principles.

$15 billion in 2006, is carefully reexamining product planning, customer service, sales and marketing, and employee training practices to prevent "being spoiled by success."[129]

Events occurring in the firm's external environment create conditions through which core competencies can become core rigidities, generate inertia, and stifle innovation. "Often the flip side, the dark side, of core capabilities is revealed due to external events when new competitors figure out a better way to serve the firm's customers, when new technologies emerge, or when political or social events shift the ground underneath."[130] However, in the final analysis, changes in the external environment do not cause core competencies to become core rigidities; rather, strategic myopia and inflexibility on the part of managers are the cause.

After studying its external environment to determine what it *might choose to do* (as explained in Chapter 2) and its internal organization to understand what it *can do* (as explained in this chapter), the firm has the information required to select a business-level strategy that will help it reach its vision and mission. We describe different business-level strategies in the next chapter.

Summary

- In the global business environment, traditional factors (e.g., labor costs and superior access to financial resources and raw materials) can still create a competitive advantage. However, these factors are less and less often a source of competitive advantage. In the new landscape, the resources, capabilities, and core competencies in the firm's internal organization may have a relatively stronger influence on its performance than do conditions in the external environment. The most effective organizations recognize that strategic competitiveness and above-average returns result only when core competencies (identified by studying the firm's internal organization) are matched with opportunities (determined by studying the firm's external environment).

- No competitive advantage lasts forever. Over time, rivals use their own unique resources, capabilities, and core competencies to form different value-creating propositions that duplicate the value-creating ability of the firm's competitive advantages. In general, the Internet's capabilities are reducing the sustainability of many competitive advantages. Because competitive advantages are not permanently sustainable, firms must exploit their current advantages while simultaneously using their resources and capabilities to form new advantages that can lead to future competitive success.

- Effectively managing core competencies requires careful analysis of the firm's resources (inputs to the production process) and capabilities (resources that have been purposely integrated to achieve a specific task or set of tasks). The knowledge possessed by human capital is among the most significant of an organization's capabilities and may ultimately be at the root of all competitive advantages. The firm must create an environment that allows people to integrate their individual knowledge with that held by others so that, collectively, the firm has significant organizational knowledge.

- Individual resources are usually not a source of competitive advantage. Capabilities are a more likely source of competitive advantages, especially relatively sustainable ones. The firm's nurturing and support of core competencies that are based on capabilities is less visible to rivals and, as such, harder to understand and imitate.

- Only when a capability is valuable, rare, costly to imitate, and nonsubstitutable is it a core competence and a source of competitive advantage. Over time, core competencies must be supported, but they cannot be allowed to become core rigidities. Core competencies are a source of competitive advantage only when they allow the firm to create value by exploiting opportunities in its external environment. When it can no longer do so, the company shifts its attention to selecting or forming other capabilities that do satisfy the four criteria of sustainable competitive advantage.

- Value chain analysis is used to identify and evaluate the competitive potential of resources and capabilities. By studying their skills relative to those associated with primary and support activities, firms can understand their cost structure and identify the activities through which they can create value.

- When the firm cannot create value in either a primary or support activity, outsourcing is considered. Used commonly in the global economy, outsourcing is the purchase of a value-creating activity from an external supplier. The firm must outsource only to companies possessing a competitive advantage in terms of the particular primary or support activity under consideration. In addition, the firm must continuously verify that it is not outsourcing activities from which it could create value.

Review Questions

1. Why is it important for a firm to study and understand its internal organization?

2. What is value? Why is it critical for the firm to create value? How does it do so?

3. What are the differences between tangible and intangible resources? Why is it important for decision makers to understand these differences? Are tangible resources linked more closely to the creation of competitive advantages than are intangible resources, or is the reverse true? Why?

4. What are capabilities? What must firms do to create capabilities?

5. What are the four criteria used to determine which of a firm's capabilities are core competencies? Why is it important for these criteria to be used?

6. What is value chain analysis? What does the firm gain when it successfully uses this tool?

7. What is outsourcing? Why do firms outsource? Will outsourcing's importance grow in the twenty-first century? If so, why?

8. How do firms identify internal strengths and weaknesses? Why is it vital that managers have a clear understanding of their firm's strengths and weaknesses?

Notes

1. M. E. Mangelsdorf, 2007, Beyond enterprise 2.0, *MIT Sloan Management Review*, 48(3): 50–55.

2. J. G. Covin & M. P. Miles, 2007, Strategic use of corporate venturing, *Entrepreneurship Theory and Practice*, 31, 183–207; R. R. Wiggins & T. W. Ruefli, 2002, Sustained competitive advantage: Temporal dynamics and the incidence of persistence of superior economic performance, *Organization Science*, 13: 82–105.

3. W. M. Becker & V. M. Freeman, 2006, Going from global trends to corporate strategy, *McKinsey Quarterly*, Number 3: 17–27; S. K. McEvily, K. M. Eisenhardt, & J. E. Prescott, 2004, The global acquisition, leverage, and protection of technological competencies, *Strategic Management Journal*, 25: 713–722.

4. J. Quittner, 2007, Selling pet owners peace of mind, *Business Week*, May 8, 48.

5. N. T. Sheehan & N. J. Foss, 2007, Enhancing the prescriptiveness of the resource-based view through Porterian activity analysis, *Management Decision*, 45: 450–461; S. Dutta, M. J. Zbaracki, & M. Bergen, 2003, Pricing process as a capability: A resource-based perspective, *Strategic Management Journal*, 24: 615–630; A. M. Knott, 2003, Persistent heterogeneity and sustainable innovation, *Strategic Management Journal*, 24: 687–705.

6. C. G. Brush, P. G. Greene, & M. M. Hart, 2001, From initial idea to unique advantage: The entrepreneurial challenge of constructing a resource base, *Academy of Management Executive*, 15(1): 64–78.

7. R. L. Priem, 2007, A consumer perspective on value creation, *Academy of Management Review*, 32: 219–235.

8. D. G. Sirmon, M. A. Hitt, & R. D. Ireland, 2007, Managing firm resources in dynamic markets to create value: Looking inside the black box, *Academy of Management Review*, 32: 273–292.

9. S. C. Kang, S. S. Morris, & S. A. Snell, 2007, Relational archetypes, organizational learning, and value creation: Extending the human resource architecture, *Academy of Management Review*, 32: 236–256.

10. S. Raisch & G. von Krog, 2007, Navigating a path to smart growth, *MIT Sloan Management Review*, 48(3): 65–72.

11. D. DePass, 2006, Cuts in incentives upset 3M supervisors, *Star Tribune*, December 16.

12. C. D. Zatzick & R. D. Iverson, 2007, High-involvement management and workforce reduction: Competitive advantage or disadvantage? *Academy of Management Journal*, 49: 999–1015.

13. R. Florida, 2005, *The Flight of the Creative Class*, New York: HarperBusiness.

14. A. W. King, 2007, Disentangling interfirm and intrafirm causal ambiguity: A conceptual model of causal ambiguity and sustainable competitive advantage, *Academy of Management Review*, 32: 156–178; J. Shamsie, 2003, The context of dominance: An industry-driven framework for exploiting reputation, *Strategic Management Journal*, 24: 199–215.

15. U. Ljungquist, 2007, Core competency beyond identification: Presentation of a model, *Management Decision*, 45: 393–402; M. Makhija, 2003, Comparing the resource-based and market-based view of the firm: Empirical evidence from Czech privatization, *Strategic Management Journal*, 24: 433–451.

16. R. D. Ireland & J. W. Webb, 2007, Strategic entrepreneurship: Creating competitive advantage through streams of innovation, *Business Horizons*, 50: 49–59.

17. M. A. Peteraf & J. B. Barney, 2003, Unraveling the resource-based tangle, *Managerial and Decision Economics*, 24: 309–323; J. B. Barney, 2001, Is the resource-based "view" a useful perspective for strategic management research? Yes, *Academy of Management Review*, 26: 41–56.

18. D. P. Lepak, K. G. Smith, & M. Susan Taylor, 2007, Value creation and value capture: A multilevel perspective, *Academy of Management Review*, 32: 180–194.

19. G. Katz, 2007, Assembling a future, *Houston Chronicle*, July 5, D1, D4.

20. T. M. Begley & D. P. Boyd, 2003, The need for a corporate global mind-set, *MIT Sloan Management Review*, 44(2): 25–32.

21. L. Gratton, 2007, Handling hot spots, *Business Strategy Review*, 18(2): 9–14.

22. O. Levy, S. Beechler, S. Taylor, & N. A. Boyacigiller, 2007, What we talk about when we talk about "global mindset": Managerial cognition in multinational corporations, *Journal of International Business Studies*, 38: 231–258.

23. Sirmon, Hitt, & Ireland, Managing resources in a dynamic environment.

24. D. A. Chmielewski & A. Paladino, 2007, Driving a resource orientation: Reviewing the role of resource and capability characteristics, *Managerial Decision*, 45: 462–483; Barney, Is the resource-based "view" a useful perspective for strategic management research? Yes.

25. K. J. Mayer & R. M. Salomon, 2006, Capabilities, contractual hazards, and governance: Integrating resource-based and transaction cost perspectives, *Academy of Management Journal*, 49: 942–959.

26. S. K. McEvily & B. Chakravarthy, 2002, The persistence of knowledge-based advantage: An empirical test for product performance and technological

knowledge, *Strategic Management Journal*, 23: 285–305.

27. D. Kaplan, 2007, A new look for Luby's, *Houston Chronicle*, July 4, D1, D5.

28. J. L. Morrow, Jr., D. G. Sirmon, M. A. Hitt, & T. R. Holcomb, 2007, Creating value in the face of declining performance: Firm strategies and organizational recovery, *Strategic Management Journal*, 28: 271–283.

29. E. Danneels, 2007, The process of technological competence leveraging, *Strategic Management Journal*, 28: 511–533; S. Nambisan, 2002, Designing virtual customer environments for new product development: Toward a theory, *Academy of Management Review*, 27: 392–413.

30. J. J. Neff, 2007, What drives consumers not to buy cars, *BusinessWeek*, July 9, 16.

31. K. Chaharbaghi, 2007, The problematic of strategy: A way of seeing is also a way of not seeing, *Management Decision*, 45: 327–339.

32. V. Shankar & B. L. Bayus, 2003, Network effects and competition: An empirical analysis of the home video game industry, *Strategic Management Journal*, 24: 375–384.

33. Morrow, Sirmon, Hitt, & Holcomb, Creating value in the face of declining performance; G. Hawawini, V. Subramanian, & P. Verdin, 2003, Is performance driven by industry- or firm-specific factors? A new look at the evidence, *Strategic Management Journal*, 24: 1–16.

34. M. R. Haas & M. T. Hansen, 2005, When using knowledge can hurt performance: The value of organizational capabilities in a management consulting company, *Strategic Management Journal*, 26: 1–24.

35. C. M. Christensen, 2001, The past and future of competitive advantage, *Sloan Management Review*, 42(2): 105–109.

36. O. Gottschalg & M. Zollo, 2007, Interest alignment and competitive advantage, *Academy of Management Review*, 32: 418–437.

37. D. P. Forbes, 2007, Reconsidering the strategic implications of decision comprehensiveness, *Academy of Management Review*, 32: 361–376; J. R. Hough & M. A. White, 2003, Environmental dynamism and strategic decision-making rationality: An examination at the decision level, *Strategic Management Journal*, 24: 481–489.

38. T. M. Jones, W. Felps, & G. A. Bigley, 2007, Ethical theory and stakeholder-related decisions: The role of stakeholder culture, *Academy of Management Review*, 32: 137–155; D. C. Kayes, D. Stirling, & T. M. Nielsen, 2007, Building organizational integrity, *Business Horizons*, 50: 61–70.

39. Y. Deutsch, T. Keil, & T. Laamanen, 2007, Decision making in acquisitions: The effect of outside directors' compensation on acquisition patterns, *Journal of Management*, 33: 30–56.

40. M. De Rond & R. A. Thietart, 2007, Choice, chance, and inevitability in strategy, *Strategic Management Journal*, 28: 535–551.

41. C. C. Miller & R. D. Ireland, 2005, Intuition in strategic decision making: Friend or foe in the fast-paced 21st century? *Academy of Management Executive*, 19(1): 19–30; P. Westhead, M. Wright, & D. Ucbasaran, 2001, The internationalization of new and small firms: A resource-based view, *Journal of Business Venturing*, 16: 333–358.

42. L. M. Lodish & C. F. Mela, 2007, If brands are built over years, why are they managed over quarters? *Harvard Business Review*, 85(7/8): 104–112; H. J. Smith, 2003, The shareholders vs. stakeholders debate, *MIT Sloan Management Review*, 44(4): 85–90.

43. P. C. Nutt, 2002, *Why Decisions Fail*, San Francisco: Berrett-Koehler Publishers.

44. R. Martin, 2007, How successful leaders think, 85(6): *Harvard Business Review*, 61–67.

45. Polaroid Corporation, 2007, Wikipedia, http://en.wikipedia.org/wiki/Polaroid_Corporation, July 5.

46. J. M. Mezias & W. H. Starbuck, 2003, What do managers know, anyway? *Harvard Business Review*, 81(5): 16–17.

47. P. G. Audia, E. Locke, & K. G. Smith, 2000, The paradox of success: An archival and a laboratory study of strategic persistence following radical environmental change, *Academy of Management Journal*, 43: 837–853; R. G. McGrath, 1999, Falling forward: Real options reasoning and entrepreneurial failure, *Academy of Management Review*, 24: 13–30.

48. C. O. Longenecker, M. J. Neubert, & L. S. Fink, 2007, Causes and consequences of managerial failure in rapidly changing organizations, *Business Horizons*, 50: 145–155; G. P. West III & J. DeCastro, 2001, The Achilles' heel of firm strategy: Resource weaknesses and distinctive inadequacies, *Journal of Management Studies*, 38: 417–442; G. Gavetti & D. Levinthal, 2000, Looking forward and looking backward: Cognitive and experimental search, *Administrative Science Quarterly*, 45: 113–137.

49. K. K. Reardon, 2007, Courage as a skill, *Harvard Business Review*, 85(1): 58–64.

50. R. Amit & P. J. H. Schoemaker, 1993, Strategic assets and organizational rent, *Strategic Management Journal*, 14: 33–46.

51. S. J. Carson, A. Madhok, & T. Wu, 2006, Uncertainty, opportunism, and governance: The effects of volatility and ambiguity on formal and relational contracting, *Academy of Management Journal*, 49: 1058–1077; R. E. Hoskisson & L. W. Busenitz, 2001, Market uncertainty and learning distance in corporate entrepreneurship entry mode choice, in M. A. Hitt, R. D. Ireland, S. M. Camp, & D. L. Sexton (eds.), *Strategic Entrepreneurship: Creating a New Integrated Mindset*, Oxford, UK: Blackwell Publishers, 151–172.

52. C. M. Fiol & E. J. O'Connor, 2003, Waking up! Mindfulness in the face of bandwagons, *Academy of Management Review*, 28: 54–70.

53. N. Byrnes & A. Aston, 2007, Coal? Yes, coal, *Business Week*, May 7, 60–63.

54. G. P. West, III, 2007, Collective cognition: When entrepreneurial teams, not individuals, make decisions, *Entrepreneurship Theory and Practice*, 31: 77–102.

55. N. J. Hiller & D. C. Hambrick, 2005, Conceptualizing executive hubris: The role of (hyper-) core self-evaluations in strategic decision making, *Strategic Management Journal*, 26: 297–319.

56. C. Stadler, 2007, The four principles of enduring success, *Harvard Business Review*, 85(7/8): 62–72.

57. C. Pasariello, 2007, Is Hermes out of fashion? *Wall Street Journal Online*, June 7, http://online.wsj.com.

58. Forbes, Reconsidering the strategic implications.

59. Mayer & Salomon, Capabilities, contractual hazards, and governance; D. M. De Carolis, 2003, Competencies and imitability in the pharmaceutical industry: An analysis of their relationship with firm performance, *Journal of Management*, 29: 27–50.

60. G. Ahuja & R. Katila, 2004, Where do resources come from? The role of idiosyncratic situations, *Strategic Management Journal*, 25: 887–907.

61. J. McGree & H. Thomas, 2007, Knowledge as a lens on the jigsaw puzzle of strategy, *Management Decision*, 45: 539–563.

62. Sirmon, Hitt, & Ireland, Managing firm resources in dynamic environments; S. Berman, J. Down, & C. Hill, 2002, Tacit knowledge as a source of competitive advantage in the National Basketball Association, *Academy of Management Journal*, 45: 13–31.

63. 2007, Borders. Teamed with Amazon.com, July 7, http://www.amazon.com.

64. K. G. Smith, C. J. Collins, & K. D. Clark, 2005, Existing knowledge, knowledge creation capability, and the rate of new product introduction in high-technology firms, *Academy of Management Journal*, 48: 346–357; S. G. Winter, 2005, Developing evolutionary theory for economics and management, in K. G. Smith and M. A. Hitt (eds.), *Great Minds in Management: The Process of Theory Development*. Oxford, UK: Oxford University Press, 509–546.

65. J. A. Dubin, 2007, Valuing intangible assets with a nested logit market share model, *Journal of Econometrics*, 139: 285–302.

66. A. M. Webber, 2000, New math for a new economy, *Fast Company*, January/February, 214–224.

67. M. Song, C. Droge, S. Hanvanich, & R. Calantone, 2005, Marketing and technology resource complementarity: An analysis of their interaction effect in two environmental contexts, *Strategic Management Journal*, 26: 259–276; R. G. Schroeder, K. A. Bates, & M. A. Junttila, 2002, A resource-based view of manufacturing strategy and the relationship to manufacturing

performance, *Strategic Management Journal,* 23: 105–117.

68. M. A. Hitt & R. D. Ireland, 2002, The essence of strategic leadership: Managing human and social capital, *Journal of Leadership and Organization Studies,* 9(1): 3–14.

69. J. B. Quinn, P. Anderson, & S. Finkelstein, 1996, Making the most of the best, *Harvard Business Review,* 74(2): 71–80.

70. N. Stieglitz & K. Heine, 2007, Innovations and the role of complementarities in a strategic theory of the firm, *Strategic Management Journal,* 28: 1–15.

71. R. D. Ireland, M. A. Hitt, & D. Vaidyanath, 2002, Managing strategic alliances to achieve a competitive advantage, *Journal of Management,* 28: 416–446.

72. E. Fischer & R. Reuber, 2007, The good, the bad, and the unfamiliar: The challenges of reputation formation facing new firms, *Entrepreneurship Theory and Practice,* 31: 53–75.

73. D. L. Deephouse, 2000, Media reputation as a strategic resource: An integration of mass communication and resource-based theories, *Journal of Management,* 26: 1091–1112.

74. P. Engardio & M. Arndt, 2007, What price reputation? *BusinessWeek,* July 9, 70–79.

75. P. Berthon, M. B. Holbrook, & J. M. Hulbert, 2003, Understanding and managing the brand space, *MIT Sloan Management Review,* 44(2): 49–54; D. B. Holt, 2003, What becomes an icon most? *Harvard Business Review,* 81(3): 43–49.

76. J. Blasberg & V. Vishwanath, 2003, Making cool brands hot, *Harvard Business Review,* 81(6): 20–22.

77. 2007, Harley-Davidson MotorClothes Merchandise, July 7, http://www.harley-davidson.com.

78. D. Roberts & S. Holmes, 2005, China's real sports contest, *BusinessWeek Online,* http://www.businessweek.com, March 14.

79. S. Dutta, O. Narasimhan, & S. Rajiv, 2005, Conceptualizing and measuring capabilities: Methodology and empirical application, *Strategic Management Journal,* 26: 277–285.

80. J. Bitar & T. Hafsi, 2007, Strategizing through the capability lens: Sources and outcomes of integration, *Management Decision,* 45: 403–419; M. A. Hitt, R. D. Ireland, & H. Lee, 2000, Technological learning, knowledge management, firm growth and performance: An introductory essay, *Journal of Engineering and Technology Management,* 17: 231–246.

81. S. K. Ethiraj, P. Kale, M. S. Krishnan, & J. V. Singh, 2005, Where do capabilities come from and do they matter? A study in the software services industry, *Strategic Management Journal,* 26: 25–45.

82. M. G. Jacobides & S. G. Winter, 2005, The co-evolution of capabilities and transaction costs: Explaining the institutional structure of production, *Strategic Management Journal,* 26: 395–413.

83. R. W. Coff & P. M. Lee, 2003, Insider trading as a vehicle to appropriate rent from R&D, *Strategic Management Journal,* 24: 183–190.

84. T. A. Stewart & A. P. Raman, 2007, Lessons from Toyota's long drive, *Harvard Business Review,* 85(7/8): 74–83.

85. Y. Liu, J. G. Combs, D. J. Ketchen, Jr., & R. D. Ireland, 2007, The value of human resource management for organizational performance, *Business Horizons,* in press; D. L. Deeds, 2003, Alternative strategies for acquiring knowledge, in S. E. Jackson, M. A. Hitt, & A. S. DeNisi (eds.), *Managing Knowledge for Sustained Competitive Advantage,* San Francisco: Jossey-Bass, 37–63.

86. B. Connelly, M. A. Hitt, A. S. DeNisi, & R. D. Ireland, 2007, Expatriates and corporate-level international strategy: Governing with the knowledge contract, *Management Decision,* 45: 564–581.

87. M. J. Tippins & R. S. Sohi, 2003, IT competency and firm performance: Is organizational learning a missing link? *Strategic Management Journal,* 24: 745–761.

88. C. Zott, 2003, Dynamic capabilities and the emergence of intraindustry differential firm performance: Insights from a simulation study, *Strategic Management Journal,* 24: 97–125.

89. K. Hafeez, Y. B. Zhang, & N. Malak, 2002, Core competence for sustainable competitive advantage: A structured methodology for identifying core competence, *IEEE Transactions on Engineering Management,* 49(1): 28–35; C. K. Prahalad & G. Hamel, 1990, The core competence of the corporation, *Harvard Business Review,* 68(3): 79–93.

90. G. Colvin, 2007, Xerox's inventor-in-chief, *Fortune,* July 9, 65–72.

91. 2006, Xerox Annual Report, December, http://www.zerox.com.

92. Quittner, Selling pet owners peace of mind.

93. 2005, Jack Welch: It's all in the sauce, *Fortune Online,* April 4, http://www.fortune.com.

94. J. B. Barney, 1995, Looking inside for competitive advantage, *Academy of Management Executive,* 9(4): 49–60.

95. Ibid., 53.

96. J. B. Barney, 1991, Firm resources and sustained competitive advantage, *Journal of Management,* 17: 99–120.

97. L. E. Tetrick & N. Da Silva, 2003, Assessing the culture and climate for organizational learning, in S. E. Jackson, M. A. Hitt, & A. S. DeNisi (eds.), *Managing Knowledge for Sustained Competitive Advantage,* San Francisco: Jossey-Bass, 333–359.

98. L. Soupata, 2001, Managing culture for competitive advantage at United Parcel Service, *Journal of Organizational Excellence,* 20(3): 19–26.

99. K. Stinebaker, 2007, Global company puts focus on people, *Houston Chronicle Online,* February 18, http://www.chron.com.

100. A. W. King & C. P. Zeithaml, 2001, Competencies and firm performance: Examining the causal ambiguity paradox, *Strategic Management Journal,* 22: 75–99.

101. 2007, Ryanair, Wikipedia, July 7, http://en.wikipedia.org/wiki/ryanair.

102. Barney, Firm resources, 111.

103. M. J. Benner & M. L. Tushman, 2003, Exploitation, exploration, and process management: The productivity dilemma revisited, *Academy of Management Review,* 28: 238–256; S. K. McEvily, S. Das, & K. McCabe, 2000, Avoiding competence substitution through knowledge sharing, *Academy of Management Review,* 25: 294–311.

104. D. J. Ketchen, Jr., & G. T. M. Hult, 2007, Bridging organization theory and supply chain management: The case of best value supply chains, *Journal of Operations Management,* 25: 573–580.

105. M. E. Porter, 1985, *Competitive Advantage,* New York: Free Press, 33–61.

106. J. Alcacer, 2006, Location choices across the value chain: How activity and capability influence co-location, *Management Science,* 52: 1457–1471.

107. 2007, Riding the global value chain, *Chief Executive Online,* January/February, http://www.chiefexecutive.net.

108. R. Locke & M. Romis, 2007, Global supply chain, *MIT Sloan Management Review,* 48(2): 54–62.

109. R. Amit & C. Zott, 2001, Value creation in e-business, *Strategic Management Journal,* 22 (Special Issue): 493–520; M. E. Porter, 2001, Strategy and the Internet, *Harvard Business Review,* 79(3): 62–78.

110. M. J. Power, K. C. DeSouze, & C. Bonifazi, 2006, *The Outsourcing Handbook: How to Implement a Successful Outsourcing Process,* Philadelphia: Kogan Page.

111. P.-W. Tam, 2007, Business technology: Outsourcing finds new niche, *Wall Street Journal,* April 17, B5.

112. S. Nambisan & M. Sawhney, 2007, A buyer's guide to the innovation bazaar, *Harvard Business Review,* 85(6): 109–118.

113. Y. Shi, 2007, Today's solution and tomorrow's problem: The business process outsourcing risk management puzzle, *California Management Review,* 49(3): 27–44.

114. A. Tiwana & M. Keil, 2007, Does peripheral knowledge complement control? An empirical test in technology outsourcing alliances, *Strategic Management Journal,* 28: 623–634; M. J. Leiblein, J. J. Reuer, & F. Dalsace, 2002, Do make or buy decisions matter? The influence of organizational governance on technological performance, *Strategic Management Journal,* 23: 817–833.

115. J. C. Linder, S. Jarvenpaa, & T. H. Davenport, 2003, Toward an innovation sourcing strategy, *MIT Sloan Management Review,* 44(4): 43–49.

116. S. Lohr, 2007, At IBM, a smarter way to outsource, *New York Times Online,* July 5, http://nytimes.com.

117. M. Useem & J. Harder, 2000, Leading laterally in company outsourcing, *Sloan Management Review,* 41(2): 25–36.

118. R. C. Insinga & M. J. Werle, 2000, Linking outsourcing to business strategy, *Academy of Management Executive,* 14(4): 58–70.

119. B. Arrunada & X. H. Vazquez, 2006, When your contract manufacturer becomes your competitor, *Harvard Business Review,* 84(9): 135–144.

120. E. Perez & J. Karp, 2007, U.S. to probe outsourcing after ITT case, *Wall Street Journal* (Eastern Edition), March 28, A3, A6.

121. M. J. Mol, P. Pauwels, P. Matthyssens, & L. Quintens, 2004, A technological contingency perspective on the depth and scope of international outsourcing, *Journal of International Management,* 10: 287–305.

122. S. Thurm, 2007, Beyond outsourcing: Promise and pitfalls, *Wall Street Journal* (Eastern Edition), February 26, B3, B6.

123. M. A. Hitt, D. Ahlstrom, M. T. Dacin, E. Levitas, & L. Svobodina, 2004, The institutional effects on strategic alliance partner selection in transition economies: China versus Russia, *Organization Science,* 15: 173–185.

124. T. Felin & W. S. Hesterly, 2007, The knowledge-based view, nested heterogeneity, and new value creation: Philosophical considerations on the locus of knowledge, *Academy of Management Review,* 32: 195–218; Y. Mishina, T. G. Pollock, & J. F. Porac, 2004, Are more resources always better for growth? Resource stickiness in market and product expansion, *Strategic Management Journal,* 25: 1179–1197.

125. M. Gibbert, M. Hoegl, & L. Valikangas, 2007, In praise of resource constraints, *MIT Sloan Management Review,* 48(3): 15–17.

126. D. S. Elenkov & I. M. Manev, 2005, Top management leadership and influence in innovation: The role of sociocultural context, *Journal of Management,* 31: 381–402.

127. M. Katz, 2001, Planning ahead for manufacturing facility changes: A case study in outsourcing, *Pharmaceutical Technology,* March: 160–164.

128. D. Kiley, 2007, The new heat on Ford, *BusinessWeek,* June 4, 32–37.

129. D. Welch, 2007, Staying paranoid at Toyota, *BusinessWeek,* July 2, 80–82.

130. Leonard-Barton, *Wellsprings of Knowledge,* 30–31.

Part 2

Strategic Actions: Strategy Formulation

Chapter 4
Building and Sustaining Competitive Advantage, 96

Chapter 5
Strategy at the Business Level, 122

Chapter 6
Corporate-Level Strategy, 152

Chapter 7
Acquisition and Restructuring Strategies, 180

Chapter 8
International Strategy, 210

Chapter 9
Cooperative Strategy, 244

Building and Sustaining Competitive Advantage

4

Studying this chapter should provide you with the strategic management knowledge needed to:

1. Define competitors, competitive rivalry, competitive behavior, and competitive dynamics.

2. Describe market commonality and resource similarity as the building blocks of a competitor analysis.

3. Explain awareness, motivation, and ability as drivers of competitive behavior.

4. Discuss factors affecting the likelihood a competitor will take competitive actions.

5. Discuss factors affecting the likelihood a competitor will respond to actions taken against it.

6. Explain competitive dynamics in slow-cycle, fast-cycle, and standard-cycle markets.

Competition Between Hewlett-Packard and Dell: The Battle Rages On

"I'm going to be the CEO for the next several years. We're going to fix this business." Michael Dell's words suggest that Dell Inc.'s founder and newly reinstalled CEO intends to do everything he can to correct the problems that led to the loss of the position as the top seller of personal computers (PCs) on a global basis. Indeed, at the close of 2006, Hewlett-Packard (HP) commanded 18.1 percent of the global PC market while Dell's share slipped to 14.7 percent. The market share loss seemingly contributed to the 32 percent total decline in the value of Dell Inc.'s stock during 2005 and 2006. (HP's stock doubled in value over the same time period.)

The performance declines were a new experience for Dell, which grew from an initial $1,000 investment in 1984 to a $56 billion dollar business in 2007. Dell's growth was founded on a "stroke of genius—to bypass the middle-man and sell custom-built computers directly to the consumer." Some analysts consider this approach, which became known as the "Dell Way," to be "one of the revolutionary business models of the late 20th century." But this approach no longer creates value to the degree that has been the case historically. The reasons for the change flow out of a tale of competitive actions and competitive reactions.

Over time, Dell and its competitive actions focused on finding ways to use its business model to continuously lower its costs and hence the prices of its products. Concentrating on a single business model can lead to quick growth when demand for a firm's products continues to expand. Across time though, innovation and reinvention are the foundation for continued success.

Over the past several years, HP found ways to innovate and reinvent itself. After examining its business model, Todd Bradely, the executive who now heads HP's PC operations, concluded that "HP was fighting on the wrong battlefield. HP was concentrating its resources to fight Dell where Dell was strong, in direct sales over the Internet and phone. Instead (Bradely) decided, HP should focus on its strength, retail stores, where Dell had no presence at all." To successfully change its focus, HP developed close relationships with retailers, even trying to "personalize" PCs. Consistent with a "The Computer Is Personal Again" campaign, HP features celebrities (e.g., fashion designer Vera Wang and hip-hop mogul Jay-Z) in its advertisements and is producing unique products for different retailers. For example, HP worked with Best Buy to design and produce a white-and-silver notebook computer. Aimed at attracting female customers, this machine was priced at $1,100 and was one of Best Buy's top-selling notebooks during the 2006 holiday season.

Dell's decision to venture into retail selling is a competitive reaction to HP's actions. Dell is now partnering with a Japanese retailer (Bic Camera Inc.) to sell notebooks and desktops throughout Japan. Additionally, Dell is experimenting with its own retail stores, opening its first one in Dallas, Texas, in July 2007. (Other Dell retail outlets are in the planning stages.) Dell is also committing additional monies to research and development (to find product innovations) and is restructuring some of its advertising campaigns "to remind consumers of the benefits of customizing computers."

Sources: M. Bartiromo, 2007, Will Dell be a comeback kid? *BusinessWeek*, February 26, 128; N. Byrnes & P. Burrows, 2007, Where Dell went wrong, *BusinessWeek*, February 19, 62–66; C. Lawton, 2007, How H-P reclaimed its PC lead over Dell, *Wall Street Journal Online*, http://online.wsj.com/article, June 5; L. Lee & P. Burrows, 2007, Is Dell too big for Michael Dell? *BusinessWeek*, February 12, 33; R. Mullins, 2007, Dell goes retail in Japan, *PCWorld*, http://www.pcworld.com, July 28.

Competitors are firms operating in the same market, offering similar products, and targeting similar customers.

Firms operating in the same market, offering similar products, and targeting similar customers are **competitors**.[1] Southwest Airlines, Delta, United, Continental, and JetBlue are competitors, as are PepsiCo and Coca-Cola Company. As described in the Opening Case, Dell Inc. and Hewlett-Packard (HP) are competitors who are actively engaging each other in competitive battles. Even though Dell's "build-to-order" business model served it well for many years, it seems that adjustments to this model are necessary because of the recent success of competitors such as HP. At a minimum, Dell's CEO, Michael Dell, says that his firm is "looking to expand services (and is) likely to do more internationally"[2] in order to improve its competitive position.

Firms interact with their competitors as part of the broad context within which they operate while attempting to earn above-average returns.[3] The decisions firms make about their interactions with their competitors significantly affect their ability to earn above-average returns.[4] Because 80 to 90 percent of new firms fail, learning how to select the markets in which to compete and how to best compete within them is highly important.[5]

Competitive rivalry is the ongoing set of competitive actions and competitive responses that occur among firms as they maneuver for an advantageous market position.

Competitive rivalry is the ongoing set of competitive actions and competitive responses that occur among firms as they maneuver for an advantageous market position.[6] Especially in highly competitive industries, firms constantly jockey for advantage as they launch strategic actions and respond or react to rivals' moves.[7] It is important for those leading organizations to understand competitive rivalry, in that "the central, brute empirical fact in strategy is that some firms outperform others,"[8] meaning that competitive rivalry influences an individual firm's ability to gain and sustain competitive advantages.[9]

Competitive behavior is the set of competitive actions and competitive responses the firm takes to build or defend its competitive advantages and to improve its market position.

A sequence of firm-level moves, rivalry results from firms initiating their own competitive actions and then responding to actions taken by competitors. **Competitive behavior** is the set of competitive actions and competitive responses the firm takes to build or defend its competitive advantages and to improve its market position.[10] Through competitive behavior, the firm tries to successfully position itself relative to the five forces of competition (see Chapter 2) and to defend current competitive advantages while building advantages for the future (see Chapter 3). Increasingly, competitors engage in competitive actions and responses in more than one market.[11] Firms competing against each other in several product or geographic markets are engaged in **multimarket competition**.[12] All competitive behavior—that is, the total set of actions and responses taken by all firms competing within a market—is called **competitive dynamics**. The relationships among these key concepts are shown in Figure 4.1.

Multimarket competition occurs when firms compete against each other in several product or geographic markets.

Competitive dynamics refer to all competitive behaviors—that is, the total set of actions and responses taken by all firms competing within a market.

This chapter focuses on competitive rivalry and competitive dynamics. The essence of these important topics is that a firm's strategies are dynamic in nature. Actions taken by one firm elicit responses from competitors that, in turn, typically result in responses from the firm that took the initial action.[13] As explained in the Opening Case, this sequence of action and reaction is occurring between Dell and HP. To change how it competes with Dell, HP developed highly personalized relationships with retailers selling its PCs. Noting that customers were responding favorably to the opportunity to personally "touch" and

Figure 4.1 From Competitors to Competitive Dynamics

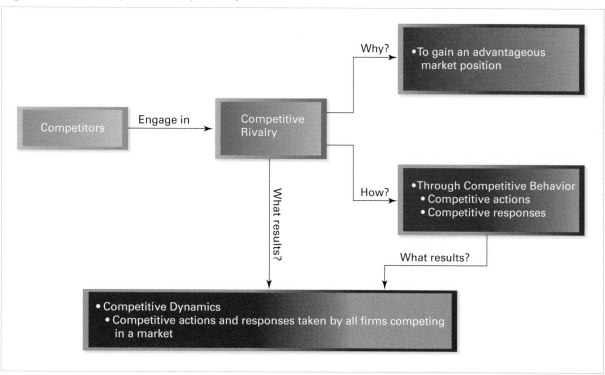

Source: Adapted from M. J. Chen, 1996, Competitor analysis and interfirm rivalry: Toward a theoretical integration, *Academy of Management Review*, 21: 100–134.

"interact" with a PC prior to making a purchase decision, Dell starting experimenting with its own retail outlets and decided to sell its PCs through retailers including 3,500 Wal-Mart stores located in Canada and the United States.[14]

Another way of highlighting competitive rivalry's effect on the firm's strategies is to say that a strategy's success is determined not only by the firm's initial competitive actions but also by how well it anticipates competitors' responses to them *and* by how well the firm anticipates and responds to its competitors' initial actions (also called attacks).[15] Although competitive rivalry affects all types of strategies (e.g., corporate-level, acquisition, and international), its most dominant influence is on the firm's business-level strategy or strategies. Indeed, firms' actions and responses to those of their rivals are the basic building block of business-level strategies.[16] Recall from Chapter 4 that business-level strategy is concerned with what the firm does to successfully use its competitive advantages in specific product markets. In the global economy, competitive rivalry is intensifying,[17] meaning that the significance of its effect on firms' business-level strategies is increasing. Rivalry is intensifying in the flat panel television market, for example. One reason is the price competition created by the price cuts of up to 40 percent below the leading brands' products by firms such as Westinghouse and Maxent.[18] However, firms that develop and use effective business-level strategies tend to outperform competitors in individual product markets, even when experiencing intense competitive rivalry that price cuts bring about.[19]

A Model of Competitive Rivalry

Over time, firms take many competitive actions and responses. As noted earlier, competitive rivalry evolves from this pattern of actions and responses as one firm's competitive actions have noticeable effects on competitors, eliciting competitive responses from them.[20]

This pattern shows that firms are mutually interdependent, that they feel each other's actions and responses, and that marketplace success is a function of both individual strategies and the consequences of their use.[21] Increasingly, too, executives recognize that competitive rivalry can have a major and direct effect on the firm's financial performance:[22] Research shows that intensified rivalry within an industry results in decreased average profitability for the competing firms.[23]

Figure 4.2 presents a straightforward model of competitive rivalry at the firm level; this type of rivalry is usually dynamic and complex.[24] The competitive actions and responses the firm takes are the foundation for successfully building and using its capabilities and core competencies to gain an advantageous market position.[25] The model in Figure 4.2 presents the sequence of activities commonly involved in competition between a particular firm and each of its competitors. Companies can use the model to understand how to be able to predict competitors' behavior (actions and responses) and reduce the uncertainty associated with competitors' actions.[26] Being able to predict competitors' actions and responses has a positive effect on the firm's market position and its subsequent financial performance.[27] The sum of all the individual rivalries modeled in Figure 4.2 that occur in a particular market reflects the competitive dynamics in that market.

The remainder of the chapter explains components of the model shown in Figure 4.2. We first describe market commonality and resource similarity as the building blocks of a competitor analysis. Next, we discuss the effects of three organizational characteristics—awareness, motivation, and ability—on the firm's competitive behavior. We then examine competitive rivalry between firms, or interfirm rivalry, in detail by describing the factors that affect the likelihood a firm will take a competitive action and the factors that affect the likelihood a firm will respond to a competitor's action. In the chapter's final section, we turn our attention to competitive dynamics to describe how market characteristics affect competitive rivalry in slow-cycle, fast-cycle, and standard-cycle markets.

Competitor Analysis

As previously noted, a competitor analysis is the first step the firm takes to be able to predict the extent and nature of its rivalry with each competitor. Recall that a competitor is a firm operating in the same market, offering similar products, and targeting similar customers. The number of markets in which firms compete against each other (called market commonality, defined on the following pages) and the similarity in their resources (called

Figure 4.2 A Model of Competitive Rivalry

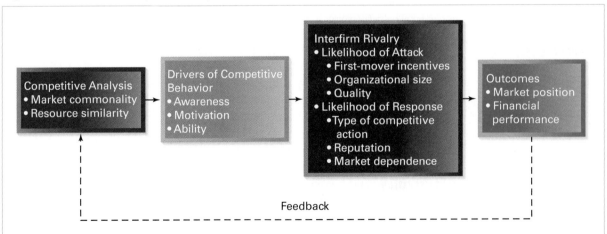

Source: Adapted from M. J. Chen, 1996, Competitor analysis and interfirm rivalry: Toward a theoretical integration, *Academy of Management Review*, 21: 100–134.

resource similarity, also defined in the following section) determine the extent to which the firms are competitors. Firms with high market commonality and highly similar resources are "clearly direct and mutually acknowledged competitors."[28] As is suggested in the Opening Case, Dell and HP are direct competitors as are Acer and Lenovo. The direct competition between Acer and Lenovo to claim the third largest share of the global PC market is quite intense with "Acer gaining ground thanks to low-cost machines and unconventional distribution" practices.[29] However, being direct competitors does not necessarily mean that the rivalry between the firms will be intense as is the case between Dell and HP and between Acer and Lenovo. The drivers of competitive behavior—as well as factors influencing the likelihood that a competitor will initiate competitive actions and will respond to its competitor's actions—influence the intensity of rivalry, even for direct competitors.[30]

Lenova and Acer are intense competitors for the global market share of personal computers.

In Chapter 2, we discussed competitor analysis as a technique firms use to understand their competitive environment. Together, the general, industry, and competitive environments comprise the firm's external environment. We also described how competitor analysis is used to help the firm *understand* its competitors. This understanding results from studying competitors' future objectives, current strategies, assumptions, and capabilities (see Figure 2.3, on page 59). In this chapter, the discussion of competitor analysis is extended to describe what firms study to be able to *predict* competitors' behavior in the form of their competitive actions and responses. The discussions of competitor analysis in Chapter 2 and in this chapter are complementary in that firms must first *understand* competitors (Chapter 2) before their competitive actions and competitive responses can be *predicted* (this chapter).

Market Commonality

Each industry is composed of various markets. The financial services industry has markets for insurance, brokerage services, banks, and so forth. To concentrate on the needs of different, unique customer groups, markets can be further subdivided. The insurance market, for example, could be broken into market segments (such as commercial and consumer), product segments (such as health insurance and life insurance), and geographic markets (such as Western Europe and Southeast Asia). In general, the capabilities the Internet's technologies generate help to shape the nature of industries' markets along with the competition among firms operating in them.[31] For example, widely available electronic news sources affect how traditional print news distributors such as newspapers conduct their business.

Competitors tend to agree about the different characteristics of individual markets that form an industry.[32] For example, in the transportation industry, the understanding is that the commercial air travel market differs from the ground transportation market, which is served by such firms as YRC Worldwide (one of the largest transportation service providers in the world)[33] and major YRC competitors Arkansas Best, Con-way Inc., and FedEx Freight.[34] Although differences exist, most industries' markets are somewhat related in terms of technologies used or core competencies needed to develop a competitive advantage. For example, different types of transportation companies need to provide reliable and timely service. Commercial air carriers such as Southwest, Continental, and JetBlue must therefore develop service competencies to satisfy their passengers, while YRC and its major competitors must develop such competencies to serve the needs of those using their fleets to ship goods.

© AFP/Getty Images

Market commonality is concerned with the number of markets with which the firm and a competitor are jointly involved and the degree of importance of the individual markets to each.

Heineken faces market commonality on many fronts with its competitor Anheuser-Busch.

Resource similarity is the extent to which the firm's tangible and intangible resources are comparable to a competitor's in terms of both type and amount.

Firms sometimes compete against each other in several markets that are in different industries. This situation finds competitors coming into contact with each other several times, a condition called market commonality. More formally, **market commonality** is concerned with the number of markets with which the firm and a competitor are jointly involved and the degree of importance of the individual markets to each.[35] Firms competing against one another in several or many markets engage in multimarket competition.[36] McDonald's and Burger King compete against each other in multiple geographic markets across the world,[37] Prudential Insurance and Cigna Insurance Corporation compete against each other in several market segments (such as institutional and retail) as well as product markets (such as life insurance and health insurance),[38] and Anheuser-Busch Cos. and Dutch brewer Heineken compete in multiple global and product (i.e., premium and light beer) markets.[39] Airlines, chemicals, pharmaceuticals, and consumer foods are examples of other industries in which firms often simultaneously compete against each other in multiple markets.

Firms competing in several markets have the potential to respond to a competitor's actions not only within the market in which the actions are taken, but also in other markets where they compete with the rival. This potential creates a complicated competitive mosaic in which "the moves an organization makes in one market are designed to achieve goals in another market in ways that aren't immediately apparent to its rivals."[40] This potential complicates the rivalry between competitors. In fact, research suggests that "a firm with greater multimarket contact is less likely to initiate an attack, but more likely to move (respond) aggressively when attacked."[41] Thus, in general, multimarket competition reduces competitive rivalry.[42]

Resource Similarity

Resource similarity is the extent to which the firm's tangible and intangible resources are comparable to a competitor's in terms of both type and amount.[43] Firms with similar types and amounts of resources are likely to have similar strengths and weaknesses and use similar strategies.[44] The competition between FedEx and United Parcel Service (UPS) to find the most effective ways to use information technology to improve the efficiency of their operations and to reduce costs demonstrates these expectations. Pursuing similar strategies that are supported by similar resource profiles, personnel in these firms work at a feverish pace to receive, sort, and ship packages. At a UPS hub, for example, "workers have less than four hours (on a peak night) to process more than a million packages from at least 100 planes and probably 160 trucks."[45] (FedEx employees face the same receiving, sorting, and shipping challenges.) FedEx and UPS are both spending more than $1 billion annually on research and development (R&D) to find ways to improve efficiency and reduce costs. According to an analyst, these firms engage in such R&D because "when you handle millions of packages, a minute's delay can cost a fortune."[46]

When performing a competitor analysis, a firm analyzes each of its competitors in terms of market commonality and resource similarity. The results of these analyses can be mapped for visual comparisons. In Figure 4.3, we show different hypothetical intersections between the firm and individual competitors in terms of market commonality and resource similarity. These intersections indicate the extent to which the firm and those with which it is compared are competitors. For example, the firm and its competitor displayed in quadrant I of Figure 4.3 have similar types and amounts of resources (i.e., the two firms have a similar portfolio of resources). The firm and its competitor in quadrant I would use their similar resource portfolios

Figure 4.3 A Framework of Competitor Analysis

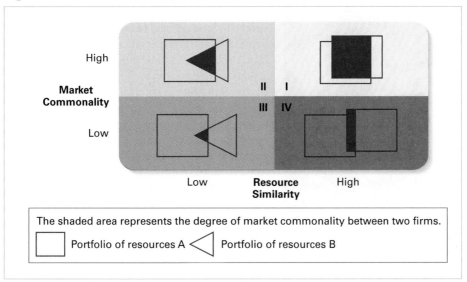

Source: Adapted from M. J. Chen, 1996, Competitor analysis and interfirm rivalry: Toward a theoretical integration, *Academy of Management Review,* 21: 100–134.

to compete against each other in many markets that are important to each. These conditions lead to the conclusion that the firms modeled in quadrant I are direct and mutually acknowledged competitors (e.g., FedEx and UPS). In contrast, the firm and its competitor shown in quadrant III share few markets and have little similarity in their resources, indicating that they aren't direct and mutually acknowledged competitors. Thus, a small local, family-owned Italian restaurant does not compete directly against Olive Garden nor does it have resources that are similar to those of Darden Restaurants, Inc. (Olive Garden's owner). The firm's mapping of its competitive relationship with rivals is fluid as firms enter and exit markets and as companies' resources change in type and amount. Thus, the companies with which the firm is a direct competitor change across time.

Drivers of Competitive Actions and Responses

As shown in Figure 4.2 (on page 100) market commonality and resource similarity influence the drivers (awareness, motivation, and ability) of competitive behavior. In turn, the drivers influence the firm's competitive behavior, as shown by the actions and responses it takes while engaged in competitive rivalry.[47]

Awareness, which is a prerequisite to any competitive action or response taken by a firm, refers to the extent to which competitors recognize the degree of their mutual interdependence that results from market commonality and resource similarity.[48] Awareness tends to be greatest when firms have highly similar resources (in terms of types and amounts) to use while competing against each other in multiple markets. Komatsu Ltd., Japan's top construction machinery maker and U.S.-based Caterpillar Inc. have similar resources and are certainly aware of each other's actions.[49] The same is true for Wal-Mart and France's Carrefour, the two largest supermarket groups in the world. The last two firms' joint awareness has increased as they use similar resources to compete against each other for dominant positions in multiple European and South American markets.[50] Awareness affects the extent to which the firm understands the consequences of its competitive actions and responses. A lack of awareness can lead to excessive competition, resulting in a negative effect on all competitors' performance.[51]

Komatsu Ltd., Japan's top construction machinery maker, and U.S.-based Caterpillar Inc. have similar resources and compete against each other in multiple markets.

As explained in the Strategic Focus, rivals Netflix and Blockbuster are acutely aware of each other's competitive actions and responses. Indeed, the rivalry between these firms is quite intense. As you will see from reading about these firms and their competitive actions and responses, both are highly motivated to engage each other in competitive battles.

Motivation, which concerns the firm's incentive to take action or to respond to a competitor's attack, relates to perceived gains and losses. Thus, a firm may be aware of competitors but may not be motivated to engage in rivalry with them if it perceives that its position will not improve or that its market position won't be damaged if it doesn't respond.[52]

Market commonality affects the firm's perceptions and resulting motivation. For example, all else being equal, the firm is more likely to attack the rival with whom it has low market commonality than the one with whom it competes in multiple markets. The primary reason is the high stakes involved in trying to gain a more advantageous position over a rival with whom the firm shares many markets. As we mentioned earlier, multimarket competition can find a competitor responding to the firm's action in a market different from the one in which the initial action was taken. Actions and responses of this type can cause both firms to lose focus on core markets and to battle each other with resources that had been allocated for other purposes. Because of the high stakes of competition under the condition of market commonality, the probability is high that the attacked firm will respond to its competitor's action in an effort to protect its position in one or more markets.[53]

In some instances, the firm may be aware of the large number of markets it shares with a competitor and may be motivated to respond to an attack by that competitor, but it lacks the ability to do so. *Ability* relates to each firm's resources and the flexibility they provide. Without available resources (such as financial capital and people), the firm lacks the ability to attack a competitor or respond to its actions. However, similar resources suggest similar abilities to attack and respond. When a firm faces a competitor with similar resources, careful study of a possible attack before initiating it is essential because the similarly resourced competitor is likely to respond to that action.[54]

Resource *dissimilarity* also influences competitive actions and responses between firms, in that "the greater is the resource imbalance between the acting firm and competitors or potential responders, the greater will be the delay in response"[55] by the firm with a resource disadvantage. For example, Wal-Mart initially used a focused cost leadership strategy to compete only in small communities (those with a population of 25,000 or less). Using sophisticated logistics systems and extremely efficient purchasing practices as advantages, among others, Wal-Mart created what was at that time a new type of value (primarily in the form of wide selections of products at the lowest competitive prices) for customers in small retail markets. Local competitors lacked the ability to marshal needed resources at the pace required to respond quickly and effectively. However, even when facing competitors with greater resources (greater ability) or more attractive market positions, firms should eventually respond, no matter how daunting the task seems. Choosing not to respond can ultimately result in failure, as happened with at least some local retailers who didn't respond to Wal-Mart's competitive actions.

Who Will Win the Competitive Battles Between Netflix and Blockbuster?

Netflix pioneered the online movie rental business. Offering customers different plans, one of which allows them to rent up to three movies at a time with no time limit on each title's return, the firm grew rapidly during its first eight years.

From the beginning, Netflix's growth was fueled by adding subscribers. In late 2004, Netflix founder and CEO Reed Hastings decided to reduce the prices of his firm's plans in order to continue adding subscribers. The pricing strategy worked. Moreover, because the firm's margins were attractive at the plans' 2004 price levels (levels that were essentially unchanged in early 2007), Netflix's profits grew from $6.5 million in 2003 to $49 million in 2006. But Blockbuster, Netflix's major rival, is aware of every competitive action its chief competitor takes. Moreover, Blockbuster is now responding aggressively to Netflix's marketplace actions. In the eyes of some, the competition between these firms has become "ugly." Even worse, it may be that the firms are now "locked into (a) mutually destructive competitive situation."

Evidence suggests that Netflix's momentum tapped out somewhat dramatically when Blockbuster launched a new option in its online rental service in 2006. Called "Total Access," subscribers pay an additional $1 per month for the ability to return and check out rentals in Blockbuster's physical stores as well as handle these transactions online. This convenience is one that Netflix cannot offer customers because its products are delivered only through the mail. Fully aware of this competitive action, Netflix responded in mid-2007 with still lower prices for its plans. The disadvantage in this response is that the lower prices cut into the firm's profits. However, Netflix also started its "Watch Now" movie downloading service in 2007. This service uses high-speed Internet connections to allow customers to download movies and watch them on their television sets or PCs.

In the continuing saga of competition between competitors who are keenly aware of each other and their actions and responses, one might wonder how Blockbuster will react to Netflix's "Watch Now" service. It seems that Blockbuster could easily imitate this service, meaning that it will be difficult for Netflix to gain a competitive advantage by using it. And both firms will have to decide how long they are willing to engage in competitive battles that are severely damaging their ability to earn profits. The window for this level of destructive competition may soon close. In mid-2007, Blockbuster stated in a Securities and Exchange Commission filing that the firm would modify its online service "to strike the appropriate balance between continued subscriber growth and enhanced profitability."

Sources: 2007, Netflix to cut rental fees in battle with Blockbuster, *USA Today Online*, http://usatoday.com, July 31; D. King, 2007, Netflix trims forecast amid war with Blockbuster, *Houston Chronicle Online*, http://www.chron.com, July 23; M. Liedtke, 2007, Netflix gives up profit to gain business, *Houston Chronicle Online*, http://www.chron.com, July 23; B. Steverman, 2007, Netflix battle with Blockbuster gets ugly, *BusinessWeek Online*, http://businessweek.com, July 24.

Competitive Rivalry

The ongoing competitive action/response sequence between a firm and a competitor affects the performance of both firms;[56] thus it is important for companies to carefully study competitive rivalry to select and implement successful strategies. Understanding a competitor's awareness, motivation, and ability helps the firm to predict the likelihood of an attack by that competitor and the probability that a competitor will respond to actions taken against it.

As we described earlier, the predictions drawn from studying competitors in terms of awareness, motivation, and ability are grounded in market commonality and resource similarity. These predictions are fairly general. The value of the final set of predictions

A **competitive action** is a strategic or tactical action the firm takes to build or defend its competitive advantages or improve its market position.

A **competitive response** is a strategic or tactical action the firm takes to counter the effects of a competitor's competitive action.

A **strategic action or a strategic response** is a market-based move that involves a significant commitment of organizational resources and is difficult to implement and reverse.

A **tactical action or a tactical response** is a market-based move that is taken to fine-tune a strategy; it involves fewer resources and is relatively easy to implement and reverse.

the firm develops about each of its competitors' competitive actions and responses is enhanced by studying the "Likelihood of Attack" factors (such as first-mover incentives and organizational size) and the "Likelihood of Response" factors (such as the actor's reputation) that are shown in Figure 4.2. Evaluating and understanding these factors allows the firm to refine the predictions it makes about its competitors' actions and responses.

Strategic and Tactical Actions

Firms use both strategic and tactical actions when forming their competitive actions and competitive responses in the course of engaging in competitive rivalry.[57] A **competitive action** is a strategic or tactical action the firm takes to build or defend its competitive advantages or improve its market position. A **competitive response** is a strategic or tactical action the firm takes to counter the effects of a competitor's competitive action. A **strategic action or a strategic response** is a market-based move that involves a significant commitment of organizational resources and is difficult to implement and reverse. A **tactical action or a tactical response** is a market-based move that is taken to fine-tune a strategy; it involves fewer resources and is relatively easy to implement and reverse.

The decision a few years ago by newly installed leaders at Guess Inc. to take their firm's brand of denims and related products upscale rather than dilute the brand more by lowering prices when Guess was losing market share is an example of a strategic response.[58] And Boeing's decision to commit the resources required to build the super-efficient 787 midsized jetliner for delivery in 2008[59] demonstrates a strategic action. Changes in airfares are somewhat frequently announced by airlines. As tactical actions that are easily reversed, pricing decisions are often taken by these firms to increase demand in certain markets during certain periods.

Jamba Juice has recently begun changing the texture of some of its smoothies. This change may not require a strategic response from its competitors.

As discussed in the Strategic Focus, Wal-Mart prices aggressively as a means of increasing revenues and gaining market share at the expense of competitors. But discounted prices and higher expenses (which the firm is incurring in order to upgrade its stores) weigh on margins and slow profit growth. Although pricing aggressively is at the core of what Wal-Mart is and how it competes, can the tactical action of aggressive pricing continue to lead to the competitive success the firm has enjoyed historically? Is Wal-Mart achieving the type of balance between strategic and tactical competitive actions and competitive responses that is a foundation for all firms' success in marketplace competitions?

When engaging rivals in competition, firms must recognize the differences between strategic and tactical actions and responses and should develop an effective balance between the two types of competitive actions and responses. Airbus, Boeing's major competitor in terms of commercial airliners, should note that its competitor is strongly committed to taking actions it believes are necessary to successfully launch the 787 jetliner, because deciding to design, build, and launch the 787 is a major strategic action. On the other hand, Jamba Juice's recent attempts to develop different textures for its smoothie drinks is a tactical action that may not demand a strategic response from competitors such as Zuka Juice.[60]

Likelihood of Attack

In addition to market commonality, resource similarity, and the drivers of awareness, motivation, and ability, other factors affect the likelihood a competitor will use strategic

Using Aggressive Pricing as a Tactical Action at Wal-Mart

"Every Day Low Prices." People throughout the world are familiar with Wal-Mart's famous slogan—a slogan on which the firm's business model is built. This model has led to remarkable success. In mid-2007, Wal-Mart had 6,775 stores and was on track to exceed $350 billion in sales for the year. With roughly 40 percent of its sales revenue being earned outside the United States, Wal-Mart continues to expand internationally and is the number one retailer in Canada and Mexico. Some analysts believe that Wal-Mart's business model will prove compelling in a number of emerging markets although the firm is struggling to operate profitably in some developed markets such as Japan and Germany. Europe's Carrefour, Costco Wholesale, and Target are Wal-Mart's major competitors, although a number of other companies (including Kohl's, J.C. Penney, and BJ's Wholesale Club) also compete against the retailing giant.

As a tactical action, Wal-Mart prices some products to increase overall sales revenue and to attract customers to its stores in hopes that they will purchase other items as well. Aggressive pricing works (for Wal-Mart and others such as Costco Wholesale using the practice) when reduced prices generate sales revenues in excess of revenues that would have been generated without the price cuts and when customers buy other higher-margin items while shopping. Recently, both Wal-Mart and Costco added gasoline to their operations as another means of attracting customers to their stores. Both stores are pricing gasoline attractively in hopes of enticing customers to buy other items located in their stores.

As a tactical action, aggressive pricing is used with virtually all products that Wal-Mart sells. (Some analysts describe Wal-Mart's price cuts as "taking a knife to prices.") Toys and electronics (i.e., flat panel televisions, PCs, and telephones) are priced aggressively during holiday seasons. More recently, Wal-Mart aggressively priced appliances in order to compete against Best Buy, Home Depot, and Lowe's in this product category. For the back-to-school season, Wal-Mart often cuts prices (anywhere from 10 percent to 50 percent) on as many as 16,000 school-related items.

Firms must carefully evaluate the effectiveness of all of their competitive actions and competitive responses. Some feel that Wal-Mart's emphasis on low prices is preventing the firm from allocating sufficient resources to remodel aging stores and to upgrade the quality of its merchandising mix. Competitors Kohl's and Costco appear to be attracting some of Wal-Mart's customers by offering more appealing mixes of merchandise and a marginally more pleasant shopping experience that modernized facilities provide. Thus, Wal-Mart must carefully assess the degree to which its tactical action of aggressive pricing is allowing it to successfully engage competitors in marketplace competitions.

Sources: M. Barbaro, 2007, Wal-Mart and Studios in film deal, *New York Times Online*, http://www.nytimes.com, February 6; A. D'Innocenzio, 2007, Wal-Mart sets in motion a price-cutting campaign, *Houston Chronicle Online*, http://www.chron.com, July 23; A. Feldman, 2007, The tiger in Costco's tank, *Fast Company*, July/August, 38–40; R. Fuhrmann, 2007, Wal-Mart vs. AT&T: Wal-Mart, *Motley Fool Stock Advisor*, http://www.fool.com, March, 15; 2007, Wal-Mart Stores, Inc., *Hoovers*, http://www.hovers.com, July 31.

© Don Hammond/Design Pics/Corbis

actions and tactical actions to attack its competitors. Three of these factors—first-mover incentives, organizational size, and quality—are discussed next.

First-Mover Incentives

A **first mover** is a firm that takes an initial competitive action in order to build or defend its competitive advantages or to improve its market position. The first-mover concept has been influenced by the work of the famous economist Joseph Schumpeter, who argued that firms achieve competitive advantage by taking innovative actions[61] (innovation is

A **first mover** is a firm that takes an initial competitive action in order to build or defend its competitive advantages or to improve its market position.

defined and described in detail in Chapter 13). In general, first movers "allocate funds for product innovation and development, aggressive advertising, and advanced research and development."[62]

The benefits of being a successful first mover can be substantial.[63] Especially in fast-cycle markets (discussed later in the chapter), where changes occur rapidly and where it is virtually impossible to sustain a competitive advantage for any length of time, "a first mover may experience five to ten times the valuation and revenue of a second mover."[64] This evidence suggests that although first-mover benefits are never absolute, they are often critical to a firm's success in industries experiencing rapid technological developments and relatively short product life cycles.[65] In addition to earning above-average returns until its competitors respond to its successful competitive action, the first mover can gain (1) the loyalty of customers who may become committed to the goods or services of the firm that first made them available, and (2) market share that can be difficult for competitors to take during future competitive rivalry.[66] The general evidence that first movers have greater survival rates than later market entrants[67] is perhaps the culmination of first-mover benefits.

The firm trying to predict its competitors' competitive actions might conclude that they will take aggressive strategic actions to gain first movers' benefits. However, even though a firm's competitors might be motivated to be first movers, they may lack the ability to do so. First movers tend to be aggressive and willing to experiment with innovation and take higher, yet reasonable, levels of risk.[68] To be a first mover, the firm must have readily available the resources to significantly invest in R&D as well as to rapidly and successfully produce and market a stream of innovative products.[69]

Organizational slack makes it possible for firms to have the ability (as measured by available resources) to be first movers. *Slack* is the buffer or cushion provided by actual or obtainable resources that aren't currently in use and are in excess of the minimum resources needed to produce a given level of organizational output.[70] As a liquid resource, slack can quickly be allocated to support competitive actions, such as R&D investments and aggressive marketing campaigns that lead to first-mover advantages. This relationship between slack and the ability to be a first mover allows the firm to predict that a competitor who is a first mover likely has available slack and will probably take aggressive competitive actions to continuously introduce innovative products. Furthermore, the firm can predict that as a first mover, a competitor will try to rapidly gain market share and customer loyalty in order to earn above-average returns until its competitors are able to effectively respond to its first move.

Firms evaluating their competitors should realize that being a first mover carries risk. For example, it is difficult to accurately estimate the returns that will be earned from introducing product innovations to the marketplace.[71] Additionally, the first mover's cost to develop a product innovation can be substantial, reducing the slack available to support further innovation. Thus, the firm should carefully study the results a competitor achieves as a first mover. Continuous success by the competitor suggests additional product innovations, while lack of product acceptance over the course of the competitor's innovations may indicate less willingness in the future to accept the risks of being a first mover.

A **second mover** is a firm that responds to the first mover's competitive action, typically through imitation. More cautious than the first mover, the second mover studies customers' reactions to product innovations. In the course of doing so, the second mover also tries to find any mistakes the first mover made so that it can avoid them and the problems they created. Often, successful imitation of the first mover's innovations allows the second mover "to avoid both the mistakes and the huge spending of the pioneers [first movers]."[72]

Second movers also have the time to develop processes and technologies that are more efficient than those used by the first mover or that create additional value for consumers.[73] Through a project with a code name of Goya, Kodak is developing a consumer inkjet printer. The product is based on "droplets of a new ink Kodak scientists produced (that) yield photo prints with vivid colors lasting a lifetime."[74] Commenting about the daunting task Kodak faces as a new entrant to the $50 billion printer business

A **second mover** is a firm that responds to the first mover's competitive action, typically through imitation.

that HP dominants, Kodak's CEO took the following position: "We're very proud that we're coming to market 20 years late. We think it will give us an opportunity to disrupt the industry's business model and address consumers' key dissatisfaction: the high cost of ink."[75] Overall, the outcomes of the first mover's competitive actions may provide an effective blueprint for second and even late movers as they determine the nature and timing of their competitive responses.[76] Kodak may experience the benefits of this effectiveness as it enters the inkjet printer business after carefully studying HP's actions as a first mover in this competitive arena.

Determining whether a competitor is an effective second mover (based on its past actions) allows a first-mover firm to predict that the competitor will respond quickly to successful, innovation-based market entries. The first mover can expect a successful second-mover competitor to study its market entries and to respond with its own new entry into the market within a short time period. As a second mover, the competitor will try to respond with a product that provides greater customer value than does the first mover's product. The most successful second movers are able to rapidly and meaningfully interpret market feedback to respond quickly, yet successfully, to the first mover's successful innovations.

A **late mover** is a firm that responds to a competitive action a significant amount of time after the first mover's action and the second mover's response. Typically, a late response is better than no response at all, although any success achieved from the late competitive response tends to be considerably less than that achieved by first and second movers. With an anticipated price of under $10,000, it is possible that the Chevy Trax, Beat, and Groove are late as entries to the small, super-efficient segment of automobiles. These cars are competitors for Honda's Fit, Toyota's Yaris, and Nissan's Versa, among others.[77]

The firm competing against a late mover can predict that the competitor will likely enter a particular market only after both the first and second movers have achieved success in that market. Moreover, on a relative basis, the firm can predict that the late mover's competitive action will allow it to earn average returns only after the considerable time required for it to understand how to create at least as much customer value as that offered by the first and second movers' products. Although exceptions exist, most of the late mover's competitive actions will be ineffective relative to those initiated by first and second movers.

Kodak is trying to use a second-mover strategy with the introduction of its new ink jet printer.

A **late mover** is a firm that responds to a competitive action a significant amount of time after the first mover's action and the second mover's response.

Organizational Size

An organization's size affects the likelihood it will take competitive actions as well as the types and timing of those actions.[78] In general, small firms are more likely than large companies to launch competitive actions and tend to do it more quickly. Smaller firms are thus perceived as nimble and flexible competitors who rely on speed and surprise to defend their competitive advantages or develop new ones while engaged in competitive rivalry, especially with large companies, to gain an advantageous market position.[79] Small firms' flexibility and nimbleness allow them to develop variety in their competitive actions; large firms tend to limit the types of competitive actions used.[80]

Large firms, however, are likely to initiate more competitive actions along with more strategic actions during a given period.[81] Thus, when studying its competitors in terms of organizational size, the firm should use a measurement such as total sales revenue or total number of employees. The competitive actions the firm likely will encounter from competitors larger than it is will be different from the competitive actions it will encounter from smaller competitors.

The organizational size factor adds another layer of complexity. When engaging in competitive rivalry, the firm often prefers a large number of unique competitive actions. Ideally, the organization has the amount of slack resources held by a large firm to launch a greater *number* of competitive actions and a small firm's flexibility to launch a greater *variety* of competitive actions. Herb Kelleher, cofounder and former CEO of Southwest Airlines, addressed this matter: "Think and act big and we'll get smaller. Think and act small and we'll get bigger."[82]

In the context of competitive rivalry, Kelleher's statement can be interpreted to mean that relying on a limited number or types of competitive actions (which is the large firm's tendency) can lead to reduced competitive success across time, partly because competitors learn how to effectively respond to the predictable. In contrast, remaining flexible and nimble (which is the small firm's tendency) in order to develop and use a wide variety of competitive actions contributes to success against rivals.

As explained in the Strategic Focus, Wal-Mart is a huge firm and generates annual sales revenue that makes it the world's largest company. Partly because of its size, Wal-Mart has the flexibility required to take many types of competitive actions. In the 2007 back-to-school selling season, for example, Wal-Mart hired a new advertising agency to help it "emphasize its product selection while striking a chord with customers." This message was seen as a sharp departure from the firm's typical "price-centric pitches." This campaign was undertaken partly in response to a disappointing spring sales season in 2007. Demonstrating its flexibility, the firm decided that, at least for the back-to-school season, it wanted customers to see that Wal-Mart had "the brands you want at the price you want" to pay.[83] Demonstrating this type of flexibility in terms of competitive actions may prove critical to Wal-Mart's battles with competitors such as Costco, Kohl's, and Target among others.

Quality

Quality has many definitions, including well-established ones relating it to the production of goods or services with zero defects[84] and seeing it as a never-ending cycle of continuous improvement.[85] From a strategic perspective, we consider quality to be an outcome of how the firm completes primary and support activities (see Chapter 3). Thus, **quality** exists when the firm's goods or services meet or exceed customers' expectations. Some evidence suggests that quality may be the most critical component in satisfying the firm's customers.[86]

In the eyes of customers, quality is about doing the right things relative to performance measures that are important to them.[87] Customers may be interested in measuring the quality of a firm's goods and services against a broad range of dimensions. Sample quality dimensions in which customers commonly express an interest are shown in Table 4.1. Quality is possible only when top-level managers support it and when its importance is institutionalized throughout the entire organization.[88] When quality is institutionalized and valued by all, employees and managers alike become vigilant about continuously finding ways to improve quality.[89]

Quality is a universal theme in the global economy and is a necessary but not sufficient condition for competitive success.[90] Without quality, a firm's products lack credibility, meaning that customers don't think of them as viable options. Indeed, customers won't consider buying a product until they believe that it can satisfy at least their base-level expectations in terms of quality dimensions that are important to them. Thus, Great Wall Motor Company, a Chinese manufacturer of low-cost automobiles, can anticipate difficulty in its efforts to sell cars in Europe until customers believe that the firm's cars have at least acceptable levels of quality.[91]

Quality affects competitive rivalry. The firm evaluating a competitor whose products suffer from poor quality can predict declines in the competitor's sales revenue until the quality issues are resolved. In addition, the firm can predict that the competitor likely won't be aggressive in its competitive actions until the quality problems are corrected in order to gain credibility with customers. However, after the problems are corrected, that competitor is likely to take more aggressive competitive actions. Additionally, a firm

Quality exists when the firm's goods or services meet or exceed customers' expectations.

Table 4.1 Quality Dimensions of Goods and Services

Product Quality Dimensions

1. *Performance*—Operating characteristics

2. *Features*—Important special characteristics

3. *Flexibility*—Meeting operating specifications over some period of time

4. *Durability*—Amount of use before performance deteriorates

5. *Conformance*—Match with preestablished standards

6. *Serviceability*—Ease and speed of repair

7. *Aesthetics*—How a product looks and feels

8. *Perceived quality*—Subjective assessment of characteristics (product image)

Service Quality Dimensions

1. *Timeliness*—Performed in the promised period of time

2. *Courtesy*—Performed cheerfully

3. *Consistency*—Giving all customers similar experiences each time

4. *Convenience*—Accessibility to customers

5. *Completeness*—Fully serviced, as required

6. *Accuracy*—Performed correctly each time

Source: Adapted from J. Evans, 2008, *Managing for Quality and Performance,* 7th ed., Mason, OH: Thomson Publishing.

can predict that a competitor for whom quality has always been important will act to regain its ability to produce products recognized for their quality, as may be the case for Mercedes-Benz automobiles.

Historically, Mercedes-Benz automobiles were known for their quality and engineering. Indeed, product quality was a competitive advantage for DaimlerBenz. However, it seems that acquiring Chrysler Corporation and becoming DaimlerChrysler negatively affected the quality of Mercedes-Benz cars. In fact, between 2003 and early 2006, company officials admitted that Mercedes' products were on a "downward spiral" in terms of quality. In 2004 and 2005, for example, difficulties with cars' electronics led to widespread recalls. A failure to recognize the rather urgent need to modernize the firm's facilities and manufacturing techniques contributed to the decline in product quality. It is possible that the attention being devoted to integrating the two formerly independent companies contributed to the relative inattention paid to Mercedes' needs. However, the decision to sell the Chrysler unit immediately resulted in changes for Mercedes' cars. Thousands of stress tests are now being made during manufacturing processes to catch problems before the cars are distributed, facilities have been upgraded, and efforts are underway to fully engage suppliers with Mercedes' personnel to increase quality and manufacturing efficiency.[92] Given these developments, competitors such as BMW and Lexus can expect that Mercedes will again promote the quality of its products as it competes with them.

Likelihood of Response

The success of a firm's competitive action is affected by the likelihood that a competitor will respond to it as well as by the type (strategic or tactical) and effectiveness of that response. As noted earlier, a competitive response is a strategic or tactical action the firm takes to counter the effects of a competitor's competitive action. In general, a firm is likely to respond to a competitor's action when (1) the action leads to better use of the competitor's capabilities to gain or produce stronger competitive advantages or an improvement in its market position, (2) the action damages the firm's ability to use its capabilities to create or maintain an advantage, or (3) the firm's market position becomes less defensible.[93]

In addition to market commonality and resource similarity and awareness, motivation, and ability, firms evaluate three other factors—type of competitive action, reputation, and market dependence—to predict how a competitor is likely to respond to competitive actions (see Figure 4.2, on page 100).

Type of Competitive Action

Competitive responses to strategic actions differ from responses to tactical actions. These differences allow the firm to predict a competitor's likely response to a competitive action that has been launched against it. In general, strategic actions receive strategic responses and tactical actions receive tactical responses.

In general, strategic actions elicit fewer total competitive responses because strategic responses, such as market-based moves, involve a significant commitment of resources and are difficult to implement and reverse.[94] Palm Inc.'s decision to sell 25 percent of itself to Elevation Partners, a private equity firm, is a strategic action that will be difficult to reverse. However, the infusion of $325 million provided the capability Palm required to grow in the highly competitive smartphone market.[95]

Another reason that strategic actions elicit fewer responses than do tactical actions is that the time needed to implement a strategic action and to assess its effectiveness can delay the competitor's response to that action.[96] In contrast, a competitor likely will respond quickly to a tactical action, such as when an airline company almost immediately matches a competitor's tactical action of reducing prices in certain markets. Either strategic actions or tactical actions that target a large number of a rival's customers are likely to elicit strong responses.[97] In fact, if the effects of a competitor's strategic action on the focal firm are significant (e.g., loss of market share, loss of major resources such as critical employees), a response is likely to be swift and strong.[98]

Actor's Reputation

In the context of competitive rivalry, an *actor* is the firm taking an action or a response while *reputation* is "the positive or negative attribute ascribed by one rival to another based on past competitive behavior."[99] A positive reputation may be a source of above-average returns, especially for consumer goods producers.[100] Thus, a positive corporate reputation is of strategic value[101] and affects competitive rivalry. To predict the likelihood of a competitor's response to a current or planned action, firms evaluate the responses that the competitor has taken previously when attacked—past behavior is assumed to be a predictor of future behavior.

Competitors are more likely to respond to strategic or tactical actions when they are taken by a market leader.[102] In particular, evidence suggests that commonly successful actions, especially strategic actions, will be quickly imitated. For example, although a second mover, IBM committed significant resources to enter the PC market. When IBM was immediately successful in this endeavor, competitors such as Dell, Compaq, HP, and Gateway responded with strategic actions to enter the market. IBM's reputation as well as its successful strategic action strongly influenced entry by these competitors. However, the competitive landscape has changed dramatically over time. As explained in the Opening Case, HP now holds the largest share of the global PC market. Dell is seeking to regain its edge in the marketplace; Compaq merged with HP some years ago; Gateway is struggling to survive; and Lenovo, a Chinese firm, paid $1.75 billion in 2005 to buy IBM's PC division.

In contrast to a firm with a strong reputation such as IBM, competitors are less likely to take responses against a company with a reputation for competitive behavior that is risky, complex, and unpredictable. The firm with a reputation as a price predator (an actor that frequently reduces prices to gain or maintain market share) generates few responses to its pricing tactical actions because price predators, which typically increase prices once their market share objective is reached, lack credibility with their competitors.[103]

Dependence on the Market

Market dependence denotes the extent to which a firm's revenues or profits are derived from a particular market.[104] In general, firms can predict that competitors with high market dependence are likely to respond strongly to attacks threatening their market position.[105] Interestingly, the threatened firm in these instances may not always respond quickly, even though an effective response to an attack on the firm's position in a critical market is important.

Sargento Foods is a family-owned company based in Wisconsin. The firm is a leading packager and marketer of "shredded, snack and specialty cheeses (that are) sold under the Sargento brand, cheese and non-cheese snack food items and ethnic sauces." With sales exceeding $600 million annually, Sargento's business is founded on a passion for cheese. Because Sargento's business operations revolve strictly around cheese products, it is totally dependent on the market for cheese. As such, any competitor that chooses to attack Sargento and its market positions can anticipate a strong response to its competitive actions.

Competitive Dynamics

Whereas competitive rivalry concerns the ongoing actions and responses between a firm and its competitors for an advantageous market position, competitive dynamics concern the ongoing actions and responses taking place among *all* firms competing within a market for advantageous positions.

To explain competitive rivalry, we described (1) factors that determine the degree to which firms are competitors (market commonality and resource similarity), (2) the drivers of competitive behavior for individual firms (awareness, motivation, and ability) and (3) factors affecting the likelihood that a competitor will act or attack (first-mover incentives, organizational size, and quality) and respond (type of competitive action, reputation, and market dependence). Building and sustaining competitive advantages are at the core of competitive rivalry, in that advantages are the key to creating value for shareholders.[106]

To explain competitive dynamics, we discuss the effects of varying rates of competitive speed in different markets (called slow-cycle, fast-cycle, and standard-cycle markets) on the behavior (actions and responses) of all competitors within a given market. Competitive behaviors as well as the reasons or logic for taking them are similar within each market type, but differ across market types.[107] Thus, competitive dynamics differ in slow-cycle, fast-cycle, and standard-cycle markets. The sustainability of the firm's competitive advantages differs across the three market types.

As noted in Chapter 1, firms want to sustain their competitive advantages for as long as possible, although no advantage is permanently sustainable. The degree of sustainability is affected by how quickly competitive advantages can be imitated and how costly it is to do so.

Slow-Cycle Markets

Slow-cycle markets are those in which the firm's competitive advantages are shielded from imitation commonly for long periods of time and where imitation is costly.[108] Thus, competitive advantages are sustainable in slow-cycle markets.

Building a unique and proprietary capability produces a competitive advantage and success in a slow-cycle market. This type of advantage is difficult for competitors to understand. As discussed in Chapter 3, a difficult-to-understand and costly-to-imitate resource or capability usually results from unique historical conditions, causal ambiguity, and/or social complexity. Copyrights, geography, patents, and ownership of an information resource are examples of resources.[109] After a proprietary advantage is developed, the firm's competitive behavior in a slow-cycle market is oriented to protecting, maintaining, and extending that advantage. Thus, the competitive dynamics in slow-cycle markets

Slow-cycle markets are those in which the firm's competitive advantages are shielded from imitation commonly for long periods of time and where imitation is costly.

usually concentrate on competitive actions and responses that enable firms to protect, maintain, and extend their competitive advantage. Major strategic actions in these markets, such acquisitions, usually carry less risk than in faster cycle markets.[110]

Walt Disney Co. continues to extend its proprietary characters, such as Mickey Mouse, Minnie Mouse, and Goofy. These characters have a unique historical development as a result of Walt and Roy Disney's creativity and vision for entertaining people. Products based on the characters seen in Disney's animated films are sold through Disney's theme park shops as well as freestanding retail outlets called Disney Stores. Because copyrights shield it, the proprietary nature of Disney's advantage in terms of animated character trademarks protects the firm from imitation by competitors.

Consistent with another attribute of competition in a slow-cycle market, Disney protects its exclusive rights to its characters and their use as shown by the fact that "the company once sued a day-care center, forcing it to remove the likeness of Mickey Mouse from a wall of the facility."[111] As with all firms competing in slow-cycle markets, Disney's competitive actions (such as building theme parks in France, Japan, and China) and responses (such as lawsuits to protect its right to fully control use of its animated characters) maintain and extend its proprietary competitive advantage while protecting it.

Patent laws and regulatory requirements such as those in the United States requiring FDA (Food and Drug Administration) approval to launch new products shield pharmaceutical companies' positions. Competitors in this market try to extend patents on their drugs to maintain advantageous positions that the patents provide. However, after a patent expires, the firm is no longer shielded from competition, allowing generic imitations and usually leading to a loss of sales.

The competitive dynamics generated by firms competing in slow-cycle markets are shown in Figure 4.4. In slow-cycle markets, firms launch a product (e.g., a new drug) that has been developed through a proprietary advantage (e.g., R&D) and then exploit it for as long as possible while the product is shielded from competition. Eventually, competitors respond to the action with a counterattack. In markets for drugs, this counterattack commonly occurs as patents expire or are broken through legal means, creating the need for another product launch by the firm seeking a protected market position.

Fast-Cycle Markets

Fast-cycle markets are markets in which the firm's capabilities that contribute to competitive advantages aren't shielded from imitation and where imitation is often rapid and inexpensive. Thus, competitive advantages aren't sustainable in fast-cycle markets. Firms

Fast-cycle markets are markets in which the firm's capabilities that contribute to competitive advantages aren't shielded from imitation and where imitation is often rapid and inexpensive.

Figure 4.4 Gradual Erosion of a Sustained Competitive Advantage

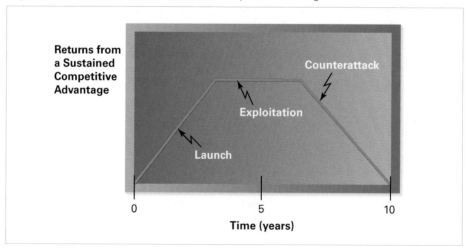

Source: Adapted from I. C. MacMillan, 1988, Controlling competitive dynamics by taking strategic initiative, *Academy of Management Executive*, II(2): 111–118.

competing in fast-cycle markets recognize the importance of speed; these companies appreciate that "time is as precious a business resource as money or head count—and that the costs of hesitation and delay are just as steep as going over budget or missing a financial forecast."[112] Such high-velocity environments place considerable pressures on top managers to quickly make strategic decisions that are also effective.[113] The often substantial competition and technology-based strategic focus make the strategic decision complex, increasing the need for a comprehensive approach integrated with decision speed, two often-conflicting characteristics of the strategic decision process.[114]

Reverse engineering and the rate of technology diffusion in fast-cycle markets facilitate rapid imitation. A competitor uses reverse engineering to quickly gain the knowledge required to imitate or improve the firm's products. Technology is diffused rapidly in fast-cycle markets, making it available to competitors in a short period. The technology often used by fast-cycle competitors isn't proprietary, nor is it protected by patents as is the technology used by firms competing in slow-cycle markets. For example, only a few hundred parts, which are readily available on the open market, are required to build a PC. Patents protect only a few of these parts, such as microprocessor chips.[115]

Fast-cycle markets are more volatile than slow-cycle and standard-cycle markets. Indeed, the pace of competition in fast-cycle markets is almost frenzied, as companies rely on innovations as the engines of their growth. Because prices fall quickly in these markets, companies need to profit quickly from their product innovations. Imitation of many fast-cycle products is relatively easy, as demonstrated by Dell and HP, along with a host of local PC vendors, that have partly or largely imitated the original PC design to create their products. Continuous declines in the costs of parts, as well as the fact that the information required to assemble a PC isn't especially complicated and is readily available, make it possible for additional competitors to enter this market without significant difficulty.[116]

The fast-cycle market characteristics just described make it virtually impossible for companies in this type of market to develop sustainable competitive advantages. Recognizing this reality, firms avoid "loyalty" to any of their products, preferring to cannibalize their own before competitors learn how to do so through successful imitation. This emphasis creates competitive dynamics that differ substantially from those found in slow-cycle markets. Instead of concentrating on protecting, maintaining, and extending competitive advantages, as in slow-cycle markets, companies competing in fast-cycle markets focus on learning how to rapidly and continuously develop new competitive advantages that are superior to those they replace. Commonly, they search for fast and effective means of developing new products. For example, it is common in some industries for firms to use strategic alliances to gain access to new technologies and thereby develop and introduce more new products into the market.[117]

The competitive behavior of firms competing in fast-cycle markets is shown in Figure 4.5. As suggested by the figure, competitive dynamics in this market type entail taking actions and responses that are oriented to rapid and continuous product introductions and the development of a stream of ever-changing competitive advantages. The firm launches a product to achieve a competitive action and then exploits the advantage for as long as possible. However, the firm also tries to develop another temporary competitive advantage before competitors can respond to the first one (see Figure 4.5). Thus, competitive dynamics in fast-cycle markets often result in rapid product upgrades as well as quick product innovations.[118]

As our discussion suggests, innovation plays a dominant role in the competitive dynamics in fast-cycle markets. For individual firms, then, innovation is a key source of competitive advantage. Through innovation, the firm can cannibalize its own products before competitors successfully imitate them.

Standard-Cycle Markets

Standard-cycle markets are markets in which the firm's competitive advantages are moderately shielded from imitation and where imitation is moderately costly. Competitive advantages are partially sustainable in standard-cycle markets, but only when the firm is

Standard-cycle markets are markets in which the firm's competitive advantages are moderately shielded from imitation and where imitation is moderately costly.

Figure 4.5 Developing Temporary Advantages to Create Sustained Advantage

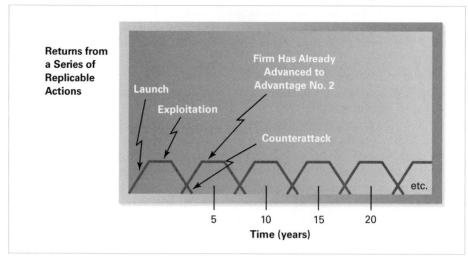

Source: Adapted from I. C. MacMillan, 1988, Controlling competitive dynamics by taking strategic initiative, *Academy of Management Executive*, II(2): 111–118.

able to continuously upgrade the quality of its capabilities, making the competitive advantages dynamic. The competitive actions and responses that form a standard-cycle market's competitive dynamics are designed to seek large market shares, to gain customer loyalty through brand names, and to carefully control a firm's operations in order to consistently provide the same positive experience for customers.[119]

Standard-cycle companies serve many customers in competitive markets. Because the capabilities and core competencies on which their competitive advantages are based are less specialized, imitation is faster and less costly for standard-cycle firms than for those competing in slow-cycle markets. However, imitation is slower and more expensive in these markets than in fast-cycle markets. Thus, competitive dynamics in standard-cycle markets rest midway between the characteristics of dynamics in slow-cycle and fast-cycle markets. Imitation comes less quickly and is more expensive for standard-cycle competitors when a firm is able to develop economies of scale by combining coordinated and integrated design and manufacturing processes with a large sales volume for its products.

Because of large volumes, the size of mass markets, and the need to develop scale economies, the competition for market share is intense in standard-cycle markets. This form of competition is readily evident in the battles among consumer foods' producers. Recently, companies such as Frito-Lay, Pepperidge Farm, Nabisco, and Hershey started "placing bigger bets on smaller packages."[120] Essentially, these firms are offering products that they already offer to consumers in smaller packages. Beef Jerky (Frito-Lay), Goldfish (Pepperidge Farm), Animals Choco Crackers (Nabisco), and Twizzlers (Hershey) are examples of food items being offered in 100-calorie per package servings. For the firms, this rapidly developing market is attractive in that they can take an existing product, put smaller amounts of it into single-serving bags, and then "sell several of the bags for about the same or more as a regular-sized package."[121] Package design and ease of availability are examples of the competitive dimensions on which these firms are now competing in efforts to outperform their rivals in this attractive market segment.

Innovation can also drive competitive actions and responses in standard-cycle markets, especially when rivalry is intense. Some innovations in standard-cycle markets are incremental rather than radical in nature (incremental and radical innovations are discussed in Chapter 13). For example, consumer foods' producers are innovating in terms of healthy products. Believing that "brown is better," Kraft Foods recently introduced the DiGiorno Harvest Wheat Crust frozen pizza under its "Sensible Solution" banner. General Mills' bakery division is using white whole wheat flour to make products such as cinnamon rolls, puff pastries, and croissants. Finally, Kellogg introduced a new Tiger

Power brand of whole-grain wheat cereal for kids featuring Tony the Tiger on the box.[122] Overall, these firms are relying on innovation as a means of competing in standard-cycle markets and to earn above-average returns.

In the final analysis, innovation has a substantial influence on competitive dynamics as it affects the actions and responses of all companies competing within a slow-cycle, fast-cycle, or standard-cycle market. We have emphasized the importance of innovation to the firm's strategic competitiveness in earlier chapters and do so again in Chapter 13. Our discussion of innovation in terms of competitive dynamics extends the earlier discussions by showing its importance in all types of markets in which firms compete.

Summary

- Competitors are firms competing in the same market, offering similar products, and targeting similar customers. Competitive rivalry is the ongoing set of competitive actions and competitive responses occurring between competitors as they compete against each other for an advantageous market position. The outcomes of competitive rivalry influence the firm's ability to sustain its competitive advantages as well as the level (average, below average, or above average) of its financial returns.

- For the individual firm, the set of competitive actions and responses it takes while engaged in competitive rivalry is called competitive behavior. Competitive dynamics is the set of actions and responses taken by all firms that are competitors within a particular market.

- Firms study competitive rivalry in order to be able to predict the competitive actions and responses that each of their competitors likely will take. Competitive actions are either strategic or tactical in nature. The firm takes competitive actions to defend or build its competitive advantages or to improve its market position. Competitive responses are taken to counter the effects of a competitor's competitive action. A strategic action or a strategic response requires a significant commitment of organizational resources, is difficult to successfully implement, and is difficult to reverse. In contrast, a tactical action or a tactical response requires fewer organizational resources and is easier to implement and reverse. For an airline company, for example, entering major new markets is an example of a strategic action or a strategic response; changing its prices in a particular market is an example of a tactical action or a tactical response.

- A competitor analysis is the first step the firm takes to be able to predict its competitors' actions and responses. In Chapter 2, we discussed what firms do to *understand* competitors. This discussion was extended in this chapter as we described what the firm does to *predict* competitors' market-based actions. Thus, understanding precedes prediction. Market commonality (the number of markets with which competitors are jointly involved and their importance to each) and resource similarity (how comparable competitors' resources are in terms of type and amount) are studied to complete a competitor analysis. In general, the greater the market commonality and resource

similarity, the more firms acknowledge that they are direct competitors.

- Market commonality and resource similarity shape the firm's awareness (the degree to which it and its competitor understand their mutual interdependence), motivation (the firm's incentive to attack or respond), and ability (the quality of the resources available to the firm to attack and respond). Having knowledge of a competitor in terms of these characteristics increases the quality of the firm's predictions about that competitor's actions and responses.

- In addition to market commonality and resource similarity and awareness, motivation, and ability, three more specific factors affect the likelihood a competitor will take competitive actions. The first of these concerns first-mover incentives. First movers, those taking an initial competitive action, often earn above-average returns until competitors can successfully respond to their action and gain loyal customers. Not all firms can be first movers in that they may lack the awareness, motivation, or ability required to engage in this type of competitive behavior. Moreover, some firms prefer to be a second mover (the firm responding to the first mover's action). One reason for this is that second movers, especially those acting quickly, can successfully compete against the first mover. By evaluating the first mover's product, customers' reactions to it, and the responses of other competitors to the first mover, the second mover can avoid the early entrant's mistakes and find ways to improve upon the value created for customers by the first mover's good or service. Late movers (those that respond a long time after the original action was taken) commonly are lower performers and are much less competitive.

- Organizational size, the second factor, tends to reduce the variety of competitive actions that large firms launch while it increases the variety of actions undertaken by smaller competitors. Ideally, the firm would like to initiate a large number of diverse actions when engaged in competitive rivalry. The third factor, quality, is a base denominator to successful competition in the global economy. It is a necessary prerequisite to achieve competitive parity. It is a necessary but insufficient condition for gaining an advantage.

- The type of action (strategic or tactical) the firm took, the competitor's reputation for the nature of its competitor behavior, and that competitor's dependence on the market in which the action was taken are studied to predict a competitor's response to the firm's action. In general, the number of tactical responses taken exceeds the number of strategic responses. Competitors respond more frequently to the actions taken by the firm with a reputation for predictable and understandable competitive behavior, especially if that firm is a market leader. In general, the firm can predict that when its competitor is highly dependent for its revenue and profitability in the market in which the firm took a competitive action, that competitor is likely to launch a strong response. However, firms that are more diversified across markets are less likely to respond to a particular action that affects only one of the markets in which they compete.

- Competitive dynamics concerns the ongoing competitive behavior occurring among all firms competing in a market for advantageous positions. Market characteristics affect the set of actions and responses firms take while competing in a given market as well as the sustainability of firms' competitive advantages. In slow-cycle markets, where competitive advantages can be maintained, competitive dynamics finds firms taking actions and responses that are intended to protect, maintain, and extend their proprietary advantages. In fast-cycle markets, competition is almost frenzied as firms concentrate on developing a series of temporary competitive advantages. This emphasis is necessary because firms' advantages in fast-cycle markets aren't proprietary and, as such, are subject to rapid and relatively inexpensive imitation. Standard-cycle markets experience competition between slow-cycle and fast-cycle markets; firms are moderately shielded from competition in these markets as they use capabilities that produce competitive advantages that are moderately sustainable. Competitors in standard-cycle markets serve mass markets and try to develop economies of scale to enhance their profitability. Innovation is vital to competitive success in each of the three types of markets. Companies should recognize that the set of competitive actions and responses taken by all firms differs by type of market.

Review Questions

1. Who are competitors? How are competitive rivalry, competitive behavior, and competitive dynamics defined in the chapter?

2. What is market commonality? What is resource similarity? What does it mean to say that these concepts are the building blocks for a competitor analysis?

3. How do awareness, motivation, and ability affect the firm's competitive behavior?

4. What factors affect the likelihood a firm will take a competitive action?

5. What factors affect the likelihood a firm will initiate a competitive response to the action taken by a competitor?

6. What competitive dynamics can be expected among firms competing in slow-cycle markets? In fast-cycle markets? In standard-cycle markets?

Notes

1. D. F. Spulber, 2004, *Management Strategy*, Boston: McGraw-Hill/Irwin, 87–88; M.-J. Chen, 1996, Competitor analysis and interfirm rivalry: Toward a theoretical integration, *Academy of Management Review*, 21: 100–134.
2. M. Bartiromo, 2007, Will Dell be a comeback kid? *BusinessWeek*, February 26, 128.
3. M. Schrage, 2007, The myth of commoditization, *MIT Sloan Management Review*, 48(2): 10–14; T. Galvin, 2002, Examining institutional change: Evidence from the founding dynamics of U.S. health care interest associations, *Academy of Management Journal*, 45: 673–696.
4. R. D. Ireland & J. W. Webb, 2007, Strategic entrepreneurship: Creating competitive advantage through streams of innovation, *Business Horizons*, 50: 49–59.
5. B. R. Barringer & R. D. Ireland, 2008, *Entrepreneurship: Successfully Launching New Ventures*, 2nd ed., Upper Saddle River, NJ: Prentice Hall; A. M. Knott & H. E. Posen, 2005, Is failure good? *Strategic Management Journal*, 26: 617–641.
6. C. M. Grimm, H. Lee, & K. G. Smith, 2006, *Strategy as Action: Competitive Dynamics and Competitive Advantage*, New York: Oxford University Press.
7. J. W. Selsky, J. Goes, & O. N. Baburoglu, 2007, Contrasting perspectives of strategy making: Applications in "hyper" environments, *Organization Studies*, 28(1): 71–94; A. Nair & L. Filer, 2003, Cointegration of firm strategies within groups: A long-run analysis of firm behavior in the Japanese steel industry, *Strategic Management Journal*, 24: 145–159.
8. T. C. Powell, 2003, Varieties of competitive parity, *Strategic Management Journal*, 24: 61–86.
9. J. Rodriguez-Pinto, J. Gutierrez-Cillan, & A. I. Rodriguez-Escudero, 2007, Order and scale market entry, firm resources, and performance, *European Journal of Marketing*, 41: 590–607; S. Jayachandran, J. Gimeno, & P. R. Varadarajan, 1999, Theory of multimarket competition: A synthesis and implications for marketing strategy, *Journal of Marketing*, 63: 49–66.
10. Grimm, Lee & Smith, *Strategy as Action*; G. Young, K. G. Smith, C. M. Grimm, & D. Simon, 2000, Multimarket contact and resource dissimilarity: A competitive dynamics perspective, *Journal of Management*, 26: 1217–1236.

11. T. L. Sorenson, 2007, Credible collusion in multimarket oligopoly, *Managerial and Decision Economics*, 28(2): 115-128; H. A. Haveman & L. Nonnemaker, 2000, Competition in multiple geographic markets: The impact on growth and market entry, *Administrative Science Quarterly*, 45: 232–267.

12. K. G. Smith, W. J. Ferrier, & H. Ndofor, 2001, Competitive dynamics research: Critique and future directions, in M. A. Hitt, R. E. Freeman, & J. S. Harrison (eds.), *Handbook of Strategic Management*, Oxford, UK: Blackwell Publishers, 326.

13. G. Young, K. G. Smith, & C. M. Grimm, 1996, "Austrian" and industrial organization perspectives on firm-level competitive activity and performance, *Organization Science*, 73: 243–254.

14. 2007, Dell to sell PCs at Wal-Mart in retail drive, http://www.reuters.com, May 24.

15. H. D. Hopkins, 2003, The response strategies of dominant U.S. firms to Japanese challengers, *Journal of Management*, 29: 5–25; G. S. Day & D. J. Reibstein, 1997, The dynamic challenges for theory and practice, in G. S. Day & D. J. Reibstein (eds.), *Wharton on Competitive Strategy*, New York: John Wiley & Sons, 2.

16. M.-J. Chen & D. C. Hambrick, 1995, Speed, stealth, and selective attack: How small firms differ from large firms in competitive behavior, *Academy of Management Journal*, 38: 453–482.

17. T. Dewett & S. David, 2007, Innovators and imitators in novelty-intensive markets: A research agenda, *Creativity and Innovation Management*, 16(1): 80–92.

18. P. Engardio, 2007, Flat panels, thin margins, *BusinessWeek*, February 26, 50–51.

19. A. Sahay, 2007, How to reap higher profits with dynamic pricing, *MIT Sloan Management Review*, 48(4): 53–60; T. J. Douglas & J. A. Ryman, 2003, Understanding competitive advantage in the general hospital industry: Evaluating strategic competencies, *Strategic Management Journal*, 24: 333–347.

20. T. Yu & A. A. Cannella, Jr., 2007, Rivalry between multinational enterprises: An event history approach, *Academy of Management Journal*, 50: 665–686; W. J. Ferrier, 2001, Navigating the competitive landscape: The drivers and consequences of competitive aggressiveness, *Academy of Management Journal*, 44: 858–877.

21. Smith, Ferrier, & Ndofor, Competitive dynamics research, 319.

22. J. Shamsie, 2003, The context of dominance: An industry-driven framework for exploiting reputation, *Strategic Management Journal*, 24: 199–215; K. Ramaswamy, 2001, Organizational ownership, competitive intensity, and firm performance: An empirical study of the Indian manufacturing sector, *Strategic Management Journal*, 22: 989–998.

23. K. Cool, L. H. Roller, & B. Leleux, 1999, The relative impact of actual and potential rivalry on firm profitability in the pharmaceutical industry, *Strategic Management Journal*, 20: 1–14.

24. G. Leask & D. Parker, 2007, Strategic groups, competitive groups and performance within the U.K. pharmaceutical industry: Improving our understanding of the competitive process, *Strategic Management Journal*, 28: 723–745; D. R. Gnyawali & R. Madhavan, 2001, Cooperative networks and competitive dynamics: A structural embeddedness perspective, *Academy of Management Review*, 26: 431–445.

25. Y. Y. Kor & J. T. Mahoney, 2005, How dynamics, management, and governance of resource deployments influence firm-level performance, *Strategic Management Journal*, 26: 489–496.

26. R. L. Priem, L. G. Love, & M. A. Shaffer, 2002, Executives' perceptions of uncertainty scores: A numerical taxonomy and underlying dimensions, *Journal of Management*, 28: 725–746.

27. J. C. Bou & A. Satorra, 2007, The persistence of abnormal returns at industry and firm levels: Evidence from Spain, *Strategic Management Journal*, 28: 707–722.

28. Chen, Competitor analysis, 108.

29. B. Einhorn, 2007, A racer called Acer, *BusinessWeek*, February 26, 72.

30. Chen, Competitor analysis, 109.

31. K. Uhlenbruck, M. A. Hitt, & M. Semadeni, 2005, Market value effects of acquisitions of Internet firms: A resource-based analysis, working paper, University of Montana; A. Afuah, 2003, Redefining firm boundaries in the face of the Internet: Are firms really shrinking? *Academy of Management Review*, 28: 34–53.

32. H. Gebauer, 2007, Entering low-end markets: A new strategy for Swiss companies, *Journal of Business Strategy*, 27(5): 23–31.

33. 2007, YRC Worldwide, http://www.yrcw.com, July 30.

34. 2007, YRC Worldwide Inc., *Hoovers*, http://www.hoovers.com/yrc-worldwide, July 30.

35. Chen, Competitor analysis, 106.

36. M. J. Chen, K.-H. Su, & W. Tsai, 2007, Competitive tension: The awareness-motivation-capability perspective, *Academy of Management Journal*, 50: 101–118; J. Gimeno & C. Y. Woo, 1999, Multimarket contact, economies of scope, and firm performance, *Academy of Management Journal*, 42: 239–259.

37. M. Arndt, 2007, McDonald's, *BusinessWeek*, February 5, 64–72.

38. 2007, Prudential Financial Inc., *Standard & Poor's Stock Reports*, http://www.standardandpoors.com, July 12.

39. A. Carter, 2007, A shining light for Heineken, *BusinessWeek*, January 15, 46.

40. I. C. MacMillan, A. B. van Putten, & R. S. McGrath, 2003, Global gamesmanship, *Harvard Business Review*, 81(5): 62–71.

41. Young, Smith, Grimm, & Simon, Multimarket contact, 1230.

42. J. Gimeno, 1999, Reciprocal threats in multimarket rivalry: Staking out "spheres of influence" in the U.S. airline industry, *Strategic Management Journal*, 20: 101–128; N. Fernandez & P. L. Marin, 1998, Market power and multimarket contact: Some evidence from the Spanish hotel industry, *Journal of Industrial Economics*, 46: 301–315.

43. Jayachandran, Gimeno, & Varadarajan, Theory of multimarket competition, 59; Chen, Competitor analysis, 107.

44. J. Gimeno & C. Y. Woo, 1996, Hypercompetition in a multimarket environment: The role of strategic similarity and multimarket contact on competitive de-escalation, *Organization Science*, 7: 322–341.

45. C. H. Deutsch, 2007, UPS embraces high-tech delivery methods, *New York Times Online*, http://www.nytimes.com, July 12.

46. Ibid.

47. Chen, Su & Tsai, Competitive tension; Chen, Competitor analysis, 110.

48. Ibid.; W. Ocasio, 1997, Towards an attention-based view of the firm, *Strategic Management Journal*, 18 (Special Issue): 187–206; Smith, Ferrier, & Ndofor, Competitive dynamics research, 320.

49. 2007, Komatsu lifts outlook, outdoes rival Caterpillar, *New York Times Online*, http://www.nytimes.com, July 30.

50. 2007, Carrefour battles Wal-Mart in South America, Elsevier Food International, http://www.foodinternational.net, July 31.

51. S. Tallman, M. Jenkins, N. Henry, & S. Pinch, 2004, Knowledge, clusters and competitive advantage, *Academy of Management Review*, 29: 258–271; J. F. Porac & H. Thomas, 1994, Cognitive categorization and subjective rivalry among retailers in a small city, *Journal of Applied Psychology*, 79: 54–66.

52. S. H. Park & D. Zhou, 2005, Firm heterogeneity and competitive dynamics in alliance formation, *Academy of Management Review*, 30: 531–554.

53. Chen, Competitor analysis, 113.

54. R. Belderbos & L. Sleuwaegen, 2005, Competitive drivers and international plant configuration strategies: A product-level test, *Strategic Management Journal*, 26: 577–593.

55. C. M. Grimm & K. G. Smith, 1997, *Strategy as Action: Industry Rivalry and Coordination*, Cincinnati: South-Western Publishing Co., 125.

56. B. Webber, 2007, Volatile markets, *Business Strategy Review*, 18(2): 60–67; K. G. Smith, W. J. Ferrier, & C. M. Grimm, 2001, King of the hill: Dethroning the industry leader, *Academy of Management Executive*, 15(2): 59–70.

57. W. J. Ferrier & H. Lee, 2003, Strategic aggressiveness, variation, and surprise: How the sequential pattern of competitive rivalry influences stock market returns, *Journal of Managerial Issues*, 14: 162–180.

58. C. Palmeri, 2007, How Guess got its groove back, *BusinessWeek*, July 23, 126.

59. S. Holmes, 2007, Better living at 30,000 feet, *BusinessWeek*, August 6, 76–77.

60. L. Lee, 2007, A smoothie you can chew on, *BusinessWeek*, June 11, 64–65.

61. J. Schumpeter, 1934, *The Theory of Economic Development*, Cambridge, MA: Harvard University Press.

62. J. L. C. Cheng & I. F. Kesner, 1997, Organizational slack and response to environmental shifts: The impact of resource allocation patterns, *Journal of Management*, 23: 1–18.

63. F. F. Suarez & G. Lanzolla, 2007, The role of environmental dynamics in building a first mover advantage theory, *Academy of Management Review*, 32: 377–392.

64. F. Wang, 2000, Too appealing to overlook, *America's Network*, December, 10–12.

65. D. P. Forbes, 2005, Managerial determinants of decision speed in new ventures, *Strategic Management Journal*, 26: 355–366.

66. W. T. Robinson & S. Min, 2002, Is the first to market the first to fail? Empirical evidence for industrial goods businesses, *Journal of Marketing Research*, 39: 120–128.

67. T. Cottrell & B. R. Nault, 2004, *Strategic Management Journal*, 25: 1005–1025; R. Agarwal, M. B. Sarkar, & R. Echambadi, 2002, The conditioning effect of time on firm survival: An industry life cycle approach, *Academy of Management Journal*, 45: 971–994.

68. A. Srivastava & H. Lee, 2005, Predicting order and timing of new product moves: The role of top management in corporate entrepreneurship, *Journal of Business Venturing*, 20: 459–481; A. Nerer & P. W. Roberts, 2004, Technological and product-market experience and the success of new product introductions in the pharmaceutical industry, *Strategic Management Journal*, 25: 779–799.

69. M. S. Giarratana & A. Fosfuri, 2007, Product strategies and survival in Schumpeterian environments: Evidence from the U.S. security software industry, *Organization Studies*, 28(6): 909–929; J. W. Spencer & T. P. Murtha, 2005, How do governments matter to new industry creation? *Academy of Management Review*, 30: 321–337.

70. Z. Simsek, J. F. Veiga, & M. H. Lubatkin, 2007, The impact of managerial environmental perceptions on corporate entrepreneurship: Toward understanding discretionary slack's pivotal role, *Journal of Management Studies*, in press; S. W. Geiger & L. H. Cashen, 2002, A multidimensional examination of slack and its impact on innovation, *Journal of Managerial Issues*, 14: 68–84.

71. B.-S. Teng, 2007, Corporate entrepreneurship activities through strategic alliances: A resource-based approach toward competitive advantage, *Journal of Management Studies*, 44: 119–142; M. B. Lieberman & D. B. Montgomery, 1988, First-mover advantages, *Strategic Management Journal*, 9: 41–58.

72. 2001, Older, wiser, webbier, *The Economist*, June 30, 10.

73. M. Shank, 2002, Executive strategy report, IBM business strategy consulting, http://www.ibm.com, March 14; W. Boulding & M. Christen, 2001, First-mover disadvantage, *Harvard Business Review*, 79(9): 20–21.

74. S. Hamm, 2007, Kodak's moment of truth, *BusinessWeek*, February 19, 42–49.

75. Ibid., 42.

76. J. Gimeno, R. E. Hoskisson, B. B. Beal, & W. P. Wan, 2005, Explaining the clustering of international expansion moves: A critical test in the U.S. telecommunications industry, *Academy of Management Journal*, 48: 297–319; K. G. Smith, C. M. Grimm, & M. J. Gannon, 1992, *Dynamics of Competitive Strategy*, Newberry Park, CA.: Sage Publications.

77. E. Schine, 2007, GM's big move to small Chevrolets, *BusinessWeek*, April 9, 9.

78. S. D. Dobrev & G. R. Carroll, 2003, Size (and competition) among organizations: Modeling scale-based selection among automobile producers in four major countries, 1885–1981, *Strategic Management Journal*, 24: 541–558.

79. F. K. Pil & M. Hoiweg, 2003, Exploring scale: The advantage of thinking small, *The McKinsey Quarterly*, 44(2): 33–39; Chen & Hambrick, Speed, stealth, and selective attack.

80. M. A. Hitt, L. Bierman & J. D. Collins, 2007, The strategic evolution of U.S. law firms, *Business Horizons*, 50: 17–28; D. Miller & M. J. Chen, 1996, The simplicity of competitive repertoires: An empirical analysis, *Strategic Management Journal*, 17: 419–440.

81. Young, Smith, & Grimm, "Austrian" and industrial organization perspectives.

82. B. A. Melcher, 1993, How Goliaths can act like Davids, *BusinessWeek*, Special Issue, 193.

83. G. McWilliams & S. Vranica, 2007, Wal-Mart raises its emotional pitch, *Wall Street Journal Online*, http://online.wsj.com, July 20.

84. P. B. Crosby, 1980, *Quality Is Free*, New York: Penguin.

84. W. E. Deming, 1986, *Out of the Crisis*, Cambridge, MA: MIT Press.

86. D. A. Mollenkopf, E. Rabinovich, T. M. Laseter, & K. K. Boyer, 2007, Managing Internet product returns: A focus on effective service operations, *Decision Sciences*, 38: 215–250; L. B. Crosby, R. DeVito, & J. M. Pearson, 2003, Manage your customers' perception of quality, *Review of Business*, 24(1): 18–24.

87. K. Watanabe, 2007, Lessons from Toyota's long drive, *Harvard Business Review*, 85(7/8): 74–83; R. S. Kaplan & D. P. Norton, 2001, *The Strategy-Focused Organization*, Boston: Harvard Business School Press.

88. O. Bayazit & B. Karpak, 2007, An analytical network process-based framework for successful total quality management (TQM): An assessment of Turkish manufacturing industry readiness, *International Journal of Production Economics*, 105(1): 79–96.

89. K. E. Weick & K. M. Sutcliffe, 2001, *Managing the Unexpected*, San Francisco: Jossey-Bass, 81–82.

90. G. Macintosh, 2007, Customer orientation, relationship quality, and relational benefits to the firm, *Journal of Services Marketing*, 21(3): 150–159; G. Yeung & V. Mok, 2005, What are the impacts of implementing ISOs on the competitiveness of manufacturing industry in China, *Journal of World Business*, 40: 139–157.

91. J. Tagliabue, 2007, Low-cost Chinese cars making restrained entry to European market, *New York Times Online*, http://www.nytimes.com, July 13.

92. G. Edmondson, 2006, Mercedes gets back up to speed, *BusinessWeek*, November 13, 46–47.

93. J. Schumpeter, 1950, *Capitalism, Socialism and Democracy*, New York: Harper; Smith, Ferrier, & Ndofor, Competitive dynamics research, 323.

94. M. J. Chen & I. C. MacMillan, 1992, Nonresponse and delayed response to competitive moves, *Academy of Management Journal*, 35: 539–570; Smith, Ferrier, & Ndofor, Competitive dynamics research, 335.

95. M. Wong, 2007, Battling rivals, Palm sells 25% to Elevation, *The Salt Lake Tribune Online*, http://www.sltrib.com, June 4.

96. M. J. Chen, K. G. Smith, & C. M. Grimm, 1992, Action characteristics as predictors of competitive responses, *Management Science*, 38: 439–455.

97. M. J. Chen & D. Miller, 1994, Competitive attack, retaliation and performance: An expectancy-valence framework, *Strategic Management Journal*, 15: 85–102.

98. T. Gardner, 2005, Interfirm competition for human resources: Evidence from the software industry, *Academy of Management Journal*, 48: 237–258; N. Huyghebaert & L. M. van de Gucht, 2004, Incumbent strategic behavior in financial markets and the exit of entrepreneurial start-ups, *Strategic Management Journal*, 25: 669–688.

99. Smith, Ferrier, & Ndofor, Competitive dynamics research, 333.

100. V. P. Rindova, A. P. Petkova, & S. Kotha, 2007, Standing out: How firms in emerging markets build reputation, *Strategic Organization*, 5: 31–70; J. Shamsie, 2003, The context of dominance: An industry-driven framework for exploiting reputation, *Strategic Management Journal*, 24: 199–215.

101. A. D. Smith, 2007, Making the case for the competitive advantage of corporate social responsibility, *Business Strategy Series*, 8(3): 186–195; P. W. Roberts & G. R. Dowling, 2003, Corporate reputation and sustained superior financial performance, *Strategic Management Journal*, 24: 1077–1093.

102. W. J. Ferrier, K. G. Smith, & C. M. Grimm, 1999, The role of competitive actions in market share erosion and industry dethronement: A study of industry leaders and challengers, *Academy of Management Journal*, 42: 372–388.

103. Smith, Grimm, & Gannon, *Dynamics of Competitive Strategy*.

104. A. Karnani & B. Wernerfelt, 1985, Multiple point competition, *Strategic Management Journal*, 6: 87–97.

105. Smith, Ferrier, & Ndofor, Competitive dynamics research, 330.

106. S. L. Newbert, 2007, Empirical research on the resource-based view of the firm: An assessment and suggestions for future research, *Strategic Management Journal*, 28: 121–146; G. McNamara, P. M. Vaaler, & C. Devers, 2003, Same as it ever was: The search for evidence of increasing hypercompetition, *Strategic Management Journal*, 24: 261–278.

107. A. Kalnins & W. Chung, 2004, Resource-seeking agglomeration: A study of market entry in the lodging industry, *Strategic Management Journal*, 25: 689–699.

108. J. R. Williams, 1992, How sustainable is your competitive advantage? *California Management Review*, 34(3): 29–51.

109. D. A. Chmielewski & A. Paladino, 2007, Driving a resource orientation: Reviewing the role of resources and capability characteristics, *Management Decision*, 45: 462–483.

110. N. Pangarkar & J. R. Lie, 2004, The impact of market cycle on the performance of Singapore acquirers, *Strategic Management Journal*, 25: 1209–1216.

111. Ibid., 57.

112. 2003, How fast is your company? *Fast Company*, June, 18.

113. D. P. Forbes, 2007, Reconsidering the strategic implications of decision comprehensiveness, *Academy of Management Review*, 32: 361–376; T. Talaulicar, J. Grundei, & A. V. Werder, 2005, Strategic decision making in start-ups: The effect of top management team organization and processes on speed and comprehensiveness, *Journal of Business Venturing*, 20: 519–541.

114. M. Song, C. Droge, S. Hanvanich, & R. Calantone, 2005, Marketing and technology resource complementarity: An analysis of their interaction effect in two environmental contexts, *Strategic Management Journal*, 26: 259–276.

115. R. Williams, 1999, Renewable advantage: Crafting strategy through economic time, New York: Free Press, 8.

116. Ibid.

117. D. Li, L. E. Eden, M. A. Hitt, & R. D. Ireland, 2008, Friends, acquaintances or strangers? Partner selection in R&D alliances, *Academy of Management Journal*, in press; D. Gerwin, 2004, Coordinating new product development in strategic alliances, *Academy of Management Review*, 29: 241–257.

118. P. Carbonell & A. I. Rodriguez, 2006, The impact of market characteristics and innovation speed on perceptions of positional advantage and new product performance, *International Journal of Research in Marketing*, 23(1): 1–12; R. Sanchez, 1995, Strategic flexibility in production competition, *Strategic Management Journal*, 16 (Special Issue): 9–26.

119. Williams, *Renewable Advantage*, 7.

120. J. W. Peters, 2007, In small packages, fewer calories and more profit, *New York Times Online*, http://www.nytimes.com, July 7.

121. Ibid.

122. P. Bhatnagar, 2006, What's for dinner in 2006? *CNNMoney*, http://cnnmoney.com, January 11.

Strategy at the Business Level

Studying this chapter should provide you with the strategic management knowledge needed to:

1. Define business-level strategy.

2. Discuss the relationship between customers and business-level strategies in terms of *who, what,* and *how.*

3. Explain the differences among business-level strategies.

4. Use the five forces of competition model to explain how above-average returns can be earned through each business-level strategy.

5. Describe the risks of using each of the business-level strategies.

From Pet Food to PetSmart

From Pet Food to PetSmart, this company has remained on top of the pet care industry in spite of fierce competition from PETCO (number 2), and major retailers Wal-Mart and Target by focusing on customer service. Although PetSmart began with a warehouse format and strategy, the company changed when research indicated that the average dog owner could spend more than $15,000 over the lifetime of the pet, if all available services were purchased. Thus, the "Engaging the Enthusiast" strategy emerged, along with a new vision: "to provide Total Lifetime Care for every pet, every parent, every time."

PetSmart first opened its doors in 1987, with two stores that operated under the name of PetFood Warehouse. Over the next two years the company changed its warehouse strategy to become a "MART for PETs that's SMART about PETs." The name and logo also changed to "PetsMart." The main focus was providing the best selection of products at the best prices. In 1993 PetsMart went public, and by 1994 had changed its slogan to "Where pets are family." By 2000 the company realized the importance of its services to pet owners (referred to as "pet parents") and developed a new vision statement: To provide Total Lifetime Care for every pet, every parent, every time. In 2001 PetsMart began an extensive customer training program for its associates (the company's name for employees). Associates were trained to identify customers' needs and how to provide solutions.

By 2005 top executives decided to leave behind the "mart" concept and move to a new focus on providing "Smart" solutions and information. The name was changed to PetSmart and a new logo was created.

Specialized services and dedication to the community distinguish PetSmart from its competitors. Services available at most PetSmart stores include pet training classes where the customer is allowed to retake the class if not 100% satisfied, grooming facilities with certified pet groomers, PetsHotels that provide daycare and extended stay facilities with 24-hour caregivers on duty, full-service pet hospitals, pet adoption centers, and new pet centers. More than 2.9 million pets have been adopted through the adoption service. In addition to services, PetSmart has implemented a universal return policy, which means that it will accept returned merchandise even if it was purchased from a competitor. Through its PetPerks customer loyalty program, customers use a card such as the ones used in many grocery stores to track customer purchases and to help develop effective marketing strategies. In return customers receive special discount offers and communications to help them become more knowledgeable about caring for their pets. PetSmart Charities, an independent nonprofit animal welfare association, was started in 1994 and has donated more than $52 million to animal welfare programs.

In addition to its traditional brick-and-mortar stores, PetSmart offers products and services through both catalog sales and on the Internet at www.petsmart.com. At PetSmart.com, customer service is taken a step further. Customers can order merchandise, learn about the company, and donate to PetSmart Charities. PetSmart is the largest online retailer of pet products and services.

PetSmart continues to increase its focus on customer service and continues to grow. Currently the firm has about 39,000 trained associates, most of them pet owners, and more than 13,000 different products are available for purchase, all at low prices, at more than 900 stores in 45 states. The market for pets and pet services continues to grow in the United States as the baby boomers and empty nesters acquire pets to fill the void left by children who have moved away, and younger Americans are choosing to wait longer to have children. PetSmart offers "Total Lifetime Care" for their new family members.

Sources: V. L. Facenda, 2000, Pet-opia, *Retail Merchandiser*, 40(7): 11; 2000, Calling all returns, *Chain Store Age*, 76(4): 41; J. Covert, 2005, PetSmart focuses on big returns by coming up with new services, *Wall Street Journal*, June 1, A1; 2007, PetSmart Fact Sheet, http://www.petsmart.com, May; 2007, PetSmart pet experts, http://www.petsmart.com/global/customerservice; T. Sullivan, 2006, Fido's at the front desk, as PetSmart adds "hotels," *Wall Street Journal Online*, http://online.wsj.com, October 8.

Increasingly important to firm success,[1] strategy is concerned with making choices among two or more alternatives.[2] As we noted in Chapter 1, when choosing a strategy, the firm decides to pursue one course of action instead of others. The choices are influenced by opportunities and threats in the firm's external environment[3] (see Chapter 2) as well as the nature and quality of its internal resources, capabilities, and core competencies[4] (see Chapter 3). PetSmart identified a large potential market that was being underserved. It developed the capabilities to offer a portfolio of goods and services that provided pet owners one-stop shopping for all of their pet needs. The full service offerings of the firm provide differentiation from and an advantage over competitors.

The fundamental objective of using any type of strategy (see Figure 1.1) is to gain strategic competitiveness and earn above-average returns.[5] Strategies are purposeful, precede the taking of actions to which they apply, and demonstrate a shared understanding of the firm's vision and mission.[6] An effectively formulated strategy marshals, integrates, and allocates the firm's resources, capabilities, and competencies so that it will be properly aligned with its external environment.[7] A properly developed strategy also rationalizes the firm's vision and mission along with the actions taken to achieve them.[8] Information about a host of variables including markets, customers, technology, worldwide finance, and the changing world economy must be collected and analyzed to properly form and use strategies. In the final analysis, sound strategic choices that reduce uncertainty regarding outcomes[9] are the foundation on which successful strategies are built.[10]

A **business-level strategy** is an integrated and coordinated set of commitments and actions the firm uses to gain a competitive advantage by exploiting core competencies in specific product markets.

Business-level strategy, this chapter's focus, is an integrated and coordinated set of commitments and actions the firm uses to gain a competitive advantage by exploiting core competencies in specific product markets.[11] Business-level strategy indicates the choices the firm has made about how it intends to compete in individual product markets. The choices are important because long-term performance is linked to a firm's strategies.[12] Given the complexity of successfully competing in the global economy, these choices are often quite difficult to make.[13] For example, to increase the effectiveness of its differentiation business-level strategy (we define and discuss this strategy later in the chapter), Kimberly-Clark executives decided to close some manufacturing facilities and to reduce its labor force. Describing these decisions, the firm's CEO said: "These are tough decisions, and these are ones that we don't take lightly. But I believe they are absolutely necessary to improve our competitive position."[14] Decisions made at Frederick Cooper, such as the closing of the manufacturing facility, were also difficult.

Every firm must form and use a business-level strategy.[15] However, every firm may not use all the strategies—corporate-level, acquisition and restructuring, international, and cooperative—that we examine in Chapters 6 through 9. A firm competing in a single-product market area in a single geographic location does not need a corporate-level strategy to deal with product diversity or an international strategy to deal with geographic diversity. In contrast, a diversified firm will use one of the corporate-level strategies as well as choose a separate business-level strategy for each product market area in which it competes. Every firm—from the local dry cleaner to the multinational corporation—chooses at least one business-level strategy. Thus business-level strategy is the *core* strategy—the strategy that the firm forms to describe how it intends to compete in a product market.[16]

We discuss several topics as we examine business-level strategies. Because customers are the foundation of successful business-level strategies and should never be taken for granted,[17] we present information about customers relevant to business-level strategies. In terms of customers, when selecting a business-level strategy the firm determines (1) *who* will be served, (2) *what* needs those target customers have that it will satisfy, and (3) *how* those needs will be satisfied. Selecting customers and deciding which of their needs the firm will try to satisfy, as well as how it will do so, are challenging tasks. Global competition has created many attractive options for customers thus making it difficult to determine the strategy to best serve them. Effective global competitors have become adept at identifying the needs of customers in different cultures and geographic regions as well as learning how to quickly and successfully adapt the functionality of the firms' good or service to meet those needs.

Descriptions of the purpose of business-level strategies—and of the five business-level strategies—follows the discussion of customers. The five strategies we examine are called *generic* because they can be used in any organization competing in any industry.[18] Our analysis describes how effective use of each strategy allows the firm to favorably position itself relative to the five competitive forces in the industry (see Chapter 2). In addition, we use the value chain (see Chapter 3) to show examples of the primary and support activities necessary to implement specific business-level strategies. Because no strategy is risk-free,[19] we also describe the different risks the firm may encounter when using these strategies.

In Chapter 11, we explain the organizational structures and controls linked with the successful use of each business-level strategy.

Customers: Their Relationship with Business-Level Strategies

Strategic competitiveness results only when the firm is able to satisfy a group of customers by using its competitive advantages as the basis for competing in individual product markets.[20] A key reason firms must satisfy customers with their business-level strategy is that returns earned from relationships with customers are the lifeblood of all organizations.[21]

The most successful companies try to find new ways to satisfy current customers and/or to meet the needs of new customers. Dell captured a significant market share in the personal computer market during the 1990s by using a low-cost strategy while simultaneously satisfying customer needs. It became the largest seller of PCs. However, it lost much of its customer focus by overemphasizing cost reduction through its supply chain. In so doing, Hewlett-Packard (HP) began to capture greater market share. HP learned how to manage its supply chain to lower costs, thereby gaining competitive parity with Dell. But it also provided a broader portfolio of goods and services that better satisfied customer needs and thereby captured customers from Dell.[22] Many

Recently, Hewlett-Packard overtook Dell in total number of sales of PCs.

firms attempt to imitate the capabilities of their competitors, as HP did in building capabilities to manage its supply chain activities similar to Dell, in order to gain competitive parity.[23] Yet firms can continue to build and leverage their tacit knowledge to avoid imitation.[24] Dell became too inward-focused and did not take actions to avoid the imitation of the capabilities that had provided it a competitive advantage. Thus, it lost that advantage and significant market share with it.

Effectively Managing Relationships with Customers

The firm's relationships with its customers are strengthened when it delivers superior value to them. Strong interactive relationships with customers often provide the foundation for the firm's efforts to profitably serve customers' unique needs.

Harrah's Entertainment believes that it provides superior value to customers by "being the most service-oriented, geographically diversified company in gaming."[25] Importantly, delivering superior value often results in increased customer loyalty. In turn, customer loyalty has a positive relationship with profitability. However, more choices and easily accessible information about the functionality of firms' products are creating increasingly sophisticated and knowledgeable customers, making it difficult to earn their loyalty.[26]

A number of companies have become skilled at the art of *managing* all aspects of their relationship with their customers.[27] For example, Amazon.com is an Internet-based venture widely recognized for the quality of information it maintains about its customers, the services it renders, and its ability to anticipate customers' needs.[28] Using the information it has, Amazon tries to serve what it believes are the unique needs of each customer. Based in Mexico, CEMEX SA is the "leading building-solutions company in the world." It is a global producer and marketer of quality cement and ready-mix concrete.[29] CEMEX uses the Internet to link its customers, cement plants, and main control room, allowing the firm to automate orders and optimize truck deliveries in highly congested Mexico City. Analysts believe that CEMEX's integration of Web technology with its cost leadership strategy differentiates it from competitors. As a result, CEMEX has become the largest cement producer in North America and one of the largest in the world.[30]

As we discuss next, firms' relationships with customers are characterized by three dimensions. Companies such as Amazon.com and CEMEX understand these dimensions and manage their relationships with customers in light of them.

Reach, Richness, and Affiliation

The *reach* dimension of relationships with customers is concerned with the firm's access and connection to customers. For instance, the largest physical retailer in bookstores, Barnes & Noble, carries 200,000-plus titles in 793 stores that average 25,000 square feet.[31] By contrast, Amazon.com offers more than 4.5 million titles and is located on tens of millions of computer screens with additional customer connections being established across the globe. Indeed, Amazon "has virtually unlimited online shelf space and can offer customers a vast selection of products through an efficient search and retrieval interface."[32] Even though Barnes & Noble also has an Internet presence (barnesandnoble.com), Amazon.com's reach is significantly greater. In general, firms seek to extend their reach, adding customers in the process of doing so.

Richness, the second dimension, is concerned with the depth and detail of the two-way flow of information between the firm and the customer. The potential of the richness dimension to help the firm establish a competitive advantage in its relationship with customers led many firms to offer online services in order to better manage information exchanges with their customers. Broader and deeper information-based exchanges allow firms to better understand their customers and their needs. Such exchanges also enable customers to become more knowledgeable about how the firm can satisfy them. Internet technology and e-commerce transactions have substantially reduced the costs of meaningful information exchanges with current and potential customers. Amazon.com is the leader in using the Internet to build relationships with customers. In fact, it bills itself as

STRATEGY RIGHT NOW

the most "customer-centric company" on earth. Executives at Amazon.com suggest that the company starts with the customer and works backwards.[33]

Affiliation, the third dimension, is concerned with facilitating useful interactions with customers. Internet navigators such as Microsoft's MSN Autos helps online clients find and sort information. MSN Autos provides data and software to prospective car buyers that enable them to compare car models along multiple objective specifications. The program can supply this information at no charge to the consumer because Internet technology allows a great deal of information to be collected from a variety of sources at a low cost. A prospective buyer who has selected a specific car based on comparisons of different models can then be linked to dealers that meet the customer's needs and purchasing requirements. Because its revenues come not from the final customer or end user but from other sources (such as advertisements on its Web site, hyperlinks, and associated products and services), MSN Autos represents the customer's interests, a service that fosters affiliation.[34] Viewing the world through the customer's eyes and constantly seeking ways to create more value for the customer have positive effects in terms of affiliation.

As we discuss next, effective management of customer relationships (along the dimensions of reach, richness, and affiliation) helps the firm answer questions related to the issues of *who, what,* and *how.*

Who: Determining the Customers to Serve

Deciding *who* the target customer is that the firm intends to serve with its business-level strategy is an important decision.[35] Companies divide customers into groups based on differences in the customers' needs (needs are discussed further in the next section) to make this decision. Dividing customers into groups based on their needs is called **market segmentation,** which is a process that clusters people with similar needs into individual and identifiable groups.[36] In the animal health business, for example, the needs for food products of owners of companion pets (e.g., dogs and cats) differ from the needs for food products of those owning production animals (e.g., livestock).[37] PetSmart serves the market segment for companion pets and not for the livestock segment. As part of its business-level strategy, the firm develops a marketing program to effectively sell products to its particular target customer group.[38]

Almost any identifiable human or organizational characteristic can be used to subdivide a market into segments that differ from one another on a given characteristic. Common characteristics on which customers' needs vary are illustrated in Table 5.1. Based on their internal core competencies and opportunities in the external environment, companies choose a business-level strategy to deliver value to target customers and satisfy their specific needs.

Customer characteristics are often combined to segment markets into specific groups that have unique needs. In the consumer clothing market, for example, Gap learned that its female and male customers want different shopping experiences. In a company official's words, "Research showed that men want to come and go easily, while women want an exploration."[39] In light of these research results, women's sections in Gap stores are organized by occasion (e.g., work, entertainment) with accessories for those occasions scattered throughout the section to facilitate browsing. The men's sections of Gap stores are more straightforward, with signs directing male customers to clothing items that are commonly stacked by size. Thus, Gap is using its understanding of some of the psychological factors (see Table 5.1) influencing its customers' purchasing intentions to better serve unique groups' needs.

Demographic factors (see Table 5.1 and the discussion in Chapter 2) can also be used to segment markets into generations with unique interests and needs. Evidence suggests, for example, that direct mail is an effective communication medium for the World War II generation (those born before 1932). The Swing generation (those born between 1933 and 1945) values taking cruises and purchasing second homes. Once financially conservative but now willing to spend money, members of this generation seek product information

Market segmentation is a process used to cluster people with similar needs into individual and identifiable groups.

Table 5.1 Basis for Customer Segmentation

Consumer Markets

1. Demographic factors (age, income, sex, etc.)
2. Socioeconomic factors (social class, stage in the family life cycle)
3. Geographic factors (cultural, regional, and national differences)
4. Psychological factors (lifestyle, personality traits)
5. Consumption patterns (heavy, moderate, and light users)
6. Perceptual factors (benefit segmentation, perceptual mapping)

Industrial Markets

1. End-use segments (identified by SIC code)
2. Product segments (based on technological differences or production economics)
3. Geographic segments (defined by boundaries between countries or by regional differences within them)
4. Common buying factor segments (cut across product market and geographic segments)
5. Customer size segments

Source: Adapted from S. C. Jain, 2000, *Marketing Planning and Strategy*, Cincinnati: South-Western College Publishing, 120.

from knowledgeable sources. The Baby Boom generation (born between 1946 and 1964) desires products that reduce the stress generated by trying to balance career demands and the needs of older parents with those of their own children. Ellen Tracy clothes, known for their consistency of fit and color, are targeted to Baby Boomer women. More conscious of hype, the 60-million-plus people in Generation X (born between 1965 and 1976) want products that deliver as promised. The Xers use the Internet as a primary shopping tool and expect visually compelling marketing. Members of this group are the fastest-growing segment of mutual-fund shareholders, with their holdings overwhelmingly invested in stock funds. As employees, the top priorities of Xers are to work in a creative learning environment, to receive constant feedback from managers, and to be rewarded for using their technical skills.[40] Different marketing campaigns and distribution channels (e.g., the Internet for Generation X customers, direct mail for the World War II generation) affect the implementation of strategies for those companies interested in serving the needs of different generations.

What: Determining Which Customer Needs to Satisfy

After the firm decides *who* it will serve, it must identify the targeted customer group's needs that its goods or services can satisfy. Successful firms learn how to deliver to customers what they want and when they want it.[41] In a general sense, *needs (what)* are related to a product's benefits and features.[42] Having close and frequent interactions with both current and potential customers helps the firm identify those individuals' and groups' current and future needs.[43] From a strategic perspective, a basic need of all customers is to buy products that create value for them. The generalized forms of value that goods or services provide are either low cost with acceptable features or highly differentiated features with acceptable cost. The most effective firms continuously strive to anticipate changes in customers' needs. Failure to anticipate results in the loss of customers to competitors who are offering greater value in terms of product features and functionalities. For example, some analysts believe that discounters, department stores, and other home furnishing chains are taking customers away from Pier 1 Imports Inc., which suggests that Pier 1 has not anticipated changes in its customers' needs in as timely a manner as should be the case.

In any given industry, consumers' needs often vary a great deal.[44] The need some consumers have for high-quality, fresh sandwiches is what Jason's Deli seeks to satisfy with its menu items. In contrast, many large fast-food companies satisfy customer needs for lower-cost food items with acceptable quality that are delivered quickly. Diversified food and soft-drink producer PepsiCo believes that "any one consumer has different needs at different times of the day." Through its soft drinks (Pepsi products), snacks (Frito-Lay), juices (Tropicana), and cereals (Quaker), PepsiCo is developing new products from breakfast bars to healthier potato chips "to make certain that it covers all those needs."[45] In general, and across multiple product groups (e.g., automobiles, clothing, food), evidence suggests that middle-market consumers in the United States want to trade up to higher levels of quality and taste. These customers are willing to pay large premiums for well-designed, well-engineered, and well-crafted goods.[46] These needs represent opportunities for some firms to pursue through their business-level strategies.

To ensure success, a firm must be able to fully understand the needs of the customers in the target group it has selected to serve. The company translates these needs into features and performance capabilities of their products designed to serve those customers. The most effective firms are committed to understanding the customers' current as well as future needs.

How: Determining Core Competencies Necessary to Satisfy Customer Needs

As explained in Chapters 1 and 3, *core competencies* are resources and capabilities that serve as a source of competitive advantage for the firm over its rivals. Firms use core competencies (*how*) to implement value-creating strategies and thereby satisfy customers' needs. Only those firms with the capacity to continuously improve, innovate, and upgrade their competencies can expect to meet and hopefully exceed customers' expectations across time.[47]

Companies draw from a wide range of core competencies to produce goods or services that can satisfy customers' needs. SAS Institute is the world's largest privately owned software company and is the leader in business intelligence and analytics. Customers use SAS's programs for data warehousing, data mining, and decision support purposes. Allocating more than 30 percent of revenues to research and development (R&D), SAS relies on its core competence in R&D to satisfy the data-related needs of such customers as the U.S. Census Bureau and a host of consumer goods firms (e.g., hotels, banks, and catalog companies).[48] Vans Inc. relies on its core competencies in innovation and marketing to design and sell skateboards and other products. The firm also pioneered thick-soled, slip-on sneakers that can absorb the shock of five-foot leaps on wheels. The company uses an unusual marketing mix to capitalize on its pioneering products. In lieu of mass media ads, the firm sponsors skateboarding events, and is building skateboard parks at malls around the country. In 2007, the company sponsored Vans Warped Tour in a variety of cities across North America to promote skateboarding and its related product lines.[49]

All organizations, including SAS and Vans Inc., must use their core competencies (the *how*) to satisfy the needs (the *what*) of the target group of customers (the *who*) the firm has chosen to serve by using its business-level strategy. Recent research suggests that firms should carefully identify clues from customers regarding the quality of their service provided and use simple as well as sophisticated means of assessing customer satisfaction.[50]

Next, we describe the formal purpose of a business-level strategy and then the five business-level strategies available to all firms.

The Purpose of a Business-Level Strategy

The purpose of a business-level strategy is to create differences between the firm's position and those of its competitors.[51] To position itself differently from competitors, a firm must decide whether it intends to *perform activities differently* or to *perform different activities*. In fact, "choosing to perform activities differently or to perform different activities than

Figure 5.1 Southwest Airlines' Activity System

rivals" is the essence of business-level strategy.[52] Thus, the firm's business-level strategy is a deliberate choice about how it will perform the value chain's primary and support activities to create unique value. Indeed, in the complex twenty-first–century competitive landscape, successful use of a business-level strategy results only when the firm learns how to integrate the activities it performs in ways that create superior value for customers and thus contribute to competitive advantages.

Firms develop an activity map to show how they integrate the activities they perform. We show Southwest Airlines' activity map in Figure 5.1. The manner in which Southwest has integrated its activities is the foundation for the successful use of its integrated cost leadership/differentiation strategy (this strategy is discussed later in the chapter).[53] The tight integration among Southwest's activities is a key source of the firm's ability to operate more profitably than its competitors. In fact, in 2007, Southwest announced its sixty-fourth consecutive quarter of profitability, unprecedented in the industry.[54]

As shown in Figure 5.1, Southwest Airlines has configured the activities it performs into six strategic themes—limited passenger service; frequent, reliable departures; lean, highly productive ground and gate crews; high aircraft utilization; very low ticket prices; and short-haul, point-to-point routes between midsized cities and secondary airports. Individual clusters of tightly linked activities make it possible for the outcome of a strategic theme to be achieved. For example, no meals, no seat assignments, and no baggage transfers form a cluster of individual activities that support the strategic theme of limited passenger service (see Figure 5.1).

Southwest's tightly integrated activities make it difficult for competitors to imitate the firm's integrated cost leadership/differentiation strategy. The firm's culture influences these activities and their integration and contributes to the firm's ability to continuously identify additional ways to differentiate Southwest's service from its competitors' as well as to lower its costs. In fact, the firm's unique culture and customer service, both of which are sources of competitive advantages, are features that rivals have been unable to imitate, although some have tried. US Airways' MetroJet subsidiary, United Airlines' United Shuttle, Delta's Song and Continental Airlines' Continental Lite all failed in attempts to imitate Southwest's strategy. Hindsight shows that these competitors offered low prices to customers, but weren't able to operate at costs close to those of Southwest or to provide customers with any notable sources of differentiation, such as a unique experience while in the air.

Fit among activities is a key to the sustainability of competitive advantage for all firms, including Southwest Airlines. As Michael Porter comments, "Strategic fit among many activities is fundamental not only to competitive advantage but also to the sustainability of that advantage. It is harder for a rival to match an array of interlocked activities than it is merely to imitate a particular sales-force approach, match a process technology, or replicate a set of product features. Positions built on systems of activities are far more sustainable than those built on individual activities."[55]

Types of Business-Level Strategies

Firms choose from among five business-level strategies to establish and defend their desired strategic position against competitors: *cost leadership, differentiation, focused cost leadership, focused differentiation,* and *integrated cost leadership/differentiation* (see Figure 5.2). Each business-level strategy helps the firm to establish and exploit a particular *competitive advantage* within a particular *competitive scope.* How firms integrate the activities they perform within each different business-level strategy demonstrates how they differ from one another.[56] For example, firms have different activity maps, and thus, a Southwest Airlines' activity map differs from those of competitors JetBlue, Continental, American Airlines, and so forth. Superior integration of activities increases the likelihood of being able to gain an advantage over competitors and to earn above-average returns.

When selecting a business-level strategy, firms evaluate two types of potential competitive advantage: "lower cost than rivals, or the ability to differentiate and command a premium price that exceeds the extra cost of doing so."[57] Having lower cost derives from

Figure 5.2 Five Business-Level Strategies

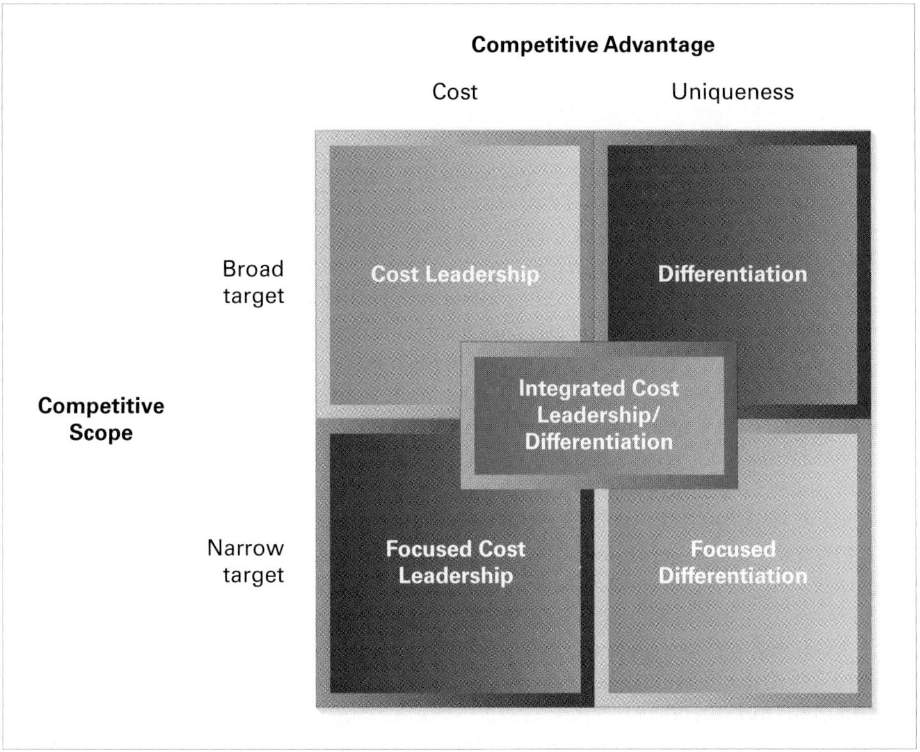

Source: Adapted with the permission of The Free Press, an imprint of Simon & Schuster Adult Publishing Group, from *Competitive Advantage: Creating and Sustaining Superior Performance,* by Michael E. Porter, 12. Copyright © 1985, 1998 by Michael E. Porter.

the firm's ability to perform activities differently than rivals; being able to differentiate indicates the firm's capacity to perform different (and valuable) activities.[58] Thus, based on the nature and quality of its internal resources, capabilities, and core competencies, a firm seeks to form either a cost competitive advantage or a uniqueness competitive advantage as the basis for implementing its business-level strategy.

Two types of competitive scope are broad target and narrow target (see Figure 5.2). Firms serving a broad target market seek to use their competitive advantage on an industry-wide basis. A narrow competitive scope means that the firm intends to serve the needs of a narrow target customer group. With focus strategies, the firm "selects a segment or group of segments in the industry and tailors its strategy to serving them to the exclusion of others."[59] Buyers with special needs and buyers located in specific geographic regions are examples of narrow target customer groups. As shown in Figure 5.2, a firm could also strive to develop a combined cost/uniqueness competitive advantage as the foundation for serving a target customer group that is larger than a narrow segment but not as comprehensive as a broad (or industry-wide) customer group. In this instance, the firm uses the integrated cost leadership/differentiation strategy. None of the five business-level strategies shown in Figure 5.2 is inherently or universally superior to the others.[60] The effectiveness of each strategy is contingent both on the opportunities and threats in a firm's external environment and on the strengths and weaknesses derived from the firm's resource portfolio. It is critical, therefore, for the firm to select a business-level strategy that is based on a match between the opportunities and threats in its external environment and the strengths of its internal environment as shown by its core competencies.

Cost Leadership Strategy

The **cost leadership strategy** is an integrated set of actions taken to produce goods or services with features that are acceptable to customers at the lowest cost, relative to that of competitors.

The **cost leadership strategy** is an integrated set of actions taken to produce goods or services with features that are acceptable to customers at the lowest cost, relative to that of competitors.[61] Firms using the cost leadership strategy commonly sell standardized goods or services (but with competitive levels of quality) to the industry's most typical customers. Cost leaders' goods and services must have competitive levels of quality (and often differentiation in terms of features) that create value for customers. At the extreme, concentrating only on reducing costs could result in the firm efficiently producing products that no customer wants to purchase. In fact, such extremes could lead to limited potential for innovation, employment of lower-skilled workers, poor conditions on the production line, accidents, and a poor quality of work-life for employees.[62]

As shown in Figure 5.2, the firm using the cost leadership strategy targets a broad customer segment or group. Cost leaders concentrate on finding ways to lower their costs relative to those of their competitors by constantly rethinking how to complete their primary and support activities to reduce costs still further while maintaining competitive levels of differentiation.[63] Cost leader Greyhound Lines Inc., for example, continuously seeks ways to reduce the costs it incurs to provide bus service while offering customers an acceptable experience. Recently Greyhound sought to improve the quality of the experience customers have when paying the firm's low prices for its services by "refurbishing buses, updating terminals, adding greeters and improving customer service training." Greyhound enjoys economies of scale by serving more than 20 million passengers annually with about 1,700 destinations in the United States and operating 1,500 buses.[64]

As primary activities, inbound logistics (e.g., materials handling, warehousing, and inventory control) and outbound logistics (e.g., collecting, storing, and distributing products to customers) often account for significant portions of the total cost to produce some goods and services. Research suggests that having a competitive advantage in terms of logistics creates more value when using the cost leadership strategy than when using the differentiation strategy.[65] Thus, cost leaders seeking competitively valuable ways to reduce costs may want to concentrate on the primary activities of inbound logistics and outbound logistics. In so doing many now outsource the operations (often manufacturing) to low-cost firms with low-wage employees (e.g., China).[66]

Cost leaders also carefully examine all support activities to find additional sources of potential cost reductions. Developing new systems for finding the optimal combination of low cost and acceptable quality in the raw materials required to produce the firm's goods or services is an example of how the procurement support activity can facilitate successful use of the cost leadership strategy.

Big Lots Inc. uses the cost leadership strategy. With its vision of being "The World's Best Bargain Place," Big Lots is the largest closeout discount chain in the United States. The firm strives constantly to drive its costs lower by relying on what some analysts see as a highly disciplined merchandise cost and inventory management system.[67] The firm's stores sell name-brand products at prices that are 20 to 40 percent below those of discount

Big Lots uses a cost leadership strategy by selling name brand merchandise at a lower cost.

retailers and roughly 70 percent below those of traditional retailers.[68] Big Lots' buyers search for manufacturer overruns and discontinued styles to find goods priced well below wholesale prices. In addition, the firm buys from overseas suppliers. Big Lots satisfies the customers' need to access the differentiated features and capabilities of brand-name products, but at a fraction of their initial cost. The tight integration of purchasing and inventory management activities across its full set of stores (slightly under 1,400 stores) is the main core competence Big Lots uses to satisfy its customers' needs.

As described in Chapter 3, firms use value-chain analysis to determine the parts of the company's operations that create value and those that do not. Figure 5.3 demonstrates the primary and support activities that allow a firm to create value through the cost leadership strategy. Companies unable to link the activities shown in this figure through the activity map they form typically lack the core competencies needed to successfully use the cost leadership strategy.

Effective use of the cost leadership strategy allows a firm to earn above-average returns in spite of the presence of strong competitive forces (see Chapter 2). The next sections (one for each of the five forces) explain how firms implement a cost leadership strategy.

Rivalry with Existing Competitors

Having the low-cost position is valuable to deal with rivals. Because of the cost leader's advantageous position, rivals hesitate to compete on the basis of price, especially before evaluating the potential outcomes of such competition.[69] Wal-Mart is known for its ability to both control and reduce costs, making it difficult for firms to compete against it on the basis of costs. The discount retailer achieves strict cost control in several ways: "Wal-Mart's 660,000-square-foot main headquarters, with its drab gray interiors and frayed carpets, looks more like a government building than the home of one of the world's largest corporations. Business often is done in the no-frills cafeteria, and suppliers meet with managers in stark, cramped rooms. Employees have to throw out their own garbage at the end of the day and double up in hotel rooms on business trips."[70] The former Kmart's decision to compete against Wal-Mart on the basis of cost contributed to the firm's failure and subsequent bankruptcy filing. Its competitively inferior distribution system—an inefficient and high-cost system compared to Wal-Mart's—is one of the factors that prevented Kmart from having a competitive cost structure.

Bargaining Power of Buyers (Customers)

Powerful customers can force a cost leader to reduce its prices, but not below the level at which the cost leader's next-most-efficient industry competitor can earn average returns. Although powerful customers might be able to force the cost leader to reduce prices even below this level, they probably would not choose to do so. Prices that are low enough to

Figure 5.3 Examples of Value-Creating Activities Associated with the Cost Leadership Strategy

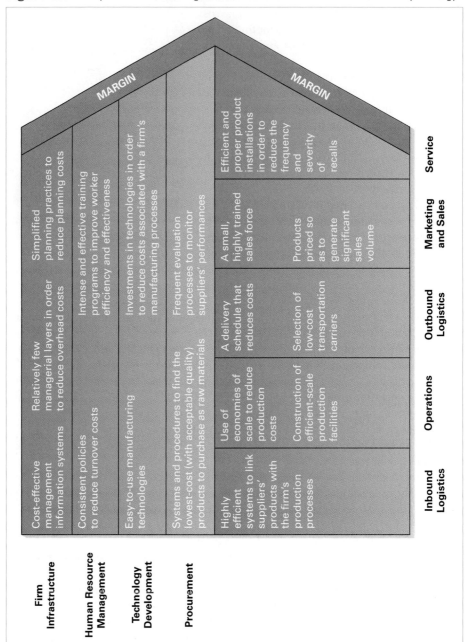

Source: Adapted with the permission of The Free Press, an imprint of Simon & Schuster Adult Publishing Group, from *Competitive Advantage: Creating and Sustaining Superior Performance,* by Michael E. Porter, 47. Copyright © 1985, 1998 by Michael E. Porter.

prevent the next-most-efficient competitor from earning average returns would force that firm to exit the market, leaving the cost leader with less competition and in an even stronger position. Customers would thus lose their power and pay higher prices if they were forced to purchase from a single firm operating in an industry without rivals. Consider Wal-Mart in this regard. Part of the reason this firm's prices continue to be the lowest available is that Wal-Mart continuously searches for ways to reduce its costs relative to competitors who try to implement a cost leadership strategy (such as Costco). Thus, customers benefit by Wal-Mart having to compete against others trying to use the cost leadership strategy and lowering its prices to engage in competitive battles.

Bargaining Power of Suppliers

The cost leader operates with margins greater than those of competitors. Among other benefits, higher margins relative to those of competitors make it possible for the cost leader to absorb its suppliers' price increases. When an industry faces substantial increases in the cost of its supplies, only the cost leader may be able to pay the higher prices and continue to earn either average or above-average returns. Alternatively, a powerful cost leader may be able to force its suppliers to hold down their prices, which would reduce the suppliers' margins in the process. Wal-Mart uses its power with suppliers (gained because it buys such large quantities from many suppliers) to extract lower prices from them. These savings are then passed on to customers in the form of lower prices, which further strengthens Wal-Mart's position relative to competitors lacking the power to extract lower prices from suppliers. Wal-Mart has significant market power. It controls 29 percent of the nonfood grocery sales, 30 percent of the health and beauty aids sales, and 45 percent of the general merchandise sales in the total U.S. retail market.[71] Of course, other firms may use alliances with suppliers to gain access to complementary resources that help them keep their overall costs low. In other words, they can share the costs with others helping them to maintain a low-cost structure.[72]

Potential Entrants

Through continuous efforts to reduce costs to levels that are lower than competitors', a cost leader becomes highly efficient. Because ever-improving levels of efficiency (e.g., economies of scale) enhance profit margins, they serve as a significant entry barrier to potential competitors.[73] New entrants must be willing and able to accept no-better-than-average returns until they gain the experience required to approach the cost leader's efficiency. To earn even average returns, new entrants must have the competencies required to match the cost levels of competitors other than the cost leader. The low profit margins (relative to margins earned by firms implementing the differentiation strategy) make it necessary for the cost leader to sell large volumes of its product to earn above-average returns. However, firms striving to be the cost leader must avoid pricing their products so low that their ability to operate profitably is reduced, even though volume increases.

Product Substitutes

Compared with its industry rivals, the cost leader also holds an attractive position in terms of product substitutes. A product substitute becomes an issue for the cost leader when its features and characteristics, in terms of cost and differentiated features, are potentially attractive to the firm's customers. When faced with possible substitutes, the cost leader has more flexibility than its competitors. To retain customers, it can reduce the price of its good or service. With still lower prices and competitive levels of differentiation, the cost leader increases the probability that customers will prefer its product rather than a substitute.

Competitive Risks of the Cost Leadership Strategy

The cost leadership strategy is not risk free. One risk is that the processes used by the cost leader to produce and distribute its good or service could become obsolete because of competitors' innovations. These innovations may allow rivals to produce at costs lower than those of the original cost leader, or to provide additional differentiated features without increasing the product's price to customers.

A second risk is that too much focus by the cost leader on cost reductions may occur at the expense of trying to understand customers' perceptions of "competitive levels of differentiation." However, Wal-Mart has begun to experience problems exemplified by Costco's ability to out-compete Wal-Mart's Sam's Club. Costco does it with an appropriate combination of low cost and quality—differentiated products.[74] A final risk of the cost leadership strategy concerns imitation. Using their own core competencies, competitors sometimes learn how to successfully imitate the cost leader's strategy. When this imitation occurs, the cost leader must increase the value that its good or service provides to customers. Commonly, value is increased by selling the current product at an even lower price or by adding differentiated features that customers value while maintaining price.

Differentiation Strategy

The **differentiation strategy** is an integrated set of actions taken to produce goods or services (at an acceptable cost) that customers perceive as being different in ways that are important to them.[75] While cost leaders serve a typical customer in an industry, differentiators target customers for whom value is created by the manner in which the firm's products differ from those produced and marketed by competitors.

> The **differentiation strategy** is an integrated set of actions taken to produce goods or services (at an acceptable cost) that customers perceive as being different in ways that are important to them.

Firms must be able to produce differentiated products at competitive costs to reduce upward pressure on the price that customers pay. When a product's differentiated features are produced at noncompetitive costs, the price for the product can exceed what the firm's target customers are willing to pay. When the firm has a thorough understanding of what its target customers value, the relative importance they attach to the satisfaction of different needs, and for what they are willing to pay a premium, the differentiation strategy can be successful.

Through the differentiation strategy, the firm produces nonstandardized products for customers who value differentiated features more than they value low cost. For example, superior product reliability and durability and high-performance sound systems are among the differentiated features of Toyota Motor Corporation's Lexus products. The Lexus promotional statement—"We pursue perfection, so you can pursue living"—suggests a strong commitment to overall product quality as a source of differentiation. However, Lexus offers its vehicles to customers at a competitive purchase price. As with Lexus products, a good's or service's unique attributes, rather than its purchase price, provide the value for which customers are willing to pay.

A Robert Talbott shirt and tie is differentiated from the market by its quality, craftsmanship, and attention to detail.

Continuous success with the differentiation strategy results when the firm consistently upgrades differentiated features that customers value and/or creates new ones (innovates) without significant cost increases.[76] This approach requires firms to constantly change their product lines.[77] Such firms may also offer a portfolio of products that complement each other, thereby enriching the differentiation for the customer and perhaps satisfying a portfolio of consumer needs.[78] Because a differentiated product satisfies customers' unique needs, firms following the differentiation strategy are able to charge premium prices. For customers to be willing to pay a premium price, however, a "firm must truly be unique at something or be perceived as unique."[79] The ability to sell a good or service at a price that substantially exceeds the cost of creating its differentiated features allows the firm to outperform rivals and earn above-average returns. For example, shirt and neckwear manufacturer Robert Talbott follows stringent standards of craftsmanship and pays meticulous attention to every detail of production. The firm imports exclusive fabrics from the world's finest mills to make men's dress shirts and neckwear. Single-needle tailoring is used, and precise collar cuts are made to produce shirts. According to the company, customers purchasing one of its products can be assured that they are being provided with the finest fabrics available.[80] Thus, Robert Talbott's success rests on the firm's ability to produce and sell its differentiated products at a price significantly higher than the costs of imported fabrics and its unique manufacturing processes.

Rather than costs, a firm using the differentiation strategy always concentrates on investing in and developing features that differentiate a good or service in ways that customers value. Robert Talbott, for example, uses the finest silks from Europe and Asia to produce its "Best of Class" collection of ties. Overall, a firm using the differentiation strategy seeks to be different from its competitors on as many dimensions as possible. The less similarity between a firm's goods or services and those of competitors, the more buffered it is from rivals' actions. Commonly recognized differentiated goods include Toyota's Lexus, Ralph Lauren's wide array of product lines, and Caterpillar's heavy-duty earth-moving equipment. Thought by some to be the world's most expensive and prestigious consulting firm, McKinsey & Co. is a well-known example of a firm that offers differentiated services.

A good or service can be differentiated in many ways. Unusual features, responsive customer service, rapid product innovations and technological leadership, perceived prestige and status, different tastes, and engineering design and performance are examples of approaches to differentiation.[81] The number of ways to reduce costs may be limited (as demonstrated by successful use of the cost leadership strategy). In contrast, virtually anything a firm can do to create real or perceived value is a basis for differentiation. Consider product design as a case in point. Because it can create a positive experience for customers, design is becoming an increasingly important source of differentiation and hopefully for firms emphasizing it, of competitive advantage.[82] Apple is often cited as the firm that sets the standard in design (see the Strategic Focus in Chapter 1). The iPod is a good case in point, and the iPhone, introduced in 2007, provides another example of Apple's creativity and design capabilities.[83]

A firm's value chain can be analyzed to determine whether the firm is able to link the activities required to create value by using the differentiation strategy. Examples of primary and support activities that are commonly used to differentiate a good or service are shown in Figure 5.4. Companies without the skills needed to link these activities cannot expect to successfully use the differentiation strategy. Next, we explain how firms using the differentiation strategy can successfully position themselves in terms of the five forces of competition (see Chapter 2) to earn above-average returns.

Rivalry with Existing Competitors

Customers tend to be loyal purchasers of products differentiated in ways that are meaningful to them. As their loyalty to a brand increases, customers' sensitivity to price increases is reduced. The relationship between brand loyalty and price sensitivity insulates a firm from competitive rivalry. Thus, Robert Talbott's "Best of Class" neckwear line is insulated from competition, even on the basis of price, as long as the company continues to satisfy the differentiated needs of its target customer group. Likewise, Bose is insulated from intense rivalry as long as customers continue to perceive that its stereo equipment offers superior sound quality at a competitive purchase price. Both Robert Talbot and Bose have strong positive reputations for the high quality and unique products that they provide. Thus, reputations can sustain the competitive advantage of firms following a differentiation strategy.[84]

Bargaining Power of Buyers (Customers)

The uniqueness of differentiated goods or services reduces customers' sensitivity to price increases. Customers are willing to accept a price increase when a product still satisfies their perceived unique needs better than a competitor's offering can. Thus, the golfer whose needs are uniquely satisfied by Callaway golf clubs will likely continue buying those products even if their cost increases. Similarly, the customer who has been highly satisfied with a 10-year-old Louis Vuitton wallet will probably replace that wallet with another one made by the same company even though the purchase price is higher than the original one. Purchasers of brand-name food items (e.g., Heinz ketchup and Kleenex tissues) will accept price increases in those products as long as they continue to perceive that the product satisfies their unique needs at an acceptable cost. In all of these instances, the customers are relatively insensitive to price increases because they do not think that an acceptable product alternative exists.

Figure 5.4 Examples of Value-Creating Activities Associated with the Differentiation Strategy

MARGIN

MARGIN

Firm Infrastructure — Highly developed information systems to better understand customers' purchasing preferences — A company-wide emphasis on the importance of producing high-quality products

Human Resource Management — Compensation programs intended to encourage worker creativity and productivity — Somewhat extensive use of subjective rather than objective performance measures — Superior personnel training

Technology Development — Strong capability in basic research — Investments in technologies that will allow the firm to produce highly differentiated products

Procurement — Systems and procedures used to find the highest-quality raw materials — Purchase of highest-quality replacement parts

Inbound Logistics — Superior handling of incoming raw materials so as to minimize damage and to improve the quality of the final product

Operations — Consistent manufacturing of attractive products — Rapid responses to customers' unique manufacturing specifications

Outbound Logistics — Accurate and responsive order-processing procedures — Rapid and timely product deliveries to customers

Marketing and Sales — Extensive granting of credit buying arrangements for customers — Extensive personal relationships with buyers and suppliers

Service — Extensive buyer training to assure high-quality product installations — Complete field stocking of replacement parts

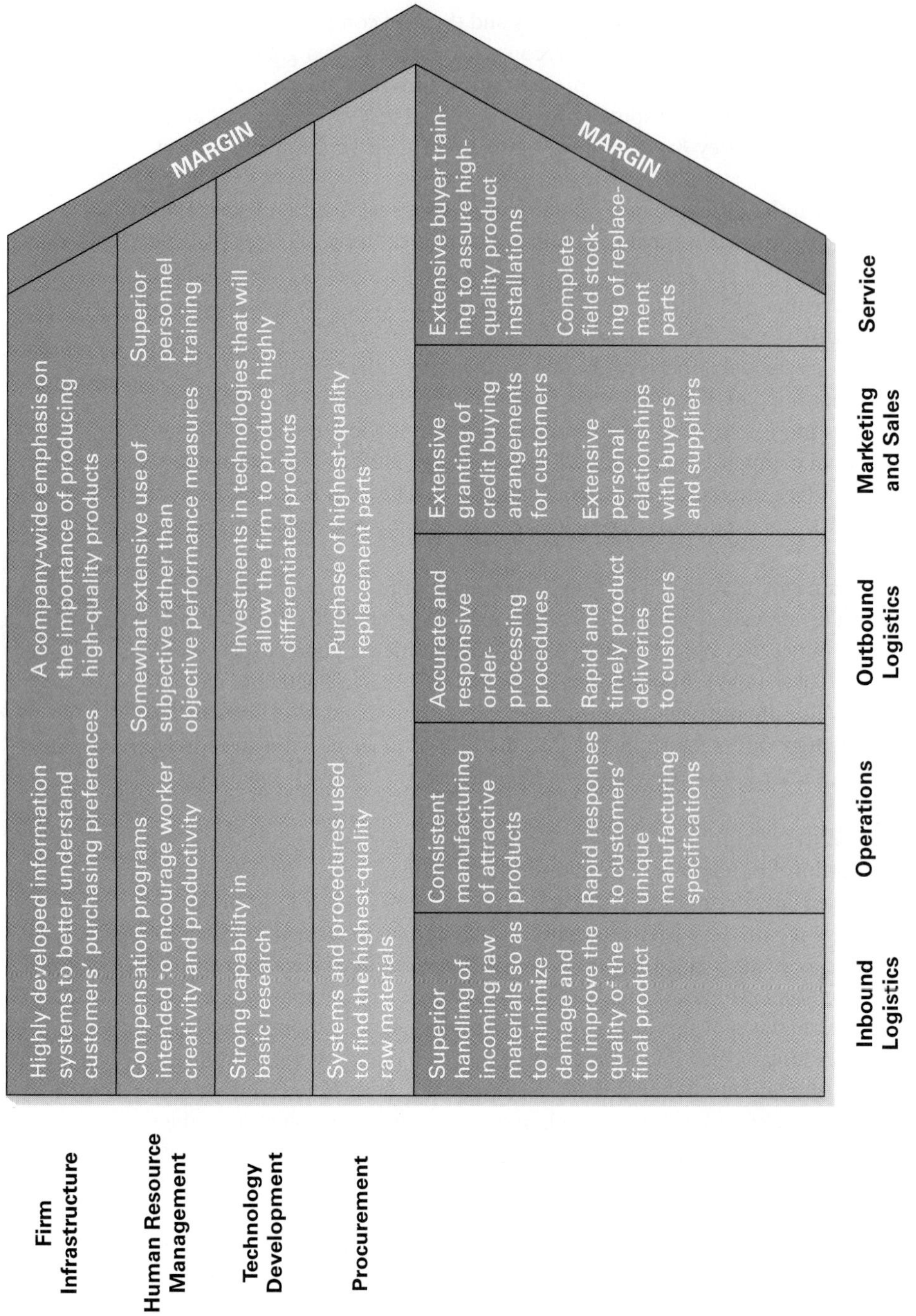

Source: Adapted with the permission of The Free Press, an imprint of Simon & Schuster Adult Publishing Group, from *Competitive Advantage: Creating and Sustaining Superior Performance*, by Michael E. Porter, 47. Copyright © 1985, 1998 by Michael E. Porter.

Bargaining Power of Suppliers

Because the firm using the differentiation strategy charges a premium price for its products, suppliers must provide high-quality components, driving up the firm's costs. However, the high margins the firm earns in these cases partially insulate it from the influence of suppliers in that higher supplier costs can be paid through these margins. Alternatively, because of buyers' relative insensitivity to price increases, the differentiated firm might choose to pass the additional cost of supplies on to the customer by increasing the price of its unique product.

Potential Entrants

Customer loyalty and the need to overcome the uniqueness of a differentiated product present substantial barriers to potential entrants. Entering an industry under these conditions typically demands significant investments of resources and patience while seeking customers' loyalty.

Product Substitutes

Firms selling brand-name goods and services to loyal customers are positioned effectively against product substitutes. In contrast, companies without brand loyalty face a higher probability of their customers switching either to products that offer differentiated features that serve the same function (particularly if the substitute has a lower price) or to products that offer more features and perform more attractive functions.

Competitive Risks of the Differentiation Strategy

As with the other business-level strategies, the differentiation strategy is not risk free. One risk is that customers might decide that the price differential between the differentiator's product and the cost leader's product is too large. In this instance, a firm may be offering differentiated features that exceed target customers' needs. The firm then becomes vulnerable to competitors that are able to offer customers a combination of features and price that is more consistent with their needs.

Another risk of the differentiation strategy is that a firm's means of differentiation may cease to provide value for which customers are willing to pay. A differentiated product becomes less valuable if imitation by rivals causes customers to perceive that competitors offer essentially the same good or service, but at a lower price.[85] For example, Walt Disney Company operates different theme parks, including The Magic Kingdom, Epcot Center, and the newly developed Animal Kingdom. Each park offers entertainment and educational opportunities. However, Disney's competitors, such as Six Flags Corporation, also offer entertainment and educational experiences similar to those available at Disney's locations. To ensure that its facilities create value for which customers will be willing to pay, Disney continuously reinvests in its operations to more crisply differentiate them from those of its rivals.[86]

A third risk of the differentiation strategy is that experience can narrow customers' perceptions of the value of a product's differentiated features. For example, customers having positive experiences with generic tissues may decide that the differentiated features of the Kleenex product are not worth the extra cost. Similarly, while a customer may be impressed with the quality of a Robert Talbott "Best of Class" tie, positive experiences with less expensive ties may lead to a conclusion that the price of the "Best of Class" tie exceeds the benefit. To counter this risk, firms must continue to meaningfully differentiate their product for customers at a price they are willing to pay.

Counterfeiting is the differentiation strategy's fourth risk. Makers of counterfeit goods—products that attempt to convey a firm's differentiated features to customers at significantly reduced prices—represent a concern for many firms using the differentiation strategy.

Caribou Coffee has taken several actions to differentiate its goods and services from Starbucks and other competitors. As explained in the Strategic Focus, Caribou has been innovative in the type of coffee offered (environmentally friendly) and in the services extended to customers. Innovation is important for differentiation strategies, particularly in the development of complementary goods and services (e.g., free WiFi).[87]

Focus Strategies

Firms choose a focus strategy when they intend to use their core competencies to serve the needs of a particular industry segment or niche to the exclusion of others. Examples

Caribou Coffee: When You Are Number Two, You Try Harder

If you're number 2, how do you compete with number 1? Caribou Coffee, has tried to differentiate as much as possible from number 1, Starbucks.

The concept for Caribou Coffee began with an idea in 1990, when engaged Dartmouth graduates Kim Whitehead and John Puckett were on vacation in Denali National Park in Alaska. The vast beauty of the environment so impressed them that as they looked down upon a herd of caribou running through a valley, they decided to start a business that would make a difference in the world.

Caribou Coffee has several differentiation strategies including free WiFi and a family-friendly atmosphere.

Caribou Coffee Company, Inc., founded in 1992 in Minneapolis, Minnesota, is the second largest specialty coffee company and coffeehouse operator in the United States. Caribou Coffee went public in 2005 and currently owns more than 430 stores, including more than 20 franchises, in 18 states plus the District of Columbia. Its coffeehouses are located predominantly in the central and eastern United States, and it employs more than 5,000 people. The company's mission is "to provide an experience that makes the day better."

Even though both Caribou Coffee and Starbucks are dedicated to providing the highest quality products and customer service, their methods of delivering them are quite different. Starbucks provides a comfortable setting for urban customers who prefer references to sizes such as "venti" and "grande." Caribou has chosen to use the more common names of "small," "medium," and "large" that are familiar to most customers. Caribou's coffeehouses are designed with a focus on customer comfort and are modeled after mountain ski lodges and Alaskan cabins. Décor includes fireplaces, wooden ceiling beams, and comfortable furniture such as large chairs and sofas. They also provide a children's play area with toys and games, contributing to a family-friendly atmosphere.

In 2006 Caribou formed an alliance with Wandering WiFi to become the first coffee company to offer free WiFi service and the latest security technology to its customers. Wandering WiFi president, John Marshall believes that Caribou Coffee is committed to providing the most customer convenience, excellent coffee, and a comfortable atmosphere.

Caribou also formed an alliance with Apple Computer to offer a podcast version of an instant win game from Caribou's CEO Michael Coles, called "Wake Up and Smell the Music." In this game customers can win iTunes, iPods, and coffee. Michael Coles emphasizes the synergies between Apple and Caribou, calling them both "challenger brands" that offer desirable products and compete through innovation to provide a unique customer experience. In March 2006, Caribou provided free live music for customers in celebration of the first day of spring. Caribou has alliances with a number of other firms such as Frontier Airlines, USA Today, General Mills (Caribou Coffee Bars), Lifetime Fitness, Kemps (Caribou Coffee Ice Cream), and Mall of America. Finally, in January 2007 Caribou entered a partnership with Keurig, Inc., a leading manufacturer of single-cup coffee makers for home and office use. In the summer of 2007, Caribou Coffee and Coca-Cola launched new Caribou Coffee ready-to-drink products.

Caribou Coffee is dedicated to the environment. For example, in 1996 Caribou supported the Wilderness Society in its efforts to persuade Congress to protect the Arctic National

Wildlife Refuge by displaying petitions in the coffeehouses. More than 100,000 caribou travel to the refuge each spring to give birth to their young. Caribou Coffee also supported preservation efforts for the Boundary Waters Canoe Area and similar areas in U.S. national parks. In May 2007 the Rainforest Alliance awarded the Corporate Green Globe Award to Caribou Coffee for its efforts in utilizing "sustainably grown" coffee beans from Rainforest Alliance Certified farms. Caribou made the further commitment that half of its coffee will come from such farms in 2008 and beyond.

Because of its differentiation efforts Caribou Coffee continues to enjoy its success as the number 2 specialty coffee company in the United States, a position it intends to further solidify in the future. The company has positioned itself for expansion across multiple business channels as a base for profitable growth in the future.

Sources: S. Reeves, 2005, Caribou Coffee's robust IPO, *Forbes*, http://www.forbes.com/strategies, September 23; G. Hayes, 2006, Caribou Coffee offers free WiFi service for customers, Caribou Coffee, http://www.cariboucoffee.com, August 28; G. Hayes, 2006, Coffee CEO podcast relays power of branding and music, Caribou Coffee, http://www .cariboucoffee.com, March 16; 2007, Caribou Coffee Company plans for continued business expansion, 2006 operating highlights and 2007 guidance, *Business Wire*, January 8; 2000, A different kind of bottom line, *Wilderness*, May 23; 2007, Rainforest alliance bestows corporate green globe award on Caribou Coffee, *PR Newswire US*, May 22.

of specific market segments that can be targeted by a focus strategy include (1) a particular buyer group (e.g., youths or senior citizens), (2) a different segment of a product line (e.g., products for professional painters or the do-it-yourself group), or (3) a different geographic market (e.g., the East or the West in the United States).[88] Thus, the **focus strategy** is an integrated set of actions taken to produce goods or services that serve the needs of a particular competitive segment.

To satisfy the needs of a certain size of company competing in a particular geographic market, firms often specialize, such as an investment bank.[89] Los Angeles–based investment banking firm Greif & Company positions itself as "The Entrepreneur's Investment Bank." Greif & Company is a leader in providing merger and acquisition advice to medium-sized businesses located in the western United States.[90] Goya Foods is the largest U.S.-based Hispanic-owned food company in the United States. Segmenting the Hispanic market into unique groups, Goya offers more than 1,500 products to consumers. The firm seeks "to be the be-all for the Latin community."[91] By successfully using a focus strategy, firms such as Greif & Company and Goya Foods gain a competitive advantage in specific market niches or segments, even though they do not possess an industry-wide competitive advantage.

Although the breadth of a target is clearly a matter of degree, the essence of the focus strategy "is the exploitation of a narrow target's differences from the balance of the industry."[92] Firms using the focus strategy intend to serve a particular segment of an industry more effectively than can industry-wide competitors. They succeed when they effectively serve a segment whose unique needs are so specialized that broad-based competitors choose not to serve that segment or when they satisfy the needs of a segment being served poorly by industry-wide competitors.[93]

Firms can create value for customers in specific and unique market segments by using the focused cost leadership strategy or the focused differentiation strategy.

Focused Cost Leadership Strategy

Based in Sweden, IKEA, a global furniture retailer with locations in 44 countries and sales revenue of $23.5 billion in 2006, follows the focused cost leadership strategy. The firm's vision is "Good design and function at low prices."[94] Young buyers desiring style at a low cost are IKEA's target customers.[95] For these customers, the firm offers home furnishings that combine good design, function, and acceptable quality with low prices. According to the firm, "Low cost is always in focus. This applies to every phase of our activities."[96]

IKEA emphasizes several activities to keep its costs low.[97] For example, instead of relying primarily on third-party manufacturers, the firm's engineers design low-cost,

> The **focus strategy** is an integrated set of actions taken to produce goods or services that serve the needs of a particular competitive segment.

IKEA, known for its low-priced home furnishings, has continued to distinguish itself using focused cost leadership strategies.

modular furniture ready for assembly by customers. To eliminate the need for sales associates or decorators, IKEA positions the products in its stores so that customers can view different living combinations (complete with sofas, chairs, tables, etc.) in a single room-like setting, which helps the customer imagine how a grouping of furniture will look in the home. A third practice that helps keep IKEA's costs low is requiring customers to transport their own purchases rather than providing delivery service.

Although it is a cost leader, IKEA also offers some differentiated features that appeal to its target customers, including its unique furniture designs, in-store playrooms for children, wheelchairs for customer use, and extended hours. IKEA believes that these services and products "are uniquely aligned with the needs of [its] customers, who are young, are not wealthy, are likely to have children (but no nanny), and, because they work, have a need to shop at odd hours."[98] Thus, IKEA's focused cost leadership strategy also includes some differentiated features with its low-cost products.

Focused Differentiation Strategy

Other firms implement the focused differentiation strategy. As noted earlier, firms can differentiate their products in many ways. The Internet furniture venture Casketfurniture. com, for example, targets Gen-Xers who are interested in using the Internet as a shopping vehicle and who want to buy items with multiple purposes. The company considers itself to be "The Internet's Leading Provider of Top Quality Furniture Products." Casketfurniture. com offers a collection of products, including display cabinets, coffee tables, and entertainment centers, that can be easily converted into coffins if desired. The firm also makes custom casket products for customers.[99]

An example of a specialty firm is a Chinese food restaurant. Interestingly, most Chinese food restaurants offer similar fare and thus end up competing largely on price. At least, these competitive conditions exist for Chinese restaurants in the San Gabriel Valley in California. It is so competitive that some restaurants send "spies" into their competitors' kitchens to gain information on their recipes and cooking practices. David Gong, owner of Alhambra's Kitchen believes that the "cutthroat" competition and price wars have reduced the quality of food served in many Chinese food restaurants (he is president of the American Chinese Restaurant Association). Gong's goal is to elevate the status of Chinese food. He hired a chef from Sydney, Australia, to be his food director for the restaurant. His focus is on preparing and serving the finest Chinese food possible. And his food has been rated by food critics as the finest in the San Gabriel Valley.[100]

With a focus strategy, firms must be able to complete various primary and support activities in a competitively superior manner to develop and sustain a competitive advantage and earn above-average returns. The activities required to use the focused cost leadership strategy are virtually identical to those of the industry-wide cost leadership strategy (Figure 5.3), and activities required to use the focused differentiation strategy are largely identical to those of the industry-wide differentiation strategy (Figure 5.4). Similarly, the manner in which each of the two focus strategies allows a firm to deal successfully with the five competitive forces parallels those of the two broad strategies. The only difference is in the firm's competitive scope; the firm focuses on a narrow industry segment. Thus, Figures 5.3 and 5.4 and the text regarding the five competitive forces also describe the relationship between each of the two focus strategies and competitive advantage.

Competitive Risks of Focus Strategies

With either focus strategy, the firm faces the same general risks as does the company using the cost leadership or the differentiation strategy, respectively, on an industry-wide basis. However, focus strategies have three additional risks.

First, a competitor may be able to focus on a more narrowly defined competitive segment and "outfocus" the focuser. For example, Confederate Motor Co. is producing a highly differentiated motorcycle that might appeal to some of Harley-Davidson's customers. Obsessed with making a "fiercely American motorcycle" (one that is even more American than Harley's products), Confederate's motorcycles are produced solely by hand labor. In fact, a full week is required to make a single bike. Digital technology is used to design Confederate's products, which have a radical appearance. At a price of $62,000 or above, the firm's products likely will appeal only to customers wanting to buy a truly differentiated product such as the new B120 Wraith introduced in 2007 (which is receiving "rave reviews in the motorcycling press").[101]

Confederate Motor Company's new B120 Wraith motorcycle is hand-manufactured and much different than its competitors' offerings.

Second, a company competing on an industry-wide basis may decide that the market segment served by the focus strategy firm is attractive and worthy of competitive pursuit. Consider the possibility that other manufacturers and marketers of women's clothing might determine that the profit potential in the narrow segment being served by Anne Fontaine is attractive. Companies such as Gap Inc., for example, have tried to design and market products that would compete with Anne Fontaine's product lines.

The third risk involved with a focus strategy is that the needs of customers within a narrow competitive segment may become more similar to those of industry-wide customers as a whole over time. As a result, the advantages of a focus strategy are either reduced or eliminated. At some point, for example, the needs of IKEA's customers for stylish furniture may dissipate, although their desire to buy relatively inexpensive furnishings may not. If this change in needs occurred, IKEA's customers might buy from large chain stores that sell more standardized furniture at low costs.

Integrated Cost Leadership/Differentiation Strategy

As stated earlier, many consumers have high expectations when purchasing a good or service. In a strategic context, these customers want to purchase low-priced, differentiated products. Because of these customer expectations, a number of firms engage in primary and support activities that allow them to simultaneously pursue low cost and differentiation. Firms with this type of activity map use the **integrated cost leadership/differentiation strategy**. The objective of using this strategy is to efficiently produce products with differentiated attributes. Efficient production is the source of maintaining low costs while differentiation is the source of unique value. Firms that successfully use the integrated cost leadership/differentiation strategy usually adapt quickly to new technologies and rapid changes in their external environments. Simultaneously concentrating on developing two sources of competitive advantage (cost and differentiation) increases the number of primary and support activities in which the firm must become competent. Such firms often have strong networks with external parties that perform some of the primary and support activities.[102] In turn, having skills in a larger number of activities makes a firm more flexible.

Concentrating on the needs of its core customer group (higher-income, fashion-conscious discount shoppers), Target Stores uses an integrated cost leadership/differentiation strategy. The company's annual report describes this strategy: "Through careful nurturing and an intense focus on consistency and coordination throughout our organization, Target has built a strong, distinctive brand. At the core of our brand is our

The **integrated cost leadership/differentiation strategy** involves engaging in primary and support activities that allow a firm to simultaneously pursue low cost and differentiation.

STRATEGY RIGHT NOW

Zara: Integrating Both Sides of the Coin

Zara is one of seven chains owned by Europe's largest specialty clothing company, Inditex SA of Spain. Early in 2007, Inditex received the Global Retailer of the Year award from the World Retail Congress. The first Zara store opened in 1975. It moved overseas about 1990. Currently Zara operates more than 1,000 stores located in 64 countries, including China and Russia.

Zara follows an integrated cost leadership differentiation strategy with its low-cost fashion goods.

Zara sells what has been referred to as "fast" fashion, or "disposable" fashion, fashion "on demand" and "fashion that you wear 10 times." It copies runway fashions and produces quality goods and sells them at affordable prices. The actual prices are market based. Zara determines the existing market price for a product, and then establishes a price below the lowest competitor's price for a similar product.

Zara is vertically integrated and controls its products from the design decision to the point of sale. This level of control allows Zara to keep the costs low. Designers closely monitor popular fashions, styles that celebrities are seen wearing, clothes worn on MTV, and so on. A just-in-time manufacturing system was implemented, and its most fashion sensitive items are produced internally. Zara has the ability to develop and begin manufacturing a new product line in three weeks compared to an industry average of nine months. Approximately 10,000 separate items are produced annually, all shipped directly from a central distribution center twice each week. Thus, no warehouses are needed because inventories are minimal. Only a limited number of products are shipped to its stores, to maintain the perception of scarcity. The most fashionable items are considered riskier and are produced in smaller quantities. The rapid product turnover also keeps customers coming back to the stores more frequently.

Zara locates attractive storefronts in prime locations in major shopping districts and designs them with the comfort of customers in mind. An emphasis on an attractive decor motivates customers to return frequently. Salespeople frequently change the location of items in the stores, which also contributes to the perception of scarcity. Information downloaded on a daily basis from each store enables designers to better monitor customer preferences.

Zara spends a relatively small amount on advertising—usually only for its end-of-season sales—compared to its major competitors such as Benetton, The Gap, and H&M of Sweden.

Sources: 2007, Zara, http://www.zara.com, July 5; 2007, Inditex, http://www.inditex.com, July 5; 2006, Inditex SA: Net climbs 22% amid cuts in costs, store openings, *Wall Street Journal*, December 14, B10; C. Rohwedder, 2006, Can Inditex stock stay as hip as its "fast fashion" clothes? *Wall Street Journal*, September 21, C14; L. Yaeger, 2003, Fete accompli, *Village Voice*, December 17, 12; 2003, Zara creates a ready to wear business: Leading fashion label designs its whole operation to fit the customer, *Strategic Direction*, November/December, 19(11): 24; L. Yaeger, 2002, Spring breaks, *Village Voice*, April 23, 14; B. Jones, 2001, Madrid: Zara pioneers fashion on demand, *Europe*, September, 43; 2001, Business: Floating on air, *Economist*, May 19, 56; C. Vitzthum, 2001, Just-in-time fashion—Spanish retailer Zara makes low-cost lines in weeks by running its own show, *Wall Street Journal*, May 18, B1.

commitment to deliver the right balance of differentiation and value through our 'Expect More. Pay Less' brand promise."[103] Target relies on its relationships with, among others, Sonia Kashuk in cosmetics, Mossimo in apparel, Eddie Bauer in camping and outdoor gear, and Michael Graves in home, garden, and electronics products to offer differentiated products at discounted prices. Committed to presenting a consistent upscale image, the firm has 1,500 stores in 47 states, including more than 175 SuperTarget stores that provide upscale grocery items. In addition most Target stores provide customers photo processing, a pharmacy, and Food Avenue restaurants.[104]

Evidence suggests a relationship between successful use of the integrated strategy and above-average returns.[105] Thus, firms able to produce relatively differentiated products at relatively low costs can expect to perform well.[106] Researchers have discovered that "businesses which combined multiple forms of competitive advantage outperformed businesses that only were identified with a single form."[107] Firms using this strategy must search for the appropriate balance between the two strategies. Because of trade-offs between the strategies, firms rarely can optimize both of them.[108]

Zara follows an integrated cost leadership/differentiation strategy. It offers current and desirable fashions goods at relatively low prices. To implement this strategy effectively requires sophisticated designers and effective means of managing costs, which well fits Zara's capabilities. Zara can design and begin manufacturing a new fashion in three weeks, which suggests a highly flexible organization that can adapt easily to changes in the market or with competitors.

Flexibility is required for firms to complete primary and support activities in ways that allow them to produce somewhat differentiated products at relatively low costs. Flexible manufacturing systems, information networks, and total quality management systems are three sources of flexibility that are particularly useful for firms trying to balance the objectives of continuous cost reductions and continuous enhancements to sources of differentiation as called for by the integrated strategy.

Flexible Manufacturing Systems

A flexible manufacturing system (FMS) increases the "flexibilities of human, physical, and information resources"[109] that the firm integrates to create relatively differentiated products at relatively low costs. A significant technological advance, FMS is a computer-controlled process used to produce a variety of products in moderate, flexible quantities with a minimum of manual intervention.[110] Often the flexibility is derived from modularization of the manufacturing process (and sometimes other value chain activities as well).[111]

The goal of an FMS is to eliminate the "low cost versus product variety" trade-off that is inherent in traditional manufacturing technologies. Firms use an FMS to change quickly and easily from making one product to making another.[112] Used properly, an FMS allows the firm to respond more effectively to changes in its customers' needs, while retaining low-cost advantages and consistent product quality.[113] Because an FMS also enables the firm to reduce the lot size needed to manufacture a product efficiently, the firm's capacity to serve the unique needs of a narrow competitive scope is higher. In industries of all types, effective mixes of the firm's tangible assets (e.g., machines) and intangible assets (e.g., people's skills) facilitate implementation of complex competitive strategies, especially the integrated cost leadership/differentiation strategy.[114]

Information Networks

By linking companies with their suppliers, distributors, and customers, information networks provide another source of flexibility. These networks, when used effectively, help the firm to satisfy customer expectations in terms of product quality and delivery speed.[115] International subsidiaries also must draw on their parent firm's knowledge to effectively serve their customers (integrating the parent's knowledge with understanding of the local market and environment).[116]

Earlier, we discussed the importance of managing the firm's relationships with its customers in order to understand their needs. Customer relationship management (CRM) is one form of an information-based network process that firms use for this purpose.[117] An effective CRM system provides a 360-degree view of the company's relationship with customers, encompassing all contact points, business processes, and communication media and sales channels.[118] The firm can then use this information to determine the trade-offs its customers are willing to make between differentiated features and low cost—an assessment that is vital for companies using the integrated cost leadership/differentiation strategy.

Thus, to make comprehensive strategic decisions with effective knowledge of the organization's context, good information flow is essential. Better quality managerial decisions require accurate information on the firm's environment.[119]

Total Quality Management Systems

Total quality management (TQM) is a "managerial innovation that emphasizes an organization's total commitment to the customer and to continuous improvement of every process through the use of data-driven, problem-solving approaches based on empowerment of employee groups and teams."[120] Firms develop and use TQM systems in order to (1) increase customer satisfaction, (2) cut costs, and (3) reduce the amount of time required to introduce innovative products to the marketplace.[121] Most firms use TQM to improve product and service quality.[122] U.S. auto manufacturers have made progress using TQM in this way, but they "still lag behind some foreign competitors, primarily the Japanese, by most quality measures."[123]

Firms able to simultaneously reduce costs while enhancing their ability to develop innovative products increase their flexibility, an outcome that is particularly helpful to firms implementing the integrated cost leadership/differentiation strategy. Exceeding customers' expectations regarding quality is a differentiating feature, and eliminating process inefficiencies to cut costs allows the firm to offer that quality to customers at a relatively low price. Thus, an effective TQM system helps the firm develop the flexibility needed to spot opportunities to simultaneously increase differentiation and reduce costs. Yet, TQM systems are available to all competitors. So they may help firms maintain competitive parity, but rarely alone will they lead to a competitive advantage.[124]

Competitive Risks of the Integrated Cost Leadership/ Differentiation Strategy

The potential to earn above-average returns by successfully using the integrated cost leadership/differentiation strategy is appealing. However, it is a risky strategy, because firms find it difficult to perform primary and support activities in ways that allow them to produce relatively inexpensive products with levels of differentiation that create value for the target customer. Moreover, to properly use this strategy across time, firms must be able to simultaneously reduce costs incurred to produce products (as required by the cost leadership strategy) while increasing products' differentiation (as required by the differentiation strategy).

Firms that fail to perform the primary and support activities in an optimum manner become "stuck in the middle."[125] Being stuck in the middle means that the firm's cost structure is not low enough to allow it to attractively price its products and that its products are not sufficiently differentiated to create value for the target customer. These firms will not earn above-average returns and will earn average returns only when the structure of the industry in which it competes is highly favorable.[126] Thus, companies implementing the integrated cost leadership/differentiation strategy must be able to perform the primary and support activities in ways that allow them to produce products that offer the target customer some differentiated features at a relatively low cost/price. As explained earlier, Southwest Airlines follows this strategy and has avoided becoming stuck in the middle.

Firms can also become stuck in the middle when they fail to successfully implement *either* the cost leadership *or* the differentiation strategy. In other words, industry-wide competitors too can become stuck in the middle. Trying to use the integrated strategy is costly in that firms must pursue both low costs and differentiation. Firms may need to form alliances with other firms to achieve differentiation, yet alliance partners may extract prices for the use of their resources that make it difficult to be a cost leader.[127] Firms may be motivated to make acquisitions to maintain their differentiation through innovation or to add products to their portfolio not offered by competitors.[128] Recent research suggests that firms using "pure strategies," either cost leadership or differentiation, often outperform firms attempting to use a "hybrid strategy" (i.e., integrated cost leadership/differentiation strategy). But sometimes firms using integrated strategies also performed equally well as those using pure strategies. This research suggests the risky nature of using an integrated strategy.[129] However, the integrated strategy is becoming more common and perhaps necessary in many industries due to technological advances and global competition.

Summary

- A business-level strategy is an integrated and coordinated set of commitments and actions the firm uses to gain a competitive advantage by exploiting core competencies in specific product markets. Five business-level strategies (cost leadership, differentiation, focused cost leadership, focused differentiation, and integrated cost leadership/differentiation) are examined in the chapter.

- Customers are the foundation of successful business-level strategies. When considering customers, a firm simultaneously examines three issues: *who, what,* and *how.* These issues, respectively, refer to the customer groups to be served, the needs those customers have that the firm seeks to satisfy, and the core competencies the firm will use to satisfy customers' needs. Increasing segmentation of markets throughout the global economy creates opportunities for firms to identify more unique customer needs they can serve with one of the business-level strategies.

- Firms seeking competitive advantage through the cost leadership strategy produce no-frills, standardized products for an industry's typical customer. However, these low-cost products must be offered with competitive levels of differentiation. Above-average returns are earned when firms continuously emphasize efficiency such that their costs are lower than those of their competitors, while providing customers with products that have acceptable levels of differentiated features.

- Competitive risks associated with the cost leadership strategy include (1) a loss of competitive advantage to newer technologies, (2) a failure to detect changes in customers' needs, and (3) the ability of competitors to imitate the cost leader's competitive advantage through their own unique strategic actions.

- Through the differentiation strategy, firms provide customers with products that have different (and valued) features. Differentiated products must be sold at a cost that customers believe is competitive relative to the product's features as compared to the cost/feature combinations available from competitors' goods. Because of their uniqueness, differentiated goods or services are sold at a premium price. Products can be differentiated along any dimension that some customer group values. Firms using this strategy seek to differentiate their products from competitors' goods or services along as many dimensions as possible. The less similarity to competitors' products, the more buffered a firm is from competition with its rivals.

- Risks associated with the differentiation strategy include (1) a customer group's decision that the differences between the differentiated product and the cost leader's goods or services are no longer worth a premium price, (2) the inability of a differentiated product to create the type of value for which customers are willing to pay a premium price, (3) the ability of competitors to provide customers with products that have features similar to those of the differentiated product, but at a lower cost, and (4) the threat of counterfeiting, whereby firms produce a cheap "knockoff" of a differentiated good or service.

- Through the cost leadership and the differentiated focus strategies, firms serve the needs of a narrow competitive segment (e.g., a buyer group, product segment, or geographic area). This strategy is successful when firms have the core competencies required to provide value to a specialized market segment that exceeds the value available from firms serving customers on an industry-wide basis.

- The competitive risks of focus strategies include (1) a competitor's ability to use its core competencies to "outfocus" the focuser by serving an even more narrowly defined market segment, (2) decisions by industry-wide competitors to focus on a customer group's specialized needs, and (3) a reduction in differences of the needs between customers in a narrow market segment and the industry-wide market.

- Firms using the integrated cost leadership/differentiation strategy strive to provide customers with relatively low-cost products that also have valued differentiated features. Flexibility is required for the firm to learn how to use primary and support activities in ways that allow them to produce differentiated products at relatively low costs. The primary risk of this strategy is that a firm might produce products that do not offer sufficient value in terms of either low cost or differentiation. In such cases, the company is "stuck in the middle." Firms stuck in the middle compete at a disadvantage and are unable to earn more than average returns.

Review Questions

1. What is a business-level strategy?

2. What is the relationship between a firm's customers and its business-level strategy in terms of *who, what,* and *how*? Why is this relationship important?

3. What are the differences among the cost leadership, differentiation, focused cost leadership, focused differentiation, and integrated cost leadership/differentiation business-level strategies?

4. How can each one of the business-level strategies be used to position the firm relative to the five forces of competition in a way that helps the firm earn above-average returns?

5. What are the specific risks associated with using each business-level strategy?

Notes

1. V. F. Misangyi, H. Elms, T. Greckhamer, & J. A. LePine, 2006, A new perspective on a fundamental debate: A multilevel approach to industry, corporate, and business unit effects, *Strategic Management Journal,* 27: 571–590; G. Gavetti & J. W. Rivkin, 2005, How strategists really think, *Harvard Business Review, 83*(4): 54–63.

2. G. Gavetti, D. A. Levinthal, & J. W. Rivkin, 2005, Strategy making in novel and complex worlds: The power of analogy, *Strategic Management Journal, 26:* 691–712.

3. S. Elbanna & J. Child, 2007, The influence of decision, environmental and firm characteristics on the rationality of strategic decision-making, *Journal of Management Studies,* 44: 561–591; T. Yu & A. A. Cannella, Jr., 2007, Rivalry between multinational enterprises: An event history approach, *Academy of Management Journal,* 50: 665–686.

4. J. Tan & D. Tan, 2005, Environment-strategy co-evolution and co-alignment: A staged model of Chinese SOEs under transition, *Strategic Management Journal,* 26: 141–157.

5. P. Megicks, 2007, Levels of strategy and performance in UK small retail businesses, *Management Decision,* 45: 484–502; G. George, J. Wiklund, & S. A. Zahra, 2005, Ownership and the internationalization of small firms, *Journal of Management,* 31: 210–233.

6. E. Kim, D. Nam, & J. L. Stimpert, 2004, The applicability of Porter's generic strategies in the digital age: Assumptions, conjectures, and suggestions, *Journal of Management,* 30: 569–589; R. D. Ireland, M. A. Hitt, S. M. Camp, & D. L. Sexton, 2001, Integrating entrepreneurship and strategic management actions to create firm wealth, *Academy of Management Executive,* 15(1): 49–63.

7. K. Shimizu & M. A. Hitt, 2004, Strategic flexibility: Organizational preparedness to reverse ineffective strategic decisions, *Academy of Management Executive,* 18(4): 44–59.

8. D. J. Ketchen Jr., C. C. Snow, & V. L. Street, 2004, Improving firm performance by matching strategic decision-making processes to competitive dynamics, *Academy of Management Executive,* 18(4): 29–43.

9. Elbanna & Child, The influence of decision, environmental and firm characteristics on the rationality of strategic decision-making; J. J. Janney & G. G. Dess, 2004, Can real-options analysis improve decision-making? Promises and pitfalls, *Academy of Management Executive,* 18(4): 60–75.

10. R. D. Ireland & C. C. Miller, 2005, Decision-making and firm success, *Academy of Management Executive,* 18(4): 8–12.

11. J.R. Hough, 2006, Business segment performance redux: A multilevel approach, *Strategic Management Journal,* 27: 45-61; N. Park, J. M. Mezias, & J. Song, 2004, Increasing returns, strategic alliances, and the values of E-commerce firms, *Journal of Management,* 30: 7–27.

12. M. C. Mankins & R. Steele, 2005, Turning great strategy into great performance, *Harvard Business Review, 83*(7): 65–72; T. J. Douglas & J. A. Ryman, 2003, Understanding competitive advantage in the general hospital industry: Evaluating strategic competencies, *Strategic Management Journal,* 24: 333–347.

13. D. Lei & J. W. Slocum, 2005, Strategic and organizational requirements for competitive advantage, *Academy of Management Executive,* 19(1): 31–45.

14. B. M. Case, 2005, Irving firm to cut jobs, *Dallas Morning News,* July 23, D1, D9.

15. J. B. Barney & T. B. Mackey, 2005, Testing resource-based theory, in D. J. Ketchen Jr. & D. D. Bergh (eds.), *Research Methodology in Strategy and Management,* 2nd ed., London: Elsevier, 1–13.

16. C. B. Dobni & G. Luffman, 2003, Determining the scope and impact of market orientation profiles on strategy implementation and performance, *Strategic Management Journal,* 24: 577–585.

17. R. Priem, 2007, A consumer perspective on value creation, *Academy of Management Review,* 32: 219–235; R. Gulati & J. B. Oldroyd, 2005, The quest for customer focus, *Harvard Business Review, 83*(4): 92–101.

18. M. E. Porter, 1980, *Competitive Strategy,* New York: Free Press.

19. A. J. Slywotzky & J. Drzik, 2005, Countering the biggest risk of all, *Harvard Business Review, 83*(4): 78–88.

20. D. G. Sirmon, M. A. Hitt, & R. D. Ireland, 2007, Managing firm resources in dynamic environments to create value: Inside the black box, *Academy of Management Review,* 32: 273–292.

21. F. E. Webster Jr., A. J. Malter, & S. Ganesan, 2005, The decline and dispersion of marketing competence, *MIT Sloan Management Review,* 6(4): 35–43.

22. K. Allison & R. Waters, 2007, Hewlett-Packard comes back fighting, *Financial Times,* http://www.ft.com, April 29.

23. M. B. Lieberman & S. Asaba, 2006, Why do firms imitate each other? *Academy of Management Review,* 31: 366–385.

24. R. W. Coff, D. C. Coff, & R. Eastvold, 2006, The knowledge-leveraging paradox: How to achieve scale without making knowledge imitable, *Academy of Management Review,* 31: 452–465.

25. 2007, About us, Harrah's Entertainment, http://www.harrahs.com, July 1.

26. P. R. Berthon, L. F. Pitt, I. McCarthy, & S. M. Kates, 2007, When customers get clever: Managerial approaches to dealing with creative customers, *Business Horizons,* 50(1): 39–47; J. E. Blose, W. B. Tankersley, & L. R. Flynn, 2005, Managing service quality using data envelopment analysis, http://www.asq.org, June.

27. R. Dhar & R. Glazer, 2003, Hedging customers, *Harvard Business Review,* 81(5): 86–92.

28. 2005, Amazon.com, *Standard & Poor's Stock Report,* http://www.standardandpoors.com, June 25.

29. 2007, This is CEMEX, CEMEX, http://www.cemex.com, July 1.

30. 2003, Fitch Mexico assigns AA qualifications to certificates of CEMEX, *Emerging Markets Economy,* April 8, 3; L. Walker, 2001, Plugged in for maximum efficiency, *Washington Post,* June 20, G1, G4.

31. 2007, Our company, Barnes & Noble, Inc., http://www.barnesandnobleinc.com, July 1.

32. 2005, Amazon.com, *Standard & Poor's Stock Reports,* http://www.standardandpoors.com, July 16.

33. 2007, Amazon.com annual shareholders meeting, http://library.corporate-ir.net/library/97/976/97664/items/249939/2007_Shareholder.pdf June 14.

34. 2007, http://www.autos.msn.com, July 1.

35. G. Dowell, 2006, Product-line strategies of new entrants in an established industry: Evidence from the U.S. bicycle industry, *Strategic Management Journal,* 27: 959–979; A. Reed II & L. E. Bolton, 2005, The complexity of identity, *MIT Sloan Management Review,* 46(3): 18–22.

36. C. W. Lamb Jr., J. F. Hair Jr., & C. McDaniel, 2006, *Marketing,* 8th ed., Mason, OH: Thomson South-Western, 224; A. Dutra, J. Frary, & R. Wise, 2004, Higher-order needs drive new growth in mature consumer markets, *Journal of Business Strategy,* 25(5): 26–34.

37. A. Baur, S. P. Hehner, & G. Nederegger, 2003, Pharma for Fido, *The McKinsey Quarterly,* Number 2, 7–10.

38. S. S. Hassan & S. H. Craft, 2005, Linking global market segmentation decisions with strategic positioning options, *Journal of Consumer Marketing,* 22(2/3): 81–88.

39. S. Hamner, 2005, Filling the Gap, *Business 2.0,* July, 30.

40. 2003, Unions and Gen-X: What does the future hold? *HR Focus,* March, 3; F. Marshall, 2003, Storehouse wakes up to Gen-X employees, *Furniture Today,* February 10, 2–3; J. Pereira, 2003, Best on the street, *Wall Street Journal,* May 12, R7; C. Burritt, 2001, Aging boomers reshape resort segment, *Lodging Hospitality,* 57(3): 31–32; J. D. Zbar, 2001, On a segmented dial, digital cuts wire finer, *Advertising Age,* 72(16): S12.

41. P. D. Ellis, 2006, Market orientation and performance: A meta-analysis and cross-national comparisons, *Journal of Management Studies,* 43: 1089–1107; J. P. Womack, 2005, Lean consumption, *Harvard Business Review,* 83(3): 58–68.

42. A. Panjwani, 2005, Open source vs. proprietary software: The pluses and minuses, *The Financial Express online,* http://www.financialexpress.com, May 2.

43. M. E. Raynor & H. S. Weinberg, 2004, Beyond segmentation, *Marketing Management,* 13(6): 22–29.

44. W. Reinartz, J. S. Thomas, & V. Kumar, 2005, Balancing acquisition and retention resources to maximize customer profitability, *Journal of Marketing,* 69: 63–85.

45. D. Foust, F. F. Jespersen, F. Katzenberg, A. Barrett, & R. O. Crockett, 2003, The best performers, *BusinessWeek Online,* http://www.businessweek.com, March 24.

46. M. J. Silverstein & N. Fiske, 2003, Luxury for the masses, *Harvard Business Review,* 81(4): 48–57.

47. C. W. L. Hill & F. T. Rothaermel, 2003, The performance of incumbent firms in the face of radical technological innovation, *Academy of Management Review,* 28: 257–274; A. W. King, S. W. Fowler, & C. P. Zeithaml, 2001, Managing organizational competencies for competitive advantage: The middle-management edge, *Academy of Management Executive,* 15(2): 95–106.

48. 2007, SAS Institute, http://www.sas.com, July 2.

49. 2007, Vans warped tour, http://www.vans.com; A. Weintraub & G. Khermouch, 2001, Chairman of the board, *BusinessWeek,* May 28, 94.

50. P. B. Barger & A. A. Grandry, 2006, Service with a smile and encounter satisfaction: Emotional contagion and appraisal mechanisms, *Academy of Management Journal,* 49: 1229–1238; L. L. Berry, E. A. Wall, & L. P. Carbone, 2006, Service clues and customer assessment of the service experience, *Academy of Management Perspective,* 20(2): 43–57.

51. M. E. Porter, 1985, *Competitive Advantage,* New York: Free Press, 26.

52. M. E. Porter, 1996, What is strategy? *Harvard Business Review,* 74(6): 61–78.

53. S. Warren & E. Perez, 2005, Southwest's net rises by 41%; Delta lifts cap on some fares, *Wall Street Journal Online,* http://www.wsj.com, July 15.

54. D. Cameron, 2007, Southwest seeks new sources of revenue, *Financial Times,* http://www.ft.com, April 19.

55. Porter, What is strategy?

56. C. Zott, 2003, Dynamic capabilities and the emergence of intraindustry differential firm performance: Insights from a simulation study, *Strategic Management Journal,* 24: 97–125.

57. M. E. Porter, 1994, Toward a dynamic theory of strategy, in R. P. Rumelt, D. E. Schendel, & D. J. Teece (eds.), *Fundamental Issues in Strategy,* Boston: Harvard Business School Press, 423–461.

58. Porter, What is strategy?, 62.

59. Porter, *Competitive Advantage,* 15.

60. G. G. Dess, G. T. Lumpkin, & J. E. McGee, 1999, Linking corporate entrepreneurship to strategy, structure, and process: Suggested research directions, *Entrepreneurship: Theory & Practice,* 23(3): 85–102; P. M. Wright, D. L. Smart, & G. C. McMahan, 1995, Matches between human resources and strategy among NCAA basketball teams, *Academy of Management Journal,* 38: 1052–1074.

61. Porter, *Competitive Strategy,* 35–40.

62. D. Mehri, 2006, The dark side of lean: An insider's perspective on the realities of the Toyota production system, *Academy of Management Perspectives,* 20(2): 21–42.

63. D. F. Spulber, 2004, *Management Strategy,* New York: McGrawHill/Irwin, 175.

64. 2007, Greyhound Lines, Inc. fact sheet, Hoovers, http://www.hoovers.com/greyhound, July 3; K. Yung, 2005, Greyhound taking new direction, *Dallas Morning News,* http://www.dallasnews.com, June 26.

65. D. F. Lynch, S. B. Keller, & J. Ozment, 2000, The effects of logistics capabilities and strategy on firm performance, *Journal of Business Logistics,* 21(2): 47–68.

66. P. Edwards & M. Ram, 2006, Surviving on the margins of the economy: Working relationships in small, low-wage firms, *Journal of Management Studies,* 43: 895–916.

67. 2005, Big Lots, *Standard & Poor's Stock Reports,* http://www.standardandpoors.com, July 16.

68. 2007, Big Lots, Inc, Hoovers profile, http://www.answers.com, July 3; 2005, Big Lots Inc. names Steve Fishman chairman, chief executive officer, and president, *Reuters,* http://www.reuters.com, June 10.

69. L. K. Johnson, 2003, Dueling pricing strategies, *The McKinsey Quarterly,* 44(3): 10–11.

70. A. D'Innocenzio, 2001, We are paranoid, *Richmond Times-Dispatch,* June 10, E1, E2.

71. A. Bianco, 2007, Wal-Mart's midlife crisis, *BusinessWeek,* April 30: 46-56; M. Maier, 2005, How to beat Wal-Mart, *Business 2.0,* May, 108–114.

72. D. Lavie, 2006, The competitive advantage of interconnected firms: An extension of the resource-based view, *Academy of Management Review,* 31: 638–658.

73. J. Bercovitz & W. Mitchell, 2007, When is more better? The impact of business scale and scope on long-term business survival, while controlling for profitability, *Strategic Management Journal,* 28: 61–79.

74. Bianco, Wal-Mart's midlife crisis.

75. Porter, *Competitive Strategy,* 35–40.

76. D. Ashmos Plowman, L. T. Baker, T. E. Beck, M. Kulkarni, S. Thomas-Solansky, & D. V. Travis, 2007, Radical change accidentally: The emergence and amplification of small change, *Academy of Management Journal,* 50: 515–543; A. Wadhwa & S. Kotha, 2006, Knowledge creation through external venturing: Evidence from the telecommunications equipment manufacturing industry, *Academy of Management Journal,* 49: 819–835.

77. M. J. Benner, 2007, The incumbent discount: Stock market categories and response to radical technological change, *Academy of Management Review,* 32:703–720.

78. F. T. Rothaermel, M. A. Hitt, & L. A. Jobe, 2006, Balancing vertical integration and strategic outsourcing: Effects on product portfolio, product success and firm performance, *Strategic Management Journal,* 27: 1033–1056; A. V. Mainkar, M. Lubatkin, & W. S. Schulze, 2006, Toward a product-proliferation theory of entry barriers, *Academy of Management Review,* 31: 1062–1075.

79. Porter, *Competitive Advantage,* 14.

80. 2007, History, http://www.roberttalbott.com, July 3.

81. W. C. Bogner & P. Bansal, 2007, Knowledge management as a basis for sustained high performance, *Journal of Management Studies,* 44:165–188;

M. Semadeni, 2006, Minding your distance: How management consulting firms use service marks to position competitively, *Strategic Management Journal,* 27: 169–187.

82. J. A. Byrne, 2005, The power of great design, *Fast Company,* June, 14.

83. W. Mossberg, 2007, iPod, iPhone, iTunes, Apple tv: Where Steve Jobs sees them all heading, *Wall Street Journal,* http://www.online.wsj.com, June 18; J. Scanlon, 2007, Apple sets the design standard, *BusinessWeek,* http://www.businessweek.com, January 8.

84. V. P. Rindova, T. G. Pollock, & M. A. Hayward, 2006, Celebrity firms: The social construction of market popularity, *Academy of Management Review,* 31: 50–71.

85. F. K. Pil & S. K. Cohen, 2006, Modularity: Implications for imitation, innovation, and sustained advantage, *Academy of Management Review,* 31: 995–1011.

86. Barney, *Gaining and Sustaining Competitive Advantage,* 268.

87. N. Stieglitz & K. Heine, 2007, Innovations and the role of complementarities in a strategic theory of the firm, *Strategic Management Journal,* 28: 1–15; S. K. Ethiraj, 2007, Allocation of inventive effort in complex product systems, *Strategic Management Journal,* 28: 563–584.

88. Porter, *Competitive Strategy,* 98.

89. A. V. Shipilov, 2006, Network strategies and performance of Canadian investment banks, *Academy of Management Journal,* 49: 590–604.

90. 2007, Greif & Co., http://www.greifco.com, July 4.

91. 2007, About Goya foods, http://www.goyafoods.com, July 4; D. Kaplan, 2005, Lots of food for diverse culture, *Houston Chronicle,* July 19, D2.

92. Porter, *Competitive Advantage,* 15.

93. Ibid., 15–16.

94. 2007, About IKEA, http://www.ikeagroup.ikea.com/corporate, July 4.

95. K. Kling & I. Goteman, 2003, IKEA CEO Andres Dahlvig on international growth and IKEA's unique corporate culture and brand identity, *Academy of Management Executive,* 17(1): 31–37.

96. About IKEA, http://www.ikeagroup.ikea.com/corporate.

97. P. Szuchman, 2005, Can this kitchen be saved? *Wall Street Journal Online,* http://www.wsj.com, April 29.

98. G. Evans, 2003, Why some stores strike me as special, *Furniture Today,* 27(24): 91; Porter, What is strategy?, 65.

99. 2007, About Casket Furniture, http://www.casketfurniture.com, July 4.

100. D. Pierson, 2007, An experiment in Alhambra's Kitchen, *Los Angeles Times,* http://www.latimes.com, April 22.

101. 2007, The art of rebellion, http://www.confederate.com, July 4; 2006, Paparazzi magnet, *Los Angeles Times,* December 20, G1–G2; B. Breen, 2005, Rebel yell, *Fast Company,* August, 60–61.

102. J. H. Dyer & N. W. Hatch, 2006, Relation-specific capabilities and barriers to knowledge transfers: Creating advantage through network relationships, *Strategic Management Journal,* 27: 701–719.

103. 2006, Annual Report, Target Corporation, http://www.target.com, July 5.

104. 2007, Target, http://www.target.com, July 5; 2001, The engine that drives differentiation, *DSN Retailing Today,* April 2, 52.

105. Dess, Lumpkin, & McGee, Linking corporate entrepreneurship to strategy, 89.

106. P. Ghemawat, 2001, *Strategy and the Business Landscape,* Upper Saddle River, NJ: Prentice Hall, 56.

107. Dess, Gupta, Hennart, & Hill, Conducting and integrating strategy research, 377.

108. M. L. Barnett, 2006, Finding a working balance between competitive and communal strategies, *Journal of Management Studies,* 43: 1753–1773.

109. R. Sanchez, 1995, Strategic flexibility in product competition, *Strategic Management Journal,* 16 (Special Issue): 140.

110. A. Faria, P. Fenn, & A. Bruce, 2005, Production technologies and technical efficiency: Evidence from Portuguese manufacturing industry, *Applied Economics,* 37: 1037–1046.

111. M. Kotabe, R. Parente, & J. Y. Murray, 2007, Antecedents and outcomes of modular production in the Brazilian automobile industry: A grounded theory approach, *Journal of International Business Studies,* 38: 84–106.

112. J. Baljko, 2003, Built for speed—When putting the reams of supply chain data they've amassed to use, companies are discovering that agility counts, *EBN,* 1352: 25–28.

113. E. K. Bish, A. Muriel, & S. Biller, 2005, Managing flexible capacity in a make-to-order environment, *Management Science,* 51: 167–180.

114. S. M. Iravani, M. P. van Oyen, & K. T. Sims, 2005, Structural flexibility: A new perspective on the design of manufacturing and service operations, *Management Science,* 51: 151–166.

115. F. Mattern, S. Schonwalder, & W. Stein, 2003, Fighting complexity in IT, *The McKinsey Quarterly,* no. 1, 57–65.

116. M. A. Lyles & J. E. Salk, 2007, Knowledge acquisition from foreign parents in international joint ventures: An empirical examination in the Hungarian context, *Journal of International Business Studies,* 38: 3–18.

117. S. W. Brown, 2003, The employee experience, *Marketing Management,* 12(2): 12–13.

118. S. Isaac & R. N. Tooker, 2001, The many faces of CRM, *LIMRA's MarketFacts Quarterly,* 20(1): 84–89.

119. D. P. Forbes, 2007, Reconsidering the strategic implications of decision comprehensiveness, *Academy of Management Review,* 32: 361–376.

120. J. D. Westphal, R. Gulati, & S. M. Shortell, 1997, Customization or conformity: An institutional and network perspective on the content and consequences of TQM adoption, *Administrative Science Quarterly,* 42: 366–394.

121. V. W. S. Yeung & R. W. Armstrong, 2003, A key to TQM benefits: Manager involvement in customer processes, *International Journal of Services Technology and Management,* 4(1): 14–29.

122. D. Welch, K. Kerwin, & C. Tierney, 2003, Way to go, Detroit—Now go a lot farther, *BusinessWeek,* May 26, 44.

123. N. Ganguli, T. V. Kumaresh, & A. Satpathy, 2003, Detroit's new quality gap, *The McKinsey Quarterly,* no. 1, 148–151.

124. R. J. David & S. Strang, 2006, When fashion is fleeting: Transitory collective beliefs and the dynamics of TQM consulting, *Academy of Management Journal,* 49: 215–233.

125. Porter, *Competitive Advantage,* 16.

126. Ibid., 17.

127. M. A. Hitt, L. Bierman, K. Uhlenbruck, & K. Shimizu, 2006, The importance of resources in the internationalization of professional service firms: The good, the bad, and the ugly, *Academy of Management Journal,* 49: 1137–1157.

128. P. Puranam, H. Singh, & M. Zollo, 2006, Organizing for innovation: Managing the coordination-autonomy dilemma in technology acquisitions, *Academy of Management Journal,* 49: 263–280.

129. S. Thornhill & R. E. White, 2007, Strategic purity: A multi-industry evaluation of pure vs. hybrid business strategies, *Strategic Management Journal,* 28: 553–561.

Corporate-Level Strategy

Studying this chapter should provide you with the strategic management knowledge needed to:

1. Define corporate-level strategy and discuss its purpose.

2. Describe different levels of diversification with different corporate-level strategies.

3. Explain three primary reasons firms diversify.

4. Describe how firms can create value by using a related diversification strategy.

5. Explain the two ways value can be created with an unrelated diversification strategy.

6. Discuss the incentives and resources that encourage diversification.

7. Describe motives that can encourage managers to overdiversify a firm.

Procter and Gamble's Diversification Strategy

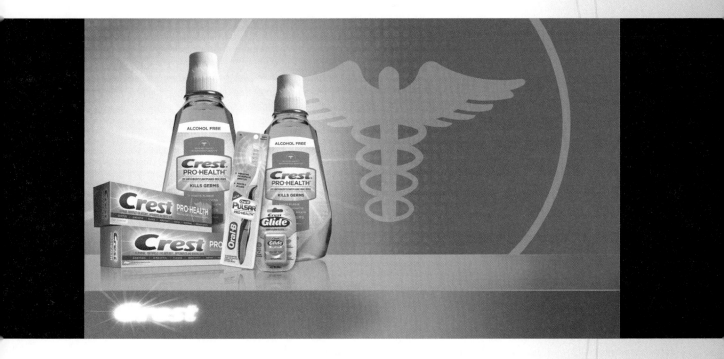

As firms grow they often seek to use the expertise and knowledge that they have gained in one business by diversifying into a business where this knowledge can be used in a related way. Economists call it "economizing on the scope of the firm," or more succinctly economies of scope (this concept will be defined more formally in the chapter). Once a firm is able to diversify using its previous expertise in other businesses, it applies a concept known as synergy, where the value added by the corporate office adds up to more than the value would be if the different businesses in the corporate portfolio were separate and independent. However, creating synergistic relationships between businesses is often more difficult than it appears. Procter & Gamble (P&G) has been seeking to create relatedness between various consumer product businesses for many years.

In 2005, Procter & Gamble Companies acquired the Gillette Company with high expectations to create synergies between these businesses. Because Gillette's consumer health care products—including products marketed under Gillette, Braun, Duracell and Oral-B brands, among others—were focused mainly on more masculine market areas and P&G had more focus on beauty products for women and baby care products, management saw complementary opportunities between these two corporations. To complete the merger, however, both businesses needed

to sell off other product lines to meet antitrust requirements. For example, Gillette had to sell off its Rembrandt toothpaste brand and P&G had to sell off its Spin Brush toothbrush brand.

One area in which they sought to create the potential synergy was combining the toothbrush and toothpaste businesses. Colgate had recently surpassed P&G's previously leading brand—Crest toothpaste. In a strategy designed to regain the lead, P&G sought to combine the Crest Toothpaste brand with the Oral-B Toothbrush using the "Pro-Health" label in seeking to sell both these complementary products. Previously the oral care retail shelves were fragmented with toothbrushes in one area and toothpaste in another. This arrangement is different from hair care or skin care products where the brands usually can be located together. As such, the combined approach may provide P&G an advantage that allows retailers to save precious shelf space and makes it easier for customers to find the separate products. However, because they had to sell off some of the other leading brands in the oral health segment, they lost some prospective market power.

Although this strategy appeared to have potential, it was much more difficult to create actual operational relatedness between the products (operational relatedness will be defined more clearly later in the chapter) than either P&G or Gillette had expected. First, Bruce Cleverly (from Gillette) and Charlie Pierce (from P&G), decided that they needed to commingle the employees in one place. Accordingly, they moved the essence of the operations to Cincinnati, Ohio, near P&G's headquarters. In the process, however, many of the Boston-area Gillette employees decided not to move, leading to an exit of talent. Second, P&G and Gillette had different ways of making business decisions. Although Cleverly was in charge, he was used to having freedom to make decisions, whereas the culture of P&G was more of a consensus-seeking process in making major decisions. Ultimately, Cleverly retired and turned the decision making over to Pierce. The business cultures never truly united, even after the combination of employees in Cincinnati, because these firms had previously been competitors.

The combination of the research unit in charge of providing new products for the Pro-Health project proceeded much better than the combination of the production and marketing personnel in Ohio. The most likely reason is that the research unit employees were able to stay in their general locations and collaborate through conferences and electronic means. Despite the difficulties, in 2007 the combined P&G brands overtook Colgate in market share with 35 percent to Colgate's 32 percent. As this case illustrates, merging two diverse firms to create operational relatedness or synergy between products can be more difficult to achieve than is apparent in the design phase.

Sources: 2007, P&G to be divided into three global units, Gillette will no longer be a separate unit, *FireWire*, May 15,1; E. Byron, 2007, Colgate's changing of the guard, *Wall Street Journal*, July 2, B7; E. Byron, 2007, Merger challenge: Unite toothbrush, toothpaste: P&G and Gillette find creating synergy can be harder than it looks, *Wall Street Journal*, April 24, A1, A17; J. Chang, 2007, Design to sell, *Sales and Working Management*, May; J. Neff, 2007, P&G struggles to hang on to top Gillette talent, *Advertising Age*, May 28, 28–29; J. Neff, 2007, Who wins? *Advertising Age*, June 18, 36–37; S. Brangen & C. Huxham, 2006, Achieving a collaborative advantage: Understanding the challenge and making it happen, *Strategic Direction*, 22(2): 3–5.

Our discussions of business-level strategies (Chapter 5) and the competitive rivalry and competitive dynamics associated with them (Chapter 4) concentrate on firms competing in a single industry or product market.[1] In this chapter, we introduce you to corporate-level strategies, which are strategies firms use to *diversify* their operations from a single business competing in a single market into several product markets and, most commonly, into several businesses. Thus, a **corporate-level strategy** specifies actions a firm takes to gain a competitive advantage by selecting and managing a group of different businesses competing in different product markets. Corporate-level strategies help companies select new strategic positions—positions that are expected to increase the firm's value.[2] As explained in the Opening Case, Procter & Gamble (P&G) competes in a number of different consumer product markets and often uses related diversification as illustrated through combining two of its brands, Crest toothpaste and Oral-B toothbrushes (part of the Gillette acquisition in 2005), into the Crest Pro-Health label to jointly market its products.

As is the case with P&G, firms use corporate-level strategies as a means to grow revenues and profits. But the decision to take actions to pursue growth is never a risk-free choice for firms to make. Indeed, as the Opening Case illustrated, P&G experienced difficulty in integrating the Crest and Oral-B brand operations to produce the Pro-Health products. Effective firms carefully evaluate their growth options (including the different corporate-level strategies) before committing firm resources to any of them.[3]

Because the diversified firm operates in several different and unique product markets and likely in several businesses, it forms two types of strategies: corporate level (or company-wide) and business level (or competitive).[4] Corporate-level strategy is concerned with two key issues: in what product markets and businesses the firm should compete and how corporate headquarters should manage those businesses.[5] For the diversified corporation, a business-level strategy (see Chapter 5) must be selected for each of the businesses in which the firm has decided to compete. In this regard, each of P&G's products or businesses uses a differentiation business-level strategy.

As is the case with a business-level strategy, a corporate-level strategy is expected to help the firm earn above-average returns by creating value.[6] Some suggest that few corporate-level strategies actually create value.[7] As the Opening Case indicates, realizing

A **corporate-level strategy** specifies actions a firm takes to gain a competitive advantage by selecting and managing a group of different businesses competing in different product markets.

value through a corporate strategy can be difficult to achieve. In fact, the degree to which corporate-level strategies create value beyond the sum of the value created by all of a firm's business units remains an important research question.[8]

Evidence suggests that a corporate-level strategy's value is ultimately determined by the degree to which "the businesses in the portfolio are worth more under the management of the company than they would be under any other ownership."[9] Thus, an effective corporate-level strategy creates, across all of a firm's businesses, aggregate returns that exceed what those returns would be without the strategy[10] and contributes to the firm's strategic competitiveness and its ability to earn above-average returns.[11]

Product diversification, a primary form of corporate-level strategies, concerns the scope of the markets and industries in which the firm competes as well as "how managers buy, create and sell different businesses to match skills and strengths with opportunities presented to the firm."[12] Successful diversification is expected to reduce variability in the firm's profitability as earnings are generated from different businesses.[13] Because firms incur development and monitoring costs when diversifying, the ideal portfolio of businesses balances diversification's costs and benefits. CEOs and their top-management teams are responsible for determining the ideal portfolio for their company.[14]

We begin this chapter by examining different levels of diversification (from low to high). After describing the different reasons firms diversify their operations, we focus on two types of related diversification (related diversification signifies a moderate to a high level of diversification for the firm). When properly used, these strategies help create value in the diversified firm, either through the sharing of resources (the related constrained strategy) or the transferring of core competencies across the firm's different businesses (the related linked strategy). We then discuss unrelated diversification, which is another corporate-level strategy that can create value. The chapter then shifts to the topic of incentives and resources that may stimulate diversification which is value neutral. However, managerial motives to diversify, the final topic in the chapter, can actually destroy some of the firm's value.

Levels of Diversification

Diversified firms vary according to their level of diversification and the connections between and among their businesses. Figure 6.1 lists and defines five categories of businesses according to increasing levels of diversification. The single- and dominant-business categories denote relatively low levels of diversification; more fully diversified firms are classified into related and unrelated categories. A firm is related through its diversification when its businesses share several links; for example, businesses may share products (goods or services), technologies, or distribution channels. The more links among businesses, the more "constrained" is the relatedness of diversification. Unrelatedness refers to the absence of direct links between businesses.

Low Levels of Diversification

A firm pursing a low level of diversification uses either a single- or a dominant-business, corporate-level diversification strategy. A *single-business diversification strategy* is a corporate-level strategy wherein the firm generates 95 percent or more of its sales revenue from its core business area.[15] For example, Wm. Wrigley Jr. Company, the world's largest producer of chewing and bubble gums, historically used a single-business strategy while operating in relatively few product markets. Wrigley's trademark chewing gum brands include Spearmint, Doublemint, and Juicy Fruit, although the firm produces other products as well. Sugar-free Extra, which currently holds the largest share of the U.S. chewing gum market, was introduced in 1984.

Wrigley is beginning to diversify its product portfolio to become an important player in the confectionery market. In 2005, Wrigley acquired certain confectionery assets from

Figure 6.1 Levels and Types of Diversification

Low Levels of Diversification

Single business:	95% or more of revenue comes from a single business.	 Ⓐ
Dominant business:	Between 70% and 95% of revenue comes from a single business.	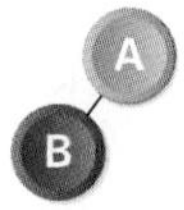 Ⓐ Ⓑ

Moderate to High Levels of Diversification

Related constrained:	Less than 70% of revenue comes from the dominant business, and all businesses share product, technological, and distribution linkages.	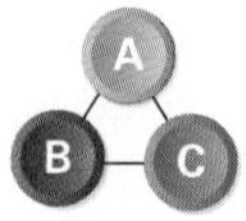 Ⓐ Ⓑ–Ⓒ
Related linked (mixed related and unrelated):	Less than 70% of revenue comes from the dominant business, and there are only limited links between businesses.	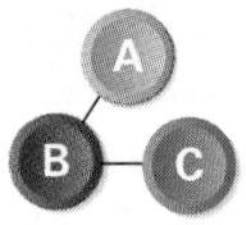 Ⓐ Ⓑ–Ⓒ

Very High Levels of Diversification

Unrelated:	Less than 70% of revenue comes from the dominant business, and there are no common links between businesses.	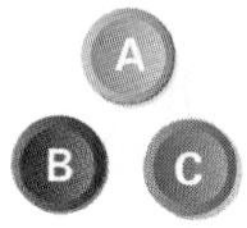 Ⓐ Ⓑ Ⓒ

Source: Adapted from R. P. Rumelt,1974, *Strategy, Structure and Economic Performance,* Boston: Harvard Business School.

Kraft Foods Inc., including the well-known brands Life Savers and Altoids. Apparently, Wrigley management has had a difficult time integrating this acquisition because Wrigley's share price has since decreased in value. Hershey recently offered to merge with Cadbury Schweppe's gum brands. If in response Wrigley tried to buy Hershey, it would probably have to pay a high premium for the Hershey assets. Alternatively, it may be in an even more "sticky" situation if Cadbury is able to acquire Hershey's assets. Thus, diversification strategies can be risky whether a company or its rival buys the assets of a firm.[16] With increasing diversification of its product lines, Wrigley may soon begin using the dominant-business corporate-level strategy.

With the *dominant-business diversification strategy,* the firm generates between 70 and 95 percent of its total revenue within a single business area. United Parcel Service (UPS) uses this strategy. Recently UPS generated 74 percent of its revenue from its U.S. package delivery business and 17 percent from its international package business, with the remaining 9 percent coming from the firm's non-package business.[17] Though the U.S. package delivery business currently generates the largest percentage of UPS's sales revenue, the firm anticipates that in the future its other two businesses will account for the majority of revenue growth. This expectation suggests that UPS may become more diversified, both in terms of its goods and services and in the number of countries in which those goods and services are offered.

Moderate and High Levels of Diversification

A firm generating more than 30 percent of its revenue outside a dominant business and whose businesses are related to each other in some manner uses a related diversification corporate-level strategy. When the links between the diversified firm's businesses are rather direct, a *related constrained diversification strategy* is being used. Campbell Soup, Procter & Gamble, Kodak, and Merck & Company all use a related constrained strategy, as do some large cable companies. With a related constrained strategy, a firm shares resources and activities between its businesses.

The diversified company with a portfolio of businesses that have only a few links between them is called a mixed related and unrelated firm and is using the *related linked diversification strategy* (see Figure 6.1). Johnson & Johnson, Procter & Gamble, and General Electric (GE) use this corporate-level diversification strategy. Compared with related constrained firms, related linked firms share fewer resources and assets between their businesses, concentrating instead on transferring knowledge and core competencies between the businesses. As with firms using each type of diversification strategy, companies implementing the related linked strategy constantly adjust the mix in their portfolio of businesses as well as make decisions about how to manage these businesses.

Li Ka-Shing (center), CEO of Hutchison Whampoa Limited (HWL), runs a conglomerate that follows an unrelated diversification strategy.

A highly diversified firm that has no relationships between its businesses follows an *unrelated diversification strategy*. United Technologies, Textron, Samsung, and Hutchison Whampoa Limited (HWL) are examples of firms using this type of corporate-level strategy. Commonly, firms using this strategy are called *conglomerates*.

HWL is a leading international corporation committed to innovation and technology with businesses spanning the globe.[18] Ports and related services, telecommunications, property and hotels, retail and manufacturing, and energy and infrastructure are HWL's five core businesses. These businesses are not related to each other, and the firm makes no efforts to share activities or to transfer core competencies between or among them. Each of these five businesses is quite large; for example, the retailing arm of the retail and manufacturing business has more than 6,200 stores in 31 countries. Groceries, cosmetics, electronics, wine, and airline tickets are some of the product categories featured in these stores. This firm's size and diversity suggest the challenge of successfully managing the unrelated diversification strategy. However, Hutchison's CEO Li Ka-shing, has been successful at not only making smart acquisitions, but also at divesting businesses at good prices.[19]

Reasons for Diversification

A firm uses a corporate-level diversification strategy for a variety of reasons (see Table 6.1). Typically, a diversification strategy is used to increase the firm's value by improving its overall performance. Value is created either through related diversification or through unrelated diversification when the strategy allows a company's businesses to increase revenues or reduce costs while implementing their business-level strategies.

Other reasons for using a diversification strategy may have nothing to do with increasing the firm's value; in fact, diversification can have neutral effects or even reduce a firm's value. Value-neutral reasons for diversification include those of a desire to match and thereby neutralize a competitor's market power (such as to neutralize another firm's advantage by acquiring a similar distribution outlet). Decisions to expand a firm's portfolio of businesses to reduce managerial risk can have a negative effect on the firm's value. Greater amounts of diversification reduce managerial risk in that if one of the businesses in a diversified firm fails, the top executive of that business does not risk total failure by the corporation. As such, this reduces the top executives' employment risk. In addition, because diversification can increase a firm's size and thus managerial compensation, managers have motives to diversify a firm to a level that reduces its value.[20] Diversification rationales that may have a neutral or negative effect on the firm's value are discussed later in the chapter.

Operational relatedness and corporate relatedness are two ways diversification strategies can create value (see Figure 6.2 on page 159). Studies of these independent relatedness

Table 6.1 Reasons for Diversification

Value-Creating Diversification

- Economies of scope (related diversification)
  - Sharing activities
  - Transferring core competencies
- Market power (related diversification)
  - Blocking competitors through multipoint competition
  - Vertical integration
- Financial economies (unrelated diversification)
  - Efficient internal capital allocation
  - Business restructuring

Value-Neutral Diversification

- Antitrust regulation
- Tax laws
- Low performance
- Uncertain future cash flows
- Risk reduction for firm
- Tangible resources
- Intangible resources

Value-Reducing Diversification

- Diversifying managerial employment risk
- Increasing managerial compensation

dimensions show the importance of resources and key competencies.[21] The figure's vertical dimension depicts opportunities to share operational activities between businesses (operational relatedness) while the horizontal dimension suggests opportunities for transferring corporate-level core competencies (corporate relatedness). The firm with a strong capability in managing operational synergy, especially in sharing assets between its businesses, falls in the upper left quadrant, which also represents vertical sharing of assets through vertical integration. The lower right quadrant represents a highly developed corporate capability for transferring one or more core competencies across businesses. This capability is located primarily in the corporate headquarters office. Unrelated diversification is also illustrated in Figure 6.2 in the lower left quadrant. Financial economies (discussed later), rather than either operational or corporate relatedness, are the source of value creation for firms using the unrelated diversification strategy.

Value-Creating Diversification: Related Constrained and Related Linked Diversification

With the related diversification corporate-level strategy, the firm builds upon or extends its resources and capabilities to create value.[22] The company using the related diversification strategy wants to develop and exploit economies of scope between its businesses.[23] Available to companies operating in multiple product markets or industries,[24] **economies of scope** are cost savings that the firm creates by successfully sharing some of its resources and capabilities or transferring one or more corporate-level core competencies that were developed in one of its businesses to another of its businesses.

Economies of scope are cost savings that the firm creates by successfully sharing some of its resources and capabilities or transferring one or more corporate-level core competencies that were developed in one of its businesses to another of its businesses.

Figure 6.2 Value-Creating Diversification Strategies: Operational and Corporate Relatedness

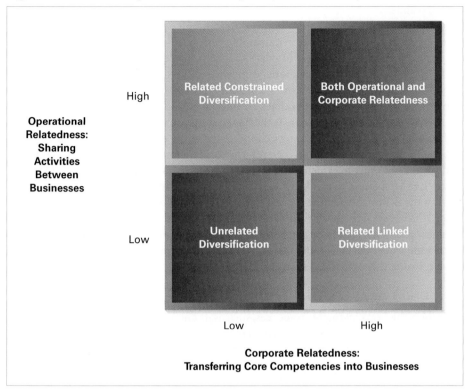

As illustrated in Figure 6.2, firms seek to create value from economies of scope through two basic kinds of operational economies: sharing activities (operational relatedness) and transferring corporate-level core competencies (corporate relatedness). The difference between sharing activities and transferring competencies is based on how separate resources are jointly used to create economies of scope. To create economies of scope tangible resources, such as plant and equipment or other business-unit physical assets, often must be shared. Less tangible resources, such as manufacturing know-how can also be shared. However, know-how transferred between separate activities with no physical or tangible resource involved is a transfer of a corporate-level core competence, not an operational sharing of activities.[25]

Operational Relatedness: Sharing Activities

Firms can create operational relatedness by sharing either a primary activity (such as inventory delivery systems) or a support activity (such as purchasing practices)—see Chapter 3's discussion of the value chain. Firms using the related constrained diversification strategy share activities in order to create value. Procter & Gamble (P&G) uses this corporate-level strategy. P&G's paper towel business and baby diaper business both use paper products as a primary input to the manufacturing process. The firm's paper production plant produces inputs for both businesses and is an example of a shared activity. In addition, because they both produce consumer products, these two businesses are likely to share distribution channels and sales networks.

As noted in the Opening Case, P&G acquired Gillette Co. Operational relatedness has been necessary in the research and marketing activities needed for the creation of Crest Pro-Health label through combining the Crest and Oral-B brands. To further foster operational relatedness, many of the people associated with the production operations of Oral-B toothbrush products were relocated to Cincinnati, near the Crest division operations as well P&G headquarters.[26] Firms expect activity sharing among units to result in increased strategic competitiveness and improved financial returns.[27] Through its shared product approach, P&G has improved its market share position. However, as previously mentioned, pursuing operational relatedness is not easy, and often synergies are not realized as planned.

Activity sharing is also risky because ties among a firm's businesses create links between outcomes. For instance, if demand for one business's product is reduced, it may not generate sufficient revenues to cover the fixed costs required to operate the shared facilities. These types of organizational difficulties can reduce activity-sharing success.[28]

Although activity sharing across businesses is not risk-free, research shows that it can create value. For example, studies that examined acquisitions of firms in the same industry (horizontal acquisitions), such as the banking industry, found that sharing resources and activities and thereby creating economies of scope contributed to postacquisition increases in performance and higher returns to shareholders.[29] Additionally, firms that sold off related units in which resource sharing was a possible source of economies of scope have been found to produce lower returns than those that sold off businesses unrelated to the firm's core business.[30] Still other research discovered that firms with closely related businesses have lower risk.[31] These results suggest that gaining economies of scope by sharing activities across a firm's businesses may be important in reducing risk and in creating value. Further, more attractive results are obtained through activity sharing when a strong corporate headquarters office facilitates it.[32]

Corporate Relatedness: Transferring of Core Competencies

Over time, the firm's intangible resources, such as its know-how, become the foundation of core competencies. **Corporate-level core competencies** are complex sets of resources and capabilities that link different businesses, primarily through managerial and technological knowledge, experience, and expertise.[33] The ability to successfully price new products in all of the firm's businesses is an example of what research has shown to be a value-creating, corporate-level competence.[34] Firms seeking to create value through corporate relatedness use the related linked diversification strategy.

In at least two ways, the related linked diversification strategy helps firms to create value.[35] First, because the expense of developing a core competence has been incurred in one of the firm's businesses, transferring it to a second business eliminates the need for that second business to allocate resources to develop it. Such is the case at Hewlett-Packard (HP), where the firm transferred its competence in ink printers to high-end copiers. Rather than the standard laser printing technology in most high-end copiers, HP is using ink-based technology. One manager liked the product because, as he noted, "We are able to do a lot better quality at less price."[36] This capability will also give HP the opportunity to sell more ink products, which is how it has been able to create higher profit margins.

Resource intangibility is a second source of value creation through corporate relatedness. Intangible resources are difficult for competitors to understand and imitate. Because of this difficulty, the unit receiving a transferred corporate-level competence often gains an immediate competitive advantage over its rivals.[37]

A number of firms have successfully transferred one or more corporate-level core competencies across their businesses. Virgin Group Ltd. transfers its marketing core competence across travel, cosmetics, music, drinks, mobile phones, health clubs, and a number of other businesses.[38] Thermo Electron uses its entrepreneurial core competence to start new ventures and maintain a new-venture network.[39] Honda has developed and transferred its competence in engine design and manufacturing to its businesses making products such as motorcycles,

Corporate-level core competencies are complex sets of resources and capabilities that link different businesses, primarily through managerial and technological knowledge, experience, and expertise.

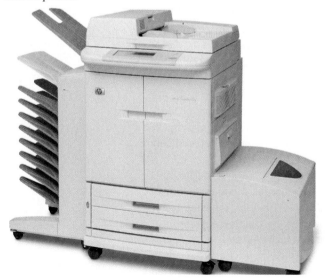

Hewlett-Packard's high-end copiers are a result of the firm's transferring competence from ink printers to this new product.

lawnmowers, and cars and trucks. With respect to smaller engines, for example, the transfers of the corporate-level competence in terms of engine design and manufacturing have been successful; company officials indicate that "Honda is the world's largest manufacturer of engines and has earned its reputation for unsurpassed quality, performance and reliability."[40]

One way managers facilitate the transfer of corporate-level core competencies is by moving key people into new management positions.[41] However, the manager of an older business may be reluctant to transfer key people who have accumulated knowledge and experience critical to the business's success. Thus, managers with the ability to facilitate the transfer of a core competence may come at a premium, or the key people involved may not want to transfer. Additionally, the top-level managers from the transferring business may not want the competencies transferred to a new business to fulfill the firm's diversification objectives. As the Strategic Focus on Smith & Wesson indicates, corporate competencies were bolstered by hiring a number of managers from outside the firm to facilitate improvement in the transfer of desired corporate competencies. Moreover, it seems that businesses in which performance does improve often demonstrate a corporate-wide passion for pursuing skill transfer and appropriate coordination mechanisms for realizing economies of scope.

Market Power

Firms using a related diversification strategy may gain market power when successfully using their related constrained or related linked strategy. **Market power** exists when a firm is able to sell its products above the existing competitive level or to reduce the costs of its primary and support activities below the competitive level, or both.[42] Nestlé SA, a large food company, will increase its market share for its baby-food line through the acquisition of Gerber Products from Novartis AG. Although Nestlé has a large baby-food position in emerging economies such as Brazil and China, it lacks a presence in the United States. Gerber has nearly an 80 percent share of baby foods in the United States. This opportunity materialized for Nestlé because Novartis decided to focus on three main areas: new prescription medicine, low-cost generic medicine, and over-the-counter medicine. Due to market and governance pressures many firms are focusing on a narrower set of businesses (see the Strategic Focus later in the chapter on the Revival of the Unrelated Strategy). This trend among pharmaceutical firms such as Novartis created an opportunity for Nestlé to buy the divested business. Certainly through this move, Nestlé will substantially increase its market power worldwide.[43]

In addition to efforts to gain scale as a means of increasing market power, as Nestlé is attempting to do by acquiring Gerber Products, firms can create market power through multipoint competition[44] and vertical integration. **Multipoint competition** exists when two or more diversified firms simultaneously compete in the same product areas or geographic markets.[45] The actions taken by United Parcel Service (UPS) and FedEx in two markets, overnight delivery and ground shipping, illustrate multipoint competition. UPS has moved into overnight delivery, FedEx's stronghold; FedEx has been buying trucking and ground shipping assets to move into ground shipping, UPS's stronghold. Moreover, geographic competition for markets increases as DHL, the strongest shipping company in Europe, tries to move into the U.S. market. All three competitors (UPS, FedEx, and DHL) are trying to move into large foreign markets to either gain a stake in a market or to expand their existing share of a market. For instance, because China was allowed into the World Trade Organization (WTO) and government officials have declared the market more open to foreign competition, the battle for global market share among these three top shippers is raging in China and other countries throughout the world.[46] If one of these firms successfully gains strong positions in several markets while competing against its rivals, its market power may increase.

Market power exists when a firm is able to sell its products above the existing competitive level or to reduce the costs of its primary and support activities below the competitive level, or both.

Multipoint competition exists when two or more diversified firms simultaneously compete in the same product areas or geographical markets.

Vertical integration
exists when a company produces its own inputs (backward integration) or owns its own source of output distribution (forward integration).

Some firms using a related diversification strategy engage in vertical integration to gain market power. **Vertical integration** exists when a company produces its own inputs (backward integration) or owns its own source of output distribution (forward integration). In some instances, firms partially integrate their operations, producing and selling their products by using company businesses as well as outside sources.[47]

Vertical integration is commonly used in the firm's core business to gain market power over rivals. Market power is gained as the firm develops the ability to save on its operations, avoid market costs, improve product quality, and, possibly, protect its technology from imitation by rivals.[48] Market power also is created when firms have strong ties between their assets for which no market prices exist. Establishing a market price would result in high search and transaction costs, so firms seek to vertically integrate rather than remain separate businesses.[49]

Vertical integration has its limitations. For example, an outside supplier may produce the product at a lower cost. As a result, internal transactions from vertical integration may be expensive and reduce profitability relative to competitors. Also, bureaucratic costs may occur with vertical integration. And, because vertical integration can require substantial investments in specific technologies, it may reduce the firm's flexibility, especially when technology changes quickly. Finally, changes in demand create capacity balance and coordination problems. If one business is building a part for another internal business, but achieving economies of scale requires the first division to manufacture quantities that are beyond the capacity of the internal buyer to absorb, it would be necessary to sell the parts outside the firm as well as to the internal business. Thus, although vertical integration can create value, especially through market power over competitors, it is not without risks and costs.[50]

CVS, which recently merged with Caremark, demonstrates a vertical integration strategy for growth and competition.

For example, CVS, a drug store competitor to Walgreens, recently merged with Caremark, a large pharmaceutical benefits manager. For CVS this merger represents a forward vertical move broadening its business from retail into health care. However, Medco a competitor to Caremark indicates that competitor companies to CVS "are more comfortable with [their] neutral position than they are with the concept of a combination" between CVS and Caremark.[51] Thus, although CVS may gain some market power, it risks alienating rivals such as Walgreens who may choose to collaborate with other benefit managers such as Medco or Express Scripts.

Many manufacturing firms no longer pursue vertical integration as a means of gaining market power.[52] In fact, deintegration is the focus of most manufacturing firms, such as Intel and Dell, and even some large auto companies, such as Ford and General Motors, as they develop independent supplier networks.[53] Flextronics, an electronics contract manufacturer, represents a new breed of large contract manufacturers that is helping to foster this revolution in supply-chain management. Flextronics itself is diversifying with a proposed acquisition with Solectron Corp., another contract manufacturer with a complementary portfolio of businesses.[54] Such firms often manage their customers' entire product lines and offer services ranging from inventory management to delivery and after-sales service. Conducting business through e-commerce also allows vertical integration to be changed into "virtual integration."[55] Thus, closer relationships are possible with suppliers and customers through virtual integration or electronic means of integration, allowing firms to reduce the costs of processing transactions while improving their supply-chain management skills and tightening the control of their inventories. This evidence suggests that *virtual integration* rather than *vertical integration* may be a more common source of market power gains for today's firms.

Simultaneous Operational Relatedness and Corporate Relatedness

As Figure 6.2 suggests, some firms simultaneously seek operational and corporate relatedness to create economies of scope.[56] The ability to simultaneously create economies of scope by sharing activities (operational relatedness) and transferring core competencies (corporate relatedness) is difficult for competitors to understand and learn how to imitate. However, firms that fail in their efforts to simultaneously obtain operational and corporate relatedness may create the opposite of what they seek—namely, diseconomies of scope instead of economies of scope.[57]

As the Strategic Focus on Smith & Wesson and Luxottica suggests, both of these companies have used a strategy that combines operational and corporate relatedness with some success. Likewise, Walt Disney Co. uses a related diversification strategy to simultaneously create economies of scope through operational and corporate relatedness. Within the firm's Studio Entertainment business, for example, Disney can gain economies of scope by sharing activities among its different movie distribution companies such as Touchstone Pictures, Hollywood Pictures, and Dimension Films, among others. Broad and deep knowledge about its customers is a capability on which Disney relies to develop corporate-level core competencies in terms of advertising and marketing. With these competencies, Disney is able to create economies of scope through corporate relatedness as it cross-sells products that are highlighted in its movies through the distribution channels that are part of its Parks and Resorts and Consumer Products businesses. Thus, characters created in movies (think of those in *The Lion King*) become figures that are marketed through Disney's retail stores (which are part of the Consumer Products business). In addition, themes established in movies become the source of new rides in the firm's theme parks, which are part of the Parks and Resorts business.[58]

As we described, Smith & Wesson, Luxottica, and Walt Disney Co. have been able to successfully use related diversification as a corporate-level strategy through which they create economies of scope by sharing some activities and by transferring core competencies. However, it can be difficult for investors to actually observe the value created by a firm (such as Walt Disney Co.) as it shares activities and transfers core competencies. For this reason, the value of the assets of a firm using a diversification strategy to create economies of scope in this manner tends to be discounted by investors. For example, analysts have complained that both Citibank and UBS, two large multiplatform banks, have underperformed their more focused counterparts in regard to stock market appreciation. In fact, both banks have heard calls for breaking up their separate businesses in insurance, hedge funds, consumer lending, and investment banking.[59] One analyst speaking of Citigroup suggested that "creating real synergy between its divisions has been hard," implying that Citigroup's related diversification strategy suffered from some possible diseconomies of scale.[60]

STRATEGY RIGHT NOW

Unrelated Diversification

Firms do not seek either operational relatedness or corporate relatedness when using the unrelated diversification corporate-level strategy. An unrelated diversification strategy (see Figure 6.2) can create value through two types of financial economies. **Financial economies** are cost savings realized through improved allocations of financial resources based on investments inside or outside the firm.[61]

Efficient internal capital allocations can lead to financial economies. Efficient internal capital allocations reduce risk among the firm's businesses—for example, by leading to the development of a portfolio of businesses with different risk profiles. The second type of financial economy concerns the restructuring of acquired assets. Here, the diversified firm buys another company, restructures that company's assets in ways that allow it to

Financial economies are cost savings realized through improved allocations of financial resources based on investments inside or outside the firm.

Operational and Corporate Relatedness: Smith & Wesson and Luxottica

Both Smith & Wesson Holding Company, a traditional handgun manufacturer, and Luxottica, a luxury sunglass producer, have been pursuing the combined operational and corporate relatedness strategy. Smith & Wesson Holding Company is one of the most recognized brands in the world, made famous partly because of the use of its .44 magnum in the movie *Dirty Harry*. Interestingly, until a short time ago Smith & Wesson did not have other weapon-related products besides handguns. But recently it moved beyond its traditional handgun market into producing shotguns and rifles, which are weekend and hunting products. These products are close to its roots in operational, technological, and marketing areas. Michael F. Golden who took over as CEO in 2004, initiated this operationally related diversification strategy by purchasing Thompson/Center Arms Company for $1.1 billion. Thompson's manufacturing expertise has helped accelerate Smith & Wesson's growth in longer barrel markets.

Golden, who did not know much about guns when he took over as CEO, had helped Black & Decker expand its tool business through improved marketing of its hardware products. Similarly in developing corporate relatedness areas for Smith & Wesson, Golden pushed into licensing agreements where the Smith & Wesson brand is now used for product advertisements such as men's cologne. "Marketing surveys showed gun buyers were interested in purchasing shotguns, hunting rifles, ammunition, even security alarm services from Smith & Wesson." To develop this strategy Golden hired executives with marketing backgrounds from Coca-Cola, Frito Lay, Stanley Works, and Harley-Davidson. Its licensing revenues rose 17 percent in the second quarter of 2007. With its dual diversification strategy (using both operational and corporate relatedness), Smith & Wesson expects sales gains of "40 percent or more for fiscal 2007 and 2008."

Luxotica used related diversification as a corporate-level strategy in acquiring Oakley, Inc., sports-brand sunglasses.

Additionally Smith & Wesson with a new .45 caliber–sized handgun expects to increase sales to the military for government contracts previously held by Beretta. This contract alone could be worth $500 million in sales. Also, through innovation of a high-tech, lightweight, yet high-strength plastic, it plans to manufacture a handgun that is likely to appeal to police departments and increase its sales to law enforcement agencies.

Similarly Luxottica moved from a focus on fashion to sports brand sunglasses. To make this shift, Luxottica acquired Oakley, Inc., which is primarily focused in the sports eyewear segment. Operationally, due to synergies between these two businesses, Luxottica expects to see proposed savings over three years equivalent to $932 million due to opportunities for operational relatedness, which is higher than the premium paid of $663 million for Oakley. The big question is whether it can manage the brand change from fashion to sports using a corporate relatedness strategy given its image as a fashion sunglass manufacturer. Another concern is that the acquisition will make Luxottica 80 percent focused on retail markets in the United States. It had signaled earlier that it would like to expand its retail outlets in more affluent markets. Thus it has risked being overly focused in the U.S. market. In summary, both Smith & Wesson and Luxottica are examples of firms that are pursuing both operational and corporate relatedness as they diversify to increase their opportunities for growth.

Sources: 2007, Cheap sunglasses? Not for Luxottica: The Italian optics giant snares performance eyewear maker Oakley in a $2.1 billion deal, *BusinessWeek*, http://www.businessweek.com, June 21; R. Owen, 2007, Oakley goes to Luxottica in $2 bn deal, *The Times*, http://www.business.timesonline.co.uk, June 22; A. Pressman, 2007, Smith & Wesson: A gun maker loaded with offshoots, *BusinessWeek*, June 4, 66; S. Walters & R. Stone, 2007, The trouble with rose-colored sunglasses, *Barron's*, 25, M10; C. Hajim, 2006, A stock with fire power: Smith & Wesson, *Fortune*, http://www.cnnMoney.com, October 9.

operate more profitably, and then sells the company for a profit in the external market.[62] Next, we discuss the two types of financial economies in greater detail.

Efficient Internal Capital Market Allocation

In a market economy, capital markets are thought to efficiently allocate capital. Efficiency results as investors take equity positions (ownership) with high expected future cash-flow values. Capital is also allocated through debt as shareholders and debtholders try to improve the value of their investments by taking stakes in businesses with high growth and profitability prospects.

In large diversified firms, the corporate headquarters office distributes capital to its businesses to create value for the overall corporation. The nature of these distributions may generate gains from internal capital market allocations that exceed the gains that would accrue to shareholders as a result of capital being allocated by the external capital market.[63] Because those in a firm's corporate headquarters generally have access to detailed and accurate information regarding the actual and prospective performance of the company's portfolio of businesses, they have the best information to make capital distribution decisions.

Compared with corporate office personnel, external investors have relatively limited access to internal information and can only estimate the performances of individual businesses as well as their future prospects. Moreover, although businesses seeking capital must provide information to potential suppliers (such as banks or insurance companies), firms with internal capital markets may have at least two informational advantages. First, information provided to capital markets through annual reports and other sources may not include negative information, instead emphasizing positive prospects and outcomes. External sources of capital have limited ability to understand the operational dynamics of large organizations. Even external shareholders who have access to information have no guarantee of full and complete disclosure.[64] Second, although a firm must disseminate information, that information also becomes simultaneously available to the firm's current and potential competitors. With insights gained by studying such information, competitors might attempt to duplicate a firm's value-creating strategy. Thus, an ability to efficiently allocate capital through an internal market may help the firm protect the competitive advantages it develops while using its corporate-level strategy as well as its various business-unit level strategies.

If intervention from outside the firm is required to make corrections to capital allocations, only significant changes are possible, such as forcing the firm into bankruptcy or changing the top management team. Alternatively, in an internal capital market, the corporate headquarters office can fine-tune its corrections, such as choosing to adjust managerial incentives or suggesting strategic changes in one of the firm's businesses. Thus, capital can be allocated according to more specific criteria than is possible with external market allocations. Because it has less accurate information, the external capital market may fail to allocate resources adequately to high-potential investments. The corporate headquarters office of a diversified company can more effectively perform such tasks as disciplining underperforming management teams through resource allocations.[65]

Large highly diversified businesses often face what is known as the "conglomerate discount." This discount results from analysts not knowing how to value a vast array of large businesses with complex financial reports. For instance, one analyst suggested in regard to figuring out GE's financial results in its quarterly report, "A rubik's cube may in fact be easier to figure out."[66] To overcome this discount many unrelated diversified or industrial conglomerates have sought to establish a brand for the parent company. For instance, recent advertisements by BASF AG, a diversified German chemical company, have included a campaign ad/slogan: "We don't make a lot of the products you buy. We make a lot of the products you buy better." General Electric and others, besides BASF AG, have been successful to varying degrees, in running such ad campaigns. More recently United Technologies initiated a brand development approach with the slogan

"United Technologies. You can see everything from here." United Technologies suggested that its earnings multiple (PE ratio) compared to its stock price is only average even though its performance has been better than other conglomerates in its group. It is hoping that the "umbrella" brand advertisement will raise its PE to a level comparable to its competitors.[67]

In spite of the challenges associated with it, a number of corporations continue to use the unrelated diversification strategy, especially in Europe and in emerging markets. Siemens, for example, is a large German conglomerate with a highly diversified approach. The former CEO argued that "When you are in an up-cycle and the capital markets have plenty of opportunities to invest in single-industry companies . . . investors savor those opportunities. But when things change pure plays go down faster than you can look."[68]

The Achilles' heel for firms using the unrelated diversification strategy in a developed economy is that competitors can imitate financial economies more easily than they can replicate the value gained from the economies of scope developed through operational relatedness and corporate relatedness. This issue is less of a problem in emerging economies, where the absence of a "soft infrastructure" (including effective financial intermediaries, sound regulations, and contract laws) supports and encourages use of the unrelated diversification strategy.[69] In fact, in emerging economies such as those in India and Chile, research has shown that diversification increases the performance of firms affiliated with large diversified business groups.[70]

Restructuring of Assets

Financial economies can also be created when firms learn how to create value by buying, restructuring, and then selling other companies' assets in the external market.[71] As in the real estate business, buying assets at low prices, restructuring them, and selling them at a price that exceeds their cost generates a positive return on the firm's invested capital.[72]

As the Strategic Focus on unrelated diversified companies who pursue this strategy suggests, creating financial economies by acquiring and restructuring other companies' assets requires an understanding of significant trade-offs. As in the ITW case, for example, success usually calls for a focus on mature, low-technology businesses because of the uncertainty of demand for high-technology products. In high-technology businesses, resource allocation decisions become too complex, creating information-processing overload on the small corporate headquarters offices that are common in unrelated diversified firms. High-technology businesses are often human-resource dependent; these people can leave or demand higher pay and thus appropriate or deplete the value of an acquired firm.[73]

Buying and then restructuring service-based assets so they can be profitably sold in the external market is also difficult. Here, sales often are a product of close personal relationships between a client and the representative of the firm being restructured. Thus, for both high-technology firms and service-based companies, relatively few tangible assets can be restructured to create value and profitably sold. It is difficult to restructure intangible assets such as human capital and effective relationships that have evolved over time between buyers (customers) and sellers (firm personnel).

Value-Neutral Diversification: Incentives and Resources

The objectives firms seek when using related diversification and unrelated diversification strategies all have the potential to help the firm create value by using a corporate-level strategy. However, these strategies, as well as single- and dominant-business diversification strategies, are sometimes used with value-neutral rather than value-creating objectives in mind. As we discuss next, different incentives to diversify sometimes surface, and the quality of the firm's resources may permit only diversification that is value neutral rather than value creating.

Revival of the Unrelated Strategy (Conglomerate): Small Firms Acquire Castoffs from Large Firms and Seek to Improve Their Value

Shareholders with significant ownership positions are exerting pressure on many large diversified firms to focus their portfolios and to divest previously high-selling brands, especially those

associated with a vast array of products. As these restructuring castoffs have become available, a number of small unrelated firms, besides private equity firms, have been purchasing them. Jarden Corporation, for instance, acquired Coleman Camping Goods in 2005 after its previous owner had gone into bankruptcy. At that point, Jarden's CEO Martin Franklin was able to transact a low price in a friendly takeover of this firm that had otherwise been pressured by competitors. Franklin stated, "We look for brands that are market leaders but haven't been innovative." Similar acquisitions by Jarden include Ball Canning Jars, Bicycle Playing Cards, and Crock-Pot Cookers.

Jarden Corporation has acquired many recognizable brand labels that it feels have the potential for renewed success with a bit of innovation.

Prestige Brands Holdings, Inc., is also a regular player in buying these castoffs. Prestige has been buying castoffs from large consumer product companies, such as Procter & Gamble, Unilever, and Colgate-Palmolive, as they sell their underperforming brands such as Sure and Right Guard deodorants, Comet Cleaner, Aqua Net standard products, Pert Plus Shampoo, and Rit Dye. Prestige also sought to revive Cutex Nail Polish Remover and Spic-n-Span cleaner, among other brands. Henkel KGaA, a German firm, follows a similar strategy. Under its Dial platform, it acquired Right Guard, Soft-n-Dry, and Dry Idea from Procter & Gamble (which it was later forced by the Federal Trade Commission to divest when it acquired Gillette). To differentiate Right Guard in its new brand, RGX, it sought to establish a target market of older men whereas TAG and Unilever's Axe brands battle over younger adolescent males.

Innovative Brands, in partnership with promotional agent Ten United, bought and revived old brands such as Cloraseptic Sore Throat Treatment and Pert Shampoo. This restructuring strategy is attractive to these firms because less money is required to get their products out on the shelves by reviving old brands than starting from scratch. However, one of the risks associated with this strategy is that retailers are often limited to holding just a few leading brands, plus their own private label brands, in their inventory. This practice often squeezes companies that have acquired these brands because powerful retailers such as Wal-Mart present them with narrowing shelf space opportunity.

This diversification strategy is not only found in consumer product industries, but also in the clothing, hardware, and tool industries. For instance CEO Mackey J. McDonald transformed VF Corporation from a manufacturer of Lee and Wrangler Jeans and Vanity Fair underwear labels into the largest apparel maker in the world. VF Brands also include Reef, JanSport, Nautica, and John Varvatos. VF Corporation seeks to maintain an entrepreneurial approach by keeping the founders of the business and managers, if possible, and giving them lots of autonomy, but at the same time alerting them that they will be under the tight financial control systems of the corporation to make sure that the entrepreneurs know how things will operate after the acquisition.

Illinois Tool Works (ITW) started out as a tool maker and tripled its size in the past decade to 750 business units worldwide. Its acquisition and diversification strategy focuses on small, low-margin but mature industrial businesses. Examples of its products include screws, auto parts, deli-slicers, and the plastic rings that hold together soft drink cans. It seeks to restructure each business it acquires in order to increase the business unit's profit margins

STRATEGY RIGHT NOW

by focusing on a narrowly defined product range and targeting the most lucrative products and customers using the 80/20 concept, where 80 percent of the revenues are derived by 20 percent of the customers. Most of its acquisitions are under $100 million, and the price is usually relatively cheap. The firms exampled in this strategic focus often seek to buy low, restructure, and operate, as well as selectively divest after the restructuring.

Sources: R. Brat, 2007, Turning managers into take over artists: How conglomerate ITW mints new deal makers to fuel its expansion, *Wall Street Journal*, April 6, A1, A8; E. Byron, 2007, How to turn trash into treasure, *Wall Street Journal*, April 13, B1, B2; A. Cordeiro, 2007, Jarden's bargain hunting wins fans on Wall Street, *Wall Street Journal*, May 23, B3; M. Kanellos, 2007, Corporate castoffs bring new light to VC, CNet News, http://www.news.com, April 11; R.A. Smith, 2007, Boss talk, A special report; VF's new man: (Strong entrepreneurs) + (Financial controls) = Growth, January 22, R4; 2007, Ten United to help revive Sure and Pert Plus: Agency to renew interest in two heritage brands, Press Release, http://www.tenunited.com, January 24; 2006, Henkel successfully concludes the acquisition of deodorant brands in the USA, Henkel Press Release Archive, http://www.henkel.com, May 2.

Incentives to Diversify

Incentives to diversify come from both the external environment and a firm's internal environment. External incentives include antitrust regulations and tax laws. Internal incentives include low performance, uncertain future cash flows, and the pursuit of synergy and reduction of risk for the firm.

Antitrust Regulation and Tax Laws

Government antitrust policies and tax laws provided incentives for U.S. firms to diversify in the 1960s and 1970s.[74] Antitrust laws prohibiting mergers that created increased market power (via either vertical or horizontal integration) were stringently enforced during that period.[75] Merger activity that produced conglomerate diversification was encouraged primarily by the Celler-Kefauver Antimerger Act (1950), which discouraged horizontal and vertical mergers. As a result, many of the mergers during the 1960s and 1970s were "conglomerate" in character, involving companies pursuing different lines of business. Between 1973 and 1977, 79.1 percent of all mergers were conglomerate.[76]

During the 1980s, antitrust enforcement lessened, resulting in more and larger horizontal mergers (acquisitions of target firms in the same line of business, such as a merger between two oil companies).[77] In addition, investment bankers became more open to the kinds of mergers facilitated by regulation changes; as a consequence, takeovers increased to unprecedented numbers.[78] The conglomerates, or highly diversified firms, of the 1960s and 1970s became more "focused" in the 1980s and early 1990s as merger constraints were relaxed and restructuring was implemented.[79]

In the late 1990s and early 2000s, antitrust concerns emerged again with the large volume of mergers and acquisitions (see Chapter 7).[80] Mergers are now receiving more scrutiny than they did in the 1980s and through the early 1990s.[81] For example, in the merger between P&G and Gillette (see the Opening Case), regulators required that each firm divest certain businesses before they were allowed to secure the deal.

The tax effects of diversification stem not only from corporate tax changes, but also from individual tax rates. Some companies (especially mature ones) generate more cash from their operations than they can reinvest profitably. Some argue that *free cash flows* (liquid financial assets for which investments in current businesses are no longer economically viable) should be redistributed to shareholders as dividends.[82] However, in the 1960s and 1970s, dividends were taxed more heavily than were capital gains. As a result, before 1980, shareholders preferred that firms use free cash flows to buy and build companies in high-performance industries. If the firm's stock value appreciated over the long term, shareholders might receive a better return on those funds than if the funds had been redistributed as dividends, because returns from stock sales would be taxed more lightly than dividends would.

Under the 1986 Tax Reform Act, however, the top individual ordinary income tax rate was reduced from 50 to 28 percent, and the special capital gains tax was changed to treat capital gains as ordinary income. These changes created an incentive for shareholders to stop encouraging firms to retain funds for purposes of diversification. These tax law changes also influenced an increase in divestitures of unrelated business units after 1984. Thus, while individual tax rates for capital gains and dividends created a shareholder incentive to increase diversification before 1986, they encouraged less diversification after 1986, unless it was funded by tax-deductible debt. The elimination of personal interest deductions, as well as the lower attractiveness of retained earnings to shareholders, might prompt the use of more leverage by firms, for which interest expense is tax deductible.

Corporate tax laws also affect diversification. Acquisitions typically increase a firm's depreciable asset allowances. Increased depreciation (a non-cash-flow expense) produces lower taxable income, thereby providing an additional incentive for acquisitions. Before 1986, acquisitions may have been the most attractive means for securing tax benefits,[83] but the 1986 Tax Reform Act diminished some of the corporate tax advantages of diversification.[84] The recent changes recommended by the Financial Accounting Standards Board—eliminating the "pooling of interests" method for accounting for the acquired firm's assets and eliminating the write-off for research and development in process—reduced some of the incentives to make acquisitions, especially acquisitions in related high-technology industries (these changes are discussed further in Chapter 7).[85]

Although federal regulations were loosened somewhat in the 1980s and then retightened in the late 1990s, a number of industries experienced increased merger activity due to industry-specific deregulation activity, including banking, telecommunications, oil and gas, and electric utilities. For instance, in banking the Garns–St. Germain Deposit Institutions Act of 1982 (GDIA) and the Competitive Equality Banking Act of 1987 (CEBA) reshaped the acquisition frequency in banking by relaxing the regulations that limited interstate bank acquisitions.[86] Regulations changes have also affected convergence between media and telecommunications industries, which has allowed a number of mergers, such as the successive Time Warner and AOL mergers. The Federal Communications Commission (FCC) made a highly contested ruling "allowing broadcasters to own TV stations that reach 45 percent of U.S. households, up from 35 percent, own three stations in the largest markets (up from two) and own a TV station and newspaper in the same town."[87] Thus, regulatory changes such as the ones we have described create incentives for diversification.

Low Performance

Some research shows that low returns are related to greater levels of diversification.[88] If "high performance eliminates the need for greater diversification,"[89] then low performance may provide an incentive for diversification. eBay looked to diversify beyond its auction business because its auction growth had slowed and it shut down its stand-alone Web sites in China and Japan. It then created a Web site for online shoppers called eBay Express. This site sells only fixed price items and appeals to online shoppers who are not comfortable bidding for items from a stranger. This business has not flourished as hoped and part of the problem may be eBay's image as an auction site and that some of the traditional customers prefer to have control over the purchase price. A large number of rivals, such as Amazon.com, which can offer low prices as well as free shipping, might also have reduced the success of the eBay Express diversification strategy.[90]

Research evidence and the experience of a number of firms suggest that an overall curvilinear relationship, as illustrated in Figure 6.3, may exist between diversification and performance.[91] Although low performance can be an incentive to

eBay's fixed-price site, eBay Express, hasn't flourished as its creators had hoped.

© AP Photo/Jae C. Hong

Figure 6.3 The Curvilinear Relationship between Diversification and Performance

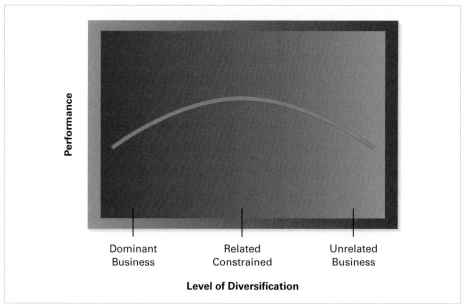

diversify, firms that are more broadly diversified compared to their competitors may have overall lower performance. Further, broadly based banks, such as Citigroup and UBS as noted earlier, have been under pressure to "break up" because they seem to underperform compared to their peer banks. Japanese firm Sanyo Electric felt the need to restructure because it had too many businesses to manage. Its portfolio ranged from Internet service providers, financial and recruiting services, a retirement home, and a golf course to semiconductors and batteries. Due to poor performance, Sanyo required a $2.6 billion restructuring loan from a consortium of lenders led by investment bank Goldman Sachs Group. Since 2004 when it began its restructuring, Sanyo has laid off 15 percent of its personnel, closed factories, and divested unprofitable businesses.[92]

Uncertain Future Cash Flows

As a firm's product line matures or is threatened, diversification may be taken as an important defensive strategy.[93] Small firms and companies in mature or maturing industries sometimes find it necessary to diversify for long-term survival.[94] For example, uncertainty was one of the dominant reasons for diversification among railroad firms during the 1960s and 1970s. Railroads diversified primarily because of the trucking industry's potential to substantially affect the rail business in a negative way. The trucking industry created uncertainty for railroad operators regarding the future levels of demand for their services.

Diversifying into other product markets or into other businesses can reduce the uncertainty about a firm's future cash flows. Thomson Corp., a large Canadian company, once owned 130 local newspapers across North America including Toronto's *Globe and Mail,* besides owning the *Times* of London in the United Kingdom. In 1997, the CEO saw two major threats: "the disappearance of its traditional small retailer advertisers across the United States, which were being gobbled up by large store chains, and the loss of classified-advertising revenue to the Internet."[95] Accordingly, the company embarked on a $30 billion acquisition strategy to move away from its dominant business. Thomson recently reached an agreement to purchase rival Reuters Group along with its other businesses, providing professionals with electronic data in finance, law, and health care.

Synergy and Firm Risk Reduction

Diversified firms pursuing economies of scope often have investments that are too inflexible to realize synergy between business units. As a result, a number of problems may arise. **Synergy** exists when the value created by business units working together exceeds the value that those same units create working independently. But as a firm increases its relatedness between business units, it also increases its risk of corporate failure, because synergy produces joint interdependence between businesses that constrains the firm's flexibility to respond. This threat may force two basic decisions.

First, the firm may reduce its level of technological change by operating in environments that are more certain. This behavior may make the firm risk averse and thus uninterested in pursuing new product lines that have potential, but are not proven. Alternatively, the firm may constrain its level of activity sharing and forgo synergy's potential benefits. Either or both decisions may lead to further diversification. The former would lead to related diversification into industries in which more certainty exists. The latter may produce additional, but unrelated, diversification.[96] Research suggests that a firm using a related diversification strategy is more careful in bidding for new businesses, whereas a firm pursuing an unrelated diversification strategy may be more likely to overprice its bid, because an unrelated bidder may not have full information about the acquired firm.[97] However, firms using either a related or an unrelated diversification strategy must understand the consequences of paying large premiums. For example, even though the P&G and Gillette transaction is being viewed positively, as noted in the Opening Case, the annual growth rate of Gillette's product lines in the newly created company will need to average 12.1 percent or more for P&G's shareholders to benefit financially from the additional diversification resulting from this merger.[98]

Resources and Diversification

As already discussed, firms may have several value-neutral incentives as well as value-creating incentives (such as the ability to create economies of scope) to diversify. However, even when incentives to diversify exist, a firm must have the types and levels of resources and capabilities needed to successfully use a corporate-level diversification strategy.[99] Although both tangible and intangible resources facilitate diversification, they vary in their ability to create value. Indeed, the degree to which resources are valuable, rare, difficult to imitate, and nonsubstitutable (see Chapter 3) influence a firm's ability to create value through diversification. For instance, free cash flows are a tangible, financial resource that may be used to diversify the firm. However, compared with diversification that is grounded in intangible resources, diversification based on financial resources only is more visible to competitors and thus more imitable and less likely to create value on a long-term basis.[100]

Tangible resources usually include the plant and equipment necessary to produce a product and tend to be less-flexible assets. Any excess capacity often can be used only for closely related products, especially those requiring highly similar manufacturing technologies. For example, some firms in the memory chip-making business examined the market and found that demand for standard memory products for DRAMs (Dynamic Random-Access Memory chips) used in personal computers was likely to decrease. Some firms such as Samsung Electronics and Hynix Semiconductors, both from South Korea, diversified their businesses into NAND flash memory chips used in MP3 players, digital cameras, and other products based on the their tangible assets in manufacturing chips. The chip makers who diversified into flash chips performed better than those who maintained their focus on DRAM chip output including U.S. firm Micron Technology, Germany's Infineon AG, and Japan's Elpida Memory. As such, Samsung and Hynix earnings were cushioned by the higher profit margins from the NAND product.[101]

Excess capacity of other tangible resources, such as a sales force, can be used to diversify more easily. Again, excess capacity in a sales force is more effective with related diversification, because it may be utilized to sell similar products. The sales force would be more knowledgeable about related-product characteristics, customers, and distribution channels.[102] Tangible resources may create resource interrelationships in

Synergy exists when the value created by business units working together exceeds the value that those same units create working independently.

production, marketing, procurement, and technology, defined earlier as activity sharing. Intangible resources are more flexible than tangible physical assets in facilitating diversification. Although the sharing of tangible resources may induce diversification, intangible resources such as tacit knowledge could encourage even more diversification.[103]

Sometimes, however, the benefits expected from using resources to diversify the firm for either value-creating or value-neutral reasons are not gained.[104] For example, as noted in the Opening Case, implementing operational relatedness has been difficult for P&G and Gillette in recasting the Crest Pro-Health brand, creating jointly marketed dental hygiene products (e.g., toothpaste and toothbrushes). Also, Sara Lee found that it could not realize synergy between its diversified portfolio and subsequently shed businesses accounting for 40 percent of is revenue to focus on food and food-related products to more readily achieve synergy.[105]

Value-Reducing Diversification: Managerial Motives to Diversify

Managerial motives to diversify can exist independently of value-neutral reasons (i.e., incentives and resources) and value-creating reasons (e.g., economies of scope). The desire for increased compensation and reduced managerial risk are two motives for top-level executives to diversify their firm beyond value-creating and value-neutral levels.[106] In slightly different words, top-level executives may diversify a firm in order to diversify their own employment risk, as long as profitability does not suffer excessively.[107]

Diversification provides additional benefits to top-level managers that shareholders do not enjoy. Research evidence shows that diversification and firm size are highly correlated, and as firm size increases, so does executive compensation.[108] Because large firms are complex, difficult-to-manage organizations, top-level managers commonly receive substantial levels of compensation to lead them.[109] Greater levels of diversification can increase a firm's complexity, resulting in still more compensation for executives to lead an increasingly diversified organization. Governance mechanisms, such as the board of directors, monitoring by owners, executive compensation practices, and the market for corporate control, may limit managerial tendencies to overdiversify. These mechanisms are discussed in more detail in Chapter 10.

In some instances, though, a firm's governance mechanisms may not be strong, resulting in a situation in which executives may diversify the firm to the point that it fails to earn even average returns.[110] The loss of adequate internal governance may result in poor relative performance, thereby triggering a threat of takeover. Although takeovers may improve efficiency by replacing ineffective managerial teams, managers may avoid takeovers through defensive tactics, such as "poison pills," or may reduce their own exposure with "golden parachute" agreements.[111] Therefore, an external governance threat, although restraining managers, does not flawlessly control managerial motives for diversification.[112]

Most large publicly held firms are profitable because the managers leading them are positive stewards of firm resources, and many of their strategic actions, including those related to selecting a corporate-level diversification strategy, contribute to the firm's success.[113] As mentioned, governance mechanisms should be designed to deal with exceptions to the managerial norms of making decisions and taking actions that will increase the firm's ability to earn above-average returns. Thus, it is overly pessimistic to assume that managers usually act in their own self-interest as opposed to their firm's interest.[114]

Top-level executives' diversification decisions may also be held in check by concerns for their reputation. If a positive reputation facilitates development and use of managerial power, a poor reputation may reduce it. Likewise, a strong external market for managerial talent may deter managers from pursuing inappropriate diversification.[115] In addition, a diversified firm may police other firms by acquiring those that are poorly managed in order to restructure its own asset base. Knowing that their firms could be acquired if they are not managed successfully encourages executives to use value-creating, diversification strategies.

As shown in Figure 6.4, the level of diversification that can be expected to have the greatest positive effect on performance is based partly on how the interaction of resources, managerial motives, and incentives affects the adoption of particular diversification strategies. As indicated earlier, the greater the incentives and the more flexible the resources, the higher the level of expected diversification. Financial resources (the most flexible) should have a stronger relationship to the extent of diversification than either tangible or intangible resources. Tangible resources (the most inflexible) are useful primarily for related diversification.

As discussed in this chapter, firms can create more value by effectively using diversification strategies. However, diversification must be kept in check by corporate governance (see Chapter 10). Appropriate strategy implementation tools, such as organizational structures, are also important (see Chapter 11).

We have described corporate-level strategies in this chapter. In the next one, we discuss mergers and acquisitions as prominent means for firms to diversify and to grow profitably while doing so.[116] These trends toward more diversification through acquisitions, which have been partially reversed due to restructuring (see Chapter 7), indicate that learning has taken place regarding corporate-level diversification strategies.[117] Accordingly, firms that diversify should do so cautiously, choosing to focus on relatively few, rather than many, businesses. In fact, research suggests that although unrelated diversification has decreased, related diversification has increased, possibly due to the

Figure 6.4 Summary Model of the Relationship between Diversification and Firm Performance

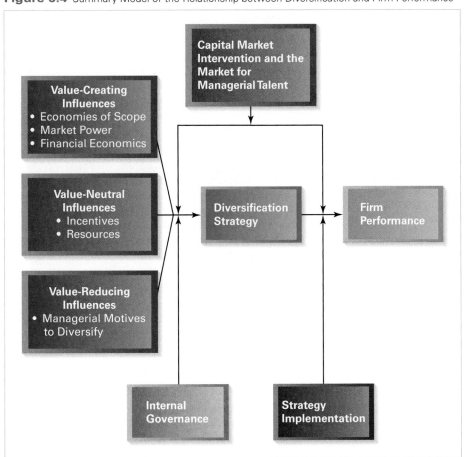

Source: Adapted from R. E. Hoskisson & M. A. Hitt, 1990, Antecedents and performance outcomes of diversification: A review and critique of theoretical perspectives, *Journal of Management,* 16: 498.

restructuring that continued into the 1990s and early twenty-first century. This sequence of diversification followed by restructuring is now taking place in Europe and other places such as Korea, mirroring actions of firms in the United States and the United Kingdom.[118] Firms can improve their strategic competitiveness when they pursue a level of diversification that is appropriate for their resources (especially financial resources) and core competencies and the opportunities and threats in their country's institutional and competitive environments.[119]

Summary

- The primary reason a firm uses a corporate-level strategy to become more diversified is to create additional value. Using a single- or dominant-business corporate-level strategy may be preferable to seeking a more diversified strategy, unless a corporation can develop economies of scope or financial economies between businesses, or unless it can obtain market power through additional levels of diversification. Economies of scope and market power are the main sources of value creation when the firm diversifies by using a corporate-level strategy with moderate to high levels of diversification.

- The corporate-level strategy of related diversification helps the firm to create value by sharing activities or transferring competencies between different businesses in the company's portfolio.

- Sharing activities usually involves sharing tangible resources between businesses. Transferring core competencies involves transferring core competencies developed in one business to another business. It also may involve transferring competencies between the corporate headquarter's office and a business unit.

- Sharing activities is usually associated with the related constrained diversification corporate-level strategy. Activity sharing is costly to implement and coordinate, may create unequal benefits for the divisions involved in the sharing, and may lead to fewer managerial risk-taking behaviors.

- Transferring core competencies is often associated with related linked (or mixed related and unrelated) diversification,

although firms pursuing both sharing activities and transferring core competencies can also use the related linked strategy.

- Efficiently allocating resources or restructuring a target firm's assets and placing them under rigorous financial controls are two ways to accomplish successful unrelated diversification. Firms using the unrelated diversification strategy focus on creating financial economies to generate value.

- Diversification is sometimes pursued for value-neutral reasons. Incentives from tax and antitrust government policies, performance disappointments, or uncertainties about future cash flow are examples of value-neutral reasons that firms may choose to become more diversified.

- Managerial motives to diversify (including to increase compensation) can lead to overdiversification and a subsequent reduction in a firm's ability to create value. Evidence suggests, however, that certainly the majority of top-level executives seek to be good stewards of the firm's assets and to avoid diversifying the firm in ways and amounts that destroy value.

- Managers need to pay attention to their firm's internal organization and its external environment when making decisions about the optimum level of diversification for their company. Of course, internal resources are important determinants of the direction that diversification should take. However, conditions in the firm's external environment may facilitate additional levels of diversification, as might unexpected threats from competitors.

Review Questions

1. What is corporate-level strategy and why is it important?

2. What are the different levels of diversification firms can pursue by using different corporate-level strategies?

3. What are three reasons firms choose to diversify their operations?

4. How do firms create value when using a related diversification strategy?

5. What are the two ways to obtain financial economies when using an unrelated diversification strategy?

6. What incentives and resources encourage diversification?

7. What motives might encourage managers to overdiversify their firm?

1. M. E. Porter, 1980, *Competitive Strategy,* New York: The Free Press, xvi.

2. A. Pehrsson, 2006, Business relatedness and performance: A study of managerial perceptions, *Strategic Management Journal,* 27: 265–282.

3. N. J. Moss, 2005, The relative value of growth, *Harvard Business Review,* 83(4): 102–112.

4. M. E. Porter, 1987, From competitive advantage to corporate strategy, *Harvard Business Review,* 65(3): 43–59.

5. Ibid.; C. A. Montgomery, 1994, Corporate diversification, *Journal of Economic Perspectives,* 8: 163–178.

6. J. R. Hough, 2006, Business segment performance redux: A multilevel approach, *Strategic Management Journal,* 27: 45–61; M. Kwak, 2002, Maximizing value through diversification, *MIT Sloan Management Review,* 43(2): 10.

7. M. Ammann & M. Verhofen, 2006, The conglomerate discount: A new explanation based on credit risk, 9(8): 1201–1214; S. A. Mansi & D. M. Reeb, 2002, Corporate diversification: What gets discounted? *Journal of Finance,* 57: 2167–2183; C. C. Markides & P. J. Williamson, 1996, Corporate diversification and organizational structure: A resource-based view, *Academy of Management Journal,* 39: 340–367.

8. C. E. Helfat & K. M. Eisenhardt, 2004, Intertemporal economies of scope organizational modularity, and the dynamics of diversification, *Strategic Management Journal,* 25: 1217–1232.

9. A. Campbell, M. Goold, & M. Alexander, 1995, Corporate strategy: The question for parenting advantage, *Harvard Business Review,* 73(2): 120–132.

10. D. Collis, D. Young, & M. Goold, 2007, The size, structure, and performance of corporate headquarters, *Strategic Management Journal,* 28: 283–405; M. Goold & A. Campbell, 2002, Parenting in complex structures, *Long Range Planning,* 35(3): 219–243; T. H. Brush, P. Bromiley, & M. Hendrickx, 1999, The relative influence of industry and corporation on business segment performance: An alternative estimate, *Strategic Management Journal,* 20: 519–547.

11. D. Miller, 2006, Technological diversity, related diversification, and firm performance, *Strategic Management Journal,* 27: 601–619; D. J. Miller, 2004, Firms' technological resources and the performance effects of diversification: A longitudinal study, *Strategic Management Journal,* 25: 1097–1119.

12. D. D. Bergh, 2001, Diversification strategy research at a crossroads: Established, emerging and anticipated paths, in M. A. Hitt, R. E. Freeman, & J. S. Harrison (eds.), *Handbook of Strategic Management,* Oxford, UK: Blackwell Publishers, 363–383.

13. H. C. Wang & J. B. Barney, 2006, Employee incentives to make firm-specific investments: Implications for resource-based theories of corporate diversification, *Academy of Management Journal,* 31: 466–476.

14. A. J. Ward, M. J. Lankau, A. C. Amason, J. A. Sonnenfeld, & B. R. Agle, 2007, Improving the performance of top management teams, *MIT Sloan Management Review,* 48(3): 85–90.

15. R. P. Rumelt, *Strategy, Structure, and Economic Performance,* Boston: Harvard Business School, 1974; L. Wrigley, 1970, *Divisional Autonomy and Diversification* (Ph.D. dissertation), Harvard Business School.

16. J. Christy, R. Cox, & A. Currie, 2007, Wrigley is in a sticky spot, *Wall Street Journal,* April 4, C12.

17. A. Ward, 2006, UPS tries to boost delivery to investors; parcels group has struggled to integrate acquisitions and justify its strategy since going public, *Financial Times,* November 28, 21.

18. J. Spencer, 2007, Hutchison's Li Looks to make well-timed exit; Indian wireless assets may yield a windfall; a bigger risk to buyers, *Wall Street Journal,* January 29, B4.

19. 2007, What has Superman got up his sleeve? *Euroweek,* February 23, 1.

20. S. W. Geiger & L. H. Cashen, 2007, Organizational size and CEO compensation: The moderating effect of diversification in downscoping organizations, *Journal of Managerial Issues,* 9(2): 233–252; R. K. Aggarwal & A. A. Samwick, 2003, Why do managers diversify their firms? Agency reconsidered, *Journal of Finance,* 58: 71–118.

21. D. J. Miller, M. J. Fern, & L. B. Cardinal, 2007, The use of knowledge for technological innovation within diversified firms, *Academy of Management Journal,* 50: 308–326.

22. M. S. Gary, 2005, Implementation strategy and performance outcomes in related diversification, *Strategic Management Journal,* 26: 643–664; H. Tanriverdi & N. Venkatraman, 2005, Knowledge relatedness and the performance of multibusiness firms, *Strategic Management Journal,* 26: 97–119.

23. H. Tanriverdi, 2006, Performance effects of information technology synergies in multibusiness firms, *MIS Quarterly,* 30(1): 57–78.

24. M. E. Porter, 1985, *Competitive Advantage,* New York: The Free Press, 328.

25. D. Miller, 2006, Technological diversity, related diversification, and firm performance, *Strategic Management Journal,* 27: 601–619.

26. E. Byron, 2007, Merger challenge: Unite toothbrush, toothpaste: P&G and Gillette find creating synergy can be harder than it looks, *Wall Street Journal,* April 24, A1, A17.

27. Tanriverdi, Performance effects of information technology synergies in multibusiness firms; D. Gupta & Y. Gerchak, 2002, Quantifying operational synergies in a merger/acquisition, *Management Science,* 48: 517–533.

28. M. L. Marks & P. H. Mirvis, 2000, Managing mergers, acquisitions, and alliances: Creating an effective transition structure, *Organizational Dynamics,* 28(3): 35–47.

29. P. Puranam & K Srikanth, 2007, What they know vs. what they do: How acquirers leverage technology acquisitions, *Strategic Management Journal,* 28: 805–825; C. Park, 2003, Prior performance characteristics of related and unrelated acquirers, *Strategic Management Journal,* 24: 471–480; G. Delong, 2001, Stockholder gains from focusing versus diversifying bank mergers, *Journal of Financial Economics,* 2: 221–252; T. H. Brush, 1996, Predicted change in operational synergy and post-acquisition performance of acquired businesses, *Strategic Management Journal,* 17.

30. D. D. Bergh, 1995, Size and relatedness of units sold: An agency theory and resource-based perspective, *Strategic Management Journal,* 16: 221–239.

31. M. Lubatkin & S. Chatterjee, 1994, Extending modern portfolio theory into the domain of corporate diversification: Does it apply? *Academy of Management Journal,* 37: 109–136.

32. A. Van Oijen, 2001, Product diversification, corporate management instruments, resource sharing, and performance, *Academy of Management Best Paper Proceedings* (on CD-ROM, Business Policy and Strategy Division); T. Kono, 1999, A strong head office makes a strong company, *Long Range Planning,* 32(2): 225.

33. Puranam & Srikanth, What they know vs. what they do; F. T. Rothaermel, M. A. Hitt, & L. A. Jobe, 2006, Balancing vertical integration and strategic outsourcing: effects on product portfolio, product success, and firm performance, *Strategic Management Journal,* 27: 1033–1056; L. Capron, P. Dussauge, & W. Mitchell, 1998, Resource redeployment following horizontal acquisitions in Europe and the United States, 1988–1992, *Strategic Management Journal,* 19: 631–661; S. Chatterjee & B. Wernerfelt, 1991, The link between resources and type of diversification: Theory and evidence,

Strategic Management Journal, 12: 33–48.

34. S. Dutta, M. J. Zbaracki, & M. Bergen, 2003, Pricing process as a capability: A resource-based perspective, *Strategic Management Journal*, 24: 615–630.

35. A. Rodríguez-Duarte, F. D. Sandulli, B. Minguela-Rata, & J. I. López-Sánchez, 2007, The endogenous relationship between innovation and diversification, and the impact of technological resources on the form of diversification, *Research Policy*, 36: 652–664; L. Capron & N. Pistre, 2002, When do acquirers earn abnormal returns? *Strategic Management Journal*, 23: 781–794.

36. C. Lawton, 2007, H-P begins push into high-end copiers, *Wall Street Journal*, April 24, B3.

37. Miller, Fern, & Cardinal, The use of knowledge for technological innovation within diversified firms; J. W. Spencer, 2003, Firms' knowledge-sharing strategies in the global innovation system: Empirical evidence from the flat panel display industry, *Strategic Management Journal*, 24: 217–233.

38. 2007, Virgin Group Ltd., *Hoovers*, www.hoovers.com, July 6.

39. 2007, Thermo Fisher Scientific, Thermo Fisher Scientiific Home Page, www.thermofisher.com, July 6.

40. 2007, Honda engines, Honda Motor Company Home Page, http://www.honda.com, July 6.

41. L. C. Thang, C. Rowley, T. Quang, & M. Warner, 2007, To what extent can management practices be transferred between countries?: The case of human resource management in Vietnam, *Journal of World Business*, 42(1): 113–127; G. Stalk Jr., 2005, Rotate the core, *Harvard Business Review*, 83(3): 18–19.

42. S. Chatterjee & J. Singh, 1999, Are trade-offs inherent in diversification moves? A simultaneous model for type of diversification and mode of expansion decisions, *Management Science*, 45: 25–41.

43. J. Whalen, 2007, Nestle Bolsters baby-food line, *Wall Street Journal*, April 12, A3.

44. Bergh, Diversification strategy research at a crossroads, 369.

45. L. Fuentelsaz & J. Gomez, 2006, Multi-point competition, strategic similarity and entry into geographic markets, *Strategic Management Journal*, 27: 477–499; J. Gimeno & C. Y. Woo, 1999, Multimarket contact, economies of scope, and firm performance, *Academy of Management Journal*, 42: 239–259.

46. R. Kwong, 2007, Big four hope expansion will deliver the goods, *Financial Times*, May 23, 15.

47. T. A. Shervani, G. Frazier, & G. Challagalla, 2007, The moderating influence of firm market power on the transaction cost economics model: An empirical test in a forward channel integration context, *Strategic Management Journal*, 28: 635–652; R. Gulati, P. R. Lawrence, & P. Puranam,

2005, Adaptation in vertical relationships: Beyond incentive conflict, *Strategic Management Journal*, 26: 415–440.

48. D. A. Griffin, A. Chandra, & T. Fealey, 2005, Strategically employing natural channels in an emerging market, *Thunderbird International Business Review*, 47(3): 287–311; A. Darr & I. Talmud, 2003, The structure of knowledge and seller-buyer networks in markets for emergent technologies, *Organization Studies*, 24: 443–461.

49. R. Carter & G. M. Hodgson, 2006, The impact of empirical tests of transaction cost economics on the debate on the nature of the firm, *Strategic Management Journal*, 27: 461–476; O. E. Williamson, 1996, Economics and organization: A primer, *California Management Review*, 38(2): 131–146.

50. Rothaermel, Hitt, & Jobe, Balancing vertical integration and strategic outsourcing; M. G. Jacobides, 2005, Industry change through vertical disintegration: How and why markets emerged in mortgage banking, *Academy of Management Journal*, 48: 465–498.

51. W. D. Brin, 2007, Earnings digest—Health care: As rivals tussle, Medco sees gains; drug-benefit manager cites competitive edge due to business model, *Wall Street Journal*, February 22, C6.

52. L. R. Kopczak & M. E. Johnson, 2003, The supply-chain management effect, *MIT Sloan Management Review*, 3: 27–34; K.R. Harrigan, 2001, Strategic flexibility in the old and new economies, in M. A. Hitt, R. E. Freeman, & J. S. Harrison (eds.), *Handbook of Strategic Management*, Oxford, UK: Blackwell Publishers, 97–123.

53. G. Smith, 2007, Factories go south. So does pay; Mexico's auto industry is booming, but parts outsourcing is keeping a lid on wages, *BusinessWeek*, April 9, 76.

54. D. Clark, 2007, Flextronics-Solectron deal unites assembling titans, *Wall Street Journal*, June 5, A3.

55. P. Kothandaraman & D. T. Wilson, 2001, The future of competition: Value-creating networks, *Industrial Marketing Management*, 30: 379–389.

56. K. M. Eisenhardt & D. C. Galunic, 2000, Coevolving: At last, a way to make synergies work, *Harvard Business Review*, 78(1): 91–111.

57. A. Willem, 2006, The role of inter-unit coordination mechanisms in knowledge sharing: A case study of a British MNC, *Journal of Information Scinece*, 32: 539–561; R. Schoenberg, 2001, Knowledge transfer and resource sharing as value creation mechanisms in inbound continental European acquisitions, *Journal of Euro-Marketing*, 10: 99–114.

58. M. Marr, 2007, The magic kingdom looks to hit the road, *Wall Street Journal*, http://www.wsj.com, February 8.

59. E. Taylor & J. Singer, 2007, New UBS chief keeps strategy intact, *Wall Street Journal*, July 7, A3.

60. 2007, Breakingviews.com: Citi to world: Drop "group," *Wall Street Journal*, January 17, C16.

61. D. D. Bergh, 1997, Predicting divestiture of unrelated acquisitions: An integrative model of ex ante conditions, *Strategic Management Journal*, 18: 715–731; C. W. L. Hill, 1994, Diversification and economic performance: Bringing structure and corporate management back into the picture, in R. P. Rumelt, D. E. Schendel, & D. J. Teece (eds.), *Fundamental Issues in Strategy*, Boston: Harvard Business School Press, 297–321.

62. Porter, *Competitive Advantage*.

63. D. Collis, D. Young, & M. Goold, 2007, The size, structure, and performance of corporate headquarters, *Strategic Management Journal*, 28: 283–405; O. E. Williamson, 1975, *Markets and Hierarchies: Analysis and Antitrust Implications*, New York: Macmillan Free Press.

64. R. J. Indjejikian, 2007, Discussion of accounting information, disclosure, and the cost of capital, *Journal of Accounting Research*, 45(2): 421–426.

65. D. Miller, R. Eisenstat, & N. Foote, 2002, Strategy from the inside out: Building capability-creating organizations, *California Management Review*, 44(3): 37–54; M. E. Raynor & J. L. Bower, 2001, Lead from the center: How to manage divisions dynamically, *Harvard Business Review*, 79(5): 92–100; P. Taylor & J. Lowe, 1995, A note on corporate strategy and capital structure, *Strategic Management Journal*, 16: 411–414.

66. K. Kranhold, 2007, GE report raises doubts, *Wall Street Journal*, January 20–21, A3.

67. J. Lunsford & B. Steinberg, 2006, Conglomerates' conundrum, *Wall Street Journal*, B1, B7.

68. F. Guerrera, Siemens chief makes the case for conglomerates, *Financial Times*, http://www.ft.com, February 5.

69. M. W. Peng & A. Delios, 2006, What determines the scope of the firm over time and around the world? An Asia Pacific perspective, *Asia Pacific Journal of Management*, 23: 385–405; T. Khanna, K. G. Palepu, & J. Sinha, 2005, Strategies that fit emerging markets, *Harvard Business Review*, 83(6): 63–76.

70. A. Chakrabarti, K. Singh, & I. Mahmood, 2006, Diversification and performance: Evidence from East Asian firms, *Strategic Management Journal*, 28: 101–120. T. Khanna & K. Palepu, 2000, Is group affiliation profitable in emerging markets? An analysis of diversified Indian business groups, *Journal of Finance*, 55: 867–892; T. Khanna & K. Palepu, 2000, The future of business groups in emerging markets: Long-run evidence from Chile, *Academy of Management Journal*, 43: 268–285.

71. C. Decker & M. Mellewigt, 2007, Thirty years after Michael E. Porter: What do we know about business exit? *Academy of Management Perspectives*, 2: 41–55; R. E. Hoskisson, R. A. Johnson, D. Yiu, & W. P. Wan, 2001, Restructuring

strategies and diversified business groups: Differences associated with country institutional environments, in M. A. Hitt, R. E. Freeman, & J. S. Harrison (eds.), *Handbook of Strategic Management,* Oxford, UK: Blackwell Publishers, 433–463; S. J. Chang & H. Singh, 1999, The impact of entry and resource fit on modes of exit by multibusiness firms, *Strategic Management Journal,* 20: 1019–1035.

72. W. Ng & C. de Cock, 2002, Battle in the boardroom: A discursive perspective, *Journal of Management Studies,* 39: 23–49.

73. R. Coff, 2003, Bidding wars over R&D-intensive firms: Knowledge, opportunism, and the market for corporate control, *Academy of Management Journal,* 46: 74–85.

74. M. Lubatkin, H. Merchant, & M. Srinivasan, 1997, Merger strategies and shareholder value during times of relaxed antitrust enforcement: The case of large mergers during the 1980s, *Journal of Management,* 23: 61–81.

75. D. P. Champlin & J. T. Knoedler, 1999, Restructuring by design? Government's complicity in corporate restructuring, *Journal of Economic Issues,* 33(1): 41–57.

76. R. M. Scherer & D. Ross, 1990, *Industrial Market Structure and Economic Performance,* Boston: Houghton Mifflin.

77. A. Shleifer & R. W. Vishny, 1994, Takeovers in the 1960s and 1980s: Evidence and implications, in R. P. Rumelt, D. E. Schendel, & D. J. Teece (eds.), *Fundamental Issues in Strategy,* Boston: Harvard Business School Press, 403–422.

78. S. Chatterjee, J. S. Harrison, & D. D. Bergh, 2003, Failed takeover attempts, corporate governance and refocusing, *Strategic Management Journal,* 24: 87–96; Lubatkin, Merchant, & Srinivasan, Merger strategies and shareholder value; D. J. Ravenscraft & R. M. Scherer, 1987, *Mergers, Sell-Offs and Economic Efficiency,* Washington, DC: Brookings Institution, 22.

79. D. A. Zalewski, 2001, Corporate takeovers, fairness, and public policy, *Journal of Economic Issues,* 35: 431–437; P. L. Zweig, J. P. Kline, S. A. Forest, & K. Gudridge, 1995, The case against mergers, *BusinessWeek,* October 30, 122–130; J. R. Williams, B. L. Paez, & L. Sanders, 1988, Conglomerates revisited, *Strategic Management Journal,* 9: 403–414.

80. E. J. Lopez, 2001, New anti-merger theories: A critique, *Cato Journal,* 20: 359–378; 1998, The trustbusters' new tools, *The Economist,* May 2, 62–64.

81. R. Croyle & P. Kager, 2002, Giving mergers a head start, *Harvard Business Review,* 80(10): 20–21.

82. M. C. Jensen, 1986, Agency costs of free cash flow, corporate finance, and takeovers, *American Economic Review,* 76: 323–329.

83. R. Gilson, M. Scholes, & M. Wolfson, 1988, Taxation and the dynamics of corporate control: The uncertain case for tax motivated acquisitions, in J. C. Coffee, L. Lowenstein, & S. Rose-Ackerman (eds.), *Knights, Raiders, and Targets: The Impact of the Hostile Takeover,* New York: Oxford University Press, 271–299.

84. C. Steindel, 1986, Tax reform and the merger and acquisition market: The repeal of the general utilities, *Federal Reserve Bank of New York Quarterly Review,* 11(3): 31–35.

85. M. A. Hitt, J. S. Harrison, & R. D. Ireland, 2001, *Mergers and Acquisitions: A Guide to Creating Value for Stakeholders,* New York: Oxford University Press.

86. J. Haleblian; J.-Y. Kim, & N. Rajagopalan, 2006, The influence of acquisition experience and performance on acquisition behavior: Evidence from the U.S. commercial banking industry, *Academy of Management Journal,* 49: 357–370.

87. D. B. Wilkerson & R. Britt, 2003, It's showtime for media deals: Radio lessons fuel debate over control of TV, newspapers, *MarketWatch,* http://www.marketwatch.com, May 30.

88. J. M. Shaver, 2006, A paradox of synergy: Contagion and capacity effects in mergers and acquisitions, *Academy of Management Journal,* 31: 962–976; C. Park, 2002, The effects of prior performance on the choice between related and unrelated acquisitions: Implications for the performance consequences of diversification strategy, *Journal of Management Studies,* 39: 1003–1019.

89. Rumelt, *Strategy, Structure and Economic Performance,* 125.

90. V. Vara, 2006, eBay's bid to go beyond auctions isn't selling well, *Wall Street Journal,* December 20, B1.

91. L. E. Palich, L. B. Cardinal, & C. C. Miller, 2000, Curvilinearity in the diversification-performance linkage: An examination of over three decades of research, *Strategic Management Journal,* 21: 155–174.

92. Y. I. Kane, 2007, Sanyo ends era of family rule, *Wall Street Journal,* March 29, B4.

93. D. G. Sirmon, M. A. Hitt, & R. D. Ireland, 2007, Managing firm resources in dynamic environments to create value: Looking inside the black box, *Academy of Management Review,* 32: 273–292; A. E. Bernardo & B. Chowdhry, 2002, Resources, real options, and corporate strategy, *Journal of Financial Economics,* 63: 211–234.

94. N. W. C. Harper & S. P. Viguerie, 2002, Are you too focused? *McKinsey Quarterly,* Mid-Summer, 29–38; J. C. Sandvig & L. Coakley, 1998, Best practices in small firm diversification, *Business Horizons,* 41(3): 33–40; C. G. Smith & A. C. Cooper, 1988, Established companies diversifying into young industries: A comparison of firms with different levels of performance, *Strategic Management Journal,* 9: 111–121.

95. C. Bryan-Low, 2007, How old Thomson stayed fresh, *Wall Street Journal,* June 12, A10.

96. N. M. Kay & A. Diamantopoulos, 1987, Uncertainty and synergy: Towards a formal model of corporate strategy, *Managerial and Decision Economics,* 8: 121–130.

97. R. W. Coff, 1999, How buyers cope with uncertainty when acquiring firms in knowledge-intensive industries: Caveat emptor, *Organization Science,* 10: 144–161.

98. S. Tully, 2005, The urge to merge, *Fortune,* February 21, 21–22.

99. S. J. Chatterjee & B. Wernerfelt, 1991, The link between resources and type of diversification: Theory and evidence, *Strategic Management Journal,* 12: 33–48.

100. W. Keuslein, 2003, The Ebitda folly, *Forbes,* March 17, 165–167; Kochhar & Hitt, Linking corporate strategy to capital structure.

101. Y.-H. Kim, 2005, Chipmakers find diversity pays, *Wall Street Journal,* August 4, B4.

102. L. Capron & J. Hulland, 1999, Redeployment of brands, sales forces, and general marketing management expertise following horizontal acquisitions: A resource-based view, *Journal of Marketing,* 63(2): 41–54.

103. A. M. Knott, D. J. Bryce, & H. E. Posen, 2003, On the strategic accumulation of intangible assets, *Organization Science,* 14: 192–207; J. Castillo, 2002, A note on the concept of tacit knowledge, *Journal of Management Inquiry,* 11(1): 46–57; R. D. Smith, 2000, Intangible strategic assets and firm performance: A multi-industry study of the resource-based view, *Journal of Business Strategies,* 17(2): 91–117.

104. K. Shimizu & M. A. Hitt, 2005, What constrains or facilitates divestitures of formerly acquired firms? The effects of organizational inertia, *Journal of Management,* 31: 50–72.

105. J. Jargon & J. Vuocolo, 2007, Sara Lee CEO challenged on antitakeover defenses, *Wall Street Journal,* May 11, B4.

106. J. G. Combs & M. S. Skill, 2003, Managerialist and human capital explanation for key executive pay premiums: A contingency perspective, *Academy of Management Journal,* 46: 63–73; M. A. Geletkanycz, B. K. Boyd, & S. Finkelstein, 2001, The strategic value of CEO external directorate networks: Implications for CEO compensation, *Strategic Management Journal,* 9: 889–898; W. Grossman & R. E. Hoskisson, 1998, CEO pay at the crossroads of Wall Street and Main: Toward the strategic design of executive compensation, *Academy of Management Executive,* 12(1): 43–57.

107. W. Shen & A. A. Cannella Jr., 2002, Power dynamics within top management and their impacts on CEO dismissal followed by inside succession, *Academy of Management Journal,* 45: 1195–1206; P. J. Lane, A. A. Cannella Jr., & M. H. Lubatkin, 1998, Agency problems

as antecedents to unrelated mergers and diversification: Amihud and Lev reconsidered, *Strategic Management Journal,* 19: 555–578; D. L. May, 1995, Do managerial motives influence firm risk reduction strategies? *Journal of Finance,* 50: 1291–1308.

108. Geiger & Cashen, Organizational size and CEO compensation; J. J. Cordeiro & R. Veliyath, 2003, Beyond pay for performance: A panel study of the determinants of CEO compensation, *American Business Review,* 21(1): 56–66; Wright, Kroll, & Elenkov, Acquisition returns, increase in firm size, and chief executive officer compensation; S. R. Gray & A. A. Cannella Jr., 1997, The role of risk in executive compensation, *Journal of Management,* 23: 517–540.

109. R. Bliss & R. Rosen, 2001, CEO compensation and bank mergers, *Journal of Financial Economics,* 1: 107–138; W. G. Sanders & M. A. Carpenter, 1998, Internationalization and firm governance: The roles of CEO compensation, top team composition, and board structure, *Academy of Management Journal,* 41: 158–178.

110. J. J. Janney, 2002, Eat or get eaten? How equity ownership and diversification shape CEO risk-taking, *Academy of Management Executive,* 14(4): 157–158; J. W. Lorsch, A. S. Zelleke, & K. Pick, 2001, Unbalanced boards, *Harvard Business Review,* 79(2): 28–30; R. E. Hoskisson & T. Turk, 1990, Corporate restructuring: Governance

and control limits of the internal market, *Academy of Management Review,* 15: 459–477.

111. M. Kahan & E. B. Rock, 2002, How I learned to stop worrying and love the pill: Adaptive responses to takeover law, *University of Chicago Law Review,* 69(3): 871–915.

112. R. C. Anderson, T. W. Bates, J. M. Bizjak, & M. L. Lemmon, 2000, Corporate governance and firm diversification, *Financial Management,* 29(1): 5–22; J. D. Westphal, 1998, Board games: How CEOs adapt to increases in structural board independence from management, *Administrative Science Quarterly,* 43: 511–537; J. K. Seward & J. P. Walsh, 1996, The governance and control of voluntary corporate spin offs, *Strategic Management Journal,* 17: 25–39; J. P. Walsh & J. K. Seward, 1990, On the efficiency of internal and external corporate control mechanisms, *Academy of Management Review,* 15: 421–458.

113. M. Wiersema, 2002, Holes at the top: Why CEO firings backfire, *Harvard Business Review,* 80(12): 70–77.

114. N. Wasserman, 2006, Stewards, agents, and the founder discount: Executive compensation in new ventures, *Academy of Management Journal,* 49: 960–976; V. Kisfalvi & P. Pitcher, 2003, Doing what feels right: The influence of CEO character and emotions on top management team dynamics, *Journal of Management Inquiry,* 12(10): 42–66; W. G. Rowe, 2001, Creating wealth in organizations:

The role of strategic leadership, *Academy of Management Executive,* 15(1): 81–94.

115. E. F. Fama, 1980, Agency problems and the theory of the firm, *Journal of Political Economy,* 88: 288–307.

116. R. Ettenson & J. Knowles, 2007, M&A blind spot; When negotiating a merger, leave a seat at the table for a marketing expert, *Wall Street Journal,* June 16, R4; F. Vermeulen, 2005, How acquisitions can revitalize companies, *MIT Sloan Management Review,* 46(4): 45–51.

117. M. L. A. Hayward, 2002, When do firms learn from their acquisition experience? Evidence from 1990–1995, *Strategic Management Journal,* 23: 21–39; L. Capron, W. Mitchell, & A. Swaminathan, 2001, Asset divestiture following horizontal acquisitions: A dynamic view, *Strategic Management Journal,* 22: 817–844.

118. R. E. Hoskisson, R. A. Johnson, L. Tihan yi, & R. E. White, 2005, Diversified business groups and corporate refocusing in emerging economies, *Journal of Management,* 31: 941–965.

119. Chakrabarti, Singh, & Mahmood, Diversification and performance: Evidence from East Asian firms; W. P. Wan & R. E. Hoskisson, 2003, Home country environments, corporate diversification strategies, and firm performance, *Academy of Management Journal,* 46: 27–45.

Acquisition and Restructuring Strategies

Studying this chapter should provide you with the strategic management knowledge needed to:

1. Explain the popularity of acquisition strategies in firms competing in the global economy.

2. Discuss reasons why firms use an acquisition strategy to achieve strategic competitiveness.

3. Describe seven problems that work against developing a competitive advantage using an acquisition strategy.

4. Name and describe attributes of effective acquisitions.

5. Define the restructuring strategy and distinguish among its common forms.

6. Explain the short- and long-term outcomes of the different types of restructuring strategies.

The Increased Trend Toward Cross-Border Acquisitions

The number of cross-border acquisitions illustrates the increasingly globalized nature of conducting business affairs in globally competitive markets. The increase is especially apparent as one looks at the number of foreign acquisitions in large, developed markets such as in the United States and the United Kingdom. Foreign direct investments increased 6.7 percent to $161.5 billion in 2006 from $91.4 billion the previous year in the United States. This level was the highest since 2000 when totals reached $335.6 billion at the peak of the dot.com boom. Even though a protectionist mood characterizes the U.S. Congress, investments in the United States appear to remain attractive. Two thirds, or $147.8 billion, of total foreign investment is due to foreign acquisitions of U.S. affiliates.

The United Kingdom has also benefited enormously from having open borders and open markets that allow foreign capital to purchase domestic U.K assets and from the foreign managerial talent associated with managing such acquired assets. However, concerns have surfaced about whether or not foreign acquisitions will make it much harder for British employees to become top-level managers. Furthermore, some industry watchers wonder if foreign takeovers will reduce intellectual property, such that foreign firms will reduce the long-term viability of British industry firms with foreign firms spending their R&D investment in their home countries. The takeover boom affected even significant icons such as Manchester United, which was purchased by Malcolm Glazer, a U.S. sports tycoon.

Other European firms such as those from Spain have been purchasing a significant number of foreign firms. Spanish firms gained experience through an international push in Latin America decades ago. Particularly Telefonica, a large telecommunication firm, purchased a number of telecommunication companies that had been privatized in Latin America. Similarly Spanish banks grew in Latin America through a number of purchases. This experience has now been transferred across Europe not only in the merging of telecommunication firms and banks, but also in merging train and airport management services, and infrastructure management services. For instance Ferrobial sought to buy BAA, the largest train and airport manager in the United Kingdom, which was recently privatized. Furthermore Banco Santander was looking to purchase Abbey National in the United Kingdom, as well as a number of other banks. Recently Abertis sought to takeover Autostrade SpA, which will provide the Spanish firm control over the train routes in Italy and other countries in Europe.

Japanese firms have also become active in large overseas takeovers after being somewhat inactive for a number of years. For example, Japan Tobacco Inc. recently acquired Gallaher Group PLC for $14.7 billion. The acquisition of this British tobacco firm will greatly increase Japan Tobacco's overseas revenues. Interestingly, much of the acquisition activity by European and Japanese firms have been driven by currency valuations, especially relative to the United States, because the dollar is much lower in value than either the euro or the Japanese yen currencies compared to the 1990s.

Emerging economies, for example, from India have become quite aggressive in overseas transactions as well. India's Tata Group won the bid for British steel maker Corus Group PLC for $13.2 billion. Similarly, Hindalco Industries Ltd. purchased Novelis Inc., an aluminum producer that manufactures products such as beer cans and rolled automobile aluminum, for $5.73 billion. Novelis was spun off from Alcan, the second largest (in size) aluminum producer next to Alcoa, and is incorporated in Canada but headquartered in Atlanta. Although pursuing smaller acquisitions, Infosys Technologies Ltd., another India-based company which provides software services, increased its growth 9 percent a year by acquiring small software providers.

Similarly many Latin American firms have been buying U.S. firms. In fact, the largest producers of cement in the United States are all owned by foreign producers, including France's Lafarge SA, Switzerland's Holcim Ltd, and Mexico's Cemex SA. Besides these large global players, a number of medium-sized producers such as Brazil's Botoratin Cinentos SA and Colombia's Cementos Argos SA have been buying North American assets and fleets of mixing trucks to deliver the concrete. Similarly a regional Mexican producer, Grupo Cementos de Chihuahua SA, made additional acquisitions in Colorado and Oklahoma following purchases in Minnesota and South Dakota. Many of these purchases were driven by the high consumption rate for cement during the building boom when cement was in a seller's market. With a slowdown in housing, it is likely this acquisition activity will slow down as well.

In summary the number of cross-border deals continues to increase, leading many emerging-country firms to pursue acquisitions in developed countries, especially in the United States, the United Kingdom, and other places in Europe. These developed economies have more open policies that allow the emerging-country economies to make inroads, especially in mature globalizing businesses such as steel, aluminum, and cement, or basic services including managing airports and railroads, or infrastructure management services such as managing toll roads.

Sources: 2007, Marauding Maharajahs; India's acquisitive companies, *Economist*, March, 86; D. K. Berman, 2007, Mergers hit record, with few stop signs, *Wall Street Journal*, C11; S. Daneshkhu, 2007, FDI flow into richest countries set to rise 20% this year, *Financial Times*, June 22, 7; J. McCary, 2007, Foreign investments rise, *Wall Street Journal*, June 6, A5; J. Saigol, M&A activity gets off to a sprinting start, *Financial Times*, June 30, 18; L. R. McNeil, 2007, Foreign direct investment in the United States: New investment in 2006, *Survey of Current Business*, 87(6): 44–48; J. Singer, K. Johnson & V. O'Connell, 2007, Tobacco consolidation speeds, *Wall Street Journal*, March 16, A3; A. Thompson, 2007, Foreign acquisitions: Success at home has bred victory abroad, *Financial Times*, May 9, 6; P. Wonacott & P. Glader, 2007, Hindalco pact to buy Novelis underlines India's push overseas, *Wall Street Journal*, February 12, A11; A. Galloni, 2006, European acquisition creates toll-road giant, *Wall Street Journal*, April 24, A3; K. Johnson, 2006, Spain emerges as M&A powerhouse, *Wall Street Journal*, September 26, A6; J. Millman, 2006, Cement demand paves path to takeovers, *Wall Street Journal*, May 23, A8; P. Engardio, M. Arndt & G. Smith, 2006, Emerging giants, *BusinessWeek*, July 31, 40.

In Chapter 6 we studied corporate-level strategies, focusing on types and levels of product diversification strategies that are derived from core competencies and create competitive advantage. As noted in that chapter, diversification allows a firm to create value by productively using excess resources.[1] In this chapter, we explore mergers and acquisitions, often combined with a diversification strategy, as a prominent strategy employed by firms throughout the world. As described in the Opening Case many firms, not only from developed countries, but also from emerging economies are increasingly becoming involved in merger and acquisition activities.

In the latter half of the twentieth century, acquisition became a prominent strategy used by major corporations to achieve growth and meet competitive challenges. Even smaller and more focused firms began employing acquisition strategies to grow and to enter new markets.[2] However, acquisition strategies are not without problems; some acquisitions fail. Thus, we focus on how acquisitions can be used to produce value for a firm's stakeholders.[3] Before describing attributes associated with effective acquisitions, we examine the most prominent problems companies experience when using an acquisition strategy. For example, when acquisitions contribute to poor performance, a firm may deem it necessary to restructure its operations as explained in the Strategic Focus on the DaimlerChrysler divestiture of Chrysler. Closing the chapter are descriptions of three restructuring strategies, as well as the short- and long-term outcomes resulting from their use. Setting the stage for these topics is an examination of the popularity of mergers and acquisitions and a discussion of the differences among mergers, acquisitions, and takeovers.

The Popularity of Merger and Acquisition Strategies

The acquisition strategy has been a popular strategy among U.S. firms for many years. Some believe that this strategy played a central role in an effective restructuring of U.S. businesses during the 1980s and 1990s and into the twenty-first century.[4] Increasingly, as the Opening Case reveals, acquisition strategies are becoming more popular with firms in other nations and economic regions, including Europe and other emerging economies such as India, China, and Brazil. In fact, a large percentage of the acquisitions in recent years have been made across country borders (i.e., a firm headquartered in one country acquiring a firm headquartered in another country).

For instance, spending on global deals totaled $3.6 trillion in 2006, the best year on record.[5] However, by July 2007 the quantity of deals was ahead of the 2006 amount by nearly 25 percent. The Organization for Economic Co-operation and Development (OECD) reported, "If the months January through May are indicative of the year 2007 as a whole, then the total value of cross-border M&As in OECD countries will exceed $1 trillion."[6] Interestingly, 20 percent of the deals worldwide have been funded by private equity, largely through the use of debt. It is also worthy to note that this volume increased to 40 percent of the deal total when focused on deals originating in the United States alone.[7]

An acquisition strategy is sometimes used because of the uncertainty in the competitive landscape. A firm may make an acquisition to increase its market power because of a competitive threat, to enter a new market because of the opportunity available in that market, or to spread the risk due to the uncertain environment.[8] In addition, as volatility brings undesirable changes to its primary markets, a firm may acquire other companies to shift its core business into different markets. Such options may arise because of industry or regulatory changes. For instance, as mentioned in Chapter 6, Thomson, a large media conglomerate headquartered in Toronto, Canada, shifted it business model from a focus on newspapers to a focus on selling electronic data services, especially to provide support for firms needing legal and financial data and analysis.[9]

The strategic management process (see Figure 1.1, on page 5) calls for an acquisition strategy to increase a firm's strategic competitiveness as well as its returns to shareholders. Thus, an acquisition strategy should be used only when the acquiring firm will be able to increase its value through ownership of the acquired firm and the use of its assets.[10]

However, evidence suggests that, at least for the acquiring firms, acquisition strategies may not always result in these desirable outcomes.[11] Researchers have found that shareholders of acquired firms often earn above-average returns from an acquisition, while shareholders of acquiring firms typically earn returns from the transaction that are close to zero. These results may suggest that for large firms, it is now more difficult to create sustainable value by using an acquisition strategy to buy publicly traded companies.[12] In approximately two-thirds of all acquisitions, the acquiring firm's stock price falls immediately after the intended transaction is announced. This negative response is an indication of investors' skepticism about the likelihood that the acquirer will be able to achieve the synergies required to justify the premium.[13]

A **merger** is a strategy through which two firms agree to integrate their operations on a relatively coequal basis.

An **acquisition** is a strategy through which one firm buys a controlling, or 100 percent, interest in another firm with the intent of making the acquired firm a subsidiary business within its portfolio.

A **takeover** is a special type of an acquisition strategy wherein the target firm does not solicit the acquiring firm's bid.

Mergers, Acquisitions, and Takeovers: What Are the Differences?

A **merger** is a strategy through which two firms agree to integrate their operations on a relatively coequal basis. Few true mergers actually occur, because one party is usually dominant in regard to market share or firm size. DaimlerChrysler AG was termed a "merger of equals" and, although Daimler-Benz was the dominant party in the automakers' transaction, Chrysler managers would not allow the business deal to be completed unless it was termed a *merger*. However, a merger of equals does not always last as Daimler of the former DaimlerChrysler is changing its name to Daimler AG as it sells off the Chrysler assets, as indicated in the Strategic Focus later in the chapter.[14]

An **acquisition** is a strategy through which one firm buys a controlling, or 100 percent, interest in another firm with the intent of making the acquired firm a subsidiary business within its portfolio. In this case, the management of the acquired firm reports to the management of the acquiring firm. Although most mergers are friendly transactions, acquisitions can be friendly or unfriendly.

A **takeover** is a special type of an acquisition strategy wherein the target firm does not solicit the acquiring firm's bid. The number of unsolicited takeover bids increased in the economic downturn of 2001–2002, a common occurrence in economic recessions, because the poorly managed firms that are undervalued relative to their assets are more easily identified.[15] Many takeover attempts are not desired by the target firm's managers and are referred to as hostile. In a few cases, unsolicited offers may come from parties familiar and possibly friendly to the target firm. However, research has "found that hostile acquirers deliver significantly higher shareholder value than friendly acquirers" for the acquiring firm.[16]

On a comparative basis, acquisitions are more common than mergers and takeovers. Accordingly, this chapter focuses on acquisitions.

Reasons for Acquisitions

In this section, we discuss reasons that support the use of an acquisition strategy. Although each reason can provide a legitimate rationale for an acquisition, the acquisition may not necessarily lead to a competitive advantage.

Increased Market Power

A primary reason for acquisitions is to achieve greater market power.[17] Defined in Chapter 6, *market power* exists when a firm is able to sell its goods or services above competitive levels or when the costs of its primary or support activities are lower than those of its competitors. Market power usually is derived from the size of the firm and its resources and capabilities to compete in the marketplace.[18] It is also affected by the firm's share of the market. Therefore, most acquisitions that are designed to achieve greater market power entail buying a competitor, a supplier, a distributor, or a business in a highly related industry to allow the exercise of a core competence and to gain competitive advantage in the acquiring firm's primary market. One goal in achieving market power is to become a market leader. As noted in Chapter 6, Nestlé SA, will increase its market share for its baby-food line through the acquisition of Gerber Products from Novartis AG.[19] Gerber has nearly an 80 percent share of baby foods in the United States, and through this acquisition Nestlé will substantially increase its market power worldwide. Research in marketing suggests that performance of the merged firm increases if marketing-related issues are involved. The performance improvement of the merged firm subsequent to a horizontal acquisition is even more significant than the average potential cost savings if marketing of the combined firms improves economies of scope.[20] To increase their market power, firms often use horizontal, vertical, and related acquisitions.

Oracle Makes a Series of Horizontal Acquisitions While CVS Makes a Vertical Acquisition

Oracle, SAP, and Microsoft compete in the database management software area. Currently SAP is leading at approximately 22 percent market share, while Oracle and Microsoft have 10 percent and 5 percent, respectively. Rivalry between these firms has heated up as they compete for customer firms that have not yet integrated their firm's business units using database software. Once a database software configuration is in place, significant switching costs to move to another software platform exist. This point has led Oracle to pursue growth through horizontal acquisition strategy. Oracle's acquisition strategy facilitates growth because each new firm acquired has existing customers that will likely be retained, a sales force that can be integrated into Oracle's existing sales force to pursue new sales, and new software applications that can be applied in industries where Oracle may not yet be involved, but with which the target firm will already have a clientele.

Larry Ellison, CEO of Oracle, has been the architect of Oracle's acquisition strategy in the corporate-software industry.

In 2004 Oracle acquired PeopleSoft for $10.3 billion through a hostile takeover. This acquisition also gave it the rights to J.D. Edwards, another industry rival that PeopleSoft had previously acquired. Oracle's acquisition strategy began when Larry Ellison decided that the corporate-software industry had matured and needed consolidation. Since then Oracle has spent $24 billion to buy a number of companies, including the recent $3.3 billion takeover of Hyperion Solutions. This series of acquisitions led to Oracle's revenue increase of 50 percent to $17.7 billion in the fiscal year ending May 2007. The acquisitions also enabled Oracle to develop a refined set of industry focuses with applications in retail, financial services, utilities, communications, and government service.

As an example, Oracle acquired Retek Inc. as well as ProfitLogic and 360Commerce to put together a set of retail software applications. These acquisitions allowed Oracle to win 30 new retail customers in 2006 and 2007 such as Wal-Mart, Nordstrom, and Perry Ellis International. Perry Ellis's CIO indicated that the company expects to save more than $20 million a year in improved just-in-time inventory controls, improved merchandising efficiency, and software that helps to adapts its pricing by store and region efficiently through the application of the newly integrated Oracle software applications.

Comparatively, SAP is ahead in specific industry applications. It has applications in 26 industries compared to Oracle's five. Also, beyond large corporations in specific industries, both companies are pursuing growth in small- to medium-sized enterprises. The equalizer for Oracle has been its acquisition strategy. However, facilitating alignment and integrating the operations of these firms with Oracle is no easy task, but Oracle's increasing acquisition experience has made for improved acquisition integration processes.

In a vertical merger, CVS Corporation, a drugstore chain, purchased pharmacy-benefits manager (PBM) Caremark RX, Inc., for $21 billion in 2007. The combined company will have $75 billion in annual sales, far higher than any other competitor, including Walgreens and comparable PBMs such as Medco Health. In this vertical acquisition CVS is purchasing a powerful customer that negotiates on behalf of large companies and their health insurance providers. One of the incentives for this vertical merger is that PBMs have put pressure on drugstores by negotiating prices on behalf of their clients and forcing firms into mail-order plans for prescription drugs. The merger will help CVS obtain large deals with big companies by offering significant discounts to employees for CVS private-label products. When Wal-Mart began charging much lower prices for generic drugs in many of their stores, drugstores and

PBM firms felt additional pressure for mergers. Walgreens, a large competitor of CVS, also plans to increase its PMB business, but it has not signaled whether it will use an acquisition process.

These two examples represent horizontal and vertical mergers that seek to simultaneously gain market power and reduce costs due to potential synergy and/or complementarity.

Sources: S. Hamm, 2007, Oracle; Larry Ellison engineered a string of acquisitions that have given boost to the software giant's revenues, *BusinessWeek*, March 26, 64–65; G. Marcial, 2007, Hail to CVS/Caremark, 2007, *BusinessWeek*, April 9, 99; A. Ricadela, 2007, Oracle vs. SAP: Sound or fiery? *BusinessWeek*, April 9, 38; V. Vara, 2007, Oracle adds business-intelligence from Hyperion, *Wall Street Journal*, March 2, B3; V. Vara, 2007, Oracle's profit shows acquisition spree is paying off, *Wall Street Journal*, June 27, A3; K. Whitehouse, 2007, CVS/Caremark directors win election, *Wall Street Journal*, May 10, B6; D. Armstrong & B. Martinez, 2006, CVS, Caremark deal to create drug-sale giant, *Wall Street Journal*, November 2, B1, B2; D. K. Berman, W. M. Bulkeley, & S. Hensley, 2006, Higher bid lifts Caremark, for now, *Wall Street Journal*, December 19, A2; S. Pritchard, 2006, How Oracle and SAP are moving down "The Tail," *Financial Times*, October 18, 5.

Horizontal Acquisitions

The acquisition of a company competing in the same industry as the acquiring firm is referred to as a *horizontal acquisition*. Horizontal acquisitions increase a firm's market power by exploiting cost-based and revenue-based synergies.[21] Research suggests that horizontal acquisitions result in higher performance when the firms have similar characteristics.[22] Examples of important similar characteristics include strategy, managerial styles, and resource allocation patterns. Similarities in these characteristics make the integration of the two firms proceed more smoothly.[23] Horizontal acquisitions are often most effective when the acquiring firm integrates the acquired firm's assets with its own assets, but only after evaluating and divesting excess capacity and assets that do not complement the newly combined firm's core competencies.[24] As the Strategic Focus illustrates, Oracle has pursued a strategy of horizontal acquisitions of other software firms quite successfully in its competition with SAP and IBM.

Vertical Acquisitions

A *vertical acquisition* refers to a firm acquiring a supplier or distributor of one or more of its goods or services.[25] A firm becomes vertically integrated through this type of acquisition in that it controls additional parts of the value chain (see Chapters 3 and 6).[26] As the Strategic Focus indicates, the acquisition of Caremark, a pharmacy-benefits manager (PBM), will allow an increase in market power for drugstore chain CVS because it will have more power to negotiate deals with large companies who have been putting pricing pressure on drug store chains through their PBMs and insurance providers.

Google's acquisition of DoubleClick is a vertical acquisition designed to allow Google to provide better quality on-line advertising.

Vertical acquisitions also occur with online businesses. For instance, Google's acquisition of DoubleClick will allow it to provide better-quality online advertisements than it can produce on its own. DoubleClick specializes in providing online display advertisements, especially customer pop-ups and video, while Google specializes in online and text banner ads. As such, Google is buying one of its suppliers in an area where it has been weak on its own. Interestingly, Microsoft complained about the deal, suggesting that it would give Google excessive market power, even though Microsoft was outbid by Google for DoubleClick.[27]

Related Acquisitions

The acquisition of a firm in a highly related industry is referred to as a *related acquisition.* IBM's traditional core business has been selling computer hardware. More recently it moved into services that have become its dominant sales growth engine. However, to sell service solutions, it must have software applications. As such, IBM has been purchasing smaller server and software providers in order to stay competitive. Of course, the software providers are related to IBM's hardware and service businesses. "Since 2003, IBM has spent $11.8 billion on 54 acquisitions: 36 software and 18 services companies."[28] However, because of the difficulty in achieving synergy, related acquisitions are often difficult to value.[29]

Acquisitions intended to increase market power are subject to regulatory review as well as to analysis by financial markets.[30] For example, as noted in the Opening Case in Chapter 6, the successful takeover of Gillette by Procter & Gamble was subjected to a significant amount of government scrutiny as well as close examination by financial analysts. Ultimately, P&G had to sell off several businesses to gain the Federal Trade Commission's approval for the acquisition. Thus, firms seeking growth and market power through acquisitions must understand the political/legal segment of the general environment (see Chapter 2) in order to successfully use an acquisition strategy.

Overcoming Entry Barriers

Barriers to entry (introduced in Chapter 2) are factors associated with the market or with the firms currently operating in it, which increase the expense and difficulty faced by new ventures trying to enter that particular market. For example, well-established competitors may have substantial economies of scale in the manufacture or service of their products. In addition, enduring relationships with customers often create product loyalties that are difficult for new entrants to overcome. When facing differentiated products, new entrants typically must spend considerable resources to advertise their goods or services and may find it necessary to sell at prices below competitors' to entice new customers.

Facing the entry barriers created by economies of scale and differentiated products, a new entrant may find acquiring an established company to be more effective than entering the market as a competitor offering a good or service that is unfamiliar to current buyers. In fact, the higher the barriers to market entry, the greater the probability that a firm will acquire an existing firm to overcome them. Although an acquisition can be expensive, it does provide the new entrant with immediate market access.

For example, as the Opening Case illustrated, many of the cross-border acquisitions, especially of firms in developing countries, are utilized to overcome entry barriers. A notable example is the cement companies, including France's Lafarge SA, Switzerland's Holcim Ltd, and Mexico's Cemex SA, which are now the largest producers of cement in the United States.

In addition, acquisitions are a commonly used method to overcome barriers to enter international markets.[31] Large multinational corporations from developed economies seek to enter emerging economies such as Brazil, Russia, India, and China (BRIC) because they are among the fastest growing economies in the world.[32] As discussed next, purchasing a local target allows a firm to enter these fast-growing economies more rapidly than learning about the local institutional barriers on its own through a greenfield or internally derived venture.

Cross-Border Acquisitions

Acquisitions made between companies with headquarters in different countries are called *cross-border acquisitions.* As mentioned previously, these acquisitions are often made to overcome entry barriers. In Chapter 9, we examine cross-border alliances and the reasons for their use. Compared with a cross-border alliance, a cross-border acquisition gives a firm more control over its international operations.[33]

Historically, U.S. firms have been the most active acquirers of companies outside their domestic market.[34] However, in the global economy, companies throughout the world are choosing this strategic option with increasing frequency.[35] In recent years, cross-border acquisitions represented as much as 40 percent of the annual total number of acquisitions.[36] Because of relaxed regulations, the amount of cross-border activity among nations within the European community also continues to increase. Many large European corporations have approached the limits of growth within their domestic markets and thus seek growth in other markets, which is what some analysts believe accounts for the growth in the range of cross-border acquisitions.

Many European and U.S. firms participated in cross-border acquisitions across Asian countries that experienced a financial crisis due to significant currency devaluations in 1997. Research indicates that these acquisitions facilitated the survival and restructuring of many large Asian companies, which enabled these economies to recover more quickly than they would have without the cross-border acquisitions.[37]

Although cross-border acquisitions are taking place across a wide variety of industries to overcome entry barriers (see the Opening Case), such acquisitions can be difficult to negotiate and operate because of the differences in foreign cultures.[38]

Cost of New Product Development and Increased Speed to Market

Developing new products internally and successfully introducing them into the marketplace often requires significant investment of a firm's resources, including time, making it difficult to quickly earn a profitable return.[39] Because an estimated 88 percent of innovations fail to achieve adequate returns, firm managers are also concerned with achieving adequate returns from the capital invested to develop and commercialize new products. Perhaps contributing to these less-than-desirable rates of return is the successful imitation of approximately 60 percent of innovations within four years after the patents are obtained. These types of outcomes may lead managers to perceive internal product development as a high-risk activity.[40]

Acquisitions are another means a firm can use to gain access to new products and to current products that are new to the firm. Compared with internal product development processes, acquisitions provide more predictable returns as well as faster market entry. Returns are more predictable because the performance of the acquired firm's products can be assessed prior to completing the acquisition.[41] For these reasons, extensive bidding wars and acquisitions are more frequent in high-technology industries.[42]

Acquisition activity is also extensive throughout the pharmaceutical industry, where firms frequently use acquisitions to enter markets quickly, to overcome the high costs of developing products internally and to increase the predictability of returns on their investments. Usually it is larger biotech or pharmaceutical firms acquiring smaller biotech firms that have drug opportunities close to market entry. For example, Gilead Sciences emerged as a leader in drugs that treat AIDS, one of the world's leading causes of death. However, with its $2.5 billion acquisition of Myogen, Inc., a smaller biotech company and one other acquisition, the company has quickly been able to diversify its pipeline into hypertension (high blood pressure), as well as drugs that treat other respiratory and heart diseases, all lines of development with high potential demand and growth.[43]

Besides quick entry into new product markets compared with internal product development, acquisitions often represent the fastest means to enter international markets and help firms overcome the liabilities associated with such strategic moves.[44] Acquisitions provide rapid access both to new markets and to new capabilities. Using new

Gilead's recent acquisition of Myogen, Inc. was a strategy designed to allow for quick entry into the pharmaceutical hypertension market.

© AP Photo/Paul Sakuma

capabilities to pioneer new products and to enter markets quickly can create advantageous market positions.[45] Pharmaceutical firms, for example, access new products through acquisitions of other drug manufacturers. They also acquire biotechnology firms both for new products and for new technological capabilities. Pharmaceutical firms often provide the manufacturing and marketing capabilities to take the new products developed by biotechnology firms to the market.[46]

Lower Risk Compared to Developing New Products

Because the outcomes of an acquisition can be estimated more easily and accurately than the outcomes of an internal product development process, managers may view acquisitions as lowering risk.[47] The difference in risk between an internal product development process and an acquisition can be seen in the results of Gilead Sciences' strategy just described.

As with other strategic actions discussed in this book, the firm must exercise caution when using a strategy of acquiring new products rather than developing them internally. Even though research suggests that they have become a common means of avoiding risky internal ventures (and therefore risky R&D investments), acquisitions may also become a substitute for innovation.[48] Also, risks are associated with acquisitions where the target firm misrepresents its assets or capabilities.[49] Thus, acquisitions are not a risk-free alternative to entering new markets through internally developed products.

Increased Diversification

Acquisitions are also used to diversify firms. Based on experience and the insights resulting from it, firms typically find it easier to develop and introduce new products in markets currently served by the firm. In contrast, it is difficult for companies to develop products that differ from their current lines for markets in which they lack experience.[50] Thus, it is uncommon for a firm to develop new products internally to diversify its product lines.[51] Cisco Systems has historically pursued many acquisitions, several of which have helped build its network components business focused on producing hardware. Recently, however, Cisco purchased IronPort Systems Inc., a company focused on producing security software for networks. This acquisition will help Cisco expand beyond its original expertise in network hardware and basic software. Cisco previously acquired technology in the security area through its purchase of Riverhead Networks Inc., Protego Networks Inc., and Perfigo Inc. However, the IronPort deal provides software service in networks that can help guard against spam and viruses that travel through e-mail and Web-based traffic. Accordingly, Cisco could make other acquisitions in service-based offerings connected to its other products. Thus the IronPort Group acquisition represents a diversifying acquisition for Cisco.[52]

Both related diversification and unrelated diversification strategies can be implemented through acquisitions.[53] For example, United Technologies Corp. (UTC) has used acquisitions to build a conglomerate. Since the mid-1970s it has been building a portfolio of stable and noncyclical businesses, including Otis Elevator Co. and Carrier Corporation (air conditioners), in order to reduce its dependence on the volatile aerospace industry. Its main businesses have been Pratt & Whitney (jet engines), Sikorsky (helicopters), and Hamilton Sundstrand (aerospace parts). UTC has also acquired a hydrogen-fuel-cell business. Perceiving an opportunity in security caused by problems at airports and because security has become a top concern both for governments and for corporations, United Technologies in 2003 acquired Chubb PLC, a British electronic-security company, for $1 billion. With its acquisition of Kidde PLC in 2004 for $2.84 billion and the security unit of Rentokil Initial PLC for $1.6 billion in 2007, UTC will have obtained a significant portion of the world's market share in electronic security and become the leading firm in the Netherlands and second-largest electronic-security provider in both Britain and France.[54] All businesses UTC purchases are involved in manufacturing industrial and commercial products. However, many have a relatively low focus on technology (e.g., elevators, air conditioners, and security systems).[55]

Although acquisitions can be either related or unrelated, research has shown that the more related the acquired firm is to the acquiring firm, the greater the probability is that the acquisition will be successful.[56] Thus, horizontal acquisitions (through which a firm acquires a competitor) and related acquisitions tend to contribute more to the firm's strategic competitiveness than would the acquisition of a company that operates in product markets quite different from those in which the acquiring firm competes.[57]

Reshaping the Firm's Competitive Scope

As discussed in Chapter 2, the intensity of competitive rivalry is an industry characteristic that affects the firm's profitability.[58] To reduce the negative effect of an intense rivalry on their financial performance, firms may use acquisitions to lessen their dependence on one or more products or markets. Reducing a company's dependence on specific markets alters the firm's competitive scope.

As the Strategic Focus illustrated, Oracle's acquisition strategy helped it shift its scope through purchasing firms with application software in order to create industry service specializations in retail, financial services, utilities, communications, and government service. These capabilities are helping Oracle compete against other leading database management providers such as SAP. Similarly, GE reduced its emphasis in the electronics market many years ago by making acquisitions in the financial services industry. Today, GE is considered a service firm because a majority of its revenue now comes from services instead of from industrial products.[59] Furthermore, as the example of Thomson suggested, acquisitions helped the company shift from a focus primarily on newspapers (with classified ad revenues declining due to online competition from the likes of Craig's List) to having most of its revenues derived from selling electronic data services in finance and law.[60]

Learning and Developing New Capabilities

Some acquisitions are made to gain capabilities that the firm does not possess. For example, acquisitions may be used to acquire a special technological capability. Research has shown that firms can broaden their knowledge base and reduce inertia through acquisitions.[61] Therefore, acquiring a firm with skills and capabilities that differ from its own helps the acquiring firm to gain access to new knowledge and remain agile.[62] For example, research suggests that firms increase the potential of their capabilities when they acquire diverse talent through cross-border acquisitions. This greater value is created through the international expansion versus a simple acquisition without such diversity and resource creation potential.[63] Of course, firms are better able to learn these capabilities if they share some similar properties with the firm's current capabilities. Thus, firms should seek to acquire companies with different but related and complementary capabilities in order to build their own knowledge base.[64]

A number of large pharmaceutical firms are acquiring the ability to create "large molecule" drugs, also known as biological drugs, by buying biotechnology firms. Thus, these firms are not only seeking the pipeline of possible drugs, but also the capabilities that these firms have to produce such drugs. Such capabilities are important for large pharmaceutical firms because these biological drugs are more difficult to duplicate by chemistry alone (the historical basis on which most pharmaceutical firms have expertise). These capabilities will allow generic drug makers to be more successful after chemistry-based drug patents expire. To illustrate the difference between these types of drugs, David Brennen, CEO of British drug maker AstraZeneca, suggested, "Some of these [biological-based drugs] have demonstrated that they're not just symptomatic treatments but that

David Brennen, CEO of British drug maker AstraZeneca, orchestrated the acquisition of MedImmune, Inc. and Cambridge Antibody Technology in order to build up AstraZeneca's biological drug production process.

they actually alter the course of the disease."[65] Furthermore, biological drugs must clear more regulatory barriers or hurdles, which, when accomplished, add more to a firm's advantage. For example, AstraZeneca bought biological-drug producer MedImmune Inc. for $15.6 billion in 2007 and a small biologic-centered firm, Cambridge Antibody Technology, for $1.6 billion in 2006 in order to build up its capabilities in biological-based drug production processes.

Problems in Achieving Acquisition Success

Acquisition strategies based on reasons described in this chapter can increase strategic competitiveness and help firms earn above-average returns. However, acquisition strategies are not risk-free. Reasons for the use of acquisition strategies and potential problems with such strategies are shown in Figure 7.1.

Figure 7.1 Reasons for Acquisitions and Problems in Achieving Success

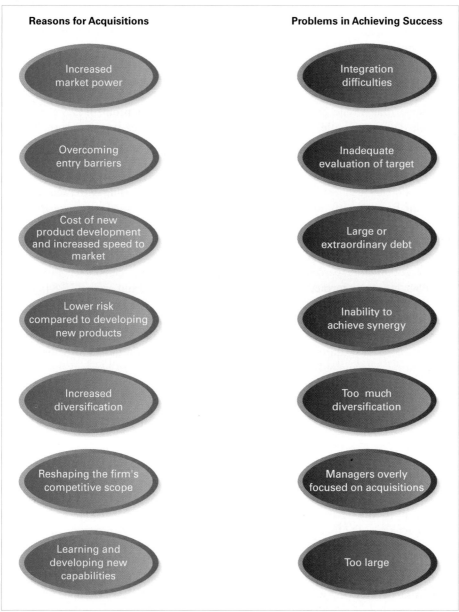

Reasons for Acquisitions

- Increased market power
- Overcoming entry barriers
- Cost of new product development and increased speed to market
- Lower risk compared to developing new products
- Increased diversification
- Reshaping the firm's competitive scope
- Learning and developing new capabilities

Problems in Achieving Success

- Integration difficulties
- Inadequate evaluation of target
- Large or extraordinary debt
- Inability to achieve synergy
- Too much diversification
- Managers overly focused on acquisitions
- Too large

Research suggests that perhaps 20 percent of all mergers and acquisitions are successful, approximately 60 percent produce disappointing results, and the remaining 20 percent are clear failures.[66] Successful acquisitions generally involve having a well-conceived strategy for selecting the target, not paying too high a premium (doing appropriate due diligence), and employing an effective integration process.[67] As shown in Figure 7.1, several problems may prevent successful acquisitions.

Integration Difficulties

Integrating two companies following an acquisition can be quite difficult. Integration challenges include melding two disparate corporate cultures, linking different financial and control systems, building effective working relationships (particularly when management styles differ), and resolving problems regarding the status of the newly acquired firm's executives.[68]

The importance of a successful integration should not be underestimated.[69] Without it, an acquisition is unlikely to produce positive returns. Thus, as suggested by a researcher studying the process, "Managerial practice and academic writings show that the post-acquisition integration phase is probably the single most important determinant of shareholder value creation (and equally of value destruction) in mergers and acquisitions."[70]

Integration is complex and involves a large number of activities, which if overlooked can lead to significant difficulties. For example, when United Parcel Service (UPS) acquired Mail Boxes Etc., a large retail shipping chain, it appeared to be a complementary merger that would provide benefits to both firms. The problem is that most of the Mail Boxes Etc. outlets were owned by franchisees. Once the merger took place the franchisees lost the ability to deal with other shipping companies such as FedEx, which reduced their competitiveness. Furthermore, franchisees complained that UPS often built company-owned shipping stores close by franchisee outlets of Mail Boxes Etc. Additionally, a culture clash evolved between the free-wheeling entrepreneurs who owned the franchises of Mail Boxes Etc. and the efficiency-oriented corporate approach of the UPS operation, which focused on managing a large fleet of trucks and an information system to efficiently pick up and deliver packages. Also, Mail Boxes Etc. was focused on retail traffic, whereas UPS was focused more on the logistics of wholesale pickup and delivery. Although 87 percent of Mail Boxes Etc. franchisees decided to rebrand under the UPS name, many formed an owner's group and even filed suit against UPS in regard to the unfavorable nature of the franchisee contract.[71]

It is important to maintain the human capital of the target firm after the acquisition. Much of an organization's knowledge is contained in its human capital.[72] Turnover of key personnel from the acquired firm can have a negative effect on the performance of the merged firm.[73] The loss of key personnel, such as critical managers, weakens the acquired firm's capabilities and reduces its value. When a deal for an acquisition is being considered, completing due diligence on the human capital to make sure that key people—who are necessary to help run the company after the integration process—will not leave is an important consideration.[74] If implemented effectively, the integration process can have a positive effect on target firm managers and reduce the probability that they will leave.[75]

Inadequate Evaluation of Target

Due diligence is a process through which a potential acquirer evaluates a target firm for acquisition. In an effective due-diligence process, hundreds of items are examined in areas as diverse as the financing for the intended transaction, differences in cultures between the acquiring and target firm, tax consequences of the transaction, and actions that would be necessary to successfully meld the two workforces. Due diligence is commonly performed by investment bankers, accountants, lawyers, and management consultants specializing in that activity, although firms actively pursuing acquisitions may form their own internal due-diligence team.[76]

The failure to complete an effective due-diligence process may easily result in the acquiring firm paying an excessive premium for the target company. Interestingly, research shows that in times of high or increasing stock prices due diligence is relaxed; firms often overpay during these periods and long-run performance of the merged firm suffers.[77] Research also shows that without due diligence, "the purchase price is driven by the pricing of other 'comparable' acquisitions rather than by a rigorous assessment of where, when, and how management can drive real performance gains. [In these cases], the price paid may have little to do with achievable value."[78]

Many firms use investment banks to perform their due diligence, but in the post-Enron era the process is increasingly performed in-house. Although investment bankers such as Credit Suisse First Boston and Citibank still play a large role in due diligence for large mergers and acquisitions, their role in smaller mergers and acquisitions seems to be decreasing.[79] However, when it comes to financing the deal, investment banks are critical to the process, whether the firm remains public or is taken private by a private equity firm.

Large or Extraordinary Debt

To finance a number of acquisitions completed during the 1980s and 1990s, some companies significantly increased their levels of debt. A financial innovation called junk bonds helped make this increase possible. *Junk bonds* are a financing option through which risky acquisitions are financed with money (debt) that provides a large potential return to lenders (bondholders). Because junk bonds are unsecured obligations that are not tied to specific assets for collateral, interest rates for these high-risk debt instruments sometimes reached between 18 and 20 percent during the 1980s.[80] Some prominent financial economists viewed debt as a means to discipline managers, causing them to act in the shareholders' best interests.[81]

Junk bonds are now used less frequently to finance acquisitions, and the conviction that debt disciplines managers is less strong. Nonetheless, some firms still take on significant debt to acquire companies. For example, more debt is being used in cross-border acquisitions such as the deal between India's Tata Steel and Corus Group PLC of the United Kingdom mentioned in the Opening Case. First, the deal went through nine rounds of bidding with two main contenders Tata Steel and Brazil's Cia Siderurgica Nacional, or CSN, which increased the price 34 percent above Tata Steel's initial offer to $11.3 billion. However, Tata proposed financing the deal using a debt approach, and its shares fell 11 percent upon this announcement because, as one analyst suggested, "Tata was paying too much for Corus and that debt incurred to fund the acquisition could affect the company's earnings for years to come."[82]

High debt can have several negative effects on the firm. For example, because high debt increases the likelihood of bankruptcy, it can lead to a downgrade in the firm's credit rating by agencies such as Moody's and Standard & Poor's.[83] In fact, in the Tata-Corus deal just noted, the stock price drop was influenced by a warning from Standard & Poor's that it might downgrade Tata's debt rating, which would effectively raise its cost of debt. In addition, high debt may preclude needed investment in activities that contribute to the firm's long-term success, such as R&D, human resources training, and marketing.[84] Still, leverage can be a positive force in a firm's development, allowing it to take advantage of attractive expansion opportunities. However, too much leverage (such as extraordinary debt) can lead to negative outcomes, including postponing or eliminating investments, such as R&D expenditures, that are necessary to maintain strategic competitiveness over the long term.

Inability to Achieve Synergy

Derived from *synergos,* a Greek word that means "working together," *synergy* exists when the value created by units working together exceeds the value those units could create working independently (see Chapter 6). That is, synergy exists when assets are worth more when used in conjunction with each other than when they are used separately.[85] For shareholders, synergy generates gains in their wealth that they could not duplicate or exceed through their own portfolio diversification decisions.[86] Synergy is created by the efficiencies derived from economies of scale and economies of scope and by sharing resources (e.g., human capital and knowledge) across the businesses in the merged firm.[87]

A firm develops a competitive advantage through an acquisition strategy only when a transaction generates private synergy. *Private synergy* is created when the combination and integration of the acquiring and acquired firms' assets yield capabilities and core competencies that could not be developed by combining and integrating either firm's assets with another company. Private synergy is possible when firms' assets are complementary in unique ways; that is, the unique type of asset complementarity is not possible by combining either company's assets with another firm's assets.[88] Because of its uniqueness, private synergy is difficult for competitors to understand and imitate. However, private synergy is difficult to create.

A firm's ability to account for costs that are necessary to create anticipated revenue- and cost-based synergies affects the acquisition's success. Firms experience several expenses when trying to create private synergy through acquisitions. Called transaction costs, these expenses are incurred when firms use acquisition strategies to create synergy.[89] Transaction costs may be direct or indirect. Direct costs include legal fees and charges from investment bankers who complete due diligence for the acquiring firm. Indirect costs include managerial time to evaluate target firms and then to complete negotiations, as well as the loss of key managers and employees following an acquisition.[90] Firms tend to underestimate the sum of indirect costs when the value of the synergy that may be created by combining and integrating the acquired firm's assets with the acquiring firm's assets is calculated.

As the Strategic Focus later in the chapter on the sale of Chrysler by Daimler points out, synergies are often difficult to achieve. In this regard, Dieter Zetsche, Daimler's CEO and a former head of Chrysler, pointedly notes: "Obviously we overestimated the potential for synergies (between Mercedes and Chrysler). Given the very different nature of the markets we operate in, the gap between luxury and volume was too great."[91] One analyst noted as well, "What once seemed like a perfect fit now just seems like a mistaken vision."[92]

Too Much Diversification

As explained in Chapter 6, diversification strategies can lead to strategic competitiveness and above-average returns. In general, firms using related diversification strategies outperform those employing unrelated diversification strategies. However, conglomerates formed by using an unrelated diversification strategy also can be successful, as demonstrated by United Technologies Corp.

At some point, however, firms can become overdiversified. The level at which overdiversification occurs varies across companies because each firm has different capabilities to manage diversification. Recall from Chapter 6 that related diversification requires more information processing than does unrelated diversification. Because of this additional information processing, related diversified firms become overdiversified with a smaller number of business units than do firms using an unrelated diversification strategy.[93] Regardless of the type of diversification strategy implemented, however, overdiversification leads to a decline in performance, after which business units are often divested.[94] There seems to be a pattern of excessive diversification followed by divestments of underperforming business units previously acquired in the automobile industry. We discuss this issue later in a Strategic Focus on DaimlerChrysler. Not only is Daimler divesting assets (Chrysler), but Ford and other companies have been unwinding previous acquisitions. Ford acquired Volvo, beating out Fiat and Volkswagen in a bidding war at a cost of $6.5 billion. However, Ford is now seeking to sell the Volvo assets and has likewise considered selling its other luxury brands that it acquired (Jaguar, Aston Martin, and

Land Rover). General Motors has also reversed acquisitions by selling off stakes in foreign companies such as Fiat and Fuji Heavy Industries.[95] These cycles were also frequent among U.S. firms during the 1960s through the 1980s.[96]

Even when a firm is not overdiversified, a high level of diversification can have a negative effect on the firm's long-term performance. For example, the scope created by additional amounts of diversification often causes managers to rely on financial rather than strategic controls to evaluate business units' performance (financial and strategic controls are defined and explained in Chapters 11 and 12). Top-level executives often rely on financial controls to assess the performance of business units when they do not have a rich understanding of business units' objectives and strategies. Use of financial controls, such as return on investment (ROI), causes individual business-unit managers to focus on short-term outcomes at the expense of long-term investments. When long-term investments are reduced to increase short-term profits, a firm's overall strategic competitiveness may be harmed.[97]

Another problem resulting from too much diversification is the tendency for acquisitions to become substitutes for innovation. Typically, managers do not intend acquisitions to be used in that way. However, a reinforcing cycle evolves. Costs associated with acquisitions may result in fewer allocations to activities, such as R&D, that are linked to innovation. Without adequate support, a firm's innovation skills begin to atrophy. Without internal innovation skills, the only option available to a firm to gain access to innovation is to complete still more acquisitions. Evidence suggests that a firm using acquisitions as a substitute for internal innovations eventually encounters performance problems.[98]

Managers Overly Focused on Acquisitions

Typically, a considerable amount of managerial time and energy is required for acquisition strategies to contribute to the firm's strategic competitiveness. Activities with which managers become involved include (1) searching for viable acquisition candidates, (2) completing effective due-diligence processes, (3) preparing for negotiations, and (4) managing the integration process after the acquisition is completed.

Liz Claiborne's CEO, William McComb, has indicated that the company will be shedding up to 16 brands due to being overly focused on making acquisitions.

Top-level managers do not personally gather all of the data and information required to make acquisitions. However, these executives do make critical decisions on the firms to be targeted, the nature of the negotiations, and so forth. Company experiences show that participating in and overseeing the activities required for making acquisitions can divert managerial attention from other matters that are necessary for long-term competitive success, such as identifying and taking advantage of other opportunities and interacting with important external stakeholders.[99]

Both theory and research suggest that managers can become overly involved in the process of making acquisitions.[100] One observer suggested, "Some executives can become preoccupied with making deals—and the thrill of selecting, chasing and seizing a target."[101] The overinvolvement can be surmounted by learning from mistakes and by not having too much agreement in the board room. Dissent is helpful to make sure that all sides of a question are considered (see Chapter 10).[102] When failure does occur, leaders may be tempted to blame the failure on others and on unforeseen circumstances rather than on their excessive involvement in the acquisition process.

© AP Photo/Gino Domenico

An example of being overly focused on making acquisitions is Liz Claiborne Inc. Over a number of years Claiborne's leadership made a number of acquisitions in sportswear apparel and grew from

16 to 36 brands; with sales beginning at $800 million and topping off at approximately $5 billion. However, while its managers were focused on making acquisitions, changes were taking place that created problems, given its number of brands. Most Claiborne sales were focused on traditional department stores, but consolidations through acquisitions in this sector left less room for as many brands, given the purchasing habits of the large department stores. Also, specialty stores, such as Coach, with their own brands were on the increase, leaving fewer sales available for established brands. As such, Claiborne's new CEO William McComb plans to divest up to 16 brands and emphasize brands with more potential.[103]

Too Large

Most acquisitions create a larger firm, which should help increase its economies of scale. These economies can then lead to more efficient operations—for example, two sales organizations can be integrated using fewer sales representative because such sales personnel can sell the products of both firms (particularly if the products of the acquiring and target firms are highly related).[104]

Many firms seek increases in size because of the potential economies of scale and enhanced market power (discussed earlier). At some level, the additional costs required to manage the larger firm will exceed the benefits of the economies of scale and additional market power. The complexities generated by the larger size often lead managers to implement more bureaucratic controls to manage the combined firm's operations. *Bureaucratic controls* are formalized supervisory and behavioral rules and policies designed to ensure consistency of decisions and actions across different units of a firm. However, through time, formalized controls often lead to relatively rigid and standardized managerial behavior. Certainly, in the long run, the diminished flexibility that accompanies rigid and standardized managerial behavior may produce less innovation. Because of innovation's importance to competitive success, the bureaucratic controls resulting from a large organization (i.e., built by acquisitions) can have a detrimental effect on performance. As one analyst noted, "Striving for size per se is not necessarily going to make a company more successful. In fact, a strategy in which acquisitions are undertaken as a substitute for organic growth has a bad track record in terms of adding value."[105]

Citigroup is the world's largest financial services company with $270 billion in market value. However, the company has been pressured to sell some of its assets to reduce the complexity associated with managing so many different financial service businesses because its stock price has not appreciated as much as other large but less complex bank organizations. The cross-selling between insurance and banking services has not created as much value as expected.[106]

Effective Acquisitions

Earlier in the chapter, we noted that acquisition strategies do not consistently produce above-average returns for the acquiring firm's shareholders.[107] Nonetheless, some companies are able to create value when using an acquisition strategy.[108] For example, few companies have grown as successfully by acquisition as Cisco. A number of other network companies pursued acquisitions to build up their ability to sell into the network equipment binge, but only Cisco retained much of its value in the post-bubble era. Many firms, such as Lucent, Nortel, and Ericsson, teetered on the edge of bankruptcy after the dot.com bubble burst. When it makes an acquisition, "Cisco has gone much further in its thinking about integration. Not only is retention important, but Cisco also works to minimize the distractions caused by an acquisition. This is important, because the speed of change is so great, that even if the target firm's product development teams are distracted, they will be slowed, contributing to acquisition failure. So, integration must be rapid and reassuring."[109]

Results from a research study shed light on the differences between unsuccessful and successful acquisition strategies and suggest that a pattern of actions can improve the probability of acquisition success.[110] The study shows that when the target firm's assets are complementary to the acquired firm's assets, an acquisition is more successful. With complementary assets, the integration of two firms' operations has a higher probability of creating synergy. In fact, integrating two firms with complementary assets frequently produces unique capabilities and core competencies.[111] With complementary assets, the acquiring firm can maintain its focus on core businesses and leverage the complementary assets and capabilities from the acquired firm. Often, targets were selected and "groomed" by establishing a working relationship prior to the acquisition.[112] As discussed in Chapter 9, strategic alliances are sometimes used to test the feasibility of a future merger or acquisition between the involved firms.[113]

The study's results also show that friendly acquisitions facilitate integration of the firms involved in an acquisition. Through friendly acquisitions, firms work together to find ways to integrate their operations to create synergy.[114] In hostile takeovers, animosity often results between the two top-management teams, a condition that in turn affects working relationships in the newly created firm. As a result, more key personnel in the acquired firm may be lost, and those who remain may resist the changes necessary to integrate the two firms.[115] With effort, cultural clashes can be overcome, and fewer key managers and employees will become discouraged and leave.[116]

Additionally, effective due-diligence processes involving the deliberate and careful selection of target firms and an evaluation of the relative health of those firms (financial health, cultural fit, and the value of human resources) contribute to successful acquisitions.[117] Financial slack in the form of debt equity or cash, in both the acquiring and acquired firms, also frequently contributes to success in acquisitions. Even though financial slack provides access to financing for the acquisition, it is still important to maintain a low or moderate level of debt after the acquisition to keep debt costs low. When substantial debt was used to finance the acquisition, companies with successful acquisitions reduced the debt quickly, partly by selling off assets from the acquired firm, especially noncomplementary or poorly performing assets. For these firms, debt costs do not prevent long-term investments such as R&D, and managerial discretion in the use of cash flow is relatively flexible.

Another attribute of successful acquisition strategies is an emphasis on innovation, as demonstrated by continuing investments in R&D activities. Significant R&D investments show a strong managerial commitment to innovation, a characteristic that is increasingly important to overall competitiveness, as well as acquisition success.

Flexibility and adaptability are the final two attributes of successful acquisitions. When executives of both the acquiring and the target firms have experience in managing change and learning from acquisitions, they will be more skilled at adapting their capabilities to new environments.[118] As a result, they will be more adept at integrating the two organizations, which is particularly important when firms have different organizational cultures.

Efficient and effective integration may quickly produce the desired synergy in the newly created firm. Effective integration allows the acquiring firm to keep valuable human resources in the acquired firm from leaving.[119]

The attributes and results of successful acquisitions are summarized in Table 7.1. Managers seeking acquisition success should emphasize the seven attributes that are listed. Berkshire Hathaway is a conglomerate holding company for Warren Buffett, one of the world's richest men. The company operates widely in the insurance industry and also has stakes in gems, candy, apparel, pilot training, and shoes. The company owns an interest in such well-known firms as Wal-Mart, American Express, Coca-Cola, The Washington Post Company, and Wells Fargo. Also, Buffett has bought an interest in: a U.S. utility firm, PacifiCorp.; Russell, a clothing manufacturer; Iscar, an Israeli tool manufacturer; and most recently invested $3 billion in Burlington Northern Santa Fe, a

Table 7.1 Attributes of Successful Acquisitions

Attributes	Results
1. Acquired firm has assets or resources that are complementary to the acquiring firm's core business	1. High probability of synergy and competitive advantage by maintaining strengths
2. Acquisition is friendly	2. Faster and more effective integration and possibly lower premiums
3. Acquiring firm conducts effective due diligence to select target firms and evaluate the target firm's health (financial, cultural, and human resources)	3. Firms with strongest complementarities are acquired and overpayment is avoided
4. Acquiring firm has financial slack (cash or a favorable debt position)	4. Financing (debt or equity) is easier and less costly to obtain
5. Merged firm maintains low to moderate debt position	5. Lower financing cost, lower risk (e.g., of bankruptcy), and avoidance of trade-offs that are associated with high debt
6. Acquiring firm has sustained and consistent emphasis on R&D and innovation	6. Maintain long-term competitive advantage in markets
7. Acquiring firm manages change well and is flexible and adaptable	7. Faster and more effective integration facilitates achievement of synergy

large Texas-based railroad and freight company.[120] His acquisition strategy in insurance and other business has been particularly successful because he has followed many of the suggestions in Table 7.1.

As we have learned, some acquisitions enhance strategic competitiveness. However, the majority of acquisitions that took place from the 1970s through the 1990s did not enhance firms' strategic competitiveness. In fact, "history shows that anywhere between one-third [and] more than half of all acquisitions are ultimately divested or spun-off."[121] Thus, firms often use restructuring strategies to correct the failure of a merger or an acquisition.

Restructuring

Restructuring is a strategy through which a firm changes its set of businesses or its financial structure.

Defined formally, **restructuring** is a strategy through which a firm changes its set of businesses or its financial structure.[122] From the 1970s into the 2000s, divesting businesses from company portfolios and downsizing accounted for a large percentage of firms' restructuring strategies. Restructuring is a global phenomenon.[123]

The failure of an acquisition strategy is often followed by a restructuring strategy. The Strategic Focus highlights the acquisition of Chrysler by Daimler and how an acquisition that looked like an excellent opportunity turned into a financial disaster for Daimler. Daimler subsequently sold the Chrysler assets to a private equity firm, Cerberus Capital Management LP, in order to cut its significant losses.

In other instances, however, firms use a restructuring strategy because of changes in their external and internal environments. For example, opportunities sometimes surface in the external environment that are particularly attractive to the diversified firm in light of its core competencies. In such cases, restructuring may be appropriate to position the firm to create more value for stakeholders, given the environmental changes.[124]

DaimlerChrysler Is Now Daimler AG: The Failed Merger with Chrysler Corporation

Daimler Benz acquired Chrysler in 1998 for $36 billion. In May 2007 DaimlerChrysler, the merged firm, sold the Chrysler business to a consortium of private equity investors led by Cerberus Capital Management LP for $7.4 billion. Through this deal, Daimler Chrysler changed its name to Daimler AG and retained only 20 percent of the ownership of Chrysler assets. Of the $7.4 billion provided by the private equity firm, $5 billion will be put into the operations of Chrysler and approximately $1 billion into Chrysler Financial Services with the rest going to pay miscellaneous expenses. Interestingly, DaimlerChrysler will only get $1.35 billion, but Daimler also expects to pay Chrysler $1.6 billion before the deal closes to subsidize its current negative cash flow. The bottom line is that Daimler will not get much out of its original $32 billion investment other than to unload $18 billion in pension and health care liabilities from its books. Many of the problems with the merger are derived from the labor and health care legacy cost differences, which have been estimated to be as high as $1,500 per vehicle on average, compared to an estimated $250 per vehicle for foreign firms such as Toyota.

This deal failure is reminiscent of the failed acquisition of Rover by BMW. BMW ultimately sold the Rover assets for little in return except that BMW was able to unload debt off its books. The Rover assets were similarly acquired by private equity firms with additional investment from a Chinese firm, Nanjing Automobile, which wished to gain entry into more developed markets such as those in Europe and the United States.

The former Daimler CEO, Jurgen Scrempp, the mastermind behind the acquisition of Chrysler had likewise made acquisitions in Asia by acquiring controlling interest in Japan's Mitsubishi Motors Corp. and with Korea's Hyundai Motors Corp. These investments also had problems, and Daimler divested the Mitsubishi assets in 2004 and likewise in the same year sold its 10 percent stake in Hyundai because of significant losses after the recession of 2000.

Dieter Zetsche, CEO of Daimler and former head of Chrysler, has admitted that perceived synergies between the two companies never came to fruition and the differences in markets for the companies was too much to overcome.

In many private equity deals, like the Chrysler deal, in recent years, private equity firms buy up a large array of businesses across a wide variety of industries in automobiles, steel, natural resources, and even electronics. (Phillips Electronics recently sold pieces of its firm to private equity operations.) The finance industry is able to facilitate the restructuring of these industrial assets due to the availability of debt, which is substituted for equity in publicly traded firms.

The hope in Detroit among the other auto firms is that the financial experts associated with private equity firms will help the Big Three auto firms (GM, Ford, and Chrysler) in the United States deal with their excessive cost structure associated with union pensions and health care costs, which make up the bulk of the cost differences between U.S. and foreign firms. If they are not able to restructure the cost situation, the next step will be bankruptcy, the method used by many other firms in the airline and steel industries to restructure these costs. Private equity firms were also involved with these deals, especially after they came out of bankruptcy.

One potential opportunity for Chrysler is the area of financing auto and other purchases. Previous to the Chrysler deal, Cerberus purchased 51 percent ownership in the GMAC assets from General Motors Corporation. GMAC is the financing line of General Motors. Likewise in the Chrysler deal, Cerberus gains control of the Chrysler finance operation. In combination with the GMAC assets, once the financial unit activities are extracted from the operations of Chrysler, Cerberus hopes to develop a strong financing business, not only in financing automobiles but also potentially in financing opportunities such as mortgages. This move may lead them to a broader set of business-level financial offerings similar to the operation of GE Capital. The combined operations will have nearly $14.3 billion of book value, whereas GE Capital will have book value at $54.1 billion. Compared to the automobile operations, the financing arms are already profitable even with the problems that GMAC is having with its subprime home lending unit, Residential Capital Corp.

The Chrysler example represents many important aspects of this chapter: the riskiness of acquisitions, the difficulty of integration, as well as what happens with failed acquisitions leading to divestiture and how private equity firms are involved in the process. Chrysler illustrates the potential for success as well as the risk of failure, and how firms deal with exit when an acquisition strategy fails.

Sources: J. Fox, 2007, Buying a used Chrysler, *Time*, May 28, 46; J. S. Gordon, 2007, Back to the future, Detroit-style *Barron's*, June 25, 45; S. Power, 2007, After pact to shed Chrysler, Daimler turns focus to other challenges, *Wall Street Journal*, May 15, A14; J. Reed, 2007, Nanjing Automobile begins UK production of MG cars, *Financial Times*, May 30, 20; B. Simon, 2007, "New" Chrysler ready to party, *Financial Times*, July 5, 26; A. Taylor III, 2007, America's best car company, *Fortune*, March 19, 98; D. Welch, N. Byrnes, & A. Bianco, 2007, A deal that could save Detroit: A Chrysler sale to Cerberus may spark a plan to eliminate most of the health care liabilities crushing carmakers, *BusinessWeek*, May 28, 30; B. White, 2007, Chrysler's coy guardian: The Cerberus head has an onerous task turning round the carmaker, says Ben White, *Financial Times*, May 19, 9; G. Zuckerman, S. Ng, & D. Cimilluca, 2007, Cerberus finds luster in Detroit, *Wall Street Journal*, May 15, C1–C2; A. Sloan, 2006, A tough race for GM against Toyota, *Newsweek*, http://www.msnbc.msn.com, March 6.

As discussed next, three restructuring strategies are used: downsizing, downscoping, and leveraged buyouts.

Downsizing

Once thought to be an indicator of organizational decline, downsizing is now recognized as a legitimate restructuring strategy.[125] *Downsizing* is a reduction in the number of a firm's employees and, sometimes, in the number of its operating units, but it may or may not change the composition of businesses in the company's portfolio. Thus, downsizing is an intentional proactive management strategy, whereas "decline is an environmental or organizational phenomenon that occurs involuntarily and results in erosion of an organization's resource base."[126] Downsizing has been shown to be associated with acquisitions, especially when excessive premiums are paid.[127]

In the late 1980s, early 1990s, and early 2000s, thousands of jobs were lost in private and public organizations within the United States. One study estimates that 85 percent of *Fortune* 1000 firms have used downsizing as a restructuring strategy.[128] Moreover, *Fortune* 500 firms laid off more than 1 million employees, or 4 percent of their collective workforce, in 2001 and into the first few weeks of 2002.[129] This trend continues in many industries. As noted earlier, Citigroup, and its CEO Charles Prince, has been under pressure to restructure its operations. To deal in part with this pressure, Citigroup signaled in 2007 that it would cut 15,000 jobs and possibly up to 5 percent of its 327,000 worldwide workforce (equivalent to more than 30,000 jobs) over time. In the process, it would take a $1 billion charge.[130]

Downscoping

Downscoping has a more positive effect on firm performance than downsizing does.[131] *Downscoping* refers to divestiture, spin-off, or some other means of eliminating businesses that are unrelated to a firm's core businesses. Commonly, downscoping is described as a set of actions that causes a firm to strategically refocus on its core businesses.[132] American Standard Companies decided to refocus on its air-conditioning systems and services business through its flagship brand line, Trane. It will accomplish this by splitting into three businesses and spinning its vehicle control systems business into a publicly traded company to be named Wabco. Furthermore, it will sell off its original business focused on bath and kitchen fixtures. The breakup and refocus has become necessary because the bath and kitchen business has underperformed compared to the other two businesses, Trane and Wabco.[133]

A firm that downscopes often also downsizes simultaneously. However, it does not eliminate key employees from its primary businesses in the process, because such action could lead to a loss of one or more core competencies. Instead, a firm that is simultaneously downscoping and downsizing becomes smaller by reducing the diversity of businesses in its portfolio.[134]

By refocusing on its core businesses, the firm can be managed more effectively by the top management team. Managerial effectiveness increases because the firm has become less diversified, allowing the top management team to better understand and manage the remaining businesses.[135]

In general, U.S. firms use downscoping as a restructuring strategy more frequently than European companies do, while the trend in Europe, Latin America, and Asia has been to build conglomerates. In Latin America, these conglomerates are called *grupos*. Many Asian and Latin American conglomerates have begun to adopt Western corporate strategies in recent years and have been refocusing on their core businesses. This downscoping has occurred simultaneously with increasing globalization and with more open markets that have greatly enhanced the competition. By downscoping, these firms have been able to focus on their core businesses and improve their competitiveness.[136]

Downscoping has been practiced recently by many emerging market firms. For example, the Tata Group, founded by Jamsetji Nusserwanji Tata in 1868 as a private trading firm and now India's largest business group, includes 91 firms in a wide range of industries. The group covers chemicals, communications, consumer products, energy, engineering, information systems, materials, and services industries. The group's revenue in 2003–2004 was $14.25 billion, about 2.6 percent of India's GDP. Tata's member companies employ about 220,000 people and export their products to 140 countries. However, as India has changed, Tata executives have sought to restructure its member businesses to "build a more focused company without abandoning the best of Tata's manufacturing tradition."[137] Over a 10-year period Tata restructured to retain 91 businesses down from 250. However, with the Tata Steel acquisition of Corus mentioned earlier, it has begun to build global businesses as well.[138]

Leveraged Buyouts

Traditionally, leveraged buyouts were used as a restructuring strategy to correct for managerial mistakes or because the firm's managers were making decisions that primarily served their own interests rather than those of shareholders.[139] A *leveraged buyout* (LBO) is a restructuring strategy whereby a party buys all of a firm's assets in order to take the firm private. Once the transaction is completed, the company's stock is no longer traded publicly. Firms that facilitate or engage in taking public firms, or a business unit of a firm, private are called *private equity firms*. However, some firms are using buyouts to build firm resources and expand rather than simply restructure distressed assets as the Tata Steel acquisition of Corus illustrates.[140]

Usually, significant amounts of debt are incurred to finance a buyout; hence the term *leveraged* buyout. To support debt payments and to downscope the company to concentrate on the firm's core businesses, the new owners may immediately sell a number of assets.[141] It is not uncommon for those buying a firm through an LBO to restructure the firm to the point that it can be sold at a profit within a five- to eight-year period.

Management buyouts (MBOs), employee buyouts (EBOs), and whole-firm buyouts, in which one company or partnership purchases an entire company instead of a part of it, are the three types of LBOs. In part because of managerial incentives, MBOs, more so than EBOs and whole-firm buyouts, have been found to lead to downscoping, increased strategic focus, and improved performance.[142] Research has shown that management buyouts can also lead to greater entrepreneurial activity and growth.[143]

Among the different reasons for a buyout is protecting against a capricious financial market, and allowing the owners to focus on developing innovations and bringing them to the market.[144] As such, buyouts can represent a form of firm rebirth to facilitate entrepreneurial efforts and stimulate strategic growth.[145]

Restructuring Outcomes

The short-term and long-term outcomes resulting from the three restructuring strategies are shown in Figure 7.2. As indicated, downsizing does not commonly lead to higher firm performance.[146] Still, in free-market-based societies at large, downsizing has generated an incentive for individuals who have been laid off to start their own businesses.

Research has shown that downsizing contributed to lower returns for both U.S. and Japanese firms. The stock markets in the firms' respective nations evaluated downsizing negatively. Investors concluded that downsizing would have a negative effect on companies' ability to achieve strategic competitiveness in the long term. Investors also seem to assume that downsizing occurs as a consequence of other problems in a company.[147] This assumption may be caused by a firm's diminished corporate reputation when a major downsizing is announced.[148] These issues were clearly part of the Citigroup layoffs mentioned earlier.

An unintentional outcome of downsizing, however, is that laid-off employees often start new businesses in order to live through the disruption in their lives. Accordingly, downsizing has generated a host of new entrepreneurial ventures.

As shown in Figure 7.2, downsizing tends to result in a loss of human capital in the long term. Losing employees with many years of experience with the firm represents a major loss of knowledge. As noted in Chapter 3, knowledge is vital to competitive success in the global economy. Thus, in general, research evidence and corporate experience suggest that downsizing may be of more tactical (or short-term) value than strategic (or long-term) value.[149]

Downscoping generally leads to more positive outcomes in both the short- and the long-term than does downsizing or engaging in a leveraged buyout (see Figure 7.2). Downscoping's desirable long-term outcome of higher performance is a product of

Figure 7.2 Restructuring and Outcomes

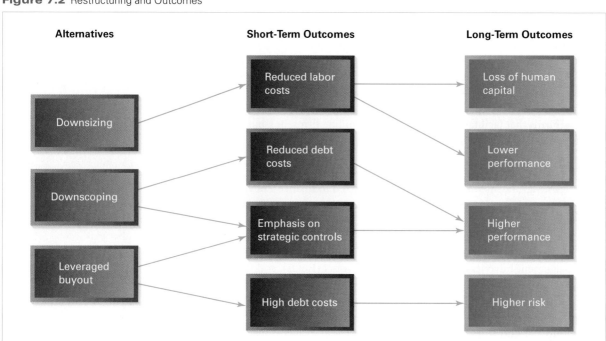

reduced debt costs and the emphasis on strategic controls derived from concentrating on the firm's core businesses. In so doing, the refocused firm should be able to increase its ability to compete.[150]

Although whole-firm LBOs have been hailed as a significant innovation in the financial restructuring of firms, they can involve negative trade-offs.[151] First, the resulting large debt increases the financial risk of the firm, as is evidenced by the number of companies that filed for bankruptcy in the 1990s after executing a whole-firm LBO. Sometimes, the intent of the owners to increase the efficiency of the bought-out firm and then sell it within five to eight years creates a short-term and risk-averse managerial focus.[152] As a result, these firms may fail to invest adequately in R&D or take other major actions designed to maintain or improve the company's core competence.[153] Research also suggests that in firms with an entrepreneurial mind-set, buyouts can lead to greater innovation, especially if the debt load is not too great.[154] However, because buyouts more often result in significant debt, most LBOs have taken place in mature industries where stable cash flows are possible. This situation enables the buyout firm to meet the recurring debt payments as exemplified by Tata Steel's buyout of Corus in the steel industry described in the Opening Case and expanded on later in the chapter.

Summary

- Acquisition strategies are increasingly popular. Because of globalization, deregulation of multiple industries in many different economies, and favorable legislation, the number and size of domestic and cross-border acquisitions continues to increase, especially from emerging economies.

- Firms use acquisition strategies to (1) increase market power, (2) overcome entry barriers to new markets or regions, (3) avoid the costs of developing new products and increase the speed of new market entries, (4) reduce the risk of entering a new business, (5) become more diversified, (6) reshape their competitive scope by developing a different portfolio of businesses, and (7) enhance their learning, thereby adding to their knowledge base.

- Among the problems associated with the use of an acquisition strategy are (1) the difficulty of effectively integrating the firms involved, (2) incorrectly evaluating the target firm's value, (3) creating debt loads that preclude adequate long-term investments (e.g., R&D), (4) overestimating the potential for synergy, (5) creating a firm that is too diversified, (6) creating an internal environment in which managers devote increasing amounts of their time and energy to analyzing and completing the acquisition, and (7) developing a combined firm that is too large, necessitating extensive use of bureaucratic, rather than strategic, controls.

- Effective acquisitions have the following characteristics: (1) the acquiring and target firms have complementary resources that can be the basis of core competencies in the newly created firm; (2) the acquisition is friendly, thereby facilitating integration of the two firms' resources; (3) the target firm is selected and purchased based on thorough due diligence; (4) the acquiring and target firms have considerable slack in the form of cash or debt capacity; (5) the merged firm maintains a low or moderate level of debt by selling off portions of the acquired

firm or some of the acquiring firm's poorly performing units; (6) the acquiring and acquired firms have experience in terms of adapting to change; and (7) R&D and innovation are emphasized in the new firm.

- Restructuring is used to improve a firm's performance by correcting for problems created by ineffective management. Restructuring by downsizing involves reducing the number of employees and hierarchical levels in the firm. Although it can lead to short-term cost reductions, they may be realized at the expense of long-term success, because of the loss of valuable human resources (and knowledge) and overall corporate reputation.

- The goal of restructuring through downscoping is to reduce the firm's level of diversification. Often, the firm divests unrelated businesses to achieve this goal. Eliminating unrelated businesses makes it easier for the firm and its top-level managers to refocus on the core businesses.

- Leveraged buyouts (LBOs) represent an additional restructuring strategy by private equity firms such as KKR or Blackstone Group. Through an LBO, a firm is purchased so that it can become a private entity. LBOs usually are financed largely through debt. The three types of LBOs are management buyouts (MBOs), employee buyouts (EBOs), and whole-firm LBOs. Because they provide clear managerial incentives, MBOs have been the most successful of the three. Often, the intent of a buyout is to improve efficiency and performance to the point where the firm can be sold successfully within five to eight years.

- Commonly, restructuring's primary goal is gaining or reestablishing effective strategic control of the firm. Of the three restructuring strategies, downscoping is aligned most closely with establishing and using strategic controls and usually improves performance more on a comparative basis.

1. Why are acquisition strategies popular in many firms competing in the global economy?

2. What reasons account for firms' decisions to use acquisition strategies as a means to achieving strategic competitiveness?

3. What are the seven primary problems that affect a firm's efforts to successfully use an acquisition strategy?

4. What are the attributes associated with a successful acquisition strategy?

5. What is the restructuring strategy, and what are its common forms?

6. What are the short- and long-term outcomes associated with the different restructuring strategies?

Notes

1. K. Uhlenbruck, M. A. Hitt, & M. Semadeni, 2006, Market value effects of acquisitions involving Internet firms: A resource-based analysis, *Strategic Management Journal,* 27: 899–913; J. Anand, 2004, Redeployment of corporate resources: A study of acquisition strategies in the U.S. defense industries, 1978–1996, *Managerial and Decision Economics,* 25: 383–400; L. Capron & N. Pistre, 2002, When do acquirers earn abnormal returns? *Strategic Management Journal,* 23: 781–794.

2. C.-C. Lu, 2006, Growth strategies and merger patterns among small and medium-sized enterprises: An empirical study, *International Journal of Management,* 23: 529–547.

3. J. Haleblian; J.-Y. Kim, & N. Rajagopalan, 2006, The influence of acquisition experience and performance on acquisition behavior: Evidence from the U.S. commercial banking industry, *Academy of Management Journal,* 49: 357–370; H. Shahrur, 2005, Industry structure and horizontal takeovers: Analysis of wealth effects on rivals, suppliers, and corporate customers, *Journal of Financial Economics,* 76: 61–98; M. A. Hitt, J. S. Harrison, & R. D. Ireland, 2001, *Mergers and Acquisitions: A Guide to Creating Value for Stakeholders,* New York: Oxford University Press.

4. R. Dobbs & V. Tortorici, 2007, Cool heads will bring in the best deals; Boardroom discipline is vital if the M&A boom is to benefit shareholders, *Financial Times,* February 28, 6.

5. D. Cimilluca, 2007, Buyout firms fuel a record; Pace of M&A pacts could start to slow amid tighter credit, *Wall Street Journal,* July 2, C8.

6. S. Daneshkhu, 2007, FDI flow into richest countries set to rise 20% this year, *Financial Times,* June 22, 7.

7. Cimilluca, Buyout firms fuel a record.

8. A. G. Warner, J. F. Fairbank, & H. K. Steensma, 2006, Managing uncertainty in a formal standards-based industry: A real

options perspective on acquisition timing, *Journal of Management,* 32: 279–298; R. Coff, 2003, Bidding wars over R&D-intensive firms: Knowledge, opportunism, and the market for corporate control, *Academy of Management Journal,* 46: 74–85; P. Chattopadhyay, W. H. Glick, & G. P. Huber, 2001, Organizational actions in response to threats and opportunities, *Academy of Management Journal,* 44: 937–955.

9. C. Bryan-Low, 2007, Thomson evolution takes next step; Reuters deal, emphasis on data services mark latest efforts to adapt, *Wall Street Journal,* June 13, A10.

10. G. Cullinan, J.-M. Le Roux, & R.-M. Weddigen, 2004, When to walk away from a deal, *Harvard Business Review,* 82(4): 96–104; L. Selden & G. Colvin, 2003, M&A needn't be a loser's game, *Harvard Business Review,* 81(6): 70–73.

11. J. J. Reuer, 2005, Avoiding lemons in M&A deals, *MIT Sloan Management Review,* 46(3): 15–17; M. C. Jensen, 1988, Takeovers: Their causes and consequences, *Journal of Economic Perspectives,* 1(2): 21–48.

12. C. Tuch & N. O'Sullivan, 2007, The impact of acquisitions on firm performance: A review of the evidence, *International Journal of Management Review,* 9(2): 141–170.

13. K. Cool & M. Van de Laar, 2006, The performance of acquisitive companies in the U.S. In L. Renneboog, (ed.), *Advances in Corporate Finance and Asset Pricing,* Amsterdam, Netherlands: Elsevier Science, 77–105; D. K. Berman, 2005, Mergers horror II: The rhetoric, *Wall Street Journal,* May 24, C1; T. Wright, M. Kroll, A. Lado, & B. Van Ness, 2002, The structure of ownership and corporate acquisition strategies, *Strategic Management Journal,* 23: 41–53; A. Rappaport & M. L. Sirower, 1999, Stock or cash? *Harvard Business Review,* 77(6): 147–158.

14. 2007, Happily never after mergers, like marriages, fail without a meeting of minds, *Financial Times,* May 15, 14.

15. E. Thornton, F. Keenan, C. Palmeri, & L. Himelstein, 2002, It sure is getting hostile, *BusinessWeek,* January 14, 28–30.

16. S. Sudarsanam & A. A. Mahate, 2006, Are friendly acquisitions too bad for shareholders and managers? Long-term value creation and top management turnover in hostile and friendly acquirers, *British Journal of Management: Supplement,* 17(1): S7–S30.

17. A. M. Marino & J. Zábojník, 2006, Merger, ease of entry and entry deterrence in a dynamic model, *Journal of Industrial Economics,* 54: 397–423; P. Haspeslagh, 1999, Managing the mating dance in equal mergers, "Mastering Strategy" (Part Five), *Financial Times,* October 25, 14–15.

18. P. Wright, M. Kroll, & D. Elenkov, 2002, Acquisition returns, increase in firm size and chief executive officer compensation: The moderating role of monitoring, *Academy of Management Journal,* 45: 599–608.

19. J. Whalen, 2007, Nestle bolsters baby-food line, *Wall Street Journal,* April 12, A3.

20. R. W. Palmatier, C. F. Miao, & E. Fang, 2007, Sales channel integration after mergers and acquisitions: A methodological approach for avoiding common pitfalls, *Industrial Marketing Management,* 36(5): 589–603; C. Hamburg & M. Bucerius, 2005, A marketing perspective on mergers and acquisitions: How marketing integration affects post-merger performance, *Journal of Marketing,* 69: 95–113.

21. E. Gal-Or & A. Dukes, 2006, On the profitability of media mergers, *Journal of Business,* 79: 489–525; Capron & Pistre, When do acquirers earn abnormal returns?; L. Capron, 1999, Horizontal acquisitions: The benefits and risks to long-term performance, *Strategic Management Journal,* 20: 987–1018.

22. C. E. Fee & S. Thomas, 2004, Sources of gains in horizontal mergers: Evidence from customer, supplier, and rival firms, *Journal of Financial Economics,* 74: 423–460.

23. M. Lubatkin, W. S. Schulze, A. Mainkar, & R. W. Cotterill, 2001, Ecological investigation of firm effects in horizontal mergers, *Strategic Management Journal,* 22: 335–357; K. Ramaswamy, 1997, The performance impact of strategic similarity in horizontal mergers: Evidence from the U.S. banking industry, *Academy of Management Journal,* 40: 697–715.

24. L. Capron, W. Mitchell, & A. Swaminathan, 2001, Asset divestiture following horizontal acquisitions: A dynamic view, *Strategic Management Journal,* 22: 817–844.

25. J. P. H. Fan & V. K. Goyal, 2006, On the patterns and wealth effects of vertical mergers, *Journal of Business,* 79: 877–902; F. T. Rothaermel, M. A. Hitt, & L. A. Jobe, 2006, Balancing vertical integration and strategic outsourcing: Effects on product portfolio, product success, and firm performance, *Strategic Management Journal,* 27: 1033–1056.

26. A. Parmigiani, 2007, Why do firms both make and buy? An investigation of concurrent sourcing, *Strategic Management Journal,* 28: 285–311.

27. J. B. Stewart, 2007, Common sense: Google's DoubleClick play still makes it a good bet, *Wall Street Journal,* April 18, D3.

28. S. Lohr, 2007, I.B.M. showing that giants can be nimble, *New York Times,* http://www.nyt.com, July 18.

29. D. Gupta & Y. Gerchak, 2002, Quantifying operational synergies in a merger/acquisition, *Management Science,* 48: 517–533.

30. R. Sinha, 2006, Regulation: The market for corporate control and corporate governance, *Global Finance Journal,* 16(3): 264–282; D. E. M. Sappington, 2003, Regulating horizontal diversification, *International Journal of Industrial Organization,* 21: 291–315.

31. S.-F. S. Chen & M. Zeng, 2004, Japanese investors' choice of acquisitions vs. startups in the U.S.: The role of reputation barriers and advertising outlays, *International Journal of Research in Marketing,* 21(2): 123–136; S. J. Chang & P. M. Rosenzweig, 2001, The choice of entry mode in sequential foreign direct investment, *Strategic Management Journal,* 22: 747–776.

32. S. McGee, 2007, Seeking value in BRICs, *Barron's,* July 9, L10–L11.

33. B. Villalonga & A. M. Mcgahan, 2005, The choice among acquisitions, alliances, and divestitures, *Strategic Management Journal,* 26: 1183–1208; K. Shimizu, M. A. Hitt, D. Vaidyanath, & V. Pisano, 2004, Theoretical foundations of cross-border mergers and acquisitions: A review of current research and recommendations for the future, *Journal of International Management,* 10: 307–353; J. A. Doukas & L. H. P. Lang, 2003, Foreign direct investment, diversification and firm performance, *Journal of International Business Studies,* 34: 153–172; M. A. Hitt, J. S. Harrison, & R. D. Ireland, 2001, *Mergers and Acquisitions: A Guide*

to Creating Value for Stakeholders, New York: Oxford University Press, Chapter 10.

34. A. Seth, K. P. Song, & R. R. Pettit, 2002, Value creation and destruction in cross-border acquisitions: An empirical analysis of foreign acquisitions of U.S. firms, *Strategic Management Journal,* 23: 921–940.

35. M. W. Peng & A. Delios, 2006, What determines the scope of the firm over time and around the world? An Asia Pacific perspective, *Asia Pacific Journal of Management,* 23: 385–405.

36. J. A. Schmidt, 2002, Business perspective on mergers and acquisitions, in J. A. Schmidt (ed.), *Making Mergers Work,* Alexandria, VA: Society for Human Resource Management, 23–46.

37. T. Clissold, 2006, The strange paradox of economic nationalism, *Financial Times,* August 10, 13; A. M. Agami, 2002, The role that foreign acquisitions of Asian companies played in the recovery of the Asian financial crisis, *Multinational Business Review,* 10(1): 11–20.

38. C. Firstbrook, 2007, Transnational mergers and acquisitions: How to beat the odds of disaster, *Journal of Business Strategy,* 28(1): 53–56; P. Quah & S. Young, 2005, Post-acquisition management: A phases approach for cross-border M&As, *European Management Journal,* 17(1), 65–75; J. K. Sebenius, 2002, The hidden challenge of cross-border negotiations, *Harvard Business Review,* 80(3): 76–85.

39. C. Homburg & M. Bucerius, 2006, Is speed of integration really a success factor of mergers and acquisitions? An analysis of the role of internal and external relatedness, *Strategic Management Journal,* 27: 347–367; V. Bannert & H. Tschirky, 2004, Integration planning for technology intensive acquisitions, *R&D Management,* 34(5): 481–494; W. Vanhaverbeke, G. Duysters, & N. Noorderhaven, 2002, External technology sourcing through alliances or acquisitions: An analysis of the application-specific integrated circuits industry, *Organization Science,* 6: 714–733.

40. S. Karim, 2006, Modularity in organizational structure: The reconfiguration of internally developed and acquired business units, *Strategic Management Journal,* 27: 799–823; H. Gatignon, M. L. Tushman, W. Smith, & P. Anderson, 2002, A structural approach to assessing innovation: Construct development of innovation locus, type, and characteristics, *Management Science,* 48: 1103–1122; Hitt, Harrison, & Ireland, *Mergers and Acquisitions.*

41. R. E. Hoskisson & L. W. Busenitz, 2002, Market uncertainty and learning distance in corporate entrepreneurship entry mode choice, in M. A. Hitt, R. D. Ireland, S. M. Camp, & D. L. Sexton (eds.), *Strategic Entrepreneurship: Creating a New Mindset,* Oxford, U.K.: Blackwell Publishers, 151–172; M. A. Hitt, R. E. Hoskisson, R. A. Johnson, & D. D. Moesel, 1996, The market for corporate control and firm innovation, *Academy of Management Journal,* 39: 1084–1119.

42. Coff, Bidding wars over R&D-intensive firms: Knowledge, opportunism, and the market for corporate control.

43. J. Palmer, 2007, Gilead's War on AIDS, *Barron's,* July 9, 25.

44. R. Mudambi & S. A. Zahra, 2007, The survival of international new ventures, *Journal of International Business Studies,* 38: 333–352; Y. Luo, O. Shenkar, & M.-K. Nyaw, 2002, Mitigating liabilities of foreignness: Defensive versus offensive approaches, *Journal of International Management,* 8: 283–300.

45. Uhlenbruck, Hitt, & Semadeni, Market value effects of acquisitions involving Internet firms: A resource-based analysis; C. W. L. Hill & F. T. Rothaermel, 2003, The performance of incumbent firms in the face of radical technological innovation, *Academy of Management Review,* 28: 257–274.

46. F. Rothaermel, 2001, Incumbent's advantage through exploiting complementary assets via interfirm cooperation, *Strategic Management Journal,* 22 (Special Issue): 687–699.

47. L.-F. Hsieh & Y.-T. Tsai, 2005, Technology investment mode of innovative technological corporations: M&A strategy intended to facilitate innovation, *Journal of American Academy of Business,* 6(1): 185–194; G. Ahuja & R. Katila, 2001, Technological acquisitions and the innovation performance of acquiring firms: A longitudinal study, *Strategic Management Journal,* 22: 197–220; M. A. Hitt, R. E. Hoskisson, & R. D. Ireland, 1990, Mergers and acquisitions and managerial commitment to innovation in M-form firms, *Strategic Management Journal,* 11 (Special Issue): 29–47.

48. Hitt, Hoskisson, Johnson, & Moesel, The market for corporate control.

49. P. Parvinen & H. Tikkanen, 2007, Incentive asymmetries in the mergers and acquisitions process, *Journal of Management Studies,* 44: 759–787; P. Strebel & A.-V. Ohlsson, 2006, The art of making smart big moves, *MIT Sloan Management Review,* 47(2): 79–83.

50. Hoskisson & Busenitz, Market uncertainty and learning distance in corporate entrepreneurship entry mode choice; Hill & Rothaermel, The performance of incumbent firms in the face of radical technological innovation.

51. F. Vermeulen, 2005, How acquisitions can revitalize companies, *MIT Sloan Management Review,* 46(4): 45–51; M. A. Hitt, R. E. Hoskisson, R. D. Ireland, & J. S. Harrison, 1991, Effects of acquisitions on R&D inputs and outputs, *Academy of Management Journal,* 34: 693–706.

52. B. White, 2007, Cisco to buy IronPort, a network-security firm, *Wall Street Journal,* January 4, A10.

53. C. E. Helfat & K. M. Eisenhardt, 2004, Inter-temporal economies of scope, organizational modularity, and the dynamics of diversification, *Strategic Management Journal,* 25: 1217–1232;

C. Park, 2003, Prior performance characteristics of related and unrelated acquirers, *Strategic Management Journal,* 24: 471–480.

54. J. L. Lunsford, 2007, United Technologies reaches a deal to buy Rentokil's security division, *Wall Street Journal,* March 30, C3.

55. J. L. Lunsford, 2007, Boss talk: Transformer in transition; He turned UTC into giant; now, CEO George David carefully prepares successor, *Wall Street Journal,* May 17, B1.

56. D. J. Miller, M. J. Fern, & L. B. Cardinal, 2007, The use of knowledge for technological innovation within diversified firms, *Academy of Management Journal,* 50: 308–326; Krishnan, Hitt, & Park, Acquisition premiums, subsequent workforce reductions and post-acquisition performance; Hitt, Harrison, & Ireland, *Mergers and Acquisitions.*

57. J. Anand & H. Singh, 1997, Asset redeployment, acquisitions and corporate strategy in declining industries, *Strategic Management Journal,* 18 (Special Issue): 99–118.

58. Helfat & Eisenhardt, Inter-temporal economies of scope, organizational modularity, and the dynamics of diversification; W. J. Ferrier, 2001, Navigating the competitive landscape: The drivers and consequences of competitive aggressiveness, *Academy of Management Journal,* 44: 858–877.

59. F. Guerrera, 2007, M&A vision highlights change of focus at House that Jack Built, *Financial Times,* January 16, 19.

60. Bryan-Low, Thomson evolution takes next step.

61. P. Puranam & K. Srikanth, 2007, What they know vs. what they do: How acquirers leverage technology acquisitions, *Strategic Management Journal,* 28: 805–825; F. Vermeulen & H. Barkema, 2001, Learning through acquisitions, *Academy of Management Journal,* 44: 457–476.

62. Vermeulen, How acquisitions can revitalize firms; J. Gammelgaard, 2004, Access to competence: An emerging acquisition motive, *European Business Forum,* Spring, 44–40; M. L. A. Hayward, 2002, When do firms learn from their acquisition experience? Evidence from 1990–1995, *Strategic Management Journal,* 23: 21–39.

63. J. Anand, L. Capron, & W. Mitchell, 2005, Using acquisitions to access multinational diversity: Thinking beyond the domestic versus cross-border M&A comparison, *Industrial and Corporate Change,* 14(2): 191–224.

64. J. S. Harrison, M. A. Hitt, R. E. Hoskisson, & R. D. Ireland, 2001, Resource complementarity in business combinations: Extending the logic to organizational alliances, *Journal of Management,* 27: 679–690.

65. J. Whalen, 2007, AstraZeneca thinks bigger; new chief increases commitment to 'large molecule' biological drugs, *Wall Street Journal,* May 22, A7.

66. Schmidt, Business perspective on mergers and acquisitions.

67. M. Zollo & H. Singh, 2004, Deliberate learning in corporate acquisitions: Post-acquisition strategies and integration capability in U.S. bank mergers, *Strategic Management Journal,* 25: 1233–1256; P. Mallette, C. L. Fowler, & C. Hayes, 2003, The acquisition process map: Blueprint for a successful deal, *Southern Business Review,* 28(2): 1–13; Hitt, Harrison, & Ireland, *Mergers and Acquisitions.*

68. J. Harrison, 2007, Why integration success eludes many buyers, *Mergers and Acquisitions,* 42(3): 18–20; R. A. Weber & C. F. Camerer, 2003, Cultural conflict and merger failure: An experimental approach, *Management Science,* 49: 400–415; J. Vester, 2002, Lessons learned about integrating acquisitions, *Research Technology Management,* 45(3): 33–41; D. K. Datta, 1991, Organizational fit and acquisition performance: Effects of post-acquisition integration, *Strategic Management Journal,* 12: 281–297.

69. F. Vermeulen, 2007, Business insight (a special report); bad deals: Eight warning signs that an acquisition may not pay off, *Wall Street Journal,* April 28, R10; J. R. Carleton & C. S. Lineberry, 2004, *Achieving Post-Merger Success,* New York: John Wiley & Sons; Y. Weber & E. Menipaz, 2003, Measuring cultural fit in mergers and acquisitions, *International Journal of Business Performance Management,* 5(1): 54–72.

70. M. Zollo, 1999, M&A—The challenge of learning to integrate, "Mastering Strategy" (Part Eleven), *Financial Times,* December 6, 14–15.

71. R. Gibson, 2006, Package deal; UPS's purchase of Mail Boxes Etc. looked great on paper. Then came the culture clash., *Wall Street Journal,* May 8, R13.

72. M. A. Hitt, L. Bierman, K. Shimizu, & R. Kochhar, 2001, Direct and moderating effects of human capital on strategy and performance in professional service firms, *Academy of Management Journal,* 44: 13–28.

73. J. A. Krug, 2003, Why do they keep leaving? *Harvard Business Review,* 81(2): 14–15; H. A. Krishnan & D. Park, 2002, The impact of workforce reduction on subsequent performance in major mergers and acquisitions: An exploratory study, *Journal of Business Research,* 55(4): 285–292; G. G. Dess & J. D. Shaw, 2001, Voluntary turnover, social capital and organizational performance, *Academy of Management Review,* 26: 446–456.

74. D. Harding & T. Rouse, 2007, Human due diligence, *Harvard Business Review,* 85(4): 124–131.

75. T. McIntyre, 2004, A model of levels of involvement and strategic roles of human resource development (HRD) professionals as facilitators of due diligence and the integration process, *Human Resource Development Review,* 3(2): 173–182; J. A. Krug & H. Hegarty, 2001, Predicting who stays and leaves after an acquisition: A study of top managers in multinational firms, *Strategic Management Journal,* 22: 185–196.

76. G. Cullinan, J.-M. Le Roux, & R.-M. Weddigen, 2004, When to walk away from a deal, *Harvard Business Review,* 82(4): 96–104.

77. R. J. Rosen, 2006, Merger momentum and investor sentiment: The stock market reaction to merger announcements, *Journal of Business,* 79: 987–1017.

78. Rappaport & Sirower, Stock or cash? 149.

79. E. Thornton, 2003, Bypassing the street, *BusinessWeek,* June 2, 79.

80. G. Yago, 1991, *Junk Bonds: How High Yield Securities Restructured Corporate America,* New York: Oxford University Press, 146–148.

81. M. C. Jensen, 1986, Agency costs of free cash flow, corporate finance, and takeovers, *American Economic Review,* 76: 323–329.

82. E. Bellman, 2007, Tata's Corus deal raises fears about likely heavy debt load, *Wall Street Journal,* February 1, C7.

83. T. H. Noe & M. J. Rebello, 2006, The role of debt purchases in takeovers: A tale of two retailers, *Journal of Economics & Management Strategy,* 15 (3): 609–648; M. A. Hitt & D. L. Smart, 1994, Debt: A disciplining force for managers or a debilitating force for organizations? *Journal of Management Inquiry,* 3: 144–152.

84. Hitt, Harrison, & Ireland, *Mergers and Acquisitions.*

85. T. N. Hubbard, 1999, Integration strategies and the scope of the company, "Mastering Strategy" (Part Eleven), *Financial Times,* December 6, 8–10.

86. Hitt, Harrison, & Ireland, *Mergers and Acquisitions.*

87. A. B. Sorescu, R. K. Chandy, & J. C. Prabhu, 2007, Why some acquisitions do better than others: Product capital as a driver of long-term stock returns, *Journal of Marketing Research,* 44(1): 57–72; T. Saxton & M. Dollinger, 2004, Target reputation and appropriability: Picking and deploying resources in acquisitions, *Journal of Management,* 30: 123–147.

88. Harrison, Hitt, Hoskisson & Ireland, Resource complementarity in business combinations; J. B. Barney, 1988, Returns to bidding firms in mergers and acquisitions: Reconsidering the relatedness hypothesis, *Strategic Management Journal,* 9 (Special Issue): 71–78.

89. O. E. Williamson, 1999, Strategy research: Governance and competence perspectives, *Strategic Management Journal,* 20: 1087–1108.

90. S. Chatterjee, 2007, Why is synergy so difficult in mergers of related businesses? *Strategy & Leadership,* 35(2): 46–52; Hitt, Hoskisson, Johnson, & Moesel, The market for corporate control.

91. 2007, Divorce puts paid to carmaking dream, *Financial Times,* May 15, 28.

92. Ibid.

93. C. W. L. Hill & R. E. Hoskisson, 1987, Strategy and structure in the multiproduct

firm, *Academy of Management Review,* 12: 331–341.

94. M. L. A. Hayward & K. Shimizu, 2006, De-commitment to losing strategic action: Evidence from the divestiture of poorly performing acquisitions, *Strategic Management Journal,* 27: 541–557; R. A. Johnson, R. E. Hoskisson, & M. A. Hitt, 1993, Board of director involvement in restructuring: The effects of board versus managerial controls and characteristics, *Strategic Management Journal,* 14 (Special Issue): 33–50; C. C. Markides, 1992, Consequences of corporate refocusing: Ex ante evidence, *Academy of Management Journal,* 35: 398–412.

95. M. Maynard, 2007, Ford seeking a future by going backward, *New York Times,* http://www.nytimes.com, July 16.

96. M. Brauer, 2006, What have we acquired and what should we acquire in divestiture research? A review and research agenda, *Journal of Management,* 32: 751–785; D. Palmer & B. N. Barber, 2001, Challengers, elites and families: A social class theory of corporate acquisitions, *Administrative Science Quarterly,* 46: 87–120.

97. Hitt, Harrison, & Ireland, *Mergers and Acquisitions;* R. E. Hoskisson & R. A. Johnson, 1992, Corporate restructuring and strategic change: The effect on diversification strategy and R&D intensity, *Strategic Management Journal,* 13: 625–634.

98. Ibid.

99. Vermeulen, Business insight (a special report); bad deals: Eight warning signs that an acquisition may not pay off; Hughes, Lang, Mester, Moon, & Pagano, Do bankers sacrifice value to build empires? Managerial incentives, industry consolidation, and financial performance; Hitt, Hoskisson, Johnson, & Moesel, The market for corporate control; Hitt, Hoskisson, & Ireland, Mergers and acquisitions and managerial commitment to innovation in M-form firms.

100. M. L. A. Hayward & D. C. Hambrick, 1997, Explaining the premiums paid for large acquisitions: Evidence of CEO hubris, *Administrative Science Quarterly* 42: 103–127; R. Roll, 1986, The hubris hypothesis of corporate takeovers, *Journal of Business,* 59: 197–216.

101. Vermeulen, Business insight (a special report); bad deals: Eight warning signs that an acquisition may not pay off.

102. Haleblian, Kim, & Rajagopalan, The influence of acquisition experience and performance on acquisition behavior; Hayward, When do firms learn from their acquisition experience?

103. R. Dobbs, 2007, Claiborne seeks to shed 16 apparel brands, *Wall Street Journal,* July 11, B1, B2.

104. Palmatier, Miao, & Fang, Sales channel integration after mergers and acquisitions.

105. Vermeulen, Business insight (a special report); bad deals: Eight warning signs that an acquisition may not pay off.

106. D. Enrich, 2007, Moving the market: Will chorus grow at Citi?; Lampert may join calls for shake-up after buying stake, *Wall Street Journal,* May 17, C3.

107. Cool & Van de Laar, The performance of acquisitive companies in the U.S.

108. C. Duncan & M. Mtar, 2006, Determinants of international acquisition success: Lessons from FirstGroup in North America, *European Management Journal,* 24(6): 396-41; Reuer, Avoiding lemons in M&A deals; R. M. Di Gregorio, 2003, Making mergers and acquisitions work: What we know and don't know— Part II, *Journal of Change Management,* 3(3): 259–274.

109. D. Mayer & M. Kenney, 2004, Economic action does not take place in a vacuum: Understanding Cisco's acquisition and development strategy, *Industry and Innovation,* 11(4): 299–325.

110. M. A. Hitt, R. D. Ireland, J. S. Harrison, & A. Best, 1998, Attributes of successful and unsuccessful acquisitions of U.S. firms, *British Journal of Management,* 9: 91–114.

111. Harrison, Hitt, Hoskisson, & Ireland, Resource complementarity in business combinations.

112. Uhlenbruck, Hitt, & Semadeni, Market value effects of acquisitions involving Internet firms: A resource-based analysis; J. Hagedoorn & G. Dysters, 2002, External sources of innovative capabilities: The preference for strategic alliances or mergers and acquisitions, *Journal of Management Studies,* 39: 167–188.

113. J. J. Reuer & R. Ragozzino, 2006, Agency hazards and alliance portfolios, *Strategic Management Journal,* 27: 27–43; P. Porrini, 2004, Can a previous alliance between an acquirer and a target affect acquisition performance? *Journal of Management,* 30: 545–562.

114. R. J. Aiello & M. D. Watkins, 2000, The fine art of friendly acquisition, *Harvard Business Review,* 78(6): 100–107.

115. Krishnan, Hitt, & Park, Acquisition premiums, subsequent workforce reductions and post-acquisition performance; P. Gwynne, 2002, Keeping the right people, *MIT Sloan Management Review,* 43(2): 19; D. D. Bergh, 2001, Executive retention and acquisition outcomes: A test of opposing views on the influence of organizational tenure, *Journal of Management,* 27: 603–622; J. P. Walsh, 1989, Doing a deal: Merger and acquisition negotiations and their impact upon target company top management turnover, *Strategic Management Journal,* 10: 307–322.

116. G. Lodorfos & A. Boateng, 2006, The role of culture in the merger and acquisition process: Evidence from the European chemical industry, *Management Decision,* 44(10):1405–1421; M. L. Marks & P. H. Mirvis, 2001, Making mergers and acquisitions work: Strategic and psychological preparation, *Academy of Management Executive,* 15(2): 80–92.

117. Cullinan, Le Roux, & Weddigen, When to walk away from a deal; S. Rovit &

C. Lemire, 2003, Your best M&A strategy, *Harvard Business Review,* 81(3): 16–17.

118. C. Terranova, 2007, Assessing culture during an acquisition, *Organization Development Journal,* 25(2): P43–P48; Hitt, Harrison, & Ireland, *Mergers and Acquisitions;* Q. N. Huy, 2001, Time, temporal capability and planned change, *Academy of Management Review,* 26: 601–623; L. Markoczy, 2001, Consensus formation during strategic change, *Strategic Management Journal,* 22: 1013–1031.

119. Harding & Rouse, Human due diligence.

120. J. B. Steward, 2007, Buffett stake may signal railroad to be corn fed, *Wall Street Journal,* http://www.wsj.com, April 11.

121. J. Anand, 1999, How many matches are made in heaven, Mastering Strategy (Part Five), *Financial Times,* October 25, 6–7.

122. J.-K. Kang, J.-M. Kim, W.-L. Liu, & S. Yi, 2006, Post-takeover restructuring and the sources of gains in foreign takeovers: Evidence from U.S. targets, *Journal of Business,* 79(5): 2503–2537; R. A. Johnson, 1996, Antecedents and outcomes of corporate refocusing, *Journal of Management,* 22: 437–481; J. E. Bethel & J. Liebeskind, 1993, The effects of ownership structure on corporate restructuring, *Strategic Management Journal,* 14 (Special Issue): 15–31.

123. K. E. Meyer, 2006, Globalfocusing: From domestic conglomerates to global specialists, *Journal of Management Studies,* 43: 1109–1144; R. E. Hoskisson, A. A. Cannella, L. Tihanyi, & R. Faraci, 2004. Asset restructuring and business group affiliation in French civil law countries, *Strategic Management Journal,* 25: 525–539.

124. J. L. Morrow Jr., D. G. Sirmon, M. A. Hitt, & T. R. Holcomb, 2007, Creating value in the face of declining performance: Firm strategies and organizational recovery, *Strategic Management Journal,* 28: 271–283; J. L. Morrow Jr., R. A. Johnson, & L. W. Busenitz, 2004, The effects of cost and asset retrenchment on firm performance: The overlooked role of a firm's competitive environment, *Journal of Management,* 30: 189–208.

125. R. D. Nixon, M. A. Hitt, H.-U. Lee, & E. Jeong, 2004, Market reactions to announcements of corporate downsizing actions and implementation strategies, *Strategic Management Journal,* 25: 1121–1129.

126. G. J. Castrogiovanni & G. D. Bruton, 2000, Business turnaround processes following acquisitions: Reconsidering the role of retrenchment, *Journal of Business Research,* 48: 25–34; W. McKinley, J. Zhao, & K. G. Rust, 2000, A sociocognitive interpretation of organizational downsizing, *Academy of Management Review,* 25: 227–243.

127. H. A. Krishnan, M. A. Hitt, & D. Park, 2007, Acquisition premiums, subsequent workforce reductions and post-acquisition performance, *Journal of Management,* 44: 709–732.

128. W. McKinley, C. M. Sanchez, & A. G. Schick, 1995, Organizational downsizing: Constraining, cloning, learning, *Academy of Management Executive*, 9(3): 32–44.

129. P. Patsuris, 2002, Forbes.com layoff tracker surpasses 1M mark, *Forbes*, http://www.forbes.com, January 16.

130. D. Enrich, C. Mollenkamp, & M. Langley, 2007, Citigroup likely to propose cuts of 15,000 jobs; revamp plan may call for charge of $1 billion; high stakes for Prince, *Wall Street Journal*, http://www.wsj.com, March 26, A1, A11.

131. R. E. Hoskisson & M. A. Hitt, 1994, *Downscoping: How to Tame the Diversified Firm*, New York: Oxford University Press.

132. L. Dranikoff, T. Koller, & A. Schneider, 2002, Divestiture: Strategy's missing link, *Harvard Business Review*, 80(5): 74–83.

133. B. Sechler & J. Rose, 2007, American Standard to split businesses, sell unit, *Wall Street Journal*, February 2, A14.

134. Brauer, What have we acquired and what should we acquire in divestiture research; M. Rajand & M. Forsyth, 2002, Hostile bidders, long-term performance, and restructuring methods: Evidence from the UK, *American Business Review*, 20(1): 71–81.

135. Johnson, Hoskisson, & Hitt, Board of director involvement; R. E. Hoskisson & M. A. Hitt, 1990, Antecedents and performance outcomes of diversification: A review and critique of theoretical perspectives, *Journal of Management*, 16: 461–509.

136. R. E. Hoskisson, R. A. Johnson, L. Tihanyi, & R. E. White, 2005, Diversified business groups and corporate refocusing in emerging economies, *Journal of Management*, 31: 941–965.

137. M. Kripalani, 2004, Ratan Tata: No one's doubting now, *Business Week*, July 26, 50–51.

138. Bellman, Tata's Corus deal raises fears about likely heavy debt load.

139. J. Krasoff & J. O'Neill, 2006, The role of distressed investing and hedge funds in turnarounds and buyouts and how this affects middle-market companies, *Journal of Private Equity*, 9(2): 17–23; C. C. Markides & H. Singh, 1997, Corporate restructuring: A symptom of poor governance or a solution to past managerial mistakes? *European Management Journal*, 15: 213–219.

140. J. Mair & C. Moschieri, 2006, Unbundling frees business for take off, *Financial Times*, October 19, 2.

141. M. F. Wiersema & J. P. Liebeskind, 1995, The effects of leveraged buyouts on corporate growth and diversification in large firms, *Strategic Management Journal*, 16: 447–460.

142. R. Harris, D. S. Siegel, & M. Wright, 2005, Assessing the impact of management buyouts on economic efficiency: Plant-level evidence from the United Kingdom, *Review of Economics and Statistics*, 87: 148–153; A. Seth & J. Easterwood, 1995, Strategic redirection in large management buyouts: The evidence from post-buyout restructuring activity, *Strategic Management Journal*, 14: 251–274; P. H. Phan & C. W. L. Hill, 1995, Organizational restructuring and economic performance in leveraged buyouts: An ex-post study, *Academy of Management Journal*, 38: 704–739.

143. C. M. Daily, P. P. McDougall, J. G. Covin, & D. R. Dalton, 2002, Governance and strategic leadership in entrepreneurial firms, *Journal of Management*, 3: 387–412.

144. M. Wright, R. E. Hoskisson, L. W. Busenitz, & J. Dial, 2000, Entrepreneurial growth through privatization: The upside of management buyouts, *Academy of Management Review*, 25: 591–601.

145. W. Kiechel III, 2007, Private equity's long view, *Harvard Business Review*, 85(8): 18–20.; M. Wright, R. E. Hoskisson, & L. W. Busenitz, 2001, Firm rebirth: Buyouts as facilitators of strategic growth and entrepreneurship, *Academy of Management Executive*, 15(1): 111–125.

146. Krishnan, Hitt, & Park, Acquisition premiums, subsequent workforce reductions and post-acquisition performance; Bergh, Executive retention and acquisition outcomes: A test of opposing views on the influence of organizational tenure.

147. H. A. Krishnan & D. Park, 2002, The impact of work force reduction on subsequent performance in major mergers and acquisitions: An exploratory study, *Journal of Business Research*, 55(4): 285–292; P. M. Lee, 1997, A comparative analysis of layoff announcements and stock price reactions in the United States and Japan, *Strategic Management Journal*, 18: 879–894.

148. D. J. Flanagan & K. C. O'Shaughnessy, 2005, The effect of layoffs on firm reputation, *Journal of Management*, 31: 445–463.

149. C. D. Zatzick & R. D. Iverson, 2006, High-involvement management and workforce reduction: Competitive advantage or disadvantage? *Academy of Management Journal*, 49: 999–1015; N. Mirabal & R. DeYoung, 2005, Downsizing as a Strategic Intervention, *Journal of American Academy of Business*, 6(1): 39–45.

150. Brauer, What have we acquired and what should we acquire in divestiture research? K. Shimizu & M. A. Hitt, 2005, What constrains or facilitates divestitures of formerly acquired firms? The effects of organizational inertia, *Journal of Management*, 31: 50–72.

151. S. Toms & M. Wright, 2005, Divergence and convergence within Anglo-American corporate governance systems: Evidence from the US and UK, 1950–2000, *Business History*, 47(2): 267–295.

152. A.-L. Le Nadant & F. Perdreau, 2006, Financial profile of leveraged buy-out targets: Some French evidence, *Review of Accounting and Finance*, (4): 370–392.

153. G. D. Bruton, J. K. Keels, & E. L. Scifres, 2002, Corporate restructuring and performance: An agency perspective on the complete buyout cycle, *Journal of Business Research*, 55: 709–724; W. F. Long & D. J. Ravenscraft, 1993, LBOs, debt, and R&D intensity, *Strategic Management Journal*, 14 (Special Issue): 119–135.

154. Wright, Hoskisson, Busenitz, & Dial, Entrepreneurial growth through privatization; S. A. Zahra, 1995, Corporate entrepreneurship and financial performance: The case of management leveraged buyouts, *Journal of Business Venturing*, 10: 225–248.

International Strategy

Studying this chapter should provide you with the strategic management knowledge needed to:

1. Explain traditional and emerging motives for firms to pursue international diversification.

2. Identify the four major benefits of an international strategy.

3. Explore the four factors that provide a basis for international business-level strategies.

4. Describe the three international corporate-level strategies: multidomestic, global, and transnational.

5. Discuss the environmental trends affecting international strategy, especially liability of foreignness and regionalization.

6. Name and describe the five alternative modes for entering international markets.

7. Explain the effects of international diversification on firm returns and innovation.

8. Name and describe two major risks of international diversification.

Shanghai Automotive Industry Corporation: Reaching for Global Markets

The Shanghai Automotive Industry Corporation (SAIC) is one of China's oldest and largest automotive companies. The company's 50 manufacturing plants in China produce autos, tractors, motorcycles, trucks, buses, and automobile parts (wholesale and retail). The company is also involved in car leasing and financing. SAIC has had highly successful joint ventures with General Motors and Volkswagen to produce GM and VW automobiles for the growing Chinese automobile market. The majority of SAIC's sales in the 1990s and 2000s have come from these joint ventures. In fact, driving in any major city in China shows the popularity of the GM (e.g., Buick) and VW autos in that country. Yet, some analysts believe that GM and VW may have become too dependent on SAIC.

SAIC also owns almost 51 percent of the Korean automaker, SSangyong, and the intellectual property rights to the Rover 25 and 75 models, as well as the K-series engine. SAIC started manufacturing the Rover 75 (redesigned for the Chinese market) in 2007.

SAIC learned much from its partnerships, and with the licensed technology, it decided to launch and promote its own branded vehicles. The Chinese government is emphasizing the importance of Chinese companies to develop their own brands partly because foreign brands are controlling many of the Chinese markets. Additionally, for these firms to become successful globally competitive companies, they need their own brands. In keeping with this goal, Chinese executives have a favorite term, *zizhu pinpai*, meaning self-owned brand. Actually, *zizhu* means to be one's own master. In 2007, SAIC began selling its own automobile brand, named the Roewe, in Chinese markets.

SAIC is currently among the top three automobile companies in China, and it has a goal of becoming among the top 10 global auto competitors. To do so, it has a goal of entering and competing effectively in the U.S. auto market, which is the largest such market in the world. It hired Philip Murtaugh, former chairman of GM China, to head its Shanghai Motor subsidiary.

This goal represents a major challenge for SAIC because all major automobile companies compete in the U.S. auto market. Hyundai discovered this challenge with its major efforts to compete more successfully in the U.S. market. Despite major improvements in quality and lower prices than competitors for comparable automobiles, Hyundai has been unable to capture the share of the U.S. market that it desires. Although its relative ranking in the market is a little higher than in 2005, its market share has remained stable at just under 3 percent.

Few Chinese autos have been exported in general and even fewer exported to the United States. Although the market share of U.S. automakers has been falling for the last several years, most of the gains in market share have been obtained by Japanese auto manufacturers, especially Toyota. Chinese exports are expected to be about 500,000 autos in 2007, but most are targeted for South America, Southeast Asia, and Eastern Europe. Yet, analysts predict Chinese automakers' success in global markets, including the United States, over time, and SAIC is likely to be one of the leaders.

Sources: A. Webb, 2007, China needs strong automakers—not more. *Automotive News,* http://www.autonews.com, July 20: 2007, China's SAIC says first half sales up 23 percent, Reuters, http://www.reuters.com, July 12; A. K. Gupta & H. Wang, 2007, How to get China and India right: Western companies need to become smarter—and they need to do it quickly, *Wall Street Journal,* April 28, R4; G. Dyer & J. Reed, 2007, SAIC plans to develop five new car classes, *Financial Times,* April 20, 23; C. Isidore, 2007, Cars from China: Not so fast, CNNMoney, http://www.cnnmoney.com, January 27; N. Madden, 2006, Chinese carmaker's push threatens Western rivals, *Advertising Age,* 77(50): 28; M. Vaughn, 2005, Refined Hyundai takes on the big boys, *Globe and Mail Update,* http://www.theglobeandmail.com, August 11.

As the Opening Case indicates, China's firms are building their competitive capabilities and seeking to enter foreign markets. China's entrance into the World Trade Organization (WTO) brought change not only to China and its trading partners but also to industries and firms throughout the world. Despite its underdeveloped market and institutional environment, Chinese firms such as the Shanghai Automotive Industry Corporation (SAIC) are taking advantage of the growing size of the Chinese market to attract foreign partners from whom they can learn new technologies and managerial capabilities.

Many firms choose direct investment in assets (e.g., establishing new subsidiaries, making acquisitions or building joint ventures) over indirect investment because it provides better protection for their assets.[1] Domestic Chinese firms are becoming more competitive and building their capabilities. As indicated in the Opening Case, Chinese firms are developing their manufacturing capabilities and building their own branded products (e.g., SAIC's Roewe auto). As such, the potential global market power of Chinese firms is astounding.[2]

As foreign firms enter China and as Chinese firms enter into other foreign markets, both opportunities and threats for firms competing in global markets are exemplified. This chapter examines opportunities facing firms as they seek to develop and exploit core competencies by diversifying into global markets. In addition, we discuss different problems, complexities, and threats that might accompany a firm's international strategy.[3] Although national boundaries, cultural differences, and geographical distances all pose barriers to entry into many markets, significant opportunities motivate businesses to enter international markets. A business that plans to operate globally must formulate a successful strategy to take advantage of these global opportunities.[4] Furthermore, to mold their firms into truly global companies, managers must develop global mind-sets.[5] As firms move into international markets, they develop relationships with suppliers, customers, and partners, and learn from these relationships. For example, SAIC learned new capabilities from its partnerships with General Motors and Volkswagen.

As illustrated in Figure 1.1, on page 5, we discuss the importance of international strategy as a source of strategic competitiveness and above-average returns. The chapter focuses on the incentives to internationalize. After a firm decides to compete internationally, it must select its strategy and choose a mode of entry into international markets. It may enter international markets by exporting from domestic-based operations, licensing some of its products or services, forming joint ventures with international partners, acquiring a foreign-based firm, or establishing a new subsidiary. Such international diversification can extend product life cycles, provide incentives for more innovation, and produce above-average returns. These benefits are tempered by political and economic risks and the problems of managing a complex international firm with operations in multiple countries.

Figure 8.1 provides an overview of the various choices and outcomes of strategic competitiveness. The relationships among international opportunities, the resources and

Figure 8.1 Opportunities and Outcomes of International Strategy

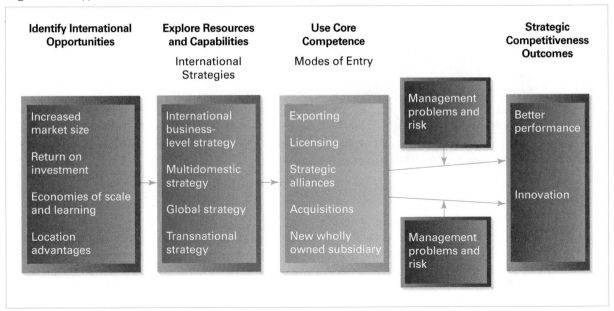

capabilities that result in strategies, and the modes of entry that are based on core competencies are explored in this chapter.

Identifying International Opportunities: Incentives to Use an International Strategy

An **international strategy** is a strategy through which the firm sells its goods or services outside its domestic market.[6] One of the primary reasons for implementing an international strategy (as opposed to a strategy focused on the domestic market) is that international markets yield potential new opportunities.[7]

Raymond Vernon captured the classic rationale for international diversification.[8] He suggested that typically a firm discovers an innovation in its home-country market, especially in an advanced economy such as that of the United States. Often demand for the product then develops in other countries, and exports are provided by domestic operations. Increased demand in foreign countries justifies making investments in foreign operations, especially to fend off foreign competitors. Vernon, therefore, observed that one reason why firms pursue international diversification is to extend a product's life cycle.

Another traditional motive for firms to become multinational is to secure needed resources. Key supplies of raw material—especially minerals and energy—are important in some industries. Other industries, such as clothing, electronics, watch making, and many others, have moved portions of their operations to foreign locations in pursuit of lower production costs. Clearly one of the reasons for Chinese firms' international expansion is to gain access to important resources.[9]

Although these traditional motives persist, other emerging motivations also drive international expansion (see Chapter 1). For instance, pressure has increased for a global integration of operations, mostly driven by more universal product demand. As nations industrialize, the demand for some products and commodities appears to become more similar. This borderless demand for globally branded products may be due to similarities in lifestyle in developed nations. Increases in global communication media also facilitate the ability of people in different countries to visualize and model lifestyles in

An **international strategy** is a strategy through which the firm sells its goods or services outside its domestic market.

IKEA has become a global brand using an international strategy for selling furniture.

different cultures.[10] IKEA, for example, has become a global brand by selling furniture in 44 countries through almost 300 stores that it owns and operates through franchisees. It generated $22.2 billion in sales in 2006. All of its furniture is sold in components that can be packaged in flat packs and assembled by the consumer after purchase. This arrangement has allowed for easier shipping and handling than fully assembled units and has facilitated the development of the global brand.[11]

In some industries, technology drives globalization because the economies of scale necessary to reduce costs to the lowest level often require an investment greater than that needed to meet domestic market demand. Companies also experience pressure for cost reductions, achieved by purchasing from the lowest-cost global suppliers. For instance, research and development expertise for an emerging business start-up may not exist in the domestic market.[12]

New large-scale, emerging markets, such as China and India, provide a strong internationalization incentive based on their high potential demand for consumer products and services.[13] Because of currency fluctuations, firms may also choose to distribute their operations across many countries, including emerging ones, in order to reduce the risk of devaluation in one country.[14] However, the uniqueness of emerging markets presents both opportunities and challenges.[15] Even though India, for example, differs from Western countries in many respects, including culture, politics, and the precepts of its economic system, it also offers a huge potential market and its government is becoming more supportive of foreign direct investment.[16] However, the differences between China and India and Western countries pose serious challenges to Western competitive paradigms that emphasize the skills needed to manage financial, economic, and political risks.[17]

Employment contracts and labor forces differ significantly in international markets. For example, it is more difficult to layoff employees in Europe than in the United States because of employment contract differences. In many cases, host governments demand joint ownership with a local company in order to invest in local operations, which allows the foreign firm to avoid tariffs. Also, host governments frequently require a high percentage of procurements, manufacturing, and R&D to use local sources.[18] These issues increase the need for local investment and responsiveness as opposed to seeking global economies of scale.

We've discussed incentives that influence firms to use international strategies. When these strategies are successful, firms can derive four basic benefits: (1) increased market size; (2) greater returns on major capital investments or on investments in new products and processes; (3) greater economies of scale, scope, or learning; and (4) a competitive advantage through location (e.g., access to low-cost labor, critical resources, or customers). We examine these benefits in terms of both their costs (such as higher coordination expenses and limited access to knowledge about host country political influences[19] and their managerial challenges.

Increased Market Size

Firms can expand the size of their potential market—sometimes dramatically—by moving into international markets. Pharmaceutical firms have been doing significant foreign direct investment into China due to the size of the market. One researcher found that approximately 85 percent of the pharmaceutical firms studied used a joint venture with a local Chinese partner as their entry mode for the Chinese market and the remaining firms established their own subsidiary in China.[20]

Although changing consumer tastes and practices linked to cultural values or traditions is not simple, following an international strategy is a particularly attractive option to firms competing in domestic markets that have limited growth opportunities. For example, firms in the domestic soft drink industry have been searching for growth in foreign markets for some time now. Major competitors Pepsi and Coca-Cola have had relatively stable market shares in the U.S. market for several years. Most of their growth in sales has come from foreign markets. In recent times, Pepsi has been using highly tailored soft drinks to capture more sales and profits in the Japanese market. For example, it introduced a limited run of "Ice Cucumber" and sold 4.8 million bottles of it before withdrawing it from the market. It has introduced several such drinks in Japan (e.g., Pepsi Blue, a berry-flavored soda) and had significant success. The limited edition drinks are designed for the Japanese consumers.[21]

Pepsi's Ice Cucumber drink is sold in the Japanese market.

The size of an international market also affects a firm's willingness to invest in R&D to build competitive advantages in that market.[22] Larger markets usually offer higher potential returns and thus pose less risk for a firm's investments. The strength of the science base in the country in question also can affect a firm's foreign R&D investments. Most firms prefer to invest more heavily in those countries with the scientific knowledge and talent to produce value-creating products and processes from their R&D activities.[23] Research suggests that German multinationals are increasingly investing in international R&D opportunities for resource development and learning purposes as opposed to market-seeking motives.[24]

Return on Investment

Large markets may be crucial for earning a return on significant investments, such as plant and capital equipment or R&D. Therefore, most R&D-intensive industries such as electronics are international. In addition to the need for a large market to recoup heavy investment in R&D, the development pace for new technology is increasing. New products become obsolete more rapidly, and therefore investments need to be recouped more quickly. Moreover, firms' abilities to develop new technologies are expanding, and because of different patent laws across country borders, imitation by competitors is more likely. Through reverse engineering, competitors are able to take apart a product, learn the new technology, and develop a similar product. Because their competitors can imitate the new technology relatively quickly, firms need to recoup new product development costs even more rapidly. Consequently, the larger markets provided by international expansion are particularly attractive in many industries such as pharmaceutical firms, because they expand the opportunity for the firm to recoup significant capital investments and large-scale R&D expenditures.[25]

Regardless of other issues, however, the primary reason for investing in international markets is to generate above-average returns on investments. Still, firms from different countries have different expectations and use different criteria to decide whether to invest in international markets.[26]

Economies of Scale and Learning

By expanding their markets, firms may be able to enjoy economies of scale, particularly in their manufacturing operations. To the extent that a firm can standardize its products across country borders and use the same or similar production facilities, thereby coordinating critical resource functions, it is more likely to achieve optimal economies of scale.[27]

Does General Motors' Survival Depend on International Markets?

For 76 years, General Motors (GM) was the global industry sales leader. In 2006, GM sold approximately 9.1 million vehicles, yet its global market share has been declining for a number of years. In fact, in 2007, Toyota became the world's largest automaker. In addition, GM has been struggling to earn positive returns in recent years. It finally returned to profitability in 2007 after experiencing several years of significant losses. Many of GM's problems stem from its competitive capabilities in the North American market, where Toyota and other foreign automakers have made substantial gains.

Interestingly, GM's return to profitability is not due to success in its North American operations. It continues to lose money there, although the losses are smaller than in past years because of a major program to reduce costs. Its recent profits have come from GM's international operations, especially its sales in the Chinese market. GM invested more than $2 billion in China, and these investments have resulted in positive returns. Sales of 7.2 million light trucks and automobiles were achieved in the Chinese market in 2006. China surpassed Japan to become the second largest vehicle market in the world. GM has the second highest market share in the Chinese market behind Volkswagen.

The Buick Excelle is one of the General Motors cars being produced as part of the General Motors and Shanghai Automotive Industry Corporation (SAIC) joint venture named Shanghai General Motors.

GM's sales in China come from a 50-50 joint venture with the Shanghai Automotive Industry Corporation (SAIC) named Shanghai General Motors. In 2006, this joint venture manufactured more than 400,000 passenger automobiles. GM predicts that Shanghai General Motors will produce 1 million passenger cars by 2010. Of course, the Chinese market for autos continues to grow and is expected to eventually become the largest auto market in the world. Through all of its joint ventures, GM sold more than 875,000 cars in China during 2006. GM's competitive advantage is clear because Toyota sold slightly more than 275,000 cars during the same period. Thus, GM has made large investments in Asia to offset Toyota's gains elsewhere.

GM's operations in Europe have been downsized. To help offset these changes, GM is investing about $500 million in Brazil to build new manufacturing facilities. Even as GM is experiencing success in Asia and is hoping for more in Latin America, it will experience a number of challenges in the next decade. Importantly, its partner in China may become a critical competitor. The transfer to technology and managerial capabilities to SAIC through the joint venture has helped it to develop its own branded auto that will compete with the GM Buicks sold in China. Furthermore, Toyota plans to double its production capacity in China by 2010. As a result, GM must employ effective strategies to maintain its current competitive advantages in China and other Asian markets, and it also must try to stem the tide of lost market share in other markets (e.g., the United States and Western Europe).

Sources: Investing in China, 2007, General Motors, http://www.gm.com, July 31; General Motors gives it stick, 2007, *The Detroit News,* http://www.detroitnews.net, July 31; Rising in the East: General Motors, 2007, *The Economist,* April 28, 82; G. Dyer, 2007, Foreign marks' lead narrows, *Financial Times,* April 25, 15; G. Dyer & J. Reed, 2007, Groups in race to sell alternative fuel cars, *Financial Times,* April 23, 22; G. Fairclough, Passing lane: GM's Chinese partner looms as a new rival; Learning from Detroit, Shanghai Automotive pushes past its own cars, *Wall Street Journal,* April 20, A.1; J. B. While & S. Power, 2007, GM retrenches in Europe, shifts gaze east, *Wall Street Journal,* April 18, A.4.

Economies of scale are critical in the global auto industry. China's decision to join the World Trade Organization has allowed carmakers from other countries to enter the country and for lower tariffs to be charged (in the past, Chinese carmakers have had an advantage over foreign carmakers due to tariffs). Ford, Honda, General Motors, and Volkswagen are each producing an economy car to compete with the existing cars in China. Because of global economies of scale (allowing them to price their products competitively) and local investments in China, all of these companies are likely to obtain significant market share in China. Alternatively, the SAIC is developing its own branded vehicles to compete with the foreign automakers (as explained in the Opening Case). SAIC's joint ventures with both GM and Volkswagen have been highly successful for SAIC and its partners. However as explained in the Opening Case, SAIC is seeking to export vehicles overseas and perhaps enter foreign markets in other ways. It aspires to be one of the 10 largest automakers by 2012 and among the top 6 in the world by 2020.[28]

Firms may also be able to exploit core competencies in international markets through resource and knowledge sharing between units and network partners across country borders.[29] This sharing generates synergy, which helps the firm produce higher-quality goods or services at lower cost. In addition, working across international markets provides the firm with new learning opportunities.[30] Multinational firms have substantial occasions to learn from the different practices they encounter in separate international markets. However, research finds that to take advantage of the international R&D investments, firms need to already have a strong R&D system in place to absorb the knowledge.[31]

Location Advantages

Firms may locate facilities in other countries to lower the basic costs of the goods or services they provide. These facilities may provide easier access to lower-cost labor, energy, and other natural resources. Other location advantages include access to critical supplies and to customers.[32] Once positioned favorably with an attractive location, firms must manage their facilities effectively to gain the full benefit of a location advantage.

Such location advantages can be influenced by costs of production and transportation requirements as well as by the needs of the intended customers.[33] Cultural influences may also affect location advantages and disadvantages. If there is a strong match between the cultures in which international transactions are carried out, the liability of foreignness is lower than if there is high cultural distance.[34] Research also suggests that regulation distances influence the ownership positions of multinational firms as well as their strategies for managing expatriate human resources.[35]

As suggested in the Strategic Focus, General Motors (GM) entered international markets to expand its market size. It is also earning positive returns on its international investments, but primarily in Asia. In fact, GM's recent return to profitability is due to its Asian operations, primarily in China. While GM has lost its position as the world's largest automaker after 76 years in the lead, it has major expansion plans for its China ventures. Still, GM faces a number of challenges from domestic Chinese competitors, such its partner SAIC, and from foreign competitors, such as Toyota and Volkswagen. It will have to formulate and implement a successful strategy for the Chinese market to maintain its current competitive advantage there.

International Strategies

Firms choose to use one or both of two basic types of international strategies: business-level international strategy and corporate-level international strategy. At the business level, firms follow generic strategies: cost leadership, differentiation, focused cost leadership, focused differentiation, or integrated cost leadership/differentiation. The three corporate-level international strategies are multidomestic, global, or transnational (a combination of multidomestic and global). To create competitive advantage, each strategy must utilize a core competence based on difficult-to-imitate resources and capabilities.[36] As discussed in Chapters 5 and 6, firms expect to create value through the implementation of a business-level strategy and a corporate-level strategy.[37]

International Business-Level Strategy

Each business must develop a competitive strategy focused on its own domestic market. We discussed competitive rivalry and competitive dynamics in Chapter 4 and business-level strategies in Chapter 5. International business-level strategies have some unique features. In an international business-level strategy, the home country of operation is often the most important source of competitive advantage.[38] The resources and capabilities established in the home country frequently allow the firm to pursue the strategy into markets located in other countries.[39] However, research indicates that as a firm continues its growth into multiple international locations, the country of origin is less important for competitive advantage.[40]

Michael Porter's model, illustrated in Figure 8.2, describes the factors contributing to the advantage of firms in a dominant global industry and associated with a specific home country or regional environment.[41] The first dimension in Porter's model is the factors of production. This dimension refers to the inputs necessary to compete in any industry—labor, land, natural resources, capital, and infrastructure (such as transportation, postal, and communication systems). There are basic factors (for example, natural and labor resources) and advanced factors (such as digital communication systems and a highly educated workforce). Other production factors are generalized (highway systems and the supply of debt capital) and specialized (skilled personnel in a specific industry, such as the workers in a port that specialize in handling bulk chemicals). If a country has both advanced and specialized production factors, it is likely to serve an industry well by spawning strong home-country competitors that also can be successful global competitors.

Ironically, countries often develop advanced and specialized factors because they lack critical basic resources. For example, some Asian countries, such as South Korea, lack

Figure 8.2 Determinants of National Advantage

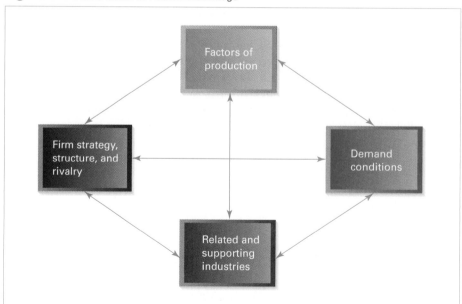

abundant natural resources but offer a strong work ethic, a large number of engineers, and systems of large firms to create an expertise in manufacturing. Similarly, Germany developed a strong chemical industry, partially because Hoechst and BASF spent years creating a synthetic indigo dye to reduce their dependence on imports, unlike Britain, whose colonies provided large supplies of natural indigo.[42]

The second dimension in Porter's model, demand conditions, is characterized by the nature and size of buyers' needs in the home market for the industry's goods or services. A large market segment can produce the demand necessary to create scale-efficient facilities.

Chinese manufacturing companies have spent years focused on building their businesses in China, but are now beginning to look at markets beyond their borders, as described in the Opening Case about SAIC. As mentioned, SAIC (along with other Chinese firms) has begun the challenging process of building its brand equity in China but especially in other countries. In doing so, most Chinese firms begin in the Far East with the intention to move into Western markets when ready to do so. Companies such as SAIC have been helped by China's entry to the World Trade Organization. Of course, interests of companies such as SAIC in entering international markets are to increase their market share and profits.

Related and supporting industries are the third dimension in Porter's model. Italy has become the leader in the shoe industry because of related and supporting industries; a well-established leather-processing industry provides the leather needed to construct shoes and related products. Also, many people travel to Italy to purchase leather goods, providing support in distribution. Supporting industries in leather-working machinery and design services also contribute to the success of the shoe industry. In fact, the design services industry supports its own related industries, such as ski boots, fashion apparel, and furniture. In Japan, cameras and copiers are related industries. Similarly, it is argued that the "creative resources nurtured by [the] popular cartoons and animation sector, combined with technological knowledge accumulated in the consumer electronics industry, facilitated the emergence of a successful video game industry in Japan."[43]

Firm strategy, structure, and rivalry make up the final country dimension and also foster the growth of certain industries. The types of strategy, structure, and rivalry among firms vary greatly from nation to nation. The excellent technical training system in Germany fosters a strong emphasis on continuous product and process improvements. In Japan, unusual cooperative and competitive systems have facilitated the cross-functional management of complex assembly operations. In Italy, the national pride of the country's designers has spawned strong industries in sports cars, fashion apparel, and furniture. In the United States, competition among computer manufacturers and software producers has contributed to the development of these industries.

The four basic dimensions of the "diamond" model in Figure 8.2 emphasize the environmental or structural attributes of a national economy that contribute to national advantage. Government policy also clearly contributes to the success and failure of many firms and industries. For example, the Chinese government has provided incentives for Chinese firms such as SAIC to develop their own branded products and to develop the capabilities necessary to compete effectively in international markets.

Although each firm must create its own success, not all firms will survive to become global competitors—not even those operating with the same country factors that spawned other successful firms. The actual strategic choices managers make may be the most compelling reason for success or failure. Accordingly, the factors illustrated in Figure 8.2 are likely to produce competitive advantages only when the firm develops and implements an appropriate strategy that takes advantage of distinct country factors. Thus, these distinct country factors must be given thorough consideration when making a decision regarding the business-level strategy to use (i.e., cost leadership, differentiation, focused cost leadership, focused differentiation, and integrated cost leadership/differentiation, discussed in Chapter 5) in an international context. However, pursuing an international strategy leads to more adjustment and learning as the firm adjusts to competition in the host country. Such adjustments are continuous as illustrated by GM's operations in the Chinese market. It must adapt to the increasing competition from its partner, SAIC, and its major competitor in global markets, Toyota.

International Corporate-Level Strategy

The international business-level strategies are based at least partially on the type of international corporate-level strategy the firm has chosen. Some corporate strategies give individual country units the authority to develop their own business-level strategies; other corporate strategies dictate the business-level strategies in order to standardize the firm's products and sharing of resources across countries.[44] International corporate-level strategy focuses on the scope of a firm's operations through both product and geographic diversification.[45] International corporate-level strategy is required when the firm operates in multiple industries and multiple countries or regions.[46] The headquarters unit guides the strategy, although business- or country-level managers can have substantial strategic input, depending on the type of international corporate-level strategy followed. The three international corporate-level strategies are multidomestic, global, and transnational, as shown in Figure 8.3.

Multidomestic Strategy

A **multidomestic strategy** is an international strategy in which strategic and operating decisions are decentralized to the strategic business unit in each country so as to allow that unit to tailor products to the local market.[47] A multidomestic strategy focuses on competition within each country. It assumes that the markets differ and therefore are segmented by country boundaries. The multidomestic strategy uses a highly decentralized approach, allowing each division to focus on a geographic area, region, or country.[48] In other words,

A **multidomestic strategy** is an international strategy in which strategic and operating decisions are decentralized to the strategic business unit in each country so as to allow that unit to tailor products to the local market.

Figure 8.3 International Corporate-Level Strategies

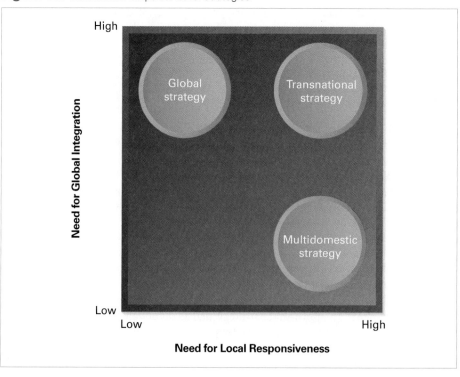

consumer needs and desires, industry conditions (e.g., the number and type of competitors), political and legal structures, and social norms vary by country. With multidomestic strategies, the country managers have the autonomy to customize the firm's products as necessary to meet the specific needs and preferences of local customers. Therefore, these strategies should maximize a firm's competitive response to the idiosyncratic requirements of each market.[49]

The use of multidomestic strategies usually expands the firm's local market share because the firm can pay attention to the needs of the local clientele.[50] However, the use of these strategies results in more uncertainty for the corporation as a whole, because of the differences across markets and thus the different strategies employed by local country units.[51] Moreover, multidomestic strategies do not allow the development of economies of scale and thus can be more costly. As a result, firms employing a multidomestic strategy decentralize their strategic and operating decisions to the business units operating in each country. Historically, Unilever, a large European consumer products firm, has had a highly decentralized approach to managing its international operations. This approach allows regional managers considerable autonomy to adapt the product offerings to fit the market needs.[52]

Global Strategy

In contrast to a multidomestic strategy, a global strategy assumes more standardization of products across country markets.[53] As a result, a global strategy is centralized and controlled by the home office. The strategic business units operating in each country are assumed to be interdependent, and the home office attempts to achieve integration across these businesses.[54] The firm uses a **global strategy** to offer standardized products across country markets, with competitive strategy being dictated by the home office. Thus, a global strategy emphasizes economies of scale and offers greater opportunities to take innovations developed at the corporate level or in one country and utilize them in other markets.[55] Improvements in global accounting and financial reporting standards are facilitating this strategy.[56]

Although a global strategy produces lower risk, it may cause the firm to forgo growth opportunities in local markets, either because those markets are less likely to be identified as opportunities or because the opportunities require that products be adapted to the local market.[57] The global strategy is not as responsive to local markets and is difficult to manage because of the need to coordinate strategies and operating decisions across country borders. Yahoo! and eBay experienced these challenges when they moved into specific Asian markets. For example, eBay was unsuccessful in both the Japanese and Chinese markets when attempting to export its business model and approach from North America to these two countries. It has reentered China but Meg Whitman, CEO of eBay, suggested that she had no current plans to reenter the Japanese market. Yahoo! has had rough times in China, going through several CEOs and trying to find the right formula to compete effectively in the Chinese market.[58]

Achieving efficient operations with a global strategy requires sharing resources and facilitating coordination and cooperation across country boundaries, which in turn require centralization and headquarters control. Furthermore, research suggests that the performance of the global strategy is enhanced if it deploys in areas where regional integration among countries is occurring, such as the European Union.[59] Many Japanese firms have successfully used the global strategy.[60]

CEMEX is the third largest cement company in the world, behind France's Lafarge and Switzerland's Holcim, and is the largest producer of ready mix, a prepackaged product that contains all the ingredients needed to make localized cement products.

CEMEX has strong market power in the Americas as well as in Europe. CEMEX serves customers in more than 50 countries with more than 50,000 employees globally. Because CEMEX pursues a global strategy effectively, its centralization process has facilitated the integration of several businesses it acquired in the United States,

A **global strategy** is an international strategy through which the firm offers standardized products across country markets, with competitive strategy being dictated by the home office.

STRATEGY RIGHT NOW

Cemex, a Mexican company, operates successfully all over the world, including in the United States.

A **transnational strategy** is an international strategy through which the firm seeks to achieve both global efficiency and local responsiveness.

Europe, and Asia. To integrate its businesses globally, CEMEX uses the Internet to improve logistics and manage an extensive supply network thereby increasing revenue and reducing costs. Connectivity between the operations in different countries and universal standards dominates its approach.[61] Because of increasing global competition and the need to be cost efficient while simultaneously provide high-quality differentiated products, a number of firms have begun to pursue the transnational strategy, which is described next.

Transnational Strategy

A **transnational strategy** is an international strategy through which the firm seeks to achieve both global efficiency and local responsiveness. Realizing these goals is difficult: One requires close global coordination while the other requires local flexibility. "Flexible coordination"—building a shared vision and individual commitment through an integrated network—is required to implement the transnational strategy. Such integrated networks allow a firm to manage its connections with customers, suppliers, partners, and other parties more efficiently rather than using arm's-length transactions.[62] The transnational strategy is difficult to use because of its conflicting goals (see Chapter 11 for more on the implementation of this and other corporate-level international strategies). On the positive side, the effective implementation of a transnational strategy often produces higher performance than does the implementation of either the multidomestic or global international corporate-level strategies.[63]

Transnational strategies are challenging to implement but are becoming increasingly necessary to compete in international markets. The growing number of global competitors heightens the requirement to hold costs down. However, the increasing sophistication of markets with greater information flow (e.g., based on the diffusion of the Internet) and the desire for specialized products to meet consumers' needs pressures firms to differentiate and even customize their products in local markets. Differences in culture and institutional environments also require firms to adapt their products and approaches to local environments.[64] As a result, more firms are increasingly using a transnational strategy.

Environmental Trends

Although the transnational strategy is difficult to implement, emphasis on global efficiency is increasing as more industries begin to experience global competition. To add to the problem, an increased emphasis on local requirements means that global goods and services often demand some customization to meet government regulations within particular countries or to fit customer tastes and preferences. In addition, most multinational firms desire coordination and sharing of resources across country markets to hold down costs, as illustrated by the CEMEX example.[65] Furthermore, some products and industries may be more suited than others for standardization across country borders.

As a result, some large multinational firms with diverse products employ a multidomestic strategy with certain product lines and a global strategy with others. Many multinational firms may require this type of flexibility if they are to be strategically competitive, in part due to trends that change over time. Two important trends are the liability of foreignness, which has increased since the terrorist attacks and the war in Iraq, and regionalization.

Liability of Foreignness

The dramatic success of Japanese firms such as Toyota and Sony in the United States and other international markets in the 1980s was a powerful jolt to U.S. managers and awakened them to the importance of international competition in markets that were rapidly becoming global markets. In the twenty-first century, China, India, Brazil, and Russia represent potential major international market opportunities for firms from many countries, including the United States, Japan, Korea, and the European Union.[66] However, there are legitimate concerns about the relative attractiveness of global strategies, as illustrated by the experience of Walt Disney Company in opening theme parks in foreign countries. For example, Disney suffered "lawsuits in France, at Disneyland Paris, because of the lack of fit between its transferred personnel policies and the French employees charged to enact them."[67] Disney executives learned from this experience in building the firm's newest theme park in Hong Kong.

Research shows that global strategies are not as prevalent as they once were and are still difficult to implement, even when using Internet-based strategies.[68] The September 11, 2001, attacks and the 2003 war in Iraq are two explanations for these concerns.[69] In addition, the amount of competition vying for a limited amount of resources and customers can limit firms' focus to regional rather than global markets. A regional focus allows firms to marshal their resources to compete effectively in regional markets rather than spreading their limited resources across many international markets.[70]

Lands' End has adapted regionally from a direct-mail catalog to having a presence both online and in retail stores.

As such, firms may focus less on truly global markets and more on regional adaptation. Although parallel developments in the Internet and mobile telecommunication facilitate communications across the globe, as noted earlier, the implementation of Web-based strategies also requires local adaptation.

The globalization of businesses with local strategies is demonstrated by the online operation of Lands' End, Inc., which uses local Internet portals to offer its products for sale. Lands' End, formerly a direct-mail catalog business and now a part of Sears, Roebuck and Co., launched the Web-based portion of its business in 1995. The firm established Web sites in the United Kingdom and Germany in 1999 and in France, Italy, and Ireland in 2000 prior to initiating a catalog business in those countries. With word-of-mouth and limited online advertising, a Web site business can be built in a foreign country without a lot of initial marketing expenses. After the online business becomes large enough, a catalog business can be launched with mailings targeted to customers who have used the business online. Thus, even smaller companies can sell their goods and services globally when facilitated by electronic infrastructure without having significant (brick-and-mortar) facilities outside of their home location. Lands' End and other retailers are going further by creating personal customization for fitting apparel sizes over the Internet. Service can be enhanced by being able to order online and pick up at a store. Even with custom ordering systems, significant local adaptation is still needed in each country or region.[71]

Regionalization

Regionalization is a second trend that has become more common in global markets. Because a firm's location can affect its strategic competitiveness,[72] it must decide whether to compete in all or many global markets, or to focus on a particular region or regions. Competing in all markets provides economies that can be achieved because of the combined market size. Research suggests that firms that compete in risky emerging markets can also have higher performance.[73]

However, a firm that competes in industries where the international markets differ greatly (in which it must employ a multidomestic strategy) may wish to narrow its focus to a particular region of the world. In so doing, it can better understand the cultures, legal and social norms, and other factors that are important for effective competition in those markets. For example, a firm may focus on Far East markets only rather than competing simultaneously in the Middle East, Europe, and the Far East. Or the firm may choose a region of the world where the markets are more similar and some coordination and sharing of resources would be possible. In this way, the firm may be able not only to better understand the markets in which it competes, but also to achieve some economies, even though it may have to employ a multidomestic strategy. For instance, research suggests that most large retailers are better at focusing on a particular region rather than being truly global.[74] Firms commonly focus much of their international market entries into countries adjacent to their home country, which might be referred to as their home region.[75]

Countries that develop trade agreements to increase the economic power of their regions may promote regional strategies. The European Union (EU) and South America's Organization of American States (OAS) are country associations that developed trade agreements to promote the flow of trade across country boundaries within their respective regions.[76] Many European firms acquire and integrate their businesses in Europe to better coordinate pan-European brands as the EU creates more unity in European markets. With this process likely to continue as new countries are added to the agreement, some international firms may prefer to pursue regional strategies versus global strategies because the size of the market is increasing.[77]

The North American Free Trade Agreement (NAFTA), signed by the United States, Canada, and Mexico, facilitates free trade across country borders in North America. NAFTA loosens restrictions on international strategies within this region and provides greater opportunity for regional international strategies. NAFTA does not exist for the sole purpose of U.S. businesses moving across its borders. In fact, Mexico is the number two trading partner of the United States, and NAFTA greatly increased Mexico's exports to the United States. Research suggests that managers of small and medium-sized firms are influenced by the strategy they implement (those with a differentiation strategy are more positively disposed to the agreement than are those pursuing a cost leadership strategy) and by their experience and rivalry with exporting firms.[78]

Most firms enter regional markets sequentially, beginning in markets with which they are more familiar. They also introduce their largest and strongest lines of business into these markets first, followed by their other lines of business once the first lines achieve success. They also usually invest in the same area as their original investment location.[79]

After the firm selects its international strategies and decides whether to employ them in regional or world markets, it must choose a market entry mode.[80]

Choice of International Entry Mode

International expansion is accomplished by exporting products, participating in licensing arrangements, forming strategic alliances, making acquisitions, and establishing new wholly owned subsidiaries. These means of entering international markets and their characteristics are shown in Table 8.1. Each means of market entry has its advantages and disadvantages. Thus, choosing the appropriate mode or path to enter international markets affects the firm's performance in those markets.[81]

Table 8.1 Global Market Entry: Choice of Entry

Type of Entry	Characteristics
Exporting	High cost, low control
Licensing	Low cost, low risk, little control, low returns
Strategic alliances	Shared costs, shared resources, shared risks, problems of integration (e.g., two corporate cultures)
Acquisition	Quick access to new market, high cost, complex negotiations, problems of merging with domestic operations
New wholly owned subsidiary	Complex, often costly, time consuming, high risk, maximum control, potential above-average returns

Exporting

Many industrial firms begin their international expansion by exporting goods or services to other countries.[82] Exporting does not require the expense of establishing operations in the host countries, but exporters must establish some means of marketing and distributing their products. Usually, exporting firms develop contractual arrangements with host-country firms.

The disadvantages of exporting include the often high costs of transportation and tariffs placed on some incoming goods. Furthermore, the exporter has less control over the marketing and distribution of its products in the host country and must either pay the distributor or allow the distributor to add to the price to recoup its costs and earn a profit.[83] As a result, it may be difficult to market a competitive product through exporting or to provide a product that is customized to each international market.[84] However, evidence suggests that cost leadership strategies enhance the performance of exports in developed countries, whereas differentiation strategies are more successful in emerging economies.[85]

Firms export mostly to countries that are closest to their facilities because of the lower transportation costs and the usually greater similarity between geographic neighbors. For example, U.S. NAFTA partners Mexico and Canada account for more than half of the goods exported from Texas. The Internet has also made exporting easier, as illustrated by the Lands' End system described earlier.[86] Even small firms can access critical information about foreign markets, examine a target market, research the competition, and find lists of potential customers.[87] Governments also use the Internet to facilitate applications for export and import licenses. Although the terrorist threat is likely to slow its progress, high-speed technology is still the wave of the future.[88]

Small businesses are most likely to use the exporting mode of international entry.[89] Currency exchange rates are one of the most significant problems small businesses face. The Bush administration has supported a weak dollar against the euro, which makes imports to the United States more expensive to U.S. consumers and U.S. goods less costly to foreign buyers, thus providing some economic relief for U.S. exporters.[90]

Licensing

Licensing is an increasingly common form of organizational network, particularly among smaller firms.[91] A licensing arrangement allows a foreign company to purchase the right to manufacture and sell the firm's products within a host country or set of countries.[92] The licensor is normally paid a royalty on each unit produced and sold. The licensee takes the risks and makes the monetary investments in facilities for manufacturing, marketing, and distributing the goods or services. As a result, licensing is possibly the least costly form of international expansion.

China is a large and growing market for cigarettes, while the U.S. market is shrinking due to health concerns. But U.S. cigarette firms have had trouble entering the Chinese market because state-owned tobacco firms have lobbied against such entry. As such, cigarette firms such as Altria Group, parent company of Philip Morris International, had an incentive to form a deal with these state-owned firms. Such an agreement provides the state-owned firms access to the most famous brand in the world, Marlboro. Accordingly, both the Chinese firms and Philip Morris have formed a licensing agreement to take advantage of the opportunity as China opens its markets more fully.[93] Because it is a licensing agreement rather than a foreign direct investment by Philip Morris, China maintains control of the distribution.

Licensing is also a way to expand returns based on prior innovations.[94] Even if product life cycles are short, licensing may be a useful tool. For instance, because the toy industry faces relentless change and an unpredictable buying public, licensing is used and contracts are often completed in foreign markets where labor may be less expensive.[95] The Sesame Street Workshop, creator of the Muppet figures, has created a large business by licensing figures such as Elmo, Snuffleupagus, and the Count to Target and other specialty stores focused on apparel for "a previously untapped teen/adult market."[96]

Licensing also has disadvantages. For example, it gives the firm little control over the manufacture and marketing of its products in other countries. Thus, license deals must be structured properly.[97] In addition, licensing provides the least potential returns, because returns must be shared between the licensor and the licensee. Additionally, the international firm may learn the technology and produce and sell a similar competitive product after the license expires. Komatsu, for example, first licensed much of its technology from International Harvester, Bucyrus-Erie, and Cummins Engine to compete against Caterpillar in the earthmoving equipment business. Komatsu then dropped these licenses and developed its own products using the technology it had gained from the U.S. companies.[98] Marriott International Inc. has achieved distinction as a franchise licensor of hotel chains. By the middle of 2007, Marriott operated or franchised almost 2,900 lodging properties in the United States and 67 other countries.[99] However, Marriott owns less than 3 percent of the properties, unlike Hilton and Starwood (St. Regis, Sheraton, and Westin hotel chains), which own more than 30 percent. Although Marriott has used franchise licensing successfully, if a firm wants to move to a different ownership arrangement, licensing may create some inflexibility. Thus, it is important that a firm think ahead and consider sequential forms of entry in international markets.[100]

Marriott Hotels, which operates as a franchise licensor, has many hotel properties all over the world but fully owns less than 5 percent of these properties.

Strategic Alliances

In recent years, strategic alliances have become a popular means of international expansion.[101] Strategic alliances allow firms to share the risks and the resources required to enter international markets.[102] Moreover, strategic alliances can facilitate the development of new core competencies that contribute to the firm's future strategic competitiveness.[103]

As explained in the Opening Case and the recent Strategic Focus, GM formed a joint venture with SAIC to produce Buick and Cadillac autos for the Chinese market. The alliance has been highly successful for both firms. Similar to this example, most international strategic alliances are formed with a host-country firm that knows and understands the competitive conditions, legal and social norms, and cultural idiosyncrasies of the country, which helps the expanding firm manufacture and market a competitive product. Often, firms in emerging economies want to form international alliances and ventures to gain access to sophisticated technologies that are new to them. Gaining access to new technologies was one of SAIC's goals in the alliance with GM. This type of arrangement can benefit the non-emerging economy firm as well, in that it gains access to a new market and doesn't have to pay tariffs to do so (because it is partnering with a local company).[104] In return, the host-country firm may find its new access to the expanding firm's technology and innovative products attractive.

Each partner in an alliance brings knowledge or resources to the partnership.[105] Indeed, partners often enter an alliance with the purpose of learning new capabilities. Common among those desired capabilities are technological skills. However, for technological knowledge to be transferred in an alliance usually requires trust between the partners.[106] Managing these expectations can facilitate improved performance.

The alliance between GM and SAIC has been successful over the years because of the way it was managed. In fact, both firms are pleased with the outcomes. Research suggests that company executives need to know their own firm well, understand factors that determine the norms in different countries, know how the firm is seen by other partners in the venture, and learn to adapt while remaining consistent with their own company cultural values. Such a multifaceted and versatile approach has helped the GM and SAIC alliance succeed.

Not all alliances are successful; in fact, many fail.[107] The primary reasons for failure include incompatible partners and conflict between the partners.[108] International strategic alliances are especially difficult to manage.[109] Several factors may cause a relationship to sour. Trust between the partners is critical and is affected by at least four fundamental issues: the initial condition of the relationship, the negotiation process to arrive at an agreement, partner interactions, and external events.[110] Trust is also influenced by the country cultures involved in the alliance or joint venture.[111]

Research has shown that equity-based alliances, over which a firm has more control, tend to produce more positive returns.[112] (Strategic alliances are discussed in greater depth in Chapter 9.) However, if trust is required to develop new capabilities in a research collaboration, equity can serve as a barrier to the necessary relationship building.[113] If conflict in a strategic alliance or joint venture is not manageable, an acquisition may be a better option.[114] Research suggests that alliances are more favorable in the face of high uncertainty and where cooperation is needed to share knowledge between partners and where strategic flexibility is important, such as with small and medium-sized firms.[115] Acquisitions are better in situations with less need for strategic flexibility and when the transaction is used to maintain economies of scale or scope.[116] Alliances can also lead to an acquisition, which is discussed next.

Acquisitions

As free trade has continued to expand in global markets, cross-border acquisitions have also been increasing significantly. In recent years, cross-border acquisitions have comprised more than 45 percent of all acquisitions completed worldwide.[117] As explained in Chapter 7, acquisitions can provide quick access to a new market. In fact, acquisitions often provide the fastest and the largest initial international expansion of any of the alternatives.[118] Thus, entry is much quicker than by other modes. For example, Wal-Mart entered Germany and the United Kingdom by acquiring local firms. Later, Wal-Mart withdrew from Germany.[119] Also, acquisitions are the mode used by many firms to enter Eastern European markets.

Although acquisitions have become a popular mode of entering international markets, they are not without costs. International acquisitions carry some of the disadvantages of domestic acquisitions (also see Chapter 7). In addition, they can be expensive and also often require debt financing, which carries an extra cost. International negotiations for acquisitions can be exceedingly complex and are generally more complicated than domestic acquisitions. For example, it is estimated that only 20 percent of cross-border bids lead to a completed acquisition, compared with 40 percent of bids for domestic acquisitions.[120]

Interestingly, acquirers make fewer acquisitions in countries with significant corruption. In fact, when they do acquire firms in such countries, acquirers commonly pay smaller premiums to buy the target firms.[121]

Dealing with the legal and regulatory requirements in the target firm's country and obtaining appropriate information to negotiate an agreement frequently present significant problems. Finally, the problems of merging the new firm into the acquiring firm often are more complex than in domestic acquisitions. The acquiring firm must deal not only with different corporate cultures, but also with potentially different social cultures and practices.[122] These differences make the integration of the two firms after the acquisition more challenging; it is difficult to capture the potential synergy when integration is slowed or stymied because of cultural differences.[123] Therefore, while international acquisitions have been popular because of the rapid access to new markets they provide, they also carry with them important costs and multiple risks.

As explained in the Opening Case, SAIC, a China-based automobile producer, acquired assets of the MG Rover Group, a historic British auto producer, which was in insolvency at the time. This acquisition gave the Chinese firm an entry point into Europe and an opportunity to establish its own brand through the MG Rover label. SAIC previously considered a joint venture but decided to make the acquisition bid, worth $104 million.[124] However, SAIC experienced formidable government opposition in the United Kingdom and had to clear extra regulatory hurdles to receive approval.

New Wholly Owned Subsidiary

The establishment of a new wholly owned subsidiary is referred to as a **greenfield venture.**

The establishment of a new wholly owned subsidiary is referred to as a **greenfield venture**. The process of creating such ventures is often complex and potentially costly, but it affords maximum control to the firm and has the most potential to provide above-average returns. This potential is especially true of firms with strong intangible capabilities that might be leveraged through a greenfield venture.[125] A firm maintains full control of its operations with a greenfield venture. More control is especially advantageous if the firm has proprietary technology. Research also suggests that "wholly owned subsidiaries and expatriate staff are preferred" in service industries where "close contacts with end customers" and "high levels of professional skills, specialized know-how, and customization" are required.[126] Other research suggests that greenfield investments are more prominent where physical capital-intensive plants are planned and that acquisitions are more likely preferred when a firm is human capital intensive—that is, where a strong local degree of unionization and high cultural distance would cause difficulty in transferring knowledge to a host nation through a greenfield approach.[127]

The risks are also high, however, because of the costs of establishing a new business operation in a new country. The firm may have to acquire the knowledge and expertise of the existing market by hiring either host-country nationals, possibly from competitors, or consultants, which can be costly. Still, the firm maintains control over the technology, marketing, and distribution of its products.[128] Furthermore, the company must build new manufacturing facilities, establish distribution networks, and learn and implement appropriate marketing strategies to compete in the new market.[129] Research also suggests that when the country risk is high, firms prefer to enter with joint ventures instead of greenfield investments in order to manage the risk. However, if they have previous experience in a country, they prefer to use a wholly owned greenfield venture rather than a joint venture.[130]

The globalization of the air cargo industry has implications for companies such as UPS and FedEx. The impact of this globalization is especially pertinent to the China and the Asia Pacific region. China's air cargo market is expected to grow 11 percent per year through 2023. Accordingly, both UPS and FedEx recently opened new hub operations in Shanghai and Hangzhou, respectively. FedEx opened its Hangzhou subsidiary in late May 2007 serving more than 200 cities throughout China and connecting businesses in China with others across the globe. Almost concurrently, UPS started construction of its

Has the Largest Automaker in the World Made Mistakes with Its International Strategy?

In 2007, three years ahead of its goal, Toyota became the largest automaker in the world. Toyota sold 2.35 million vehicles in the first quarter of 2007, 900,000 more than General Motors. It was the first time in many years that a company other than GM had sold the most vehicles in any one time period. Many analysts praised the automaker for accomplishing its goal. Toyota has many positive attributes. The Toyota brand has come to mean reliability at an affordable price. Furthermore, while sales of Toyota vehicles have leveled off in Europe due to European Union policies designed to limit sales of Toyota products, the company plans to build five more large assembly plants in North America by 2016. That would bring Toyota's total to 13 plants and 50,000 employees in North America.

Though Toyota is now manufacturing and selling its larger automobiles in China—as well as its new hybrid Prius—it is still only third in automobile sales in China behind VW and GM.

Toyota first entered the Chinese market with exported cars built in Japan in the 1960s. Interestingly, it did not begin manufacturing autos in China for the Chinese market until 2002, 10 years after Volkswagen did. The two leaders in the Chinese auto market are VW and GM. Toyota built manufacturing facilities in China as a part of a joint venture with FAW China. Toyota began pushing the sales of a small, modestly priced auto, the Vios, a similar strategy used for many emerging economy countries. Although its initial sales were positive, they weakened as Chinese customers seemed more interested in luxury cars. However, Toyota rebounded quickly with the introduction in 2006 of the Camry, a popular auto in many international markets. Its sales reached 150,000 units in 2007. Toyota also formed other joint ventures in China, such as one with Guangzhou Automotive Group to manufacture engines. Still Toyota must build its brand name in China and also has to fend off anti-Japanese sentiment left over from Japanese government's actions in World War II. For these reasons and its late start, it has a large gap in sales to overtake the market leaders.

Toyota is also experiencing some problems in other international markets. For example, in North America, the number of recalls of its vehicles has tripled in recent years. And customer satisfaction has declined with the J.D. Powers ratings listing Toyota 28th out of 36 in customer experience. Analysts suggest that the reason for these outcomes is Toyota's relentless pressure to increase sales, sometimes at the expense of customer satisfaction. Because of these problems, Toyota has begun a new program in North America named EM[2], Everything Matters Exponentially. The emphasis is on improving product planning, customer service, sales and marketing, along with the car dealerships.

China's major international initiative in the 2000s has been the Chinese market. Thus, it may have "taken its eye off of the North American market a little. However, it cannot afford to slip in the lucrative North American market while it fights for market share in China. Thus, it will be interesting to observe whether Toyota can regain its customer satisfaction in North America, continue to build market share there, and make gains in the Chinese market simultaneously.

Sources: 2007, Toyota, *Hoover's Company Information*, Hoover's, Inc.; D. Welch, 2007, Staying paranoid at Toyota: Fearful of "big-company disease," the No. 1 carmaker keeps scrambling to retool itself, *BusinessWeek*, July 02, 80; R. Regassa & A. Ahmadian, 2007, Comparative study of American and Japanese auto industry: General Motors versus Toyota Motors Corporations, *The Business Review, Cambridge*, Summer, 8(1): 1–11; A. Chozick, 2007, Japan's auto giants steer toward China; Toyota, Nissan, Honda refocus their efforts as U.S. demand slows, *Wall Street Journal*, May 16, A 12; M. Zimmerman, 2007, Autos; Toyota ends GM's reign as car sales leader, *Los Angeles Times*, April 25, C.1; G. Dyer & D. Pilling, 2007, Toyota: Ready to accelerate the Chinese market, *Financial Times*, April 23, 22; M. Dickerson, 2007, Global capital; Picking up steam in Mexico; Japanese automakers are gaining on their U.S. counterparts in what is becoming a key market, *Los Angeles Times*, April 21, C.1; N. Shirouzu, 2006, Toyota speeds up push to expand in China, India; Strategy takes aim at emerging markets with low-cost cars, *Wall Street Journal Asia*, November 13, 1.

new Shanghai subsidiary offices in August 2007. In the five years prior to the establishment of its Shanghai operations, UPS had invested approximately $600 million in China. These investments are wholly owned because these firms need to maintain the integrity of their IT and logistics systems in order to maximize efficiency. Greenfield ventures also help the firms to maintain the proprietary nature of their systems.[131]

2007年4月12日·中国 上海
12 April, 2007 · Shanghai, China

Globalization has resulted in UPS signing agreements to open a new hub operation in China. Construction began on the first UPS subsidiary in Shanghai in August of 2007.

As explained in the Strategic Focus, Toyota has become the largest automaker in the world. Its success is because of many positive actions including entry into and effective competition in international markets such as those in Europe and North America. Yet, while it was an early foreign entrant into the Chinese market with exports, it was late to build manufacturing facilities in China. It formed a joint venture with a Chinese firm to manufacture autos in China. It had been reluctant to manufacture cars in China for several reasons. Importantly it wanted to protect its technology and manufacturing processes from falling into the hands of Chinese competitors. Because of its reluctance, Toyota has allowed Volkswagen and General Motors to become the market leaders in the Chinese market. And Toyota faces an uphill battle to gain significant market share in this market. Since 2000, Toyota has invested significant financial resources and effort in China, but doing so may be partly responsible for its problems with quality and customer satisfaction declines in the North American market. Toyota's experiences suggest that operating in international markets can be a substantial challenge, even for a resourceful and powerful multinational company.

Dynamics of Mode of Entry

A firm's choice of mode of entry into international markets is affected by a number of factors.[132] Initially, market entry is often achieved through export, which requires no foreign manufacturing expertise and investment only in distribution. Licensing can facilitate the product improvements necessary to enter foreign markets, as in the Komatsu example. Strategic alliances have been popular because they allow a firm to connect with an experienced partner already in the targeted market. Strategic alliances also reduce risk through the sharing of costs. Therefore, all three modes—export, licensing, and strategic alliance—are good tactics for early market development. Also, the strategic alliance is often used in more uncertain situations, such as an emerging economy where there is significant risk, such as Colombia.[133] However, if intellectual property rights in the emerging economy are not well protected, the number of firms in the industry is growing fast, and the need for global integration is high, the wholly owned subsidiary entry mode is preferred.[134]

To secure a stronger presence in international markets, acquisitions or greenfield ventures may be required. Large aerospace firms Airbus and Boeing have used joint ventures, while military equipment firms such as Thales SA have used acquisitions to build a global presence.[135] Japanese auto manufacturers, such as Toyota, have gained a presence in the United States through both greenfield ventures and joint ventures.[136] Because of Toyota's highly efficient manufacturing process, it wants to maintain control over its auto manufacturing where possible. It has engaged in a joint venture in the United States, but most of its manufacturing facilities are greenfield investments. Therefore, Toyota uses some form of foreign direct investment (e.g., greenfield ventures, joint ventures) rather than another mode of entry (although it may use exporting early in new markets as it did in China). Both acquisitions and greenfield ventures are likely to come at later stages in the development of an international strategy. In addition, both strategies tend to be more successful when the firm making the investment possesses valuable core competencies.[137] Large diversified business groups, often found in emerging economies, not only gain resources through diversification but also have specialized abilities in managing differences in inward and outward flows of foreign direct investment.[138] Multinational firms can engage in substantial competitive rivalry in international markets as evidenced by the battles for market share among GM, Toyota, and VW in China.[139]

Thus, to enter a global market, a firm selects the entry mode that is best suited to the situation at hand. In some instances, the various options will be followed sequentially, beginning with exporting and ending with greenfield ventures. In other cases, the firm may use several, but not all, of the different entry modes, each in different markets. The decision regarding which entry mode to use is primarily a result of the industry's competitive conditions, the country's situation and government policies, and the firm's unique set of resources, capabilities, and core competencies.

Strategic Competitive Outcomes

After its international strategy and mode of entry have been selected, the firm turns its attention to implementation issues (see Chapter 11). Implementation is highly important, because international expansion is risky, making it difficult to achieve a competitive advantage (see Figure 8.1 on p. 213). The probability the firm will be successful with an international strategy increases when it is effectively implemented.

International Diversification and Returns

Firms have numerous reasons to diversify internationally.[140] **International diversification** is a strategy through which a firm expands the sales of its goods or services across the borders of global regions and countries into different geographic locations or markets. Because of its potential advantages, international diversification should be related positively to firms' returns. Research has shown that, as international diversification increases, firms' returns decrease initially but then increase quickly as firms learn to manage international expansion.[141] In fact, the stock market is particularly sensitive to investments in international markets. Firms that are broadly diversified into multiple international markets usually achieve the most positive stock returns, especially when they diversify geographically into core business areas.[142] Many factors contribute to the positive effects of international diversification, such as potential economies of scale and experience, location advantages, increased market size, and the opportunity to stabilize returns. The stabilization of returns helps reduce a firm's overall risk.[143] All of these outcomes can be achieved by smaller and newer ventures, as well as by larger and established firms.

Toyota has found that international diversification allows it to better exploit its core competencies, because sharing knowledge resources across subsidiaries can produce synergy.[144] Also, a firm's returns may affect its decision to diversify internationally. For example, poor returns in a domestic market may encourage a firm to expand internationally in order to enhance its profit potential. In addition, internationally diversified firms may have access to more flexible labor markets, as the Japanese do in the United States, and may thereby benefit from scanning international markets for competition and market opportunities. Also, through global networks with assets in many countries, firms can develop more flexible structures to adjust to changes that might occur. "Offshore outsourcing" has created significant value-creation opportunities for firms engaged in it, especially as firms move into markets with more flexible labor markets. Furthermore, offshoring increases exports to firms that receive the offshoring contract.[145]

International diversification is a strategy through which a firm expands the sales of its goods or services across the borders of global regions and countries into different geographic locations or markets.

International Diversification and Innovation

In Chapter 1, we indicated that the development of new technology is at the heart of strategic competitiveness. As noted in Porter's model (see Figure 8.2 on p. 218), a nation's competitiveness depends, in part, on the capacity of its industry to innovate. Eventually and inevitably, competitors outperform firms that fail to innovate and improve their operations and products. Therefore, the only way to sustain a competitive advantage is to upgrade it continually.[146]

International diversification provides the potential for firms to achieve greater returns on their innovations (through larger or more numerous markets) and reduces the often substantial risks of R&D investments. Therefore, international diversification provides incentives for firms to innovate. Additionally, the firm uses its primary resources and capabilities to diversify internationally and thus earn further returns on these capabilities (e.g., capability to innovate).[147]

In addition, international diversification may be necessary to generate the resources required to sustain a large-scale R&D operation. An environment of rapid technological obsolescence makes it difficult to invest in new technology and the capital-intensive operations necessary to compete in this environment. Firms operating solely in domestic markets may find such investments difficult because of the length of time required to recoup the original investment. If the time is extended, it may not be possible to recover the investment before the technology becomes obsolete.[148] However, international diversification improves a firm's ability to appropriate additional returns from innovation before competitors can overcome the initial competitive advantage created by the innovation. In addition, firms moving into international markets are exposed to new products and processes. If they learn about those products and processes and integrate this knowledge into their operations, further innovation can be developed. To incorporate the learning into their own R&D processes, firms must manage those processes effectively in order to absorb and use the new knowledge to create further innovations.[149]

The relationship among international diversification, innovation, and returns is complex. Some level of performance is necessary to provide the resources to generate international diversification, which in turn provides incentives and resources to invest in research and development. The latter, if done appropriately, should enhance the returns of the firm, which then provides more resources for continued international diversification and investment in R&D.[150]

Because of the potential positive effects of international diversification on performance and innovation, such diversification may even enhance returns in product-diversified firms. International diversification increases market potential in each of these firms' product lines, but the complexity of managing a firm that is both product-diversified and internationally diversified is significant. Research indicates that media firms gain from both product and geographic diversification. However, international diversification often contributes more than product diversification for firms in developed countries.[151] Research also suggests that firms in less developed countries gain more from being product-diversified than firms in developed countries, especially when partnering with multinational firms from a more developed country that desire to enter less developed country markets. [152]

Evidence suggests that more culturally diverse top management teams often have a greater knowledge of international markets and their idiosyncrasies.[153] (Top management teams are discussed further in Chapter 12.) Moreover, an in-depth understanding of diverse markets among top-level managers facilitates intrafirm coordination and the use of long-term, strategically relevant criteria to evaluate the performance of managers and their units.[154] In turn, this approach facilitates improved innovation and performance. [155]

Complexity of Managing Multinational Firms

Although firms can realize many benefits by implementing an international strategy, doing so is complex and can produce greater uncertainty.[156] For example, multiple risks are involved when a firm operates in several different countries. Firms can grow only so large and diverse before becoming unmanageable, or before the costs of managing them exceed their benefits.[157] Managers are constrained by the complexity and sometimes by the culture and institutional systems within which they must operate.[158] The complexities involved in managing diverse international operations are shown in the problems experienced by even high-performing firms such as Toyota. The Strategic Focus explains that Toyota became overly focused on sales in the North American market and began to experience quality problems (i.e., increased number of recalls) and reduced customer satisfaction. It also was late in entering the Chinese market with manufacturing and as a result, it is now behind the market leaders, VW and GM (in the Chinese market).[159] Other complexities include the highly competitive nature of global markets, multiple cultural environments, potentially rapid shifts in the value of different currencies, and the instability of some national governments.

Risks in an International Environment

International diversification carries multiple risks.[160] Because of these risks, international expansion is difficult to implement and manage. The chief risks are political and economic. Specific examples of political and economic risks are shown in Figure 8.4.

Figure 8.4 Risk in the International Environment

Political Risks

- War in Iraq and Afghanistan following the September 11, 2001, terrorist attacks
- Continual warfare between the Palestinians and Israel
- Potential of war between Pakistan and India
- Potential of integration between North and South Korea

Economic Risks

- Failure of the Argentine economy and devaluation of the peso
- Challenges for China in implementing the World Trade Organization agreements
- The proposed constitution as well as entry of new countries into the European Union strengthening the euro currency and uniting Europe more tightly with existing and new partner countries
- Success of privatization and firm restructuring among Eastern European countries

Sources: 2003, Finance and economics: The perils of convergence; Economics focus, *The Economist,* April 5, 71; K. D. Brouthers, 2003, Institutional, cultural and transaction cost influences on entry mode choice and performance, *Journal of International Business Studies,* 33: 203–221; F. Bruni, 2003, With a constitution to ponder, Europeans gather in Greece, *New York Times,* http://www.nytimes.com, June 20; B. Davis, R. Buckman, & C. Rhoads, 2003, A global journal report: For global economy, much rides on how the U. S. war plays out, *Wall Street Journal,* March 20, A1; J. Flint, 2003, China: How big, how fast, how dangerous? *Forbes,* http://www.forbes.com, July 1; G. A. Fowler, 2003, Copies 'R' Us—Pirates in China move fast to pilfer toy makers' ideas, *Wall Street Journal,* January 31, B1; W. Rugg, 2003, A down dollar's lure—and peril, *BusinessWeek Online,* http://www.businessweek.com, May 22; J. H. Zhao, S. H. Kim, & J. Du, 2003, The impact of corruption and transparency on foreign direct investment: An empirical analysis, *Management International Review,* 43(1): 41–62.

Political Risks

Political risks are risks related to instability in national governments and to war, both civil and international. Instability in a national government creates numerous problems, including economic risks and uncertainty created by government regulation; the existence of many, possibly conflicting, legal authorities or corruption; and the potential nationalization of private assets.[161] Foreign firms that invest in another country may have concerns about the stability of the national government and the effects of unrest and government instability on their investments or assets.[162]

Russia has experienced a relatively high level of institutional instability in the years following its revolutionary transition to a more democratic government. Decentralized political control and frequent changes in policies created chaos for many, but especially for those in the business landscape. In an effort to regain more central control and reduce the chaos, Russian leaders took actions such as prosecuting powerful private firm executives, seeking to gain state control of firm assets, and not approving some foreign acquisitions of Russian businesses. The initial institutional instability, followed by the actions of the central government, caused some firms delay or negated significant foreign direct investment in Russia. Although Vladimir Putin, Russia's president, tried to reassure potential investors about their property rights, prior actions, and the fact that other laws (e.g., environmental and employee laws) are weak, many Russian firms keep double books to hide information from tax collectors and the mafia, and the fact that government corruption is common makes firms leery of investing in Russia.[163]

Economic Risks

As illustrated in the example of Russian institutional instability and property rights, economic risks are interdependent with political risks. If firms cannot protect their intellectual property, they are highly unlikely to make foreign direct investments. Countries therefore need to create and sustain strong intellectual property rights and enforce them in order to attract desired foreign direct investment. Another economic risk is the security risk posed by terrorists. For instance, concerns about terrorism in Indonesia have kept firms from investing in the Indonesian economy. Although many foreign investors in the energy and mining sectors have kept their investments in Indonesia through political and economic instability, the nation needs new investors to sustain economic growth. Indonesia has difficulty competing for investment against the comparatively faster growth in China and India, which have fewer security risks.[164]

As noted earlier, foremost among the economic risks of international diversification are the differences and fluctuations in the value of different currencies.[165] The value of the dollar relative to other currencies determines the value of the international assets and earnings of U.S. firms; for example, an increase in the value of the U.S. dollar can reduce the value of U.S. multinational firms' international assets and earnings in other countries. Furthermore, the value of different currencies can also, at times, dramatically affect a firm's competitiveness in global markets because of its effect on the prices of goods manufactured in different countries.[166] An increase in the value of the dollar can harm U.S. firms' exports to international markets because of the price differential of the products. Thus, government oversight and control of economic and financial capital in the country affect not only local economic activity but also foreign investments in the country.[167]

eBay is the market leader in the Internet auction markets in the United States and Europe. However, its expansion to Asian countries has experienced

eBay reenters the Chinese market in a joint venture with a Chinese partner, Tom Online Inc.

difficulties. As noted earlier, its first ventures into the Japanese and Chinese markets failed and they withdrew. In 2007, Meg Whitman, CEO of eBay, announced that the company planned to reenter the Chinese market with a new partner. It learned from its previous failure and is entering with tighter restrictions to stop the sales of counterfeit goods through eBay's service. So the firm is taking actions to assure trust and safety in the sale and purchase of goods through eBay in the Chinese market.[168]

Limits to International Expansion: Management Problems

After learning how to operate effectively in international markets, firms tend to earn positive returns on international diversification. But, the returns often level off and become negative as the diversification increases past some point.[169] Several reasons explain the limits to the positive effects of international diversification. First, greater geographic dispersion across country borders increases the costs of coordination between units and the distribution of products. Second, trade barriers, logistical costs, cultural diversity, and other differences by country (e.g., access to raw materials and different employee skill levels) greatly complicate the implementation of an international diversification strategy.[170]

Institutional and cultural factors can present strong barriers to the transfer of a firm's competitive advantages from one country to another.[171] Marketing programs often have to be redesigned and new distribution networks established when firms expand into new countries. In addition, firms may encounter different labor costs and capital charges. In general, it is difficult to effectively implement, manage, and control a firm's international operations.[172]

The amount of international diversification that can be managed varies from firm to firm and according to the abilities of each firm's managers. The problems of central coordination and integration are mitigated if the firm diversifies into more friendly countries that are geographically close and have cultures similar to its own country's culture. In that case, the firm is likely to encounter fewer trade barriers, the laws and customs are better understood, and the product is easier to adapt to local markets.[173] For example, U.S. firms may find it less difficult to expand their operations into Mexico, Canada, and Western European countries than into Asian countries.

Companies also do not generally accept poor returns from international expansion. If they experience poor returns, they usually try to change the structure or management approaches to enhance the returns received on foreign investments. For example, IBM reorganized and changed its structure from a multidomestic to a transnational approach. In doing so, it created a more "seamless" organization, allowing it to capitalize on its core competencies.

Management must also be concerned with the relationship between the host government and the multinational corporation.[174] Although government policy and regulations are often barriers, many firms, such as Toyota and General Motors, have turned to strategic alliances, as they did in China, to overcome those barriers. By forming interorganizational networks, such as strategic alliances (see Chapter 9), firms can share resources and risks but also build flexibility. However, large networks can be difficult to manage.[175]

STRATEGY RIGHT NOW

Summary

- The use of international strategies is increasing. Traditional motives include extending the product life cycle, securing key resources, and having access to low-cost labor. Emerging motives include the integration of the Internet and mobile telecommunications, which facilitates global transactions. Also, firms experience increased pressure for global integration as the demand for commodities becomes borderless, and yet they feel simultaneous pressure for local country responsiveness.

- An international strategy is commonly designed primarily to capitalize on four benefits: increased market size; earning a return on large investments; economies of scale and learning; and advantages of location.

- International business-level strategies are usually grounded in one or more home-country advantages, as Porter's model suggests. Porter's model emphasizes four determinants: factors of production; demand conditions; related and supporting industries; and patterns of firm strategy, structure, and rivalry.

- There are three types of international corporate-level strategies. A multidomestic strategy focuses on competition within each country in which the firm competes. Firms using a multidomestic strategy decentralize strategic and operating decisions to the business units operating in each country, so that each unit can tailor its goods and services to the local market. A global strategy assumes more standardization of products across country boundaries; therefore, competitive strategy is centralized and controlled by the home office. A transnational strategy seeks to integrate characteristics of both multidomestic and global strategies to emphasize both local responsiveness and global integration and coordination. This strategy is difficult to implement, requiring an integrated network and a culture of individual commitment.

- Although the transnational strategy's implementation is a challenge, environmental trends are causing many multinational firms to consider the need for both global efficiency and local responsiveness. Many large multinational firms, particularly those with many diverse products, use a multidomestic strategy with some product lines and a global strategy with others.

- The threat of wars and terrorist attacks increase the risks and costs of international strategies. Furthermore, research suggests that the liability of foreignness is more difficult to overcome than once thought.

- Some firms decide to compete only in certain regions of the world, as opposed to viewing all markets in the world as potential opportunities. Competing in regional markets allows firms and managers to focus their learning on specific markets, cultures, locations, resources, and other factors.

- Firms may enter international markets in one of several ways, including exporting, licensing, forming strategic alliances, making acquisitions, and establishing new wholly owned subsidiaries, often referred to as greenfield ventures. Most firms begin with exporting or licensing, because of their lower costs and risks, but later they might use strategic alliances and acquisitions to expand internationally. The most expensive and risky means of entering a new international market is through the establishment of a new wholly owned subsidiary. On the other hand, such subsidiaries provide the advantages of maximum control by the firm and, if it is successful, the greatest returns.

- International diversification facilitates innovation in a firm, because it provides a larger market to gain more and faster returns from investments in innovation. In addition, international diversification may generate the resources necessary to sustain a large-scale R&D program.

- In general, international diversification is related to above average returns, but this assumes that the diversification is effectively implemented and that the firm's international operations are well managed. International diversification provides greater economies of scope and learning, which, along with greater innovation, help produce above-average returns.

- Several risks are involved with managing multinational operations. Among these are political risks (e.g., instability of national governments) and economic risks (e.g., fluctuations in the value of a country's currency).

- Some limits also constrain the ability to manage international expansion effectively. International diversification increases coordination and distribution costs, and management problems are exacerbated by trade barriers, logistical costs, and cultural diversity, among other factors.

Review Questions

1. What are the traditional and emerging motives that cause firms to expand internationally?

2. What are the four primary benefits of an international strategy?

3. What four factors provide a basis for international business-level strategies?

4. What are the three international corporate-level strategies? How do they differ from each other? What factors lead to their development?

5. What environmental trends are affecting international strategy?

6. What five modes of international expansion are available, and what is the normal sequence of their use?

7. What is the relationship between international diversification and innovation? How does international diversification affect innovation? What is the effect of international diversification on a firm's returns?

8. What are the risks of international diversification? What are the challenges of managing multinational firms?

1. S. Li, 2005, Why a poor governance environment does not deter foreign direct investment: The case of China and its implications for investment protection, *Business Horizons*, 48(4): 297–302.

2. A. K. Gupta & H. Wang, 2007, How to get China and India right: Western companies need to become smarter—and they need to do it quickly, *Wall Street Journal*, April 28, R4.

3. H. J. Sapienza, E. Autio, G. George, & S. A. Zahra, 2006, A capabilities perspective on the effects of early internationalization on firm survival and growth, *Academy of Management Review*, 31: 914–933; W. P. Wan, 2005, Country resource environments, firm capabilities, and corporate diversification strategies. *Journal of Management Studies*, 42: 161–182.

4. F. T. Rothaermel, S. Kotha, & H. K. Steensma, 2006, International market entry by U.S. Internet firms: An empirical analysis of country risk, national culture and market size, *Journal of Management*, 32: 56–82; R. E. Hoskisson, H. Kim, R. E. White, & L. Tihanyi, 2004, A framework for understanding international diversification by business groups from emerging economies, in M. A. Hitt & J. L. C. Cheng (eds.), *Theories of the Multinational Enterprise: Diversity, Complexity, and Relevance. Advances in International Management*, Oxford, UK: Elsevier/JAI Press, 137–163.

5. M. Javidan, R. Steers, & M. A. Hitt (eds.), 2007, *The Global Mindset*. Oxford, UK: Elsevier Publishing; T. M. Begley & D. P. Boyd, 2003, The need for a corporate global mind-set, *MIT Sloan Management Review*, 44(2): 25–32.

6. M. A. Hitt, L. Tihanyi, T. Miller, & B. Connelly, 2006, International diversification: Antecedents, outcomes and moderators, *Journal of Management*, 32: 831–867; L. Tongll, E. J. Ping, & W. K. C. Chiu, 2005, International diversification and performance: Evidence from Singapore, *Asia Pacific Journal of Management* 22: 65–88.

7. Y. Luo & R. L. Tung, 2007, International expansion of emerging market enterprises: A springboard perspective, *Journal of International Business Studies* 38: 481–498; J. E. Ricart, M. J. Enright, P. Ghemawat, S. L. Hart, & T. Khanna, 2004, New frontiers in international strategy, *Journal of International Business Studies*, 35: 175–200.

8. R. Vernon, 1996, International investment and international trade in the product cycle, *Quarterly Journal of Economics*, 80: 190–207.

9. P. J. Buckley, L. J. Clegg, A. R. Cross, X. Liu, H. Voss, & P. Zheng, 2006, The determinants of Chinese outward foreign direct investment, *Journal of International Business Studies*, 38: 499–518.

10. L. Yu, 2003, The global-brand advantage, *MIT Sloan Management Review*, 44(3): 13.

11. IKEA, 2007, Wikipedia, http://en.wikipedia .org.wiki/IKEA, August 1; 2005, IKEA, a household name, *Journal of Commerce*, May 30, 1.

12. D. Rigby & C. Zook, 2003, Open-market innovation, *Harvard Business Review*, 89(10): 80–89; J-R. Lee & J.-S. Chen, 2003, Internationalization, local adaptation and subsidiary's entrepreneurship: An exploratory study on Taiwanese manufacturing firms in Indonesia and Malaysia, *Asia Pacific Journal of Management*, 20: 51–72.

13. Gupta & Wang, How to get China and India right; Y. Luo, 2003, Market-seeking MNEs in an emerging market: How parent-subsidiary links shape overseas success, *Journal of International Business Studies*, 34(3): 290–309.

14. I. Filatotchev, R. Strange, J. Piesse, & Y.-C. Lien, 2007, FDI by firms from newly industrialized economies in emerging markets: Corporate governance, entry mode and location, *Journal of International Business Studies*, 38(4): 556–572; C. C. Y. Kwok & D. M. Reeb, 2000, Internationalization and firm risk: An upstream-downstream hypothesis, *Journal of International Business Studies*, 31: 611–629.

15. M. Wright, I. Filatotchev, R. E. Hoskisson, & M. W. Peng, 2005, Strategy research in emerging economies: Challenging the conventional wisdom, *Journal of Management Studies*, 42: 1–30; T. London & S. Hart, 2004, Reinventing strategies for emerging markets: Beyond the transnational model, *Journal of International Business Studies*, 35: 350–370; R. E. Hoskisson, L. Eden, C. M. Lau, & M. Wright, 2000, Strategy in emerging economies, *Academy of Management Journal*, 43: 249–267.

16. H. Sender, 2005, The economy; the outlook: India comes of age, as focus on returns lures foreign capital, *Wall Street Journal*, June 6, A2.

17. M. A. Witt & A. Y. Lewin, 2007, Outward foreign direct investment as escape to home country institutional constraints, *Journal of International Business Studies*, 38: 579–594; M. W. Peng, S.-H. Lee, & D. Y. L. Wang, 2005, What determines the scope of the firm over time? A focus on institutional relatedness, *Academy of Management Review*, 30: 622–633.

18. J. W. Spencer, T. P. Murtha, & S. A. Lenway, 2005, How governments matter to new industry creation, *Academy of Management Review*, 30: 321–337; I. P. Mahmood & C. Rufin, 2005, Government's dilemma: The role of government in imitation and innovation, *Academy of Management Review*, 30: 338–360.

19. L. Eden & S. Miller, 2004, Distance matters: Liability of foreignness, institutional distance and ownership strategy, in M. A. Hitt & J. L. Cheng (eds.), *Advances in International Management*, Oxford, UK: Elsevier/JAI Press, 187–221; T. Kostova & S. Zaheer, 1999, Organizational legitimacy under conditions of complexity: The case of the multinational enterprise, *Academy of Management Review*, 24: 64–81.

20. F. Jiang, 2005, Driving forces of international pharmaceutical firms' FDI into China, *Journal of Business Research*, 22(1): 21–39.

21. K. Hall, 2007, Fad marketing's balancing act, *BusinessWeek*, August 6, 42.

22. K. Asakawa & M. Lehrer, 2003, Managing local knowledge assets globally: The role of regional innovation relays, *Journal of World Business*, 38: 31–42.

23. J. Cantwell, J. Dunning, & O. Janne, 2004, Towards a technology-seeking explanation of U.S. direct investment in the United Kingdom, *Journal of International Management*, 10: 5–20; W. Chung & J. Alcacer, 2002, Knowledge seeking and location choice of foreign direct investment in the United States, *Management Science*, 48(12): 1534–1554.

24. B. Ambos, 2005, Foreign direct investment in industrial research and development: A study of German MNCs, *Research Policy*, 34: 395–410.

25. Jiang, Driving forces of international pharmaceutical firms' FDI into China.

26. M. D. R. Chari, S. Devaraj, & P. David, 2007, International diversification and firm performance: Role of information technology investments, *Journal of World Business*, 42: 184–197; W. Chung, 2001, Identifying technology transfer in foreign direct investment: Influence of industry conditions and investing firm motives, *Journal of International Business Studies*, 32: 211–229.

27. K. J. Petersen, R. B. Handfield, & G. L. Ragatz, 2005, Supplier integration into new product development: Coordinating product process and supply chain design, *Journal of Operations Management*, 23: 371–388; S. Prasad, J. Tata, & M. Madan, 2005, Build to order supply chains in developed and developing countries, *Journal of Operations Management*, 23: 551–568.

28. A. Webb, 2007, China needs strong automakers—not more. *Automotive News*, http://www.autonews.com, July 20; China's SAIC says first half sales up 23 percent. 2007, Reuters, http://www.reuters.com, July 12; A. Taylor,

2004, Shanghai Auto wants to be the world's next great car company, *Fortune*, October 4, 103–109.

29. L. Zhou, W.-P. Wu, & X. Luo, 2007, Internationalization and the performance of born-global SMEs: The mediating role of social networks, *Journal of International Business Studies*, 38: 673–690; W. Kuemmerle, 2002, Home base and knowledge management in international ventures, *Journal of Business Venturing*, 2: 99–122.

30. H. Berry, 2006, Leaders, laggards, and the pursuit of foreign knowledge, *Strategic Management Journal*, 27: 151–168; Cantwell, Dunning, & Janne, Towards a technology-seeking explanation of U.S. direct investment in the United Kingdom.

31. J. Penner-Hahn & J. M. Shaver, 2005, Does international research increase patent output? An analysis of Japanese pharmaceutical firms, *Strategic Management Journal*, 26: 121–140.

32. G. K. Lee, 2007, The significance of network resources in the race to enter emerging product markets: The convergence of telephony, communications, and computer networking, *Strategic Management Journal*, 28: 17–37; K. Ito & E. L. Rose, 2002, Foreign direct investment location strategies in the tire industry, *Journal of International Business Studies*, 33(3): 593–602.

33. R. Tahir & J. Larimo, 2004, Understanding the location strategies of the European firms in Asian countries, *Journal of American Academy of Business*, 5: 102–110.

34. D. Xu & O. Shenkar, 2004, Institutional distance and the multinational enterprise, *Academy of Management Review*, 27: 608–618.

35. D. Xu, Y. Pan, & P. W. Beamish, 2004, The effect of regulative and normative distances on MNE ownership and expatriate strategies, *Management International Review*, 44(3): 285–307.

36. Tallman & Fladmoe-Lindquist, Internationalization, globalization, and capability-based strategy; D. A. Griffith & M. G. Harvey, 2001, A resource perspective of global dynamic capabilities, *Journal of International Business Studies*, 32: 597–606; Y. Luo, 2000, Dynamic capabilities in international expansion, *Journal of World Business*, 35(4): 355–378.

37. D. Tan & J. T. Mahoney, 2005, Examining the Penrose effect in an international business context: The dynamics of Japanese firm growth in U.S. industries, *Managerial and Decision Economics*, 26(2): 113–127; K. Uhlenbruck, 2004, Developing acquired foreign subsidiaries: The experience of MNEs for multinationals in transition economies, *Journal of International Business Studies*, 35: 109–123.

38. J. Gimeno, R. E. Hoskisson, B.D. Beal, & W. P. Wan, 2005, Explaining the clustering of international expansion moves: A critical test in the U.S. telecommunications industry, *Academy of Management Journal*, 48: 297–319.

39. M. A. Hitt, L. Bierman, K. Uhlenbruck, & K. Shimizu, 2006, The importance of resources in the internationalization of professional service firms: The good, the bad and the ugly, *Academy of Management Journal*, 49: 1137–1157.

40. L. Nachum, 2001, The impact of home countries on the competitiveness of advertising TNCs, *Management International Review*, 41(1): 77–98.

41. M. E. Porter, 1990, *The Competitive Advantage of Nations*, New York: The Free Press.

42. Ibid., 84.

43. Y. Aoyama & H. Izushi, 2003, Hardware gimmick or cultural innovation? Technological, cultural, and social foundations of the Japanese video game industry, *Research Policy*, 32: 423–443.

44. A. Tempel & P. Walgenbach, 2007, Global standardization of organizational forms and management practices? What new institutionalism and business systems approach can learn from each other, *Journal of Management Studies*, 44: 1–24; P. Ghemawat, 2004, Global standardization vs. localization: A case study and model, in J. A. Quelch & R. Deshpande (eds.), *The Global Market: Developing a Strategy to Manage Across Borders*, New York: Jossey-Bass.

45. W. P. Wan & R. E. Hoskisson, 2003, Home country environments, corporate diversification strategies and firm performance, *Academy of Management Journal*, 46: 27–45; J. M. Geringer, S. Tallman, & D. M. Olsen, 2000, Product and international diversification among Japanese multinational firms, *Strategic Management Journal*, 21: 51–80.

46. Wan & Hoskisson, Home country environments, corporate diversification strategies and firm performance; M. A. Hitt, R. E. Hoskisson, & R. D. Ireland, 1994, A mid-range theory of the interactive effects of international and product diversification on innovation and performance, *Journal of Management*, 20: 297–326.

47. L. Li, 2005, Is regional strategy more effective than global strategy in the U.S. service industries? *Management International Review*, 45: 37–57; B. B. Alred & K. S. Swan, 2004, Global versus multidomestic: Culture's consequences on innovation, *Management International Review*, 44: 81–105.

48. A. Ferner, P. Almond, I. Clark, T. Colling, & T. Edwards, 2004, The dynamics of central control and subsidiary anatomy in the management of human resources: Case study evidence from US MNCs in the UK, *Organization Studies*, 25: 363–392.

49. B. Connelly, M. A. Hitt, A. S. DeNisi, & R. D. Ireland, 2007, Expatriates and corporate-level international strategy: Governing with the knowledge contract, *Management Decision*, 45: 564–581; L. Nachum, 2003, Does nationality of ownership make any difference and if so, under what circumstances? Professional service MNEs in global competition, *Journal of International Management*, 9: 1–32.

50. Y. Luo, 2001, Determinants of local responsiveness: Perspectives from foreign subsidiaries in an emerging market, *Journal of Management*, 27: 451–477.

51. M. Geppert, K. Williams, & D. Matten, 2003, The social construction of contextual rationalities in MNCs: An Anglo-German comparison of subsidiary choice, *Journal of Management Studies*, 40: 617–641; M. Carpenter & J. Fredrickson, 2001, Top management teams, global strategic posture, and the moderating role of uncertainty, *Academy of Management Journal*, 44: 533–545.

52. About the Company, 2007, Unilever, http://www.unilever.com, August 2; G. Jones, 2002, Control, performance, and knowledge transfers in large multinationals: Unilever in the United States, 1945–1980, *Business History Review*, 76(3): 435–478.

53. Tempel & Walgenbach, Global standardization of organizational forms and management practices; Li, Is regional strategy more effective than global strategy in the U.S. service industries?

54. M. Zellmer-Braun & C. Gibson, 2006, Multinational organization context: Implications for team learning and performance, *Academy of Management Journal*, 49:501–518; I. C. MacMillan, A. B. van Putten, & R. G. McGrath, 2003, Global gamesmanship, *Harvard Business Review*, 81(5): 62–71.

55. Connelly, Hitt, DeNisi, & Ireland, Expatriates and corporate-level international strategy; J.F.L. Hong, M. Easterby-Smith, & R.S. Snell, 2006, Transferring organizational learning systems to Japanese subsidiaries in China, *Journal of Management Studies*, 43: 1027–1058.

56. R. G. Barker, 2003, Trend: Global accounting is coming, *Harvard Business Review*, 81 (4): 24–25.

57. A. Yaprak, 2002, Globalization: Strategies to build a great global firm in the new economy, *Thunderbird International Business Review*, 44(2): 297–302; D. G. McKendrick, 2001, Global strategy and population level learning: The case of hard disk drives, *Strategic Management Journal*, 22: 307–334.

58. V. Shannon, 2007, eBay is preparing to re-enter the China auction business, *New York Times*, http://www.nytimes.com, June 22; B Einhorn, 2007, A break in Yahoo's China clouds? *BusinessWeek*, http://wwwbusinessweek.com, June 20.

59. K. E. Meyer, 2006, Globalfocusing: From domestic conglomerates to global specialists, *Journal of Management Studies*, 43: 1109–1144; A. Delios & P. W. Beamish, 2005, Regional and global strategies of Japanese firms, *Management International Review*, 45: 19–36.

60. H. D. Hopkins, 2003, The response strategies of dominant US firms to

Japanese challengers, *Journal of Management*, 29: 5–25; S. Massini, A. Y. Lewin, T. Numagami, & A. Pettigrew, 2002, The evolution of organizational routines among large Western and Japanese firms, *Research Policy*, 31(8,9): 1333–1348.

61. 2006 annual report, 2007, CEMEX, http://www.cemex.com, August 2; K. A. Garrett, 2005, Cemex, *Business Mexico*, April 23.

62. B. Elango & C. Pattnaik, 2007, Building capabilities for international operations through networks: A study of Indian firms, *Journal of International Business Studies*, 38: 541–555; T. B. Lawrence, E. A. Morse, & S. W. Fowler, 2005, Managing your portfolio of connections, *MIT Sloan Management Review*, 46(2): 59–65; C. A. Bartlett & S. Ghoshal, 1989, *Managing across Borders: The Transnational Solution*, Boston: Harvard Business School Press.

63. A. Abbott & K. Banerji, 2003, Strategic flexibility and firm performance: The case of US based transnational corporations, *Global Journal of Flexible Systems Management*, 4(1/2): 1–7; J. Child & Y. Van, 2001, National and transnational effects in international business: Indications from Sino-foreign joint ventures, *Management International Review*, 41(1): 53–75.

64. W. Barner-Rasmussen & I. Bjorkman, 2007, Language fluency, socialization and inter-unit relationships in Chinese and Finnish subsidiaries, *Management and Organization Review*, 3:105–128; A.S. Cui, D.A. Griffith, S.T. Cavusgil, & M. Dabic, 2006, The influence of market and cultural environmental factors on technology transfer between foreign MNCs and local subsidiaries: A Croatian illustration, *Journal of World Business*, 41: 100–111.

65. A. M. Rugman & A. Verbeke, 2003, Extending the theory of the multinational enterprise: Internalization and strategic management perspectives, *Journal of International Business Studies*, 34: 125–137.

66. H. F. Cheng, M. Gutierrez, A. Mahajan, Y. Shachmurove, & M. Shahrokhi, 2007, A future global economy to be built by BRICs, *Global Finance Journal*, in press; Wright, Filatotchev, Hoskisson, & Peng, Strategy research in emerging economies: Challenging the conventional wisdom.

67. N. Y. Brannen, 2004, When Mickey loses face: Recontextualization, semantic fit and semiotics of foreignness, *Academy of Management Review*, 29: 593–616.

68. A. M. Rugman & A. Verbeke, 2007, Liabilities of foreignness and the use of firm-level versus country-level data: A response to Dunning et al. (2007), *Journal of International Business Studies*, 38: 200–205; S. Zaheer & A. Zaheer, 2001, Market microstructure in a global B2B network, *Strategic Management Journal*, 22: 859–873.

69. J. A. Trachtenberg & B. Steinberg, 2003, Plan B for Marketers-in a time of global

conflict, companies consider changing how they push products, *Wall Street Journal*, March 20, B7.

70. S. R. Miller & L. Eden, 2006, Local density and foreign subsidiary performance, *Academy of Management Journal*, 49: 341–355.

71. About Lands' End, 2007, Lands' End, http://www.landsend.com, August 2; J. Schlosser, 2004, Cashing in on the new world of me, *Fortune,* December, 13, 244–248.

72. C. H. Oh & A. M. Rugman, 2007, Regional multinationals and the Korean cosmetics industry, *Asia Pacific Journal of Management*, 24: 27–42; A. Rugman & A. Verbeke, 2004, A perspective on regional and global strategies of multinational enterprises, *Journal of International Business Studies*, 35: 3–18.

73. C. Pantzalis, 2001, Does location matter? An empirical analysis of geographic scope and MNC market valuation, *Journal of International Business Studies*, 32: 133–155.

74. A. Rugman & S. Girod, 2003, Retail multinationals and globalization: The evidence is regional, *European Management Journal*, 21(1): 24–37.

75. D. E. Westney, 2006. Review of the regional multinationals: MNEs and global strategic management, *Journal of International Business Studies*, 37: 445–449.

76. R. D. Ludema, 2002, Increasing returns, multinationals and geography of preferential trade agreements, *Journal of International Economics*, 56: 329–358.

77. Meyer, Globalfocusing: From domestic conglomerates to global specialists; Delios & Beamish, Regional and global strategies of Japanese firms.

78. T. L. Pett & J. A. Wolff, 2003, Firm characteristic and managerial perceptions of NAFTA: An assessment of export implications for U.S. SMEs, *Journal of Small Business Management*, 41(2): 117–132.

79. W. Chung & J. Song, 2004, Sequential investment, firm motives, and agglomeration of Japanese electronics firms in the United States, *Journal of Economics and Management Strategy*, 13: 539–560; D. Xu & O. Shenkar, 2002, Institutional distance and the multinational enterprise, *Academy of Management Review*, 27(4): 608–618.

80. K. D. Brouthers, L. E. Brouthers, & S. Werner, 2003, Industrial sector, perceived environmental uncertainty and entry mode strategy, *Journal of Business Research*, 55: 495–507.

81. H. Zhao, Y. Luo, & T. Suh, 2004, Transaction costs determinants and ownership-based entry mode choice: A meta-analytical review, *Journal of International Business Studies*, 35: 524–544; K. D. Brouthers, 2003, Institutional, cultural and transaction cost influences on entry mode choice and performance, *Journal of International Business Studies*, 33: 203–221.

82. C. Lages, C. R. Lages, & L. F. Lages, 2005, The RELQUAL scale: A measure of relationship quality in export market ventures, *Journal of Business Research*, 58: 1040–1048; R. Isaak, 2002, Using trading firms to export: What can the French experience teach us? *Academy of Management Executive*, 16(4): 155–156.

83. Y. Chui, 2002, The structure of the multinational firm: The role of ownership characteristics and technology transfer, *International Journal of Management*, 19(3):472–477.

84. Luo, Determinants of local responsiveness.

85. L. E. Brouthers & K. Xu, 2002, Product stereotypes, strategy and performance satisfaction: The case of Chinese exporters, *Journal of International Business Studies*, 33: 657–677; M. A. Raymond, J. Kim, & A. T. Shao, 2001, Export strategy and performance: A comparison of exporters in a developed market and an emerging market, *Journal of Global Marketing*, 15(2): 5–29.

86. W. Dou, U. Nielsen, & C. M. Tan, 2003, Using corporate Web sites for export marketing, *Journal of Advertising Research*, 42(5): 105–115.

87. A. Haahti, V. Madupu, U. Yavas, & E. Babakus, 2005, Cooperative strategy, knowledge intensity and export performance of small and medium-sized enterprises, *Journal of World Business*, 40(2): 124–138.

88. K. A. Houghton & H. Winklhofer, 2004, The effect of Web site and ecommerce adoption on the relationship between SMEs and their export intermediaries, *International Small Business Journal*, 22: 369–385.

89. P. Westhead, M. Wright, & D. Ucbasaran, 2001, The internationalization of new and small firms: A resource-based view, *Journal of Business Venturing*, 16: 333–358.

90. The U.S. dollar weakened to a new two-year low against the euro, 2007, Union Bank of California, http://www.fxstreet.com, April 17; M. N. Bailey & R. Z. Lawrence, 2005, Don't blame trade for U.S. job losses, *The McKinsey Quarterly*, 1: 86.

91. D. Kline, 2003, Sharing the corporate crown jewels, *MIT Sloan Management Review*, 44(3): 83–88; M. A. Hitt & R. D. Ireland, 2000, The intersection of entrepreneurship and strategic management research, in D. L. Sexton & H. Landstrom (eds.), *Handbook of Entrepreneurship*, Oxford, UK: Blackwell Publishers, 45–63.

92. A. Arora & A. Fosfuri, 2000, Wholly owned subsidiary versus technology licensing in the worldwide chemical industry, *Journal of International Business Studies*, 31: 555–572.

93. N. Zamiska & V. O'Connell, 2005, Philip Morris is in talks to make Marlboros in China, *Wall Street Journal*, April 21, B1, B2.

94. Y. J. Kim, 2005, The impact of firm and industry characteristics on technology

licensing, *S.A.M. Advanced Management Journal*, 70(1): 42–49.

95. M. Johnson, 2001, Learning from toys: Lessons in managing supply chain risk from the toy industry, *California Management Review*, 43(3): 106–124.

96. B. Ebenkamp, 2005, Tamra Seldin, *Brandweek*, April 11, 40, 50.

97. Rigby & Zook, Open-market innovation.

98. C. A. Bartlett & S. Rangan, 1992, Komatsu limited, in C. A. Bartlett & S. Ghoshal (eds.), *Transnational Management: Text, Cases and Readings in Cross-Border Management*, Homewood, IL: Irwin, 311–326.

99. Profile: Marriott International, Inc., 2007, Yahoo! Finance, http://finance.yahoo.com, August 2; Fitch, 2004, Soft pillows and sharp elbows, *Forbes*, May 10, 66.

100. J. J. Reuer & T. W. Tong, 2005, Real options in international joint ventures, *Journal of Management* 31: 403–423; B. Petersen, D. E. Welch, & L. S. Welch, 2000, Creating meaningful switching options in international operations, *Long Range Planning*, 33(5): 688–705.

101. M. Nippa, S. Beechler, & A. Klossek, 2007, Success factors for managing international joint ventures: A review and an integrative framework, *Management and Organization Review*, 3: 277–310; R. Larsson, K. R. Brousseau, M. J. Driver, & M. Homqvist, 2003, International growth through cooperation: Brand-driven strategies, leadership, and career development in Sweden, *Academy of Management Executive*, 17(1): 7–21.

102. J. S. Harrison, M. A. Hitt, R. E. Hoskisson, & R. D. Ireland, 2001, Resource complementarity in business combinations: Extending the logic to organization alliances, *Journal of Management*, 27: 679–690; T. Das & B. Teng, 2000, A resource-based theory of strategic alliances, *Journal of Management*, 26: 31–61.

103. M. A. Hitt, D. Ahlstrom, M. T. Dacin, E. Levitas, & L. Svobodina, 2004, The institutional effects on strategic alliance partner selection in transition economies: China versus Russia, *Organization Science*, 15: 173–185; M. Peng, 2001, The resource-based view and international business, *Journal of Management*, 27: 803–829.

104. J. Bamford, D. Ernst, & D. G. Fubini, 2004, Launching a world-class joint venture, *Harvard Business Review*, 82(2): 91–100.

105. M. A. Lyles & J. E. Salk, 2007, Knowledge acquisition from foreign parents in international joint ventures: An empirical examination in the Hungarian context, *Journal of International Business Studies*, 38: 3–18; E. W. K. Tsang, 2002, Acquiring knowledge by foreign partners for international joint ventures in a transition economy: Learning-by-doing and learning myopia, *Strategic Management Journal*, 23(9): 835–854; P. J. Lane, J. E. Salk, & M. A. Lyles, 2002, Absorptive capacity learning and performance in international joint ventures, *Strategic Management Journal*, 22: 1139–1161.

106. S. Zaheer & A. Zaheer, 2007, Trust across borders, *Journal of International Business Studies*, 38: 21–29; P. Almeida, J. Song, & R. M. Grant, 2002, Are firms superior to alliances and markets? An empirical test of cross-border knowledge building, *Organization Science*, 13(2): 147–161; M. A. Hitt, M. T. Dacin, E. Levitas, J. L. Arregle, & A. Borza, 2000, Partner selection in emerging and developed market contexts: Resource-based and organizational learning perspectives, *Academy of Management Journal*, 43: 449–467.

107. M. W. Peng & O. Shenkar, 2002, Joint venture dissolution as corporate divorce, *Academy of Management Executive*, 16(2): 92–105; O. Shenkar & A. Van, 2002, Failure as a consequence of partner politics: Learning from the life and death of an international cooperative venture, *Human Relations*, 55: 565–601.

108. J. A. Robins, S. Tallman, & K. Fladmoe-Lindquist, 2002, Autonomy and dependence of international cooperative ventures: An exploration of the strategic performance of U.S. ventures in Mexico, *Strategic Management Journal*, 23(10): 881–901; Y. Gong, O. Shenkar, Y. Luo, & M.-K. Nyaw, 2001, Role conflict and ambiguity of CEOs in international joint ventures: A transaction cost perspective, *Journal of Applied Psychology*. 86: 764–773.

109. P. K. Jagersma, 2005, Cross-border alliances: Advice from the executive suite, *Journal of Business Strategy*, 26(1): 41–50; D. C. Hambrick, J. Li, K. Xin, & A. S. Tsui, 2001, Compositional gaps and downward spirals in international joint venture management groups, *Strategic Management Journal*, 22: 1033–1053.

110. A. Madhok, 2006, Revisiting multinational firms' tolerance for joint ventures: A trust-based approach, *Journal of International Business Studies*, 37: 30–43; J. Child & Y. Van, 2003, Predicting the performance of international joint ventures: An investigation in China, *Journal of Management Studies*, 40(2): 283–320; J. P. Johnson, M. A. Korsgaard, & H. J. Sapienza, 2002, Perceived fairness, decision control, and commitment in international joint venture management teams, *Strategic Management Journal*, 23(12): 1141–1160.

111. L. Huff & L. Kelley, 2003, Levels of organizational trust in individualist versus collectivist societies: A seven-nation study, *Organization Science*, 14(1): 81–90.

112. D. Li, L. Eden, M. A. Hitt, & R. D. Ireland, 2008, Friends, acquaintances and strangers? Partner selection in R&D alliances, *Academy of Management Journal*, in press; Y. Pan & D. K. Tse, 2000, The hierarchical model of market entry modes, *Journal of International Business Studies*, 31: 535–554.

113. J. J. Reuer & M. Zollo, 2005, Termination outcomes of research alliances, *Research Policy*, 34(1): 101–115.

114. P. Porrini, 2004, Can a previous alliance between an acquirer and a target affect acquisition performance? *Journal of Management*, 30: 545–562; J. J. Reuer, 2002, Incremental corporate reconfiguration through international joint venture buyouts and selloffs, *Management International Review*, 42: 237–260.

115. J. J. Reuer, 2005, Avoiding lemons in M&A deals, *MIT Sloan Management Review*; 46(3): 15–17; G. A. Knight & P. W. Liesch, 2002, Information internalization in internationalizing the firm, *Journal of Business Research*, 55(12): 981–995.

116. S. G. Lazzarini, 2007, The impact of membership in competing alliance constellations: Evidence on the operational performance of global airlines, *Strategic Management Journal*, 28: 345–367; J. H. Dyer, P. Kale, & H. Singh, 2004, When to ally and when to acquire, *Harvard Business Review*, 82(7): 108–117.

117. K. Shimizu, M. A. Hitt, D. Vaidyanath, & V. Pisano, 2004, Theoretical foundations of cross-border mergers and acquisitions: A review of current research and recommendations for the future, *Journal of International Management*, 10: 307–353; M. A. Hitt, J. S. Harrison, & R. D. Ireland, 2001, *Mergers and Acquisitions: A Guide to Creating Value for Stakeholders,* New York: Oxford University Press.

118. M. A. Hitt & V. Pisano, 2003, The cross-border merger and acquisition strategy, *Management Research*, 1: 133–144.

119. International operational fact sheet, 2007, http://www.walmartfacts.com, July; J. Levine, 2004, Europe: Gold mines and quicksand, *Forbes*, April 12, 76.

120. 1999, French dressing, *The Economist*, July 10, 53–54.

121. U. Weitzel & S. Berns, 2006, Cross-border takeovers, corruption, and related aspects of governance, *Journal of International Business Studies*, 37: 786–806.

122. A. H. L. Slangen, 2006, National cultural distance and initial foreign acquisition performance: The moderating effect of integration, *Journal of World Business*, 41: 161–170.

123. I. Bjorkman, G. K. Stahl, & E. Vaara, 2007, Cultural differences and capability transfer in cross-border acquisitions: The mediating roles of capability complementarity, absorptive capacity, and social integration, *Journal of International Business Studies*, 38: 658–672.

124. C. Buckley, 2005, SAIC to fund MG Rover bid, *The Times of London*, http://www.timesonline.co.uk, July 18.

125. A.-W. Harzing, 2002, Acquisitions versus greenfield investments: International strategy and management of entry modes, *Strategic Management Journal*, 23: 211–227; K. D. Brouthers & L. E. Brouthers, 2000, Acquisition or greenfield start-up? Institutional, cultural and transaction cost influences, *Strategic Management Journal*, 21: 89–97.

126. C. Bouquet, L. Hebert, & A. Delios, 2004, Foreign expansion in service industries: Separability and human capital intensity, *Journal of Business Research*, 57: 35–46.

127. D. Elango, 2005, The influence of plant characteristics on the entry mode choice of overseas firms, *Journal of Operations Management*, 23(1): 65–79.

128. P. Deng, 2003, Determinants of full-control mode in China: An integrative approach, *American Business Review*, 21(1): 113–123.

129. R. Belderbos, 2003, Entry mode, organizational learning, and R&D in foreign affiliates: Evidence from Japanese firms, *Strategic Management Journal*, 34: 235–259.

130. S. Mani, K. D. Antia & A. Rindfleisch, 2007, Entry mode and equity level: A multilevel examination of foreign direct investment ownership structure, *Strategic Management Journal*, 28: 857–866.

131. Construction starts on UPS air hub in Shanghai, 2007, United Parcel Service, http://ups.com/pressroom, August 9; FedEx announces next-business-day domestic express service in China, 2007, FedEx Corporation, http://home .businesswire.com/portal/site/fedex—corp/index, March 19; B. Stanley, 2005, United Parcel Service to open a hub in Shanghai, *Wall Street Journal*, July 8, B2; B. Stanley, 2005, FedEx plans hub in Guangzhou: Facility to begin operation in 2008 as cargo industry tries to claim turf in Asia, *Asian Wall Street Journal*, July 14, A3.

132. V. Gaba, Y. Pan, & G. R. Ungson, 2002, Timing of entry in international market: An empirical study of U.S. Fortune 500 firms in China, *Journal of International Business Studies*, 33(1): 39–55; S.-J. Chang & P. Rosenzweig, 2001, The choice of entry mode in sequential foreign direct investment, *Strategic Management Journal*, 22: 747–776.

133. R. Farzad, 2007, Extreme investing: Inside Colombia, *BusinessWeek*, May 28, 50–58; K. E. Myer, 2001, Institutions, transaction costs, and entry mode choice in Eastern Europe, *Journal of International Business Studies*, 32: 357–367.

134. S. Li, 2004, Why are property rights protections lacking in China? An institutional explanation, *California Management Review*, 46(3): 100–115; Y. Luo, 2001, Determinants of entry in an emerging economy: A multilevel approach, *Journal of Management Studies*, 38: 443–472.

135. A. Antoine, C. B. Frank, H. Murata, & E. Roberts, 2003, Acquisitions and alliances in the aerospace industry: An unusual triad, *International Journal of Technology Management*, 25(8): 779–790.

136. M. Zimmerman, 2007, Toyota ends GM's reign as car sales leader, *Los Angeles Times*, April 25, 2007, C.1; L. J. Howell & J. C. Hsu, 2002, Globalization within the auto industry, *Research Technology Management*, 45(4): 43–49.

137. J. Hagedoorn & G. Dysters, 2002, External sources of innovative capabilities: The preference for strategic alliances or mergers and acquisitions, *Journal of Management Studies*, 39: 167–188; H. Chen, 1999, International performance of multinationals: A hybrid model, *Journal of World Business*, 34: 157–170.

138. A. Chacar & B. Vissa, 2005, Are emerging economies less efficient? Performance persistence and the impact of business group affiliation, *Strategic Management Journal*, 26: 933–946; Hoskisson, Kim, Tihanyi, & White, A framework for understanding international diversification by business groups from emerging economies.

139. T. Yu & A. A. Cannella, 2007, Rivalry between multinational enterprises: An event history approach, *Academy of Management Journal*, 50: 665–686.

140. M. F. Wiersma & H. P. Bowen, 2007, Corporate diversification: The impact of foreign competition, industry globalization and product diversification, *Strategic Management Journal*, 28: in press.

141. L. Li, 2007, Multinationality and performance: A synthetic review and research agenda, *International Journal of Management Reviews*, 9: 117–139; J. A. Doukas & O. B. Kan, 2006, Does global diversification destroy firm value, *Journal of International Business Studies*, 37: 352–371; J. W. Lu & P. W. Beamish, 2004, International diversification and firm performance: The S-curve hypothesis, *Academy of Management Journal*, 47: 598–609.

142. S. E. Christophe & H. Lee, 2005, What matters about internationalization: A market-based assessment, *Journal of Business Research*. 58: 536–643; J. A. Doukas & L. H. P. Lang, 2003, Foreign direct investment, diversification and firm performance, *Journal of International Business Studies*, 34: 153–172.

143. Hitt, Tihanyi, Miller, & Connelly, International diversification; Kwok & Reeb, Internationalization and firm risk.

144. Y. Fang, M. Wade, A. Delios, & P. W. Beamish, 2007, International diversification, subsidiary performance, and the mobility of knowledge resources, *Strategic Management Journal*, 28: in press.

145. T. R. Holcomb & M. A. Hitt, 2007, Toward a model of strategic outsourcing, *Journal of Operations Management*, 25: 464–481; J. P. Doh, 2005, Offshore outsourcing: Implications for international business and strategic management theory and practice, *Journal of Management Studies*, 42: 695–704.

146. J. Penner-Hahn & J. M. Shaver, 2005, Does international research and development increase patent output? An analysis of Japanese pharmaceutical firms, *Strategic Management Journal*, 26: 121–140; Hagedoorn & Dysters, External sources of innovative capabilities.

147. Hitt, Bierman, Uhlenbruck, & Shimizu, The importance of resources in the internationalization of professional service firms; L. Tihanyi, R. A. Johnson, R. E. Hoskisson, & M. A. Hitt, 2003, Institutional ownership differences and international diversification: The effects of board of directors and technological opportunity, *Academy of Management Journal*, 46:195–211.

148. Ambos, Foreign direct investment in industrial research and development; F. Bradley & M. Gannon, 2000, Does the firm's technology and marketing profile affect foreign market entry? *Journal of International Marketing*, 8(4): 12–36.

149. B. Ambos & B. B. Schlegelmilch, 2007, Innovation and control in the multinational firm: A comparison of political and contingency approaches, *Strategic Management Journal*, 28: 473–486; Asakawa & Lehrer, Managing local knowledge assets globally: The role of regional innovation relays.

150. O. E. M. Janne, 2002, The emergence of corporate integrated innovation systems across regions: The case of the chemical and pharmaceutical industry in Germany, the UK and Belgium, *Journal of International Management*, 8: 97–119.

151. Wiersema & Bowen, Corporate diversification; J. Jung & S. M. Chan-Olmsted, 2005, Impacts of media conglomerates' dual diversification on financial performance, *Journal of Media Economics*, 18(3): 183–202.

152. Wan & Hoskisson, Home country environments, corporate diversification strategies and firm performance.

153. D. S. Elenkov, W. Judge, & P. Wright, 2005, Strategic leadership and executive innovation influence: An international multi-cluster comparative study, *Strategic Management Journal*, 26: 665–682; P. Herrmann, 2002, The influence of CEO characteristics on the international diversification of manufacturing firms: An empirical study in the United States, *International Journal of Management*, 19(2): 279–289.

154. H. A. Krishnan & D. Park, 2003, Power in acquired top management teams and post-acquisition performance: A conceptual framework, *International Journal of Management*, 20: 75–80; A. McWilliams, D. D. Van Fleet, & P. M. Wright, 2001, Strategic management of human resources for global competitive advantage, *Journal of Business Strategies*, 18(1): 1–24.

155. M. A. Hitt, R. E. Hoskisson, & H. Kim, 1997, International diversification: Effects on innovation and firm performance in product-diversified firms, *Academy of Management Journal*, 40: 767–798.

156. J. Child, L. Chung, & H. Davies, 2003, The performance of cross-border units in China: A test of natural selection, strategic choice and contingency theories, *Journal of International Business Studies*, 34: 242–254.

157. Y.-H. Chiu, 2003, The impact of conglomerate firm diversification on corporate performance: An empirical study in Taiwan, *International Journal of Management*, 19: 231–237; Luo, Market-seeking MNEs in an emerging market: How parent-subsidiary links shape overseas success.

158. C. Crossland & D. C. Hambrick, 2007, How national systems differ in their constraints on corporate executives: A study of CEO effects in three countries, *Strategic Management Journal,* 28: 767–789; M. Javidan, P. W. Dorfman, M. S. de Luque, & R. J. House, 2006, In the eye of the beholder: Cross-cultural lessons in leadership from Project GLOBE, *Academy of Management Perspectives,* 20 (1): 67–90.

159. 2005, Keeping IT together, *Chain Store Age,* June, 48.

160. Y. Paik, 2005, Risk management of strategic alliances and acquisitions between western MNCs and companies in central Europe, *Thunderbird International Business Review,* 47(4): 489–511; A. Delios & W. J. Henisz, 2003, Policy uncertainty and the sequence of entry by Japanese firms, 1980–1998, *Journal of International Business Studies,* 34: 227–241.

161. P. Rodriguez. K. Uhlenbruck, & L. Eden, 2005, Government corruption and the entry strategies of multinationals, *Academy of Management Review,* 30: 383–396; J. H. Zhao, S. H. Kim, & J. Du, 2003, The impact of corruption and transparency on foreign direct investment: An empirical analysis, *Management International Review,* 43(1): 41–62.

162. P. S. Ring, G. A. Bigley, T. D'aunno, & T. Khanna, 2005, Perspectives on how governments matter, *Academy of Management Review,* 30: 308–320; S. Globerman & D. Shapiro, 2003, Governance infrastructure and U.S. foreign direct investment, *Journal of International Business Studies,* 34(1): 19–39.

163. W. Bailey & A. Spicer, 2007, When does identity matter? Convergence and divergence in international business ethics, *Academy of Management Journal,* 50: in press; Hitt, Ahlstrom, Dacin, Levitas, & Svobodina, The institutional effects

on strategic alliance partner selection in transition economies.

164. Y. Lu & J. Yao, 2006, Impact of state ownership and control mechanisms on the performance of group-affiliated companies in China, *Asia Pacific Journal of Management,* 23: 485–503; T. Mapes, 2005, Terror still keeps foreign investors out of Indonesia, *Wall Street Journal,* May 31, AI4.

165. T. Vestring, T. Rouse, & U. Reinert, 2005, Hedging your offshoring bets, *MIT Sloan Management Review,* 46(3): 26–29; L. L. Jacque & P. M. Vaaler, 2001, The international control conundrum with exchange risk: An EVA framework, *Journal of International Business Studies,* 32: 813–832.

166. T. G. Andrews & N. Chompusri, 2005, Temporal dynamics of crossvergence: Institutionalizing MNC integration strategies in post-crisis ASEAN, *Asia Pacific Journal of Management,* 22(1): 5–22; S. Mudd, R. Grosse, & J. Mathis, 2002, Dealing with financial crises in emerging markets, *Thunderbird International Business Review,* 44(3): 399–430.

167. L. Tihanyi & W. H. Hegarty, 2007, Political interests and the emergence of commercial banking in transition economies, *Journal of Management Studies,* 44: 789–813.

168. Shannon, eBay is preparing to reenter the Chinese auction business.

169. Lu & Beamish, International diversification and firm performance: The s-curve hypothesis; Wan & Hoskisson, Home country environments, corporate diversification strategies and firm performance; Hitt, Hoskisson, & Kim, International diversification.

170. C. C. Kwok & S. Tadesse, 2006, The MNC as an agent of change for host-country institutions: FDI and corruption, *Journal of International Business Studies,* 37: 767–785; F. J. Contractor, S. K. Kundu, &

C. C. Hsu, 2003, A three-stage theory of international expansion: The link between multinationality and performance in the service sector, *Journal of International Business Studies,* 34(1): 5–19.

171. I. Bjorkman, W. Barner-Rasmussen, & L. Li, 2004, Managing knowledge transfer in MNCs: The impact of headquarters control mechanisms, *Journal of International Business Studies,* 35: 443–455.

172. C. M. Chan & S. Makino, 2007, Legitimacy and multi-level institutional environments: Implications for foreign subsidiary ownership structure, *Journal of International Business Studies,* 38:621–638; S. Li & H. Scullion, 2006, Bridging the distance: Managing cross-border knowledge holders, *Asia Pacific Journal of Management,* 23: 71–92.

173. D. W. Yiu, C. M. Lau & G. D. Bruton, 2007, International venturing by emerging economy firms: The effects of firm capabilities, home country networks, and corporate entrepreneurship, *Journal of International Business Studies,* 38: 519–540; P. S. Barr & M. A. Glynn, 2004, Cultural variations in strategic issue interpretation: Relating cultural uncertainty avoidance to controllability in discriminating threat and opportunity, *Strategic Management Journal,* 25: 59–67.

174. W. P. J. Henisz & B. A. Zeiner, 2005, Legitimacy, interest group pressures and change in emergent institutions, the case of foreign investors and host country governments, *Academy of Management Review,* 30: 361–382; T. P. Blumentritt & D. Nigh, 2002, The integration of subsidiary political activities in multinational corporations, *Journal of International Business Studies,* 33: 57–77.

175. S.-J. Chang & S. Park, 2005, Types of firms generating network externalities and MNCs' co-location decisions, *Strategic Management Journal,* 26: 595–616.

Cooperative Strategy

9

Studying this chapter should provide you with the strategic management knowledge needed to:

1. Define cooperative strategies and explain why firms use them.

2. Define and discuss three types of strategic alliances.

3. Name the business-level cooperative strategies and describe their use.

4. Discuss the use of corporate-level cooperative strategies in diversified firms.

5. Understand the importance of cross-border strategic alliances as an international cooperative strategy.

6. Explain cooperative strategies' risks.

7. Describe two approaches used to manage cooperative strategies.

Using Cooperative Strategies at IBM

A company widely known throughout the world, IBM's 350,000-plus employees design, manufacturer, sell, and service advanced information technologies such as computer systems, storage systems, software, and microelectronics. The firm's extensive lineup of products and services is grouped into three core business units— Systems and Financing, Software, and Services.

As is true for all companies, IBM uses three means to grow—internal developments (primarily through innovation), mergers and acquisitions (such as IBM's recent purchase of Internet Security Systems to boost its ability to deliver security solutions to corporations), and cooperative strategies. By cooperating with other companies, IBM is able to leverage its core competencies to grow and improve its performance.

Through cooperative strategies (e.g., strategic alliances and joint ventures, both of which are defined and discussed in this chapter), IBM finds itself working with a variety of firms in order to deliver products and services. However, IBM has specific performance-related objectives it wants to accomplish as it engages in an array of cooperative arrangements. Some of the firm's cooperative relationships are with competitors. (Actually, deciding to cooperate with a competitor in order to compete in a particular market or market segment is becoming increasingly common.) In late 2007, IBM teamed with longtime

computing rival Sun Microsystems. Expectations for this corporate-level cooperative strategy (corporate-level cooperative strategies are discussed later in the chapter) were high in that executives in the two companies labeled it a "comprehensive relationship" that represented a "tectonic shift in the market landscape." Essentially, the firms intended to cooperate on server technologies so that Sun's Solaris operating system could run on IBM's servers and eventually on its mainframes. Gaining ground on Hewlett-Packard in the battle for leadership in the global server market is a key objective for this cooperative arrangement.

In other instances, IBM cooperates with companies to serve the needs of certain-sized firms. For example, IBM's collaboration with SAP (the world's leading provider of business software) seeks to serve the needs that midsized companies in 12 countries have for world-class business applications built on reliable infrastructures. An estimated 80 million small and midsized firms on a global basis can benefit from the joint services of IBM and SAP. These possibilities from working together support the firms' intention of expanding their cooperative relationship. IBM also has a global alliance with Lenovo, the company that purchased its personal computer (PC) business. With a focus on firms in certain industries (health care, financial services, education, retail, and government), IBM and Lenovo are cooperating to deliver end-to-end technology solutions to solve customers' problems. Some of IBM's cooperative arrangements such as the one with Cisco Systems are long-lived. The partners in this strategic alliance, formed in 1997, focus on providing solutions and services to help customers "transform" their businesses by using competitive advantages that result from the interactions of IBM and Cisco personnel.

As one might anticipate, a firm the size and diversity of IBM is involved with a number of cooperative relationships such as those already mentioned. Given the challenges associated with achieving and maintaining superior performance, and in light of its general success with cooperative relationships, one might anticipate that IBM will continue to use cooperative strategies as a path toward growth and enhanced performance.

Sources: B. Bergstein, 2007, IBM and Sun join forces in server technologies, *Houston Chronicle,* http://chron.com, August 17; D. Kawamoto, 2007, IBM to buy ISS for $1.3 billion, http://news.com, May 24; 2007, International Business Machines, *Market Edge Research,* http://marketedgeresearch.com, August 27; 2007, Lenovo and IBM expand global alliance, http://ibm.com, May 22; 2007, IBM and SAP expand partnership to reach midsize companies in Europe and Asia-Pacific, http://ibm.com, April 23; 2007, Cisco and IBM Strategic alliance, http://cisco.com, August 15; 2006, Cognos and IBM form global strategic alliance to deliver integrated solutions to boost customer performance, http://ibm.com, March 7.

As noted in the Opening Case, firms use three means to grow and improve their performance—internal development, mergers and acquisitions, and cooperation. In each of these cases, the firm seeks to use its resources in ways that will create the greatest amount of value for stakeholders.[1]

A **cooperative strategy** is a strategy in which firms work together to achieve a shared objective.

Recognized as a viable engine of firm growth,[2] **cooperative strategy** is a strategy in which firms work together to achieve a shared objective.[3] Thus, cooperating with other firms is another strategy firms use to create value for a customer that exceeds the cost of providing that value and to establish a favorable position relative to competition.[4]

As explained in the Opening Case, IBM is involved with a number of cooperative arrangements. The intention of serving customers better than competitors serve them and of gaining an advantageous position relative to competitors drive this firm's use of cooperative strategies. IBM's corporate-level cooperative strategy with Sun Microsystems, for example, finds it seeking to deliver server technologies in ways that maximize customer value while improving the firm's position relative to Hewlett-Packard as these companies battle for the leadership position in the global server market. The business-level alliance with Lenovo finds IBM and its partner focusing on what the firms believe are the unique personal computer (PC) needs of customers competing in particular industries. The objectives IBM and its various partners seek by working together highlight the reality that in the twenty-first century landscape, firms must develop the skills required to successfully use cooperative strategies as a complement to their abilities to grow and improve performance through internal developments and mergers and acquisitions.[5]

We examine several topics in this chapter. First, we define and offer examples of different strategic alliances as primary types of cooperative strategies. Next, we discuss the extensive use of cooperative strategies in the global economy and reasons for them. In succession, we then describe business-level (including collusive strategies), corporate-level, international, and network cooperative strategies. The chapter closes with discussion of the risks of using cooperative strategies as well as how effective management of them can reduce those risks.

As you will see, we focus on strategic alliances in this chapter because firms use them more frequently than other types of cooperative relationships. Although not frequently used, collusive strategies are another type of cooperative strategy discussed in this chapter. In a *collusive strategy,* two or more firms cooperate to increase prices above the fully competitive level.[6]

Strategic Alliances as a Primary Type of Cooperative Strategy

A **strategic alliance** is a cooperative strategy in which firms combine some of their resources and capabilities to create a competitive advantage.[7] Thus, strategic alliances involve firms with some degree of exchange and sharing of resources and capabilities to co-develop, sell, and service goods or services.[8] Strategic alliances allow firms to leverage their existing resources and capabilities while working with partners to develop additional resources and capabilities as the foundation for new competitive advantages.[9] To be certain, the reality today is that "strategic alliances have become a cornerstone of many firms' competitive strategy."[10]

Consider the case for Kodak. CEO Antonio Perez stated, "Kodak today is involved with partnerships that would have been unthinkable a few short years ago."[11] His comment suggests the breadth and depth of cooperative relationships with which the firm is involved. However, each of the cooperative relationships described in the Strategic Focus is intended to lead to a new competitive advantage as the source of growth and performance improvement.

A competitive advantage developed through a cooperative strategy often is called a *collaborative* or *relational* advantage.[12] As previously discussed, particularly in Chapter 5, competitive advantages enhance the firm's marketplace success. Rapid technological changes and the global economy are examples of factors challenging firms to constantly upgrade current competitive advantages while they develop new ones to maintain strategic competitiveness.[13]

Many firms, especially large global competitors, establish multiple strategic alliances. Although we discussed only a few of them in the Opening Case, the reality is that IBM has formed hundreds of partnerships as it uses cooperative strategies. IBM is not alone in its decision to frequently use cooperative strategies as a means of competition. Focusing on developing advanced technologies, Lockheed Martin has formed more than 250 alliances with firms in more than 30 countries as it concentrates on its primary business of defense modernization and serving the needs of the air transportation industry. Recently, Lockheed Martin and Boeing formed a strategic alliance with the purpose of integrating their capabilities to "accelerate solutions for a growing air traffic capacity problem."[14] Xerox is another large firm relying on hundreds of cooperative arrangements to grow and outperform its rivals as it competes in what the firm sees as a rapidly changing competitive environment.[15] For all cooperative arrangements, including those we are describing here, success is more likely when partners behave cooperatively when interacting with one another. Actively solving problems, being trustworthy, and consistently pursuing ways to combine partners' resources and capabilities to create value are examples of cooperative behavior known to contribute to alliance success.[16]

Increasingly, public-sector agencies are using strategic alliances as well to improve the quality of their work. The recent alliance formed between the Office of the State Comptroller (OSC) and the Division of the Budget (DOB) with the purpose of cooperating to better coordinate the "implementation of a financial system for New York State" is an example of this phenomenon.[17]

Three Types of Strategic Alliances

The three major types of strategic alliances include joint venture, equity strategic alliance, and nonequity strategic alliance.

A **joint venture** is a strategic alliance in which two or more firms create a legally independent company to share some of their resources and capabilities to develop a competitive advantage.[18] Joint ventures, which are often formed to improve firms' abilities to compete in uncertain competitive environments,[19] are effective in establishing long-term relationships and in transferring tacit knowledge. Because it can't be codified, tacit knowledge is learned through experiences[20] such as those taking place when people from

A **strategic alliance** is a cooperative strategy in which firms combine some of their resources and capabilities to create a competitive advantage.

A **joint venture** is a strategic alliance in which two or more firms create a legally independent company to share some of their resources and capabilities to develop a competitive advantage.

Strategic Focus   Strategic Focus   Strategic Focus

Partnering for Success at Kodak

Founded in 1892, Eastman Kodak Company (Kodak) has a rich history with consumers world-wide for its photographic film products. Currently though, Kodak is focusing its competitive efforts on three main businesses—digital photography, health imaging, and printing. Kodak remains the world's leading producer of silver halide (AgX) paper that is used for printing film and digital images. However, it no longer manufactures or licenses its names to others to produce traditional film cameras. This strategic action highlights Kodak's emphasis on grow-ing in digital markets.

As a large firm, Kodak uses internal development, mergers and acquisitions, and coopera-tive strategies to grow and enhance its performance. Sony, Canon, and Fuji are just a few of the firms with whom Kodak has developed cooperative relationships. As is common for firms using cooperative strategies, Kodak is also partnering with competitors such as Hewlett-Packard (HP) and Xerox. While competing with Xerox in commercial printing, Kodak partners with that firm to supply the controllers that Xerox uses in its iGen3 digital presses. The Kodak-Creo unit supplies the workflow for HP's Indigo printer as the firms compete in the commercial and home printing markets.

The array of individual cooperative arrangements Kodak has formed is interesting as well as impressive. Recently, Sony Corporation and Kodak entered into a technology cross-license agreement that "will allow broad access to the other's patent portfolio." Simultaneously, Kodak formed another technology alliance with Sony Ericsson. This arrangement called for the sharing of technologies and technological capabilities between the partners. Kodak views these arrangements as validation of the quality of its intellectual property portfolio while allowing it access to technologies that it believes are capable of stimulating digitally oriented innovation and subsequent product developments. Kodak also has formed collaborations with companies (such as Real D and Barco) to effectively serve the worldwide digital camera market with a "full menu of products, systems, and services, including installation and support."

In addition to cooperative relationships with large, well-established companies, Kodak has formed a unit that is responsible for organizing strategic relationships with universi-ties, government labs, and early-stage companies. This unit is considered vital to Kodak's efforts to use cooperative relationships to leverage its innovation and technological capa-bilities on a global basis. Calling these cooperative relationships Early-Stage Firm Alliances, Kodak believes they will complement its internal development processes while providing access to new technologies, products, and services. Licensing agreements and joint de-velopment agreements are examples of the cooperative relationships Kodak is willing to form with early start-up ventures in addition to more traditional strategic alliances and joint ventures.

Although diverse in nature, all of the relationships Kodak is establishing by using coopera-tive strategies are designed to facilitate its growth and performance as a digitally oriented firm. As we have seen, some of these relationships are with large, established firms while others are being formed with start-up ventures. In all cases though, the focus is on digitaliza-tion as the path to Kodak's growth and enhanced performance.

Sources: R. E. Hoskisson, M. A. Hitt, R. D. Ireland, & J. S. Harrison, 2008, *Competing for Advantage,* 2nd ed., Thomson South-Western; 2007, Eastman Kodak, Wikipedia, http://en.wikipedia.org, August 26; 2007, Kodak external alliances, http://kodak.com, August 26; 2005, Kodak and Barco forge strategic alliance to serve the worldwide digital cinema market, *Digital Content Producer.com,* http://digitalcontenproducer.com, June 22; 2005, Kodak and Real D strategic alliance for 3D cinema, http://letsgodigital.org, December 20.

partner firms work together in a joint venture. As discussed in Chapter 3, tacit knowledge is an important source of competitive advantage for many firms.[21]

Typically, partners in a joint venture own equal percentages and contribute equally to the venture's operations. In the joint venture that Polo Ralph Lauren Corp. and Geneva-based watch and jewelry company Compagnie Financiere Richemont AG formed, each firm owns 50 percent of a new entity they are creating. Called Polo Ralph Lauren Watch and Jewelry Co., the partners intend to use this new entity to develop and distribute products through Ralph Lauren boutique stores as well as independent watch and jewelry stores throughout the world. This joint venture is "Polo's first foray into the fine jewelry and luxury watch business and is Richemont's first joint venture with a fashion designer."[22] Overall, evidence suggests that a joint venture may be the optimal type of cooperative arrangement when firms need to combine their resources and capabilities to create a competitive advantage that is substantially different from any they possess individually and when the partners intend to enter highly uncertain markets.[23] These conditions influenced the two independent companies' decision to form the Polo Ralph Lauren Watch and Jewelry Co.

**STRATEGY
RIGHT NOW**

Polo Ralph Lauren Corp. and Geneva-based watch and jewelry company Richemont recently entered into a joint venture, which will be named Polo Ralph Lauren Watch and Jewelry Co. Products will be distributed through Ralph Lauren boutique stores as well as via independent watch and jewelry stores throughout the world.

An **equity strategic alliance** is an alliance in which two or more firms own different percentages of the company they have formed by combining some of their resources and capabilities to create a competitive advantage. Many foreign direct investments, such as those made by Japanese and U.S. companies in China, are completed through equity strategic alliances.[24]

For example, Citigroup Inc. and Nikko Cordial Corporation formed a comprehensive strategic alliance with the intention of creating "one of Japan's leading financial services groups and to enable the combined franchise to pursue important new growth opportunities, giving due respect to Japanese culture and business practices."[25] Citigroup was to have the majority ownership stake in this alliance. Retail businesses, asset management, and capital markets and banking businesses are examples of the product and service domains in which the two firms intend to integrate what they believe are highly complementary capabilities as the foundation for serving many types of customers.

A **nonequity strategic alliance** is an alliance in which two or more firms develop a contractual relationship to share some of their unique resources and capabilities to create a competitive advantage.[26] In this type of alliance, firms do not establish a separate independent company and therefore do not take equity positions. For this reason, nonequity strategic alliances are less formal and demand fewer partner commitments than do joint ventures and equity strategic alliances.[27] The relative informality and lower commitment levels characterizing nonequity strategic alliances make them unsuitable for complex projects where success requires effective transfers of tacit knowledge between partners.[28]

Forms of nonequity strategic alliances include licensing agreements, distribution agreements, and supply contracts. Hewlett-Packard (HP), which actively "partners to create new markets . . . and new business models," licenses some of its intellectual property through strategic alliances.[29] Typically, outsourcing commitments are specified in the form of a nonequity strategic alliance. (Discussed in Chapter 3, *outsourcing* is the purchase of a value-creating primary or support activity from another firm.) Dell Inc. and most other computer firms outsource most or all of their production of laptop computers and often form nonequity strategic alliances to detail the nature of the relationship with firms to whom they outsource. Increasingly, state governments in the United States are outsourcing incarceration to private contractors. Corrections Corp. of America and

An **equity strategic alliance** is an alliance in which two or more firms own different percentages of the company they have formed by combining some of their resources and capabilities to create a competitive advantage.

A **nonequity strategic alliance** is an alliance in which two or more firms develop a contractual-relationship to share some of their unique resources and capabilities to create a competitive advantage.

© AP Photo/Sigi Tischler

Geo Group Inc. are two of the largest of these contractors. State governments are forming these relationships to reduce costs and improve services.[30]

Reasons Firms Develop Strategic Alliances

As our discussion to this point implies, cooperative strategies are an integral part of the competitive landscape and are quite important to many companies and even to educational institutions. In educational institutions, for example, the number of libraries cooperating to improve their services continues to expand.[31] In for-profit organizations, many executives believe that strategic alliances are central to their firm's success.[32] One executive's position that "you have to partner today or you will miss the next wave . . . and that . . . you cannot possibly acquire the technology fast enough, so partnering is essential"[33] highlights this belief.

Motorola has recently formed alliances with Suning and Gome Appliances to sell Motorola mobile phones in China. Gome, China's largest electronics retail chain, will open Motorola shop-within-shops inside 30 of its largest stores in China.

Among other benefits, strategic alliances allow partners to create value that they couldn't develop by acting independently[34] and to enter markets more quickly and with greater market penetration possibilities.[35] Moreover, most (if not all) firms lack the full set of resources and capabilities needed to reach their objectives, which indicates that partnering with others will increase the probability of reaching firm-specific performance objectives.[36] Motorola recently formed strategic alliances with Suning, a firm that will be Motorola's first direct supply retailing partner in China, and with Gome Appliances, which will sell Motorola products using a store-within-a-store concept. Through these partnerships, Motorola seeks to increase its share of the Chinese mobile phone market more rapidly than it could as an independent company.[37]

The effects of the greater use of cooperative strategies—particularly in the form of strategic alliances—are noticeable. In large firms, for example, alliances can account for 25 percent or more of sales revenue. And many executives believe that alliances are a prime vehicle for firm growth.[38] In some industries, alliance versus alliance is becoming more prominent than firm versus firm as a point of competition. In the global airline industry, for example, competition is increasingly between large alliances rather than between airlines.[39]

In summary, we can note that firms form strategic alliances to reduce competition, enhance their competitive capabilities, gain access to resources, take advantage of opportunities, build strategic flexibility, and innovate. To achieve these objectives, they must select the right partners and develop trust.[40] Thus, firms attempt to develop a network portfolio of alliances in which they create social capital that affords them flexibility.[41] Because of the social capital, they can call on their partners for help when needed. Of course, social capital means reciprocity exists: Partners can ask them for help as well (and they are expected to provide it).[42]

The individually unique competitive conditions of slow-cycle, fast-cycle, and standard-cycle markets[43] find firms using cooperative strategies to achieve slightly different objectives (see Table 9.1). We discussed these three market types in Chapter 4 while examining competitive rivalry and competitive dynamics. *Slow-cycle markets* are markets where the firm's competitive advantages are shielded from imitation for relatively long periods of time and where imitation is costly. These markets are close to monopolistic conditions. Railroads and, historically, telecommunications, utilities, and financial services are examples of industries characterized as slow-cycle markets. In *fast-cycle markets,* the firm's competitive advantages aren't shielded from imitation, preventing their long-term sustainability. Competitive advantages are moderately shielded from imitation in *standard-cycle markets,* typically allowing them to be sustained for a longer period of time than in fast-cycle market situations, but for a shorter period of time than in slow-cycle markets.

Table 9.1 Reasons for Strategic Alliances by Market Type

Market	Reason
Slow-Cycle	• Gain access to a restricted market
	• Establish a franchise in a new market
	• Maintain market stability (e.g., establishing standards)
Fast-Cycle	• Speed up development of new goods or services
	• Speed up new market entry
	• Maintain market leadership
	• Form an industry technology standard
	• Share risky R&D expenses
	• Overcome uncertainty
Standard-Cycle	• Gain market power (reduce industry overcapacity)
	• Gain access to complementary resources
	• Establish better economies of scale
	• Overcome trade barriers
	• Meet competitive challenges from other competitors
	• Pool resources for very large capital projects
	• Learn new business techniques

Slow-Cycle Markets

Firms in slow-cycle markets often use strategic alliances to enter restricted markets or to establish franchises in new markets. For example, because of consolidating acquisitions that have occurred over the last dozen or so years, the American steel industry has only two remaining major players: U.S. Steel and Nucor. To improve their ability to compete successfully in the global steel market, these companies are forming cooperative relationships. They have formed strategic alliances in Europe and Asia and are invested in ventures in South America and Australia. Simultaneously however, companies based in countries other than the United States are forming or expanding alliances to enhance their presence in the partially restricted U.S. steel markets. For example, ArcelorMittal, the world's leading steel manufacturer, recently enhanced its strategic alliance with Japan's Nippon Steel Corporation. Expanding the partners' ability to gain share of the automotive sheet steel business in the United States is one of the key objectives of this alliance.[44]

The truth of the matter is that slow-cycle markets are becoming rare in the twenty-first century competitive landscape for several reasons, including the privatization of industries and economies, the rapid expansion of the Internet's capabilities for the quick dissemination of information, and the speed with which advancing technologies make quickly imitating even complex products possible.[45] Firms competing in slow-cycle markets, including steel manufacturers, should recognize the future likelihood that they'll encounter situations in which their competitive advantages become partially sustainable (in the instance of a standard-cycle market) or unsustainable (in the case of a fast-cycle market). Cooperative strategies can be helpful to firms transitioning from relatively sheltered markets to more competitive ones.[46]

Fast-Cycle Markets

Fast-cycle markets are unstable, unpredictable, and complex.[47] Combined, these conditions virtually preclude establishing long-lasting competitive advantages, forcing firms to constantly seek sources of new competitive advantages while creating value by using current ones. Alliances between firms with current excess resources and capabilities and those with promising capabilities help companies competing in fast-cycle markets to effectively transition from the present to the future and to gain rapid entry to new markets.

The information technology (IT) industry is a fast-cycle market, motivating firms to form partnerships as a way to effectively cope with the changes occurring in this market setting. In 2006, Microsoft and Novell (a leader in enterprise-wide operating systems based on Linux) formed a partnership with the intention of building, marketing, and supporting new solutions to improve interoperability and intellectual property assurance. Subsequently, Dell Inc. joined this collaboration in 2007. As the first major systems provider to join the Microsoft/Novell partnership, Dell agreed to "purchase SUSE Linux Enterprise Server certificates from Microsoft and establish a service and marketing program to migrate existing Linux users who are not Dell Linux customers to SUSE Linux Enterprise Server."[48] This expanded partnership was formed because the involved parties believe that Windows and Linux are the platforms on which a majority of applications using hardware will be based in the future.

Standard-Cycle Markets

In standard-cycle markets, alliances are more likely to be made by partners with complementary resources and capabilities. Even though airline alliances were originally set up to increase revenue,[49] airlines have realized that they can also be used to reduce costs. SkyTeam (chaired by Delta and Air France) developed an internal Web site to speed joint buying and let member carriers swap tips on pricing. Managers at Oneworld (American Airlines and British Airways) say the alliance's members have already saved more than $200 million through joint purchasing, and Star Alliance (United and Lufthansa) estimates that its member airlines save up to 25 percent on joint orders.

Given the geographic areas where markets are growing, these global alliances are adding partners from Asia. Recently, China Southern Airlines joined the SkyTeam alliance, Air China and Shanghai Airlines were added to the Star Alliance, and Dragonair joined as an affiliate of Oneworld. The following comment from an Air China executive demonstrates why firms choose to join airline alliances: "In order to survive and develop, airlines have to cooperate with other partners in various forms including multilateral alliance cooperation."[50] As is the case with airline companies, economies of scale are a key objective firms seek when forming alliances in standard-cycle markets.[51] The fact that the Oneworld, SkyTeam, and Star Alliances account for more than 60 percent of the world's airline capacity suggests that firms participating as members of these alliances have gained scale economies.

Business-Level Cooperative Strategy

> A firm uses a **business-level cooperative strategy** to grow and improve its performance in individual product markets.

A firm uses a **business-level cooperative strategy** to grow and improve its performance in individual product markets. As discussed in Chapter 5, business-level strategy details what the firm intends to do to gain a competitive advantage in specific product markets. Thus, the firm forms a business-level cooperative strategy when it believes that combining its resources and capabilities with those of one or more partners will create competitive advantages that it can't create by itself and that will lead to success in a specific product market. The four business-level cooperative strategies are listed in Figure 9.1.

Complementary Strategic Alliances

> **Complementary strategic alliances** are business-level alliances in which firms share some of their resources and capabilities in complementary ways to develop competitive advantages.

Complementary strategic alliances are business-level alliances in which firms share some of their resources and capabilities in complementary ways to develop competitive advantages.[52] Vertical and horizontal are the two types of complementary strategic alliances (see Figure 9.1).

Vertical Complementary Strategic Alliance

In a *vertical complementary strategic alliance,* firms share their resources and capabilities from different stages of the value chain to create a competitive advantage

Figure 9.1 Business-Level Cooperative Strategies

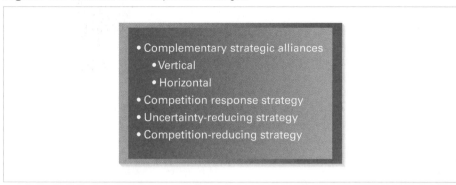

- Complementary strategic alliances
  - Vertical
  - Horizontal
- Competition response strategy
- Uncertainty-reducing strategy
- Competition-reducing strategy

(see Figure 9.2).[53] Oftentimes, vertical complementary alliances are formed to adapt to environmental changes;[54] sometimes, as is the case for General Electric (GE) and Konica Minolta, the changes represent an opportunity for partnering firms to innovate while adapting.[55]

GE and Konica Minolta formed an alliance with the intention of combining their "substantial resources and expertise to accelerate the development of this transformational technology."[56] Organic Light Emitting Diodes (OLED), which are thin, organic materials sandwiched between two electronic conductors, is the transformational technology the two firms seek to develop. The firms expect this technology to be capable of driving creative lighting applications. Formed in mid-2007, the partners hoped to introduce OLED-based lighting applications to the marketplace by 2010. Konica Minolta's imaging capabilities were to be combined with GE's lighting products' capabilities for this purpose. Even though both companies had been working on the technology in their own research and development (R&D) laboratories, they concluded that the most promising path was to use their different skills to collaborate to develop superior outcomes in the form of innovative products.

Horizontal Complementary Strategic Alliance

A *horizontal complementary strategic alliance* is an alliance in which firms share some of their resources and capabilities from the same stage (or stages) of the value chain to create a competitive advantage (see Figure 9.2). Commonly, firms use complementary strategic alliances to focus on long-term product development and distribution opportunities.[57] Sprint has formed a number of these alliances as part of its objective of redefining the telecommunications industry.[58] One of these alliances finds Sprint partnering with Lucent to develop wireless data services including mobile broadband and the delivery of network-based VoIP solutions.[59]

The automotive manufacturing industry is one in which many horizontal complementary strategic alliances are formed. In fact, virtually all global automobile manufacturers use cooperative strategies to form scores of cooperative relationships. As we explain in the Strategic Focus, the Renault-Nissan alliance, signed on March 27, 1999, is a prominent example of a horizontal complementary strategic alliance. Thought to be successful, the challenge is to integrate the partners' operations to create value while maintaining their unique cultures.

Competition Response Strategy

As discussed in Chapter 4, competitors initiate competitive actions to attack rivals and launch competitive responses to their competitors' actions. Strategic alliances can be used at the business level to respond to competitors' attacks. Because they can be difficult to reverse and expensive to operate, strategic alliances are primarily formed to take strategic rather than tactical actions and to respond to competitors' actions in a like manner.

Figure 9.2 Vertical and Horizontal Complementary Strategic Alliances

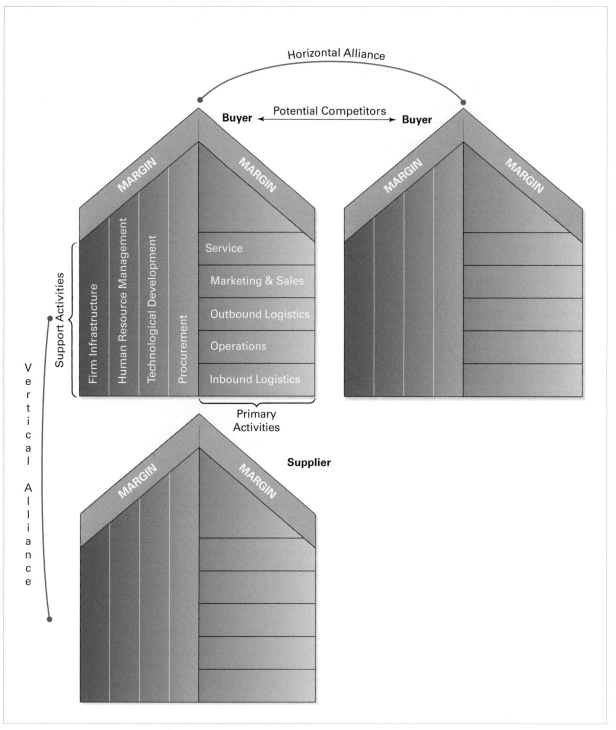

France Telecom and Microsoft, for example, formed an alliance with two initial major projects. The first project found the partners developing a series of phones based on Microsoft technology that uses Internet services. The phones are designed to be used as traditional cell phones or to access the Internet while at home or on the road. This project was a response to the announcement by BT Group PLC of a new hybrid fixed-line and mobile phone service using short-range wireless technology called Bluetooth. The France Telecom–Microsoft alliance will use the more powerful Wireless Fidelity (WiFi)

Using Complementary Resources and Capabilities to Succeed in the Global Automobile Industry

The degree of success a company can achieve as an automobile manufacturer is influenced by its ability to create *economies of scale* (generated when an increase in the scale of the firm's production process causes a decrease in the long-run average cost of each unit produced) and *economies of scope* (generated when the firm earns more sales or reduces its costs by increasing the scope of its activities such as marketing and distribution as well as the number of products sold). Indeed, an inability to generate scale and scope economies places a global automobile manufacturer at a competitive disadvantage. In particular, scale economies can be created by combining firms' resources and capabilities to complete particular activities in the value chain.

The SM3 is one of the new cars that has been produced as a result of the Renault/Nissan alliance.

Because of their relatively small size, the 1990s found Nissan and Renault's cost structures at noncompetitive levels; and their ability to provide multiple innovative products was diminished as well. To deal with their joint and similar problems, these firms finalized the details of a unique strategic alliance in March 1999. This alliance was the first of its kind to involve a Japanese and French company, each with its own corporate culture and brand identity. Horizontal in nature, the Nissan/Renault partnership is an example of an equity strategic alliance. Renault holds a 44.4 percent stake in Nissan which in turn holds 15 percent of Renault's shares. Carlos Ghosn serves as CEO for both companies.

To date, the alliance is deemed successful. "Nissan—Japan's second biggest carmaker and the world's ninth—has produced some hefty profits in recent years, a major turnaround from the late 1990s when the company was in serious financial trouble." Renault is now the world's tenth largest car manufacturer and intends to become Europe's most profitable mass volume producer by 2010. The alliance now accounts for 9.8 percent of the world-wide automobile market.

The firms participate in a number of joint activities to create scale and scope economies. Sharing production platforms (the partners intend to share 10 platforms by 2010) and powertrains (engines and transmissions) are examples of how scale economies are being created as is the alliance's work with Cisco Systems to deliver cost-effective systems and optimized infrastructure capabilities to the partners' IS/IT departments. To generate scope economies, the firms combine their resources and capabilities to cooperate in several activities including sales, purchasing, and the use of common distribution channels in Europe. In a comprehensive and summarized sense, this alliance finds Nissan and Renault cooperating in terms of "global product development, financial policy, and corporate strategy." To facilitate efforts to achieve the alliance's objectives, the partners have formed a number of cross-company teams (employees from both companies looking for ways to create additional synergies in terms of developing new products and manufacturing current ones) and functional task teams (employees from both companies seeking ways to contribute to synergies in support functions such as legal and tax and cost management and control).

The alliance partners continue to seek ways to enhance the performance of their cooperative relationship. For example, the partners examined the possibility of acquiring Ford

Motor Company's Jaguar and Land Rover businesses when those units became available for purchase in 2007. After evaluating the matter, the partners chose not to bid for Jaguar or Land Rover. Across time though, the challenge of managing relationships between partners who are sharing resources and capabilities in various value chain activities remains notable.

Sources: A. English, 2007, No news is bad news, http://telegraphc.co.uk, June 16; S. O'Grady, 2007, Jaguar and Land Rover: Marques on the market, *The Independent on Sunday,* http://news.independent.co.uk, September 2; 2007, The Renault-Nissan alliance, http://renault.com, August 20; 2007, Topics of the alliance, http://nissan.com, August 20; 2006, Q&A: GM-Renault-Nissan alliance, BBC News, http://news.bbc.co.uk, July 4; 2005, Renault and Nissan: Forging a global alliance that is creating more than the sum of its parts, http://cisco.com.

technology. Didier Lombard, CEO of France Telecom, stated that the telecom industry is undergoing rapid changes and current members must also act rapidly to adapt. The partnership with Microsoft is designed to respond to these changes.[60]

Uncertainty-Reducing Strategy

Some firms use business-level strategic alliances to hedge against risk and uncertainty, especially in fast-cycle markets.[61] Also, they are used where uncertainty exists, such as in entering new product markets or emerging economies. The long-term uncertainty about the continuing availability of fossil fuels is a reason ConocoPhillips and Tyson Foods formed a strategic alliance to produce "next generation" renewable diesel fuel. This product is intended to supplement the use of traditional petroleum-based diesel fuel. By-product fats that Tyson generates while processing beef, pork, and poultry are the raw ingredients to be used to create a transportation fuel. This effort is part of the partners' overall goal of collaborating to "leverage Tyson's advanced knowledge in protein chemistry and production with ConocoPhillips' processing and marketing expertise to introduce a renewable diesel to the United States."[62]

In other instances, firms form business-level strategic alliances to reduce the uncertainty associated with developing new products or establishing a technology standard. Interestingly, the alliance between France Telecom and Microsoft (mentioned earlier) is a competition response alliance for France Telecom but is an uncertainty-reducing alliance for Microsoft. Microsoft is using the alliance to learn more about the telecom industry and business. It wants to learn how it can develop software to satisfy needs in this industry. By partnering with a firm in this industry, it is reducing its uncertainty about the market and software needs. And the alliance is clearly designed to develop new products so the alliance reduces the uncertainty for both firms by combining their knowledge and capabilities.

Competition-Reducing Strategy

Used to reduce competition, collusive strategies differ from strategic alliances in that collusive strategies are often an illegal type of cooperative strategy. Two types of collusive strategies are explicit collusion and tacit collusion.

When two or more firms negotiate directly with the intention of jointly agreeing about the amount to produce and the price of the products that are produced, *explicit collusion* exists.[63] Explicit collusion strategies are illegal in the United States and most developed economies (except in regulated industries).

Firms that use explicit collusion strategies may find others challenging their competitive actions. In late 2006, for example, the British Office of Fair Trading and the U.S. Department of Justice joined forces to investigate alleged "price coordination" among American Airlines, United Airlines, and British Airways. The probe was conducted to investigate possible explicit collusion among the airlines in terms of passenger airfares, cargo shipping prices, and various surcharges.[64] In mid-2007, Green Oil, a bio-product company based in Illinois in the United States, alleged that LUKOIL, Russia's largest producer of crude oil, joined forces with Saudi Arabian and Venezuelan companies to manipulate production quotas and the prices of their products in the United States. All companies involved with Green Oil's allegations rejected the charges as baseless and false.[65] As these examples suggest, any firm that may use explicit collusion as a strategy should recognize that competitors and regulatory bodies might challenge the acceptability of their competitive actions.

Tacit collusion exists when several firms in an industry indirectly coordinate their production and pricing decisions by observing each other's competitive actions and responses.[66] Tacit collusion results in production output that is below fully competitive levels and above fully competitive prices. Unlike explicit collusion, firms engaging in tacit collusion do not directly negotiate output and pricing decisions.

Tacit collusion tends to be used as a business-level, competition-reducing strategy in highly concentrated industries, such as breakfast cereals. Firms in these industries recognize that they are interdependent and that their competitive actions and responses significantly affect competitors' behavior toward them. Understanding this interdependence and carefully observing competitors because of it tend to lead to tacit collusion.

Four firms (Kellogg, General Mills, Post, and Quaker) have accounted for as much as 80 percent of sales volume in the ready-to-eat segment of the U.S. cereal market.[67] Some believe that this high degree of concentration results in "prices for branded cereals that are well above [the] costs of production."[68] Prices above the competitive level in this industry suggest the possibility that the dominant firms use a tacit collusion cooperative strategy.

Discussed in Chapter 6, *mutual forbearance* is a form of tacit collusion in which firms do not take competitive actions against rivals they meet in multiple markets. Rivals learn a great deal about each other when engaging in multimarket competition, including how to deter the effects of their rival's competitive attacks and responses. Given what they know about each other as a competitor, firms choose not to engage in what could be destructive competitions in multiple product markets.[69]

In general, governments in free-market economies need to determine how rivals can collaborate to increase their competitiveness without violating established regulations.[70] However, this task is challenging when evaluating collusive strategies, particularly tacit ones. For example, regulation of pharmaceutical and biotech firms who collaborate to meet global competition might lead to too much price fixing and, therefore, regulation is required to make sure that the balance is right, although sometimes the regulation gets in the way of efficient markets.[71] Individual companies must analyze the effect of a competition-reducing strategy on their performance and competitiveness.

Assessment of Business-Level Cooperative Strategies

Firms use business-level strategies to develop competitive advantages that can contribute to successful positions and performance in individual product markets. To develop a competitive advantage using an alliance, the resources and capabilities that are integrated through the alliance must be valuable, rare, imperfectly imitable, and nonsubstitutable (see Chapter 3).

Evidence suggests that complementary business-level strategic alliances, especially vertical ones, have the greatest probability of creating a sustainable competitive advantage.[72] Horizontal complementary alliances are sometimes difficult to maintain because they are often between rivalrous competitors. In this instance, firms may feel a "push" toward and a "pull" from alliances. Airline firms, for example, want to compete aggressively against others serving their markets and target customers. However, the need to develop scale economies and to share resources and capabilities (such as scheduling systems) dictates that alliances be formed so the firms can compete by using cooperative actions and responses while they simultaneously compete against one another through competitive actions and responses. The challenge in these instances is for each firm to find ways to create the greatest amount of value from both their competitive and cooperative actions. It seems that Nissan and Renault have learned how to achieve this balance.

Although strategic alliances designed to respond to competition and to reduce uncertainty can also create competitive advantages, these advantages often are more temporary than those developed through complementary (both vertical and horizontal) strategic alliances. The primary reason is that complementary alliances have a stronger focus on creating value than do competition-reducing and uncertainty-reducing alliances, which are formed to respond to competitors' actions or reduce uncertainty rather than to attack competitors.

Of the four business-level cooperative strategies, the competition-reducing strategy has the lowest probability of creating a sustainable competitive advantage. For example, research suggests that firms following a foreign direct investment strategy using alliances as a follow-the-leader imitation approach may not have strong strategic or learning goals. Thus, such investment could be attributable to tacit collusion among the participating firms rather than to forming a competitive advantage (which should be the core objective).

Corporate-Level Cooperative Strategy

A firm uses a **corporate-level cooperative strategy** to help it diversify in terms of products offered or markets served, or both.

A firm uses a **corporate-level cooperative strategy** to help it diversify in terms of products offered or markets served, or both. Diversifying alliances, synergistic alliances, and franchising are the most commonly used corporate-level cooperative strategies (see Figure 9.3).

Firms use diversifying alliances and synergistic alliances to grow and improve performance by diversifying their operations through a means other than a merger or an acquisition.[73] When a firm seeks to diversify into markets in which the host nation's government prevents mergers and acquisitions, alliances become an especially appropriate option. Corporate-level strategic alliances are also attractive compared with mergers and particularly acquisitions, because they require fewer resource commitments[74] and permit greater flexibility in terms of efforts to diversify partners' operations.[75] An alliance can be used as a way to determine whether the partners might benefit from a future merger or acquisition between them. This "testing" process often characterizes alliances formed to combine firms' unique technological resources and capabilities.[76]

Diversifying Strategic Alliance

A **diversifying strategic alliance** is a corporate-level cooperative strategy in which firms share some of their resources and capabilities to diversify into new product or market areas.

A **diversifying strategic alliance** is a corporate-level cooperative strategy in which firms share some of their resources and capabilities to diversify into new product or market areas. Recently, Marriott International Inc., Miller Global Properties, and Nickelodeon decided to combine some of their resources and capabilities to create value that their firms could not create without each other. In this case, entertainment giant Nickelodeon (which is owned by Viacom International) is providing its brand name to establish Nickelodeon-themed hotels. Marriott's contribution to this diversifying strategic alliance is to manage the hotels

Figure 9.3 Corporate-Level Cooperative Strategies

- Diversifying alliances
- Synergistic alliances
- Franchising

while Miller Global Properties owns them. These partners formed this relationship to take advantage of the growing trend of families desiring to travel to theme-oriented facilities. Nickelodeon believes that it can derive two benefits by its decision to diversity into the hotel business through this alliance: (1) sales of Nickelodeon merchandise (e.g., books, DVDs, toys, and clothes) can be increased by using the hotels as a distribution channel and (2) hotel guests, who are continuously exposed to opportunities to view Nickelodeon programs (e.g., Nick @ Nite), may become loyal watchers of those programs.[77]

It should be noted that highly diverse networks of alliances can lead to poorer performance by partner firms.[78] However, cooperative ventures are also used to reduce diversification in firms that have overdiversified.[79] Japanese chipmakers Fujitsu, Mitsubishi Electric, Hitachi, NEC, and Toshiba have been using joint ventures to consolidate and then spin off diversified businesses that were performing poorly. For example, Fujitsu, realizing that memory chips were becoming a financial burden, dumped its flash memory business into a joint venture company controlled by Advanced Micro Devices. This alliance helped Fujitsu refocus on its core businesses.[80]

Nickelodeon-themed hotels and waterparks are the outcome of the alliance among Marriott Hotels, Miller Global Properties, and Viacom International.

Synergistic Strategic Alliance

A **synergistic strategic alliance** is a corporate-level cooperative strategy in which firms share some of their resources and capabilities to create economies of scope. Similar to the business-level horizontal complementary strategic alliance, synergistic strategic alliances create synergy across multiple functions or multiple businesses between partner firms. The cooperative relationship between IBM and Sun Microsystems we discussed in the Opening Case is a synergistic strategic alliance.

In late 2007, NBC Universal, Viacom, the News Corporation, and CBS were combining forces to establish their own Web site to compete against YouTube. (YouTube "is a video-sharing Web site where users can upload, view, and share video clips."[81]) Launched in 2006, a number of television and entertainment executives dismissed YouTube as a "flash-in-the-pan" business concept (and possibly an illegal one as well, given potential copyright infringement charges concerning content that is posted on YouTube). However, their view changed dramatically in October 2006 when Google Inc. paid $1.65 billion to purchase YouTube. At that point, the media giants decided that YouTube had tapped into customer needs with huge market potential. A number of factors were delaying completion of a cooperative relationship that analysts believed the involved companies almost desperately wanted to form. Ownership percentages and the management structure were among the issues affecting the negotiations. The fact that this type of collaboration among these large firms "would be nearly unprecedented" also increased the complexity of finalizing the proposed alliance's details. In spite of this, analysts expected the alliance to be formed as a means of allowing the media giants to have a competitive platform in what appeared to be an increasingly important distribution channel for their products—online video.[82] Thus, a synergistic strategic alliance such as the one among NBC Universal, Viacom, the News Corporation, and CBS is different from a complementary business-level alliance in that it diversifies the involved firms into a new business, but in a synergistic way.

Franchising

Franchising is a corporate-level cooperative strategy in which a firm (the franchisor) uses a franchise as a contractual relationship to describe and control the sharing of

A **synergistic strategic alliance** is a corporate-level cooperative strategy in which firms share some of their resources and capabilities to create economies of scope.

Franchising is a corporate-level cooperative strategy in which a firm (the franchisor) uses a franchise as a contractual relationship to describe and control the sharing of its resources and capabilities with partners (the franchisees).

its resources and capabilities with partners (the franchisees).[83] A *franchise* is a "contractual agreement between two legally independent companies whereby the franchisor grants the right to the franchisee to sell the franchisor's product or do business under its trademarks in a given location for a specified period of time."[84] In strategic management terminology, "franchising is a strategic alliance between groups of people who have specific relationships and responsibilities with a common goal to dominate markets."[85]

Subway, a firm using franchising as a cooperative strategy, is one of the fastest growing businesses in the United States.

Franchising (from the French for honesty or freedom[86]) is a popular strategy. In the United States alone, more than 2,500 franchise systems are located in more than 75 industries; and those operating franchising outlets generate roughly one-third of all U.S. retail sales.[87] Already frequently used in developed nations, franchising is expected to account for significant portions of growth in emerging economies in the twenty-first century as well.[88] As with diversifying and synergistic strategic alliances, franchising is an alternative to pursuing growth through mergers and acquisitions. McDonald's, Hilton International, Mrs. Fields Cookies, Subway, and Ace Hardware are well-known examples of firms using the franchising corporate-level cooperative strategy.

Franchising is a particularly attractive strategy to use in fragmented industries, such as retailing and commercial printing. In fragmented industries, a large number of small and medium-sized firms compete as rivals; however, no firm or small set of firms has a dominant share, making it possible for a company to gain a large market share by consolidating independent companies through contractual relationships.

In the most successful franchising strategy, the partners (the franchisor and the franchisees) work closely together.[89] A primary responsibility of the franchisor is to develop programs to transfer to the franchisees the knowledge and skills that are needed to successfully compete at the local level.[90] In return, franchisees should provide feedback to the franchisor regarding how their units could become more effective and efficient.[91] Working cooperatively, the franchisor and its franchisees find ways to strengthen the core company's brand name, which is often the most important competitive advantage for franchisees operating in their local markets.[92]

Assessment of Corporate-Level Cooperative Strategies

Costs are incurred with each type of cooperative strategy.[93] Compared with those at the business-level, corporate-level cooperative strategies commonly are broader in scope and more complex, making them relatively more costly. Those forming and using cooperative strategies, especially corporate-level ones, should be aware of alliance costs and carefully monitor them.

In spite of these costs, firms can create competitive advantages and value when they effectively form and use corporate-level cooperative strategies.[94] The likelihood of being able to parlay strategy into advantage increases when successful alliance experiences are internalized. In other words, those involved with forming and using corporate-level cooperative strategies can also use them to develop useful knowledge about how to succeed in the future. To gain maximum value from this knowledge, firms should organize it and verify that it is always properly distributed to those involved with forming and using alliances.[95]

We explain in Chapter 6 that firms answer two questions to form a corporate-level strategy—in which businesses will the diversified firm compete and how will those businesses be managed? These questions are also answered as firms form corporate-level cooperative strategies. Thus, firms able to develop corporate-level cooperative strategies and manage them in ways that are valuable, rare, imperfectly imitable, and nonsubstitutable (see Chapter 3) develop a competitive advantage that is in addition to advantages gained through the activities of individual cooperative strategies. (Later in the chapter, we further describe alliance management as another potential competitive advantage.)

International Cooperative Strategy

A **cross-border strategic alliance** is an international cooperative strategy in which firms with headquarters in different nations decide to combine some of their resources and capabilities to create a competitive advantage. Taking place in virtually all industries, the number of cross-border alliances continues to increase.[96] These alliances too are sometimes formed instead of mergers and acquisitions (which can be riskier).[97] Even though cross-border alliances can themselves be complex and hard to manage,[98] they have the potential to help firms use their resources and capabilities to create value in locations outside their home market.

> A **cross-border strategic alliance** is an international cooperative strategy in which firms with headquarters in different nations decide to combine some of their resources and capabilities to create a competitive advantage.

The joint venture formed by Sony Corporation and Ericsson is a collaborative relationship through which each company is effectively using its capabilities to create value outside its home market. Founded in 2001, the joint venture is called Sony Ericsson. Combining Sony's consumer electronics expertise with Ericsson's technological leadership in the communications sector, this relationship was formed to make mobile phones. This cross-border alliance has been successful in that at the end of 2006, Sony Ericsson had a 9 percent share of the global mobile phone market, trailing only Nokia, Motorola, and Samsung, and was generating profits.[99]

Several reasons explain the increasing use of cross-border strategic alliances, including the fact that in general, multinational corporations outperform domestic-only firms.[100] What takes place with a cross-border alliance is that a firm leverages core competencies that are the foundation of its domestic success in international markets.[101] Nike provides an example as it leverages its core competence with celebrity marketing to expand globally with its diverse line of athletic goods and apparel. With a $2 billion celebrity endorsement budget, Nike has formed relationships with athletes having global appeal. Tiger Woods, Michael Jordan, seven-time Tour de France winner Lance Armstrong, and Magic Johnson are examples of these types of individuals. In addition, Nike has endorsement relationships with star athletes and organizations outside the United States such as Brazilian soccer star Ronaldo Nazario and Manchester United, the world's most popular soccer team.[102] Coupling these alliances with Nike's powerful global brand name helps the firm apply its marketing competencies in markets outside the United States.

Nike, a U. S.-based company, has endorsement alliances with the Manchester United Soccer team from The United Kingdom.

Limited domestic growth opportunities and foreign government economic policies are additional reasons firms use cross-border alliances. As discussed in Chapter 8, local ownership is an important national policy objective in some nations. In India and China, for example, governmental policies reflect a strong preference to license local companies. Thus, in some countries, the full range of entry mode choices that we described in Chapter 8 may not be available to firms seeking to diversify internationally. Indeed, investment by foreign firms in these instances may be allowed only through a partnership with a local firm, such as in a cross-border alliance. Especially important, strategic alliances with local partners can help firms overcome certain liabilities of moving into a foreign country, such as lack of knowledge of the local culture or institutional norms.[103] A cross-border strategic alliance can also be helpful to foreign partners from an operational perspective, because the local partner has significantly more information about factors contributing to competitive success such as local markets, sources of capital, legal procedures, and politics.[104]

In general, cross-border alliances are more complex and risky than domestic strategic alliances.[105] However, the fact that firms competing internationally tend to outperform domestic-only competitors suggests the importance of learning how to diversify into international markets. Compared with mergers and acquisitions, cross-border alliances may be a better way to learn this process, especially in the early stages of the firms' geographic diversification efforts. Starbucks is a case in point.

When Starbucks sought overseas expansion, it wanted to do so quickly as a means of supporting its strong orientation to continuous growth through expansion. Thus, it agreed to a complex series of joint ventures in many countries in the interest of speed. While the company receives a percentage of the revenues and profits as well as licensing fees for supplying its coffee, controlling costs abroad is more difficult than in the United States. Starbucks is learning from the results achieved from the collaborative relationships it established initially. In light of what it has learned, the firm continues to evaluate its opportunities to collaborate with others in different countries including China, a market that company officials believe "will eventually be the largest international market for Starbucks."[106] Among other actions, Starbucks is seeking to take larger equity positions in some of the joint ventures with which it is now involved in different countries (such as China).

Network Cooperative Strategy

A **network cooperative strategy** is a cooperative strategy wherein several firms agree to form multiple partnerships to achieve shared objectives.

Increasingly, firms use several cooperative strategies. In addition to forming their own alliances with individual companies, a growing number of firms are joining forces in multiple networks.[107] A **network cooperative strategy** is a cooperative strategy wherein several firms agree to form multiple partnerships to achieve shared objectives. IBM and Cisco have multiple cooperative arrangements as do Toyota and General Motors. Demonstrating the complexity of network cooperative strategies is the fact that Cisco also has a set of unique collaborations with both Hewlett-Packard and Dell Inc. The fact is that the number of network cooperative strategies being formed today continues to increase as firms seek to find the best ways to create value by offering multiple goods and services in multiple geographic (domestic and international) locations.

A network cooperative strategy is particularly effective when it is formed by geographically clustered firms,[108] as in California's Silicon Valley (where "the culture of Silicon Valley encourages collaborative webs"[109]) and Singapore's Silicon Island.[110] Effective social relationships and interactions among partners while sharing their resources and capabilities make it more likely that a network cooperative strategy will be successful,[111] as does having a productive *strategic center firm* (we discuss strategic center firms in detail in Chapter 11). Firms involved in networks gain information and knowledge from multiple sources. They can use these heterogeneous knowledge sets to produce more and better innovation. As a result, firms involved in networks of alliances tend to be more innovative.[112] However, there are disadvantages to participating in networks as a firm can be locked in to its partners, precluding the development of alliances with others. In certain types of networks, such as Japanese *keiretsus,* firms in the network are expected to help other firms in the network whenever they need aid. Such expectations can become a burden and reduce the focal firm's performance over time.[113]

Alliance Network Types

An important advantage of a network cooperative strategy is that firms gain access to their partners' other partners. Having access to multiple collaborations increases the likelihood that additional competitive advantages will be formed as the set of shared resources and capabilities expands.[114] In turn, being able to develop new capabilities further stimulates product innovations that are so critical to strategic competitiveness in the global economy.[115]

The set of strategic alliance partnerships resulting from the use of a network cooperative strategy is commonly called an *alliance network.* The alliance networks that companies develop vary by industry conditions. A *stable alliance network* is formed in mature industries where demand is relatively constant and predictable. Through a stable alliance network, firms try to extend their competitive advantages to other settings while continuing to profit from operations in their core, relatively mature industry. Thus, stable networks are built primarily to *exploit* the economies (scale and/or scope) that exist between the partners.[116] *Dynamic alliance networks* are used in industries characterized by frequent product innovations and short product life cycles.[117] For instance, the pace of innovation in the information technology (IT) industry (as well as other industries that are characterized by fast-cycle markets) is too fast for any one company to be successful across time if it only competes independently. In dynamic alliance networks, partners typically *explore* new ideas and possibilities with the potential to lead to product innovations, entries to new markets, and the development of new markets.[118] Often, large firms in such industries as software and pharmaceuticals create networks of relationships with smaller entrepreneurial start-up firms in their search for innovation-based outcomes.[119] An important outcome for small firms successfully partnering with larger firms in an alliance network is the credibility they build by being associated with their larger collaborators.[120]

SunPower Corp. CEO Thomas Warner is photographed holding a solar panel next to the panels on the roof of SunPower's building in San Jose. Silicon Valley is leveraging its expertise in computer chips to design and manufacture the solar cells needed to convert sunlight into electricity. As prices for fossil fuels rise and demand for renewable energy grows, the region known for its silicon-based semiconductors is emerging as a key center for solar power technology.

Competitive Risks with Cooperative Strategies

Stated simply, many cooperative strategies fail. In fact, evidence shows that two-thirds of cooperative strategies have serious problems in their first two years and that as many as 70 percent of them fail. This failure rate suggests that even when the partnership has potential complementarities and synergies, alliance success is elusive.[121] Although failure is undesirable, it can be a valuable learning experience, meaning that firms should carefully study a cooperative strategy's failure to gain insights with respect to how to form and manage future cooperative arrangements.[122] We show prominent cooperative strategy risks in Figure 9.4.

One cooperative strategy risk is that a partner may act opportunistically. Opportunistic behaviors surface either when formal contracts fail to prevent them or when an alliance is based on a false perception of partner trustworthiness. Not infrequently, the opportunistic firm wants to acquire as much of its partner's tacit knowledge as it can.[123] Full awareness of what a partner wants in a cooperative strategy reduces the likelihood that a firm will suffer from another's opportunistic actions.[124]

The situation in late 2007 with a joint venture British Petroleum (BP) formed in 2003 with oil tycoons Mikhail Fridman, Viktor Vekeselberg, and Len Blavatnik seems to demonstrate opportunistic behavior as well as political risks. Called TNK-BP, the cooperative relationship in question is unique in that BP and the three oilmen each

Figure 9.4 Managing Competitive Risks in Cooperative Strategies

own 50 percent of the venture "that gave the Western company unprecedented access to vital Russian oil and gas." The Kremlin's increasing involvement in the nation's energy production activities and its claim that TNK-BP has failed to fulfill all of the terms of its license regarding production at one field (the Kovykta field) are threatening the venture. Part of the license requires the venture to produce 9 billion cubic meters of gas per year at Kovykta; the actual production is roughly 18 times less than this figure. Some speculate that Gazprom, the state-run gas giant, may join the venture as a partner to deal with the production shortfall. If this were to happen, "the question is what TNK-BP might be able to get for its stake." For its part, BP seeks to maintain good relationships with the Russian government; BP's plan to invest $1.25 billion in TNK-BP in 2007 demonstrates this commitment. Additionally, in light of the available oil and gas reserves in Russia, BP is forming other cooperative relationships including the minority stake it took in 2007 "in a venture with state oil giant Rosneft to drill for crude on Sakhalin Island."[125] Nonetheless, as we see, BP's cooperative strategies with Russian companies are not risk free.

Some cooperative strategies fail when it is discovered that a firm has misrepresented the competencies it can bring to the partnership. The risk of competence misrepresentation is more common when the partner's contribution is grounded in some of its intangible assets. Superior knowledge of local conditions is an example of an intangible asset that partners often fail to deliver. Asking the partner to provide evidence that it does possess the resources and capabilities (even when they are largely intangible) it is to share in the cooperative strategy may be an effective way to deal with this risk.

Another risk is a firm failing to make available to its partners the resources and capabilities (such as the most sophisticated technologies) that it committed to the cooperative strategy.[126] This risk surfaces most commonly when firms form an international cooperative strategy. In these instances, different cultures and languages can cause misinterpretations of contractual terms or trust-based expectations.

A final risk is that one firm may make investments that are specific to the alliance while its partner does not. For example, the firm might commit resources and capabilities to develop manufacturing equipment that can be used only to produce items coming from the alliance. If the partner isn't also making alliance-specific investments, the firm is at a relative disadvantage in terms of returns earned from the alliance compared with investments made to earn the returns. Issues such as these led to problems with the cooperative relationship that was formed between Pixar and Walt Disney Company.

Pixar (a computer animation studio) and entertainment giant Walt Disney Company partnered to develop and market several computer-animated features, including *Toy Story, Monsters Inc.,* and *Cars,* all of which were box-office hits. However, Disney perceived risks in its partnership with Pixar, largely because the films Pixar made without Disney were greater successes at the box office than were the films Disney made through its own studio operations. Moreover, the films Disney made with Pixar accounted for a substantial percentage of the profits Disney earned from its studio operations (35 percent in 2002). Thus, it seemed that Disney may have been making more alliance-specific commitments to the relationship than was Pixar.

Subsequently, ineffective communications between Pixar's chairman, Steve Jobs, and then-current Disney CEO (Michael Eisner) led to a breakdown of negotiations for a revised partnership arrangement in mid-2004. After some time and Eisner's departure as Disney's CEO, negotiations between the two firms resumed in September 2005. These negotiations led to Disney's purchase of Pixar in January 2006. The purchase was an all-stock transaction valued at $7.4 billion. Given that he owned 50.1 percent of Pixar, this transaction made Steve Jobs Disney's largest single shareholder. Currently, Disney is working on sequels to some of the box office successes that it had with Pixar (*Toy Story 3*, for example, will be in theaters in 2010).[127]

Managing Cooperative Strategies

Although cooperative strategies are an important means of firm growth and enhanced performance, managing these strategies is challenging. Learning how to effectively manage cooperative strategies is important however, in that being able to do so can be a source of competitive advantage.[128] Because the ability to effectively manage cooperative strategies is unevenly distributed across organizations in general, assigning managerial responsibility for a firm's cooperative strategies to a high-level executive or to a team improves the likelihood that the strategies will be well managed.

Those responsible for managing the firm's set of cooperative strategies should take the actions necessary to coordinate activities, categorize knowledge learned from previous experiences, and make certain that what the firm knows about how to effectively form and use cooperative strategies is in the hands of the right people at the right time. And firms must learn how to manage both the tangible assets and the intangible assets (such as knowledge) that are involved with a cooperative arrangement. Too often, partners concentrate on managing tangible assets at the expense of taking action to also manage a cooperative relationship's intangible assets.[129]

Two primary approaches are used to manage cooperative strategies—cost minimization and opportunity maximization[130] (see Figure 9.4). In the *cost minimization* management approach, the firm develops formal contracts with its partners. These contracts specify how the cooperative strategy is to be monitored and how partner behavior is to be controlled. The TNK-BP joint venture discussed previously is managed through contractual agreements. The goal of the cost minimization approach is to minimize the cooperative strategy's cost and to prevent opportunistic behavior by a partner. The focus of the second managerial approach—*opportunity maximization*—is on maximizing a partnership's value-creation opportunities. In this case, partners are prepared to take advantage of unexpected opportunities to learn from each other and to explore additional marketplace possibilities. Less formal contracts, with fewer constraints on partners' behaviors, make it possible for partners to explore how their resources and capabilities can be shared in multiple value-creating ways.

Firms can successfully use both approaches to manage cooperative strategies. However, the costs to monitor the cooperative strategy are greater with cost minimization, in that writing detailed contracts and using extensive monitoring mechanisms is expensive, even though the approach is intended to reduce alliance costs. Although monitoring systems may prevent partners from acting in their own best interests, they also often preclude positive responses to new opportunities that surface to use the alliance's competitive advantages. Thus, formal contracts and extensive monitoring systems tend to stifle partners' efforts to gain maximum value from their participation in a cooperative strategy and require significant resources to put into place and use.[131]

The relative lack of detail and formality that is a part of the contract developed by firms using the second management approach of opportunity maximization means that firms need to trust each other to act in the partnership's best interests. A psychological state, *trust* in the context of cooperative arrangements is "the expectation held by one firm that another will not exploit its vulnerabilities when faced with the opportunity to do so."[132] When partners trust each other, there is less need to write detailed formal contracts to specify each firm's alliance behaviors,[133] and the cooperative relationship tends to be more stable.[134] On a relative basis, trust tends to be more difficult to establish in international cooperative strategies compared with domestic ones. Differences in trade policies, cultures, laws, and politics that are part of cross-border alliances account for the increased difficulty. When trust exists, partners' monitoring costs are reduced and opportunities to create value are maximized. Essentially, in these cases, the firms have built social capital.[135] According to company officials, the alliance between Renault and Nissan that we examined in the Strategic Focus on page 255 is built on "mutual trust between the two partners . . . together with operating and confidentiality rules."[136]

Research showing that trust between partners increases the likelihood of alliance success seems to highlight the benefits of the opportunity maximization approach to managing cooperative strategies. Trust may also be the most efficient way to influence and control alliance partners' behaviors. Research indicates that trust can be a capability that is valuable, rare, imperfectly imitable, and often nonsubstitutable.[137] Thus, firms known to be trustworthy can have a competitive advantage in terms of how they develop and use cooperative strategies.[138] One reason is that it is impossible to specify all operational details of a cooperative strategy in a formal contract. Confidence that its partner can be trusted reduces the firm's concern about the inability to contractually control all alliance details.

Summary

- A cooperative strategy is one where firms work together to achieve a shared objective. Strategic alliances, where firms combine some of their resources and capabilities to create a competitive advantage, are the primary form of cooperative strategies. Joint ventures (where firms create and own equal shares of a new venture that is intended to develop competitive advantages), equity strategic alliances (where firms own different shares of a newly created venture), and nonequity strategic alliances (where firms cooperate through a contractual relationship) are the three basic types of strategic alliances. Outsourcing, discussed in Chapter 3, commonly occurs as firms form nonequity strategic alliances.

- Collusive strategies are the second type of cooperative strategies (with strategic alliances being the other). In many economies, explicit collusive strategies are illegal unless sanctioned by government policies. Increasing globalization has led to fewer government-sanctioned situations of explicit collusion. Tacit collusion, also called mutual forbearance, is a cooperative strategy through which firms tacitly cooperate to reduce industry output below the potential competitive output level, thereby raising prices above the competitive level.

- The reasons firms use cooperative strategies vary by slow-cycle, fast-cycle, and standard-cycle market conditions. To enter restricted markets (slow-cycle), to move quickly from

one competitive advantage to another (fast-cycle), and to gain market power (standard-cycle) are among the reasons why firms choose to use cooperative strategies.

- Four business-level cooperative strategies are used to help the firm improve its performance in individual product markets. (1) Through vertical and horizontal complementary alliances, companies combine their resources and capabilities to create value in different parts (vertical) or the same parts (horizontal) of the value chain. (2) Competition-responding strategies are formed to respond to competitors' actions, especially strategic ones. (3) Competition-reducing strategies are used to avoid excessive competition while the firm marshals its resources and capabilities to improve its competitiveness. (4) Uncertainty-reducing strategies are used to hedge against the risks created by the conditions of uncertain competitive environments (such as new product markets). Complementary alliances have the highest probability of yielding a sustainable competitive advantage; competition-reducing alliances have the lowest probability of doing so.

- Firms use corporate-level cooperative strategies to engage in product and/or geographic diversification. Through diversifying strategic alliances, firms agree to share some of their resources and capabilities to enter new markets or produce new products. Synergistic alliances are ones where firms share resources and capabilities to develop economies of scope. This alliance is similar to the business-level horizontal complementary alliance where firms try to develop operational synergy, except that synergistic alliances are used to develop synergy at the corporate level. Franchising is a corporate-level cooperative strategy where the franchisor uses a franchise as a contractual relationship to specify how resources and capabilities will be shared with franchisees.

- As an international cooperative strategy, a cross-border alliance is used for several reasons, including the performance superiority of firms competing in markets outside their domestic market and governmental restrictions on growth through mergers and acquisitions. Commonly, cross-border alliances are riskier than their domestic counterparts, particularly when partners aren't fully aware of each other's purpose for participating in the partnership.

- In a network cooperative strategy, several firms agree to form multiple partnerships to achieve shared objectives. A primary benefit of a network cooperative strategy is the firm's opportunity to gain access "to its partner's other partnerships." When this happens, the probability greatly increases that partners

will find unique ways to share their resources and capabilities to form competitive advantages. Network cooperative strategies are used to form either a stable alliance network or a dynamic alliance network. Used in mature industries, partners use stable networks to extend competitive advantages into new areas. In rapidly changing environments where frequent product innovations occur, dynamic networks are primarily used as a tool of innovation.

- Cooperative strategies aren't risk free. If a contract is not developed appropriately, or if a partner misrepresents its competencies or fails to make them available, failure is likely. Furthermore, a firm may be held hostage through asset-specific investments made in conjunction with a partner, which may be exploited.

- Trust is an increasingly important aspect of successful cooperative strategies. Firms recognize the value of partnering with companies known for their trustworthiness. When trust exists, a cooperative strategy is managed to maximize the pursuit of opportunities between partners. Without trust, formal contracts and extensive monitoring systems are used to manage cooperative strategies. In this case, the interest is to minimize costs rather than to maximize opportunities by participating in a cooperative strategy.

Review Questions

1. What is the definition of cooperative strategy, and why is this strategy important to firms competing in the twenty-first century competitive landscape?

2. What is a strategic alliance? What are the three types of strategic alliances firms use to develop a competitive advantage?

3. What are the four business-level cooperative strategies, and what are the differences among them?

4. What are the three corporate-level cooperative strategies? How do firms use each one to create a competitive advantage?

5. Why do firms use cross-border strategic alliances?

6. What risks are firms likely to experience as they use cooperative strategies?

7. What are the differences between the cost-minimization approach and the opportunity-maximization approach to managing cooperative strategies?

Notes

1. J. L. Morrow, Jr., D. G. Sirmon, M. A. Hitt, & T. R. Holcomb, 2007, Creating value in the face of declining performance: Firm strategies and organizational recovery, *Strategic Management Journal*, 28: 271–283.
2. 2007, Small-to-midsize firms often form alliances to kick start growth, *The Conference Board*, Release #5149, July 12.
3. R. C. Fink, L. F. Edelman, & K. J. Hatten, 2007, Supplier performance improvements in relational exchanges, *Journal of Business & Industrial Marketing*, 22: 29–40.

4. P. E. Bierly, III & S. Gallagher, 2007, Explaining alliance partner selection: Fit, trust and strategic expediency, *Long Range Planning*, 40: 134–153; K. Singh & W. Mitchell, 2005, Growth dynamics: The bidirectional relationship between interfirm collaboration and business sales in entrant and incumbent alliances, *Strategic Management Journal*, 26: 497–521.
5. P. M. Senge, B. B. Lichtenstein, K. Kaeufer, H. Bradbury, & J. Carroll, 2007, Collaborating for systemic change, *MIT Sloan Management Review*, 48(2): 44–53; C. Hardy, T. B. Lawrence, & D. Grant, 2005, Discourse and collaboration: The role

of conversations and collective identity, *Academy of Management Review*, 30: 58–77; R. Vassolo, J. Anand, & T. B. Folta, 2004, Non-additivity in portfolios of exploration activities: A real options-based analysis of equity alliances in biotechnology, *Strategic Management Journal*, 25: 1045–1061.
6. T. L. Sorenson, 2007, Credible collusion in multimarket oligopoly, *Managerial and Decision Economics*, 28: 115–128.
7. R. D. Ireland, M. A. Hitt, & D. Vaidyanath, 2002, Alliance management as a source of competitive advantage, *Journal of Management*, 28: 413–446; J. G. Coombs

& D. J. Ketchen, 1999, Exploring interfirm cooperation and performance: Toward a reconciliation of predictions from the resource-based view and organizational economics, *Strategic Management Journal,* 20: 867–888.

8. J. J. Reuer & A. Arino, 2007, Strategic alliance contracts: Dimensions and determinants of contractual complexity, *Strategic Management Journal,* 28: 313–330; M. R. Subramani & N. Venkatraman, 2003, Safeguarding investments in asymmetric interorganizational relationships: Theory and evidence, *Academy of Management Journal,* 46(1): 46–62.

9. R. Krishnan, X Martin, & N. G. Noorderhaven, 2007, When does trust matter to alliance performance? *Academy of Management Journal,* 49: 894–917; P. Kale, J. H. Dyer, & H. Singh, 2002, Alliance capability, stock market response, and long-term alliance success: The role of the alliance function, *Strategic Management Journal,* 23: 747–767.

10. K. H. Heimeriks & G. Duysters, 2007, Alliance capability as a mediator between experience and alliance performance: An empirical investigation into the alliance capability development process, *Journal of Management Studies,* 44: 25–49.

11. R. E. Hoskisson, M. A. Hitt, R. D. Ireland, & J. S. Harrison, 2008, *Competing for Advantage,* 2nd ed., Thomson/Southwestern, 184.

12. R. Seppanen, K. Blomqvist, & S. Sundqvist, 2007, Measuring interorganizational trust—A critical review of the empirical research in 1990–2003, *Industrial Marketing Management,* 36: 249–265; T. K. Das & B.-S. Teng, 2001, A risk perception model of alliance structuring, *Journal of International Management,* 7: 1–29.

13. F. F. Suarez & G. Lanzolla, 2007, The role of environmental dynamics in building a first mover advantage theory, *Academy of Management Review,* 32: 377–392; M. A. Geletkanycz & S. S. Black, 2001, Bound by the past? Experience-based effects on commitment to the strategic status quo, *Journal of Management,* 27: 3–21.

14. 2007, Lockheed Martin and Boeing form strategic alliance, http://www.lockheedmartin.com, January 22.

15. T. Wailgum & D. Kleiman, 2007, Picture perfect, *Continental.com Magazine,* June, 76–79.

16. D. Gerwin, 2004, Coordinating new product development in strategic alliances, *Academy of Management Review,* 29: 241–257; Ireland, Hitt, & Vaidyanath, Alliance management as a source of competitive advantage.

17. 2007, Strategic alliance formed between OSC and DOB, http://www.nyfms.state.ny.us, April 23.

18. 2007, Strategic alliances and joint ventures: A how to guide, *New Zealand Trade & Enterprise,* http://exportyear.co.nz, March.

19. Y. Luo, 2007, Are joint venture partners more opportunistic in a more volatile environment? *Strategic Management Journal,* 28: 39–60.

20. S. L. Berman, J. Down, & C. W. L. Hill, 2002, Tacit knowledge as a source of competitive advantage in the National Basketball Association, *Academy of Management Journal,* 45: 13–31.

21. R. W. Coff, D. C. Coff & R. Eastvold, 2007, The knowledge-leveraging paradox: How to achieve scale without making knowledge imitable, *Academy of Management Review,* 31: 452–465; H. Hoang & F. T. Rothaermel, 2005, The effect of general and partner-specific alliance experience on joint R&D project performance, *Academy of Management Journal,* 48: 332–345.

22. T. Agins, 2007, Polo, Richemont team up in watch and jewelry venture, *Wall Street Journal Online,* http://online.wsj.com, March 5.

23. L. G. Zucker, M. R. Darby, J. Furner, & R. C. Liu, 2007, Minerva unbound: Knowledge flows and new knowledge production, *Research Policy,* 36: 850–863; R. E. Hoskisson & L. W. Busenitz, 2002, Market uncertainty and learning distance in corporate entrepreneurship entry mode choice, in M. A. Hitt, R. D. Ireland, S. M. Camp, & D. L. Sexton (eds.), *Strategic Entrepreneurship: Creating a New Mindset,* Oxford, UK: Blackwell Publishers, 151–172.

24. D. Greenaway & R. Kneller, 2007, Firm heterogeneity, exporting and foreign direct investment, *The Economic Journal,* 117: F134–F161; A.-W. Harzing, 2002, Acquisitions versus greenfield investments: International strategy and management of entry modes, *Strategic Management Journal,* 23: 211–227.

25. 2007, Citigroup and Nikko Cordial agree on comprehensive strategic alliance, http://www.citi.com/domain/index.htm, March 6.

26. Y. Wang & S. Nicholas, 2007, The formation and evolution of nonequity strategic alliances in China, *Asia Pacific Journal of Management,* 24: 131–150.

27. R. Kumar & T. K. Das, 2007, Interpartner legitimacy in the alliance development process, *Journal of Management Studies,* in press.

28. S. Comino, P. Mariel, & J. Sandonis, 2007, Joint ventures versus contractual agreements: An empirical investigation, *Spanish Economic Journal,* 9: 159–175.

29. 2007, Intellectual property licensing, http://hp.com, August 30.

30. M. Lifsher, 2007, Companies say they can build prisons cheaper, faster than government, *Bryan-College Station Eagle,* September 2, E1, E2.

31. L. M. Anglada, 2007, Collaborations and alliances: Social intelligence applied to academic libraries, *Library Management,* 28: 406–415.

32. M. J. Kelly, J.-L. Schaan, & H. Jonacas, 2002, Managing alliance relationships: Key challenges in the early stages of collaboration, *R&D Management,* 32(1): 11–22.

33. A. C. Inkpen & J. Ross, 2001, Why do some strategic alliances persist beyond their useful life? *California Management Review,* 44(1): 132–148.

34. M. Haiken, Innovative partnering, 2007, http://money.cnn.com, February 28; C. Hardy, N. Phillips, & T. B. Lawrence, 2003, Resources, knowledge and influence: The organizational effects of interorganizational collaboration, *Journal of Management Studies,* 40(2): 321–347.

35. F. Rothaermel & D. L. Deeds, 2006, Alliance type, alliance experience and alliance management capability in high-technology ventures, *Journal of Business Venturing,* 21: 429–460; L. Fuentelsaz, J. Gomez, & Y. Polo, 2002, Followers' entry timing: Evidence from the Spanish banking sector after deregulation, *Strategic Management Journal,* 23: 245–264.

36. B. L. Bourdeau, J. J. Cronink, Jr., & C. M. Voorhees, 2007, Modeling service alliances: An exploratory investigation of spillover effects in service partnerships, *Strategic Management Journal,* 28: 609–622.

37. 2007, Motorola enters strategic alliance with Suning, *ChinaTechNews,* http://chinatechnews.com, April 17.

38. A. Arino, P. Olk, & J. J. Reuer, 2008, *Entrepreneurial Strategic Alliances,* Prentice Hall, in press.

39. S. G. Lazzarini, 2007, The impact of membership in competing alliance constellations: Evidence on the operational performance of global airlines, *Strategic Management Journal,* 28: 345–367.

40. M. A. Hitt, D. Ahlstrom, M. T. Dacin, E. Levitas, & L. Svobodina, 2004, The institutional effects of strategic alliance partner selection in transition economies: China versus Russia, *Organization Science,* 15: 173–185; P. A. Saparito, C. C. Chen, & H. J. Sapienza, 2004, The role of relational trust in bank-small firm relationships, *Academy of Management Journal,* 47: 400–410.

41. A. C. Inkpen & E. W. K. Tsang, 2005, Social capital, networks and knowledge transfer, *Academy of Management Review,* 30: 146–165.

42. M. Hughes, R. D. Ireland, & R. E. Morgan, 2007, Stimulating dynamic value: Social capital and business incubation as a pathway to competitive success, *Long Range Planning,* 40(2): 154-177; T. G. Pollock, J. F. Porac, & J. B. Wade, 2004, Constructing deal networks: Brokers as network "architects" in the U.S. IPO market and other examples, *Academy of Management Review,* 29: 50–72.

43. J. R. Williams, 1998, *Renewable Advantage: Crafting Strategy Through Economic Time,* New York: The Free Press.

44. 2007, ArcelorMittal broadens strategic alliance with Nippon Steel, http://reuters.com, July 12.

45. S. A. Zahra, R. D. Ireland, I. Gutierrez, & M. A. Hitt, 2000, Privatization and entrepreneurial transformation: Emerging issues and a future research agenda, *Academy of Management Review,* 25: 509–524.

46. I. Filatotchev, M. Wright, K. Uhlenbruck, L. Tihanyi, & R. E. Hoskisson, 2003, Governance, organizational capabilities, and restructuring in transition economies, *Journal of World Business,* 38(4): 331–347.

47. J. Lash & F. Wellington, 2007, Competitive advantage on a warming planet, *Harvard Business Review,* 85(3): 94–102; K. M. Eisenhardt, 2002, Has strategy changed? *MIT Sloan Management Review,* 43(2): 88–91.

48. 2007, Dell joins Microsoft and Novell collaboration, http://novell.com, May 7.

49. C. Czipura & D. R. Jolly, 2007, Global airline alliances: Sparking profitability for a troubled industry, *Journal of Business Strategy,* 28(2): 57–64.

50. 2007, Tourism futures international, http://tourismfuturesintl.com, August 26.

51. 2007, Airline alliance, Wikipedia, http://en.wikipedia.org, August 26; D. Michaels & J. L. Lunsford, 2003, Airlines move toward buying planes jointly, *Wall Street Journal,* May 20, A3.

52. D. R. King, J. G. Covin, & H. Hegarty, 2003, Complementary resources and the exploitation of technological innovations, *Journal of Management,* 29: 589–606; J. S. Harrison, M. A. Hitt, R. E. Hoskisson, & R. D. Ireland, 2001, Resource complementarity in business combinations: Extending the logic to organizational alliances, *Journal of Management,* 27: 679–699.

53. F. T. Rothaermel, M. A. Hitt, & L. A. Jobe, 2006, Balancing vertical integration and strategic outsourcing: Effects on product portfolio, product success, and firm performance, *Strategic Management Journal,* 27: 1033–1056.

54. R. Gulati, P. R. Lawrence, & P. Puranam, 2005, Adaptation in vertical relationships beyond incentive conflict, *Strategic Management Journal,* 26: 415–440.

55. B.-S. Teng, 2007, Corporate entrepreneurship activities through strategic alliances: A resource-based approach toward competitive advantage, *Journal of Management Studies,* 44: 119–142.

56. 2007, Konica Minolta and GE form strategic alliance to accelerate the commercialization of OLED lighting, http://konicaminolta.com, March 27.

57. F. T. Rothaermel & M. Thursby, 2007, The nanotech versus the biotech revolution: Sources of productivity in incumbent firm research, *Research Policy,* 36: 832–849; T. H. Oum, J.-H. Park, K. Kim & C. Yu, 2004, The effect of horizontal alliances on firm productivity and profitability: Evidence from the global airline industry; *Journal of Business Research,* 57: 844–853.

58. S. Nelson, 2007, Strategic alliances are channels for innovation at Sprint Nextel, *Global Business and Organizational Excellence,* 26(5): 6–12.

59. 2007, Strategic alliances, http://sprint.com, August 30.

60. C. Bryan-Low & B. Lagrotteria, 2005, France Telecom and Microsoft forge product alliance, *Wall Street Journal Online,* http://online.wsj.com, July 7.

61. J. J. Reuer & T. W. Tong, 2005, Real options in international joint ventures, *Journal of Management,* 31: 403–423; S. Chatterjee, R. M. Wiseman, A. Fiegenbaum, & C. E. Devers, 2003, Integrating behavioral and economic concepts of risk into strategic management: The twain shall meet, *Long Range Planning,* 36(1), 61–80.

62. 2007, ConocoPhillips and Tyson Foods announce strategic alliance, http://conocophillips.com, April 16.

63. L. Tesfatsion, 2007, Agents come to bits: Toward a constructive comprehensive taxonomy of economic entities, *Journal of Economic Behavior & Organization,* 63: 333–346.

64. M. Adams, 2006, Airline price-fixing allegations raised, *USA Today,* http://usatoday.com, June 23.

65. 2007, LUKOIL dismisses charges of price fixing in U.S., RIA Novosti, http://en.rian.ru/business.com, June 8.

66. C. d'Aspremont, R. D. S. Ferreira & L.-A. Gerard-Varet, 2007, Competition for market share or for market size: Oligopolistic equilibria with varying competitive toughness, *International Economic Review,* 48: 761–784.

67. G. K. Price & J. M. Connor, 2003, Modeling coupon values for ready-to-eat breakfast cereals, *Agribusiness,* 19(2): 223–244.

68. G. K. Price, 2000, Cereal sales soggy despite price cuts and reduced couponing, *Food Review,* 23(2): 21–28.

69. J. Hagedoorn & G. Hesen, 2007, Contract law and the governance of interfirm technology partnerships—An analysis of different modes of partnering and their contractual implications, *Journal of Management Studies,* 44: 342–366; B. R. Golden & H. Ma, 2003, Mutual forbearance: The role of intrafirm integration and rewards, *Academy of Management Review,* 28: 479–493.

70. J. Apesteguia, M. Dufwenberg, & R. Selton, 2007, Blowing the whistle, *Economic Theory,* 31: 127–142.

71. J. H. Johnson & G. K. Leonard, 2007, Economics and the rigorous analysis of class certification in antitrust cases, *Journal of Competition Law and Economics,* http://jcle.oxfordjournals.org, June 26.

72. P. Dussauge, B. Garrette, & W. Mitchell, 2004, Asymmetric performances: The market share impact of scale ad link alliances in global auto industry, *Strategic Management Journal,* 25: 701–711.

73. Harrison, Hitt, Hoskisson, & Ireland, Resource complementarity, 684–685.

74. R. Grunwald & A. Kieser, 2007, Learning to reduce interorganizational learning: An analysis of architectural product innovation in strategic alliances, *Journal of Product Innovation Management,* 24: 369–391; A. E. Bernardo & B. Chowdhry, 2002, Resources, real options, and

corporate strategy, *Journal of Financial Economics,* 63: 211–234; Inkpen, Strategic alliances, 413.

75. J. L. Johnson, R. P.-W. Lee, A. Saini, & B. Grohmann, 2003, Market-focused strategic flexibility: Conceptual advances and an integrative model, *Academy of Marketing Science Journal,* 31: 74–90.

76. C. C. Pegels & Y. I. Song, 2007, Market competition and cooperation: Identifying competitive/cooperative interaction groups, *International Journal of Services Technology and Management,* 2/3: 139–154; Folta & Miller, Real options in equity partnerships, 77.

77. S. Berfield, 2007, Room service, send up some slime, *BusinessWeek,* June 11, 38.

78. A. Goerzen & P. W. Beamish, 2005, The effect of alliance network diversity on multinational enterprise performance, *Strategic Management Journal,* 333–354.

79. M. V. Shyam Kumar, 2005, The value from acquiring and divesting a joint venture: A real options approach, *Strategic Management Journal,* 26: 321–331.

80. J. Yang, 2003, One step forward for Japan's chipmakers, *BusinessWeek Online,* http://www.businessweek.com, July 7.

81. 2007, YouTube, Wikipedia, http://en.wikipedia.org, August 31.

82. R. Siklos & B. Carter, 2006, Old model versus a speedster, *New York Times Online,* http://nytimes.com, December 18.

83. M. Tuunanen & F. Hoy, 2007, Franchising—multifaceted form of entrepreneurship, *International Journal of Entrepreneurship and Small Business,* 4: 52–67; J. G. Combs & D. J. Ketchen Jr., 2003, Why do firms use franchising as an entrepreneurial strategy? A meta-analysis, *Journal of Management,* 29: 427–443.

84. F. Lafontaine, 1999, Myths and strengths of franchising, "Mastering Strategy" (Part Nine), *Financial Times,* November 22, 8–10.

85. 2007, What is franchising? *Franchising.com,* http://franchising.com, August 31.

86. 2007, Franchising, Wikipedia, http://en.wikipedia.org, August 31.

87. B. Barringer & R. D. Ireland, 2008, *Entrepreneurship: Successfully Launching New Ventures,* 2nd ed., Prentice Hall, 440.

88. 2007, Global trends in franchising, *DCStrategy,* http://dcstrategy.com, August 23.

89. R. B. DiPietro, D. H. B. Welsh, P. V. Raven, & D. Severt, 2007, A message of hope in franchises systems: Assessing franchisees, top executives, and franchisors, *Journal of Leadership & Organizational Studies,* 13(3): 59–66; S. C. Michael, 2002, Can a franchise chain coordinate? *Journal of Business Venturing,* 17: 325–342.

90. J. Barthelemy, 2004, The administrative productivity of U.S. franchisors: An empirical investigation, *Economics Letters,* 83(1): 115–121.

91. J. Torikka, 2007, Franchisees can be made: Empirical evidence from a follow-up study, *International Journal of*

Entrepreneurship and Small Business, 4: 68–96; P. J. Kaufmann & S. Eroglu, 1999, Standardization and adaptation in business format franchising, *Journal of Business Venturing,* 14: 69–85.

92. S. C. Michael, 2002, First mover advantage through franchising, *Journal of Business Venturing,* 18: 61–81.

93. M. Zollo, J. J. Reuer, & H. Singh, 2002, Interorganizational routines and performance in strategic alliances, *Organization Science,* 13: 701–714.

94. Ireland, Hitt, & Vaidyanath, Alliance management.

95. A. V. Shipilov, 2007, Network strategies and performance of Canadian investment banks, *Academy of Management Journal,* 49: 590–604; P. Almeida, G. Dokko, & L. Rosenkopf, 2003, Startup size and the mechanisms of external learning: Increasing opportunity and decreasing ability? *Research Policy,* 32(2): 301–316.

96. R. Narula & G. Duysters, 2004, Globalization and trends in international R&D alliances, *Journal of International Management,* 10: 199–218; M. A. Hitt, M. T. Dacin, E. Levitas, J.-L. Arregle, & A. Borza, 2000, Partner selection in emerging and developed market contexts: Resource-based and organizational learning perspectives, *Academy of Management Journal,* 43: 449–467.

97. J. H. Dyer, P. Kale, & H. Singh, 2004, When to ally & when to acquire, *Harvard Business Review,* 81(7/8): 109–115.

98. P. Ghemawat, 2007, Managing differences: The central challenge of global strategy, *Harvard Business Review,* 85(3): 59–68.

99. 2007, Sony Ericsson, *Wikipedia,* http://en.wikipedia.org, August 28.

100. L. Dong & K.W. Glaister, 2007, National and corporate culture differences in international strategic alliances: Perceptions of Chinese partners, *Asia Pacific Journal of Management,* 24: 191–205; I. M. Manev, 2003, The managerial network in a multinational enterprise and the resource profiles of subsidiaries, *Journal of International Management,* 9: 133–152.

101. P. H. Dickson, K. M. Weaver, & F. Hoy, 2006, Opportunism in the R&D alliances of SMEs: The roles of the institutional environment and SME size, *Journal of Business Venturing,* 21: 487–513; H. K. Steensma, L. Tihanyi, M. A. Lyles, & C. Dhanaraj, 2005, The evolving value of foreign partnerships in transitioning economies, *Academy of Management Journal,* 48: 213–235.

102. 2007, Branding and celebrity endorsements, *VentureRepublic,* http://venturerepublic.com, August 31.

103. Y. Luo, O. Shenkar, & M.-K. Nyaw, 2002, Mitigating the liabilities of foreignness: Defensive versus offensive approaches, *Journal of International Management,* 8: 283–300.

104. S. R. Miller & A. Parkhe, 2002, Is there a liability of foreignness in global banking? An empirical test of banks' x-efficiency,

Strategic Management Journal, 23: 55–75; Y. Luo, 2001, Determinants of local responsiveness: Perspectives from foreign subsidiaries in an emerging market, *Journal of Management,* 27: 451–477.

105. D. Li, L. E. Eden, M. A. Hitt, & R. D. Ireland, 2008, Friends, acquaintances or strangers? Partner selection in R&D alliances, *Academy of Management Journal,* in press; J. E. Oxley & R. C. Sampson, 2004, The scope and governance of international R&D alliances, *Strategic Management Journal,* 25: 723–749.

106. 2006, Starbucks acquires control of China joint venture, *Apostille US,* http://apostille.us.com, October 25.

107. D. Lavie, C. Lechner, & H. Singh, 2007, The performance implications of timing of entry and involvement in multipartner alliances, *Academy of Management Journal,* 49: 569–604; Z. Zhao, J. Anand, & W. Mitchell, 2005, A dual networks perspective on inter-organizational transfer of R&D capabilities: International joint ventures in the Chinese automotive industry, *Journal of Management Studies,* 42: 127–160.

108. A. Nosella & G. Petroni, 2007, Multiple network leadership as a strategic asset: The Carlo Gavazzi space case, *Long Range Planning,* 40: 178–201.

109. K. Sawyer, 2007, Strength in webs, *The Conference Board,* July/August, 9–11.

110. A. H. Van de Ven & H. J. Sapienza, 2008, Entrepreneurial pursuits of self and collective interests in resource mobilization and running in packs, *Strategic Entrepreneurship Journal,* in press; M. Ferrary, 2003, Managing the disruptive technologies life cycle by externalizing the research: Social network and corporate venturing in the Silicon Valley, *International Journal of Technology Management,* 25(1,2): 165–180.

111. G. K. Lee, 2007, The significance of network resources in the race to enter emerging product markets: The convergence of telephony communications and computer networking, 1989–2001, *Strategic Management Journal,* 28: 17–37; A. C. Cooper, 2002, Networks, alliances, and entrepreneurship, in M. A. Hitt, R. D. Ireland, S. M. Camp, & D. L. Sexton (eds.), *Strategic Entrepreneurship: Creating a New Mindset,* Oxford, UK: Blackwell Publishers, 203–222.

112. G. G. Bell, 2005, Clusters, networks, and firm innovativeness, *Strategic Management Journal,* 26: 287–295.

113. H. Kim, R. E. Hoskisson, & W. P. Wan, 2004, Power, dependence, diversification strategy and performance in keiretsu member firms, *Strategic Management Journal,* 25: 613–636.

114. M. Rudberg & J. Olhager, 2003, Manufacturing networks and supply chains: An operations strategy perspective, *Omega,* 31(1): 29–39.

115. E. J. Kleinschmidt, U. de Brentani, & S. Salomo, 2007, Programs: A resource-

based view, *Journal of Product Innovation Management,* 24: 419–441; G. J. Young, M. P. Charns, & S. M. Shortell, 2001, Top manager and network effects on the adoption of innovative management practices: A study of TQM in a public hospital system, *Strategic Management Journal,* 22: 935–951.

116. E. Garcia-Canal, C. L. Duarte, J. R. Criado, & A. V. Llaneza, 2002, Accelerating international expansion through global alliances: A typology of cooperative strategies, *Journal of World Business,* 37(2): 91–107; F. T. Rothaermel, 2001, Complementary assets, strategic alliances, and the incumbent's advantage: An empirical study of industry and firm effects in the biopharmaceutical industry, *Research Policy,* 30: 1235–1251.

117. V. Shankar & B. L. Bayus, 2003, Network effects and competition: An empirical analysis of the home video game industry, *Strategic Management Journal,* 24: 375–384.

118. Z. Simsek, M. H. Lubatkin, & D. Kandemir, 2003, Inter-firm networks and entrepreneurial behavior: A structural embeddedness perspective, *Journal of Management,* 29: 401–426.

119. P. Puranam & K. Srikanth, 2007, What they know vs. what they do: How acquirers leverage technology acquisitions, *Strategic Management Journal,* 28: 805–825; M. Moensted, 2007, Strategic networking in small high-tech firms, *The International Entrepreneurship and Management Journal,* 3: 15–27.

120. C. T. Street & A.-F. Cameron, 2007, External relationships and the small business: A review of small business alliance and network research, *Journal of Small Business Management,* 45: 239–266.

121. T. K. Das & R. Kumar, 2007, Learning dynamics in the alliance development process, *Management Decision,* 45: 684–707.

122. J.-Y. Kim & A. S. Miner, 2007, Vicarious learning from the failures and near-failures of others: Evidence from the U.S. commercial banking industry, *Academy of Management Journal,* 49: 687–714.

123. P. M. Norman, 2002, Protecting knowledge in strategic alliances— Resource and relational characteristics, *Journal of High Technology Management Research,* 13(2): 177–202; P. M. Norman, 2001, Are your secrets safe? Knowledge protection in strategic alliances, *Business Horizons,* November–December, 51–60.

124. J. Connell & R. Voola, 2007, Strategic alliances and knowledge sharing: Synergies or silos? *Journal of Knowledge Management,* 11: 52–66.

125. J. Bush, 2007, The Kremlin's big squeeze, *BusinessWeek,* April 30, 42–43.

126. P. D. Cousins & B. Lawson, 2007, Sourcing strategy, supplier relationships and firm performance: An empirical investigation of UK organizations, *British Journal of Management,* 18(2): 123–137; P. Lane, J. E. Salk, & M. A. Lyles, 2001, Absorptive capacity, learning,

and performance in international joint ventures, *Strategic Management Journal,* 22: 1139–1161.

127. 2007, Pixar, *Wikipedia,* http://en.wikipedia.org, September 2.

128. K. G. Provan & P. Kenis, 2007, Modes of network governance: Structure, management, and effectiveness, *Journal of Public Administration Research and Theory,* in press; J. H. Dyer, P. Kale, & H. Singh, 2001, How to make strategic alliances work, *MIT Sloan Management Review,* 42(4): 37–43.

129. Connell & Voola, Strategic alliances and knowledge sharing.

130. J. H. Dyer, 1997, Effective interfirm collaboration: How firms minimize transaction costs and maximize transaction value, *Strategic Management Journal,* 18: 535–556.

131. J. H. Dyer & C. Wujin, 2003, The role of trustworthiness in reducing transaction costs and improving performance: Empirical evidence from the United States, Japan, and Korea, *Organization Science,* 14: 57–69.

132. Krishnan, Martin, & Noorderhaven, When does trust matter to alliance performance?

133. M. Lundin, 2007, Explaining cooperation: How resource interdependence, goal congruence, and trust affect joint actions in policy implementation, *Journal of Public Administration Research and Theory,* in press.

134. V. Perrone, A. Zaheer, & B. McEvily, 2003, Free to be trusted? Boundary constraints on trust in boundary spanners, *Organization Science,* 14: 422–439; H. K. Steensma, L. Marino, & K. M. Weaver, 2000, Attitudes toward cooperative strategies: A cross-cultural analysis of entrepreneurs, *Journal of International Business Studies,* 31: 591–609.

135. R. D. Ireland & J. W. Webb, 2007, A multi-theoretic perspective on trust and power in strategic supply chains, *Journal of Operations Management,* 25: 482–497.

136. 2007, The principles of the alliance, http://renault.com, August 26.

137. F. D. Schoorman, R. C. Mayer, & J. H. Davis, 2007, An integrative model of organizational trust: Past, present, and future, *Academy of Management Review,* 344–354; J. H. Davis, F. D. Schoorman, R. C. Mayer, & H. H. Tan, 2000, The trusted general manager and business unit performance: Empirical evidence of a competitive advantage, *Strategic Management Journal,* 21: 563–576.

138. B. Hillebrand & W. G. Biemans, 2003, The relationship between internal and external cooperation: Literature review and propositions, *Journal of Business Research,* 56: 735–744.

Part 3

Strategic Actions: Strategy Implementation

Chapter 10
Corporate Governance, 274

Chapter 11
Organizational Structure and Controls, 306

Chapter 12
Strategic Leadership, 338

Chapter 13
Strategic Entrepreneurship, 366

Corporate Governance

10

Studying this chapter should provide you with the strategic management knowledge needed to:

1. Define corporate governance and explain why it is used to monitor and control managers' strategic decisions.

2. Explain why ownership has been largely separated from managerial control in the modern corporation.

3. Define an agency relationship and managerial opportunism and describe their strategic implications.

4. Explain how three internal governance mechanisms—ownership concentration, the board of directors, and executive compensation—are used to monitor and control managerial decisions.

5. Discuss the types of compensation executives receive and their effects on strategic decisions.

6. Describe how the external corporate governance mechanism—the market for corporate control—acts as a restraint on top-level managers' strategic decisions.

7. Discuss the use of corporate governance in international settings, especially in Germany and Japan.

8. Describe how corporate governance fosters ethical strategic decisions and the importance of such behaviors on the part of top-level executives.

How Has Increasingly Intensive Corporate Governance Affected the Lives of CEOs?

In 2006, a record number of CEOs left their jobs through dismissal, retirement, or recruitment to another firm. This notable exodus is due in part to increasing scrutiny by boards, governance activists, and increased pressure from the market for corporate control (other firms considering an ownership position or outright purchase of an under-performing target firm), especially by private equity firms and activist hedge funds. Although many CEOs still hold the title of chair and chief executive officer, the day of the "Imperial CEO" is over as board members are pressured to challenge the views of the CEO if they appear to be headed in a direction that will not benefit all stakeholders. As such, outside directors are also more forthright. Nell Minow, a corporate governance expert, indicated, "It used to be that it was considered somehow impolite or improper (for a board member) to ask a tough question, now it is considered irresponsible not to ask a tough question."

Also, the controversy and scrutiny in the media, by government agencies such as the Security and Exchange Commission (SEC), and from activist shareholders (e.g., pension funds) over executive pay is increasing. The Sarbanes-Oxley legislation (passed in 2002) caused U.S. corporate governance policies to be more intense. This scrutiny translates into a zero tolerance for any form of corruption, conflict of interest, or other forms of wrong-doing or inappropriate behavior.

On the other hand, all of this scrutiny may have a price. Interestingly, the average tenure of CEOs is now down to 18–24 months because so many new CEOs have been appointed. An article in the *Harvard Business Review* reported, "At the current rate, almost 50 percent of the largest U.S. firms will have a new CEO in the next four years." This trend presents a true challenge for a CEO who comes from the outside to make the business profitable in a short period of time without inside knowledge of how to run the business. Because of the high turnover and shorter tenures, CEOs are focusing more and more on short-term turnaround corporate strategies and contractually looking to their inevitable departure. Ironically, the increases in governance controls have led to an increase in CEO pay and severance perks, including golden parachutes that often pay three years of annual salary if a CEO exits before his/her contract expires because the firm is taken over. If the SEC sets a limit on exit pay, CEOs will likely arrange more pay upfront to compensate for the risks they are taking, given the shorter CEO tenures in most firms.

Additionally, CEOs are now serving on fewer external boards in order to focus on their own firms' activities. However, the result is less external governance experience for CEOs to understand a large complex operation associated with most S&P 500 or *Fortune* 500–type firms. Author of the book *Built to Last*, Jim Collins, found that inside CEOs are able to provide information that is idiosyncratic and allows the firm to experience longer-term profitability and above-average returns. The problem, he argues, is that on average it took about seven years into a CEO's tenure to help a firm achieve profitability, which does not bode well for most CEOs who are "resigning" much sooner than seven years. Collins suggests, "If we're systematically looking for saviors and shortening the amount of time a CEO gets, we're on a systematic path toward increased mediocrity."

In summary, corporate governance is a double-edged sword. On the one hand, it is necessary to put an end to scandals such as the Enron disaster, which led to a significant loss for all of the stakeholders involved, including employees. Also, CEO compensation is quite excessive relative to other managers and employees. On the other hand, governance that is overly restrictive can reduce managerial risk taking and increase governance costs excessively as well as constrain the CEO's decision-making authority. Ironically, it inadvertently leads to increased pay for CEOs, which many governance activists rail against. Although corporate governance is a necessity, it is also important to make sure that it is executed properly to avoid the problems noted here.

Sources: N. Byrnes & J. Sasseen, 2007, Board of hard knocks: Activist shareholders, tougher rules and anger over CEO pay have put directors on the hot seat, *BusinessWeek*, January 22, 37–39; K. P. Coyne & E. J. Coyne, Sr., 2007, Surviving your CEO, *Harvard Business Review*, 85(5): 1–9; D. R. Dalton & C. M. Dalton, 2007, CEO succession: Best practices in a changing environment, *Journal of Business Strategy*, 28(2): 11–13; L. Dittmar, 2007, Raising the bar on governance: Are boards up to the task? *Financial Executive*, 23(2): 50–53; D. Eichinger, 2007, Do you know where your next CEO is? *BusinessWeek*, http://www.businessweek.com, July 31; F. Guerrera, 2007, Once-mighty U.S. chiefs feel the heat, *Financial Times*, January 3, 22; C. Hymowitz, 2007, Personal boundaries shrink as companies punish bad behavior, *Wall Street Journal*, June 18, B1; K. Kelly, 2007, Roller coaster leadership, *Business Strategy Review*, 18(1): 22–27; 2006, Why corporate boardrooms are in turmoil, *Wall Street Journal*, September 16, A7; N. Byrnes, D. Kiley, R. O. Crockett, & T. Lowry, 2006, The great CEO exodus, *BusinessWeek*, October 30, 78.

As the Opening Case illustrates, making sure that the governance devices used to oversee firms are appropriately applied is an increasingly important part of the strategic management process.[1] If the board makes the wrong decisions in selecting, governing, and compensating the firm's strategic leader (e.g., CEO), the shareholders and the firm suffer. When CEOs are motivated to act in the best interest of the firm—in particular, the shareholders—the firm's value should increase.

Although some critics argue that CEOs in the United States are paid too much, the hefty increases in their incentive compensation in recent years ostensibly come from linking pay to their firms' performance, and U.S. firms have performed better than many companies in other countries. However, research also suggests that firms with a smaller pay gap between the CEO and other top executives perform better, especially when collaboration among top management team members is more important.[2] The performance improvement is attributed to better cooperation among the top management team members. Other research suggests that CEOs receive excessive compensation when corporate governance is the weakest.[3]

Corporate governance
is the set of mechanisms used to manage the relationship among stakeholders and to determine and control the strategic direction and performance of organizations.

Corporate governance is the set of mechanisms used to manage the relationship among stakeholders and to determine and control the strategic direction and performance of organizations.[4] At its core, corporate governance is concerned with identifying ways to ensure that strategic decisions are made effectively.[5] Governance can also be thought of as a means corporations use to establish order between parties (the firm's owners and its top-level managers) whose interests may conflict. Thus, corporate governance reflects and enforces the company's values.[6] In modern corporations—especially those in the United States and the United Kingdom—a primary objective of corporate governance is to ensure that the interests of top-level managers are aligned with the interests of the shareholders. Corporate governance involves oversight in areas where owners, managers, and members of boards of directors may have conflicts of interest. As the Opening Case illustrates, these areas include the election of directors, the general supervision of CEO pay and more focused supervision of director pay, and the corporation's overall structure and strategic direction.[7]

Recent emphasis on corporate governance stems mainly from the occasional failure of corporate governance mechanisms to adequately monitor and control top-level managers' decisions. This situation results in changes in governance mechanisms in corporations throughout the world, especially with respect to efforts intended to improve the performance of boards of directors. These changes often cause confusion about the proper role of the board. According to one observer, "Depending on the company, you get very different perspectives: Some boards are settling for checking the boxes on compliance regulations, while others are thinking about changing the fundamental way they govern, and some worry that they've gotten themselves into micromanaging the CEO and company. There's a fair amount of turmoil and collective searching going on."[8] A second and more positive reason for this interest comes from evidence that suggests that a well-functioning corporate governance and control system can create a competitive advantage for an individual firm.[9] For example, one governance mechanism—the board of directors—has been suggested to be rapidly evolving into a major strategic force in U.S. business firms.[10] Thus, in this chapter, we describe actions designed to implement strategies that focus on monitoring and controlling mechanisms, which can help to ensure that top-level managerial actions contribute to the firm's strategic competitiveness and its ability to earn above-average returns.

Effective corporate governance is also of interest to nations.[11] Although corporate governance reflects company standards, it also collectively reflects country societal standards.[12] As with these firms and their boards, nations that effectively govern their corporations may gain a competitive advantage over rival countries. In a range of countries, but especially in the United States and the United Kingdom, the fundamental goal of business organizations is to maximize shareholder value.[13] Traditionally, shareholders are treated as the firm's key stakeholders, because they are the company's legal owners. The firm's owners expect top-level managers and others influencing the corporation's actions (e.g., the board of directors) to make decisions that will maximize the company's value and, hence, the owners' wealth.[14] Interestingly, research shows that in cross-border acquisitions target firms from countries with weak governance (e.g., lower shareholder protections) are devalued relative to targets from countries with stronger governance regimes.[15]

In the first section of this chapter, we describe the relationship that is the foundation on which the modern corporation is built: the relationship between owners and managers. The majority of this chapter is used to explain various mechanisms owners use to govern managers and to ensure that they comply with their responsibility to maximize shareholder value.

Three internal governance mechanisms and a single external one are used in the modern corporation. The three internal governance mechanisms we describe in this chapter are (1) ownership concentration, as represented by types of shareholders and their different incentives to monitor managers; (2) the board of directors; and (3) executive compensation. We then consider the market for corporate control, an external corporate governance mechanism. Essentially, this market is a set of potential owners seeking to acquire undervalued firms and earn above-average returns on their investments by replacing ineffective top-level management teams.[16] The chapter's focus then shifts to the issue of international corporate governance. We briefly describe governance approaches used in German and Japanese firms whose traditional governance structures are being affected by the realities of global competition. In part, this discussion suggests that the structures used to govern global companies in many different countries, including Germany, Japan, the United Kingdom, and the United States, as well as emerging economies, are becoming more, rather than less, similar. Closing our analysis of corporate governance is a consideration of the need for these control mechanisms to encourage and support ethical behavior in organizations.

Importantly, the mechanisms discussed in this chapter can positively influence the governance of the modern corporation, which has placed significant responsibility and authority in the hands of top-level managers. With multiple governance mechanisms operating simultaneously, however, it is also possible for some of the governance mechanisms to be in conflict.[17] Later, we review how these conflicts can occur.

Separation of Ownership and Managerial Control

Historically, U.S. firms were managed by the founder-owners and their descendants. In these cases, corporate ownership and control resided in the same persons. As firms grew larger, "the managerial revolution led to a separation of ownership and control in most large corporations, where control of the firm shifted from entrepreneurs to professional managers while ownership became dispersed among thousands of unorganized stockholders who were removed from the day-to-day management of the firm."[18] These changes created the modern public corporation, which is based on the efficient separation of ownership and managerial control. Supporting the separation is a basic legal premise suggesting that the primary objective of a firm's activities is to increase the corporation's profit and, thereby, the financial gains of the owners (the shareholders).[19]

The separation of ownership and managerial control allows shareholders to purchase stock, which entitles them to income (residual returns) from the firm's operations after paying expenses. This right, however, requires that they also take a risk that the firm's expenses may exceed its revenues. To manage this investment risk, shareholders maintain a diversified portfolio by investing in several companies to reduce their overall risk.[20] As shareholders diversify their investments over a number of corporations, their risk declines. The poor performance or failure of any one firm in which they invest has less overall effect. Thus, shareholders specialize in managing their investment risk.

In small firms, managers often are high percentage owners, which means less separation between ownership and managerial control. In fact, in a large number of family-owned firms, ownership and managerial control are not separated. In the United States, at least one-third of the S&P 500 firms have substantial family ownership, holding on average about 18 percent of the outstanding equity. And family-owned firms perform better when a member of the family is the CEO than when the CEO is an outsider.[21] In many countries outside the United States, such as in Latin America, Asia, and some European countries, family-owned firms represent the dominant form.[22] The primary purpose of most of these firms is to increase the family's wealth, which explains why a family CEO often is better than an outside CEO.

Family-controlled firms face at least two critical issues. First, as they grow, they may not have access to all of the skills needed to effectively manage the firm and maximize its returns for the family. Thus, they may need outsiders. Also, as they grow, they may need to seek outside capital and thus give up some of the ownership. In these cases, protection of the minority owners' rights becomes important.[23] To avoid these potential problems, when these firms grow and become more complex, their owner-managers may contract with managerial specialists. These managers make major decisions in the owners' firm and are compensated on the basis of their decision-making skills. As decision-making specialists, managers are agents of the firm's owners and are expected to use their decision-making skills to operate the owners' firm in ways that will maximize the return on their investment.[24]

Without owner (shareholder) specialization in risk bearing and management specialization in decision making, a firm may be limited by the abilities of its owners to manage and make effective strategic decisions. Thus, the separation and specialization of ownership (risk bearing) and managerial control (decision making) should produce the highest returns for the firm's owners.

Shareholder value is reflected by the price of the firm's stock. As stated earlier, corporate governance mechanisms, such as the board of directors, or compensation based on the performance of a firm is the reason that CEOs show general concern about the firm's stock price.

Agency Relationships

The separation between owners and managers creates an agency relationship. An **agency relationship** exists when one or more persons (the principal or principals) hire another person or persons (the agent or agents) as decision-making specialists to perform a service.[25] Thus, an agency relationship exists when one party delegates decision-making responsibility to a second party for compensation (see Figure 10.1).[26] In addition to shareholders and top executives, other examples of agency relationships are consultants and clients and insured and insurer. Moreover, within organizations, an agency relationship exists between managers and their employees, as well as between top executives and the firm's owners.[27] In the modern corporation, managers must understand the links between these relationships and the firm's effectiveness.[28] Although the agency relationship between managers and their employees is important, in this chapter we focus on the agency relationship between the firm's owners (the principals) and top-level managers (the principals' agents), because this relationship is related directly to how the firm's strategies are implemented.[29]

The separation between ownership and managerial control can be problematic. Research evidence documents a variety of agency problems in the modern corporation.[30] Problems can surface because the principal and the agent have different interests and goals, or because shareholders lack direct control of large publicly traded corporations. Problems also arise when an agent makes decisions that result in the pursuit of goals that conflict with those of the principals. Thus, the separation of ownership and control potentially allows divergent interests (between principals and agents) to surface, which can lead to managerial opportunism.

Managerial opportunism is the seeking of self-interest with guile (i.e., cunning or deceit).[31] Opportunism is both an attitude (e.g., an inclination) and a set of behaviors (i.e., specific acts of self-interest).[32] It is not possible for principals to know beforehand which

> An **agency relationship** exists when one or more persons (the principal or principals) hire another person or persons (the agent or agents) as decision-making specialists to perform a service.

> **Managerial opportunism** is the seeking of self-interest with guile (i.e., cunning or deceit).

Figure 10.1 An Agency Relationship

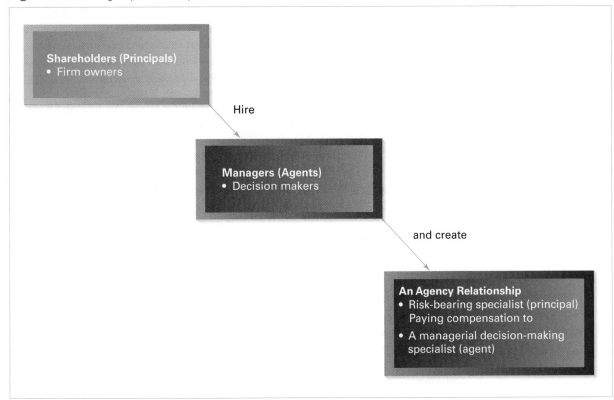

agents will or will not act opportunistically. The reputations of top executives are an imperfect predictor, and opportunistic behavior cannot be observed until it has occurred. Thus, principals establish governance and control mechanisms to prevent agents from acting opportunistically, even though only a few are likely to do so. Any time that principals delegate decision-making responsibilities to agents, the opportunity for conflicts of interest exists. Top executives, for example, may make strategic decisions that maximize their personal welfare and minimize their personal risk.[33] Decisions such as these prevent the maximization of shareholder wealth. Decisions regarding product diversification demonstrate these possibilities.

Product Diversification as an Example of an Agency Problem

As explained in Chapter 6, a corporate-level strategy to diversify the firm's product lines can enhance a firm's strategic competitiveness and increase its returns, both of which serve the interests of shareholders and the top executives. However, product diversification can result in two benefits to managers that shareholders do not enjoy, so top executives may prefer product diversification more than shareholders do.[34]

First, diversification usually increases the size of a firm, and size is positively related to executive compensation. Also, diversification increases the complexity of managing a firm and its network of businesses, possibly requiring more pay because of this complexity.[35] Thus, increased product diversification provides an opportunity for top executives to increase their compensation.[36]

Second, product diversification and the resulting diversification of the firm's portfolio of businesses can reduce top executives' employment risk. Managerial employment risk is the risk of job loss, loss of compensation, and loss of managerial reputation.[37] These risks are reduced with increased diversification, because a firm and its upper-level managers are less vulnerable to the reduction in demand associated with a single or limited number of product lines or businesses. For example, Kellogg Co. was almost entirely focused on breakfast cereal in 2001 when it suffered its first-ever market share leadership loss to perennial number two, General Mills, Inc. Upon appointing Carlos Gutierrez, a longtime manager at Kellogg, to the CEO position, the company embarked on a new strategy to overcome its poor performance. A *BusinessWeek* article outlined his strategy results as follows: "To drive sales, Gutierrez unveiled such novel products as Special K snack bars, bought cookie maker Keebler Co., and ramped up Kellogg's health-foods presence by snapping up Worthington Foods Inc., a maker of soy and vegetarian products, and cereal maker Kashi. He pushed net earnings up 77 percent, to $890.6 million, from 1998 to 2004, as sales rose 42 percent, to $9.6 billion; no wonder the stock soared 54 percent, to some $42 a share."[38] In 2006, Kellogg revenues were at $10.9 billion a year and the stock was close to $52. Kellogg's diversified scope increased, and through this strategy the CEO's risk of job loss was substantially reduced.

Another concern that may represent an agency problem is a firm's free cash flows over which top executives have control. Free cash flows are resources remaining after the firm has invested in all projects that have positive net present value within its current businesses.[39] In anticipation of positive returns, managers may decide to invest these funds in products that are not associated with the firm's current lines of business to increase the firm's level of diversification. The managerial decision to use free cash flows to overdiversify the firm is an example of self-serving and opportunistic managerial behavior. In contrast to managers, shareholders may prefer that free cash flows be distributed to them as dividends, so they can control how the cash is invested.[40]

Curve *S* in Figure 10.2 depicts the shareholders' optimal level of diversification. Owners seek the level of diversification that reduces the risk of the firm's total failure while simultaneously increasing the company's value through the development of economies of scale and scope (see Chapter 6). Of the four corporate-level diversification strategies shown in Figure 10.2, shareholders likely prefer the diversified position

STRATEGY RIGHT NOW

Figure 10.2 Manager and Shareholder Risk and Diversification

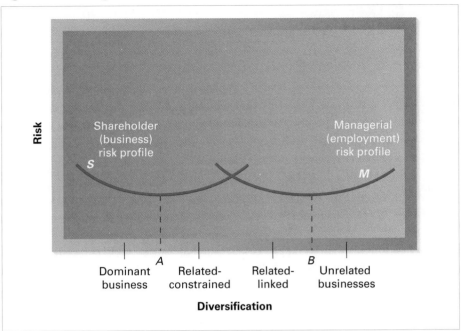

noted by point *A* on curve *S*—a position that is located between the dominant business and related-constrained diversification strategies. Of course, the optimum level of diversification owners seek varies from firm to firm.[41] Factors that affect shareholders' preferences include the firm's primary industry, the intensity of rivalry among competitors in that industry, and the top management team's experience with implementing diversification strategies.

As do principals, upper-level executives—as agents—also seek an optimal level of diversification. Declining performance resulting from too much product diversification increases the probability that corporate control of the firm will be acquired in the market. After a firm is acquired, the employment risk for the firm's top executives increases substantially. Furthermore, a manager's employment opportunities in the external managerial labor market (discussed in Chapter 12) are affected negatively by a firm's poor performance. Therefore, top executives prefer diversification, but not to a point that it increases their employment risk and reduces their employment opportunities.[42] Curve *M* in Figure 10.2 shows that executives prefer higher levels of product diversification than do shareholders. Top executives might prefer the level of diversification shown by point *B* on curve *M*.

In general, shareholders prefer riskier strategies and more focused diversification. They reduce their risk through holding a diversified portfolio of equity investments. Alternatively, managers obviously cannot balance their employment risk by working for a diverse portfolio of firms. Therefore, top executives may prefer a level of diversification that maximizes firm size and their compensation and that reduces their employment risk. Product diversification, therefore, is a potential agency problem that could result in principals incurring costs to control their agents' behaviors.

Agency Costs and Governance Mechanisms

The potential conflict illustrated by Figure 10.2, coupled with the fact that principals do not know which managers might act opportunistically, demonstrates why principals establish governance mechanisms. However, the firm incurs costs when it uses one or more governance mechanisms. **Agency costs** are the sum of incentive costs, monitoring costs, enforcement costs, and individual financial losses incurred by principals

Agency costs are the sum of incentive costs, monitoring costs, enforcement costs, and individual financial losses incurred by principals because governance mechanisms cannot guarantee total compliance by the agent.

Securities and Exchange Commission Chairman Christopher Cox holds up a copy of the "Sarbanes-Oxley for Dummies" book while testifying on Capitol Hill in Washington, before the House Financial Services Committee.

because governance mechanisms cannot guarantee total compliance by the agent. If a firm is diversified, governance costs increase because it is more difficult to monitor what is going on inside the firm.[43]

In general, managerial interests may prevail when governance mechanisms are weak, as is exemplified by allowing managers a significant amount of autonomy to make strategic decisions. If, however, the board of directors controls managerial autonomy, or if other strong governance mechanisms are used, the firm's strategies should better reflect the interests of the shareholders. More recently, governance observers have been concerned about more egregious behavior beyond inefficient corporate strategy.

Due to fraudulent behavior such as that found at Enron and WorldCom, concerns regarding corporate governance continue to grow. In 2002, the U.S. Congress enacted the Sarbanes-Oxley (SOX) Act, which increased the intensity of corporate governance mechanisms.[44]

Since the implementation of the Sarbanes-Oxley Act in 2002 a significant controversy centers around whether its effect on the economy is positive or negative. On the positive side, many analysts argue that it is a set of regulations that is being copied in democracies and other economies throughout the world. Furthermore, the stock market value increased dramatically since the implementation of SOX because the act helps increase confidence in the stock market due to the reduced possibility of fraud by corporate executives. Section 404 of SOX, which prescribes significant transparency improvement on internal controls associated with accounting and auditing, has arguably improved the internal auditing scrutiny and thereby trust in such financial reporting. In fact a recent study indicated that internal controls associated with Section 404 have increased shareholder value.[45]

On the other hand, many argue that the act, especially Section 404, creates excessive costs for firms. Certainly, information systems audit corporations experience increased revenues, and it has been a boon for such firms.[46] Others also argue that a decrease in foreign firms listing on U.S. stock exchanges occurred at the same time as listing on foreign exchanges increased. In part, this shift may be due to the costs associated with listing on U.S. exchanges associated with requirements of SOX. In fact, figures show that fewer foreign companies are listed on both their domestic and the U.S. exchange, and that more listings have been done in countries where there are less restrictive regulations. Interestingly, this view was supported by Henry Paulson, U.S. Treasury Secretary.[47]

These criticisms led the Bush administration to seek to lessen the affects of the Sarbanes-Oxley Act by adjusting the legislation. As such Bush indicated, "Government should not decide the compensation for America's corporate executives." However he did note that "the salaries and bonuses of CEOs should be based on their success in improving the companies and bringing value to their shareholders."[48]

More intensive application of governance mechanisms may produce significant changes in strategies. For example, because of more intense governance, firms may take on fewer risky projects and thus decrease potential shareholder wealth significantly. As the Opening Case indicates, CEOs and directors have been distracted from more important strategic issues in order to meet detailed compliance deadlines provided by the Sarbanes-Oxley Act and increased governance intensity and media scrutiny. Next, we explain the effects of different governance mechanisms on the decisions managers make about the choice and the use of the firm's strategies.

Ownership Concentration

Both the number of large-block shareholders and the total percentage of shares they own define **ownership concentration. Large-block shareholders** typically own at least 5 percent of a corporation's issued shares. Ownership concentration as a governance mechanism has received considerable interest because large-block shareholders are increasingly active in their demands that corporations adopt effective governance mechanisms to control managerial decisions.[49]

In general, diffuse ownership (a large number of shareholders with small holdings and few, if any, large-block shareholders) produces weak monitoring of managers' decisions. Among other problems, diffuse ownership makes it difficult for owners to effectively coordinate their actions. Diversification of the firm's product lines beyond the shareholders' optimum level can result from ineffective monitoring of managers' decisions. Higher levels of monitoring could encourage managers to avoid strategic decisions that harm shareholder value. In fact, research evidence shows that ownership concentration is associated with lower levels of firm product diversification.[50] Thus, with high degrees of ownership concentration, the probability is greater that managers' strategic decisions will be intended to maximize shareholder value.[51]

As noted, such concentration of ownership has an influence on strategies and firm value. Interestingly, research in Spain showed a curvilinear relationship between shareholder concentration and firm value. At moderate levels of shareholder concentration, firm value increased; at high levels of concentration, firm value decreased for shareholders, especially minority shareholders.[52] When large shareholders have a high degree of wealth, they have power relative to minority shareholders in extracting wealth from the firm, especially when they are in managerial positions. The importance of boards of directors in mitigating expropriation of minority shareholder value has been found in the United States relative to strong family ownership wherein lays incentive to appropriate shareholder wealth, especially in the second generation after the founder has left.[53] Such expropriation is often found in countries such as Korea where minority shareholder rights are not as protected as they are in the United States.[54] However, in the United States much of this concentration has come from increasing equity ownership by institutional investors.

The Growing Influence of Institutional Owners

A classic work published in the 1930s argued that the "modern" corporation had become characterized by a separation of ownership and control.[55] This change occurred primarily because growth prevented founders-owners from maintaining their dual positions in their increasingly complex companies. More recently, another shift has occurred: Ownership of many modern corporations is now concentrated in the hands of institutional investors rather than individual shareholders.[56]

Institutional owners are financial institutions such as stock mutual funds and pension funds that control large-block shareholder positions. Because of their prominent ownership positions, institutional owners, as large-block shareholders, are a powerful governance mechanism. Institutions of these types now own more than 50 percent of the stock in large U.S. corporations, and of the top 1,000 corporations, they own, on average, 56 percent of the stock. Pension funds alone control at least one-half of corporate equity.[57]

These ownership percentages suggest that as investors, institutional owners have both the size and the incentive to discipline ineffective top-level managers and can significantly influence a firm's choice of strategies and overall strategic decisions.[58] Research evidence indicates that institutional and other large-block shareholders are becoming more active in their efforts to influence a corporation's strategic decisions, unless they have a business relationship with the firm. Initially, these shareholder activists and institutional investors concentrated on the performance and accountability of CEOs and contributed

Both the number of large-block shareholders and the total percentage of shares they own define **ownership concentration.**

Large-block shareholders typically own at least 5 percent of a corporation's issued shares.

Institutional owners are financial institutions such as stock mutual funds and pension funds that control large-block shareholder positions.

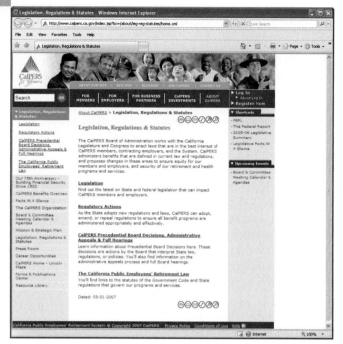

CalPERS, the largest public employee pension fund in the United States, acts boldly to promote regulations and improve firm governance that it believes will enhance shareholder value in companies in which it invests.

to the dismissal of a number of them. They are now targeting actions of boards more directly via proxy vote proposals that are intended to give shareholders more decision rights because they believe board processes have been ineffective.[59]

For example, CalPERS provides retirement and health coverage to more than 1.3 million current and retired public employees. As the largest public employee pension fund in the United States, CalPERS is generally thought to act aggressively to promote governance decisions and actions that it believes will enhance shareholder value in companies in which it invests. For instance, the *Financial Times* indicated that CalPERS "filed 33 'shareowner proposals' as of June 30 [2007], compared with 17 for the previous year [2006]."[60] The shareholder proposals referred to are usually proposed governance changes (say on executive compensation) put forward and supported by significant shareholders on annual proxy ballots that also include new board member nominations. Six of CalPERS's proposals that appeared on proxy ballots in the first half of 2007 received shareholder votes averaging more than 60 percent. The largest institutional investor, TIAA-CREF, has taken actions similar to those of CalPERS, but with a less publicly aggressive stance. To date, research suggests that this institutional activism may not have a direct effect on firm performance, but that its influence may be indirect through its effects on important strategic decisions, such as those concerned with international diversification and innovation.[61] With the increased intensity of governance associated with the passage of the SOX Act, institutional investors as well as other groups have been emboldened in their activism. But this activism may also depend on the country context. For example, one analyst was disappointed in the activism of Indian institutional investors who were also on the board of key firms.[62]

Board of Directors

Typically, shareholders monitor the managerial decisions and actions of a firm through the board of directors. Shareholders elect members to their firm's board. Those who are elected are expected to oversee managers and to ensure that the corporation is operated in ways that will maximize its shareholders' wealth. Even with large institutional investors having major equity ownership in U.S. firms, diffuse ownership continues to exist in most firms, which means that in large corporations, monitoring and control of managers by individual shareholders is limited. Furthermore, large financial institutions, such as banks, are prevented from directly owning stock in firms and from having representatives on companies' boards of directors, although this restriction is not the case in Europe and elsewhere.[63] These conditions highlight the importance of the board of directors for corporate governance. Unfortunately, over time, boards of directors have not been highly effective in monitoring and controlling top management's actions.[64] As noted in the Opening Case, boards are experiencing increasing pressure from shareholders, lawmakers, and regulators to become more forceful in their oversight role and thereby forestall inappropriate actions by top executives. Furthermore, boards not only serve a monitoring role, but they also provide resources to firms. These resources include their personal knowledge and expertise as well as their access to resources of other firms through their external contacts and relationships.[65]

Table 10.1 Classifications of Board of Director Members

Insiders

- The firm's CEO and other top-level managers

Related outsiders

- Individuals not involved with the firm's day-to-day operations, but who have a relationship with the company

Outsiders

- Individuals who are independent of the firm in terms of day-to-day operations and other relationships

The **board of directors** is a group of elected individuals whose primary responsibility is to act in the owners' best interests by formally monitoring and controlling the corporation's top-level executives.[66] Boards have the power to direct the affairs of the organization, punish and reward managers, and protect shareholders' rights and interests. Thus, an appropriately structured and effective board of directors protects owners from managerial opportunism such as that found at Enron and WorldCom where shareholders and employees encountered significant losses. Board members are seen as stewards of their company's resources, and the way they carry out these responsibilities affects the society in which their firm operates. For instance, research suggests that better governance encourages increased flow of foreign direct investment into emerging economies.[67]

Generally, board members (often called directors) are classified into one of three groups (see Table 10.1). *Insiders* are active top-level managers in the corporation who are elected to the board because they are a source of information about the firm's day-to-day operations.[68] *Related outsiders* have some relationship with the firm, contractual or otherwise, that may create questions about their independence, but these individuals are not involved with the corporation's day-to-day activities. *Outsiders* provide independent counsel to the firm and may hold top-level managerial positions in other companies or may have been elected to the board prior to the beginning of the current CEO's tenure.[69]

Historically boards of directors were primarily dominated by inside managers. A widely accepted view is that a board with a significant percentage of its membership drawn from the firm's top executives tends to provide relatively weak monitoring and control of managerial decisions.[70] Managers have been suspected of using their power to select and compensate directors and exploit their personal ties with them. In response to the SEC's proposal to require audit committees to be made up of outside directors, in 1984, the New York Stock Exchange, possibly to preempt formal legislation, implemented an audit committee rule requiring outside directors to head the audit committee. Subsequently, other rules required important committees such as the compensation committee and the nomination committee to be headed by independent outside directors.[71] These other requirements were instituted after the Sarbanes-Oxley Act was passed, and policies of the New York Stock Exchange as well as the American Exchange now require companies to maintain boards of directors that are composed of a majority of outside independent directors and to maintain full independent audit committees. Thus one can clearly see that corporate governance is becoming more intense through the board of directors mechanism.

Critics advocate reforms to ensure that independent outside directors represent a significant majority of the total membership of a board, which research suggests has been accomplished.[72] On the other hand, others argue that having outside directors is not enough to resolve the problems; it depends on the power of the CEO. One proposal to reduce the power of the CEO is to separate the chairperson's role and the CEO's role on the board so that the same person does not hold both positions.[73]

The **board of directors** is a group of elected individuals whose primary responsibility is to act in the owners' interests by formally monitoring and controlling the corporation's top-level executives.

Because of previous scandals in board rooms, the trend toward separating the roles of the CEO and the chairperson continues, which provides more power and independence to the independent outside directors relative to the CEOs. As the Opening Case indicates, this shift has led to more CEO dismissals when things go wrong, such as the dismissal of Robert Nardelli (see the Strategic Focus on page 288). Because of recent problems associated with the egregious use of CEO power, CEOs now must meet tougher standards.[74] Although the Sarbanes-Oxley Act has created stronger scrutiny in regard to finances, the legislation and concern in the media have heightened scrutiny on a range of candidate traits beyond the leader's actual ability to run the company's businesses.[75]

Alternatively, having a large number of outside board members can also create some problems. Outsiders do not have contact with the firm's day-to-day operations and typically do not have easy access to the level of information about managers and their skills that is required to effectively evaluate managerial decisions and initiatives.[76] Outsiders can, however, obtain valuable information through frequent interactions with inside board members, during board meetings and otherwise. Insiders possess such information by virtue of their organizational positions. Thus, boards with a critical mass of insiders typically are better informed about intended strategic initiatives, the reasons for the initiatives, and the outcomes expected from them.[77] Without this type of information, outsider-dominated boards may emphasize the use of financial, as opposed to strategic, controls to gather performance information to evaluate managers' and business units' performances. A virtually exclusive reliance on financial evaluations shifts risk to top-level managers, who, in turn, may make decisions to maximize their interests and reduce their employment risk. Reductions in R&D investments, additional diversification of the firm, and the pursuit of greater levels of compensation are some of the results of managers' actions to achieve financial goals set by outsider-dominated boards.[78]

Enhancing the Effectiveness of the Board of Directors

Because of the importance of boards of directors in corporate governance and as a result of increased scrutiny from shareholders—in particular, large institutional investors—the performances of individual board members and of entire boards are being evaluated more formally and with greater intensity.[79] Given the demand for greater accountability and improved performance, many boards have initiated voluntary changes. Among these changes are (1) increases in the diversity of the backgrounds of board members (e.g., a greater number of directors from public service, academic, and scientific settings; a greater percentage of ethnic minorities and women; and members from different countries on boards of U.S. firms), (2) the strengthening of internal management and accounting control systems, and (3) the establishment and consistent use of formal processes to evaluate the board's performance.[80] Additional changes include (4) the creation of a "lead director" role that has strong powers with regard to the board agenda and oversight of nonmanagement board member activities, and (5) modification of the compensation of directors, especially reducing or eliminating stock options as a part of the package. Activists shareholders such as CalPERS are also lobbying that "directors be elected by a majority of votes cast rather than by a plurality."[81]

Boards have become more involved in the strategic decision-making process, so they must work collaboratively. Some argue that improving the processes used by boards to make decisions and monitor managers and firm outcomes is the key to increasing board effectiveness.[82] Moreover, because of the increased pressure from owners and the potential conflict among board members, procedures are necessary to help boards function effectively in facilitating the strategic decision-making process.

Increasingly, outside directors are being required to own significant equity stakes as a prerequisite to holding a board seat. In fact, some research suggests that firms perform better if outside directors have such a stake; the trend is toward higher pay for directors with more stock ownership, but less stock options.[83] However, other research suggests that too much ownership can cause problems of less independence and lead to problems for the firm.[84] Additionally, other research suggests that diverse boards help firms make more effective strategic decisions and perform better over time.[85] Although questions remain about whether more independent and diverse boards are more effective, it is likely that board independence and increasing diversity are likely to continue. Also, activist shareholders are likely to continue to put forward shareholder proposals as evidenced by their increased level of activity in the Opening Case. As such, boards need to work on being more effective under this situation.

Executive Compensation

As the Opening Case and Strategic Focus illustrate, the compensation of top-level managers, and especially of CEOs, generates a great deal of interest and strongly held opinions. One reason for this widespread interest can be traced to a natural curiosity about extremes and excesses. For example, the *Los Angeles Times* reported that "CEO compensation tripled from 1990 to 2004, rising at more than three times the rate of corporate earnings. CEOs at 11 of the largest U.S. companies received $865 million in a five-year period while presiding over losses in shareholder value."[86] Another stems from a more substantive view that CEO pay is tied in an indirect but tangible way to the fundamental governance processes in large corporations: Who has power? What are the bases of power? How and when do owners and managers exert their relative preferences? How vigilant are boards? Who is taking advantage of whom?[87]

Executive compensation is a governance mechanism that seeks to align the interests of managers and owners through salaries, bonuses, and long-term incentive compensation, such as stock awards and options.[88] Long-term incentive plans have become a critical part of compensation packages in U.S. firms. The use of longer-term pay theoretically helps firms cope with or avoid potential agency problems by linking managerial wealth to the wealth of common shareholders.[89]

Sometimes the use of a long-term incentive plan prevents major stockholders (e.g., institutional investors) from pressing for changes in the composition of the board of directors, because they assume that the long-term incentives will ensure that top executives will act in shareholders' best interests. Alternatively, stockholders largely assume that top-executive pay and the performance of a firm are more closely aligned when firms have boards that are dominated by outside members. However, research shows that fraudulent behavior can be associated with stock option incentives, especially if board members also hold stock options and the CEO also holds the board chair position.[90]

Recently, the persistence of institutional investors has paid off in regard to questioning actions of boards regarding executive pay packages. As the Strategic Focus on executive compensation indicates, the persistent questions of activists and the media led to the dismissal of CEO Robert Nardelli at Home Depot.

Effectively using executive compensation as a governance mechanism is particularly challenging to firms implementing international strategies. For example, the interests of owners of multinational corporations may be best served by less uniformity among the firm's foreign subsidiaries' compensation plans.[91] Developing an array of unique compensation plans requires additional monitoring and increases the firm's potential agency costs. Importantly, levels of pay vary by regions of the world. For example, managerial pay is highest in the United States and much lower in Asia. Compensation is lower in India partly because many of the largest firms have strong family ownership and control.[92] As corporations acquire firms in other countries, the managerial compensation puzzle for boards becomes more complex and may cause additional governance problems.[93]

Executive compensation is a governance mechanism that seeks to align the interests of managers and owners through salaries, bonuses, and long-term incentive compensation, such as stock awards and options.

STRATEGY RIGHT NOW

Executive Compensation Is Increasingly Becoming a Target for Media, Activist Shareholders, and Government Regulators

In April 2007 the *Wall Street Journal* developed a special report on executive compensation. The lead article was entitled "Ten ways to restore investor confidence in compensation: What words can do to ease shareholder anger over pay packages." Amid growing outrage over excessive executive compensation, a number of outside entities, including the media, shareholder activists, and government regulators, are seeking to reduce the increases in CEO and other executive compensation pay packages.

The reason for this outrage can be illustrated by the compensation package for former Home Depot CEO Robert Nardelli. Home Depot awarded Mr. Nardelli $245 million over his five-year stint. However during his tenure the company's stock price slid 12 percent, while the stock price of its most important rival, Lowe's, increased 173 percent. When Nardelli was hired by Home Depot, he successfully negotiated a package relative to what his future earnings would have been at General Electric (GE). As such, he was awarded $25 million in vested shares on his start date. Additionally, he received a new car every three years (similar price to a Mercedes-Benz S series), the opportunity to use the company jet for personal trips, as well as a $10 million loan at an annual interest of 5.8 percent that would be forgiven over five years.

The board argued that to hire such a high-profile candidate as Nardelli was a significant achievement for Home Depot because he could move to another job quite readily as indicated by Gerard R. Roche, a high-profile recruiter who brought Nardelli to the attention of Home Depot's board: "I can tell you there are a number of companies telling me to find them another Nardelli." In part, due to his perception as a top-level executive, when Mr. Nardelli did not reach his performance goals, the board changed the long-term incentive plan and lowered his target goals in order for him to reach his goals and obtain his negotiated compensation.

Besides the competition for high-profile CEOs such as Nardelli, what are other reasons that a board would approve such compensation packages as received by Robert Nardelli? A *New York Times* article suggested that the six-member compensation committee was composed of other CEOs, one of which had an even higher compensation package than Nardelli. Others were suggested to have had associations with Nardelli, directly or indirectly, through his previous employer GE. As such, it would be hard for his associates to lower Nardelli's pay, especially when one board member was making more than he was.

However, increased pressure comes from a number of sources, as noted previously, including the media, the government, and activist shareholders. In July 2006 the Securities and Exchange Commission overhauled the rules regarding requirements for disclosure of information provided to shareholders in proxy statements about executive compensation. This increased information disclosure as well as the number of scandals associated with backdating options (using hindsight to set an option price at the lowest or near the lowest stock price during the year, which is illegal) have made board executive compensation committees (and boards in general) a focus of activist investors and have increased government scrutiny. Certainly Home Depot was a target for much of this scrutiny, which forced the board to oust Nardelli from his position when he would not accept a lower pay package.

Frank Blake, the new CEO at Home Depot received a salary and long-term incentive package much less than that of his predecessor, Robert Nardelli.

The new Home Depot CEO, Frank Blake, has a pay package that is significantly less than his predecessor. Interestingly, Blake rejected the retailer's first offer because it included too much pay. He refused getting restricted stock that retains value even if the share price declines. In other words, he wanted to make sure that his pay package was in line with the desires of Home Depot shareholders. In the end, Blake received a pay package worth as much as $8 million, which is roughly one third of the $24 million (excluding stock options) that Robert Nardelli earned annually during his six-year term at the home improvement chain. At least in the case of Home Depot, it appears that increased scrutiny, activist shareholder monitoring, and executive pay disclosure rules are having a significant effect in bringing CEO pay in line.

However, a large discrepancy still remains between executive and other nonunion employee pay increases. In 2006 salary and bonus compensation increased 7.1 percent in the largest 350 U.S. corporations while it increased 3.6 percent for nonunion employees. However, executive long-term incentive pay increased 8.1 percent, even more than the salary and bonus increase. It is important to note that corporate profits jumped 14.4 percent in 2006. At least it appears that overall compensation is keeping pace with profits in the latest year available.

Sources: M. Byrnes & J. Sasseen, 2007, Board of hard knocks, activists shareholders, tough rules and anger over CEO pay have the directors on the hot seat, *BusinessWeek,* January 22, 37; G. Colvin, 2007, A tie goes to the Managers, *Fortune,* May 28, 34; G. Colvin, A gadfly in the ivory tower, 2007, *Fortune,* April 16, 40; J. S. Lublin, 2007, Ten ways to restore investor confidence in compensation: What boards can do to ease shareholder anger over pay packages, *Wall Street Journal,* April 9, R1, R3; J. S. Lublin, 2007, The pace of pay gains: A survey overview, *Wall Street Journal,* April 9, R1; J. S. Lublin & A. Zimmerman, 2007, Home Depot CEO takes stand on pay, *Wall Street Journal,* B7; S. Lueck, 2007, Executive pay looks to take hit, *Wall Street Journal,* January 30, A4; J. McGregor, 2007, Activist investors get more respect, *BusinessWeek,* June 11, 34; G. Morgenson, 2007, Panel to look at conflicts in consulting, *New York Times,* http://www.nyt.com, May 11; M. Orey & M. Arndt, 2007, Jumping without a parachute, *BusinessWeek,* April 16, 16; J. Sasseen, 2007, A better look at the bosses pay: New SEC rules require greater disclosure but don't expect CEOs to take a hit, *BusinessWeek,* February 26, 44; E. White & A. O. Patrick, 2007, Shareholders push for vote on executive pay, *Wall Street Journal,* February 26, B1, B3; G. Wright, 2007, Home Depot reports pay for its CEOs, *Wall Street Journal,* April 16, B5; J. Creswell, 2006, With links to board, Chief saw his pay soar, *New York Times,* http://www.nyt.com, May 24.

The Effectiveness of Executive Compensation

Executive compensation—especially long-term incentive compensation—is complicated for several reasons. First, the strategic decisions made by top-level managers are typically complex and nonroutine, so direct supervision of executives is inappropriate for judging the quality of their decisions. The result is a tendency to link the compensation of top-level managers to measurable outcomes, such as the firm's financial performance. Second, an executive's decision often affects a firm's financial outcomes over an extended period, making it difficult to assess the effect of current decisions on the corporation's performance. In fact, strategic decisions are more likely to have long-term, rather than short-term, effects on a company's strategic outcomes. Third, a number of other factors affect a firm's performance besides top-level managerial decisions and behavior. Unpredictable economic, social, or legal changes (see Chapter 2) make it difficult to discern the effects of strategic decisions. Thus, as indicated in the Strategic Focus, although performance-based compensation may provide incentives to top management teams to make decisions that best serve shareholders' interests, such compensation plans alone are imperfect in their ability to monitor and control managers. Still, incentive compensation represents a significant portion of many executives' total pay.

Although incentive compensation plans may increase the value of a firm in line with shareholder expectations, such plans are subject to managerial manipulation as the Home Depot example illustrates. Additionally, annual bonuses may provide incentives to pursue short-run objectives at the expense of the firm's long-term interests. Although long-term, performance-based incentives may reduce the temptation to under-invest in the short run, they increase executive exposure to risks associated with uncontrollable events, such as market fluctuations and industry decline. The longer term the focus of incentive compensation, the greater are the long-term risks borne by top-level managers. Also, because long-term incentives tie a manager's overall wealth to the firm in a way that is inflexible, such incentives and ownership may not be valued as highly by a manager as by outside investors who have the opportunity to diversify their wealth in a number of other financial investments.[94] Thus, firms may have to overcompensate for managers using long-term incentives.

Even though some stock option–based compensation plans are well designed with option strike prices substantially higher than current stock prices, too many have been designed simply to give executives more wealth. Research of stock option repricing where the strike price value of the option has been lowered from its original position suggests that action is taken more frequently in high-risk situations.[95] However, repricing also happens when firm performance is poor, to restore the incentive effect for the option. Evidence also suggests that politics are often involved, which has resulted in "option backdating."[96] Interestingly, institutional investors prefer compensation schemes that link pay with performance, including the use of stock options.[97] Again, this evidence shows that no internal governance mechanism is perfect.

Stock options became highly popular as a means of compensating top executives and linking pay with performance, but they also have become controversial of late as indicated in the Opening Case. Because all internal governance mechanisms are imperfect, external mechanisms are also needed. One such governance device is discussed next.

Market for Corporate Control

The **market for corporate control** is an external governance mechanism that becomes active when a firm's internal controls fail.[98] The market for corporate control is composed of individuals and firms that buy ownership positions in or take over potentially undervalued corporations so they can form new divisions in established diversified companies or merge two previously separate firms. Because the undervalued firm's executives are assumed to be responsible for formulating and implementing the strategy that led to poor performance, they are usually replaced. Thus, when the market for corporate control operates effectively, it ensures that managers who are ineffective or act opportunistically are disciplined.[99]

The market for corporate control is often viewed as a "court of last resort."[100] The takeover market as a source of external discipline is used only when internal governance mechanisms are relatively weak and have proven to be ineffective. Alternatively, other research suggests that the rationale for takeovers as a corporate governance strategy is not as strong as the rationale for takeovers as an ownership investment in target candidates where the firm is performing well and does not need discipline.[101] A study of active corporate raiders in the 1980s showed that takeover attempts often were focused on above-average performance firms in an industry.[102] Taken together, this research suggests that takeover targets are not always low performers with weak governance. As such, it also suggests that the market for corporate control may not be as efficient as a governance device as theory suggests. At the very least, internal governance controls would be much more precise relative to this external control mechanism.

Hedge funds are also becoming a source of activist investors as noted in Chapter 7 and in the Opening Case. An enormous amount of money is invested in hedge funds, and because it is becoming significantly more difficult to gain high returns in the market, hedge funds have turned to activism. Likewise in a competitive environment characterized by a greater willingness on part of investors to hold under-performing managers accountable, hedge funds have been given license for increased activity.[103] Traditionally, hedge funds are a portfolio of stocks or bonds, or both, managed by an individual or a team on behalf of a large number of investors. Hedge funds usually engage in faster turnaround investments than traditional mutual funds. Hedge fund managers often invest in futures,

The **market for corporate control** is an external governance mechanism that becomes active when a firm's internal controls fail.

derivatives, and other riskier investment strategies to take advantage of rapid changes in the market. Activism allows them to influence the market by taking a large position in seeking to drive the stock price up in a short period of time and then sell. More recently this activity is done through proxy votes, where they seek to get a fund representative voted to be a member of the board of directors. Hedge fund managers are allowed to sit on boards because they do not manage a traditional mutual or pension fund (whereas mutual fund managers or financial institutions do not have this privilege by law). Most hedge funds are unregulated relative to the Securities and Exchange Commission because they represent a set of private investors. However, more recently these private investors represent large public pension funds. Many pension funds have an average of 6 percent of their portfolio invested in hedge funds as well as private equity funds.[104]

Although the market for corporate control may be a blunt instrument as far as corporate governance is concerned, the takeover market has continued to be active as noted in Chapter 7. In fact, research suggests that the more intense governance environment may have fostered an increasingly active takeover market. Because institutional investors have more concentrated ownership, they may be interested in firms that are targeted for acquisition. Target firms earn a substantial premium over the acquiring firm.[105] At the same time, managers who have ownership positions or stock options are likely to gain in making a transaction with an acquiring firm. Even more evidence indicates that this type of gain may be the case, given the increasing number of firms that have golden parachutes that allow up to three years of additional compensation plus other incentives if a firm is taken over. These compensation contracts reduce the risk for managers if a firm is taken over. Private equity firms often seek to obtain a lower price in the market through initiating friendly takeover deals. The target firm's executives may be amenable to such "friendly" deals because not only do they get the payout through a golden parachute, but at their next firm they may get a "golden hello" as a signing bonus to work for the new firm.[106] Golden parachutes help them leave, but "golden hellos are increasingly needed to get them in the door" of the next firm.[107] For instance, W. James McNerney Jr., a former executive of General Electric received such outsized pay packages by moving to 3M in 2000 and then again to Boeing in 2005. When he moved from 3M to Boeing he received "a pay package worth more than $52 million, which included $25.3 million of restricted shares and $22 million to replace his 3M pension."[108] Although the 1980s had more defenses put up against hostile takeovers, the current environment has been much friendlier, most likely due to the increased intensity of the governance devices on both the buyer (institutional investor) side as well as the corporate management side. The idea that CEOs who have substantial ownership or stock options in the target firm do well in the friendly transactions in the 1990s and into the twenty-first century is also supported by research.[109]

The market for corporate control governance mechanisms should be triggered by a firm's poor performance relative to industry competitors. A firm's poor performance, often demonstrated by the firm's below-average returns, is an indicator that internal governance mechanisms have failed; that is, their use did not result in managerial decisions that maximized shareholder value. This market has been active for some time. As noted in Chapter 7, the years 2005 and 2006 produced the largest number and value of mergers and acquisitions. Additionally, the number of mergers and acquisitions began to increase and the market for corporate control has become increasingly international, with more than 40 percent of the merger and acquisition activity involving firms from different countries.[110]

Although some acquisition attempts are intended to obtain resources important to the acquiring firm, most *hostile* takeover attempts are due to the target firm's poor performance.[111] Therefore, target firm managers and members of the boards of directors are highly sensitive about hostile takeover bids. It frequently means that they have not done an effective job in managing the company. If they accept the offer, they are likely to lose their jobs; the acquiring firm will insert its own management. If they reject the offer and fend off the takeover attempt, they must improve the performance of the firm or risk losing their jobs as well.[112]

Managerial Defense Tactics

Hostile takeovers are the major activity in the market for corporate control governance mechanism. Not all hostile takeovers are prompted by poorly performing targets, and firms targeted for hostile takeovers may use multiple defense tactics to fend off the takeover attempt. Historically, the increased use of the market for corporate control has enhanced the sophistication and variety of managerial defense tactics that are used to reduce the influence of this governance mechanism. The market for corporate control tends to increase risk for managers. As a result, managerial pay is often augmented indirectly through golden parachutes (wherein, as mentioned, a CEO can receive up to three years' salary if his or her firm is taken over). Golden parachutes, similar to most other defense tactics, are controversial.

Among other outcomes, takeover defenses increase the costs of mounting a takeover, causing the incumbent management to become entrenched, while reducing the chances of introducing a new management team.[113] One takeover defense is traditionally known as a "poison pill." This defense mechanism usually allows shareholders (other than the acquirer) to convert "shareholders' rights" into a large number of common shares if anyone acquires more than a set amount of the target's stock (typically 10–20%.) This move dilutes the percentage of shares that the acquiring firm must purchase at a premium and in effect raises the cost of the deal for the acquiring firm.

Many firms have been pressured to reduce such takeover defenses. Sara Lee Corporation restructured its operations, as noted in Chapter 7, and shed approximately 40 percent of its revenue through divestitures and spinoffs. It also has a plan to buy back its own stock worth approximately $3 billion to facilitate an increase in share price. In addition, shareholders voted to terminate Sara Lee's "poison pill" takeover defense in an effort to increase shareholder benefits if a bid for the firm is presented.[114]

Sara Lee Corporation is currently using managerial defense tactics to restructure its capital structure and operations for the purpose of increased shareholder benefits in the event that a bid is made for the company.

Table 10.2 lists a number of additional takeover defense strategies. Some defense tactics necessitate only changes in the financial structure of the firm, such as repurchasing shares of the firm's outstanding stock.[115] Some tactics (e.g., reincorporation of the firm in another state) require shareholder approval, but the green-mail tactic, wherein money is used to repurchase stock from a corporate raider to avoid the takeover of the firm, does not. Some firms use rotating board member elections as a defense tactic where only one third of members are up for reelection each year. Research shows that this results in managerial entrenchment and reduced vulnerability to hostile takeovers.[116] These defense tactics are controversial, and the research on their effects is inconclusive.

Most institutional investors oppose the use of defense tactics. TIAA-CREF and CalPERS have taken actions to have several firms' poison pills eliminated. Many institutional investors also oppose severance packages (golden parachutes), and the opposition is growing significantly in Europe as well.[117] But, as previously noted, an advantage to severance packages is that they may encourage executives to accept takeover bids that are attractive to shareholders.[118] Also, as in the case of Robert Nardelli at Home Depot, a severance package may encourage a CEO doing a poor job to depart.[119]

A potential problem with the market for corporate control is that it may not be totally efficient. A study of several of the most active corporate raiders in the 1980s showed that approximately 50 percent of their takeover attempts targeted firms with above-average

Table 10.2 Hostile Takeover Defense Strategies

Defense strategy	Category	Popularity among firms	Effectiveness as a defense	Stockholder wealth effects
Poison pill Preferred stock in the merged firm offered to shareholders at a highly attractive rate of exchange.	Preventive	High	High	Positive
Corporate charter amendment An amendment to stagger the elections of members to the board of directors of the attacked firm so that all are not elected during the same year, which prevents a bidder from installing a completely new board in the same year.	Preventive	Medium	Very low	Negative
Golden parachute Lump-sum payments of cash that are distributed to a select group of senior executives when the firm is acquired in a takeover bid.	Preventive	Medium	Low	Negligible
Litigation Lawsuits that help a target company stall hostile attacks; areas may include antitrust, fraud, inadequate disclosure.	Reactive	Medium	Low	Positive
Greenmail The repurchase of shares of stock that have been acquired by the aggressor at a premium in exchange for an agreement that the aggressor will no longer target the company for takeover.	Reactive	Very low	Medium	Negative
Standstill agreement Contract between the parties in which the pursuer agrees not to acquire any more stock of the target firm for a specified period of time in exchange for the firm paying the pursuer a fee.	Reactive	Low	Low	Negative
Capital structure change Dilution of stock, making it more costly for a bidder to acquire; may include employee stock option plans (ESOPs), recapitalization, new debt, stock selling, share buybacks.	Reactive	Medium	Medium	Inconclusive

Source: J. A. Pearce II & R. B. Robinson, Jr., 2004, Hostile takeover defenses that maximize shareholder wealth, *Business Horizons*, 47(5): 15–24.

performance in their industry—corporations that were neither undervalued nor poorly managed.[120] The targeting of high-performance businesses may lead to acquisitions at premium prices and to decisions by managers of the targeted firm to establish what may prove to be costly takeover defense tactics to protect their corporate positions.[121]

Although the market for corporate control lacks the precision of internal governance mechanisms, the fear of acquisition and influence by corporate raiders is an effective constraint on the managerial-growth motive. The market for corporate control has been responsible for significant changes in many firms' strategies and, when used appropriately, has served shareholders' interests. But this market and other means of corporate governance vary by region of the world and by country. Accordingly, we next address the topic of international corporate governance.

International Corporate Governance

Understanding the corporate governance structure of the United Kingdom and the United States is inadequate for a multinational firm in today's global economy.[122] The stability associated with German and Japanese governance structures has historically been viewed as an asset, but the governance systems in these countries are changing, just as they are in other parts of the world.[123] These changes are partly the result of multinational firms operating in many different countries and attempting to develop a more global governance system.[124] Although the similarity among national governance systems is increasing, significant differences remain evident, and firms employing an international strategy must understand these differences in order to operate effectively in different international markets.[125]

Corporate Governance in Germany

In many private German firms, the owner and manager may still be the same individual. In these instances, agency problems are not present.[126] Even in publicly traded German corporations, a single shareholder is often dominant. Thus, the concentration of ownership is an important means of corporate governance in Germany, as it is in the United States.[127]

Historically, banks occupied the center of the German corporate governance structure, as is also the case in many other European countries, such as Italy and France. As lenders, banks become major shareholders when companies they financed earlier seek funding on the stock market or default on loans. Although the stakes are usually less than 10 percent, the only legal limit on how much of a firm's stock banks can hold is that a single ownership position cannot exceed 15 percent of the bank's capital. Through their shareholdings, and by casting proxy votes for individual shareholders who retain their shares with the banks, three banks in particular—Deutsche, Dresdner, and Commerzbank—exercise significant power. Although shareholders can tell the banks how to vote their ownership position, they generally do not do so. A combination of their own holdings and their proxies results in majority positions for these three banks in many German companies. Those banks, along with others, monitor and control managers, both as lenders and as shareholders, by electing representatives to supervisory boards.

German firms with more than 2,000 employees are required to have a two-tiered board structure that places the responsibility for monitoring and controlling managerial (or supervisory) decisions and actions in the hands of a separate group.[128] All the functions of direction and management are the responsibility of the management board (the Vorstand), but appointment to the Vorstand is the responsibility of the supervisory tier (the Aufsichtsrat). Employees, union members, and shareholders appoint members to the Aufsichtsrat. Proponents of the German structure suggest that it helps prevent corporate wrongdoing and rash decisions by "dictatorial CEOs." However, critics maintain that it slows decision making and often ties a CEO's hands. In Germany the power sharing may have gone too far because it includes representation from the local community as well as unions. Accordingly, the corporate governance framework in Germany has made it difficult to restructure companies as quickly as can be done in the United States when performance suffers. Such is the case with EADS, the parent of Airbus. Part of Airbus's difficulties stem from the challenges it encountered in restructuring due to the complexities of corporate governance not only in Germany, but also in France.[129]

Because of the role of local government (through the board structure) and the power of banks in Germany's corporate governance structure, private shareholders rarely have major ownership positions in German firms. Large institutional investors, such as pension funds and insurance companies, are also relatively insignificant owners of corporate stock. Thus, at least historically, German executives generally have not been dedicated to the maximization of shareholder value that occurs in many countries.[130]

However, corporate governance in Germany is changing, at least partially, because of the increasing globalization of business. Many German firms are beginning to gravitate toward the U.S. system. Recent research suggests that the traditional system produced some agency costs because of a lack of external ownership power. According to research, countries that traditionally have more relationship-oriented capital markets such as Germany whose firms are exposed and required to meet governance aspects of financial capitalism due stock exchange listing requirements (perhaps in the United States) often begin to adopt such governance requirements. For example, German firms with such exposure have increasingly adopted executive stock option compensation as a long-term incentive pay policy.[131]

Corporate Governance in Japan

Attitudes toward corporate governance in Japan are affected by the concepts of obligation, family, and consensus.[132] In Japan, an obligation "may be to return a service for one rendered or it may derive from a more general relationship, for example, to one's family or old alumni, or one's company (or Ministry), or the country. This sense of particular obligation is common elsewhere but it feels stronger in Japan."[133] As part of a company family, individuals are members of a unit that envelops their lives; families command the attention and allegiance of parties throughout corporations. Moreover, a *keiretsu* (a group of firms tied together by cross-shareholdings) is more than an economic concept; it, too, is a family. Consensus, an important influence in Japanese corporate governance, calls for the expenditure of significant amounts of energy to win the hearts and minds of people whenever possible, as opposed to top executives issuing edicts.[134] Consensus is highly valued, even when it results in a slow and cumbersome decision-making process.

As in Germany, banks in Japan play an important role in financing and monitoring large public firms.[135] The bank owning the largest share of stocks and the largest amount of debt—the main bank—has the closest relationship with the company's top executives. The main bank provides financial advice to the firm and also closely monitors managers. Thus, Japan has a bank-based financial and corporate governance structure, whereas the United States has a market-based financial and governance structure.[136]

Aside from lending money, a Japanese bank can hold up to 5 percent of a firm's total stock; a group of related financial institutions can hold up to 40 percent. In many cases, main-bank relationships are part of a horizontal keiretsu. A keiretsu firm usually owns less than 2 percent of any other member firm; however, each company typically has a stake of that size in every firm in the keiretsu. As a result, somewhere between 30 and 90 percent of a firm is owned by other members of the keiretsu. Thus, a keiretsu is a system of relationship investments.

As is the case in Germany, Japan's structure of corporate governance is changing. For example, because of Japanese banks' continuing development as economic organizations, their role in the monitoring and control of managerial behavior and firm outcomes is less significant than in the past.[137] In fact, research indicates that it increased the cost of governance due the entrenchment of poor management. Also, deregulation in the financial sector reduced the cost of mounting hostile takeovers.[138] As such, deregulation facilitated more activity in Japan's market for corporate control, which was nonexistent in past years.[139]

Also, as noted in the following Strategic Focus, activist shareholders have also been lobbying for governance changes. With foreign shareholders accounting for 28 percent of the overall ownership among Japanese firms, their opinions are being heard in shareholder meetings where votes on proposition for change are voiced. Outside directors are increasing their influence, and activist shareholders have become aggressive with their increased ownership positions as illustrated in the Strategic Focus.

It will be interesting to see how this activism influences the long-term orientation of Japanese firms. Research suggests that the Japanese stewardship-management approach, historically dominated by inside managers, produces greater investments in long-term R&D projects than does the more financially oriented system in the United States.[140] As the potential for a stronger takeover market increases, some Japanese firms are considering delisting and taking their firms private in order to maintain long-term "strategic flexibility."[141] Interestingly, research suggests that the SOX Act in the United States has created an increase in delisting.[142]

Shareholder Activists Invade Japan's Large Firms Traditionally Focused on "Stakeholder" Capitalism

Japanese firms have recently begun experiencing activist shareholders who seek to increase returns through improved dividend policy.

Japan has traditionally focused on relationship-capitalism, built on the premise that firms help each other when they are weak and facilitate each other's success when they are strong. This relationship-capitalism created a system of protection against "outside" owners by having a close-knit group of insiders who manage the firm as well as a larger set of interlocking shareholders who are mutually bonded by owning each other's stock. This arrangement largely prevented outsiders from "taking over" Japanese corporations. In the 1980s such cross-shareholdings between banks, companies, and insurers accounted for approximately 50 percent of equity. Over the recent term, however, ownership has changed with cross-shareholdings currently accounting for only about 20 percent. As this change occurred and with deregulation allowing more foreign ownership, foreign ownership of Japanese firms has increased from approximately 4.7 percent in 1990 to 28 percent in 2007.

A parallel trend is the increase in activist foreign shareholders making proposals in governing the firms differently. Many of the publicly traded firms in Japan hold their annual shareholder meetings in the latter part of June. In 2007, at many of the shareholder meetings, Japanese managers faced increasing activism, especially by foreign shareholders. Interestingly, in Japan, shareholders can vote directly on dividends and executive pay. Thus, on the surface it would appear that Japanese stock market policies are more shareholder-friendly than those in the United States or the United Kingdom. Furthermore, shareholders can vote to dismiss the entire board without cause. However, Japanese investors do not take up this power readily and most often defer to executive proposals.

These practices are changing now that 28 percent of Japanese shares are held by foreign institutional investors. At the June 2007 annual shareholders' meeting, companies faced 30 shareholder resolutions, nearly twice as many as in 2006, which is threatening to Japanese managers who are seeking to maintain the tight-knit business culture that exists in Japan. For example, the activist shareholders brought to light the large cash reserves that sizeable corporations hold as well as a reluctance to restructure operations that would require layoffs. The large cash reserves are sought by the activist shareholders to increase returns through improved dividend policy and increase overall stock prices by restructuring operations to improve return on equity. For example, returns have languished in Japan at about 9 percent compared to 14 percent and 17 percent in the United States and Europe, respectively. In fact, these figures suggest that Japanese managers could profitably put their cash reserves to better use or return the money to shareholders through stock buybacks or improved dividends.

Not surprisingly many of the large Japanese firms are fighting back by encouraging politicians and media outlets to "demonize" the activists as "financial criminals" who seek short-term gain over long-term health. Similar accusations were made in the European press in 2005 when private equity firms were making hostile acquisitions called *locusts*. However, it appears that the long-term health of Japanese firms might be improved, given that Japanese firms hold cash and securities equivalent to 16 percent of GDP, whereas American firms' long-term average of cash and securities is about 5 percent. Although these slack resources in Japan may facilitate a longer-term view, from the eyes of the

activist shareholders they represents underutilization of potential capital, which, if not utilized, should be returned to shareholders through dividends or stock buybacks.

Sources: 2007, Business: In the locust position; shareholder activism in Japan, *Economist*, June 30, 80; S. Moffett, 2007, Signs of hope for Japan's activists, *Wall Street Journal*, July 13, C3; M. Nakamoto, 2007, Corporate Japan needs the activist touch, *Financial Times*, June 25, 13; D. Pilling, 2007, Japan's outsiders can come in from the cold, *Financial Times*, June 28, 9; A. Scott, Japanese companies get an ear full; activist funds try to muscle cash out of big firms, *Wall Street Journal*, March 27, C5; L. Santini, 2006, Investor activism grows globally, but wins are rare, *Wall Street Journal*, July 3, C1.

Global Corporate Governance

As noted in the Strategic Focus, foreign investors are becoming increasingly important to shareholders in economies around the world, even in emerging economies. Although many times domestic shareholders will vote with management, as activist foreign investors enter a country it gives domestic institutional investors courage to become more active in shareholder proposals, which will increase shareholder welfare.

For example, Steel Partners, LLC, focused its attention on Korean cigarette maker KT&G. Warren Lichtenstein of Steel Partners and Carl Icahn pressured KT&G to increase its market value. Lichtenstein and Icahn began their activism in February 2006, by nominating a slate of board directors as well as pushing KT&G to sell off its lucrative Ginseng unit, which manufactures popular herbal products in Korea. They also demanded that the company sell off its real estate assets, raise its dividends, and buy back common shares. Lichtenstein and Icahn threatened a hostile tender offer if their demands were not met. Shareholders showed support for Steel Partners' activism such that they elected Mr. Lichtenstein to KT&G's board. In 2006 Mr. Icahn sold his 4.74 percent ownership in KT&G and received a 33 percent return. Mr. Lichtenstein opposed KT&G's offer in 2007 to acquire 1 percent of Korea's Shinhan Financial Group, Korea's second-largest banking institution. However, it was approved by 11 of KT&G's 12 other board members, thus Lichtenstein threatened to remove the CEO, Kwak Young-kyoon, if KT&G completed the deal. Interestingly, in support of Mr. Lichtenstein's opposition, the stock price decreased by 2.2 percent. Activist hedge funds, such as Steel Partners, have found fertile ground in Korean companies and other emerging economies because of low valuations relative to their global peers.[143]

The trends toward improved governance are reaching even Chinese firms, which are primarily government owned. China has been seeking to demonstrate increased openness in advance of the Olympic Games in Beijing in August 2008. Accordingly it has created regulations for greater firm transparency that will go into effect May 1, 2008. Although this regulatory action is meant to broaden the transparency of all aspects of Chinese society, it does have an impact on corporate governance aspects to allow better disclosure of financial information. However, because of the dominance of a central communist party system in China, some areas are considered "too sensitive" to disclose and the government has a "screening" system for protecting certain information. Many government-owned firms will find cover using these means and not disclose more information.[144]

Not only has the legislation that produced the Sarbanes-Oxley Act in 2002 increased the intensity of corporate governance in the United States,[145] but other governments around the world are seeking to increase the transparency and intensity of corporate governance to prevent the type of scandals found in the United States and other places around the world. For example, the British government in 2003 implemented the findings of the Derek Higgs report, which increased governance intensity mandated by the United Kingdom's Combined Code on Corporate Governance. Similarly, Japan is considering drafting legislation entitled "Financial Instruments and Exchange Law," which will be dubbed "J-Sox" because of its similarity to the U.S. Sarbanes-Oxley Act. This legislation is expected to pass by the middle of 2008. Also the European Union enacted what is known as the Transparency Directive, which is aimed at enhancing reporting and the disclosure of financial reports by firms within the European capital markets. Another European Union initiative labeled "Modernizing Company Law and Enhancing Corporate Governance" promises to improve the responsibility and liability of executive officers, board members, and others to important stakeholders such as shareholders, creditors, and members of the public at large.[146] Thus, governance is becoming more intense around the world.

Governance Mechanisms and Ethical Behavior

The governance mechanisms described in this chapter are designed to ensure that the agents of the firm's owners—the corporation's top executives—make strategic decisions that best serve the interests of the entire group of stakeholders, as described in Chapter 1. In the United States, shareholders are recognized as a company's most significant stakeholder. Thus, governance mechanisms focus on the control of managerial decisions to ensure that shareholders' interests will be served, but product market stakeholders (e.g., customers, suppliers, and host communities) and organizational stakeholders (e.g., managerial and nonmanagerial employees) are important as well.[147] Therefore, at least the minimal interests or needs of all stakeholders must be satisfied through the firm's actions. Otherwise, dissatisfied stakeholders will withdraw their support from one firm and provide it to another (e.g., customers will purchase products from a supplier offering an acceptable substitute).

The firm's strategic competitiveness is enhanced when its governance mechanisms take into consideration the interests of all stakeholders. Although the idea is subject to debate, some believe that ethically responsible companies design and use governance mechanisms that serve all stakeholders' interests. The more critical relationship, however, is found between ethical behavior and corporate governance mechanisms. The Enron disaster illustrates the devastating effect of poor ethical behavior not only on a firm's stakeholders, but also on other firms. This issue is being taken seriously in other countries. The trend toward increased governance scrutiny continues to spread around the world.[148]

For instance, SK Corporation in South Korea faced a shareholder-led proposal to oust or significantly reshape the company's CEO position. Although the CEO was not replaced (despite being convicted of accounting fraud) because he is the dominant family owner, they did force change in some of the ways that the corporation was governed.[149]

In addition to Enron, scandals at WorldCom, HealthSouth, and Tyco show that all corporate owners are vulnerable to unethical behaviors by their employees, including top-level managers—the agents who have been hired to make decisions that are in shareholders' best interests. The decisions and actions of a corporation's board of directors can be an effective deterrent to these behaviors. In fact, some believe that the most effective boards participate actively to set boundaries for their firms' business ethics and values.[150] Once formulated, the board's expectations related to ethical decisions and actions of all of the firm's stakeholders must be clearly communicated to its top-level managers. Moreover, as shareholders' agents, these managers must understand that the board will hold them fully accountable for the development and support of an organizational culture that allows unethical decisions and behaviors. As will be explained in Chapter 12, CEOs can be positive role models for improved ethical behavior.

Dennis Kozlowski was sentenced to up to 25 years in prison and fined $70 million for his fraudulent behavior when he was the CEO of Tyco.

© AP Photo/Suzanne Plunkett

Only when the proper corporate governance is exercised can strategies be formulated and implemented that will help the firm achieve strategic competitiveness and earn above-average returns. As the discussion in this chapter suggests, corporate governance mechanisms are a vital, yet imperfect, part of firms' efforts to select and successfully use strategies.

Summary

- Corporate governance is a relationship among stakeholders that is used to determine a firm's direction and control its performance. How firms monitor and control top-level managers' decisions and actions affects the implementation of strategies. Effective governance that aligns managers' decisions with shareholders' interests can help produce a competitive advantage.

- Three internal governance mechanisms in the modern corporation include (1) ownership concentration, (2) the board of directors, and (3) executive compensation. The market for corporate control is the single external governance mechanism influencing managers' decisions and the outcomes resulting from them.

- Ownership is separated from control in the modern corporation. Owners (principals) hire managers (agents) to make decisions that maximize the firm's value. As risk-bearing specialists, owners diversify their risk by investing in multiple corporations with different risk profiles. As decision-making specialists, owners expect their agents (the firm's top-level managers) to make decisions that will lead to maximization of the value of their firm. Thus, modern corporations are characterized by an agency relationship that is created when one party (the firm's owners) hires and pays another party (top-level managers) to use its decision-making skills.

- Separation of ownership and control creates an agency problem when an agent pursues goals that conflict with principals' goals. Principals establish and use governance mechanisms to control this problem.

- Ownership concentration is based on the number of large-block shareholders and the percentage of shares they own. With significant ownership percentages, such as those held by large mutual funds and pension funds, institutional investors often are able to influence top executives' strategic decisions and actions. Thus, unlike diffuse ownership, which tends to result in relatively weak monitoring and control of managerial decisions, concentrated ownership produces more active and effective monitoring. Institutional investors are an increasingly powerful force in corporate America and actively use their positions of concentrated ownership to force managers and boards of directors to make decisions that maximize a firm's value.

- In the United States and the United Kingdom, a firm's board of directors, composed of insiders, related outsiders, and outsiders, is a governance mechanism expected to represent shareholders' collective interests. The percentage of outside directors on many boards now exceeds the percentage of inside directors. Through the implementation of the SOX Act, outsiders are expected to be more independent of a firm's top-level managers compared with directors selected from inside the firm.

- Executive compensation is a highly visible and often criticized governance mechanism. Salary, bonuses, and long-term incentives are used to strengthen the alignment between managers' and shareholders' interests. A firm's board of directors is responsible for determining the effectiveness of the firm's executive compensation system. An effective system elicits managerial decisions that are in shareholders' best interests.

- In general, evidence suggests that shareholders and boards of directors have become more vigilant in their control of managerial decisions. Nonetheless, these mechanisms are insufficient to govern managerial behavior in many large companies. Therefore, the market for corporate control is an important governance mechanism. Although it, too, is imperfect, the market for corporate control has been effective in causing corporations to combat inefficient diversification and to implement more effective strategic decisions.

- Corporate governance structures used in Germany and Japan differ from each other and from the structure used in the United States. Historically, the U.S. governance structure focused on maximizing shareholder value. In Germany, employees, as a stakeholder group, take a more prominent role in governance. By contrast, until recently, Japanese shareholders played virtually no role in the monitoring and control of top-level managers. However, now Japanese firms are being challenged by "activist" shareholders. Internationally, all these systems are becoming increasingly similar, as are many governance systems both in developed countries, such as France and Spain, and in transitional economies, such as Russia and China.

- Effective governance mechanisms ensure that the interests of all stakeholders are served. Thus, long-term strategic success results when firms are governed in ways that permit at least minimal satisfaction of capital market stakeholders (e.g., shareholders), product market stakeholders (e.g., customers and suppliers), and organizational stakeholders (managerial and nonmanagerial employees; see Chapter 2). Moreover, effective governance produces ethical behavior in the formulation and implementation of strategies.

Review Questions

1. What is corporate governance? What factors account for the considerable amount of attention corporate governance receives from several parties, including shareholder activists, business press writers, and academic scholars? Why is governance necessary to control managers' decisions?

2. What does it mean to say that ownership is separated from managerial control in the modern corporation? Why does this separation exist?

3. What is an agency relationship? What is managerial opportunism? What assumptions do owners of modern corporations make about managers as agents?

4. How is each of the three internal governance mechanisms—ownership concentration, boards of directors, and executive

compensation—used to align the interests of managerial agents with those of the firm's owners?

5. What trends exist regarding executive compensation? What is the effect of the increased use of long-term incentives on executives' strategic decisions?

6. What is the market for corporate control? What conditions generally cause this external governance mechanism to become active? How does the mechanism constrain top executives' decisions and actions?

7. What is the nature of corporate governance in Germany and Japan as well as in emerging economies?

8. How can corporate governance foster ethical strategic decisions and behaviors on the part of managers as agents?

Notes

1. C. Thomas, D. Kidd, & C. Fernández-Aráoz, 2007, Are you underutilizing your board? *MIT Sloan Management Review*, 48(2): 71–76; D. C. Carey &, M. Patsalos-Fox, 2006, Shaping strategy from the boardroom. *McKinsey Quarterly*, (3): 90–94; K. Hendry & G. C. Kiel, 2004, The role of the board in firm strategy: Integrating agency and organizational control perspectives, *Corporate Governance*, 12(4), 500–520.

2. J. B. Wade, C. A. O'Reilly, & T. G. Pollock, 2006, Overpaid CEOs and underpaid managers: Fairness and executive compensation, *Organization Science*, 17: 527–544; A. Henderson & J. Fredrickson, 2001, Top management team coordination needs and the CEO pay gap: A competitive test of economic and behavioral views, *Academy of Management Journal*, 44: 96–117.

3. A. D. F. Penalva, 2006, Governance structure and the weighting of performance measures in CEO compensation, *Review of Accounting Studies*, 11: 463–493; S. Werner, H. L. Tosi, & L. Gomez-Mejia, 2005, Organizational governance and employee pay: How ownership structure affects the firm's compensation strategy, *Strategic Management Journal*, 26: 377–384.

4. C. Crossland & D. C. Hambrick, 2007, How national systems differ in their constraints on corporate executives: A study of CEO effects in three countries, *Strategic Management Journal*, 28: 767–789; M. D. Lynall, B. R. Golden, & A. J. Hillman, 2003, Board composition from adolescence to maturity: A multitheoretic view, *Academy of Management Review*, 28: 416–431.

5. M. A. Rutherford, A. K. Buchholtz, & J. A. Brown, 2007, Examining the relationships between monitoring and incentives in corporate governance, *Journal of Management Studies* 44: 414–430; C. M. Daily, D. R. Dalton, & A. A. Cannella, 2003, Corporate governance: Decades of dialogue and data, *Academy of Management Review*, 28: 371–382; P. Stiles, 2001, The impact of the board on strategy: An empirical examination, *Journal of Management Studies*, 38: 627–650.

6. C. J. Prince, 2006, When bad things happen to good CEOs, *Chief Executive*, October, 52–55; M. S. Schwartz, T. W. Dunfee, & M. J. Kline, 2005, Tone at the top: An ethics code for directors? *Journal of Business Ethics*, 58: 79–100; D. Finegold, E. E. Lawler III, & J. Conger, 2001, Building a better board, *Journal of Business Strategy*, 22(6): 33–37.

7. E. F. Fama & M. C. Jensen, 1983, Separation of ownership and control, *Journal of Law and Economics*, 26: 301–325.

8. C. Hymowitz, 2004, Corporate Governance (a special report); Experiments in corporate governance: Finding the right way to improve board oversight isn't easy; but plenty of companies are trying, *Wall Street Journal*, June 21, R1.

9. I. Le Breton-Miller & D. Miller, 2006, Why do some family businesses out-compete? Governance, long-term orientations, and sustainable capability, *Entrepreneurship Theory and Practice*, 30: 731–746; M. Carney, 2005, Corporate governance and competitive advantage in family-controlled firms, *Entrepreneurship Theory and Practice*, 29: 249–265; R. Charan, 1998,

How Corporate Boards Create Competitive Advantage, San Francisco: Jossey-Bass.

10. G. J. Nicholson & G. C. Kiel, 2007, Can directors impact performance? A case-based test of three theories of corporate governance, *Corporate Governance*, 15(4): 585–608; G. J. Nicholson & G. C. Kiel, 2004, Breakthrough board performance: How to harness your board's intellectual capital, *Corporate Governance*, 4(1): 5–23; A. Cannella Jr., A. Pettigrew, & D. Hambrick, 2001, Upper echelons: Donald Hambrick on executives and strategy, *Academy of Management Executive*, 15(3): 36–52.

11. X. Wu, 2005, Corporate governance and corruption: A cross-country analysis, *Governance*, 18(2): 151–170; J. McGuire & S. Dow, 2002, The Japanese keiretsu system: An empirical analysis, *Journal of Business Research*, 55: 33–40.

12. R. E. Hoskisson, D. Yiu, & H. Kim, 2004, Corporate governance systems: Effects of capital and labor market congruency on corporate Innovation and global competitiveness, *Journal of High Technology Management*, 15: 293–315.

13. Crossland & Hambrick, How national systems differ in their constraints on corporate executives; R. Aguilera & G. Jackson, 2003, The cross-national diversity of corporate governance: Dimensions and determinants, *Academy of Management Review*, 28: 447–465.

14. R. P. Wright, 2004, Top managers' strategic cognitions of the strategy making process: Differences between high and low performing firms, *Journal of General Management*, 30(1): 61–78.

15. A. Bris & C. Cabous, 2006, In a merger, two companies come together and

integrate their distribution lines, brands, work forces, management teams, strategies and cultures, *Financial Times*, October 6, 1.

16. S. Sudarsanam & A. A. Mahate, 2006, Are friendly acquisitions too bad for shareholders and managers? Long-term value creation and top management turnover in hostile and friendly acquirers, *British Journal of Management: Supplement*, 17(1): S7–S30; T. Moeller, 2005, Let's make a deal! How shareholder control impacts merger payoffs, *Journal of Financial Economics*, 76(1): 167–190; M. A. Hitt, R. E. Hoskisson, R. A. Johnson, & D. D. Moesel, 1996, The market for corporate control and firm innovation, *Academy of Management Journal*, 39: 1084–1119.

17. R. E. Hoskisson, M. A. Hitt, R. A. Johnson, & W. Grossman, 2002, Conflicting voices: The effects of ownership heterogeneity and internal governance on corporate strategy, *Academy of Management Journal*, 45: 697–716.

18. G. E. Davis & T. A. Thompson, 1994, A social movement perspective on corporate control, *Administrative Science Quarterly*, 39: 141–173.

19. R. Bricker & N. Chandar, 2000, Where Berle and Means went wrong: A reassessment of capital market agency and financial reporting, *Accounting, Organizations, and Society*, 25: 529–554; M. A. Eisenberg, 1989, The structure of corporation law, *Columbia Law Review*, 89(7): 1461, as cited in R. A. G. Monks & N. Minow, 1995, *Corporate Governance*, Cambridge, MA: Blackwell Business, 7.

20. R. M. Wiseman & L. R. Gomez-Mejia, 1999, A behavioral agency model of managerial risk taking, *Academy of Management Review*, 23: 133–153.

21. T. Zellweger, 2007, Time horizon, costs of equity capital, and generic investment strategies of firms, *Family Business Review*, 20(1): 1–15; R. C. Anderson & D. M. Reeb, 2004, Board composition: Balancing family influence in S&P 500 firms, *Administrative Science Quarterly*, 49: 209–237.

22. Carney, Corporate governance and competitive advantage in family-controlled firms; N. Anthanassiou, W. F. Crittenden, L. M. Kelly, & P. Marquez, 2002, Founder centrality effects on the Mexican family firm's top management group: Firm culture, strategic vision and goals and firm performance, *Journal of World Business*, 37: 139–150.

23. M. Santiago-Castro & C. J. Brown, 2007, Ownership structure and minority rights: A Latin American view, *Journal of Economics and Business*, 59: 430–442; M. Carney & E. Gedajlovic, 2003, Strategic innovation and the administrative heritage of East Asian family business groups, *Asia Pacific Journal of Management*, 20: 5–26; D. Miller & I. Le Breton-Miller, 2003, Challenge versus advantage in family business, *Strategic Organization*, 1: 127–134.

24. E. E. Fama, 1980, Agency problems and the theory of the firm, *Journal of Political Economy*, 88: 288–307.

25. Rutherford, Buchholtz, & Brown, Examining the relationships between monitoring and incentives in corporate governance; D. Dalton, C. Daily, T. Certo, & R. Roengpitya, 2003, Meta-analyses of financial performance and equity: Fusion or confusion? *Academy of Management Journal*, 46: 13–26; M. Jensen & W. Meckling, 1976, Theory of the firm: Managerial behavior, agency costs, and ownership structure, *Journal of Financial Economics*, 11: 305–360.

26. G. C. Rodríguez, C. A.-D. Espejo, & R. Valle Cabrera, 2007, Incentives management during privatization: An agency perspective, *Journal of Management Studies*, 44: 536–560; D. C. Hambrick, S. Finkelstein, & A. C. Mooney, 2005, Executive job demands: New insights for explaining strategic decisions and leader behaviors, *Academy of Management Review*, 30: 472–491.

27. T. G. Habbershon, 2006, Commentary: A framework for managing the familiness and agency advantages in family firms, *Entrepreneurship Theory and Practice*, 30: 879–886; M. G. Jacobides & D. C. Croson, 2001, Information policy: Shaping the value of agency relationships, *Academy of Management Review*, 26: 202–223.

28. S.-H. Kang, P. Kumar, & H. Lee, 2006, Agency and corporate investment: The role of executive compensation and corporate governance, *Journal of Business*, 79: 1127–1147; H. E. Ryan Jr. & R. A. Wiggins III, 2004, Who is in whose pocket? Director compensation, board independence, and barriers to effective monitoring, *Journal of Financial Economics*, 73: 497–524.

29. Y. Y. Kor, 2006, Direct and interaction effects of top management team and board compositions on R&D investment strategy, *Strategic Management Journal*, 27: 1081–1099.

30. A. Ghosh, D. Moon, & K. Tandon, 2007, CEO ownership and discretionary investments, *Journal of Business Finance & Accounting*, 34: 819–839; M. W. Peng, 2004, Outside directors and firm performance during institutional transitions, *Strategic Management Journal*, 25: 453–471; A. J. Hillman & T. Dalziel, 2003, Boards of directors and firm performance: Integrating agency and resource dependence perspectives, *Academy of Management Review*, 28: 383–396.

31. S. Ghoshal & P. Moran, 1996, Bad for practice: A critique of the transaction cost theory, *Academy of Management Review*, 21: 13–47; O. E. Williamson, 1996, *The Mechanisms of Governance*, New York: Oxford University Press, 6.

32. E. Kang, 2006, Investors' perceptions of managerial opportunism in corporate acquisitions: The moderating role of environmental condition, *Corporate Governance*, 14: 377–387; R. W. Coff & P. M. Lee, 2003, Insider trading as a vehicle

to appropriate rent from R&D. *Strategic Management Journal*, 24: 183–190; C. C. Chen, M. W. Peng, & P. A. Saparito, 2002, Individualism, collectivism, and opportunism: A cultural perspective on transaction cost economics, *Journal of Management*, 28: 567–583.

33. Fama, Agency problems and the theory of the firm.

34. P. Jiraporn, Y. Sang Kim, W. N. Davidson, & M. Singh, 2006, Corporate governance, shareholder rights and firm diversification: An empirical analysis, *Journal of Banking & Finance*, 30: 947–963; R. C. Anderson, T. W. Bates, J. M. Bizjak, & M. L. Lemmon, 2000, Corporate governance and firm diversification, *Financial Management*, 29(1): 5–22; R. E. Hoskisson & T. A. Turk, 1990, Corporate restructuring: Governance and control limits of the internal market, *Academy of Management Review*, 15: 459–477.

35. G. P. Baker & B. J. Hall, 2004, CEO incentives and firm size, *Journal of Labor Economics*, 22: 767–798; R. Bushman, Q. Chen, E. Engel, & A. Smith, 2004, Financial accounting information, organizational complexity and corporate governance systems, *Journal of Accounting & Economics*, 7: 167–201; M. A. Geletkanycz, B. K. Boyd, & S. Finkelstein, 2001, The strategic value of CEO external directorate networks: Implications for CEO compensation, *Strategic Management Journal*, 9: 889–898.

36. S. W. Geiger & L. H. Cashen, 2007, Organizational size and CEO compensation: The moderating effect of diversification in downscoping organizations, *Journal of Managerial Issues*, 9(2): 233–252; Y. Grinstein & P. Hribar, 2004, CEO compensation and incentives: Evidence from M&A bonuses, *Journal of Financial Economics*, 73: 119–143; P. Wright, M. Kroll, & D. Elenkov, 2002, Acquisition returns, increase in firm size and chief executive officer compensation: The moderating role of monitoring, *Academy of Management Journal*, 45: 599–608.

37. S. Rajgopal, T. Shevlin, & V. Zamora, 2006, CEOs' outside employment opportunities and the lack of relative performance evaluation in compensation contracts, *Journal of Finance*, 61: 1813–1844; Gomez-Mejia, Nunez-Nickel, & Gutierrez, The role of family ties in agency contracts.

38. J. Weber, 2007, The accidental CEO (well, not really), Kellogg needed a new boss, fast. Here's how it groomed insider David Mackay, *BusinessWeek*, April 23, 65.

39. M. S. Jensen, 1986, Agency costs of free cash flow, corporate finance, and takeovers, *American Economic Review*, 76: 323–329.

40. A. V. Douglas, 2007, Managerial opportunism and proportional corporate payout policies, *Managerial Finance*, 33(1): 26–42; M. Jensen & E. Zajac, 2004, Corporate elites and corporate strategy: How demographic preferences and structural position shape the scope of the firm, *Strategic Management Journal*,

25: 507–524; T. H. Brush, P. Bromiley, & M. Hendrickx, 2000, The free cash flow hypothesis for sales growth and firm performance, *Strategic Management Journal*, 21: 455–472.

41. J. Lunsford & B. Steinberg, 2006, Conglomerates' conundrum, *Wall Street Journal*, September 14, B1, B7; K. Ramaswamy, M. Li, & B. S. P. Petitt, 2004, Who drives unrelated diversification? A study of Indian manufacturing firms, *Asia Pacific Journal of Management*, 21: 403–423; Ramaswamy, Li, & Veliyath, Variations in ownership behavior and propensity to diversify.

42. K. B. Lee, M. W. Peng & K. Lee, 2007, From diversification premium to diversification discount during institutional transitions, *Journal of World Business*, forthcoming; A. Desai, M. Kroll, & P. Wright, 2005, Outside board monitoring and the economic outcomes of acquisitions: A test of the substitution hypothesis, *Journal of Business Research*, 58: 926–934; P. Wright, M. Kroll, A. Lado, & B. Van Ness, 2002, The structure of ownership and corporate acquisition strategies, *Strategic Management Journal*, 23: 41–53.

43. T. K. Berry, J. M. Bizjak, M. L. Lemmon, & L. Naveen, 2006, Organizational complexity and CEO labor markets: Evidence from diversified firms, *Journal of Corporate Finance*, 12: 797–817; R. Rajan, H. Servaes, & L. Zingales, 2001, The cost of diversity: The diversification discount and inefficient investment, *Journal of Finance*, 55: 35–79; A. Sharma, 1997, Professional as agent: Knowledge asymmetry in agency exchange, *Academy of Management Review*, 22: 758–798.

44. V. Chhaochharia & Y. Grinstein, 2007, Corporate governance and firm value: The impact of the 2002 governance rules, *Journal of Finance*, 62: 1789–1825; A. Borrus, L. Lavelle, D. Brady, M. Arndt, & J. Weber, 2005, Death, taxes and Sarbanes-Oxley? Executives may be frustrated with the law's burdens, but corporate performance is here to stay, *BusinessWeek*, January 17, 28–31.

45. D. Reilly, 2006, Checks on internal controls pay off, *Wall Street Journal*, August 10, C3.

46. S. E. Needleman, 2006, Sarbanes-Oxley creates special demand, *Wall Street Journal*, May 16, B8; T. J. Healey, 2007, Sarbox was the right medicine, *Wall Street Journal*, August 9, A13.

47. G. Ip, 2006, Is a U.S. listing worth the effort?; Premiums paid for shares in foreign firms are reduced since crackdown, study finds, *Wall Street Journal*, November 28, C1.

48. J. D. McKinnon & C. Conkey, 2007, Bush gives hope to foes of Sarbanes-Oxley law, *Wall Street Journal*, February 1, A4.

49. F. Navissi & V. Naiker, 2006, Institutional ownership and corporate value, *Managerial Finance*, 32: 247–256; A. de Miguel, J. Pindado, & C. de la Torre, 2004, Ownership structure and firm value: New evidence from Spain, *Strategic Management Journal*, 25: 1199–1207; J. Coles, N. Sen, & V. McWilliams, 2001,

An examination of the relationship of governance mechanisms to performance, *Journal of Management*, 27: 23–50.

50. Jiraporn, Kim, Davidson, & Singh, Corporate governance, shareholder rights and firm diversification; M. Singh, I. Mathur, & K. C. Gleason, 2004, Governance and performance implications of diversification strategies: Evidence from large U.S. firms, *Financial Review*, 39: 489–526; R. E. Hoskisson, R. A. Johnson, & D. D. Moesel, 1994, Corporate divestiture intensity in restructuring firms: Effects of governance, strategy, and performance, *Academy of Management Journal*, 37: 1207–1251.

51. G. Iannotta, G. Nocera, & A. Sironi, 2007, Ownership structure, risk and performance in the European banking industry, *Journal of Banking & Finance*, 31: 2127–2149.

52. De Miguel, Pindado, & de la Torre, Ownership structure and firm value: New evidence from Spain.

53. B. Villalonga & R. Amit, 2006, How do family ownership, control and management affect firm value? *Journal of Financial Economics*, 80: 385–417; R. C. Anderson & D. M. Reeb, 2004, Board composition: Balancing family influence in S&P 500 firms, *Administrative Science Quarterly*, 49: 209–237.

54. S. J. Chang, 2003, Ownership structure, expropriation and performance of group-affiliated companies in Korea, *Academy of Management Journal*, 46: 238–253.

55. A. Berle & G. Means, 1932, *The Modern Corporation and Private Property*, New York: Macmillan.

56. M. Gietzmann, 2006, Disclosure of timely and forward-looking statements and strategic management of major institutional ownership, *Long Range Planning*, 39(4): 409–427; B. Ajinkya, S. Bhojraj, & P. Sengupta, 2005, The association between outside directors, institutional investors and the properties of management earnings forecasts, *Journal of Accounting Research*, 43: 343–376; M. P. Smith, 1996, Shareholder activism by institutional investors: Evidence from CalPERS, *Journal of Finance*, 51: 227–252.

57. Hoskisson, Hitt, Johnson, & Grossman, Conflicting voices; C. M. Daily, 1996, Governance patterns in bankruptcy reorganizations, *Strategic Management Journal*, 17: 355–375.

58. M. M. Cornett, A. J. Marcus, A. Saunders, & H. Tehranian, 2007, The impact of institutional ownership on corporate operating performance, *Journal of Banking & Finance*, 3: 1771–1794; A. Picou & M. J. Rubach, 2006, Does good governance matter to institutional investors? Evidence from the enactment of corporate governance guidelines, *Journal of Business Ethics*, 65(1), 55–67.

59. T. W. Briggs, 2007, Corporate governance and the new hedge fund activism: An empirical analysis. *Journal of Corporation Law*, 32(4): 681–723,725–738; K. Rebeiz, 2001, Corporate governance effectiveness in American corporations: A survey, *International Management Journal*, 18(1): 74–80.

60. J. Grant & F. Guerrera, 2007, CalPERS files twice as many "shareholder proposals," *Financial Times*, August 14, 19.

61. S. Thurm, When investor activism doesn't pay, *Wall Street Journal*, September 12, A2; S. M. Jacoby, 2007, Principles and agents: CalPERS and corporate governance in Japan, *Corporate Governance*, 15(1): 5–15; L. Tihanyi, R. A. Johnson, R. E. Hoskisson, & M. A. Hitt, 2003, Institutional ownership differences and international diversification: The effects of boards of directors and technological opportunity, *Academy of Management Journal*, 46: 195–211; Hoskisson, Hitt, Johnson, & Grossman, Conflicting voices; P. David, M. A. Hitt, & J. Gimeno, 2001, The role of institutional investors in influencing R&D, *Academy of Management Journal*, 44: 144–157.

62. M. A. A. Khan, 2006, Corporate governance and the role of institutional investors in India, *Journal of Asia-Pacific Business*, 7(2): 37–54.

63. V. Krivogorsky, 2006, Ownership, board structure, and performance in continental Europe, *International Journal of Accounting*, 41(2): 176–197; S. Thomsen & T. Pedersen, 2000, Ownership structure and economic performance in the largest European companies, *Strategic Management Journal*, 21: 689–705.

64. C. M. Dalton & D. R. Dalton, 2006, Corporate governance best practices: The proof is in the process, *Journal of Business Strategy*, 27(4), 5–7; R. V. Aguilera, 2005, Corporate governance and director accountability: An institutional comparative perspective, *British Journal of Management*, 16(S1), S39–S53; E. H. Fram, 2004, Governance reform: It's only just begun, *Business Horizons*, 47(6): 10–14.

65. Thomas, Kidd, & Fernández-Aráoz, Are you underutilizing your board?; Hillman & Dalziel, Boards of directors and firm performance.

66. L. Bonazzi, & S. M. N. Islam, 2007, Agency theory and corporate governance: A study of the effectiveness of board in their monitoring of the CEO, *Journal of Modeling in Management*, 2(1): 7–23; Rebeiz, Corporate governance effectiveness in American corporations.

67. N. Chipalkatti, Q. V. Le, & M. Rishi, 2007, Portfolio flows to emerging capital markets: Do corporate transparency and public governance matter? *Business and Society Review*, 112(2): 227–249; J. Chidley, 2001, Why boards matter, *Canadian Business*, October 29, 6; D. P. Forbes & F. J. Milliken, 1999, Cognition and corporate governance: Understanding boards of directors as strategic decision-making groups, *Academy of Management Review*, 24: 489–505.

68. Krivogorsky, Ownership, board structure, and performance in continental Europe; Hoskisson, Hitt, Johnson, & Grossman, Conflicting voices; B. D. Baysinger & R. E. Hoskisson, 1990, The composition of

boards of directors and strategic control: Effects on corporate strategy, *Academy of Management Review*, 15: 72–87.

69. E. E. Lawler III & D. Finegold, 2006, Who's in the boardroom and does it matter: The impact of having non-director executives attend board meetings, *Organizational Dynamics*, 35(1): 106–115; M. Carpenter & J. Westphal, 2001, Strategic context of external network ties: Examining the impact of director appointments on board involvement in strategic decision making, *Academy of Management Journal*, 44: 639–660; E. J. Zajac & J. D. Westphal, 1996, Director reputation, CEO-board power, and the dynamics of board interlocks, *Administrative Science Quarterly*, 41: 507–529.

70. E. M. Fich & A. Shivdasani, 2006, Are busy boards effective monitors? *Journal of Finance*, 61: 689–724; J. Westphal & L. Milton, 2000, How experience and network ties affect the influence of demographic minorities on corporate boards, *Administrative Science Quarterly*, 45(2): 366–398.

71. Fich & Shivdasani, Are busy boards effective monitors; S. T. Petra, 2005, Do outside independent directors strengthen corporate boards? *Corporate Governance*, 5(1): 55–65.

72. S. K. Lee & L. R. Carlson, 2007, The changing board of directors: Board independence in S & P 500 Firm, *Journal of Organizational Culture, Communication and Conflict*, 11(1): 31–41.

73. R. C. Pozen, 2006, Before you split that CEO/Chair, *Harvard Business Review*, 84(4): 26–28; J. W. Lorsch & A. Zelleke, 2005, Should the CEO be the Chairman, *MIT Sloan Management Review*, 46(2): 71–74.

74. A. Murray, 2007, *Revolt in the Boardroom: The New Rules of Power in Corporate America*, New York: HarperCollins.

75. E. White & T. Herrick, 2006, Ethical breaches pose dilemma for boards: When to fire a CEO? *Wall Street Journal*, February 16, B1.

76. Fich & Shivdasani, Are busy boards effective monitors; J. Roberts, T. McNulty, &, P. Stiles, 2005, Beyond agency conceptions of the work of the non-executive director: Creating accountability in the boardroom, *British Journal of Management*, 16(S1): S5–S26.

77. Fich & Shivdasani, Are busy boards effective monitors; S. Zahra, 1996, Governance, ownership and corporate entrepreneurship among the *Fortune* 500: The moderating impact of industry technological opportunity, *Academy of Management Journal*, 39: 1713–1735.

78. Baysinger, & Hoskisson, Board composition and strategic control: The effect on corporate strategy.

79. Lawler & Finegold, Who's in the boardroom and does it matter?; E. E. Lawler III & D. L. Finegold, 2005, The changing face of corporate boards, *MIT Sloan Management Review*, 46(2): 67–70; A. Conger, E. E. Lawler, & D. L. Finegold, 2001, *Corporate Boards: New Strategies for Adding Value at the Top*, San Francisco: Jossey-Bass; J. A. Conger, D. Finegold, & E. E. Lawler III, 1998, Appraising boardroom performance, *Harvard Business Review*, 76(1): 136–148.

80. A. L. Boone, L. C. Field, J. M. Karpoff, & C. G. Raheja, 2007, The determinants of corporate board size and composition: An empirical analysis, *Journal of Financial Economics*, 85(1): 66–101; J. Marshall, 2001, As boards shrink, responsibilities grow, *Financial Executive*, 17(4): 36–39.

81. L. Brannen, 2007, A center lane for governance, *Business Finance*, August, 25.

82. T. Long, 2007, The evolution of FTSE 250 boards of directors: Key factors influencing board performance and effectiveness, *Journal of General Management*, 32(3): 45–60; S. Finkelstein & A. C. Mooney, 2003, Not the usual suspects: How to use board process to make boards better, *Academy of Management Executive*, 17: 101–113.

83. J. L. Koors, 2006 Director pay: A work in progress, *The Corporate Governance Advisor*, 14(5): 25–31; W. Shen, 2005, Improve board effectiveness: The need for incentives, *British Journal of Management*, 16(S1): S81–S89; M. Gerety, C. Hoi, & A. Robin, 2001, Do shareholders benefit from the adoption of incentive pay for directors? *Financial Management*, 30: 45–61; D. C. Hambrick & E. M. Jackson, 2000, Outside directors with a stake: The linchpin in improving governance, *California Management Review*, 42(4): 108–127.

84. Y. Deutsch, T. Keil, & T. Laamanen, 2007, Decision making in acquisitions: the effect of outside directors' compensation on acquisition patterns, *Journal of Management*, 33(1): 30–56.

85. A. J. Hillman, C. Shropshire, & A. A. Cannella, Jr. 2007, Organizational predictors of women on corporate boards, *Academy of Management Journal*, 50: 941–952; I. Filatotchev & S. Toms, 2003, Corporate governance, strategy and survival in a declining industry: A study of UK cotton textile companies, *Journal of Management Studies*, 40: 895–920.

86. 2007, Wall St. Roundup: pay increases for CEOs fall below 10% in 2006, *Los Angeles Times*, April 3, C4.

87. L. A. Bebchuk & J. M. Fried, 2006, Pay without performance: Overview of the issues, *Academy of Management Perspectives*, 20(1): 5–24; L. A. Bebchuk & J. M. Fried, 2004, *Pay Without Performance: The Unfulfilled Promise of Executive Compensation*, Cambridge, MA: Harvard University Press; M. A. Carpenter & W. G. Sanders, 2002, Top management team compensation: The missing link between CEO pay and firm performance, *Strategic Management Journal*, 23: 367–375.

88. K. Rehbein, 2007, Explaining CEO compensation: How do talent, governance, and markets fit in? *Academy of Management Perspectives*, 21(1): 75–77; J. S. Miller, R. M. Wiseman, & L. R. Gomez-Mejia, 2002, The fit between CEO compensation design and firm risk, *Academy of Management Journal*, 45: 745–756; L. Gomez-Mejia & R. M. Wiseman, 1997, Reframing executive compensation: An assessment and outlook, *Journal of Management*, 23: 291–374.

89. M. Larraza-Kintana, R. M. Wiseman, L. R. Gomez-Mejia, & T. M. Welbourne, 2007, Disentangling compensation and employment risks using the behavioral agency model, *Strategic Management Journal*, 28: 1001–1019; J. McGuire & E. Matta, 2003, CEO stock options: The silent dimension of ownership, *Academy of Management Journal*, 46: 255–265; W. G. Sanders & M. A. Carpenter, 1998, Internationalization and firm governance: The roles of CEO compensation, top team composition and board structure, *Academy of Management Journal*, 41: 158–178.

90. J. P. O'Connor, R. L. Priem, J. E. Coombs, & K. M. Gilley, 2006, Do CEO stock options prevent or promote fraudulent financial reporting? *Academy of Management Journal*, 49: 483–500.

91. S. O'Donnell, 2000, Managing foreign subsidiaries: Agents of headquarters, or an interdependent network? *Strategic Management Journal*, 21: 521–548; K. Roth & S. O'Donnell, 1996, Foreign subsidiary compensation: An agency theory perspective, *Academy of Management Journal*, 39: 678–703.

92. A. Ghosh, 2006, Determination of executive compensation in an emerging economy: Evidence from India, *Emerging Markets, Finance & Trade*, 42(3): 66–90; K. Ramaswamy, R. Veliyath, & L. Gomes, 2000, A study of the determinants of CEO compensation in India, *Management International Review*, 40(2): 167–191.

93. C. L. Staples, 2007, Board globalization in the world's largest TNCs 1993–2005, *Corporate Governance*, 15(2): 311–32.

94. L. K. Meulbroek, 2001, The efficiency of equity-linked compensation: Understanding the full cost of awarding executive stock options, *Financial Management*, 30(2): 5–44.

95. C. E. Devers, R. M. Wiseman, & R. M. Holmes Jr., 2007, The effects of endowment and loss aversion in managerial stock option valuation, *Academy of Management Journal*, 50: 191–208; J. C. Bettis, J. M. Biziak, & M. L. Lemmon, 2005, Exercise behavior, valuation and the incentive effects of employee stock options, *Journal of Financial Economics*, 76: 445–470.

96. M. Klausner, 2007, Reducing directors' legal risk, *Harvard Business Review*, 85(4), 28; T. G. Pollock, H. M. Fischer, & J. B. Wade, 2002, The role of politics in repricing executive options, *Academy of Management Journal*, 45: 1172–1182; M. E. Carter & L. J. Lynch, 2001, An examination of executive stock option repricing, *Journal of Financial Economics*, 59: 207–225; D. Chance, R. Kumar, & R. Todd, 2001, The "repricing" of executive stock options, *Journal of Financial Economics*, 59: 129–154.

97. Picou & Rubach, Does good governance matter to institutional investors? Evidence from the enactment of corporate governance guidelines; J. C. Hartzell & L. T. Starks, 2003, Institutional investors and executive compensation, *Journal of Finance,* 58: 2351–2374.

98. R. Sinha, 2006, Regulation: The market for corporate control and corporate governance, *Global Finance Journal,* 16(3): 264–282; R. Coff, 2002, Bidding wars over R&D intensive firms: Knowledge, opportunism and the market for corporate control, *Academy of Management Journal,* 46: 74–85; Hitt, Hoskisson, Johnson, & Moesel, The market for corporate control and firm innovation.

99. R. W. Masulis, C. Wang, & F. Xie, 2007, Corporate governance and acquirer returns, *Journal of Finance,* 62(4), 1851–1889; R. Sinha, 2004, The role of hostile takeovers in corporate governance, *Applied Financial Economics,* 14: 1291–1305; D. Goldstein, 2000, Hostile takeovers as corporate governance? Evidence from 1980s, *Review of Political Economy,* 12: 381–402.

100. O. Kini, W. Kracaw, & S. Mian, 2004, The nature of discipline by corporate takeovers, *Journal of Finance,* 59: 1511–1551.

101. Masulis, Wang, & Xie, Corporate governance and acquirer returns.

102. J. P. Walsh & R. Kosnik, 1993, Corporate raiders and their disciplinary role in the market for corporate control, *Academy of Management Journal,* 36: 671–700.

103. T. W. Briggs, 2007, Corporate governance and a new hedge fund activism: *Empirical Analysis,* 32(4): 681–723.

104. N. Naik & M. Tapley, 2007, Demystifying hedge funds, *Business Strategy Review,* 18(2): 68–72.

105. Thurm, When investor activism doesn't pay.

106. R. B. Adams & D. Ferreira, 2007, A theory of friendly boards, *Journal of Finance,* 62: 217–250.

107. J Cresswell, 2006, Gilded paychecks: Pay packages allow executives to jump ship with less risk, *New York Times,* http://www.nyt.com, December 29.

108. Ibid.

109. M. Maremont, 2007, Scholars link success of firms to lives of CEOs, *Wall Street Journal,* September 5, A1, A15; J. Hartzell, E. Ofek, & D. Yermack, 2004, What's in it for me? CEOs whose firms are acquired, *Review of Financial Studies,* 17: 37–61.

110. J. McCary, 2007, Foreign investments rise, *Wall Street Journal,* June 6, A5; K. Shimizu, M. A. Hitt, D. Vaidyanath, & P. Vincenzo, 2004, Theoretical foundations of cross-border mergers and acquisitions: A review of current research and recommendations for the future, *Journal of International Management,* 10: 307–353; M. A. Hitt & V. Pisano, 2003, The cross-border merger and acquisition strategy, *Management Research,* 1: 133–144.

111. Sinha, Regulation: The market for corporate control and corporate governance; J. Anand & A. Delios, 2002,

Absolute and relative resources as determinants of international acquisitions, *Strategic Management Journal,* 23: 119–134.

112. J. Harford, 2003, Takeover bids and target directors' incentives: The impact of a bid on directors' wealth and board seats, *Journal of Financial Economics,* 69: 51–83; S. Chatterjee, J. S. Harrison, & D. D. Bergh, 2003, Failed takeover attempts, corporate governance, and refocusing, *Strategic Management Journal,* 24: 87–96.

113. E. Webb, 2006, Relationships between board structure and takeover defenses, *Corporate Governance,* 6(3): 268–180; C. Sundaramurthy, J. M. Mahoney, & J. T. Mahoney, 1997, Board structure, antitakeover provisions, and stockholder wealth, *Strategic Management Journal,* 18: 231–246.

114. J. Jargon & J. Vuocolo, 2007, Sara Lee CEO challenged on anti-takeover defenses, *Wall Street Journal,* May 11, B4.

115. W. G. Sanders & M. A. Carpenter, 2003, Strategic satisficing? A behavioral-agency theory perspective on stock repurchase program announcements, *Academy of Management Journal,* 46: 160–178; J. Westphal & E. Zajac, 2001, Decoupling policy from practice: The case of stock repurchase programs, *Administrative Science Quarterly,* 46: 202–228.

116. O. Faleye, 2007, Classified boards, firm value, and managerial entrenchment, *Journal of Financial Economics,* 83: 501–529.

117. 2007, Leaders: Pay slips; management in Europe, *Economist,* June 23, 14: A. Cala, 2005, Carrying golden parachutes; France joins EU trend to reign in executive severance deals, *Wall Street Journal,* June 8, A13.

118. J. A. Pearce II & R. B. Robinson Jr., 2004, Hostile takeover defenses that maximize shareholder wealth, *Business Horizons,* 47(5): 15–24.

119. G. Wright, 2007, Home Depot reports pay for its CEOs, *Wall Street Journal,* April 16, B5.

120. Walsh & Kosnik, Corporate raiders.

121. A. Chakraborty & R. Arnott, 2001, Takeover defenses and dilution: A welfare analysis, *Journal of Financial and Quantitative Analysis,* 36: 311–334.

122. M Wolf, 2007, The new capitalism: How unfettered finance is fast reshaping the global economy, *Financial Times,* June 19, 13: C. Millar, T. I. Eldomiaty, C. J. Choi, & B. Hilton, 2005, Corporate governance and institutional transparency in emerging markets, *Journal of Business Ethics,* 59: 163–174; D. Norburn, B. K. Boyd, M. Fox, & M. Muth, 2000, International corporate governance reform, *European Business Journal,* 12(3): 116–133; M. Useem, 1998, Corporate leadership in a globalizing equity market, *Academy of Management Executive,* 12(3): 43–59.

123. S. M. Jacoby, 2004, *The Embedded Corporation: Corporate Governance and Employment Relations in Japan and the*

United States, Princeton, NJ: Princeton University Press.

124. P. Witt, 2004, The competition of international corporate governance systems—A German perspective, *Management International Review,* 44: 309–333; L. Nachum, 2003, Does nationality of ownership make any difference and if so, under what circumstances? Professional service MNEs in global competition, *Journal of International Management,* 9: 1–32.

125. Crossland & Hambrick, How national systems differ in their constraints on corporate executives; Aguilera & Jackson, The cross-national diversity of corporate governance: Dimensions and determinants.

126. Carney, Corporate governance and competitive advantage in family-controlled firms; S. Klein, 2000, Family businesses in Germany: Significance and structure, *Family Business Review,* 13: 157–181.

127. A. Tuschke & W. G. Sanders, 2003, Antecedents and consequences of corporate governance reform: The case of Germany, *Strategic Management Journal,* 24: 631–649; J. Edwards & M. Nibler, 2000, Corporate governance in Germany: The role of banks and ownership concentration, *Economic Policy,* 31: 237–268; E. R. Gedajlovic & D. M. Shapiro, 1998, Management and ownership effects: Evidence from five countries, *Strategic Management Journal,* 19: 533–553.

128. P. C. Fiss, 2006, Social influence effects and managerial compensation evidence from Germany, *Strategic Management Journal,* 27: 1013–1031; S. Douma, 1997, The two-tier system of corporate governance, *Long Range Planning,* 30(4): 612–615.

129. K Done, 2007, Tackling the many challenges of Airbus, *Financial Times,* July 17, 22.

130. P. C. Fiss & E. J. Zajac, 2004, The diffusion of ideas over contested terrain: The (non) adoption of a shareholder value orientation among German firms, *Administrative Science Quarterly,* 49: 501–534.

131. W. G. Sanders & A. C. Tuschke, 2007, The adoption of the institutionally contested organizational practices: The emergence of stock option pay in Germany, *Academy of Management Journal,* 57: 33–56.

132. T. Hoshi, A. K. Kashyap, & S. Fischer, 2001, *Corporate Financing and Governance in Japan,* Boston: MIT Press.

133. J. P. Charkham, 1994. *Keeping Good Companies: A Study of Corporate Governance in Five Countries.* New York: Oxford University Press, 70.

134. M. A. Hitt, H. Lee, & E. Yucel, 2002, The importance of social capital to the management of multinational enterprises: Relational networks among Asian and Western Firms, *Asia Pacific Journal of Management,* 19: 353–372.

135. W. P. Wan, D. W. Yiu, R. E. Hoskisson, & H. Kim, 2008, The performance implications of relationship banking during macroeconomic expansion and contraction: A study of Japanese banks' social relationships and overseas

expansion, *Journal of International Business Studies,* forthcoming.

136. Jacoby, *The embedded corporation;* P. M. Lee & H. M. O'Neill, 2003, Ownership structures and R&D investments of U.S. and Japanese firms: Agency and stewardship perspectives, *Academy of Management Journal,* 46: 212–225.

137. I. S. Dinc, 2006, Monitoring the monitors: The corporate governance in Japanese banks and their real estate lending in the 1980s, *Journal of Business,* 79(6): 3057–3081; A. Kawaura, 2004, Deregulation and governance: Plight of Japanese banks in the 1990s, *Applied Economics,* 36: 479–484; B. Bremner, 2001, Cleaning up the banks—finally, *BusinessWeek,* December 17, 86; 2000, Business: Japan's corporate-governance U-turn, *The Economist,* November 18, 73.

138. N. Isagawa, 2007, A theory of unwinding of cross-shareholding under managerial entrenchment, *Journal of Financial Research,* 30: 163–179.

139. C. L. Ahmadjian & G. E. Robbins, 2005, A clash of capitalisms: Foreign shareholders and corporate restructuring in 1990s Japan, *American Sociological Review,* 70: 451–471.

140. P. M. Lee, 2004, A comparison of ownership structures and innovations of

U.S. and Japanese firms, *Managerial and Decision Economics,* 26(1): 39–50; Lee & O'Neill, Ownership structures and R&D investments of U.S. and Japanese firms.

141. Y. Hayashi, 2005, Japan firms ponder private life, *Wall Street Journal,* August 1, C14.

142. E. Engel, R. M. Hayes, & X. Wang, 2007, The Sarbanes-Oxley Act and firms' going-private decisions, *Journal of Accounting & Economics,* 44(1/2): 116–145.

143. L. Santini, 2007, Rematch: KT&G vs. Steel Partners: Korean cigarette maker again angers an activist fund, *Wall Street Journal,* June 22, C5.

144. G. A. Fowler & J. Quin, 2007, China moves to boost transparency, but much is kept hidden, *Wall Street Journal,* April 25, A6.

145. T. J. Healey, 2007, Sarbox was the right medicine, *Wall Street Journal,* August 9, A13.

146. J. D. Hughes & J. H. Lee, 2007, The changing landscape of D & O liability, *Risk Management Journal,* January, 18–22.

147. C. Shropshire & A. J. Hillman, 2007, A longitudinal study of significant change in stakeholder management, *Business and Society,* 46(1): 63–87; S. Sharma & I. Henriques, 2005, Stakeholder influences on sustainability practices in the Canadian Forest products industry, *Strategic*

Management Journal, 26: 159–180; A. J. Hillman, G. D. Keim, & R. A. Luce, 2001, Board composition and stakeholder performance: Do stakeholder directors make a difference? *Business and Society,* 40: 295–314.

148. D. L. Gold & J. W. Dienhart, 2007, Business ethics in the corporate governance era: Domestic and international trends in transparency, regulation, and corporate governance, *Business and Society Review,* 112(2): 163–170; N. Demise, 2005, Business ethics and corporate governance in Japan, *Business and Society,* 44: 211–217.

149. L. Santini, 2006, Investor activism grows globally, but wins are rare, *Wall Street Journal,* July 3, C1.

150. R. V. Aguilera, D. E. Rupp, C. A. Williams, & J. Ganapathi, 2007, Putting the S back in corporate social responsibility: A multilevel theory of social change in organizations, *Academy of Management Review,* 32(3): 836–863; Caldwell & Karri, Organizational governance and ethical systems: A covenantal approach to building trust; A. Felo, 2001, Ethics programs, board involvement, and potential conflicts of interest in corporate governance, *Journal of Business Ethics,* 32: 205–218.

Organizational Structure and Controls

11

Studying this chapter should provide you with the strategic management knowledge needed to:

1. **Define organizational structure and controls and discuss the difference between strategic and financial controls.**

2. **Describe the relationship between strategy and structure.**

3. **Discuss the functional structures used to implement business-level strategies.**

4. **Explain the use of three versions of the multidivisional (M-form) structure to implement different diversification strategies.**

5. **Discuss the organizational structures used to implement three international strategies.**

6. **Define strategic networks and discuss how strategic center firms implement such networks at the business, corporate, and international levels.**

Are Strategy and Structural Changes in the Cards for GE?

GE is the only company listed in the Dow Jones Industrial Index today that was also included in the original index in 1896. This fact highlights the quality of General Electric's performance for more than a century. The firm's 2006 financial results ($163 billion in revenue and $20.7 billion of earnings) also appear to validate the view that GE is performing extremely well. Today, GE serves customers in more than 100 countries, employs more than 300,000 people worldwide, and generates in excess of 50 percent of its revenues from outside the United States. Committed to innovation as an important source of profitable growth, GE spent $5.7 billion in research and development (R&D) in 2006. But in some analysts' and investors' eyes, all is not well at GE. To respond to these concerns, changes to GE's corporate-level strategy and structure may be in the making.

In mid-2005, slightly less than four years after taking over from Jack Welch as CEO, Jeffrey Immelt changed GE's structure so that the firm operated with 6 rather than 11 business units. (Commercial Finance, Healthcare, Industrial, Infrastructure, Money, and NBC Universal were the six businesses forming the new structure. Infrastructure accounts for the largest percentage of total firm revenue with NBC Universal generating the smallest percentage of total revenue.) In announcing his decision, Immelt said that "these changes will accelerate GE's growth in key

industries" while simultaneously helping the firm become more focused on emerging technologies with significant commercial potential. Even with this reorganization, GE continued using the related-linked diversification strategy at the corporate level (see Chapter 6); the SBU form of the multidivisional structure (discussed in this chapter) remained the structure in place to facilitate use of the related-linked strategy.

Let's move forward to mid-2007, a time when a prominent analyst appeared to speak for many of his peers and some investors when he called for GE to sell one or more of its six businesses. Specifically, the call was for GE to sell noncore businesses such as NBC Universal and Money (formerly called Consumer Finance) to "raise billions (and) make this colossus a heck of a lot easier for one man to manage." The thought is that these two businesses have relatively little in common with the other four, and having them in GE's portfolio of businesses takes attention away from developing additional synergies (primarily in the form of economies of scope—see Chapter 6) across the four businesses with greater similarities. Immelt and Welch both reacted less than positively to this suggestion with Welch saying that following this advice "would be a tragedy of enormous proportions."

If these two businesses were sold, GE's corporate-level strategy would change from related linked to related constrained. If this change in strategy were to occur, the firm's structure would also need to be changed from the SBU form of the multidivisional structure to the cooperative form of the multidivisional structure. From the perspective of strategic management, the important outcome is that a change to organizational structure accompany a decision to change a firm's strategy. The reason for making such a change is that a mismatch between strategy and structure negatively affects performance.

Sources: 2007, Our businesses, http://www.ge.com, September 2; 2007, The weight of one observer's words, *New York Times Online*, http://www.nytimes.com, July 22; N. D. Schwartz, 2007, Is GE too big for its own good? *New York Times Online*, http://www.nytimes.com, July 22; G. Colvin, 2006, Lafley and Immelt: In search of billions, *Fortune*, December 11, 70–82.

As we explain in Chapter 5, all firms use one or more business-level strategies. In Chapters 6–9, we discuss other strategies firms may choose to use (corporate-level, international, and cooperative). Once selected, strategies are not implemented in a vacuum. Organizational structure and controls, this chapter's topic, provide the framework within which strategies are used in both for-profit organizations and not-for-profit agencies.[1] However, as we explain, separate structures and controls are required to successfully implement different strategies. In all organizations, top-level managers have the final responsibility for ensuring that the firm has matched each of its strategies with the appropriate organizational structure and that changes to both occur when necessary. Thus, Jeffrey Immelt is responsible for changing GE's organizational structure if the firm decides to use a different corporate-level strategy. The match or degree of fit between strategy and structure influences the firm's attempts to earn above-average returns.[2] Thus, the ability to select an appropriate strategy and match it with the appropriate structure is an important characteristic of effective strategic leadership.[3]

This chapter opens with an introduction to organizational structure and controls. We then provide more details about the need for the firm's strategy and structure to be properly matched. Affecting firms' efforts to match strategy and structure is their influence on each other.[4] As we discuss, strategy has a more important influence on structure, although once in place, structure influences strategy.[5] Next, we describe the relationship between growth and structural change successful firms experience. We then discuss the different organizational structures firms use to implement the separate business-level, corporate-level, international, and cooperative strategies. A series of figures highlights the different structures firms match with strategies. Across time and based on their experiences, organizations, especially large and complex ones, customize these general structures to meet their unique needs.[6] Typically, the firm tries to form a structure that is complex enough to facilitate use of its strategies but simple enough for all parties to understand and implement.[7] When structures become too complicated, firms try to reduce that complexity. This process is happening at Yahoo! through its efforts to flatten the organization's hierarchies so the firm will be closer to the customer as it battles rivals such as Google.[8]

Organizational Structure and Controls

Research shows that organizational structure and the controls that are a part of the structure affect firm performance.[9] In particular, evidence suggests that performance declines when the firm's strategy is not matched with the most appropriate structure and controls.[10] Even though mismatches between strategy and structure do occur, research indicates that managers try to act rationally when forming or changing their firm's structure.[11] His record of success at GE suggests that Jeffrey Immelt will pay close attention to the need to make certain that strategy and structure remained matched in his firm if a decision is made to divest one or more businesses.

Organizational Structure

Organizational structure specifies the firm's formal reporting relationships, procedures, controls, and authority and decision-making processes.[12] Developing an organizational structure that effectively supports the firm's strategy is difficult,[13] especially because of the uncertainty (or unpredictable variation[14]) about cause-effect relationships in the global economy's rapidly changing and dynamic competitive environments.[15] When a structure's elements (e.g., reporting relationships, procedures, etc.) are properly aligned with one another, the structure facilitates effective use of the firm's strategies.[16] Thus, organizational structure is a critical component of effective strategy implementation processes.[17]

A firm's structure specifies the work to be done and how to do it, given the firm's strategy or strategies.[18] Thus, organizational structure influences how managers work and the decisions resulting from that work.[19] Supporting the implementation of strategies, structure is concerned with processes used to complete organizational tasks.[20] Sometimes, firms develop creative processes for employees to use while completing their work. This appears to be the case at Best Buy. As we explain in the Strategic Focus, the firm's ROWE (Results-Only Work Environment) program is unique and is generating positive outcomes for Best Buy as a company and for participating employees. However, Best Buy and all firms must recognize that in general, changing processes detailing how work is to be performed is challenging and may be resisted for a variety of reasons.[21]

Effective structures provide the stability a firm needs to successfully implement its strategies and maintain its current competitive advantages while simultaneously providing the flexibility to develop advantages it will need in the future.[22] *Structural stability* provides the capacity the firm requires to consistently and predictably manage its daily work routines[23] while *structural flexibility* provides the opportunity to explore competitive possibilities and then allocate resources to activities that will shape the competitive advantages the firm will need to be successful in the future.[24] An effectively flexible organizational structure allows the firm to *exploit* current competitive advantages while *developing* new ones[25] that can potentially be used in the future.[26] For example, at Bavarian Motor Works (BMW) the firm's structure is thought to be "flat, flexible, entrepreneurial, and fast";[27] these structural characteristics contribute positively to efforts to exploit current advantages while exploring for new ones. For Best Buy, the long-term success of its ROWE program may be a function of the degree to which its use simultaneously enhances the firm's structural stability and structural flexibility.

Modifications to the firm's current strategy or selection of a new strategy call for changes to its organizational structure. However, research shows that once in place, organizational inertia often inhibits efforts to change structure, even when the firm's performance suggests that it is time to do so.[28] In his pioneering work, Alfred Chandler found that organizations change their structures when inefficiencies force them to do so.[29] Firms seem to prefer the structural status quo and its familiar working relationships until the firm's performance declines to the point where change is absolutely necessary.[30] Necessity may be the case at Samsung Electronics Co. Some analysts think that "Samsung is at a crossroads." A faltering corporate-level strategy and the use of the structure supporting that strategy may be contributing to the firm's difficulties.[31]

In addition to the issues we already mentioned, it is important to note that top-level managers hesitate to conclude that the firm's structure (or its strategy, for that matter) are the problem, in that doing so suggests that their previous choices were not the best ones. Because of these inertial tendencies, structural change is often induced instead by actions from stakeholders (e.g., those from the capital market and customers—see Chapter 2) who are no longer willing to tolerate the firm's performance. Evidence shows that appropriate timing of structural change happens when top-level managers recognize that a current organizational structure no longer provides the coordination and direction needed for the firm to successfully implement its strategies.[32]

Organizational structure specifies the firm's formal reporting relationships, procedures, controls, and authority and decision-making processes.

Best Buy is the largest U.S. consumer electronics retailer with more than 100,000 employees and roughly 800 stores. In addition to its well-known flagship stores, Best Buy owns Future Shop (Canada's largest and fastest-growing retailer of consumer electronics) and Magnolia (a high-end electronics retailer concentrating on audio and video packages for homes, cars, and businesses). The firm's Geek Squads are located in each Best Buy store and are offered as self-standing units in some cities such as Atlanta, Dallas, and Minneapolis (the firm's headquarters).

The Results-Only Work Environment (ROWE) program, created to improve job satisfaction and productivity, is being used in multiple parts of Best Buy's operations, including the Geek Squad.

To improve job satisfaction, employee productivity, and the firm's performance, Best Buy continues to experiment with ROWE (Results-Only Work Environment). Developed in-house, ROWE was rolled out in 2002 with approximately 4,000 headquarters' employees participating in the experiment. Results achieved through this program are impressive in that "Productivity has increased an average of 35 percent within six to nine months in Best Buy units implementing ROWE, a figure based on metrics reported or estimated by managers using the new system. Voluntary turnover has dropped between 52 percent and 90 percent in three Best Buy locations being studied." Survey results also indicate that employees take more ownership of their work and express much greater satisfaction with what they do as well as how they complete the tasks associated with their jobs.

Redesigns of how work activities are performed are at the core of ROWE. Essentially, employees have the freedom and responsibility to decide when and where they will work. Those supervising employees empowered in this manner believe that they are managing outcomes rather than directly managing the people expected to reach the desired outcomes. A designer of the program describes one of ROWE's objectives in this manner: "We want people to stop thinking of work as someplace you go to, five days a week from 8 to 5, and start thinking of work as something you do."

This paradigm shift in work activities that is becoming a more central part of Best Buy's organizational structure is guided by 13 commandments. Because Best Buy has established a division (CultureRX) that is selling the ROWE program to other companies, only three of the commandments, as follows, are public information: "(1) There are no work schedules, (2) Every meeting is optional, and (3) Employees should render no judgment about how colleagues spend their time." Employee performance is judged strictly on the basis of tasks completed, even if none of them were handled in the office. In this results-only environment, the work design allows people to come and go as they please. But the trade-off is that employees are clearly held accountable for their work to be completed successfully and on time. Excuses are not tolerated; and, for employees, it is important to understand that the "guidelines that signal where work ends and leisure begins" become blurred.

Given its success, the challenge for Best Buy's executives is to determine how to adapt ROWE for use across other tasks that are a part of its organizational structure. Can the results-only approach be adapted to all of Best Buy's work processes? This important question remains unanswered.

Sources: J. Brandon, 2007, Rethinking the clock, *Business 2.0*, March, 24–29; F. Jossi, 2007, Clocking out, *HR Magazine*, June, 47–50; C. Penttila, 2007, Flexibility is the workstyle of the future, *Entrepreneur*, May, 47; M. Conlin, 2006, Smashing the clock, *BusinessWeek*, December 11, 60–68; P. J. Kiger, 2006, Throwing out the rules of work, *WorkForce Management*, September 25, 16–23.

Chandler's contributions to our understanding of organizational structure and its relationship to strategies and performance are quite significant. Indeed, some believe that Chandler's emphasis on "organizational structure so transformed the field of business history that some call the period before Dr. Chandler's publications "B.C.," meaning "before Chandler." [33] As we discuss next, effective organizational controls help managers recognize when it is time to adjust the firm's structure.

Organizational Controls

Organizational controls are an important aspect of structure.[34] **Organizational controls** guide the use of strategy, indicate how to compare actual results with expected results, and suggest corrective actions to take when the difference is unacceptable. When fewer differences separate actual from expected outcomes, the organization's controls are more effective.[35] It is difficult for the company to successfully exploit its competitive advantages without effective organizational controls.[36] Properly designed organizational controls provide clear insights regarding behaviors that enhance firm performance.[37] Firms use both strategic controls and financial controls to support using their strategies.

Strategic controls are largely subjective criteria intended to verify that the firm is using appropriate strategies for the conditions in the external environment and the company's competitive advantages. Thus, strategic controls are concerned with examining the fit between what the firm *might do* (as suggested by opportunities in its external environment) and what it *can do* (as indicated by its competitive advantages). Effective strategic controls help the firm understand what it takes to be successful.[38] Strategic controls demand rich communications between managers responsible for using them to judge the firm's performance and those with primary responsibility for implementing the firm's strategies (such as middle and first-level managers). These frequent exchanges are both formal and informal in nature.[39]

Strategic controls are also used to evaluate the degree to which the firm focuses on the requirements to implement its strategies. For a business-level strategy, for example, the strategic controls are used to study primary and support activities (see Tables 3.6 and 3.7, on page 86) to verify that the critical activities are being emphasized and properly executed. With related corporate-level strategies, strategic controls are used to verify the sharing of appropriate strategic factors such as knowledge, markets, and technologies across businesses. To effectively use strategic controls when evaluating related diversification strategies, executives must have a deep understanding of each unit's business-level strategy.[40]

As we described in the Opening Case, GE's CEO Jeffrey Immelt allocates a great deal of his time and energy to issues related to strategic control. Constantly challenged to "deliver profitable growth," executives rely on innovative strategies and appropriate organizational structures as the path to improved performance. To facilitate a focus on what he believes are key technologies (e.g., renewable energy and nanotechnology), Immelt has changed GE's structure by jettisoning "much of GE's insurance business while bulking up in health care, water, security, and other areas." Similarly, Procter & Gamble's CEO A. G. Lafley is restructuring parts of P&G. Deciding to work with external partners to develop innovative products while divesting well-known brands such as Crisco, Jif, Pert Plus, and Sure while acquiring giants Gillette, Clairol, and Wella are products of this restructuring effort. The exact structural changes necessary to accommodate these acquisitions remain a work in progress at P&G. In both firms though, the CEOs are using strategic controls to support their chosen strategies.[41]

Financial controls are largely objective criteria used to measure the firm's performance against previously established quantitative standards. Accounting-based measures

P&G's recent acquisition of Gillette, a giant in the personal grooming arena, is a result of restructuring efforts designed to exert strategic controls on P&G's future growth.

Organizational controls guide the use of strategy, indicate how to compare actual results with expected results, and suggest corrective actions to take when the difference is unacceptable.

Strategic controls are largely subjective criteria intended to verify that the firm is using appropriate strategies for the conditions in the external environment and the company's competitive advantages.

Financial controls are largely objective criteria used to measure the firm's performance against previously established quantitative standards.

such as return on investment (ROI) and return on assets (ROA) as well as market-based measures such as economic value added are examples of financial controls. Partly because strategic controls are difficult to use with extensive diversification,[42] financial controls are emphasized to evaluate the performance of the firm using the unrelated diversification strategy. The unrelated diversification strategy's focus on financial outcomes (see Chapter 6) requires using standardized financial controls to compare performances between units and managers.[43]

When using financial controls, firms evaluate their current performance against previous outcomes as well as against competitors' performance and industry averages. In the global economy, technological advances are being used to develop highly sophisticated financial controls, making it possible for firms to more thoroughly analyze their performance results and to assure compliance with regulations. Companies such as Oracle and SAP sell software tools that automate processes firms can use to meet the financial reporting requirements specified by the Sarbanes-Oxley Act. (As noted in Chapter 10, this act requires a firm's principal executive and financial officers to certify corporate financial and related information in quarterly and annual reports submitted to the Securities and Exchange Commission.)

Both strategic and financial controls are important aspects of each organizational structure, and as we noted previously, any structure's effectiveness is determined by using a combination of strategic and financial controls. However, the relative use of controls varies by type of strategy. For example, companies and business units of large diversified firms using the cost leadership strategy emphasize financial controls (such as quantitative cost goals), while companies and business units using the differentiation strategy emphasize strategic controls (such as subjective measures of the effectiveness of product development teams).[44] As previously explained, a corporate-wide emphasis on sharing among business units (as called for by related diversification strategies) results in an emphasis on strategic controls, while financial controls are emphasized for strategies in which activities or capabilities are not shared (e.g., in an unrelated diversification strategy).

As firms consider controls, the important point is to properly balance the use of strategic and financial controls. Indeed, overemphasizing one at the expense of the other can lead to performance declines. According to Michael Dell, an overemphasis on financial controls to produce attractive short-term results contributed to recent performance difficulties at Dell Inc. In addressing this issue, Dell said the following: "The company was too focused on the short term, and the balance of priorities was way too leaning toward things that deliver short-term results."[45] Dell is now restructuring his firm to achieve a proper emphasis on the long term as well as the short term. A greater emphasis on strategic controls is resulting from this restructuring.

Relationships between Strategy and Structure

Strategy and structure have a reciprocal relationship.[46] This relationship highlights the interconnectedness between strategy formulation (Chapters 5–9) and strategy implementation (Chapters 10–13). In general, this reciprocal relationship finds structure flowing from or following selection of the firm's strategy. Once in place though, structure can influence current strategic actions as well as choices about future strategies. Consider, for example, the possible influences of the ROWE program on Best Buy's current and future strategies (see the Strategic Focus).

The general nature of the strategy/structure relationship means that changes to the firm's strategy create the need to change how the organization completes its work. In the "structure influences strategy" direction, firms must be vigilant in their efforts to verify that how their structure calls for work to be completed remains consistent with the implementation requirements of chosen strategies. Research shows, however, that "strategy has a much more important influence on structure than the reverse."[47]

Regardless of the strength of the reciprocal relationships between strategy and structure, those choosing the firm's strategy and structure should be committed to matching each strategy with a structure that provides the stability needed to use current competitive advantages as well as the flexibility required to develop future advantages. Therefore, when changing strategies, the firm should simultaneously consider the structure that will be needed to support use of the new strategy; properly matching strategy and structure can create a competitive advantage.[48]

Evolutionary Patterns of Strategy and Organizational Structure

Research suggests that most firms experience a certain pattern of relationships between strategy and structure. Chandler[49] found that firms tend to grow in somewhat predictable patterns: "first by volume, then by geography, then integration (vertical, horizontal), and finally through product/business diversification"[50] (see Figure 11.1). Chandler interpreted his findings as an indication that firms' growth patterns determine their structural form.

As shown in Figure 11.1, sales growth creates coordination and control problems the existing organizational structure cannot efficiently handle. Organizational growth

Figure 11.1 Strategy and Structure Growth Pattern

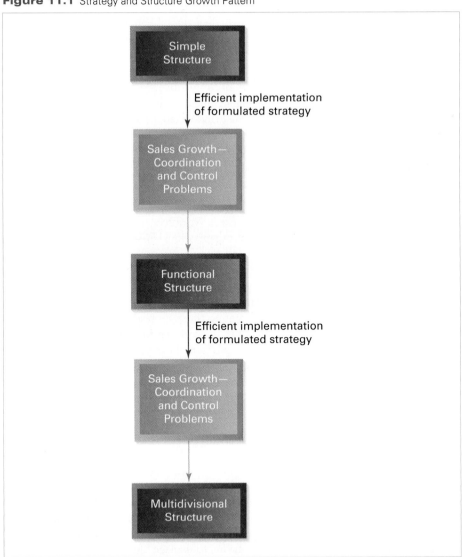

creates the opportunity for the firm to change its strategy to try to become even more successful. However, the existing structure's formal reporting relationships, procedures, controls, and authority and decision-making processes lack the sophistication required to support using the new strategy.[51] A new structure is needed to help decision makers gain access to the knowledge and understanding required to effectively integrate and coordinate actions to implement the new strategy.[52]

Firms choose from among three major types of organizational structures—simple, functional, and multidivisional—to implement strategies. Across time, successful firms move from the simple to the functional to the multidivisional structure to support changes in their growth strategies.[53]

Simple Structure

The **simple structure** is a structure in which the owner-manager makes all major decisions and monitors all activities while the staff serves as an extension of the manager's supervisory authority.[54] Typically, the owner-manager actively works in the business on a daily basis. Informal relationships, few rules, limited task specialization, and unsophisticated information systems characterize this structure. Frequent and informal communications between the owner-manager and employees make coordinating the work to be done relatively easy. The simple structure is matched with focus strategies and business-level strategies, as firms implementing these strategies commonly compete by offering a single product line in a single geographic market. Local restaurants, repair businesses, and other specialized enterprises are examples of firms using the simple structure.

As the small firm grows larger and becomes more complex, managerial and structural challenges emerge. For example, the amount of competitively relevant information requiring analysis substantially increases, placing significant pressure on the owner-manager. Additional growth and success may cause the firm to change its strategy. Even if the strategy remains the same, the firm's larger size dictates the need for more sophisticated workflows and integrating mechanisms. At this evolutionary point, firms tend to move from the simple structure to a functional organizational structure.[55]

Functional Structure

The **functional structure** consists of a chief executive officer and a limited corporate staff, with functional line managers in dominant organizational areas such as production, accounting, marketing, R&D, engineering, and human resources.[56] This structure allows for functional specialization,[57] thereby facilitating active sharing of knowledge within each functional area. Knowledge sharing facilitates career paths as well as professional development of functional specialists. However, a functional orientation can negatively affect communication and coordination among those representing different organizational functions. For this reason, the CEO must work hard to verify that the decisions and actions of individual business functions promote the entire firm rather than a single function.[58] The functional structure supports implementing business-level strategies and some corporate-level strategies (e.g., single or dominant business) with low levels of diversification. When changing from a simple to a functional structure, firms want to avoid introducing value-destroying bureaucratic procedures such as failing to promote innovation and creativity.[59]

Multidivisional Structure

With continuing growth and success, firms often consider greater levels of diversification. Successfully using a diversification strategy requires analyzing substantially greater amounts of data and information when the firm offers the same products in different markets (market or geographic diversification) or offers different products in several markets (product diversification). In addition, trying to manage high levels of diversification

The **simple structure** is a structure in which the owner-manager makes all major decisions and monitors all activities while the staff serves as an extension of the manager's supervisory authority.

The **functional structure** consists of a chief executive officer and a limited corporate staff, with functional line managers in dominant organizational areas such as production, accounting, marketing, R&D, engineering, and human resources.

through functional structures creates serious coordination and control problems,[60] a fact that commonly leads to a new structural form.[61]

The **multidivisional (M-form) structure** consists of operating divisions, each representing a separate business or profit center in which the top corporate officer delegates responsibilities for day-to-day operations and business-unit strategy to division managers. Each division represents a distinct, self-contained business with its own functional hierarchy.[62] As initially designed, the M-form was thought to have three major benefits: "(1) it enabled corporate officers to more accurately monitor the performance of each business, which simplified the problem of control; (2) it facilitated comparisons between divisions, which improved the resource allocation process; and (3) it stimulated managers of poorly performing divisions to look for ways of improving performance."[63] Active monitoring of performance through the M-form increases the likelihood that decisions made by managers heading individual units will be in stakeholders' best interests. Because diversification is a dominant corporate-level strategy used in the global economy, the M-form is a widely adopted organizational structure.[64]

Used to support implementation of related and unrelated diversification strategies, the M-form helps firms successfully manage diversification's many demands.[65] Chandler viewed the M-form as an innovative response to coordination and control problems that surfaced during the 1920s in the functional structures then used by large firms such as DuPont and General Motors.[66] Research shows that the M-form is appropriate when the firm grows through diversification.[67] Partly because of its value to diversified corporations, some consider the multidivisional structure to be one of the twentieth century's most significant organizational innovations.[68]

No one organizational structure (simple, functional, or multidivisional) is inherently superior to the others.[69] Peter Drucker says the following about this matter: "There is no one right organization. . . . Rather the task . . . is to select the organization for the particular task and mission at hand."[70] In our context, Drucker is saying that the firm must select a structure that is "right" for successfully using the chosen strategy. Because no single structure is optimal in all instances, managers concentrate on developing proper matches between strategies and organizational structures rather than searching for an "optimal" structure. This matching of structure and strategy is taking place at Pfizer, Inc. Noting that the firm's current organizational structure was not serving it well, CEO David Shedlarz is changing the firm's structure so it will be easier for company personnel to openly collaborate to develop new products, form effective alliances, and identify ideal companies to acquire (all of these actions are necessary to implement the firm's strategies).[71]

We now describe the strategy/structure matches that evidence shows positively contribute to firm performance.

The **multidivisional (M-form) structure** consists of operating divisions, each representing a separate business or profit center in which the top corporate officer delegates responsibilities for day-to-day operations and business-unit strategy to division managers.

Pfizer CEO David Shedlarz is working to change Pfizer's corporate structure for more effective sharing of ideas, resources, and personnel.

Matches between Business-Level Strategies and the Functional Structure

Firms use different forms of the functional organizational structure to support implementing the cost leadership, differentiation, and integrated cost leadership/differentiation strategies. The differences in these forms are accounted for primarily by different uses of three important structural characteristics: *specialization* (concerned with the type and number of jobs required to complete work[72]), *centralization* (the degree to which decision-making authority is retained at higher managerial levels[73]), and *formalization* (the degree to which formal rules and procedures govern work[74]).

© AP Photo/Henny Ray Abrams

Using the Functional Structure to Implement the Cost Leadership Strategy

Firms using the cost leadership strategy sell large quantities of standardized products to an industry's typical customer. Simple reporting relationships, few layers in the decision-making and authority structure, a centralized corporate staff, and a strong focus on process improvements through the manufacturing function rather than the development of new products by emphasizing product R&D characterize the cost leadership form of the functional structure[75] (see Figure 11.2). This structure contributes to the emergence of a low-cost culture—a culture in which employees constantly try to find ways to reduce the costs incurred to complete their work.[76]

In terms of centralization, decision-making authority is centralized in a staff function to maintain a cost-reducing emphasis within each organizational function (engineering, marketing, etc.). While encouraging continuous cost reductions, the centralized staff also verifies that further cuts in costs in one function won't adversely affect the productivity levels in other functions.[77]

Jobs are highly specialized in the cost leadership functional structure; work is divided into homogeneous subgroups. Organizational functions are the most common subgroup, although work is sometimes batched on the basis of products produced or clients served. Specializing in their work allows employees to increase their efficiency, reducing costs as a result. Guiding individuals' work in this structure are highly formalized rules and procedures, which often emanate from the centralized staff.

Wal-Mart Stores Inc. uses the functional structure to implement cost leadership strategies in each of its three segments (Wal-Mart Stores, Sam's Clubs, and International). In the Wal-Mart Stores segment (which generates the largest share of the firm's total sales), the cost leadership strategy is used in the firm's Supercenter, Discount, and Neighborhood Market retailing formats.[78] Long known for its "Always Low Prices" slogan (which was used for 19 years), Wal-Mart recently changed to a new slogan—"Save Money, Live

Figure 11.2 Functional Structure for Implementing a Cost Leadership Strategy

Notes:
• Operations is the main function
• Process engineering is emphasized rather than new product R&D
• Relatively large centralized staff coordinates functions
• Formalized procedures allow for emergence of a low-cost culture
• Overall structure is mechanistic; job roles are highly structured

Better."[79] Although the slogan is new, Wal-Mart continues using the functional organizational structure in its divisions to drive costs lower. As discussed in Chapter 5, competitors' efforts to duplicate the success of Wal-Mart's cost leadership strategies have generally failed, partly because of the effective strategy/structure matches in each of the firm's segments.

Using the Functional Structure to Implement the Differentiation Strategy

Firms using the differentiation strategy produce products customers perceive as being different in ways that create value for them. With this strategy, the firm wants to sell nonstandardized products to customers with unique needs. Relatively complex and flexible reporting relationships, frequent use of cross-functional product development teams, and a strong focus on marketing and product R&D rather than manufacturing and process R&D (as with the cost leadership form of the functional structure) characterize the differentiation form of the functional structure (see Figure 11.3). From this structure emerges a development-oriented culture in which employees try to find ways to further differentiate current products and to develop new, highly differentiated products.[80]

Wal-Mart Stores Inc. uses the functional structure to implement cost leadership strategies in each of its three segments (ASDA is part of Wal-Mart's International segment).

Continuous product innovation demands that people throughout the firm interpret and take action based on information that is often ambiguous, incomplete, and uncertain. Following a strong focus on the external environment to identify new opportunities, employees often gather this information from people outside the firm (e.g., customers and suppliers). Commonly, rapid responses to the possibilities indicated by the collected

Figure 11.3 Functional Structure for Implementing a Differentiation Strategy

Notes:
• Marketing is the main function for keeping track of new product ideas
• New product R&D is emphasized
• Most functions are decentralized, but R&D and marketing may have centralized staffs that work closely with each other
• Formalization is limited so that new product ideas can emerge easily and change is more readily accomplished
• Overall structure is organic; job roles are less structured

© Steven Lunetta Photography, 2007

information are necessary, suggesting the need for decentralized decision-making responsibility and authority. To support creativity and the continuous pursuit of new sources of differentiation and new products, jobs in this structure are not highly specialized. This lack of specialization means that workers have a relatively large number of tasks in their job descriptions. Few formal rules and procedures also characterize this structure. Low formalization, decentralization of decision-making authority and responsibility, and low specialization of work tasks combine to create a structure in which people interact frequently to exchange ideas about how to further differentiate current products while developing ideas for new products that can be crisply differentiated.

Using the Functional Structure to Implement the Integrated Cost Leadership/Differentiation Strategy

Firms using the integrated cost leadership/differentiation strategy sell products that create value because of their relatively low cost and reasonable sources of differentiation. The cost of these products is low "relative" to the cost leader's prices while their differentiation is "reasonable" when compared with the clearly unique features of the differentiator's products.

Although challenging to implement, the integrated cost leadership/differentiation strategy is used frequently in the global economy. The challenge of using this structure is due largely to the fact that different primary and support activities (see Chapter 3) are emphasized when using the cost leadership and differentiation strategies. To achieve the cost leadership position, production and process engineering are emphasized, with infrequent product changes. To achieve a differentiated position, marketing and new product R&D are emphasized while production and process engineering are not. Thus, effective use of the integrated strategy depends on the firm's successful combination of activities intended to reduce costs with activities intended to create additional differentiation features. As a result, the integrated form of the functional structure must have decision-making patterns that are partially centralized and partially decentralized. Additionally, jobs are semispecialized, and rules and procedures call for some formal and some informal job behavior.

Matches between Corporate-Level Strategies and the Multidivisional Structure

As explained earlier, Chandler's research shows that the firm's continuing success leads to product or market diversification or both.[81] The firm's level of diversification is a function of decisions about the number and type of businesses in which it will compete as well as how it will manage the businesses (see Chapter 6). Geared to managing individual organizational functions, increasing diversification eventually creates information processing, coordination, and control problems that the functional structure cannot handle. Thus, using a diversification strategy requires the firm to change from the functional structure to the multidivisional structure to develop an appropriate strategy/structure match.

As defined in Figure 6.1, on page 156, corporate-level strategies have different degrees of product and market diversification. The demands created by different levels of diversification highlight the need for a unique organizational structure to effectively implement each strategy (see Figure 11.4).

Using the Cooperative Form of the Multidivisional Structure to Implement the Related Constrained Strategy

The **cooperative form** is a structure in which horizontal integration is used to bring about interdivisional cooperation. Divisions in a firm using the related constrained diversification strategy commonly are formed around products, markets, or both. In Figure 11.5, we use product divisions as part of the representation of the cooperative form of the multidivisional

The **cooperative form** is a structure in which horizontal integration is used to bring about interdivisional cooperation.

Figure 11.4 Three Variations of the Multidivisional Structure

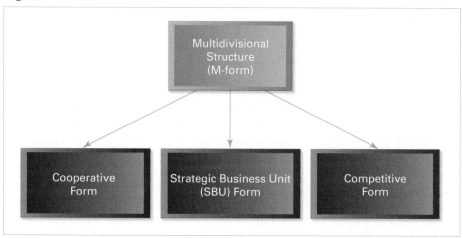

structure, although market divisions could be used instead of or in addition to product divisions to develop the figure.

Using this structure, Harley-Davidson, Inc., has two divisions or segments: Motorcycles & Related Products and Financial Services. These divisions "are managed separately based on the fundamental differences in their operations." However, the divisions are "related" because they share the firm's brand name and reputation.[82]

Figure 11.5 Cooperative Form of the Multidivisional Structure for Implementing a Related Constrained Strategy

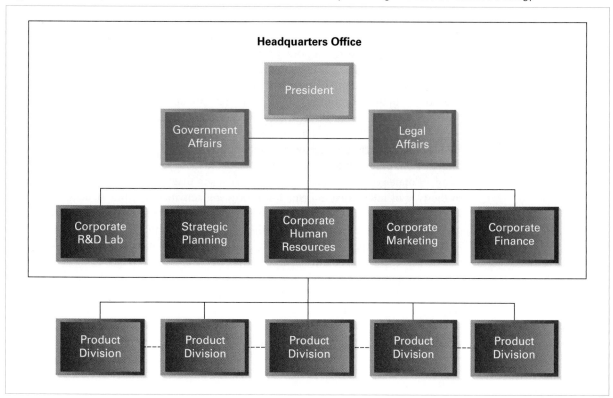

Notes:
• Structural integration devices create tight links among all divisions
• Corporate office emphasizes centralized strategic planning, human resources, and marketing to foster cooperation between divisions
• R&D is likely to be centralized
• Rewards are subjective and tend to emphasize overall corporate performance in addition to divisional performance
• Culture emphasizes cooperative sharing

As is the case at Harley-Davidson, all divisions in a related constrained firm share one or more corporate strengths.[83] Outback Steakhouse, Inc., for example, shares its real estate development, purchasing and leasing strengths, and its expertise in running franchise operations across its eight food concepts (Outback Steakhouse, Carrabba's Italian Grill, Roy's Restaurant, Bonefish Grill, Fleming's Prime Steakhouse & Wine Bar, Lee Roy Selmon's, Cheeseburger in Paradise, and Blue Coral Seafood & Spirits).[84] Colgate-Palmolive's use of the cooperative M-form finds the firm's oral care, personal care, and pet food divisions sharing marketing and manufacturing skills.[85] Sharing divisional competencies facilitates the corporation's efforts to develop economies of scope. As explained in Chapter 6, economies of scope (cost savings resulting from the sharing of competencies developed in one division with another division) are linked with successful use of the related constrained strategy. Interdivisional sharing of competencies depends on cooperation, suggesting the use of the cooperative form of the multidivisional structure.[86] Increasingly, it is important that the links resulting from effectively using integrating mechanisms support the cooperative sharing of both intangible resources (such as knowledge) and tangible resources (such as facilities and equipment).[87]

The cooperative structure uses different characteristics of structure (centralization, standardization, and formalization) as integrating mechanisms to facilitate interdivisional cooperation. Centralizing real estate development at the corporate level allows Outback Steakhouse, Inc., for example, to use these skills across its eight food concepts.[88] Frequent, direct contact between division managers, another integrating mechanism, encourages and supports cooperation and the sharing of competencies or resources that could be used to create new advantages. Sometimes, liaison roles are established in each division to reduce the time division managers spend integrating and coordinating their unit's work with the work occurring in other divisions. Temporary teams or task forces may be formed around projects whose success depends on sharing competencies that are embedded within several divisions. Formal integration departments might be established in firms frequently using temporary teams or task forces.

Ultimately, a matrix organization may evolve in firms implementing the related constrained strategy. A *matrix organization* is an organizational structure in which there is a dual structure combining both functional specialization and business product or project specialization.[89] Although complicated, an effective matrix structure can lead to improved coordination among a firm's divisions.[90]

The success of the cooperative multidivisional structure is significantly affected by how well divisions process information. However, because cooperation among divisions implies a loss of managerial autonomy, division managers may not readily commit themselves to the type of integrative information-processing activities that this structure demands. Moreover, coordination among divisions sometimes results in an unequal flow of positive outcomes to divisional managers. In other words, when managerial rewards are based at least in part on the performance of individual divisions, the manager of the division that is able to benefit the most by the sharing of corporate competencies might be viewed as receiving relative gains at others' expense. Strategic controls are important in these instances, as divisional managers' performance can be evaluated at least partly on the basis of how well they have facilitated interdivisional cooperative efforts. In addition, using reward systems that emphasize overall company performance, besides outcomes achieved by individual divisions, helps overcome problems associated with the cooperative form.

Using the Strategic Business Unit Form of the Multidivisional Structure to Implement the Related Linked Strategy

The **strategic business unit (SBU) form** consists of three levels: corporate headquarters, strategic business units (SBUs), and SBU divisions.

Firms with fewer links or less constrained links among their divisions use the related linked diversification strategy. The strategic business unit form of the multidivisional structure supports implementation of this strategy. The **strategic business unit (SBU) form** consists of three levels: corporate headquarters, strategic business units (SBUs), and SBU divisions (see Figure 11.6). The SBU structure is used by large firms and can be complex, with the complexity reflected by the organization's size and product and market diversity.

The divisions within each SBU are related in terms of shared products or markets or both, but the divisions of one SBU have little in common with the divisions of the other SBUs. Divisions within each SBU share product or market competencies to develop economies of scope and possibly economies of scale. The integrating mechanisms used by the divisions in this structure can be equally well used by the divisions within the individual strategic business units that are part of the SBU form of the multidivisional structure. In this structure, each SBU is a profit center that is controlled and evaluated by the headquarters office. Although both financial and strategic controls are important, on a relative basis financial controls are vital to headquarters' evaluation of each SBU; strategic controls are critical when the heads of SBUs evaluate their divisions' performances. Strategic controls are also critical to the headquarters' efforts to determine whether the company has formed an effective portfolio of businesses and whether those businesses are being successfully managed.

Sharing competencies among units within an SBU is an important characteristic of the SBU form of the multidivisional structure (see the notes to Figure 11.6). A drawback to the SBU structure is that multifaceted businesses often have difficulties in communicating this complex business model to stockholders.[91] Furthermore, if coordination between SBUs is needed, problems can arise because the SBU structure, similar to the competitive form discussed next, does not readily foster cooperation across SBUs.

Figure 11.6 SBU Form of the Multidivisional Structure for Implementing a Related Linked Strategy

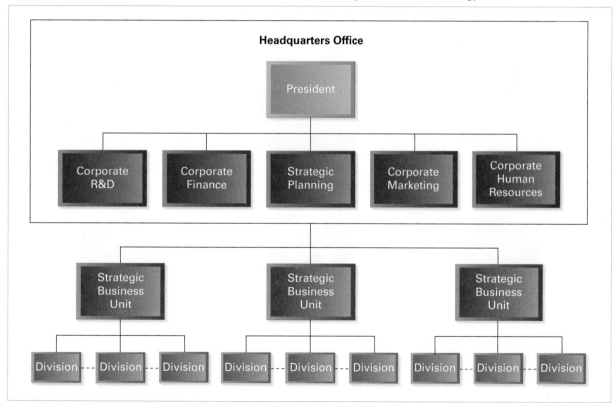

Notes:
• Structural integration among divisions within SBUs, but independence across SBUs
• Strategic planning may be the most prominent function in headquarters for managing the strategic planning approval process of SBUs for the president
• Each SBU may have its own budget for staff to foster integration
• Corporate headquarters staff serve as consultants to SBUs and divisions, rather than having direct input to product strategy, as in the cooperative form

Using the Competitive Form of the Multidivisional Structure to Implement the Unrelated Diversification Strategy

Firms using the unrelated diversification strategy want to create value through efficient internal capital allocations or by restructuring, buying, and selling businesses.[92] The competitive form of the multidivisional structure supports implementation of this strategy.

The **competitive form** is a structure characterized by complete independence among the firm's divisions (see Figure 11.7). Unlike the divisions included in the cooperative structure, divisions that are part of the competitive structure do not share common corporate strengths. Because strengths are not shared, integrating devices are not developed for use by the divisions included in the competitive structure.

The efficient internal capital market that is the foundation for using the unrelated diversification strategy requires organizational arrangements emphasizing divisional competition rather than cooperation.[93] Three benefits are expected from the internal competition. First, internal competition creates flexibility (e.g., corporate headquarters can have divisions working on different technologies and projects to identify those with the greatest potential). Resources can then be allocated to the division appearing to have the most potential to fuel the entire firm's success. Second, internal competition challenges the status quo and inertia, because division heads know that future resource allocations are a product of excellent current performance as well as superior positioning in terms of future performance. Last, internal competition motivates effort in that the challenge of competing against internal peers can be as great as the challenge of competing against external rivals.[94] In this structure, organizational controls (primarily financial controls) are used to emphasize and support internal competition among separate divisions and as the basis for allocating corporate capital based on divisions' performances.

> The **competitive form** is a structure characterized by complete independence among the firm's divisions.

Figure 11.7 Competitive Form of the Multidivisional Structure for Implementing an Unrelated Strategy

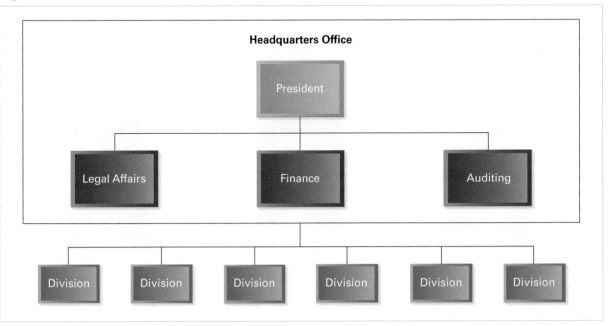

Notes:
- Corporate headquarters has a small staff
- Finance and auditing are the most prominent functions in the headquarters office to manage cash flow and assure the accuracy of performance data coming from divisions
- The legal affairs function becomes important when the firm acquires or divests assets
- Divisions are independent and separate for financial evaluation purposes
- Divisions retain strategic control, but cash is managed by the corporate office
- Divisions compete for corporate resources

Textron Inc., a large "multi-industry" company seeks "to identify, research, select, acquire and integrate companies, and has developed a set of rigorous criteria to guide decision making." Textron continuously looks "to enhance and reshape its portfolio by divesting non-core assets and acquiring branded businesses in attractive industries with substantial long-term growth potential." Textron operates four independent businesses—Bell Helicopter (29% of revenue), Cessna Aircraft (35%), Finance (6%), and Industrial (30%). The firm uses return on invested capital (ROIC) as the "compass for guiding" the evaluation of its diversified set of businesses as they compete internally for resources.[95]

Textron, Inc., owner of Bell Helicopter, uses the competitive form of the multidivisional structure to encourage the best performance from its four business units.

To emphasize competitiveness among divisions, the headquarters office maintains an arm's-length relationship with them, intervening in divisional affairs only to audit operations and discipline managers whose divisions perform poorly. In emphasizing competition between divisions, the headquarters office relies on strategic controls to set rate-of-return targets and financial controls to monitor divisional performance relative to those targets. The headquarters office then allocates cash flow on a competitive basis, rather than automatically returning cash to the division that produced it. Thus, the focus of the headquarters' work is on performance appraisal, resource allocation, and long-range planning to verify that the firm's portfolio of businesses will lead to financial success.[96]

The three major forms of the multidivisional structure should each be paired with a particular corporate-level strategy. Table 11.1 shows these structures' characteristics. Differences exist in the degree of centralization, the focus of the performance appraisal, the horizontal structures (integrating mechanisms), and the incentive compensation schemes. The most centralized and most costly structural form is the cooperative structure. The least centralized, with the lowest bureaucratic costs, is the competitive structure. The SBU structure requires partial centralization and involves some of the mechanisms

Table 11.1 Characteristics of the Structures Necessary to Implement the Related Constrained, Related Linked, and Unrelated Diversification Strategies

	Overall Structural Form		
Structural Characteristics	Cooperative M-Form (Related Constrained Strategy)[a]	SBU M-Form (Related Linked Strategy)[a]	Competitive M-Form (Unrelated Diversification Strategy)[a]
Centralization of operations	Centralized at corporate office	Partially centralized (in SBUs)	Decentralized to divisions
Use of integration mechanisms	Extensive	Moderate	Nonexistent
Divisional performance appraisals	Emphasize subjective (strategic) criteria	Use a mixture of subjective (strategic) and objective (financial) criteria	Emphasize objective (financial) criteria
Divisional incentive compensation	Linked to overall corporate performance	Mixed linkage to corporate, SBU, and divisional performance	Linked to divisional performance

[a]Strategy implemented with structural form.

necessary to implement the relatedness between divisions. Also, the divisional incentive compensation awards are allocated according to both SBUs and corporate performance.

Matches between International Strategies and Worldwide Structure

As explained in Chapter 8, international strategies are becoming increasingly important for long-term competitive success[97] in what continues to become an increasingly borderless global economy.[98] Among other benefits, international strategies allow the firm to search for new markets, resources, core competencies, and technologies as part of its efforts to outperform competitors.[99]

As with business-level and corporate-level strategies, unique organizational structures are necessary to successfully implement the different international strategies.[100] Forming proper matches between international strategies and organizational structures facilitates the firm's efforts to effectively coordinate and control its global operations. More importantly, research findings confirm the validity of the international strategy/ structure matches we discuss here.[101]

Using the Worldwide Geographic Area Structure to Implement the Multidomestic Strategy

The *multidomestic strategy* decentralizes the firm's strategic and operating decisions to business units in each country so that product characteristics can be tailored to local preferences. Firms using this strategy try to isolate themselves from global competitive forces by establishing protected market positions or by competing in industry segments that are most affected by differences among local countries. The worldwide geographic area structure is used to implement this strategy. The **worldwide geographic area structure** emphasizes national interests and facilitates the firm's efforts to satisfy local differences (see Figure 11.8).

> The **worldwide geographic area structure** emphasizes national interests and facilitates the firm's efforts to satisfy local differences.

Figure 11.8 Worldwide Geographic Area Structure for Implementing a Multidomestic Strategy

Notes:
- The perimeter circles indicate decentralization of operations
- Emphasis is on differentiation by local demand to fit an area or country culture
- Corporate headquarters coordinates financial resources among independent subsidiaries
- The organization is like a decentralized federation

Xerox Corporation is a technology and services company helping "businesses deploy smart document management strategies and find better ways to work." The firm emphasizes product innovation to best serve customers' needs and process innovations to simultaneously improve quality and reduce its production costs. Allocating more than 6 percent of total revenues to research and development (R&D), Xerox's Innovation Group collaborates with personnel across the firm's business units to facilitate development of product and process innovations.

Xerox focuses its efforts on three primary markets: (1) high-end production and commercial print environments, (2) networked offices from small to large and (3) value-added services. Document color and solutions "that tailor Xerox devices to solve a customer's problem" are the unifying themes that guide the firm's actions in these three markets.

Xerox is using the multidomestic strategy to serve customers in its three primary markets. One reason for using this strategy is so the firm can apply its service capabilities to solve the unique problems of customers in different geographic locations. Although customers throughout the world have needs for documents and document services, the specific nature of their needs varies on the basis of business culture and the sophistication of the local business environment. Because of this reality, Xerox uses the worldwide geographic area structure to support its multidomestic strategy. Global Services, North America, Europe, and Developing Markets Operations are the four business groups that make up Xerox's organizational structure. Supporting these units' efforts to serve the unique needs of customers in different regions are groups such as Innovation, Corporate Strategy/Alliances, and Human Resources/Ethics. Xerox relies on the match between its international strategy and structure as a key driver of profitable growth.

Sources: M. Bushman, 2007, Functional, divisional and matrix organizational structures, *The People's Media Company*, http://www.associatedcontent.com, January 18; 2007, Xerox fact sheet, http://www.xerox.com, September 14; 2006, Aligning the organization with the market: Focusing on the customer's total experience, *Knowledge@Wharton*, http://knowledge.wharton.upenn.edu, May 31; 2006, Xerox annual report, http://www.xerox.com.

As explained in the Strategic Focus, Xerox Corporation uses the worldwide geographic area structure to support implementation of its multidomestic strategy. In 2006, 52 percent of the firm's revenue was generated in the United States while 34 percent was earned in Europe. The remaining 13.2 percent of Xerox's 2006 revenue came from sales in developing markets.

Using the multidomestic strategy requires little coordination between different country markets, meaning that integrating mechanisms among divisions in the worldwide geographic area structure are not needed. Hence, formalization is low, and coordination among units in a firm's worldwide geographic area structure is often informal.

The multidomestic strategy/worldwide geographic area structure match evolved as a natural outgrowth of the multicultural European marketplace. Friends and family members of the main business who were sent as expatriates into foreign countries to develop the independent country subsidiary often used this structure for the main business. The relationship to corporate headquarters by divisions took place through informal communication among "family members."[102]

Just as Xerox Corporation does, SABMiller uses the worldwide geographic area structure. SABMiller is one of the world's largest brewers with distribution agreements and brewing interests in more than 60 countries involving six continents. It is also one of the world's largest bottlers of Coca-Cola products. SABMiller was created in 2002 through a

SABMiller, created by a merger of two companies in 2002, uses a multidomestic strategy to sell its premium beers around the world.

merger of South African Breweries and Miller Brewing. Currently, SABMiller owns several premium international beers including Pilsner Urquell, Peroni Nastro Azzurro, and Miller Genuine Draft. Six of its brands are among the world's top 50 beer brands. In late 2007, the firm planned to launch its premium Italian beer (Peroni Nastro Azzurro) in Japan (its first foray into the East Asian market). Complementing these international brands are dominant locally prominent beers such as Aquila, Snow, and Tyskie, which are also part of SABMiller's product lines. Committed to profitable growth, SABMiller uses the multidomestic strategy to expand its product offerings and geographic locations. Acquisitions and cooperative strategies figure prominently in the firm's use of this strategy. In late 2007, for example, SABMiller's joint venture with China Resources Enterprises, Limited (called CRE), announced that it was acquiring four breweries in China.[103] Global brewers Inbev and Heineken have also acquired firms and formed cooperative relationships as a means of implementing their multidomestic strategies.[104]

To implement its multidomestic strategy, SABMiller uses the worldwide geographic area structure with regional and country division headquarters throughout the world. Decentralization to these regional and country headquarters allows for strong marketing to adapt the acquired brands to the local cultures and for some improved cost structures, especially in avoiding significant transportation costs across geographic regions. SABMiller expects to make further acquisitions in developing markets, such as India, to contribute to future growth. The strategy/structure match we are describing likely contributes to this firm's positive financial performance.[105]

A key disadvantage of the multidomestic strategy/worldwide geographic area structure match is the inability to create strong global efficiency. With an increasing emphasis on lower-cost products in international markets, the need to pursue worldwide economies of scale has also increased. These changes foster use of the global strategy and its structural match, the worldwide product divisional structure.

Using the Worldwide Product Divisional Structure to Implement the Global Strategy

With the corporation's home office dictating competitive strategy, the *global strategy* is one through which the firm offers standardized products across country markets. The firm's success depends on its ability to develop economies of scope and economies of scale on a global level. Decisions to outsource some primary or support activities to the world's best providers are particularly helpful when the firm tries to develop economies of scale.[106]

The worldwide product divisional structure supports use of the global strategy. In the **worldwide product divisional structure,** decision-making authority is centralized in the worldwide division headquarters to coordinate and integrate decisions and actions among divisional business units (see Figure 11.9). This structure is often used in rapidly growing firms seeking to manage their diversified product lines effectively. Avon Products, Inc. is an example of a firm using the worldwide product divisional structure.

In the **worldwide product divisional structure,** decision-making authority is centralized in the worldwide division headquarters to coordinate and integrate decisions and actions among divisional business units.

Avon is a global brand leader in products for women such as lipsticks, fragrances, and anti-aging skincare. Committed to "empowering women all over the world since 1886," Avon relies on product innovation to be a first-mover in its markets. For years, Avon used the multidomestic strategy. However, the firm's growth came to a screeching halt in 2006. Contributing to this decline were simultaneous stumbles in sales revenues in emerging markets (e.g., Russia and Central Europe), the United States, and Mexico. To cope with its problems, the firm changed to a global strategy and to the worldwide product divisional structure to support its use. Commenting on this change, CEO Andrea Jung noted that, "Previously, Avon managers from Poland to Mexico ran their own plants,

Figure 11.9 Worldwide Product Divisional Structure for Implementing a Global Strategy

Notes:
• The headquarters'circle indicates centralization to coordinate information flow among worldwide products
• Corporate headquarters uses many intercoordination devices to facilitate global economies of scale and scope
• Corporate headquarters also allocates financial resources in a cooperative way
• The organization is like a centralized federation

developed new products, and created their own ads, often relying as much on gut as numbers."[107] Today, Avon is organized around product divisions including Avon Color, the firm's "flagship global color cosmetics brand, which offers a variety of color cosmetics products, including foundations, powders, lips, eye, and nail products," Skincare, Bath & Body, Hair Care, Wellness, and Fragrance. The analysis of these product divisions' performances is conducted by individuals in the firm's New York headquarters. One of the purposes of changing strategy and structure is for Avon to control its costs and gain additional scale economies as paths to performance improvements.[108]

Integrating mechanisms are important in the effective use of the worldwide product divisional structure. Direct contact between managers, liaison roles between departments, and temporary task forces as well as permanent teams are examples of these mechanisms. One researcher describes the use of these mechanisms in the worldwide structure: "There is exten-

sive and formal use of task forces and operating committees to supplement communication and coordination of worldwide operations."[109] The disadvantages of the global strategy/worldwide structure combination are the difficulty involved with coordinating decisions and actions across country borders and the inability to quickly respond to local needs and preferences.

To deal with these types of disadvantages, Avon takes several actions including completing surveys with women on a global basis. In 2005, for example, Avon surveyed more than 20,000 women in 22 countries to better understand their opinions about skincare, physical appearance, and self-indulgence. With this information, the firm is better able to develop innovative products that will appeal to women on a global basis.[110]

Avon has recently moved from a multidomestic strategy to a global strategy and to the worldwide product divisional structure in order to control costs and develop economies of scale.

© AP Photo/Gregory Bull

Using the Combination Structure to Implement the Transnational Strategy

The *transnational strategy* calls for the firm to combine the multidomestic strategy's local responsiveness with the global strategy's efficiency. Firms using this strategy are trying to gain the advantages of both local responsiveness and global efficiency. The combination structure is used to implement the transnational strategy. The **combination structure** is a structure drawing characteristics and mechanisms from both the worldwide geographic area structure and the worldwide product divisional structure. The transnational strategy is often implemented through two possible combination structures: a global matrix structure and a hybrid global design.[111]

> The **combination structure** is a structure drawing characteristics and mechanisms from both the worldwide geographic area structure and the worldwide product divisional structure.

The global matrix design brings together both local market and product expertise into teams that develop and respond to the global marketplace. The global matrix design (the basic matrix structure was defined earlier) promotes flexibility in designing products and responding to customer needs. However, it has severe limitations in that it places employees in a position of being accountable to more than one manager. At any given time, an employee may be a member of several functional or product group teams. Relationships that evolve from multiple memberships can make it difficult for employees to be simultaneously loyal to all of them. Although the matrix places authority in the hands of managers who are most able to use it, it creates problems in regard to corporate reporting relationships that are so complex and vague that it is difficult and time-consuming to receive approval for major decisions.

We illustrate the hybrid structure in Figure 11.10. In this design, some divisions are oriented toward products while others are oriented toward market areas. Thus, in some cases when the geographic area is more important, the division managers are area-oriented. In other divisions where worldwide product coordination and efficiencies are more important, the division manager is more product oriented.

Individual managers seek synergies as they simultaneously work to discharge their geographic- or product-centered responsibilities. In the case of Procter & Gamble (P&G), the firm's structure includes global business units (product focused) and market development organizations (geography or location focused). At P&G, those managing these units seek to define the brand's equity while at the same time applying that equity within the context of different tastes in various geographic regions.[112]

The fits between the multidomestic strategy and the worldwide geographic area structure and between the global strategy and the worldwide product divisional structure are apparent. However, when a firm wants to implement the multidomestic and the global strategies simultaneously through a combination structure, the appropriate integrating

Figure 11.10 Hybrid Form of the Combination Structure for Implementing a Transnational Strategy

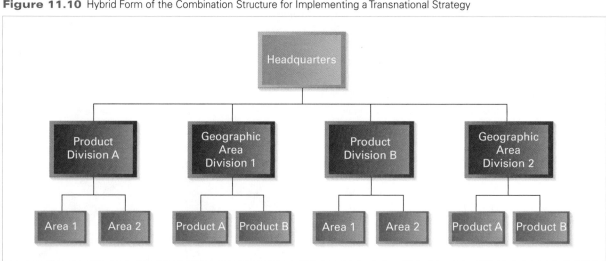

mechanisms are less obvious. The structure used to implement the transnational strategy must be simultaneously centralized and decentralized; integrated and nonintegrated; formalized and nonformalized. These seemingly opposite characteristics must be managed by an overall structure that is capable of encouraging all employees to understand the effects of cultural and geographic diversity on a firm's operations.

Matches between Cooperative Strategies and Network Structures

As discussed in Chapter 9, a network strategy exists when partners form several alliances in order to improve the performance of the alliance network itself through cooperative endeavors.[113] The greater levels of environmental complexity and uncertainty facing companies in today's competitive environment are causing more firms to use cooperative strategies such as strategic alliances and joint ventures.[114]

The breadth and scope of firms' operations in the global economy create many opportunities for firms to cooperate.[115] In fact, a firm can develop cooperative relationships with many of its stakeholders, including customers, suppliers, and competitors. When a firm becomes involved with combinations of cooperative relationships, it is part of a strategic network, or what others call an alliance constellation.[116]

A *strategic network* is a group of firms that has been formed to create value by participating in multiple cooperative arrangements. An effective strategic network facilitates discovering opportunities beyond those identified by individual network participants.[117] A strategic network can be a source of competitive advantage for its members when its operations create value that is difficult for competitors to duplicate and that network members can't create by themselves.[118] Strategic networks are used to implement business-level, corporate-level, and international cooperative strategies.

Commonly, a strategic network is a loose federation of partners participating in the network's operations on a flexible basis. At the core or center of the strategic network, the *strategic center firm* is the one around which the network's cooperative relationships revolve (see Figure 11.11).

Figure 11.11 A Strategic Network

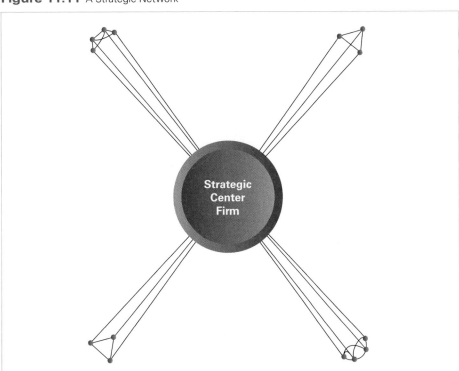

Because of its central position, the strategic center firm is the foundation for the strategic network's structure. Concerned with various aspects of organizational structure, such as formal reporting relationships and procedures, the strategic center firm manages what are often complex, cooperative interactions among network partners. To perform the tasks discussed next, the strategic center firm must make sure that incentives for participating in the network are aligned so that network firms continue to have a reason to remain connected.[119] The strategic center firm is engaged in four primary tasks as it manages the strategic network and controls its operations:[120]

Strategic outsourcing. The strategic center firm outsources and partners with more firms than do other network members. At the same time, the strategic center firm requires network partners to be more than contractors. Members are expected to find opportunities for the network to create value through its cooperative work.

Competencies. To increase network effectiveness, the strategic center firm seeks ways to support each member's efforts to develop core competencies with the potential of benefiting the network.

Technology. The strategic center firm is responsible for managing the development and sharing of technology-based ideas among network members. The structural requirement that members submit formal reports detailing the technology-oriented outcomes of their efforts to the strategic center firm facilitates this activity.[121]

Race to learn. The strategic center firm emphasizes that the principal dimensions of competition are between value chains and between networks of value chains. Because of this interconnection, the strategic network is only as strong as its weakest value-chain link. With its centralized decision-making authority and responsibility, the strategic center firm guides participants in efforts to form network-specific competitive advantages. The need for each participant to have capabilities that can be the foundation for the network's competitive advantages encourages friendly rivalry among participants seeking to develop the skills needed to quickly form new capabilities that create value for the network.[122]

Interestingly, strategic networks are being used more frequently, partly because of the ability of a strategic center firm to execute a strategy that effectively and efficiently links partner firms. Improved information systems and communication capabilities (e.g., the Internet) make such networks possible.[123]

Implementing Business-Level Cooperative Strategies

As noted in Chapter 9, the two types of business-level complementary alliances are vertical and horizontal. Firms with competencies in different stages of the value chain form a vertical alliance to cooperatively integrate their different, but complementary, skills. Firms combining their competencies to create value in the same stage of the value chain are using a horizontal alliance. Vertical complementary strategic alliances such as those developed by Toyota Motor Company are formed more frequently than horizontal alliances.[124]

A strategic network of vertical relationships such as the network in Japan between Toyota and its suppliers often involves a number of implementation issues.[125] First, the strategic center firm encourages subcontractors to modernize their facilities and provides them with technical and financial assistance to do so, if necessary. Second, the strategic center firm reduces its transaction costs by promoting longer-term contracts with subcontractors, so that supplier-partners increase their long-term productivity. This approach is diametrically opposed to that of continually negotiating short-term contracts based on unit pricing. Third, the strategic center firm enables engineers in upstream companies (suppliers) to have better communication with those companies with whom it has contracts for services. As a result, suppliers and the strategic center firm become more interdependent and less independent.[126]

The lean production system (a vertical complementary strategic alliance) pioneered by Toyota and others has been diffused throughout the global auto industry.[127] However, no auto company has learned how to duplicate the manufacturing effectiveness and efficiency Toyota derives from the cooperative arrangements in its strategic network.[128] A key factor accounting for Toyota's manufacturing-based competitive advantage is the cost other firms would incur to imitate the structural form used to support Toyota's application. In part, then, the structure of Toyota's strategic network that it created as the strategic center firm facilitates cooperative actions among network participants that competitors can't fully understand or duplicate.

In vertical complementary strategic alliances, such as the one between Toyota and its suppliers, the strategic center firm is obvious, as is the structure that firm establishes. However, the same is not always true with horizontal complementary strategic alliances where firms try to create value in the same part of the value chain, as with airline alliances that are commonly formed to create value in the marketing and sales primary activity segment of the value chain (see Table 3.6). Because air carriers commonly participate in multiple horizontal complementary alliances such as the Star Alliance between Lufthansa, United, Thai, Air Canada, SAS, and others, it is difficult to determine the strategic center firm. Moreover, participating in several alliances can cause firms to question partners' true loyalties and intentions. Also, if rivals band together in too many collaborative activities, one or more governments may suspect the possibility of illegal collusive activities. For these reasons, horizontal complementary alliances are used less frequently than their vertical counterpart.

Implementing Corporate-Level Cooperative Strategies

Corporate-level cooperative strategies (such as franchising) are used to facilitate product and market diversification. As a cooperative strategy, franchising allows the firm to use its competencies to extend or diversify its product or market reach, but without completing a merger or an acquisition.[129] Research suggests that knowledge embedded in corporate-level cooperative strategies facilitates synergy.[130] For example, "McDonald's Corporation primarily franchises and operates McDonald's restaurants in the food service industry. These restaurants serve a varied, yet limited value-priced menu in more than 100 countries around the world."[131] The McDonald's franchising system is a strategic network. McDonald's headquarters office serves as the strategic center firm for the network's franchisees. The headquarters office uses strategic controls and financial controls to verify that the franchisees' operations create the greatest value for the entire network.

An important strategic control issue for McDonald's is the location of its franchisee units. Because it believes that its greatest expansion opportunities are outside the United States, the firm has decided to continue expanding in countries such as China where it is a "partner of the 2008 Summer Olympic Games in Beijing."[132] Thus, as the strategic center firm around the globe for its restaurants, McDonald's is devoting the majority of its capital expenditures to develop units in non–U.S. markets.

Implementing International Cooperative Strategies

Strategic networks formed to implement international cooperative strategies result in firms competing in several countries.[133] Differences among countries' regulatory environments increase the challenge of managing international networks and verifying that at a minimum, the network's operations comply with all legal requirements.[134]

Distributed strategic networks are the organizational structure used to manage international cooperative strategies. As shown in Figure 11.12, several regional strategic center firms are included in the distributed network to manage partner firms' multiple cooperative arrangements.[135]

Figure 11.12 A Distributed Strategic Network

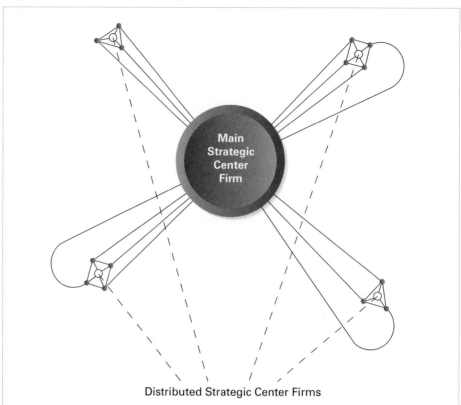

Distributed Strategic Center Firms

The EDS Agility Alliance is an example of a distributed strategic network. This alliance is "built on the basis that all of the Alliance members will jointly deliver solutions—committing resources to a project and collaborating with each other to get the job done."[136] EDS is the main strategic center firm in this alliance and has two dedicated centers that are the hubs for jointly developing initiatives with its partners. Cisco, SAP, Sun, Xerox, Oracle, EMC, and Microsoft are members of this distributed strategic network. Working together, EDS and its partners "collaborate to design, build and run a market-leading services platform and develop technology-based services that deliver tangible results to clients."[137] EDS's partners each work with their own networks to complete projects that are a part of the Agility Alliance. As this example demonstrates, the structure used to implement the international cooperative strategy is complex and demands careful attention to be used successfully.

Summary

- Organizational structure specifies the firm's formal reporting relationships, procedures, controls, and authority and decision-making processes. Essentially, organizational structure details the work to be done in a firm and how that work is to be accomplished. Organizational controls guide the use of strategy, indicate how to compare actual and expected results, and suggest actions to take to improve performance when it falls below expectations. A proper match between strategy and structure can lead to a competitive advantage.

- Strategic controls (largely subjective criteria) and financial controls (largely objective criteria) are the two types of organizational controls used to implement a strategy. Both controls are critical, although their degree of emphasis varies based on individual matches between strategy and structure.

- Strategy and structure influence each other; overall though, strategy has a stronger influence on structure. Research indicates that firms tend to change structure when declining performance forces them to do so. Effective managers anticipate the need for structural change and quickly modify structure to better accommodate the firm's strategy when evidence calls for that action.

- The functional structure is used to implement business-level strategies. The cost leadership strategy requires a centralized functional structure—one in which manufacturing efficiency and process engineering are emphasized. The differentiation strategy's functional structure decentralizes implementation-related decisions, especially those concerned with marketing, to those involved with individual organizational functions. Focus strategies, often used in small firms, require a simple structure until such time that the firm diversifies in terms of products and/or markets.

- Unique combinations of different forms of the multidivisional structure are matched with different corporate-level diversification strategies to properly implement these strategies. The cooperative M-form, used to implement the related constrained corporate-level strategy, has a centralized corporate office and extensive integrating mechanisms. Divisional incentives are linked to overall corporate performance. The related linked SBU M-form structure establishes separate profit centers within the diversified firm. Each profit center may have divisions offering similar products, but the centers are unrelated to each other. The competitive M-form structure, used to implement the unrelated diversification strategy, is highly

decentralized, lacks integrating mechanisms, and utilizes objective financial criteria to evaluate each unit's performance.

- The multidomestic strategy, implemented through the worldwide geographic area structure, emphasizes decentralization and locates all functional activities in the host country or geographic area. The worldwide product divisional structure is used to implement the global strategy. This structure is centralized in order to coordinate and integrate different functions' activities so as to gain global economies of scope and economies of scale. Decision-making authority is centralized in the firm's worldwide division headquarters.

- The transnational strategy—a strategy through which the firm seeks the local responsiveness of the multidomestic strategy and the global efficiency of the global strategy—is implemented through the combination structure. Because it must be simultaneously centralized and decentralized, integrated and nonintegrated, and formalized and nonformalized, the combination structure is difficult to organize and successfully manage. However, two structural designs are suggested: the matrix and the hybrid structure with both geographic and product-oriented divisions.

- Increasingly important to competitive success, cooperative strategies are implemented through organizational structures framed around strategic networks. Strategic center firms play a critical role in managing strategic networks.

Review Questions

1. What is organizational structure and what are organizational controls? What are the differences between strategic controls and financial controls? What is the importance of these differences?

2. What does it mean to say that strategy and structure have a reciprocal relationship?

3. What are the characteristics of the functional structures used to implement the cost leadership, differentiation, integrated cost leadership/differentiation, and focused business-level strategies?

4. What are the differences among the three versions of the multidivisional (M-form) organizational structures that are used to implement the related constrained, the related linked, and the unrelated corporate-level diversification strategies?

5. What organizational structures are used to implement the multidomestic, global, and transnational international strategies?

6. What is a strategic network? What is a strategic center firm?

Notes

1. B. Ambos & B. B. Schlegelmilch, 2007, Innovation and control in the multinational firm: A comparison of political and contingency approaches, *Strategic Management Journal,* 28: 473–486; S. Kumar, S. Kant, & T. L. Amburgey, 2007, Pubic agencies and collaborative management approaches, *Administration & Society,* 39: 569–610.

2. R. C. Sampson, 2007, R&D alliances and firm performance: The impact of

technological diversity and alliance organization on innovation, *Academy of Management Journal,* 50: 364–386; R. E. Miles & C. C. Snow, 1978, *Organizational Strategy, Structure and Process,* New York: McGraw-Hill.

3. E. M. Olson, S. F. Slater, & G. T. M. Hult, 2007, The importance of structure and process to strategy implementation, *Business Horizons,* 48(1): 47–54; D. N. Sull & C. Spinosa, 2007,

Promise-based management, *Harvard Business Review,* 85(4):79–86.

4. T. Amburgey & T. Dacin, 1994, As the left foot follows the right? The dynamics of strategic and structural change, *Academy of Management Journal,* 37: 1427–1452.

5. P. Ghemawat, 2007, Managing differences: The central challenge of global strategy, *Harvard BusinessReview,* 85(3): 59–68; B. Keats & H. O'Neill, 2001, Organizational structure: Looking through a

strategy lens, in M. A. Hitt, R. E. Freeman, & J. S. Harrison (eds.), *Handbook of Strategic Management,* Oxford, UK: Blackwell Publishers, 520–542.

6. P. J. Brews & C. L. Tucci, 2007, The structural and performance effects of internetworking, *Long Range Planning,* 40: 223–243; R. E. Hoskisson, C. W. L. Hill, & H. Kim, 1993, The multidivisional structure: Organizational fossil or source of value? *Journal of Management,* 19: 269–298.

7. E. M. Olson, S. F. Slater, G. Tomas, & G. T. M. Hult, 2005, The performance implications of fit among business strategy, marketing organization structure, and strategic behavior, *Journal of Marketing,* 69(3): 49–65.

8. R. D. Hof, 2007, Back to the future at Yahoo! *BusinessWeek,* July 2, 35–36.

9. T. Burns & G. M. Stalker, 1961, *The Management of Innovation,* London: Tavistok; P. R. Lawrence & J. W. Lorsch, 1967, *Organization and Environment,* Homewood, IL: Richard D. Irwin; J. Woodward, 1965, *Industrial Organization: Theory and Practice,* London: Oxford University Press.

10. H. Kim, R. E. Hoskisson, L. Tihanyi, & J. Hong, 2004, Evolution and restructuring of diversified business groups in emerging markets: The lessons from chaebols in Korea, *Asia Pacific Journal of Management,* 21: 25–48.

11. R. Kathuria, M. P. Joshi, & S. J. Porth, 2007, Organizational alignment and performance: Past, present and future, *Management Decision,* 45: 503–517.

12. A. Tempel & P. Walgenbach, 2007, Global standardization of organizational forms and management practices: What new institutionalism and the business-systems approach can learn from each other, *Journal of Management Studies,* 44: 1–24; Keats & O'Neill, Organizational structure, 533.

13. M. Buchanan, 2007, Questioning authority, *The Conference Board Review,* July/August, 59; H. J. Leavitt, 2003, Why hierarchies thrive, *Harvard Business Review,* 81(3): 96–102.

14. J. S. McMullen & D. A. Shepherd, 2006, Entrepreneurial action and the role of uncertainty in the theory of the entrepreneur, *Academy of Management Review,* 31: 132–152; R. L. Priem, L. G. Love, & M. A. Shaffer, 2002, Executives' perceptions of uncertainty sources: A numerical taxonomy and underlying dimensions, *Journal of Management,* 28: 725–746.

15. W. R. Chen & K. D. Miller, 2007, Situational and institutional determinants of firms' R&D search intensity, *Strategic Management Journal,* 28: 369–381; S. K. Ethiraj & D. Levinthal, 2004, Bounded rationality and the search for organizational architecture: An evolutionary perspective on the design of organizations and their evolvability, *Administrative Science Quarterly,* 49: 404–437.

16. J. G. Covin, D. P. Slevin, & M. B. Heeley, 2001, Strategic decision making in an intuitive vs. technocratic mode: Structural

and environmental consideration, *Journal of Business Research,* 52: 51–67.

17. E. M. Olson, S. F. Slater, & G. T. M. Hult, 2005, The importance of structure and process to strategy implementation, *Business Horizons,* 48(1): 47–54; H. Barkema, J. A. C. Baum, & E. A. Mannix, 2002, Management challenges in a new time, *Academy of Management Journal,* 45: 916–930.

18. L. Donaldson, 2001, *The contingency theory of organizations,* Thousand Oaks, CA: Sage; Jenster & Hussey, *Company Analysis,* 169.

19. M. A. Schilling & H. K. Steensma, 2001, The use of modular organizational forms: An industry-level analysis, *Academy of Management Journal,* 44: 1149–1168.

20. C. B. Dobni & G. Luffman, 2003, Determining the scope and impact of market orientation profiles on strategy implementation and performance, *Strategic Management Journal,* 24: 577–585; D. C. Hambrick & J. W. Fredrickson, 2001, Are you sure you have a strategy? *Academy of Management Executive,* 15(4): 48–59.

21. M. Hammer, 2007, The process audit, *Harvard Business Review,* 85(4): 111–123.

22. R. D. Ireland & J. W. Webb, 2007, Strategic entrepreneurship: Creating competitive advantage through streams of innovation, *Business Horizons,* 50: 49–59; T. J. Andersen, 2004, Integrating decentralized strategy making and strategic planning processes in dynamic environments, *Journal of Management Studies,* 41: 1271–1299.

23. J. Rivkin & N. Siggelkow, 2003, Balancing search and stability: Interdependencies among elements of organizational design, *Management Science,* 49: 290–321; G. A. Bigley & K. H. Roberts, 2001, The incident command system: High-reliability organizing for complex and volatile task environments, *Academy of Management Journal,* 44: 1281–1299.

24. S. Nadkarni & V. K. Narayanan, 2007, Strategic schemas, strategic flexibility, and firm performance: The moderating role of industry clockspeed, *Strategic Management Journal,* 28: 243–270; K. D. Miller & A. T. Arikan, 2004, Technology search investments: Evolutionary, option reasoning, and option pricing approaches, *Strategic Management Journal,* 25: 473–485.

25. S. K. Ethiraj & D. Levinthal, 2004, Modularity and innovation in complex systems, *Management Science,* 50: 159–173; T. W. Malnight, 2001, Emerging structural patterns within multinational corporations: Toward process-based structures, *Academy of Management Journal,* 44: 1187–1210; H. A. Simon, 1991, Bounded rationality and organizational learning, *Organization Science,* 2: 125–134.

26. C. Zook, 2007, Finding your next core business, *Harvard Business Review,* 85(4): 66–75.

27. G. Edmondson, 2006, BMW's dream factory, *BusinessWeek,* October 16, 70–78.

28. S. K. Maheshwari & D. Ahlstrom, 2004, Turning around a state owned enterprise: The case of Scooters India Limited, *Asia Pacific Journal of Management,* 21(1–2): 75–101; B. W. Keats & M. A. Hitt, 1988, A causal model of linkages among environmental dimensions, macroorganizational characteristics, and performance, *Academy of Management Journal,* 31: 570–598.

29. A. Chandler, 1962, *Strategy and Structure,* Cambridge, MA: MIT Press.

30. R. E. Hoskisson, R. A. Johnson, L. Tihanyi, & R. E. White, 2005, Diversified business groups and corporate refocusing in emerging economies, *Journal of Management,* 31: 941–965; J. D. Day, E. Lawson, & K. Leslie, 2003, When reorganization works, *The McKinsey Quarterly,* (2), 20–29.

31. M. Ihlwan, 2007, Samsung is having a Sony moment, *BusinessWeek,* July 30, 38.

32. S. K. Ethiraj, 2007, Allocation of inventive effort in complex product systems, *Strategic Management Journal,* 28: 563–584.

33. D. Martin, 2007, Alfred D. Chandler, Jr., a business historian, dies at 88, *New York Times Online,* http://www.nytimes.com, May 12.

34. A. Weibel, 2007, Formal control and trustworthiness, *Group & Organization Management,* 32: 500–517; P. K. Mills & G. R. Ungson, 2003, Reassessing the limits of structural empowerment: Organizational constitution and trust as controls, *Academy of Management Review,* 28: 143–153.

35. M. Santala & P. Parvinen, 2007, From strategic fit to customer fit, *Management Decision,* 45: 582–601; R. Reed, W. J. Donoher, & S. F. Barnes, 2004, Predicting misleading disclosures: The effects of control, pressure, and compensation, *Journal of Managerial Issues,* 16: 322–336.

36. T. Galpin, R. Hilpirt, & B. Evans, 2007, The connected enterprise: Beyond division of labor, *Journal of Business Strategy,* 28(2): 38–47; C. Sundaramurthy & M. Lewis, 2003, Control and collaboration: Paradoxes of governance, *Academy of Management Review,* 28: 397–415.

37. Y. Li, L. Li, Y. Liu, & L. Wang, 2005, Linking management control system with product development and process decisions to cope with environment complexity, *International Journal of Production Research,* 43: 2577–2591; D. F. Kuratko, R. D. Ireland, & J. S. Hornsby, 2001, Improving firm performance through entrepreneurial actions: Acordia's corporate entrepreneurship strategy, *Academy of Management Executive,* 15(4): 60–71.

38. G. J. M. Braam & E. J. Nijssen, 2004, Performance effects of using the Balanced Scorecard: A note on the Dutch experience, *Long Range Planning,* 37: 335–349; S. D. Julian & E. Scifres, 2002, An interpretive perspective on the role of strategic control in triggering strategic

change, *Journal of Business Strategies,* 19: 141–159.

39. D. F. Kuratko, R. D. Ireland, & J. S. Hornsby, 2004, Corporate entrepreneurship behavior among managers: A review of theory, research, and practice, in J. A. Katz & D. A. Shepherd (Eds.), *Advances in Entrepreneurship: Firm Emergence and Growth: Corporate Entrepreneurship,* Oxford, UK: Elsevier Publishing, 7–45; R. E. Hoskisson, M. A. Hitt, & R. D. Ireland, 1994, The effects of acquisitions and restructuring strategies (strategic refocusing) on innovation, in G. von Krogh, A. Sinatra, & H. Singh (eds.), *Managing Corporate Acquisition,* London: MacMillan, 144–169.

40. K. L. Turner & M. V. Makhija, 2006, The role of organizational controls in managing knowledge, *Academy of Management Review,* 31: 197–217; M. A. Hitt, R. E. Hoskisson, R. A. Johnson, & D. D. Moesel, 1996, The market for corporate control and firm innovation, *Academy of Management Journal,* 39: 1084–1119.

41. C. Witkin, 2006, Lafley and Immelt: In search of billions, *Fortune,* December 11, 70–81.

42. M. A. Hitt, L. Tihanyi, T. Miller, & B. Connelly, 2006, Internatioanl diversification: Antecedents, outcomes, and moderators, *Journal of Management,* 32:831–867; R. E. Hoskisson & M. A. Hitt, 1988, Strategic control and relative R&D investment in multiproduct firms, *Strategic Management Journal,* 9: 605–621.

43. D. Collis, D. Young, & M. Goold, 2007, The size, structure, and performance of corporate headquarters, *Strategic Management Journal,* 28: 383–405.

44. K. Chaharbaghi, 2007, The problematic of strategy: A way of seeing is also a way of not seeing, *Management Decision,* 45: 327–339; J. B. Barney, 2002, *Gaining and Sustaining Competitive Advantage,* 2nd ed., Upper Saddle River, NJ: Prentice Hall.

45. S. Lohr, 2007, Can Michael Dell refocus his namesake? *New York Times Online,* http://www.nytimes.com, September 9.

46. X. Yin & E. J. Zajac, 2004, The strategy/ governance structure fit relationship: Theory and evidence in franchising arrangements, *Strategic Management Journal,* 25: 365–383.

47. Keats & O'Neill, Organizational structure, 531.

48. Olson, Slater, & Hult, The importance of structure and process to strategy implementation; D. Miller & J. O. Whitney, 1999, Beyond strategy: Configuration as a pillar of competitive advantage, *Business Horizons,* 42(3): 5–17.

49. Chandler, *Strategy and Structure.*

50. Keats & O'Neill, Organizational structure, 524.

51. M. E. Sosa, S. D. Eppinger, & C. M. Rowles, 2004, The misalignment of product architecture and organizational structure in complex product development, *Management Science,* 50: 1674–1689.

52. S. Karim & W. Mitchell, 2004, Innovating through acquisition and internal development: A quarter-century of boundary evolution at Johnson & Johnson, *Long Range Planning,* 37: 525–547; C. Williams & W. Mitchell, 2004, Focusing firm evolution: The impact of information infrastructure on market entry by U.S. telecommunications companies, 1984–1998, *Management Science,* 50: 1561–1575.

53. I. Daizadeh, 2006, Using intellectual property to map the organizational evolution of firms: Tracing a biotechnology company from startup to bureaucracy to a multidivisional firm, *Journal of Commercial Biotechnology,* 13: 28–36.

54. C. Levicki, 1999, *The Interactive Strategy Workout,* 2nd ed., London: Prentice Hall.

55. E. E. Entin, F. J. Diedrich, & B. Rubineau, 2003, Adaptive communication patterns in different organizational structures, *Human Factors and Ergonomics Society Annual Meeting Proceedings,* 405–409; H. M. O'Neill, R. W. Pouder, & A. K. Buchholtz, 1998, Patterns in the diffusion of strategies across organizations: Insights from the innovation diffusion literature, *Academy of Management Review,* 23: 98–114.

56. 2007, Organizational structure, *Wikipedia,* http://en.wikipedia.org; Gallbraith, *Designing Organizations,* 25.

57. Keats & O'Neill, Organizational structure, 539.

58. T. J. Andersen & A. H. Segars, 2001, The impact of IT on decision structure and firm performance: Evidence from the textile and apparel industry, *Information & Management,* 39: 85–100; Lawrence & Lorsch, *Organization and Environment.*

59. J. Welch & S. Welch, 2006, Growing up but staying young, *BusinessWeek,* December 11, 112.

60. O. E. Williamson, 1975, *Markets and Hierarchies: Analysis and Anti-Trust Implications,* New York: The Free Press.

61. B. Harstad, 2007, Organizational form and the market for talent, *Journal of Labor Economics,* 25: 581–611; Chandler, *Strategy and Structure.*

62. R. Inderst, H. M. Muller, & K. Warneryd, 2007, Distributional conflict in organizations, *European Economic Review,* 51: 385–402; J. Greco, 1999, Alfred P. Sloan Jr. (1875–1966): The original organizational man, *Journal of Business Strategy,* 20(5): 30–31.

63. Hoskisson, Hill, & Kim, The multidivisional structure, 269–298.

64. H. Zhou, 2005, Market structure and organizational form, *Southern Economic Journal,* 71: 705–719; W. G. Rowe & P. M. Wright, 1997, Related and unrelated diversification and their effect on human resource management controls, *Strategic Management Journal,* 18: 329–338.

65. C. E. Helfat & K. M. Eisenhardt, 2004, Inter-temporal economies of scope, organizational modularity, and the dynamics of diversification, *Strategic Management Journal,* 25: 1217–1232;

A. D. Chandler, 1994, The functions of the HQ unit in the multibusiness firm, in R. P. Rumelt, D. E. Schendel, & D. J. Teece (eds.), *Fundamental Issues in Strategy,* Cambridge, MA: Harvard Business School Press, 327.

66. O. E. Williamson, 1994, Strategizing, economizing, and economic organization, in R. P. Rumelt, D. E. Schendel, & D. J. Teece (eds.), *Fundamental Issues in Strategy,* Cambridge, MA: Harvard Business School Press, 361–401.

67. R. M. Burton & B. Obel, 1980, A computer simulation test of the M-form hypothesis, *Administrative Science Quarterly,* 25: 457–476.

68. O. E. Williamson, 1985, *The Economic Institutions of Capitalism: Firms, Markets, and Relational Contracting,* New York: Macmillan.

69. Keats & O'Neill, Organizational structure, 532.

70. M. F. Wolff, 1999, In the organization of the future, competitive advantage will be inspired, *Research Technology Management,* 42(4): 2–4.

71. A. Weintraub, 2006, The big rethink at Pfizer, *BusinessWeek,* December 18, 42.

72. R. H. Hall, 1996, *Organizations: Structures, Processes, and Outcomes,* 6th ed., Englewood Cliffs, NJ: Prentice Hall, 13; S. Baiman, D. F. Larcker, & M. V. Rajan, 1995, Organizational design for business units, *Journal of Accounting Research,* 33: 205–229.

73. L. G. Love, R. L. Priem, & G. T. Lumpkin, 2002, Explicitly articulated strategy and firm performance under alternative levels of centralization, *Journal of Management,* 28: 611–627.

74. Hall, *Organizations,* 64–75.

75. Barney, *Gaining and Sustaining Competitive Advantage,* 257.

76. H. Karandikar & S. Nidamarthi, 2007, Implementing a platform strategy for a systems business via standardization, *Journal of Manufacturing Technology Management,* 18: 267–280.

77. Olson, Slater, Tomas, & Hult, The performance implications of fit.

78. 2007, Wal-Mart Stores, Inc, *New York Times Online,* http://www.nytimes.com, July 21.

79. 2007, Wal-Mart rolling out new company slogan, *New York Times Online,* http://www.nytimes.com, July 12.

80. Olson, Slater, Tomas & Hult, The performance implications of fit.

81. Chandler, *Strategy and Structure.*

82. 2007, Harley-Davidson, Inc., *New York Times Online,* http://www.nytimes.com, July 19.

83. R. Rumelt, 1974, *Strategy, Structure and Economic Performance,* Boston: Harvard University Press.

84. 2007, Outback Steakhouse, http://www.outback.com, September 21; R. Gibson, 2005, Outback tries to diversify in new strategy, *Wall Street Journal,* April 27, B8.

85. 2007, Restructuring boosts Colgate profit, *CNNMoney.com,* http://cnnmoney.com, July 25.

86. C. C. Markides & P. J. Williamson, 1996, Corporate diversification and organizational structure: A resource-based view, *Academy of Management Journal,* 39: 340–367; C. W. L. Hill, M. A. Hitt, & R. E. Hoskisson, 1992, Cooperative versus competitive structures in related and unrelated diversified firms, *Organization Science,* 3: 501–521.

87. P. F. Drucker, 2002, They're not employees, they're people, *Harvard Business Review,* 80(2): 70–77; J. Robins & M. E. Wiersema, 1995, A resource-based approach to the multibusiness firm: Empirical analysis of portfolio interrelationships and corporate financial performance, *Strategic Management Journal,* 16: 277–299.

88. J. R. Baum & S. Wally, 2003, Strategic decision speed and firm performance, *Strategic Management Journal,* 24: 1107–1129.

89. J. G. March, 1994, *A Primer on Decision Making: How Decisions Happen,* New York: The Free Press, 117–118.

90. M. Goold & A. Campbell, 2003, Structured networks: Towards the well designed matrix, *Long Range Planning,* 36(5): 427–439.

91. P. A. Argenti, R. A. Howell, & K. A. Beck, 2005, The strategic communication imperative, *MIT Sloan Management Review,* 46(3): 84–89.

92. R. E. Hoskisson & M. A. Hitt, 1990, Antecedents and performance outcomes of diversification: A review and critique of theoretical perspectives, *Journal of Management,* 16: 461–509.

93. Hill, Hitt, & Hoskisson, Cooperative versus competitive structures, 512.

94. J. Birkinshaw, 2001, Strategies for managing internal competition, *California Management Review,* 44(1): 21–38.

95. 2007, Textron Inc., *Wikipedia,* http://en.wikipedia.org, September 21; 2007, Textron profile, http://www.textron.com, September 21.

96. M. Maremont, 2004, Leadership; more can be more: Is the conglomerate a dinosaur from a bygone era? The answer is no—with a caveat, *Wall Street Journal,* October 24, R4; T. R. Eisenmann & J. L. Bower, 2000, The entrepreneurial M-form: Strategic integration in global media firms, *Organization Science,* 11: 348–355.

97. T. Yu & A. A. Cannella, Jr., 2007, Rivalry bwetween multinational enterprises: An event history approach, *Academy of Management Journal,* 50: 665–686; S. E. Christophe & H. Lee, 2005, What matters about internationalization: A market-based assessment, *Journal of Business Research,* 58: 636–643; Y. Luo, 2002, Product diversification in international joint ventures: Performance implications in an emerging market, *Strategic Management Journal,* 23: 1–20.

98. M. Mandel, 2007, Globalization vs. immigration reform, *BusinessWeek,* June 4, 40.

99. T. M. Begley & D. P. Boyd, 2003, The need for a corporate global mind-set, *MIT Sloan Management Review,* 44(2): 25–32; Tallman, Global strategic management, 467.

100. T. Kostova & K. Roth, 2003, Social capital in multinational corporations and a micro-macro model of its formation, *Academy of Management Review,* 28: 297–317.

101. J. Jermias & L. Gani, 2005, Ownership structure, contingent-fit, and business-unit performance: A research model and evidence, *The International Journal of Accounting,* 40: 65–85; J. Wolf & W. G. Egelhoff, 2002, A reexamination and extension of international strategy-structure theory, *Strategic Management Journal,* 23: 181–189.

102. C. A. Bartlett & S. Ghoshal, 1989, *Managing Across Borders: The Transnational Solution,* Boston: Harvard Business School Press.

103. 2007, SABMiller joint venture to buy 4 Chinese breweries for $79M, *St. Louis Buisness Journal,* http://www.mlive.com, August 24.

104. 2007, Netherlands: Heineken, InBev, SABMiller benefit from coverge review, *Just-Drinks,* http://www.just-drinks.com, September 18.

105. 2007, About SABMiller, http://www.sabmiller.com, September 21.

106. S. T. Cavusgil, S. Yeniyurt, & J. D. Townsend, 2004, The framework of a global company: A conceptualization and preliminary validation, *Industrial Marketing Management,* 33: 711–716.

107. N. Byrnes, 2007, Avon: More than cosmetic changes, *BusinessWeek,* March 12, 62–63.

108. 2007, Avon's Products, http://www.avon.com, September 20.

109. Malnight, Emerging structural patterns, 1197.

110. 2007, Avon 2005 Global Women's Survey, http://www.avon.com, September 22.

111. B. Connelly, M. A. Hitt, A. DeNisi, & R. D. Ireland, 2007, Expatriates and corporate-level international strategy: Governing with the knowledge contract, *Management Decision,* 45: 564–581.

112. 2007, P&G Corporate information—Structure, http://www.pg.com, September 21.

113. S. G. Lazzarini, 2007, The impact of membership in competing alliance constellations: Evidence on the operational performance of global airlines, *Strategic Management Journal,* 28: 345–367; Y. L. Doz & G. Hamel, 1998, *Alliance Advantage: The Art of Creating Value through Partnering,* Boston: Harvard Business School Press, 222.

114. Y. Luo, 2007, Are joint venture partners more opportunistic in a more volatile environment? *Strategic Management Journal,* 28: 39–60; K. Moller, A. Rajala, & S. Svahn, 2005, Strategic business nets—their type and management, *Journal of Business Research,* 58: 1274–1284.

115. D. Li, L. E. Eden, M. A. Hitt, & R. D. Ireland, 2008, Friends, acquaintances or strangers? *Academy of Management Journal,* in press.

116. B. Comes-Casseres, 2003, Competitive advantage in alliance constellations, *Strategic Organization,* 1: 327–335; T. K. Das & B. S. Teng, 2002, Alliance constellations: A social exchange perspective, *Academy of Management Review,* 27: 445–456.

117. S. Tallman, M. Jenkins, N. Henry, & S. Pinch, 2004, Knowledge, clusters, and competitive advantage, *Academy of Management Review,* 29: 258–271; C. Lee, K. Lee, & J. M. Pennings, 2001, Internal capabilities, external networks, and performance: A study on technology-based ventures, *Strategic Management Journal,* 22: 615–640.

118. A. Capaldo, 2007, Network structure and innovation: The leveraging of a dualnetwork as a distinctive relational capability, *Strategic Management Journal,* 28: 585–608; A. Zaheer & G. G. Bell, 2005, Benefiting from network position: Firm capabilities, structural holes, and performance, *Strategic Management Journal,* 26: 809–825; M. B. Sarkar, R. Echambadi, & J. S. Harrison, 2001, Alliance entrepreneurship and firm market performance, *Strategic Management Journal,* 22: 701–711.

119. R. D. Ireland & J. W. Webb, 2007, A multi-theoretic perspective on trust and power in strategic supply chains, *Journal of Operations Management,* 25: 482–497; V. G. Narayanan & A. Raman, 2004, Aligning incentives in supply chains, *Harvard Business Review,* 82(11): 94–102.

120. S. Harrison, 1998, *Japanese Technology and Innovation Management,* Northampton, MA: Edward Elgar.

121. T. Keil, 2004, Building external corporate venturing capability, *Journal of Management Studies,* 41: 799–825.

122. P. Dussauge, B. Garrette, & W. Mitchell, 2004, Learning from competing partners: Outcomes and duration of scale and link alliances in Europe, North America and Asia, *Strategic Management Journal,* 21: 99–126; G. Lorenzoni & C. Baden-Fuller, 1995, Creating a strategic center to manage a web of partners, *California Management Review,* 37(3): 146–163.

123. N. C. Carr, 2005, In praise of walls, *MIT Sloan Management Review,* 45(3): 10–13.

124. T. A. Stewart & A. P. Raman, 2007, Lessons from Toyota's long drive, *Harvard Business Review,* 85(7/8): 74–83; J. H. Dyer & K. Nobeoka, 2000, Creating and managing a high-performance knowledge-sharing network: The Toyota case, *Strategic Management Journal,* 21: 345–367.

125. K. G. Provan & P. Kenis, 2007, Modes of network governance: Structure, management, and effectiveness, *Journal of Public Administration Research and Theory,* http://www.oxfordjournals.org, September 21; M. Kotabe, X. Martin, & H. Domoto, 2003, Gaining from vertical partnerships: Knowledge transfer, relationship duration and supplier performance improvement in the U.S. and Japanese automotive industries,

Strategic Management Journal, 24: 293–316.

126. T. Nishiguchi, 1994, *Strategic Industrial Sourcing: The Japanese Advantage,* New York: Oxford University Press.

127. P. Dussauge, B. Garrette, & W. Mitchell, 2004, Asymmetric performance: The market share impact of scale and link alliances in the global auto industry, *Strategic Management Journal,* 25: 701–711.

128. C. Dawson & K. N. Anhalt, 2005, A "China price" for Toyota, *BusinessWeek,* February 21, 50–51; W. M. Fruin, 1992, *The Japanese Enterprise System,* New York: Oxford University Press.

129. M. Tuunanen & F. Hoy, 2007, Franchising: Multifaceted form of entrepreneurship, *International Journal of Entrepreneurship and Small Business,* 4: 52–67.

130. B. B. Nielsen, 2005, The role of knowledge embeddedness in the creation of synergies in strategic alliances, *Journal of Business Research,* 58: 1194–1204.

131. 2007, McDonald's Corporation, http://www.reuters.com, September 21.

132. 2007, McDonald's: China Olympics, http://www.mcchronicles.blogspot.com, September 21.

133. P. H. Andersen & P. R. Christensen, 2005, Bridges over troubled water: Suppliers as connective nodes in global supply networks, *Journal of Business Research,* 58: 1261–1273; C. Jones, W. S. Hesterly, & S. P. Borgatti, 1997, A general theory of network governance: Exchange conditions and social mechanisms, *Academy of Management Review,* 22: 911–945.

134. A. Goerzen, 2005, Managing alliance networks: Emerging practices of multinational corporations, *Academy of Management Executive,* 19(2): 94–107; J. M. Mezias, 2002, Identifying liabilities of foreignness and strategies to minimize their effects: The case of labor lawsuit judgments in the United States, *Strategic Management Journal,* 23: 229–244.

135. R. E. Miles, C. C. Snow, J. A. Mathews, G. Miles, & J. J. Coleman Jr., 1997, Organizing in the knowledge age: Anticipating the cellular form, *Academy of Management Executive,* 11(4): 7–20.

136. 2005, EDS and the ability alliance, http://www.ovum.com.

137. 2007, EDG Agility Alliance, http://www.eds.com, September 21.

Strategic Leadership

12

Studying this chapter should provide you with the strategic management knowledge needed to:

1. Define strategic leadership and describe top-level managers' importance.

2. Define top management teams and explain their effects on firm performance.

3. Describe the managerial succession process using internal and external managerial labor markets.

4. Discuss the value of strategic leadership in determining the firm's strategic direction.

5. Describe the importance of strategic leaders in managing the firm's resources.

6. Define organizational culture and explain what must be done to sustain an effective culture.

7. Explain what strategic leaders can do to establish and emphasize ethical practices.

8. Discuss the importance and use of organizational controls.

How Long Can I Have the Job?
The Short Lives of CEOs and
Top-Level Strategic Leaders

Evidence shows that the shelf life of a CEO is not long, and it continues to get shorter. In 1995, the average CEO tenure was 9.5 years. This average fell to 7.3 years in 2005 and is becoming even shorter today.

In ways, these averages dealing with CEO tenure do not tell the full story in that other top-level leaders sometimes last for only a short amount of time as well. Consider the following tenures as examples of this phenomenon: (1) Craig Monaghan, Sears CFO, five months, (2) Tom Taylor, Home Depot Marketing and Merchandising Chief, 11 months, (3) Catherine West, JCPenny COO, 7 months, (4) Charles Champion, Airbus Chief Operating Officer, 13 months, and (5) Xie Wen, Yahoo! China President, 42 days. Thus, short tenure for some top-level leaders is not specific to an industry, a job title, or duties.

What accounts for the brevity of some CEOs and top-level managers' tenure as strategic leaders? Without a doubt, the high stress levels and significant performance expectations cause some CEOs and top-level managers to voluntarily resign their positions more rapidly than historically was the case (we say more about this issue in the chapter's last Strategic Focus). However, other reasons play a role as well.

Peter Boneparth recently resigned as CEO of Jones Apparel Group, which owns brands such as Anne Klein, Jones New York, and Nine West. Disagreements between Boneparth and the firm's board of directors about the firm's strategy (and the future Boneparth envisioned for Jones using different strategies) led to his resignation. Chosen from the external managerial labor market (described in this chapter), Boneparth "spent much of his six years at Jones diversifying its clothing offerings through acquisitions, including a hostile takeover of the Maxwell Shoe Company, the purchase of Gloria Vanderbilt, and later, Barneys New York." The firm's board of directors seemingly felt that the company had lost contact with its core customers and that it had become too diversified through actions Boneparth took and championed. Accordingly, Jones sold Barneys New York and considered selling itself to a private equity firm. No search was conducted to replace Boneparth; instead, an insider who had been at Jones since 1990 was chosen as the new CEO.

Lasting roughly five years, Paul Pressler was tapped from Disney in the fall of 2002 to become Gap Inc.'s new CEO. In part, Pressler was chosen because he was known to be a "hard-nosed operations wizard," the type of disciplined leader Gap's board believed would reign in the firm's cost structure and improve its performance. As it turned out though, critics contend that Pressler never learned to appreciate the nuances of the fashion business. For this reason, Gap's creative artists and designers felt constrained by what they thought was an overemphasis on controlling costs and using strict financial controls. After the departure, a former Gap executive said that although talented, Pressler may have been "the wrong guy at the wrong time."

These examples appear to imply the superiority of internal successions to top-level positions; but, such an assumption is not the case. Selecting people from inside the company, with rich experience and even deep understandings of the firm's traditions as top-level strategic leaders can also lead to quick departures and less-than-expected outcomes.

Sources: N. Byrnes & D. Kiley, 2007, Hello, you must be going, *BusinessWeek,* February 12, 30–32; L. Lee, 2007, Paul Pressler's fall from the Gap, *BusinessWeek,* February 26, 80–84; J. L. Story, 2007, Chief executive steps down at Jones Apparel, *New York Times Online,* http://www.nytimes.com, July 13.

As the Opening Case implies, strategic leaders' work is demanding, challenging, and may end rapidly. Regardless of how long they remain in their positions though, strategic leaders (and most prominently CEOs) can make a major difference in how a firm performs. If a strategic leader can create a strategic vision for the firm using forward thinking, she may be able to energize the firm's human capital and achieve positive outcomes. However, the challenge of strategic leadership is significant. For example, a great deal of publicity accompanied Hewlett-Packard's (HP) hiring of Carly Fiorina; and she operated under the media spotlight during much of the six years she served as HP's CEO. The controversial acquisition of Compaq and the attempts to change the company appeared to be unsuccessful as the firm suffered weakening performance. Fiorina paid the ultimate price: losing her job. Her replacement (Mark Hurd) is unlike Fiorina in many ways and is focusing on improving HP's operational performance—a task some believe is necessary to realize benefits from acquiring Compaq. In late 2007 though, HP was outperforming major rival Dell Inc. in the PC business (see Chapter 4's Opening Case). An intriguing question to consider is the amount of credit that should go to Fiorina rather than to Hurd for this turnaround.

A major message in this chapter is that effective strategic leadership is the foundation for successfully using the strategic management process. As is implied in Figure 1.1 (on page 5), strategic leaders guide the firm in ways that result in forming a vision and mission (see Chapter 1). Often, this guidance finds leaders thinking of ways to create goals that stretch everyone in the organization to improve performance.[1] Moreover, strategic leaders facilitate the development of appropriate strategic actions and determine how to implement them. As we show in Figure 12.1, these actions are the path to strategic competitiveness and above-average returns.[2]

We begin this chapter with a definition of strategic leadership; we then discuss its importance as a potential source of competitive advantage as well as effective strategic leadership styles. Next, we examine top management teams and their effects on innovation, strategic change, and firm performance. Following this discussion, we analyze the internal and external managerial labor markets from which strategic leaders are selected. Closing the chapter are descriptions of the five key components of effective strategic leadership: determining a strategic direction, effectively managing the firm's resource portfolio (which includes exploiting and maintaining core competencies along with developing human capital and social capital), sustaining an effective organizational culture, emphasizing ethical practices, and establishing balanced organizational controls.

Strategic Leadership and Style

Strategic leadership
is the ability to anticipate, envision, maintain flexibility, and empower others to create strategic change as necessary.

Strategic leadership is the ability to anticipate, envision, maintain flexibility, and empower others to create strategic change as necessary. Multifunctional in nature, strategic leadership involves managing through others, managing an entire enterprise rather than a functional subunit, and coping with change that continues to increase in the global

Figure 12.1 Strategic Leadership and the Strategic Management Process

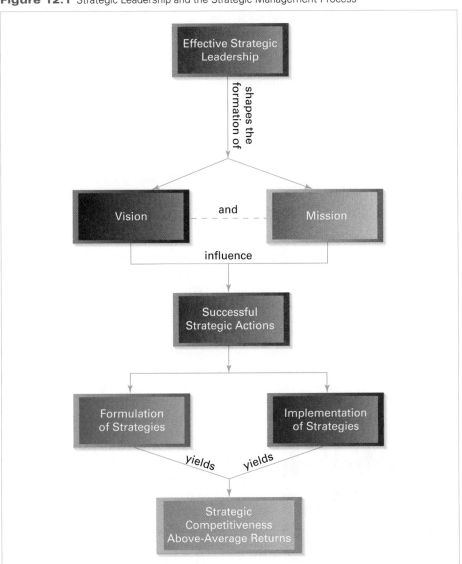

economy. Because of the global economy's complexity, strategic leaders must learn how to effectively influence human behavior, often in uncertain environments. By word or by personal example, and through their ability to envision the future, effective strategic leaders meaningfully influence the behaviors, thoughts, and feelings of those with whom they work.[3]

The ability to attract and then manage human capital may be the most critical of the strategic leader's skills,[4] especially in light of the fact that not being able to fill key positions with talented human capital constrains firm growth.[5] Increasingly, leaders throughout the global economy possess or are developing this skill. Some believe, for example, that leaders now surfacing in Chinese companies understand the rules of competition in market-based economies and are leading in ways that will develop their firm's human capital.[6] However, for some of these leaders, learning how to successfully compete in market-based economies creates a great deal of stress, causing some analysts to say that "progress, as always, comes with a price."[7]

In the twenty-first century, intellectual capital that the firm's human capital possesses, including the ability to manage knowledge and create and commercialize innovation,

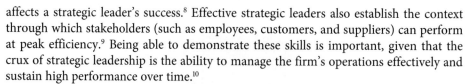

affects a strategic leader's success.[8] Effective strategic leaders also establish the context through which stakeholders (such as employees, customers, and suppliers) can perform at peak efficiency.[9] Being able to demonstrate these skills is important, given that the crux of strategic leadership is the ability to manage the firm's operations effectively and sustain high performance over time.[10]

A firm's ability to achieve a competitive advantage and earn above-average returns is compromised when strategic leaders fail to respond appropriately and quickly to changes in the complex global competitive environment. The inability to respond or to identify the need for change in the competitive environment is one of the reasons some CEOs fail. Therefore, strategic leaders must learn how to deal with diverse and complex environmental situations. Individual judgment is an important part of learning about and analyzing the firm's competitive environment.[11] However, strategic leaders also make mistakes when evaluating competitive conditions in their firm's external environment. Effective strategic leaders have the courage to admit to and accept responsibility for such decision errors and then to ask for corrective feedback from peers, superiors, and employees.[12]

The primary responsibility for effective strategic leadership rests at the top, in particular with the CEO. Other commonly recognized strategic leaders include members of the board of directors, the top management team, and divisional general managers. In truth, any individual with responsibility for the performance of human capital and/or a part of the firm (e.g., a production unit) is a strategic leader. Regardless of their title and organizational function, strategic leaders have substantial decision-making responsibilities that cannot be delegated.[13] Strategic leadership is a complex but critical form of leadership. Strategies cannot be formulated and implemented for the purpose of achieving above-average returns without effective strategic leaders.

McDonald's founder, Ray Kroc, was a strategic leader known for his high degree of integrity.

The styles used to provide leadership often affect the productivity of those being led. Transformational leadership is the most effective strategic leadership style. This style entails motivating followers to exceed the expectations others have of them, to continuously enrich their capabilities, and to place the interests of the organization above their own.[14] Transformational leaders develop and communicate a vision for the organization and formulate a strategy to achieve the vision. They make followers aware of the need to achieve valued organizational outcomes. And they encourage followers to continuously strive for higher levels of achievement. These types of leaders have a high degree of integrity (Roy Kroc, founder of McDonald's was a strategic leader valued for his high degree of integrity)[15] and character. Speaking about character, one CEO said the following: "Leaders are shaped and defined by character. Leaders inspire and enable others to do excellent work and realize their potential. As a result, they build successful, enduring organizations."[16] Additionally, transformational leaders have emotional intelligence. Emotionally intelligent leaders understand themselves well, have strong motivation, are empathetic with others, and have effective interpersonal skills.[17] At Procter & Gamble (P&G), emotional intelligence is thought of as having an "in-touch capability."[18]

Doug Conant, CEO of Campbell Soup Co., appears to be a transformational leader. We present evidence supporting this possibility in the Strategic Focus. Notice that among other characteristics of a transformational leader, Conant has established a vision and mission for the firm and is committed to supporting the firm's employees—a resource that he believes is critical to his firm's continuing success. While reading the Strategic Focus, make a list of the characteristics or qualities that allow you to conclude that Conant is a transformational leader.

STRATEGY RIGHT NOW

Doug Conant: Providing Effective Strategic Leadership at Campbell Soup Co.

"In just under six years since he came on board, Conant, 55, has transformed Campbell from a beleaguered old brand rumored to be on the auction block to one of the food industry's best performers." Obviously, the accomplishments these words suggest are quite noteworthy. Although cutting costs contributed to this positive outcome, smart product innovations and actions to empower and reinvigorate the workforce are playing a more important role in the Conant-led turnaround at Campbell. Additionally, Conant constantly evaluates the synergies within his firm's portfolio of consumer goods. Recently, he concluded that the Godiva unit no longer fits with Campbell's "strategic focus on simple meals, including soup, baked snacks, and vegetable-based beverages." As a result, Godiva became available for sale in the third quarter of 2007.

Many of the actions Conant is taking as well as how he takes those actions are consistent with the attributes of transformational leadership. Consider that he happily gives credit to others for the firm's achievements and continuously deflects praise about his role in Campbell's turnaround. During his tenure, he sent (to date) more than 16,000 handwritten thank you notes to employees and others to highlight an achievement. He makes this effort to celebrate "what's right" about a person's work or attitudes. He readily admits mistakes (saying "I can do better"), largely because he realizes he doesn't have all the answers. Framing an inspiring vision and mission statements were among the first actions he took as CEO. He believes strongly in workforce diversity, saying that "Our goal as a company is to cultivate a diverse employee population that brings new and richer perspectives to their jobs and enables us to better understand, anticipate and respond to the changed marketplace." Part of the reason for announcing that Campbell would expand its corporate headquarters building (as well as construct other facilities at its headquarters site) in Camden, New Jersey, is Conant's belief that companies need to be good citizens in the communities in which they are located.

Several principles guide Conant's work as a strategic leader. Using a personal touch to interact with people, working with individuals to jointly set their performance expectations, and creating opportunities for every person to succeed are some of the direction-providing principles Conant follows as a strategic leader.

Sources: 2007, Diversity, passion, innovation, growth, http://www.campbellsoupcompany.com, September 30; 2007, Executive team, http://www.campbellsoupcompany.com, September 30; 2007, Doug Conant remarks to press announcing plan for Campbell to expand world headquarters facilities, http://www.campbellsoupcompany.com, September 30; B. Dorman, 2007, Campbell Soup considers selling Godiva unit, *USA Today Online*, http://www .usatoday.com, August 9; A. Carter, 2006, Lighting a fire under Campbell, *BusinessWeek*, December 4, 96–100.

The Role of Top-Level Managers

Top-level managers play a critical role in that they are charged to make certain their firm is able to effectively formulate and implement strategies.[19] Top-level managers' strategic decisions influence how the firm is designed and goals will be achieved. Thus, a critical element of organizational success is having a top management team with superior managerial skills.[20]

Managers often use their discretion (or latitude for action) when making strategic decisions, including those concerned with effectively implementing strategies.[21] Managerial discretion differs significantly across industries. The primary factors that determine the amount of decision-making discretion held by a manager (especially a top-level manager) are (1) external environmental sources such as the industry structure, the rate of market growth in the firm's primary industry, and the degree to which products can be differentiated; (2) characteristics of the organization, including its size, age, resources, and culture; and (3) characteristics of the manager, including commitment to the firm and its strategic outcomes, tolerance for ambiguity, skills in working with different people, and aspiration levels (see Figure 12.2). Because strategic leaders' decisions are intended to help the firm gain a competitive advantage, how managers exercise discretion when determining appropriate strategic actions is critical to the firm's success.[22]

In addition to determining new strategic initiatives, top-level managers develop a firm's organizational structure and reward systems. Top executives also have a major effect on a firm's culture. Evidence suggests that managers' values are critical in shaping a firm's cultural values.[23] Accordingly, top-level managers have an important effect on organizational activities and performance.[24] Because of the challenges top executives face, they often are more effective when they operate as top management teams.

Top Management Teams

In most firms, the complexity of challenges and the need for substantial amounts of information and knowledge require strategic leadership by a team of executives. Using a team to make strategic decisions also helps to avoid another potential problem when these decisions are made by the CEO alone: managerial hubris. Research evidence

Figure 12.2 Factors Affecting Managerial Discretion

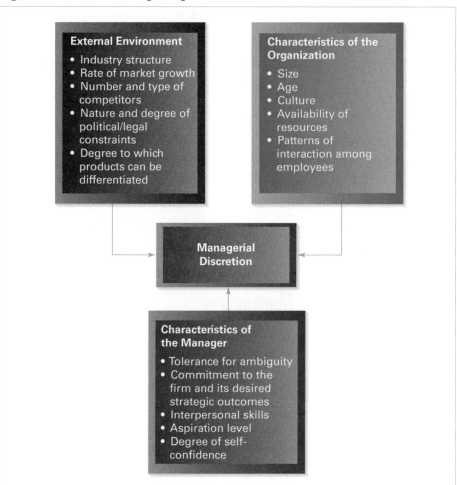

Source: Adapted from S.Finkelstein & D. C. Hambrick, 1996, *Strategic Leadership: Top Executives and Their Effects on Organizations*, St. Paul, MN: West Publishing Company.

shows that when CEOs begin to believe glowing press accounts and to feel that they are unlikely to make errors, they are more likely to make poor strategic decisions.[25] Top executives need to have self-confidence but must guard against allowing it to become arrogance and a false belief in their own invincibility.[26] To guard against CEO over-confidence and poor strategic decisions, firms often use the top management team to consider strategic opportunities and problems and to make strategic decisions. The **top management team** is composed of the key individuals who are responsible for selecting and implementing the firm's strategies. Typically, the top management team includes the officers of the corporation, defined by the title of vice president and above or by service as a member of the board of directors.[27] The quality of the strategic decisions made by a top management team affects the firm's ability to innovate and engage in effective strategic change.[28]

> The **top management team** is composed of the key individuals who are responsible for selecting and implementing the firm's strategies.

Top Management Team, Firm Performance, and Strategic Change

The job of top-level executives is complex and requires a broad knowledge of the firm's operations, as well as the three key parts of the firm's external environment—the general, industry, and competitor environments, as discussed in Chapter 2. Therefore, firms try to form a top management team with knowledge and expertise needed to operate the internal organization, yet that also can deal with all the firm's stakeholders as well as its competitors.[29] To have these characteristics normally requires a heterogeneous top management team. A **heterogeneous top management team** is composed of individuals with different functional backgrounds, experience, and education.

> A **heterogeneous top management team** is composed of individuals with different functional backgrounds, experience, and education.

Members of a heterogeneous top management team benefit from discussing the different perspectives advanced by team members.[30] In many cases, these discussions increase the quality of the team's decisions, especially when a synthesis emerges within the team after evaluating the diverse perspectives.[31] The net benefit of such actions by heterogeneous teams has been positive in terms of market share and above-average returns. Research shows that more heterogeneity among top management team members promotes debate, which often leads to better strategic decisions. In turn, better strategic decisions produce higher firm performance.[32]

It is also important for top management team members to function cohesively. In general, the more heterogeneous and larger the top management team is, the more difficult it is for the team to effectively implement strategies.[33] Comprehensive and long-term strategic plans can be inhibited by communication difficulties among top executives who have different backgrounds and different cognitive skills.[34] Alternatively, communication among diverse top management team members can be facilitated through electronic communications, sometimes reducing the barriers before face-to-face meetings.[35] However, a group of top executives with diverse backgrounds may inhibit the process of decision making if it is not effectively managed. In these cases, top management teams may fail to comprehensively examine threats and opportunities, leading to a suboptimal strategic decision. Thus, the CEO must attempt to achieve behavioral integration among the team members.[36]

Having members with substantive expertise in the firm's core functions and businesses is also important to a top management team's effectiveness. In a high-technology industry, it may be critical for a firm's top management team members to have R&D expertise, particularly when growth strategies are being implemented.[37] Yet their eventual effect on strategic decisions depends not only on their expertise and the way the team is managed but also on the context in which they make the decisions (the governance structure, incentive compensation, etc.).[38]

The characteristics of top management teams are related to innovation and strategic change.[39] For example, more heterogeneous top management teams are positively associated with innovation and strategic change. The heterogeneity may force the team or some of its members to "think outside of the box" and thus be more creative in making decisions. Therefore, firms that need to change their strategies are more likely to do so if they have top management teams with diverse backgrounds and expertise. When a new CEO is hired from outside the industry, the probability of strategic change is greater than if the new CEO is from inside the firm or inside the industry.[40] Although hiring a new CEO from outside the industry adds diversity to the team, the top management team must be managed effectively to use the diversity in a positive way. Thus, to successfully create strategic change, the CEO should exercise transformational leadership.[41] A top management team with various areas of expertise is more likely to identify environmental changes (opportunities and threats) or changes within the firm, suggesting the need for a different strategic direction.

The CEO and Top Management Team Power

As noted in Chapter 10, the board of directors is an important governance mechanism for monitoring a firm's strategic direction and for representing stakeholders' interests, especially those of shareholders.[42] In fact, higher performance normally is achieved when the board of directors is more directly involved in shaping a firm's strategic direction.[43]

Boards of directors, however, may find it difficult to direct the strategic actions of powerful CEOs and top management teams.[44] Often, a powerful CEO appoints a number of sympathetic outside members to the board or may have inside board members who are also on the top management team and report to her or him.[45] In either case, the CEO may significantly influence the board's actions. Thus, the amount of discretion a CEO has in making strategic decisions is related to the board of directors and how it chooses to oversee the actions of the CEO and the top management team.[46]

CEOs and top management team members can achieve power in other ways. A CEO who also holds the position of chairperson of the board usually has more power than the CEO who does not.[47] Some analysts and corporate "watchdogs" criticize the practice of CEO duality (when the CEO and the chairperson of the board are the same). A reason for this criticism is that CEO duality has been blamed for poor performance and slow response to change in a number of firms.[48]

Although it varies across industries, CEO duality occurs most commonly in larger firms. Increased shareholder activism, however, has brought CEO duality under scrutiny and attack in both U.S. and European firms. Historically, an independent board leadership structure in which the same person did not hold the positions of CEO and chair was believed to enhance a board's ability to monitor top-level managers' decisions and actions, particularly with respect to financial performance.[49] And, as reported in Chapter 10, many believe these two positions should be separate in most companies to make the board more independent from the CEO. Stewardship theory, on the other hand, suggests that CEO duality facilitates effective decisions and actions. In these instances, the increased effectiveness gained through CEO duality accrues from the individual who wants to perform effectively and desires to be the best possible steward of the firm's assets. Because of this person's positive orientation and actions, extra governance and the coordination costs resulting from an independent board leadership structure would be unnecessary.[50]

Top management team members and CEOs who have long tenure—on the team and in the organization—have a greater influence on board decisions. And CEOs with greater influence may take actions in their own best interests, the outcomes of which increase their compensation from the company.[51] In response to this concern, U.S. lawmakers voted in the latter part of 2007 to "require public companies to put executive pay packages before shareholders for an advisory vote." Most analysts expected the bill to face an uphill battle, meaning that the final outcome for this proposed legislation was uncertain.[52]

In general, long tenure is thought to constrain the breadth of an executive's knowledge base. Some evidence suggests that with the limited perspectives associated with a restricted knowledge base, long-tenured top executives typically develop fewer alternatives to evaluate in making strategic decisions.[53] However, long-tenured managers also may be able to exercise more effective strategic control, thereby obviating the need for board members' involvement because effective strategic control generally produces higher performance.[54] Intriguingly, recent findings suggest that "the liabilities of short tenure . . . appear to exceed the advantages, while the advantages of long tenure—firm-specific human and social capital, knowledge, and power—seem to outweigh the disadvantages of rigidity and maintaining the status quo."[55] Overall then the relationship between CEO tenure and firm performance is complex, indicating that to strengthen the firm, boards of directors should develop an effective relationship with the top management team.

In summary, the relative degrees of power held by the board and top management team members should be examined in light of an individual firm's situation. For example, the abundance of resources in a firm's external environment and the volatility of that environment may affect the ideal balance of power between the board and the top management teams. Moreover, a volatile and uncertain environment may create a situation where a powerful CEO is needed to move quickly, but a diverse top management team may create less cohesion among team members and prevent or stall necessary strategic actions. With effective working relationships, boards, CEOs, and other top management team members have the foundation required to select arrangements with the highest probability of best serving stakeholders' interests.[56]

Managerial Succession

The choice of top executives—especially CEOs—is a critical decision with important implications for the firm's performance.[57] Many companies use leadership screening systems to identify individuals with managerial and strategic leadership potential as well as to determine the criteria individuals should satisfy to be candidates for the CEO position.[58] The most effective of these systems assess people within the firm and gain valuable information about the capabilities of other companies' managers, particularly their strategic leaders.[59] Based on the results of these assessments, training and development programs are provided for current individuals in an attempt to preselect and shape the skills of people who may become tomorrow's leaders. Because of the quality of its programs, General Electric "is famous for developing leaders who are dedicated to turning imaginative ideas into leading products and services."[60]

Organizations select managers and strategic leaders from two types of managerial labor markets—internal and external.[61] An **internal managerial labor market** consists of a firm's opportunities for managerial positions and the qualified employees within that firm. An **external managerial labor market** is the collection of managerial career opportunities and the qualified people who are external to the organization in which the opportunities exist.

Several benefits are thought to accrue to a firm when the internal labor market is used to select an insider as the new CEO. Because of their experience with the firm and the industry environment in which it competes, insiders are familiar with company products, markets, technologies, and operating procedures. Also, internal hiring produces lower turnover among existing personnel, many of whom possess valuable firm-specific knowledge. When the firm is performing well, internal succession is favored to sustain high performance. It is assumed that hiring from inside keeps the important knowledge necessary to sustain performance.

An **internal managerial labor market** consists of a firm's opportunities for managerial positions and the qualified employees within that firm.

An **external managerial labor market** is the collection of managerial career opportunities and the qualified people who are external to the organization in which the opportunities exist.

Kellogg's has consistently been named one of the most ethical companies in the world. David Mackay, CEO of Kellogg's, has worked hard to maintain founder W. K. Kellogg's philosophy of integrity and doing good things for people through good nutrition.

Alan Mulally (pictured here), Ford's new CEO, was an outside hire. In fact, all of Detroit's big three companies are now headed by new CEOs hired from outside their organizations.

Results of work completed by management consultant Jim Collins support the value of using the internal labor market when selecting a CEO. Collins found that high-performing firms almost always appoint an insider to be the new CEO. He argues that bringing in a well-known outsider, to whom he refers as a "white knight," is a recipe for mediocrity.[62] The nature of Collins's results may account for recent succession decisions made at General Electric (GE) and Kellogg Co. Given the phenomenal success of GE and the firm's highly effective management and leadership development programs insider Jeffrey Immelt was chosen to succeed Jack Welch. The succession process led to an identical outcome at Kellogg. "Even though Mackay was not quite ready to assume the top job, the directors did not want to entrust the nearly 100-year-old company to someone who hadn't spent his professional life hip-deep in corn flakes, Rice Krispies, and Froot Loops." Given their view, Kellogg's board of directors chose insider David Mackay as its new CEO. However, one of its own board members served as interim CEO for two years, a time period during which Mackay fully acquainted himself with the nature and rigors of his new position.[63]

It is not unusual for employees to strongly prefer using the internal managerial labor market when selecting top management team members and the CEO. In the past, companies have also had a preference for insiders to fill top-level management positions because of a desire for continuity and a continuing commitment to the firm's current vision, mission, and chosen strategies.[64] However, because of a changing competitive landscape and varying levels of performance, an increasing number of boards of directors are turning to outsiders to succeed CEOs. A firm often has valid reasons to select an outsider as its new CEO: In some situations for example, long tenure with a firm may reduce strategic leaders' level of commitment to push innovation throughout the firm. Given innovation's importance to firm success (see Chapter 13), this hesitation could be a liability for a strategic leader.

In a break from tradition, the recent choices of CEOs in U.S. automobile manufacturers (Chrysler, Ford, and General Motors) have come from the external labor market. Some analysts see these choices as an indication that "it is no longer a requirement to have 'motor oil in your veins'. . . to run a car company."[65] However, as is the case with using the internal market, deciding to select top-level leaders from the external market does not guarantee success. Consider Wal-Mart's recent experiences. Facing a "mid-life" crisis,[66] Wal-Mart recruited Claire Watts from the external market and appointed her as senior vice president for merchandising. Having worked at Limited Brands and May Department Stores, Watts was asked to lead Wal-Mart's foray into fashionable clothing and home décor. Stated simply, this effort never approached the levels of success Wal-Mart envisioned, resulting in Watts's decision to resign.[67] Although the exact causes of this failure are probably many, some who have worked at Wal-Mart allege that the firm's culture is too resistant to new programs[68] and that the resistance likely created problems for Watts and those working with her.

Figure 12.3 Effects of CEO Succession and Top Management Team Composition on Strategy

In Figure 12.3, we show how the composition of the top management team and the CEO succession (managerial labor market) interact to affect strategy. For example, when the top management team is homogeneous (its members have similar functional experiences and educational backgrounds) and a new CEO is selected from inside the firm, the firm's current strategy is unlikely to change. Alternatively, when a new CEO is selected from outside the firm and the top management team is heterogeneous, the probability is high that strategy will change. When the new CEO is from inside the firm and a heterogeneous top management team is in place, the strategy may not change, but innovation is likely to continue. An external CEO succession with a homogeneous team creates a more ambiguous situation. The recent selection of Sir Howard Stringer as CEO of Sony suggests changes in that firm's future. He is not only an outsider but also a foreigner. His selection as Sony's new CEO may be a result of increasing globalization and may be a harbinger of future appointments.[69]

Including talent from all parts of both the internal and external labor markets increases the likelihood that the firm will be able to form an effective top-management team. Evidence suggests that women are a qualified source of talent as strategic leaders that have been somewhat overlooked. In light of the success of a growing number of female executives, the foundation for change may be established. Trailblazers such as Catherine Elizabeth Hughes (the first African-American woman to head a firm that was publicly traded on a U.S. stock exchange), Muriel Siebert (the first woman to purchase a seat on the New York Stock Exchange), and publisher Judith Regan have made important contributions as strategic leaders. Prominent female CEOs are also receiving deserved recognition for their accomplishments. Anne Mulcahy (Xerox Corporation), Meg Whitman (eBay), and Andrea Jung (Avon Products) are examples of these individuals.

Despite the progress already made, work remains. Recent evidence shows, for example, "that investor reactions to the announcements of female CEOs are significantly more negative than those of their male counterparts."[70] Other evidence suggests that "women continue to be markedly underrepresented in leadership positions in organizations."[71] The important point for strategic leaders to recall is that empowering all individuals in the workforce increases the opportunities for them to fully develop their skills, expanding the size of the internal and external managerial labor markets as a result of doing so.[72]

Key Strategic Leadership Actions

Certain actions characterize effective strategic leadership; we present the most important ones in Figure 12.4. Many of the actions interact with each other. For example, managing the firm's resources effectively includes developing human capital and contributes to establishing a strategic direction, fostering an effective culture, exploiting core competencies, using effective organizational control systems, and establishing ethical practices. While studying these actions, notice that all of them find strategic leaders making decisions about the firm's direction, about how to use resources, and so forth.[73] The most effective strategic leaders create viable options when dealing with each of the key strategic leadership action situations as the foundation for making effective decisions.[74]

Determining Strategic Direction

Determining the strategic direction involves specifying the image and character the firm seeks to develop over time.[75] The strategic direction is framed within the context of the conditions (i.e., opportunities and threats) strategic leaders expect their firm to face in roughly the next three to five years.

The ideal long-term strategic direction has two parts: a core ideology and an envisioned future. The core ideology motivates employees through the company's heritage, but the envisioned future encourages employees to stretch beyond their expectations of accomplishment and requires significant change and progress to be realized.[76] The envisioned future serves as a guide to many aspects of a firm's strategy implementation process, including motivation, leadership, employee empowerment, and organizational design.

Most changes in strategic direction are difficult to design and implement; however, CEO Jeffrey Immelt has an even greater challenge at GE. GE performed exceptionally well under Jack Welch's leadership. Although change is necessary because the competitive landscape is shifting, stakeholders accustomed to Jack Welch and high performance may not readily accept Immelt's changes (e.g., changes to the firm's corporate-level strategy and structure we discussed in Chapter 11). Immelt is trying to effect critical changes in the firm's culture, strategy, and governance and simultaneously gain stakeholders'

Determining the strategic direction involves specifying the image and character the firm seeks to develop over time.

Figure 12.4 Exercise of Effective Strategic Leadership

commitment to them. As is true for all leaders trying to change a firm's strategic direction, Immelt needs to win people's hearts and minds while encouraging them to "tackle unscalable heights and make them understand why change is necessary, passionately explaining what's in it for the company—and employees."[77] Additionally, information regarding the firm's strategic direction must be consistently and clearly communicated to all affected parties.[78]

A charismatic CEO may foster stakeholders' commitment to a new vision and strategic direction. Nonetheless, it is important not to lose sight of the organization's strengths when making changes required by a new strategic direction. Immelt, for example, needs to use GE's strengths to ensure continued positive performance. The goal is to pursue the firm's short-term need to adjust to a new vision and strategic direction while maintaining its long-term survivability by effectively managing its portfolio of resources.

Effectively Managing the Firm's Resource Portfolio

Effectively managing the firm's portfolio of resources may be the most important strategic leadership task. The firm's resources are categorized as financial capital, human capital, social capital, and organizational capital (including organizational culture).[79]

Clearly, financial capital is critical to organizational success; strategic leaders understand this reality.[80] However, the most effective strategic leaders recognize the equivalent importance of managing each remaining type of resource as well as managing the integration of resources (e.g., using financial capital to provide training opportunities through which human capital is able to learn and maximize its performance). Most importantly, effective strategic leaders manage the firm's resource portfolio by organizing them into capabilities, structuring the firm to facilitate using those capabilities, and choosing strategies through which the capabilities are successfully leveraged to create value for customers. Exploiting and maintaining core competencies and developing and retaining the firm's human and social capital are actions taken to reach these important objectives.

Exploiting and Maintaining Core Competencies

Examined in Chapters 1 and 3, *core competencies* are capabilities that serve as a source of competitive advantage for a firm over its rivals. Typically, core competencies relate to an organization's functional skills, such as manufacturing, finance, marketing, and research and development. Strategic leaders must verify that the firm's competencies are emphasized when implementing strategies. Intel, for example, has core competencies of *competitive agility* (an ability to act in a variety of competitively relevant ways) and *competitive speed* (an ability to act quickly when facing environmental and competitive pressures).[81] Capabilities are developed over time as firms learn from their actions and enhance their knowledge about specific actions needed. For example, through repeated interactions, some firms have formed a capability allowing them to fully understand customers' needs as they change.[82] Firms with capabilities in R&D that develop into core competencies are rewarded by the market because of the critical nature of innovation in many industries.[83]

Through its purchase of Quaker Foods (which owned Gatorade), PepsiCo was able to use its competence in distribution systems to exploit the Quaker assets and to increase the nutritional value of all of its food offerings.

In many large firms, and certainly in related diversified ones, core competencies are effectively exploited when they are developed and applied across different organizational units (see Chapter 6). For example, PepsiCo purchased Quaker Oats (now called Quaker Foods), which makes the

© AP Photo/John Keating, ho

sports drink Gatorade. PepsiCo uses its competence in distribution systems to exploit the Quaker assets. In this instance, Pepsi soft drinks (e.g., Pepsi Cola and Mountain Dew) and Gatorade share the logistics activity. Similarly, PepsiCo uses this competence to distribute Quaker's healthy snacks and Frito-Lay salty snacks through the same channels. Today, PepsiCo seeks to increase the nutritional value of all of its food items while trying to "ensure consumers never have to trade off nutrition and taste."[84]

Firms must continuously develop and when appropriate, change their core competencies to outperform rivals. If they have a competence that provides an advantage but do not change it, competitors will eventually imitate that competence and reduce or eliminate the firm's competitive advantage. Additionally, firms must guard against the competence becoming a liability, thereby preventing change.

As we discuss next, human capital is critical to a firm's success. One reason it's so critical is that human capital is the resource through which core competencies are developed and used.

Developing Human Capital and Social Capital

Human capital refers to the knowledge and skills of a firm's entire workforce. From the perspective of human capital, employees are viewed as a capital resource requiring continuous investment.[85] At PepsiCo, people are identified as the key to the firm's continuing success. Given the need to "sustain its talent," PepsiCo invests in its human capital in the form of a host of programs and development-oriented experiences.[86]

Investments such as those being made at PepsiCo are productive, in that much of the development of U.S. industry can be attributed to the effectiveness of its human capital. This fact suggests that "as the dynamics of competition accelerate, people are perhaps the only truly sustainable source of competitive advantage."[87] In all types of organizations—large and small, new and established, and so forth—human capital's increasing importance suggests a significant role for the firm's human resource management activities.[88] As a support activity (see Chapter 3), human resource management practices facilitate people's efforts to successfully select and especially to use the firm's strategies.[89]

Effective training and development programs increase the probability of individuals becoming successful strategic leaders.[90] These programs are increasingly linked to firm success as knowledge becomes more integral to gaining and sustaining a competitive advantage.[91] Additionally, such programs build knowledge and skills, inculcate a common set of core values, and offer a systematic view of the organization, thus promoting the firm's vision and organizational cohesion. At McDonald's, the firm is trying to build an "employment brand," which suggests that individuals can begin their McDonald's career as a teenager and, through hard work and the company's training programs, become a strategic leader. This career path is the one Karen King, who is the president of McDonald's USA East Division, has experienced.[92]

Effective training and development programs also contribute positively to the firm's efforts to form core competencies.[93] Furthermore, they help strategic leaders improve skills that are critical to completing other tasks associated with effective strategic leadership, such as determining the firm's strategic direction, exploiting and maintaining the firm's core competencies, and developing an organizational culture that supports ethical practices. Thus, building human capital is vital to the effective execution of strategic leadership. Indeed, some argue that the world's "best companies are realizing that no matter what business they're in, their real business is building leaders."[94]

Strategic leaders must acquire the skills necessary to help develop human capital in their areas of responsibility.[95] When human capital investments are successful, the result is a workforce capable of learning continuously. Continuous learning and leveraging the firm's expanding knowledge base are linked with strategic success.[96]

Human capital refers to the knowledge and skills of a firm's entire workforce.

STRATEGY RIGHT NOW

An important aspect of leveraging a firm's knowledge is for retiring employees to convey their knowledge to their successors. Increasingly, firms are putting formal programs into place through which knowledge from human capital that is retiring is successfully transferred to human capital that is the firm's future.[97]

Learning also can preclude making errors. Strategic leaders tend to learn more from their failures than their successes because they sometimes make the wrong attributions for the successes.[98] For example, the effectiveness of certain approaches and knowledge can be context specific.[99] Some "best practices," for example, may not work well in all situations. We know that using teams to make decisions can be effective, but sometimes it is better for leaders to make decisions alone, especially when the decisions must be made and implemented quickly (e.g., in crisis situations).[100]

Thus, effective strategic leaders recognize the importance of learning from success *and* from failure. Although Disney Co.'s strategic leaders have learned from many successes, they have a current opportunity to learn from failure. Only briefly after launching Disney cell phone service and the ESPN cell phone company,

Walt Disney's strategic leaders learned that trying to sell cell phone service directly to customers was difficult and would not work.

Disney closed both businesses. The decision to rely on brand names to sell cell phones and cell phone services directly to customers simply did not work as efforts to compete against the major carriers and to use big box retailers such as Best Buy as distribution channels were unsuccessful. Learning from these failures, Disney is now seeking to partner with others (e.g., Verizon Wireless) to find ways to distribute its content.[101]

Learning and building knowledge are important for creating innovation in firms.[102] Innovation leads to competitive advantage.[103] Overall, firms that create and maintain greater knowledge usually achieve and maintain competitive advantages. However, as noted with core competencies, strategic leaders must guard against allowing high levels of knowledge in one area to lead to myopia and overlooking knowledge development opportunities in other important areas of the business.[104]

When facing challenging conditions, firms sometimes decide to lay off some of their human capital. Strategic leaders must recognize though that layoffs can result in a significant loss of the knowledge possessed by the firm's human capital. Research evidence shows that moderate-sized layoffs may improve firm performance, but large layoffs produce stronger performance downturns in firms because of the loss of human capital.[105] Although it is also not uncommon for restructuring firms to reduce their expenditures on or investments in training and development programs, restructuring may actually be an important time to increase investments in these programs. The reason for increased focus on training and development is that restructuring firms have less slack and cannot absorb as many errors; moreover, the employees who remain after layoffs may find themselves in positions without all the skills or knowledge they need to perform the required tasks effectively.

Viewing employees as a resource to be maximized rather than as a cost to be minimized facilitates successful implementation of a firm's strategies as does the strategic leader's ability to approach layoffs in a manner that employees believe is fair and equitable.[106] A critical issue for employees is the fairness in the layoffs and in treatment in their jobs.[107]

Social capital involves relationships inside and outside the firm that help the firm accomplish tasks and create value for customers and shareholders.[108] Social capital is a critical asset for a firm. Inside the firm, employees and units must cooperate to get the work done. In multinational organizations, employees often find themselves cooperating across country boundaries on activities such as R&D to achieve performance objectives (e.g., developing new products).[109]

Social capital involves relationships inside and outside the firm that help the firm accomplish tasks and create value for customers and shareholders.

External social capital is increasingly critical to firm success. The reason for this is that few if any companies have all of the resources they need to successfully compete against their rivals. Firms can use cooperative strategies such as strategic alliances (see Chapter 9) to develop social capital. Social capital can develop in strategic alliances as firms share complementary resources. Resource sharing must be effectively managed, though, to ensure that the partner trusts the firm and is willing to share the desired resources.[110]

Research evidence suggests that the success of many types of firms may partially depend on social capital. Large multinational firms often must establish alliances in order to enter new foreign markets. Likewise, entrepreneurial firms often must establish alliances to gain access to resources, venture capital, or other types of resources (e.g., special expertise that the entrepreneurial firm cannot afford to maintain in-house).[111] Retaining quality human capital and maintaining strong internal social capital can be affected strongly by the firm's culture.

Sustaining an Effective Organizational Culture

An **organizational culture** consists of a complex set of ideologies, symbols, and core values that are shared throughout the firm and influence the way business is conducted.

In Chapter 1, we define **organizational culture** as a complex set of ideologies, symbols, and core values that are shared throughout the firm and influence the way business is conducted. Evidence suggests that a firm can develop core competencies in terms of both the capabilities it possesses and the way the capabilities are leveraged when implementing strategies to produce desired outcomes. In other words, because the organizational culture influences how the firm conducts its business and helps regulate and control employees' behavior, it can be a source of competitive advantage[112] and is a "critical factor in promoting innovation."[113] Given its importance, it may be that a vibrant organizational culture is the most valuable competitive differentiator for business organizations.[114] Thus, shaping the context within which the firm formulates and implements its strategies—that is, shaping the organizational culture—is an essential strategic leadership action.[115]

Entrepreneurial Mind-Set

Especially in large organizations, an organizational culture often encourages (or discourages) strategic leaders from pursuing (or not pursuing) entrepreneurial opportunities.[116] This issue is important because entrepreneurial opportunities are a vital source of growth and innovation.[117] Therefore, a key role of strategic leaders is to encourage and promote innovation by pursuing entrepreneurial opportunities.[118]

One way to encourage innovation is to invest in opportunities as real options—that is, invest in an opportunity in order to provide the potential option of taking advantage of the opportunity at some point in the future.[119] For example, a firm might buy a piece of land to have the option to build on it at some time in the future should the company need more space and should that location increase in value to the company. Firms might enter strategic alliances for similar reasons. In this instance, a firm might form an alliance to have the option of acquiring the partner later or of building a stronger relationship with it (e.g., developing a joint new venture).[120]

In Chapter 13, we describe how large firms use strategic entrepreneurship to pursue entrepreneurial opportunities and to gain first-mover advantages. Small and medium-sized firms also rely on strategic entrepreneurship when trying to develop innovations as the foundation for profitable growth. In firms of all sizes, strategic entrepreneurship is more likely to be successful when employees have an entrepreneurial mind-set.[121] Five dimensions characterize a firm's entrepreneurial mind-set: autonomy, innovativeness, risk taking, proactiveness, and competitive aggressiveness.[122] In combination, these dimensions influence the actions a firm takes to be innovative and launch new ventures. In sum, strategic leaders with an entrepreneurial mind-set are committed to pursuing profitable growth.[123]

Autonomy, the first of an entrepreneurial orientation's five dimensions, allows employees to take actions that are free of organizational constraints and permits individuals and groups to be self-directed. The second dimension, *innovativeness,* "reflects a firm's tendency to engage in and support new ideas, novelty, experimentation, and creative processes that may result in new products, services, or technological processes."[124] Cultures with a tendency toward innovativeness encourage employees to think beyond existing knowledge, technologies, and parameters to find creative ways to add value. *Risk taking* reflects a willingness by employees and their firm to accept risks when pursuing entrepreneurial opportunities. Assuming significant levels of debt and allocating large amounts of other resources (e.g., people) to projects that may not be completed are examples of these risks. The fourth dimension of an entrepreneurial orientation, *proactiveness,* describes a firm's ability to be a market leader rather than a follower. Proactive organizational cultures constantly use processes to anticipate future market needs and to satisfy them before competitors learn how to do so. Finally, *competitive aggressiveness* is a firm's propensity to take actions that allow it to consistently and substantially outperform its rivals.[125]

Changing the Organizational Culture and Restructuring

Changing a firm's organizational culture is more difficult than maintaining it; however, effective strategic leaders recognize when change is needed. Incremental changes to the firm's culture typically are used to implement strategies.[126] More significant and sometimes even radical changes to organizational culture support selecting strategies that differ from those the firm has implemented historically. Regardless of the reasons for change, shaping and reinforcing a new culture require effective communication and problem solving, along with selecting the right people (those who have the values desired for the organization), engaging in effective performance appraisals (establishing goals and measuring individual performance toward goals that fit in with the new core values), and using appropriate reward systems (rewarding the desired behaviors that reflect the new core values).[127]

Evidence suggests that cultural changes succeed only when the firm's CEO, other key top management team members, and middle-level managers actively support them.[128] To effect change, middle-level managers in particular need to be highly disciplined to energize the culture and foster alignment with the strategic vision.[129]

Emphasizing Ethical Practices

The effectiveness of processes used to implement the firm's strategies increases when they are based on ethical practices. Ethical companies encourage and enable people at all organizational levels to act ethically when doing what is necessary to implement strategies. In turn, ethical practices and the judgment on which they are based create "social capital" in the organization, increasing the "goodwill available to individuals and groups" in the organization.[130] Alternatively, when unethical practices evolve in an organization, they may become acceptable to many managers and employees. One study found that in these circumstances, managers were particularly likely to engage in unethical practices to meet their goals when current efforts to meet them were insufficient.[131]

To properly influence employees' judgment and behavior, ethical practices must shape the firm's decision-making process and must be an integral part of organizational culture. In fact, research evidence suggests that a value-based culture is the most effective means of ensuring that employees comply with the firm's ethical requirements.[132] As we explained in Chapter 10, managers may act opportunistically, making decisions that are in their own best interests but not in the firm's best interests when facing lax expectations regarding ethical behavior. In other words, managers acting opportunistically take advantage of their positions, making decisions that benefit themselves to the detriment of the firm's stakeholders.[133] But strategic leaders are most likely to integrate ethical values into their decisions when the company has explicit ethics codes, the code is integrated into the business through extensive ethics training, and shareholders expect ethical behavior.[134]

Firms should employ ethical strategic leaders—leaders who include ethical practices as part of their strategic direction for the firm, who desire to do the right thing, and for whom honesty, trust, and integrity are important.[135] Strategic leaders who consistently display these qualities inspire employees as they work with others to develop and support an organizational culture in which ethical practices are the expected behavioral norms.[136]

Strategic leaders can take several actions to develop an ethical organizational culture. Examples of these actions include (1) establishing and communicating specific goals to describe the firm's ethical standards (e.g., developing and disseminating a code of conduct); (2) continuously revising and updating the code of conduct, based on inputs from people throughout the firm and from other stakeholders (e.g., customers and suppliers); (3) disseminating the code of conduct to all stakeholders to inform them of the firm's ethical standards and practices; (4) developing and implementing methods and procedures to use in achieving the firm's ethical standards (e.g., using internal auditing practices that are consistent with the standards); (5) creating and using explicit reward systems that recognize acts of courage (e.g., rewarding those who use proper channels and procedures to report observed wrongdoings); and (6) creating a work environment in which all people are treated with dignity.[137] The effectiveness of these actions increases when they are taken simultaneously and thereby are mutually supportive. When strategic leaders and others throughout the firm fail to take actions such as these—perhaps because an ethical culture has not been created—problems are likely to occur. As we discuss next, formal organizational controls can help prevent further problems and reinforce better ethical practices.[138]

Establishing Balanced Organizational Controls

Organizational controls are basic to a capitalistic system and have long been viewed as an important part of strategy implementation processes.[139] Controls are necessary to help ensure that firms achieve their desired outcomes.[140] Defined as the "formal, information-based . . . procedures used by managers to maintain or alter patterns in organizational activities," controls help strategic leaders build credibility, demonstrate the value of strategies to the firm's stakeholders, and promote and support strategic change.[141] Most critically, controls provide the parameters for implementing strategies as well as the corrective actions to be taken when implementation-related adjustments are required.

In this chapter, we focus on two organizational controls—strategic and financial—that were introduced in Chapter 11. Our discussion of organizational controls here emphasizes strategic and financial controls because strategic leaders, especially those at the top of the organization, are responsible for their development and effective use.

As we explained in Chapter 11, financial control focuses on short-term financial outcomes. In contrast, strategic control focuses on the *content* of strategic actions rather than their *outcomes*. Some strategic actions can be correct but still result in poor financial outcomes because of external conditions such as a recession in the economy, unexpected domestic or foreign government actions, or natural disasters. Therefore, emphasizing financial controls often produces more short-term and risk-averse managerial decisions, because financial outcomes may be caused by events beyond managers' direct control. Alternatively, strategic control encourages lower-level managers to make decisions that incorporate moderate and acceptable levels of risk because outcomes are shared between the business-level executives making strategic proposals and the corporate-level executives evaluating them.

The challenge strategic leaders face is to verify that their firm is emphasizing financial and strategic controls so that firm performance improves. The Balanced Scorecard is a tool that helps strategic leaders assess the effectiveness of the controls.

The Balanced Scorecard

The **balanced scorecard** is a framework firms can use to verify that they have established both strategic and financial controls to assess their performance.[142] This technique is most appropriate for use when dealing with business-level strategies; however, it can also be used with the other strategies firms may choose to implement (e.g., corporate level, international, and cooperative).

The underlying premise of the balanced scorecard is that firms jeopardize their future performance possibilities when financial controls are emphasized at the expense of strategic controls,[143] in that financial controls provide feedback about outcomes achieved from past actions, but do not communicate the drivers of future performance.[144] Thus, an overemphasis on financial controls has the potential to promote managerial behavior that sacrifices the firm's long-term, value-creating potential for short-term performance gains.[145] An appropriate balance of strategic controls and financial controls, rather than an overemphasis on either, allows firms to effectively monitor their performance.

Four perspectives are integrated to form the balanced scorecard framework: *financial* (concerned with growth, profitability, and risk from the shareholders' perspective), *customer* (concerned with the amount of value customers perceive was created by the firm's products), *internal business processes* (with a focus on the priorities for various business processes that create customer and shareholder satisfaction), and *learning and growth* (concerned with the firm's effort to create a climate that supports change, innovation, and growth). Thus, using the balanced scorecard framework allows the firm to understand how it looks to shareholders (financial perspective), how customers view it (customer perspective), the processes it must emphasize to successfully use its competitive advantage (internal perspective), and what it can do to improve its performance in order to grow (learning and growth perspective).[146] Generally speaking, strategic controls tend to be emphasized when the firm assesses its performance relative to the learning and growth perspective, whereas financial controls are emphasized when assessing performance in terms of the financial perspective.

Firms use different criteria to measure their standing relative to the scorecard's four perspectives. We show sample criteria in Figure 12.5. The firm should select the number of criteria that will allow it to have both a strategic understanding and a financial understanding of its performance without becoming immersed in too many details.[147] For example, we know from research that a firm's innovation, quality of its goods and services, growth of its sales, and its profitability are all interrelated.[148]

Strategic leaders play an important role in determining a proper balance between strategic controls and financial controls, whether they are in single-business firms or large diversified firms. A proper balance between controls is important, in that "wealth creation for organizations where strategic leadership is exercised is possible because these leaders make appropriate investments for future viability [through strategic control], while maintaining an appropriate level of financial stability in the present [through financial control]."[149] In fact, most corporate restructuring is designed to refocus the firm on its core businesses, thereby allowing top executives to reestablish strategic control of their separate business units.[150]

Successfully using strategic control frequently is integrated with appropriate autonomy for the various subunits so that they can gain a competitive advantage in their respective markets.[151] Strategic control can be used to promote the sharing of both tangible and intangible resources among interdependent businesses within a firm's portfolio. In addition, the autonomy provided allows the flexibility necessary to take advantage of

The **balanced scorecard** is a framework firms can use to verify that they have established both strategic and financial controls to assess their performance.

Figure 12.5 Strategic Controls and Financial Controls in a Balanced Scorecard Framework

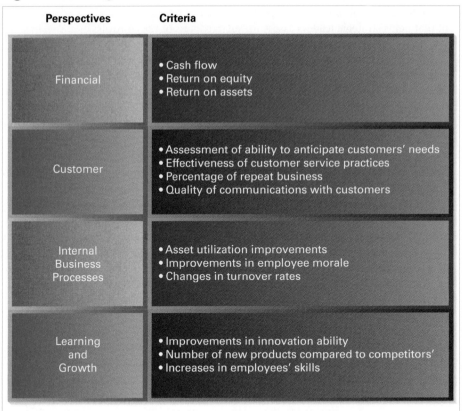

Perspectives	Criteria
Financial	• Cash flow • Return on equity • Return on assets
Customer	• Assessment of ability to anticipate customers' needs • Effectiveness of customer service practices • Percentage of repeat business • Quality of communications with customers
Internal Business Processes	• Asset utilization improvements • Improvements in employee morale • Changes in turnover rates
Learning and Growth	• Improvements in innovation ability • Number of new products compared to competitors' • Increases in employees' skills

specific marketplace opportunities. As a result, strategic leadership promotes simultaneous use of strategic control and autonomy.[152]

The balanced scorecard is being used by car manufacturer Porsche. After this manufacturer of sought-after sports cars regained its market-leading position, it implemented a balanced scorecard approach in an effort to maintain this position. In particular, Porsche used the balanced scorecard to promote learning and continuously improve the business. For example, knowledge was collected from all Porsche dealerships throughout the world. The instrument used to collect the information was referred to as "Porsche Key Performance Indicators." The fact that Porsche is now the world's most profitable automaker suggests the value the firm gained and is gaining by using the balanced scorecard as a foundation for simultaneously emphasizing strategic and financial controls.[153]

Porsche used the balanced scorecard to promote learning and continuously improve the business.

As we have explained, strategic leaders are critical to a firm's ability to successfully use all parts of the strategic management process. What does the future hold for strategic leaders? We try to describe that future in the Strategic Focus. As you will see, the future for strategic leaders is likely to be challenging. At the same time, the work of strategic leaders will remain exciting and will still be a set of actions that, when executed successfully, has a strong possibility of creating positive outcomes for all of a firm's stakeholders.

© AP Photo/Porsche

What's Next? Strategic Leadership in the Future

The essence of the expectations for a firm's key strategic leaders is captured by the details of the strategic management process. Stated simply, strategic leaders must design a process (such as the one shown in Figure 1.1, on page 5) their firm will use as the foundation for earning above-average returns and consistently outperforming rivals. The simplicity of this statement belies its complexity though, whether we are talking about strategic management today or strategic management for tomorrow.

What do we know about the future of strategic leadership and the tasks future strategic leaders may encounter? Even though predicting the future is risky, several realities and expectations seem likely.

First, it is likely that tomorrow's strategic leaders will feel even more stress than do their counterparts of today. One reason for this expectation is that those for whom a firm's key strategic leaders work (the board of directors in the case of the CEO and the CEO in the instance of top-level executives) rightfully have significant expectations of strategic leaders. The past successes of individuals chosen as strategic leaders are assumed to predict even greater success in the future. Strategic leadership's demands create stress that leaders must acknowledge and with which they must learn how to cope if they are to successfully discharge their responsibilities.

Another reasonably safe prediction is that all stakeholders will continue to expect the firm's board of directors to better represent their interests. Even today, board members are on the "hot seat" to improve their performance as agents for each stakeholder group. In turn, the expectation of better board performance will find board members holding strategic leaders more accountable for achieving positive outcomes with respect to (1) strategy formulation and execution, (2) the effective handling of crises, particularly financial ones, (3) being able to meaningfully link top-level managerial pay to performance, and (4) representing the company's best interests at all times. Tomorrow's board members and a firm's strategic leaders will undoubtedly continue to face high levels of accountability for their actions and the outcomes they achieve or fail to achieve.

What can individuals do to enhance their ability to be an effective strategic leader in tomorrow's organizations? We'll identify a few actions here. First, strategic leaders should be continuously curious so that they will have the foundation for seeking to learn everything they can from every person with whom they have contact. Greater diversity of what a person "knows" increases the likelihood an individual will examine the widest possible range of issues when making decisions related to effective strategic management. Strategic leaders should rely on their curiosity to spot patterns that suggest future conditions. Once spotted, these individuals should think deeply about the implications of those patterns for their firm's success. Additionally, tomorrow's strategic leaders should place even greater emphasis on the "simple rules" of effective strategic leadership than is the case today. These simply yet vital rules are the following:

1. Leaders make work about others, not about themselves. Once a person becomes a strategic leader, everything that person does is about "them" (the stakeholders, but especially employees) while nothing is about the leader.
2. Leaders learn everything possible about their company from both strategic and tactical perspectives.
3. Leaders hold individuals accountable for their outcomes. However, leaders must make themselves the most accountable for overall performance.
4. Leaders shoulder all responsibility for all parts of their job; they always take the blame for mistakes and distribute the credit for successes to others.

Sources: N. Byrnes & J. Sasseen, 2007, Board of hard knocks, *BusinessWeek*, January 22, 36–39; K. Sulkowicz, 2007, Stressed for success, *BusinessWeek*, May 21, 18; J. Useem, 2007, What's next? *Fortune*, February 5, 44–54; M. Heffernan, 2006, Lessons from a great thinker, *Fast Company Online*, http://www.fastcompany.com, January 2; L. Lavelle, 2005, Three simple rules Carly ignored, *BusinessWeek*, February 28, 46.

Summary

- Effective strategic leadership is a prerequisite to successfully using the strategic management process. Strategic leadership entails the ability to anticipate events, envision possibilities, maintain flexibility, and empower others to create strategic change.

- Top-level managers are an important resource for firms to develop and exploit competitive advantages. In addition, when they and their work are valuable, rare, imperfectly imitable, and nonsubstitutable, strategic leaders can themselves be a source of competitive advantage.

- The top management team is composed of key managers who play a critical role in selecting and implementing the firm's strategies. Generally, they are officers of the corporation or members of the board of directors.

- The top management team's characteristics, a firm's strategies, and its performance are all interrelated. For example, a top management team with significant marketing and R&D knowledge positively contributes to the firm's use of growth strategies. Overall, having diverse skills increases most top management teams' effectiveness.

- Typically, performance improves when the board of directors is involved in shaping a firm's strategic direction. However, when the CEO has a great deal of power, the board may be less involved in decisions about strategy formulation and implementation. By appointing people to the board and simultaneously serving as CEO and chair of the board, CEOs increase their power.

- In managerial succession, strategic leaders are selected from either the internal or the external managerial labor market. Because of the effect on performance, selection of strategic leaders has implications for a firm's effectiveness. Companies use a variety of reasons for looking either internally or externally when choosing the firm's strategic leaders. In most instances, the internal market is used to select the CEO; but the number of outsiders chosen is increasing. Outsiders often are selected to initiate changes.

- Effective strategic leadership has five major components: determining the firm's strategic direction, effectively managing the firm's resource portfolio (including exploiting and maintaining core competencies and managing human capital and social capital), sustaining an effective organizational culture, emphasizing ethical practices, and establishing balanced organizational controls.

- Strategic leaders must develop the firm's strategic direction. The strategic direction specifies the image and character the firm wants to develop over time. To form the strategic direction, strategic leaders evaluate the conditions (e.g., opportunities and threats in the external environment) they expect their firm to face over the next three to five years.

- Strategic leaders must ensure that their firm exploits its core competencies, which are used to produce and deliver products that create value for customers, when implementing its strategies. In related diversified and large firms in particular, core competencies are exploited by sharing them across units and products.

- The ability to manage the firm's resource portfolio is a critical element of strategic leadership and processes used to effectively implement the firm's strategy. Managing the resource portfolio includes integrating resources to create capabilities and leveraging those capabilities through strategies to build competitive advantages. Human capital and social capital are perhaps the most important resources.

- As a part of managing the firm's resources, strategic leaders must develop a firm's human capital. Effective strategic leaders view human capital as a resource to be maximized—not as a cost to be minimized. Resulting from this perspective is the development and use of programs intended to train current and future strategic leaders to build the skills needed to nurture the rest of the firm's human capital.

- Effective strategic leaders also build and maintain internal and external social capital. Internal social capital promotes cooperation and coordination within and across units in the firm. External social capital provides access to resources the firm needs to compete effectively.

- Shaping the firm's culture is a central task of effective strategic leadership. An appropriate organizational culture encourages the development of an entrepreneurial orientation among employees and an ability to change the culture as necessary.

- In ethical organizations, employees are encouraged to exercise ethical judgment and to always act ethically. Improved ethical practices foster social capital. Setting specific goals to describe the firm's ethical standards, using a code of conduct, rewarding ethical behaviors, and creating a work environment where all people are treated with dignity are examples of actions facilitating and supporting ethical behavior.

- Developing and using balanced organizational controls is the final component of effective strategic leadership. The balanced scorecard is a tool that measures the effectiveness of the firm's strategic and financial controls. An effective balance between strategic and financial controls allows for flexible use of core competencies, but within the parameters of the firm's financial position.

Review Questions

1. What is strategic leadership? In what ways are top executives considered important resources for an organization?

2. What is a top management team, and how does it affect a firm's performance and its abilities to innovate and make effective strategic changes?

3. How do the internal and external managerial labor markets affect the managerial succession process?

4. What is the effect of strategic leadership on determining the firm's strategic direction?

5. How do strategic leaders effectively manage their firm's resource portfolio such that its core competencies are exploited and the human capital and social capital are leveraged to achieve a competitive advantage?

6. What is organizational culture? What must strategic leaders do to develop and sustain an effective organizational culture?

7. As a strategic leader, what actions could you take to establish and emphasize ethical practices in your firm?

8. What are organizational controls? Why are strategic controls and financial controls important aspects of the strategic management process?

Notes

1. E. F. Goldman, 2007, Strategic thinking at the top, *MIT Sloan Management Review*, 48(4): 75–81.

2. L. Bassi & D. McMurrer, 2007, Maximizing your return on people, *Harvard Business Review*, 85(3): 115–123; R. D. Ireland & M. A. Hitt, 2005, Achieving and maintaining strategic competitiveness in the 21st century: The role of strategic leadership, *Academy of Management Executive*, 19: 63–77.

3. J. P. Kotter, 2007, Leading change: Why transformation efforts fail, *Harvard Business Review*, 85(1): 96–103.

4. M. A. Hitt, C. Miller, & A. Collella, 2009, *Organizational Behavior: A Strategic Approach*, 2nd ed., New York: John Wiley & Sons; M. A. Hitt & R. D. Ireland, 2002, The essence of strategic leadership: Managing human and social capital, *Journal of Leadership and Organizational Studies*, 9: 3–14.

5. D. A. Ready & J. A. Conger, 2007, Make your company a talent factory, *Harvard Business Review*, 85(6): 69–77.

6. D. Roberts & C.-C. Tschang, 2007, China's rising leaders, *BusinessWeek*, October 1, 33–35.

7. M. Conlin, 2007, Go-go—going to pieces in China, *BusinessWeek*, April 23, 88.

8. P. A. Gloor & S. M. Cooper, 2007, The new principles of a swarm business, *MIT Sloan Management Review*, 48(3): 81–85; A. S. DeNisi, M. A. Hitt, & S. E. Jackson, 2003, The knowledge-based approach to sustainable competitive advantage, in S. E. Jackson, M. A. Hitt, & A. S. DeNisi (eds.), *Managing Knowledge for Sustained Competitive Advantage*, San Francisco: Jossey-Bass, 3–33.

9. L. Bossidy, 2007, What your leader expects of you: And what you should expect in return, *Harvard Business Review*, 85(4): 58–65; J. E. Post, L. E. Preston, & S. Sachs, 2002, Managing the extended enterprise: The new stakeholder view, *California Management Review*, 45(1): 6–28.

10. A. McKee & D. Massimilian, 2007, Resonant leadership: A new kind of leadership for the digital age, *Journal of Business Strategy*, 27(5): 45–49.

11. E. Baraldi, R. Brennan, D. Harrison, A. Tunisini, & J. Zolkiewski, 2007, Strategic thinking and the IMP approach: A comparative analysis, *Industrial Marketing Management*, 36: 879–894; C. L. Shook, R. L. Priem, & J. E. McGee, 2003, Venture creation and the enterprising individual: A review and synthesis, *Journal of Management*, 29: 379–399.

12. K. K. Reardon, 2007, Courage as a skill, *Harvard Business Review*, 85(1): 48–564.

13. R. A. Burgleman & A. S. Grove, 2007, Let chaos reign, then rein in chaos—repeatedly: Managing strategic dynamics for corporate longevity, *Strategic Management Journal*, 28: 965–979.

14. S. Borener, S. A. Eisenbeliss, & D. Griesser, 2007, Follower behavior and organizational performance: The impact of transformational leaders, *Journal of Leadership & Organizational Studies*, 13(3): 15–26; D. Vera & M. Crossan, 2004, Strategic leadership and organizational learning, *Academy of Management Review*, 29: 222–240.

15. T. G. Buchholz, 2007, The Kroc legacy at McDonald's, *The Conference Review Board*, July/August, 14–15.

16. H. S. Givray, 2007, When CEOs aren't leaders, *BusinessWeek*, September 3, 102.

17. D. Goleman, 2004, What makes a leader? *Harvard Business Review*, 82(1): 82–91.

18. 2007, How they do it, *Fortune*, October 1, 111.

19. J. L. Morrow, Jr., D. G. Sirmon, M. A. Hitt, & T. R. Holcomb, 2007, Creating value in the face of declining performance: Firm strategies and organizational recovery, *Strategic Management Journal*, 28: 271–283; R. Castanias & C. Helfat, 2001, The managerial rents model: Theory and empirical analysis, *Journal of Management*, 27: 661–678.

20. H. G. Barkema & O. Shvyrkov, 2007, Does top management team diversity promote or hamper foreign expansion? *Strategic Management Journal*, 28: 663–680; M. Beer & R. Eisenstat, 2000, The silent killers of strategy implementation and learning, *Sloan Management Review*, 41(4): 29–40.

21. V. Santos & T. Garcia, 2007, The complexity of the organizational renewal decision: The management role, *Leadership & Organization Development Journal*, 28: 336–355; M. Wright, R. E. Hoskisson, L. W. Busenitz, & J. Dial, 2000, Entrepreneurial growth through privatization: The upside of management buyouts, *Academy of Management Review*, 25: 591–601; N. Rajagopalan, A. M. Rasheed, & D. K. Datta, 1993, Strategic decision processes: Critical review and future directions, *Journal of Management*, 19: 349–384.

22. Y. L. Doz & M. Kosonen, 2007, The new deal at the top, *Harvard Business Review*, 85(6): 98–104; W. G. Rowe, 2001, Creating wealth in organizations: The role of strategic leadership, *Academy of Management Executive*, 15(1): 81–94.

23. A. S. Tsui, Z.-X. Zhang, H. Wang, K. R. Xin, & J. B. Wu, 2006, Unpacking the relationship between CEO leadership behavior and organizational culture, *The Leadership Quarterly*, 17: 113–137; J. A. Petrick & J. F. Quinn, 2001, The

challenge of leadership accountability for integrity capacity as a strategic asset, *Journal of Business Ethics,* 34: 331–343.

24. D. G. Sirmon, S. Gove, & M. A. Hitt, 2008, Resource management in dyadic competitive rivalry: The effects of resource bundling and deployment, *Academy of Management Journal,* in press; R. Martin, 2007, How successful leaders think, *Harvard Business Review,* 85(6): 60–67.

25. M. L. A. Hayward, V. P. Rindova, & T. G. Pollock, 2004, Believing one's own press: The causes and consequences of CEO celebrity, *Strategic Management Journal,* 25: 637–653.

26. N. J. Hiller & D. C. Hambrick, 2005, Conceptualizing executive hubris: The role of (hyper-) core self-evaluations in strategic decision making, *Strategic Management Journal,* 26: 297–319.

27. A. M. L. Raes, U. Glunk, M. G. Heijitjes, & R. A. Roe, 2007, Top management team and middle managers, *Small Group Research,* 38: 360–386; I. Goll, R. Sambharya, & L. Tucci, 2001, Top management team composition, corporate ideology, and firm performance, *Management International Review,* 41(2): 109–129.

28. J. Bunderson, 2003, Team member functional background and involvement in management teams: Direct effects and the moderating role of power and centralization, *Academy of Management Journal,* 46: 458–474; L. Markoczy, 2001, Consensus formation during strategic change, *Strategic Management Journal,* 22: 1013–1031.

29. C. Pegels, Y. Song, & B. Yang, 2000, Management heterogeneity, competitive interaction groups, and firm performance, *Strategic Management Journal,* 21: 911–923.

30. R. Rico, E. Molleman, M. Sanchez-Manzanares, & G. S. Van der Vegt, 2007, The effects of diversity faultlines and team task autonomy on decision quality and social integration, *Journal of Management,* 33: 111–132.

31. A. Srivastava, K. M. Bartol, & E. A. Locke, 2006, Empowering leadership in management teams: Effects on knowledge sharing, efficacy, and performance, *Academy of Management Journal,* 49: 1239–1251; D. Knight, C. L. Pearce, K. G. Smith, J. D. Olian, H. P. Sims, K. A. Smith, & P. Flood, 1999, Top management team diversity, group process, and strategic consensus, *Strategic Management Journal,* 20: 446–465.

32. B. J. Olson, S. Parayitam, & Y. Bao, 2007, Strategic decision making: The effects of cognitive diversity, conflict, and trust on decision outcomes, *Journal of Management,* 33: 196–222; T. Simons, L. H. Pelled, & K. A. Smith, 1999, Making use of difference: diversity, debate, and decision comprehensiveness in top management teams, *Academy of Management Journal,* 42: 662–673.

33. S. Finkelstein, D. C. Hambrick, & A. A. Cannella, Jr., 2008, *Strategic Leadership: Top Executives and Their Effects on Organizations,* New York: Oxford University Press.

34. S. Barsade, A. Ward, J. Turner, & J. Sonnenfeld, 2000, To your heart's content: A model of affective diversity in top management teams, *Administrative Science Quarterly,* 45: 802–836; C. C. Miller, L. M. Burke, & W. H. Glick, 1998, Cognitive diversity among upper-echelon executives: Implications for strategic decision processes, *Strategic Management Journal,* 19: 39–58.

35. B. J. Avolio & S. S. Kahai, 2002, Adding the "e" to e-leadership: How it may impact your leadership, *Organizational Dynamics,* 31: 325–338.

36. Z. Simsek, J. F. Veiga, M. L. Lubatkin, & R. H. Dino, 2005, Modeling the multilevel determinants of top management team behavioral integration, *Academy of Management Journal,* 48: 69–84.

37. U. Daellenbach, A. McCarthy, & T. Schoenecker, 1999, Commitment to innovation: The impact of top management team characteristics, *R&D Management,* 29(3): 199–208; D. K. Datta & J. P. Guthrie, 1994, Executive succession: Organizational antecedents of CEO characteristics, *Strategic Management Journal,* 15: 569–577.

38. M. Jensen & E. J. Zajac, 2004, Corporate elites and corporate strategy: How demographic preferences and structural position shape the scope of the firm, *Strategic Management Journal,* 25: 507–524.

39. W. B. Werther, 2003, Strategic change and leader-follower alignment, *Organizational Dynamics,* 32: 32–45; S. Wally & M. Becerra, 2001, Top management team characteristics and strategic changes in international diversification: The case of U.S. multinationals in the European community, *Group & Organization Management,* 26: 165–188.

40. Y. Zhang & N. Rajagopalan, 2003, Explaining the new CEO origin: Firm versus industry antecedents, *Academy of Management Journal,* 46: 327–338.

41. T. Dvir, D. Eden, B. J. Avolio, & B. Shamir, 2002, Impact of transformational leadership on follower development and performance: A field experiment, *Academy of Management Journal,* 45: 735–744.

42. C. Thomas, D. Kidd, & C. Fernandez-Araoz, 2007, Are you underutilizing your board? *MIT Sloan Management Review,* 48(2): 71–76.

43. F. Adjaoud, D. Zeghal & S. Andaleeb, 2007, The effect of board's quality on performance: A study of Canadian firms, *Corporate Governance: An International Review,* 15: 623–635; L. Tihanyi, R. A. Johnson, R. E. Hoskisson, & M. A. Hitt, 2003, Institutional ownership and international diversification: The effects of boards of directors and technological opportunity, *Academy of Management Journal,* 46: 195–211.

44. B. R. Golden & E. J. Zajac, 2001, When will boards influence strategy? Inclination times power equals strategic change, *Strategic Management Journal,* 22: 1087–1111.

45. M. Carpenter & J. Westphal, 2001, Strategic context of external network ties: Examining the impact of director appointments on board involvement in strategic decision making, *Academy of Management Journal,* 44: 639–660.

46. M. A. Rutherford & A. K. Buchholtz, 2007, Investigating the relationship between board characteristics and board information, *Corporate Governance: An International Review,* 15: 576–584.

47. X. Huafang & Y. Jianguo, 2007, Ownership structure, board composition and corporate voluntary disclosure: Evidence from listed companies in China, *Managerial Auditing Journal,* 22: 604–619.

48. J. Coles, N. Sen, & V. McWilliams, 2001, An examination of the relationship of governance mechanisms to performance, *Journal of Management,* 27: 23–50; J. Coles & W. Hesterly, 2000, Independence of the chairman and board composition: Firm choices and shareholder value, *Journal of Management,* 26: 195–214.

49. C. M. Daily & D. R. Dalton, 1995, CEO and director turnover in failing firms: An illusion of change? *Strategic Management Journal,* 16: 393–400.

50. D. Miller, I. LeBreton-Miller, & B. Scholnick, 2007, Stewardship vs. stagnation: An empirical comparison of small family and non-family businesses, *Journal of Management Studies,* in press; G. J. Nicholson & G. C. Kiel, 2007, Can directors impact performance? A case-based test of three theories of corporate governance, *Corporate Govenance: An International Review,* 15: 585–608; J. H. Davis, F. D. Schoorman, & L. Donaldson, 1997, Toward a stewardship theory of management, *Academy of Management Review,* 22: 20–47.

51. J. G. Combs & M. S. Skill, 2003, Managerialist and human capital explanations for key executive pay premiums: A contingency perspective, *Academy of Management Journal,* 46: 63–73.

52. J. Peterson, 2007, House wants investors to vote on executive pay, *Los Angeles Times Online,* http://www.latimes.com, April 27.

53. N. Rajagopalan & D. Datta, 1996, CEO characteristics: Does industry matter? *Academy of Management Journal,* 39: 197–215.

54. R. A. Johnson, R. E. Hoskisson, & M. A. Hitt, 1993, Board involvement in restructuring: The effect of board versus managerial controls and characteristics, *Strategic Management Journal,* 14 (Special Issue): 33–50.

55. Z. Simsek, 2007, CEO tenure and organiza-tional performance: An intervening model, *Strategic Management Journal,* 28: 653–662.

56. M. Schneider, 2002, A stakeholder model of organizational leadership, *Organization Science,* 13: 209–220.

57. M. Sorcher & J. Brant, 2002, Are you picking the right leaders? *Harvard Business*

Review, 80(2): 78–85; D. A. Waldman, G. G. Ramirez, R. J. House, & P. Puranam, 2001, Does leadership matter? CEO leadership attributes and profitability under conditions of perceived environmental uncertainty, *Academy of Management Journal,* 44: 134–143.

58. J. Werdigier, 2007, UBS not willing to talk about departure of chief, *New York Times Online,* http://www.nytimes.com, July 7.

59. W. Shen & A. A. Cannella, 2002, Revisiting the performance consequences of CEO succession: The impacts of successor type, postsuccession senior executive turnover, and departing CEO tenure, *Academy of Management Journal,* 45: 717–734.

60. D. Ulrich & N. Smallwood, 2007, Building a leadership brand, *Harvard Business Review,* 85(7/8): 93–100.

61. G. A. Ballinger & F. D. Schoorman, 2007, Individual reactions to leadership succession in workgroups, *Academy of Management Review,* 32: 116–136; R. E. Hoskisson, D. Yiu, & H. Kim, 2000, Capital and labor market congruence and corporate governance: Effects on corporate innovation and global competitiveness, in S. S. Cohen & G. Boyd (eds.), *Corporate Governance and Globalization,* Northampton, MA: Edward Elgar, 129–154.

62. M. Hurlbert, 2005, Lo! A white knight! So why isn't the market cheering? *New York Times Online,* http://www.nytimes.com, March 27.

63. J. Weber, 2007, The accidental CEO, *BusinessWeek,* April 23, 64–72.

64. W. Shen & A. A. Cannella, 2003, Will succession planning increase shareholder wealth? Evidence from investor reactions to relay CEO successions, *Strategic Management Journal,* 24: 191–198.

65. M. Maynard, 2007, Importing chiefs, Detroit reflects in its "car guys," *New York Times Online,* http://www.nytimes.com, August 12.

66. A. Bianco, 2007, Wal-Mart's midlife crisis, *BusinessWeek,* April 30, 46–56.

67. M. Barbaro, 2007, Wal-Mart apparel chief resigns as sales lag, *New York Times Online,* http://nytimes.com, July 21.

68. R. Berner, 2007, My year at Wal-Mart, *BusinessWeek,* February 12, 70–73.

69. K. Belson & T. Zaun, 2005, Land of the rising gaijin chief executive, *New York Times Online,* http://www.nytimes.com, March 27.

70. P. M. Lee & E. H. James, 2007, She'-E-Os: Gender effects and investor reactions to the announcements of top executive appointments, *Strategic Management Journal,* 28: 227–41.

71. M. K. Ryan & S. A. Haslam, 2007, The glass cliff: Exploring the dynamics surrounding the appointment of women to precarious leadership positions, *Academy of Management Review,* 32: 549–572.

72. D. Brady, 2007, Getting to the corner office, *BusinessWeek,* March 12, 104.

73. J. Welch & S. Welch, 2007, Bosses who get it all wrong, *BusinessWeek,* July 23, 88.

74. J. O'Toole & E. E. Lawler, Jr., 2006, The choices managers make—or don't make, *The Conference Board,* September/October, 24–29.

75. M. A. Hitt, B. W. Keats, & E. Yucel, 2003, Strategic leadership in global business organizations, in W. H. Mobley & P. W. Dorfman (eds.), *Advances in Global Leadership,* Oxford, UK: Elsevier Science, Ltd., 9–35.

76. I. M. Levin, 2000, Vision revisited, *Journal of Applied Behavioral Science,* 36: 91–107.

77. J. Welch & S. Welch, 2006, It's not about empty suits, *BusinessWeek,* October 16, 132.

78. J. Welch & S. Welch, 2007, When to talk, when to balk, *BusinessWeek,* April 30, 102.

79. J. Barney & A. M. Arikan, 2001, The resource-based view: Origins and implications, in M. A. Hitt, R. E. Freeman, & J. S. Harrison (eds.), *Handbook of Strategic Management,* Oxford, UK: Blackwell Publishers, 124–188.

80. E. T. Prince, 2005, The fiscal behavior of CEOs, *Managerial Economics,* 46(3): 23–26.

81. R. A. Burgelman, 2001, *Strategy Is Destiny: How Strategy-Making Shapes a Company's Future,* New York: The Free Press.

82. D. J. Ketchen, Jr., G. T. M. Hult, & S. F. Slater, 2007, Toward greater understanding of market orientation and the resource-based view, *Strategic Management Journal,* 28: 961–964; S. K. Ethiraj, P. Kale, M. S. Krishnan, & J. V. Singh, 2005, Where do capabilities come from and how do they matter? A study in the software services industry, *Strategic Management Journal,* 26: 25–45.

83. S. K. Ethiraj, 2007, Allocation of inventive effort in complex product systems, *Strategic Management Journal,* 28: 563–584; S. Dutta, O. Narasimhan, & S. Rajiv, 2005, Conceptualizing and measuring capabilities: Methodology and empirical application, *Strategic Management Journal,* 26: 277–285.

84. 2006, PepsiCo Annual Report, http://www.pepsico.com, September.

85. M. Larson & F. Luthans, 2006, Potential added value of psychological capital in predicting work attitudes, *Journal of Leadership & Organizational Studies,* 13: 45–62; N. W. Hatch & J. H. Dyer, 2004, Human capital and learning as a source of sustainable competitive advantage, *Strategic Management Journal,* 25: 1155–1178.

86. 2006, PepsiCo Annual Report, http://www.pepsico.com, September.

87. M. A. Hitt, L. Bierman, K. Shimizu, & R. Kochhar, 2001, Direct and moderating effects of human capital on strategy and performance in professional service firms: A resource-based perspective, *Academy of Management Journal,* 44: 13–28.

88. S. E. Jackson, M. A. Hitt, & A. S. DeNisi (eds.), 2003, *Managing Knowledge for Sustained Competitive Advantage: Designing Strategies for Effective Human Resource Management,* Oxford, UK: Elsevier Science, Ltd.

89. B. E. Becker & M. A. Huselid, 2007, Strategic human resources management:

Where do we go from here? *Journal of Management,* 32: 898–925.

90. R. E. Ployhart, 2007, Staffing in the 21st century: New challenges and strategic opportunities, *Journal of Management,* 32: 868–897.

91. R. A. Noe, J. A. Colquitt, M. J. Simmering, & S. A. Alvarez, 2003, Knowledge management: Developing intellectual and social capital, in S. E. Jackson, M. A. Hitt, & A. S. DeNisi (eds.), 2003, *Managing Knowledge for Sustained Competitive Advantage: Designing Strategies for Effective Human Resource Management,* Oxford, UK: Elsevier Science, Ltd., 209–242.

92. B. Helm & M. Arndt, 2007, It's not a McJob, it's a McCalling, *BusinessWeek,* June 4, 13.

93. G. P. Hollenbeck & M. W. McCall Jr. 2003, Competence, not competencies: Making a global executive development work, in W. H. Mobley & P. W. Dorfman (eds.), *Advances in Global Leadership,* Oxford, UK: Elsevier Science, Ltd., 101–119; J. Sandberg, 2000, Understanding human competence at work: An interpretative approach, *Academy of Management Journal,* 43: 9–25.

94. G. Colvin, 2007, Leader machines, *Fortune,* October 1, 100–106.

95. Y. Liu, J. G. Combs, D. A. Ketchen, Jr., & R. D. Ireland, 2007, The value of human resource management for organizational performance, *Business Horizons,* in press.

96. J. S. Bunderson & K. M. Sutcliffe, 2003, Management team learning orientation and business unit performance, *Journal of Applied Psychology,* 88: 552–560; C. R. James, 2003, Designing learning organizations, *Organizational Dynamics,* 32(1): 46–61.

97. A. Fisher, 2006, Retain your brains, *Fortune,* July 24, 49.

98. J. D. Bragger, D. A. Hantula, D. Bragger, J. Kirnan, & E. Kutcher, 2003, When success breeds failure: History, hysteresis, and delayed exit decisions, *Journal of Applied Psychology,* 88: 6–14.

99. M. R. Haas & M. T. Hansen, 2005, When using knowledge can hurt performance: The value of organizational capabilities in a management consulting company, *Strategic Management Journal,* 26: 1–24; G. Ahuja & R. Katila, 2004, Where do resources come from? The role of idiosyncratic situations, *Strategic Management Journal,* 25: 887–907.

100. Hitt, Miller, & Colella, *Organizational Behavior.*

101. M. Marr, 2007, Disney will shut down cellphone service, *Wall Street Journal,* September 28, B3.

102. J. W. Spencer, 2003, Firms' knowledge-sharing strategies in the global innovation system: Empirical evidence from the flat-panel display industry, *Strategic Management Journal,* 24: 217–233; M. Harvey & M. M. Novicevic, 2002, The hypercompetitive global marketplace: The importance of intuition and creativity in expatriate managers, *Journal of World Business,* 37: 127–138.

103. S. Rodan & C. Galunic, 2004, More than network structure: How knowledge heterogeneity influences managerial performance and innovativeness, *Strategic Management Journal*, 25: 541–562; S. K. McEvily & B. Charavarthy, 2002, The persistence of knowledge-based advantage: An empirical test for product performance and technological knowledge, *Strategic Management Journal*, 23: 285–305.

104. K. D. Miller, 2002, Knowledge inventories and managerial myopia, *Strategic Management Journal*, 23: 689–706.

105. R. D. Nixon, M. A. Hitt, H. Lee, & E. Jeong, 2004, Market reactions to corporate announcements of downsizing actions and implementation strategies, *Strategic Management Journal*, 25: 1121–1129.

106. Nixon, Hitt, Lee, & Jeong, Market reactions to corporate announcements of downsizing actions.

107. T. Simons & Q. Roberson, 2003, Why managers should care about fairness: The effects of aggregate justice perceptions on organizational outcomes, *Journal of Applied Psychology*, 88: 432–443; M. L. Ambrose & R. Cropanzano, 2003, A longitudinal analysis of organizational fairness: An examination of reactions to tenure and promotion decisions, *Journal of Applied Psychology*, 88: 266–275.

108. P. S. Adler & S.-W. Kwon, 2002, Social capital: Prospects for a new concept, *Academy of Management Review*, 27: 17–40.

109. C. Williams, 2007, Transfer in context: Replication and adaptation in knowledge transfer relationships, *Strategic Management Journal*, 28: 867–889; A. Mendez, 2003, The coordination of globalized R&D activities through project teams organization: An exploratory empirical study, *Journal of World Business*, 38: 96–109.

110. W. H. Hoffmann, 2007, Strategies for managing a portfolio of alliances, *Strategic Management Journal*, 28: 827–856; R. D. Ireland, M. A. Hitt, & D. Vaidyanath, 2002, Managing strategic alliances to achieve a competitive advantage, *Journal of Management*, 28: 413–446.

111. J. Florin, M. Lubatkin, & W. Schulze, 2003, *Academy of Management Journal*, 46: 374–384; P. Davidsson & B. Honig, 2003, The role of social and human capital among nascent entrepreneurs, *Journal of Business Venturing*, 18: 301–331.

112. C. M. Fiol, 1991, Managing culture as a competitive resource: An identity-based view of sustainable competitive advantage, *Journal of Management*, 17: 191–211; J. B. Barney, 1986, Organizational culture: Can it be a source of sustained competitive advantage? *Academy of Management Review*, 11: 656–665.

113. 2006, Connecting the dots between innovation and leadership, *Knowledge@ wharton*, http: //www.knowledge.wharton .upenn.edu, October 4.

114. S. Cawood, 2007, Culture as a competitive advantage, *Talent Management*, http:// www.talentmgt.com, July.

115. M.-F. Lai & G.-G Lee, Relationships of organizational culture toward knowledge

activities, *Business Process Management Journal*, 13: 306–322; V. Govindarajan & A. K. Gupta, 2001, Building an effective global business team, *Sloan Management Review*, 42(4): 63–71; S. Ghoshal & C. A. Bartlett, 1994, Linking organizational context and managerial action: The dimensions of quality of management, *Strategic Management Journal*, 15: 91–112.

116. R. D. Ireland, J. G. Covin, & D. F. Kuratko, 2008, Conceptualizing corporate entrepreneurship strategy, *Entrepreneurship Theory and Practice*, in press; D. F. Kuratko, R. D. Ireland, & J. S. Hornsby, 2001, Improving firm performance through entrepreneurial actions: Acordia's corporate entrepreneurship strategy, *Academy of Management Executive*, 15(4): 60–71.

117. R. D. Ireland & J. W. Webb, 2007, Strategic entrepreneurship: Creating competitive advantage through streams of innovation, *Business Horizons*, 50: 49–49; T. E. Brown, P. Davidsson, & J. Wiklund, 2001, An operationalization of Stevenson's conceptualization of entrepreneurship as opportunity-based firm behavior, *Strategic Management Journal*, 22: 953–968.

118. S. Ko & J. E. Butler, 2007, Creativity: A key to entrepreneurial behavior, *Business Horizons*, 50: 365–372; D. S. Elenkov, W. Judge, & P. Wright, 2005, Strategic leadership and executive innovation influence: An international multi-cluster comparative study, *Strategic Management Journal*, 26: 665–682.

119. R. E. Hoskisson, M. A. Hitt, R. D. Ireland, & J. S. Harrison, 2008, *Competing for Advantage*, 2nd ed., Thomson Publishing; R. G. McGrath, W. J. Ferrier, & A. L. Mendelow, 2004, Real options as engines of choice and heterogeneity, *Academy of Management Review*, 29: 86–101.

120. R. S. Vassolo, J. Anand, & T. B. Folta, 2004, Non-additivity in portfolios of exploration activities: A real options analysis of equity alliances in biotechnology, *Strategic Management Journal*, 25: 1045–1061.

121. R. D. Ireland, M. A. Hitt, & D. Sirmon, 2003, A model of strategic entrepreneurship: The construct and its dimensions, *Journal of Management*, 29: 963–989.

122. G. T. Lumpkin & G. G. Dess, 1996, Clarifying the entrepreneurial orientation construct and linking it to performance, *Academy of Management Review*, 21: 135–172; R. G. McGrath & I. MacMillan, 2000, *The Entrepreneurial Mindset*, Boston: Harvard Business School Press.

123. C. Heath & D. Heath, 2007, Leadership is a muscle, *Fast Company*, July/August, 62–63.

124. Lumpkin & Dess, Clarifying the entrepreneurial orientation construct, 142.

125. Ibid., 137.

126. P. Pyoria, 2007, Informal organizational culture: The foundation of knowledge workers' performance, *Journal of Knowledge Management*, 11(3): 16–30; R. R. Sims, 2000, Changing an

organization's culture under new leadership, *Journal of Business Ethics*, 25: 65–78.

127. C. M. Christensen & S. D. Anthony, 2007, Put investors in their place, *BusinessWeek*, May 28, 108; R. A. Burgelman & Y. L. Doz, 2001, The power of strategic integration, *Sloan Management Review*, 42(3): 28–38.

128. J. S. Hornsby, D. F. Kuratko, & S. A. Zahra, 2002, Middle managers' perception of the internal environment for corporate entrepreneurship: Assessing a measurement scale, *Journal of Business Venturing*, 17: 253–273.

129. D. F Kuratko, R. D. Ireland, J. G. Covin, & J. S. Hornsby, 2005, A model of middle-level managers' entrepreneurial behavior, *Entrepreneurship Theory and Practice*, 29: 699–716.

130. Adler & Kwon, Social capital.

131. M. E. Scheitzer, L. Ordonez, & M. Hoegl, 2004, Goal setting as a motivator of unethical behavior, *Academy of Management Journal*, 47: 422–432.

132. D. C. Kayes, D. Stirling, & T. M. Nielsen, 2007, Building organizational integrity, *Business Horizons*, 50: 61–70; L. K. Trevino, G. R. Weaver, D. G. Toffler, & B. Ley, 1999, Managing ethics and legal compliance: What works and what hurts, *California Management Review*, 41(2): 131–151.

133. M. A. Hitt & J. D. Collins, 2007, Business ethics, strategic decision making, and firm performance, *Business Horizons*, 50: 353–357; C. W. L. Hill, 1990, Cooperation, opportunism, and the invisible hand: Implications for transaction cost theory, *Academy of Management Review*, 15: 500–513.

134. J. M. Stevens, H. K. Steensma, D. A. Harrison, & P. L. Cochran, 2005, Symbolic or substantive document? Influence of ethics codes on financial executives' decisions, *Strategic Management Journal*, 26: 181–195.

135. C. Driscoll & M. McKee, 2007, Restorying a culture of ethical and spiritual values: A role for leader storytelling, *Journal of Business Ethics*, 73: 205–217; C. J. Robertson & W. F. Crittenden, 2003, Mapping moral philosophies: Strategic implications for multinational firms, *Strategic Management Journal*, 24: 385–392; E. Soule, 2002, Managerial moral strategies—In search of a few good principles, *Academy of Management Review*, 27: 114–124.

136. C. Caldwell & L. A. Hayes, 2007, Leadership, trustworthiness, and the mediating lens, *Journal of Management Development*, 26: 261–281.

137. M. Schminke, A. Arnaud, & M. Kuenzi, 2007, The power of ethical work climates, *Organizational Dynamics*, 36: 171–186; L. B. Ncube & M. H. Wasburn, 2006, Strategic collaboration for ethical leadership: A mentoring framework for business and organizational decision making, *Journal of Leadership & Organizational Studies*, 13: 77–92;

P. E. Murphy, 1995, Corporate ethics statements: Current status and future prospects, *Journal of Business Ethics,* 14: 727–740.

138. J. Welch & S. Welch, 2007, Flying solo: A reality check, *BusinessWeek,* June 4, 116.

139. A. Weibel, 2007, Formal control and trustworthiness, *Group & Organization Management,* 32: 500–517; G. Redding, 2002, The capitalistic business system of China and its rationale, *Asia Pacific Journal of Management,* 19: 221–249.

140. A. C. Costa, 2007, Trust and control interrelations, *Group & Organization Management,* 32: 392–406; J. H. Gittell, 2000, Paradox of coordination and control, *California Management Review,* 42(3): 101–117.

141. M. D. Shields, F. J. Deng, & Y. Kato, 2000, The design and effects of control systems: Tests of direct- and indirect-effects models, *Accounting, Organizations and Society,* 25: 185–202.

142. R. S. Kaplan & D. P. Norton, 2001, The strategy-focused organization, *Strategy & Leadership,* 29(3): 41–42; R. S. Kaplan &

D. P. Norton, 2000, *The Strategy-Focused Organization: How Balanced Scorecard Companies Thrive in the New Business Environment,* Boston: Harvard Business School Press.

143. B. E. Becker, M. A. Huselid, & D. Ulrich, 2001, *The HR Scorecard: Linking People, Strategy, and Performance,* Boston: Harvard Business School Press, 21.

144. Kaplan & Norton, The strategy-focused organization.

145. R. S. Kaplan & D. P. Norton, 2001, Transforming the balanced scorecard from performance measurement to strategic management: Part I, *Accounting Horizons,* 15(1): 87–104.

146. R. S. Kaplan & D. P. Norton, 1992, The balanced scorecard—measures that drive performance, *Harvard Business Review,* 70(1): 71–79.

147. M. A. Mische, 2001, *Strategic Renewal: Becoming a High-Performance Organization,* Upper Saddle River, NJ: Prentice Hall, 181.

148. H.-J. Cho & V. Pucik, 2005, Relationship between innovativeness, quality,

growth, profitability and market value, *Strategic Management Journal,* 26: 555–575.

149. Rowe, Creating wealth in organizations: The role of strategic leadership.

150. R. E. Hoskisson, R. A. Johnson, D. Yiu, & W. P. Wan, 2001, Restructuring strategies of diversified business groups: Differences associated with country institutional environments, in M. A. Hitt, R. E. Freeman, & J. S. Harrison (eds.), *Handbook of Strategic Management,* Oxford, UK: Blackwell Publishers, 433–463.

151. J. Birkinshaw & N. Hood, 2001, Unleash innovation in foreign subsidiaries, *Harvard Business Review,* 79(3): 131–137.

152. Ireland & Hitt, Achieving and maintaining strategic competitiveness.

153. G. Edmondson, 2007, Pedal to the metal at Porsche, *BusinessWeek,* September 3, 68; J. D. Gunkel & G. Probst, 2003, Implementation of the balanced scorecard as a means of corporate learning: The Porsche case, European Case Clearing House, Cranfield, UK.

Strategic Entrepreneurship

13

Studying this chapter should provide you with the strategic management knowledge needed to:

1. Define strategic entrepreneurship and corporate entrepreneurship.

2. Define entrepreneurship and entrepreneurial opportunities and explain their importance.

3. Define invention, innovation, and imitation, and describe the relationship among them.

4. Describe entrepreneurs and the entrepreneurial mind-set.

5. Explain international entrepreneurship and its importance.

6. Describe how firms internally develop innovations.

7. Explain how firms use cooperative strategies to innovate.

8. Describe how firms use acquisitions as a means of innovation.

9. Explain how strategic entrepreneurship helps firms create value.

© Don Hammond/Design Pics/Corbis

Googling Innovation!

Google has become an entrepreneurial sensation with rapid and phenomenal success as an Internet search engine. In 2007 it had more than 380 million people accessing its services in 35 different languages globally. It has become so popular that a new term has entered our lexicon. People refer to searching for information on the Internet using a Google search engine as *googling*.

Google actually provides a number of services. In addition to its well-known search engines, it also provides Web portal services such as Webmail, blogging, photo sharing, and instant messaging. It also provides a number of other tools such as interactive maps, discussion groups, comparison shopping, and an image library. Google has expanded the services that it provides through acquisitions (e.g., YouTube, DoubleClick) and extended its reach to different markets through strategic alliances (e.g., with Sun Microsystems, MTV, News Corporation's Fox Interactive Media).

However, Google is perhaps best known as an innovative company because it constantly develops and introduces to the market new services. Google has a corporate culture that promotes creativity and innovation. For example, all employees are allowed 20 percent of their time to work on projects of their choosing. Also, Google has a flat organization structure and few managers. Even project teams have no permanent leader. Team members rotate as the project leader. Google is a relaxed and fun place to work with free snacks and meals and video games available for break times. The attractiveness of its culture is shown by the fact that Google has almost no turnover.

Google has found a way to harness all of the ideas created by its employees and its motivational workplace. First, to harness the many ideas, Google established an internal Web page for tracking new ideas. Each "idea creator" set up a special Web page for her/his new idea. This information was posted on the intranet, which allowed others in the company to test the idea. Second, Marissa Mayer was made vice president of search products and user experience. Her responsibility is to recommend if and when a particular product is ready for release to the market. Thus, she has an internal gatekeeper role. Marissa also plays a role in helping to develop good ideas. She is able to span the boundary between the technical ("geeks") and the markets (marketing and sales). One former colleague described it as "her clothes match but she is also a geek." She helps to determine when projects are adequately developed and tested to present to the company's other top managers. To further test new "product" ideas, Google launched Google Labs where the public was invited to test new product ideas, providing feedback on new technology and service prototypes.

Google Labs also provides an initial way to build demand for a new product so that it has a customer base when the product is formally introduced to the market.

Google has launched what some analysts refer to as "category killers," such as Google Checkout, which have become major successes. This phenomenon is especially true for its new search products. Some believe that the best services it offers outside of search have come through acquisitions and strategic alliances. Regardless, Google uses innovation as a way to beat its competition even in international markets such as China. The market leader in China is Baidu.com. But Google developed a research center in Beijing to develop new products for the Chinese market and introduced a Chinese-language brand name to compete effectively in this market.

Sources: 2007, Marissa Mayer, *Wikipedia,* http://wikipedia.org, September 2; 2007, It's not journalism; Google's latest effort highlights the difference between what it does and what newspapers and magazines do, *Los Angeles Times,* August 17, 30; D. Clark, 2007, Google begins to distribute Sun's Staroffice software, *Wall Street Journal,* August 16, B4; K. J. Delaney & A. LaVallee, 2007, Google news offers rebuttal time; Articles' subjects, sources allowed to post comments; Verifying identity an issue, *Wall Street Journal.* August 9, B2; L. Garrigues, 2007, Surui partner with Google Earth to map territory, *Indian Country Today,* July 4, *27*(4): A5; 2007, Reclaiming the web from YouTube, *Investors Chronicle,* May 29, 1; J. Murphy, 2007, Google prepares to fend off army of "YouTube killers," *Media,* April 20, 14; A. Pham, 2007, Google spends oodles again; The Internet behemoth agrees to pay $3.1 billion for ad firm and once more uses its financial strength to head off rivals, *Los Angeles Times,* April 14, C1; A. Schein, 2007, Google, Inc. (NASDAQ (GS): GOOG), http://www.google.com; 2006. Inside Google's new-product process. *BusinessWeek,* http://businessweek.com, June 30; 2006, Google, BSkyB plan online video deal, *Wall Street Journal* (Eastern edition), December 6, B4; M. Hitt, C. Miller, & A. Collela, 2006, *Organizational Behavior,* New York: John Wiley & Sons, 469–476; B. Elgin, 2005, Managing Google's idea factory, *BusinessWeek,* http://businessweek.com, October 3.

In Chapter 1, we indicated that *organizational culture* refers to the complex set of ideologies, symbols, and core values that are shared throughout the firm and that influence how the firm conducts business. Thus, culture is the social energy that drives—or fails to drive—the organization. This chapter's Opening Case explains that Google's culture encourages and supports continuous product innovations. Increasingly, a firm's ability to engage in innovation makes the difference in gaining and maintaining a competitive advantage and achieving performance targets.[1]

Google is clearly an entrepreneurial and innovative company. Not only is Google the leading Internet search engine in the world, but it also consistently produces product innovations. In addition to the internal development of new products, Google has diversified its product offerings and the markets served by making carefully planned acquisitions and participating in strategic alliances. From reading this chapter, you will understand that Google's ability to innovate shows that it successfully practices strategic entrepreneurship.

Strategic entrepre-neurship is taking entre-preneurial actions using a strategic perspective.

Strategic entrepreneurship is taking entrepreneurial actions using a strategic perspective. When engaging in strategic entrepreneurship, the firm simultaneously focuses on finding opportunities in its external environment that it can try to exploit through innovations. Identifying opportunities to exploit through innovations is the *entrepreneurship* dimension of strategic entrepreneurship, while determining the best way to manage the firm's innovation efforts is the *strategic* dimension. Thus, firms engaging in strategic entrepreneurship integrate their actions to find opportunities and to successfully innovate as a primary means of pursuing them.[2] In the twenty-first–century competitive landscape, firm survival and success depend on a firm's ability to continuously find new opportunities and quickly produce innovations to pursue them.[3]

To examine strategic entrepreneurship, we consider several topics in this chapter. First, we examine entrepreneurship and innovation in a strategic context. Definitions of entrepreneurship, entrepreneurial opportunities, and entrepreneurs as those who engage in entrepreneurship to pursue entrepreneurial opportunities are included as parts of this analysis. We then describe international entrepreneurship, a phenomenon reflecting the increased use of entrepreneurship in economies throughout the world. After this discussion, the chapter shifts to descriptions of the three ways firms innovate. Internally, firms innovate through either autonomous or induced strategic behavior. We then describe actions firms take to implement the innovations resulting from those two types of strategic behavior.

In addition to innovating through internal activities, firms can develop innovations by using cooperative strategies, such as strategic alliances, and by acquiring other companies to gain access to their innovations and innovative capabilities. Most large, complex firms use all three methods to innovate. The method the firm chooses to innovate can be affected by the firm's governance mechanisms. Research evidence suggests, for example, that inside board directors with equity positions favor internal innovation while outside directors with equity positions prefer acquiring innovation.[4] The chapter closes with summary comments about how firms use strategic entrepreneurship to create value and earn above-average returns.

As you will see from studying this chapter, innovation and entrepreneurship are vital for young and old and for large and small firms, for service companies as well as manufacturing firms, and for high-technology ventures.[5] In the global competitive landscape, the long-term success of new ventures and established firms is a function of the ability to meld entrepreneurship with strategic management.[6]

A major portion of the material in this chapter is on innovation and entrepreneurship within established organizations. This phenomenon is called **corporate entrepreneurship**, which is the use or application of entrepreneurship within an established firm.[7] An important part of the entrepreneurship discipline, corporate entrepreneurship increasingly is thought to be linked to survival and success of established organizations.[8] Indeed, established firms use entrepreneurship to strengthen their performance and to enhance growth opportunities.[9] Of course, innovation and entrepreneurship play a critical role in the degree of success achieved by start-up entrepreneurial ventures as well. Much of the content examined in this chapter is equally important in entrepreneurial ventures (sometimes called "start-ups") and established organizations.[10]

> **Corporate entrepreneurship** is the use or application of entrepreneurship within an established firm.

Entrepreneurship and Entrepreneurial Opportunities

Entrepreneurship is the process by which individuals or groups identify and pursue entrepreneurial opportunities without being immediately constrained by the resources they currently control.[11] **Entrepreneurial opportunities** are conditions in which new goods or services can satisfy a need in the market. These opportunities exist because of competitive imperfections in markets and among the factors of production used to produce them[12] and when information about these imperfections is distributed asymmetrically (i.e., not equally) among individuals.[13] Entrepreneurial opportunities come in a host of forms such as the chance to develop and sell a new product and the chance to sell an existing product in a new market.[14] Firms should be receptive to pursuing entrepreneurial opportunities whenever and wherever they may surface.[15]

As these two definitions suggest, the essence of entrepreneurship is to identify and exploit entrepreneurial opportunities—that is, opportunities others do not see or for which they do not recognize the commercial potential.[16] As a process, entrepreneurship results in the "creative destruction" of existing products (goods or services) or methods of producing them and replaces them with new products and production methods.[17] Thus, firms engaging in entrepreneurship place high value on individual innovations as well as the ability to continuously innovate across time.[18]

We study entrepreneurship at the level of the individual firm. However, evidence suggests that entrepreneurship is the economic engine driving many nations' economies in the global competitive landscape.[19] Thus, entrepreneurship, and the innovation it spawns, is important for companies competing in the global economy and for countries seeking to stimulate economic climates with the potential to enhance the

> **Entrepreneurship** is the process by which individuals or groups identify and pursue entrepreneurial opportunities without being immediately constrained by the resources they currently control.

> **Entrepreneurial opportunities** are conditions in which new goods or services can satisfy a need in the market.

living standard of their citizens.[20] A recent study conducted by the Boston Consulting Group and the Small Business Division of Intuit found that 10 million people in the United States were considering starting a new business. About one-third of those who do will expand into international markets. The study suggested that by 2017 the number of entrepreneurs will increase, and the entrepreneurs will be younger and include more women and immigrants. Thus, even though the importance of entrepreneurship continues to grow, the "face" of those who start new ventures is also changing.[21]

Innovation

Peter Drucker argued that "innovation is the specific function of entrepreneurship, whether in an existing business, a public service institution, or a new venture started by a lone individual."[22] Moreover, Drucker suggested that innovation is "the means by which the entrepreneur either creates new wealth-producing resources or endows existing resources with enhanced potential for creating wealth."[23] Thus, entrepreneurship and the innovation resulting from it are important for large and small firms, as well as for start-up ventures, as they compete in the twenty-first–century competitive landscape. In fact, some argue that firms failing to innovate will stagnate.[24] The realities of competition in the competitive landscape of the twenty-first century suggest that to be market leaders, companies must regularly develop innovative products desired by customers. This means that innovation should be an intrinsic part of virtually all of a firm's activities.[25]

Innovation is a key outcome firms seek through entrepreneurship and is often the source of competitive success, especially in turbulent, highly competitive environments.[26] For example, research results show that firms competing in global industries that invest more in innovation also achieve the highest returns.[27] In fact, investors often react positively to the introduction of a new product, thereby increasing the price of a firm's stock. Furthermore, "innovation may be required to maintain or achieve competitive parity, much less a competitive advantage in many global markets."[28] Investing in the development of new technologies can increase the performance of firms that operate in different but related product markets (refer to the discussion of related diversification in Chapter 6). In this way, the innovations can be used in multiple markets, and return on the investments is earned more quickly.[29]

In his classic work, Schumpeter argued that firms engage in three types of innovative activity.[30] **Invention** is the act of creating or developing a new product or process. **Innovation** is the process of creating a commercial product from an invention. Innovation begins after an invention is chosen for development.[31] Thus, an invention brings something new into being, while an innovation brings something new into use. Accordingly, technical criteria are used to determine the success of an invention, whereas commercial criteria are used to determine the success of an innovation.[32] Finally, **imitation** is the adoption of a similar innovation by different firms. Imitation usually leads to product or process standardization, and products based on imitation often are offered at lower prices, but without as many features. Entrepreneurship is critical to innovative activity in that it acts as the linchpin between invention and innovation.[33]

In the United States in particular, innovation is the most critical of the three types of innovative activity. Many companies are able to create ideas that lead to inventions, but commercializing those inventions has, at times, proved difficult. This difficulty is suggested by the fact that approximately 80 percent of R&D occurs in large firms, but these same firms produce fewer than 50 percent of the patents.[34] Patents are a strategic asset and the ability to regularly produce them can be an important source of

Invention is the act of creating or developing a new product or process.

Innovation is the process of creating a commercial product from an invention.

Imitation is the adoption of a similar innovation by different firms.

competitive advantage, especially for firms competing in knowledge-intensive industries (e.g., pharmaceuticals).[35]

Entrepreneurs

Entrepreneurs are individuals, acting independently or as part of an organization, who see an entrepreneurial opportunity and then take risks to develop an innovation to pursue it. Entrepreneurs are found throughout an organization—from top-level managers to those working to produce a firm's goods or services. Entrepreneurs are found throughout Google, for example. Recall from the Opening Case that all Google employees are encouraged to use roughly 20 percent of their time to develop innovations. Entrepreneurs tend to demonstrate several characteristics: They are highly motivated, willing to take responsibility for their projects, and self-confident.[36] In addition, entrepreneurs tend to be passionate and emotional about the value and importance of their innovation-based ideas.[37] They are able to deal with uncertainty and are more alert to opportunities than others.[38]

Evidence suggests that successful entrepreneurs have an entrepreneurial mind-set. The person with an **entrepreneurial mind-set** values uncertainty in the marketplace and seeks to continuously identify opportunities with the potential to lead to important innovations.[39] Because it has the potential to lead to continuous innovations, an individual's entrepreneurial mind-set can be a source of competitive advantage for a firm.[40] Howard Schultz, founder of Starbucks, and his management team at the company have an entrepreneurial mind-set. Making music a meaningful part of Starbucks' customers' experiences is an example of an evolving product offering resulting from an entrepreneurial mind-set. In Schultz's words: "The music world is changing, and Starbucks and Starbucks Hear Music will continue to be an innovator in the industry. It takes passion, commitment, and even a bit of experimentation to maintain that position."[41] Expanding its reach into the music market, Starbucks formed an alliance with Concord Music Group to help market its new Hear Music label. The alliance seems to be successful: Paul McCartney's new album on this label sold more than 1 million copies in the first two months after its release. Starbucks is also extending its package of products to other forms of entertainment, including movies. It signed a deal to jointly distribute the family movie, *Akeelah and the Bee.*[42]

> **Entrepreneurs** are individuals, acting independently or as part of an organization, who see an entrepreneurial opportunity and then take risks to develop an innovation to exploit it.

> The person with an **entrepreneurial mind-set** values uncertainty in the marketplace and seeks to continuously identify opportunities with the potential to lead to important innovations.

Starbucks Hear Music™ is a result of the entrepreneurial mindset of Starbucks Chairman Howard Schultz and his management team. Here Schultz and executive Don MacKinnon unveil the first Hear Music media bar.

Entrepreneurial mind-sets are fostered and supported when knowledge is readily available throughout a firm. Indeed, research has shown that units within firms are more innovative when they have access to new knowledge.[43] Transferring knowledge, however, can be difficult, often because the receiving party must have adequate absorptive capacity (or the ability) to learn the knowledge.[44] Learning requires that the new knowledge be linked to the existing knowledge. Thus, managers need to develop the capabilities of their human capital to build on their current knowledge base while incrementally expanding that knowledge.[45]

Recent actions at Coca-Cola are designed to acquire and better use knowledge to enter new product markets. In 2007, Coca-Cola announced a reorganization of its North American operations, with special focus on its beverage units. It created a special unit with the purpose of developing new products outside the soft drink market. It also acquired Fuze Beverages, maker of teas and juices, to enlarge its product portfolio and to gain knowledge about other beverage markets.[46]

International Entrepreneurship

International entrepreneurship is a process in which firms creatively discover and exploit opportunities that are outside their domestic markets in order to develop a competitive advantage.[47] As the practices suggested by this definition show, entrepreneurship is a global phenomenon.[48] As noted earlier, approximately one-third of new ventures move into international markets early in their life cycle. Most large established companies have significant foreign operations and often start new ventures in domestic and international markets. Large multinational companies, for example, generate approximately 54 percent of their sales outside their domestic market, and more than 50 percent of their employees work outside of the company's home country.[49]

A key reason that entrepreneurship has become a global phenomenon is that in general, internationalization leads to improved firm performance.[50] Nonetheless, decision makers should recognize that the decision to internationalize exposes their firms to various risks, including those of unstable foreign currencies, problems with market efficiencies, insufficient infrastructures to support businesses, and limitations on market size.[51] Thus, the decision to engage in international entrepreneurship should be a product of careful analysis.

Because of its positive benefits, entrepreneurship is at the top of public policy agendas in many of the world's countries, including Finland, Germany, Ireland, and Israel. Some argue that placing entrepreneurship on these agendas may be appropriate in that regulation hindering innovation and entrepreneurship is the root cause of Europe's productivity problems.[52] In Ireland, for example, the government is "particularly focused on encouraging new innovative enterprises that have growth potential and are export oriented."[53]

Even though entrepreneurship is a global phenomenon, the rate of entrepreneurship differs across countries. A study of 42 countries found that the percentage of adults involved in entrepreneurial activity ranged from a high of more than 40 percent in Peru to a low of approximately 3 percent in Belgium. The United States had a rate slightly more than 10 percent. Importantly, this study also found a strong positive relationship between the rate of entrepreneurial activity and economic development in a country.[54]

Culture is one of the reasons for the differences in rates of entrepreneurship among different countries. The research suggests that a balance between individual initiative and a spirit of cooperation and group ownership of innovation is needed to encourage entrepreneurial behavior. For firms to be entrepreneurial, they must provide appropriate autonomy and incentives for individual initiative to surface, but also promote cooperation and group ownership of an innovation if it is to be implemented successfully. Thus, international entrepreneurship often requires teams of people with unique skills and resources, especially in cultures that highly value individualism or collectivism. In addition to a balance of values for individual initiative and cooperative behaviors, firms must build the capabilities to be innovative and acquire the resources needed to support innovative activities.[55]

The level of investment outside of the home country made by young ventures is also an important dimension of international entrepreneurship. In fact, with increasing globalization, a greater number of new ventures have been "born global."[56] Research has shown that new ventures that enter international markets increase their learning of new technological knowledge and thereby enhance their performance.[57] Because of the positive outcomes associated with its use, the amount of international entrepreneurship has been increasing in recent years.[58]

The probability of entering international markets increases when the firm has top executives with international experience, which increases the likelihood of the firm successfully competing in those markets.[59] Because of the learning and economies of scale and scope afforded by operating in international markets, both young and established internationally diversified firms often are stronger competitors in their domestic market

---

International entrepreneurship is a process in which firms creatively discover and exploit opportunities that are outside their domestic markets in order to develop a competitive advantage.

as well. Additionally, as research has shown, internationally diversified firms are generally more innovative.[60]

Next, we discuss the three ways firms innovate.

Internal Innovation

In established organizations, most innovation comes from efforts in research and development (R&D). Effective R&D often leads to firms' filing for patents to protect their innovative work. Increasingly, successful R&D results from integrating the skills available in the global workforce. Firms seeking internal innovations through their R&D must understand that "Talent and ideas are flourishing everywhere—from Bangalore to Shanghai to Kiev—and no company, regardless of geography, can hesitate to go wherever those ideas are."[61] Thus, in the years to come, the ability to have a competitive advantage based on innovation may accrue to firms able to meld the talent of human capital from countries around the world.

Motorola has been a highly innovative firm over time as explained in the Strategic Focus on page 374. In fact, because of its significant innovation efforts, it was awarded the National Medal of Technology. It has created many radical (handheld cellular phone) and incremental (e.g., Razr2) innovations. And its Razr cell phone sold more units than any cell phone in history. Additionally, it has R&D operations all over the world. Yet, it was caught with an incomplete product portfolio recently and competitors took market share away from it. This example suggests the critical nature and importance of innovation to firm success.

Increasingly, it seems possible that in the twenty-first century competitive landscape, R&D may be the most critical factor in gaining and sustaining a competitive advantage in some industries, such as pharmaceuticals. Larger, established firms, certainly those competing globally, often try to use their R&D labs to create competence-destroying new technologies and products.[62] Being able to innovate in this manner can create a competitive advantage for a firm in many industries.[63] Although critical to long-term corporate success, the outcomes of R&D investments are uncertain and often not achieved in the short term,[64] meaning that patience is required as firms evaluate the outcomes of their R&D efforts.

Incremental and Radical Innovation

Firms produce two types of internal innovations—incremental and radical innovations—when using their R&D activities. Most innovations are *incremental*—that is, they build on existing knowledge bases and provide small improvements in the current product lines. Incremental innovations are evolutionary and linear in nature.[65] "The markets for incremental innovations are well-defined, product characteristics are well understood, profit margins tend to be lower, production technologies are efficient, and competition is primarily on the basis of price."[66] Adding a different kind of whitening agent to a soap detergent is an example of an incremental innovation, as are improvements in televisions over the last few decades (moving from black-and-white to color, improving existing audio capabilities, etc.). Motorola's launch of the Razr2 is an example of incremental innovation. Companies launch far more incremental innovations than radical innovations.[67]

In contrast to incremental innovations, *radical innovations* usually provide significant technological breakthroughs and create new knowledge.[68] Radical innovations, which are revolutionary and nonlinear in nature typically use new technologies to serve newly created markets. The development of the original personal computer (PC) is an example of a radical innovation. Reinventing the computer by developing a "radically new computer-brain chip" (e.g., with the capability to process a trillion calculations per second) is an example of what could be a radical innovation. Obviously, such a radical innovation would seem to have the capacity to revolutionize the tasks computers could perform.

The Razr's Edge: R&D and Innovation at Motorola

Motorola has been known for its innovative products since its inception as Galvin Manufacturing Corporation. In fact, it introduced the first car radios in 1930. Importantly, Motorola developed the first handheld cellular phone in 1984. It is a *Fortune* 100 company with $42.6 billion of sales in 2006. It has received many awards for its innovations, including these recent ones:

2004 National Medal of Technology

2006 IEEE-Standards Association Corporate Award

2006 CES Mark of Excellence Award (for the best home wireless product)

2006 Best of ITS Award for Research and Innovation

2006 Nano 50th Award for Nano Emissive Display Technology

The National Medal of Technology is presented by the White House and is the highest honor in the United States for technological innovation. This medal was awarded "for over 75 years of technological achievement and leadership in the development of innovation in electronic solutions, which have enabled portable and mobile communications to become the standard across society."

In recent years, however, Motorola is perhaps best known to the mass markets for its Razr wireless cell phone introduced in 2005. The Razr is an ultraslim phone with a highly attractive design. In fact, it became popular as a fashion item and at one time sold for more than $500 per phone. Its popularity led to Motorola selling its 100 millionth Razr in the summer of 2007, only three years after its introduction. The Razr helped Motorola to increase its market share in this market from 13 percent in 2003 to 22 percent in 2006. To produce products such as the Razr, Motorola has a labyrinth of R&D laboratories and complementary units. These units work in a cross-functional manner to develop new product ideas, test them, and then commercialize the best ones. The company makes use of the best technology minds globally with research units in North, Central, and South America, Europe, and Asia. These research units are operating on the cutting edge of technology and may have some radical new products on the horizon (e.g., a special writing keypad).

Although Motorola has been a technology leader, it has also suffered from some strategic errors in the past. Most recently, Motorola's market share declined and it was supplanted as the number two handset manufacturer by Samsung. It posted a loss in the first quarter of 2007. The reason for this drop in the market was a move to gain market share by cutting costs and prices rather than continuing to introduce new products to the market. Motorola's CEO Ed Zander admitted this mistake. As a result, the company was caught with a weak product portfolio at a time when competitors were introducing a host of new products.

Motorola moved its R&D processes into high gear to correct these problems. In May 2007, Motorola introduced five new handset products. The most important of its new products is the Razr2. Even more sleek than the Razr, the Razr2 has the most up-to-date technology including the 3G network technology.

Because of the negative outcomes it experienced, Motorola took other actions to solidify its position. For example, Motorola acquired Symbol Technologies, Inc., to gain access to products and systems for enterprise mobility solutions, advanced data capture,

In 2004, Motorola received the National Medal of Technology for over 75 years of technological achievement and leadership. Recently however, Motorola's market share has declined because they were not putting enough money into R&D. Motorola is again emphasizing the R&D process and has already introduced 5 new products.

and radio frequency identification. Additionally, it acquired Good Technology to move into the markets for "smartphones." Finally, it acquired Terayon to build Motorola's capabilities to provide next-generation services (e.g., targeted advertising).

Sources: Motorola Technology: Global R&D and Software Development Organization, http://www.motorola.com/innovators/pdfs/Motorola-Technology-FactSheet05142007.pdf, fact sheet, accessed September 7; J. Palmer, 2007, Our gadget of the week: A better Razr, *Barron's*, August 27, 87(35): 40; M. Palmer & P. Taylor, 2007, Loss of market share adds to pressure on Motorola chief, *Financial Times*, August 23, 21; P. Taylor, 2007, Gloom over Motorola's results, *Financial Times*, July 19, 23; R. O. Crockett, 2007, Honing the Razr edge: Motorola stops trying to reinvent the wheel, *BusinessWeek*, May 28, 38; R. Martin, 2007, With Razr2, Motorola returns to what's worked before, *Information Week*, May 21, 36; M. Reardon, 2007, Is Motorola's cell phone revamp enough? CNET.com, http://www.news.com, May 15.

Because they establish new functionalities for users, radical innovations have strong potential to lead to significant growth in revenue and profits.[69] Developing new processes is a critical part of producing radical innovations. Both types of innovation can create value, meaning that firms should determine when it is appropriate to emphasize either incremental or radical innovation.[70] However, radical innovations have the potential to contribute more significantly to a firm's efforts to earn above-average returns.

Radical innovations are rare because of the difficulty and risk involved in developing them. The value of the technology and the market opportunities are highly uncertain.[71] Because radical innovation creates new knowledge and uses only some or little of a firm's current product or technological knowledge, creativity is required. However, creativity does not produce something from nothing. Rather, creativity discovers, combines, or synthesizes current knowledge, often from diverse areas.[72] This knowledge is then used to develop new products that can be used in an entrepreneurial manner to move into new markets, capture new customers, and gain access to new resources.[73] Such innovations are often developed in separate business units that start internal ventures.[74]

Internally developed incremental and radical innovations result from deliberate efforts. These deliberate efforts are called *internal corporate venturing*, which is the set of activities firms use to develop internal inventions and especially innovations.[75] As shown in Figure 13.1, autonomous and induced strategic behaviors are the two types of internal corporate venturing. Each venturing type facilitates incremental and radical innovations. However, a larger number of radical innovations spring from autonomous

Figure 13.1 Model of Internal Corporate Venturing

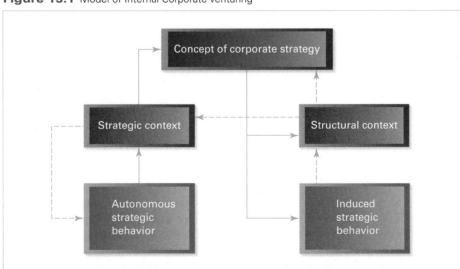

Source: Adapted from R. A. Burgelman, 1983, A model of the interactions of strategic behavior, corporate context, and the concept of strategy, *Academy of Management Review*, 8: 65.

strategic behavior while the greatest percentage of incremental innovations come from induced strategic behavior.

Autonomous Strategic Behavior

Autonomous strategic behavior is a bottom-up process in which product champions pursue new ideas, often through a political process, by means of which they develop and coordinate the commercialization of a new good or service until it achieves success in the marketplace. A *product champion* is an organizational member with an entrepreneurial vision of a new good or service who seeks to create support for its commercialization. Product champions play critical roles in moving innovations forward.[76] Indeed, in many corporations, "Champions are widely acknowledged as pivotal to innovation speed and success."[77] Champions are vital to sell the ideas to others in the organization so that the innovations will be commercialized. Commonly, product champions use their social capital to develop informal networks within the firm. As progress is made, these networks become more formal as a means of pushing an innovation to the point of successful commercialization.[78] Internal innovations springing from autonomous strategic behavior frequently differ from the firm's current strategy, taking it into new markets and perhaps new ways of creating value for customers and other stakeholders.

Autonomous strategic behavior is based on a firm's wellspring of knowledge and resources that are the sources of the firm's innovation. Thus, a firm's technological capabilities and competencies are the basis for new products and processes.[79] Obviously, Motorola has depended to a degree on autonomous strategic behavior over the years to identify new technologies and products that can better serve its customers. The iPod likely resulted from autonomous strategic behavior in Apple. Yet, the development of the iPhone likely was more the result of induced strategic behavior discussed in the next section.

Changing the concept of corporate-level strategy through autonomous strategic behavior results when a product is championed within strategic and structural contexts (see Figure 13.1). Such a transformation occurred with the development of the iPod and introduction of iTunes at Apple. The strategic context is the process used to arrive at strategic decisions (often requiring political processes to gain acceptance). The best firms keep changing their strategic context and strategies because of the continuous changes in the current competitive landscape. Thus, some believe that the most competitively successful firms reinvent their industry or develop a completely new one across time as they compete with current and future rivals.[80]

To be effective, an autonomous process for developing new products requires that new knowledge be continuously diffused throughout the firm. In particular, the diffusion of tacit knowledge is important for development of more effective new products.[81] Interestingly, some of the processes important for the promotion of autonomous new product development behavior vary by the environment and country in which a firm operates. For example, the Japanese culture is high on uncertainty avoidance. As such, research has found that Japanese firms are more likely to engage in autonomous behaviors under conditions of low uncertainty.[82]

Induced Strategic Behavior

The second of the two forms of internal corporate venturing, *induced strategic behavior,* is a top-down process whereby the firm's current strategy and structure foster innovations that are closely associated with that strategy and structure.[83] In this form of venturing, the strategy in place is filtered through a matching structural hierarchy. In essence, induced strategic behavior results in internal innovations that are highly consistent with the firm's current strategy.

While the iPod likely resulted from autonomous strategic behavior, the iPhone is probably a result of induced strategic behavior.

Nokia, one of Motorola's chief competitors in the global cell phone market, is using an induced strategic approach to developing new mobile phones. For example, its strategic goal is to add 2 billion new customers by the end of 2010 by focusing on emerging markets. Thus, its decentralized R&D units in China, Brazil, and India are integrating attributes that are important and attractive to the local culture (e.g., design features) with major technologies developed in the Finnish R&D laboratories at its headquarters. Interestingly, these design teams include not only engineers but also anthropologists and psychologists who study cultures and behaviors in the search for early signals of changes in behavior patterns that may be important for the design of cell phones (or even the need for new technologies). They are especially sensitive to country-specific trends. These actions and approaches at Nokia are intended to keep the firm number one in the global market.[84]

STRATEGY RIGHT NOW

Implementing Internal Innovations

An entrepreneurial mind-set is required to be innovative and to develop successful internal corporate ventures. When valuing environmental and market uncertainty, which are key parts of an entrepreneurial mind-set, individuals and firms demonstrate their willingness to take risks to commercialize innovations. Although they must continuously attempt to identify opportunities, they must also select and pursue the best opportunities and do so with discipline. Employing an entrepreneurial mind-set entails not only developing new products and markets but also placing an emphasis on execution. Often, firms provide incentives to managers to be entrepreneurial and to commercialize innovations.[85]

Having processes and structures in place through which a firm can successfully implement the outcomes of internal corporate ventures and commercialize the innovations is critical. Indeed, the successful introduction of innovations into the marketplace reflects implementation effectiveness.[86] In the context of internal corporate ventures, managers must allocate resources, coordinate activities, communicate with many different parties in the organization, and make a series of decisions to convert the innovations resulting from either autonomous or induced strategic behaviors into successful market entries.[87] As we describe in Chapter 11, organizational structures are the sets of formal relationships that support processes managers use to commercialize innovations.

Effective integration of the various functions involved in innovation processes— from engineering to manufacturing and, ultimately, market distribution—is required to implement the incremental and radical innovations resulting from internal corporate ventures.[88] Increasingly, product development teams are being used to integrate the activities associated with different organizational functions. Such integration involves coordinating and applying the knowledge and skills of different functional areas in order to maximize innovation.[89] Teams must help to make decisions as to which projects should be commercialized and which ones should end. Although ending a project is difficult, sometimes because of emotional commitments to innovation-based projects, effective teams recognize when conditions change such that the innovation cannot create value as originally anticipated.

Cross-Functional Product Development Teams

Cross-functional teams facilitate efforts to integrate activities associated with different organizational functions, such as design, manufacturing, and marketing.[90] In addition, new product development processes can be completed more quickly and the products more easily commercialized when cross-functional teams work effectively.[91] Using cross-functional teams, product development stages are grouped into parallel or overlapping processes to allow the firm to tailor its product development efforts to its unique core competencies and to the needs of the market.

Horizontal organizational structures support the use of cross-functional teams in their efforts to integrate innovation-based activities across organizational functions.[92] Therefore, instead of being designed around vertical hierarchical functions or departments, the organization is built around core horizontal processes that are used to produce and manage innovations. Some of the core horizontal processes that are critical to innovation efforts are formal; they may be defined and documented as procedures and practices. More commonly, however, these processes are informal: "They are routines or ways of working that evolve over time."[93] Often invisible, informal processes are critical to successful innovations and are supported properly through horizontal organizational structures more so than through vertical organizational structures.

Two primary barriers that may prevent the successful use of cross-functional teams as a means of integrating organizational functions are independent frames of reference of team members and organizational politics.[94] Team members working within a distinct specialization (e.g., a particular organizational function) may have an independent frame of reference typically based on common backgrounds and experiences. They are likely to use the same decision criteria to evaluate issues such as product development efforts as they do within their functional units. Research suggests that functional departments vary along four dimensions: time orientation, interpersonal orientation, goal orientation, and formality of structure.[95] Thus, individuals from different functional departments having different orientations on these dimensions can be expected to perceive product development activities in different ways. For example, a design engineer may consider the characteristics that make a product functional and workable to be the most important of the product's characteristics. Alternatively, a person from the marketing function may hold characteristics that satisfy customer needs most important. These different orientations can create barriers to effective communication across functions and even produce conflict in the team at times.[96]

Organizational politics is the second potential barrier to effective integration in cross-functional teams. In some organizations, considerable political activity may center on allocating resources to different functions. Interunit conflict may result from aggressive competition for resources among those representing different organizational functions. This dysfunctional conflict between functions creates a barrier to their integration.[97] Methods must be found to achieve cross-functional integration without excessive political conflict and without changing the basic structural characteristics necessary for task specialization and efficiency.

Facilitating Integration and Innovation

Shared values and effective leadership are important for achieving cross-functional integration and implementing innovation.[98] Highly effective shared values are framed around the firm's vision and mission, and become the glue that promotes integration between functional units. Thus, the firm's culture promotes unity and internal innovation.[99]

Strategic leadership is also highly important for achieving cross-functional integration and promoting innovation. Leaders set the goals and allocate resources. The goals include integrated development and commercialization of new goods and services. Effective strategic leaders also ensure a high-quality communication system to facilitate cross-functional integration. A critical benefit of effective communication is the sharing of knowledge among team members. Effective communication thus helps create synergy and gains team members' commitment to an innovation throughout the organization. Shared values and leadership practices shape the communication systems that are formed to support the development and commercialization of new products.[100]

Creating Value from Internal Innovation

The model in Figure 13.2 shows how firms can create value from the internal corporate venturing processes they use to develop and commercialize new goods and services. An

Figure 13.2 Creating Value Through Internal Innovation Processes

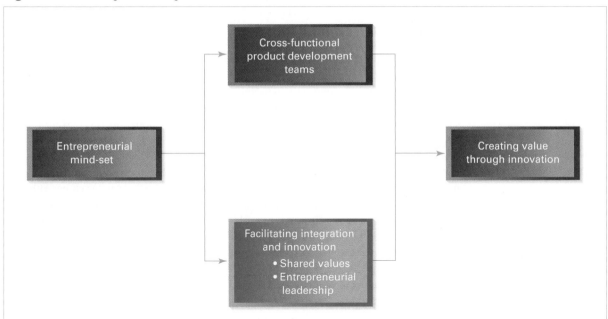

entrepreneurial mind-set is necessary so that managers and employees will consistently try to identify entrepreneurial opportunities the firm can pursue by developing new goods and services and new markets. Cross-functional teams are important for promoting integrated new product design ideas and commitment to their subsequent implementation. Effective leadership and shared values promote integration and vision for innovation and commitment to it. The end result for the firm is the creation of value for the customers and shareholders by developing and commercializing new products.[101] We should acknowledge that not all entrepreneurial efforts succeed, even with effective management. Sometimes managers must decide to exit the market as well to avoid value decline.[102]

In the next two sections, we discuss the other ways firms innovate—by using cooperative strategies and by acquiring companies.

Innovation Through Cooperative Strategies

Virtually all firms lack the breadth and depth of resources (e.g., human capital and social capital) in their R&D activities needed to internally develop a sufficient number of innovations to meet the needs of the market and remain competitive. As such, firms must be open to using external resources to help produce innovations.[103] Alliances with other firms can contribute to innovations in several ways. First, they provide information on new business opportunities and how to exploit them.[104] In other instances, firms use cooperative strategies to align what they believe are complementary assets with the potential to lead to future innovations.[105]

The rapidly changing technologies of the twenty-first–century competitive landscape, globalization, and the need to innovate at world-class levels are primary influences on firms' decisions to innovate by cooperating with other companies. Evidence shows that the skills and knowledge contributed by firms

IBM now has full partnerships with several companies to research, develop, and manufacture, next generation computer chips.

forming a cooperative strategy to innovate tend to be technology-based, a fact suggesting how technologies and their applications continue to influence the choices firms make while competing in the twenty-first–century competitive landscape.[106] Indeed, some believe that because of these conditions, firms are becoming increasingly dependent on cooperative strategies as a path to successful competition in the global economy.[107] Even venerable old firms such as IBM have learned that they need help to create innovations necessary to be competitive in a twenty-first–century environment. In 2002, IBM's chip business lost $1 billion and IBM management decided it had to make major changes. As such, it decided to open its innovation processes and invite full partners to cooperate. It is partnering with Sony, Toshiba, and Albany Nanotech in R&D on cell chips. It is working with AMD and Freescale on R&D to develop manufacturing processes for high-performance chips. It also has a number of partners with which it is doing research to produce next-generation materials and processes to achieve breakthroughs in science on computer chips. Although the process has not been simple, in 2007 it had a number of partners that invested almost $1 billion of their resources in working with IBM to produce innovations.[108]

Both entrepreneurial firms and established firms use cooperative strategies (e.g., strategic alliances and joint ventures) to innovate. An entrepreneurial firm, for example, may seek investment capital as well as established firms' distribution capabilities to successfully introduce one of its innovative products to the market.[109] Alternatively, more-established companies may need new technological knowledge and can gain access to it by forming a cooperative strategy with entrepreneurial ventures.[110] Alliances between large pharmaceutical firms and biotechnology companies increasingly have been formed to integrate the knowledge and resources of both to develop new products and bring them to market.[111]

Because of the importance of strategic alliances, particularly in the development of new technology and in commercializing innovations, firms are beginning to build networks of alliances that represent a form of social capital to them.[112] Building social capital in the form of relationships with other firms provides access to the knowledge and other resources necessary to develop innovations.[113] Knowledge from these alliances helps firms develop new capabilities.[114] Some firms now even allow other companies to participate in their internal new product development processes. It is not uncommon, for example, for firms to have supplier representatives on their cross-functional innovation teams because of the importance of the suppliers' input to ensure quality materials for any new product developed.[115]

However, alliances formed for the purpose of innovation are not without risks. In addition to conflict that is natural when firms try to work together to reach a mutual goal,[116] cooperative strategy participants also take a risk that a partner will appropriate a firm's technology or knowledge and use it to enhance its own competitive abilities.[117] To prevent or at least minimize this risk, firms, particularly new ventures, need to select their partners carefully. The ideal partnership is one in which the firms have complementary skills as well as compatible strategic goals.[118] However, because companies are operating in a network of firms and thus may be participating in multiple alliances simultaneously, they encounter challenges in managing the alliances.[119] Research has shown that firms can become involved in too many alliances, which can harm rather than facilitate their innovation capabilities.[120] Thus, effectively managing a cooperative strategy to produce innovation is critical.

As explained in the Strategic Focus, Whole Foods is a successful and innovative company. However, not all of the innovation is developed solely by Whole Foods' employees and managers. One innovative concept introduced is the result of an alliance between Lord & Taylor and Whole Foods. Located in the same redevelopment, they are working on opportunities for cross-selling goods. Whole Foods has made a number of acquisitions as listed in the Strategic Focus. Thus, Whole Foods' offerings to customers are the result of organic growth (internal innovation), shared resources (alliances), and acquired products and locations (acquisitions).

STRATEGY
RIGHT NOW

Does Whole Foods Really Obtain Innovation in Unnatural Ways?

Whole Foods pioneered the natural and organic food supermarket and almost single-handedly made organic food a household term. Whole Foods started as a small organic food retailer in Austin, Texas, in 1980. In 2006, it operated more than 300 stores and had sales of $5.6 billion. It has become the world's largest natural food retailer. It markets more than 1,500 items, two-thirds of which are perishable.

Over the years, Whole Foods introduced a number of unique products and concepts, and it stands alone at the top of its industry. Most of the new products and concepts introduced in its stores were developed from internal ideas. For example, in 2005, Whole Foods developed a new stand-alone store named Lifestyle Store. It sells environment-friendly goods ranging from clothes to housewares. The products are composed of all organic materials. For example, Lenore Bags and Totes are made from old phone books and other recycled materials. The stores also have organic clothing for babies, and departments that serve other personal and home needs of customers.

Yet, not all of its new product introductions come from internal ideas. For example, Whole Foods acquired Allegro Coffee Company and entered the specialty coffee market. Allegro Coffee is sold in all of the Whole Foods stores. Likewise in 2007 Whole Foods formed an alliance with Lord & Taylor to serve as anchors of a redevelopment project in Stamford, Connecticut. They are promoting it as a distinctive shopping experience that integrates department store *chic* with supermarket *hip*. They believe that both have unique cross-selling opportunities.

Interestingly for a natural food retailer that has grown largely through organic (internal) means, it has completed an interesting number of acquisitions over time. In addition to Allegro, Whole Foods acquired Wellspring Grocery, Bread & Circus, Mrs. Gooch's, Fresh Fields, Bread of Life, Amrion, Merchant of Vino, WholePeople.com (e-commerce subsidiary), Nature's Heartland, Food For Thought, Harry's Farmers Market, Select Fish, Fresh & Wild, Tiny Trapeze, and most recently, Wild Oats. Undoubtedly, these businesses provide not only growth, new customers and outlets, but also add new products to the Whole Foods portfolio. Whole Foods used acquisitions as a means to enter international markets, buying a small natural food chain in the United Kingdom. It then opened its first large new retail outlet in London in 2007.

Regardless of the use of alliances and acquisitions, Whole Foods continues to be innovative. It opened a restaurant in its Chicago store and it became so popular for dinner among customers that it has now opened restaurants in other store locations. The restaurants promote the organic foods sold in the stores. Interestingly, Whole Foods has been listed on the best companies to work for during the period of 1998–2007.

While Whole Foods began as a natural and organic food supermarket, they have continued to expand through innovation, acquisition, and strategic alliances.

Sources: 2007, Whole Foods Market, Inc., http://www.hoovers.com/company-information, September 2; 2007, Whole Foods Market, Inc., http://www.wikipedia.org, September 2; 2007, Whole Foods, http://www.wholefoodsmarket.com, September 2; K. Field, 2007, Vertically championed, *Chain Store Age*, August, 83(8): 158; S. Armstrong, 2007, Make way for Big Organic, *New Statesman*, April 2, 136(4838): 32; D. Desjardins, 2005, Whole Foods goes Hollywood with Lifestyle store, *DSN Retailing Today*, November 7, 44(21): 4; D. Howell, 2005, Whole Foods goes whole hog with landmark Austin store, *DSN Retailing Today*, October 10, 44(5): 3.

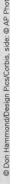

Innovation Through Acquisitions

Firms sometimes acquire companies to gain access to their innovations and to their innovative capabilities. One reason companies make these acquisitions is that the capital market values growth; acquisitions provide a means to rapidly extend one or more product lines and increase the firm's revenues. Acquisitions pursued for this reason should, nonetheless, have a strategic rationale. For example, several large pharmaceutical firms have made acquisitions in recent years for several reasons such as enhancing growth. However, a primary reason for acquisitions in this industry has been to acquire innovation, new drugs that can be commercialized. In this way they strengthen their new product pipeline.[121]

Similar to internal corporate venturing and strategic alliances, acquisitions are not a risk-free approach to innovating. A key risk of acquisitions is that a firm may substitute an ability to buy innovations for an ability to produce innovations internally. In support of this contention, research shows that firms engaging in acquisitions introduce fewer new products into the market.[122] This substitution may take place because firms lose strategic control and focus instead on financial control of their original and especially of their acquired business units.

We note in Chapter 7 that companies can also learn new capabilities from firms they acquire. Thus, firms may gain capabilities to produce innovation from an acquired company. Additionally, firms that emphasize innovation and carefully select companies for acquisition that also emphasize innovation are likely to remain innovative.[123] Likewise, firms must manage well the integration of the acquired firms' technical capabilities so that they remain productive and continue to produce innovation after the acquired firm is merged into the acquiring firm.[124] Cisco has been highly successful with the integration of acquired technology firms. Cisco managers take great care not to lose key personnel in the acquired firm, realizing they are the source of many innovations.

This chapter closes with an assessment of how strategic entrepreneurship, as we have discussed it, helps firms create value for stakeholders through its operations.

Creating Value Through Strategic Entrepreneurship

Newer entrepreneurial firms often are more effective than larger established firms in the identification of entrepreneurial opportunities.[125] As a consequence, entrepreneurial ventures produce more radical innovations than do their larger, more established counterparts. Entrepreneurial ventures' strategic flexibility and willingness to take risks at least partially account for their ability to identify opportunities and then develop radical innovations to exploit them.

Alternatively, larger and well-established firms often have more resources and capabilities to exploit identified opportunities.[126] Younger, entrepreneurial firms generally excel in the opportunity-seeking dimension of strategic entrepreneurship while more established firms generally excel in the advantage-seeking dimension. However, to compete effectively in the twenty-first–century competitive landscape, firms must not only identify and exploit opportunities but do so while achieving and sustaining a competitive advantage.[127] Thus, on a relative basis, newer entrepreneurial firms must learn how to gain a competitive advantage (advantage-seeking behaviors), and older, more established firms must relearn how to identify entrepreneurial opportunities (opportunity-seeking skills).

In some large organizations, action is being taken to deal with these matters. For example, an increasing number of widely known, large firms, including Williams-Sonoma, Inc., Wendy's International, AstraZeneca, and Choice Hotels, have created a new, top-level managerial position commonly called president or executive vice president of emerging brands. The essential responsibility for people holding these positions is to find entrepreneurial opportunities for their firms. If a decision is made to pursue one or more of the identified opportunities, this person also leads the analysis to determine whether the innovations should be internally developed, pursued through a cooperative venture, or acquired. The objective is to help firms develop successful incremental and radical innovations.

To be entrepreneurial, firms must develop an entrepreneurial mind-set among their managers and employees. Managers must emphasize the management of their resources, particularly human capital and social capital.[128] The importance of knowledge to identify and exploit opportunities as well as to gain and sustain a competitive advantage suggests that firms must have strong human capital.[129] Social capital is critical for access to complementary resources from partners in order to compete effectively in domestic and international markets.[130]

Many entrepreneurial opportunities continue to surface in international markets, a reality that is contributing to firms' willingness to engage in international entrepreneurship. By entering global markets that are new to them, firms can learn new technologies and management practices and diffuse this knowledge throughout the entire enterprise. Furthermore, the knowledge firms gain can contribute to their innovations. Research has shown that firms operating in international markets tend to be more innovative.[131] Entrepreneurial ventures and large firms now regularly enter international markets. Both types of firms must also be innovative to compete effectively. Thus, by developing resources (human and social capital), taking advantage of opportunities in domestic and international markets, and using the resources and knowledge gained in these markets to be innovative, firms achieve competitive advantages.[132] In so doing, they create value for their customers and shareholders.

Firms practicing strategic entrepreneurship contribute to a country's economic development. In fact, some countries such as Ireland have made dramatic economic progress by changing the institutional rules for businesses operating in the country. This approach could be construed as a form of institutional entrepreneurship. Likewise, firms that seek to establish their technology as a standard, also representing institutional entrepreneurship, are engaging in strategic entrepreneurship because creating a standard produces a competitive advantage for the firm.[133]

Research shows that because of its economic importance and individual motives, entrepreneurial activity is increasing around the globe. Furthermore, more women are becoming entrepreneurs because of the economic opportunity entrepreneurship provides and the individual independence it affords. Recent research showed that about one-third of all entrepreneurs are now women[134] In the United States, for example, women are the nation's fastest-growing group of entrepreneurs.[135] In future years, entrepreneurial activity may increase the wealth of less-affluent countries and continue to contribute to the economic development of the more-affluent countries. Regardless, the entrepreneurial ventures and large, established firms that choose to practice strategic entrepreneurship are likely to be the winners in the twenty-first century.[136]

After identifying opportunities, entrepreneurs must act to develop capabilities that will become the basis of their firm's core competencies and competitive advantages. The process of identifying opportunities is entrepreneurial, but this activity alone is not sufficient to create maximum wealth or even to survive over time.[137] As we learned in Chapter 3, to successfully exploit opportunities, a firm must develop capabilities that are valuable, rare, difficult to imitate, and nonsubstitutable. When capabilities satisfy these four criteria, the firm has one or more competitive advantages to exploit the identified opportunities (as described in Chapter 3). Without a competitive advantage, the firm's success will be only temporary (as explained in Chapter 1). An innovation may be valuable and rare early in its life, if a market perspective is used in its development. However, competitive actions must be taken to introduce the new product to the market and protect its position in the market against competitors to gain a competitive advantage. These actions combined represent strategic entrepreneurship.

Summary

- Strategic entrepreneurship is taking entrepreneurial actions using a strategic perspective. Firms engaging in strategic entrepreneurship simultaneously engage in opportunity-seeking and advantage-seeking behaviors. The purpose is to continuously find new opportunities and quickly develop innovations to exploit them.

- Entrepreneurship is a process used by individuals and groups to identify entrepreneurial opportunities without being immediately constrained by the resources they control. Corporate entrepreneurship is the application of entrepreneurship (including the identification of entrepreneurial opportunities) within ongoing, established organizations. Entrepreneurial opportunities are conditions in which new goods or services can satisfy a need in the market. Increasingly, entrepreneurship positively contributes to individual firms' performance and stimulates growth in countries' economies.

- Firms engage in three types of innovative activity: (1) invention, which is the act of creating a new good or process, (2) innovation, or the process of creating a commercial product from an invention, and (3) imitation, which is the adoption of similar innovations by different firms. Invention brings something new into being while innovation brings something new into use.

- Entrepreneurs see or envision entrepreneurial opportunities and then take actions to develop innovations to exploit them. The most successful entrepreneurs (whether they are establishing their own venture or are working in an ongoing organization) have an entrepreneurial mind-set, which is an orientation that values the potential opportunities available because of marketplace uncertainties.

- International entrepreneurship, or the process of identifying and exploiting entrepreneurial opportunities outside the firm's domestic markets, has become important to firms around the globe. Evidence suggests that firms capable of effectively engaging in international entrepreneurship outperform those competing only in their domestic markets.

- Three basic approaches are used to produce innovation: (1) internal innovation, which involves R&D and forming

internal corporate ventures, (2) cooperative strategies such as strategic alliances, and (3) acquisitions. Autonomous strategic behavior and induced strategic behavior are the two forms of internal corporate venturing. Autonomous strategic behavior is a bottom-up process through which a product champion facilitates the commercialization of an innovative good or service. Induced strategic behavior is a top-down process in which a firm's current strategy and structure facilitate the development and implementation of product or process innovations. Thus, induced strategic behavior is driven by the organization's current corporate strategy and structure while autonomous strategic behavior can result in a change to the firm's current strategy and structure arrangements.

- Firms create two types of innovation—incremental and radical—through internal innovation that takes place in the form of autonomous strategic behavior or induced strategic behavior. Overall, firms produce more incremental innovations although radical innovations have a higher probability of significantly increasing sales revenue and profits. Increasingly, cross-functional integration is vital to a firm's efforts to develop and implement internal corporate venturing activities and to commercialize the resulting innovation. Additionally, integration and innovation can be facilitated by developing shared values and effectively using strategic leadership.

- To gain access to the specialized knowledge that often is required to innovate in the complex global economy, firms may form a cooperative relationship such as a strategic alliance with other companies, some of which may be competitors.

- Acquisitions are another means firms use to obtain innovation. Innovation can be acquired through direct acquisition, or firms can learn new capabilities from an acquisition, thereby enriching their internal innovation abilities.

- The practice of strategic entrepreneurship by all types of firms, large and small, new and more established, creates value for all stakeholders, especially for shareholders and customers. Strategic entrepreneurship also contributes to the economic development of countries.

Review Questions

1. What is strategic entrepreneurship? What is corporate entrepreneurship?

2. What is entrepreneurship, and what are entrepreneurial opportunities? Why are they important for firms competing in the twenty-first–century competitive landscape?

3. What are invention, innovation, and imitation? How are these concepts interrelated?

4. What is an entrepreneur, and what is an entrepreneurial mind-set?

5. What is international entrepreneurship? Why is it important?

6. How do firms develop innovations internally?

7. How do firms use cooperative strategies to innovate and to have access to innovative capabilities?

8. How does a firm acquire other companies to increase the number of innovations it produces and improve its capability to produce innovations?

9. How does strategic entrepreneurship help firms to create value?

1. D. J. Miller, M. J. Fern, & L. B. Cardinal, 2007, The use of knowledge for technological innovation within diversified firms, *Academy of Management Journal*, 50: 308–326; D. S. Elenkov & I. M. Manev, 2005, Top management leadership and influence on innovation: The role of sociocultural context, *Journal of Management*, 31: 381–402.

2. R. D. Ireland & J. W. Webb, 2007, Strategic entrepreneurship: Creating competitive advantage through streams of innovation, *Business Horizons*, 50(4): 49–59; M. A. Hitt, R. D. Ireland, S. M. Camp, & D. L. Sexton, 2002, Strategic entrepreneurship: Integrating entrepreneurial and strategic management perspectives, in M. A. Hitt, R. D. Ireland, S. M. Camp, & D. L. Sexton (eds.), *Strategic Entrepreneurship: Creating a New Mindset*, Oxford, UK: Blackwell Publishers, 1–16; M. A. Hitt, R. D. Ireland, S. M. Camp, & D. L. Sexton, 2001, Strategic entrepreneurship: Entrepreneurial strategies for wealth creation, *Strategic Management Journal*, 22 (Special Issue): 479–491.

3. C. E. Helfat, 2006, Review of Open innovation: The new imperative for creating and profiting from technology, *Academy of Management Perspectives*, 20(2): 86–88; D. A. Shepherd & D. R. DeTienne, 2005, Prior knowledge, potential financial reward, and opportunity identification, *Entrepreneurship Theory and Practice*, 29(1): 91–112.

4. R. E. Hoskisson, M. A. Hitt, R. A. Johnson, & W. Grossman, 2002, Conflicting voices: The effects of institutional ownership heterogeneity and internal governance on corporate innovation strategies, *Academy of Management Journal*, 45: 697–716.

5. J. L. Morrow, D. G. Sirmon, M. A. Hitt & T. R. Holcomb, 2007, Creating value in the face of declining performance: Firm strategies and organizational recovery, *Strategic Management Journal*, 28: 271–283; K. G. Smith, C. J. Collins, & K. D. Clark, 2005, Existing knowledge, knowledge creation capability, and the rate of new product introduction in high-technology firms, *Academy of Management Journal*, 48: 346–357.

6. D. F. Kuratko, 2007, Entrepreneurial leadership in the 21st century, *Journal of Leadership and Organizational Studies*, 13(4): 1–11; R. D. Ireland, M. A. Hitt, & D. G. Sirmon, 2003, A model of strategic entrepreneurship: The construct and its dimensions, *Journal of Management*, 29: 963–989.

7. B. R. Barringer & R. D. Ireland, 2008, *Entrepreneurship: Successfully Launching New Ventures*, Upper Saddle River, NJ: Pearson Prentice Hall, 5; D. T. Holt, M. W. Rutherford, & G. R. Clohessy, 2007,

Corporate entrepreneurship: An empirical look at individual characteristics, context and process, *Journal of Leadership and Organizational Studies*, 13(4): 40–54.

8. M. H. Morris, S. Coombes, & M. Schindehutte, 2007, Antecedents and outcomes of entrepreneurial and market orientations in a non-profit context: Theoretical and empirical insights, *Journal of Leadership and Organizational Studies*, 13(4): 12–39; H. A. Schildt, M. V. J. Maula, & T. Keil, 2005, Explorative and exploitative learning from external corporate ventures, *Entrepreneurship Theory and Practice*, 29: 493–515.

9. G. T. Lumpkin & B. B. Lichtenstein, 2005, The role of organizational learning in the opportunity-recognition process, *Entrepreneurship Theory and Practice*, 29: 451–472.

10. B. A. Gilbert, P. P. McDougall, & D. B. Audretsch, 2006, New venture growth: A review and extension, *Journal of Management*, 32: 926–950.

11. Barringer & Ireland, *Entrepreneurship*; S. A. Zahra, H. J. Sapienza, & P. Davidsson, 2006, Entrepreneurship and dynamic capabilities: A review, model and research agenda, *Journal of Management Studies*, 43: 917–955.

12. S. A. Alvarez & J. B. Barney, 2005, Organizing rent generation and appropriation: Toward a theory of the entrepreneurial firm, *Journal of Business Venturing*, 19: 621–635.

13. M. Minniti, 2005, Entrepreneurial alertness and asymmetric information in a spin-glass model, *Journal of Business Venturing*, 19: 637–658.

14. W. Kuemmerle, 2005, The entrepreneur's path to global expansion, *MIT Sloan Management Review*, 46(2): 42–49.

15. C. Marquis & M. Lounsbury, 2007, Vive la resistance: Competing logics and the consolidation of U.S. community banking, *Academy of Management Journal*, 50: 799–820; S.-H. Lee, M. W. Peng, & J. B. Barney, 2007, Bankruptcy law and entrepreneurship development: A real-options perspective, *Academy of Management Review*, 32: 257–272.

16. N. Wasserman, 2006, Stewards, agents, and the founder discount: Executive compensation in new ventures, *Academy of Management Journal*, 49: 960–976; S. Shane & S. Venkataraman, 2000, The promise of entrepreneurship as a field of research, *Academy of Management Review*, 25: 217–226.

17. J. Schumpeter, 1934, *The Theory of Economic Development*, Cambridge, MA: Harvard University Press.

18. R. Greenwood & R. Suddaby, 2006, Institutional entrepreneurship in mature fields: The big five accounting firms, *Academy of Management Journal*, 49:

27–48; R. Katila, 2002, New product search over time: Past ideas in their prime? *Academy of Management Journal*, 45: 995–1010.

19. W. J. Baumol, R. E. Litan, & C. J. Schramm, 2007, *Good capitalism, bad capitalism, and the economics of growth and prosperity*, New Haven: Yale University Press; R. G. Holcombe, 2003, The origins of entrepreneurial opportunities, *Review of Austrian Economics*, 16: 25–54.

20. R. D. Ireland, J. W. Webb, & J. E. Coombs, 2005, Theory and methodology in entrepreneurship research, in D. J. Ketchen Jr. & D. D. Bergh (eds.), *Research Methodology in Strategy and Management* (Volume 2), San Diego: Elsevier Publishers, 111–141; S. D. Sarasvathy, 2005, The questions we ask and the questions we care about: Reformulating some problems in entrepreneurship research, *Journal of Business Venturing*, 19: 707–717.

21. K. E. Klein, 2007, The face of entre-preneurship in 2017, *BusinessWeek*, http://www.businessweek.com, January 31.

22. P. F. Drucker, 1998, The discipline of innovation, *Harvard Business Review*, 76(6): 149–157.

23. Ibid.

24. K. Karnik, 2005, Innovation's importance: Powering economic growth, *National Association of Software and Service Companies*, http://www.nasscom.org, January 24.

25. M. Subramaniam & M. A. Youndt, 2005, The influence of intellectual capital on the types of innovative capabilities, *Academy of Management Journal*, 48: 450–463.

26. F. F. Suarez & G. Lanzolla, 2007, The role of environmental dynamics in building a first mover advantage theory, *Academy of Management Review*, 32: 377–392.

27. R. Price, 1996, Technology and strategic advantage, *California Management Review*, 38(3): 38–56; L. G. Franko, 1989, Global corporate competition: Who's winning, who's losing and the R&D factor as one reason why, *Strategic Management Journal*, 10: 449–474.

28. M. A. Hitt, R. D. Nixon, R. E. Hoskisson, & R. Kochhar, 1999, Corporate entrepreneurship and cross-functional fertilization: Activation, process and disintegration of a new product design team, *Entrepreneurship: Theory and Practice*, 23(3): 145–167.

29. D. J. Miller, 2006, Technological diversity, related diversification, and firm performance, *Strategic Management Journal*, 27: 601–619.

30. Schumpeter, *The Theory of Economic Development*.

31. R. Katila & S. Shane, 2005, When does lack of resources make new firms

innovative? *Academy of Management Journal*, 48: 814–829.

32. P. Sharma & J. L. Chrisman, 1999, Toward a reconciliation of the definitional issues in the field of corporate entrepreneurship, *Entrepreneurship: Theory and Practice*, 23(3): 11–27; R. A. Burgelman & L. R. Sayles, 1986, *Inside Corporate Innovation: Strategy, Structure, and Managerial Skills*, New York: Free Press.

33. D. K. Dutta & M. M. Crossan, 2005, The nature of entrepreneurial opportunities: Understanding the process using the 4I organizational learning framework, *Entrepreneurship Theory and Practice* 29: 425–449.

34. R. E. Hoskisson & L. W. Busenitz, 2002, Market uncertainty and learning distance in corporate entrepreneurship entry mode choice, in M. A. Hitt, R. D. Ireland, S. M. Camp, & D. L. Sexton (eds.), *Strategic Entrepreneurship: Creating a New Mindset*, Oxford, UK: Blackwell Publishers, 151–172.

35. S. Thornhill, 2006, Knowledge, innovation, and firm performance in high- and low-technology regimes, *Journal of Business Venturing*, 21: 687–703; D. Somaya, 2003, Strategic determinants of decisions not to settle patent litigation, *Strategic Management Journal*, 24: 17–38.

36. F. Luthans & E. S. Ibrayeva, 2006, Entrepreneurial self-efficacy in central Asian transition economies: Quantitative and qualitative analyses, *Journal of International Business Studies*, 37: 92–110; D. Duffy, 2004, Corporate entrepreneurship: Entrepreneurial skills for personal and corporate success, *Center for Excellence*, http://www.centerforexcellence.net, June 14.

37. M. S. Cardon, C. Zietsma, P. Saparito, B. P. Matheren, & C. Davis, 2005, A tale of passion: New insights into entrepreneurship from a parenthood metaphor, *Journal of Business Venturing*, 19: 23–45.

38. J. O. Fiet, 2007, A prescriptive analysis of search and discovery, *Journal of Management Studies*, 44: 592–611; J. S. McMullen & D. A. Shepherd, 2006, Entrepreneurial action and the role of uncertainty in the theory of the entrepreneur, *Academy of Management Review*, 31: 132–152.

39. R. A. Baron, 2006, Opportunity recognition as pattern recognition: How entrepreneurs "connect the dots" to identify new business opportunities, *Academy of Management Perspectives*, 20(1): 104–119; R. G. McGrath & I. MacMillan, 2000, *The Entrepreneurial Mindset*, Boston, MA: Harvard Business School Press.

40. R. D. Ireland, M. A. Hitt, & J. W. Webb, 2005, Entrepreneurial alliances and networks, in O. Shenkar and J. J. Reuer (eds.), *Handbook of Strategic Alliances*, Thousand Oaks, CA: Sage Publications, 333–352; T. M. Begley & D. P. Boyd, 2003, The need for a corporate global mind-set, *MIT Sloan Management Review*, 44(2): 25–32.

41. H. D. Schultz, 2005, Starbucks' founder on innovation in the music biz, *BusinessWeek*, July 4, 16–17.

42. P. Sexton, 2007, Mocha and music as Starbucks serves up a record label, *Financial Times*, http://www.ft.com, August 27; Starbucks to launch music label, 2007, CBC Arts, http://www.cbc.ca/consumer story, March 13.

43. W. Tsai, 2001, Knowledge transfer in intraorganizational networks: Effects of network position and absorptive capacity on business unit innovation and performance, *Academy of Management Journal*, 44: 996–1004.

44. S. A. Zahra & G. George, 2002, Absorptive capacity: A review, reconceptualization, and extension, *Academy of Management Review*, 27: 185–203.

45. M. A. Hitt, L. Bierman, K. Uhlenbruck, & K. Shimizu, 2006, The importance of resources in the internationalization of professional service firms: The good, the bad and the ugly, *Academy of Management Journal*, 49: 1137–1157; M. A. Hitt, L. Bierman, K. Shimizu, & R. Kochhar, 2001, Direct and moderating effects of human capital on strategy and performance in professional service firms, *Academy of Management Journal*, 44: 13–28.

46. A. Ward, 2007, Coca-Cola looks beyond the fizz, *Financial Times*, http://www.ft.com, March 10.

47. Zahra & George, Absorptive capacity: 261.

48. H. J. Sapienza, E. Autio, G. George, & S. A. Zahra, 2006, A capabilities perspective on the effects of early internationalization on firm survival and growth, *Academy of Management Review*, 31: 914–933; T. M. Begley, W.-L. Tan, & H. Schoch, 2005, Politico-economic factors associated with interest in starting a business: A multi-country study, *Entrepreneurship Theory and Practice*, 29: 35–52.

49. M. Javidan, R. M. Steers, & M. A. Hitt, 2007, *The Global Mindset*, Amsterdam: Elsevier Ltd.

50. Hitt, Bierman, Uhlenbruck, Shimizu, The importance of resources in the internationalization of professional service firms; L. Tihanyi, R. A. Johnson, R. E. Hoskisson, & M. A. Hitt, 2003, Institutional ownership differences and international diversification: The effects of boards of directors and technological opportunity, *Academy of Management Journal*, 46: 195–211.

51. Q. Yang & C. X. Jiang, 2007, Location advantages and subsidiaries' R&D activities in emerging economies: Exploring the effect of employee mobility, *Asia Pacific Journal of Management*, 24: 341–358; R. D. Ireland & J. W. Webb, 2006, International entrepreneurship in emerging economies: A resource-based perspective, in S. Alvarez, A. Carrera, L. Mesquita, & R. Vassolo (eds.), *Entrepreneurship and Innovation in Emerging Economies*, Oxford, UK: Blackwell Publishers, in press.

52. D. Farrell, H. Fassbender, T. Kneip, S. Kriesel, & E. Labaye, 2003, Reviving

French and German productivity, *The McKinsey Quarterly*, (1), 40–53.

53. 2004, *GEM 2004 Irish Report*, http://www.gemconsortium.org/download, July 13.

54. N. Bosma & R. Harding, 2007, 2006 *Global Entrepreneurship Monitor*, Babson College, http://www3.babson.edu/ESHIP/research-publications/gem.cfm, March 1.

55. D. W. Yiu, C. M. Lau, & G. D. Bruton, 2007, International venturing by emerging economy firms: The effects of firm capabilities, home country networks, and corporate entrepreneurship, *Journal of International Business Studies*, 38: 519–540; M. H. Morris, 1998, *Entrepreneurial Intensity: Sustainable Advantages for Individuals, Organizations, and Societies*, Westport, CT: Quorum Books, 85–86.

56. N. Nummeia, S. Saarenketo, & K. Puumalainen, 2005, Rapidly with a rifle or more slowly with a shotgun? Stretching the company boundaries of internationalizing ICT firms, *Journal of International Entrepreneurship*, 2: 275–288; S. A. Zahra & G. George, 2002, International entrepreneurship: The state of the field and future research agenda, in M. A. Hitt, R. D. Ireland, S. M. Camp, & D. L. Sexton (eds.), *Strategic Entrepreneurship: Creating a New Mindset*, Oxford, UK: Blackwell Publishers, 255–288.

57. S. A. Zahra, R. D. Ireland, & M. A. Hitt, 2000, International expansion by new venture firms: International diversity, mode of market entry, technological learning and performance, *Academy of Management Journal*, 43: 925–950.

58. R. Mudambi & S.A. Zahra, 2007, The survival of international new ventures, *Journal of International Business Studies*, 38: 333-352; P. P. McDougall & B. M. Oviatt, 2000, International entrepreneurship: The intersection of two paths, *Academy of Management Journal*, 43: 902–908.

59. H. Barkema, & O. Chvyrkov, 2007, Does top management team diversity promote or hamper foreign expansion? *Strategic Management Journal*, 28: 663–680; A. Yan, G. Zhu, & D. T. Hall, 2002, International assignments for career building: A model of agency relationships and psychological contracts, *Academy of Management Review*, 27: 373–391.

60. T. S. Frost, 2001, The geographic sources of foreign subsidiaries' innovations, *Strategic Management Journal*, 22: 101–122.

61. R. Underwood, 2005, Walking the talk? *Fast Company*, March, 25–26.

62. J. Battelle, 2005, Turning the page, *Business 2.0*, July, 98–100.

63. J. Santos, Y. Doz, & P. Williamson, 2004, Is your innovation process global? *MIT Sloan Management Review*, 45(4): 31–37; C. D. Charitou & C. C. Markides, 2003, Responses to disruptive strategic innovation, *MIT Sloan Management Review*, 44(2): 55–63.

64. J. A. Fraser, 2004, A return to basics at Kellogg, *MIT Sloan Management Review*,

45(4): 27–30; P. M. Lee & H. M. O'Neill, 2003, Ownership structures and R&D investments of U.S. and Japanese firms: Agency and stewardship perspectives, *Academy of Management Journal,* 46: 212–225.

65. F. K. Pil & S. K. Cohen, 2006, Modularity: Implications for imitation, innovation, and sustained advantage, *Academy of Management Review,* 31: 995–1011; S. Kola-Nystrom, 2003, Theory of conceptualizing the challenge of corporate renewal, Lappeenranta University of Technology, working paper.

66. 2005, Radical and incremental innovation styles, *Strategies 2 innovate,* http://www.strategies2innovate.com, July 12.

67. W. C. Kim & R. Mauborgne, 2005, Navigating toward blue oceans, *Optimize,* February, 44–52.

68. G. Ahuja & M. Lampert, 2001, Entrepreneurship in the large corporation: A longitudinal study of how established firms create breakthrough inventions, *Strategic Management Journal,* 22 (Special Issue): 521–543.

69. 2005, Getting an edge on innovation, *BusinessWeek,* March 21, 124.

70. J. E. Ashton, F. X. Cook Jr., & P. Schmitz, 2003, Uncovering hidden value in a midsize manufacturing company, *Harvard Business Review,* 81(6): 111–119; L. Fleming & O. Sorenson, 2003, Navigating the technology landscape of innovation, *MIT Sloan Management Review,* 44(2): 15–23.

71. J. Goldenberg, R. Horowitz, A. Levav, & D. Mazursky, 2003, Finding your innovation sweet spot, *Harvard Business Review,* 81(3): 120–129; G. C. O'Connor, R. Hendricks, & M. P. Rice, 2002, Assessing transition readiness for radical innovation, *Research Technology Management,* 45(6): 50–56.

72. C. E. Shalley & J. E. Perry-Smith, 2008, Team creativity and creative cognition: Interactive effects of social and cognitive networks, *Strategic Entrepreneurship Journal,* 1: in press; R. I. Sutton, 2002, Weird ideas that spark innovation, *MIT Sloan Management Review,* 43(2): 83–87.

73. K. G. Smith & D. Di Gregorio, 2002, Bisociation, discovery, and the role of entrepreneurial action, in M. A. Hitt, R. D. Ireland, S. M. Camp, & D. L. Sexton (eds.), *Strategic Entrepreneurship: Creating a New Mindset,* Oxford, UK: Blackwell Publishers, 129–150.

74. J. G. Covin, R. D. Ireland, & D. F. Kuratko, 2005, Exploration through internal corporate ventures, Indiana University, working paper; Hoskisson & Busenitz, Market uncertainty and learning distance.

75. R. A. Burgelman, 1995, *Strategic Management of Technology and Innovation,* Boston: Irwin.

76. S. K. Markham, 2002, Moving technologies from lab to market, *Research Technology Management,* 45(6): 31–42.

77. J. M. Howell, 2005, The right stuff: Identifying and developing effective champions of innovation, *Academy of Management Executive,* 19(2): 108–119.

78. M. D. Hutt & T. W. Seph, 2004, *Business Marketing Management,* 8th ed., Cincinnati, OH: Thomson South-Western.

79. S. K. Ethiraj, 2007, Allocation of inventive effort in complex product systems, *Strategic Management Journal,* 28: 563–584; M. A. Hitt, R. D. Ireland, & H. Lee, 2000, Technological learning, knowledge management, firm growth and performance, *Journal of Engineering and Technology Management,* 17: 231–246.

80. H. W. Chesbrough, 2002, Making sense of corporate venture capital, *Harvard Business Review,* 80(3): 90–99.

81. M. Subramaniam & N. Venkatraman, 2001, Determinants of transnational new product development capability: Testing the influence of transferring and deploying tacit overseas knowledge, *Strategic Management Journal,* 22: 359–378.

82. M. Song & M. M. Montoya-Weiss, 2001, The effect of perceived technological uncertainty on Japanese new product development, *Academy of Management Journal,* 44: 61–80.

83. B. Ambos & B. B. Schegelmilch, 2007, Innovation and control in the multinational firm: A comparison of political and contingency approaches, *Strategic Management Journal,* 28: 473–486.

84. N. Lakshman, 2007, Nokia: It takes a village to design a phone for emerging markets, *BusinessWeek,* September, 12–14.

85. M. Makri, P. J. Lane, & L. R. Gomez-Mejia, 2006, CEO incentives, innovation and performance in technology-intensive firms: A reconciliation of outcome and behavior-based incentive schemes, *Strategic Management Journal,* 27: 1057–1080.

86. Multinational knowledge spillovers with decentralized R&D: A game theoretic approach, *Journal of International Business Studies,* 2007, 38: 47–63; 2002, Building scientific networks for effective innovation, *MIT Sloan Management Review,* 43(3): 14.

87. E. Danneels, 2007, The process of technological competence leveraging, *Strategic Management Journal,* 28: 511–533; C. M. Christensen & M. Overdorf, 2000, Meeting the challenge of disruptive change, *Harvard Business Review,* 78(2): 66–77.

88. L. Yu, 2002, Marketers and engineers: Why can't we just get along? *MIT Sloan Management Review,* 43(1): 13.

89. A. Somech, 2006, The effects of leadership style and team process on performance and innovation in functionally hetergeneous teams, *Journal of Management,* 32: 132–157.

90. P. Evans & B. Wolf, 2005, Collaboration rules, *Harvard Business Review,* 83(7): 96–104.

91. B. Fischer & A. Boynton, 2005, Virtuoso teams, *Harvard Business Review,* 83(7): 116–123.

92. Hitt, Nixon, Hoskisson, & Kochhar, Corporate entrepreneurship.

93. Christensen & Overdorf, Meeting the challenge of disruptive change.

94. Hitt, Nixon, Hoskisson, & Kochhar, Corporate entrepreneurship.

95. A. C. Amason, 1996, Distinguishing the effects of functional and dysfunctional conflict on strategic decision making: Resolving a paradox for top management teams, *Academy of Management Journal,* 39: 123–148; P. R. Lawrence & J. W. Lorsch, 1969, *Organization and Environment,* Homewood, IL: Richard D. Irwin.

96. M. A. Cronin & L. R. Weingart, 2007, Representational gaps, information processing, and conflict in functionally heterogeneous teams, *Academy of Management Review,* 32: 761–773; D. Dougherty, L. Borrelli, K. Muncir, & A. O'Sullivan, 2000, Systems of organizational sensemaking for sustained product innovation, *Journal of Engineering and Technology Management,* 17: 321–355.

97. Hitt, Nixon, Hoskisson, & Kochhar, Corporate entrepreneurship.

98. E. C. Wenger & W. M. Snyder, 2000, Communities of practice: The organizational frontier, *Harvard Business Review,* 78(1): 139–144.

99. Gary Hamel, 2000, *Leading the Revolution,* Boston: Harvard Business School Press.

100. Q. M. Roberson & J. A. Colquitt, 2005, Shared and configural justice: A social network model of justice in teams, *Academy of Management Review,* 30: 595–607.

101. N. Stieglitz & L. Heine, 2007, Innovations and the role of complementarities in a strategic theory of the firm, *Strategic Management Journal,* 28: 1–15; S. W. Fowler, A. W. King, S. J. Marsh, & B. Victor, 2000, Beyond products: New strategic imperatives for developing competencies in dynamic environments, *Journal of Engineering and Technology Management,* 17: 357–377.

102. M. B. Sarkar, R. Echamabadi, R. Agarwal, & B. Sen, 2006, The effect of the innovative environment on exit of entrepreneurial firms, *Strategic Management Journal,* 27: 519–539.

103. K. Larsen & A. Salter, 2006, Open for innovation: The role of openness in explaining innovation performance among U.K. manufacturing firms, *Strategic Management Journal,* 27: 131–150.

104. A. Tiwana & M. Keil, 2007, Does peripheral knowledge complement control? An empirical test in technology outsourcing alliances, *Strategic Management Journal,* 28: 623–634; A.V. Shipilov, 2006, Network strategies and performance of Canadian investment banks, *Academy of Management Journal,* 49: 590–604.

105. C. Dhanaraj & A. Parkhe, 2006, Orchestrating innovation networks, *Academy of Management Review,* 31: 659–669.

106. F. T. Rothaermel & D. L. Deeds, 2004, Exploration and exploitation alliances in biotechnology: A system of new product development, *Strategic Management Journal,* 25: 201–221; R. Gulati & M. C. Higgins, 2003, Which ties matter when? The contingent effects of interorganizational partnerships on IPO

success, *Strategic Management Journal,* 24: 127–144.

107. F. T. Rothaermel, M. A. Hitt & L. A. Jobe, 2006, Balancing vertical integration and strategic outsourcing: Effects on product portfolio, product success and firm performance, *Strategic Management Journal,* 27: 1033–1056; J. Hagel III & J. S. Brown, 2005, Productive friction, *Harvard Business Review,* 83(2): 82–91.

108. S. Hamm, 2007, Radical Collaboration: Lessons from IBM's innovation factory, *BusinessWeek,* September 10, 17–22.

109. A. C. Cooper, 2002, Networks, alliances and entrepreneurship, in M. A. Hitt, R. D. Ireland, S. M. Camp, & D. L. Sexton (eds.), *Strategic Entrepreneurship: Creating a New Mindset,* Oxford, UK: Blackwell Publishers, 204–222.

110. B.-S. Teng, 2007, Corporate entrepreneurship activities through strategic alliances: A resource-based approach toward competitive advantage, *Journal of Management Studies,* 44: 119–142; S. A. Alvarez & J. B. Barney, 2001, How entrepreneurial firms can benefit from alliances with large partners, *Academy of Management Executive,* 15(1): 139–148.

111. F. T. Rothaermel, 2001, Incumbent's advantage through exploiting complementary assets via interfirm cooperation, *Strategic Management Journal,* 22 (Special Issue): 687–699.

112. A. Capaldo, 2007, Network structure and innovation: The leveraging of a dual network as a distinctive capability, *Strategic Management Journal,* 28: 585–608.

113. H. Yli-Renko, E. Autio, & H. J. Sapienza, 2001, Social capital, knowledge acquisition and knowledge exploitation in young technology-based firms, *Strategic Management Journal,* 22 (Special Issue): 587–613.

114. C. Lee, K. Lee, & J. M. Pennings, 2001, Internal capabilities, external networks and performance: A study of technology-based ventures, *Strategic Management Journal,* 22 (Special Issue): 615–640.

115. A. Takeishi, 2001, Bridging inter- and intra-firm boundaries: Management of supplier involvement in automobile product development, *Strategic Management Journal,* 22: 403–433.

116. R. C. Sampson, 2007, R&D alliances and firm performance: The impact of technological diversity and alliance organization on innovation, *Academy of Management Journal,* 50: 364–386; J. Weiss & J. Hughes, 2005, Want collaboration? Accept—and actively manage—conflict, *Harvard Business Review,* 83(3): 92–101.

117. R. D. Ireland, M. A. Hitt, & D. Vaidyanath, 2002, Strategic alliances as a pathway to competitive success, *Journal of Management,* 28: 413–446.

118. M. A. Hitt, M. T. Dacin, E. Levitas, J. -L. Arregle, & A. Borza, 2000, Partner selection in emerging and developed market contexts: Resource-based and organizational learning perspectives, *Academy of Management Journal,* 43: 449–467.

119. J. J. Reuer, M. Zollo, & H. Singh, 2002, Post-formation dynamics in strategic alliances, *Strategic Management Journal,* 23: 135–151.

120. F. Rothaermel & D. Deeds, 2002, More good things are not always necessarily better: An empirical study of strategic alliances, experience effects, and new product development in high-technology start-ups, in M. A. Hitt, R. Amit, C. Lucier, & R. Nixon (eds.), *Creating Value: Winners in the New Business Environment,* Oxford, UK: Blackwell Publishers, 85–103.

121. 2005, Novartis announces completion of Hexal AG acquisition, http://www.novartis.com, June 6; 2005, Pfizer sees sustained long-term growth, http://www.pfizer.com, April 5.

122. M. A. Hitt, R. E. Hoskisson, R. A. Johnson, & D. D. Moesel, 1996, The market for corporate control and firm innovation, *Academy of Management Journal,* 39: 1084–1119.

123. P. Puranam & K. Srikanth, 2007, What they know vs. what they do: How acquirers leverage technology acquisitions, *Strategic Management Journal,* 28: 805–825; M. A. Hitt, J. S. Harrison, & R. D. Ireland, 2001, *Mergers and Acquisitions: A Guide to Creating Value for Stakeholders,* New York: Oxford University Press.

124. P. Puranam, H. Singh & M. Zollo, 2006, Organizing for innovation: Managing the coordination-autonomy dilemma in technology, *Academy of Management Journal,* 49: 263–280.

125. Ireland, Hitt, & Sirmon, A model of strategic entrepreneurship.

126. Ibid.

127. Hitt, Ireland, Camp, & Sexton, Strategic entrepreneurship.

128. D. G. Sirmon, M. A. Hitt, & R. D. Ireland, 2007, Managing firm resources in dynamic environment to create value: Looking inside the black box, *Academy of Management Review,* 32: 273–292.

129. Hitt, Bierman, Shimizu, & Kochhar, Direct and moderating effects of human capital.

130. Hitt, Bierman, Uhlenbruck, & Shimizu, The importance of resources in the internationalization of professional service firms; M. A. Hitt, H. Lee, & E. Yucel, 2002, The importance of social capital to the management of multinational enterprises: Relational networks among Asian and Western firms, *Asia Pacific Journal of Management,* 19: 353–372.

131. M. A. Hitt, R. E. Hoskisson, & H. Kim, 1997, International diversification: Effects on innovation and firm performance in product diversified firms, *Academy of Management Journal,* 40: 767–798.

132. M. A. Hitt & R. D. Ireland, 2002, The essence of strategic leadership: Managing human and social capital, *Journal of Leadership and Organization Studies,* 9(1): 3–14.

133. Baumol, Litan, & Schramm, *Good capitalism, bad capitalism*; R. Garud, S. Jain, & A. Kumaraswamy, 2002, Institutional entrepreneurship in the sponsorship of common technological standards: The case of Sun Microsystems and JAVA, *Academy of Management Journal,* 45: 196–214.

134. I. E. Allen, N. Langowitz, & M. Minniti, 2007, Global entrepreneurship monitor: 2006 report on women in entrepreneurship, Babson College, http://www3.babson.edu/ESHIP/research-publications/gem.cfm, March 1.

135. J. D. Jardins, 2005, I am woman (I think), *Fast Company,* May, 25–26.

136. Hitt, Ireland, Camp, & Sexton, Strategic entrepreneurship.

137. C. W. L. Hill & F. T. Rothaermel, 2003, The performance of incumbent firms in the face of radical technological innovation, *Academy of Management Review,* 28: 257–274.

Case Studies

Case 1
3M: Cultivating Core Competency, 1

Case 2
A-1 Lanes and the Currency Crisis of
the East Asian Tigers, 13

Case 3
AMD vs. Intel: Competitive Challenges, 25

Case 4
Boeing: Redefining Strategies to Manage
the Competitive Market, 33

Case 5
Carrefour in Asia, 49

Case 6
Dell: From a Low-Cost PC Maker to an
Innovative Company, 61

Case 7
Ford Motor Company, 75

Case 8
Jack Welch and Jeffrey Immelt:
Continuity and Change in Strategy,
Style, and Culture at GE, 91

Case 9
The Home Depot, 105

Case 10
China's Home Improvement Market: Should
Home Depot Enter or Will it Have a Late-Mover
(Dis)advantage?, 117

Case 11
Huawei: Cisco's Chinese Challenger, 133

Case 12
ING DIRECT: Rebel in the Banking Industry, 145

Case 13
JetBlue Airways: Challenges Ahead, 157

Case 14
Lufthansa: Going Global, but How to Manage
Complexity?, 175

Case 15
Microsoft's Diversification Strategy, 185

Case 16
Nestlé: Sustaining Growth in Mature Markets, 203

Case 17
An Entrepreneur Seeks the Holy Grail of Retailing, 217

Case 18
PSA Peugeot Citroën: Strategic Alliances for
Competitive Advantage?, 221

Case 19
Sun Microsystems, 233

Case 20
Teleflex Canada: A Culture of Innovation, 241

Case 21
Tyco International: A Case of Corporate Malfeasance, 249

Case 22
Vodafone: Out of Many, One, 263

Case 23
Wal-Mart Stores, Inc. (WMT), 281

Case 24
WD-40 Company: The Squeak, Smell, and
Dirt Business (A), 309

What to Expect From In-Class Case Discussions

As you will learn, classroom discussions of cases differ significantly from lectures. The case method calls for your instructor to guide the discussion and to solicit alternative views as a way of encouraging your active participation when analyzing a case. When alternative views are not forthcoming, your instructor might take a position just to challenge you and your peers to respond thoughtfully as a way of generating still additional alternatives. Often, instructors will evaluate your work in terms of both the quantity and the quality of your contributions to in-class case discussions. The in-class discussions are important in that you can derive significant benefit by having your ideas and recommendations examined against those of your peers and by responding to thoughtful challenges by other class members and/or the instructor.

During case discussions, your instructor will likely listen, question, and probe to extend the analysis of case issues. In the course of these actions, your peers and/or your instructor may challenge an individual's views and the validity of alternative perspectives that have been expressed. These challenges are offered in a constructive manner; their intent is to help all parties involved with analyzing a case develop their analytical and communication skills. Developing these skills is important in that they will serve you well when working for all types of organizations. Commonly, instructors will encourage you and your peers to be innovative and original when developing and presenting ideas. Over the course of an individual discussion, you are likely to form a more complex view of the case as a result of listening to and thinking about the diverse inputs offered by your peers and instructor. Among other benefits, experience with multiple case discussions will increase your knowledge of the advantages and disadvantages of group decision-making processes.

Both your peers and instructor will value comments that contribute to identifying problems as well as solutions to them. To offer relevant contributions, you are encouraged to think independently and, through discussions with your peers outside of class, to refine your thinking. We also encourage you to avoid using "I think," "I believe," and "I feel" to discuss your inputs to a case analysis process. Instead, consider using a less emotion laden phrase, such as "My analysis shows. . . ." This highlights the logical nature of the approach you have taken to analyze a case. When preparing for an in-class case discussion, you should plan to use the case data to explain your assessment of the situation. Assume that your peers and instructor are familiar with the basic facts included in the case. In addition, it is good practice to prepare notes regarding your analysis of case facts before class discussions and use them when explaining your perspectives. Effective notes signal to classmates and the instructor that you are prepared to engage in a thorough discussion of a case. Moreover, comprehensive and detailed notes eliminate the need for you to memorize the facts and figures needed to successfully discuss a case.

The case analysis process described above will help prepare you effectively to discuss a case during class meetings. Using this process results in consideration of the issues required to identify a focal firm's problems and to propose strategic actions through which the firm can increase the probability it will outperform its rivals. In some instances, your instructor may ask you to prepare either an oral or a written analysis of a particular case. Typically, such an assignment demands even more thorough study and analysis of the case contents. At your instructor's discretion, oral and written analyses may be completed by individuals or by groups of three or more people. The information and insights gained by completing the six steps shown in Table 1 often are of value when developing an oral or a written analysis. However, when preparing an oral or written presentation, you must

Table 1 An Effective Case Analysis Process

Step 1: Gaining Familiarity	a. In general—determine who, what, how, where, and when (the critical facts of the case).
	b. In detail—identify the places, persons, activities, and contexts of the situation.
	c. Recognize the degree of certainty/uncertainty of acquired information.
Step 2: Recognizing Symptoms	a. List all indicators (including stated "problems") that something is not as expected or as desired.
	b. Ensure that symptoms are not assumed to be the problem (symptoms should lead to identification of the problem).
Step 3: Identifying Goals	a. Identify critical statements by major parties (for example, people, groups, the work unit, and so on).
	b. List all goals of the major parties that exist or can be reasonably inferred.
Step 4: Conducting the Analysis	a. Decide which ideas, models, and theories seem useful.
	b. Apply these conceptual tools to the situation.
	c. As new information is revealed, cycle back to substeps a and b.
Step 5: Making the Diagnosis	a. Identify predicaments (goal inconsistencies).
	b. Identify problems (discrepancies between goals and performance).
	c. Prioritize predicaments/problems regarding timing, importance, and so on.
Step 6: Doing the Action Planning	a. Specify and prioritize the criteria used to choose action alternatives.
	b. Discover or invent feasible action alternatives.
	c. Examine the probable consequences of action alternatives.
	d. Select a course of action.
	e. Design an implementation plan/schedule.
	f. Create a plan for assessing the action to be implemented.

Source: C. C. Lundberg and C. Enz, 1993, A framework for student case preparation, *Case Research Journal*, 13 (Summer): 144. Reprinted by permission of NACRA, North American Case Research Association.

consider the overall framework in which your information and inputs will be presented. Such a framework is the focus of the next section.

Preparing an Oral/Written Case Presentation

Experience shows that two types of thinking (analysis and synthesis) are necessary to develop an effective oral or written presentation (see Exhibit 1). In the analysis stage, you should first analyze the general external environmental issues affecting the firm. Next, your environmental analysis should focus on the particular industry (or industries, in the case of a diversified company) in which a firm operates. Finally, you should examine companies against which the focal firm competes. By studying the three levels of the external environment (general, industry, and competitor), you will be able to identify a firm's opportunities and threats. Following the external environmental analysis is the analysis of the firm's internal organization. This analysis provides the insights needed to identify the firm's strengths and weaknesses.

As noted in Exhibit 1, you must then change the focus from analysis to synthesis. Specifically, you must synthesize information gained from your analysis of the firm's external environment and internal organization. Synthesizing information allows you to generate alternatives that can resolve the significant problems or challenges facing the focal firm. Once you identify a best alternative, from an evaluation based on predetermined criteria and goals, you must explore implementation actions.

In Table 2, we outline the sections that should be included in either an oral or a written presentation: strategic profile and case analysis purpose, situation analysis, statements of strengths/weaknesses and opportunities/threats, strategy formulation, and strategy implementation. These sections are described in the following discussion. Familiarity with the contents of your book's thirteen chapters is helpful because the general outline for an oral or a written presentation shown in Table 2 is based on an understanding of the strategic management process detailed in those chapters. We follow the discussions of the parts of Table 2 with a few comments about the "process" to use to present the results of your case analysis in either a written or oral format.

Exhibit 1 Types of Thinking in Case Preparation: Analysis and Synthesis

Table 2 General Outline for an Oral or Written Presentation

I. Strategic Profile and Case Analysis Purpose

II. Situation Analysis
   A. General environmental analysis
   B. Industry analysis
   C. Competitor analysis
   D. Internal analysis

III. Identification of Environmental Opportunities and Threats and Firm Strengths and Weaknesses (SWOT Analysis)

IV. Strategy Formulation
   A. Strategic alternatives
   B. Alternative evaluation
   C. Alternative choice

V. Strategic Alternative Implementation
   A. Action items
   B. Action plan

Strategic Profile and Case Analysis Purpose

You will use the strategic profile to briefly present the critical facts from the case that have affected the focal firm's historical strategic direction and performance. The case facts should not be restated in the profile; rather, these comments should show how the critical facts lead to a particular focus for your analysis. This primary focus should be emphasized in this section's conclusion. In addition, this section should state important assumptions about case facts on which your analyses are based.

Situation Analysis

As shown in Table 2, a general starting place for completing a situation analysis is the general environment.

General Environmental Analysis. Your analysis of the general environment should focus on trends in the six segments of the general environment (see Table 3). Many of the segment issues shown in Table 3 for the six segments are explained more fully in Chapter two of your book. The objective you should have in evaluating these trends is to be able to *predict* the segments that you expect to have the most significant influence on your focal firm over the next several years (say three to five years) and to explain your reasoning for your predictions.

Table 3 Sample General Environmental Categories

Technological Trends
- Information technology continues to become cheaper with more practical applications
- Database technology enables organization of complex data and distribution of information
- Telecommunications technology and networks increasingly provide fast transmission of all sources of data, including voice, written communications, and video information
- Computerized design and manufacturing technologies continue to facilitate quality and flexibility

Demographic Trends
- Regional changes in population due to migration
- Changing ethnic composition of the population
- Aging of the population
- Aging of the "baby boom" generation

Economic Trends
- Interest rates
- Inflation rates
- Savings rates
- Exchange rates
- Trade deficits
- Budget deficits

Political/Legal Trends
- Antitrust enforcement
- Tax policy changes
- Environmental protection laws
- Extent of regulation/deregulation
- Privatizing state monopolies
- State-owned industries

Sociocultural Trends
- Women in the workforce
- Awareness of health and fitness issues
- Concern for the environment
- Concern for customers

Global Trends
- Currency exchange rates
- Free-trade agreements
- Trade deficits

Industry Analysis. Porter's five force model is a useful tool for analyzing the industry (or industries) in which your firm competes. We explain how to use this tool in Chapter 2. In this part of your analysis, you want to determine the attractiveness of an industry (or a segment of an industry) in which your firm is competing. As attractiveness increases, so does the possibility your firm will be able to earn profits by using its chosen strategies. After evaluating the power of the five forces relative to your firm, you should make a judgment as to *how* attractive the industry is in which your firm is competing.

Competitor Analysis. Firms also need to analyze each of their primary competitors. This analysis should identify competitors' current strategies, strategic intent, strategic mission, capabilities, core competencies, and a competitive response profile (see Chapter 2). This information is useful to the focal firm in formulating an appropriate strategy and in predicting competitors'

probable responses. Sources that can be used to gather information about an industry and companies with whom the focal firm competes are listed in Appendix I. Included in this list is a wide range of publications, such as periodicals, newspapers, bibliographies, directories of companies, industry ratios, forecasts, rankings/ratings, and other valuable statistics.

Internal Analysis. Assessing a firm's strengths and weaknesses through a value chain analysis facilitates moving from the external environment to the internal organization. Analysis of the primary and support activities of the value chain provides opportunities to understand how external environmental trends affect the specific activities of a firm. Such analysis helps highlight strengths and weaknesses (see Chapter 3 for an explanation and use of the value chain).

For purposes of preparing an oral or a written presentation, it is important to note that strengths are internal resources and capabilities that have the potential to be core competencies. Weaknesses, on the other hand, are internal resources and capabilities that have the potential to place a firm at a competitive disadvantage relative to its rivals. Thus, some of a firm's resources and capabilities are strengths; others are weaknesses.

When evaluating the internal characteristics of the firm, your analysis of the functional activities emphasized is critical. For instance, if the strategy of the firm is primarily technology driven, it is important to evaluate the firm's R&D activities. If the strategy is market driven, marketing functional activities are of paramount importance. If a firm has financial difficulties, critical financial ratios would require careful evaluation. In fact, because of the importance of financial health, most cases require financial analyses. Appendix II lists and operationally defines several common financial ratios. Included are tables describing profitability, liquidity, leverage, activity, and shareholders' return ratios. Leadership, organizational culture, structure, and control systems are other characteristics of firms you should examine to fully understand the "internal" part of your firm.

Identification of Environmental Opportunities and Threats and Firm Strengths and Weaknesses (SWOT Analysis).
The outcome of the situation analysis is the identification of a firm's strengths and weaknesses and its environmental threats and opportunities. The next step requires that you analyze the strengths and weaknesses and the opportunities and threats for configurations that benefit or do not benefit your firm's efforts to perform well. Case analysts and organizational strategists as well, seek to match a firm's strengths with its opportunities. In addition, strengths are chosen to prevent any serious environmental threat from negatively affecting the firm's performance. The key objective of conducting a SWOT analysis is to determine how to position the firm so it can take advantage of opportunities, while simultaneously avoiding or minimizing environmental threats. Results from a SWOT analysis yield valuable insights into the selection of a firm's strategies. The analysis of a case should not be overemphasized relative to the synthesis of results gained from your analytical efforts. There may be a temptation to spend most of your oral or written case analysis on results from the analysis. It is important, however, that you make an equal effort to develop and evaluate alternatives and to design implementation of the chosen strategy.

Strategy Formulation-Strategic Alternatives, Alternative Evaluation, and Alternative Choice.
Developing alternatives is often one of the most difficult steps in preparing an oral or a written presentation. Developing three to four alternative strategies is common (see Chapter 5 for business-level strategy alternatives and Chapter 6 for corporate-level strategy alternatives). Each alternative should be feasible (i.e., it should match the firm's strengths, capabilities, and especially core competencies),

and feasibility should be demonstrated. In addition, you should show how each alternative takes advantage of the environmental opportunity or avoids/buffers against environmental threats. Developing carefully thought out alternatives requires synthesis of your analyses' results and creates greater credibility in oral and written case presentations.

Once you develop strong alternatives, you must evaluate the set to choose the best one. Your choice should be defensible and provide benefits over the other alternatives. Thus, it is important that both alternative development and evaluation of alternatives be thorough. The choice of the best alternative should be explained and defended.

Strategic Alternative Implementation-Action Items and Action Plan.
After selecting the most appropriate strategy (that is, the strategy with the highest probability of helping your firm in its efforts to earn profits), implementation issues require attention. Effective synthesis is important to ensure that you have considered and evaluated all critical implementation issues. Issues you might consider include the structural changes necessary to implement the new strategy. In addition, leadership changes and new controls or incentives may be necessary to implement strategic actions. The implementation actions you recommend should be explicit and thoroughly explained. Occasionally, careful evaluation of implementation actions may show the strategy to be less favorable than you thought originally. A strategy is only as good as the firm's ability to implement it.

Process Issues.
You should ensure that your presentation (either oral or written) has logical consistency throughout. For example, if your presentation identifies one purpose, but your analysis focuses on issues that differ from the stated purpose, the logical inconsistency will be apparent. Likewise, your alternatives should flow from the configuration of strengths, weaknesses, opportunities, and threats you identified by analyzing your firm's external environment and internal organization.

Thoroughness and clarity also are critical to an effective presentation. Thoroughness is represented by the comprehensiveness of the analysis and alternative generation. Furthermore, clarity in the results of the analyses, selection of the best alternative strategy, and design of implementation actions are important. For example, your statement of the strengths and weaknesses should flow clearly and logically from your analysis of your firm's internal organization.

Presentations (oral or written) that show logical consistency, thoroughness, and clarity of purpose, effective analyses, and feasible recommendations (strategy and implementation) are more effective and are likely to be more positively received by your instructor and peers. Furthermore, developing the skills necessary to make such presentations will enhance your future job performance and career success.

Appendix I Sources for Industry and Competitor Analyses

Abstracts and Indexes

Periodicals	ABI/*Inform*
	Business Periodicals Index
	InfoTrac Custom Journals
	InfoTrac Custom Newspapers
	InfoTrac OneFile
	EBSCO Business Source Premiere
	Lexis/Nexis Academic
	Public Affairs Information Service Bulletin (PAIS)
	Reader's Guide to Periodical Literature
Newspapers	*NewsBank—Foreign Broadcast Information*
	NewsBank-Global NewsBank
	New York Times Index
	Wall Street Journal Index
	Wall Street Journal/Barron's Index
	Washington Post Index

Bibliographies

	Encyclopedia of Business Information Sources

Directories

Companies—General	*America's Corporate Families and International Affiliates*
	Hoover's Online: The Business Network www.hoovers.com/free
	D&B *Million Dollar Directory (databases:* http://www.dnbmdd.com)
	Standard & Poor's Corporation Records
	Standard & Poor's Register of Corporations, Directors, and Executives (http://www.netadvantage.standardandpoors.com *for all of Standard & Poor's)*
	Ward's Business Directory of Largest U.S. Companies
Companies—International	*America's Corporate Families and International Affiliates*
	Business Asia
	Business China
	Business Eastern Europe
	Business Europe
	Business International
	Business International Money Report
	Business Latin America
	Directory of American Firms Operating in Foreign Countries
	Directory of Foreign Firms Operating in the United States
	Hoover's Handbook of World Business
	International Directory of Company Histories
	Mergent International Manual
	Mergent Online (http://www.fisonline.com—for "Business and Financial Information Connection to the World")
	Who Owns Whom
Companies—Manufacturers	*Thomas Register of AmericanManufacturers*
	U.S. Office of Management and Budget, Executive Office of the President, *Standard Industrial Classification Manual*
	U.S. *Manufacturer's Directory, Manufacturing & Distribution, USA*
Companies—Private	*D&B Million Dollar Directory*
	Ward's Business Directory of Largest U.S. Companies

Companies—Public	Annual Reports and 10-K Reports *Disclosure*(corporate reports) *Q-File* Security and Exchange Commision Filings & Forms (EDGAR) *http://www.sec.gov/edgar.shtml* *Mergent's Manuals:* • *Mergent's Bank and Finance Manual* • *Mergent's Industrial Manual* • *Mergent's International Manual* • *Mergent's Municipal and Government Manual* • *Mergent's OTC Industrial Manual* • *Mergent's OTC Unlisted Manual* • *Mergent's Public Utility Manual* • *Mergent's Transportation Manual* Standard & Poor Corporation, *Standard Corporation Descriptions: http://www* *.netadvantage.standardandpoors.com* • *Standard & Poor's Analyst Handbook* • *Standard & Poor's Industry Surveys* • *Standard & Poor's Statistical Service*
Companies—Subsidiaries and Affiliates	*America's Corporate Families and International Affiliates* *Ward's Directory* *Who Owns Whom* *Mergent's Industry Review* *Standard & Poor's Analyst's Handbook* *Standard & Poor's Industry Surveys* (2 volumes) U.S. Department of Commerce, *U.S. Industrial Outlook*
Industry Ratios	Dun & Bradstreet, *Industry Norms and Key Business Ratios* *RMA's Annual Statement Studies* *Troy Almanac of Business and Industrial Financial Ratios—*
Industry Forecasts	International Trade Administration, *U.S. Industry & Trade Outlook*
Rankings & Ratings	Annual Report on American Industry in *Forbes* *Business Rankings Annual* *Mergent's Industry Review http://www.worldcatlibraries.org* *Standard & Poor's Industry Report Service http://www.netadvantage* *.standardandpoors.com* *Value Line Investment Survey* *Ward's Business Directory of Largest U.S. Companies*
Statistics	*American Statistics Index (ASI)* Bureau of the Census, U.S. Department of Commerce, *Economic Census Publications* Bureau of the Census, U.S. Department of Commerce, *Statistical Abstract of the* *United States* Bureau of Economic Analysis, U.S. Department of Commerce, *Survey of Current* *Business* Internal Revenue Service, U.S. Treasury Department, *Statistics of Income:* *Corporation Income Tax Returns* *Statistical Reference Index (SRI)*

Appendix II: Financial Analysis in Case Studies

Table A-1 Profitability Ratios

Ratio	Formula	What It Shows
1. Return on total assets	$\dfrac{\text{Profits after taxes}}{\text{Total assets}}$ or $\dfrac{\text{Profits after taxes} + \text{Interest}}{\text{Total assets}}$	The net return on total investments of the firm or The return on both creditors' and shareholders' investments
2. Return on stockholder's equity (or return on net worth)	$\dfrac{\text{Profits after taxes}}{\text{Total stockholder's equity}}$	How profitably the company is utilizing shareholders' funds
3. Return on common equity	$\dfrac{\text{Profits after taxes} - \text{Preferred stock dividends}}{\text{Total stockholder's equity} - \text{Par value of preferred stock}}$	The net return to common stockholders
4. Operating profit margin (or return on sales)	$\dfrac{\text{Profits before taxes and before interest}}{\text{Sales}}$	The firm's profitability from regular operations
5. Net profit margin (or net return on sales)	$\dfrac{\text{Profits after taxes}}{\text{Sales}}$	The firm's net profit as a percentage of total sales

Table A-2 Liquidity Ratios

Ratio	Formula	What It Shows
1. Current ratio	$\dfrac{\text{Current assets}}{\text{Current liabilities}}$	The firm's ability to meet its current financial liabilities
2. Quick ratio (or acid-test ratio)	$\dfrac{\text{Current assets} - \text{Inventory}}{\text{Current liabilities}}$	The firm's ability to pay off short-term obligations without relying on sales of inventory
3. Inventory to net working capital	$\dfrac{\text{Inventory}}{\text{Current assets} - \text{Current liabilities}}$	The extent to which the firm's working capital is tied up in inventory

Table A-3 Leverage Ratios

Ratio	Formula	What It Shows
1. Debt-to-assets	$\dfrac{\text{Total debt}}{\text{Total assets}}$	Total borrowed funds as a percentage of total assets
2. Debt-to-equity	$\dfrac{\text{Total debt}}{\text{Total shareholders' equity}}$	Borrowed funds versus the funds provided by shareholders
3. Long-term debt-to-equity	$\dfrac{\text{Long-term debt}}{\text{Total shareholders' equity}}$	Leverage used by the firm
4. Times-interest-earned (or coverage ratio)	$\dfrac{\text{Profits before interest and taxes}}{\text{Total interest charges}}$	The firm's ability to meet all interest payments
5. Fixed charge coverage	$\dfrac{\text{Profits before taxes and interest} + \text{Lease obligations}}{\text{Total interest charges} + \text{Lease obligations}}$	The firm's ability to meet all fixed-charge obligations including lease payments

Table A-4 Activity Ratios

Ratio	Formula	What It Shows
1. Inventory turnover	$\dfrac{\text{Sales}}{\text{Inventory of finished goods}}$	The effectiveness of the firm in employing inventory
2. Fixed-assets turnover	$\dfrac{\text{Sales}}{\text{Fixed assets}}$	The effectiveness of the firm in utilizing plant and equipment
3. Total assets turnover	$\dfrac{\text{Sales}}{\text{Total assets}}$	The effectiveness of the firm in utilizing total assets
4. Accounts receivable turnover	$\dfrac{\text{Annual credit sales}}{\text{Accounts receivable}}$	How many times the total receivables have been collected during the accounting period
5. Average collecting period	$\dfrac{\text{Accounts receivable}}{\text{Average daily sales}}$	The average length of time the firm waits to collect payment after sales

Table A-5 Shareholders' Return Ratios

Ratio	Formula	What It Shows
1. Dividend yield on common stock	$\dfrac{\text{Annual dividend per share}}{\text{Current market price per share}}$	A measure of return to common stockholders in the form of dividends
2. Price-earnings ratio	$\dfrac{\text{Current market price per share}}{\text{After-tax earnings per share}}$	An indication of market perception of the firm; usually, the faster-growing or less risky firms tend to have higher PE ratios than the slower-growing or more risky firms
3. Dividend payout ratio	$\dfrac{\text{Annual dividends per share}}{\text{After-tax earnings per share}}$	An indication of dividends paid out as a percentage of profits
4. Cash flow per share	$\dfrac{\text{After-tax profits + Depression}}{\text{Number of common shares outstanding}}$	A measure of total cash per share available for use by the firm

Case 1

3M: Cultivating Core Competency

Mridu Verma

ICFAI Business School

One of the keys to sustainable success is unfettered and well-directed innovation. Innovation is not just about a process, it's also about imagination and people.

> **GEORGE W. BUCKLEY**[1]
> —*3M CHAIRMAN, PRESIDENT, & CEO*

Introduction

In 2006, the $21.2 billion 3M was the epitome of a high-technology/low-technology business with over 50,000 products ranging from Post-it Notes and Scotch tape to transdermal patches of nitroglycerin and optical films. 3M owed its formidable strength to its unusual corporate culture, which comfortably fostered innovation and inter-departmental cooperation, backed by a massive research and development budget, which typically exceeded $1 billion annually. Because of this, the company was a leader in—and in many cases a founder of—a number of important technologies, including pressure-sensitive tapes, sandpaper, protective chemicals, microflex circuits, reflective materials, and premium graphics. 3M operated in electronics, telecommunications, industrial, consumer and office, health care, safety, and other markets. It owned popular brands such as Post-it, Scotch-Brite, and 3M Scotchshield. Because the end-user segment for the products was diverse, the company did not fall under any of the normal industry classifications. In December 2005, the company recorded a net profit of $3.2 billion, an increase of 7 percent from 2004.

When George Buckley joined 3M as the CEO in December 2005, the company was facing criticism from analysts and investors over anemic revenue growth that had slowed to between 1 and 5 percent through parts of 2004 and 2005, even while the broader markets had been expanding. Buckley realized that he needed to generate growth, maintain premium margins, and strategically manage the company's portfolio—all without driving out 3M's culture of innovation on which both the company's fame and its long history of success rested. He needed to develop a growth strategy that was based on and enhanced 3M's core competency. What could he do to ensure that?

Background Note

Minnesota Mining and Manufacturing Company (nicknamed 3M) was formed in 1902 by five businessmen. The company's initial venture to mine a rare mineral and market it as an abrasive was unsuccessful. In 1907 and 1909, William L. McKnight[2] and A. G. Bush joined 3M and soon designed an aggressive, customer-oriented brand of salesmanship. Sales representatives, instead of dealing with a company's purchasing agent, were encouraged to proceed directly to the shop where they could talk with the people who used the products. In so doing, 3M salesmen could discover both how products could be improved and what new products might be needed. This contact resulted in some of 3M's early innovations. For instance, when Henry Ford's newly motorized assembly lines created too much friction for existing sandpapers that were designed to sand wood and static objects, the concerned 3M salesman informed the company of the customer's problem. The company devised a tougher sandpaper, and thus captured much of this niche market within the growing auto industry.

Another salesman noticed that dust from sandpaper use made the shop environment extremely unhealthy. Around the same time, a Philadelphia ink manufacturer named Francis G. Okie wrote McKnight with a request for mineral grit samples. Prompted by curiosity, McKnight approached Okie and found that he had invented a waterproof, and consequently dust-free, sandpaper. In 1921, after purchasing the patent and then solving various defects, 3M came out with Wetordry sandpaper and significantly expanded its business. It also hired the inventor as its first full-time researcher, making the creation of one of the first corporate research and development (R&D) divisions in the United States.

In 1923, a salesman in an auto body painting shop noticed that the process used to paint cars in two tones worked poorly. In response, 3M developed a successful masking tape—Scotch tape—which prevented the paints from running together. The company immediately began to develop different applications of its new technology and the transparent Scotch tape was created. Another salesman invented a portable tape dispenser, and 3M had its first large-scale consumer product. During the 1930s, it funneled 45 percent of its profits into new product research and tripled in size.

3M continued to grow during World War II by concentrating on understanding its markets and finding a niche to fill, rather than shifting to making military goods, as many U. S. corporations had done. Among the new products debuting in the immediate postwar period was Scotch magnetic audiotape, which was introduced in 1947. Under McKnight,[3] 3M grew almost 20-fold. By 1952, it had surpassed the $100 million mark and was employing approximately 10,000 people.

The new president Richard Carlton kept the company focused on product research leading to further innovations in the 1950s: the first dry-printing photocopy process, ThermoFax (1951), Scotchgard fabric and upholstery protector (1956), and Scotch-Brite scouring pads (1958). In 1959 the company marked its 20th consecutive year of increased sales. 3M doubled in size between 1963 and 1967, becoming a billion-dollar company in the process. During the 1970s, a number of obstacles interfered with its growth and the company also lost the cassette tape market to two Japanese companies, TDK and Maxell, who were engaged in price-cutting. 3M stuck to its tradition of abandoning markets where it could not set its own prices, and backed off. During the 1980s, major competitors seemed to threaten the company on all fronts. The major product innovation of the decade was Post-it—a low-tech marvel.

L. D. DeSimone[4] who became the CEO in 1991, pushed research staff to work more closely with marketers and transform existing technology into commercial products. Product turnaround time was slashed; product development rivaled basic research. Customer-driven products such as Never Rust Wool Soap Pad made from recycled plastic bottles and a laptop computer screen film that enhanced brightness without heavy battery drain were invented. In 1992, international sales accounted for aver 50 percent of total 3M sales. In 1994, more than $1 billion of the $15 billion in total sales came from first-year products. By 1997, 30 percent of total sales were generated from products introduced within the past four years. Declines in both revenues and profits in 1998 prompted restructuring, including a workforce reduction of about 5,000. 3M also reorganized into six business segments in 1999.[5] Highlighting the company's continued commitment to innovation, nearly 35 percent of revenues in 2000 came from products that had been introduced within the previous four years. Many of these products fell within higher technology areas. DeSimone's stewardship of 3M ended at the close of 2000 with his retirement.

McNerney's Balancing Act

When W. James McNerney[6]—the first outsider at the helm in the company's nearly 100 years of existence—took over as chairman and CEO in early 2001, he found 3M underperforming and relatively directionless. Its vaunted research facilities were turning out fewer and fewer commercial hits, and quarterly results were not meeting shareholders' and analysts' expectations. Though it still drew many of the world's best chemical engineers, the company's labs had not had a major breakthrough for over two decades.

One of McNerney's first initiatives was to launch Six Sigma,[7] a quality control and improvement initiative to cut costs by reducing errors or defects. During his first year, he saved more than half a billion dollars through various efforts, including the layoff of 6,500 of the company's 75,000 workers and a major streamlining of purchasing functions. Another initiative, dubbed 3M Acceleration, involved channeling more of product development funds on the most promising ideas, dropping weaker ideas earlier in the process, and in this way getting the best products to market much faster. In implementing this and other initiatives, most of which focused on making the company more efficient, McNerney had to be careful not to drive out 3M's culture of innovation. Nevertheless, one apparent victim of McNerney's efficiency drive was 3M's revered 15 Percent Rule.[8] Although the rule still existed in theory, it was increasingly difficult to act upon it within the evolving culture at 3M, which was seemingly becoming more short-term oriented.

Early in 2002 the company officially became the 3M Company. In addition to organic growth, McNerney also decided to look at acquisitions to generate growth. In December 2002, he purchased Corning Precision Lens, Inc., for $850 million. Renamed 3M Precision Optics, Inc., the acquired unit was the world's leading supplier of optical lenses used in projection televisions. In 2002, revenues increased marginally, while net income increased by about 20 percent. In early 2003, 3M reorganized yet again, this time attempting to gain improved access to larger, higher-growth markets. 3M's largest division—transportation, graphics, and safety—was split into display and graphics; safety, security, and protection services; and transportation. The specialty material segment was split up, with consumer-related products shifted to the consumer and office unit and industrial products shifted to the industrial unit. Health care became the largest unit.[9]

In October 2003, 3M implemented a major realignment of its R&D operations. Fourteen separate technology centers were closed, with the scientists at these centers shifted either to a newly formed Corporate Research Laboratory or to the company's 40 divisions, where they would be able to work closely on products within those divisions. The main goal of this R&D shakeup was to move more of 3M's R&D resources to the divisions where the products were actually developed and thereby bring the scientists closer to customers. This latest initiative was McNerney's attempt to turn a slightly ossified manufacturing company into a nimbler growth machine. In 2003, 3M posted an increase in sales and operating margin. In June 2005 McNerney resigned from 3M to become Boeing's CEO. In December 2005, George Buckley, an engineer, became the company's CEO. He was entrusted with the task of revitalizing 3M's competitive advantages.

Evaluating 3M

Buckley conducted a detailed study of the company and found that it was a highly capable scientific, engineering, and manufacturing company with deeply conservative values, participating in many successful niche markets. 3M had incredible intersegment technology sharing, where new markets were continually built through a virtual "adjacency machine"—technology sharing and transfer across products and markets. For example, Scotch-Brite Sponges, 3M Respirators, Filtrete Filters, and Thinsulate Insulation along with dozens of other 3M products, drew on nonwoven materials technology—one of more than 32 3M technology platforms (see Exhibit 2).

3M had a strong R&D capability. Its strong knowledge and understanding of technologies such as adhesives, materials science, light management, micro replication, and nonwoven materials had resulted in several innovative products. Furthermore, the company had the ability to manufacture these innovative products efficiently and consistently, on a global basis. The company had reduced cycle time to commercialization substantially from four years to two and a half years in order to realize sales faster. R&D expenses totaled $1.2 billion in 2005, $1.19 billion in 2004, and $1.14 billion in 2003. R&D expenditure as a percentage of sales stood at 6.3 percent in 2003, 5.9 percent in 2004, and 5.9 percent in 2005.

3M had diversified operations in terms of the number of industries and geographic regions served. The company's revenues were spread across its six key businesses, with health care (the largest contributor) and industrial accounting for about 21 percent and 18 percent of the total revenues, respectively. Other businesses included display and graphics; consumer and office; electro and communications; and safety, security, and protection services. The group had also maintained a regional balance in operations, with the United States accounting for 39.1 percent, Asia Pacific

Exhibit 1 How 3M Invention Machine Goes to Market

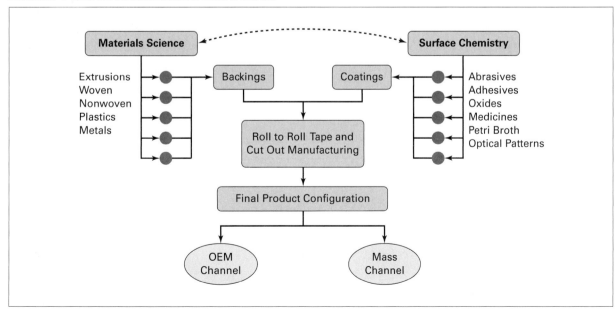

27.1 percent, Europe, Middle East, and Africa 24.7 percent, and Latin America and Canada 8.9 percent of total revenues. This diversity across industries and regions enabled the company to protect itself against demand fluctuations in industry segments and regions.

The industrial division, whose products included tapes, coated and nonwoven abrasives, adhesives, specialty materials, and supply chain execution software solutions, showed a strong performance in fiscal 2005. The acquisition of Cuno,[10] along with continued demand for industrial adhesives and tape were the growth drivers for this division. Its revenues increased by 10.5 percent from 2004 to $3.8 billion. The personal care segment was witnessing sales declines in three areas: personal care-related products,[11] drug delivery, and pharmaceutical. Sales of certain products within 3M's pharmaceuticals business, primarily comprising prescription drugs designed for inhalation, women's health, and cardiovascular, also declined due to price pressure in Europe and decreased demand for some of these older products.

Buckley observed that 3M's history was rooted in an "invent and experiment" approach or "make a little, sell a little," which had led to an incremental approach to capacity and strategic planning, with complex supply chains evolving quite naturally—extrusion processes at one plant, coating in another plant, and final conversion at yet another. Though individual plants were run with superb efficiency, interconnecting logistics were often complicated and costly, resulting in higher inventory. Buckley believed that chronic underinvestment in core capacity had led to many lost upside growth opportunities. In fact, this underinvestment in core markets had made readily available growth hard to capture. The company's strategic planning capability seemed underdeveloped, but this deficiency did not diminish the fact that the company possessed world-class manufacturing capability.

3M's world-class materials science and surface chemistry capability was built over many years. It had often entered markets only after privileged intellectual property (IP) positions were built. In early days scale was not considered important and demand and capacity were often underestimated. 3M had focused on making risk-free capital investments by using highly flexible machine tools capable of making many products in plants that served multiple businesses. The cross-business use of central technologies was encouraged by the earlier leadership, which in turn led to 3M's participation in many high-margin niche areas such as reflective material (3M Scotchlite) and sealing ground

Exhibit 2 3M Lattice : The 32 Technology Platforms

Ad Adhesives	**Am** Advanced Materials	**Bi** Biotech							**Rf** Reclosable Fasteners
Ab Abrasives	**Dd** Drug Delivery						**Mr** Micro-replication	**Pe** Predctive Engineering & Modeling	**Rp** Radiation Processing
Ac Acoustics	**Dm** Display Materials					**Nt** Nano Technology	**Nm** Nonwoven Materials	**Pm** Polymer Melt Processing	**Sm** Specialty Materials
As Application Software	**Do** Dental & Orthodontic Materials	**Fi** Films	**Fs** Filtration, Separation, Purification	**Is** Integrated Systems Design	**Md** Medical Data Mgmt	**Mi** Microbial Detection & Control	**Pc** Precision Coating	**Po** Porous Materials & Membrane	**Su** Surface Modification
Ce Ceramics	**Ep** Electronic Packaging	**Fl** Fluoro-materials	**Im** Imaging	**Lm** Light Mgmt	**Me** Metal Matrix Composites	**Mo** Molding	**Pd** Particle & Dispersion Processing	**Pr** Process Design & Control	**Wo** Wound Mgmt
Cp Chemical Power Sources	**Fc** Flexible Converting & Packaging	**Fo** Fiber Optics	**Ip** Inks & Pigments				**Pp** Precision Processing		**Vp** Vacuum Processing

Source: George Buckley's presentation to investors in May 2006; http://www.3m.com.

connections (3M Scotchcast), among others. A high degree of conservatism had become the norm. Though 3M's inward focus brought margin benefits, it often hindered growth and long-range planning.

Buckley realized a need to demystify 3M and understand the workings of the 3M Lattice. In understanding 3M, it was important to realize that the company was not a conglomerate with siloed independent business units. It was a unique model of a technology and manufacturing *adjacency lattice* that shared basic technologies and manufacturing processes across multiple businesses, markets, and product lines. Almost all of 3M's basic businesses were connected to each other in this way, from water filtration to Scotch brand tape. He opined, "In network theory, the power of a network (or lattice) is proportional to the square of the number of users.[12] It is this lattice that makes 3M so powerful and enduring as an industrial competitor. But . . . the lattice can also make 3M difficult to organize for optimal growth"[13] (see Exhibit 2).

As noted above, to encourage innovation, perhaps to deal with "latticing" the company used the 15 Percent Rule, which allowed its employees to spend up to 15 percent of company time on independent projects, a process called "bootlegging" or "scrounging."

Defining 3M's Core Competency

3M is an invention and manufacturing company. Its major strength lay in solving and delivering unique solutions for original equipment manufacturers (OEM) and mass channel customers. Its technologies could be extended into multiple markets. 3M's technology portfolio and process capability were at the core of its unique business model. This strength included technologies such as adhesives, materials science, light management; microreplication and nonwoven materials; and its ability to not only develop unique products, but also to manufacture them efficiently and consistently around the world. By sharing technologies, manufacturing operations, brands, and other resources across its businesses and geographies, it increased speed and efficiency. These technology platforms were the thread that wove together the company's diverse businesses. It was their interlocking and sometimes overlapping nature that set 3M apart from other companies. Industry observers pointed out that 3M's remarkable breadth of technologies, along with its ability to combine them to create a steady stream of groundbreaking products, made it unique.

The range of a single technology application could be seen in many areas. On one end of the adhesion spectrum were the Post-it Products—a universal communication tool that could stick practically anywhere, yet could be repositioned time and again—and on the other end was 3M Scotch-Weld Structural Adhesive that had taken the

place of metal fasteners in the production of airplanes, helping make aircraft lighter and more fuel-efficient. In the electronics industry, 3M Form-in-Place Gaskets (nonwoven technology product), were widely used in computer hard disk drive covers. This resilient, ultra-clean, adhesive-based material sealed out contaminants, while also increasing manufacturing productivity. Thinsulate Insulation—another nonwoven product—offered warmth without bulk. It was incorporated into jackets, boot, gloves, and sleeping bags. A companion product—Thinsulate Acoustic Insulation—helped in reducing road noise inside vehicles. Yet another 3M product based on nonwoven technology—3M Nomad Floor Matting—helped in keeping floors clean longer.

In applying coatings, 3M had developed world-class competencies. It modified the shapes and patterns of surface coatings in a process called microreplication, which in turn altered the fundamental behavior of a product. This micromanufacturing competency, leveraged across many markets made it difficult for 3M's competitors to beat it. For example, the technology made road signs return nearly twice as much reflected light to drivers as the brightest materials previously available. In the automotive industry, the technology (3M Paint Replacement Film) eliminated the need for paint on door pillars, window sashes, and other body trim. When combined with high-performance abrasives and fasteners, the microreplication technology enabled diapers to hold more securely and comfortably. It was also used to create channels that directed fluids across a surface using capillary action as in biotechnology products (see Exhibit 3).

According to Buckley, 3M's fundamental core competency lay in applying coatings to backings. Both the coatings and the backings were traditionally developed inside 3M. The backings could either be woven or nonwoven fabrics, paper, cloth, plastics, or metal while coatings were adhesives, abrasives, medicines, nano particles, or imprinted optical patterns. 3M applied coatings to backings in a highly precise manufacturing approach that involved the large-scale unwinding, winding, and splitting of tapes. 3M sometimes sold its coatings and backings separately configured as other products, such as face masks, Thinsulate thermal and acoustic insulation, and roofing granules. In developing backings and coatings competencies, broad know-how in adjacent technologies was built in areas such as microreplication of surface patterns, optics and light management, nanotechnology, and ceramics adhesives. 3M extended this adjacent knowledge across multiple markets in less obvious applications such as Post-it Notes (the adhesive was microreplicated) and adhesives (on which 3M's dentistry competency was based).

Interestingly, the same precision machining and materials science capabilities had also been applied in market adjacencies such as dentistry. Though experts cited

Exhibit 3 Technology Market Architecture

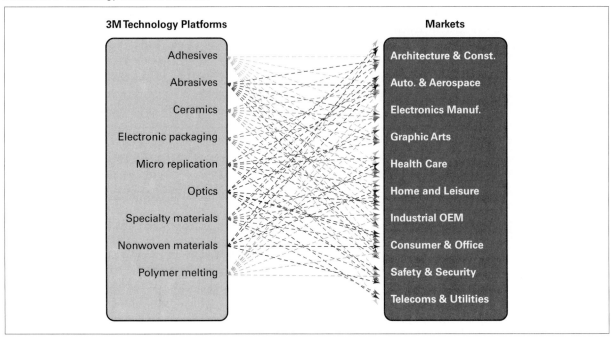

Source: George Buckley's presentation to investors in May 2006; http://www.3m.com.

innovation as 3M's main strength, Buckley felt that the company's superior manufacturing capability and know-how was equally important and a significant barrier to entry. He believed that one source of the next wave of growth would come from reinvention of the space science materials with nanotechnology. In addition to its core, 3M had six competitive platforms: low cost, which gave it a considerable edge over competition; scale share; relative share; customer value chain; pristine service; and premium brands.

Buckley's Strategy

Technology and innovation had played a key role throughout 3M's illustrious history. Buckley recognized that it was also the engine of 3M's future growth. He stressed the uniqueness of the company's shared technology model. For future growth, the company was searching for disruptive technologies as well as logical developments and extensions of its existing products. It would increasingly prospect for "just out of the garage" technology developments, which would be the key to building its core competency. The heart and soul of 3M's approach would remain technological differentiation and application across multiple lines of business. It would add digital-oriented competencies over time.

To grow its core business, the company intended to build on 3M's strengths through constant reinvention, even stronger key customer partnerships, customization, solving customers needs, entering niche segments, and capturing new segments. Buckley intended to build scale, increase market share, emphasize localization, and build long-term competency. The idea was to defend created markets against new entrants, using dual branding in the upper middle market; emphasizing product localization using a mixture of brands and local acquisitions; thoughtfully extending private labeling, and accurately planning capacity. The core product categories he had identified for building scale included Scotch-branded industrial and office tapes, abrasives, automotive, optical films, face masks and respirators, medical tapes and drapes, Post-it Notes, and traffic signage. It would aim for a relative share in areas such as dentistry, orthodontics, office supplies, roofing granules, commercial graphics, and adhesives.

3M's core strategy focused on developing and growing the existing market by using its technological prowess to invent natural substitute technology. He intended to ensure that the 15 Percent Rule was followed. To aid speed, 3M went for strategic licensing of technology, investment in small technology companies, greater university support and liaison, and encouraging the use of imagination and invention extensively. A renewed focus on innovation would encourage new products and continued international expansion and penetration with greater emphasis on localization. In mid-2006, 3M was generating more than 60 percent of its sales from outside the United States with more than 20 percent coming from emerging markets. For international growth the company was concentrating on BRICP (Brazil, Russia, India, China, and Poland), Eastern Europe, Western

Europe, Japan, and Australasia. Over time 3M intended to divest or close those businesses where it could not, over time, build scale or good relative share, or differentiate through technology. It also intended to divest in areas where the base technology was at "end of life" and could not be refreshed, or the risk profile suggested another owner could extract more value than 3M. As a part of this strategy, in November 2006, 3M sold the pharmaceutical business for $2.1 billion.

It was decided that the majority of acquisitions would closely reflect and support its strategic plan and adjacencies. Trends showed that adjacency would evolve in areas such as electronics and software, RFID/Wireless/global positioning service (GPS), minerals extraction, oil and gas, food safety, border crossing and security, and consumer electronics. The company intended to build new business through enhanced focus on emerging business opportunities with high growth potential such as filtration, track and trace, energy and minerals extraction, and food safety. The concept would be used where capability existed with ready adjacencies but no focus. Buckley outlined a clear acquisition strategy driven by a determination to quickly add value. Soon after joining the company, he told analysts that acquisitions would be one way he would grow the top line. In 2006, 3M announced 16 acquisitions, which equaled the number of acquisitions the company had made in the previous four years combined. However, these deals were smaller than many purchases made in the past years. Alfred Marcus, professor of strategic management and organization at the University of Minnesota's Carlson School of Management applauded the small "tuck-in" acquisition strategy as he felt that small buys were more likely to be successful than big ones. Big deals required a lot of time and money to integrate and took longer to pay off, he said.

No clear pattern emerged among the kind of businesses that 3M has purchased. The company made at least two acquisitions in each of its six business units. While some of the deals provided access to new geographic markets, like the UK-based Security Printing & Systems passport-printing business it bought in July 2006; other deals were just filling in capacity in channels 3M already understood, such as the acquisition of Nylonge Corp., an Elyria, Ohio-based maker of household cleaning products. Additionally, other small deals focused on acquiring new technology, such as the $95 million purchase of Brontes Technologies Inc. announced in October 2006. Brontes developed a digital tool for dentists that mapped dimensions to facilitate design of crowns, bridges, and orthodontic appliances.

Looking Ahead

In April 2006, 3M reported record first-quarter sales and profits with local-currency sales growth of over 10 percent and earnings per share increase over 20 percent. The company also raised its 2006 revenue growth guidance, and expected full-year, organic local-currency growth between 5.5 and 8 percent, up from a previous expectation of 4 to 7 percent. However in June 2006, Buckley surprised Wall Street when he announced that the company would miss its earnings target for the second quarter, sending the company's stock tumbling from a 52-week high of $88 per share in May 2006 to a 52-week low of $67 in July 2006. 3M said the problems stemmed from its display and graphics business, which had difficulties launching a new optical-film factory. It also misread demand for LCD TVs in advance of the World Cup soccer tournament. But by fall 2006, investor confidence in Buckley was restored, thanks to a convincing third-quarter turnaround that beat analysts' estimates. In the third quarter, 3M's sales increased 7.3 percent compared to the same period a year earlier. Not including acquisitions, organic sales were up 6.5 percent. Buckley was projecting 8 percent growth by 2008 and 10-plus percent by 2011.

3M's acquisitions were expected to contribute $350 million to $400 million to its expected $22.8 billion in 2006 sales. But at the end of year one, Buckley's record was exactly as advertised. Revenue growth was up, and the number of acquisitions was way up. John Roberts, an analyst at Buckingham Research believed that investors were still waiting to see growth accelerate at 3M's core businesses. Mark Henneman, a principal analyst at St. Paul-based Mairs and Powers Funds, which invested in 3M stock, credited Buckley for slowly reinvigorating 3M's engineering culture and technological foundation. "He's focusing investments on where the core competencies are, and I think that increases the chance for success going forward."[14]

Other industry observers also opined that Buckley had sparked more innovation and boosted morale. Art Fry, a retired 3M scientist who had invented Post-it Notes opined that the acquisitions were a quick way of building and adding technology to the company. But like in product development, some ventures would fail, he said. "I think basically he's more like an old-school-type 3M leader in that he's focused both on building the company and operating it. The [improved] morale is palpable; you can just feel it around 3M," Fry mentioned.[15] Fry opined that circumstances Buckley had to face due to underinvesment in growth platforms under former CEO James McNerney Jr. and an emphasis on boosting profits was "like you walk in after the feast and you have to clean up all the dirty dishes."

Buckley still had to take care of other problems also. Retailers such as Wal-Mart, Target, Staples, and Office Depot were increasingly offering branded goods (better known as private labels) at affordable prices. An increasing number of 3M's customers, particularly in the consumer and office business, had been shifting to private label products. This migration prompted 3M to target lower price points through the launch of secondary brands. Compared to margins of about 45 percent from premium-priced products, lower-priced products would only yield maximum of 20 percent. The private label products of mass market retailers lowered margins of the company.

Meanwhile, higher oil prices resulted in price increases and supply limitations of several oil-derived raw materials (see Appendixes 1–9).

As 2006 drew to a close, Buckley decided to evaluate his strategy to determine whether it would yield desired results. Would his initiatives succeed in building 3M's core competency? What else could he do?

Appendix 1 The World's Most Innovative Companies 2005

Asia	Europe	North America	Global
1. Apple	1. Apple	1. Apple	1. Apple
2. Google	2. Google	2. Google	2. Google
3. 3M	3. Nokia	3. P&G	3. 3M
4. Samsung	4. Microsoft	4. 3M	4. Toyota
5. Microsoft	5. 3M	5. Toyota	5. Microsoft
6. IBM	6. Toyota	6. GE	6. GE
7. GE	7. Virgin	7. Starbucks	7. P&G
8. Toyota	8. BMW	8. Microsoft	8. Nokia
9. Nokia	9. GE	9. IBM	9. Starbucks
10. infosys	10. eBay	10. Dell	10. IBM
11. Virgin	11. IKEA	11. Wal-Mart	11. Virgin
12. P&G	12. RyanAir	12. IDEO	12. Samsung
12. Dell	12. Sony	12. Target	13. Sony
14. Sony	14. Intel	14. Samsung	14. Dell
15. Intel	15. Porsche	15. Southwest	15. IDEO

Source: George Buckley's presentation to investors in May 2006; http://www.3m.com.

Appendix 2 3M Innovation: Process, Imagination, People

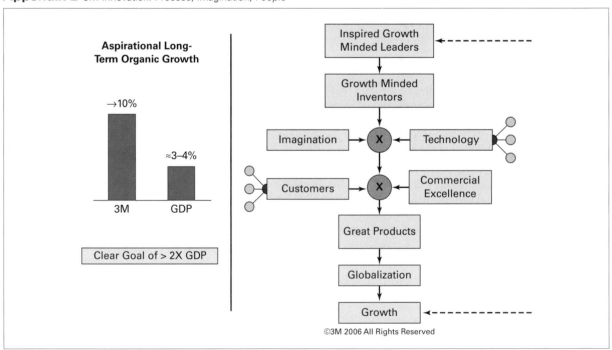

Source: George Buckley's presentation to investors in May 2006 at 3M Investor Meeting; http://www.3m.com.

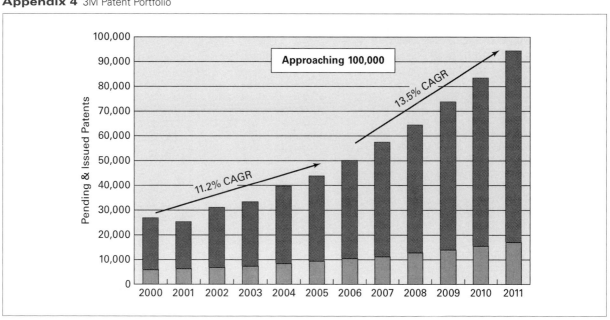

Appendix 3 Some Breakthrough 3M Products

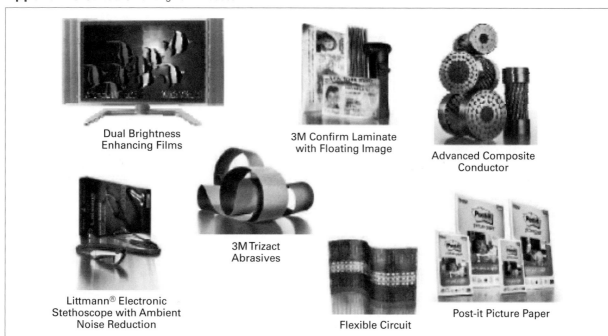

Dual Brightness Enhancing Films

3M Confirm Laminate with Floating Image

Advanced Composite Conductor

3M Trizact Abrasives

Littmann® Electronic Stethoscope with Ambient Noise Reduction

Flexible Circuit

Post-it Picture Paper

Source: George Buckley's presentation to investors in May 2006; http://www.3m.com.

Appendix 4 3M Patent Portfolio

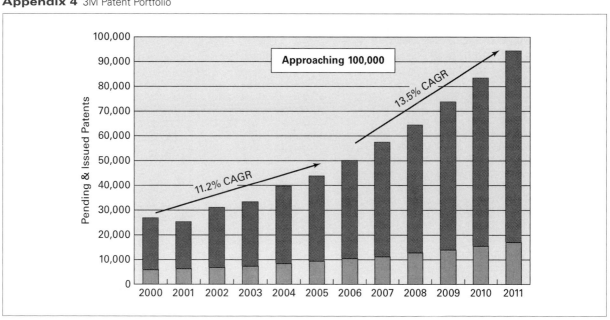

Source: George Buckley's presentation to investors in May 2006; http://www.3m.com.

Appendix 5 Building Emerging Country Capacity, End 2006

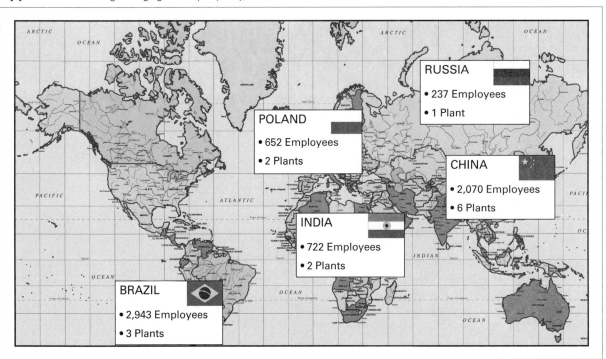

Source: George Buckley's presentation to investors in May 2006; http://www.3m.com.

Appendix 6 3M vs. Peers—Du Pont Analysis

	$\dfrac{\text{Net Income}}{\text{Sales}}$ × $\dfrac{\text{Sales}}{\text{Assets}}$ × $\dfrac{\text{Assets}}{\text{Equity}}$ = ROE%		
	Net Income Margin % ×	Asset Turn ×	Leverage =	ROE
3M	**15.3%**	**1.03x**	**2.03x**	**32.0%**
ITW	11.6%	1.13	1.52	19.8%
Danaher	11.4%	0.87	1.80	17.8%
IR	10.0%	0.90	2.04	18.3%
Emerson	8.8%	1.04	2.18	20.0%
Tyco	8.3%	0.64	1.92	10.1%
UTX	7.4%	0.93	2.70	18.6%
Eaton	7.2%	1.09	2.70	21.3%
HON	5.7%	0.86	2.87	14.0%
Textron	5.1%	0.61	5.04	15.8%
ITT	4.2%	1.05	2.59	11.5%

Source: George Buckley's presentation to investors in May 2006; http://www.3m.com.

Appendix 7 Financial Information

(In $ millions, except per share amounts)	2005	2004	2003	2002	2001
Years ended December 31:					
Net sales	$21,167	$20,011	$18,232	$16,332	$16,054
Income before cumulative effect of accounting change	3,234	2,990	2,403	1,974	1,430
Per share of common stock:					
Income before cumulative effect of accounting change—basic	4.23	3.83	3.07	2.53	1.81
Income before cumulative effect of accounting change—diluted	4.16	3.75	3.02	2.50	1.79
Cash dividends declared and paid	1.68	1.44	1.32	1.24	1.20
At December 31:					
Total assets	$20,513	$20,708	$17,600	$15,329	$14,606
Long-term debt (excluding portion due within one year) and long-term capital lease obligations	1,368	798	1,805	2,142	1,520

Source: 3M Annual Report 2005.

Appendix 8 3M SWOT Analysis

Strengths	Weaknesses
Strong R&D capability	Weak personal care segment
Diversified business portfolio	Low margins in the United States
Robust industrial business	
Opportunities	**Threats**
Growing demand for LCDs	Growth in private labels
Acquisition of brands	Higher oil prices
International expansion	Exchange rate fluctuations

Source: 2006, Datamonitor Company Report, July.

Appendix 9 A Few 3M Brands

Source: George Buckley's presentation to investors in May 2006; http://www.3m.com.

Notes

1. S. Black, Buys defines 3M CEO's first year, *Minneapolis/St. Paul Business Journal,* December 1, 2005.

2. McKnight ran 3M between 1914 and 1966, serving as general manager from 1914 to 1929, president from 1929 to 1949, and chairman of the board from 1949 to 1966. He created the general guidelines of diversification, avoiding price cuts, increasing sales by 10 percent a year, high employee morale, and quality control that fueled the company's growth and created its unique corporate culture. In some ways, the sales system overshadowed the guidelines.

3. In 1949, McKnight became chairman of the board (with A. G. Bush also moving from daily operations to the boardroom).

4. DeSimone joined 3M in 1958 as a manufacturing engineer and moved into management while working in international operations.

5. The six segments were Industrial Markets; Transportation, Graphics, and Safety; Health Care; Consumer and Office Products; Electro and Communications; and Specialty Material.

6. McNerney was a 19-year veteran of General Electric Company (GE)—like 3M a diversified, manufacturing-oriented corporation—having most recently served as head of GE Aircraft Engines. McNerney had lost out in a three-way battle to succeed legendary GE leader John F. (Jack) Welch, Jr.

7. Six Sigma was a quality control and improvement initiative that had been pioneered by Motorola, Inc., and AlliedSignal Inc. and then adopted by GE in the late 1990s. The aim of the statistics-driven program was to cut costs by reducing errors or defects.

8. The 15 Percent Rule allowed 3M employees to spend up to 15 percent of company time on independent projects, a process called "bootlegging" or "scrounging" to encourage innovation.

9. Health Care became the largest unit in terms of both revenues (22% of the total) and earnings (27%).

10. In August 2005, 3M acquired Cuno, a manufacturer of a comprehensive line of filtration products for the separation, clarification, and purification of fluids and gases. 3M and Cuno had complementary sets of filtration technologies, which enabled them to bring an even wider range of filtration solutions to customers around the world.

11. The personal care diaper closure business continued to experience significant price increases due to raw material increases. However, 3M has been unable to raise its prices sufficiently to cover raw material inflation, owing to a competitive environment in the diaper market. The company chose to manufacture lower volumes rather than suffer losses in the end.

12. Robert Metcalfe, Inventor of the Ethernet.

13. George Buckley's presentation to investors in May 2006; http://www.3m.com.

14. S. Black, Buys defines 3M CEO's first year.

15. Ibid.

Additional Readings and Reference

1. J. Webern, 2000, 3M's big clean-up, *BusinessWeek,* June 5, 96–98.

2. D. Little, 2000, 3M: Glued to the Web, *BusinessWeek,* 3708, November 20, EB64.

3. M. Arndt, 2002, 3M: A lab for growth, *BusinessWeek,* January 21, 50–51.

4. J. Useem, 2002, Jim McNerney thinks he can turn 3M from a good company into a great one—with a little help from his former employer, General Electric, *Fortune,* (3), August 12, 127–132.

5. M. Overfelt, 2003, 3M, *Fortune Small Business,* 13 (3), April, 36.

6. M. Arndt & D. Brady, 2004, 3M's rising star, *BusinessWeek,* April 12, 62–74.

7. 2004, Innovation is job one, *BusinessWeek,* April 12, 120–120.

8. M. Arndt, 2005, The new skipper at 3M's helm, *BusinessWeek,* December 19, 12.

9. H. David, 2006, Creativity pays. Here's how much, *BusinessWeek,* April 24, 76–76.

10. 2006, 3M CEO outlines strategy for growth, company press release, http://www.3m.com, May 2.

11. 2006, Tamper-indicating security seals from 3M, *Business & Commercial Aviation,* 98(6), June, 88.

12. 2006, 3M CEO outlines long-term strategy for growth, *Filtration + Separation,* 43 (5).

13. 2006, 3M puts emphasis on convenience in bandage packaging, *Drug Store News,* June 26, 48.

14. T. B. Jensen, 2006, Meeting environmental demands with pressure-sensitive tapes, *Adhesives & Sealants Industry,* 13 (7), 27–30.

15. 2006, 3M completes OMNII acquisition, *Proofs,* 89 (3), June, 46–48.

16. 2006, 3M'S Post-it sortable cards, *OfficeSolutious,* July–August, 46.

17. 2006, 3M SWOT analysis, *Datamonitor,* July.

18. A. DeRosa, 2006, 3M investing in film projects, *Plastics News,* July 17.

19. 2006, Products and services by category Hardware, *Computers in Libraries,* July–August, 12–13.

20. 2006, I. Brat, At 3M, stock slide stirs criticism, *Wall Street Journal,* July 24.

21. 2006, Quaker fabric launches safer Scotchgard fabric, *Home Textiles Today,* September 18, 10.

22. 3M Annual Report 2006.

23. 3M Annual Report 2005.

24. http://www.3m.com.

25. http://www.wikipedia.com.

26. http://www.hoovers.com.

27. http://www.fundinguniverse.com.

28. CEO Buckley's presentation to analysts in May 2006, Investor relations, http://www.3m.com.

29. Company presentation to analysts in 2003, http://www.3m.com.

30. http://www.yahoofinance.com.

A-1 Lanes and the Currency Crisis of the East Asian Tigers

Phil E. Stetz, Stephen F. Austin State University
Todd A. Finkle, The University of Akron
Larry R. O'Neil, Stephen F. Austin State University

On July 2, 1997, Rick Baker, the president and founder of A-1 Lanes (a manufacturer and an international supplier of wood and synthetic bowling lanes) was having his morning coffee when he was devastated to learn that Thailand had devalued its currency, the baht, by 11 percent. Baker had an uneasy feeling about the potential domino effect across all countries in Asia because their economies were interrelated. If that happened, Baker wondered, how would it affect the future of his company?

Baker realized that the company faced several critical issues. First, 80 percent of A-1's sales were derived from countries in and around the Asian Pacific Rim. Second, the company had more than $1 million in accounts receivable from this region. Third, in 1996 the company had taken out a loan for $500,000 on a new manufacturing facility to capitalize on the popularity and growth of bowling centers in Korea, China, and Taiwan.

The combination of these issues in conjunction with the cut-throat competition within the bowling equipment industry placed Baker in a position to make a critical decision about the future of his company. He had narrowed his decision to three options: (1) liquidate his company, (2) sell the company, or (3) stay in business and try to weather the impending storm.

Company Background

In 1985, Baker and two investors founded A-1 Lanes in a chicken house and barn in Rusk, Texas. The company's main products were high-grade wood and technologically advanced synthetic bowling lanes for domestic and international markets. According to Baker, "The key to our success is the quality of the wood and the advanced synthetic design of our bowling lanes supported with responsive service, operational efficiencies and proven accomplishments at penetrating international markets."

Although the company began with high expectations, A-1 Lanes quickly discovered that locally owned bowling centers across the United States did not have the financial resources to replace existing lanes. Instead, owners would simply sand the lanes. To complicate matters, competitors within the industry developed a synthetic overlay for existing lanes. For example, Brunswick developed a cost-effective way of refurbishing worn and damaged wood lanes that prolonged their service life by as much as 10 years. Rather than tearing out and replacing existing lanes, bowling centers could sand them down and overlay the wood with a synthetic resin, thereby restoring the old lanes to industry standards.

Because of the weakened demand for wood replacement of bowling lanes, A-1 began to concentrate on new bowling lane sales in international markets. According to Baker, "We pursued international markets because the margins were better, receivables were more reliable, and the additional volume meant a healthier bottom line." As a result, A-1 grew and moved operations into a vacant 34,000-square-foot metal building in 1987.

In the same year, A-1 Lanes began to establish relationships with distributors in other parts of the world (e.g., Mendes, a Canadian marketer of bowling lanes). In 1988, Baker and his investors forged a partnership with a company called Dacos, an established distributor of bowling equipment and accessories that was based in Europe and Korea. With a source for U.S. manufactured lanes, Dacos could offer a complete turn-key package to bowling center owners and developers all over the world. In turn, the arrangement enabled A-1 to compete directly with the largest firms in the industry, Brunswick and American Machine Foundry (AMF). It also gave A-1 an advantage over smaller competitors in the United States because those firms lacked similar distribution channels and presence in Europe and Asia.

The Bowling Industry

Archeologists discovered that bowling dates back to ancient Egypt when they found pins in a child's tomb. The sport expanded into Europe in the early 1900s, but its popularity in the United States did not thrive until after World War II. In the 1950s, television embraced bowling and the automatic pin spotter was invented. The game grew dramatically in the United States and eventually peaked in the 1960s. New markets emerged in Australia and Mexico, as well as in other Latin American countries. By the mid-1970s, the bowling boom had spread into Japan. Russia followed suit by opening its first bowling center in 1976. Interest in bowling also grew in China. The bowling boom spread into Thailand and the Asia Pacific regions during the early 1990s.

By the 1990s, bowling comprised two main industries. One involved the ownership and operation of bowling centers. The other was the manufacture of bowling equipment used in bowling centers or by bowlers. These manufactured items included automatic pin spotters, computerized automatic scoring systems, wood and synthetic bowling lanes, lane maintenance systems, masking panes, ball returns, seating, bumper bowling systems, replacement and maintenance parts, and operating supplies such as spare parts, pins, lane oils, bowling balls, bowling shoes, and other bowling accessories.

In 1996, estimates were that more than 100 million people in more than 90 countries bowled at least one game a year and bowlers in the United States spent approximately $4 billion annually on lane fees, equipment and supplies, uniforms, and food and beverage purchased within bowling centers.[1] More than 53 million Americans patronized the country's bowling centers every year,

making tenpin bowling the number one indoor participation sport in the United States.[2]

The Bowling Industry in the United States

During bowling's peak years in the 1960s and early 1970s, bowling centers were being constructed almost overnight across the country. During the early to mid-1970s white American blue-collar workers (the primary clientele of the bowling industry) moved to the suburbs, away from the city neighborhoods where most of the bowling centers had been built. Bowling began to open facilities in the suburbs while maintaining their existing centers in the cities. This strategy was not successful due to the lifestyle changes of the blue-collar workers.[3] They were simply less interested in bowling than they had been.[4]

As a result, the new suburban bowling centers were not as successful, while existing bowling centers in the cities became only marginally profitable. The number of bowling centers gradually declined, but the number of lanes increased due to the construction of large new centers and the remodeling of surviving ones.[5] Exhibit 1 shows the historical relationship between the number of centers, lanes, and population in the United States.[6]

In response to the decreasing popularity of bowling, many bowling operators started differentiating their image by renovating their alleys into entertainment centers in the early 1990s.[7] Their strategy was to market to families with children and teenagers by offering childcare, video games, laser lights, lightweight neon-glowing bowling balls, and fog machines. They also devised bumper bowling, in which gutters are filled with plastic tubes to keep the balls on the lane. This strategy proved to be profitable and operators were able to restore their revenues to the levels of the 1960s.[8]

Many analysts thought operators had created a "double-edged sword" by pampering one market segment and alienating another. The upgraded facilities with flashy, loud, and

Exhibit 1 U.S. Bowling Centers, 1955–1995

Year	Centers	Lanes	Lanes per Center	Population	
				Total (000)	Per Center
1955	7,062	60,648	8.6	165,275	23,403
1965	11,363	165,601	14.5	193,460	17,025
1975	8,974	144,829	16.1	215,973	24,046
1985	8,629	159,394	18.5	237,950	27,575
1995	7,331	144,187	19.7	262,755	35,841

Source: A-1 Lanes company literature.

modern atmospheres were the opposite of the dark, quiet, smoky lanes to which league bowlers were accustomed. Evidence indicated that league bowlers, a steady source of revenue for bowling centers, further dwindled due to these changes.[9] A league bowler commented, "The centers have all of these great gimmicks and are giving financial breaks to families and people that really do not bowl that much. Meanwhile, they're raising the prices for league bowlers, the true loyal customers, and driving them away."[10]

The U.S. bowling center industry (see Exhibit 2) was highly fragmented. The top eight operators, including AMF, accounted for less than 10 percent of U.S. bowling centers. The two largest, AMF and Brunswick Corporation ("Brunswick") owned approximately 340 and 111 U.S. bowling centers, respectively.[11] Four medium-sized chains together accounted for 70 bowling centers. More than 5,300 bowling centers were owned by single-center and small-chain operators, which typically owned four or fewer centers.

By 1997, the U.S. bowling center industry was considered mature and was characterized by a continual contraction in the number of bowling centers. Nevertheless, the decreasing lineage (games per lane per day) was offset by an increasing average price per game and by revenue from ancillary sources. Bowling centers derived their revenues from bowling (60.2%), food and beverage (25.4%)[12], and other sources such as rentals, amusement games, billiards, and pro shops (14.4%).[13]

According to the 1997 Economic Census, 619 establishments existed with 17,109 employees in the

Exhibit 2 Operators of U.S. Bowling Centers in 1997

Operator	Number of Bowling Centers	Percent of Total
AMF	370	6.3
Brunswick	111	1.9
Bowl America	23	0.4
Active West	16	0.3
Mark Voight	16	0.3
Bowl New England	15	0.2
Subtotal:	551	9.4
Single-center & small-chain operators	5,302	90.6
Total	5,853	100.0%

Source: AMF Bowling Worldwide Inc. (1997). Annual Report: 10-K, Period ending December 31.

hardwood dimension and flooring mills classification (NAICS 321912).[14] However, only a few companies operated in the bowling lane and equipment supply business (see Exhibit 3).[15] Some of the competitors

Exhibit 3 Major Competitors in the Bowling Equipment Industry in 1997

Company Name	Product Line	Total Employees	Estimated Sales ($M)	Headquarters
Brunswick Corp.	Bowling Equipment*	1,000	$350.0	Lake Forest, IL
AMF	Bowling Equipment*	635	$250.0	Richmond, VA
Heddon Bowling Corporation	Synthetic Lanes	50	$ 40.0	Tampa, FL
Hodge Lumber Company	Wood Lanes	40	$ 30.0	New Knoxville, OH
Mendes	Synthetic Lanes	40	$ 30.0	Quebec City, Canada
Murrey International	Synthetic Lanes	35	$ 30.0	Los Angeles, CA
A-1 Lanes	Wood & Synthetic Lanes	35	$ 12.5	Rusk, TX

*Equipment includes bowling lanes, automatic pinsetters, ball returns, computerized scoring equipment, business systems, and other industrial equipment and supplies sold to bowling centers in addition to resale products, such as bowling balls, bags, shoes, and other bowlers' aids, sold primarily through pro shops.

Source: From A-1 Lanes 1997 company estimates.

Exhibit 4 Selected Markets in the International Bowling Industry in 1997

Country	Centers	Lanes	Lanes per Center	Population Total (000)	Population Per Lane*
Japan	1,123	32,200	29	125,000	3,900
Korea	1,104	16,300	15	45,350	2,800
Taiwan	370	11,567	31	21,120	1,800
United Kingdom	210	4,400	21	58,160	12,900

*The population per lane is an industry statistic that enables a bowling lane distributor to get an idea of the number customers per lane per city or area. This statistic is better than "bowling centers" because it gives an idea of literally how many people can actually bowl and a good indication of a saturation point for bowling centers in a given area.

Source: From A-1 Lanes company literature.

manufactured a broad range of products; others produced only a specific line of equipment. All competitors were active in both the domestic and international markets.

Foreign-based competition in the bowling lane manufacturing industry was almost nonexistent due to the lack of key raw materials. For example, lane construction required the use of specific types and grades of maple and pine. The necessary maple is found only in the United States and the preferred southern yellow pine is found only in the southeastern region of the United States. Furthermore, Asian bowling operators showed little interest in purchasing bowling lanes or other bowling products and accessories manufactured outside the United States. They considered bowling an American sport and the equipment had to be manufactured in the United States.

Bowling in Asia

In the late 1980s, because of the saturation of bowling lane markets in the United States and Europe, Brunswick and AMF began to expand into the Asian Pacific Rim by developing bowling centers throughout the region. The pivotal event that triggered Asian interest was the inclusion of bowling as a trial event in the 1988 Olympics in Seoul, South Korea.[16] After the Olympics, a bowling boom began in East Asia.

U.S. bowling exports increased by 27 percent from 1988 through 1993, and sales to China accounted for almost one-third of sales. An estimated 15,000 lanes were already in use in China, and most industry analysts expected this demand to blossom into a 100,000+ lane market. With a population of 1.3 billion, 100,000 lanes would amount to approximately one lane per 13,000 people,

much lower than the United States rate of one lane per 1,800 people. Exhibit 4 estimates the population per lane for selected international markets in 1997.[17]

Asian Cultures

Asian cultures reflected numerous influences. Their business practices differed in many ways from those in the United States. Conducting business in Asia required a long-term perspective through the formulation of strong bonds and ties with potential business partners. Patience was important and connections were crucial. Asia, particularly China, was a gift-giving culture and the giving of gifts was a means to solidify personal ties.[18]

Many social and cultural demographics helped to explain the popularity of bowling in Asia. Half the Asian population was younger than 25, an optimal age range for introducing the sport to new bowlers. A bowling enthusiast and Asian market analyst, Mort Luby Jr., explained bowling's popularity:

Bowling is popular in the Asian market because many young urban people complain there isn't much to do with their leisure time (and increased disposable income). Disco is dead, the nightclubs are intimidating, the bars are full of AIDS, and foreign movies are expensive and largely incomprehensible. There are very few mid-price restaurants. Bowling has filled this recreational void with a vengeance.[19]

Asian Economies

Following the rapid growth in the 1980s of Taiwan, Korea, Singapore, and Hong Kong, the so-called Four Tigers, a new wave of economic growth swept across Asia. This wave was driven primarily by the newly industrializing economies of Malaysia, Thailand, Indonesia, and others. Thailand's growth was especially noticeable. The *Nation*,

Bangkok's independent newspaper, predicted that Thailand would become known as the "Fifth Tiger" during the 1990s. The Asian Development Bank predicted that Asia's economy would grow at a pace twice as fast as other world regions. Some suggested that the new millennium would begin the "Asian Century."[20]

The early 1990s also marked the globalization of financial markets. With slow growth and competitive home markets, private capital flows turned to these emerging markets that offered higher interest rates and robust economic growth.[21] From 1990 to 1997, capital flows to developing countries rose more than five-fold. While world trade grew by about 5 percent annually, private capital flows grew annually by 30 percent. The most mobile forms of flow, commercial bank debt and portfolio investments, set the pace,[22] with East Asia absorbing nearly 60 percent of all short-term capital.[23]

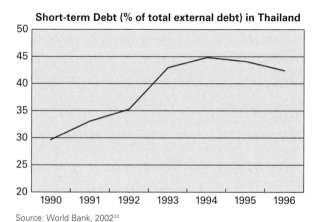

Short-term Debt (% of total external debt) in Thailand

Source: World Bank, 2002[24]

Thailand attempted to "become the regional financial hub" for neighboring economies. The government enacted policies in 1993 that allowed some foreign and local banks to make loans in U.S. dollars and other currencies through what was called the Bangkok International Banking Facilities (BIBF).[25] However, with the Thai government continuing to maintain high interest rates on baht-denominated loans to keep inflation in check,[26] the policy was in reality a conduit by which local Thai companies could obtain special foreign loans at far lower interest rates than could be borrowed in baht.[27]

For example, in the mid-1990s, an investor could borrow yen at nearly 0 percent interest and invest in Bangkok skyscrapers, where the expected annual return was 20 percent.[28] With access to low-interest loans and readily available capital, and high demand, foreign capital flowed into the region and accounted for as much as 13 percent of Thailand's GDP, reaching a peak of $25.5 billion in 1995. Nearly 75 percent of these foreign capital inflows were from international banks in the form of

bank loans with maturities of less than one year. The majority of these loans were made to Thai banks and finance companies, which in turn made domestic loans of much longer duration.[29]

The dramatic influx of cheap capital spurred investment in the domestic infrastructure, such as chemical and steel plants. Developers counted on the continuation of strong growth. Luxury hotels and high-rises became plentiful as development companies borrowed and invested at a breakneck pace.[30]

The year 1996 marked the beginning of an economic downturn in Thailand.[31] Exports began to stagnate and growth slowed.[32] The Asian Development Bank attributed the decline in exports to several factors, including a slump in the electronic sector, tight monetary policies in other countries, and the appreciation of the U.S. dollar against the Japanese yen.[33]

The appreciation of the U.S. dollar had a serious effect on Thailand's economy because the Thai baht was "pegged" to a basket of currencies with strong ties to the U.S. dollar.[34] As the dollar strengthened, so did the baht. Meanwhile Japanese exports, priced in yen, became more attractive to consumers in the United States.[35] Another disadvantage of letting the baht remain on par with the U.S. dollar was that Thai interest rates were far above U.S. rates, which caused distortion of the real worth of the baht. Nevertheless, the combination of exchange-rate stability and high interest rates continued to attract vast capital inflows.[36]

In light of an economic slowdown and the accumulation of aggressive investment, heavy borrowing, and wasteful use of resources, the International Monetary Fund (IMF), on September 1996, warned that several Southeast Asian economies "current growth rates may be above their sustainable long-term trends." The report also suggested that a key economic problem confronting the developing countries was how to prevent big foreign-capital inflows from fueling inflation, blowing out their current accounts and producing a repeat of Mexico's financial-market crunch. The report also stated that the rapid growth of spending on real estate—a classic sign of speculative excess—in Indonesia, Malaysia, and Thailand and the appearance of skilled-labor bottlenecks in the region were early signs of overheating.[37] Following the IMF's warning of impending peril, senior Asian central bankers met on November 20, 1996, at the World Economic Forum to discuss how to prevent a "financial crisis from hitting the region."[38]

In the first and second quarters of 1997, Thailand's banks experienced a net $6 billion outflow of foreign investment. Short-term loans were not being renewed by foreign banks. During this time, Baker watched the exchange rate and was confident the Thai government would be able to maintain the value of the baht, therefore preserving the existing dollar/baht pegged exchange rate. However, the Bank of Thailand began to run out of reserves in its attempt to maintain the baht's value. On July 2, 1997, the Thailand government devalued its currency.[39]

Because the Asian Pacific economies were interconnected,[40] this event was likely to affect the currencies of the whole Asian Pacific region.[41] For American bowling manufacturers exporting to East Asia, the baht devaluation was a major concern on three accounts. First, U.S. firms feared that their Asian customers would be unable to pay off their accounts (usually payable in U.S. dollars). Second, a significant devaluation would make U.S. exports substantially more expensive across the entire region. Finally, governments usually raise interest rates in conjunction with any devaluation to assist in the stabilization of their currency. Manufacturers worried that the higher prices of capital equipment and higher interest rates could quash Asian investment in bowling centers (and new bowling equipment) almost overnight, especially if governments acted quickly.

A-1's International Expansion

Following the 1988 Olympics, A-1 began shipping lanes to Taiwan. From 1990 to 1992, the company concentrated on developing contacts through Dacos' Asian networks. Increasing sales to Korea and Taiwan more than offset A-1's declining sales to Europe, where the market was saturated. Baker saw a distinctive Asian business mind-set: "They were much more aggressive than we are in the West," he said, "They would actually build a bowling alley next to an existing one to drive out a local competitor."

By the end of 1992, Taiwan and South Korea were also reaching a saturation point for new wood bowling lanes; however, China had a growing interest in bowling. AMF and Brunswick had already developed centers in China. A-1 was able to penetrate this market in 1993 and 1994, mainly through its partnership with Dacos. A-1 had developed a synthetic lane called UltraLane, a popular substitute for wood flooring. As a result of this innovation, A-1 Lanes was one of only three companies in the world to supply both wood and synthetic lanes. By 1995, Asia was the company's main market. In 1996, A-1's sales increased to $12.4 million, 33 percent above the previous year.

In 1995–1996, AMF attempted to consolidate the highly fragmented bowling equipment industry by slashing the prices of its capital equipment, especially wood and synthetic flooring. The aggressive move drove down prices and profitability across the industry. A-1 matched AMF's pricing, but its profits suffered substantially.

In spite of the region's problems, Baker and his Asian distributors saw increasing interest in bowling in Singapore and Malaysia. They thought these markets were promising, and the additional volume could possibly offset the smaller profit per unit and thereby restore net income to its 1995 level. At this time, A-1 had 80 percent of its sales volume in the Asian markets and 20 percent in the United States.

A-1's Situation

As Rick Baker contemplated the changes in the international market, he could not help but think about his own firm's viability. A-1's domestic sales were primarily of synthetic overlay systems. He wondered how A-1 could survive an Asian crash and continue to make a profit, or at the very least, generate a positive cash flow. To understand his company's financial health he began to assess its activities, assets, and capabilities.

A-1 Lanes had become an important player in the international bowling industry within 10 years of its chicken-house origin. In Baker's view, his company strived to provide competitively priced, premium-quality bowling lanes and related equipment to the domestic and international markets, and this had earned a favorable industry reputation. More than 30 capital equipment distributors used A-1 as a source for bowling lanes.

Manufacturing Facilities

A-1 was operating at about 60 percent of the capacity of its state-of-the-art plant. The company could expand production quickly to meet the demand in Singapore and Malaysia. More than 160 companies supplied the materials A-1 used to produce its bowling lanes and complementary components and accessories, such as gutters, capping, and return tracks. Rusk, Texas, was an ideal location because of its proximity to southern yellow pine. In Baker's mind, its location gave A-1 a distinct advantage over rivals in the northern states due to low inbound costs of lumber and easy access to the mills.

Products and Innovation

Wood lanes were constructed of the highest quality southern yellow pine and hard maple boards, which were routed and milled to specification, and shipped either pre-nailed or loose to be installed by the ultimate buyer. According to Baker:

The specifications for building wood lanes are very strict concerning the orientation and grain of the wood. Some wood is not appropriate, so there are many rejected boards. To aid in lowering the rejection rate and our costs, we have trained graders in local sawmills to grade lumber for use in our manufacturing process.

Exhibit 5 Breakdown of A-1's Sales in 1996

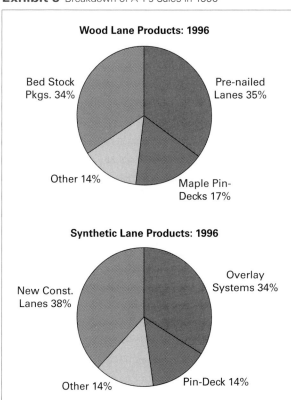

Wood Lane Products: 1996

Bed Stock Pkgs. 34%
Pre-nailed Lanes 35%
Other 14%
Maple Pin-Decks 17%

Synthetic Lane Products: 1996

New Const. Lanes 38%
Overlay Systems 34%
Other 14%
Pin-Deck 14%

By 1996, synthetic sales accounted for 42 percent of A-1 Lanes' total revenue, up from 25 percent of total sales in 1994. New synthetic lanes sold by the company were typically shipped in sections, installed on site, and cost $7,000 per lane. Exhibit 5 shows the breakdown of revenue from various synthetic lane products sold by A-1 Lanes.

In addition to UltraLane, Baker and his team continuously developed innovative products to complement or improve their existing products. For instance, A-1 developed a unique "snap on" ball return capping system and engineered changes in lane components that made the system less costly to manufacture. The capping system, made of high-impact plastic, covers (caps) the gutter dividers (A) and ball returns (B) that are positioned alternately between lanes.

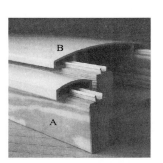

Overview of bowling lanes. The "capped ball" return (B) begins in the foreground and extends to the back of the lane.

Close-up of Capping System. A divider (A) and a ball return system (B) are made of wood and then covered (capped).

Once purchased, the lanes were shipped from the plant and assembled on site by highly skilled carpenters who specialized in the installation of bowling lanes.

Wood lanes and various derivatives accounted for 58 percent of A-1's revenues in 1996. Each wood lane cost $6,250 including accessories. A breakdown of revenue from the company's various products is shown in Exhibit 5.

To address some of the shortcomings associated with wood lanes, such as marring and gouging (deep etching), synthetic lanes were introduced during the 1980s. However, A-1 did not introduce its first synthetic flooring, UltraLane, until 1992. Baker was especially proud that this innovation was developed within the company and that the resin could be used not only for the construction of new lanes, but also for refurbishing existing wood lanes (overlay system). He elaborated,

The advantage of UltraLane is its improvement to the approach surface. Our competitors' synthetic flooring used the same product on the approach and the lane. The lane material was not slick enough for the approach. Bowlers' shoes stubbed on the material, and some lawsuits have been filed over injuries. UltraLane's approach has an orange peel texture that is very slick to the bowling shoe and allows it to slide properly.

Baker believed that continuously improving A-1's products was crucial to being competitive, even survival. Technological enhancements could alter the entire bowling equipment industry, bringing changes that could accelerate the development of bowling in foreign markets. Baker thought it ironic that the entire industry could be undermined by the recent currency devaluation rather than by a radical innovation.

Marketing

"We need to do little advertising because the coverage of our company in trade publications is very positive due to our quality of products and reputation," Baker said. However, to stay in continual contact with its customers, A-1 bought display space at trade shows and at regional and international meetings of national bowling associations.

A-1's ongoing relationship with Dacos was a "win-win situation," he thought. It allowed Dacos to offer a complete bowling center package that included pinsetters and bowling lanes supplied by A-1. By 1996, 50 percent of A-1's sales were channeled through this partnership. Dacos was formulating plans for developing bowling centers in Malaysia and Singapore, thereby enabling A-1 to be at the forefront of bowling's continuing growth in Asia.

Service and Sales

A-1's sales force was smaller than those of most competitors. The company's top three executives were its sales force and had been with the company since its inception. Baker thought that its sales force was an advantage for A-1 because competitors' sales forces were generally not very experienced. Furthermore, because of the knowledge and experience of its sales team, A-1 was able to provided consistent and reliable service. In Baker's mind, such service was especially important because business in Asia was primarily based on relationships.

Being small brought another advantage, he believed. Asians were insulted when larger companies sent middle managers to negotiate deals. Because A-1 was so small, all encounters with the company were with executives. Baker remembered that when he gave his Asian customers his business card and introduced himself as the president of A-1 Lanes, they would respond as if he were the president of AMF. When Baker traveled to Asia, he was treated "like royalty."

Performance Metrics

According to Baker, "It is amazing how a small firm in a rural community could sell millions of dollars of product to customers halfway around the world." Even so, Baker felt helpless in the currency crisis. Feeling a sense of urgency in his company's financial situation, Baker thought, "I wonder what story the financial statements might tell me?" (See Exhibits 6 through 8.)

A-1 Lanes' net profit reached an all-time high in 1995. Baker was sure that his decision to cut prices had hurt the bottom line, but he surmised that everyone in the industry was experiencing the slimmer margins. The real question, he figured, was how long AMF would pursue its price-cutting policy.

Another troublesome aspect of the financials was the increase in operating expenses as a percent of sales. Baker knew that these expenditures were needed to modernize A-1's facilities and enable the firm to meet the expected increase in sales. In fact, A-1 had increased production to bring its finished inventory to 25 percent of projected sales. Baker reasoned that if A-1 were unable to meet demand, customers could easily go elsewhere. The outlay of $554,000 to modernize the plant was financed by a 10 percent note payable over 10 years.

Credit and Currency Risk

Although sales contracts with foreign customers specified payment in U.S. dollars, the fluctuations of foreign currencies against the dollar produced risk for both the customer and A-1. A large appreciation in the U.S. dollar could affect the collectability of foreign accounts receivable. Standard industry practice was to ship to foreign customers only after receipt of full payment in U.S. dollars, or upon presentation of irrevocable letters of credit. However, Baker did make exceptions for long-standing customers that were key accounts. The exception applied to several major Asian customers, and Baker wondered whether this decision had been a smart one. He thought that hedging techniques to reduce A-1's transaction exposure would entail too much work; already he was too busy growing his business and filling orders. Besides, he had irrevocable letters of credit.

A-1's Future

Although Baker knew he did not fully understand the story within A-1's financials, he was growing uncomfortable with how the crash in Asian currency markets could affect his company. Should he have monitored the Asian economic environment more closely? Should he have expanded manufacturing operations in 1996? Should he have extended credit to his selected foreign customers? How could he have protected his company?

Exhibit 6 A-1 Lanes Income Statement, 1994–1996

	1996	1995	1994
Sales	$12,359,561	$9,326,649	$7,781,131
Cost of Goods Sold	9,887,649	6,460,768	6,035,549
Gross Profit	**2,471,912**	**2,865,881**	**1,745,582**
Operating Expenses	1,680,900	1,325,557	742,081
Earnings Before Interest and Taxes	**791,012**	**1,540,324**	**1,003,501**
Interest Expense	111,340	45,113	70,322
Income Tax Expense	203,902	447,779	317,281
Net Income	**$ 475,770**	**$1,047,432**	**$ 615,898**

Exhibit 7 A-1 Lanes Balance Sheet, 1994–1996

	1996	1995	1994
Cash	$ 296,603	$ 114,847	$ 73,411
Accounts Receivable	2,101,125	1,416,523	950,180
Inventory	2,050,636	2,418,940	1,571,758
Other Current	84,622	58,752	25,000
Total Current Assets	**4,532,986**	**4,009,062**	**2,620,349**
Fixed Assets	1,121,783	567,877	462,939
Accumulated Depreciation	(496,993)	(301,163)	(258,981)
Net Fixed Assets	624,790	266,714	203,958
TOTAL ASSETS	**$5,157,776**	**$4,275,776**	**$2,824,307**
Accounts Payable	$1,382,526	$1,440,354	$1,043,776
Short-Term Notes Payable	0	0	249,000
Taxes Payable	11,711	271,529	336,905
Other Current Liabilities	38,008	56,083	227,957
Total Current Liabilities	**1,432,245**	**1,767,966**	**1,857,638**
Long-Term Notes Payable	1,289,400	547,449	72,740
Common Stock	15,000	15,000	15,000
Excess of Par	60,000	60,000	60,000
Retained Earnings	2,361,131	1,885,361	818,929
Total Equity	**2,436,131**	**1,960,361**	**893,929**
TOTAL LIABILITIES & EQUITY	**$ 5,157,776**	**$4,275,776**	**$2,824,307**

Exhibit 8 A-1 Lanes Cash Flow Statement, 1994–1996

	1996	1995	1994
Cash Flow from Operating Activities			
Net Income	$475,770	$1,047,432	$615,898
Depreciation	195,830	42,182	55,108
(Increase) Accounts Receivable	(684,602)	(466,343)	(350,218)
Other Current	(25,870)	(33,752)	(31,654)
(Increase) Decrease Inventory	368,304	(847,182)	(355,916)
Increase (Decrease) Accounts Payable	(57,828)	396,578	115,530
Taxes Payable	(259,818)	(65,376)	(32,126)
Net Cash from Operating Activities	**11,786**	**73,539**	**48,276**
Purchase of Fixed Assets	**(553,906)**	**(104,938)**	**(74,136)**
Financial Proceeds			
Decrease Short-Term Notes	0	(249,000)	(250,000)
Increase Long-Term Debt	741,951	474,709	434,742
(Decrease) Other Current Liabilities	(18,075)	(171,874)	(91,279)
Total Proceeds (Payments)	**723,876**	**53,835**	**19,327**
Net Change in Cash	**$181,756**	**$ 22,436**	**$ 28,949**

Exhibit 9 A-1 Lanes Financial Ratios versus Industry[1] Averages

	A-1 Lanes			Industry[2]			1996[4] Sales $10–$25 M
	1996	**1995**	**1994**	**1996**	**1995**	**1994**	
1. Firm Liquidity Current Ratio	3.16	2.27	1.41	1.80	1.70	1.70	1.8
Average Collection Period for Accounts Receivable	62.05	55.44	44.57	NA	NA	NA	NA
2. Operating Profitability Operating Income Return on Investment	15.34%	36.02%	35.53%	7.20%	11.10%	9.30%	10.00%
Operating Profit Margin	6.40%	16.52%	12.90%	3.60%	4.63%	4.43%	5.56%
Total Asset Turnover	2.40	2.18	2.76	2.00	2.40	2.10	1.8
Accounts Receivable Turnover	5.88	6.58	8.19	13.00	12.50	12.20	12.9
Inventory Turnover	4.82	2.67	3.84	5.10	6.30	5.90	7.00
Fixed Assets Turnover	19.78	34.97	38.15	7.20	6.60	6.50	6.80
3. Financing Decisions Debt Ratio	25.00%	12.80%	2.58%	20.10	20.30%	20.80%	15.6%
Times Interest Earned	7.10	34.14	14.27	3.10	4.50	6.00	14.6
4. Return on Equity Return on Equity[3]	32.47%	78.57%	112.26%	17.31%	25.06%	23.13%	18.28%

1. SIC 2426; NAICS 321918 Manufacturing, Other Millwork (including Flooring).
2. Source: Robert Morris & Associates (1996). *Annual Statement Studies: Financial Ratio Benchmarks.* Philadelphia, PA.
3. RMA does not report net income (after taxes) nor stockholders equity. Therefore, a derivative was used (Profit before taxes/net worth) as an indicant for return on equity.
4. This information is reported for the current year (1996) of firms with sales of $10–$25 million.

Baker recalled that his old management professor at college once told him that behind each set of financial statements is a story—especially when you compare your company with the industry averages. Baker visited the library and collected the ratios pertaining to his industry. Now he laid them on a table next to A-1's financial statements (see Exhibit 9). He grabbed an ice cream bar from the freezer and sat down to ponder his next move.

Notes

1. C. Pezzano, 1996, The push is on for olympic status, *The Record* (New Jersey), January 7: S17.
2. 1997, AMF Bowling looks to equity markets going public, *The IPO Reporter,* September 1, Securities Data Publishing.
3. C. Stooksbury, 1998, Bowling boasts lengthy history as popular pastime, *Amusement Business,* May: 20.
4. Bowling centers. *Encyclopedia of American Industries,* 2001: 2.
5. N. King, 1997, Bowling must learn by its mistakes, *The Ledger* (Lakeland, Florida), July 20: C2.
6. A-1 Lanes company literature.
7. S. Hansell, *Overview of the Bowling Industry.* http://www .ltfun.com/documents/hansell_article.pdf (accessed January 7, 2006).
8. M. Matzer, 1996, Bowling for dollars, *Brandweek,* August: 18.
9. S. Hansell, 1998, A double-edged sword, *International Bowling Industry,* July: 37.
10. I. P. Murphy, 1997, Bowling industry rolls out unified marketing plan, *Sports Marketing,* January: 2.
11. 1997, AMF Bowling Worldwide Inc., 1997 Annual Report: 10-K, Period ending December 31.

12. Food and beverage includes bar sales. On average, bar sales would account for 55 percent of these sales.

13. I. P. Murphy, 1997, Bowling industry rolls out unified marketing plan, *Sports Marketing,* January: 2.

14. 1997 Economic Census: Bridge Between NAICS and SIC Manufacturing. http://www.census.gov/epcd/ec97brdg/E97B1321. HTM#321918 (accessed August 25, 2004).

15. From A-1 Lanes 1997 company estimates.

16. M. Cooper, 1998, On the shining paths of tenpin, *The Nation,* 267, August 10: 35.

17. From A-1 Lanes company literature.

18. M. Luby, Jr., 1998, Asia's malaise is only temporary, *Bowler's Journal International,* January: 12. http://www.census.gov/epcd/naics/ NAICS32A.HTM#N321918.

19. Ibid.

20. 1990, Wave of growth sweeping across Asia, Jiji Press Ltd., June 7.

21. M. N. Baily, D. Farrel, & S. Lund, 2000, The color of hot money, *Foreign Affairs,* 79(2), March/April: 99–110.

22. 1998, East Asia: The road to recovery, World Bank, Washington, DC.

23. WEO, cited in East Asia: The road to recovery, 1998, World Bank, Washington, DC.

24. World Development Indicators on CD-ROM, 2002, World Bank.

25. B. Einhorn & R. Corben, 1997, One tired tiger, *Business Week* (International Edition), March 24.

26. 1997, Thailand finally lets its currency float, *Wall Street Journal,* July 3.

27. J. Sapsford, 1997, Asia's financial shock: How it began, and what comes next, *Wall Street Journal,* November 26.

28. World Development Indicators on CD-ROM, 2002, World Bank.

29. M. N. Baily, D. Farrel, & S. Lund, 2000, The color of hot money, *Foreign Affairs,* 79(2), March/April: 99–110.

30. C. Lebourgre, 1997, Thailand: "Tis an ill wind that blows nobody any good," *Banque Paribas Conjoncture,* May.

31. Thailand, http://www.infoplease.com/ipa/A0108034.html.

32. C. Lebourgre, 1997, Thailand: "Tis an ill wind that blows nobody any good," *Banque Paribas Conjoncture,* May.

33. 1997, Asia-Pacific to grow at slower pace in '97 and '98, Japan Economic News Wire. *Kyodo News Service,* April 17.

34. H. Sender, 1997, Get a grip: Can Thailand's Central Bank handle the baht crisis? *Far Eastern Economic Review,* 160(13): March 27.

35. 1997, Several European bourses float at lofty levels: Tokyo shares rise following pause for holiday, *Wall Street Journal,* January 17.

36. H. Sender, 1997, Get a grip: Can Thailand's Central Bank handle the baht crisis? *Far Eastern Economic Review,* 160(13): March 27.

37. P. Kandiah, 1996, Malaysia warned over possibility of Mexico-style crash, *The Nikkei Weekly,* September 30, *http://web.lexis-nexis .com/universe/document* (accessed April 23, 2003).

38. S. Kohli, 1996, Bankers fear Asian "Mexico" crisis, *South China Morning Post,* November 21, *http://web.lexis-nexis.com/universe/ document* (accessed April 10, 2003).

39. M. N. Baily, D. Farrel, & S. Lund, 2000, The color of hot money, *Foreign Affairs,* 79(2), March/April: 99–110.

40. R. Y. C. Wong, 1999, Lessons from the Asian financial crisis, *Cato Journal,* 18(3), Winter: 391–398.

41. A. Brummer, 1996, East Asian tigers are endangered, *The Guardian* (London), October 16. *http://web.lexis-nexis.com/universe/document* (accessed April 1, 2003).

Case 3

AMD vs. Intel: Competitive Challenges

Siddhartha Paul

ICFAI Business School

What can still hurt us the most, frankly, is Intel's antitrust practices. That's the largest obstacle for us to get where we need to go.

> —HECTOR RUIZ,
> CHAIRPERSON AND CEO OF AMD[1]

The competitive challenges between the top two chip makers Intel and AMD took on a new dimension due to different strategic initiatives of both companies. AMD, the second largest chip maker, challenged the market leader Intel with its server chips. Intel had faced stiff competition from the Opteron chip manufactured by AMD ever since its launch in 2003. AMD's revenue increased from $3.5 billion in 2003 to $5.8 billion in 2005 (see Exhibit 1). Moreover, in 2006, AMD announced its plan to acquire Array Technologies Incorporated (ATI) for $5.4 billion. The merger between AMD and ATI posed a threat and challenge to Intel. Still, AMD was worried about Intel's antitrust practices. AMD blamed Intel for its illegal discount program that resulted in AMD's PC market share drop in Japan. Therefore, analysts were skeptical about whether AMD could overcome Intel's monopolistic practices (see Appendix 1).

Company Background

AMD

AMD was founded by Jerry Sanders and seven friends on May 1, 1969. During its early years, the company's major products were outsourced from other companies that were redesigned and upgraded for better speed and efficiency. In 1975, AMD launched its first memory product—a random access memory (RAM)[2] chip known as Am9102. In the same year the company developed a reverse-engineered[3] version of 8080A standard processor. This product brought AMD into the microprocessor[4]

arena. The company's business grew to $168 million by the end of 1975. During the 1980s, AMD ventured into the overseas market with the establishment of facilities in Singapore and Thailand. Since the rise in the personal computer industry, in the early 1980s, AMD played an important role by providing high-quality x86 processors.[5] In 1986, AMD launched the industry's first 1-million bit EPROM (erasable programmable read-only memory).[6] In the following year the company merged with Monolithic Memories,[7] the pioneer in field-programmable logic.[8]

Exhibit 1 Net Sales of AMD (in $ billions)

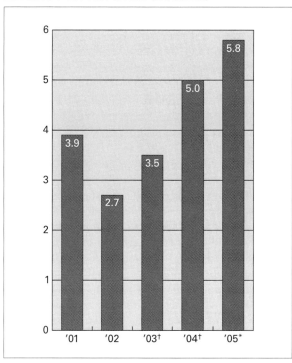

Source: http://annualreport.amd.com.

Since the early 1990s, AMD introduced various products, including microprocessors compatible with IBM computers, networking and communication chips, programmable logic devices, and high-performance memory. During the same period, AMD introduced new products in the microprocessor category including the AM386 and AM486. During the same period (1990), flash memory[9] took over the EEPROM (electrically erasable programmable read-only memory) market by serving as a nonvolatile[10] memory solution. AMD launched the first economically viable single-voltage flash memory device and, in 1993, established a joint venture with Fujitsu Limited[11] and formed Fujitsu AMD Semiconductor Limited, or Spansion. In 1994, AMD formed an alliance with Compaq Computer Corp. under which AMD's microprocessors were part of Compaq computers. The company released its AMD-K6 processors in 1997 and AMD Athlon processors in 1999. In February 2002, AMD acquired Alchemy Semiconductor,[12] which designed microprocessors for personal connectivity. In the following year, the company formed a new flash memory semiconductor joint venture with Fujitsu. Both the companies offered their flash memory solutions under the global brand name Spansion. In 2005, AMD introduced the dual core processor for desktop PCs. AMD achieved sales of $5.8 billion in the year 2005, which was an increase of 17 percent compared to 2004. AMD's business divisions consisted of computation products (microprocessors), memory products (flash memory devices), and personal connectivity solutions (embedded microprocessors for commercial and consumer markets).

INTEL

In 1968, Intel was founded by Robert Noyce and Gordon Moore as Integrated Electronics Corporation. During its initial years the company manufactured semiconductor[13] memory for mini computers and mainframe computers. In 1969, it launched the world's first metal oxide semiconductor (MOS)[14] static RAM, followed by the Schottky[15] bipolar 64-bit[16] static random access memory (SRAM)[17] chip. By 1970 the company became the market leader in the highly competitive DRAM,[18] SRAM, and ROM[19] market. In 1971, Intel introduced the world's first microprocessor. The company continued with its improvements and came up with the 8086 microprocessors in 1978, which became the industry standard. In 1981, Intel entered into a strategic alliance with IBM,[20] in which IBM would use Intel's microprocessor for its desktops models. After this deal, Intel became a dominant player in the desktop PC segment. In 1982, Intel continued to develop innovative products and launched the high-performance 16-bit microprocessor (80286). Further developments led to the 386 microprocessors and then the 486 microprocessors in 1989. Beginning in 1991, Intel started its brand building with the slogan "Intel Inside" to connect personal computers with the Intel microprocessor in users' minds. According to Dataquest,[21] Intel became the largest semiconductor supplier in 1992. The company changed the industry standard the following year by launching the Pentium processors (Pentium I), which were 300 times faster than the microprocessors used in IBM desktops. Intel continued its strategy of upgrading the models of the Pentium processors and launched Pentium-II, Pentium-III, and Pentium-IV. In 1998, the company segmented its product portfolio according to customer profile. The company introduced the Celeron processor for the household PC segment, and the Pentium II Xeon processor for workstations[22] and servers.[23] During the same time, it introduced high-performance StrongARM technology[24] for handheld computing and communication devices. In 2003, the company came up with its Centrino[25] mobile technology for laptop PCs.

In 2005, Intel recorded revenue of $38.8 billion, and the company's product portfolio included microprocessors, chipsets, motherboards, and flash memory. It also had communications infrastructure components, network processors, applications and cellular baseband processors, and products for network storage.

Chip Industry Overview

The chip industry's major customers were manufacturers of computers, digital consumer appliances, and mobile communications. This industry experienced growing demand due to the increasing semiconductor content of electronic products. World Semiconductor Trade Statistics (WSTS)[26] estimated that the global chip revenue would rise by 10.1 percent in 2006 over its 2005 mark of $227.5 billion.[27] Analysts predicted that the chip industry would reach a new height during the next three years due to the growth of wireless and consumer electronics and computers. WSTS predicted that the global chip industry would accelerate to 11 percent in 2007 and 12.8 percent by 2008.[28]

Computers were the biggest user of semiconductor chips and would continue to drive demand in the semiconductor industry. According to analysts, about 41 percent of all semiconductors produced were consumed by computers (see Exhibit 2). But the demand for chipsets in other sectors also grew. Jean-Philippe Dauvin, chief economist for semiconductor supplier STMicroelectronics,[29] stated, "Cell phones, laptops, DVD players and automotive electronics are traditional applications for semiconductors and those applications are in a renewal mode in the United States, Europe and Japan." He was also of the opinion that the electronics market in China, India, and Eastern Europe was growing and would boost the semiconductor demand.

Exhibit 2 Where Semiconductors Are Consumed

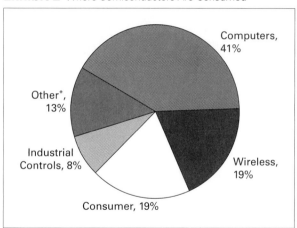

* "Other" includes automotive, wired components, and multichip packages.

Source: http://www.purchasing.com/article/CA6361157.html.

Exhibit 3 Gartner's Worldwide PC Vendor Unit Shipment Second Quarter 2006

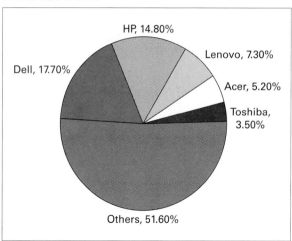

Note: Percentages include desktop PCs, mobile PCs, and x86 servers.

Source: http://computers.tekrati.com/research/news.asp?id=7475.

Analysts expected chip demand within the computer industry to increase due to Vista, Microsoft's new operating system.[30] Vista required that the computers be equipped with more DRAMs. Analysts opined that due to Vista, the amount of DRAM in a PC would double. Therefore, according to Tom Trill, director of DRAM marketing for Samsung Semiconductor, "Overall, Vista is good news for everyone in the PC industry. PC growth is robust, and megabytes of DRAM per system is growing"[31] Moreover, analysts also felt that cell phones, MP3 players, and personal digital assistants (PDAs) would drive demand for chipsets due to more innovative features. The number of chips in mobile phones was increasing as more functions were added. According to Dauvin of STMicroelectronics, the voice-centric phones had about $12 of semiconductor content whereas the 3G phones equipped with camera, video, and audio features had about $65 of chip content. The chip companies manufacturing NAND flash[32] would benefit the most due to increased usage of NAND in the cell phones. Analysts predicted that the NAND market was expected to grow from $10.5 billion in 2005 to $14.8 billion in 2009.

According to WSTS, the Asia-Pacific market would be the largest and fastest-growing regional market in chip revenue with 12.4 percent in 2006 and 12.8 percent in 2007. WSTS predicted that the Asia-Pacific segment would rise by 15 percent to $150 billion in 2008.[33]

Battle Intensified: AMD vs. Intel

Intel, the world leader in making chipsets, faced intense competition from its competitor AMD. The company achieved its biggest victory when Dell, the largest PC

maker worldwide (see Exhibit 3), announced in May 2006 that it would start using AMD's server chips. This announcement was a major setback for Intel; Dell had been its largest customer. Dell opted for AMD's Opteron chips in the high-end server segment. In view of Technology Business Research[34] analyst, Martin Kariithi, this was a major blow to Intel. As Intel's largest customer, Dell accounted for almost one-fourth of Intel's processor shipment per quarter. Hewlett-Packard (HP), the world's second-largest PC manufacturer, used AMD chips in their machines. Whereas Lenovo, the third-largest manufacturer and already a strong AMD customer in China, planned to use AMD chips in its business desktop PCs for the United States.

Intel began losing market share. According to the analysts, the company's market share declined from 74.3 percent in the first quarter of 2006 to 72.9 percent in the third quarter. Whereas, AMD's share grew by half a point from 21.1 percent in the first quarter of 2006 to 21.6 percent in the third quarter. However, from 2005 onward, AMD followed a more aggressive approach that ate away at Intel's market share until Intel's share of the chip market was 72.9 percent (2006), down from 82.2 percent a year earlier (2005), according to Mercury Research.[35] AMD's third quarter sales increased by 9 percent in 2006 from its previous quarter, and by 32 percent from the prior year (see Exhibit 4). At the same time, Intel's revenue declined by 12 percent to $8.74 billion from $9.96 billion a year earlier (2005). However, Intel's CFO Andy Bryant felt that the company had been recovering market share from AMD.

Exhibit 4 AMD's Third Quarter Results, 2006

	Q3 2006	Q2 2006	Q3 2005	Change Q3 2006 vs. Q2 2006	Q3 2006 vs. Q3 2005
Net Sales (billions)	$1.33	$1.22	$1.01	9%	32%
Operating Income (millions)	$119	$102	$129	17%	(8)%
Gross Margin	51.4%	56.8%	55.4%	(5.4)%	(4.0)%

Source: http://www.amd.com/us-en/Corporate/VirtualPressRoom/0,,51_104_543~113657,00.html.

According to him, "We lost market share and were under price pressure. We still have to live with tough year-over-year comparisons . . . but we think the worst is behind us." The company was in a restructuring mode that included the elimination of 10,500 jobs through layoffs, attrition, and the sale of underperforming business groups. This elimination was about 10 percent of its total workforce. Intel expected that this restructuring would save the company $5 billion by 2008. As Intel lost market share to AMD, it slashed prices of many products. In July 2006, Intel dropped the price of its Pentium 4 desktop chip to $84 from $218. The company also reduced its price for the expensive Pentium D desktop chip by 40 percent, which had been priced at $530 to $316. According to an analyst at the Enderle Group,[36] both AMD and Intel were hit massively hard by the price war. Intel's average selling price revenue of its processor was lower even though the total processor unit sales were high in the third quarter (2006). AMD also faced the same consequence of the price war—the higher desktop microprocessor sales reflected a lower average selling price during the same period.

AMD's Opteron chip aimed for the corporate server market was launched in 2003. This chip boosted AMD's revenue from $3.5 billion in 2003 to $5.8 billion in 2005. The company also kept the momentum going for its Opteron processors as its market share rose from 22.1 percent in the first quarter of 2006 to 25.9 percent in the second quarter of 2006, according to Mercury Research. But Intel reacted by its release of Xeon 5100 chip for servers. Intel claimed that its Xeon chip was 71 percent better than AMD's Opteron and also had an 84 percent improvement over AMD's power consumption. Moreover, Intel launched its Core 2 Duo processor in July 2006 and planned to release a microprocessor that had four computing engines on a single chip (Core 2 Extreme quad-core). The company felt that its restructuring in addition to its new product development would win back market share from AMD.

Intel's Antitrust

AMD had been in the growth stage of its product life cycle with its Opteron processors, which boosted the company's revenue. But still AMD was worried about Intel's exclusionary practices in Britain, Germany, and Japan. Especially in Japan, AMD began to lose market share, beginning in 2002. According to Gartner Dataquest, AMD's unit share slid from 25 percent in mid-2002 to 9 percent in mid-2004 (see Exhibit 5). AMD's portion of Sony's business dropped from 23 percent in 2002 to zero by 2004, and its total share of NEC[37] business dropped by 35 percent during the same period. During early 2004, AMD brought these figures to the notice of the Japan Fair Trade Commission,[38] and in April of the same year, the commission's agents raided Intel's Japan office. In the next year, the commission ruled that, since May 2002, Intel had violated Japanese law by offering rebates to computer manufacturers upon the purchase of a high percentage of Intel processors.

According to Tom McCoy, AMD executive vice president of legal affairs, "Intel went into Japan and just blew us out as a matter of sheer exercise of monopoly power." He believed that Intel gave Japanese computer makers millions of dollars in rebates for exclusivity. He felt that this rebate sometimes amounted to 100 percent. Therefore, in June 2005, AMD filed a historic antitrust suit against Intel. AMD accused Intel of illegally preserving its monopoly on x86 processors through an illegal discounting program. According to McCoy, "Our customers were telling us, 'The only thing that prevents us from buying more technology from you is the fact that we don't think we can withstand the punishment Intel will put on us.' What the industry needed was antitrust cover to try to back Intel off its practices. With the regulatory spotlight being turned on bright, the industry would be more courageous in building market share with us."

Analysts explained the so-called rebates offered by Intel: If a computer maker bought 100 chips in the last

Exhibit 5 AMD Share in Japanese PC Market

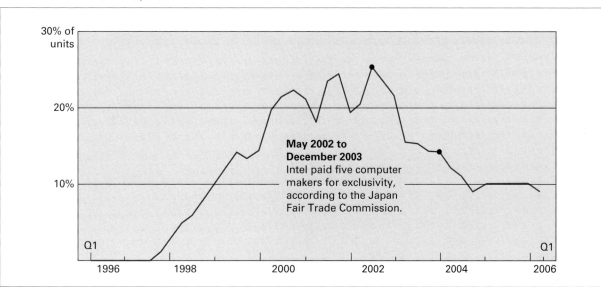

May 2002 to December 2003
Intel paid five computer makers for exclusivity, according to the Japan Fair Trade Commission.

Source: Roger Parloff, Intel's Worst Nightmare, *Fortune,* September 4, 2006.

quarter, of which 90 units were supplied by Intel and the rest from AMD, then in the new quarter AMD might bid for 20 units to increase its share. But Intel might dash AMD's hopes by offering illegal discounting. According to the analysts, if the price per processor was $90, then Intel would offer it at $80 if the computer maker was buying more than 80 percent of its processors from Intel. Moreover, the rebate was not only applied to the processors over the 80 percent target but to every processor that the company was buying from Intel in that quarter. According to AMD's outside lawyer, "Effectively, what Intel's saying is, if you don't buy those ten incremental units from AMD, we'll give you them for free." He explained that 80 processors at $90 each cost the same as 90 processors at $80 each and so he felt that "AMD has to give away product for free. It's pretty axiomatic that you can't stay in any business if you're giving away your product free to pick up the market share." But Intel reacted by labeling it as a simple discounting program that was a part of its trade promotion. If a computer manufacturer purchased less than 20 percent of its chips from Intel, a discount price was not offered, but if it bought between 20 and 40 percent, then a discount price was offered. However, if this figure rose to 80 percent to 100 percent, then the company enjoyed the highest discount rate. In Intel's view, this arrangement was a traditional discount program that increased with volume.

Analysts opined that the case against Intel would not be tried before 2008 because the findings for the case would be monumental; but in September 2006, a federal judge dismissed a major portion of AMD's antitrust lawsuit against Intel. According to him, AMD could not sue Intel in the U.S. courts for its monopolistic tactics in other countries. Moreover, the judge ruled that AMD could not prove that Intel's illegal tactics abroad had an effect on AMD's operations in the United States. However, the judge also ruled that AMD could ask the court to reconsider its decision by presenting foreign evidence that would be a part of the domestic trial. Intel was happy with the proceedings and its spokesperson Chuck Mulloy said, "We are pleased that the judge understood and agreed with our argument and analysis of the law. Nonetheless, we plan to vigorously defend ourselves on the remaining portions of this case." Tom McCoy, on the other hand, felt that "Intel cannot escape antitrust scrutiny for its conduct. As this U.S. litigation is joined by global antitrust investigations, it is clear that Intel cannot escape the consequences of its illegal monopoly abuses." Therefore, the conflict continued between the top two chip makers and analysts were undecided about who would emerge as the winner in this legal war (see Appendix 2).

The Road Ahead

AMD has grown steadily in the server market with its Opteron chips. According to IDC, the global server market was expected to grow by 11 percent per year with 11.8 million unit shipments by 2010.[39] Marty Seyer, AMD vice president and head of the server chip division, said that the company was aiming for a 40 percent global market share for server chips by 2009, which was already 26 percent in the second quarter of 2006, according to IDC analyst Shan Rau. Moreover, AMD

Appendix 1 Market Share Ranking of the Top 20 Semiconductors, 2005

Rank 2005	Rank 2004	Company	Country of origin
1	1	Intel	United States
2	2	Samsung Semiconductors	South Korea
3	3	Texas Instruments	United States
4	7	Toshiba Semiconductors	Japan
5	6	STMicroelectronics	Europe
6	4	Infineon (spin-off from Siemens Semiconductors)	Europe
7	5	Renesas (merger of Mitsubishi and Hitachi Semiconductors)	Japan
8	8	NEC Semiconductors	Japan
9	9	Philips Semiconductors	Europe
10	10	Freescale (ex Motorola Semiconductors)	United States
11	14	Hynix	South Korea
12	13	Micron Technology	United States
13	15	Sony Semiconductors	Japan
14	12	Matsushita Semiconductors	Japan
15	11	AMD (1)	United States
16	17	Qualcomm (3) (fabless)	United States
17	16	Sharp Semiconductors	Japan
18	19	Rohm	Japan
19	20	IBM Microelectronics (2)	United States
20	22	Broadcom (3) (fabless)	United States

Source: http://en.wikipedia.org.

has aggressively challenged Intel by diversifying into the graphics chip category with its acquisition of ATI Technologies in a $5.4 billion deal. Still, AMD's alleged antitrust suit against Intel continued to worry AMD when it considered what effects Intel's practices might have on AMD's growth in other countries, but especially in Japan. Because AMD felt that this practice by Intel was anticompetitive, it filed an antitrust law suit against Intel. Analysts felt that if these claims were proven, then AMD would have a winning hand. However, the same analysts were skeptical that AMD would win the legal battle against Intel based on AMD's setback that happened when a federal judge dismissed a major portion of AMD's antitrust lawsuit against Intel.

Appendix 2 Intel and AMD: Parallel Time Lines

AMD's product introductions followed carefully behind Intel's—until the Athlon arrived.
Today, AMD is in the enviable position of having Intel clone its 64-bit x86 extensions.

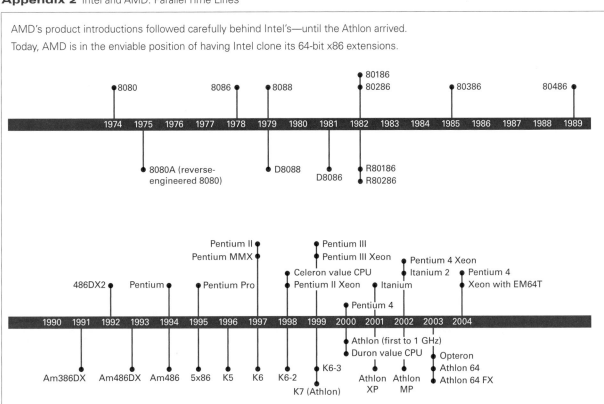

Source: http://www.infoworld.com/infoworld/img/35FEamd-in.gif.

Notes

1. R. Parloff, Intel's worst nightmare, *Fortune*, September 4, 2006.
2. Random access memory (RAM) refers to data storage formats and equipment that allow the stored data to be accessed in any order—that is, at random, not just in sequence.
3. Reverse engineering (RE) is the process of discovering the technological principles of a mechanical application through analysis of its structure, function, and operation.
4. A microprocessor is a digital electronic component with transistors on a single semiconductor integrated circuit (IC). One or more microprocessors typically serve as a central processing unit (CPU) in a computer system or handheld device.
5. x86 is the generic name of a microprocessor architecture. The architecture is called x86 because the earliest processors in this family were identified by model numbers ending in the sequence "86": the 8086, the 80186, the 80286, the 386, and the 486.
6. EPROM, or erasable programmable read-only memory, is a type of computer chip that retains its data when its power supply is switched off. In other words, it is nonvolatile.
7. Monolithic Memories, Inc. (MMI), produced bipolar PROMs, programmable logic devices, and logic circuits. MMI invented Programmable Array Logic (PAL) devices. MMI was eventually acquired by AMD.
8. The company produces a family of programmable logic device semiconductors used to implement logic functions in digital circuits.
9. Flash memory ash is a form of nonvolatile computer memory that can be electrically erased and reprogrammed.
10. Nonvolatile memory retains its contents even if power is turned off.
11. Fujitsu is a Japanese company specializing in semiconductors, computers (supercomputers, personal computers, servers), telecommunications, and services, and is headquartered in Tokyo.
12. This privately held company designed microprocessors for personal connectivity devices.
13. A semiconductor is a material with an electrical conductivity and acts as an intermediate between an insulator and a conductor.
14. A metal oxide semiconductor (MOS) structure is obtained by depositing a layer of silicon dioxide (SiO2) and a layer of metal (polycrystalline silicon is actually used instead of metal) on top of a semiconductor die.
15. A Schottky barrier is a metal-semiconductor junction.
16. A bit refers to a digit in the binary numeral system (base 2).
17. Static random access memory (SRAM) is a type of semiconductor memory. The word *static* indicates that the memory retains its contents as long as power remains applied, unlike dynamic RAM (DRAM) that needs to be periodically refreshed.
18. Dynamic random access memory (DRAM) is a type of random access memory that stores each bit of data in a separate capacitor.
19. Read-only memory (ROM) is a class of storage media used in computers and other electronic devices that can only be read.
20. IBM (International Business Machines Corporation) manufactures and sells computer hardware, software, infrastructure services, hosting services, and consulting services.
21. Dataguest is a leading provider of market research, statistical, and forecasting data to IT vendors, manufacturers, and investors.

22. A workstation (Unix workstation, RISC workstation, or engineering workstation) is a high-end technical computing desktop microcomputer designed primarily to be used by one person at a time, but can also be connected remotely to other users when necessary.
23. A server is a computer system that provides services to other computing systems—called clients—over a network.
24. StrongARM technology was designed to accelerate the development of advanced handheld computing products, enable new classes of low-power, high-performance Internet access devices, and enhance Internet backbone products.
25. Centrino is a platform marketing initiative from Intel for a particular combination of CPU, main board chipset, and wireless network interface in the design of a laptop personal computer.
26. WSTS Inc. is a nonprofit mutual benefit corporation whose charter and bylaws define services for the world semiconductor industry, including management of the collection and publication of trade net shipments and semiconductor industry forecasts. WSTS headquarters are incorporated and located in San Jose, California.
27. Global chip growth forecast for 2006 revised up, http://www.webwereld.nl, May 31, 2006.
28. Ibid.
29. STMicroelectronics is a leading international supplier of semiconductors.
30. Microsoft Windows Vista is the next major version of Microsoft Windows, the proprietary operating system developed by Microsoft.
31. Chip growth reaches new heights, http://www.purchasing.com/article/CA6361157.html, August 17, 2006.
32. Flash memory is a form of nonvolatile computer memory that can be electrically erased and reprogrammed.
33. Global chip growth forecast for 2006 revised up, http://www.webwereld.nl, May 31, 2006.
34. Technology Business Research is an information and market research organization that analyzes computer and networking equipment companies.
35. Mercury Research is a small, focused research firm that provides detailed information for PC-related semiconductor and components markets.
36. This research organization provides perspectives for the technology leaders.
37. NEC, part of the Sumitomo Group, provides information technology (IT) and network solutions to business enterprises, communications services providers, and government. Their business is divided into the three principal segments: IT Solutions, Network Solutions, and Electronic Devices.
38. Fair Trade Commission is the name for the government unit charged with ensuring the fairness of trade.
39. AMD aims for 40 percent of server market, http://news.com.com, August 22, 2006.

References

R. Parloff, 2006, Intel's worst nightmare, *Fortune,* September 4.

J. Robertson, 2006, Judge dismisses key part of AMD lawsuit, http://www.businessweek.com, September 27.

J. Robertson, 2006, AMD earns 27 cents per share in 3Q, http://www.businessweek.com, October 18.

Intel shares up after beating street, http://www.businessweek.com, October 18, 2006.

Ahead of the Bell: Intel, http://www.businessweek.com, October 18, 2006.

R. Konrad, 2006, Intel plans quad-core chip in late 2006, http://www.businessweek.com, September 26.

HSBC sees limit on AMD's sales, http://www.businessweek.com, October 9, 2006.

M. Kanellos, 2006, AMD, Intel trim processor pricing, http://news.com.com, October 25.

J. Davis, 2006, AMD, Intel margins suffer on price war, http://www.edn.com, October 24.

S. Hillis, 2006, AMD profit margins fall amid Intel price war, http://news.yahoo.com, October 18.

J. G. Spooner, 2006, AMD, Intel brace for third-quarter showdown, http://www.eweek.com, August 1.

AMD reports third quarter results, http://www.amd.com, October 18, 2006.

AMD's third quarter earnings were good, but the stock took a hit as its competition with Intel heats up, http://www.tmcnet.com, October 18, 2006.

Intel profit plunges by 35% in third quarter, http://www.finfacts.com, October 17, 2006.

Intel shows signs of chip comeback, http://cnnmoney.com, October 17, 2006.

A. Hesseldahl, 2006, Intel's AMD troubles continue, http://www.businessweek.com, October 17.

M. Andrejczak, 2006, AMD quarterly profit up 77% on chip demand, http://www.newsalert.com, October 18.

A. Hesseldahl, 2006, AMD's race for server space, http://www.businessweek.com, August 22.

AMD shoots for 40 percent of server market, http://money.cnn.com, August 22, 2006.

Chip sales may increase by 10 percent, WSTS says, http://www.taipeitimes.com/News/biz/archives, May 31, 2006.

D. Goodin, 2006, AMD to buy chip-maker ATI for $5.4B, http://www.businessweek.com, July 24.

http://en.wikipedia.org.

http://www.amd.com.

http://www.intel.com.

Case 4

Boeing: Redefining Strategies to Manage the Competitive Market

Ryan Gust, Brandon Barth, Joey O'Donnell, Drew Forsberg, Robin Chapman

Arizona State University

Introduction

In 1992 Boeing and Airbus parent, EADS, agreed to conduct a joint study on the prospects for a superjumbo airplane. With a forecasted 5 percent annual growth in air travel, both companies saw the need for a new aircraft large enough to support this growth. However, the world will not be permitted to see what the brain trust of the two aerospace industry giants could have produced. Airbus and Boeing reached different conclusions concerning market trends, and the joint effort was called off.

The average size of aircraft grew until the late 1990s; however, this trend began to change as carriers shifted their primary focus to profits as opposed to market share. Strong competition among airlines prompted ticket prices to fall in recent years. As a result, carriers dramatically reduced costs and aggressively expanded their networks. The assumption reached by many carriers was that in order to become more flexible, a smaller aircraft must be used to reach many regional airports rather than larger aircraft that can only access hub airports in major cities.[1]

As both companies considered which options to pursue in order to satisfy the growing market, Airbus speculated that the hub-and-spoke system would prove to be the future for airlines and decided to launch the A-380 project in December 2000. Boeing's aircraft, dubbed the 787, was launched in 2005. This aircraft represents a fundamentally different vision, one anchored in the belief that the point-to-point system is the most sensible growth platform.

What is at stake for Boeing and Airbus? Boeing invested more than $8 billion in development for the 787, while Airbus went over budget, investing more than $14 billion and experienced a two-year delay in delivery to its customers. Boeing received solid orders for the midsized 787 and is determined to deliver the 787 in May 2008 as promised to avoid the problems that have plagued its competitor. Some manufacturing problems threatened to delay delivery, however, and are minimizing Boeing's margin for error.[2]

This case discusses the history of Boeing and the salient industry forces affecting the company, leading to the critical decisions faced by both competitors. The key strategic issues driving Boeing's competitive strategies are also outlined along with a discussion of strategies used to manage the competitive environment by both Boeing and Airbus, and the challenges facing both companies.

Boeing's History

William E. Boeing originally worked in the timber industry, and his knowledge of wooden structures led him to design and build an airplane, the B&W Seaplane. When the B&W was ready to fly, the test pilot was late and Mr. Boeing grew impatient, which prompted him to pilot the aircraft himself.[3] This example illustrates Mr. Boeing's level of determination, a key quality of his character, which was incorporated into his airplane manufacturing company.

Established on July 15, 1916, the company was originally called Pacific Aero Products Company. A year later Mr. Boeing changed the name to what is now the Boeing Airplane Company. Edgar Gott, William Boeing's first cousin, became president of the company in 1922.[4] Gott helped Boeing Co. obtain business contracts with the military; succeeding presidents, Philip G. Johnson and Clairmont L. Egtvedt, maintained this relationship with the government throughout WWII. Boeing became a powerhouse in large part due to its war effort, essentially because the military ordered numerous B-17 Bombers.

After the war many of the Bomber orders were canceled, so Boeing's management team tried to recover by

The authors would like to thank Professor Robert E. Hoskisson for his support and under whose direction the case was developed. The case solely provides material for class discussion. The authors do not intend to illustrate either effective or ineffective handling of a managerial situation. This case was developed with contributions from Hal Hardy and Emily Little.

diversifying its product offerings. Boeing began selling a luxurious four-engine commercial aircraft known as the Stratocruiser.[5] However, this aircraft was not the commercial success Boeing had hoped for and as a result, Boeing once again found itself at the drawing board.

William M. Allen took control of Boeing in 1945 and oversaw the building of the United States' first commercial jet airliner, the 707. The 707 had capacity for 156 passengers and helped the United States become a leader in commercial jet manufacturing. The 720 jet plane, which was faster, soon followed, but it had a shorter flying range. A demand for planes capable of flying long routes led Boeing to develop the 727.[6] This aircraft utilized one less engine than previous models and was thought to be significantly more comfortable and reliable than competitors' products.[7] Because most models are eventually discontinued to allocate resources to "new and improved models," the 727 was discontinued in 1984; however, by the beginning of 2000 almost 1,300 of these planes were still in service. Boeing achieved additional commercial success in 1967 and 1968 with the production of the 737 and 747. The 737 would become the best-selling commercial jet aircraft in history while the 747 would hold the passenger seating capacity record for 35 years. The 747 utilizes a double-decker configuration, allowing for a maximum of 524 passengers on board.[8]

In 1994, under the leadership of Frank Shrontz, Boeing developed the 777. This aircraft would actually be the first aircraft designed entirely by computer. "Throughout the design process, the airplane was 'pre-assembled' on the computer, eliminating the need for a costly, full-scale mock-up."[9] This aircraft became the longest range twin-engine aircraft in the world.

Thornton "T" Wilson became president of Boeing in 1968 and continued as CEO until 1986. Malcolm T. Stamper became president in 1972 and, in collaboration with Mr. Wilson, he led Boeing's development of the single-aisle 757 and the larger twin-aisle 767 in the wake of a new European competitor, Airbus. During these years Boeing also participated in space programs and military projects, such as the International Space Station and the development of new sophisticated missiles. Today, "Boeing is organized into two business units: Boeing Commercial Airplanes and Boeing Integrated Defense Systems," with the latter making Boeing the world's second-largest defense company.[10]

Philip M. Condit took over in 1996 but was quickly relieved of his position in 1997 because he underestimated Airbus's ability to compete with Boeing. Harry Stonecipher succeeded Condit and faced even more intense rivalry with Airbus. By 2003, Airbus had become the market leader, sending Boeing scrambling frantically to pursue new projects, such as the Sonic Cruiser. The Sonic Cruiser aimed to please customers with a faster, more comfortable ride for long-distance travel. The Cruiser would cut an hour off traditional travel time by flying at a higher elevation and a Mach speed of .98 (most aircraft fly at Mach .80).[11] When Lew Platt became board chair in December of 2003, Boeing abandoned the Sonic Cruiser project in order to focus its efforts on the 787 Dreamliner. Airlines were favoring planes that boasted fuel efficiency over those that offered faster speed. The Dreamliner, slated to fly in May 2008, is popular in the industry because of its potential fuel economy, one-piece composite fuselage sections, and eco-friendliness. It will cost slightly more than half of Airbus's complementary product, and currently has more than twice as much order-book value.[12]

Although each of Boeing's leaders sought to improve the organization during his tenure (for additional biographical information on Boeing's previous leadership, please refer to Exhibit 1), the rivalry with Boeing's key competitor is still intense.

Airbus: Boeing's Key Competitor

The industry for large commercial aircraft (LCA) is a duopoly composed of Boeing Co. and Airbus Industries. These two manufacturing giants have emerged in an unsteady industry whose fortune is based upon strategic timing and luck. Market share is overwhelmingly the most important consideration for each company when making strategic decisions. Essentially, market share determines success. Airbus, once considered a small player, swiftly emerged as an industry giant by focusing on the needs of the market, a standard product line, efficient production methods, and successful marketing ploys. Other players such as Douglas Aircraft Corporation and Lockheed Martin, who were successful and competitive corporations, fell from their positions due to failure in their demand forecast strategies and they merged with other competitors; especially significant was the merger between McDonnell Douglas and Boeing.[13]

Airplanes are grouped into families based on size, range, and technology. At the low end of the market are two single-aisle airplanes; the Boeing 737 and the Airbus A-320, which both seat about 190 people. These planes have each been extremely successful in generating sales, but fall short as revenue earners for both companies. The most profitable market segment has been the middle market, filled with the medium-sized aircraft, which seat from 200 to 300 passengers. Boeing's 757 and Airbus's A330-200 are the most popular planes in this segment. High-end jumbo airplanes fill the remaining segment of the market and are characterized by long-range flight capability, 300+ seats, and maximum use of technology. Each company attempts to develop its products to match the forecasted market demands by producing an airplane

Exhibit 1 Biographical Information on Boeing's Previous Leadership

Walter James McNerney Jr.
President, Chief Executive Officer, and Chairman of the Board of Directors of The Boeing Company, 2005–Present

McNerney received a BA from Yale University in 1971 and an MBA from Harvard in 1975. While receiving his education, McNerney played varsity baseball and hockey. McNerney started his executive career at General Electric in 1982. Over the next 19 years he held many positions including president and CEO of GE Aircraft Engines, GE Lighting, and GE Electrical Distribution and Control. He also spent time as president of GE Asia-Pacific and GE Information Services, and executive vice president of GE Capital. In 2001 McNerney joined 3M as CEO. After turning down two offers in two years, 3M CEO McNerney finally accepted the position as CEO and chairman of The Boeing Company in June of 2005. McNerney had already been a member of the board of directors at Boeing since 2001. He is the chair of the U.S.-China Business Council and serves on the World Business Council for Sustainable Development.

James A. Bell
Interim Chief Executive Officer of the Boeing Company, March 2005–June 2005; Chief Financial Officer, 2004–Present

James A. Bell received a BA in accounting from California State University. Mr. Bell started his career as an accountant at The Rockwell Company. He advanced through management at Rockwell, holding positions as senior internal auditor, accounting manager, and manager of general and cost accounting. When Rockwell's aerospace division was acquired by Boeing in 1996, Bell moved with it. At Boeing, Bell held positions as the vice president of contracts and pricing for the company's space and communications division, as well as senior vice president of finance and corporate controller. In 2004, following the firing of Michel M. Sears (due to a government contract scandal), Bell accepted the position as the chief financial officer of The Boeing Company. Bell also served as an interim CEO for a few months in 2005 between the time that Harry Stonecipher was forced to resign and James McNerney Jr. accepted the position.

Harry C. Stonecipher
President; 1997–2005; Chief Executive Officer of The Boeing Company, 2003–2005

Harry C. Stonecipher received a BS in physics from Tennessee Technological University in 1960. He began his career as a lab technician at General Motors. He then moved to GE's large engine division and worked his way up to become a vice president and then a division head. He left GE to go to Sundstrand where he became president and CEO after two years. After that he served as president and CEO of McDonnell Douglas until the merger with Boeing in 1997. At Boeing he served as the president and COO until 2003 when he filled the shoes of Philip M. Condit as CEO. In 2005, however, Stonecipher resigned at the request of the board after news of a "consensual relationship" with a female board member surfaced (violating Boeing's Code of Conduct).

Philip Murray Condit
Chief Executive Officer, 1996–2003; Chairman of the Board, 1997–2003 of The Boeing Company

Condit earned a Bachelor's degree in mechanical engineering from the University of California, Berkley; a master's degree in Aeronautical Engineering from Princeton; an MBA from the MIT Sloan School of Management; and a PhD in engineering from Science University of Tokyo. Condit started at Boeing in 1965 as an aerodynamics engineer, he then advanced to a lead engineer and soon after became a marketing manager. After a short break to earn his MBA he returned to Boeing, working through a myriad of leadership positions until he ascended to CEO in 1996 and board chair in 1997. His time as CEO and chairperson was characterized by a number of mergers and acquisitions as well as a struggle with increasing competition with Airbus. Condit was forced to resign in 2003 amidst corruption charges involving his freezing of a contract with the U.S. Air Force in 1997.

Thornton "T" A. Wilson
President, 1968–1972; Chief Executive Officer, 1969–1986; Chairman of the Board, 1972–1987; Chairman Emeritus of The Boeing Company, 1987–1993

Wilson received an aeronautical engineering degree from Iowa State University in 1943 and a master's degree in aeronautical engineering from the California Institute of Technology in 1948. Wilson begins his career with Boeing in 1943 and advanced rapidly. His first assignment of note was as project engineer on the B-52 and then was general manager of the proposal team for the Minuteman intercontinental ballistic missile program. Wilson became a vice president in 1963 and was put in charge of planning the Boeing corporate headquarters in 1964. He was named executive vice president in 1966 and president in 1968. Wilson became the CEO in 1969 and board chair in 1972.

Louis Gallois
Chief Executive Officer of Airbus, 2006–Present

Gallois graduated from both the Ecole Des Hautes Etudes Commerciales (where he received an education in economic science) and the Ecole Nationale de l'Administration. In 1972 Gallois started with the Treasury Department of the French government. During 1982–1987, Gallois worked his way up at the Cabinet Office of the Ministry of Research. His appointment as the Head of Civil and Military Cabinet Office of the French Ministry of Defense took place in 1988. It was in 1989 that Gallois shifted his career from government to the private sector when be became board chair and CEO of SNECMA, an airplane engine manufacturer. He then moved to Aerospatiale, another aerospace manufacture, as board chair and CEO. Gallois was chair of the French National Railways from 1996 to 2006. In October 2006, Gallois became CEO of Airbus.

Source: Executive Biographies, Wikipedia, http://en.wikipedia.org; http://www.boeing.com.

that offers the appropriate size, range, fuel efficiency, and technology. These forecasts are based on huge uncertainties, such as what size of airplane will airlines need in order to carry an unknown amount of people to and from large hub airports or smaller regional airports. These variables make accurate short-term projections and assumptions key to long-term success in an industry that is constantly changing.[14]

Airbus became a competitive global manufacturer of LCAs with the help of "launch aid," a form of government subsidies implemented to help a company, such as Airbus, compete and survive in industries where competitive giants such as Boeing have established distribution networks and economies of scale. Airbus was able to establish a significant market share and a brand name by making airplanes that addressed the needs of the market. Airlines had been "crying" for midsized cost efficient airplanes, and Airbus answered by building the A-320. The "commonality" that the A-320 had with other Airbus airplanes was attractive to airlines because of its potential to reduce pilot and attendant training costs as well as improve airplane turnaround time.[15]

Despite Airbus's strategy, Boeing had not embraced commonality among its products because of the changes and high costs that would be incurred at its current stage. As a result, the manufacturing giant fell from its number one position. In order for Boeing to survive its newfound misfortune, it needed to make serious changes in its strategy and business processes. The first aspect considered for business-process change would be its relationships with suppliers.

Suppliers

The importance of suppliers to aircraft manufacturers has shifted with advancements in technology. Chuck Agne, a former director of supplier management for Boeing's Integrated Defense Systems, said in 2004 that Boeing's strategy was to "move up the value chain," meaning that Boeing was going to focus less on the many details and more on their core competence, integration, and assembly. As part of this strategy, Boeing consolidated its supplier list and managed relationships only with those that provide quality products with the best value. Agne said, "What we have found is, the suppliers we're sticking with are the ones who are able to move up that value chain with us."[16]

Traditionally, most manufacturers similar to Boeing completed all research and production in-house. Technological research and development is seen as a competitive advantage that must be closely guarded within the airplane production industry. Boeing's key technical expertise—such as wing technology and new lightweight materials such as composites—are considered its core competencies. Boeing traditionally believed that outsourcing these components to suppliers would give the suppliers control over manufacturing and ultimately place the supplier in control when determining its share of revenue. However, it is no longer a sensible option for Boeing to keep an entire production line in-house. Thus, a new trend emerged in the production of new aircraft, such as the 787 Dreamliner. For the first time Boeing announced it would "offload" (Boeing's term for *outsourcing*)[17] the design of it wings and parts of its fuselage to Japan, and also outsource its fuselage panel work to an Italian company. It is estimated that now 70 percent of the components of a given airplane are outsourced. As such, Boeing is responsible for plane assembly, assuming the title of "Systems Integrator."[18]

Boeing also sought strategic partnerships globally in an effort to reduce costs and perhaps generate sales. By outsourcing to countries such as China and India, Boeing entered what is called an "offset agreement," such that they obtain aircraft sales in return for manufacturing work. This arrangement allowed Boeing to gain more substantial entry into two of the largest and fastest growing airplane markets (China and India).[19]

One of the main attractions for establishing strategic partnerships is the ability to distribute some of the risk associated with the large investment required to build an airplane. By outsourcing, LCA manufacturers are able to share risks and focus their efforts on marketing and supplier relationships. By developing components of the 787 Dreamliner in Japan, Boeing also acquires support from Asian Airlines through the purchase of planes, aided by Japanese government incentives. Another indirect financial benefit to Boeing is the fact that the Japanese and Italian companies are all subsidized by their governments. If successful, the projects present multiple opportunities for Boeing to develop and market their product in an entirely new way.[20] However, risk sharing also equates to profit sharing.

In addition to diminished profits, other implications related to outsourcing are worth noting. First of all, many Boeing employees, including the engineers, are against the outsourcing for obvious reasons; they feel that their jobs are at stake and believe that Boeing has lost sight of its larger interests.[21] Former CEO Harry Stonecipher countered outsourcing concerns by stating, "We have to understand that the go-it-alone approach doesn't work in today's world. Companies will increasingly focus on their core competencies. As they do, they will outsource (a) where the markets are, and (b) where the best people to do the job are."[22] Eventually union leaders and employees were able to acknowledge that outsourcing is about more than just cutting jobs, it is about competing efficiently in a global industry.[23]

Additional controversy centers on whether Boeing is transferring knowledge vital to U.S. military security and commercial competitiveness. The United States has given Boeing's aerospace and defense divisions many subsidies to develop technology. Some of this technology has presumably been transferred to Boeing's aircraft manufacturing division. Japanese suppliers may use the technology shared by Boeing to eventually design their own airplanes. Over the past three years, "The Japanese government and its heavy industrial firms have openly sought to establish Japan as an aerospace power for generations."[24] A Japanese aerospace giant would pose a huge threat to both Boeing and Airbus because it would be able to capitalize on political and trade ties with the flourishing Asia-Pacific markets.[25]

Comparatively, Airbus has kept tighter control over the knowledge it shares with suppliers. In fact, in late 2005 Airbus tightened control over tier one suppliers, directing them to outsource only minimal amounts of work to Asian countries.[26] As such, most of their suppliers are associated with European Union countries, most of which have some ownership in Airbus's parent, EADS. Airbus models its relationship with suppliers after Wal-Mart and utilizes JIT, just-in-time delivery. To further develop efficiencies it follows the approach of the auto industry and requests that its suppliers deliver all components in prepackaged trays that can be loaded onto carts similar to a chest of drawers. Assembly line workers are able to get everything they need without having to leave their stations. As a result, some of Airbus's assembly lines have nearly doubled their efficiency in the past two years.[27]

Clearly, Airbus and Boeing are utilizing relatively different strategies concerning value chain logistics. Consequently, the question remains: Which strategic approach to value chain management will provide better efficiency and long-run strategic advantage? Boeing must continuously monitor and evaluate over time these key concerns in order to maintain positive relations with its stakeholders, specifically its customers and employees.

Customers

Boeing's mission statement signifies that one of its core competencies lays in "detailed customer knowledge and focus."[28] Customers have the choice of buying new or used planes and to license them or purchase them entirely. The customers for Boeing's commercial division are the airlines of the world, and governments are the customers for the defense division. For the commercial division, carriers in China and India are becoming valuable overseas customers, as income rises in these countries along with a forecasted air traffic growth of 8.8 percent in China through the year 2024, and 25 percent growth yearly in India.[29] Half of the orders for the Boeing 787 Dreamliner are from Asia-Pacific clients. Although it is early in the process, the Airbus A-380 currently has

not been purchased by any American carriers, which may suggest that Boeing will dominate the superjumbo aircraft market within the United States.[30] Australia's carrier, Qantas, has indicated it will purchase 115 of its 787 Dreamliners valued at more than $14 billion.[31]

United Airlines has traditionally been Boeing's largest domestic customer,[32] and low-cost airlines have also been key clients for Boeing. However, successful sales campaigns by Airbus resulted in some lost sales for Boeing with the low-cost airlines. JetBlue, when it first emerged in the low-cost industry, announced its decision to purchase Airbus's A-320 over Boeing's 737.[33] JetBlue liked the wider seats, more leg room, and more overhead storage that the A-320 could offer its passengers.

Through early 2004, a major problem seemed to lay in the fact that Boeing had a weak sales force and Airbus was consistently pricing its products below Boeing's prices.[34] These factors, coupled with superior technology in the A-320, won Airbus a considerable amount of Boeing's previous contracts. Boeing's list of lost deals was getting longer and longer, with notable losses to Airbus from United Airlines, AirBerlin, Air Asia, and Southwest. The situation became extremely alarming to Boeing, and in the latter half of 2004 and the beginning of 2005, numerous changes were made in Boeing's sales force. Senior executives and board members were sent into the field to garner sales, decision making was sped up, and the salespeople were empowered to take more risks in pricing.[35]

Frustration with the two-year delay in delivery of the Airbus A-380 (as discussed later in the case) allowed Boeing to acquire some valuable customers from Airbus, including FedEx. FedEx is experiencing growing demand for international freight shipments and needs more planes in its fleet sooner than Airbus can deliver, which resulted in a $2.3 billion loss for Airbus and a $3.6 billion gain for Boeing in new orders.[36] Virgin, also frustrated with the Airbus delays, canceled its order for the A-380 and partnered with Boeing, ordering 15 of its 787s.[37]

In addition to the battle for sales, Boeing and Airbus have been engaged in an ongoing dispute concerning the role that governments play in the success of the two companies.

Government Issues

Boeing attributes much of Airbus's success to its extensive financial support through subsidies called "launch aid" from Spain, France, Germany, and Great Britain, the four member countries that have ownership interests in EADS, the parent of Airbus. During the 1980s Airbus was able to create its multitude of products because of the financial support it relied on from these countries. Airbus still receives a debatable amount, thought to be $1.7 billion for the year 2005.[38]

Boeing was able to further its case against "launch aid" when Airbus released plans to develop the A-350 in response to Boeing's 787, which suspiciously will be developed despite the huge financial losses Airbus accumulated due the problems associated with its A-380 superjumbo jet.[39] Boeing sought protection from the World Trade Organization from these subsidies because they threaten its competitiveness in the global economy. Conversely, Airbus fired back, claiming that Boeing also receives subsidies from the U.S. government. This financial aid comes in the form of "federal research and development contracts from NASA and the Pentagon and, more recently, tax breaks from Washington State."[40] Those in support of Boeing counter with the argument that these contracts are business deals associated with its defense business (not its commercial airlines business) and for which other companies can compete and therefore are not defined as subsidies.[41] Nonetheless, Airbus argues that the government funded technology assists in commercial plane development because such technology is transferable.

For example, about half of the 787 will consist of composites of which knowledge can be directly drawn from Boeing's experience with the B-2 stealth bomber program. However, Airbus also has the ability to draw on military technology from its parent company EADS, so the true validity within this argument is uncertain. Both companies decided to file complaints with the WTO in 2004. The acceptance of government subsidies by global corporations, known as "extraterritorial income," is deemed illegal by the WTO. In reality both companies receive almost equal support from their governments, and tracking or even ending these funds is difficult. The WTO has little judicial power and really only provides leverage to settle disputes.

It is understood that WTO cases are fraught with risk and have uncertain outcomes and often last for years. Also, the European Union and the United States, the two sides in this dispute, are the strongest members in the WTO. The outcome is yet to be determined, but the ultimate conclusion is likely to have an impact on the finances of both firms.[42]

Financials

Boeing's revenue increased nearly 15 percent from 2005 to 2006 ($53,621 million to $61,530 million). In part, this extraordinary growth can be attributed to the record-breaking number of orders and a one-third increase in production capacity. Boeing's net profit on this revenue more than doubled from $464 million in 2005 to $980 million in 2006. This jump equates to net change of 111.2 percent. For investors it is great news. It allowed Boeing to increase its earnings per share (EPS) from $0.59 in 2005 to $1.28 in 2006 (see Exhibits 2, 3, and 4).

Boeing's financial margins indicate how well the organization is utilizing sales dollars. Boeing's gross margin increased at the end of 2006 to 17.6 percent from 14.6 percent in 2005. Gross margin provides insight into the profit available from the sales dollars. Generally, the higher the percentage of gross margin, the more flexible the organization can be in its operating decisions. The gross margin for the industry average is 13.8 percent for 2006 (see Exhibits 2, 3, and 4). Due to its increased flexibility Boeing increased its spending for R&D by nearly $1 billion.

Operating margin (or operating profit margin) increased 2.7 percentage points in 2006 from 2005, moving from 3.9 percent to 6.6 percent. This ratio is useful in determining the earnings before taxes (EBIT) on each dollar. The stronger the ratio, the better, and when coupled with growth year over year, this ratio equates to a favorable analysis. Net margin also increased from 2005 (3.3%) to 2006 (5.6%) for a net change of 2.3 percentage points, indicating that Boeing is doing a better job at controlling its costs and converting its revenue dollars into profit (see Exhibits 2, 3, and 4). Cash flow grew to be 12 percent of revenues, up $.5 billion from $7 billion in 2005 (see Exhibit 7).

Boeing is heavily leveraged compared to its industry; its debt-to-equity ratio is 2.01, compared to the industry average of 0.96. However, when building products with budgets discussed in terms of billions of U.S. dollars, leveraging perhaps allows for better use of assets. This rationale can be seen in Boeing's 2006 credit rating of A3, as provided by Moody's Investors Service.[43] Despite the positive credit rating it is especially important for Boeing to contain its debt levels and use its financial resources wisely in order to come out on top with its strategy versus Airbus's strategy. (For a broader picture of Boeing's financial condition and a comparison of Airbus's financials please refer to Exhibits 5, 6, 7, and 8.)

Opposing Strategies

In comparing the strategies of Boeing and Airbus, one analyst concluded the following: "In today's marketplace, distinct differences in the way competitive products work have become increasingly rare. But functional product differentiation is exactly what the rivalry between the Airbus A-380 and the Boeing 787 Dreamliner is all about: Two companies with fundamentally different products, based on diametrically opposite visions of the future."[44] Boeing maintains that increased fragmentation in the form of point-to-point travel will not only solve the problem of airport congestion, but also appeal to travelers. Airbus on the other hand believes that hub-to-hub travel, especially between major cities will continue to grow—with an emphasis on the Asian markets.

Exhibit 2 Boeing Financial Ratios with Contrast

Growth Rates %	Company	Industry	S&P 500
Sales (Qtr vs year ago qtr)	26.20	16.40	13.60
Net Income (YTD vs YTD)	−14.00	28.10	24.40
Net Income (Qtr vs year ago qtr)	111.20	57.40	80.80
Sales (5-Year Annual Avg.)	1.12	8.39	13.12
Net Income (5-Year Annual Avg.)	−4.83	58.28	22.42
Dividends (5-Year Annual Avg.)	12.03	11.41	9.95

Price Ratios	Company	Industry	S&P 500
Current P/E Ratio	33.1	22.2	21.9
P/E Ratio 5-Year High	65.3	88.0	61.3
P/E Ratio 5-Year Low	9.0	20.9	14.8
Price/Sales Ratio	1.20	1.28	2.77
Price/Book Value	15.63	7.46	4.06
Price/Cash Flow Ratio	19.80	16.10	14.80

Profit Margins %	Company	Industry	S&P 500
Gross Margin	18.0	13.8	36.8
Pre-Tax Margin	5.2	5.1	19.1
Net Profit Margin	3.6	2.7	13.4
5Yr Gross Margin (5-Year Avg.)	15.3	14.5	35.6
5Yr PreTax Margin (5-Year Avg.)	4.3	5.5	17.2
5Yr Net Profit Margin (5-Year Avg.)	3.5	4.0	11.8

Financial Condition	Company	Industry	S&P 500
Debt/Equity Ratio	2.01	0.96	1.32
Current Ratio	0.8	1.2	1.2
Quick Ratio	0.5	0.8	1.0
Interest Coverage	12.5	11.1	24.7
Leverage Ratio	10.9	5.5	4.6
Book Value/Share	6.01	18.51	19.14

Investment Returns %	Company	Industry	S&P 500
Return On Equity	27.9	24.5	21.6
Return On Assets	3.9	5.5	8.0
Return On Capital	8.2	9.8	10.5
Return On Equity (5-Year Avg.)	20.8	16.5	20.2
Return On Assets (5-Year Avg.)	3.5	4.0	6.6
Return On Capital (5-Year Avg.)	6.1	6.5	8.7

Management Efficiency	Company	Industry	S&P 500
Income/Employee	14,325	18,312	104,736
Revenue/Employee	399,546	315,545	856,844
Receivable Turnover	11.7	19.5	17.5
Inventory Turnover	6.3	9.6	8.9
Asset Turnover	1.1	1.1	0.8

Source: Boeing Company Financial Ratios, *Reuters,* http://stocks.us.reuters.com/stocks/ratios.asp?symbol=BA&WT.

Exhibit 3 Boeing Performance Summary, 10 years

	Avg P/E	Price/Sales	Price/Book	Net Profit Margin (%)
12/06	28.20	1.14	14.79	3.6
12/05	19.50	1.05	5.08	4.8
12/04	21.30	0.82	3.82	3.5
12/03	39.50	0.68	4.36	1.4
12/02	13.90	0.50	3.43	4.3
12/01	15.10	0.55	2.86	4.9
12/00	19.90	1.12	5.01	4.1
12/99	16.50	0.66	3.15	4.0
12/98	37.70	0.57	2.48	2.0
12/97	−286.40	1.04	3.68	−0.4

	Book Value/Share	Debt/Equity	Return on Equity (%)	Return on Assets (%)	Interest Coverage
12/06	$6.01	2.01	46.5	4.3	12.0
12/05	$13.82	0.97	23.2	4.3	9.3
12/04	$13.56	1.08	16.1	3.2	5.7
12/03	$9.67	1.77	8.4	1.3	NA
12/02	$9.62	1.87	29.8	4.4	10.9
12/01	$13.57	1.13	26.1	5.8	10.7
12/00	$13.18	0.80	19.3	5.0	6.7
12/99	$13.16	0.59	20.1	6.4	7.3
12/98	$13.13	0.57	9.1	3.0	3.6
12/97	$13.31	0.53	−1.4	−0.5	−0.4

Source: Boeing Company Financial Ratios, *Reuters,* http://stocks.us.reuters.com/stocks/ratios.asp?symbol=BA.

The solution for Boeing is the 787 Dreamliner, a midsized twin-engine airplane with long-haul capabilities, longer than any of Boeing's previous models. Boeing has championed the 787 as "revolutionary," encompassing major changes in all aspects of the airplane including design, production, and finance. Based on a decade of focus groups and scientific studies, the objective for the 787 has been to offer the passenger the most comfortable point-to-point travel experience with as few intermediate stops as possible. The 787 will have more standing room, larger windows and bathrooms, ambient light settings in the cabin to adjust to the time of day, and the cabin will also be set at a higher humidity level. For the airlines it is an attractive product because it is fuel efficient (burning 27 percent less fuel per passenger than the A-380[45]), made from lightweight composite materials, and simple to operate.[46]

Airbus's offering is dubbed the A-380, or commonly referred to as the "superjumbo." The A-380 will be the largest aircraft in the world, 35 percent larger than the current largest, the Boeing 747-400. The A-380 is 239 feet long and stands over 80 feet tall.[47] It can be configured with bars and specialty boutiques. With a wing span of almost 300 feet, the A-380 can transport 550 passengers

in a typical three-class layout.[48] Airbus claims the A-380 will allow 10 million additional passengers per year to fly between airports with no increase in flights.[49] Despite a size that provides boasting rights, it also creates challenges because the A-380 will only be able to utilize the largest airports—most facilities are unable to accommodate this aircraft. Airports are having to spend millions of dollars to accommodate this new superjumbo plane. For example, London's Heathrow airport has already spent $909 million for upgrades to prepare for the A-380.[50] Thus, Boeing has the opportunity to exploit smaller airports. The success of Boeing's strategy will depend largely upon its marketing approach. (See Exhibits 9 and 10 to view the differences in features and success between the 787 and A-380.)

Marketing Approach

As a result of the billions of dollars already spent, and the future of the firm at stake, Boeing has marketed the 787 extensively. Boeing recognized that as its products became more sophisticated, it needed to revamp its marketing approach. Rob Pollack, vice president of branding at Boeing, said, "We realized that if you have the most

Exhibit 4 Financial Highlights

Financial Highlights			
Sales	61.53Bil	Revenue/Share	78.68
Income	2.21Bil	Earnings/Share	2.85
Net Profit Margin	3.59%	Book Value/Share	6.01
Return on Equity	27.93%	Dividend Rate	1.40
Debt/Equity Ratio	2.01	Payout Ratio	43.00%

Revenue–Quarterly Results (in Millions)			
	FY (12/06)	FY (12/05)	FY (12/04)
1st Qtr	14,264.0	12,681.0	12,903.0
2nd Qtr	14,986.0	14,684.0	13,088.0
3rd Qtr	14,739.0	12,355.0	13,152.0
4th Qtr	17,541.0	13,901.0	13,314.0
Total	61,530.0	53,621.0	52,457.0

Earnings Per Share–Quarterly Results			
	FY (12/06)	FY (12/05)	FY (12/04)
1st Qtr	$0.91	$0.68	$0.77
2nd Qtr	−$0.21	$0.71	$0.75
3rd Qtr	$0.90	$1.28	$0.56
4th Qtr	$1.30	$0.62	$0.24
Total	$2.90	$3.29	$2.32

Qtr. over Qtr. EPS Growth Rate			
	FY (12/06)	FY (12/05)	FY (12/04)
1st Qtr	47%	183%	—
2nd Qtr	NA	4%	−3%
3rd Qtr	NA	80%	−25%
4th Qtr	44%	−52%	−57%

Yr. over Yr. EPS Growth Rate		
	FY (12/06)	FY (12/05)
1st Qtr	34%	−12%
2nd Qtr	NA	−5%
3rd Qtr	−30%	129%
4th Qtr	110%	158%

Source: Boeing Company Financial Highlights, *Reuters*, http://stocks.us.reuters.com/stocks/financialHighlights.asp?symbol=BA.

state-of-the-art products in the world, how you represent yourself has to be done with state-of-the-art marketing techniques." The new strategy presents Boeing as not just a manufacturer, but a "life cycle partner," providing its customers with business solutions through the full lifespan of its products.[51] "Trade shows are now more about creating an immersion than a spectacle. Media is designed to bring the brand to life. Press events strive to stamp an indelible message."[52] Prospective clients are now invited to Boeing's Customer Experience Center, a 30,000-square-foot facility that allows an interactive experience in which Boeing's sales force can address the needs, concerns, and challenges of its customers. "The studio is facilitating discussions that might never have taken place between Boeing and its clients."[53]

The effort taken to improve its marketing and sales approach will hopefully prove to benefit Boeing as it strives to overcome the challenges that lay ahead.

The Challenges Ahead

As previously mentioned, Airbus has experienced significant delays and other problems surrounding the A-380 project. Not only has Airbus run 50 percent over

budget, but they also face hundreds of millions of dollars in penalties for delays. EADS's earnings will decrease by $6 billion over the next four years, and the share price has declined 21 percent in the past year (2006). Additionally, Christian Streiff was forced to quit after only three months in his position as CEO.[54] The problems started when mechanics spent weeks routing 348 miles of bundled electrical wiring in each plane, but came up short when attempting to connect one section to another. The cause was determined to be the fact that engineers in Hamburg were drawing on two-dimensional computer programs whereas engineers in Toulouse were using three-dimensional programs.[55]

Multiple redesigns of the proposed A-350 model intended to compete with Boeing's 787 Dreamliner have been delayed as well, resulting in more bad press for Airbus. Six years ago, Airbus executives said the company would need to sell 250 A-380s to break even on the investment. This number has now risen to more than 400 due to delays and cancelations. The company has ramped up production of its A-320 model, the single-aisle aircraft purchased by many low-cost carriers, in an effort to earn badly needed cash. This tactic could prove disastrous if suppliers are not able to keep up with Airbus's schedule.

Exhibit 5 Boeing Income Statement

Boeing	2006	2005	2004	2003	2002
Period End Date	12/31/2006	12/31/2005	12/31/2004	12/31/2003	12/31/2002
Period Length	12 Months	12 Months	12 Months	12 Months	12 Months
Stmt Source	10-K	10-K	10-K	10-K	10-K
Stmt Source Date	2/16/2007	2/16/2007	2/16/2007	2/28/2005	2/28/2005
Stmt Update Type	Updated	Reclassified	Reclassified	Restated	Restated
Revenue	61,530.00	53,621.00	51,400.00	50,256.00	53,831.00
Total Revenue	**61,530.00**	**53,621.00**	**51,400.00**	**50,256.00**	**53,831.00**
Cost of Revenue, Total	50,437.00	44,984.00	43,968.00	44,150.00	45,804.00
Gross Profit	**11,093.00**	**8,637.00**	**7,432.00**	**6,106.00**	**8,027.00**
Selling/General/Administrative Expenses, Total	4,171.00	4,228.00	3,657.00	3,200.00	2,959.00
Research & Development	3,257.00	2,205.00	1,879.00	1,651.00	1,639.00
Depreciation/Amortization	0	0	3	0	0
Interest Expense (Income), Net Operating	−146	−88	−91	−28	49
Unusual Expense (Income)	571	0	0	892	−2
Other Operating Expenses, Total	226	−520	−23	−7	−44
Operating Income	**3,014.00**	**2,812.00**	**2,007.00**	**398**	**3,426.00**
Interest Income (Expense), Net Non-Operating	−240	−294	−335	−358	−320
Gain (Loss) on Sale of Assets	0	0	0	0	0
Other, Net	420	301	288	460	37
Income Before Tax	**3,194.00**	**2,819.00**	**1,960.00**	**500**	**3,143.00**
Income Tax, Total	988	257	140	−185	847
Income After Tax	**2,206.00**	**2,562.00**	**1,820.00**	**685**	**2,296.00**
Minority Interest	0	0	0	0	0
Equity In Affiliates	0	0	0	0	0
U.S. GAAP Adjustment	0	0	0	0	0
Net Income Before Extra Items	**2,206.00**	**2,562.00**	**1,820.00**	**685**	**2,296.00**
Total Extraordinary Items	9	10	52	33	−1,804.00
Accounting Change	0	17	0	0	−1,827.00
Discontinued Operations	9	−7	52	33	23
Net Income	**2,215.00**	**2,572.00**	**1,872.00**	**718**	**492**
Total Adjustments to Net Income	0	0	0	0	0

Source: Boeing Company Financial Statements, *Reuters*, http://stocks.us.reuters.com/stocks/incomeStatement.asp.

Exhibit 6 Boeing Balance Sheet

Boeing	2006	2005	2004	2003	2002
Period End Date	12/31/2006	12/31/2005	12/31/2004	12/31/2003	12/31/2002
Stmt Source	10-K	10-K	10-K	10-K	10-K
Stmt Source Date	2/16/2007	2/16/2007	2/28/2006	2/28/2005	2/27/2003
Stmt Update Type	Updated	Restated	Restated	Restated	Updated
Assets					
Cash and Short-Term Investments	6,386.00	5,966.00	3,523.00	4,633.00	2,333.00
Cash & Equivalents	6,118.00	5,412.00	3,204.00	4,633.00	2,333.00
Short-Term Investments	268	554	319	0	0
Total Receivables, Net	5,655.00	5,613.00	5,269.00	5,522.00	6,296.00
Accounts Receivable—Trade, Net	5,285.00	5,246.00	4,653.00	4,466.00	5,007.00
Accounts Receivable—Trade, Gross	5,368.00	5,336.00	0	0	0
Provision for Doubtful Accounts	−83	−90	0	0	0
Notes Receivable—Short-Term	370	367	616	857	1,289.00
Receivables—Other	0	0	0	199	0
Total Inventory	8,105.00	7,878.00	6,508.00	5,338.00	6,184.00
Prepaid Expenses	0	0	0	0	0
Other Current Assets, Total	2,837.00	2,449.00	2,061.00	3,798.00	2,042.00
Total Current Assets	**22,983.00**	**21,906.00**	**17,361.00**	**19,291.00**	**16,855.00**
Property/Plant/Equipment, Total—Net	7,675.00	8,420.00	8,443.00	8,597.00	8,765.00
Goodwill, Net	3,047.00	1,924.00	1,948.00	1,913.00	2,760.00
Intangibles, Net	1,426.00	671	955	1,035.00	1,128.00
Long-Term Investments	4,085.00	2,852.00	3,050.00	646	0
Note Receivable—Long-Term	8,520.00	9,639.00	10,385.00	10,057.00	10,922.00
Other Long-Term Assets, Total	4,058.00	14,584.00	14,082.00	11,447.00	11,912.00
Other Assets, Total	0	0	0	0	0
Total Assets	**51,794.00**	**59,996.00**	**56,224.00**	**52,986.00**	**52,342.00**
Liabilities and Shareholders' Equity					
Accounts Payable	16,201.00	16,513.00	14,869.00	13,514.00	13,739.00
Payable/Accrued	0	0	0	0	0
Accrued Expenses	0	0	0	0	0
Notes Payable/Short-Term Debt	0	0	0	0	0
Current Port. of LT Debt/Capital Leases	1,381.00	1,189.00	1,321.00	1,144.00	1,814.00
Other Current Liabilities, Total	12,119.00	10,424.00	6,906.00	3,741.00	4,257.00
Total Current Liabilities	**29,701.00**	**28,126.00**	**23,096.00**	**18,399.00**	**19,810.00**
Total Long-Term Debt	8,157.00	9,538.00	10,879.00	13,299.00	12,589.00
Long-Term Debt	8,157.00	9,538.00	10,879.00	13,299.00	12,589.00
Deferred Income Tax	0	2,067.00	1,090.00	0	0

(continued)

Exhibit 6 Boeing Balance Sheet *(continued)*

Boeing	2006	2005	2004	2003	2002
Minority Interest	0	0	0	0	0
Other Liabilities, Total	9,197.00	9,206.00	9,873.00	13,149.00	12,247.00
Total Liabilities	**47,055.00**	**48,937.00**	**44,938.00**	**44,847.00**	**44,646.00**
Redeemable Preferred Stock	0	0	0	0	0
Preferred Stock—Non Redeemable, Net	0	0	0	0	0
Common Stock	5,061.00	5,061.00	5,059.00	5,059.00	5,059.00
Additional Paid-In Capital	4,655.00	4,371.00	3,420.00	2,880.00	2,141.00
Retained Earnings (Accumulated Deficit)	18,453.00	17,276.00	15,565.00	14,407.00	14,262.00
Treasury Stock—Common	−12,459.00	−11,075.00	−8,810.00	−8,322.00	−8,397.00
ESOP Debt Guarantee	−2,754.00	−2,796.00	−2,023.00	−1,740.00	−1,324.00
Other Equity, Total	−8,217.00	−1,778.00	−1,925.00	−4,145.00	−4,045.00
Total Equity	**4,739.00**	**11,059.00**	**11,286.00**	**8,139.00**	**7,696.00**
Total Liabilities & Shareholders' Equity	**51,794.00**	**59,996.00**	**56,224.00**	**52,986.00**	**52,342.00**
Total Common Shares Outstanding	788.74	800.17	832.18	841.48	799.66
Total Preferred Shares Outstanding	0	0	0	0	0

Source: Boeing Company Financial Statements, *Reuters,* http://stocks.us.reuters.com/stocks/balanceSheet.asp.

However, Airbus executives insist that losses will be recouped by 2010.[56]

Boeing also invested heavily in its 787 project and faced criticism over weight issues and composite construction materials. Although both firms experienced setbacks, Airbus has taken the brunt of these setbacks, as already noted. Boeing's challenges have more to do with potential production delays and meeting its massive order-backlog on time. In 2007, Boeing had already announced some delays. Boeing officials noted that "it is possible to overcome a nearly four-month delay in the 787 Dreamliner program and deliver the first jet on time in May [2008]."[57] However, "Industry observers and a number of the plane's suppliers say it would be the aerospace equivalent of hitting a hole in one on a golf course." The complexity of producing an aircraft is significant, but when you have to simultaneously bring together a large array of suppliers and the various parts that they produce to meet a deadline, the possibilities for error increase geometrically.

In the long term, Boeing must wonder whether it is going to create a new competitor in Japan and eventually in China, given its outsourcing strategy. Also, Airbus countered Boeing's 787 product strategy with the A-350 in addition to the A-380 (Boeing does not have a comparable product, unless they can effectively update the 747). Thus, both Boeing and Airbus face significant strategic challenges.

Conclusion

Both Boeing and Airbus spent billions of dollars in developing their unique strategies. Airbus bet that the way to cope with increased customer demand is to offer a platform, namely the A-380, capable of moving mass amounts of people using the hub system. Alternatively, Boeing focused on the 787 to offer consumers long-range capabilities while at the same time using direct connections. Initial trends indicate support for Boeing strategies based on accumulated orders for the 787, numbering nearly 500, whereas Airbus's A-380 has not received the amount of orders originally forecasted. Airbus also experienced major setbacks with the two-year delivery delay while running nearly 50 percent over budget[58] and losing orders from frustrated customers. Thus, Boeing currently holds the lead in the aerospace

Exhibit 7 Boeing Statement of Cash Flows

Boeing	2006	2005	2004	2003	2002
Period End Date	12/31/2006	12/31/2005	12/31/2004	12/31/2003	12/31/2002
Net Income/Starting Line	2,215.00	2,572.00	1,872.00	718	492
Depreciation/Depletion	1,445.00	1,412.00	1,412.00	1,306.00	1,362.00
Amortization	100	91	97	94	88
Non-Cash Items	1,552.00	1,807.00	1,538.00	1,737.00	2,907.00
Discontinued Operations	−14	12	−51	63	76
Unusual Items	344	−437	102	1,068.00	2,723.00
Other Non-Cash Items	1,222.00	2,232.00	1,487.00	606	108
Changes in Working Capital	2,187.00	1,118.00	−1,415.00	−1,079.00	−2,513.00
Accounts Receivable	−244	−592	−241	357	−155
Inventories	444	−1,965.00	535	191	1,507.00
Prepaid Expenses	−522	−1,862.00	−4,355.00	−1,728.00	−340
Other Assets	718	600	−425	−1,321.00	−2,038.00
Accounts Payable	−744	1,147.00	1,321.00	−132	−441
Accrued Expenses	114	30	214	311	67
Taxes Payable	933	628	1,086.00	320	322
Other Liabilities	1,677.00	3,086.00	705	876	−978
Other Operating Cash Flow	−189	46	−255	47	−457
Cash from Operating Activities	**7,499.00**	**7,000.00**	**3,504.00**	**2,776.00**	**2,336.00**
Capital Expenditures	−1,681.00	−1,547.00	−1,246.00	−836	−1,001.00
Purchase of Fixed Assets	−1,681.00	−1,547.00	−1,246.00	−836	−1,001.00
Other Investing Cash Flow Items, Total	−1,505.00	1,449.00	−200	896	−381
Acquisition of Business	−1,854.00	−172	−34	289	−22
Sale of Business	123	1,709.00	194	186	157
Sale of Fixed Assets	225	51	2,285.00	95	0
Sale/Maturity of Investment	2,850.00	2,725.00	1,323.00	203	140
Purchase of Investments	−2,815.00	−2,866.00	−4,142.00	−102	−505
Other Investing Cash Flow	−34	2	174	225	−151
Cash from Investing Activities	**−3,186.00**	**−98**	**−1,446.00**	**60**	**−1,382.00**
Financing Cash Flow Items	395	70	23	0	0
Other Financing Cash Flow	395	70	23	0	0
Total Cash Dividends Paid	−956	−820	−648	−572	−571
Issuance (Retirement) of Stock, Net	−1,404.00	−2,529.00	−654	18	67
Issuance (Retirement) of Debt, Net	−1,680.00	−1,378.00	−2,208.00	18	1,250.00
Cash from Financing Activities	**−3,645.00**	**−4,657.00**	**−3,487.00**	**−536**	**746**
Foreign Exchange Effects	38	−37	0	0	0
Net Change in Cash	**706**	**2,208.00**	**−1,429.00**	**2,300.00**	**1,700.00**
Net Cash, Beginning Balance	5,412.00	3,204.00	4,633.00	2,333.00	633
Net Cash, Ending Balance	6,118.00	5,412.00	3,204.00	4,633.00	2,333.00

Source: Boeing Financial Statements, *Reuters,* http://stocks.us.reuters.com/stocks/cashFlowStatement.

Exhibit 8 Airbus Select Financials

(Euro, million)	2006	2005	2004	2003
EBIT	(572)	2307	1919	1353
Total Revenue	25190	22179	20224	19048
Assets	33958	33226	35044	29290
Goodwill	6374	6987	6883	6342
Liabilities	24096	20553	17019	17501
Provisions	6272	4205	0	0
Capital Expenditures	1750	1864	2778	2027
Depreciation, Amortization	1140	1131	1088	1628
R&D	2035	1659	1734	1819
Exchange Rate	0.757855	0.844589	0.738788	0.793869

(U.S., million)	2006	2005	2004	2003
EBIT	(433)	1948	1418	1074
Total Revenue	19090	18732	14941	15122
Assets	25735	28062	25890	23252
Goodwill	4831	5901	5085	5035
Liabilities	18261	17359	12573	13894
Provisions	4753	3551	0	0
Capital Expenditures	1326	1574	2052	1609
Depreciation, Amortization	864	955	804	1292
R&D	1542	1401	1281	1444

Source: 2006, 2005, 2004, *EADS Annual Reports,* www.eads.com/1024/en/investor/Reports/Archive/Archives.html.

Exhibit 9 Dreamliner (787) vs. Superjumbo (A-380)

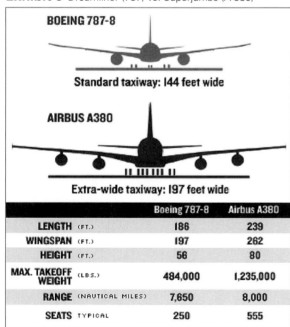

Source: 2007, Dissecting the A-380's troubles, *Fortune,* http://www.fortune.com, March 5.

Exhibit 10 Boeing vs. Airbus Orders

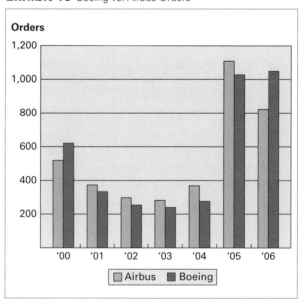

Source: 2007, Dissecting the A-380's troubles, *Fortune,* http://www.fortune.com, March 5.

industry. However, the Asian markets are growing, and demand for large aircraft to meet air traffic increases is also likely to grow. Boeing may be confident in its strategy, but recent minor delays serve as a reminder that Boeing cannot get too comfortable. The first A-380 is slated to be delivered to Singapore Airlines on October

15, 2007.[59] Will this aircraft become a sensation? Will Airbus be able to recoup its costs by 2010 and flourish in the industry? Will Boeing realize continued strategic success, given Airbus's A-350 program, which was established to compete with the 787?

Notes

1. 2001, Aviation competition: Regional jet service yet to reach many small communities, United States General Accounting Office, http://www.gao.gov, February, 5–10; D. Schlossberg, 2007, FAA fights proliferation of small planes, http://www.consumeraffairs.com, August 23.
2. J. L. Lunsford, 2007, Boeing's 787 faces less room for error: Dreamliner flight tests pushed by months; sticking to delivery date, *Wall Street Journal*, September 6, A13.
3. 2007, Boeing, *Wikipedia*, http://en.wikipedia.org/wiki/Boeing.
4. 2007, Boeing History, http://www.boeing.com/history/chronology.
5. 2007, Boeing History, http://www.boeing.com/history.
6. 2007, Boeing History: Beginnings—Building a company, *Aviation History*, http://www.wingsoverkansas.com/history/article.asp?id=404.
7. R. J. Gordon, 1983, Energy efficiency, user cost change, and the measurement of durable goods prices, The U.S. national income and product accounts: Selected topics, Chicago: University of Chicago Press, 235.
8. 2007, Boeing, *Wikipedia*, http://en.wikipedia.org/wiki/Boeing_747-8.
9. 2007, Boeing history, http://www.boeing.com/history/boeing/777.
10. 2007, Boeing, http://www.careerbuilder.com.
11. 2001, Boeing's Sonic Cruiser skirts the edge of the sound barrier, *Popular Mechanics*, http://www.popularmechanics.com, October.
12. L. Laurent, 2007, Boeing's Dreamliner, Airbus's nightmare, *Forbes*, http://www.forbes.com, July 9.
13. J. Newhouse, 2007, *Boeing Versus Airbus*, Toronto, Canada: Alfred A. Knopf.
14. Ibid.
15. Ibid.
16. J. Destefani, 2004, A look at Boeing's outsourcing strategy, *Manufacturing Engineering*, March.
17. Ibid.
18. Ibid.
19. 2006, Boeing's global strategy takes off: The aerospace titan is taking a measured approach to outsourcing, with help from local teams, *BusinessWeek*, http://www.businessweek.com, January 30.
20. Ibid.
21. Ibid.
22. Harry C. Stonecipher, 2004, Outsourcing, the real issue, Orange County Business Council Annual Meeting and Dinner, http://www.boeing.com/news/speeches, June 2.
23. 2006, Boeing's global strategy takes off.
24. E. F. Vencat, 2006, A Boeing of Asia? It could happen, now that Airbus and Boeing build planes in global factories, *Newsweek International*, http://www.msnbc.msn.com, May 15.
25. Ibid.
26. J. Newhouse, *Boeing versus Airbus*.
27. C. Matlack & S. Holmes, 2007, Airbus revs up the engines; to generate badly needed cash, it's boosting output of its popular A-320 to record levels, *BusinessWeek*, March 5, 4024: 41.
28. 2004, There where they're needed, *Boeing Frontiers*, http://www.boeing.com, December.
29. V. Kwong & A. Rothman, 2006, Boeing vs. Airbus: The next bout, *International Herald Tribune*, http://www.iht.com, February 16.
30. L. Wayne, 2007, Airbus superjumbo takes a lap around America, *New York Times*, http://www.nytimes.com, March 20.
31. A. Burgos, 2005, Qantas sets $14 billion order for Boeing planes, *Forbes*, http://www.forbes.com, December 14.
32. J. Newhouse, *Boeing versus Airbus*.
33. 1999, JetBlue chooses the Airbus A-320, Press Releases, http://www.jetblue.com, July 14.
34. L. Timmerman, 2004, Boeing sales to get new leadership, *The Seattle Times*, http://www.seattletimes.com, December 4.
35. D. Drezner, 2005, Competition has been good for Boeing, http://www.danieldrezner.com, April 13.
36. M. Schlangenstein, 2007, FedEx dumps Airbus for Boeing, *The News Tribune* (Tacoma, WA), http://www.thenewstribune.com, September 25.
37. P. Olson, 2007, Branson turns his back on Airbus, *Forbes*, http://www.forbes.com, April 25.
38. D. Ackman, 2005, Boeing, Airbus showdown at 40,000 feet, *Forbes*, http://www.forbes.com, May 31.
39. M. Adams, 2006, Airbus announces new jet to rival Boeing Dreamliner, *USA Today*, http://www.usatoday.com, July 18.
40. D. Ackman, Boeing, Airbus showdown at 40,000 feet.
41. Ibid.
42. J. Audley & K. Saleh, 2004, Boeing vs. Airbus: Trade fight could prove costly for everyone, *The Seattle Times*, http://www.seattletimes.com, December 6.
43. 2006, Moody's boosts Boeing's credit rating, *International Business Times*, http://in.ibtimes.com, March 15.
44. M. E. Babej & T. Pollak, 2006, Boeing versus Airbus, *Forbes*, http://www.forbes.com, May 24.
45. P. Olson, Branson turns his back on Airbus.
46. M. E. Babej & T. Pollak, Boeing versus Airbus.
47. 2007, Anatomy of an A-380, *Fortune*, March 5, 101–106.
48. J. Newhouse, *Boeing versus Airbus*.
49. Ibid.
50. R. Stone, 2007, Airbus A-380 promises less for big airports, *Wall Street Journal*, September 5, D7.
51. 2007, Ground Control, *Event Marketer*, http://www.eventmarketer.com, February 11.
52. Ibid.
53. Ibid.
54. N. D. Schwartz, 2007, Big plane, big problems, *Fortune*, March 5, 95–98.
55. 2007, Anatomy of an A-380.
56. G. Parkinson, 2006, Crisis at Airbus as chief quits after only 100 days, The *(London) Independent*, http://www.findarticles.com, October 10.
57. J. L. Lunsford, 2007, Boeing's tall order: On-time 787; suppliers say Dreamliner delivery could hit may target—if all goes right, *Wall Street Journal*, September 17, A8.
58. D. Michaels, 2007, More super, less jumbo for this carrier, *Wall Street Journal*, September 25, B8.
59. Ibid.

Case 5

Carrefour in Asia

Claudia Gehlen, Neil Jones, Philippe Lasserre

INSEAD

"China represents a huge market and now it has acquired its WTO membership. But there is no easy way to stand out a winner here. China is nearly as big as Europe and all areas differ from each other," declared Jean-Luc Chereau, president of Carrefour China, at the opening of the first Carrefour store in Urumqi, Xinjiang province. The Urumqi hypermarket was the forty-second to be opened by the company in China where Carrefour was the leading mass retailer, despite mounting competition.

History

In 2003 Carrefour was the second-largest mass retailer in the world with net sales totaling €70.5 billion (US$84 billion) and net profits of €1.6 billion. It operated 10,378 stores in 29 countries and employed more than 410,000 people.

Although primarily known as a hypermarket pioneer, Carrefour also operated supermarkets, hard discounts and other formats, such as convenience stores (see Exhibits 1 and 2).

Exhibit 1 Carrefour's Key Figures

Year	Revenue (in million euros)	Net Income (in million euros)	Net Profit Margin (%)	Employees	Sales Area (m²)	Annual Sales/m² in Euros
2003	70,486	1,629	2.3%	410,000	13,207	5,337
2002	68,728	1,347	2.0	396,662	9,767	7,037
2001	69,486	1,265	1.8	382,821	9,151	7,593
2000	64,802	1,065	1.6	330,247	8,130	7,971
1999	51,948	898	1.7	297,290	6,569	7,908
1998	27,408	647	2.4	132,875	3,721	7,366
1997	25,804	546	2.1	113,289	3,075	8,392
1996	23,615	476	2.0	103,600	2,727	8,660
1995	22,046	539	2.4	102,900	2,378	9,271
1994	20,778	324	1.6	95,900	2,129	9,760
1993	18,708	448	2.4	81,500	1,920	9,744

Exhibit 2 Carrefour Formats Worldwide

Format	Number of Stores	Sales (incl. taxes in million euros)	Sales % of Total	Sales Area (1000 m²)	Sales Incl. Taxes/m² in Euros
Hypermarkets	823	51,060	57.60%	6,985	7,310
Supermarkets	2,380	22,592	25.50	3,394	6,656
Hard discounts	4,456	6,692	7.60	1,459	4,586
Other stores	2,718	8,229	9.30	1,369	6,010
Total	10,378	88,572	100.00	13,207	

Note: Those figures relate to all stores operated under Carrefour's banner, including the franchises.
Source: Carrefour Annual Report, 2003.

It has always been significantly more international than most of its competitors (see Exhibit 3). Carrefour's international operations are located in three major geographical zones: Europe and the Middle East, Latin America, and Asia. In 2003, 49 percent of its hypermarket revenues were derived from markets outside France (see Exhibit 4). In Europe and China, Carrefour is the number one retailer in terms of size.

Carrefour developed the hypermarket concept of bringing nearly all types of consumer goods under one roof in 1959, when the Defforey and Fournier families created their first hypermarket in the suburbs of Paris. It built a reputation as the retailer that offered the most variety and freshness at low prices. For years its claim to fame was to offer a massive array of quality goods in one place, at reasonable prices rather than bargain-basement value.

The retailer operated exclusively in France until the late 1960s before expanding into Spain, where under the name of Pryca, it became the country's second-largest retailer. It then successfully entered Portugal, Argentina, and Brazil. However, in more mature markets its results were not so conclusive and it had to pull out of the United Kingdom, Switzerland, the United States, and Belgium (although it was later to reenter Switzerland and Belgium).

As in France during the 1960s, Carrefour was generally successful when it entered new markets that had seen dramatic changes in consumer buying habits, coupled with high growth in *per capita GNP*, suburbanization, greater participation of women in the labor force, and a large increase in the ownership of cars and refrigerators.

During the 1980s and 1990s, Carrefour continued its international expansion through a combination of organic growth and acquisitions, extending its reach into Latin America. The 1990s were characterized by a move into Asia, starting with Taiwan in 1989 and a few years later expanding to Malaysia, China, South Korea, Thailand, Singapore, Indonesia, and Japan. In all the Asian markets, hypermarkets emerged as the winning format (see Exhibit 5).

In France, due to regulatory constraints, Carrefour merged in 1999 with rival Promodès, the number two in the French market. The merger may also have been motivated by Wal-Mart's acquisition of Asda in the United Kingdom that same year. From 2000 to 2003 Carrefour wrestled with integrating Promodès' businesses into its existing operations. As a result, its performance and organic growth rate slipped during this period. Carrefour focused intensely on integration and repairing weak domestic sales and by the end of the year it had successfully repositioned itself to continue its international expansion at its historically fast pace.

Carrefour also has a foothold in the Middle East. In the United Arab Emirates (UAE), the joint venture company between Majid al Futtaim and Carrefour was the most dynamic and fast-moving hypermarket chain, with a total of eight stores in 2004. Thanks to its massive buying power, Carrefour could guarantee low prices while permanently offering about 50,000 items in stock.

In February 2004 shares in Carrefour SA jumped in value, renewing market speculation that its larger rival, Wal-Mart, was planning a bid. Wal-Mart had coveted the French market for years but its attempts to buy a French subsidiary had been stymied since its abortive courtship of the Auchan and Carrefour chains in 1999.

Adding to the speculation over Carrefour's future was the death in a plane crash in December 2003 of a member of the Halley family group, Carrefour's largest shareholder with an approximate 11.5 percent stake. Such speculation highlighted that Carrefour was vulnerable to a takeover, or at least to increased competition from international competitors like Wal-Mart and Tesco that were posting stronger domestic growth. In 2003 Carrefour's hypermarkets

Exhibit 3 Level of Internationalization of Global Retailers in 2003

Retailer	Number of Countries	Net Sales (in million US$)	Foreign Sales %
Carrefour	29	84,000	50
Metro	22	46,900	45
Ito-Yokado	12	27,238	41
Tesco	11	39,521	18
Aeon	10	24,677	17
Costco	7	37,993	16
Wal-Mart	11	205,500	16
Daiei	3	17,717	1

Source: http://www.siamfuture.com; companies reports.

Exhibit 4 Carrefour Worldwide Operations

Region	Number of Stores	Net Sales (in million euros)	Sales (% of total)	Investments Million€	%/Sales	Operating Million €	Margin %
France	1,448	35,704	50.65%	818	2.3%	2144	6.0%
Europe	3,606	25,526	36.21	1169	4.6	952	3.7
Latin America	814	4,619	6.55	295	6.4	13	0.3
Asia	199	4,637	6.58	436	9.4	143	3.1
Total	6,067	70,486	100.00	2717	3.9	3251	4.6

Source: Carrefour Annual Report, 2003.

Exhibit 5 Carrefour Formats by Region

Sales Incl. Taxes in 2003 (in million euros)					
	Hypermarkets	Supermarkets	Hard Discounts	Others	Total
France	23,948	13,151	2,037	5,576	44,912
Europe	17,900	8,302	4,405	2,453	33,060
Latin America	4,059	1,139	245	–	5,444
Asia	5,152	–	4	–	5,157
	51,060				–
Total	50,509	22,592	6,692	2,719	88,572

Number of Stores in 2003					
	Hypermarkets	Supermarkets	Hard Discounts	Others	Total
France	216	1,005	588	1,766	3,575
Europe	315	1,121	3,381	953	5,770
Latin America	147	254	432	–	833
Asia	145	–	55	–	200
Total	823	2,380	4,456	2,719	10,378

Sales Area in 2002 (thousand m²)					
	Hypermarkets	Supermarkets	Hard Discounts	Others	Total
France	1,864	1,577	343	945	4,729
Europe	2,584	1,367	959	425	5,335
Latin America	1,316	449	141	–	1,907
Asia	1,220	–	16	–	1,236
Total	6,985	3,393	1,459	1,370	13,207

Source: Carrefour Annual Report, 2003.

had a 13.9 percent share of the "fast-moving consumer goods" category in its French home market (which included food as well as household goods and health and beauty products), down from 14.4 percent in 2002. The company might have considered a defensive merger with another European retailer had Wal-Mart set its sights on Carrefour, although any merger or takeover might well run into culture clashes, integration headaches, and anti-trust concerns. As CEO Daniel Bernard put it, "Hostile bids in a 'people' sector simply don't work."

Another threat came from the growth of hard-discounters like Aldi from Germany that sold goods at rock-bottom prices. In order to fight back against the hard-discounters, Carrefour expanded its own hard discount chain, ED.

Carrefour's Approach

The basics of Carrefour's concept are (1) one-stop shopping, (2) low prices, (3) self-service, (4) quality products, (5) freshness, and (6) free parking.

Before entering a new international market, local conditions are analyzed against a set of socio-economic criteria. The size and maturity of the market, the legal framework and the openness to foreign investors are major aspects. For instance, Carrefour postponed its entry into India due to a lack of clarity on direct foreign investment. Basic figures regarding population, per capita GDP, transport networks, the level of motorization, urbanization, real estate prices, and so forth are also taken into account. However, Carrefour does not believe only in extensive market research, as Jean-Michel Arlaud, head of its Romanian operations, put it in an interview:

When we decided to set up stores in Romania, it was more an instinctive feeling than the results of a market study. If we had based our decisions on studies, we would never have come.

Once the feasibility study is conclusive, Carrefour focuses on selecting the format best suited to the particular market and adapting that format to local needs. Unprecedented in its history, Carrefour has opted in many Asian countries for an urban location for its stores due to the population density, and has positioned its hypermarkets as proximity stores rather than suburban stores, offering a limited product range but producing greater volume.

Carrefour tries to establish as many stores as possible in major urban areas in order to achieve economies

Exhibit 6 Carrefour's Virtuous Circle

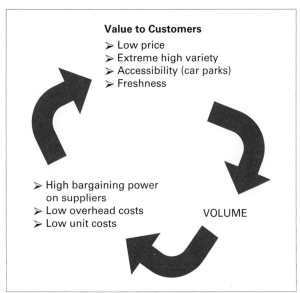

Value to Customers
➤ Low price
➤ Extreme high variety
➤ Accessibility (car parks)
➤ Freshness

➤ High bargaining power
on suppliers
➤ Low overhead costs
➤ Low unit costs

VOLUME

Source: Carrefour Annual Report, 2003; EIU Data Services.

of scale. Its challenge in each new market is to recreate the virtuous circle of "freshness + variety + low prices → high volume → high bargaining power → low costs → low prices" (see Exhibit 6).

For Carrefour, price is not simply a competitive advantage but an essential means of survival. In order to drive down prices in response to competition while maintaining high-quality brands, Carrefour advertises new promotions and discounts every day, reminding customers that they will be refunded if they find the same product cheaper elsewhere.

Taking local constraints into account, Carrefour has added new services in developing markets, such as free shuttle services for customers and play areas for children, as well as home delivery. In some markets, such as China, Carrefour has launched its own product line in home appliances and spices.

Because Carrefour operates on tiny margins (6.9 percent gross margin and 2.5 percent net margin), the slightest improvement in these translates into significant growth for the bottom line.

One important factor in cost management is its sourcing strategy. In China, for instance, more than 95 percent of its merchandise is locally sourced and the remainder is sourced through local importers or the trading office in Hong Kong. Carrefour has built big global procurement centers coordinated through Shanghai and Hong Kong.

The centralization of its IT systems and administrative procedures achieves further savings. Shared processes and systems increase operational efficiency and the introduction of international product ranges complements its locally sensitive strategy. In order to increase its profitability, in 2000 Carrefour created the GNX online supply

platform with Oracle and Sears, whereby suppliers and retailers can exchange information via the Internet and optimize the flow of merchandise, thus reducing their administrative costs. Other retailers have since joined GNX including Metro (Germany), Sainsbury's (U.K.), Kroger (U.S.) and Coles Myer (Australia).

Carrefour also works actively with local governments and nonprofit organizations to protect the environment. In 2002 Carrefour and the Chinese Packaging Corporation initiated actions to globally reduce pollution from packaging. Worldwide, Carrefour requested that its stores make less use of plastic in packaging, thereby gaining a reputation as a model in the retailing industry.

While venturing into new markets, Carrefour's human resource policy has relied on a small number of expatriates. In 2002 Carrefour employed about 200 expatriate executives with solid experience of adapting Carrefour's retailing concept to local contexts. They were mainly recruited in France but also in countries that were considered Carrefour strongholds, such as Taiwan.

When opening a new market, Carrefour operates a dual system for employing expatriates and local executives. Initially, store and department heads are experienced expatriates. Local managers receive six months' training in a country of the region where Carrefour is already successfully operating. Thereafter they work hand-in-hand: the expatriates contributing their expertise and experience and the local executives sharing their know-how of the local business environment. Carrefour's aim is to eventually promote local talent to top management.

As early as 1969 Carrefour was the first mass retailer to measure performance on the return on invested capital instead of the classic concept of gross profit margin used in traditional trade. In terms of remuneration it has a reputation for paying employees well: Department heads earn 20 percent more than they would with other supermarkets, and can earn a bonus linked to the results of the department. The pressure for sales and profit is put on department heads, as each store is a profit center. In Asia, department heads are much more autonomous than in France and are also in charge of recruiting employees and negotiating salaries.

In China, Carrefour employs 95 percent of local Chinese managers and invests heavily in their training. In 2002 Carrefour employed a total of 18,000 local employees, and 1,000 Chinese department heads were trained in retail techniques and business management.

Carrefour in Asia

In 2003 Carrefour was present in eight Asian markets, operating 144 hypermarkets and 55 hard discount stores (see Exhibits 7 and 8). The Asian zone represented

Exhibit 7 Carrefour's Asian Presence

	Year of Entry	Sales in 2002 (in million euro)	Sales growth (%)	GDP Growth in 2002 (%)	Population (millions) in 2002	Urban population (%)
Taiwan	1989	1,381.00	1.6	3.0	22.50	n.a.
Malaysia	1994	225.90	−1.7	3.5	24.00	58.7
China	1995	1,369.50	6.1	7.5	1,282.10	33.1
South Korea	1996	1,242.90	1.7	6.3	48.10	83.0
Thailand	1996	416.40	21.0	4.5	63.40	22.4
Singapore	1997	86.00	6.0	2.2	3.60	100.0
Indonesia	1998	313.20	48.6	3.5	217.10	42.9
Japan	2000	156.90	6.1	0.9	127.20	79.1
Total		**5,191.80**				

Exhibit 8 Carrefour in Asia

Expansion of Stores and Surface													Tesco	Macro	Wal-Mart
	1993	1994	1995	1996	1997	1998	1999	2000	2001	2002	2003	Surface (1000 m²)	2002	2002	2002
China			2	3	7	14	20	24	24	36	**95**	**337**	12	5	25
Hypermarkets											40	321			
Hard Discounts											55	15			
South Korea				3	3	6	12	20	22	25	27	**253**	20		9
Hong Kong				1	2	4	4								
Indonesia						1	5	7	8	10	**11**	**73**		12	
Japan								1	3	4	**7**	**65**			
Malaysia		1	1	2	3	5	6	6	6	6	**7**	**69**	1	8	
Singapore					1	1	1	1	1	1	**2**	**15**			
Taiwan	7	8	10	13	17	21	23	24	26	28	**31**	**243**	3	8	
Thailand				2	6	7	9	11	15	17	**19**	**172**	41	21	
Total	7	9	13	24	39	59	80	94	105	126	**199**	**1228**	**77**	**54**	**34**
Hypermarkets											144	1212			
Hard Discounts											55	15			

13 percent of the group's hypermarket sales and 6.7 percent of the total. Net sales revenues totaled €4,637 million and profits €143 million (4.7 percent of the total).

When first moving into Asia, Carrefour opted for joint ventures and partnerships to make up for its lack of knowledge of the Asian market. Later on it worked with financial or industrial partners only when national regulations made it necessary, as in China, Thailand, Malaysia, and Indonesia.

With the exception of Japan, Carrefour chose those countries that, despite their low GDP, had reached a sufficient level of maturity to make the transition to mass consumption. Timing was crucial to Carrefour's success because it entered these markets earlier than its competitors, who had delayed entry due to the Asian crisis. Local competition was also slow to react to this new phenomenon and was often thwarted by the onset of the Asian crisis, especially in Korea, Thailand, and Indonesia.

According to Gérard Clerc, the vice president who led Carrefour's Asian expansion, the Asian crisis did not affect the company; on the contrary, Carrefour benefited, thanks to its low price policy and emerged even stronger from the crisis with a higher market share than expected. Until the year 2000 international competition had been rather timid but was now progressing fast. International players such as Makro, Metro, Tesco, and Wal-Mart had shown a big appetite for the region.

Even though Asian customers still tended to shop daily at wet markets or "mom & pop" stores, buying patterns were slowly changing and a certain degree of Westernization of local tastes was apparent in most countries. Moreover, impulse buying was on the rise and replacing necessity purchasing. Shopping as a form of leisure was an increasing phenomenon: a visit to the French hypermarket had turned into a Sunday outing.

Carrefour in Taiwan

"It was as if the Huns had arrived in Taiwan," Gérard Clerc said of the reaction of local retailers in Taiwan to Carrefour's arrival.

In 1987 Carrefour selected Taiwan as the entry point into the vast, mainly untapped market space for hypermarkets. As René Brillet, director of the Asia region, put it: "This explains why we have roots on this continent, offering us the potential for tremendous growth, because of its size, its cultural diversity and its enormous population." Another advantage of the Taiwanese experience was that it served as a human resource hub for other Asian markets, especially China.

However, Carrefour did not have an easy start in Taiwan and it was almost two years before it finally set up a hypermarket in 1989. Carrefour, with Makro, was the first foreign retailer to establish the hypermarket concept in Taiwan. The retailer entered a partnership with a local food and retailing conglomerate, the President Group, which held 40 percent of the shares. The President Group is a dominant figure on the Taiwanese business landscape, ranking number two in size. Right from the start it accepted the role of a dormant partner but played a big role in introducing Carrefour to the political and economic establishment.

During this period real estate prices skyrocketed, making some adaptation of Carrefour's policy necessary. Traditionally, Carrefour had set up much bigger stores in suburban areas. Instead of buying the sites, Carrefour rented space to operate hypermarkets in Kaohsiung and Taipei on a much smaller scale (3,500 m²) in urban centers on two stories instead of the classic one-floor layout. In addition, in urban areas some kind of "protection" from the local secret societies had to be negotiated.

All stores consistently had pilot departments to introduce new product ranges. Study conclusions were then introduced on a national scale across all Carrefour stores in Taiwan. This cross-learning was vitally important as it spread the know-how within the company. Subsequently, Carrefour increased the size of its new stores.

In certain cases Carrefour chose industrial and commercial parks to develop the hypermarkets. Wholesale stores or "green stores" were built in industrial areas, and general retailing or "blue stores" in residential areas. By adopting this strategy Carrefour could capture both big and small accounts and grow much faster than its rival Makro.

Carrefour is pronounced Jia Le Fu in Chinese, which means "luck and happiness for the whole family." This fortunate phonetic translation unexpectedly contributed to Carrefour's success in Taiwan and later in China, where foreign names often remain unpronounceable.

However, Carrefour still had to tackle different business approaches, especially to negotiation. "For Europeans, Chinese are known to be difficult negotiators. They consider the negotiation process as a refined art which they master with intelligence and patience," Gerard Clerc explained. Managing the supply chain was another major challenge. Taiwanese suppliers lacked rigor, organization, equipment, and aggressiveness, but they were much more flexible than their Western counterparts. They sold products, not services, and often lacked information regarding basic data on their sales, inventory level, and even internal accounting.

Communication was another challenge. In Taiwan, all documents were written in Chinese while Carrefour's documentation was in English. Corporate culture, training, and company goals, among other factors, were difficult to communicate to all staff members, and promotions were only possible for English-speaking staff.

The cultural gap was also a source of misunderstanding amongst management. Rather than sharing their knowledge with their staff, local managers had the tendency to withhold information. According to one French local store manager, Philippe Ravelli, the French and the Chinese cultures do not give the same priority to the three basic elements in daily life. For the Chinese, emotion (quing) comes first, followed by reason (li), and law (fa). For the French, law comes first (the company policy), reason second, emotion last. Despite such differences, thanks to its adaptive capabilities Carrefour became the largest mass retailer on the island.

Fortunately, Taiwan was relatively spared by the Asian crisis and consumption levels continued to increase. Carrefour continued to reinforce its lead over Makro, sometimes opening new stores near existing Makro stores. By 2003 Carrefour was operating 31 stores in Taiwan, which continued to be its most important Asian market with net sales of €1,322 million.

Carrefour in South Korea

Since the liberalization of the Korean retail market in 1996, local and foreign retailers, such as Carrefour, Makro, Costco, Wal-Mart, and Metro, had struggled to stake out their territory. Local conglomerates raised the stakes and invested massively to protect the local industry. But the Asian crisis forced these local retailers to freeze their expansion plans, and some even had to file for bankruptcy. As a consequence, Carrefour further reinforced its position and recorded its first profit in 1997. Restructuring and modernization of existing stores started in 2001. Carrefour introduced a new feature with the creation of cultural centers in two stores in partnership with Korea's leading newspaper. These offered women and children weekly courses in English, dance, cooking, drawing, and other subjects. In 2003 Carrefour, now the number four food retailer, operated 27 stores, posting net sales of €1,149 million.

Carrefour in Thailand

As with Korea, Thailand seemed to present all the conditions for Carrefour to succeed and the crisis offered an opportunity to expand while costs were lower and the competition reduced. Carrefour opened two stores there in 1996. However, unlike Korea, the chain operated with two local partners and this postponed their expansion plans for a year and reduced the number of stores to be opened from five to two in 1999.

Foreign ownership laws in Thailand allowed foreign companies—except American companies—to hold no more than 49 percent of the shares. Carrefour argued that this law would favor its rival, Wal-Mart. When the Central Retail Corp. sold its 40 percent shareholding in 1998, this law made it impossible for Carrefour to purchase the shares.

In 2002 Carrefour introduced a number of sales innovations that proved successful. The fresh product concept was redesigned in order to reproduce the atmosphere and merchandising style found in street markets, while emphasizing hygienic conditions. As an example, the "pork quality line" covered the entire cycle from breeding selection and reproduction to stocking the shelves. In 2003 Carrefour Thailand counted 19 stores with net sales of €392 million.

Carrefour in Indonesia

With a population of 202 million, Indonesia was an attractive market for retailers, which Carrefour entered in 1998 at the peak of the Asian crisis. Just before the merger with Carrefour, Promodès had opened two stores in the country in 1998 and 1999, and these were subsequently integrated.

Indonesia's recovery from the Asian crisis had not been swift, unlike Korea and Thailand. The country was still facing major problems of financial sector fragility and private sector debt. Carrefour took advantage of the Indonesian crisis with its low prices. In order to offer a larger section of the population its first opportunity to purchase durable household goods, Carrefour organized two "free credit" campaigns in 2002, which were a resounding success, given that the household appliance segment represented 21 percent of total sales revenues.

In 2003 Carrefour was Indonesia's leading foreign hypermarket with 11 stores and net sales of €286 million.

In addition to consolidating its position in Jakarta, Carrefour also planned to enter other provinces in 2003.

Carrefour in Malaysia

When Carrefour entered the Malaysian market in 1994 it met with little competition. Before the Asia crisis Malaysia had experienced one of the strongest growth rates of all the Asian nations. The strong contraction of the economy after 1998 did not jeopardize Carrefour's expansion. In 1999 it opened its sixth store, and in 2003 its seventh. In 2004 it planned to open a hypermarket in Kepong, Kuala Lumpur, on three stories with 46,450m² of floorspace.

Illustrating the local adjustments necessary for this market, all products within its stores were "halal" in compliance with prevailing food requirements. Nevertheless, in order to cater to the large ethnic Chinese community it also operated a separate "non-halal" store outside its catchment zone. Alcoholic beverages received a distinct label clearly indicating the alcohol content.

In 2003 Carrefour was the number three food retailer in Malaysia but was facing increasing competition from strong local and foreign retailers, such as Tesco. Carrefour's net sales represented €226 million in 2003.

Carrefour in Singapore

Since entering this mature and sophisticated market in 1997, Carrefour succeeded in modifying both shopping habits and price expectations among the small population of 4 million Singaporeans. However, local competition remained strong and professional (NTUC) and local suppliers resisted Carrefour's methods. Singapore was not overly affected by the Asian crisis, posting a rise of more than 2 percent in GDP in 1999.

Backed by a dynamic commercial strategy with frequent and original promotional campaigns, Carrefour, No. 5 in food retail, adapted well to the local economic environment. Monthly theme promotions were introduced (French Week, Wine Fair, Japanese Week, Bicycle Week, etc). In particular, products imported from France, both fine foods and fresh produce, recorded continuing success. Its hypermarket in Suntec City registered significant sales growth, and a second store was opened in Plaza Singapura in December 2003. Net sales in 2003 amounted to €83 million (see Exhibit 9).

Carrefour in Hong Kong

Initially, Carrefour thought Hong Kong would help it penetrate the Chinese market. In contrast to Taiwan, Hong Kong's retail industry was hard hit by the Asian crisis and had yet to return to strong growth. The price slump and

Exhibit 9 Carrefour Advertisement in Singapore

suppliers' concerns over retailers' insolvency worked in Carrefour's favor and the company opened four stores by 1998. But in 1999 it experienced fierce competition and had to modify its activity. Despite its efforts, Carrefour failed to find large sites suitable for developing its hypermarket concept and to acquire a significant market share. It disposed of its four stores in 2000.

Carrefour in China

Based on the lessons learned in Taiwan, Carrefour moved into China in 1995 with its first store opening in Shanghai. In 2003 it was ranked the top foreign retailer with net sales of €1,031 million, operating 40 hypermarkets and 55 hard discount stores in all major cities. The continental Chinese market is quite different from those of Taiwan and Hong Kong because urbanization, consumption and purchasing power are steadily increasing (see Exhibit 10).

As in Taiwan, Carrefour had to deal with a different negotiation culture and at first used Taiwanese negotiators for its suppliers in China. Since 1992, foreign participation in retailing had been permitted through joint ventures with Chinese companies. At first, Carrefour's

Exhibit 10 Per Capita Annual Disposable Income of China's 10 Richest Cities, 2002–2003

	Income (in US$)	Population (in million)
Shenzhen	2,887	1.3
Guangzhou	1,812	7.1
Shanghai	1,796	13.3
Ningbo	1,724	5.4
Beijing	1,677	11.3
Xiamen	1,560	1.3
Hangzhou	1,557	6.3
Jinan	1,330	5.7
Tianjin	1,246	9.2
Nanjing	1,231	5.5

Sources: National Statistics Bureau; Ministry of Public Security.

strategy was to look for a strong local partner who could help it overcome the hurdles while keeping the majority stake and assigning a non-operational role to the partner. Its relationship with Lianhua, one of the two major local retailers, helped Carrefour to establish its leadership in China. In different provinces it used different partners.

In 1999 China's central government ruled that foreign companies could not own more than 65 percent of any retailing enterprise in China. Carrefour, which wholly owned many of its stores, was subsequently ordered to sell its excess shares (above the regulatory 65 percent limit) and in 2002 signed a deal to sell stakes to local partners.

China's retail scene differs substantially from one store type to another as well as geographically. Convenience stores and supermarkets are dominated by domestic chains such as Lianhua, whereas hypermarkets are in the firm hands of big international players. In the Shanghai region, foreign retailers such as Carrefour, Makro, Wal-Mart, and Metro generate about a third of total supermarket sales. Because most retailers concentrate their efforts in this part of China, competition is steadily increasing. As a result, Royal Ahold, which operated 46 stores until 2002, withdrew from China and eventually divested all its activities in the Asian region.

In 2000 Carrefour experienced legal tribulations due to the intricate network of central, provincial, and local authorities that resulted in lengthy negotiation procedures at many different levels. "Sometimes, we may have problems in understanding Chinese laws and regulations, but we always respond positively to the government's requirements when problems arise, by rectifying our operations to make sure that the law is fully observed," commented Jean-Luc Chereau. Even though China is officially a centralized country, local authorities seek to enforce their own sphere of influence. In its rush to achieve economies of scale, Carrefour set up hypermarkets and operated stores based on licenses obtained from local authorities, which were not approved by the central authorities. Subsequently, the SETC (State Economic and Trade Commission) threatened to shut down all the stores if Carrefour did not comply with central government regulations. As a result Carrefour had to re-apply to obtain proper licenses from the central regulator, a delay that enabled its closest foreign competitor, Wal-Mart, to make inroads into the market.

Thus from 2000 to 2002 Carrefour was not allowed to open any new stores until it had first restructured its existing outlets. "Through two-and-a-half years of effort, we have completed our revamp in China, and now we are heading into a fast growth period in the country," said Chereau. Legal restructuring was performed in collaboration with the Chinese authorities and allowed expansion to resume. In this respect, the Chinese authorities were pragmatic with regard to legislation, having first evaluated the benefits an industrial player could bring to the country.

In 2002 and 2003 Carrefour stepped up its expansion in a bid to move faster than its competitors. It opened more hypermarkets in existing and new cities as well as 55 new Dia discount stores.

In 2004 Carrefour opened its forty-second hypermarket in one of the most remote regions in China. The new Urumqi store in Xinjiang province in the northwestern part of the country shared a 6,500 m² shopping center with five other stores. For religious reasons it could not sell fresh pork, but focused on beef and lamb. This shopping center was the first to be built by a retail chain in a province earmarked by the authorities as a development priority. The store was served by 17 different bus lines. Carrefour's aim had always been to pioneer urban centers that had been ignored by competitors, as with Wuhan and Shenyang, where it opened hypermarkets in 1999 despite a 30 percent rate of unemployment.

Carrefour opened its first Champion store in Zhongguancun Beijing. This was its fifth store in Beijing, and regarded as Carrefour's flagship store in Asia after three years of dormancy in the capital. Located in an area dubbed Beijing's Silicon Valley, the outlet has floorspace of 11,600 m², much bigger than any other Carrefour store in the country. As an area lacking big shopping centers and supermarkets, Zhongguancun is attracting foreign retailers such as PriceSmart, one of Carrefour's major rivals. In the wake of the Zhongguancun store opening, Carrefour planned to open one or two more stores in Beijing in 2004 as well as a store in Jinan, the capital of east China's Shandong Province.

Carrefour is one of the world's major exporters of Chinese products. It purchased US$1.6 billion worth of goods in China in 2002 and US$2.15 billion in 2003. Since 2002 a new organization within the group has aimed to expand market outlets for its suppliers and enhance its product offering in its European stores. An "export service" was established in Shanghai, and 10 liaison offices were set up with the objective of doubling export volumes by 2005.

Carrefour also sought to participate in public welfare projects and to contribute to local communities, while cooperating closely with local authorities. Among other things, the company set up Hope primary schools, donated to disaster-hit areas, and contributed face masks during the SARS outbreak.

In 2004 China announced that it would honor its pledges to open the booming retail sector to foreign players such as Wal-Mart and Carrefour, abolishing joint-venture requirements before the end of the year. Beijing also promised to end restrictions on the location and number of foreign-owned chain stores.

With China's entry into the WTO, its main trade barriers such as import taxes had to be abolished, but nontariff trade barriers might still be put in place. Although officially welcomed, the press often blames foreign retail operations for destroying jobs and killing the local retail industry. In recent years Shanghai-based major retailers have started to defy foreign competition.

In 2004 the Bailian Group, which controlled Lianhua Supermarket Holdings, announced plans to merge with Hualian into China's largest retailer, the Brilliance Group, with the aim of creating a local giant with assets of US$721.4 million.

Carrefour has only just started making profits in all its stores, while Wal-Mart is still witnessing losses in some outlets. The company's aim is to operate 70 hypermarkets in a few years' time, but political risk remains high in China.

Carrefour in Japan

Being a different market in cultural and economic terms, Carrefour postponed entering Japan until 2000. By then, compared to the 1990s, real estate prices had become more affordable, loans more attractive, and the traditional clout of wholesalers was slowly being reduced to a more logistic function.

Compared to other Asian markets many differences still remain. Although Japan's GDP and purchasing power are much higher, refrigerators and storage space in Japanese homes are limited, so housewives tend to go shopping more often. They make it their daily routine to visit a nearby supermarket where other friends congregate, rather than to drive to a hypermarket to stock up on groceries for a week.

In addition, the Japanese have a sound marketing culture and are perfectionists. Japan is a much more advanced market with established consumer trends, local brands, and supplier networks. Consumers are sophisticated and look for quality and service.

Despite the spectacular bankruptcies of local players such as Mycal in 2002, Japan's retail sector has remained overcrowded and competition quite fierce. Japan was left with five major general merchandise store chains, namely Ito-Yokado, Aeon (parent company of Jusco), Daiei, Uny, and Seiyu, of which Wal-Mart was the largest shareholder in 2002 (see Exhibit 11).

Ito-Yokado, Japan's largest supermarket chain, had no plans to copy Carrefour or to open hypermarkets because land costs remained too high. Ito-Yokado did not reduce prices but instead emphasized higher quality. Aeon, the parent company of Jusco, was Japan's second-largest supermarket chain and took a more aggressive

and innovative approach. It operated 368 stores in 2002. Daiei, for years Japan's largest retailer, had been on the edge of bankruptcy for some time. Uny, the smallest of the four, had not been able to keep up with the rapid expansion pace of Jusco and Ito-Yokado.

One concrete barrier to entry into the Japanese market was the close network of multiple layers of intermediaries. Carrefour fell short of its original plan to persuade all of its Japanese suppliers to adopt the Carrefour direct-purchasing system, which was revolutionary by Japanese standards. Instead, local distributors launched lawsuits against Carrefour as the company opted to purchase directly rather than conform to the long-established distribution channels. After the Japanese distributors lost their case, Carrefour resumed its expansion.

When Carrefour opened its first megastore in a Tokyo suburb in December 2000, so many shoppers poured into the store that managers had to restrict entry. Two other stores, set up in Tokyo and Osaka, were similarly clogged. Junichi Kanamori, a retail analyst at Société Générale Securities Ltd. in Tokyo, explained that Carrefour's arrival was portrayed as "a foreign attack on the Japanese retail market. That made people think something French was going to arrive. Then they discovered it wasn't different from other supermarkets." It was not surprising, therefore, that after a month customers evaporated because shoppers had initially shown up purely out of curiosity.

Like other Western megastores, Carrefour had apparently swept into the Japanese market with much fanfare and little sensitivity to Japan's retail culture. The company did not adequately adjust its business to the purchasing patterns of Japanese consumers, nor did it capitalize on the curiosity of local consumers regarding products hailing from France.

There was some misconception that Carrefour was a general merchandise store that competed on price alone. Japanese supermarkets chains began slashing prices in anticipation of the "foreign threat." Thus its three stores were showing major losses and Carrefour had to review its ambitious plans to expand to 13 stores by 2003.

In 2003 Carrefour continued its adaptation to the specific requirements of the local market. Along with demonstrating its professionalism in fresh produce, the company established its first sales space specializing in French household goods at its fully renovated store in Chiba Prefecture. Named "La Maison," the 110m² store-within-a-store offered 1,000 items ranging from fragrant soaps to trendy tableware and other sundry goods, all made in France. The French-themed corner came into being after a pilot sales space in Carrefour's fourth hypermarket store at Saitama Prefecture was well received by housewives. The corner was established to grow consumer interest in certain categories of French products that were not available in Japanese

Exhibit 11 Main Japanese Retailers, February 2003

	Revenue (in million US$)	Net income (in million US$)	Net Profit Margin %	Employees
Ito-Yokado	28,435.50	178.80	0.6	125,400
Aeon	24,274.40	436.00	1.8	42,376
Daiei	18,692.20	1,151.60	6.2	26,589
Uny	8,736.90	106.70	1.2	25,095

Source: Hoover's Online.

supermarkets, and bring the "French touch" loved by the Japanese.

This approach was a clear departure from Carrefour Japan's existing policy of localizing its merchandise and the highly successful store would serve as a benchmark for future store openings. In 2003 Carrefour's stores recorded net sales of €225 million. However, rumors circulated in October 2004 in the *Asian Wall Street Journal* that, according to a consultant, Carrefour was planning to sell its eight stores in Japan due to "difficulties in acquiring real estate for new stores and the lack of touch with Japanese consumers' tastes."

Notes

1. *EuroMonitor.*
2. *Asian Wall Street Journal,* March 2004.
3. CSFB report, October 10, 2003.
4. INSEAD case Carrefour's Entry into Asia (A1), (A2), 10 years later.
5. Interview Gérard Clerc, *Reflets ESSEC* magazine.
6. Carrefour Worldwide.
7. *China Business Weekly,* March 2004.
8. Comparative Study of Asia Strategy: Wal-Mart versus Carrefour.
9. *Forbes,* March 2004.
10. *China Online,* March 2004.
11. *International Herald Tribune,* 2001.
12. *Retail Asia Online,* March 2000.

Case 6

Dell: From a Low-Cost PC Maker to an Innovative Company

Abhijit Sinha

ICFAI Business School

If you ask, Okay, is Dell in the penalty box? Yeah, Dell is in the penalty box. Then we will use this opportunity to fix everything.[1]
> —**MICHAEL DELL,**
> **CHAIRMAN, DELL INC.**

There is no perfect linear path to success. I think the stock market overreacted.[2]
> —**MICHAEL DELL,**
> **CHAIRMAN, DELL INC.**

No, the sky is not falling at Dell.[3]
> —**KEVIN B ROLLINS,**
> **CHIEF EXECUTIVE OFFICER, DELL INC.**

Dell had a humble beginning at a dorm room of the University of Texas, Austin, in 1984, where 18-year-old Michael Dell started a part-time business of computer peripherals. The company became the number one PC maker of the United States in 1999. The company's revenue grew from $546 million in 1991 to $32 billion in 2001 and $56 billion in 2005.[5] Dell and its founder, Michaell Dell, earned many laurels from both analysts and investors. When Dell became a publicly listed

company in 1989, its founder became the youngest CEO in the *Fortune* 500. The company emerged as the world's number one PC seller, enjoying strong brand equity and high customer satisfaction ratings. Its unique Dell Business Model[6] however became a debatable topic among both academicians and industry experts (see Exhibit 1).

After enjoying a heady growth since Dell's inception, both the chairperson and the CEO probably wished to hide behind a mask before announcing the company's second quarter financial performance, for FY 2006–2007. Dell's second quarter revenue and profit failed to match the expectations. Though the company posted revenue of $55.9 billion (February 3, 2006), the company failed to achieve its own forecasted target for revenue growth during the second quarter for FY 2006–2007. August 2006 was difficult month and the second quarter of FY 2006–2007 was the harshest quarter for the company. Its bottom line was its lowest ever—51 percent down, compared to the same period of the previous financial year (see Exhibit 2). Faltering on its own forecasted revenue growth target was not new for Dell. During the second quarter for FY 2005–2006, the company's revenue grew

Exhibit 1 Direct Business Model of Dell

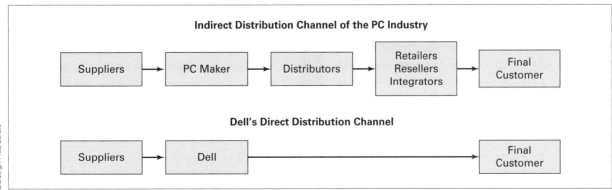

Source: 2003 Competing in Network Era, http://www.oft.osd.mil, December.

Exhibit 2 Dell's Financial Highlights (in $ million)

	August 2006	May 2006	July 2005
Net Revenue	$ 14,094	$ 14,216	$ 13,428
Cost of Revenue	11,904	11,744	10,929
Gross Margin	**2190**	**2472**	**2499**
Selling and Administrative Expenses	1457	1394	1204
Research Expenses	128	129	122
Total Operating Expenses	**1585**	**1523**	**1326**
Operating Income	605	949	1173
Income from Investment and other Income	53	50	61
PBIT	**658**	**999**	**1234**
Income Tax Provision	156	237	214
PAT	**502**	**762**	**1020**

Source: http://www.dell.com.

by 14.7 percent to $13.4 billion compared to its projected growth of 18 percent.[7] In the third quarter of the same financial year, Dell posted revenue of $13.9 billion instead of its targeted $14.5 billion. For a company like Dell, whose top line had grown consistently at the yearly average by 15 percent since 2001–2002, the decline in its growth raised questions over the success of its strategy and business model.

Following its sluggish growth, Dell's customer satisfaction rating declined in the survey conducted by the University of Michigan in 2005. The company had to write off $450 million for the installation of defective capacitors[8] in a large number of computers. In August 2006, it also had to recall 4.1 million lithium batteries that were manufactured by Sony and were used in Dell's laptops. To add to its woes, for the first time in the history of Dell Inc., the company hinted at layoffs—what it called "workforce realignment"—and the Security and Exchange Commission (SEC) launched an informal investigation against the company's accounting practices. Investors who enjoyed more than 28,000 percent gains since Dell went public 17 years ago, and the Wall Street[9] analysts who were accustomed to high revenue, increasing market share, and rocketing profits of the company, suddenly became skeptical about Dell's future. In the second quarter of FY 2006–2007, the company's stock was already down by 25 percent and had been falling further (see Exhibit 3). Before the recent setbacks in 2005 and 2006, the company had also experienced hurdles in 1989 and 1993[10] and was certainly put to a disadvantage when the NASDAQ[11] fell in 2000. Yet, during 2000–2004, the company was able to dominate the PC market. But in August 2006, it announced a 51 percent decline in its revenue for the second quarter of FY 2006–2007 compared to the same period of the previous year. Dell's top line growth, though positive, had

Exhibit 3 Declining Stock Price

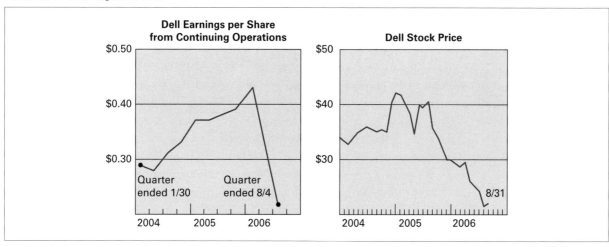

Source: http://www.fortune.com.

declined continuously during the past six quarters. The fact that the company could not meet its own modified and modest targets raised an awkward question among the stakeholders, "Could this be the end of Dell as we know it?"

Company Background

In 1984, 18-year-old Michael Dell, a student at the University of Texas, Austin, set up PCs Limited as a part-time business in his dorm room to sell IBM compatible computers built from stock components. Michael Dell started formatting hard disks for personal computers, added additional memory, disk drives, and modems with IBM clones and sold them for 40 percent less than that of the IBM machines. In 1985, the company moved up the value chain and started to assemble Dell branded PCs ("Turbo PC") instead of upgrading the machines of other manufacturers. Within one year of its operation, the company posted revenue of $6 million. Inspired by the success of the company, Michael Dell dropped out of college in 1986, to run the business full time. During this time, he renamed the company Dell Computer Corporation.

In 1984, when Michael Dell started the company (PCs Limited), the PC industry had vertically integrated companies like IBM (hardware) and software developers like Microsoft. Dell presumed that customization, fast delivery and low price would give his company a higher profit margin over IBM and HP. Contrary to the existing trends of displaying the products in retail stores or selling them through intermediaries, the company delivered its products directly to the consumers. Dell sourced the components directly from the manufacturers, assembled them according to the customer specifications and delivered them free of cost. Initially, it took orders over the telephone, followed by advertisements in magazines and dailies and later from its e-commerce platform, *www.dell.com*.

In 1989, as noted above, the company issued an IPO. In 1992, *Fortune* 500 included Dell Computer Corporation among the world's best 500 companies. In the same year, Michael Dell was also featured in *Fortune* 500 as the youngest CEO. The company forayed into the United Kingdom, and then into Australia and Japan in 1993. It set up its own manufacturing facilities in Limerick, Ireland (to serve European, Middle East, and Africa), Penang, Malaysia (1996), Xiamen, China (1998), Eldorado do Sul, Brazil (1999, to serve Latin America), and Texas and Tennessee in the United States. In 1999, Dell Computer Corporation overtook Compaq and became the largest PC seller in the United States.

Along with setting up manufacturing facilities in different markets, the company tried to improve its products according to industry trends and consumer preferences. In 1989, it launched the notebook computer, followed by the network server (1996), workstation systems (1997), network switches (2001), and projectors and printers (2002). In 2003, the company extended its product portfolio to the consumer electronics market by launching flat panel TVs, Dell Digital Jukebox, USB key drives, and Windows mobile-powered PDAs. In the same year, in recognition of its efforts at product extension, the company's name was changed to Dell Inc. The company marketed its products under different brand names to different consumer segments. OptiPlex, Latitude, and Precision were targeted at medium-sized and large consumers, whereas students and small offices were identified as the target audience for Dimension, Inspiron, and the XPS Brand.

In January 2004, Dell entered into a technology partnership with Fuji, Xerox, Kodak, and Samsung, followed by a strategic partnership with Microsoft Corporation and Oracle Inc. It set up the Dell Enterprise Command Center to support the server and storage customers in the region. In January 2005, the company entered into a contract with Bombardier Recreational Products to supply technology products and services throughout the global IT network.

U.S. PC Industry in 2006

During the 1980s IBM and Apple Computer were the leading PC manufacturers, and Microsoft, Lotus, and IBM, were the major software firms of the United States. By the end of the 1990s, the U.S. PC market had matured due to high penetration in the traditional market and stagnation in the replacement market. According to a survey conducted by U.S. Consumer Electronics Association in 2005, more than 90 percent of households in the United States had at least one PC, 36 percent had two or more PCs, and 52 percent were reluctant to purchase a new PC.[12] In the United States, PC sales surpassed 190 million in 2005 and were growing at 5 percent annually.

During 2000–2001, the U.S. PC market accounted for 34 percent of the global PC sales. However, after the slump in the industry during 2000–2001, PC sales consistently declined. For instance, the PC shipments dropped by 11 percent from 128 million in 2001 to 114 million in 2002. Between 1996 and 1999, the average growth of PC sales in the United States was 16 percent, which reduced to 3.6 percent between 2000 and 2004. Its average price also declined by 17 percent, thereby reducing industry revenue by 4 percent. Moreover, its average selling price, which had long been near $2,000, dropped down to $1,500 for both household and business segments. Analysts feared that the growth in the industry was stagnating after showing an upward trend from 1995 to 2000.

Because the PC market had matured, companies tried different strategies to improve sales. HP[13] stressed the household mass market; Gateway Computers[14] focused on semiprofessionals; and Apple and Dell sought business customers. Various sales promotion tools (discounts, easy installment plans, free gifts) were offered to attract customers. Leading PC manufacturers such as Dell, HP, and Apple offered freebies—scanners and printers—along with PCs and huge discounts to reduce the inventory. Analysts felt that consolidation was the right measure to deal with overcapacity. In 2002, the PC industry experienced the most expensive merger between HP and Compaq, valued at $25 billion. The scenario, however, did not improve. Dell, who had recorded a high profit margin previously, began to reduce prices. After the dot.com bubble burst, many corporate companies were reluctant to invest in IT, thereby reducing the profit of HP and Dell, and pushing Gateway Computers into the red.

The industry leaders realized that the PC market had matured, leaving little room for growth, so they started diversifying into other areas and new markets. While HP provided e-business services and Web site management, Dell and Apple[15] diversified into the consumer electronics business and launched music systems as well as digital and flat televisions. Dell also started working as an Internet service provider. PC makers realized the potential of developing countries (India, China, Brazil, and Russia) and forayed into these markets. HP, which first entered the Chinese market, registered a 40 percent revenue growth from the developing market in 2004. Lyle Hurst of HP commented, "The wealthest 1 billion people in the world are pretty well served and we are targeting the next 4 billion." In 2001, only 670 million people who constituted 11 percent of the global population used PCs. Considering the increasing potential of developing markets, analysts felt that PC sales would touch 1 billion in 2010.[16]

In 1984, when Michael Dell started his company, IBM and HP were ranked as the United States's number one and number three most admired companies, respectively. In those days, nobody knew Michael Dell and his company. Commodore, with $1.1 billion PC sales and a 27 percent market share in the United States, was the market leader followed by IBM, Apple, and Tandy (see Exhibit 4). But in 2006, the scenario changed. Dell topped the list of the top 10 most admired U.S. companies, while HP and IBM found no place in this list (see Exhibit 5). Dell controlled 33 percent of the U.S. market share (see Exhibit 6) (one out of three PCs shipped was of Dell) and 19 percent of the global market (see Exhibit 7). Besides being the most admired computer company in the United States (see Exhibit 8), Dell was also the number one brand in Britain, Canada, and Ireland. In 2006, the company's earnings increased to $55 billion from a modest $80,000 in its inception year (1984). Further, its

Exhibit 4 U.S. PC Companies, 1984

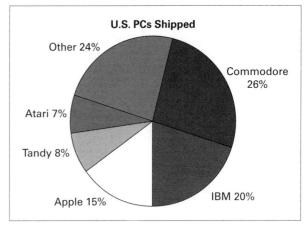

Source: http://www.fortune.com.

Exhibit 5 The Most Admired Companies, 2005

Rank	Most Admired Companies in U.S.	Most Admired Companies Globally
1.	Dell Inc.	GE
2.	GE	Wal-Mart
3.	Starbucks	Dell Inc.
4.	Wal-Mart	Microsoft
5.	SouthWest Airlines	Toyota Motor
6.	Fed Ex	Procter & Gamble
7.	Berkshire Hathaway	Johnson & Johnson
8.	Microsoft	Fed Ex
9.	Johnson & Johnson	IBM
10.	Procter & Gamble	Berkshire Hathaway

Source: http://www.fortune.com.

Exhibit 6 U.S. PC Industry, 2005

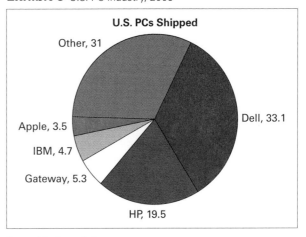

Source: http://www.fortune.com.

Exhibit 7 Top PC Makers (Global market share, first quarter 2005)

Rank	Company	Location	Market Share
1.	Dell Inc.	Texas, US	19%
2.	HP	California, US	15
3.	IBM/Lenevo	NewYork/HongKong	7
4.	Fujitsu/Siemens	Japan/Germany	5
5.	Acer	Taiwan	4
6.	Toshiba	Japan	4
7.	NEC	Japan	3
8.	Apple	California, US	2
9.	Gateway	California, US	2

Source: http://www.idc.com.

Exhibit 8 The Most Admired Computer Companies in the U.S.

YEAR		Company	Score (out of 10)
2005	2004		
1	1	IBM	7.61
2	2	Dell	7.46
3	4	Apple	6.84
4	3	Xerox	6.67
5	8	Pitney Bowes	6.52
6	6	Canon	6.49
7	7	HP	5.91
8	9	Sun Microsystems	5.81
9	10	NCR	4.92
10	5	Gateway	4.86

Source: http://www.fortune.com.

investors experienced a 28,000 percent jump in stock prices since the company went public 18 years earlier. Dell's direct business model created ripples among both the academicians and industry experts.

Dell: Facing Challenges

In 2005, the U.S. PC industry experienced many changes. IBM, the company that invented the desktop computer, sold its PC business to Lenovo in 2004; Gateway, merged with eMachines[17]; and the biggest merger in the PC industry between HP and Compaq happened in 2002. In 2003, Dell surpassed HP and emerged as a global leader with 17.6 percent market share. During 2001–2004, its average global revenue increased 19 percent, while the industry average was 12 percent. However, in 2005, after leading for almost two decades, Dell started facing problems.

During the second quarter of 2006, Dell announced that it would fall short of both its expected revenue and earnings. Though the company's bottom line was growing sluggishly, its top line growth was experiencing a decline for the last six quarters (see Exhibit 9). Between 1995 and 1999, Dell's earnings doubled on each quarter, but during the last 20 quarters, it increased by only 43 percent. It was an amazing rate according to industry standards, but a slower one when compared to its past performance. Though analysts admitted that with a turnover of $56 billion and being positioned as number 25 in the *Fortune* 500, the company was too large to replicate its previous growth rate.

In the second quarter of 2006, the company's earnings were reduced by only 1 percent, compared to the previous quarter of 2006, and it recorded revenue of $14 billion, lower than its projected $16 billion. Thus, Dell, the company that once grew more than the industry average, failed to even maintain its projected growth. In fact, it even experienced negative growth. Stakeholders felt that the shortfalls portrayed that Dell might be struggling to slash costs in order to maintain its profitability, while

Exhibit 9A Dell's Bottom Line

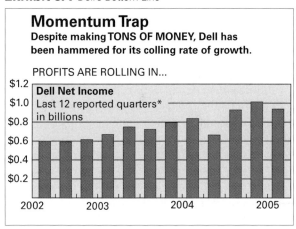

Source: http://www.fortune.com.

Exhibit 9B Dell's Top Line

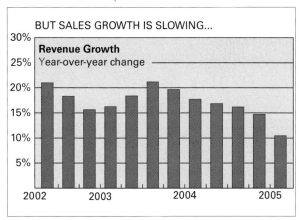

Source: http://www.fortune.com.

Exhibit 9C Dell's Revenues and Net Income (in $ million)

	2006	2005	2004	2003	2002
Revenue ($)	$55,908	$49,205	$41,444	$35,404	$31,168
Net Income ($)	3,572	3,043	2,645	2,122	1,246

Source: Compiled by the author from *Dell Annual Report* 2006.

also trying to reduce prices to increase its market share along with maintaining its top line growth. Michael Dell and Kevin Rollins, Dell's CEO, confessed that the company tried to increase its market share by reducing prices. Although the price cut helped the company to increase its shipments by 6 percent, its operating income declined by 48 percent.[18] Kevin Rollins termed the plan as a "one-time pricing and miscalculation problem" when the sales of PCs did not increase as expected. Analysts opined that Dell also failed to replace Intel chips with cheaper and better quality chips from AMD.

Apart from its top line and bottom line, Dell's growth rate in unit shipments also declined. While competitors like Acer and Fujitsu increased their global shipments in 2005, Dell's growth during that period was 17.8 percent, compared to 23.7 percent during the previous year. According to IDC, the company's unit growth rate in 2005 in the United States also declined to 12.2 percent from 16.3 percent in the 2004.[19]

Industry analysts and stakeholders felt that in the recent quarters, the company's aggressive cost cutting to meet its financial targets had compromised other performance measures, including customer support and product quality. As Jason Maxwell[20] commented, "The way is to keep customers happy in an efficient manner. Not getting the processes right can really snowball through the system quickly."[21] Michael Dell and Kevin Rollins were also worried about the unhappy customers most. Although the company once boasted its excellence in customer service, its after-sales service declined during the past couple of years. During those years, the company relocated its call centers to support its after-sales service team in India, Philippines, and Taiwan. Criticizing Dell's outsourcing strategy, Nick Donatiello, CEO of Odyssey, a San Francisco–based consulting firm commented, "They put a knife in their own heart."[22] Michael Dell also confessed, "The team was managing costs instead of managing service and quality."[23] Employees at the call centers of Dell were evaluated on the time taken to handle each call instead of the satisfaction level of the customers. Therefore, customers remained unhappy and called back angrily.

Dell also spent less on research and development (R&D) compared to HP and IBM. For instance, in 2005, Dell spent $475 million or less than 1 percent of its revenue on R&D, while HP and IBM spent 6 percent each. Meanwhile, the companies with innovative products like

Apple (with its iPod) were growing at a faster pace. Apple's stunning success with its products, iMac and the MacBook models, iPod, and the iTunes Music store virtually changed the dynamics of the industry. Dell failed to lure its customers by a traditional box slapped with Intel processors and Microsoft operating system. Even in the second quarter of 2006, HP grew faster than Dell. HP's unit growth rate was 17.9 percent, whereas Dell's was 17.8 percent. HP also proved to be more innovative than Dell. MediaSmart TV, the latest offerings from HP, could work both as conventional TV and wireless monitor for a PC, and could display photos, music, and video. HP also became more appealing and innovative than its competitors in marketing. HP's recent advertisements focus less on product features and more on the emotional aspects of using the product, feelings of the users, and the way the products changed the users' lives. Compared to its innovative competitors, Dell still positioned itself as a "value for money" PC supplier. Most of its products were alike with minor changes in configurations. Aaron Goldberg, PC industry expert of consulting firm Ziff-Davis commented, "Competitors are selling the use, the solution. But Dell's still selling products, the BQS31-S273."[24] But in a mature and consolidated industry like the PC industry, premium products, and not the basic products, contributed mostly to the company's top line and bottom line.

In the mature PC industry, the low-cost, low-style approach that made Dell number one in the PC industry seemed outdated. Contrary to cheap PCs, product design and branding also played a key role. But Dell did not have core competence in either branding or innovative product design. Analysts perceived that Dell's brand consisted of "a man and a business model." Industry analysts opined that Dell lacked in innovation and development of new businesses. Undoubtedly, for 10 years, the company's direct business model helped it to perform flawlessly, but it was a seemingly impossible approach to continue.

In 2005, Dell, which was famous for its operational efficiency, had to write off $300 million. In its shipments, most of the computers had faulty capacitors. Hence, besides $300 million for replacing them, the company had to pay $150 million extra to cover the costs associated with its recent global layoffs ("workforce realignment" according to Dell management) and the excess inventory of machine parts that Dell would not use anymore. According to a survey conducted by the University of Michigan in 2005, Dell's customer satisfaction rating fell by 6.3 percent to 74 points.

Exhibit 10 Customer Satisfaction Rating of Dell, 2005

Company	2004 (Rating)	2005 (Rating)	% Change
Apple	81	81	0%
HP (HP Brand)	71	74	2.8
Dell	79	74	−6.3
Gateway	74	72	−2.7
HP (Compaq brand)	69	67	−2.9
Others	71	74	+4.2
Industry Avg	74	74	0

Source: http://www.fortune.com.

Exhibit 11 Brand Valuation of Global Top Five Computer Companies

Rank 2005	Rank 2004	Company	Brand Value 2004	Brand Value 2005	% Change	Country of Ownership
3	3	IBM	$ 53,791	$ 51,767	4%	United States
5	5	Intel	33,499	31,112	8	United States
12	12	HP	20,978	19,860	6	United States
29	25	Dell	11,500	10,367	11	United States
43	50	Apple	6,871	5,554	24	United States

Source: http://www.interbrand.com.

However, Apple, with its innovative products, such as iPod,[25] led the list with a score of 81(see Exhibit 10). Along with the customer satisfaction rating survey, Dell received a negative ranking in the Interbrand's survey of 2005 (see Exhibit 11).

Dell faced challenges in the corporate market as well. Due to an increase in Internet traffic, the enterprising customers shifted to more powerful servers, instead of assembling lower-end models where Dell had its competence. For instance, both IBM and HP offered high-tech servers called Blade Servers, which required more sophisticated software than the stand-alone Dell machines. Dell was the only major server maker that used Intel chips in its servers. But the preference of the corporate customers was high-speed servers based on Advance Micro Devices (AMD) Opteron chip. Thus, Dell was losing out to IBM and HP. Greg Papadopoulos, chief technology officer of Sun Microsystems, commented, "Dell is stuck with only Intel, and Intel is just not competitive right now."[26]

To add to its worries, Dell experienced sluggish sales growth in Britain, where the company was the number one PC seller. According to IDC, in the Asia-Pacific region, the fastest-growing PC market (see Exhibit 12), Dell ranked third with only 7.8 percent market share. The Chinese PC group, Lenovo, which acquired IBM's PC business and had 20.4 percent market share, led the market, followed by HP with 14 percent market share. Analysts commented that because Dell could not repli-cate its direct selling business model in China, it failed to gain a significant market share in the largest emerging market of the Asia-Pacific region (see Exhibit 13). Chinese customers preferred to see and examine the products before purchasing, which meant Dell's business model was not effective in China.

Moreover, the lithium battery controversy further added to the worries of Michael Dell and Kevin Rollins. On August 14, 2006, the company announced that it would recall 4.1 million laptop computer batteries sold from April 2006 to July 2006. The batteries fitted in Dell laptops had the possibility of overheating and, in rare cases, catching fire. The lithium-ion (Li-ion) batteries used by Dell were manufactured by Sony Energy Devices Corporation. Earlier, these Li-ion batteries caused several incidents of Dell product recalls. In 2001, Dell recalled 284,000 laptop batteries and in 2005, it recalled 22,000 batteries. However, the recall of 4.1 million was the largest product battery recall in the history of the consumer electronics industry. Though Dell claimed that the recall process did not affect the Dell brand negatively, or affect the company financially, analysts had a different opinion. Analysts believed that the recall would cost the company $450 million and would have a negative impact on "Brand Dell."

Dell was no longer the high-flying company it used to be. It was not possible for a $50 billion company to

Exhibit 12 Emerging Markets

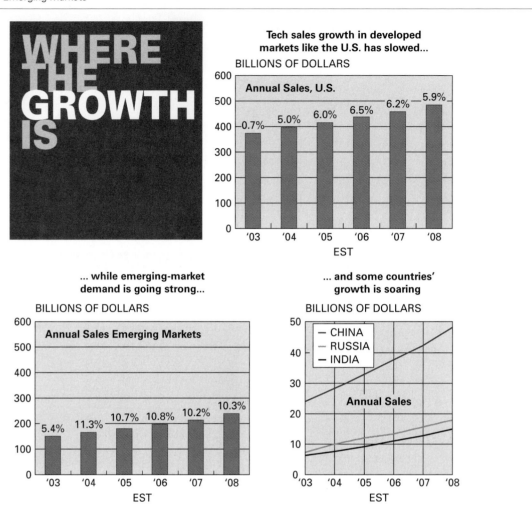

Source: http://www.fortune.com.

Exhibit 13 U.S. and Worldwide PC Market Growth

	1975	1980	1985	1990	1995	2000	2003	2005	2010
U.S. PC Sales ($ million)	$0.04	$0.76	$ 6.6	$ 9.5	$ 21.4	$ 46	$ 48.3	$ 56.6	$ 66.7
U.S. PC Revenues ($ billion)	0.05	1.50	17.2	24.5	56.8	869	78.1	84.5	86.1
Global PC Sales ($ million)	0.05	1.10	11.0	24.2	70.1	130	149.0	181.0	249.0
Global PC Revenues ($ billion)	0.06	3.60	29.5	71.3	155.0	247	243.0	270.0	302.0

Source: http://www.etforecasts.com.

ensure double-digit growth every year. The law of large numbers would eventually affect any business model, regardless of its uniqueness. "What Dell did was really brilliant,"[27] commented Phil Asmundson.[28] By developing a direct sales structure for customized PCs, Dell eliminated all kinds of inventory and intermediaries, which resulted in its phenomenal success. But even in the sluggish PC industry, this structure alone could not trigger continuous growth. In an era where every company needed to challenge and reinvent itself, the industry analysts pondered on how Dell would do this. (See Appendixes 1, 2, and 3.)

Appendix 1 Dell Products and Services

Servers   Dell's PowerEdge line of servers includes rack and tower servers for enterprise customers and aggressively priced tower servers for small organizations and workgroups/remote locations.

Storage   Dell/EMC and Dell's PowerVault lines of storage products offer hardware and software products to store, serve, and protect customer data.

Printing and Imaging Systems   Dell offers a wide array of printers, from photo printers for consumers to large multifunction lasers for corporate workgroups.

Workstations   Dell Precision desktop and mobile workstations are intended for professional users who demand exceptional performance to run sophisticated applications, such as three dimensional computer-aided design, digital content creation, geographic information systems, computer animation, software development, and financial analysis.

Notebook Computers   Dell offers two lines of notebook computer systems, namely Latitude and Inspiron.

Desktop Computers   Dell has two lines of desktop computer systems. The OptiPlex line is designed for corporate, institutional, and small-business customers. The Dimension line is designed for small businesses and home users requiring fast technology turns and high-performance computing.

Networking Products   Dell's PowerConnect switches connect computers and servers in small- to medium-sized networks.

Electronics and Accessories Products   Dell offers a range of electronics and accessories, including monitors, printers, handhelds, notebook accessories, networking and wireless products, memory, projectors, and scanners.

Managed Services   Dell also offers a wide range of IT management services, including on-site and other related services. Apart from these, Dell offers various services such as Professional Services, Deployment Services, Support Services, Training, and Certification Services.

Source: http://www.dell.com.

Appendix 2 Market Share of Top 5 PC Vendors Worldwide (Shipments in thousand units)

Rank	Company	2005 Shipments	Market Share (%)	2004 Shipments	Market Share (%)
1.	Dell	37,732	18.1	31,769	17.7
2.	HP	32,525	15.6	28,101	15.7
3.	Lenovo	12,995	6.2	4,183	2.3
4.	Acer	9,803	4.7	6,368	3.6
5.	Fujitsu/Siemens	8,489	4.1	7,187	4.0
	Others	107,041	51.3	101,573	56.7
	Total	208,586	100.0	179,181	100.0

Source: http://www.idc.com.

Appendix 3 Market Share of Top 10 Notebook Vendors Worldwide

Rank	Company	2005 Shipments (in thousand units)	Market Share (%)
1.	Dell	11,290	17.29
2.	HP	10,250	15.70
3.	Toshiba	7,156	10.96
4.	Acer	6,626	10.15
5.	Lenovo	5,376	8.23
6.	Fujitsu/Siemens	4,089	6.26
7.	Sony	2,560	3.92
8.	NEC	2,447	3.75
9.	Apple	2,171	3.32
10.	Asustek	1,552	2.38

Source: Compiled by the author from http://macdailynews.com/index.php/weblog/comments/84.

Dell's Turnaround Strategy

Until recently, Dell's business model revolved around the world's most efficient assembly and distribution of Wintel Technology. If a customer wanted a PC with an Intel chip and Microsoft software, Dell was the optimal choice for the customized PC at the lowest price. Though Dell's core business of manufacturing and selling customized PCs was a relatively low-margin commodity business, the "Wintel vendor" label had worked for the company. But growth in the PC business was slowing down, particularly in the mature U.S. market. Michael Dell understood that the company would need new growth drivers to add or move incremental business lines into profitable business lines. For instance, the markets for servers and printers, which were still relatively new to Dell, had higher margins than those of PCs. Dell moved into servers and storage, mobility products, services, software peripheral categories, and printers, thereby, becoming a diversified IT company.

In 2003 Dell introduced multifunction flat panel TVs, DJ music players, an online music download service, digital music players, and projectors. Analysts commented that the product extension into the consumer electronics market was a natural fit for the company. New products such as plasma TVs, MP3 players, and digital cameras were still in their infancy. Along with these growing lines, entertainment had become increasingly digital, making music, movies, and photos an extension of the PC. Dell's PCs ran on Intel Pentium 4 processors and the Microsoft's Windows XP Media Center System. These PCs enabled live-TV viewing and included DVD players, TiVo-style personal video recorders, and software for digital music downloading and photo management. "We are here to confirm our entry into the consumer electronics category. We are expanding our line up, even as our PC business is profitable in every segment,"[29] commented Michael Dell. The media PC occupied a middle ground between standard PCs and consumer electronics. These models were considered by the PC giants to have immense potential. Dell's Media Center PCs were a combination of PC and entertainment systems with the ability to play music, edit, play, and record videos, besides having Internet compatibility. In 2006, the company launched XPS, a high-end subbrand in the media PC segment. It also purchased gaming PC maker Alienware to strengthen its position in the media PC segment. The recently launched XPS M2010 was positioned as "A unique luggable multimedia computer designed to be carried from room to room, complete with large screen, high-quality speakers and an easy-to-access DVD player."[30]

Analysts felt that with its proven business model in the PC industry, Dell would also be able to gain a significant share in the consumer electronics industry, not only because these two segments had similar products, but also the same buying process and target customer groups. Besides the supply side, Dell was able to source components at a lower price, because a large number of OEMs were identical and in the same low cost production countries, operating in a similar industry. The fundamental difference between Dell and its competitors was that while other companies produced to match sales forecasts, Dell produced every single machine for a specific order. This approach helped Dell to reduce its inventory and prices. For instance, Dell carried only four days of inventory, compared to IBM's 20 days and HP's 28 days. The company also urged its suppliers to build raw-material inventory bases close to Dell's factories for cost sharing.

In addition to expanding its consumer electronics business, the company improved its products and launched innovative product lines to match the industry trends and tastes of its customers. With the advent of computer networking technology, the company entered into the network server market in 1999, followed by workstation systems market and storage products (2001). It also introduced network switches, projectors, and printers for corporate and consumer markets. In 2005, Dell launched new consumer PC lines. The company introduced desktop models in the $250–350 price bracket, notebooks at $500–750, midsized and business PCs at $350–400. In the PC industry, Dell waged a war against HP's printer business. Because printing was an installed base business, the revenue came from the demand of cartridges from the established customers, who would buy them for years. In 2002, Dell began to sell both inkjet and laser printers, and within three years it managed to grab 20 percent of the U.S. inkjet printer market. Analysts felt that the margins from printers were not as great as from its other businesses, but that the product with its low price had the potential to be a significant business for Dell within a few years.[31]

A new move of Dell that was appreciated by analysts was the Robins decision to use AMD microprocessors in its products. Michael Dell and Kevin Rollins also admitted that the move, though necessary, took a long time to implement. Michael Dell commented, "We overestimated Intel and under estimated AMD in prior periods."[32] Since 2004, AMD had developed processors that were faster and more energy efficient than Intel's. AMD's prices were also lower than Intel's. Despite these reasons, until May 2006, Dell was the only manufacturer who refused to use AMD's product. Michael Dell commented that Dell was an "equal opportunity processor user" and it would not restrict the use of AMD recovers to two types of server and one desktop line only, but would use AMD chips more extensively.

To improve the customer satisfaction rating, Dell took some innovative measures. Analysts felt that the customers expected a low-priced PC, along with better customer service. Stephen Dukker, founder of eMachines Inc., commented, "Customers want to have their cake and eat it too. They want a PC at $300 but expect the same support that came with a machine 10 years ago and cost $2,500."[33] The company planned to offer a one-year membership to customers so that they could opt for various levels of assistance at varied prices. For instance, one of the options was a quarterly PC tune-up, where the company personnel would clean the hard drive and check security software. The company also opened kiosks (57 kiosks in 9 states of the United States) in 2003 to enable the shoppers to acquaint themselves with its products.

For the corporate customers, the company also improved its services. In 2005, the company introduced its Premier Page Web site. This Web site was customized according to the specific needs of the corporate customers. Each company's Premier Page provided specific information about the Dell products and services it used. Orders placed through a company's Premier Page, were routed to Dell for approval and processing. The Web page helped the customers to track records of inventories and assignments through detailed purchasing reports, on the basis of geographic location, product, average unit price, and total dollar value.

In the overseas markets, Dell started taking some new initiatives. For instance, in China, the company launched the Smart PC in 2002. The Smart PC was a low-cost, high-memory basic PC, without any value-added service. It was offered at a price lower than $579, compared to the Chinese-made Tongxi PC that was priced at $628. Because most of the Chinese customers were not confident about electronic transactions, Dell worked with Chinese banks to receive payments. These innovative initiatives and products helped the company to increase its market share to 7.8 percent by 2005 from 4 percent in 2002.

If product recalls are handled properly, a company not only can keep damage to a minimum but also may find opportunities to reap unexpected benefits.[34]

Nevertheless, analysts were not convinced by the company's claims. They thought Dell, and not the battery manufacturer Sony, would face bad publicity because of the recall. According to them, in order to save its reputation among customers Dell had to be more strategic. From the perspective of industry analysts, the recall would have a bigger impact on Dell's reputation with individual customers than corporate customers. They asserted that institutional buyers "will probably take a balanced view of this." An analyst commented, "If Dell handles this well, and everything comes together with the right message, I think corporate buyers will shrug it off over time and it will be a forgotten issue a year from now."[35] On the other hand, experts warned, individual customers were expected to form a negative opinion of the company and it would be difficult for the company to change customer perceptions.

Some industry watchers felt that Dell's voluntary recall of faulty batteries would boost its efforts to improve its customer service and win back the goodwill of the customers. They pointed out that the recall was a great opportunity for Dell to prove that it acted voluntarily to protect its customers. Moreover, industry insiders said that Dell would not have any serious financial implication because Sony (the battery manufacturer) was sharing the cost of the recall with Dell. They also mentioned that the fact that Dell announced the recall first and others (Apple and Matsushita) followed, would go on to show that Dell was a company with foresight.

Despite these odds, Dell was able to retain its number one position in the PC industry across the globe. In July 2006, in a survey jointly conducted by *Investor's Business Daily* and TIPP, Dell still topped the list (50 percent of U.S. consumers who planned to buy PCs opted for Dell as their first choice). Dell had more market share in the United States (45 percent) than the combined market share of HP, Gateway, and Apple. Even though the dominance in the domestic PC market was difficult to improve dramatically, the company experienced success in selling related products and services to businesses. In the quarter ending in July 2006, the company experienced 36 percent growth in its storage business and 21 percent in its service business (see Exhibit 14).

Turnaround Strategy: Will It Do Wonders?

Dell's stakeholders were worried about the threats that its initiatives faced. Their foremost concern was the failure of Dell's business model in the consumer electronics division, which the company thought would work. According to David Naranjo of DisplaySearch, in the $130 billion consumer electronics industry, Dell was ranked number 10 in LCD TV shipments (with 2.4 percent market share) and number seven in plasma screen shipments (with 3.3 percent market share) in 2005. The much-hyped Media Center PC segment also failed to act as a growth driver. HP's HP-z500 Windows XP-based PC and Apple's Macintosh Mini were more innovative products than Dell's Media PC; hence HP and Apple were the market leaders. Though Dell offered its products at competitive prices, its business model failed to replicate the success of Dell's PCs in the consumer electronics business. The customers of the consumer electronics category preferred to compare various brands displayed in the retail stores, thereby judging the product quality before making purchasing decisions. But Dell did not have enough shelf space in its retail outlets to display its products. Dell's customers could buy only through catalogs and the Web site, which did not provide adequate demonstration value and

Exhibit 14 Dell's Net Revenue by Product Category (in $ billion)

	August 2006	April 2006	July 2005	Growth Rates	
				Sequential	Year to Year
Net Revenue by Product Category					
Desktop PC	$ 4.9	$ 5.1	$ 5.1	6%	4%
Mobility	3.7	3.7	3.4	1	8
Server	1.4	1.3	1.3	0	1
Storage	0.5	0.5	0.4	12	36
Enhanced Services	1.4	1.4	1.2	2	21
Software	2.2	2.2	2.0	2	10
Percentage of Total Net Revenue					
Desktop PC	35%	36%	37%		
Mobility	26	26	26		
Server	9	9	10		
Storage	4	3	3		
Enhanced Services	10	10	9		
Software	16	16	15		

Source: http://www.dell.com.

was the main reason for Dell's failure. Thus the company overlooked the Chinese customers' preference of touching and examining the products before purchase. While the market leader Lenovo had 4,800 retail outlets in China alone, the number of Dell's retail outlets was negligible.

Analysts were skeptical about the tech companies' idea of making successful forays into consumer markets. During the 1980s, IBM made a foray into such markets with its PC Jr. Machine but was forced to withdraw in the early 1990s. Similarly, Dell was accustomed to the PC market, but the consumer electronics category would be a tougher challenge. The retail stores, however, were packed with products from entrenched companies, including Sony, Samsung, and Phillips, and aggressive new companies such as Apex Digital. Several other PC companies—Apple, Gateway, and HP—also made forays into the consumer electronics segment. For instance, Gateway introduced 100 new products, including 11 plasma and liquid crystal display televisions, digital cameras, camcorders, MP3 music players, and DVD players.

Even the struggling U.S. consumer electronics market became a problem for Dell. Though the segment accounted for only 15 percent of the company's turnover in 2005, it was considered to be a key growth driver. The analysts predicted only 4–5 percent growth ($8 billion) in the consumer electronics segment for 2006, compared to 13 percent in 2005 and 19 percent in 2004.

Kevin Rollins acknowledged that the company had emphasized selling low-end PCs. These PCs had insignificant margins and contributed negligible amounts to the company's bottom line, but Dell did not plan to abandon its most popular $500 PC segment. However, the company, with its pricing and innovative business model, was expected to find opportunities in the up-market. It needed to identify its key growth drivers from the up-market category, including printers. But analysts felt that achieving success in the PC business and doing the same in the printer business were two different things. Dell succeeded in the PC business because it, unlike that of the printer business, was commodifying. Moreover, Dell outsourced the manufacturing of printers to Lexmark, Fuji, and Kodak, who might not be capable of producing Dell-compatible printers.

With a 19 percent share (2005) of the $1.2 trillion global IT market, the CEO and the chair of Dell predicted that the company would hit $80 billion in revenue by 2010. Analysts figured out that more than 70 percent of Dell's projected revenue would be derived from corporate customers, TVs, displays, media center PCs, and other accessories and services. Due to higher profit margins, the aggregate revenue growth of these categories would be twice that of desktop computers. The company needed a yearly growth of 15 percent to meet its target. But in the fiscal year 2005–2006, the company expected only a 10 percent growth, much less than the 20–25 percent of the 1990s. However, as always, Michael Dell was relentlessly upbeat, "Our model continues to be best in the business. We would not trade ours for anyone else's. It is also important to have a little perspective. In the past ten years our sales are up about 15 times, earnings and stock prices are up about 20 times. Not too shabby!"[36] It's difficult to refute this claim, but past performance is no guarantee of future results.

1. 2006, Dell: Under siege, *Fortune,* September 18.
2. 2006, Dell's midlife crisis, *Fortune,* November 28.
3. Ibid.
4. Fatboy Slim (born on July 16, 1963, also known as Norman Cook) is a British musician in the dance music genre. His style is known as big beat, a combination of hip hop, breakbeat, rock, and rhythm and blues.
5. Dell: Under siege.
6. Dell Inc. sells all its products to both consumers and corporate customers, using a direct sales model via the Internet Internet and telephone network. It manufactures PCs according to the customer specifications.
7. 2005, Technology's Mr. Predictable, http://www.economist.com, September, 22.
8. A capacitor is a passive electronic component that stores energy in the form of an *electrostatic field.* In its simplest form, a capacitor consists of two conducting plates separated by an insulating material called the dielectric. Capacitance is directly proportional to the surface areas of the plates, and is inversely proportional to the plates' separation.
9. Wall Street is the name of a narrow street in lower Manhattan running east from Broadway downhill to the East River. Considered to be the historical heart of the Financial District, it was the first permanent home of the New York Stock Exchange. The phrase "Wall Street" is also used to refer to American financial markets and financial institutions as a whole.
10. In 1989, Dell launched a high end product named "Olympic," which was rejected by the customers and subsequently withdrawn by the company. In 1992, Dell also faced quality problems in its notebook.
11. NASDAQ (originally an acronym for National Association of Securities Dealers Automated Quotations) is a U.S. electronic stock market. It was founded by the National Association of Securities Dealers (NASD) who divested it in a series of sales in 2000 and 2001. It is owned and operated by The Nasdaq Stock Market, Inc.
12. The consumer PC market in United States, http://www.oft.gov.uk.
13. Hewlett-Packard Company, commonly known as HP, is one of the world's largest corporations. Headquartered in Palo Alto, California, United States, it has a global presence in the fields of computing, printing, and digital imaging, and also sells software and services.
14. Gateway, Inc., is an Irvine, California-based computer company founded in 1985 by Ted Waitt. Originally called Gateway 2000, it was one of the first widely successful direct order companies, utilizing a sales model similar to that of Dell.
15. Apple Computer, Inc., is an American computer technology company. Apple was a major player in the personal computer revolution in the 1970s. The Apple II microcomputer, introduced in 1977, was a hit with home users. In 1983, Apple introduced the first commercial personal computer to use a graphical user interface (GUI), the Lisa.

In 1984, Apple introduced the revolutionary Macintosh. The Macintosh (commonly called the "Mac") was the first successful commercial implementation of a GUI, which is now used in all major computers. Apple is known for its innovative, well-designed hardware and software, such as the iPod and the iMac, as well as the well-known iTunes application (originally part of the iLife suite), and Mac OS X., its current operating system.
16. Kenellos Michael, 2005, A billion PC users on the way, CNET News, http://www.cnet.com, August 2.
17. On January 30, 2004, Gateway purchased low-cost PC maker eMachines, hoping that its outsourced manufacturing process would help Gateway cut costs and eMachines' profitable retail business would help its bottom line. Gateway announced its intention to keep the eMachines brand.
18. In the first quarter of 2006, the company posted an operating income of $949 million, which reduced to $605 million during the second quarter.
19. U.S.-based IT consulting firms provide information technology industry analysis, market data and insight, as well as strategic and tactical guidance.
20. Jason Maxwell is the portfolio manager of Los Angeles–based TCW Group, which owns 29 million shares of Dell Inc.
21. 2005, It's bad to worse at Dell, *BusinessWeek,* November.
22. 2006, Dell: Under siege, *Fortune,* September 18.
23. Ibid.
24. Ibid.
25. The iPod is a brand of portable digital media player designed and marketed by Apple Computer.
26. 2005, It's bad to worse at Dell, *BusinessWeek,* November.
27. 2005, Dell's midlife crisis, *Fortune,* November 28.
28. Phil Asmundson is the managing partner of Deloitte's United States Technology, Media, and Telecommunications global industry group specialists.
29. R. Shim & J. G. Spooner, Dell opens its doors to home electronics, CNET News.com.
30. http://www.dell.com.
31. Dell's color laser is almost half the price of an HP and the cartridge is 45 percent less.
32. 2006, Dell: Under siege, *Fortune,* September 18.
33. 2005, Hanging up on Dell, http://www.businessweek.com, October 10.
34. N. C. Smith, et al. A strategic approach to managing product recalls, *Harvard Business Review.*
35. L. Tucci, 2006, Battery recall has upside for Dell, http://searchtechtarget.techtarget.com, August 16, 2006.
36. 2005, Dell's midlife crisis, *Fortune* November 28.

Case 7

Ford Motor Company

Jeff Andress, Dennis Horton, Cody Kleven,
Mike McCullar, Hollon Stevens, Robin Chapman

Arizona State University

Introduction

William Clay Ford, Jr., was staring out the window of his office in Dearborn, Michigan, lost in thought. The future of Ford Motor Company was hanging in the balance, and no one was certain how best to save this once-great company. Question after question without any easy answers kept going through his mind. . . . How much longer can Ford survive with the large losses? Will it have to sell off assets or financially restructure? Can it cut enough costs, and where should it cut? Will the union leaders realize the situation, and how much will they be willing to help? When will Chinese competitors enter the U.S. market? How can Ford develop its product offerings to adjust for higher fuel costs? How can Ford improve its product offering to reverse or at least stop the market share losses? How much more market share will it lose?

The magnitude of the situation seemed overwhelming. In order to overcome these challenges, it seemed as if Ford would have to restructure every aspect of its business. It would require improved product offerings with cutting-edge design and high quality; improved operation with more flexibility and lower costs; and improved marketing with better brand image and customer interest. Ford was at a crossroads, and the way ahead remained shrouded in fog.

History

Ford has gone through many evolutions since its humble beginnings on June 16, 1903.[1] Henry Ford began this corporation, now synonymous with the assembly line, the Industrial Revolution, and the American Dream, with 11 business associates and $28,000 in capital.[2] Ford Motor Company continued along with minimal leadership problems until the death of its president, Edsel Ford,

in 1943. Intense dissension about who should succeed Edsel Ford continued until Henry Ford, at the age of 79, returned from retirement to lead the company. For the next two years under Henry Ford the company operated with massive losses of $10 million dollars per month.[3] Finally, in 1945, Henry Ford was forced to step down and Henry Ford II assumed the role of president.[4] Henry Ford II managed to successfully maneuver the company back to productivity and empowered Robert McNamara and his group (planning and financial analysis) to transform Ford's leadership style from a tyrannical dictatorship to a "powerful, professional oligarchy."[5] Over the next 20 years, Ford Motor Company's presidents and CEOs turned over 13 times.[6] The current CEO, Alan Mulally, was appointed in September 2006 to take over for William Clay Ford, Jr., who had served as both president and CEO since 2001. William Clay Ford, Jr., led Ford Motor Company to three straight years of profitability followed by a sharp decrease in profits marked by a $1.44 billion loss in the first half of 2006.[7] These losses motivated Ford Motor Company to search for a new CEO from outside the industry, Alan Mulally, formerly of Boeing Corporation. Mulally stood out as a qualified successor because he demonstrated the leadership skills Ford had established many years ago as critical to success.

Strategic Leadership

Ford Motor Company, recognizing the importance of human capital development in strengthening the company as a whole, developed a leadership training program in the late 1990s comprised of four separate courses, Capstone, Experienced Leader Challenge, Ford Business Associates, and New Business Leader. These programs were designed to instill the mind-set and vocabulary of

This case was developed with contributions from Melodie Bolin.

a revolutionary leader as well as to teach the tools necessary to steer a leadership and manufacturing revolution.[8] Ford also planned to use its Business Leaders Initiative to get all 100,000 salaried employees worldwide involved in "business-leadership 'cascades,' intense exercises that combine trickle-down communications with substantive team projects."[9] In 2000, Ford planned to guide 2,500 managers through one of its four leadership courses.[10] Yet in 2006, Ford Motor Company's leadership structure remained complex, highly bureaucratic, and comprised of a six-layered management scheme on which pay is based.

The former COO for the Americas affirmed, "The company has too many layers, the company is too bureaucratic, and it takes too long to get things done."[11] (See Exhibit 1 for Ford senior leadership structure.) Ford geared up for many changes under the leadership of Alan Mulally, including the replacement of many members of the top leadership team.[12]

Alan Mulally

Alan Mulally was named CEO and president of Ford Motor Company in September 2006. He is also a member

Exhibit 1 Ford's Top Management Structure

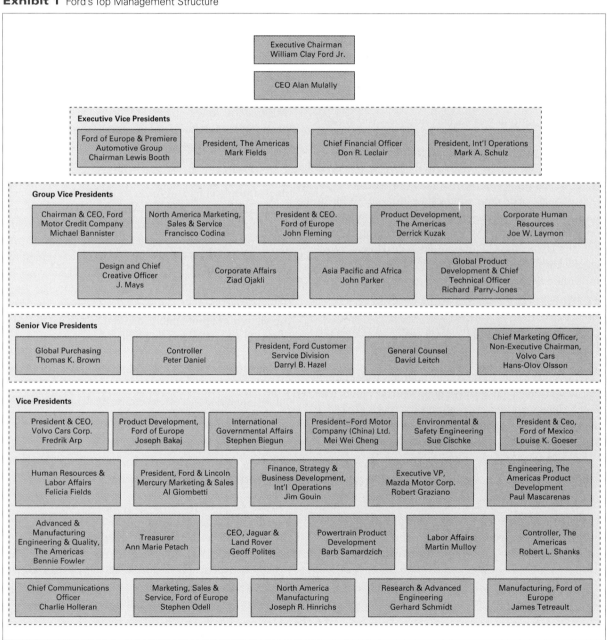

of the board of directors. Prior to joining Ford, Mulally was an executive vice president at Boeing as well as the president and CEO of Boeing Commercial Airlines. Mulally has received many accolades throughout his career and has been recognized for his contributions and industry leadership by being named one of the "Best Leaders of 2005" by *BusinessWeek* magazine. Mulally is perhaps best known for his efforts to streamline Boeing's production system and the associated transformation of the company's commercial airplanes product line.[13] Despite his many successes in the airline industry, chiefly his turnaround of Boeing's commercial airline division, it remains to be seen whether these turnaround experiences will be applicable to the turnaround Ford is seeking.

William Clay Ford, Jr.

The current executive chairperson of Ford Motor Company is William Clay Ford, Jr. William Ford has been a member of the board since 1988, and was elected to the office of chairperson on January 1, 1999. He is also the chair of the board's Finance Committee and a member of the Environmental and Public Policy Committee. William Ford also served as chief executive officer from October 2001 to September 2006. As CEO, William Ford led the company to three straight years of profitability, after experiencing a $5.5 billion loss in

2001, by focusing on improving quality, lowering costs, and delivering new products that satisfy customers."[14] On his step back from CEO to executive chairperson, William Ford said in an interview with journalist Keith Naughton of *Newsweek,* "I've always said that titles are not important to me. This company has been part of my life since the day I was born and will be until the day I die. What's important is getting this company headed in the right direction."[15] According to Ford's Web site, William Ford continues to focus on the future of Ford Motor Company and the strategies that will move it successfully into the future. He is quoted as saying, "Innovation is the compass by which Ford Motor Company sets its direction. We want to have an even bigger impact in our next 100 years than we did in our first 100."[16]

Board of Directors

Ford Motor Company's board of directors is comprised of 13 extremely diverse members who have many different corporate and personnel backgrounds, ranging from professor of physics to publishing, banking, and auditing. Three of the directors are members of the Ford family, and six have served on the board of directors for more than 10 years (see Exhibit 2). Despite the myriad of backgrounds presented in Ford's board of directors, past decisions have shown that the Ford family retains

Exhibit 2 Ford's Board of Directors

Director	Position	Member Since
William Clay Ford Jr.	Executive Chairman, Ford Motor Company	1988
John R. H. Bond	Group Chairman, HSBC Holdings plc	2000
Stephen G. Butler	Retired Chairman and CEO, KPMG, LLP	N.A.
Kimberly Casiano	President and COO, Casiano Communications, Inc.	2003
Edsel B. Ford II	Retired Vice President, Ford Motor Company Former President and COO, Ford Credit	1988
William Clay Ford	Director Emeritus	2000
Irvine O. Hockaday, Jr.	Retired President and CEO, Hallmark Cards Inc.	1987
Richard A. Manoogian	Chairman and CEO, Masco Corporation	2001
Ellen R. Marram	Managing Director, North Castle Partners, LLC	1988
Alan Mulally	President and CEO, Ford Motor Company	2006
Homer A. Neal	Director, University of Michigan ATLAS Project, Samuel A. Goudsmit Distinguished University Professor of Physics, and Interim President Emeritus, University of Michigan	1997
Jorma Ollila	Chairman, CEO, and Chairman of the Group Executive Board, Nokia Corporation	2000
John L. Thornton	Professor and Director, Global Leadership Program, Tsinghua University, Beijing, China	1996

Source: 2006, Ford Company Media, http://media.ford.com.

most of the decision-making power and influence. It was only after Ford Motor Company began to lose billions of dollars that William Clay Ford, Jr., stepped down as CEO. Even with his resignation as CEO, it is clear that William Ford still wields most of the power at Ford, as evidenced by his renaming the board chair position, "Executive Chairman." William Ford was honored as the 2006 Automotive Industry Executive of the Year, a great honor considering the trends taking place within the automotive industry.[17]

Trends in the U.S. Auto Market

Although the U.S. auto market is large, it is not a high-growth market. The average growth rate has been less than 1 percent over the past seven years. However, competitors have experienced market share shifts. Despite the fact that GM still has the dominant market share, both GM and Ford have been losing market share to foreign competition. (See Exhibit 3 and 4 for trends related to U.S. light vehicle market share from domestic, Japanese, Korean, and European producers.) In 1995, the Big Three American auto producers held 73 percent of the U.S. market share, but by third quarter 2007, that number had dropped below 50 percent.[18] Similarly, foreign firms have steadily increased production in the United States. In 1986, U.S. firms produced about 95 percent of the cars made in the United States, but by 2005, that number had fallen to 47.7 percent.[19] The trend of increased foreign

production in the United States should continue as Ford and GM continue to trim production in the United States.

Consolidation

A consolidation of auto manufacturing firms has affected both the global and domestic markets. Chrysler merged with German manufacturer Daimler-Benz in 1998 to form DaimlerChrysler, but Daimler sold Chrysler shares in 2007. Over the past several years, Ford purchased or formed agreements with Mazda, Volvo, Jaguar, and Land Rover. In 2006 GM began discussions about possible alliances with Renault and Nissan, but skeptics were relieved when these talks broke off. However, the competitive structure of the global automotive industry makes further mergers and alliances that involve firms competing in the U.S. market likely.

Market Segmentation

Another trend has been further market segmentation. With the increased number of foreign competitors and little differentiation between manufacturers, firms competing in the U.S. market have continued to target smaller customer segments, increasing the number of models each maker produces in an effort to attract each smaller customer group. Analysts predict that the number of available car models in the U.S. market will increase from 250 in 1999 to 330 by 2008. Similarly, the average annual sales of each model decreased from 106,819 to 48,626 in the years between 1985 and 2005.[20]

Exhibit 3 U.S. Light Vehicle Market Trends

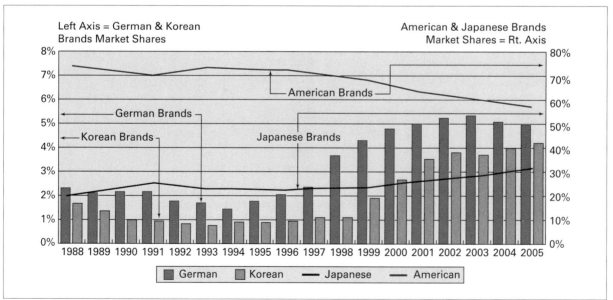

Sources: Ward's AutoInfoBank; 2006, The road ahead for the U.S. auto industry, Office of Aerospace and Automotive Industries International Trade Administration U.S. Department of Commerce, April.

Exhibit 4 North American Automotive Market Share (GM, Ford, Toyota)

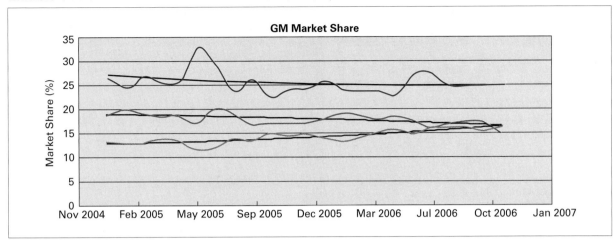

Note: Black line represents the trend of the individual automakers North American market share.

Source: 2006, North American Automotive Market Data, http://www.wardsauto.com, December 2.

Alternative Fuels

Another change is the significant trend in building cars that use alternative fuels and have higher fuel efficiency. Although hybrid cars that combine small engines with electric power currently are gaining the most attention, other alternatives such as bio diesel, electric, or hydrogen fuel cells have also been developed. Given the increasing global demand for fuel, and the recent increase in gas prices in the United States, the drive toward alternative fuels and greater efficiency should continue.

One cost-effective alternative currently being used by automakers is E85, a corn based fuel,which is a blend of 85 percent ethanol (a form of alcohol) and 15 percent gasoline. E85 provides about 25 percent less energy than traditional gasoline, but advocates argue that it will reduce U.S. dependence on foreign producers and develop a domestic industry that supports farmers.[21]

As noted previously, electric hybrid vehicles have already been commercialized and represent a significant technological change, but if hydrogen fuel cell technology can be commercialized, it would represent an even more radical technological shift. These technological innovations represent an opportunity for the auto manufacturers to differentiate themselves from the competition. Just as important as considering the current trends in the market place, automotive firms must examine the competitive environment.

U.S. Auto Industry Competitive Environment

The United States comprises the largest auto market in the world with more than 16 million vehicles sold in each of the last seven years.[22] Given its size, automakers from around the world have targeted the U.S. market for exports. Although at least 22 firms compete in the U.S. market, the four largest firms (GM, Ford, Toyota, and DaimlerChrysler) control more than 68 percent of the market and the top six firms (including Honda and Nissan) control 83.5 percent of the market.[23] See Exhibit 5 for a breakdown of light vehicle U.S. market share. General Motors (GM) and Ford are the only two domestic firms that still have a significant presence. Chrysler had been the third largest U.S. auto manufacturing firm before it merged with Daimler-Benz AG in 1998 to form DaimlerChrysler. Many of the foreign firms who compete in the U.S. market also produce vehicles in the United States. In 2006, 11 firms produced cars and light trucks in the United States (BMW, DaimlerChrysler, Ford, GM, Honda, Hyundai, Mazda, Mitsubishi, Nissan, Subaru, and Toyota).[24]

DaimlerChrysler

As mentioned, DaimlerChrysler was formed in 1998 as the result of a merger between Daimler-Benz and Chrysler. At year-end 2006 it employed approximately 360,000 people and sold almost 4.7 million vehicles (both passenger and commercial) to consumers in 200 different countries.[25] Similar to the financial struggles experienced in recent years by Ford and GM, DaimlerChrysler announced a $1.2 billion loss in 2006, a 9 percent decrease in sales, and a 0.5 percent decrease in market share to 13.5 percent.[26] The merger did not prove to be beneficial for Daimler and the majority interest of Chrysler was recently divested to a private equity group, Cerberus Capital Management (August 2007). DaimlerChrysler (to be renamed Daimler AG) continues to hold 19 percent ownership and will strive to help Chrysler succeed as a stand-alone car company.[27]

Exhibit 5 November 2006 and Year-to-Date U.S. Light Vehicle Market Share

Maker	November 2006			YTD		
	Volume	% Change	Market Share	Volume	% Change	Market Share
GM	291,061	6.0	24.3	3,698,026	(8.3)	24.5
Ford	166,397	(10.6)	13.9	2,504,151	(7.5)	16.6
Toyota	196,695	15.9	16.4	2,314,202	12.5	15.3
Chrysler	164,556	2.9	13.7	1,952,090	(7.7)	12.9
Honda	106,446	0.6	8.9	1,377,580	3.6	9.1
Nissan	76,015	(1.6)	6.3	927,474	(5.9)	6.1
Hyundai	28,417	(14.9)	2.4	418,155	1.5	2.8
BMW	25,889	(3.6)	2.2	280,186	0.7	1.9
Kia	22,203	10.5	1.9	264,298	2.8	1.7
Mazda	20,729	16.7	1.7	248,874	4.1	1.6
Mercedes	22,079	20.8	1.8	219,678	13.9	1.5
Subaru	15,800	8.8	1.3	180,090	2.3	1.2
Mitsubishi	9,256	4.0	0.8	108,648	(5.0)	0.7
Volvo	9,229	14.3	0.8	107,282	(6.3)	0.7
Suzuki	6,395	12.1	0.5	93,673	27.5	0.6
Audi	9,209	16.4	0.8	78,219	5.4	0.5
Land Rover	4,229	(7.6)	0.4	41,760	6.4	0.3
Saab	2,497	19.4	0.2	32,814	(7.8)	0.2
Porsche	2,611	(2.4)	0.2	31,377	7.9	0.2
Jaguar	1,256	(35.2)	0.1	19,130	(31.6)	0.1
Isuzu	565	(23.4)	0.0	7,977	(29.6)	0.1

Source: 2006, U.S. Light Vehicle Sales, Market Share for November.

The major brands comprising DaimlerChrysler include Mercedes-Benz, Dodge, Chrysler, Jeep, and Smart (initially only available in Europe but slated for U.S. debut). Within these brands are a wide variety of vehicle types: trucks, SUVs, sedans, compacts, and sports cars.

Like other major automobile manufacturers, Daimler-Chrysler focuses on finding alternative sources of power to gasoline. The 2006 DaimlerChrysler lineup of vehicles included five E85 capable vehicles: the Dodge Durango (SUV), Dodge Ram 1500 Series (truck), Dodge Stratus (sedan), Chrysler Sebring (sedan), and Dodge Caravan. In 2007, three additional vehicles were added to the lineup. As for hybrid technology, DaimlerChrysler is far behind U.S. and Japanese competitors, but instead has focused on clean diesel power using its BLUETEC technology that reduces nitrogen oxide levels.[28]

R&D efforts are focused on fuel cell infrastructure and vehicle development and GTL (gas to liquids) diesel. Similar to Ford and GM, DaimlerChrysler is piloting fuel cell powered vehicles; it has 60 vehicles deployed worldwide.[29] Its GTL initiatives are meant to enable DaimlerChrysler's diesel product line to produce higher-quality diesel than that made from crude.[30]

General Motors

General Motors, the world's largest automaker, was founded in 1908 and currently employs approximately 284,000 people and manufactures its cars and trucks in 33 countries.[31] While Ford suffered a 7.5 percent market share loss in the last 6 years, from 22.8 percent in 2000 to about 15.3 percent in second quarter 2007,[32] GM experienced a somewhat less significant 6 percent loss, from 28.1 percent to 22.1 percent.[33] Like Ford, GM has been working to increase profitability by decreasing costs and maintaining market share.

On November 21, 2005, GM announced plant closings and the loss of jobs that resulted in an annual reduction of expenses totaling $7 billion, and a 30 percent loss in capacity. The already depleted workforce, which has been reduced by 40 percent since 2000,[34] will continue to decline by 30,000 employees by the end of 2008.

In terms of maintaining market share in future years, General Motors has focused its R&D efforts on gasoline-alternative sources of power. It currently offers 16 E85 capable vehicles which include sedans, trucks, SUVs, and vans. In September 2006 GM announced "Project Driveway," which highlighted the Chevy Equinox Fuel Cell. The hydrogen-powered Equinox is slated to be delivered to 100 customers in the fall of 2007, in three different geographic areas: California, New York City, and Washington, D.C. Drivers will be asked to report on all aspects of their driving experience. According to GM, these customers will provide the first "meaningful market test."[35]

Another aspect of GM's effort to reduce vehicle emissions and improve fuel efficiency is the research and development of hybrid vehicles. The focus has been placed on high-volume, high fuel-consuming vehicles first, but eventually GM plans to develop 12 different hybrid models The current hybrid offerings include the 2006 Chevy Silverado Classic, 2006 GMC Sierra Classic, 2007 Saturn Vue Green Line, 2008 Chevy Tahoe, and the 2008 GMC Yukon.

Toyota

Toyota Motor Company is one of the principal competitors to Ford domestically. The Japan-based automaker has made tremendous strides in increasing market share and sales volume in the North American automotive market. Since 2000, Ford's market share has continuously fallen while Toyota continues to gain ground. In 2000 Ford and Toyota had 25 percent and 10 percent of the market respectively, while at the start of 2007 they possessed 14.8 percent and 15 percent respectively.[36] Ford sold 3.05 million vehicles during 2006 while Toyota sold 2.5 million cars and trucks.[37] Toyota's success in the United States has led to a change in the "Big Three" moniker; Ford, GM, and Chrysler have instead been designated as the "Detroit Three."[38]

Toyota's appeal is based on its vehicle lineup, quality, safety ratings, and resale value. Toyota offers a vehicle lineup that spans the breadth of the automotive market from subcompact autos to full-size SUVs. Toyota currently produces seven (7) passenger cars, six (6) SUVs, two (2) truck models, and one (1) minivan, under its flagship name, with prices ranging from $11,000 to $60,000.[39] Of the vehicles in Toyota's lineup, three, one in each category except the minivan, are offered with hybrid technology. The number of available vehicles and fuel options give the consumer a great deal of flexibility when choosing an automobile.

Toyota's flagship models are considered to be high-quality vehicles and among the safest vehicles available. The National Highway Traffic Safety Administration (NHTSA) performs safety tests on each vehicle design for a given year. For the vehicle year 2006, the NHTSA rated all but one of Toyota's vehicles, the Matrix, with at least a four-star rating. Five of Toyota's vehicles received a five-star rating, the highest possible safety rating.[40]

Innovation is another of Toyota's competitive advantages over not just Ford, but the majority of the auto industry. Booz Allen, which rates companies against their peers on research and development, rated Toyota highest among major automobile producing companies.[41] In 2005, Toyota spent $7.2 billion on R&D while Ford, which spends the most on R&D within the domestic automotive industry, spent $8 billion.[42] The Booz Allen rating indicates that Toyota achieves the highest return on its R&D expenditures.

Firms within the automotive industry have had to be wise in the battle for market share by evaluating and paying attention to important factors such as suppliers, customers, possible threats, and operating costs.

Suppliers, Customers, and Other Competitive Threats

Suppliers

The auto industry obtains resources from a wide array of firms globally. Although the number of suppliers has dropped since 2001, an estimated 450 suppliers still provide output used in each automotive plant.[43] Many of these suppliers rely heavily on the auto industry for a large percentage of their revenue. For example, Gentex Corp., who supplies high-end rearview mirrors, realizes 96 percent of its sales from the auto industry.[44] Large diversified suppliers such as BASF and Dow Chemical supply plastics, foams, paint, and other basic materials to the auto industry along with many other industries. Although the large suppliers are diversified with many products in many industries, the automotive industry is still a significant customer especially for specific divisions within the large firms.

Delphi and Visteon are two key part suppliers for the auto industry. These two firms used to be the GM and Ford parts divisions until they were spun off. Since then, both firms have struggled with high debt, burdensome union contracts, and declining sales from their primary customers (GM and Ford). In fact, Delphi which was spun off from GM in May 1999 filed for Chapter 11 bankruptcy in October 2005.[45] Visteon which was spun off from Ford in 2000 has also struggled with high debt. In November 2006, Visteon's debt rating was further cut into junk bond rating by Moody's, who also lowered Visteon's credit rating from B2 to B3.[46] Although Delphi and Visteon have remained independent, financial troubles for both suppliers create concerns for GM and Ford. First, both automakers are still dependent on their spun off parts suppliers for a large amount of their parts, so supply uncertainties are a concern.[47] Second, when the parts suppliers were spun off, certain agreements where made with the unions that leave the automakers still potentially liable for labor costs. Ford, for example, has committed to the Visteon workers that they still would have jobs if Visteon folded.[48] Although Ford and GM both have financial strains of their own, they would likely have to step in if needed to ensure that their previously spun off parts suppliers remain viable.

Customers

Auto manufacturers sell their cars to a distribution network of dealerships that then sell to the general public. Additionally, the auto manufacturers sell to fleet sales firms, such as rental car companies. Although fleet sales generally are not as profitable as sales to the general public, they do account for a significant volume of sales. With production of the Taurus being discontinued, Ford is expecting fleet sales to decrease by 175,000 vehicles in 2007.[49]

Although the auto manufacturers sell to the dealerships, they have to be able to supply products that the end customer wants to purchase from the dealers, which means the auto manufacturers have to focus on the quality, design, performance, and cost desires of the general public. In addition, auto manufacturers need to recognize the emerging challenges dealers are facing. Harsh competition has minimized profit margins, especially with the current surplus of dealerships. In fact, an article in *BusinessWeek* stated, "There are too many dealers out there. If normal economic rules applied, say industry insiders, the nation's dealer population of 21,000 (three-quarters of them Big Three stores) would be cut by at least 3,000."[50] The challenges drive down margins even farther and affect compensation of car salespeople. With the explosion of information available on the Internet, the end consumers have access to more information to compare products and determine which vehicle meets their needs. Well-informed consumers are able to shop and negotiate pricing between dealerships, which diminishes a salesperson's tactical advantage.[51]

Additional Competitive Threats

Many urban areas have considered opportunities for improved public transportation via rail or bus. Salt Lake City recently implemented a mass transit system, and built the TRAX rail in time for the 2002 Winter Olympics. Phoenix is one of the most recent to begin construction of its mass transit system in the metropolitan area.

Even though factors such as capital requirements, economies of scale, need for distribution channels, and threat of retaliation make it unlikely for a new entrant to sprout up from within the United States, history has shown that new entrants can succeed in the U.S. market. Asian automakers such as Toyota and Honda have successfully entered and established themselves as key players in the market. More recent entries from Kia and Hyundai are also making progress in the United States. Automakers that are established in foreign countries have been able to gain a foothold by exporting to the United States and targeting a niche market. Once they have established a reputation and distribution channels, they then have been able to expand into the broader market. After reaching an economic scale, they typically then establish production within the United States. Chinese auto manufacturers will likely provide the next wave of new entrants into the U.S. market. China is now the second-largest auto market in the world and has a growth rate of nearly 26 percent.[52] One Chinese auto manufacturer (Greely Automotive Holding Company) recently displayed a car at the Detroit Auto Show, and they intend to begin exporting to the United States in 2008.[53]

Operating Costs

Fueled by intense competition and excess capacity within the market, automakers feel an ongoing drive to reduce costs and improve efficiencies. These desires contributed to some of the mergers and alliances already discussed, but other activities are also ongoing to reduce expenses. Ford and GM have been working to gain concessions, especially in relation to retiree medical costs, from the United Auto Workers (UAW) association, which represents many of the automaker's hourly workers. They are also striving to shed excess capacity and reduce fixed costs by closing manufacturing sites and bringing capacity more in line with their current market share. Additionally, firms are looking for more efficient ways to produce automobiles. Several firms are implementing flexible manufacturing capabilities to increase their production flexibility. For example, GM's new plant in Delta Township, Michigan, will have the new Tru-Flex system. This system will allow them to produce vehicles that have different platforms on the same assembly line.[54]

In light of the many factors associated with the automotive industry, it is wise for Ford to continue to invest heavily in R&D.

Research and Development

In addition to developing alternative fuel vehicles and associated technology, Ford Motor Company's primary engineering efforts include developing attractive safety and convenience features.

Safety Features

Ford has been working to improve the safety features of its vehicles. In an effort to reduce the probability of a rollover, Ford developed Roll Stability Control for the Volvo XC90, Lincoln Navigator, Lincoln Aviator, Ford Explorer, Mercury Mountaineer, Ford Expedition, and Ford E-Series vans. This feature detects when drivers corner too fast and applies pressure to the brakes on the outside of the turn, reducing understeer and the likeliness of a rollover. Additionally, Ford implemented what they call AdvanceTrac, which is designed to increase vehicle stability in emergency maneuver situations. Ford also developed adaptive cruise control. This feature is available in the Jaguar S-Type and uses radar to adjust the cruise control speed to the speed of the vehicle immediately in front.

Ford-engineered safety features reduce the likelihood of serious injury or death in case of a collision. One of these features is the safety canopy: In the event of an accident, airbags not only deploy in front of the driver and front passenger, but also from the sides of the vehicle to prevent passengers from being thrown into the side glass. Additionally, Ford developed what it calls an "Intelligent Safety System." The airbag inflator and steering column absorption adjust to driver variables such as seat position, body weight, and event severity.

Convenience Features

Convenience features are also a focus of Ford engineering, both as a means of product differentiation and to customer satisfaction. McKinsey & Co. estimates that electronics will comprise 40 percent of COGS by 2015 as opposed to the present 20 percent.[55] Although a large percentage of those COGS are safety related, many are convenience related, such as the integration of PDAs and cell phones for voice-activated dialing and hands-free operation, voice integration for GPS navigation, entertainment, climate control, retractable roof, and so on. For the more adventurous consumer, Ford developed a terrain response system, currently being tested in the Land Rover Range Stormer concept vehicle, which adjusts the engine, gearbox, air suspension, driveline controls, traction control functions, and brakes according to the environment and driving requirements.

Ford can get the greatest return on investment for R&D expenditures if the company's branding and marketing strategies are taken into account.

Branding and Marketing Strategies

Ford Brands

Ford markets automobiles in the United States under the Ford, Lincoln, Mercury, Mazda, Volvo, Jaguar, Land Rover, and Aston Martin brands. Because some of the brands have been acquired in recent years, some overlap occurs between target markets, but each brand tries to differentiate itself in order to appeal to a specific customer segment. Ford groups Jaguar, Volvo, Aston Martin, and Land Rover into its Premier Automotive Group (PAG).[56] Mazda, which is a Japanese auto manufacturer, and Ford started a relationship in 1979 which has continued to evolve, and in 1996, Ford took over 33.4 percent of Mazda shares.[57] The Lincoln and Mercury brands share a long history with Ford. Historically, the

Ford brand included light trucks and cars targeted at the more price-conscious consumers. Lincoln targets higher-end consumers, and Mercury aims to fill the gap between the upper-end Lincolns and the lower-end Ford brand.

Marketing Strategies

In an effort to increase online traffic on dealership Web sites, and provide increased Web customization potential, in December 2006 Ford planned to implement new Web sites for 5,000 North American dealerships. The initiative focuses on bi-directional input, enabling customers to request key information such as quotes or test drives, as well as allowing Ford to push targeted advertisements and promotions out to customers. Ford strives to develop user-friendly, easy-to-operate dealer sites, which can be integrated with Ford's current corporate Web sites.[58]

Product Design and Positioning

Drastic product design transformation and advancement are critical to Ford's sustainability in the automotive market. The current leadership group is guiding designers to deliver product designs that demonstrate confidence. Ford's design director for passenger cars recognizes the need for Ford to research the market trends, desires, and expectations. As an example of the renewed design focus, in November 2006, Ford unveiled its Super Duty line of trucks planned for release in 2008, which offers increased towing capacity, improved interiors, and upgraded options packages to potential customers. For this line, Ford added MP3 capability, a superior tailgate step, and a stowable truck bed extender in its efforts to appeal to consumers. Further, the Super Duties incorporate Ford's Clean Diesel Technology, an advanced technology that equalizes diesel and gasoline emission levels.[59]

In addition to creating fresh product designs, Ford aims to further position its vehicles by offering attractive financing and discount options. In August 2006, Ford provided 0 percent financing to buyers with solid credit, and low rates even to those with mediocre credit.[60] Ford is offering bonus cash for purchases of specific 2007 models, including the Fusion, Escape, and Super Duty F-series.[61]

Ford continues its efforts to increase sales and enhance its tired brand image through a variety of approaches, ranging from participating in automotive exhibitions to marketing vehicles on film and television. At the Beijing International Automobile Exhibition, Ford will be the largest exhibitor.[62] The 2007 Ford Mondeo is driven by James Bond in the 2006 film *Casino Royale,* contributing to the positive branding of Ford as chic and powerful. Ford vehicles also appeared on the popular television show, *American Idol,* and the award-winning movie, *Crash.*[63]

Despite its efforts to differentiate and survive in an ever-intensifying competitive environment, the financial condition of the company has not been as strong as stakeholders would hope.

Financial Condition

Ford's declining economic performance can be attributed to two major factors, dwindling demand for its product and the rising cost of production and operational expenses. Rising fuel costs and increased competition, both domestic and foreign, have reduced Ford's sales and led to a loss of market share.[64] Ford's excess capacity and decrease in operating margins have put Ford at a financial disadvantage. (See Exhibits 6, 10, 11, 12, 13, and 14 for a comparison of select financial attributes for auto manufacturers.) One of the major underpinnings of its restructuring plan is to match capacity with demand.

Another financial constraint results from Ford's agreements with labor unions and its defined benefit plan, which spells out its obligations to provide post-retirement benefits for former employees. These benefits include pension benefits as well as life and health insurance in the United States and abroad. For example, in August of 2006, Ford announced plans to idle 10 of its production facilities as part of the Ford's Way Forward Plan, in an attempt to reduce inventory and production costs. This decision was required primarily due to the reductions in light truck and SUV sales. Even though the move will reduce the inventory levels and cost of machine operation, it will have a minimal effect on the cost of production personnel, hourly and salaried. Ford's agreement with the United Auto Workers union mandates that Ford continue to pay union employees the majority of their normal wage and Ford has further extended this to

Exhibit 6 Comparison of Select Financial Attributes (in $ millions)

Selected Auto Maker	Market Capitalization	Sales, TTM	Operating Income	Net Income, TTM
Ford Motor	15,187	170,425	2,842	1,575
Toyota Motor	194,505	186,677	16,668	12,176
Honda Motor	63,660	87,921	7,710	5,298
DaimlerChrysler AG	59,044	187,555	2,779	3,564

Source: 2006, Ford Motor Company, http://www.morningstar.com.

Exhibit 7 Performance of Ford Stock, January 2001 to December 2006

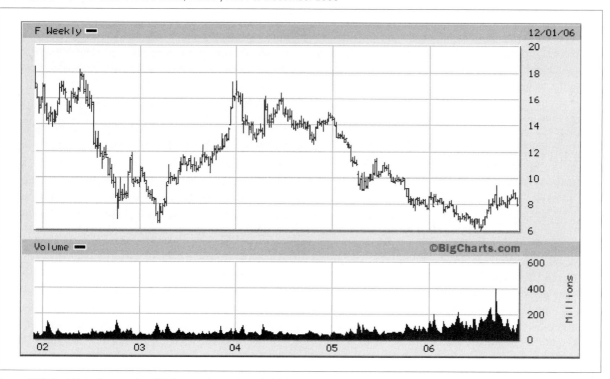

Source: 2006, Ford Motor Company, http://bigcharts.marketwatch.com/quickchart.

nonunion salaried employees.[65] These types of agreements are one of the principal causes of Ford's excessive operating costs as compared to its foreign competitors.

Ford intends to reduce operating costs through the consolidation of suppliers. To simplify its diffuse supply chain, Ford intends to consolidate the number of major parts suppliers for its automotive sector from 200 down to 100.[66] It also intends to continue to source raw materials and supplies from lower-cost geographical regions in order to improve its gross margin, which has declined 44 percent from 25.9 percent in 1996 to 14.6 percent in 2006.[67] As a comparison, the industry average is 19.2 percent,[68] representing 32 percent better performance over Ford. The narrower gross margins represent a challenge to garner adequate financial resources to mount an attack on market share against its rivals.

To further improve cash flows, Ford also stated that they will cut their dividend to shareholders of common stock in half to five cents per share and will also not be paying board member fees. Ford issued a dividend to common shareholders every year over the past 10 years, which usually yielded between 3 percent and 7 percent of earnings. The reduction in dividend payments will reduce net cash losses by $368 million per quarter.[69] (See Exhibits 7, 8, and 9 for Ford's stock performance.)

In September 2006, Ford's balance sheet showed a working capital deficit exceeding $35 billion with cash and cash equivalents balance of $25.5 billion with total current assets of $64.8 billion. In order to improve its liquidity and to allow sufficient cash reserves to fund its restructuring, Ford elected to raise an additional $18 billion. The financing includes $15 billion that is secured by current fixed assets with the balance being unsecured. In addition to funding operations, a portion of the proceeds from the new debt financing will restructure preexisting debt. It is the first time in the firm's history that Ford has been forced to secure financing with its internal assets.[70] The result of the additional debt on Ford's balance sheet resulted in further downgrades of its existing commercial paper to "junk" status. The S&P rating on Ford's senior unsecured debt was CCC-plus while Moody's assigned a Ba3 rating.[71] During the quarter ending in September 2006, Ford recorded a net loss of $5.8 billion and consumed more than $2 billion in cash.[72] Analysts anticipate that in 2007, Ford will burn through in excess of $5 billion in cash as it continues with its restructuring.[73]

An essential aspect in Ford's restructuring process is developing and understanding the corporate strategy.

Corporate Strategy

Ford's portfolio of automotive businesses includes auto manufacturers from around the world, replacement auto parts, and financial services. Ford recently hired Kenneth Leet, a former investment banker, to assist in developing a business strategy to improve business conditions. Recent

Exhibit 8 Performance of Ford Stock Versus the Dow Jones Index and GM, December 2002 to December 2006

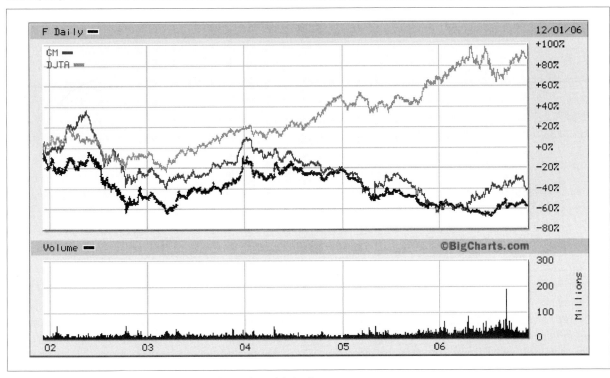

Source: 2006, Ford Motor Company, http://bigcharts.marketwatch.com/advchart/frames.

Exhibit 9 Stock Indices, 2000 to Present

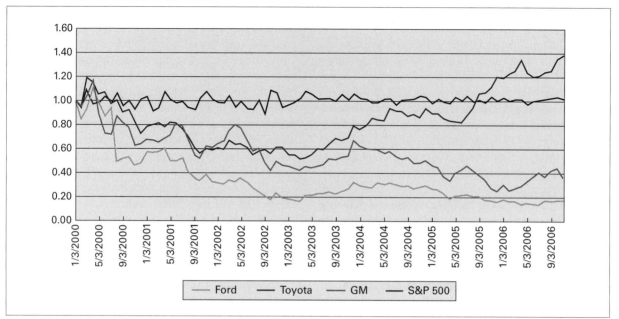

Exhibit 10 Comparative Operating Margin, 1996 to Present

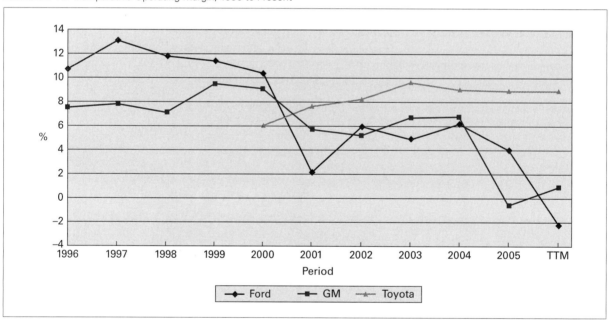

Sources: 2006, Ford Motor Company, http://www.morningstar.com; 2006, General Motors Corporation, http://www.morningstar.com; 2006, Toyota Motor Corporation, http://www.morningstar.com.

discussions include the possibility of forming alliances with other car manufacturers and selling off unprofitable divisions.[74] Due to its Premium Auto Group's pretax loss of $327 million in 2006, Ford sold off the Aston Martin brand in first quarter 2007 and is seeking to divest the Jaguar and Land Rover brands.[75]

Other rumors swirl around the idea that Ford will go private. An article in CNNMoney.com cites Ford's contemplation of going private as it restructures and

tries to return to profitability.[76] This step would help to reduce the pressure from Wall Street for short-term results and allow Ford to better focus on making solid long-term decisions. However, other sources dispute this rumor with Bill Ford stating that Ford has no interest in going private.[77]

Another option to help Ford remedy its financial struggles, declining credit ratings, and falling stock value is declaring bankruptcy, but Ford asserts that bankruptcy

Exhibit 11 Financial Comparison Summary 2005 (in $ millions)

	Ford Corporation (F)	General Motors Corporation (GM)	Toyota Motor Corporation (ADR-TM)
Net revenue	$ 177,089,000	$ 192,604,000	$ 179,083,000
Cost of revenue	144,944,000	171,033,000	144,249,000
Gross profit	32,145,000	21,571,000	34,834,000
SG&A	24,652,000	22,734,000	18,844,000
Other expenses	483,000		
Operating income/(loss)	7,010,000	(1,163,000)	15,990,000
Net Income	$ 2,024,000	$ (10,567,000)	$ 11,681,000
Total current assets	51,712,000	99,414,000	91,387,000
Total Assets	$ 269,476,000	$ 476,078,000	$ 244,587,000
Total current liabilities	95,790,000	113,973,000	85,373,000
Total Liabilities	$ 256,519,000	$ 461,481,000	$ 154,688,000
Total Stockholders Equity	$ 12,957,000	$ 14,597,000	$ 89,899,000
Cash flow from operations	21,728,000	(16,856,000)	21,414,000
Cash flow from investing activities	7,408,000	8,565,000	(28,735,000)
Cash flow from financing activities	(20,651,000)	3,480,000	7,465,000
Net Change in Cash	$ 7,989,000	$ (5,267,000)	$ 729,000

Sources: 2006, Ford Motor Company, http://www.morningstar.com; 2006, Toyota Motor Corporation, http://www.morningstar.com; 2006, General Motors Corporation, http://www.morningstar.com.

Exhibit 12 Selected Financial Ratios for Toyota Motor Corporation

	1997	1998	1999	2000	2001	2002	2003	2004	2005	2006
Revenue ($ millions)					$118,558	$114,572	$126,232	$152,237	$173,304	$186,842
Gross margin, %					19.0	20.8	20.4	19.8	19.8	19.5
Operating margin, %					6.0	7.6	8.2	9.6	9.0	8.9
Operating income					$ 7,136	$ 8,751	$ 10,355	$ 14,672	$ 15,621	$ 16,682
Net income*					6,089	4,437	6,113	10,228	10,906	12,176
Cash flow from operations					12,887	12,265	16,978	20,096	22,148	22,341
Free cash flow					2,045	(127)	3,866	6,993	4,182	(2,271)

* Unadjusted for nonrecurring above-the-line transactions.

Source: 2007, Toyota Motor Corporation, http://www.morningstar.com.

is not an option it will consider.[78] News that Chapter 11 will not be filed has led to recent improved shareholder confidence.[79]

With the new CEO in place, other changes are slated to take place in Ford's corporate strategy. Mulally is determined to decrease the influence of the finance department, which historically had significant power in determining the final product and has too often compromised an automobile's competitiveness in order to save a few dollars.[80] Mulally believes that the key to its future success is not squeezing by with fewer resources than competitors use, but "working smarter with what it has."[81] Another component of the new strategy directed by Mulally is ridding Ford of "needless complexity."[82] Mulally stated that prior to him being on board, "The company was being managed as a collection of six or seven Fords, each

Exhibit 13 Selected Financial Ratios for General Motors Corporation

	1996	1997	1998	1999	2000	2001	2002	2003	2004	2005	2006
Revenue ($ millions)	$164,069	$178,174	$161,315	$176,558	$184,632	$177,260	$186,763	$185,524	$193,517	$192,604	$207,349
Gross margin, %	24.5	27.0	26.9	28.2	21.1	18.8	17.9	18.0	17.3	11.2	20.6
Operating margin, %	7.5	7.8	7.1	9.5	9.1	5.7	5.2	6.7	6.8	(0.6)	(3.7)
Operating income	$ 12,371	$ 13,827	$ 11,505	$ 16,797	$ 16,716	$ 10,108	$ 9,795	$ 12,445	$ 13,172	$ (1,163)	$ (7,668)
Net income*	4,963	6,698	2,956	5,922	4,342	502	1,689	3,822	2,805	(10,567)	(1,978)
Cash flow from operations	18,720	16,454	17,067	27,030	19,750	9,166	17,109	7,600	13,061	(16,856)	(11,759)
Free cash flow	(9,723)	(14,939)	(16,076)	(3,519)	(11,855)	(17,505)	(6,958)	(11,491)	(9,016)	(40,531)	(19,692)

* Unadjusted for nonrecurring above-the-line transactions.

Source: 2007, General Motors Corporation, http://www.morningstar.com.

Exhibit 14 Selected Financial for Ford Motor Corporation

	1996	1997	1998	1999	2000	2001	2002	2003	2004	2005	2006
Revenue ($ millions)	$146,991	$153,627	$144,416	$162,558	$170,064	$162,412	$163,420	$164,196	$171,652	$177,089	$170,425
Gross margin, %	25.9	29.1	27.4	26.8	25.8	20.5	23.4	20.9	20.9	18.2	6.9
Operating margin, %	10.7	13.1	11.8	11.4	10.4	2.1	6.0	4.9	6.2	4.0	(5.1)
Operating income	$ 15,707	$ 20,142	$ 17,013	$ 18,592	$ 17,718	$ 3,354	$ 9,857	$ 8,118	$ 10,681	$ 7,010	$ (8,167)
Net income*	4,381	6,866	21,964	7,222	3,452	(5,468)	(995)	495	3,487	2,024	(12,613)
Cash flow from operations	19,257	27,634	23,100	29,811	33,764	22,764	18,633	20,195	24,514	21,674	9,609
Free cash flow	10,411	18,585	14,373	21,276	25,416	15,756	11,355	12,446	17,769	14,157	2,761

* Unadjusted for nonrecurring above-the-line transactions.

Source: 2007, Ford Motor Company, http://www.morningstar.com.

pursuing its own agenda."[83] Mulally's focus is to unite the company with a single business purpose.

Additionally, Ford will concentrate more on the worldwide market and customers, and work to better utilize its global assets and capabilities.[84] The global organization will streamline operations rather than differentiating processes for different countries. Already, Ford has closed plants in Wixom, Michigan; Louisville, Kentucky; and Lorain, Ohio, and will soon close its St. Louis, Missouri, plant. Ford is also attempting to increase operational efficiency by investing $2 billion in the Rouge manufacturing plant in Dearborn, Michigan, for cutting-edge manufacturing equipment and environmental features,[85] $62 million into the Buffalo plant to increase output and widen the scope of parts production, and $240 million over the next four years at its Wayne Assembly Plant.[86] To further aid with this process, Mulally organized a global product development team.

Mulally has been working closely with labor unions in an attempt to increase contributions to the retirement plans helping to relieve the financial burden as it tries to decrease operating costs. In the effort to alleviate the financial burden of the labor agreements, Ford announced that it would be offering its 75,000 domestic union workers a buyout of their existing contracts including an option to receive lump sum payment in lieu of future pension and health care obligations.[87] Economic terms of the buyouts range from $35,000 to $140,000 and are based on current compensation, occupation level, and other post-employment compensation packages elected. Ford originally anticipated that the buyout would allow them to reduce 30,000 of its hourly positions. In late November 2006, Ford reported that the acceptance rate for the buyout had exceeded the anticipated number of 30,000 and that roughly 38,000 of its U.S. employees had opted to participate.[88] The reduction in force (RIF) buyout is expected to reduce operating expenses by between $335 million to $1.1 billion.[89] The net effect of the buyouts will increase the possibility that Ford could return to profitability in 2008.[90]

Conclusion

Ford Motor Company began with Henry Ford and his revolutionary $5-a-day minimum-wage scheme and an 8-hour work day,[91] but now, Ford Motor Company is struggling to survive. From the advent of the assembly line in 1913,[92] well-designed manufacturing has played a vital role at Ford Motor Company, but now Ford is planning to eliminate 40 percent of its workforce by 2008[93] in an effort to cut manufacturing costs. Ford is also striving to improve its competitive position by driving innovation. Successful innovation in manufacturing processes, product design, marketing approach, and business structure will be needed to improve Ford's brand image, and return Ford to profitability. The only remaining question is how and if Ford can achieve the needed improvements before time runs out.

Notes

1. 2006, Ford Company History, http://www.ford.com.
2. 2006, *Wikipedia,* http://en.wikipedia.org/wiki/Henry_Ford.
3. Ibid.
4. Ibid.
5. 2006, *Fast Company,* http://www.fastcompany.com/online/33/ford.html.
6. http://www.thehenryford.org/exhibits/fmc/chrono.asp.
7. R. Jones, 2006, Ford makes bold move, but is it enough? *MSNBC,* http://www.msnbc.msn.com/id/14687037/, September 6.
8. K. Hammonds, 2000, Grassroots Leadership—Ford Motor Co., *Fast Company,* http://www.fastcompany.com/online/33/ford.html, March.
9. Ibid.
10. Ibid.
11. S. Webster, 2006, Inside Ford: Departing exec Anne Stevens says company needs to trim at top and her job is expendable, *Detroit Free Press* (Michigan), September 18.
12. S. Webster, 2006, Change looks inevitable at Ford: Analysts expect more top rank shake-ups, *Detroit Free Press* (Michigan), September 26.
13. 2006, Alan Mulally Biography, http://media.ford.com.
14. 2006, William Clay Ford Jr. Biography, http://media.ford.com.
15. 2006, New top man at Ford, http://www.carkeys.co.uk/news/2006/september/06/11258.asp, September 6.
16. 2006, William Clay Ford Jr. Biography.
17. 2006, William Clay Ford Media Articles, http://media.ford.com/people/related_articles.
18. Ibid.; 2007, Auto sales tumble amid housing slump, http://www.msnbc.msn.com, August 1.
19. A. Halperin, 2006, Does big R&D mean big returns? *BusinessWeek,* November 26.
20. Ibid.
21. 2006, R. Vartabedian, E85 getting attention, http://www.energyrefuge.com/archives/e85_getting_attention.htm, June.
22. 2006, The road ahead for the U.S. auto industry, Office of Aerospace and Automotive Industries International Trade Administration, U.S. Department of Commerce, April.
23. 2006, U.S. light vehicle sales, market share for November, http://sg.biz.yahoo.com/061201/3/45809.html, December 2.
24. 2007, The road ahead for the U.S. auto industry.
25. 2006, DaimlerChrysler: Corporate profile, http://www.daimlerchrysler.com, December 7.
26. 2007, The road ahead for the U.S. auto industry.
27. 2007, DaimlerChrysler closes transaction on transfer of majority interest in Chrysler to Cerberus, press release, http://www.daimlerchrysler.com, August 3.
28. 2006, DaimlerChrysler: Technology & Innovation, http://www.daimlerchrysler.com, December 7.
29. Ibid.
30. Ibid.
31. 2007, General Motors: Company Information, http://www.gm.com/company/corp_info/.
32. 2007, Ford makes surprise quarterly profit, MSNBC, http://www.msnbc.msn.com, July 26.
33. D. A. McIntyre, 2007, GM's market share drives off a cliff, 24/7 *Wall Street,* http://www.247wallst.com, July 7.
34. 2006, The road ahead for the U.S. auto industry.
35. 2006, General Motors: GM Advanced Technology, http://www.gm.com/company/gmability/adv_tech/100_news/fc_fleet_launch_091806.html, December 7.
36. N. Bunkley, 2006, Ford dropped to 4th place in market share last month, *New York Times,* http://www.nytimes.com, December 2.
37. A. Taylor III, 2007, America's best car company: Toyota has become a red, white, and blue role model. How? By understanding Americans better than Detroit does, *Fortune,* http://www.cnnmoney.com, March 7.
38. Ibid.
39. 2007, Toyota Vehicle Lineup, http://www.toyota.com.
40. 2007, http://www.motortrendcars.com.
41. J. Scanlon, 2006, How to turn money into innovation, *BusinessWeek,* http://www.businessweek.com, November 14.
42. A. Halperin, 2006, Does big R&D mean big returns? *Yahoo!,* http://www.uk.biz.yahoo.com, November 11.
43. 2006, Auto industry consolidation: Is there a new model on the horizon? http://knowledge.wharton.upenn.edu/article.cfm?articleid=1365&CFID=2396121&CFTOKEN=91611858, January 25.

44. 2006, Gentex Corp Investor Information, Corporate profile, http://www.gentex.com/corp_investor.html.

45. 2006, Delphi (auto parts), *Wikipedia,* http://en.wikipedia.org/wiki/Delphi_(auto_parts).

46. Associated Press, 2006, Moody's lowers Visteon credit rating, *Yahoo!,* http://biz.yahoo.com/ap/061122/visteon_rating.html?.v=1, November 22.

47. Ibid.

48. D. Welch, 2003, Ford and Visteon: Ties that bind, *BusinessWeek,* http://www.businessweek.com/magazine/content/03_16/b3829064.htm, April 21.

49. B. Koening & A. Ohnsman, 2006, Ford's U.S. sales unexpectedly fall: Toyota gains (Update 10), *Bloomberg,* http://www.bloomberg.com/apps/news?pid=20601087&sid=aYNYk.c_jNrY&refer=home, December 1.

50. D. Welch, 2006, Death of the car salesman, *BusinessWeek,* November 27, 33.

51. Ibid.

52. 2007, China car sales rev up nearly 26%, *Asia Times,* http://www.atimes.com/atimes/china_business, July 10.

53. Ibid.

54. Ibid.

55. 2006, The road ahead for the U.S. auto industry.

56. M. Krebs, 2005, Can endangered Jaguar be saved? Edmunds.com, http://www.edmunds.com/insideline/do/Columns/articleId=104594/subsubtypeId=217, February 7.

57. 2006, Ford Motor Company, http://www.ford.com/en/company/about/brands/mazda.htm.

58. R. Kisiel, 2006, Ford dealerships get new Web site designs, *Automotive News,* November 27, 43.

59. W. Leavitt, 2006, Ford debuts '08 Super Duties, *Fleet Owner,* November 1, 101(11).

60. J. Saranow & G. Chon, 2006, The return of 0% financing; auto makers pile on deals to clear swollen inventories; some hot models excluded, *Wall Street Journal,* August 31, D1.

61. A. Wilson, 2006, Ford, GM launch year-end incentives, *Automotive News,* November 20, 3.

62. 2006, Demand for autos moves into high gear, *Financial Times Information Limited - Asia Intelligence Wire,* http://www.chinadaily.com.cn, November 18.

63. 2006, Q+A: Casino Royale reaffirms 007's bond with Ford, *Brandweek.com,* http://www.brandweek.com, November 13.

64. J. Novak, 2006, Ford arranges new financing, *Morningstar Report,* November 28, 1.

65. C. Isidore, 2006, Ford slashes production, *CNN,* http://www.money.cnn.com, August 18.

66. 2005, Ford will use fewer suppliers in attempt to cut costs, *USA Today,* http://www.usatoday.com/money/autos, September 29.

67. 2006, Ford Motor Company, http://www.morningstar.com.

68. Ibid.

69. S. Jarush, 2006, Ford halves dividend, board member fees, *The Associated Press State & Local Wire,* July 13.

70. 2006, Ford plans to obtain $18 billion financing, http://www.smartmoney.com, November 27.

71. 2006, S&P, Moody's rate Ford's new credit line, http://www.reuters.com, November 29.

72. 2006, Third quarter earnings 2006 earnings review, http://media.ford.com/article_display.cfm?article_id=24527, October 23.

73. 2006, Ford plans to obtain $18 billion financing.

74. 2006, Ford review 'may spark sell-off,' http://news.bbc.co.uk/2/hi/business/5240794.stm, August 2.

75. J. Reed, 2007, Ford selling Jaguar, Land Rover, http://www.carsguide.news.com.au, June 13.

76. 2006, Report: Ford weighs going private, *CNN,* http://money.cnn.com/2006/08/24/news/companies/ford_private/, August 24.

77. 2006, Ford CEO: Bankruptcy 'not an option,' *Fox News,* http://www.foxnews.com/story/0,2933,201563,00.html, June 29.

78. Ibid.

79. D. Kiley, 2006, Lessened bankruptcy fears lift Ford shares, *BusinessWeek,* http://www.businessweek.com, December 21.

80. D. Kiley, 2007, Mulally: Ford's most important new model, *BusinessWeek,* http://www.businessweek.com, January 9.

81. Ibid.

82. Ibid.

83. D. Levin, 2007, Think Bush has had it bad, try a day as Bill Ford, Jr., *Bloomberg,* http://www.bloomberg.com, January 11.

84. 2006, Ford Motor Company, Ford announces corporate realignment, http://www.ford.com/newsroom/pressreleases, December 14.

85. 2006, Ford Motor Company: A history of innovative thinking, http://www.ford.com/en/innovation/technology/historyOfInnovativeThinking.htm, December 3.

86. 2006, Change looks inevitable at Ford: Analysts expect more top rank shake-ups.

87. J. Rodrigues, 2006, Ford employees take deep breaths, weigh options, *Virginian Pilot,* September 16.

88. 2006, Half of Ford's U.S. factory workers accept redundancy, http://www.reuters.com., November 30.

89. Ibid.

90. 2005 Ford 10-K/A SEC filing, 23.

91. http://www.time.com/time/time100/builder/profile/ford3.html.

92. 2006, Ford Motor Company: A history of innovative thinking, http://www.ford.com/en/innovation/technology/historyOfInnovativeThinking.htm, December 3.

93. J. McCracken, S. Power, & J. White, 2006, Sharp skid: Ford and Chrysler show dark outlook for U.S. car makers; Ford will drop its dividend, cut more salaried jobs; Daimler unit's loss grows; a 'Black Friday' for Detroit, *Wall Street Journal,* http://www.wsj.com, September 16.

Case 8

Jack Welch and Jeffrey Immelt: Continuity and Change in Strategy, Style, and Culture at GE

Shirisha Regani, Saji Sam George

ICFAI Center for Management Research

I'm a different generation from Jack . . . . . I have a different view of the world.

> —JEFFREY IMMELT,
> CEO OF GENERAL ELECTRIC, IN 2002.[1]

The thing that makes me most proud of Jeff is his visibility in tough times.

> —JACK WELCH,
> FORMER CEO OF GENERAL ELECTRIC, IN 2002.[2]

An Inauspicious Beginning

Jeffrey Immelt became the chief executive officer (CEO) of the General Electric Company (GE) on September 7, 2001, drawing to a close one of the longest[3] succession planning programs in corporate America. Immelt succeeded Jack Welch, who was generally acknowledged as one of the most successful CEOs in business history for his management of GE in the 20 years he headed the company.

On September 11, 2001, just four days after Immelt stepped into the job for which he had been in training for almost a year, hijackers crashed planes into the Pentagon and the twin towers of the World Trade Center. This event shocked the world and left the U.S. economy— already in bad shape from a recession and the bursting of the dot.com bubble in 2000—battered.

It was an inauspicious beginning for Immelt. As a huge, diversified company, GE had interests in several sensitive industries, including aircraft engines, plastics, and insurance, which were sure to suffer some of the after-effects of September 11.

The terrorist attacks were a harbinger of bad times to come for GE. As of early 2006, in the four and a half years that he had headed GE, Immelt dealt with a series of problems. By 2002, GE's share price had fallen to levels much below its peak in early 2001, showing no signs of improvement by mid-2006 (refer to Exhibit 1 for GE's share price).

Background

GE's origins can be traced to 1879, when Thomas Alva Edison invented the first successful incandescent electric lamp. Edison was an entrepreneur as well as an inventor and started several small businesses dealing with power stations, wiring devices, and appliances during the late 1870s and 1880s. In 1890, he brought all these businesses together and combined them under the Edison General Electric Company (EGEC).

EGEC merged with the Thomas-Houston Electric Company[4] in 1892 to form GE. The newly formed GE was then headquartered in New York. In 1894, Edison gave way to Charles Coffin, a former shoe salesman, as the CEO of GE. Coffin licensed out the electric bulb technology to other companies, thus consolidating GE's position in the emerging lighting industry. Coffin also created a formal hierarchy at the company and organized GE's various businesses in a systematic manner, arranging each unit around a product line. Coffin was also responsible for setting up financial control systems at GE.

Coffin had a long tenure at GE and eventually stepped aside in favor of Gerard Swope in 1922. Under Swope, GE launched several progressive industrial relations initiatives, setting up new policies to give employees pensions, bonuses, stock purchase options, profit sharing, and group insurance. GE also became the first company to establish an unemployment pension plan, which guaranteed laid-off workers a stipend of $7.50 per week for a period of 10 weeks after the layoff.

In 1940, Charles Wilson became the CEO of GE. Wilson was an autocratic leader and employee relations

Exhibit 1 GE's Share Prices

Source: http://www.bigcharts.com.

deteriorated during his tenure. After World War II (1939 to 1945), GE faced a major crisis in industrial relations due to the increasing clout of the trade unions. The crisis culminated in a major strike in 1948, which caused a rift between the blue-collar workers and the top management at the company.

By the 1950s, GE was a major industrial conglomerate with interests in a variety of businesses. But growth brought its own problems. From the beginning, GE was organized like a holding company, with a few executives at the headquarters monitoring the activities of the various businesses. Except for routine monitoring, each business unit enjoyed great autonomy. Over the years, the heads of individual businesses became powerful and began operating their units like independent businesses with little reference to GE's strategic intentions.

After Ralph Cordiner became the CEO in 1958, he embarked on a company-wide restructuring program to bring discipline to GE. To obtain more control over the various businesses, he strengthened bureaucracy within the company. Cordiner created a team of GE executives, outside consultants, and management experts to develop strategies to streamline the company's management practices. Cordiner was also responsible for setting up GE's management training center at Croton-on-Hudson in New York, popularly known as the Crotonville School,[5] to train future GE leaders.

Fred Borch succeeded Cordiner in 1964. Borch was an aggressive leader and was responsible for much of GE's growth in the 1960s. He added three new capital intensive lines to GE's portfolio: computers, nuclear power, and aircraft engines, all of which were considered risky investments, but with huge potential, at that time. Borch was also responsible for introducing the concept of strategic business units (SBUs),[6] and created 46 SBUs within the company in the late 1960s. (At that time GE's businesses were arranged around 10 groups with nearly 200 profit centers and 145 departments in all.)

Reginald Jones became the CEO in 1972. Jones accelerated GE's shift from electromechanical to electronic technology. He also emphasized the need to be responsive to the international environment and competition from overseas. Jones invested heavily in office automation in order to increase productivity and made some strategic decisions that involved strengthening promising business units, such as plastics, and divesting the unproductive computer businesses. Under Jones, GE became one of the most powerful conglomerates in the world.

A significant phase in GE's history began in 1981, when Welch became the CEO of the company.

Jack Welch

Welch, the son of a railway conductor, was born on November 19, 1935, in Salem, Massachusetts. He studied chemical engineering at the University of Massachusetts, where he graduated in 1957. He then moved to the University of Illinois, where he received his master's and PhD in chemical engineering.

Welch joined GE in 1960 as a junior engineer with an annual salary of $10,500. He was not happy with the excessively bureaucratic culture of the company. In 1961, soon after he completed his first year at GE, he resigned because he was disappointed with the $1,000 raise he received.[7] He accepted a job at a company called International Minerals & Chemicals Corporation.

But just a few days before he was due to leave GE, Reuben Gutoff, Welch's immediate superior, took him out to dinner and spent four hours trying to convince him to stay with GE. Gutoff promised Welch that he would try to create a good work atmosphere for him—one that would combine a "small-company environment, with big-company resources." He also assured Welch that he would keep him from getting entangled with GE's bureaucracy.

Welch apparently agreed to stay and see how things worked out. Gutoff presumably kept his word, because Welch stayed with GE and rapidly rose through the company's ranks. After he helped develop a new type of plastic called Noryl,[8] Welch was made general manager of GE's new plastics factory. A little later, he was made the head of GE's entire plastics division.

In 1972, Welch became vice president at GE (it was one of the fastest rises into senior management within GE). In 1977, he was made senior vice president and two years later vice chairman. In 1981, he was chosen as Jones's successor, becoming the youngest CEO in GE's history.

GE Under Welch

Welch's appointment as the CEO of GE was first greeted with skepticism. Several people thought that at 45, Welch was far too young and inexperienced for a post with so much responsibility. (GE was one of the largest companies in the world and had interests in a diverse range of businesses.) People also thought he was too flamboyant and far too aggressive to fit in with GE's staid culture.

In addition to these concerns, Jones had been a successful CEO, keeping GE profitable and growing, even during the recession of the late 1970s. He was also one of the most admired business leaders in the United States at that time. Therefore, stepping into Jones's shoes was not easy for Welch.

GE was widely regarded as one of the most profitable and well-managed companies in the world. However, Welch still felt the need for several changes that were aimed at making the company more nimble and profitable. He foresaw that GE was in danger of becoming complacent, and that this complacency would harm the company in the long run. In addition in the early 1980s, the United States was facing tough competition from the Japanese and the Europeans in several industries.

One of the first things Welch did as CEO of GE was to take steps to radically transform the company's bureaucratic culture. He created a flatter structure by trimming the company's nine management levels to six. The object of this exercise was to make GE more nimble and to improve communications within the company.

Over the years, GE had been following a matrix-based corporate planning system,[9] which was widely admired by management experts. However, Welch replaced it with what was known as his "Number One Number Two" strategy.

"Fix it, sell it, or close it" summarized Welch's approach to GE's businesses during this period. He insisted that GE should be one of the top two players in every segment in which it operated. If any business failed to meet this criterion, he closed it down or sold it. During his tenure, GE divested several businesses such as air-conditioning and housewares, and thousands of employees lost their jobs. Welch's willingness to retrench employees earned him the nickname "Neutron Jack."[10]

On the other hand, Welch acquired several other businesses he thought would add value to GE's portfolio. Some significant acquisitions in the 1980s and 1990s were Employers Reinsurance and Radio Corporation of America (RCA), including National Broadcasting Corporation (NBC). (When GE acquired RCA for $6.28 billion in December 1985, it was the biggest merger ever in the non-oil sector. It established Welch's reputation as a master of large business deals.) By the time Welch retired in 2001, he had supervised GE's acquisition of more than 600 companies.

Strategic planning was always accorded great importance at GE, and the company had been the birthplace of several new management concepts. Other companies often sent their managers to study the strategic planning process at GE. Until the 1980s, strategic planning was primarily a corporate function at the company. However, Welch made it a line function and vested the responsibility for strategic planning with individual business units. He felt that the business units understood their own markets and were better off doing their own planning.

Welch also cut the company's spending on research & development (R&D). Historically, from the time of Edison, GE had put great emphasis on R&D. The company had an active Global R&D Center in New York, assisted by more than 100 product-oriented labs around the world. By the 1980s, GE owned more patents than any other company in the world.

However, Welch felt that innovation and problem solving had to be incorporated into everyday work. To promote innovation, he launched a program called "Work Out," which encouraged employees at all levels of the organization to get involved with innovation and problem solving.

The Work Out program included a series of company retreats where a group of employees (usually 50 in number) of varying ranks and responsibilities got together to review company policies and processes and make suggestions for improvement. Employees were encouraged to argue with and criticize their superiors, and the superiors were required to respond to the issues raised by employees as soon as possible. Welch believed that organization-wide problem solving improved overall quality, which made better business sense for the company as it increased customer value. "We want to make our quality so special, so valuable to our customers, so important to their success, that our products become their only real value choice," said Welch.[11]

Welch also believed that involving all employees in the quality processes of the company had great potential benefits. He believed that human creativity was unlimited and that when this creativity was tapped, it could lead to tremendous value. "The idea flow from the human spirit is absolutely unlimited. All you have to do is tap into that well. I don't like to use the word *efficiency*. It's creativity. It's a belief that every person counts," he said.[12]

Welch's commitment to quality led to the adoption of Six Sigma at GE in the mid-1990s. Six Sigma was a quality initiative first developed at Motorola Inc.[13] in 1986. The program aimed at reducing production defects to less than 3.4 per million through continuous improvements (refer to Exhibit 2 for a note on Six Sigma).

Welch borrowed the idea of implementing Six Sigma from AlliedSignal Inc.,[14] where his friend Lawrence Bossidy had become the CEO in 1991. Welch heard from Bossidy about how the Six Sigma program was helping AlliedSignal cut costs and increase productivity. He invited Bossidy to present this idea to the top management at GE. The management was impressed with the concept and decided to implement a Six Sigma program at GE.

The program was launched at the company in 1995 and was applied to 200 projects in its first year.

Launching Six Sigma was not easy. The company had to invest heavily in training employees. Employees at GE were trained in Six Sigma at three levels—green belts, black belts, and master black belts, in increasing order of proficiency. Green belts were employees who took up Six Sigma implementation responsibility along with their regular work. Black belts guided green belts in the implementation of the Six Sigma programs. Black belts were completely devoted to Six Sigma without any other job responsibilities. Master black belts supervised the black belts and were responsible for identifying the projects in which Six Sigma could be implemented.

GE made it compulsory for employees to have at least green belt training and involvement in one quality control project to be eligible for promotion to management levels. Black belts and master black belts were usually at higher levels of management, and the company ensured that the best people were trained as black belts and master black belts.

To stress the importance of the Six Sigma initiative, GE linked it with compensation. Typically, 40 percent of the annual bonus of GE's top 7,000 employees was directly related to involvement in Six Sigma. By 1996, Six Sigma was applied to 3,000 projects, and this number rose to 7,000 by 1997.

Some concerns were expressed within GE that the stress placed on Six Sigma was leading to an increase in bureaucracy within the company, and employees were rigidly following established processes and were not willing to try new things. But Welch said that he was ready to put up with a little bureaucracy if it brought improved production and greater efficiency for the company.

Exhibit 2 A Note on Six Sigma

Six Sigma is based on a combination of well-established statistical quality control techniques and simple plus advanced data analysis methods. It essentially involves the systematic training of all personnel at every level of the organization involved in the targeted activity or process. It is based on the statistical concept that the output of most of the physical processes follows a normal distribution,[36] with the processes centered at the mean. As a normal result of the manufacturing process, all manufactured items are subject to item-to-item variation. Sigma is the standardized statistical measure of the variability or the dispersion within a given population of items. Six Sigma denotes 3.4 defects per million. Other Six Sigma levels include Two Sigma, Three Sigma, Four Sigma, and Five Sigma. These levels signify 308,537; 66,807; 6,200; and 233 defects per million respectively.

Six Sigma focuses on streamlining all the processes in the organization to improve productivity and reduce capital outlays while increasing the quality, speed, and efficiency of the operations. It was originally developed to be used for physical processes—those performed in manufacturing—which are easy to observe, record, analyze, and measure. However, later on it was extended to processes that were not as explicit and encompassed business areas such as bid and proposal, procurement, and contract management. Even though Six Sigma comprised strict measurements for physical processes, it involved identifying waste in the form of delays for other processes.

Six Sigma's success is measured by the extent to which it improves the quality and profitability at all levels of an organization. At the business level, Six Sigma could be used to improve profitability and market share, and also to ensure the company's long-term viability. At the process level, Six Sigma could be used to reduce defects and variation. It could also be used to enhance process capability so as to increase profitability and customer satisfaction.

Source: Compiled from various sources.

At GE management meetings, heads of businesses were frequently encouraged to talk about the quality initiatives at their own units, so that ideas and best practices could get transferred among the company's various businesses. The business heads usually spoke about the methods they used in their units to decrease costs and/or increase efficiency, so that people from other parts of the company could borrow and adapt their ideas.

Welch stressed the importance of communication at GE. He encouraged communication at all levels and in all directions (top-down, bottom-up, and lateral) within the company. Effective communication was promoted by GE's informal culture. Welch had a unique ability to communicate with and motivate people at all levels of the organization. All the company's employees called him "Jack," and were encouraged to express their opinions candidly to their superiors or to him directly. It was said that Welch tried to create the same "small-company environment, with big-company resources," atmosphere that Gutoff had created for him at the start of his career.

Welch used GE's various meetings and review sessions to great advantage in enhancing communications at the company. GE held several company events through the year. Instead of making these events just formal company gatherings, Welch transformed them into levers of leadership. The meetings gave him a chance to interact with different people in the company, listen to their opinions, and gauge their leadership potential.

Welch also used these opportunities to make sure that all GE employees knew his opinions and ideas. At the beginning of his term as CEO, Welch had realized that a CEO of a large company could not afford to communicate only with his top people and expect things to happen. Therefore, he constantly repeated his opinions and ideas at every opportunity, to all classes of employees. In turn, the business heads followed the same behavior within their units, which ensured that the lines of communication were always active. Welch's speeches were regularly video taped, translated into local languages and sent to various GE setups across the world. This practice enabled him to make his presence felt even to employees at distant locations.

Welch believed in staying visible within GE. He regularly visited different GE departments and factories where he made it a point to interact with employees. Surprise visits were also a part of his leadership style. Analysts said that it was remarkable how, at a company of GE's size, employees at even the lowest levels in the company hierarchy seemed to know Welch and his opinions.

GE as a company lost most of its staidness under Welch. Thirty of GE's top managers met just before the close of every quarter in a meeting called the Corporate Executive Council. All the business heads were required to candidly share the new developments (particularly relating to the success or failure of new initiatives) in their departments. Welch challenged and tested his business heads constantly and pushed them to do better. Reportedly, these meetings often became heated and resulted in vigorous arguments, prompting some employees to call them "food fights" and "free for alls." However, the meetings allowed Welch to keep tabs on the happenings at the different GE businesses.

Analysts said that Welch was a master of the art of motivating people and stirring them to action. One way he made his presence felt at the company was by writing notes to employees. Welch frequently wrote notes to all levels of employees, to express appreciation for their contribution to the company, or to guide, inspire, or stir them to action. These notes were faxed directly to the employees the moment they were written, and the originals were sent later by mail. This way, Welch managed to exert a tremendous amount of influence over the GE behemoth.

Naturally, Welch did not know all the GE employees personally, but he learned about them through their bosses. Employees said that it made them feel more motivated, knowing that the CEO cared about them and bothered to get in touch personally. "We're pebbles in an ocean, but he knows about us. He's able to get people to give more of themselves because of who he is," said Brian Nailor, a marketing manager at GE's Industrial Products division.[15]

William Woodburn, an employee at GE's industrial diamonds business, recalled that when he turned down a promotion just because it would also involve a transfer and he did not want to uproot his teenage daughter from her school, he received a personal note from Welch appreciating his concern for his family. "Bill, we like you for a lot of reasons—one of them is that you are a very special person. You proved it again this morning. Good for you and your lucky family," wrote Welch.[16]

Another employee at GE's Capital Services business once spent several days preparing a report on why GE should buy AT&T's Universal Card[17] division. When this report was sent to Welch, he decided within a day that the division would not add value to GE's portfolio. However, he wrote a note to the employee appreciating the effort she had put into the presentation and complimenting her work.

Welch's charisma earned him a great reputation both within and outside GE. According to analysts, his appeal was magnified by the fact that he was a self-made man and had managed to overcome several handicaps to became a great leader. (Welch had a stutter, but was a great orator. He came from a lower middle class background, but went on to become the head of one of the greatest companies in the world.) These attributes made him a role model for many Americans.

However, Welch also had another side to him that was quite the opposite of the benevolent leader. According to GE insiders, he had a tendency to jump to conclusions about people, and formed opinions too rapidly. In addition, he was an extremely demanding boss and several employees, especially those at the lowest levels, complained about the pressure that was placed on them to perform.

Reportedly, Welch had a habit of asking people things like "What have you done for me lately?" whenever he met them. In addition, rewards and promotions at GE were based strictly on performance, and Welch routinely fired nonperformers. Several employees felt that this practice put too much pressure on them. They complained that they were never sure how much was enough.

Welch was a tough task-master who created fear in his subordinates. Nonperformers did not last at GE. Welch demanded that employees perform or be prepared to forgo their jobs. It was said that Welch was never satisfied with GE's performance even when the company was growing at more than 10 percent a year.

However, good performers were rewarded well. Analysts said that under Welch, GE functioned as a true meritocracy. Promotions at the company were mainly from within, and few outsiders were ever brought in. High performers could expect quick promotions in addition to generous bonuses, pay raises, and stock options. Bonuses and stock options were also highly differentiated with high performers being rewarded far more than mediocre ones. However, rewards came with the demand that the employee do even better the next year. "There are carrots and sticks here, and he is extraordinarily good at applying both," said Gary M. Reiner, a senior vice president at the company. "When he hands you a bonus or a stock option, he lets you know exactly what he wants in the coming year."[18]

Welch was responsible for extending the stock options program to the middle and lower levels of the organization and insisted that as many people as possible should receive options. One rule Welch made was that every time options were given, at least 25 percent of the people receiving options should be getting them for the first time, and that not more than 50 percent should get more than three grants in a row.

To determine rewards at GE, Welch devised a system where people were classified under three categories. Every department had to classify its employees as the top 20 percent, the middle 70 percent and the bottom 10 percent, based on their performance. The top performers were generously rewarded, and the middle level performers were rewarded and encouraged to emulate the top performers. The bottom 10 percent, who were considered the least effective employees, were fired. Welch believed that retaining nonperformers was detrimental to the company's health and that they would probably be better off in another company where the work was more suited to their potential and inclinations.

Among the most important events at GE under Welch were the annual "C" session meetings that started in April and lasted through May. During this period, Welch along with three senior executives traveled across the United States to meet with the top managers of each of GE's 12 businesses and to review their performance over the previous year. Three thousand senior GE employees were reviewed every year during the "C" Sessions and Welch kept close tabs on the top 500 people in the organization. The purpose of these sessions was to identify and promote leadership talent within GE.

The sessions were usually conducted with the CEO of each GE business and the senior human resource executive. Each business head was expected to identify candidates with leadership potential in their units and chalk out plans to help them realize this potential. Succession planning was also done for all key jobs within each unit, and decisions were made about who to send to Crotonville for leadership training. Welch was usually given a briefing book containing details of all the employees being reviewed along with their strengths, weaknesses, and development needs. The C sessions were a good way of identifying leadership talent within the company and planning for succession. They also served as a way to recognize good performers and assist them in developing their skills.

Leadership training and executive development were given tremendous importance at GE. Usually employees in management ranks were transferred every few years between locations. This rotation was done to enable them to learn about the various businesses and obtain an overall understanding of GE's operations.

Welch's theory of leadership later came to be known as the 4E theory. The four Es stood for Energy, Energizing, Edge, and Execute. According to Welch, successful leaders had tremendous positive energy, and the edge, or the courage, to make bold decisions. They also had the ability to energize other people, and the ability to execute, or deliver results. He connected these four Es with a P that stood for Passion. Welch said that the best leaders had the four Es as well as the P. People who had the four Es, but not the P had the potential to develop into good leaders, and were encouraged to emulate the top leaders (refer to Table 1).

Welch played an active role in leadership development at GE and taught regularly at Crotonville. He said that this gave him a chance to interact directly with the future leaders of the company. At Crotonville, managers were expected to participate actively in the leadership training, ask questions, and debate issues. Welch said interacting with the participants at Crotonville helped him understand them and their ideas about GE better. Welch

Table 1 Welch's 4Es

- **Energy:** Enormous amount of positive energy and a strong bias for action. An ability to love and adapt to change.
- **Energizing:** High level of people orientation and the ability to motivate and inspire people to maximize organizational potential.
- **Edge:** The courage to make bold decisions and the conviction to stick with them. Healthy competitive spirit.
- **Execute:** The ability to give a form to vision and deliver results.

Passion: A heartfelt, deep and authentic excitement about life and work.

Source: Compiled from various sources.

also interacted with the participants informally after the sessions at the cafeteria. Typically Welch taught one class a month at Crotonville, generally at the end of the three-week program.

Welch was also familiar with each of GE's businesses, no matter what its size, and took a keen interest in operations. It was said that when a unit was not operating up to the mark, Welch became more involved with it and asked managers to send him regular reports updating him on the situation. On the other hand, when a business was functioning well, the head of the business was given a great deal of autonomy. GE business heads who showed results were sometimes given more autonomy and power than even the heads of independent companies. "It's part of living with Jack," a former GE executive said. "If you're doing well, you probably have more freedom than most CEOs of publicly traded companies. But the leash gets pulled very tightly when a unit is underperforming."[19]

Welch promoted the idea of a boundary-less corporation at GE. Not only did he break down the boundaries separating the different departments within the company to promote the exchange of ideas, but also borrowed ideas from other companies to implement at GE. Welch believed that an organization was dependent on the external environment for its success. He created a culture at GE where people were open and curious and always ready to adopt ideas and best practices from other organizations.

Analysts said that borrowing ideas from other organizations was institutionalized at GE, and any idea that was not patented or copyrighted was adopted by the company. The adoption of Six Sigma was just one of the many examples of this practice. GE also adopted ideas such as Demand Flow Technology[20] from American Standard (a customer of GE's Motors and Industrial Systems business), Bullet Train Thinking[21] from Yokogawa (GE's partner in the Medical Systems business), and Quick Market Intelligence[22] from Wal-Mart, among others.

While most analysts agreed that Welch's successes at GE were more significant than his failures, his tenure was not without a few big missteps. One of Welch's biggest failures was GE's factory automation unit started in the early 1980s. The unit was set up to tap the nascent factory automation market by offering a collection of high-technology products. However, by 1983 it had run into serious losses due to erroneous demand projections. It was then that Welch shifted focus from manufacturing to financial services and concentrated on GE Capital Services, which remained one of the most profitable units of the company, even in the early 2000s.

Welch was also criticized for the sale of GE's appliance business to Black & Decker in 1984 and the acquisition of Thomson SA, a French medical diagnostics firm in 1987. The Kidder, Peabody & Co. (a brokerage firm that GE acquired in 1986) scam of 1994 was also a source of considerable embarrassment for GE and Welch.[23]

Welch endured some flack for the failure of GE's attempt to merge with Honeywell Inc., an aerospace and industrial-equipment group. In late 2000, Welch had learned that Honeywell's board was considering a takeover offer from GE's rival United Technologies Corporation.[24] Welch apparently did not want this deal to happen and interrupted Honeywell's board meeting with a higher offer of $43 billion.

United Technologies did not wish to enter into a bidding war with the "wild man" from GE, and refrained from further bidding. Honeywell accepted Welch's offer on the condition that he would postpone his retirement until the deal went through in late 2001. (He had previously planned to retire in April 2001). The GE-Honeywell merger was to create one of the world's largest industrial companies, until the European Union's Competition Commission refused to permit it on the grounds that it would give the merged company undue competitive advantage in the aviation industry.

Between 1981 and 2001, GE's revenues increased from about $27 billion to $129.8 billion (refer to Exhibit 3). By the time Welch retired from the company, GE was not only the biggest corporation in the world, but also one of the most profitable.

Jeffrey Immelt

Immelt was born in 1956 in Cincinnati, Ohio. His father was an employee of GE's Aircraft Engines division. As a child, Immelt was active in sports and was on the football and basketball teams at his school. He majored

Exhibit 3 GE's Revenues, 1981–2000 (in $US millions)

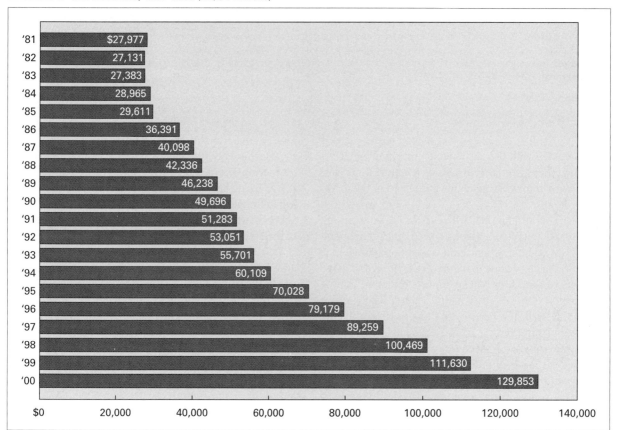

Source: http://www.ge.com.

GE Under Immelt

in mathematics at Dartmouth College in the late 1970s, after which he joined Procter & Gamble Co. (P&G) as a member of its brand management team.

After about a year with P&G, Immelt enrolled in Harvard's MBA program. On finishing his degree, he joined GE as a marketing executive in 1982 at the company's headquarters in Fairfield, Connecticut. After six months, he was transferred to GE Plastics, where he continued until the late 1990s, in various marketing positions.

In the late 1990s, Immelt, along with James McNerney and Robert Nardelli, was short listed as a possible successor to Welch as GE's CEO. In November 2000, the board of GE chose Immelt as the successor. McNerney and Nardelli subsequently left GE to become the CEOs of 3M and Home Depot, respectively. Immelt was formally appointed as the CEO of GE in September 2001. Observers thought that Immelt was chosen because he was the youngest of the three contenders and therefore, likely to have the longest term. Besides, like Welch, Immelt had also spent a major part of his career at GE in the plastics division.

Immelt became the head of GE at one of the most difficult times in American economic history. At the start of his tenure, GE lost two employees to the September 11 attacks and the company's insurance business took a $600 million hit. In addition, Aircraft Engines, one of GE's major businesses, experienced an immediate slowdown. GE Capital Aviation Services, a unit that leased aircraft to airlines, was also expected to be affected.

Immelt was in Seattle when the attacks occurred. He reacted immediately by setting up an office and command center at the small GE office in Seattle. He had to stay there for a few days because no flights were operating, so he managed through telephone and e-mail. Immelt met with investors in late September 2001 and assured them that despite the bad economic scenario, GE would still continue to post double-digit growth as it did under Welch.

However, when the New York Stock Exchange opened the week after the attacks, investors began selling their shares and the price of GE stock fell to $30 per share, 20 percent lower than the price before the attacks.

Exhibit 4 GE's Revenues and Earnings (all amounts in $US millions)

Year ended December 31	2000	2001	2002	2003	2004	2005
Revenues	130,385	126,416	132,210	134,187	151,300	148,019
Net earnings	12,735	13,684	14,118	15,002	16,593	16,353

Sources: http://www.hoovers.com; http://www.ge.com.

This lower stock price was just the beginning of a troublesome period for GE. Just a little after September 11, an anthrax[25] scare broke out when an envelope containing a brown granular substance (containing anthrax spores) was opened by NBC employee Erin O'Connor. In a few days O'Connor contracted anthrax. Over the next few months, envelopes containing anthrax spores were posted to a few prominent people in the United States, resulting in a major scare.

This incident was followed by the eruption of two of the biggest corporate scandals in U.S. business history—Enron Corporation[26] and Tyco International Corporation[27] in 2001–2002. Allegations of corporate fraud at both companies cast a shroud of doubt on all large conglomerates.

GE, being one of the largest corporations in the world, bore the full brunt of the distrust as investors started panicking and offloading their shares in the company. Investors were especially skeptical about GE's record of profitability and wanted to know how the company managed to stay profitable and fuel growth even during economic lows. They also wanted to know how much of GE's growth depended on acquisitions and how much of it was organic. The consistency that had made GE a favorite with investors now was viewed with suspicion in the early 2000s.

By early 2002, investors had started demanding more information about GE's complicated financial reports, and Immelt decided to give in to their demands. (Analysts thought that in the same situation, Welch would have ignored such rumors and demands for explanations.) GE's annual report in March 2002 was huge, giving several hitherto unknown details about the company and its financial management systems.

However, the effort did not achieve the desired outcome. In the same month, Bill Gross, the manager of Pacific Investment Management Co., which ran the largest bond fund in the world, published an article about GE's opaque finances and accused the company of inflating earnings through acquisitions and cheap debt rather than through organic growth. GE's share price fell by 6 percent after this report was published.

Investors also expressed concerns about how the company would fuel growth, when several of its units such as Aircraft Engines, Aviation Services, Plastics, and Industrial Systems were affected by the downturn in the economy. Even GE Power Systems, one of the big drivers of growth at GE, was facing large write-offs due to cancelled orders. Other concerns swirled around the debt levels of GE Capital, the company's successful financial arm, as people questioned Immelt's promises of double-digit growth. They also wondered how long it would be before GE would have to be split up, considering that at the rate of growth the management was promising, the company would reach revenues of $1 trillion by around 2020. In financial year 2002, GE's net earnings were $14.1 billion on revenues of $132 billion (refer to Exhibit 4 for GE's revenues and net profits in the early 2000s).

In an attempt to win investors over, GE redesigned its CEO compensation package in mid 2003. Under the new plan, Immelt was eligible to receive stock (performance share units) worth $7.5 million over a period of five years. Half of the performance share units would vest if GE's cash flow from operations rose at least 10 percent annually over the next five years. The other half would accrue to him if GE's stock met or exceeded the average performance of the S&P's 500 stock index[28] over the same period.

Immelt also modified the equity packages of other GE executives to link their stock options to the company's performance. "We believe that our pay should be completely transparent, that shareholders should know how we're paid. We have a philosophy on compensation that's based on performance," said Immelt.[29] He also said that while retention was an important issue in the granting of options for other GE executives, in his case, the only issue should be that of performance.

Immelt also tried to improve investor confidence by reshuffling GE's portfolio. Analysts said that he was trying to send across the message that GE was essentially a strong company and that there was no need for investors to be concerned about its business model. Immelt said that GE had acquired other companies, not simply to fuel expansion but also to improve the business portfolio. "I don't want us to be a company that does deals because we can. I want us to do the deals we need to do to improve strategically. If I didn't think this improved our business strategically for the long-term good of our shareholders, I wouldn't do it. We're not in the business of flipping assets. That's not our game," said Immelt.[30] By 2002, Immelt had started trying to beef up GE's portfolio by spinning off less-lucrative businesses and acquiring other strategically significant ones.

On October 8, 2003, GE announced the final terms of its acquisition of the French media giant Vivendi Universal's American assets in an equity deal valued at $14 billion. The combined company was expected to have $13 billion in 2003 revenues, with holdings that included film and TV studios, theme-park interests, and cable channels. Analysts were a little surprised by this acquisition, as GE had stayed away from the production business for years, despite owning the NBC television network. The company had long believed that NBC could survive without the backing of a studio and a content library. Therefore, analysts wondered whether Immelt had just been attracted by the bargain price of the deal.

On October 9, 2003, GE acquired Instrumentarium, a Finnish medical-equipment maker and immediately after that, on October 10, 2003, it purchased Amersham, a British life-sciences and medical-diagnostics company. The three deals together were valued at $25 billion. Analysts said that Immelt was trying to showcase a bold business transformation through these deals. However, they were skeptical about whether these deals would actually benefit the company or create more trouble for it.

By 2005, Immelt had sold less profitable GE businesses, including insurance, and had spent more than $60 billion to acquire businesses in new and fast-growing industries like renewable energy, cable and film entertainment, bioscience, and security. Slow-growth low-margin businesses such as lighting were also reduced to 10 percent of GE's portfolio from 33 percent in 2000 (refer to Exhibit 5 for Immelt's important acquisitions in the early 2000s).

Immelt also tried to increase GE's global orientation in the early 2000s. GE had always been a global company, but Immelt saw the potential to push it further. He invested hugely in setting up new research centers in Shanghai (China), Bangalore (India), and Munich (Germany) in 2004, and increased the company's R&D budget from $286 million in 2000 to $359 million in 2004. Immelt said that he wanted to create something like a "global brain trust" that the company could use to spur innovation, which explained the diverse locations of the facilities. Immelt also thought that globalizing

research would allow GE to stay more in touch with customer needs. (GE predicted in 2004 that 60% of the company's growth in the next 10 years would come from developing countries campared to 20% in the 1990s).

By 2003–2004, Immelt had begun to put his stamp on GE's culture, and insiders said that they could see several changes in the company. For one thing, GE had always had a culture of promoting communications within the company. But under Immelt, the company had increased its external communications. Communicating with investors and third parties had become important in the early 2000s, due to uncertain external conditions. Immelt reportedly spent more than 70 percent of his time away from his office at GE's headquarters. He was either in the field meeting employees or he was meeting with investors.

Analysts said that GE's culture had softened under Immelt. The focus had shifted from performance and strictly quantifiable results, to more abstract aspects, such as customer satisfaction and value. Immelt also tied executive compensation to factors like the ability to boost sales, to come up with innovative ideas, and to generate customer satisfaction, rather that just the ability to meet performance targets.

In a departure from the company's traditional way of basing compensation on the bottom-line results, the new GE was focused on intangible factors that were more difficult to measure. Immelt thought that removing the emphasis from the bottom line would encourage employees to take risks and come up with innovative ideas. It was his aim to stretch GE's Six Sigma quality initiative into its industrial customers' processes to help them create more value for their customers.

GE however continued with the practice of firing the least effective 10 percent of its workforce every year. But analysts said that the way the firing was done seemed to be more subtle than in the Welch era, where it was done more publicly and with a view to let the entire organization know the reasons for the firing.

Another significant change within GE was the increased number of outsiders brought into the company at senior positions. Immelt believed that bringing in

Exhibit 5 Some of GE's Business Acquisitions Under Immelt

Industry	Acquisition
Media content	Universal Entertainment
Biosciences	Amersham
Security	Edward Systems
Water	Ionics and Osmonics
Renewable energy	Enron Wind

Source: 2005 Shuffling the Portfolio, *BusinessWeek*, March 28.

people from outside brought in new ideas, creative energy, and a new perspective on the company's policies. This practice contrasted with GE's traditional policy of promoting from within. Managers within GE were also being encouraged to "develop a passion" for and become experts in industries of their interest by spending a longer time at one job, rather than moving frequently between jobs. This mind-set was also different from the Welch era where managers were transferred between industries every few years. Under Welch, the focus had been on enhancing general management skills rather than industry expertise.

Immelt focused on establishing a greater level of diversity in GE's workforce. Traditionally GE had one of the lowest levels of workforce diversity among large companies in the United States. Welch, however, maintained that this was not due to the company's policies or work environment, but because of the nature of GE's businesses, which did not seem to attract women. This pattern was changing under Immelt. In the early 2000s, 50 percent of all senior executive hires and 54 percent of new corporate officers were women, minorities, or foreign employees. Immelt also created a separate diversity forum within the company and actively encouraged mentoring programs for women, minorities, and foreigners.

Within GE, Immelt was thought to be more people-oriented than Welch. Welch was an intimidating boss, but Immelt used a "friendly, regular-guy approach"[31] in dealing with employees. He was also not as demanding as Welch, and reportedly, employees found him more approachable than his predecessor. Describing Immelt's style of functioning, an article in *BusinessWeek* stated, "He prefers to tease where Welch would taunt. Immelt likes to cheer his people on rather than chew them out."[32]

Immelt was also responsible for shifting GE's focus from production to marketing. For a long time, GE had operated on the premise that winning products sold themselves. In contrast Immelt stressed that "the best managers are great marketers and not just great operators."[33] In 2002, Immelt appointed Beth Comstock as GE's chief marketing officer with the mandate of improving the company's marketing expertise.

Comstock said that it was not easy to get the employees of the production-oriented company to take to marketing. However, she put together a commercial leadership strategy that identified the best marketers within GE and gave them extensive training by sending them across the organization for two years. (Under Welch this type of training was done for audit staff, who played an important role in maintaining financial discipline in the company). GE also designed new marketing courses to train the company's marketing executives.

GE continued with its tradition of borrowing winning ideas from other companies and in November 2004, some GE marketing executives spent time at P&G, learning how the company examined and debated strategies and issues to arrive at marketing decisions. Employees also spent time at FedEx, which was known for its exceptional customer service, in the early 2000s.

Immelt set up a high-profile group known as the Commercial Council in 2002. It consisted of a handful of the top sales and marketing executives from GE's different units as well as unit heads from critical businesses such as Consumer Finance. The Commercial Council met every quarter to discuss growth strategies and ways to reach customers innovatively, as well as evaluate new ideas from the senior staff. According to GE insiders, these meetings were generally more "collegial and experimental" than other typical GE meetings. Meetings led by Immelt were also not as aggressive as those led by Welch.

Innovation and creativity were also promoted by Immelt. Immelt was worried that the uncertain economic scenario of the early 2000s would make GE employees risk-averse and hesitant to take bold decisions. Besides, GE had been criticized as being excessively dependent on acquisitions for its growth. To combat this image, he launched a program called Innovation Breakthrough in 2003. Employees were expected to come up with ideas to improve GE's existing products or for the development of new products through the Innovation Breakthrough program.

All business leaders were expected to submit at least three innovative project ideas per year that would then be reviewed and discussed by the Commercial Council within GE. For a project to qualify under the Innovation Breakthrough program, it had to take GE into a new line of business, a new geographic area, or a new customer base. Each project also had to have the potential to give GE incremental revenue of $100 million.

Since mid 2003, when the project was launched, GE invested more than $5 billion in 80 projects that ranged from creating microjet engines and cleaner coal to desalination. The company expected to have more than 200 projects under way by 2007 and estimated that the first lot of 80 projects would generate $25 billion in revenue. Analysts said that this move was aimed at proving that GE could grow internally and organically and not just through acquisitions.

GE also wanted to develop ways to spark idea generation. Executives were encouraged to hold "idea jams," where employees from different departments came together to brainstorm. GE Energy had also set up a "virtual idea box" where employees could post ideas on the Web, and then presented Excellerator awards for the development of ideas.

Exhibit 6 Ge's Business Reorganization in 2005

GE's 11 Core Businesses before 2005	
1	Healthcare
2	Transportation
3	Energy
4	Infrastructure
5	Commercial Finance
6	Consumer Finance
7	NBC
8	Advanced Materials
9	Consumer & Industrial
10	Equipment & Other
11	Insurance

GE's 6 Core Businesses after 2005	
1	Commercial Finance
2	Consumer Finance
3	Healthcare
4	Industrial
5	Infrastructure
6	NBC Universal

Source: Adapted from http://www.ge.com.

In early 2005, Immelt reorganized GE's businesses to make them more customer focused. Toward the end of Welch's tenure, GE was organized around 11 businesses based on product lines. This number was pared down to six in 2005, and the grouping was done based on the customers served. The reorganization was done to lower costs and eliminate redundancies, as well as to implement new systems of customer management. It was expected that as opposed to a product-based grouping, customer-based grouping made it easier for GE to mine and manage customer information better. "This change allows us to leverage our exceptionally deep leadership team to accelerate growth and improve productivity," said Immelt[34] (refer to Exhibit 6).

Under Immelt GE was also becoming "cleaner and greener." In 2005, GE announced that it would double its investment in ecoimagination projects to $1.5 billion by 2010. Ecoimagination projects related to the development and use of technologies that would eventually lead to cleaner and environmentally responsible products and processes at the company. Some of the ecoimagination projects at GE included producing a diesel and electric hybrid vehicle, developing cleaner coal-fired power plants and other products that would put less strain on the environment. Immelt's acquisition of Enron Wind (the only manufacturer of utility-scale wind turbines in the United States) in 2002 reflected the company's commitment to exploring alternative sources of energy.

Immelt announced in late 2005 that by 2010, all GE businesses would aim at reducing the emission of carbon dioxide—the main greenhouse gas[35] behind global warming—by a significant percentage. The company would focus on the by-products of energy-intensive businesses such as locomotives and plastics to achieve its environmental targets, but even non-energy-based businesses like GE Capital would have to take up environmentally responsible initiatives. The company had also started evaluating managers on their involvement in environmental responsibility.

Previously GE had never displayed any special consideration for the environment. The company had long been criticized for boosting coal and nuclear power and for dumping chemicals in the Hudson River near New York. Therefore, analysts were skeptical about the company's seriousness in this initiative and were inclined to dismiss it as "greenwash." However, Immelt seemed committed to this cause. GE's new environmental mantra was "green is green" (invoking the green color of currency in America), and the company was poised to make substantial investments in environmental projects.

Immelt also initiated the process of making governance changes at GE. GE had always had a reputation for good governance, and Immelt was trying to enhance it by bringing more outside directors to the board. The company had also adopted some accounting changes in an attempt to make its financials more transparent from 2002.

Making changes at GE was not easy for Immelt for several reasons. The most important was that he was a follow-up act to Welch, and Welch had already been established as one of the greatest business managers of all time. Therefore, making changes at GE, especially those that contradicted Welch's policies would not be easily accepted at the company.

Moreover, every step he took was being analyzed in the media in terms of what Welch would have done in the same situation. In addition, Immelt had to fight an uphill battle at GE to introduce concepts such as creativity, customer satisfaction, and value to employees who were steeped in the Six Sigma culture and for years had only understood quantifiable bottom-line results.

As of mid-2006, Immelt still had several challenges before him. He had to consolidate his position at and put his personal stamp on a company that had been molded to a great extent by a strong and charismatic predecessor. He also had to operate in a difficult economic environment and yet post double-digit growth every year, and he was having to prove time and again that GE had not lost its magic after Welch left.

Notes

1. 2002, The days of Welch and roses, *BusinessWeek Online,* April 29.
2. Ibid.
3. Succession planning to identify Welch's successor had started in 1994, and the final decision was announced in November 2000.
4. The Thomas-Houston Electric Company was founded in 1879 by Elihu Thomson and Edwin J. Houston. It was a competitor to EGEC until the merger of the two companies.
5. Over the years, Crotonville became a major corporate training center. It was also the birthplace of several management techniques, including SWOT analysis, management by objectives (MBO), and strategic planning.
6. Strategic business unit, or SBU, is understood as a business unit within the overall corporate identity, which is distinguishable from other business units because it serves a defined external market where management can conduct strategic planning in relation to products and markets.
7. At that time, raises were standardized at GE and the company did not differentiate between meritorious employees and nonperformers.
8. Noryl was a modified PPO (polyphenyleneoxide)/PS blend resin that offered optimized processing and enhanced productivity for applications of business equipment and communications, and electrical and electronic appliances.
9. The GE matrix, which was based on the BCG Matrix, was developed for GE by McKinsey and Co. The GE matrix cross-referenced market attractiveness and business position using three criteria for each: high, medium, and low. The market attractiveness considered variables relating to the market itself, including the rate of market growth, market size, potential barriers to entering the market, the number and size of competitors, the actual profit margins currently enjoyed, and the technological implications of involvement in the market. The business position criteria looked at the business's strengths and weaknesses in a variety of fields. These assessments included its position in relation to its competitors, and the business's ability to handle product research, development, and ultimate production (http://www.palgrave.com).
10. In reference to the neutron bomb that killed people but left buildings standing (see 2000, The CEO Trap, *BusinessWeek* http://www .businessweek.com December 11.)
11. 2001, Assessing Jack Welch, http://beginnersinvest.about.com, September 10.
12. 1998, How Jack Welch runs GE, *BusinessWeek,* June 8.
13. Motorola was a major manufacturer of mobile phones and communication systems in the early 2000s.
14. AlliedSignal was a major business conglomerate in the 1980s and 1990s, with interests in chemicals, dyes, and aerospace products.

The company merged with Honeywell Inc., another technology and manufacturing conglomerate in 1999.
15. 1998, How Jack Welch runs GE, *BusinessWeek,* June 8.
16. Ibid.
17. AT&T's credit card division.
18. 1998, How Jack Welch runs GE, *BusinessWeek,* June 8.
19. 1998, How Jack Welch runs GE, *BusinessWeek,* June 8.
20. A system that allowed a company to have zero working capital by increasing inventory turnover rates.
21. This technique employed "out-of-the-box" thinking and cross-functional teams to remove obstacles to cost reduction.
22. QMI was a system of getting rapid feedback directly from the customer.
23. It was discovered in 1994 that a Kidder & Peabody trader named Joseph Jett had created about $350 million in phantom profits to increase his own bonuses.
24. United Technologies was one of the major manufacturers of building systems and aerospace products. It owned brands such as Carrier (air conditioners), Otis (lifts), Hamilton Sundstrand (engine controls, environmental systems, propellers, and other flight systems), etc.
25. Anthrax, also referred to as splenic fever, is an acute infectious disease caused by the bacteria bacillus anthracis and is highly lethal in some forms. It is therefore used as a weapon in biological warfare. Anthrax most commonly occurs in wild and domestic herbivores, but it can also occur in humans when they are exposed to infected animals, tissue from infected animals, or high concentrations of anthrax spores.
26. Enron Corporation was an energy company based in Houston, Texas. Prior to its bankruptcy in late 2001, Enron employed about 21,000 people and was one of the world's leading electricity, natural gas, pulp and paper, and communications companies, with claimed revenues of $101 billion in 2000. At the end of 2001, it was revealed that its prosperous financial condition was sustained mostly by institutionalized, systematic, and "creatively" planned accounting fraud. The company's European operations filed for bankruptcy on November 30, 2001, and it sought Chapter 11 protection in the United States two days later, on December 2.
27. Tyco was a major conglomerate with interests in electronic components, health care, fire safety, security, and fluid control. The company's CEO Dennis Kozlowski and CFO Mark Swartz were accused of theft of the company's funds in 2002. The case went on trial in 2004, and both men were convicted in 2005.
28. The Standard & Poor's 500 Index was one of the most watched indices of the financials among large firms in the United States.

29. 2004, On the record: Jeffrey Immelt, *The San Francisco Chronicle,* June 6.

30. 2003, Jeff Immelt: We know this world, *BusinessWeek Online,* http://www.businessweek.com, September 15.

31. 2002, The days of Welch and roses, *BusinessWeek,* April 29.

32. Ibid.

33. 2005, The Immelt Revolution, *BusinessWeek,* March 28.

34. 2005, GE begins reorganizing around the customer, http://customer .corante.com, June 23.

35. Greenhouse gases are those components in the atmosphere that contribute to the "greenhouse effect," or global warming. The main natural greenhouse gases are carbon dioxide, water vapor, and ozone.

36. The normal distribution is one of the most important distributions used in probability. It is useful for describing a variety of random processes. A normal distribution is fully described with just two parameters: its mean and standard deviation. The distribution is a continuous, bell-shaped distribution, which is symmetric about its mean and can take on values from negative infinity to positive infinity.

Case 9

The Home Depot

Dan Phillips, Bo Young Hwang, Sarah Sheets, Tristan Longstreth

Arizona State University

Introduction

The succession of CEOs, presidents, and board of directors provides a challenge for businesses as they reform, reposition, and restructure. Although these successions may provide a company with beneficial results, many experience hardship. Top company officials leave due to a variety of reasons, but a common reason is conflict with employees related to executive leadership style and the culture it creates.

Robert Nardelli, former CEO of Home Depot Inc., resigned in January 2007. Numerous factors led to Nardelli's resignation: Shareholders experienced dissatisfaction with the performance of Home Depot's stagnating stock prices; Nardelli's militaristic leadership style and centralized organizational structure affected the performance of employees resulting in excessive layoffs; and the expansion of retail stores became unmanageable. The once successful and highly valued Home Depot culture had changed, affecting Home Depot's sales and customer loyalty. Along with the change in Home Depot's business culture, it faced challenges associated with the dramatic boom and fall in the housing market. These problems affected Home Depot's employee morale, stockholders, and customers. CEO successor Frank Blake has much to address in order to reposition Home Depot as the industry giant it has been for 20 years.

History

Bernie Marcus and Arthur Blank cofounded Home Depot on June 29, 1978, after being fired from Handy Dan, a small chain of home improvement stores. Their vision was to offer "warehouse stores filled from floor to ceiling with a wide assortment of products at the lowest prices" along with superior customer service provided by a knowledgeable staff.[1] This vision became a reality after acquiring sufficient capital from a New York investment banker. They opened two Home Depot stores on June 22, 1979, in the company headquarters, Atlanta, Georgia. Home Depot grew rapidly in a short period of time and went public in 1981. In 1986 Home Depot broke the $1 billion mark in sales with 50 stores that expanded into eight markets.

Home Depot revolutionized the home improvement industry by offering a wide selection of merchandise, low prices, and superior customer service to both the professional contractor as well as the do-it-yourself patron. In-store inventory contains premium products imported from more than 40 countries, including 40,000–50,000 different types of building materials, home improvement supplies, and lawn and garden products. An additional 250,000 products are available upon special order. In addition, merchandise is localized throughout each store to match the area's specific market needs.

Today Home Depot is the largest home improvement retailer in the world.[2] The 2,100 stores located throughout the United States, Canada, China, and Mexico employ roughly 335,000 people. Home Depot also operates 34 EXPO design centers, 11 landscape supply stores, and two floor stores.[3] In addition, Home Depot has become one of the leading diversified wholesale distributors in the United States due to its former HD Supply division. HD Supply Centers caters to the professional contractor for home improvement and municipal infrastructures with nearly 1,000 locations in the United States and Canada.[4]

Marcus and Blank implemented a decentralized structure with an entrepreneurial style of management, which consisted of a laid-back organization known for

The authors would like to thank Professor Robert E. Hoskisson for his support under whose direction the case was developed. The authors do not intend to illustrate either effective or ineffective handling of a managerial situation. The case solely provides material for class discussion. This case was developed with contributions from Kevin Holmberg.

the independence of its store managers.[5] Over time the changes in leadership, structure, and management style diverged from what the originators intended.

Strategic Leaders

Robert L. Nardelli acted as president, CEO, and chairperson of the board from December 2000 until January of 2007. Nardelli received his BS in business from Western Illinois University and earned his MBA from University of Louisville. Nardelli joined General Electric in 1971 as an entry-level manufacturing engineer and by 1995 became president and CEO of GE Power Systems.

After leaving GE he was quickly hired as CEO of Home Depot despite the fact that he lacked any retail experience. From GE he brought a new management strategy based on Six Sigma to Home Depot. Using Six Sigma principles he centralized the management structure of the company by eliminating and consolidating division executives, he initiated processes and streamlined operations, such as the computerized automated inventory system, and centralized supply orders at the Atlanta headquarters. He took the focus off the retail stores, moving beyond the core U.S. big-box business to conquer new markets by building up its Home Depot Supply division, and expanded into China.[6] Under Nardelli, Home Depot's sales over a five-year period went from $45.7 in 2000 to $81.5 billion in 2005,[7] and stock prices stagnated during Nardelli's six-year reign at just over $40 per share.[8] The weak financial profits and his results-driven management style, which allegedly affected the cherished culture of the company, led to a backlash and push for his resignation in January 2007.

Frank Blake succeeded Nardelli as chair and CEO of Home Depot in January of 2007. He earned his bachelor's degree from Harvard College and a jurisprudence degree from Columbia Law School. Blake originally joined the company in 2002 as executive vice president of Business Development and Corporate Operations.[9] His responsibilities included real estate, store construction and maintenance, credit services, strategic business development, special orders and service improvement, call centers, and installation services business. Prior to this role, Blake was deputy secretary for the U.S. Department of Energy and also a former GE executive. Blake also has public sector experience, serving as general counsel for the U.S. Environmental Protection Agency, deputy counsel to Vice President George Bush, and as a law clerk to Justice Stevens of the U.S. Supreme Court.[10] As Home Depot's new leader, Blake faces significant challenges, especially when it comes to rising above competition.

Competition

Competition fuels businesses to be efficient in almost every way. Competition forces companies to control their costs, develop new products, and stay at the forefront of technology. Companies that provide similar services are required to differentiate from the rest of the pack. All of these facets of competition exist in the home improvement industry. Home Depot has more than 25 direct competitors including Lowe's, Menards, True Value, Ace Hardware, Do It Best, Sears, Target, and Wal-Mart.[11] Only a select few pose a true threat to Home Depot.

Lowe's

Lowe's is Home Depot's largest competitor and holds a significant market share. Founded in 1946, Lowe's grew from a small hardware store in North Carolina to the second largest home improvement wholesaler in the world. It currently operates 1,375 stores in 49 states and ranks 42 on the *Fortune* 500 list. Lowe's can attribute its success to a philosophy similar to Home Depot's: "Providing customers with the lowest priced and the highest quality home improvement products."[12] However, Lowe's distinguished itself from Home Depot by targeting the individual customer, especially women, as Home Depot began to focus on contractors. Lowe's will continue to differentiate from competitors by promoting and expanding through exclusive private labels or select brands. Premium kitchen cabinets and stone countertops are a few new product lines that Lowe's is implementing within their stores. Much like Home Depot, Lowe's is looking to expand by pursuing interest in installing services, special orders, and commercial sales.[13]

Menards

Menards is Home Depot's second biggest competitor.[14] Although most competitors construct their stores in a compact fashion in order to adhere to real estate constraints, Menard's is moving ahead with an opposing strategy. The midwestern home center chain has started to build two-story urban stores. "We might be No. 3 as far as store counts go, but we are a regional player and we are innovative," said Menards spokeswoman Dawn Sands. Customers navigate the two-story stores using escalators that accommodate both the customer and their shopping cart. The stores also brag a unique customer experience, including a baby grand piano that provides in-store music, new boutique departments, upscale merchandise, specialty departments, wider aisles, and lower, more convenient merchandise shelves.[15]

Home Depot's competitive position is not only affected by the strategies used by the top two competitors, but also by the relationships it maintains with suppliers.

Suppliers

Home Depot relies on 10,000 to 12,000 suppliers to keep its shelves stocked, creating a tremendous challenge in regard to the process and coordination of the logistics.[16] During the reign of CEO Robert Nardelli, Home Depot expanded at a rapid rate and failed to take the additional supply requirements into consideration,[17] and thus found its brand image in jeopardy when suppliers were unable to keep up with the increased production demands.

When Robert Nardelli became CEO, he inherited a disorganized system of suppliers that relied on archaic accounting practices, including individual product order forms and fax-only lines of communication.[18] Nardelli placed increased emphasis on renovating the Home Depot supplier networks. The first thing he did was to gradually implement the Home Depot Online Supplier Center and the Cognos 8 Scorecarding software. The Center "features continuously updated information on how to do business with Home Depot, including the corporate performance policy, updates, news, information on events and training and scorecards."[19] The Cognos 8 system gathers data from warehouse management sources, purchase orders, and contract terms, and condenses it. The data is then analyzed and each supplier is rated on various aspects of the transaction. All the information is available online via the supplier center, allowing suppliers to see what areas they should improve to become more efficient.[20]

Nardelli also held workshops for specific groups of Home Depot suppliers. For instance, Nardelli hosted meetings with Home Depot's top 15 strategic suppliers four times a year to discuss plans for new products and store promotions. The suppliers toured a Home Depot Store and gave Nardelli input on product placement.[21] Because Home Depot has such a wide variety of suppliers, including suppliers from many different countries, it offers overseas workshops to educate prospective suppliers. The latest workshop took place in Shanghai and was conducted by native speakers in an effort to educate vendors on "how to do business with Home Depot, and be a better supplier overall."[22]

Another area of innovation is Home Depot's inventory and warehousing procedure. Home Depot prefers to receive products directly from their suppliers, eliminating the need for distribution centers, which are popular with many other retail organizations.[23] This system has serious benefits and drawbacks. First, it allows Home Depot to leverage the space it has and display a multitude of products in a warehouse setting. This capability is beneficial because customers are able to see the products available and purchase them in the same visit. The major drawback to this system is that each store must have an extremely efficient and organized warehouse supply chain operation. If a store runs out of a particular item, the customer will have to wait until the supplier can produce more of that item, which can take more time than transporting an out-of-stock item from a distribution center to a local store.[24] Finally, Home Depot has utilized a system of "less than truck load" store deliveries, which allows its trucking partners to carry inventories to Home Depot stores along with products destined for other customers to save on transportation costs. But as Home Depot expands, it may switch to a dedicated trucking system with full truck loads servicing multiple stores in a specific region.[25] Home Depot has developed many innovations to help make transactions with suppliers more efficient. One of Home Depot's biggest challenges is ensuring good interactions with its customer base.

Customers

Although Home Depot was originally designed as a home improvement superstore that would cater to both individual consumers and building contractors, throughout its tumultuous history, Home Depot has changed its focus a number of times. During Nardelli's reign, cost cutting was a key focus and the individual customer was neglected in lieu of professional contractors who purchased materials in bulk amounts. Many long-time Home Depot customers have switched to competitors, mainly Lowe's, because of constant inefficiencies at Home Depot. One customer explained that he had to wait three months to get his kitchen remodeled due to errors on Home Depot's behalf and he will now "go out of [his] way to go to Lowe's."[26] This customer's experience is not unique and new CEO Frank Blake has acknowledged the magnitude of this issue. Home Depot has sold its contractors supply division, which will allow them to resume the focus on the individual customer.[27] Due to the wide range of customers it caters to, Home Depot will likely face significant competition from other firms selling substitute services that match the information provided by Home Depot in the do-it-yourself segment.

Substitute Information Services for Do-It-Yourself Customers

Most companies focus on differentiating their products and services in order to combat rivalry, but also obtain enough loyalty to dissuade customers from switching to a substitute product. Not many substitutes can realistically threaten the success of Home Depot's product sales because they offer such a wide variety of products and people will always need to build houses and desire to improve existing homes. However, Home Depot's services, such as installation, may be hampered by substitutes. Today numerous Internet sites offer "How to" information as well as structured plans for various types of home improvement projects. HGTV and other home improvement shows may also deter customers away from Home Depot's services. One way to fend off threats from rivalry and possible substitutes is for Home Depot to expand its operations internationally.

International Operations

Home Depot is the largest home improvement retailer in the world and employs 335,000 people. In light of the industry trends that are occurring, Home Depot is reaching out to new markets, which may give them additional sources of revenue as well international business experience. Stores are opening in Canada and Mexico. In Canada, Home Depot acquired Canadian hardware store Aikenhead Hardware, and has ambitions to take over its biggest Canadian competitor Rona Hardware.[28] The most recent stage of expansion includes 12 stores in China, called "The Home Way."[29] This foothold in Asia will allow them access to markets that were previously inaccessible.

The Chinese home improvement industry is a refreshing niche market with a lot of potential for new sales for Home Depot. In China, when a consumer purchases a home from a contractor, they purchase an unfinished shell. The house itself is little more than four walls and floor.[30] In order to make the house livable, Chinese consumers must pay contractors, including electricians, plumbers, and drywall experts, to renovate the house. Home Depot plans to provide Chinese consumers with the hardware and skills to do much of the renovation work themselves. In order to meet this goal Home Depot will need to train an army of knowledgeable salespeople who can provide assistance and workshops for consumers.[31] Home Depot will face a number of challenges as they expand into China. It must contend with the bureaucratic communist government that rules China. There are relatively few safeguards against nationalization, if the government decides to appropriate Home Depot assets or property. In addition the Chinese consumers may not have the desire to renovate their homes by themselves. Upper management must decide which method of entry would be most appropriate, and the most effective way to appeal to the average Chinese consumer. In addition, given the recent domestic housing recession, upper management must decide whether expansion into China is the most effective use of the firm's money. Because of the diverse ventures Home Depot is involved in, Nardelli and more recently Frank Blake adopted some basic strategies that can be applied in order to maintain the company's viability.

Strategies Used

As previously mentioned Home Depot historically used a decentralized organizational structure with an entrepreneurial management style, focusing on the retail stores. Store managers were given immense autonomy, and its stores were staffed with well-trained and knowledgeable employees who could offer advice and help customers find items they wanted quickly.[32] Home Depot used to place a huge emphasis on creating a customer-friendly atmosphere with clean aisles, organized shelves, and well-stocked inventory.

However, profit from the retail stores began to decrease as the home improvement retail industry matured and became saturated. Home Depot needed to find its next great idea that would sustain growth. Nardelli believed that the key to Home Depot's success was the acquisition and incorporation of existing business into Home Depot Supply, while simultaneously squeezing efficiencies out of its retail stores.[33]

Home Depot Retail

A critical part of Nardelli's strategy was to reshape Home Depot into a more centralized organization.[34] The centralization effort was evident in the management system that one journalist referred to as a "Command and Control Management system," with a goal to replace the old, sometimes random, management style with a strict one.[35] Management in corporate headquarters started to rank every employee on the basis of four performance metrics: financial, operational, customer, and people skills. Nardelli created an equation to measure effective performance. The equation is $VA = Q \times A \times E$: the value-added (VA) of an employee equals the quality (Q) of what the employee does, multiplied by its acceptance (A) in the company, times how well the employee executes (E) the task.[36]

Influenced by his military background, Nardelli often hired employees who had military experience. Of the 1,142 people who were hired into Home Depot's store leadership program, which consisted of a two-year training program for future store managers, 528 were junior military officers.[37] He also brought many militaristic ideas into managing Home Depot, which required his employees to carry out his "command." Home Depot began to measure everything from gross margin per labor-hour to the number of greets at its front doors to maintain better information, allowing the CEOs to improve control of the Home Depot operation.

However, this lead to many underperforming executives being routinely pushed out of their positions. Since 2001, 56 percent of job changes involved bringing new managers in from outside the company.[38] This hiring trend is quite different from the past, when managers ran Home Depot stores based on the knowledge built through the years of internal experience in Home Depot operations.

In an effort to drive down labor costs, many full-time employees were replaced by part-time employees. But this approach did more than just cut costs; it damaged employee morale, diminished the knowledgeable staff available to customers, and led to many complaints about poor customer service and understaffing. As one customer from San Fernando, California, stated:

The Home Depot at 12960 Foothill Boulevard, San Fernando, California 91342, has virtually no customer service. First I thought I couldn't find any employees to help me because I used to go after work at around 5:00 P.M. Then I tried going during my lunch hour, then during off-work week days. To my surprise, no matter what time I go, there are no present employees out on the floor. The one or two that I've seen are obtained by hassling the cashiers. Try getting help from the guy out in the garden department and he answers with "I don't know, I'm not an expert. They didn't train me." What kind of answer is this, what kind of store is this? The commercials on TV make it almost seem like a mom and pop candy store. You go in and you're by yourself. You need a refrigerator? Tough. There's nobody there to sell it to you. You need a chandelier? Tough—no one in this department to help you. What about the next department? Oh, he replies he knows nothing about the department next door. Customers beware: shop elsewhere.[39]

According to the University of Michigan's annual American Customer Satisfaction Index released on February 21, 2006, with a score of 67, down from 73 in 2004, Home Depot scored 11 points behind Lowe's. Claes Fornell, a professor at University of Michigan, stated that the drop in satisfaction was one reason why Home Depot's stock price has declined at the same time Lowe's has improved.[40]

The general appearance of Home Depot retail stores was becoming a drawback for customers. They often complained that Home Depot had become more like a "warehouse" that was unclean, unorganized, and far from the enjoyable shopping experience it had been in the past.[41] This neglect of the Home Depot's retail stores may have been the result of Nardelli shifting his focus toward new ventures, including Home Depot Supply.

Home Depot Supply

The building supply market during the early 1990s was a growing yet fragmented market segment worth $410 billion per year.[42] Nardelli saw an opportunity to enter this new market because there were few large competitors. To reduce the cannibalization of sales from its existing retail stores, he announced that Home Depot would cut retail store openings by nearly half over a five-year period.[43] Using the money saved from cutting retail store construction, Home Depot spent about $6 billion acquiring more than 25 wholesale suppliers to build up Home Depot Supply (HDS). HDS was a wholesale unit that sold pipes, custom kitchens, and building materials to contractors and municipalities.

Because Home Depot had acquired so many wholesalers, HDS became one of the leaders in the building supply industry. For example, in 2005 Home Depot purchased National Waterworks and entered the municipal water pipe market. Home Depot's biggest purchase was that of the $3.5 billion acquisition of Hughes Supply in 2006, which made Home Depot a leading distributor of electrical and plumbing supplies. HDS expected to have 1,500 supply houses with revenues of $25 billion annually by 2010.[44]

Due to the fragmentation of the building supply market, many contractors were associated with their regional suppliers based on long-standing relationships. Those regional suppliers offered a highly trained sales staff and specialized service, whereas HDS stores worked much like the standard warehouse format.[45] Home Depot was challenged to satisfy a new range of customers' needs, which were different from do-it-yourself customers. Therefore, HDS encouraged its sales employees by rewarding them, primarily in commissions, to win contracts. Furthermore, Home Depot retained most of the management of acquired suppliers, realizing the importance of cultural continuity. Nardelli insisted that top management, salespeople, and internal cultures of the acquired companies maintain their corporate names and colors on stores and delivery trucks.[46] He believed that these efforts would help them keep existing long-term relationships with contractors. HDS was expected to earn 20 percent of the company's overall sales.

As mentioned, when Blake took over as CEO he saw the need to refocus Home Depot's vision and again cater to the retail market. Therefore, in June 2007 Home Depot announced the sale of Home Depot Supply for $10 billion to a group of private equity firms (Brian Capital Partners, Carlyle Group, and Clayton, Dubilier, and Rice).[47] The proceeds from the sale will be used to implement necessary changes in Home Depot such as increased capital spending, upgrading merchandise, and hiring trained and qualified staff and sales associates.[48] The latter is especially important because many employees were beginning to feel dissatisfied with their positions, leading to a dangerously volatile corporate culture.

Corporate Culture

Home Depot's corporate culture has changed drastically as a result of Nardelli's leadership style. Due to Nardelli's military background, many of the changes he implemented were designed to create a more vertically oriented management structure. Originally each Home Depot store enjoyed a sense of autonomy, as each store director was able to set prices and promote products within that store to match the needs of the community in which it was located. Under Nardelli, each executive and store director was responsible for various financial targets, and if these targets were not met, they were immediately terminated. This expectation created a general atmosphere of fear and distrust. Throughout Nardelli's tenure as CEO, 97 percent of top executives were removed and replaced.

To further cut costs, Nardelli implemented a part-time workforce and eliminated many of the full-time employee positions. This trend caused a great deal of resentment from employees who had previously worked full time for Home Depot, because they could no longer receive medical and dental benefits. When the part-time workforce was combined with a management system that only focused on the bottom line, no time was left for taking care of the customer.

The advent of new technology had a big impact on corporate culture, and ultimately customer service. Nardelli believed that by implementing automated checkout lines, customers would be able to pay for their purchases quickly and save time. This innovation would also cut down on employee hours, and checkout personnel would no longer be used. However, this plan backfired when the automated checkout machines malfunctioned more often than they worked correctly, and the few employees who were not laid off as a result of the innovation experienced a significant amount of stress due to having to fix the checkout machines, and answer customer questions at the same time. This frustration was mirrored by customers who were unable to find sales associates when they had specific questions. In addition to significant corporate culture problems, Home Depot's financial statements were beginning to show signs of trouble for the home improvement giant.

Financial Issues

Due to the housing and home improvement boom, sales soared from $46 billion in 2000, the year Nardelli took over, to $81.5 billion in 2005, with an annual average growth rate of 12 percent.[49] The Home Depot's gross margins increased 3.5 percent from 2000 to 35.5 percent in 2005.[50]

For fiscal 2006, net sales were $90.8 billion with earnings of $5.8 billion, an 11.4 percent increase from fiscal 2005. Fiscal 2006 net sales in the retail segment were $79.0 billion, a 2.6 percent increase from 2005, which was driven by the opening of new stores. The Home Depot Supply segment contributed $12.1 billion, an increase of 161.6 percent from 2005. This increase was driven by solid organic growth and sales from acquired businesses.[51] Although Home Depot remains one of the world's largest home improvement retailers in the world, results for fiscal 2006 were disappointing, according to Frank Blake, current chair and CEO.[52] Housing slowdowns have hurt the financial goals for the retail segment of Home Depot. In the third quarter of 2006, same-store sales at Home Depot's 2,127 retail stores declined 5.1 percent.[53]

Economic and current market conditions caused a slowdown in the residential and housing market and an overall market share decline. Analysts do not expect an improvement until late 2007 or early 2008. The company's main focus for fiscal 2007 will be on the retail segment of their business, with total investments of $2.2 billion of capital spending and investments.[54] For Home Depot's income statement, balance sheet, statement of cash flows, and key ratios, see Exhibit 1. For a comparison of January 2006 and January 2007 consolidated statement of earnings, balance sheet, and segment information, see Exhibits 2, 3, and 4, on pages 112, 113, and 114, respectively.

Shareholders

Even though Nardelli was helping Home Depot achieve drastic structural changes, stock prices were affected by the lack of focus of this retail organization. Home Depot's shares were down 7 percent while archrival Lowe's stock prices had soared more than 200 percent since 2000. The poor stock performance led to anger among many of the shareholders.[55] (For a comparison of Home Depot's top competitors and their industry and market, see Exhibit 5, on page 114.)

Investment bankers are currently working on different ways to solve the share price problem such as returning $1.4 billion in cash to shareholders through dividends paid.[56] The company's dividend payout ratio is now approximately 24 percent.[57] In addition, during fiscal year 2006, Home Depot returned cash to shareholders by spending $6.7 billion to repurchase 174 million shares, or 19 percent of its outstanding shares. A stock chart is provided in Exhibit 6, on page 115, which illustrates share prices between March 27, 2006, and March 27, 2007.

Exhibit 1 Highlights of Key Financial Statements and Ratios for Home Depot

Income Statement (in US$ millions, except for per-share items)	01/28/07	01/29/06	01/30/05 Restated 01/29/06	02/01/04 Restated 01/29/06	02/02/03
Net Sales	90,837.00	81,511.00	73,094.00	64,816.00	58,247.00
Cost of Goods Sold	29,783.00	27,320.00	24,430.00	20,580.00	18,108.00
Income Before Tax	9,308.00	9,282.00	7,912.00	6,843.00	5,872.00
Net Income	5,761.00	5,838.00	5,001.00	4,304.00	3,664.00

Balance Sheet	01/28/07	01/29/06 Restated 01/28/07	01/30/05 Restated 01/29/06	02/01/04 Restated 01/30/05	02/02/03
Assets					
Total Current Assets	$18,000.00	$15,269.00	$14,273.00	$13,328.00	$11,917.00
Net PP&E	26,605.00	24,901.00	22,726.00	20,063.00	17,168.00
Total Assets	52,263.00	44,405.00	39,020.00	34,437.00	30,011.00
Liabilities and Shareholders' Equity					
Total Current Liabilities	$12,931.00	$12,706.00	$10,455.00	$ 9,554.00	$ 8,035.00
Long-Term Debt	11,643.00	2,672.00	2,148.00	856.00	1,321.00
Total Liabilities	27,233.00	17,496.00	14,862.00	12,030.00	10,209.00
Total Shareholders Equity	25,030.00	26,909.00	24,158.00	22,407.00	19,802.00
Total Liabilities & Shareholders Equity	52,263.00	44,405.00	39,020.00	34,437.00	30,011.00

Cash Flow Statement	01/29/06	01/30/05	02/01/04 Restated 01/30/05	02/02/03 Restated 01/30/05	02/03/02
Net Cash Flows from Operations	$ 6,484.00	$ 6,904.00	$ 6,545.00	$ 4,802.00	$ 5,963.00
Net Cash Flows from Investing	(4,586.00)	(4,479.00)	(4,171.00)	(2,601.00)	(3,466.00)
Net Cash Flows from Financing	(1,612.00)	(3,055.00)	(1,931.00)	(2,165.00)	(173.00)

Key Ratios	As of 03/26/07
Price/Earnings (TTM)	$13.64
Annual Dividend	.90
Annual Yield %	2.36
Quick Ratio (MRQ)	.40
Current Ratio (MRQ)	1.39
Return on Equity (TTM)	16.22
Return on Assets (TTM)	11.92
Return on Investment (TTM)	16.22

Data provided by Marketguide. Shareholder.com, the producer of this site, and The Home Depot, Inc. do not guarantee the accuracy of the information provided on this page, and will not be held liable for consequential damages arising from the use of this information.

Source: Home Depot, 2007, http://ir.homedepot.com/summary_financials.cfm.

Exhibit 2 Statement of Earnings for Home Depot

THE HOME DEPOT, INC. AND SUBSIDIARIES
CONSOLIDATED STATEMENTS OF EARNINGS
FOR THE THREE MONTHS AND YEARS ENDED JANUARY 28, 2007 AND JANUARY 29, 2006

(Unaudited)

(Amounts in Millions Except Per Share Data and as Otherwise Noted)

	Three Months Ended		% Increase (Decrease)	Years Ended		% Increase (Decrease)
	1-28-07	1-29-06		1-28-07	1-29-06	
NET SALES	$20,265	$19,489	4.0 %	$90,837	$81,511	11.4 %
Cost of Sales	13,627	12,896	5.7	61,054	54,191	12.7
GROSS PROFIT	6,638	6,593	0.7	29,783	27,320	9.0
Operating Expenses:						
Selling, General and Administrative	4,594	4,132	11.2	18,348	16,485	11.3
Depreciation and Amortization	442	413	7.0	1,762	1,472	19.7
Total Operating Expenses	5,036	4,545	10.8	20,110	17,957	12.0
OPERATING INCOME	1,602	2,048	(21.8)	9,673	9,363	3.3
Interest Income (Expense):						
Interest and Investment Income	4	8	(50.0)	27	62	(56.5)
Interest Expense	(127)	(35)	262.9	(392)	(143)	174.1
Interest, net	(123)	(27)	355.6	(365)	(81)	350.6
EARNINGS BEFORE PROVISION FOR INCOME TAXES	1,479	2,021	(26.8)	9,308	9,282	0.3
Provision for Income Taxes	554	736	(24.7)	3,547	3,444	3.0
NET EARNINGS	$ 925	$ 1,285	(28.0)%	$ 5,761	$ 5,838	(1.3)%
Weighted Average Common Shares	1,993	2,119	(5.9)%	2,054	2,138	(3.9)%
BASIC EARNINGS PER SHARE	$0.46	$0.61	(24.6)%	$2.80	$2.73	2.6%
Diluted Weighted Average Common Shares	2,004	2,128	(5.8)%	2,062	2,147	(4.0)%
DILUTED EARNINGS PER SHARE	$0.46	$0.60	(23.3)%	$2.79	$2.72	2.6%

SELECTED HIGHLIGHTS

	Three Months Ended		% Increase (Decrease)	Years Ended		% Increase (Decrease)
	1-28-07	1-29-06		1-28-07	1-29-06	
Number of Customer Transactions (1)	304	308	(1.3)%	1,330	1,330	– %
Average Ticket (1)	$56.27	$57.20	(1.6)	$58.90	$57.98	1.6
Weighted Average Weekly Sales per Operating Store (000's) (1)	$617	$676	(8.7)	$723	$763	(5.2)
Square Footage at End of Period (1)	224	215	4.2	224	215	4.2
Capital Expenditures	$1,032	$1,028	0.4	$3,542	$3,881	(8.7)
Depreciation and Amortization (2)	$476	$445	7.0%	$1,886	$1,579	19.4%

(1) Includes retail segment only.

(2) Includes depreciation of distribution centers and tool rental equipment included in Cost of Sales and amortization of deferred financing costs included in Interest Expense.

Source: Home Depot, 2007, http://www.homedepot.com.

Exhibit 3 Consolidated Balance Sheets for Home Depot

THE HOME DEPOT, INC. AND SUBSIDIARIES
CONSOLIDATED BALANCE SHEETS
AS OF JANUARY 28, 2007 AND JANUARY 29, 2006
(Amounts in Millions)

	1-28-07 (Unaudited)	1-29-06 (Audited)
ASSETS		
Cash and Short-Term Investments	$ 614	$ 807
Receivables, net	3,223	2,396
Merchandise Inventories	12,822	11,401
Other Current Assets	1,341	665
Total Current Assets	18,000	15,269
Property and Equipment, net	26,605	24,901
Goodwill	6,314	3,286
Other Assets	1,344	949
TOTAL ASSETS	$52,263	$44,405
LIABILITIES AND STOCKHOLDERS' EQUITY		
Short-Term Debt	$ –	$ 900
Accounts Payable	7,356	6,032
Accrued Salaries and Related Expenses	1,295	1,068
Current Installments of Long-Term Debt	18	513
Other Current Liabilities	4,262	4,193
Total Current Liabilities	12,931	12,706
Long-Term Debt	11,643	2,672
Other Long-Term Liabilities	2,659	2,118
Total Liabilities	27,233	17,496
Total Stockholders' Equity	25,030	26,909
TOTAL LIABILITIES AND STOCKHOLDERS' EQUITY	$52,263	$44,405

Source: Home Depot, 2007, http://www.homedepot.com.

What Should Happen to Improve Home Depot?

Home Depot has been plagued by many problems in its recent history. Robert Nardelli's strategic approach of focusing on suppliers and improving efficiency demoralized much of the human capital in its retail business, and as a result seemingly reduced the effectiveness of Home Depot's cherished organizational culture. The approach left employees afraid of their own executives, which forced them to focus on maintaining their current positions through hyperefficiency and in effect to fall short in customer service. This bottom-line thinking had drastic implications for Home Depot's customer base as more customers left Home Depot to shop at other stores such as Lowe's and Wal-Mart to meet their home improvement needs. In addition, a cyclical market and international expansion are issues that will need to be addressed. Frank Blake as the new CEO faces the monumental task of making the home improvement giant profitable again and restructuring to repair the damaged aspects of the corporation. With Blake in command, Home Depot has a good chance of leveraging its core competencies in the retail market and becoming an excellent corporation for customers and shareholders. Shareholders and employees alike anxiously await the future to see what lies in store for Home Depot.

Exhibit 4 Segment Financial Information for Home Depot

THE HOME DEPOT, INC. AND SUBSIDIARIES
SEGMENT INFORMATION
FOR THE YEARS ENDED JANUARY 28, 2007, AND JANUARY 29, 2006

(Unaudited)
(amounts in $ millions)

Year Ended January 28, 2007

	HD Retail (a)	HD Supply	Eliminations/ Other (b)	Consolidated
Net Sales	$79,027	$12,070	$(260)	$90,837
Operating Income	9,024	800	(151)	9,673
Depreciation and Amortization	1,679	197	10	1,886
Total Assets	42,094	10,021	148	52,263
Capital Expenditures	3,321	221		3,542
Payments for Businesses Acquired, net	305	3,963	–	4,268

Year Ended January 29, 2006

	HD Retail (a)	HD Supply	Eliminations/ Other (b)	Consolidated
Net Sales	$77,022	$4,614	$(125)	$81,511
Operating Income	9,058	319	(14)	9,363
Depreciation and Amortization	1,510	63	6	1,579
Total Assets	39,827	4,517	61	44,405
Capital Expenditures	3,777	104	–	3,881
Payments for Businesses Acquired, net	190	2,356	–	2,546

(a) Includes all retail stores, Home Depot Direct and retail installation services.

(b) Includes elimination of intersegment sales and unallocated corporate overhead. Operating Income for the year ended January 28, 2007, includes $129 million of cost associated with executive severance and separation agreements.

Source: Home Depot, 2007, http://www.homedepot.com.

Exhibit 5 Industry Statistics and Comparisons

	Home Depot	Lowe's	Menard	True Value
Annual Sales	$81,511	$43,243	$6,500	$2,043
Employees	345,000	185,000	35,000	2,800
Market Cap ($ millions)	$77,488	$48,852.8	0	0

Comparison of Home Depot to Industry and Stock Market

Valuation	Company	Industry[1]	Stock Market[2]
Price/Sales Ratio	0.83	0.83	2.22
Price/Earnings Ratio	12.51	12.51	18.98
Price/Book Ratio	2.70	2.93	2.16
Price/Cash Flow Ratio	12.02	12.02	13.44

[1]**Industry:** Building Materials, Hardware, Garden Supply, and Mobile Home Dealers

[2]**Market:** Public companies trading on the NYSE, AMEX, and NASDAQ

Source: © 2007, Hoover's, Inc., All Rights Reserved, http://www.hoovers.com/home-depot/—ID__11470,ticker__—/free-co-fin-factsheet.xhtml.

Exhibit 6 Home Depot Stock Chart

Source: Home Depot, Inc. (HD), http://moneycentral.msn.com/stock_
quote?Symbol=HD.

Notes

1. 2007, Home Depot, http://corporate.homedepot.com/wps/portal,
   March 28.
2. Ibid.
3. Ibid.
4. Ibid.
5. R. Farzad, D. Foust, B. Grow, E. Javers, E. Thornton, & R. Zegel, 2007,
   Out at Home Depot, *BusinessWeek,* http://www.businessweek.com,
   January 15.
6. Ibid
7. 2007, Home Depot, http://ir.homedepot.com/releaseDetail
   .cfm?ReleaseID=194738&ShSect=E, July 3.
8. Ibid.
9. 2007, Home Depot, http://corporate.homedepot.com/wps/portal,
   March 28.
10. Ibid.
11. 2007, http://www.hoovers.com, April 1.
12. 2007, Lowe's , http://www.Lowe's.com, April 1.
13. D. Howell, 2005, Lowe's hammers home growth objective: National
    in a year, http://findarticles.com/p/articles/mi_m0FNP/is_6_44/
    ai_n13726491.
14. 2007, HD: Competitors for Home Depot, *Yahoo! Finance,* July 10.
15. Ibid.
16. R. Bowman, 2006, Home Depot turns its attention to supplier
    performance management, *Global Logistics & Supply Chain Strategies,*
    http://www.glscs.com/archives/06.06.casestudy.htm?adcode=5, June.
17. Ibid.
18. Ibid.
19. Ibid.
20. Ibid.
21. Ibid.
22. Ibid.
23. R. Bowman, 2001, Global supply chain partnerships, *Global Logistics
    & Supply Chain Strategies,* http://www.glscs.com/archives/7.02
    .homedepot.htm?adcode=5, July.
24. Ibid.
25. Ibid.
26. B. Grow & S. McMillan, 2006, Home Depot: Last among shoppers,
    BusinessWeek Online, http://www.businessweek.com, June 19.
27. H. Weber, 2007, Home Depot undecided on supply business,
    BusinessWeek Online, http://www.businessweek.com, March 22.
28. 2007, Home Depot, http://en.wikipedia.org/wiki/Home_depot,
    accessed on April 17.
29. Ibid.
30. B. Grow & F. Balfour, 2006, Home Depot: One foot in China,
    BusinessWeek Online, http://www.businessweek.com, May 1.
31. Ibid.
32. D. Brady & B. Grow, 2006, Renovating Home Depot, *BusinessWeek,*
    http://www.businessweek.com, March 6, 50–56.
33. Ibid.
34. Ibid.
35. Ibid.
36. R. Farzad, D. Foust, B. Grow, E. Javers, E. Thornton, & R. Zegel, 2007,
    Out at Home Depot.
37. D. Brady & B. Grow, Renovating Home Depot.
38. Ibid.
39. 2004, http://www.complaints.com/directory/2004/june/14/15.htm.
40. D. Brady & B. Grow, Renovating Home Depot.
41. H. Weber, 2006, Home Depot needs makeover, *Washington Post,*
    http://www.washingtonpost.com, January 6.
42. 2006, Home Depot will buy building supply chain, *Winston-Salem
    Journal,* http://www.journalnow.com/servlet/Satellite?pagename=WS
    J%2FMGArticle%2FWSJ_BasicArticle&c=MGArticle&cid=11287692
    38504&path=!business&s=1037645507703%20, January 11.
43. C. Terhune, 2006, Home Depot knocks on contractors' doors, *Wall
    Street Journal,* August 7.
44. P. Bond, 2006, Commercial wholesale division doubles Home Depot's
    supply business, *The Atlanta Journal-Constitution,* August 6.
45. C. Terhune, 2007, Home Depot knocks on contractors' doors,
    Wall Street Journal Online, http://online.wsj.com/article/
    SB115491714152328447.html, July 13.
46. Ibid.
47. M. Flaherty & K. Jacobs, 2007, Bids for Home Depot Supply due
    Friday, *BNET Today,* http://www.bnet.com/2407-13071_23-88489
    .html, July 5.
48. Ibid.
49. D. Brady & B. Grow, Renovating Home Depot.
50. Ibid.
51. Home Depot, 2007, The Home Depot announces fourth quarter and
    fiscal 2006 results, http://ir.homedepot.com, February 20.
52. Home Depot, 2007, The Home Depot announces fourth quarter
    dividend, http://ir.homedepot.com, February 22.
53. R. Farzad, D. Foust, B. Grow, E. Javers, E. Thornton, & R. Zegel, 2007,
    Out at Home Depot.
54. Home Depot, 2007, The Home Depot presents 2007 key priorities
    and financial outlook, http://ir.homedepot.com, February 28.
55. D. Brady & B. Grow, Renovating Home Depot.
56. Home Depot, 2007, The Home Depot announces fourth quarter
    dividend, http://irhomedepot.com, February 22.
57. Ibid.

Case 10

China's Home Improvement Market: Should Home Depot Enter or Will it Have a Late-Mover (Dis)advantage?

R. Muthu Kumar, Nagendra Chowdary

ICFAI University

China, the fastest-growing economy in the world, is witnessing rapid growth in the private housing market after its introduction of housing reforms in 1998. As the Chinese people's income and purchasing power increases, their property investment is also on the rise. In 2005, real estate investment accounted for 8.65 percent of China's GDP and it is expected to rise to 9.3 percent in 2006.[1] As a result, the total value of property under construction in 2005 was RMB 5.1 trillion ($637.42 billion), contributing to 28 percent of China's GDP.[2] Consequently, China's home improvement market also projected great potential for growth. Many foreign home improvement retailers such as B&Q and IKEA have established their strong presence along with the domestic home improvement players.

"The home improvement market on the mainland is the most promising in the world: $50 billion in sales in 2005 and growing at 12% a year. Homeownership has skyrocketed, from near zero two decades ago, when there was virtually no private property, to 70% of all housing today," *BusinessWeek* reported.[3] However, China's home improvement market is not that easy to navigate although the potential is highly tempting.

U.S.-based Home Depot has not yet started its operations in China and its "China Strategy" is in progress. Some think it missed the bus by not being an early entrant and therefore will suffer from late mover disadvantage. Others think the delay will help shorten its learning curve and it will rise rapidly.

China's Economy and Real Estate

China is the second-largest economy in the world (see Exhibit 1) when measured by Purchasing Power Parity, with a GDP (PPP) of $9.412 trillion in 2005. When measured in USD-exchange rate terms, it is the fourth largest in 2005 (Exhibit 1) with $2.25 trillion. It is the world's fastest-growing major economy with a population of 1.3 billion (see Exhibit 2). Its per capita GDP was $1,703 in 2005 and varied for each region in China (see Exhibit 3, on page 119).

Economic Growth

China's economic evolution happened over a period of four generations (see Exhibit 4, on page 119). To speed up the industrialization process, the central government invested heavily in the 1960s and 1970s. A large share of the country's economic output was controlled by the government, which set production goals, controlled prices, and allocated resources. As a result, by 1978 nearly three-fourths of industrial production was manufactured by state-owned enterprises based on centrally planned output targets. The central government's major goal was to make China's economy self-sufficient. Foreign trade was restricted to obtain only those goods that could not be manufactured in China. Only countries that maintained diplomatic relations with China could participate in foreign trade. Though China's real GDP grew at an average annual rate of 5.3 percent from 1960 to 1978, the economy was almost inactive due to the huge population base and lack of competition. In addition, the economy was inefficient because of the few profit incentives for enterprises and workers. Price and production controls also caused widespread distortions in China's economy.[4]

Since 1978, the government had been devising strategies to shift from a centrally planned economy to a more market-oriented economy. China's economic development had occurred in two phases. The first phase began in 1979,

Exhibit 1 World Economies GDP Rankings

List of Countries by GDP (PPP)			List of Countries by GDP (Nominal)			Economy of China: 2005 Statistics	
Rank	Country	GDP (in $ billion)	Rank	Country	GDP (in $ billion)		
1	United States	12277.583	1	United States	12485.725	GDP (Nominal) Ranking	4
2	**China**	**9412.361**	2	Japan	4571.314	GDP (PPP) Ranking	2
3	Japan	3910.728	3	Germany	2797.343	GDP (Nominal)	$2.22 trillion
4	India	3633.441	4	**China**	**2224.811**	GDP (PPP)	$9.412 trillion
5	Germany	2521.699	5	United Kingdom	2201.473	GDP per capita	$1,703
6	United Kingdom	1832.792	6	France	2105.864	GDP per capita (PPP)	$6,200
7	France	1830.11	7	Italy	1766.16	GDP growth rate	9.90%
8	Italy	1668.151	8	Canada	1130.208		
9	Brazil	1576.728	9	Spain	1126.565		
10	Russia	1575.561	10	Korea	793.07		

Source: Compiled from "International Monetary Fund, World Economic Outlook Database," http://www.imf.org/external/pubs/ft/weo/2006/01/data/dbcoutm.cfm? April 2006.

Exhibit 2 Population of China (2000–2004)

	2000	2001	2002	2003	2004
Male	654.4	656.7	661.1	665.6	669.8
Female	613.1	619.6	623.4	626.7	630.1
Total (million)	**1,267.4**	**1,276.3**	**1,284.5**	**1,292.3**	**1,299.9**
% change, year on year	0.8	0.7	0.6	0.6	0.6
Urban (million)	459.1	480.6	502.1	532.8	542.8
% of total	36.2	37.7	39.1	40.5	41.7
Rural (million)	808.4	795.6	782.4	768.5	757.1
% of total	63.8	62.3	60.9	59.5	58.2

Source: "Country Profile 2006," http://www.eiu.com.

when the then Chairman Deng Xiaoping launched a series of reforms, including decollectivization of agriculture and a return to household farming.

In the 1980s, China tried to combine central planning with market-oriented reforms to increase productivity, living standards, and technological quality without exacerbating inflation, unemployment, and budget deficits. The country pursued agricultural reforms, dismantling the commune system and introducing household farming that authorized peasants with greater decision-making powers in agricultural activities. The government also encouraged non-agricultural activities, such as setting up of village enterprises in rural areas, promoting more self-management of state-owned enterprises, and increasing competition in the marketplace.

These reforms led to average annual rates of growth of 10 percent in agricultural and industrial output. Rural per capita real income doubled. Industry posted major gains especially in coastal areas, where foreign investment helped drive output of both domestic and export goods. However, beginning in 1985, agricultural output witnessed a steady decline due to subsidy cuts and rising costs of inputs.

From the 1990s, during the second phase of China's growth, as the country further opened up, many foreign companies began entering China. China's economy boomed in the early 1990s. During 1993, output and prices were accelerating, and economic expansion was fueled by the introduction of more than 2,000 special economic zones (SEZs) and the influx of foreign capital that the SEZs facilitated. But the economy slowed down in the late 1990s, influenced in part by the Asian Financial Crisis of 1998–1999. Economic growth fell from 13.6 percent in 1992 to 7.1 percent in 1999 (see Exhibit 5, on page 120). From 1995 to 1999 inflation dropped sharply, reflecting the tighter monetary policy of central banks and stronger measures to control food prices.

However, the average annual growth rate of China's GDP through 2001 had been 8.9 percent since its economic

Exhibit 3 China GDP per Person by Province, 2005

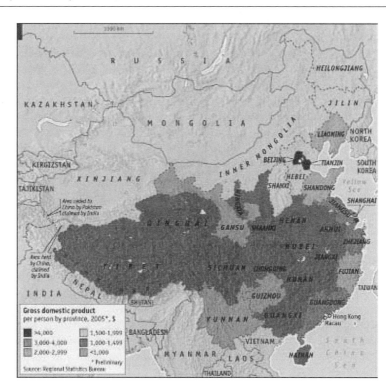

Source: "Coming out," http://www.economist.com/surveys/displaystory.cfm?story_id=5623226, March 23, 2006.

Exhibit 4 Four Generations of China's Economic Growth

Mao Era, 1949–1976

After the Communist victory in 1949, China had a strong central government for the first time since the fall of the Qing dynasty in 1911. But a succession of political campaigns, including the Great Leap Forward and the Cultural Revolution, brought famine and upheaval. Agriculture was collectivized and industry nationalized. Economic growth suffered. China largely cut itself off from the world, and relations with the United States were hostile until President Richard Nixon's 1972 visit.

Deng Era, 1978–1990s

Deng Xiaoping launched his famous economic reforms in 1978, which led to the flourishing of private enterprise in the 1980s. U.S.-China ties blossomed following the normalization of relations in 1979 and amid mutual distrust of the Soviet Union. Killings of pro-democracy Tiananmen protesters in 1989 tarnished Deng's legacy, bruised ties with the United States, and slowed reform. But Deng's 1992 call for faster reforms reignited economic growth.

Jiang Era, 1990s–2002

Catapulted from relative obscurity, Jiang consolidated his power as Deng's influence waned in the years before his death in 1997. Jiang jettisoned Marxist ideology and fostered the shift to a market-oriented economy. He expanded social freedoms for the urban elite and curbed military clout. His attempts to make the state sector more competitive and clean up the financial sector were less successful. In 2002, he oversaw China's entry into the World Trade Organization.

Fourth Generation, 2003–

Lacking revolutionary experience, this generation is the best-educated to date. Hu Jintao may be president, but no one leader will dominate, and consensus will be the rule. On the economic front, the leadership will likely focus on reforming agriculture, state-owned enterprises, and the financial sector. There is disagreement between those who favor maintaining an authoritarian approach and those who insist economic reform must be accompanied by limited democracy.

Source: Roberts Dexter and Clifford Mark L., "China's Power Shift," http://www.businessweek.com/magazine/content/02_08/b3771018.htm, February 25, 2002.

Exhibit 5 China's GDP Percentage

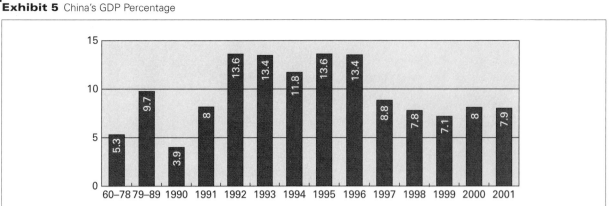

Source: Ye Xiannian, "China Real Estate Market—Economic Development," http://www.china-window.com/china_market/china_real_estate/china-real-estate-market-2.shtml, August 20, 2004.

Exhibit 6 China's GDP and the Percentage Share of GDP in Total GDP for the Three Areas (1978–2001)

	National GDP (million yuan)	Eastern Area		Central Area		Western Area	
		GDP (million yuan)	%	GDP (million yuan)	%	GDP (million yuan)	%
1978	346,354	181,832	52.5	106,466	30.7	58,056	16.8
1979	394,275	203,873	51.7	123,687	31.4	66,715	16.9
1980	439,596	229,585	52.2	136,908	31.1	73,103	16.6
1981	479,347	250,961	52.4	151,041	31.5	77,345	16.1
1982	533,108	279,868	52.5	166,131	31.2	87,109	16.3
1983	595,085	311,019	52.0	189,495	31.7	97,571	16.3
1984	712,537	373,412	52.4	223,875	31.4	115,250	16.2
1985	862,066	455,246	52.8	267,538	31.0	139,282	16.2
1986	965,648	511,314	53.0	300,087	31.1	154,247	16.0
1987	1,144,177	612,845	53.6	352,365	30.8	178,967	15.6
1988	1,445,266	786,501	54.4	434,060	30.0	224,705	15.5
1989	1,635,691	895,790	54.8	489,251	29.9	250,650	15.3
1990	1,833,023	989,966	54.0	547,920	29.9	295,137	16.1
1991	2,110,312	1,164,293	55.2	605,130	28.7	340,889	16.2
1992	2,584,738	1,459,328	56.5	725,345	28.1	400,065	15.5
1993	3,422,001	1,981,049	57.9	931,780	27.2	509,172	14.9
1994	4,521,683	2,652,547	58.7	1,212,823	26.8	656,313	14.5
1995	5,763,278	3,361,540	58.3	1,586,764	27.5	814,974	14.1
1996	6,730,552	3,970,377	59.0	1,916,757	28.5	843,418	12.5
1997	7,547,520	4,445,350	58.9	2,164,300	28.7	937,870	12.4
1998	8,106,540	4,807,090	59.3	2,287,150	28.2	1,012,300	12.5
1999	8,619,170	5,156,430	59.8	2,397,450	27.8	1,065,290	12.4
2000	9,527,990	5,752,720	60.4	2,625,020	27.6	1,150,250	12.1
2001	10,501,650	6,362,436	60.6	2,867,045	27.3	1,272,169	12.1

Source: Zhang Wei, "Can the Strategy of Western Development Narrow Down China's Regional Disparity," *Asia Economic Paper,* 2005, 3.

reforms. The pace of GDP growth in different regions was uneven due to variation in their incomes. Based on geographical location and government regulations, China can be divided into three areas—eastern coastal, central and western. The average growth rate of GDP in these areas during 1978–2001 were 10.2 percent, 9.08 percent, and 8.19 percent, respectively. The GDP share of eastern area in the total national GDP increased from 52 percent to 60 percent, while the other two areas' share decreased (see Exhibit 6).

Between 1978 and 2001, the ratio of GDP per capita in the eastern area to the average GDP per capita nationwide increased from 1.28 to 1.42, while for the other areas it decreased (see Exhibit 7).

In addition, economic inequalities between rural and urban regions were high in China. From 1994, a steep rise in unemployment had turned many rural farmers into absolute economic losers. Meanwhile, the inflow of foreign direct investment and the rise of industrial joint ventures had increased the urban-rural disparity. China's levels of inequality surpassed that of Eastern European transition economies, Western European industrialized nations, and other Asian developing nations such as India, Pakistan, and Indonesia. Since the inception of reforms in 1978, the disparities had witnessed a cyclical pattern (Appendixes I(a) and I(b)) that was attributed to urban-biased industrial development strategy over agricultural development. Since the reforms, the politically powerful urban population had pressured the government for fast income growth. As a result, the government followed an urban bias in order to preserve regime stability and political legitimacy.

The people's response to such urban-based policies has been rural social unrest and mass migration to cities in

Exhibit 7 China's GDP per Capita and the Ratio of GDP per Capita to National GDP per Capita for the Three Areas, 1978–2001

| | National GDP per Capita (yuan) | Eastern Area | | Central Area | | Western Area | |
		GDP per Capita (yuan)	R*	GDP per Capita (yuan)	R*	GDP per Capita (yuan)	R*
1978	361.4	462.2	1.28	311.0	0.86	260.7	0.72
1979	406.0	511.3	1.26	356.1	0.88	296.3	0.73
1980	447.4	569.0	1.27	389.2	0.87	321.5	0.72
1981	481.1	612.6	1.27	423.8	0.88	335.8	0.70
1982	527.1	672.4	1.28	459.3	0.87	373.1	0.71
1983	585.0	739.0	1.26	517.9	0.89	414.1	0.71
1984	689.6	877.4	1.27	604.8	0.88	485.1	0.70
1985	824.9	1,058.0	1.28	714.2	0.87	580.1	0.70
1986	911.3	1,172.0	1.29	790.2	0.87	633.1	0.69
1987	1,063.5	1,383.3	1.30	913.9	0.86	723.8	0.68
1988	1,322.7	1,750.1	1.32	1,107.2	0.84	894.4	0.68
1989	1,474.8	1,965.8	1.33	1,227.4	0.83	983.8	0.67
1990	1,611.0	2,104.0	1.31	1,345.7	0.84	1,134.6	0.70
1991	1,835.2	2,451.8	1.34	1,468.4	0.80	1,296.5	0.71
1992	2,225.2	3,042.4	1.37	1,741.7	0.78	1,507.3	0.68
1993	2,918.3	4,093.2	1.40	2,215.2	0.76	1,899.9	0.65
1994	3,819.3	5,436.9	1.42	2,854.0	0.75	2,421.3	0.63
1995	4,816.3	6,812.0	1.41	3,698.7	0.77	2,972.9	0.62
1996	5,548.9	7,946.8	1.43	4,421.2	0.80	3,014.5	0.54
1997	6,327.6	8,821.9	1.39	4,952.2	0.78	3,723.8	0.59
1998	6,743.0	9,474.2	1.41	5,194.2	0.77	3,977.6	0.59
1999	7,114.8	10,089.5	1.42	5,406.8	0.76	4,145.7	0.58
2000	7,737.7	10,728.3	1.39	5,974.1	0.77	4,497.4	0.58
2001	8,490.6	12,070.6	1.42	6,400.9	0.75	4,858.4	0.57

*R is the ratio of the GDP per capita for a given area to the national GDP per capita.

Source: Zhang Wei, "Can the Strategy of Western Development Narrow Down China's Regional Disparity," *Asia Economic Paper*, 2005, 4.

search of jobs. Many other countries including the United States had faced similar dilemmas of human displacement in the course of their development. The significant urban-rural income disparity led to massive rural-to-urban migration. Numbers of migrants peaked during the planting and harvesting seasons, desperate for jobs.

As China joined the WTO in 2001, the import quotas, subsidies, and tariffs that had traditionally protected Chinese agriculture disappeared. Some experts commented that entry into WTO would further exacerbate the issues of unemployment and inequality. But the Chinese government hoped that the WTO membership would induce more foreign investment and much-needed technology that would sustain long-term growth and would reduce the income disparity and unemployment rates. GDP growth accelerated again in early 2000s, reaching 9.3 percent in 2003, 9.4 percent in 2004, and 9.8 percent in 2005 (see Exhibits 8 (a) and 8 (b)).

In 2005, China's GDP grew by 9.8 percent. China's economy is expected to grow further with an increase in trade and the expected huge investment for the 2008 Olympics. Industry observers said that high GDP growth is coming at the expense of a gaping chasm between the rich and the poor.[5] Joe O'Mara, partner in-charge of KPMG's North America's China practice said, "It's one of the fastest-growing economies with 1.3 billion people. There is a growing middle class—over the last 20 years, per capita income has ballooned more than 700 percent."[6]

Real Estate

After the founding of People's Republic of China in 1949, the first Chairman Mao Zedong (Mao) seized land from private landowners (killing thousands of them in the process) and redistributed it to peasants.[7] To facilitate the mobilization of agricultural resources, improve the efficiency of farming, and increase government access to agricultural products in the 1950s, private land ownership was eliminated. Mao took the land away from them and put it under the "collective" ownership of communes. Peasants had become property-less members of "People's Communes."[8] Private ownership of housing in the urban areas was nearly extinguished.

The communes were dismantled in the early 1980s, a few years after Mao's death. Peasants were allocated land for farming, but ownership remained collective. Under Deng Xiaoping, agricultural production soared for the first time as peasants were allocated (but not given full ownership of) plots of land to farm independently, and marked the start of the economic transformation in the rural areas.

Since the 1990s, leases of 30 years had been granted for these tiny plots, but the peasants were not allowed to use the land as collateral for loans or to sell it. They could rent it out, but this arrangement often involved paying a fee to the village administration.

So whereas trade in land and property had become an important engine of growth in urban China (where residential leases run for 70 years and others for 40 or 50), farmers had been far removed from the effects of this boom. When land was seized, peasants were compensated for its agricultural value, which averaged about one-tenth of its market value. Out of that village administration took a cut, and so the amount received by the peasants was far less. However, in the cities, the privatization of housing since the late 1990s had created a middle class that was utilizing its property as collateral to borrow. Trading in property had become a huge source of urban wealth.

The government was alarmed that creating a free market in rural land would prompt peasants to sell their holdings to pay their debts. As a result a flood of landless farmers fled to cities that had no social security infrastructure to deal with the influx. In order for rural land reform to work, fiscal transfers from the center to the provinces required fairer reforms. This required considerable political

Exhibit 8 (a) China's Gross Domestic Product (at market prices), 2000–2004

	2000	2001	2002	2003	2004
Total (US$ bn)					
At current prices	1,080	1,159	1,304	1,471	1,720
Total (Rmb bn)					
At current prices	8,940	9,593	10,790	12,173	14,239
At constant (1990) prices	4,857	5,221	5,639	6,164	6,744
% change, year on year	8.0	7.5	8.0	9.3	9.4
Per Head (Rmb)					
At current prices	7,054	7,517	8,400	9,420	10,954
At constant (1990) prices	3,832	4,091	4,390	4,770	5,188
% change, year on year	7.2	6.8	7.3	8.7	8.8

Source: "Country Profile 2006," http://www.eiu.com.

Exhibit 8 (b) China's GDP (% increase on a year earlier), 1990–2005

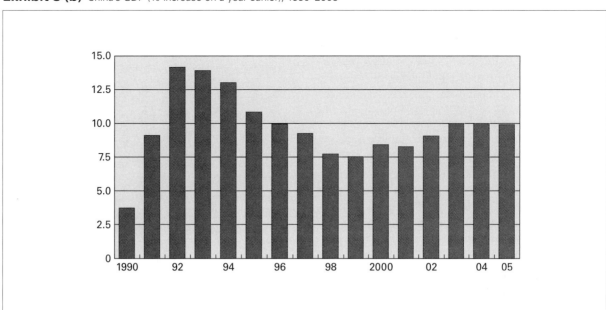

Source: "Coming out," http://www.economist.com/surveys/displaystory.cfm?story_id=5623226, March 23, 2006.

will because richer provinces would be reluctant to lose their privileges. However, in 1998, the government ordered written land-use contracts to be issued to peasants. A law introduced in 2003 restricted the right of collectives to reassign land within villages and provided a legal basis for transfer of land between peasants for farming.[9]

The leasing of land to households in the early 1980s began as an initiative that gradually gained official support. Under the 1982 Constitution, urban land in China is owned by the state and the collectives own the rural land. Since the local and central governments administer the rural collectives, it can be construed that all land ownership is under the control of the state. However, the Constitution's Amendment Act of 1988 to Article 10 adopted on April 12, 1988, states that a land use right may be transferred in accordance to law. Accordingly, a land use right was accorded with a sort of land ownership, thus making land use right likely to be privatized. Individuals, including foreigners, were allowed to hold long-term leases for land use. They were eligible to own buildings, apartments, and other structures on land, as well as own personal property.[10]

In the 1980s, almost all urban housing was owned by the state. Most of the people in China's urban centers had patronized the welfare housing system in which the government provided nearly free housing to urban residents. All employees from government agencies, academic and public institutions, and state-owned companies, received housing facilities from the government or their work units. In March 1998, Chinese Premier Zhu Rongji introduced a package of reforms that included a series of housing reforms intended

to stimulate the domestic economy. He declared that subsidized housing traditionally available to Chinese workers would be phased out and that workers would be encouraged to buy their own homes or pay rent closer to real market prices. The reforms intended for workers to utilize their savings, along with the one-time housing subsidies they received, to purchase their own houses. *The Economist* observed, "In one of the most dramatically successful economic reforms of the past quarter century in China, most housing is now privately owned. This has fostered the growth of a middle class that wants guarantees that its new assets are safe from the party's whims. Property owners are electing their own landlord committees—independent of the party—to protect their rights. A new breed of lawyers, not party stooges as most once were, is emerging to defend those whose properties are threatened by the state. Property owners want a clean environment around their homes. Green activism, which hardly existed in China a decade ago, is spurring the development of a civil society."[11]

In the 1990s, with the emergence of better public housing, improved incomes, and raised expectations of the community at large, the housing market had grown beyond the provision of shelter to the quest to provide pleasant homes tailored to the community needs.

The Chinese government began to divest state housing and create a class of homeowners, primarily in the larger cities but gradually across the country. With the proposed development of a secondary housing market in the future, eventually it is envisaged that the Chinese housing market will come to resemble that of mature private property markets.

In August 1999, the government announced that all vacant residential housing units built after January 1, 1999, were to be sold, not allocated. Since then, the private housing market has seen tremendous growth. The Chinese people, faced with a local stock market offering low returns and high-risk and looking for other ways to invest their money, poured their money into property.

The investment in China's real estate development in 1999 was RMB 401 billion ($48.43 billion), up 10 percent from 1998. From January to November of 2000, the total investment in the real estate sector reached RMB 374.4 billion ($45 billion). In 2000, commercial housing construction had increased by 17.9 percent, finished construction area increased by 22.3 percent, sales volume increased by 38.8 percent, and housing purchase increased by 44.5 percent over the same period in 1999.[12]

A study by the *Sinomonitor* and the British Market Research Bureau indicated that from 1999 to 2000 the percentage of homeowners in China's urban areas rose nearly by 10 percent, from 49.9 percent to 59 percent. The study also commented that the housing reform had boosted home purchase and construction in China.[13]

China's state banks also started lending to home buyers. From 1998 to 2003, mortgage and consumer credit liabilities rose from virtually zero to 11.6 percent of GDP.

As many middle-class families started investing in property, the real estate prices started increasing. Some believed that in some cities it was rising too fast. The government announced that it would reduce the prices in favor of construction of more affordable housing for relatively low-income earners. The government had ordered in 2005 its city leaders to contain the rising housing prices. The main target of this order was Shanghai, which had the largest and most expensive housing market in China. This order resulted in the price reduction in the range of 15 to 20 percent on average.

Consequently, the local Shanghai property speculators started moving to other cities such as Beijing and Chongqing in the west. "The problem is that China has built up this huge pile of wealth and there is nowhere else for it to go, other than into property," said Sam Crispin, a Shanghai-based property consultant.[14]

The National Bureau of Statistics says that new house prices in Beijing have gone up by 7.6 percent in the first quarter of 2006 (see Exhibit 9). Some economists argue that China faces a risky property bubble. While urban property prices are rising fast, so are incomes, and hence property is generally affordable.

China's Home Improvement Market

Since the mid-1990s, the home improvement market had grown rapidly, as housing reform encouraged home ownership in China. In 1998, the Chinese government

Exhibit 9 China Property Price Increase by City, First Quarter 2006 (% change over 2005)

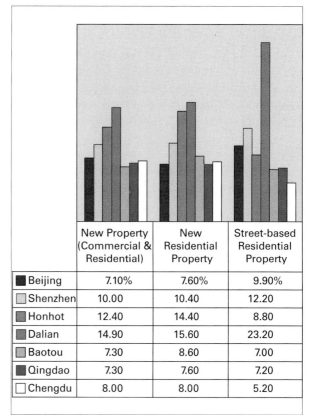

	New Property (Commercial & Residential)	New Residential Property	Street-based Residential Property
Beijing	7.10%	7.60%	9.90%
Shenzhen	10.00	10.40	12.20
Honhot	12.40	14.40	8.80
Dalian	14.90	15.60	23.20
Baotou	7.30	8.60	7.00
Qingdao	7.30	7.60	7.20
Chengdu	8.00	8.00	5.20

Source: Compiled from Browne Andrew, "China reins in real-estate sector," *Wall Street Journal*, May 19–21, 2006, 3.

made changes in its home ownership policy by getting state companies out of the business of providing housing facilities to their workers. Instead, these companies had to extend financial assistance to the employees for housing purposes, which for many raised their incomes by half. The employee could buy the work-unit flat he was already living in at a heavy discount.[15] It encouraged people to buy homes, offering low-cost mortgages or bargain prices on older apartments. Coupled with rising urban incomes, the private housing market boom in the late 1990s in Beijing, Shanghai, and other cities ushered in a new revolution in the Chinese housing sector.

New apartments were built, largely for private buyers. Private buyers bought 88 percent of the homes, compared with about 50 percent before 1995. In Shanghai, China's most sophisticated city, 10 percent of households owned their own homes in 1997, while the figure was about 25 percent in 2000.[16] However, Chinese construction industry operates quite differently.

Newly constructed homes in China do not have bathrooms, kitchens, and even interior walls. These features do not come with the new house. The Chinese contractors do not do any finishing work; they just hand over

Exhibit 10 (a) China's Home Improvement Market: Percentage Breakdown by Sector, 1996–2000

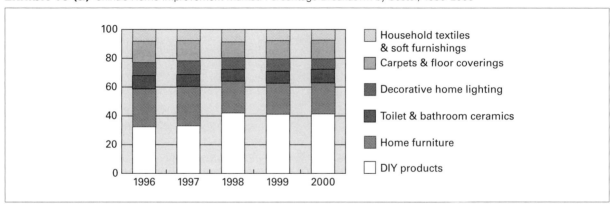

Source: "Doing it for themselves," *The Economist Intelligence Unit (Business China)*, 27(21), September 24, 2001, 9.

concrete shells. Chinese homeowners have to fix up these shells themselves. They have to install everything with the help of locally hired workers. The home improvement stores operating in China undertake to provide the necessary workforce. As a result, home purchases generated significant sales of appliances and other home improvement items. Many foreign retailers such as IKEA (1998) and B&Q[17] (1999) entered China.

China has proven to be a huge market for foreign home improvement players for more than one reason. In China, retailing is overspecialized; one store sells door handles, another paint, and yet another paintbrushes. Decorating takes loads of energy, requiring the homeowners to make trips to scores of stores, and hunt for a reliable contractor. Foreign stores profit from this activity, providing end-to-end "home solutions" under one roof with a do-it-yourself (DIY) model. B&Q can fit out an entire house, including furniture, and guarantee all the work. Another key advantage that foreign chains have is trust reposed in them by the Chinese consumers. "Chinese shoppers are used to being sold shoddy goods backed by dodgy guarantees," observed *The Economist*.[18] Chinese homeowners trust international retailers when they promise "no fakes" and money-back guarantees. B&Q even takes Chinese customers to workshops to reassure them about quality.

As a result, the homeowners began focusing on decorating and even handling home-decoration projects themselves. The sales of DIY products were on the rise compared to other home improvement products (Exhibits 10 (a) and 10 (b)). The DIY sector has become the major area of growth in the market, due to increasing demand for basic tools for household repair and decorating, as well as decorative products, such as paint, wallpaper, and tiles.

Statistics from the Ministry of Construction indicated that the business volume of interior renovation and decoration registered a 50 percent year-on-year rise in 1998 to more than RMB 75 billion. More than 60 percent

Exhibit 10 (b) China's Home Improvement Market: Growth of DIY Products, 1994–2000

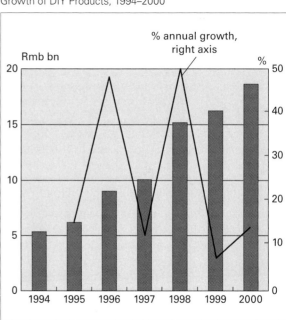

Source: "Doing it for themselves," *The Economist Intelligence Unit (Business China)*, 27(21), September 24, 2001, 9.

of urban households had spruced up their houses, with the average cost reaching RMB 20,000 per household. In 1998, Beijing residents spent more than RMB 2 billion on housing improvements.[19] It was reported that only 70 percent of the market demand was supplied in 1999.[20]

Based on a national development plan on housing construction, China will build at least 200 million square meters of residential housing annually by 2010. The plan is aimed to help 4.5 million residents to have spacious living space.[21]

In a survey, *McKinsey* found that nearly three-quarters of the respondents upgraded their furniture and home appliances when they moved into a new apartment.[22] New homeowners dug into their savings to add flooring, plumbing, and furniture to the unfinished units they had purchased. In 2000, total market value of home market was RMB 43 billion ($5.2 billion) (see Exhibit 11).[23]

In 2004, *China Construction magazine* reported that about 59 percent of the urban residents in China own their own homes. It was also reported that 21.9 percent of the residents would like to purchase new houses within five years. Family savings were the main source of financing, which was at RMB 6700 billion ($1 trillion).[24] China is expected to build 70 million houses in the coming 10 years.[25]

Home ownership has been the catalyst behind the home improvements market and has encouraged consumers to engage in home improvement/decorating activities. Industry analysts said, "As living standards improve in China and the government opens up the property market, interior decoration, design, and DIY are becoming popular pastimes in certain key markets. In line with the interest in home decoration and improvement has come a desire for better quality materials."[26] Additionally, this growth in private housing has resulted in fierce competition among domestic and foreign retailers.

Sweden-based IKEA, which opened its first store in Shanghai in 1998, opened outlets in Beijing and in the southern city of Guangzhou a year later. IKEA also plans to open a total of 10 stores within 2010, including expansion to the country's west with an outlet being built in the city of Chengdu.[27]

B&Q, which opened a store in Shanghai in 1999, later expanded to Beijing and increased its stores to 14. Its sales have doubled each year since it opened its first store in China. B&Q estimates that one-tenth of China's 400 million households have disposable income of $1,000 or more a year to spend on home improvements and it

is increasing rapidly. Government deregulation is boosting home ownership by 30 percent a year. Increased home ownership coupled with "western" levels of disposable income and lifestyles have ushered in a demand for decor. "Chinese people have the money, intention and desire to improve their homes," said David Wei, head of B&Q China.[28]

B&Q bought five outlets from PriceSmart China in November 2004 and took over the mainland operations of rival, German-based OBI, which had 13 stores in April 2005. B&Q became the biggest decorative building materials retailer in China in April 2005 (see Exhibit 12). It dominates China's home improvement market. B&Q's sales rose by nearly 48 percent to 313 million pounds ($547 million) in 2005.[29] As of early 2006, the company had 49 stores in eight Chinese cities, including Shenzhen. B&Q plans to have 75 stores in 30 Chinese cities by the end of 2008.[30] Wei said, "In the past five years, we have enjoyed average double-digit like-for-like growth and we continue to see double-digit as a trend and our forecast for our next five years. The company's market share has risen sharply, from 0.8 percent at the beginning of 2005, as B&Q has opened new stores and sales have increased at existing ones. Getting statistics in China is really difficult, but whatever figures you quote as the national market, we will probably be at 2 to 3 percent."[31] He wants to double B&Q's store count in China by 2010.

Local competitors include Home Mart, controlled by retail conglomerate Friendship Co., with about 20 outlets, and Orient Home, a part of Orient Group Inc. Foreign competition is also heating up. France's Leroy Merlin opened its first China store in Beijing in 2004 and said that it would have 20 outlets across the country by 2010. German franchiser OBI (owned by Tengelmann Warenhandelsgesellschaft) also operates four stores in China.

Exhibit 11 Growth of Total Home Improvement Market of China, 1994–2005

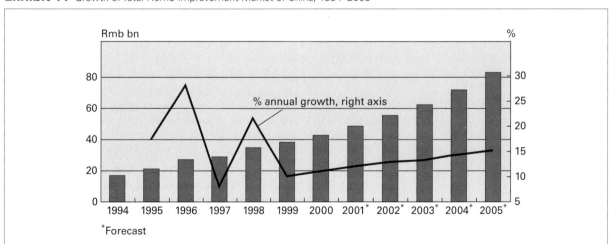

*Forecast

Source: "Doing it for themselves," *The Economist Intelligence Unit (Business China),* 27(21), September 24, 2001, 9.

Exhibit 12 China Home Improvement Market: The Major Players

Hammer Down
Competition is building in China's do-it-yourself retail market

COMPANY	DESCRIPTION	NO. OF STORES	2005 SALES
B&Q	British-owned retailer dominates the big coastal cities	49	$542 million
ORIENT HOME	Beijing-based chain is possible takeover target for Home Depot	30	$350 million*
HOMEMART	State-owned Shanghai chain has good locations but indifferent service	27	$300 million*
HOMEWAY	Tianjin-based retailer benefited from training cooperation with Home Depot	11	$215 million
HOME DEPOT	Has two global sourcing centers in China but no stores—yet	0	0

*Estimate Data: *Business Week*, companies

Source: Frederik Balfour and Brain Grow, "One Foot In China," http://www.businessweek.com/magazine/content/06_18/b3982068.htm, May 1, 2006.

"The growth has been very strong between IKEA, B&Q, even local brands like Orient Home. It's very competitive. Over 100 cities in China have more than 1 million people. If even a small percentage of these people are able to purchase home furnishings, it would be really promising," said Anna Kalifa, head of research in Beijing for consulting firm Jones Lang LaSalle.[32]

In China, housing construction is growing by 33 percent a year. In 2006, Chinese banks relaxed controls on loans to purchase houses. This would result in the growth of the home improvement market estimated at $50 billion annually.[33] It is projected that the China's home improvement market will have growth rate of 10 to 20 percent a year.[34] Wei said that it is highly fragmented industry dotted with mom-and-pop outfits, niche stores that stock one product type, and a few budding domestic one-stop shops.

After witnessing the growth of the home improvement market in China and B&Q's success, Atlanta-based Home Depot, the world's biggest DIY group, also planned to set up shops in China.[35] In June 2005, *Reuters* announced that Home Depot was seeking to buy a stake in a Chinese peer Orient Group Inc. for up to $500 million to win a foothold in the country's fast-growing home improvement market. An agreement would mark the U.S. group's entry into the Chinese home improvement market. However, it already has an indirect interest in China through its links with the Homeway chain. In 2004, Home Depot opened a business-development office in China and named Bill E. Patterson for the newly created position of president, The Home Depot Asia. Home Depot runs two procurement centers in China. Home Depot announced plans in mid-2004 to start opening retail stores in China, but has yet to set up shop.

Should Home Depot Enter or Will It Have a Late-Mover (Dis)advantage?

Amid many speculations about the Home Depot's foray into China, the company remained tight-lipped. Home Depot's China head said, "China is an incredibly exciting opportunity. We're going to make the prudent decision. We're going to make sure we have the right business model."[36] For Home Depot's CEO Robert Nardelli, China is a top priority and he said, "A successful strategy there would offset the challenge of sustaining string sales growth back home and could even boost the stock."[37] He added, "China's economy is over $1 trillion. It has GDP growth of 7% to 8%. No one has dominance there. It's a unique opportunity to get a footprint, to really be part of the expansiveness and the growth. Sixty percent of the world concrete is being consumed in China today. Surveys say that Chinese consumers are looking for Westernized products and brands."[38]

However, there are many challenges in China's home improvement market. Some of them concern Chinese consumer behavior while others have more to do with the market (competition) dynamics. Unless addressed with a clear strategic intent (as opposed to short-term), the potential virtue can become mere wishful thinking, not converting into a reality.

The big challenge facing Home Depot and its rivals in China is that most customers are not doing home improvement themselves. "Chinese DIY is still really BIY—buy it yourself,"[39] admits Wei. He added, "You need time for DIY. There aren't many public holidays or paid leave. And you need the incentive to do it. Labor is so cheap in China there's no incentive to save money by doing your own work."[40] Since the government policy is to build homes that are more finished, the foreign players have to convert DIY into more of a hobby and the Chinese into a nation of home improvers, like the Americans and British. Yet, for many middle-class Chinese, it is not befitting to build a cabinet or fit a shelf by themselves. Thanks to abundant cheap labor, they've never had to do it themselves, nor do they have the skills. "Many Chinese don't know how to wire a plug or rise to the challenge of scumble painting,"[41] observed *The Economist*. B&Q, for instance, conducts training sessions for customers, showing them how to use a drill and even teaching children the mysteries and the fun of DIY. However, to utilize the potential, B&Q has initiated CIY (create-it-yourself) that helps customers to be involved in the process of creation. B&Q staffers help customers design a floor plan and choose materials and then perform all the installation work. In Beijing and Shanghai, B&Q started to build a DIY culture starting with a DIY kids club, where on the weekends people who do not have DIY skills could come and learn some basic skills. It is provided free of cost to attract kids and parents to the stores. Also, Chinese shoppers like to handle the merchandise before buying. However, products were stacked high on shelves. They still believe that foreign retailers display the most expensive products. They are intimidated by the exorbitant rates.

Another challenge for foreign home improvement players in China is managing their supply chain. Efficient suppliers are the key to success in a low-margin industry like retailing. Getting goods into stores in China is costly and expensive. B&Q's gross margins in China are half of those of its international division. *The Economist* observed, "China's huge size and enormous regional variations mean retailers struggle to establish a national infrastructure, let alone a national brand."[42] It is almost like operations in different countries. In humid summers, laminated wood cannot survive in Shenzhen. During a winter in Beijing, aquariums freeze. (Chinese believe fish bring good luck.) The biggest retailers, therefore, "remain in thrall to regional manufacturers—and their middlemen—which raises costs."[43] For 15 of B&Q's China stores, it has 1,800 vendors, while its 350 British stores have only 600 vendors. Moreover, these middlemen enter into deals clandestinely. Even on the shop floor, vendor representatives regularly offer customers "special" prices. "This is a state-controlled economy. Price fixing is endemic. Retailers are at the bottom of the food chain in China. They have far less power than manufacturers. It is the opposite of the rest of the world,"[44] said Steve Gilman, head of B&Q international.

Another concern for foreign home improvement retailers is regarding the treatment meted out to them in China in sales tax imposition and allocation of land. Foreign retailers face discrimination. Foreign home improvement retailers are forced to pay much more sales tax than the domestic counterparts. Using *Guanxi* (connections), the tiny stores avoid paying sales tax. They are often offered the poorest sites to carry out their business operations. For instance, B&Q had to build its new Shenzhen store under a residential tower block. Low-cost labor does not translate into quality labor either, forcing the foreign home improvement retailers to employ more workers to meet the greater service levels expected and continue to win the customers' trust.

Home Depot is studying the industry environment, competitors, and searching for suitable locations. According to the company, China has few large-format home improvement stores, and the country is largely served by small outdoor markets and shopping malls. Patterson said, "About 70 percent of home improvement spending in China is for completion of interior space in new homes. We see that as a solid growth opportunity given The Home Depot's strength in merchandise and services geared to finishing out a home."[45] However,

experts say that due to the urban-rural divide and income disparity, requirements for houses are quite different due to different regions and culture. Housing consumption witnesses strong regional and multilevel characteristics.[46]

Home Depot's major rivals such as B&Q and IKEA were early entrants to the Chinese home improvement market. It has helped them gain better traction in many areas, such as government connections for getting approvals for zoning and licensing. Wei said, "Also, we have had the opportunity to recruit the best people and train them. New entrants may nick a few people, but it won't damage our management team and forces. And we understand product mix. Building relationships with suppliers and getting the pricing and supply chain right take time."[47]

In the United States, Home Depot has benefited from high labor prices for skilled labor, which encourages Americans to improve their own homes. But in China labor is low-cost and plentiful, and is often the single cost-effective element in home improvement. For this reason, some analysts say Home Depot's largest customers might not be homeowners, but interior designers and construction contractors.[48] If Home Depot decides to enter China, it has to train its employees to do installations also.

Home Depot faces stiff competition from foreign players such as B&Q and IKEA and domestic players including Homemart, Homeway, and Orient Home. Homeway, which had a brief alliance with Home Depot in the mid-1990s, adopted much of the Home Depot model, including the orange work aprons. These retail chains spent many years cultivating relationship with local suppliers and are already located in prime retail locations in the big cities. B&Q has already learned many lessons about operating in China. B&Q attracts consumers with stylish brands and more fashionable products, with an improved decorative-lighting section. Homeowners in China started switching from small local retailers to B&Q and other warehouse chains to buy flooring, cabinets, and curtain rods.

In China, due to increasing urbanization, most customers of home improvement chains are urban residents and the stores had to be located in urban centers. Locating in urban centers will require new strategies for its stores (in the United States, its stores are mostly in the suburbs). Home Depot needs to meet the unique demands of these urban customers and a multitude of challenges related to dealing with large urban markets. Analysts say, "It will be good if companies such as Home Depot learn from their experiences in China's urban markets. In Connecticut, as well as in many other parts of the United States, large retailers tend to overlook or avoid the large urban market due to what they perceive as potential problems. Perhaps companies that have

129

Case 10 • China's Home Improvement Market: Should Home Depot Enter or Will it Have a Late-Mover (Dis)advantage?

Appendix I (a) Per Capita Consumption of Rural and Urban Residents of China, 1952–1997 (Units: nominal yuan per year; Ratio: rural = 1)

Year	National Average	Rural Residents	Urban Residents	Ratio (Nominal)	Ratio (Real)
1952	76	62	149	2.4	
1953	87	69	181	2.6	
1954	89	70	183	2.6	
1955	94	76	188	2.5	
1956	99	78	197	2.5	
1957	102	79	205	2.6	
1958	105	83	195	2.4	
1959	96	65	206	3.2	
1960	102	68	214	3.2	
1961	114	82	225	2.8	
1962	117	88	226	2.6	
1963	116	89	222	2.5	
1964	120	95	234	2.5	
1965	125	100	237	2.4	
1966	132	106	244	2.3	
1967	136	110	251	2.3	
1968	132	106	250	2.4	
1969	134	108	255	2.4	
1970	140	114	260	2.3	
1971	142	116	267	2.3	
1972	147	116	295	2.6	
1973	155	123	306	2.5	
1974	155	123	313	2.6	
1975	158	124	324	2.6	
1976	161	125	340	2.7	
1977	165	124	360	2.9	
1978	175	132	383	2.9	2.9
1979	197	152	406	2.7	2.6
1980	227	173	468	2.7	2.5
1981	249	194	487	2.5	2.3
1982	267	212	500	2.4	2.1
1983	289	234	531	2.3	2.0
1984	329	266	599	2.3	2.0
1985	406	324	747	2.3	1.9
1986	451	353	850	2.4	2.0
1987	513	393	997	2.5	2.0
1988	643	480	1288	2.7	2.1
1989	700	518	1404	2.7	2.2
1990	803	571	1686	3.0	2.4
1991	896	621	1925	3.1	2.5
1992	1070	718	2356	3.3	2.5
1993	1331	855	3027	3.5	2.7
1994	1781	1138	3979	3.5	2.6
1995	2311	1479	5044	3.4	2.6
1996	2677	1756	5620	3.2	2.4
1997	2936	1930	6048	3.1	2.3

Source: Yang Dennis Tao and Fang Cai, "The Political Economy of China's Rural-Urban Divide," http://scid.stanford.edu/pdf/credpr62.pdf, August 2000.

Appendix I(b) Real Per Capita Total Income for Rural and Urban Residents of China, 1978–1997
(Units: nominal yuan per year; Ratio: rural = 1)

Year	Urban per Capita Income	Rural per Capita Income	Ratio of Urban to Rural Income
1978	454	134	3.4
1979	523	160	3.3
1980	560	190	3.0
1981	567	219	2.6
1982	597	261	2.3
1983	620	296	2.1
1984	690	330	2.1
1985	692	358	1.9
1986	784	360	2.2
1987	801	369	2.2
1988	783	370	2.1
1989	778	343	2.3
1990	855	374	2.3
1991	916	378	2.4
1992	989	399	2.5
1993	1073	413	2.6
1994	1133	443	2.6
1995	1179	487	2.4
1996	1217	551	2.2
1997	1252	584	2.1

Source: Yang Dennis Tao and Fang Cai, "The Political Economy of China's Rural-Urban Divide," http://scid.stanford.edu/pdf/credpr62.pdf, August 2000.

learned strategies in China will be able to bring back some of lessons and be more willing to invest in the potentially lucrative inner city markets."[49]

About the foray of Home Depot into China, *BusinessWeek* says, "Is Home Depot blowing it? Or is it biding its time for the right reasons? The China home improvement market is a lot tricker to navigate than those hot growth numbers would indicate. For starters, it barely resembles the do-it-yourself market back in America, where Home Depot workers dispense advice, then send customers back home to lay their own tiles and install some track lighting."[50]

As Home Depot executives try to gauge the risks and rewards in China, they do not want to get off on the wrong foot either. Home Depot's foreign forays have yielded mixed results. Although it was successful in Canada and Mexico, it had to close its stores in Chile and Argentina in 2001.

Goldman Sachs analyst Matthew Fassler said that Home Depot's reported interest in the Chinese home improvement market was "consistent" with Home Depot's goals and Wall Street expectations. He added, "We believe that an alliance . . . or minority invest-

ment with option for increased ownership would enable Home Depot to participate in China's economic development without the difficulties associated with navigating its political and cultural challenges alone."[51] Keith Davis, analyst at investment managers Farr Miller Washington, said, "It's going to take a long time to see any effects to the bottom line from an expansion into China, but in the more near term it will hopefully alleviate some concerns about opportunities for growth going forward."[52] Tian Guanyong, CEO of CGen Media,[53] said, "Home Depot had better make up its mind about China before it's too late."[54]

However, some analysts are skeptical whether Home Depot will suffer from any late-mover disadvantage and whether the early movers will enable Home Depot to compete more effectively and efficiently against them. *BusinessWeek* says, "It's likely that Home Depot will try some mix of building its own stores and buying share in China through an acquisition. Yet the longer it waits, the tougher it will be to break in. Securing the best locations requires good government connections. Getting to know the market and forging relationships with local suppliers can take years."[55]

1. A. Browne, 2006, China reins in real-estate sector, *Wall Street Journal,* May 19–21, 3.
2. Ibid.
3. F. Balfour & B. Grow, 2006, One foot in China, http://www.businessweek.com/magazine/content/06_18/b3982068.htm, May 1.
4. Ye Xiannian, 2004, China real estate market—Economic development, http://www.china-window.com/china_market/china_real_estate/china-real-estate-market—2.shtml, August 20.
5. 2004, Market for luxury brands booms in Shanghai, http://www.chinadaily.com.cn/english/doc/2004-03/13/content_314462.htm, March 13.
6. 2004, Chinese consumer markets: Exploding demand, worries, http://www.kpmginsiders.com/display_analysis.asp?cs_id=107803, July 2.
7. A peasant is a farm worker who does not own the land he farms, but pays part of the crops he grows to the owner of the land as rent. Peasants cannot ever prosper, because, if they work hard and grow a surplus, the landowner will inevitably raise the amount of the crop to be paid in "rent."
8. People's communes, in the People's Republic of China, were formerly the highest of three administrative levels in rural areas in the period from 1958 to 1982–85, when they were replaced by townships. Communes, the largest collective units, were divided in turn into production brigades and production teams. The communes had governmental, political, and economic functions.
9. 2006, Fat of the land, http://www.economist.com/surveys/displaystory.cfm?story_id=5623357, March 23.
10. China real estate market—Economic development, op.cit.
11. 2006, How to make China even richer, http://www.economist.com/opinion/displaystory.cfm?story_id=5660833, March 23.
12. Ye Xiannian, 2004, China real estate market—Housing reforms, http://www.china-window.com/china_market/china_real_estate/china-real-estate-market-4.shtml, August 12.
13. China real estate market—Housing reforms, op.cit.
14. R. McGregor, 2006, Beijing confronts calls for ceiling on spiralling property prices, http://www.ft.com, May 19.
15. 2000, Housing's great leap forward, http://www.economist.com, September 28.
16. Ibid.
17. It is a subsidiary of Europe-based Kingfisher plc, the largest home improvement retailer in Britain. It is the world's third-largest home improvement chain, with more than 650 stores in 10 countries in Europe and Asia.
18. 2003, Doing up the Middle Kingdom, http://www.economist.com, October 9.
19. 1999, Home improvement boom in China, http://www.hartford-hwp.com/archives/55/279.html, June 11.
20. Ibid.
21. Ibid.
22. K. P. Lane & I. St-Maurice, 2006, The Chinese consumer: To spend or to save? *The McKinsey Quarterly,* 1, 1, 6–8.
23. 2001, Doing it for themselves, *The Economist Intelligence Unit (Business China),* 27(21), September 24, 9.
24. China real estate market—Economic development, op.cit.
25. 2004, China's real estate industry in a boom, http://www.china-window.com/china_market/china_real_estate/chinas-real-estate-indust.shtml, March 24.
26. 2001, Home improvement in China: A market analysis, http://www.the-infoshop.com/study/ae8399_home_china.html, August.
27. J. McDonald, 2006, IKEA happily feeds China's hungry home-improvement market, http://the.honoluluadvertiser.com/article/2006/Apr/11/bz/FP604110318.html, April 11.
28. Doing up the Middle Kingdom, op.cit.
29. 2006, B&Q expects more double-digit growth, http://en.ce.cn/Business/Enterprise/200603/21/t20060321_6435244.shtml, March 21.
30. Doing up the Middle Kingdom, op.cit.
31. B&Q expects more double-digit growth, op.cit.
32. IKEA happily feeds China's hungry home-improvement market, op. cit.
33. J. Beystehner, 2005, Asia's ideas market, http://www.pressroom.ups.com/execforum/op-eds/op-ed/0,1399,52,00.html, June 1.
34. IKEA happily feeds China's hungry home-improvement market, op. cit.
35. Home Depot, which was started in the late 1970s, has grown from a single-store operation in Atlanta to a network that now boasts more than 1,700 stores with a revenue of $60 billion in 2004.
36. One foot in China, op. cit.
37. Ibid.
38. M. A. Schwarz, 2004, Fixer-uppers spruce up profit at Home Depot, http://www.usatoday.com/money/companies/management/2004-07-05-insana-nardelli_x.htm, July 7.
39. Doing up the Middle Kingdom, op. cit.
40. F. Balfour, 2006, B&Q Stores: Renovating China's attitudes, http://www.businessweek.com/globalbiz/content/apr2006/gb20060425_120572.htm?campaign_id=search, April 25.
41. Doing up the Middle Kingdom, op. cit.
42. Ibid.
43. Ibid.
44. Ibid.
45. Home Depot to establish China business operation, http://www.buildingonline.com/news/viewnews.pl?id=320306/10/2004.
46. China's real estate industry in a boom, op. cit.
47. 2006, B&Q stores: Renovating China's attitudes, http://www.businessweek.com/globalbiz/content/apr2006/gb20060425_120572.htm?campaign_id=search, April 25.
48. P. Denlinger, 2004, Home depot plans China strategy, http://www.china-ready.com/news/June2004/HomeDepotPlansChinaStrategy060804.htm, June 8.
49. Y. Zhang, 2003, Learning to pay more attention to urban consumers: What home improvement companies could learn in China, www.cerc.com/pdfs/home_improve.pdf.
50. One foot in China, op. cit.
51. 2006, Home Depot mum on China chain, http://www.foxnews.com/story/0,2933,184699,00.html, February 13.
52. 2004, U.S. DIY store in China expansion, http://news.bbc.co.uk/2/hi/business/3785871.stm, June 8.
53. A company that installs flat-panel screens that play ads in retail outlets.
54. One foot in China, op. cit.
55. Ibid.

Huawei: Cisco's Chinese Challenger

Phoebe Ho, Ali F. Farhoomand

The University of Hong Kong

Users are looking for a challenger [to Cisco] and value for money. Huawei has got the channel strategy and the pricing is right.[1]

Immaculately trimmed green lawns, basketball courts, swimming pools, ergonomically designed office spaces set in a casual yet high-tech atmosphere—images frequently associated with technology parks in Silicon Valley—were found on the outskirts of Shenzhen, China, where Huawei Technologies housed its corporate headquarters. The 1.8-square-kilometer property signified the state of exponential growth the company had gone through since its inauguration in 1988.

Huawei (pronounced Hua-way) was incorporated in 1988 as a private enterprise manufacturing telecommunications equipment for local Chinese companies at a fraction of the price of its international rivals. By 2002, the company overtook Shanghai Bell, an Alcatel joint venture, to become the dominant supplier of digital switches and routers in China. It then entered the low-end international markets, supplying routers that were 40 percent cheaper than its competitors. The company had developed a full product portfolio consisting of wireless and fixed-line networking equipment, handsets, optical communications platforms, data networking, products for virtual private networks (VPNs), and Internet protocol (IP) telephony. It boasted an annual revenue of US$6.7 billion in 2005, of which 60 percent came from international sales.[2] With 55 branch offices worldwide, eight regional headquarters, world-scale research institutes in strategic locations, and a host of customer support and training centers, the company came to be known as the Cisco of China.

In early 2006, Huawei Technologies was among the ranks of China's "National Champions," along with Haier, Lenovo TCL, and the Wanxiang Group, poised to compete with global leaders in the international marketplace.[3] As concluded by an industry analyst, Huawei's threat came not from low-cost manufacturing, but from low-cost engineering.[4] With an inexpensive and highly qualified research and development (R&D) workforce, the company was able to deliver customized, innovative solutions to global enterprises looking to reduce their capital expenditures. Could Huawei climb up the technology value chain, replicating its success in low-end telecom networking in high-technology products and services? Could it build a global brand? If so, how profound was this threat to established global leaders in the telecom equipment sector? Were there any lessons for other Chinese companies in their respective paths to globalization?

The Global Telecom Equipment Industry

The global telecom equipment industry had gone through a series of changes within the past few decades. In the 1960s and 1970s, network equipment suppliers were few and were categorized by the types of products they specialized in, primarily through in-house development. Manufacturing was largely decentralized as suppliers operated independent subsidiaries to serve different countries and regional markets around the world. With the introduction of digital technology in the 1980s, product lines proliferated and country-specific operations were integrated into single, global organizations. Manufacturing tended to become more centralized to increase production volumes and decrease unit costs. By the 1990s, the pace of technological advances, commercialization of the Internet, and privatization of telecom service providers worldwide had created an unprecedented level of competition in the industry. Telecom equipment suppliers took on the role of broad-based system integrators, building extensive product lines through third-party contracts, original equipment manufacturers (OEMs) and other partnership arrangements.[5] Service

© Don Hammond/Design Pics/Corbis

providers used acquisition-based strategies to keep pace with consumer demand and drove the market for global networking products to US$50 billion by the end of 2000, up from US$15 billion in 1995.[6]

The dotcom bubble burst in 2001 and devastated the overheated telecom industry on a global scale. Service providers had difficulty accessing capital and the industry as a whole suffered from overcapacity. Global networking suppliers had to scale back and reposition themselves in light of the market slowdown. However, technological advances in the Internet boom had persisted up to 2006, and the technology choices and service requirements of service providers such as AT&T, AOL, and PCCW were more diverse than ever (see Exhibit 1 for the worldwide equipment capital expenditures by segment). Telecom equipment suppliers could be broadly divided into five subsectors and global players tended to align themselves with two or more of these subsectors: optical transmission systems, switch systems, access systems, data communications, and mobile communications (see Table 1).

Exhibit 1 Worldwide Equipment CAPEX Spending by Segment, 2004

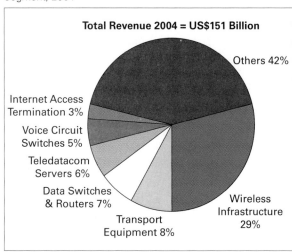

Source: 2005, In-Stat, June.

Table 1 Leading Firms in the Global Telecom Equipment Industry, 2001[7]

Subsectors	Leading Firms
Optical Transmission Systems	Alcatel, Lucent, Nortel
Switch Systems	3Com, Cisco
Access Systems	DSL: Alcatel, Siemens, Lucent Cable Modem: Motorola, Toshiba, Ambit
Data Communications	Routers: Cisco, Juniper Networks Ethernet Switches: Cisco, Nortel, Enterasys
Mobile Communications	Ericsson, Motorola, Nokia, Lucent

China's Telecom Equipment Industry

In the 1980s, China's telecom industry achieved substantial double-digit growth, and by the end of 2002, China surpassed the United States to become the largest telecom market in the world. Overall, China's telecom industry recorded US$112 billion in business transactions in 2004, with an annual growth rate of 34.9 percent, 3.7 times China's GDP growth rate of 9.5 percent.[8] Phone subscriptions had increased to 390 million mobile phone users and 348 million fixed-line users by October 2005.[9] Telecom service providers were shifting their focus from infrastructure development to network improvement and value-added service offerings. According to the Gartner research group, China's telecom equipment market would continue to grow at a compound annual rate of 10.9 percent between 2004 and 2008, from US$30 billion to US$45 billion.[10]

As the market grew, most of the leading global telecom equipment firms started operations in China in the 1980s and 1990s. Due to ownership restrictions, most foreign firms entered the market by setting up joint ventures with local Chinese companies, usually involving equity investments. They leveraged their Chinese partners' local market knowledge and distribution networks in order to reduce investment risk.[11] Among the leading multinationals in China (Motorola, Siemens, Nokia, Alcatel, Lucent Technologies, and Ericsson), Cisco was a latecomer. Cisco first entered the Chinese market in 1994, but it was not until 1998 that the company intensely focused its attention on China[12] (see Cisco's story in the next section). High-end networking products were the traditional strongholds of foreign players, with the market divided between North American, European, and Japanese vendors. American companies accounted for 75 percent of the telecom equipment market in China in 2001, within which Cisco accounted for 62 percent and 26 percent of the routers and switching markets respectively.[13]

Even though the entry of these multinational telecom enterprises had facilitated the building of China's telecom infrastructure, they had also contributed to the growth of domestic manufacturers in China. Domestic firms had progressed from being far behind foreign companies in every subsector of the industry in the 1980s, to catching up in the switch market in the middle 1990s, to capturing the access market in the late 1990s, and finally to becoming competitive in the optical transmission, data communications, and mobile technology in the new millennium. Domestic Chinese vendors started to emerge, most notably the four companies, Huawei, ZTE, DTT, and GDT, collectively known as "Great China."[14] According to the CRC-Pinnacle market research firm, domestic Chinese equipment manufacturers occupied a

Table 2 Telecom Equipment Market Share by Leading Vendors in China, 2005[15]

Company Name	Market Share (%)
Huawei*	13.5
ZTE*	12
Ericsson	12
Alcatel Shanghai Bell	7
Motorola	6.9
Nokia	6.2
UTStarcom*	6.1
Siemens	5.3
Lucent	4.7
Nortel	4
Cisco	4
Others	18.3
Total	100%

*Denotes domestic Chinese companies.

combined 32 percent of the Chinese market by 2005, of which Huawei Technologies became the market leader with 13.5 percent market share (see Table 2).

The Cisco Story[16]

Cisco started as a one-product company in 1984 when two Stanford computer scientists, Len Bosack and Sandy Lerner, a married couple, built a multi-protocol router for networking between different types of computers. The couple ran the business out of their living room and sold to networking-intensive customers such as Hewlett-Packard, the U.S. Defense Department, and American universities. By 1987, the company had outgrown its capacity and, after a period of legal battles with Stanford University, managed to secure a sizable venture capital from Silicon Valley for its large-scale expansion.

The phenomenal growth of the Internet in the 1990s precipitated the building of the Cisco empire. As communication networks grew in complexity and size, Cisco expanded from a one-product router company into a comprehensive, service-based leader in the networking business. John Chambers, Cisco's president and CEO since 1995, recognized that the company could not rely on its own R&D departments to prevail as a leader in multiple product categories. He began to take on a series of acquisitions to broaden the company's service and product portfolios. The acquisitions consisted primarily of small companies developing leading technologies in different areas within the networking industry. To move into new market segments, Cisco formed extensive strategic alliances, frequently with equity investments, with companies in the networking value chain. Chambers used these acquisitions and strategic alliances as a way to accommodate the rapid market shifts in the exploding IT sector. By the end of the 1990s, Cisco had become a virtual manufacturer of networking products, running a network of outsourced operations.

As the Internet expanded its footprint across the globe, Cisco also began to develop its global presence. Cisco opened its first offices outside of the United States in 1991, in Britain and France initially, then Canada, Japan, Belgium, Mexico, and Hong Kong. Cisco entered these markets as foreign governments invested in their public Internet infrastructures, domestic telecom markets were liberalized, and commercial investments in the sector increased. To meet global demand for its products, Cisco made alliances with local original equipment manufacturers (OEMs) and distributors, but maintained a centralized management structure by region. The Netherlands, for example, was chosen as Cisco's regional headquarters to manage its European, African, and Middle Eastern markets.

Cisco entered China in 1994 with the opening of its first office in Beijing. Its original intention was simply to establish a presence and sell its equipment in China. In 1998, the company began to intensely focus its attention on China and announced a capital expenditure of $100 million over two years to expand its business in China. Cisco's strategy in China was to focus on recruiting and training employees to service the high-end markets of telecom service providers and enterprise markets. Instead of forming joint ventures with local partners (like most of its international competitors did in China), Cisco opened its own subsidiary in China, Cisco Networking Technology Co. Ltd, to promote education, demonstration, and development of network technology. It provided its market-leading switches and routers to all the major telecom service providers in China, including China Telecom, China Unicom, and China Mobile. Cisco also embarked on a number of education initiatives to develop favorable relations with Chinese authorities and to cultivate new areas of business within China. The Cisco Network Academy was one such initiative where 157 university-based, technical schools offered free network technology education to more than 7,000 students. On the business solution side, Cisco established its Internet Business Solutions Group to help top business leaders transform their own businesses into e-businesses, enhancing their business operations using supply chain management, customer care, or workforce optimization. Recognizing the large, low-cost, and skilled labor force in China, Cisco made further commitments to invest in a new R&D center in Shanghai. The facility would employ more than 100 people after its launch in 2005. Chambers's plans for the research facility were to allow Cisco access to technology and local talent so as to buy into the local Chinese market.

In all these endeavors, Cisco insisted on maintaining its leadership position in cutting-edge technology and single-system images (SSI) throughout the world. Most of its applications, and its Web site, were hosted in the United States. The company's entire data center was constantly replicated between San Jose, California and Raleigh, North Carolina. Global standards and consistencies were maintained such that applications were designed from a structural point of view and local content was dumped into a standardized functional design.

Cisco was by far the largest telecom networking company in the world, with 35,000 employees and an annual revenue of US$22 billion in 2003–2004. Its broadened service and product portfolio meant that it was not competing head-on with Huawei; rather they were competing in the data communications subsector. Cisco's leadership position in the telecommunications equipment sector was, however, not entirely insurmountable. Chinese competitors were using their aggressive pricing strategies to expand into the international markets, and were rapidly using their low-cost advantage to move up the value chain. Both Huawei and ZTE were expected to make further inroads into international markets in the next few years, competing head-to-head with the established Western players for the same global accounts. In Chambers's own words, "China will provide even stiffer competition over the next decade. . . . Half of our top 12 competitors will be Chinese vendors."[17]

Huawei: The Home-Grown Chinese Multinational

Huawei, meaning "China achievement," was considered the model home-grown multinational company in China. Founded in 1988, Huawei Technologies was almost single-handedly created by Ren Zhengfei, a former People's Liberation Army officer and telecom engineer. Since the outset, Zhengfei's vision was to build innovation capability into the company. Contrary to the country's policy of "exchanging market for technology,"[18] Zhengfei believed that joint venturing with foreign companies would not enable the Chinese to obtain foreign technologies, and they might end up losing the domestic market to foreign players. He stated his goals as:

. . . to develop the national industry, not to set up joint ventures with foreign companies, to closely follow global cutting-edge technology, and to insist on self-development, to gain domestic market share, and to explore the international market and compete against international rivals.[19]

R&D Powerhouse

In accordance with these goals, Huawei focused its resources on building itself into an R&D powerhouse. In the early years, the company started with 500 R&D staff

and only 200 production staff. By the end of 2005, of its 24,000 employees, 48 percent were engaged in R&D. Huawei had a policy of investing no less than 10 percent of its total annual revenue in R&D (compared to 15 percent in leading foreign technology companies). Yet it was still able to establish the early winning formula for the company as its development leapfrogged into the Global Systems for Mobile Communications (GSM), obtaining almost 90 percent of the Chinese domestic market in mobile network equipment by 2002. Because of the low labor cost in China, Huawei's focused R&D strategy became a significant competitive advantage over its international competitors.

Another major foresight was its early and heavy investment in the third-generation (3G) mobile communications technology. Huawei started its own R&D in Code-Division Multiple Access (CDMA) in 1995. In the next few years, it invested more than US$370 million[20] in wide-band CDMA (WCDMA) technologies with a dedicated R&D staff of 3,500 scattered through its research centers in China and overseas. In 2006, Huawei had a 21-story research center at its corporate headquarters in Shenzhen; six other research laboratories in Beijing, Shanghai, Nanjing, Huangzhou, Xi'an, and Chengdu; a software development center in Bangalore (India) with 1,500 engineers working on-site; and research facilities in Moscow (Russia), Stockholm (Sweden), and the Silicon Valley in California (see Exhibit 2 for Huawei's R&D Institutes).

Also noteworthy was the education level of the company's employees. Huawei frequently boasted about having the most educated workforce in all of mainland China. Among its 24,000 employees, more than 85 percent had a bachelors or higher degree, and about 60 percent had a master's or PhD. As a result of its generous R&D spending and high-caliber labor pool, Huawei held an impressive record of patent ownership. By the end of 2004, its patent applications had totaled more than 8,000, of which 800 were applied for in more than 20 countries and territories, including the United States and Europe. In 2004 alone, its patent applications reached 2,000, on par with its international rivals in the telecom equipment sector.

In addition to internal development, Huawei had actively undertaken joint R&D laboratories with foreign companies, including Texas Instruments, Motorola, IBM, Intel, Sun Microsystems, and Microsoft, focusing on various telecom technologies. To Huawei, these joint development efforts were used as a complementary approach to enhancing its innovation capabilities. As one of Huawei's senior R&D officers pointed out:

Huawei does not view R&D cooperation with foreign companies as an effective mechanism to gain technological competitiveness. There is no reason for foreign firms to transfer their most advanced core technologies to a

Exhibit 2 Huawei's R&D Institutes

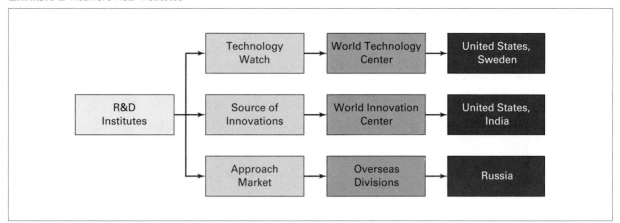

Source: J. Chen, 2005, Towards Indigenous Innovation: Pathways for Chinese Firms, Workshop of Technology Innovation and Economic Development, Zhejiang University, China, May 25–27.

Chinese partner over whom they do not have management control.[21]

The Military-Styled Wolf-Pack Enterprise

Ren Zhengfei's history with the Chinese military was a topic of much interest (and concern) in the Western world. Zhengfei's connection to the army had undoubtedly created a guanxi (relationship) network few other competitors could match. In fact, in its early years the company had relied on big contract orders from the military to secure a foothold in the telecom network market. The company visitors' book contained such influential names as Jiang Zemin, Zhu Rongji, Li Peng, Hu Jintao, Wen Jiabao, and other central military dignitaries. The company received financial support from the state-owned Chinese Development Bank in the form of a US$10 billion facility for Huawei's international expansions over five years, and an additional US$600 million from the official Export-Import Bank of China. Zhengfei was reluctant to speak of his relationship with Beijing, but did give credit to the favorable industry policies his company benefited from:

Huawei was somewhat naïve to choose telecom-equipment as its business domain in the beginning. Huawei was not prepared for such intensified competition when the company was just established. The rivals were internationally renowned companies with assets valued at tens of billions of dollars. If there had been no government policy to protect [nationally owned companies], Huawei would no longer exist.[22]

Ren Zhengfei's military background had also instilled a unique corporate culture within Huawei. He was known to frequently extol patriotism and cite Mao Zedong's thoughts in speeches and internal publications. All new employees were put through intensive military-style

Exhibit 3 2004 Average Annual Wage of Staff and Workers by Sector and Region, 2004

Region	IT and Computer Service and Software Sector
Beijing	57,412 RMB
Tianjin	38,257
Liaoning	36,976
Heilongjiang	28,554
Shanghai	58,874
Jiangsu	36,754
Zhejiang	47,690
Hubei	19,451
Guangdong	45,624
Chongqing	30,607
Yunnan	21,855
Shaanxi	30,085
Xinjiang	24,032

Source: 2005, *Chinese Statistics Year Book*.

training for a few months. Zhengfei urged his employees to learn from the behavior of wolves, who had a keen sense of smell, were aggressive, and, most importantly, hunted in packs. In Zhengfei's own words, "An enterprise needs to develop a pack of wolves. Huawei's marketing arm has to focus on organizational aggressiveness."[23]

Over time, the company developed a national recruitment system with exceptionally high pay by Chinese standards (see Exhibit 3). According to a Huawei ex-employee, the lowest monthly salary in 2000 for a bachelors degree holder was US$500.[24] With housing and other benefits, an employee's first-year compensation could total as much as US$12,500.[25] To replicate a Western model of corporate management, the company had engaged a team of foreign experts to adopt international best practices in the areas

Exhibit 4 Huawei's Corporate Management Systems

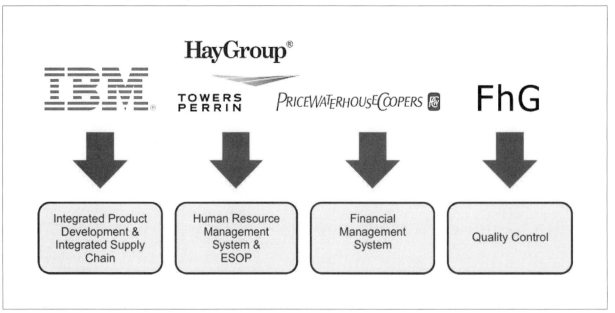

Source: J. Chen, 2005, Towards Indigenous Innovation: Pathways for Chinese Firms, Workshop of Technology Innovation and Economic Development, Zhejiang University, China, May 25–27.

of product development, supply chain integration, human resources management, financial management, and quality control (see Exhibit 4). Among these foreign consulting firms, IBM had been the most involved in reengineering Huawei's business processes and supply chains. For a while, 70 IBM consultants were working at the Huawei headquarters alongside Huawei employees and manufacturing facilities worldwide.

A Strong and Integrated Chinese Network

Huawei was undisputedly the largest Chinese telecom equipment manufacturer, with an annual revenue of US$6.7 billion in 2005, and a net profit of US$470 million. Market capitalization was estimated to be up to US$10 billion. In China, Huawei's major customers included all the big names such as China Telecom, China Mobile, China Netcom, and China Unicom. Huawei's networks in China served more than 400 million people communicating across the country,[26] occupied 25 percent market share in the mobile networks, and supplied 80 percent of all short messaging services from China Mobile.[27] The company had been selected as one of the major equipment suppliers for China Telecom's ChinaNet Next Carrying Network, or CN2, the core network for the country's next-generation business and consumer services, paving the way for China Telecom's entry into the 3G mobile market. In addition to the inexpensive R&D labor pool in China, the company had the advantage of integrating its marketing people into its

core R&D team. The needs of service providers and telephone companies could thus be communicated through the marketers to the R&D headquarters in a timely and responsive manner.

Huawei's products could be divided into the following categories (see Exhibit 5 and 6):

- Wireless network
- Fixed-line network
- Optical network
- Data communications network
- Value-added services
- Handsets and terminals (with a full series of switches and routers)

Despite the original desire to not form a joint venture with foreign firms, it became necessary to form such a relationship in order to remain a leader in the industry. In November 2003, Huawei entered a joint venture with 3Com in China and Japan, called Huawei-3Com, in which Huawei held a 51 percent stake. The joint venture was aimed at selling to corporate customers, Cisco's stronghold. Products manufactured by the joint venture were sold under the individual Huawei and 3Com brands throughout the world, except in China and Japan where the joint Huawei-3Com brand was used. In February 2006, 3Com increased its stake in the equity joint venture to 51 percent. The joint venture had captured about 35 percent of the Chinese corporate market and was expected to overtake Cisco to be the largest network equipment provider in China.

Exhibit 5 Huawei's Products Lines

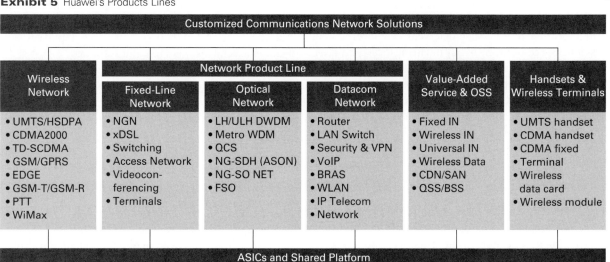

Source: J. Chen, 2005, Towards Indigenous Innovation: Pathways for Chinese Firms, Workshop of Technology Innovation and Economic Development, Zhejiang University, China, May 25–27.

EXHIBIT 6 Huawei's Sales by Technology

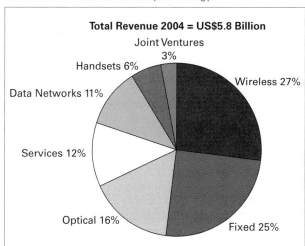

Source: EuroLAN.

As part of the joint venture arrangement, 3Com contributed US$160 million in cash, assets related to its operations in China and Japan, and licences to certain intellectual property. Moreover, the main reason Huawei entered into the joint venture with 3Com was that it wanted to leverage the latter's strong brand to increase profitability. Already a strong OEM with efficient production facilities, good R&D capabilities, and an extensive worldwide distribution network, what Huawei needed was a global name, because building a brand like 3Com's would be expensive and take a long time.

Path to Globalization

One dominant player [Cisco] has two-thirds of the market—the opportunity is there to become number two. With more than 65 percent of the market looking at one vendor, we believe some of that remaining 35 percent are unhappy and some of that 65 percent are very unhappy. We expect to be clearly number two.

—**D. RICHARDSON**
CHANNEL OPERATIONS CONSULTANT, HUAWEI UK

Huawei began considering international expansion in 1996 when it was looking for diverse sources of growth beyond the Chinese market. To avoid head-to-head competition with its international rivals such as Cisco and 3Com, the company made its initial overseas move in the markets of developing countries. Huawei made its first significant international sale to a Russian telecom service provider in 2000, which was quickly followed by Advanced Info Service, Thailand's largest mobile service provider, and Tele Norte Leste Participacoes, Brazil's fixed-line carrier.

The years between 1999 and 2001 were our breakthrough years. We would go to any country where we saw a market for telecom equipment. We invited as many prospective buyers as possible to come to our corporate headquarters, meet our people and see our products. We also went to all kinds of trade shows and exhibitions to show ourselves to the international customer base.

—**WILLIAM XU**
PRESIDENT OF HUAWEI'S EUROPEAN REGION[28]

As a newcomer battling against the perception that Chinese products were cheap and unreliable, Huawei had to use aggressive tactics to win contracts. In addition to unbeatable pricing (typically 30 percent lower than those of established suppliers), Huawei went out of its way to offer powerful incentives. To win the Neuf

Telecom contract in France in 2001, Huawei offered to build part of the customer's network free of charge and to run it for three months such that Neuf's engineers could test it before committing to buy it. Hiring local personnel was also part of Huawei's strategy to tailor technologies and services to customer's specific needs.

Major contracts won in recent years included the network upgrade contract with Etissalat, the telecommunications carrier of the United Arab Emirates, making UAE the first Arab country with 3G wireless communications. In 2004, Huawei became one of the first global communications suppliers to set up a CDMA network in Europe when it completed the construction of a project in Portugal for Denmark-based Radiometer A/S. In December that year, Huawei was selected by Telfort, the Dutch mobile operator, to build its 3G mobile phone network, signifying the company's first win in Europe's intensely competitive 3G market, and its arrival in the big league of telecom equipment suppliers. In late 2005, Huawei was selected as one of the four preferred suppliers to British Telecom's US$19 billion, five-year-long 21st Century Network upgrade project, along with the U.S.-based Ciena Corporations and Lucent Technologies, and Germany's Siemens AG. It had also signed a global framework agreement with the Vodafone Group to supply mobile phone networks to any Vodafone company worldwide. In all these countries, Huawei had taken business from global giants in the rank of Siemens and Alcatel. In 2004, of the 19 licences awarded around the world for 3G wireless networks, Huawei was involved in building 14 of them.

Struggles in the United States

Compared to Huawei's footprint in the European and other overseas markets, Huawei's presence in the United States was more limited. When it opened its first office in 2001 in Plano, Texas, the company made every effort to blend into the local culture. It shared the building with law offices, realtors, and the regional office of the lingerie company Victoria's Secret. A Texas state flag and an American receptionist welcomed visitors on the ground-floor lobby. Shortly after the U.S. launch, Huawei executives realized that Americans had difficulty pronouncing the company's name and came up with a working name, Futurewei. The new name, however, was never consistently adopted or promoted effectively. Magazines would still advertise Huawei, while trade shows, brochures, and other materials would feature Futurewei. Even though Americans had an easier time pronouncing the new name, they were confused by two different names belonging to the same company. In addition, the Chinese employees had a difficult time adapting to the Texas accent and other aspects of the local culture. The company

sought to make its public face as American as possible, and hired local telecom talent in the area to that effect, but the relationship between its U.S. employees and Huawei executives was sometimes strained.

Contrary to its success in winning deals in developing countries, Huawei had run into snags in making deals in the United States. In a mature market where phone companies and their equipment suppliers had long-term ties, customers looked for exceptional leading-edge technology and a compelling reason to switch. One telecom service provider suggested that they would consider Huawei only after putting it through exhaustive trials, a common procedure for sourcing from an unknown company. Huawei management admitted that it was not prepared for the time and effort needed to break into the U.S. market, where lower prices were often not enough to land a deal.

Six months after setting up its subsidiary in the United States, Huawei was sued by Cisco for having allegedly infringed a number of Cisco's patents and copyrights by copying Cisco's user interface, user manuals, and source code for running its low-end routers. According to Cisco, the copying was so "lavish" that Huawei's router software contained the same bugs as Cisco's.[29] Cisco was seeking stiff penalties in the lawsuit, including the discontinuation of the production of Huawei's Quidway routers, as well as impoundment and destruction of all Huawei routers and manuals in the United States. At the same time, Cisco launched a "cease and desist" order against Huawei's UK distributor, Spot Distribution. Analysts observed that Huawei's steep discounting of Cisco products in its home turf, the U.S. market, had prompted the lawsuit, which was Cisco's first intellectual property lawsuit despite its huge intellectual portfolio.

Huawei initially denied the allegations, asserting its respect of intellectual property rights and its own focus on original R&D. The company then acknowledged that it had inadvertently obtained a small amount of Cisco's source code and used it in its own products. After Huawei agreed to withdraw its Quidway routers and other related products from sale in the United States, Cisco finally dropped the lawsuit in July 2004. In the midst of the legal proceedings, numerous sales contracts that Huawei was trying to close were killed. When the allegations were finally cleared, the company stumbled again. In June 2004, a Huawei employee was caught taking pictures of the insides of some high-tech equipment from Fujitsu in a Chicago trade show. Huawei later explained that it never used those photos and that it was the employee's first time in the United States.

After these blunders, Huawei landed the first contract with a U.S. wireless carrier in February 2004. It subsequently secured several other contracts with small wireless carriers in the United States. Huawei had serious intensions for the U.S. market, but results were yet to be seen. As Albert Lin, Huawei's head of R&D for North America, explained, "We need to present ourselves better. We also have to make it clear that we are not just testing the waters in the United States."[30]

3G and Huawei's Future

The industry was of the opinion that Huawei's success as a global company eventually hinged on its performance at home.[31] China, with its huge and rapidly growing telecom market, would be the ultimate battleground for the world's telecom infrastructure suppliers. Core to the battle was the much-anticipated launch of 3G mobile phone services in early 2006. According to an estimate by China's Institute of Telecommunications Science and Technology, China's 3G users would reach 200 million by 2010, with associated revenue in the range of US$124 billion.[32] Confirmation of the 3G technology standards and the issue of licences were the two imminent issues for all players in China's much-coveted telecom market.

China was conducting standardized on-site testing on all three internationally recognized 3G technologies: the Chinese home-grown TD-SCDMA standard, the European-origined WCDMA standard, and the American CDMA2000 standard. Huawei had made heavy investments in WCDMA since 1995, formed a 3G research joint venture with Japan's NEC and Matsushita in 2003, and had deliberately entered the mobile handset market in early 2004 to prepare itself for the 3G market down the road. Concurrently, Huawei had formed a joint venture with Siemens, called TD-Tech, to test TD-SCDMA handsets and network gears. Huawei had been investing one-third of its R&D spending in 3G technologies for the past two years. To Huawei and other telecom players in China, the stakes were enormous as the launch of 3G services was expected to push the company onward to its next wave of growth and expansion.

Conclusion

It's like the global automotive industry in the 1970s and 1980s when the Japanese started to penetrate Europe and the United States with lower-cost products and then started to work their way up.

  —K. DEUTSCH
  VICE PRESIDENT, A. T. KEARNEY[33]

Incumbent Western firms should be very scared of Huawei. Its reputation as a low-cost vendor is only the visible part of the iceberg.

  —J. DOINEAU
  OVUM IT CONSULTANTS[34]

The low price is not the only reason that our customers choose us. Equipment reliability, service quality, and the company's association with long-term development are elements of its success.

  —JOHNSON HU
  VICEPRESIDENT, CORPORATE BRANDING AND
  COMMUNICATIONS, HUAWEI TECHNOLOGIES[35]

To distance itself from its low-cost image, Huawei launched its first global image-building campaign in mid-2004. To emphasise the reliability of its telecommunication networks, one print media boasted that Huawei's networks were able to withstand Siberian winters and Saharan summers.[36] In early 2005, a survey report of 100 telecom operators worldwide ranked Huawei eighth among wireline-equipment suppliers, up from eighteenth the previous year. In addition, Huawei ranked fourth in service and support. The report called Huawei's ascendancy "astounding" as it surpassed several incumbent vendors in perceived market leadership.[37] Huawei's threat to the international telecom equipment suppliers was not to be overlooked (see Exhibit 7 for select financial performance of Huawei and its global competitors).

However, the battle could only become more intense. Huawei's track record was disappointing in the United States, just short of solid distribution networks to break into the lucrative enterprise markets; the network of choice in the developed countries was still Cisco. Huawei and other Chinese peers would have a difficult time matching the brand recognition and level of service provided by Cisco and other U.S. counterparts. Network security was another major concern expressed by service providers and enterprise customers. As stated by Cisco's CEO John Chambers, "Networks would have to be capable of responding to intrusions and viruses before human operators become aware of them. And security will be the most effective and efficient if a common strategy extends through all of a corporation's wired and mobile networks." During two years' time, Cisco acquired over 14 companies involved in network security and aspired to be "not just a vendor, but a trusted business advisor."[38]

In Asia, according to research firm IDC, Cisco's share of the Asian market (excluding Japan) in routers and LAN switches was still going strong at 62 percent versus Huawei's 6.2 percent.[39] In mobile handsets, Chinese suppliers were losing ground to their foreign counterparts; market shares of the Chinese companies of the local market fell from 50 percent in 2004 to 38 percent in the first six months of 2005. Foreign suppliers were also dominating the mobile switching infrastructure market.

Huawei was a privately owned global company. The industry speculated that the company could raise up to US$1.5 billion in an initial public offering on the back of its strong growth and high penetration in international

Exhibit 7 Select Performance of Huawei and Its Global Competitors

Huawei

Calendar year	**2004**	**2003**	**2002**
Net sales (billions of $)	5.6	3.8	2.7
Net profit (billions of $)	0.47	0.38	0.11
Number of employees	22,000		

Cisco Systems

Fiscal year through	**July 2004**	**July 2003**	**July 2002**
Net sales (billions of $)	22.0	18.9	18.9
Net income (billions of $)	4.4	3.6	1.9
Number of employees	35,000		

3Com

Fiscal year through	**May 2004**	**May 2003**	**May 2002**
Net sales (billions of $)	0.699	0.933	1.259
Net income (loss) (billions of $)	(0.349)	(0.284)	(0.596)

Alcatel

Calendar year	**2003**	**2002**	**2001**
Net sales (billions of $)	9.4	12.4	19.1
Net income (loss) (billions of $)	(1.5)	(3.6)	(3.7)

Juniper Networks

Calendar year	**2003**	**2002**	**2001**
Total sales (billions of $)	0.701	0.547	0.887
Net income (loss) (billions of $)	0.039	(0.120)	(0.013)

Motorola

Calendar year	**2003**	**2002**	**2001**
Net sales (billions of $)	27.1	27.3	30.0
Net profit (loss) (billions of $)	0.9	(2.5)	(3.9)

Nokia

Calendar year	**2003**	**2002**	**2001**
Net sales (billions of $)	22.1	22.6	23.5
Net profit (billions of $)	2.7	2.5	1.7

Note: For Nokia and Alcatel, Euros were converted into U.S. dollars at the rate of €1.33 = US$1, as per the U.S. Federal Reserve Bank exchange rate on December 21, 2004.

Source: D. Normile, 2005, Chinese Telecom Companies Come Calling, *Electronic Business*, 31(2): 38–43.

telecommunications markets. Huawei stated that it had no intention to go public before 2008 because it had no urgent need for funds. The vice president of Huawei, however, expressed that the company was preparing to save more capital to look for good opportunities for overseas mergers and acquisitions in order to enhance its technical strength. The company's position was that it would seek acquisitions overseas to compete with its international rivals such as Nokia, Motorola, Alcatel, and NEC. Buying 3Com was always a possibility as the U.S. company continued to stumble in its global sales.

The general feeling was that Chinese vendors were mostly using Western engineering and not inventing much of their own. As with earlier technology migration from the United States to the Far East in the consumer electronics and personal computer businesses, Asian manufacturers were turning complex and high-profit products into standard commodities. Some had observed that Huawei's products appeared to be derived from those of other companies, either through patent-mining or reverse engineering. To become a serious global contender, Huawei would have to move beyond low-cost versions of Western gear. Its low-cost strategy seemed increasingly untenable because its reliance on local service partners in foreign markets would ultimately raise its cost of running the business. At the same time, foreign companies were increasing their manufacturing base and R&D facilities in China and would soon become equally competitive in terms of pricing.

Last but not least, Huawei's connection to the Chinese army continued to cast a shadow around Huawei's image for some overseas customers. A number of U.S. distributors remained skeptical about the potential military influence the company was subject to and were wary of any implication to international business relationships. Zhengfei's military background and the company's recent sales to Iraq had created suspicion in the eyes of the Western world. In 2005, Huawei lost its bid to acquire British telecom equipment provider Marconi to the world giant Ericsson largely because of Huawei's baffling connection with the Chinese military. Although the company was trying to improve its corporate image and increase transparency, questions of trust and reputation could undermine its efforts to win contracts with governments and international enterprises in the long run. Facing so many thorny challenges, Huawei's management had to draft a sustainable global strategy.

Notes

1. C. Walton, 2005, Huawei moves in on Cisco, MicroScope, September 5.
2. R. McGregor, 2005, Huawei reaches foreign sales milestone, *Financial Times,* London, November 30.
3. M. Zeng & P. Williamson, 2003, The hidden dragons, *Harvard Business Review,* October.
4. D. Normille, 2005, Chinese telecom companies come calling, *Electronic Business,* 31(2): 38–42.
5. K. Nissen, 2005, New world telecom: A survival guide for global equipment suppliers, *Business Communications Review,* September.
6. F.W. McFarlan, G. Chen, & D. Kiron, 2001, Cisco China, Harvard Business School Case, Harvard Business School.
7. P. Fan, 2004, Catching up through developing innovation capability: Evidence from China's telecom-equipment industry, Department of Urban Studies and Planning, MIT, November 11.
8. Annual Report, China's post and telecommunications industry 2005, Ministry of Information Industry, China.
9. 2005, China to have over 440 Million mobile phone users by end of next year, http://www.today.com.
10. A. Harney, 2005, The challenger from China: Why Huawei is making the telecoms world take notice, *Financial Times,* London, January 11.
11. A. Farhoomand, Z. Tao, Y. Jiang, & T. X. Liu, 2005, China's telecommunications industry in 2004, Asia case research center case, University of Hong Kong.
12. F. W. McFarlan, G. Chen, & D. Kiron, 2001, op. cit.
13. Ibid.
14. When the first characters of the four companies were arranged in reverse order (Ju-Great Dragon, Da-DTT, Zhong-ZTT, Hua-Huawei), the phrase "Great China" was created.
15. 2006, China's telecommunications market 2005, CRC-Pinnacle Consulting Co. Ltd., http://www.buyusainfo.net/docs/x_8130085.pdf November 13.
16. Information in this section was extracted from the following Harvard Business School cases: F. W., McFarlan, G. Chen, & D. Kiron, 2001, Cisco China, Harvard Business School Case; and G. Jones, & D. Kiron, 2005, Cisco goes to China: Routing an emerging economy, Harvard Business School Case.
17. G. Long, 2005, Power Shift, Telecom Asia, March.
18. China's "exchanging market for technology" policy encouraged foreign companies with the desired technological expertise to develop business in China, on the condition that they would share certain technical knowledge with their Chinese counterparts.
19. P. Fan, 2004, Catching up through developing innovation capability: Evidence from China's telecom-equipment industry, Department of Urban Studies and Planning, MIT, November 11.
20. US$1 = RMB 8.07 on December 29, 2005.
21. A. Smith-Gillespie, 2001, Building China's high-tech telecom equipment industry: A study of strategies in technology acquisition for competitive advantage, Masters Thesis, MIT.
22. P. Fan, 2004, Catching up through developing innovation capability: Evidence from China's telecom-equipment industry, Department of Urban Studies and Planning, MIT, November 11.
23. R. Tang, 2004, Hungry like a wolf, *The Standard,* September 24.
24. US$1 = RMB 8.07 on December 29, 2005.
25. R. Tang, Hungry like a wolf.
26. Refers to networks built with Huawei equipment in China, as noted by J. Hu, the company's vice president, corporate branding and communications.
27. J. Chen, 2005, Giant rises in the east, *National Post,* June 10.
28. C. Wu, 2004, Huawei reveals its difficult journey to globalization, http://tech.sina.com.cn/it/t/2004-08-06/0751399261/shtml.
29 2003, A New Global technology player, *Exchange,* March 14.
30. C. Rhoads & R. Buckman, 2005, Trial and error: A Chinese telecom powerhouse stumbles on road to the U.S., *Wall Street Journal,* July 28.
31 A. Harney, 2005, The challenger from China: Why Huawei is making the telecoms world take notice, *Financial Times,* London, January 11.
32. A. Farhoomand, Z. Tao, Y. Jiang, & T. X. Liu, 2005, China's telecommunications industry in 2004, Asia case research centre case, University of Hong Kong.
33. 2003, A new global technology player, *Exchange,* March 14.
34. 2005, Business: See Huawei run, *The Economist,* March 5.
35. J. Chen, 2005, Giant rises in the east, *National Post,* June 10.
36. R. Flannery, 2004, An air of mystery, *Forbes* Online, http://www.forbes.com/business/global/2004/1129/030.html.
37. 2005, Business: See Huawei run, *The Economist,* March 5.
38. D. Normile, 2005, Chinese telecom companies come calling, *Electronic Business,* 31(2): 38–43.
39. 2005, Business: See Huawei run, *The Economist,* March 5.

ING DIRECT: Rebel in the Banking Industry

Dr. Kurt Verweire
Dr. Lutgart A. A. Van den Berghe

Vlerick Leuven Gent Management School

ING DIRECT USA is built on the foundation of being unconventional. We aren't like other banks. We've not only developed a unique business model, but the way we look at the business is different than how our competitors look at it. Our purpose is to be a servant of the average person. Rather than getting people to spend more—which is what most banks do—our approach is to get Americans to save more—to return to the values of thrift, self-reliance, and building a nest egg.

ING DIRECT was born in an age of broken promises. The last thing America needed was another bank, but that didn't mean America didn't need us. ING DIRECT's mission is to make it easy to save by offering the same great values to all Americans.

> —ARKADI KUHLMANN
> PRESIDENT AND CEO, ING DIRECT
> (UNITED STATES AND CANADA)

Many organizations have tried to enter the banking industry with innovative business models. But incumbents have always been able to defend their markets successfully. Today, ING DIRECT is changing the odds. Arkadi Kuhlmann, founder of ING DIRECT, is clear about his goals: "There's no such thing as an industry that can't be reenergized!"

Customers welcomed the company with open arms. In just five years, ING DIRECT has become the largest Internet-based bank—passing E*TRADE Bank—in the United States, and one of the 30 largest banks of any sort in the country. The company adds an astonishing 100,000 customers and $1 billion in deposits every month, and in 2005 (its fifth year of operations) generated a profit of $360 million. And above all, 90 percent of the ING DIRECT customers believe it provides a much better service than the competitors.

Profile of the ING Group

ING DIRECT is one of the six business lines of ING Group, a major international financial services group. ING Group is active in more than 50 countries and is often cited as the example of an integrated financial services provider, offering a wide array of insurance, banking, and asset management services to a broad customer base: individuals, families, small businesses, large corporations, and institutions and governments.

ING Group is a financial conglomerate founded in 1991 by the merger between Nationale-Nederlanden, the Netherlands' largest insurance company, and NMB Postbank Group, one of the largest banking groups in the Netherlands. NMB Postbank Group itself was the result of a merger between the very entrepreneurial NMB Banking Group and the Postbank. Postbank had been split off from the Dutch Post Office and was privatized. Many people within ING believe that Postbank has been the true inspiration for ING DIRECT.

The merger between Nationale-Nederlanden and NMB Postbank Group created the first bancassurer in the Netherlands. Since 1991, ING has developed from a Dutch financial institution with some international businesses to a multinational with Dutch roots. It acquired banks and insurance companies in the United Kingdom (Barings Bank, 1995), Belgium (Bank Brussels Lambert, 1998), Germany (BHF-Bank, 1999), United States (Equitable of Iowa, 1997; ReliaStar, 2000; Aetna Financial Services, 2000), Canada (Wellington, 1995; Canadian Group Underwriters, 1998; Allianz of Canada, 2004), and other countries. Some of these financial institutions were sold later, such as parts of Barings and BHF-Bank. As such, ING Group has become one of the 15 largest financial institutions worldwide and top-10 in Europe

Case 12 • ING DIRECT: Rebel in the Banking Industry

Exhibit 1 20 Largest Financial Institutions Worldwide

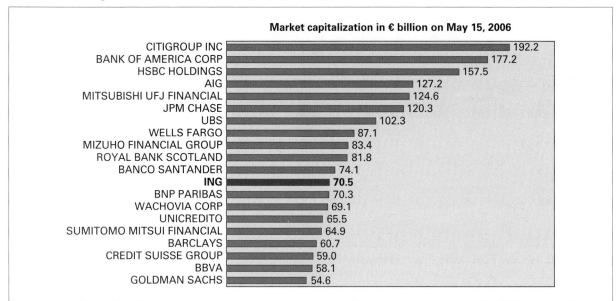

Market capitalization in € billion on May 15, 2006

CITIGROUP INC	192.2
BANK OF AMERICA CORP	177.2
HSBC HOLDINGS	157.5
AIG	127.2
MITSUBISHI UFJ FINANCIAL	124.6
JPM CHASE	120.3
UBS	102.3
WELLS FARGO	87.1
MIZUHO FINANCIAL GROUP	83.4
ROYAL BANK SCOTLAND	81.8
BANCO SANTANDER	74.1
ING	70.5
BNP PARIBAS	70.3
WACHOVIA CORP	69.1
UNICREDITO	65.5
SUMITOMO MITSUI FINANCIAL	64.9
BARCLAYS	60.7
CREDIT SUISSE GROUP	59.0
BBVA	58.1
GOLDMAN SACHS	54.6

Source: http://www.bloomberg.com

(in market capitalization). Exhibit 1 provides an overview of the 20 largest financial institutions, measured by market capitalization.

ING also used greenfields to grow the business. Greenfields were set up in the emerging markets, where ING leveraged the bancassurance concept it continued to refine in its home markets. ING Group also set up other initiatives to fuel the group's revenue and profit growth. It created a new international retail/direct banking division, which was composed of a team of Postbank's best marketing and IT people. Hans Verkoren, CEO of Postbank, became the head of this new division. This new venture was to explore to what extent Postbank's strategy could be expanded outside its Dutch home market. Postbank operated in a "branchless" manner for many years, offering simple checking accounts, savings, mortgages, consumer loans, and investment products.

This new division operated autonomously from the rest of the company. The parent company gave the new organization the necessary freedom to experiment. After detailed marketing research, the team introduced to Canada ING's first foreign direct banking experiment in 1996.

ING chose Canada because it had no presence there, and the market was dominated by a small number of players. ING agreed it was important for this new experiment to survive or fail on its own. It created optimal conditions for success by providing it with adequate financial means and a brand new management team, lead by Arkadi Kuhlmann.

A Growing Success Story in the Banking Industry

Arkadi Kuhlmann, a Harley-riding painter and poet, was a professor of International Finance and Investment Banking at the American Graduate School of International Management (Thunderbird) in Phoenix, Arizona. He also served as president of North American Trust, CEO of Deak International Incorporated, and held various executive positions at the Royal Bank of Canada. When Hans Verkoren asked him in 1996 whether he was interested to start up a new foreign bank in Canada, he accepted the challenge.

Arkadi had noticed that few foreign banks had successfully entered the North American banking industry and had built a sustainable competitive position in that market. But he realized that those incumbents were not invincible.

Traditional banks are stuck. They have high fixed costs and use technology in an inefficient way. They have rigid distribution systems. And they charge too high prices. The customer always loses. When we came in, we said: "How can we do something different?" We looked at other industries and copied some ideas from successful players in the retail and airline industry. It is true that we actually haven't defined something new. In the context of Southwest Airlines or Wal-Mart, there are similarities. For decades, Southwest Airlines has defied the industry's standard approaches to economics and customer service, and has achieved good results. And we are on our way to do the same in the banking industry. Most companies, especially in our industry, are truly boring. If you do things the way everybody else does, why do you think you're going to be any better?

ING DIRECT differentiates itself from traditional banks in many ways. But in essence, its differentiation lies in being direct.

Our biggest advantage in standing out in the financial service market from all other players is that we are direct. Anyway we can emphasize that we are direct, thereby cutting out the middleman, is a way of saving money. So being a retail business, being simple, focused and direct adds up to good value. This is a retail trend that consumers know and one we should emphasize in everything we do.

ING DIRECT is a direct-to-the-customer operation, an Internet-based savings bank, although customers can also bank by mail or telephone.

The bank operates no branches, no ATMs, just a couple of cafés in big cities where it sells coffee and mountain bikes in addition to savings accounts, a few certificates of deposit, home mortgages, home equity lines, and a handful of mutual funds.[1] The bank does not offer traditional paper-based checking accounts—that costs too much. For these accounts, ING DIRECT points customers back to their local bank. ING DIRECT charges no fees and maintains no minimum deposits for savings accounts and a limited number of product offerings.

What started as a small successful experiment in Canada in 1997 has become one of the success stories in today's financial services industry. ING DIRECT launched operations in Spain and Australia in 1999. One year later, it entered France and the United States.

Since then, ING DIRECT has entered Italy, the United Kingdom, and Germany, and it has plans to set up operations in Japan. ING DIRECT globally ended the first quarter of 2006 with €194 billion in deposits and €15,7 million customers (see Exhibit 2). In 2005, ING DIRECT's profits constituted 7 percent of ING's total profits. Exhibit 3 shows ING DIRECT's global profit progression from its creation to 2005.

Exhibit 2 ING DIRECT's Clients and Funds Base

	2005 Profit (in € millions)	Deposits (in € millions)	Customers
Canada	69.4	12,579	1,360,588
Spain	51.0	13,726	1,341,759
Australia	73.8	10,757	1,282,459
France	23.9	11,389	555,922
USA	162.9	39,031	3,785,927
Italy	29.0	13,426	699,603
Germany	242.1	57,654	5,488,865
UK	(27.7)	33,704	1,038,650
Austria	(15.6)	2,475	210,808
Total ING DIRECT	612.3	194,741	15,764,581

Source: ING DIRECT, http://www.ingdirect.com

Exhibit 3 ING DIRECT's Global Profit Progression (in € millions)

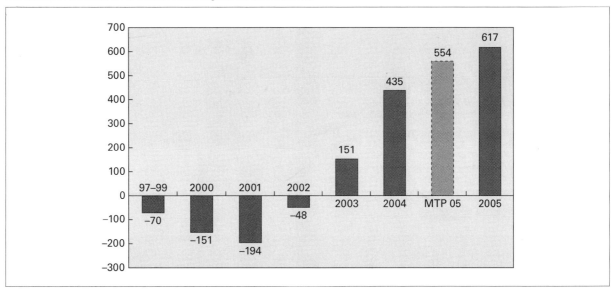

Source: ING DIRECT, http://www.ingdirect.com.

Reenergizing the U.S. Retail Banking Industry

ING DIRECT has attracted a lot of attention in the United States for several reasons. Despite the wide acceptance of the Internet in American households, online banks have not been particularly successful. Nevertheless, ING DIRECT has experienced a meteoric growth since its launch in September 2000. What is more, the venture broke-even after only two years.

More striking is the way that ING DIRECT positions itself in the U.S. banking industry. Arkadi Kuhlmann rejects the characterization of ING DIRECT as an Internet bank, even though the Web is its primary customer channel.

We're actually a pure savings bank, focusing on residential mortgages and savings accounts. You can't get any more old-fashioned than that.

In all of its communication, ING DIRECT points out that it is a federally chartered bank and that its savings are FDIC insured in order to guarantee credibility with its customers.[2] But that is where the comparison with typical retail banks stops. In fact, there is nothing typical about ING DIRECT.

ING DIRECT's Product Offering and Value Proposition

In a typical bank, first and foremost, the focus is on payments services. Once you get the payment services—such as checking, face-to-face teller services, and ATMs (automatic teller machines)—you're "owned" by the bank. But Arkadi Kuhlmann's strategy is different. The last thing he wants is to hold the traditional demand deposit accounts (i.e., checking account). These accounts typically have a large number of transactions per month and require a physical branch and a great deal of internal labor to process them. All this activity is too costly. Rather ING DIRECT wants to be "your other bank," offering a simple, high-return savings account, called the Orange Savings Account—ING's theme colour is orange. Customers are encouraged to shift money back and forth between their ING DIRECT savings account and their checking accounts with their existing bank. The account generates one of the highest rates in the market; sometimes the rate is four times higher than the industry average (see Exhibit 4). ING DIRECT sells its products with the simple slogan: "Great rates, no fees, no minimums."

ING DIRECT also offers a limited number of mutual funds. And the bulk of the assets of the bank consists of

Exhibit 4 "Great Rates, No Fees, No Minimums"

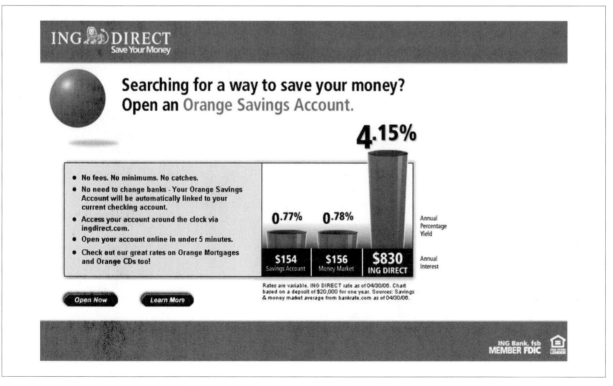

Source: ING DIRECT Web site, May 2006, http://www.ingdirect.com.

simple residential mortgages and a small percentage of home equity lines of credit and customer loans. Nearly 90 percent of the loan portfolio consists of mortgages. All products have low fees and few requirements.

But what's so unique about high rates? Arkadi Kuhlmann comments:

Nothing . . . . What is unique is that we offer consistently great rates and at the same time a high quality service. The key to deliver high quality service is simplicity: no tricks, no catches. Customers must immediately understand ING DIRECT products. Educating people about financial products is very expensive.

Although some banking professionals consider mortgages a difficult product to standardize and to sell via the Internet, Arkadi Kuhlmann disagrees:

You can turn mortgages into simple products too. But it requires that you reengineer the product and the processes behind it. And to some extent, you need to reengineer the customer as well.

And that strategy did not only attract many new customers, but also allowed the company to retain most of them.

Savings accounts can be set up in five minutes online. Mortgages take seven minutes to close (with all customer documentation available), as is demonstrated in Exhibit 5. The company tries to avoid customer contact over the phone. The Web site plays a crucial role in informing customers how to deal with the bank. ING DIRECT makes opening a savings account and transferring money extremely simple and straightforward. On the Web site, it posts: "It's that simple to earn more!" For the people who prefer human contact, ING DIRECT's U.S. operations have more than 500 call center associates in three call centers. Those associates are trained to provide fast response and prompt service to the customers. The company strives to get 80 percent of the calls answered in 20 seconds. As a matter of fact, employees have their bonuses tied to achieving this goal. In order to reach that goal, employees receive extensive training—about 20 days for five products (which is a lot compared to traditional banks). Overall, the brand strategy of ING DIRECT is best described by the acronym GRASP, "Great deals, Responsive, Accessible, Simple and easy, and Passionate."

The Target Customers

The first order of business for ING DIRECT is to introduce products that make it easy and financially rewarding for customers to save more. But part of the strategy is choosing the products it won't offer and the customers it won't serve. Unlike its traditional competitors, the company is not interested in rich Americans (unless they do what it wants them to do). "We want to *serve* the average American" as long as he/she behaves in the way ING DIRECT wants. In 2004, the company "fired" more than 3,500 customers who didn't play by the bank rules. Those customers relied too much on the call centers, or asked for too many exceptions from the standard operating procedures.

People should not come and explain their financial problems. We sell products and commodities, not solutions.

Communicating the Message

So far ING DIRECT USA has managed to communicate well the message about its rules and target customers. In five years, the bank has attracted more than 3.5 million customers. This growth can partially be explained by the huge efforts the company undertook to build the ING DIRECT brand: One third of its budget is allocated to marketing programs. Many customers are attracted by the combination of rates and a hip brand. ING DIRECT's marketing campaigns project a differentiated brand and "unbank-ness." They have a simple, clear message, and feature the bright colour orange, capturing customers' attention by communicating in a humorous, "anti-establishment" tone. Exhibit 6 presents some outdoor advertising ING DIRECT used in 2006. Some of those campaigns were locally adapted to the target markets (see Exhibit 7). (Exhibit 8 presents some marketing campaigns of ING DIRECT in other countries.) The purpose of the guerrilla marketing tactics is clear, according to Arkadi Kuhlmann:

People are sleeping. You have to shock people a little bit to get them to think differently about how they manage their money. So we wake them up with one of our marketing campaigns. They switch their money and go back to sleep.

Exhibit 5 Online Banking: It's as Easy as . . .

Source: Picture taken at ING DIRECT Café (New York), May 2006.

Exhibit 6 Outdoor Advertising from ING DIRECT USA

Source: ING DIRECT, http://www.ing.com.

Exhibit 7 Local Marketing Campaigns, ING DIRECT USA

Washington D.C.

New York

Phoenix & Philadelphia

Source: ING DIRECT, http://www.ing.com.

Exhibit 8 Marketing Campaigns, ING DIRECT in Countries Outside of the United States

Source: ING DIRECT, http://www.ing.com.

ING DIRECT does not restrict itself to the more traditional marketing campaigns. The bank continuously organizes innovative promotion campaigns to attract new customers. The company's "Save your money at the movies" campaign attracted many spectators and publicity in the press. In Baltimore and Washington, D.C., ING DIRECT surprised more than 8,000 people with a free movie at two participating Regal Cinemas. In a similar way, it offered free gas in Baltimore to 1,000 drivers at three selected Shell stations, and asked them to put that money into an Orange Savings Account. By the end of the three-hour promotion campaign cars lined up for more than three kilometres. ING Direct also let commuters ride the Boston "T" lines for free

one morning, while ING representatives danced around in orange Paul Revere costumes. Those kinds of events certainly do wake people up.

Another uncommon feature of the marketing strategy is ING DIRECT's cafés. The cafés, each located in a big city of the targeted countries—such as New York, Washington, Philadelphia, Los Angeles—are not substitutes for branches. Rather they introduce the customers to the ING DIRECT brand. When ING DIRECT started its marketing and operations in Canada, early prospects were somewhat suspicious about the new brand. So they began visiting the company's call center in Toronto to check out the new bank to verify its physical existence. The employees from ING DIRECT Canada

Exhibit 9 Pictures of ING DIRECT Cafés in New York, Los Angeles, Philadelphia, and Wilmington

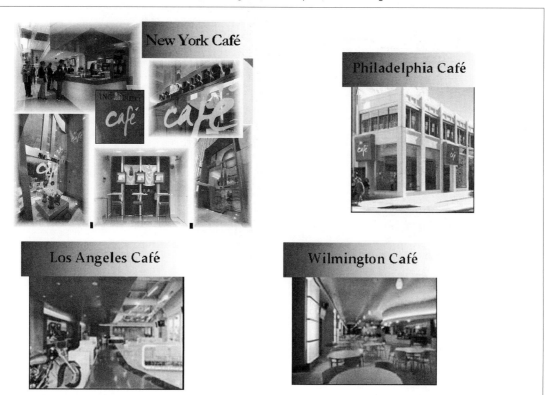

Source: ING DIRECT, http://www.ing.com.

offered those prospectors a cup of coffee in the coffee corner of the call center. That is how the idea emerged. It took Arkadi Kuhlmann some time to convince the managers at ING in Amsterdam to set up "coffee shops,"[3] but now the cafés are a typical element of ING DIRECT's marketing strategy. Pictures of the ING DIRECT cafés are shown in Exhibit 9.

The cafés sustain ING DIRECT's atypical bank image, and they offer the customers a place to go to speak with an ING DIRECT café member, each a trained banker, and experience the simplicity the brand denotes. While serving coffee, the café staff members—called sales associates—can discuss financial products or help check information on one of the online terminals located on the premises. Consistent with the brand, the coffee is much less expensive than similar coffee at Starbucks, and Internet usage at the cafés is free.

We believe saving money should be as simple as getting a cup of coffee. So we invite you to come in and experience just how refreshing it is to sip a latte, surf the Internet for free, and talk to us about how we can help Save Your Money.

Managing a Rebellious Organization

Obviously, the cafés have helped to build the brand. But it requires more than a handful of cafés to achieve the revenue and profit figures ING DIRECT has achieved so far. Behind that rebellious image is a well-oiled machine, designed to deal with high-volume, low-margin commodity products. Exhibit 10 shows the key components of the company's strategy execution. Although significant attention is paid to understand demand and increase revenues, the execution challenge also involves cost control and efficiency improvement. Even though most retail banks in the United States operate at a margin spread of 250 basis points (2.50 percentage points), ING DIRECT operates on a spread of 175 basis points. ING DIRECT is able to operate at lower costs by managing both the "front and back" offices.

Managing the Front and Back Office

A big part of its lower cost structure stems from the things that it doesn't offer, and where it doesn't have to invest. The company does not invest in an ATM network

Exhibit 10 Strategy Execution at ING DIRECT

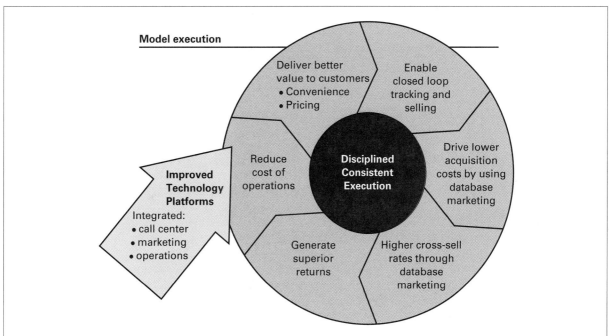

Source: ING Group, http://www.ing.com.

or in traditional branches. It encourages customers to open accounts online or by using an interactive voice response (IVR) system. Online servicing of accounts and mortgage applications cuts down on costs. The company's acquisition costs are estimated to be lower than $100. According to Jim Kelly, chief marketing officer for ING DIRECT: "It is not unusual for a bank to have customer acquisition costs of about $300–400."[4] Similarly, maintenance costs are kept low as well. Says Arkadi Kuhlmann:

If you don't have any activity in a month, we're not sending you a statement. Savings account customers who insist on a paper statement should go back to Chase.

The company also communicates to its customers that a high number of calls to the call center will lead to higher fees or lower interest rates. So customers should understand why ING DIRECT discourages telephone calls to (expensive) operators at the call center. To further discourage the use of these operators, customers who call frequently are put at the end of the operator's queue.

All of these aspects require that ING DIRECT manages its processes in a rigorous way. Processes are documented, and a large number of guidelines and procedures exist for the core processes within the organization. The company is constantly looking to simplify financial products and financial transactions, and uses tools such as Lean Six Sigma to achieve the efficiency of the manufacturing industry. In 2004, ING DIRECT Canada won a Canadian

Information Productivity Award of Excellence for its Mortgage Application Processing Solution (MAPS). This solution enabled ING DIRECT to simplify the process of obtaining a mortgage dramatically. And this new solution is also leveraged in the other ING DIRECT entities.

The sharing of best practices and materials is common within the ING DIRECT business units. For example, ING DIRECT shares marketing campaigns across all of the countries in which it has operations and reuses marketing concepts and graphic designs.

Information Technology

ING DIRECT benefited from the absence of "legacy" information technology systems. ING DIRECT started from scratch, which helped the company significantly to operate with a higher performing IT architecture at a lower cost. The challenge was to develop a flexible IT architecture providing brand uniformity across borders, but allowing for adaptation to local banking regulations.

ING DIRECT buys the IT hardware centrally, exploiting its buying power, and then makes it available to the various country organizations. For software, the company's strategy is to "re-use (from sister companies) before buy, and buy before build." This approach saves an enormous amount of money, and at the same time helps to insure a high level of service and ease in accommodating growing numbers of accounts. A central IT Group develops and maintains the IT policies and standards

Exhibit 11 Evolution of ING DIRECT's Operational Cost Base to Assets (excluding marketing)

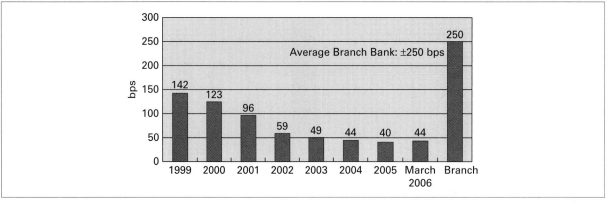

Source: ING Group, http://www.ing.com.

across the company, and works with the various countries to update and improve the systems.

ING DIRECT also strives to have its different departments in close contact with each other. The process flow is specified for the whole organization and takes into account all processes from the various departments simultaneously. Streamlining processes is a key element in ING DIRECT's business architecture, and business process orientation is a necessary element, says Arkadi Kuhlmann.

We put our marketing and IT departments in one area. If your core competencies are marketing and IT, you really have to do both of them together.

Product Development

Product development is also done in close coordination with marketing and IT. To develop and introduce a new product, a country unit would first develop a business plan that includes forecasts of demand and marketing expenditures. The plan also evaluates the operational, financial, and legal risks associated with the launch of the product. And it specifies clearly what IT and operational requirements are necessary to support the product. The hurdles for a new product are high. Brunon Bartkiewicz (former manager at ING DIRECT, now heading ING's banking operations in Poland) explains:[5]

Every new product reduces our simplicity, increases our risk and defocuses our people. A person who is working on marketing seven products cannot know all the details, all the figures, all the logic that a person focused on one product does. In the end, the whole game is efficiency: efficiency in marketing, in operations, and in systems.

Performance Measurement

Another important element of ING DIRECT's business model is the obsession for measuring how customers react to marketing campaigns and online advertising. But ING DIRECT's performance measurement doesn't stop at the marketing department. The company's operations centers compete against each other for recognition and monthly bonuses based on their ability to meet sales and service goals. Everybody in ING DIRECT measures and is measured. Some performance measures are posted daily on an intranet site, accessible to everyone within the company. The performance measures are continuously analyzed and are the input for action plans, allowing new product and process initiatives.

All operational performance measures have a direct impact on the company's five high-level targets. These targets are: (1) total profit, (2) nonmarketing expenses/ending assets, (3) net-retail funds entrusted (on balance sheet) growth, (4) net mortgage growth, and (5) call-center service level. Efficiency and cost effectiveness are monitored carefully. Exhibit 11 presents the evolution of the operational costs of ING DIRECT (all countries) from 1999 to March 2006. There we can see that the expense-to-assets ratio (excluding marketing expenses) for ING DIRECT (all countries) decreased from 96 basis points in 2001 to 40 basis points in 2006. An average branch bank has an expense-to-asset ratio of about 250 basis points. In a similar way, total assets per employee for ING DIRECT are $48 million, whereas traditional branch-based banks have an average of $5–$6 million per employee.

Those figures are impressive. But equally impressive is how ING DIRECT has "structured" its measurement processes. ING DIRECT used Microsoft Excel spreadsheets to create annual reports summarizing the company's performance until the company's fast growth necessitated a more structured approach toward measuring company performance. In 2004, the company hired a consultant who helped it set up a performance measurement system, generating enterprise-wide, relevant management information that steers the company's future growth. The powerful reporting and analysis tools help identify further cost-saving opportunities and gain in-depth visibility into the key performance metrics. In addition, the performance measurement system allows ING DIRECT to measure the effectiveness of marketing campaigns, to track market and risk exposure, and to gain a better understanding of its new and existing customer base. Arkadi Kuhlmann agrees that ING DIRECT has been getting more efficient with customer acquisition and with lowering customer acquisition costs due to the introduction of the new performance measurement system.

Leadership, People, and Culture

What really sets ING DIRECT apart from its competitors is its people. You can't be a rebel if you have all traditional bankers in your organization. That is why ING DIRECT tries to hire people who do not come from the big banks. Only for functions such as risk management, treasury, or asset-liability management does the bank hire employees with a banking background. Of course, ING DIRECT can benefit from ING's expertise in these technical matters. CEO Arkadi Kuhlmann himself is an experienced banker with a deep knowledge of all core functions within the bank. But he profiles himself as the outsider—even the bad guy—of the industry: "When the rest of the banking industry decides to zig, I zag," he says. And he ensures that the entire organization zags with him.

Arkadi Kuhlmann truly is a visionary and inspiring leader. You won't hear Arkadi talk a lot about financial metrics. Arkadi Kuhlmann is out for a more inspiring mission and vision.

We are leading the Americans back to saving. One way or another, most financial companies are telling you to spend more. That's not what we want.

In all communication, the focus is on saving. And that's why credit cards and traditional checking accounts don't fit in the product portfolio.

Above all, it is the way that Arkadi conveys the message that makes him an inspiring leader: "You can't do meaningful things without passion and a powerful idea about what you're trying to do," he argues. In the United States, he has about 1,300 people who help him on his crusade. What is striking is that the employees of ING DIRECT are as determined as the CEO himself.

But then ING DIRECT spends a lot of time and effort to ensure that it hires people willing to do things differently from the industry, and inspires them with the same set of values that it uses to connect with its customers. The company hires people with the right attitude, who can easily be trained and introduced to a competitive selling culture. But above all, people are selected based on whether their personal values fit with the values of ING DIRECT. Rick Perles, head of human resources at ING DIRECT, comments:

Everyone, no matter what level, starts in the new hire program. The new hire program used to be three days but we have expanded it to five, which is a big investment in our people and not something most companies do. All new hires take customer calls. During those first days, they'll hear a lot about culture and what ING stands for. Some people don't subscribe to it, but they realize it even before the five days are up.

The Maiden Voyage refers to the next 90 days, where we spend another week or two facilitating technical training with our sales associates. During those first 90 days, there are things the new hire has to do before coming back for the second part of new hire training. These activities include volunteering in the community, working in one of our Cafés, and reading The Alchemist *by Paulo Coelho.*[6]

Values and culture are not idle concepts within ING DIRECT. Arkadi Kuhlmann is aware that the most differentiating aspect of the whole company is situated in what is called the "Orange Code." The Orange Code specifies in 13 statements what ING DIRECT is all about and what it stands for. The Orange Code brings the vision to life and provides employees with common goals. For example, one of those statements is "We will be for everyone." In the company, this vision is made concrete by removing all titles and offices. Everybody is in the bonus program, and the metrics are the same for everybody.

The reward strategy is also particular. Employees can earn substantial bonuses, based on how they perform relative to some well-specified financial, customer, and operational targets. Bonuses can be up to half of the fixed salary. Interestingly enough, the employees' fixed salary is also higher than the industry average. Although a cost leader, the company prides itself on paying at the 75th percentile or higher. Maybe that's why in a recent employee survey, 99 percent of the employees were proud to say that they are part of ING DIRECT. The survey indicated however that the employees' positive attitude is based on other facets than the reward policy. In particular, the employees consider ING DIRECT an attractive employer for the strength of its business model, and its "nonbanking" culture. ING DIRECT is a flat organization with few management layers. And employees can provide input in the many action plans that the organization sets up. Arkadi Kuhlmann describes it as follows: "I make sure that managers tell the employees *what* to do, but not *how* to do things. This is the starting point for real empowerment."

The growth of the company and the support of the ING Group is another driving force for the employees to help fulfill ING DIRECT's ambitious goals.

The Orange Code also ensures that the employees don't become too complacent. One of the statements reads as follows: "We aren't conquerors. We are pioneers. We are not here to destroy. We are here to create!"

Challenges

The market has been created and ING DIRECT has developed an attractive position within that market. But the easy success of the online savings bank has attracted other newcomers. MetLife launched an Internet bank in late 2002 and has been heavily promoting high interest rates. And in 2006, HSBC's Internet Bank stepped in with higher rates than those of ING DIRECT. Other banks are soon to follow.

Arkadi Kuhlmann acknowledges that he will have to cope with more challenging competitors in the future. At the same time, the success of ING DIRECT has also created even higher expectations on the financial potential of its business model. A key question for the management team will be how the company can sustain its growth. What products should the company introduce? And which markets should it enter?

The company carefully analyzes what other ING DIRECT products customers will desire. In line with the general philosophy of the company, such an offer will only be made with the customers' consent. But only a small number of customers have opted into the permission marketing program. Should the company more aggressively try to cross-sell?

ING DIRECT also has to manage internal challenges. One of these challenges is how to cope with the growth the company has experienced. More customers mean increased pressure on the systems and processes. In the banking industry, size quite often implies *dis*economies of scale. Furthermore, will the company find employees who embrace its unique culture? Managing a unique culture is easier if the company is small. But it gets more challenging as the company grows.

One of the internal challenges also relates to the relationship that ING DIRECT has with its parent organization, ING Group. ING Group, known as the integrated financial services group, actively stimulates synergies between its banking, insurance, and investment entities across different countries. But Arkadi Kuhlmann has always been able to limit ING DIRECT's participation in the Mandated Synergies program to what he calls the "low hanging fruit." ING DIRECT will help to exploit the benefits of cooperation with sister companies, but not at all costs. How long will ING DIRECT's management benefit from that exceptional status? And what will be the implications if ING DIRECT becomes more integrated and incorporated within the traditional ING businesses.

One of those synergies is to integrate brand development. ING DIRECT positions itself as the rebel in the banking industry, but at the same time it wears the brand of one of the most respected, traditional financial institutions, ING. The more that ING DIRECT contributes to ING's profit increases, the greater the dilemma.

Notes

1. ING DIRECT has opened cafés in Toronto, Vancouver, Sydney, Barcelona, Madrid, New York, Philadelphia, Los Angeles, Wilmington, and a couple of other cities.
2. The Federal Deposit Insurance Corporation (FDIC) is a governance institution that insures deposits in thrift institutions and commercial banks.
3. Coffee shops have a different connotation in the Netherlands than in the United States.
4. Would you like a mortgage with your mocha? *Fast Company*, March, 68, 110.
5. ING DIRECT: Your other bank, IMD Case, IMD-3-1343, 7.
6. 2005, Interview with Rick Perles by Irene Monley, *Delaware Society for Human Resource Management*, October, 2(4).

Case 13

JetBlue Airways: Challenges Ahead

Theodore Bosley, Christopher Calton, Jeffrey Deakins, Tomoko Nakajima,
Sally Orford, Robin Pohl, Robin Chapman

Arizona State University

Introduction

We're going to bring humanity back to air travel.
  —**DAVID NEELEMAN**
    FOUNDER AND CHAIRPERSON

David Neeleman, JetBlue's founder and chairperson, sought to "bring the humanity back to air travel."[1] Since launching operations in February 2000, JetBlue distinguished itself from its competitors by providing superior customer service at low fares. The JetBlue experience included brand new airplanes, leather seats, and personal satellite TV service. The firm experienced rapid early growth. In a period when most U.S. airlines struggled in the aftermath of the September 11, 2001, terrorist attacks, JetBlue reported 18 consecutive quarterly profits.

Then in 2005, JetBlue announced its first net loss of $20 million. The disappointing results were attributed to spiraling fuel prices, aggressive competition, and increasing operating costs. Global events such as war, political turmoil, and natural disasters contributed to the rise in fuel prices. The average price for a barrel of oil in 2003 was $30, by the summer of 2005 prices had climbed above $60 per barrel. The legacy airlines were becoming more competitive after exiting bankruptcy and streamlining their operations to benefit from economies of scale.[2] Analysts speculated that JetBlue was experiencing growth pains:, their maintenance costs on aging planes were increasing, employees were becoming more senior, and new profitable routes were harder to obtain.[3] The company continued to lose money in 2006. While major competitors, such as AMR, the parent company for American Airlines, and Continental, reported higher than expected returns, JetBlue announced a narrow third-quarter loss of $500,000. Following its third-quarter loss, JetBlue announced plans to slow down growth by delaying deliveries of some aircraft, selling others, and eliminating some cross-country flights.[4] Despite these actions, in a recent interview Neeleman insisted, "We're still a growth airline."[5] It remains to be seen how JetBlue will continue to grow in the face of increasing strategic challenges.

History

Founding History of Jet Blue

David Neeleman founded JetBlue Airways Corporation in 1999, after raising $130 million in investment capital. Building on his past experiences, Neeleman hired talented executives, such as David Barger, previous vice president of the Newark, New Jersey, hub for Continental, and John Owen, previous vice president of Operations Planning and Analysis for Southwest.[6] JetBlue chose John F. Kennedy International Airport in New York as its hub and initially obtained 75 takeoff and landing slots.

Neeleman's vision was to provide "high-end customer service at low-end prices."[7] Although JetBlue imitated competitor Southwest Airlines with a single seat class, it did so with Airbus A-320 narrow-body jets instead of Boeing 737s. The A-320 provided wider cabins and wider seats for JetBlue passengers with more room for carry-on baggage.[8] JetBlue implemented innovative IT programs such as an Internet booking system that allowed customers to make reservations online or with a touch-tone phone, and a paperless cockpit to allow pilots to prepare for flight more quickly, helping planes to stay on schedule.[9] JetBlue also provided complementary, unlimited snacks and beverages, preassigned seating, and a selection of first-run movies available from Fox InFlight on flights longer than two hours. For further differentiation, JetBlue installed 36 channels of free DIRECTV programming.

The authors would like to thank Professor Robert E. Hoskisson for his support under whose direction the case was developed. The authors do not intend to illustrate either effective or ineffective handling of a managerial situation. The case solely provides material for class discussion.

Early in 2000, the first JetBlue flights departed from New York to Fort Lauderdale, with a fleet of two planes. JetBlue gradually increased its destinations during the year to include 12 additional airports in California, Florida, New York, Utah, and Vermont. By December, Neeleman announced the landmark of JetBlue's millionth customer and reported $100 million in revenues.

Rapid Growth in 2000–2004

The September 11, 2001, terrorist attacks on America resulted in a widespread fear of air travel, negatively impacting most of the airline industry. While other airlines announced millions in lost revenue following 9/11, JetBlue made a profit and within eight weeks expanded its network to include six more destinations and resumed IT spending to further improve services offered.[10] In February 2002, JetBlue won the 2002 Air Transport World "Market Development Award" for its successful first two years of service, and also was named "Best Overall Airline" by *Onboard Service* magazine.[11] On April 11, 2002, JetBlue

announced its initial public offering (IPO) of 5.86 million shares of common stock at a price of $27 per share.[12] JetBlue grew steadily between 2003 and 2004, with annual operating revenues growing from $998.4 million in 2003, to $1.27 billion in 2004. Exhibits 1 through 3 show JetBlue's financial statements for the years 2001 to 2005.

Slowed Growth in 2005–2007

In November 2005 JetBlue decided to add nine new Embraer E190s to its fleet. JetBlue ordered the aircraft with a 100-seat configuration, bigger television screens than the Airbus A-320, and 100 channels from XM Satellite Radio. Also, in late 2005, JetBlue decided to fund $80 million of an airport expansion project at John F. Kennedy Airport, which had a total budget of $875 million. The expansion would allow for more than double the number of flights at JetBlue's hub airport within three years.[13]

However, JetBlue's quarterly financial report started to show growth saturation. Quarterly growth records of operating revenue in 2005 were 29.5 percent, 34.5 percent,

Exhibit 1 Consolidated Statement of Income

JetBlue Airways Corporation (in $ millions, year ended December 31)					
	2006	2005	2004	2003	2002
Operating Revenues					
Passenger	$ 2223	$ 1620	$ 1220	$ 965	$ 615
Other	140	81	45	33	20
Total Operating Revenues	2363	1701	1265	998	635
Operating Expenses					
Salaries, wages, and benefits	553	428	337	267	162
Aircraft fuel	752	488	255	147	76
Landing fees and other rents	158	112	92	70	44
Depreciation and amortization	151	115	77	51	43
Aircraft rent	103	74	70	60	41
Sales and marketing	104	81	63	54	27
Maintenance materials and repairs	87	64	45	23	9
Other operating expenses	328	291	215	159	127
Total Operating Expenses	2236	1653	1154	831	530
Operating Income	$ 127	$ 48	$ 111	$ 167	$ 105
Other Income (Expenses)					
Interest expense	(173)	(107)	(53)	(29)	(21)
Capitalized interest	27	16	9	5	5
Interest income and other	28	19	8	8	5
government compensation				23	
Total other income (expense)	(118)	(72)	(36)	7	(10)
Income (Loss) before income taxes	9	(24)	75	174	95
Income tax expense (benefit)	10	(4)	29	71	40
Net Income (Loss)	$ (1)	$ (20)	$ 46	$ 103	$ 55

Source: JetBlue Airways Corporation 2006 Annual Report.

Exhibit 2 Consolidated Balance Sheet

JetBlue Airways Corporation
(in $ millions, except share data)

Assets	December 31				
	2006	2005	2004	2003	2002
Cash and short-term Investments	$ 699	$ 484	$ 450	$ 607.31	$ 257.85
Total receivables, net	77	94	37	16.72	11.93
Total inventory	27	21	10	8.3	4.84
Prepaid expenses	124	36	17	13.42	5.59
Other current assets, total	0	0	0	0	2.85
Total Current Assets	$ 927	$ 635	$ 514	$ 645.74	$ 283.06
Property/Plant/Equip, total	$ 3438	$ 2978	$ 2130	$ 1421	$ 997
Goodwill, net	0	0	0	0	0
Intangibles, net	32	43	54	62	68
Long-term investments	0	0	0	0	0
Note receivable long-term	0	0	0	0	0
Other long-term assets, total	446	236	99	57	30
Other assets, total	0	0	0	0	0
Total Assets	$ 4843	$ 3892	$ 2797	$ 2186	$ 1379

Liabilities and Shareholders' Equity	December 31				
	2006	2005	2004	2003	2002
Accounts payable	$ 136	$ 99	$ 71	$ 53	$ 46
Payable/Accrued	0	0	0	0	0
Accrued expenses	164	111	94	85	54
Notes payable/Short-term debt	39	64	44	30	22
Current port. of LT debt/capital	175	158	105	67	51
Leases					
Other current liabilities, total	340	243	174	135	98
Total Current Liabilities	$ 854	$ 676	$ 488	$ 370	$ 270
Long-term debt and leases	$ 2626	$ 2103	$ 1396	$ 1012	$ 640
Deferred income tax	136	116	121	99	39
Minority interest	0	0	0	0	0
Other liabilities, total	275	86	38	34	17
Total Liabilities	$ 3891	$ 2981	$ 2043	$ 1515	$ 964
Redeemable preferred stock	$ 0	$ 0	$ 0	$ 0	$ 0
Preferred stock-non	0	0	0	0	0
Common stock	2	2	1	1	1
Additional paid-in capital	813	764	581	552	407
Retained earnings	144	145	165	120	16
Other equity, total	(7)	0	7	(2)	(9)
Total Equity	952	911	754	671	415
Total Liabilities & Shareholders' Equity	$ 4843	$ 3892	$ 2797	$ 2186	$1,379

Source: JetBlue Airways Corporation 2006 Annual Report.

Exhibit 3 Consolidated Statement of Cash Flows

JetBlue Airways Corporation
(in $ millions)

	December 31				
	2006	2005	2004	2003	2002
Cash Flows from Operating Activities					
Net Income	$ (1)	$ (20)	$ 46	$ 103	$ 55
Operating Activities					
Deferred income taxes	10	(4)	29	69	40
Depreciation	136	101	67	45	25
Amortization	18	16	11	7	2
Stock-based compensation	21	9	2	2	
Changes in certain operating assets and liabilities					
Increase in receivables	(12)	(28)	(20)	(4)	7
Increase in inventories	(28)	(20)	(6)	(11)	(4)
Increase in air traffic liabilities	97	69	39	37	46
Increase in accounts payable and other accrued liabilities	33	54	21	38	35
Other, Net	0	(7)	10	1	11
Net Cash Provided by Operating Activities	274	170	199	287	216
Cash Flows from Investing Activities					
Capital expenditures	(996)	(941)	(617)	(573)	(544)
Predelivery deposits for flight equipment	(106)	(183)	(180)	(160)	(109)
Purchase of held-to-maturity investment	(23)	(5)	(19)	(26)	(11)
Proceeds from maturities of held-to-maturity investment	15	18	25	9	2
Purchase of available-for-sale securities	(1002)	(79)	76	(235)	(80)
Increase in restricted cash and other assets	(16)	(86)	(5)	(2)	(1)
Net Cash Used in Investing Activities	$ (1307)	$ (1276)	$ (720)	$ (987)	$ (744)
Cash Flows from Financing Activities					
Proceeds from:					
Issuance of common stock	28	178	20	136	174
Issuance of long-term debt	855	872	499	446	416
Aircraft sale and leaseback transactions	406	152		265	0.3
Short-term borrowings	45	68	44	33	150
Repayment of long-term debt	(390)	(117)	(77)	(57)	27
Repayment of short-term debt	(71)	(47)	(30)	(25)	(71)
Other, Net	−15	(13)	(19)	(9)	(34)
Net Cash Provided by Financing Activities	$ 1037	$ 1093	$ 437	$ 789	$ (5)
Increase in Cash and Cash Equivalents	$ 4	$ (13)	$ (84)	$ 89	$ 129
Cash and cash equivalent at beginning of period	$ 6	$ 19	$ 103	$ 14	$ 117
Cash and cash equivalent at end of period	$ 10	$ 6	$ 19	$ 103	$ 247

Source: JetBlue Airways Corporation 2006 Annual Report.

40.2 percent, and −5.2 percent, respectively. JetBlue announced a fourth quarter net loss of $42.4 million, representing a loss per share of $0.25. It was JetBlue's first quarterly net loss.[14]

In 2006, the firm announced unstable earnings, and reported a loss of $32 million, a profit of $14 million, and a loss of $0.5 million in the first three quarters, respectively.[15] Even though JetBlue served 47 destinations with up to 470 daily flights, it decided to reduce its rate of growth over the next three years by delaying the delivery of additional planes.[16] Data for destination and service commenced are listed in Exhibit 4. Effort to slow the growth rate was intended to preserve cash, enabling JetBlue to remain stable among competitors.

The first quarter of 2007 did not get off to a great start for JetBlue. Bad weather in February resulted in many

Exhibit 4 JetBlue's Destinations

Destination	Service Commenced
New York, New York	February 2000
Fort Lauderdale, Florida	February 2000
Buffalo, New York	February 2000
Tampa, Florida	March 2000
Orland, Florida	June 2000
Ontario, California	July 2000
Oakland, California	August 2000
Rochester, New York	August 2000
Burlington, Vermont	September 2000
West Palm Beach, Florida	October 2000
Salt Lake City, Utah	November 2000
Fort Myers, Florida	November 2000
Seattle, Washington	May 2001
Syracuse, New York	May 2001
Denver, Colorado	May 2001
New Orleans, Louisiana	July 2001
Long Beach, California	August 2001
Washington, D.C. (Dulles Airport)	November 2001
San Juan, Puerto Rico	May 2002
Las Vegas, Nevada	November 2002
San Diego, California	June 2003
Boston, Massachusetts	January 2004
Sacramento, California	March 2004
Aguadilla, Puerto Rico	May 2004
Santiago, Dominican Republic	June 2004
San Jose, California	June 2004
New York, New York (LGA Airport)	September 2004
Phoenix, Arizona	October 2004
Nassau, The Bahamas	November 2004
Burbank, California	May 2005
Portland, Oregon	May 2005
Ponce, Puerto Rico	June 2005
Newark, New Jersey	October 2005
Austin, Texas	January 2006
Richmond, Virginia	March 2006
Hamilton, Bermuda	May 2006
Sarasota-Bradenton, Florida	September 2006
Cancun, Mexico	November 2006
Island of Aruba	November 2006
Chicago, Illinois	January 2007
White Plains, New York	March 2007
San Francisco, California	May 2007

Source: JetBlue Airways Corporation Form 10-K, Fiscal year ending December 31, 2006.

cancelled flights and stranded passengers. The climax of the crisis occurred when nine airplanes full of angry passengers sat on the tarmac for six hours, because JetBlue leaders had expected the weather to clear and did not cancel flights. CEO David Neeleman received bad press for his management of the situation. Neeleman responded by humbly admitting "that his company's management was not strong enough. [It] was the result of a shoestring communications system that left pilots and flight attendants in the dark, and an undersize reservation system."[17] Rapid efforts were made to regain its brand image such that a JetBlue Customer Bill of Rights was created, a customer advisory council was formed, plans were made to cross-train crew members, and new communication strategies were put in place.[18] In addition JetBlue waived change fees and fare differences to assist customers who may be affected by additional storms throughout the winter of 2007. Despite his sincere efforts to bounce back from this predicament, Neeleman eventually had to step down as CEO in order to appease shareholders. David Barger, former COO succeeded Neeleman as CEO and needed to establish a strong position against JetBlue rivals.

Competitive Environment

In 1978, the Airline Deregulation Act eliminated government control over fares and routes, opening up the industry to increased competition. The airline industry is now highly competitive, consisting of 43 mainline carriers and 79 regional airlines. The U.S. Department of Transportation (DOT) classifies airlines into three categories based on annual revenue: major (revenue more than $1 billion), national (revenue between $100 million to $1 billion), and regional/commuter (revenue less than $100 million).[19] With annual revenue of $1.7 billion, JetBlue is one of the smaller major carriers and competes primarily on point-to-point routes. Its major competitors are low-cost carrier Southwest Airlines and traditional carriers, AMR Corp, United Airlines, US Airways, Continental Airlines, and Delta Air.[20]

Southwest is JetBlue's most obvious competitor, but the traditional airlines are becoming more aggressive in the low-fare market. Following recent bankruptcies, legacy airlines are emerging with clean balance sheets and lower cost structures. As the major airlines become more competitive and expand their domestic businesses, the low-cost airlines struggle to find new markets.[21]

Competition also comes from the regional carriers, which typically partner with the major airlines to share routes, risk, and costs. For example, Mesa partners with United Airlines and operates as United Express, with Delta Airlines as Delta Express, and with US Air as US Air Express. In exchange for an agreed proportion of revenue, Mesa operates flights on select local routes, while its partners handle reservations and marketing. In recent years, the regional airlines fared better than most, growing twice as fast as the national carriers.[22] However, as the competitive environment toughens, many of the large airlines are renegotiating the agreements, and in some cases—such as Atlantic Coast, a former partner of United Airlines—regional airlines are deciding to operate independently.[23]

The major airlines also form alliances—with each other and international carriers—to share marketing and scheduling capabilities. American Airlines partners with British Airways, Quantas, and various European airlines to form the One World Alliance, which serves 135 countries and operates a shared frequent flyer program. The Star Alliance, spearheaded by United Airlines, with Lufthansa, Scandinavian Air System, All Nippon Airways, and Air Canada, serves 157 countries.[24] Such alliances increase the market power of their members, and research has shown they increase passenger volume by an average of 9.4 percent.[25] Although the benefit is more significant for global carriers seeking to expand their network abroad, researchers observed an average improvement in number of tickets booked by 7.4 percent on short-haul flights.

Although JetBlue does not currently participate in any alliances, it has had discussions about forming one with international airlines in an effort to leverage its power at the hub in JFK. JetBlue does not want to enter a traditional agreement with other airlines, because many of these agreements include increased overhead costs. JetBlue is hoping to create an agreement that will increase traffic without increasing costs.[26]

Fare pricing is an important competitive factor within the industry. For many years excess capacity posed a significant problem, causing airlines to either leave planes on the ground or fly planes with empty seats. In order to avoid this dilemma, carriers try to increase market share by discounting tickets. Even the legacy airlines slash fares in order to compete on low-cost routes. Although low-cost airlines, like JetBlue, still offer the greatest number of discounted fares, some of the cheapest tickets are now available from traditional airlines, such as American, Delta, and United.[27]

Rumors of consolidation in the industry could change the competitive landscape. US Airways made a hostile bid for bankrupt Delta Airlines in fourth quarter 2006, but withdrew its offer in January 2007 due to the inability to reach financial agreement with Delta creditors.[28] The merger would have created the largest airline in a fragmented industry and would likely have triggered further consolidations.[29] Even though a wave of consolidation may create a more efficient airline industry with fewer major players, consolidations affect ticket prices, usually leading to higher ticket prices, and complicate the flight paths offered by airlines. Therefore, consolidations affect all competitors within the industry.

Key Competitors

Southwest Airlines

Southwest is the leading low-fare, no-frills, U.S. carrier. The company was founded in 1967 as a Texas-based airline to serve Dallas, Houston, and San Antonio. The airline now flies to more than 63 cities across the United States. In 2006, Southwest reported a $499 million profit and net sales of $9.86 billion.[30] Exhibit 5 compares key financial data for the major airlines. In 2005, America West's CEO, Douglas Parker, described Southwest as follows: "They really were at one point the scrawny kid who was lifting weights in his basement. Now they come out and they're bigger than anybody else and stronger than anybody else."[31]

Southwest's strategy emphasizes low costs; the firm was the first to sell tickets online and to introduce unassigned seating. It operates a single aircraft fleet of 481 Boeing 737s. The company is also lauded for its unique and friendly culture and its high level of customer service.[32] However, evidence now indicates a shift in its strategy—from serving underserved routes, to competing in major markets such as Denver and Philadelphia. Southwest is now the largest U.S. airline in terms of number of passengers (Exhibit 6), and in order to continue to grow, Southwest is competing against United in its Denver hub, and US Airways, on routes out of Philadelphia.[33]

Exhibit 5 U.S. Major Airlines' Select Financials for Year Ended 2006 (in $millions)

	JetBlue	UAL	SWA	Delta	Continental	US Airways	AMR Corp.
Total revenues	$2,363	$ 19,340	$ 9,086	$ 17,171	$13,128	$11,557	$ 22,563
Cost of revenues	1,653	14,114	6,311	14,430	11,007	9,049	17,659
Gross profit	570	5,226	2,573	1,694	1,453	1,814	4,904
Profit as % of revenue	24%	27%	28%	10%	11%	16%	22%
Operating income (loss)	127	23,381	934	(6,148)	468	558	1,060
Net income (loss)	$ (1)	$ 22,386	$ 499	$ (6,203)	$ 343	$ 304	$ 231
Total assets	$4,843	25,369	$13,460	$ 19,622	$11,308	$ 7,576	$ 29,145
Current assets	927	6,273	2,601	5,385	4,129	3,354	6,902
Total liabilities	$3,891	$ 23,221	$ 7,011	$ 33,215	$10,961	$ 6,606	$ 29,751
Current liabilities	854	7,945	2,887	5,769	3,955	2,712	8,505
Total owner equity	$ 952	$ 2,148	$ 6,449	$ (13,593)	$ 347	$ 970	$ (606)

Source: 2007, MSN Money Central, http://moneycentral.msn.com/investor/research/welcome.asp, July 24.

Exhibit 6 Top 10 U.S. Airlines, Ranked by August 2006 Domestic Scheduled Enplanements

Passenger numbers in millions

August 2006 Rank	Carrier	August 2006 Enplanements	August 2005 Rank	August 2005 Enplanements
1	Southwest	8.7	1	8.1
2	American	6.5	3	6.8
3	Delta	5.4	2	7.0
4	United	5.1	4	5.0
5	Northwest	4.1	5	4.2
6	Continental	3.1	7	2.9
7	US Airways	2.6	6	3.1
8	America West	1.8	8	1.9
9	AirTran	1.8	9	1.5
10	JetBlue	1.7	13	1.3

Note: Percentage changes based on numbers prior to rounding.

Source: Bureau of Transportation Statistics, T-100 Domestic Market.

AMR Corp.

As the world's largest airline, American Airlines (AMR's main subsidiary) offers flights to 150 destinations throughout North America, Latin America, the Caribbean, Europe, and Asia. It has had its share of success and failures; two of its planes were hijacked during the September 11, 2001, terrorist attacks and the firm barely avoided bankruptcy in 2003.[34] In 2006, AMR Corp. reported net earnings of $231 million, an improvement over its net loss of $861 million in 2005 and other significant losses in preceding years.[35] In order to return to profitability, the firm streamlined costs and expanded its routes in Asia.

United Airlines

United also lost two planes on September 11, 2001, and after several years of financial difficulties, UAL eventually filed for Chapter 11 bankruptcy in 2002.[36] UAL emerged from bankruptcy as a more competitive firm. In February 2004, United launched its own low-cost off-shoot, Ted. The firm is now looking for new ways to expand and improve profitability. Global expansion is central to UAL's strategy; in July 2006, the firm announced plans to expand its Asia/Pacific routes.[37] Recent rumors report that UAL hired Goldman Sachs to assess possible merger options.[38]

US Airways

US Airways Group is the product of a merger between US Airways and America West. CEO Parker believes this acquisition strategy is successful; when comparing the firm's post-bankruptcy performance to United, he stated, "The big difference is we were able to generate synergies that United was not able to."[39] Shareholders experienced a 45 percent increase in stock price during the first full year after the merger.[40]

Delta Air

With an 11.8% domestic market share, Delta places third among traditional airline icons.[41] Delta is strongly focused on international expansion, adding 50 new international routes in 2005–2006. Delta now serves over 450 destinations in 95 countries. Delta filed for bankruptcy and was a target acquisition by US Airways just before it emerged from bankruptcy in April 2007.

Continental Airlines

Continental targets the business traveler by serving diverse U.S. and international routes.[42] Continental has a strong balance sheet, having recently retired $100 million in debt.[43] In the third quarter of 2006, Continental followed in the path of the other legacy airlines by reporting stronger than expected results. The positive results were attributed to greatly increased number of passengers, especially on Continental's regional and Latin American routes.[44]

As well as domestic competitors, the international airline market conditions are a factor that JetBlue must consider.

International Market Conditions

The demand for international travel has increased significantly over the past decade (see Exhibit 7). The international travel growth rate is more than double the domestic travel growth rate in the United States.[45] Travel to Southeast Asia and China increases every year by about 7.3 percent and 8.0 percent. Looking forward, the number of transatlantic plane tickets purchased is expected to grow by 4.6 percent annually. Global business transactions have contributed, as well as more discretionary income for consumers, and lower airfare resulting from greater efficiencies in international travel.

The international market is attractive to many airlines because they can include fuel surcharges in the ticket price and recover some of the costs associated with higher-priced fuel.

However, the airline industry is monitored more scrupulously by the government than any other industry conducting business internationally. The government has many regulations on when, where, and how airlines can fly, how much they can charge, and how they can market international travel.[46] Many lobbyist firms and politicians in the United States have been fighting for deregulation and less restrictions on international air travel so that the United States might be more of a force in the international market. The European airline industry, more specifically AirFrance/KLM, has taken the lead in revenues for international aviation.[47]

Not only is it important for JetBlue to consider its competitive environment, but it is also important to understand the companies/industries that supply the provisions necessary to remain competitive.

Key Suppliers

Fuel

Fuel is usually the second-highest expense for an airline next to labor.[48] Therefore, fuel price increases are a major contributor to rising operating costs in the airline industry. A Merrill Lynch analyst indicated that for every $1 increase in price for a barrel of fuel, the airline industry experiences a $450 million loss in pretax profits.[49] According to the FAA, jet fuel costs rose by 20.1 percent in 2004, 40.5 percent in 2005, and 30.4 percent in 2006.[50] In 2006, fuel costs became JetBlue's largest operating expense at 33.65 percent.[51] The FAA forecasts fuel costs will remain high for the next several years. Neeleman seriously considers fuel costs and is investigating alternative sources of energy, such as liquid coal. Because the

Exhibit 7 U.S. Commercial Air Carriers Total U.S. Passenger Traffic

Fiscal Year	Revenue Passenger Enplanements (millions)			Revenue Passenger Miles (billions)		
	Domestic	International	System	Domestic	International	System
Historical*						
2000	641.2	56.4	697.6	512.8	181.8	694.6
2001	626.8	56.7	683.4	508.1	183.3	691.4
2002	574.5	51.2	625.8	473.0	158.2	631.3
2003	587.8	54.2	642.0	492.7	155.9	648.6
2004	628.5	61.4	689.9	540.2	177.4	717.7
2005	661	86.2	747.2	573.7	221.5	795.1
Forecast						
2006	660.9	89.7	750.6	577.6	232.5	810.1
2007	693.3	75.8	769.1	603.3	221.5	824.7
2008	713.8	79.8	793.6	624.6	234.5	859.0
2009	735.7	84.0	819.7	647.7	247.9	895.6
2010	758.9	88.3	847.2	671.9	262.1	934.1
2011	782.6	92.9	875.5	697.6	276.9	974.5
2012	807.7	97.6	905.2	724.5	291.9	1,016.4
2013	833.4	102.3	935.7	752.6	307.4	1,059.9
2014	860.5	107.2	967.7	782.2	323.5	1,105.7
2015	888.4	112.3	1,000.7	813.3	340.2	1,153.5
2016	917.7	117.6	1,035.3	846.1	357.5	1,203.6
2017	848.4	123.1	1,071.6	880.6	375.2	1,255.8
Average Annual Growth 2005–2017	2.9%	5.0%	3.1%	3.6%	5.5%	4.1%

Source: Forms 41 and 298-C, U.S. Department of Transportation.

United States has an abundant supply of coal, Neeleman is urging his customers to support a new bill to fund additional coal-to-liquid plants.[52]

Airlines engage in fuel hedging in order to manage unpredictable costs. However, the jet fuel commodities market is illiquid, and it is especially difficult for the large airlines to hedge sufficient quantities of fuel.[53] JetBlue is increasing its efforts to systematically hedge against future fuel needs. JetBlue also seeks more efficient fuel usage through the planes purchased and improved flight planning.[54]

Aircraft Manufacturers

The aircraft industry is dominated by two companies, Airbus and Boeing. Due to the weak economy following September 11, 2001, their orders for new commercial planes fell sharply. However, as commercial business improved, the large manufacturers profited from the buoyant space and defense markets. Embraer, the number four aircraft manufacturer, has seen lackluster commercial sales, but is benefiting from increased sales in the military sector.

Typically, the low-cost airlines operate few aircraft types, reducing their maintenance, scheduling, and training costs. JetBlue currently owns two airplane models, and its growth plans include the addition of 96 Airbus A-320s and 92 Embraer E190s.[55] Cost efficiencies would be lost if JetBlue switched suppliers, exposing the firm to any problems related to either of its aircraft suppliers. But currently more pressing for JetBlue are the challenges associated with the airline industry.

General Environment

A number of new trends are emerging in air travel. After September 11, 2001, the industry saw a drop in the number of corporate travelers, but five years later this trend appeared to be reversing. According to a survey by the National Business Travel Association, 65 percent of businesses expect employees to take more flights in 2007, and 75 percent predict an increase in the amount of business travel.[56]

Another factor in the environment of air travel is the characteristics of the airport and FAA density regulations. JetBlue experiences general performance setbacks by operating in high traffic areas such as the northeastern United States, and the airport congestion hampers performance statistics.[57] The FAA regulates airport slot (a slot is a time frame allotted for takeoff and landing)[58] allocations with the intent to ease congestion problems and enhance airport capacity. For example, recent measures at New York La Guardia airport include growth limitations, regulations encouraging use of larger aircraft, and a proposal for 10-year slot reallocation.[59]

Natural disasters and annual weather patterns also affect the performance statistics for air travel. Florida is quite popular during the winter months and the western states during summer months. Air travel is also affected by winter weather in the Northeast and tropical storms along the Atlantic and Gulf coasts.[60]

In the airline industry, more than 60 percent of employees are unionized.[61] Although JetBlue is nonunionized, it can be affected by the industry environment. In June 2006, the International Association of Machinists and Aerospace Workers campaigned to represent JetBlue's ramp service workers. The bid was unsuccessful; however JetBlue's management commented, "We can expect ongoing attempts by unions to organize groups of JetBlue crewmembers."[62]

As can be expected from the general environment, JetBlue is exposed to the widespread attraction of media coverage and negative press. One recent major incident appearing in headlines is the mechanical failure of Flight 292 landing in Los Angeles.[63] On September 21, 2005, JetBlue Flight 292 left Burbank, California, bound for JFK in New York City. Soon after takeoff, the pilot acknowledged problems with the landing gear. The decision was made to have an emergency landing at Los Angeles International Airport and after circling Orange County for three hours, to burn off fuel, Flight 292 landed safely. None of the 139 passengers or six crew members was injured during the landing. Upon landing it became certain that the nose gear had rotated 90 degrees and was locked in the down position[64] (see Exhibit 8). Although the outcome was ultimately favorable, had Flight 292 crashed or lives been lost, JetBlue's image would have suffered drastically. The perceived safety of air travel is important for all airlines.

Airlines also face a heightened sense of consumer information privacy. In 2002, JetBlue offered extensive passenger data to a data mining company, Torch, who in conjunction with the U.S. Army, tested a customer profiling system to identify high risk passengers that might threaten military installations.[65] According to the District Court,

Exhibit 8 JetBlue Airbus A-320 Flight 292 with Its Nose Landing Gear Jammed

Source: JetScott, 2005, http://www.aerospaceweb.org/question/planes/q0245a.shtml, October 2.

Eastern New York, Memorandum & Order 04-MD-1587, JetBlue was responsible for the release of "each passenger's name, address, gender, home ownership or rental status, economic status, social security number, occupation, and the number of adults and children in the passenger's family as well as the number of vehicles owned or leased."[66] With increased online purchases, all airlines are publicly pressured to protect passengers' identity.

JetBlue must make a conscious effort to rise above all of the setbacks associated with the general environment and ensure that all actions are in alignment with its corporate and business strategies.

JetBlue Strategies

Because many of the other airlines play a significant role in the low-cost carrier segment within the airline industry, JetBlue competes by differentiation. The goal is to achieve an image of far superior customer service.

Superior Customer Service

JetBlue delivers this service by offering additional preflight and on-board conveniences that other low-cost carriers do not provide as a whole package. Before traveling, customers benefit from JetBlue's simple-to-use reservation system, ticketless travel, and preassigned seating. The cabin features leather seats and an additional two inches of leg room than most carriers. As previously mentioned, on board JetBlue passengers receive free DIRECTV service, and its Embraer E190 planes have XM Satellite Radio.[67] To improve the customer experience, JetBlue added healthier snacks and, as of November 2006, offers a 100 percent transfat-free selection. All snacks are complementary and unlimited.

All passengers on "shut eye" flights receive a comfort kit from Bliss, which includes earplugs, lip balm, an eye mask, and hand lotion. Crewmembers wake customers with the smell of Dunkin' Donuts coffee and offer a hot towel service.[68]

It is valuable to customers to have their flight depart as planned. To provide customers with confidence, JetBlue focuses on its completion rate, even at the expense of its on-time rate. At the end of third quarter 2006, JetBlue had a 99.6 percent completion rate. In addition, customers want to be confident that they will have their bags at the end of the flight. At 2006 year-end, JetBlue was ranked number 1 out of the 15 busiest airlines in regard to the least number of lost or mishandled bags.[69]

A critical factor in achieving superior service is employee moral. As Neeleman has stated, the crewmembers are the "real secret weapon."[70] His philosophy is that if crew members are treated well, they will in turn treat the customers well.

Culture

Currently, David Neeleman, chairperson, and Dave Barger, CEO, are hands-on people who like to interact with employees and customers. Each week members of top management fly with 8 to 12 crew members and almost always attend new hire training to teach new crewmembers about JetBlue's brand, how the company makes money, and how crewmembers contribute to the bottom line. Whenever they fly, they help the crew clean the plane after the flight to ensure a quick turnaround time. In addition they have informal meetings with crewmembers to learn about issues and problems as crewmembers see them.[71] This management style continues to attract motivated new hires; JetBlue has a reputation as a great place to work, company profit sharing, high productivity of planes and people, and rapid advancements. In 2004 alone, JetBlue hired 1,700–1,800 people.[72]

The combined effort to provide exceptional service and instill a valued-employee culture will fulfill Neeleman's hope that JetBlue can "keep our folks fresh and keep our customers coming back."[73]

However, as proven by Delta's Song and the installation of leather seats in its planes, the "superior service" attributes can be imitated by competitors. What has also allowed JetBlue to remain one step ahead in its competitive environment is cost management.

Cost Management

JetBlue's cost-saving initiative includes electronic ticketing, paperless cockpits, and online check-in.[74] In order to achieve paperless cockpits, JetBlue supplied pilots and first officers with laptops to retrieve electronic flight manuals and make preflight load and balance calculations.[75] In the year following implementation of paperless cockpits, the company saved approximately 4,800 hours of labor.[76] One of JetBlue's more original strategies to cut costs is its

telephone reservation system. Reservation agents work from their homes in Salt Lake City, using personal computers equipped with VoIP technology. VoIP stands for Voice over Internet Protocol and utilizes the Internet to make free phone calls.[77] This system gives JetBlue flexibility to handle varying call volumes without needing a costly call center.[78]

JetBlue also uses technology to manage its marketing costs. JetBlue employs Omniture software to increase efficiency of Internet searches, decreasing associated search conversion costs by 94 percent.[79] By using animation in its television ads with its advertising agency, JetBlue produced eight ads for the standard price of one.[80]

Another value-adding initiative is BlueTurn, the name for JetBlue's ground operations. In an effort to improve the overall on-time performance statistics, BlueTurn allows crewmembers to minimize ground time and decrease the turnaround time for aircraft.[81]

JetBlue operates two aircraft types and a single travel class. This simplicity reduces training, maintenance, and operating costs relative to competitors that operate multiple aircraft types.

These cost-cutting strategies follow the standard low-cost, low-fare business model, without sacrificing the ultimate strategy of providing superior customer service with happy employees.

In order to best market its services, JetBlue has carefully considered its marketing approach.

Marketing Strategy

Neeleman believes that marketing is best accomplished by word of mouth; therefore top management aims to make sure that customers are treated well and employees feel valued.[82] Yet, they have made concerted efforts to market in other ways. To establish a media campaign, JetBlue hired J. Walter Thompson (JWT) as its advertising agency.[83] To create a fresh identity, JWT found candid statements by customers on JetBlue service. Online sources were consulted such as Craigslist and Epinions. The statements, written as short stories, were used to create eight different animated ads as testimonials to JetBlue's customer service. Other forms of direct marketing were used such as leather benches and snack bins in serviced airports. JetBlue also created comical postcards and distributed to customers to mail back their comments.[84]

In order to record customers' opinions on JetBlue service, an interactive video installation called the "JetBlue Story Booth" was set up in Rockefeller Center, and is traveling around the country to other cities served by JetBlue.[85] In the one-week New York exhibit, an estimated 20,000 people participated in the installation.[86] A vehicle called Blue Betty was created to simulate an airplane cabin and showcase in-flight amenities. As it traveled to various events across the country, visitors could enter a contest (or lottery) for ticket giveaways. JetBlue also used direct marketing to target college students with a public relations team called CrewBlue. This group used unconventional methods of posters, flyers, and chalk art to educate students about various aspects of the airline's services. Other marketing efforts include "Blue Days," where students were encouraged to wear blue and were rewarded with airline tickets through drawings. A 2005 survey indicated this marketing campaign was successful and increased JetBlue awareness by 41 percent.[87]

In addition to marketing initiatives, JetBlue on a consistent basis updates its business strategy to increase growth and revenue.

Current Strategies

In the first quarter of 2006, due to operating losses, JetBlue executives announced a turnaround plan called "Return to Profitability." Items included in this initiative were revisions to fare structures, corrections to flight capacity, and reprioritizing of flight segments (short, medium, and long haul).[88]

The growth rate has been slowed. The company expects to grow between 14 and 17 percent over the next year versus the 18 to 20 percent originally forecasted.[89]

JetBlue plans to fuel this growth by adding a number of flights on existing routes, connecting new city pairs among the destinations already served, and entering new markets usually served by higher-cost, higher-fare airlines. To determine which cities JetBlue should include in its flight pattern, executives study information made available from the Department of Transportation, which outlines the historical number of passengers, capacity, and average fares over time in all city-pair markets within North America.[90] This information along with JetBlue's historical data allows them to predict how a market will react to the introduction of JetBlue's service and lower prices.

JetBlue expects to use the new Embraer fleet to create demand in many midsized markets that could benefit from its point-to-point service.[91]

In addition, as mentioned previously, JetBlue is in the midst of some discussions about creating a partnership to enter the international market. Due to the limited type of aircraft in JetBlue's fleet, an alliance is the only way for JetBlue to capitalize on the international market opportunities, because its aircraft are not large enough to fly overseas.

The firm is also optimistic that recent moves to expand distribution channels will increase revenue. In August of 2006, the company signed a five-year agreement with Sabre Holdings and Galileo International. This arrangement will allow more than 52,000 travel agencies to purchase tickets for JetBlue travelers with a single connection. These deals are an attempt to reach a broader customer base, especially business travelers.[92]

Moreover, JetBlue is constantly striving to introduce new methods of providing superior customer service. As of March 2007 the first 11 rows in the cabin feature four inches of legroom between each row rather than the previous two inches.[93] To augment its flight services, JetBlue has established complementary products and services.

Associated Products and Services

In addition to air travel, JetBlue sells combined flight and hotel packages, which it terms "JetBlue Getaways." When JetBlue Getaways launched in November 2005, Tim Claydon, vice president of Sales and Marketing, commented, "By working with the hotels directly, rather than through an intermediary, we are able to offer our customers only the finest properties at great prices. Using the latest technology to combine the lowest JetBlue airfare with the best hotel or resort rate, we are able to offer our customers a new level of value with vacations beginning and ending on JetBlue Airways—something not available on any other online travel site."[94]

An American Express card was issued in 2005 called the "JetBlue Card," which earns TrueBlue points for members.[95] Customers earn TrueBlue points when purchasing flights, movie tickets, sporting event tickets, and gym memberships. When a customer amasses 100 TrueBlue points (equivalent to approximately five medium-length round trips), the customer earns a free round-trip valid for one year. In 2006, award travel accounted for only 2 percent of JetBlue's total revenue passenger miles.[96]

In order to sustain its business and corporate strategies, JetBlue monitors its financial situation regularly.

Financial Condition

JetBlue's current financial situation is highlighted by its short-term liquidity, long-term stability, and company profitability. Stockholder profitability signals whether JetBlue is meeting its stockholders' expectations.[97]

Short-Term Liquidity

JetBlue's balance sheet over the past five years is shown in Exhibit 2. JetBlue has struggled with financial performance since 2005. The growth of current liabilities from 2003 to 2006 is significant, compared to the growth of current assets. However, the payables turnover ratio has been increasing, which indicates that JetBlue has been able to pay its suppliers at a faster rate even though it has not been as efficient in collecting receivables as in years past. (Liquidity ratios are shown in Exhibit 9 and turnover ratios are shown in Exhibit 10.)

Long-Term Stability

Long-term financial stability will be an issue as JetBlue toils to consistently turn a profit. JetBlue has maintained

Exhibit 9 Liquidity Ratios

	2006	2005	2004	2003	2002
Current ratio	1.1	0.94	1.05	1.75	1.05
Quick ratio	1.05	0.91	1.03	1.72	1.03

Source: JetBlue Airways Corporation 2006 Annual Report.

Exhibit 10 Receivables and Payables

Receivables	2006	2005	2004	2003	2002
Receivable turnover	30.6	26	47.1	69.7	38.8
Days to collect	11.9	14.1	7.8	5.2	9.4

Payables	2006	2005	2004	2003	2002
Payable turnover	16.4	13.8	12.9	11.5	9.5
Days to pay		26.4	28.3	31.7	38.5

Source: JetBlue Airways Corporation 2006 Annual Report.

Exhibit 11 Stability Ratios

	2006	2005	2004	2003	2002
Debt/Asset ratio	0.8	0.8	0.7	0.7	0.7
Asset/Equity ratio	5.1	4	3.5	3.3	3.5
Debt/Equity (financial leverage)	4.1	3.3	2.7	2.3	2.3
Interest coverage ratio	0.7	0.7	2.7	8.4	7.1

Source: JetBlue Airways Corporation 2006 Annual Report.

Exhibit 12 Fuel Expenses

	2006	2005	2004	2003	2002
Operating revenue	$2363	$1701	$1265	$998	$635
Aircraft fuel	752	488	255	147	76
Aircraft fuel %	31	29	20	15	12
Other Costs % Revenue					
Salaries and benefits %	23	25	27	27	26
Aircraft rent %	4	4	6	6	6
Sales and Marketing %	4	5	5	5	7
Maintenance %	4	4	4	2	1

Source: JetBlue Airways Corporation 2006 Annual Report.

a fairly consistent debt-to-asset mix as most of the cash received from issuances has been invested in capital assets. The majority of JetBlue's issuances are floating rate bonds, exposing the firm to increases in the Federal Reserve's prime rate.[98] JetBlue's first quarter 2007 assets/equity ratio stood at 5.4 compared to the industry average of 3.[99] (See Exhibits 3 and 11 for details.)

Company Profitability

JetBlue's gross margins continued to decline in recent years, which can be mainly attributed to increasing fuel

Exhibit 13 Profitability

	2006	2005	2004	2003	2002
Gross margins	20%	27%	33%	40%	45%
Operating margins	5.4%	3%	9%	17%	17%
Net profit margins	0.4%	–1%	4%	10%	9%
Return on equity	0.97%	–2%	6%	19%	19%
Return on assets	2%	2%	3%	6%	6%

Source: JetBlue Airways Corporation 2006 Annual Report; 2007; http://www.finance.yahoo.com.

charges as shown in Exhibit 12. Salaries, landing fees, and other expenses remain fairly stable as a percent of revenues (most have actually decreased, see Exhibit 1). For 2006, gross margins remained 23 percent (see Exhibit 13). As stated earlier, interest expense has a negative effect on profitability.

Stockholder Profitability

In July 2007, the stock was trading at $11.01 versus $14.90[100] at the end of April 2002. In addition to the lackluster stock movement, JetBlue has never paid dividends, so the overall return for the past four years is 5.5 percent. According to moneycentral.com and Yahoo! Finance, the average analyst recommendation is "Hold" for JetBlue. The declining return on equity and inconsistency of net income appears to be having negative implications for JetBlue.

Strategic Challenges

JetBlue faces many challenges as it continues to operate in the highly competitive airline industry. The main challenges are maintaining JetBlue's culture as it grows, dealing with the surfacing complexities of two fleet types, managing maintenance expenses as airplanes and engines begin to age, and dealing with an increasingly senior labor pool. Although fuel prices are a concern, they affect the industry in the same way, and airlines have opportunities to mitigate these risks. Southwest hedged its fuel position more effectively than other airlines, but these hedges will expire and everyone will have a more level playing field when it comes to fuel prices.[101]

Maintaining the JetBlue culture will be difficult to do as the airline grows. The explosive increase in employees may hinder the ability to sustain high utilization and maintain a positive work environment. The time that top management has to interact with individual crewmembers will decrease. Neeleman stated that he would no longer be able to respond to every crewmember's e-mail.[102] This change will hinder a popular cultural component because the chairperson and CEO may no longer be seen as accessible.[103]

Multiple Aircraft Types

JetBlue will have a challenge as it continues to integrate two different types of aircraft. The firm suffered a setback when it incorporated the Embraer E190 into its fleet. JetBlue wanted to fly the new planes 14 hours a day, similar to its A-320s. However, the airplane characteristics were different from the Airbus.[104] Both pilots and mechanics needed additional time and training to understand the new plane. These factors caused flight delays and cancellations throughout the JetBlue system.[105] JetBlue had to reevaluate its plans.

Another issue associated with two types of aircraft is that JetBlue must staff two groups of pilots and flight attendants. The different aircraft require unique training and integration procedures. JetBlue will need separate inventories, training programs, and facilities to accommodate two fleet types.[106] In addition, the pay scales are different, which requires additional support from corporate employees.

Increased Maintenance Expenses

Maintenance expense will be a significant concern for JetBlue in coming years. As with a new car, new airplanes rarely need maintenance and when they do, they are covered under warranty. In 2004, JetBlue experienced a 94 percent increase in maintenance costs.[107] The increase in maintenance costs was not as significant in 2005 and 2006 at 36 percent and 42 percent, respectively (see Exhibit 1); however, as the large fleet of new planes comes due for heavy maintenance at the same time, JetBlue will experience a significant increase in maintenance costs.

Airplane operators have A, C, and D levels of scheduled maintenance and inspection intervals. A-checks occur every 400–500 hours and are similar to an oil change on a vehicle. C- and D-checks are more extensive, more expensive, and longer. The C-check schedule is every 18 months/6,000 hours/3,000 cycles.[108] Additionally, the fourth C-check consists of more inspections, and takes 10 days, compared to just 4 days for regular C-checks.[109] Furthermore, JetBlue decided to outsource maintenance to Air Canada Technical Services in Winnipeg, and Aeroman in El Salvador. Because these operations are not co-located with any of its scheduled service, JetBlue has to spend additional money ferrying planes and paying employees to work in these facilities. JetBlue spends "seven figures" each year in ferrying planes and as much as $700 per day extra for people to monitor the quality of work.[110] As JetBlue's planes enter more extensive service, the amount of time to ferry airplanes and actual maintenance will increase.

Engine expense is another huge maintenance cost for JetBlue. In July 2005, JetBlue signed a 10-year service agreement with a German company, MTU. It covers all scheduled and unscheduled repair for all A-320 engines.[111] At year-end 2006, JetBlue had more than 90 A-320 aircraft, and with two engines per plane and a healthy spares inventory, JetBlue has a significant number of engines to maintain (including its 23 E190 airplanes and engines).[112] Typical charges for a comparable engine overhaul range from $1 million to $1.5 million per heavy visit.

In addition to engines and airframes, airplane operators have additional equipment they must maintain and arrange for contract maintenance support. They have auxiliary power units, landing gear systems, environmental systems, avionics, and flight controls.

As the number of aircraft increases, the cost to maintain will increase. JetBlue may lose economies of scale because multiple aircraft types require multiple repair facilities, and they will have to employ and house multiple sets of inventory and people.

Increased Payroll Expenses

Payroll costs will multiply at JetBlue as the company ages. During 2006 salaries, wages, and benefits increased 29 percent, or $125 million, due primarily to an increased workforce (refer to Exhibit 1).[113] According to the Bureau of Transportation (see Exhibit 14), JetBlue experienced a 212 percent staff growth and ranks third among low-cost carriers for total number of employees in the United States.

Currently, all of the crewmembers are near the bottom of the pay scales, and JetBlue enjoys a relatively low-cost labor pool. However, as these people attain seniority with the company their pay level will increase.[114] Not only will salaried employees get annual pay raises, but crewmembers are paid for each hour flown, according to type of aircraft and depending on the number of years with the company (see Exhibit 15). A more senior staff means the company will start paying higher wages.

Because JetBlue desires to remain nonunionized, it will have to pay its employees well to ensure they do not become disgruntled and demand representation. Unions have not gained a foothold in JetBlue, but the Air Lines Pilot Association has JetBlue as a target. In addition to pilots, flight attendants, mechanics, ground crews, and gate agents will also receive pressure from other national unions for representation. If by chance the employees of JetBlue succumb to union pressure, union negotiators will then push for increased wages and other amenities—such as hotel requirements, time off, minimum number of flight hours per month, and so on—resulting in higher costs.

Exhibit 14 Low-Cost Carrier Full-Time Equivalent Employees, August 2002–2006

(Numbers in thousands)

Rank		2002	2003*	2004*	2005*	2006	Percent Change 2002–2006
1	Southwest	34	33	31	31	32	–4.5
2	America West	12	11	11	12	13	7.0
3	JetBlue	3	5	6	8	10	212.4
4	AirTran	5	5	6	6	7	56.9
5	Frontier	3	3	4	4	5	70.6
6	ATA	7	7	7	4	3	–61.5
7	Spirit	2	2	2	2	2	–14.4
8	Independence	N/A	4	4	3	N/A	N/A
	Total****	65	71	72	71	71	9.3

*Employment numbers in 2003, 2004, and 2005 for Independence Air, which changed its business model from a regional to low-cost carrier in mid-2004, are included with low-cost carriers. The carrier did not meet the standard for filing in previous years. The airline discontinued flights on January 5, 2006.

N/A = Not applicable because carriers did not meet the standard for filing.

Source: Bureau of Transportation Statistics.

Exhibit 15 Pay Scale Table

2004 Year	A-320 Captain	EMB190 Captain	A-320 FO	EMB190 FO
12	$126	$89	$76	$53
11	$126	$87	$76	$52
10	$126	$85	$76	$51
9	$125	$84	$75	$50
8	$124	$82	$74	$49
7	$123	$80	$74	$48
6	$122	$79	$73	$47
5	$121	$77	$72	$46
4	$118	$76	$67	$44
3	$116	$74	$61	$42
2	$113	$72	$56	$40
1	$110	$71	$51	$37

Note: Guarantee of 70 hrs/month; above 70 hours paid at 150%.

Source: 2006, Will fly for food, http://www.willflyforfood.cc/Payscales/PayScales.htm.

JetBlue's Challenge in Coming Years

David Neeleman started an airline based on previous experience and an entrepreneurial spirit. He knew what people wanted and how much they would pay for it. JetBlue attracted high-quality employees because of the unique culture that stressed customer service and differentiated offerings. Allowing at-home reservations agents, paperless cockpits, and crewmembers' easy access to executives has created an environment with which people want to associate. In addition, by purchasing brand new Airbus airplanes and having a junior staff, JetBlue has minimized labor and maintenance costs, both major operating expenses, for several years. As growth slows in the domestic market, its aircraft begin to age, and the workforce becomes more senior, the number of challenges will increase. Barger and Neeleman are faced with persistent questions about how to continue to grow the airline profitably. Does JetBlue attack Southwest, United, Delta, American, or Continental strongholds in the Midwest and/or smaller airports? Does it form an alliance in order to expand into international markets such as Europe and Asia? To minimize expenses related to airplanes, should JetBlue return to one airplane type? Finally, while unions are prevalent at every other airline, how can JetBlue maintain an environment where employees remain committed, dedicated, and satisfied?

Notes

1. 2002, JetBlue Airways Corporation, *International Directory of Company Histories,* Vol. 44. St. James Press. 2006, Reproduced in Business and Company Resource Center. Farmington Hills, Mich.: Gale Group.

2. M. Trottman & S. Carey, 2006, Legacy Airlines may outfly discount rivals, *Wall Street Journal,* October 30, C1.

3. T. Fredrickson, 2006, Middle-aged JetBlue finds it's harder to fly; Ballooning fuel costs, intense competition turn it into a loser, *Crain's New York Business,* February 13, 22(7):4.

4. J. Bernstein, 2006, JetBlue posts quarterly loss, *Newsday*, October 25.

5. J. H. Dobrzynski, 2006, We're still a growth airline, *Wall Street Journal*, November 4, A6.

6. JetBlue Airways Corporation, http://galenet.galegroup.com.ezproxy1 .lib.asu.edu/servlet/BCRC.

7. S. Overby, 2002, JetBlue skies ahead, *CIO Magazine*, http://www.cio .com, July 1.

8. 2006, Airbus, http://www.airbus.com/en/aircraftfamilies/a320/a320/.

9. S. Overby, JetBlue skies ahead.

10. Ibid.

11. 2002, JetBlue announces second quarter 2002 earnings—Low-fare carrier achieves record operating margin of 18.6%, JetBlue Airways Corporation press release, July 25.

12. 2002, JetBlue announces initial public offering of its common stock, JetBlue Airways Corporation press release, April 11.

13. 2005, JetBlue's New Terminal 5 will more than double airline's JFK capacity within three years, JetBlue Airways Corporation press release, December 7.

14. 2006, Fourth quarter of 2005, JetBlue Airways Corporation press release, February 1.

15. 2006, Third quarter of 2006, JetBlue Airways Corporation press release, October 24.

16. Ibid.

17. J. Bailey, 2007, JetBlue's C.E.O. is mortified after fliers are stranded, *New York Times*, http://www.nytimes.com, February 19; T. Keenan, 2007, JetBlue damage control, http://www.foxnews.com, February 27.

18. 2007, JetBlue announces the JetBlue Customer Bill of Rights, JetBlue Airways Corporation press release, February 20.

19. 2006, Air transportation, scheduled, *Encyclopedia of American Industries*, online ed., Thomson Gale.

20. 2006, Hoover's Company Records, JetBlue Airways Corporation, October 31.

21. R. M. Schneiderman, 2006, Legacy carriers fly back into favor, *Forbes*, http://www.forbes.com, October 20.

22. 2006, Air transportation, scheduled.

23. J. Schoen, 2006, Airline woes spark industry dogfight, http://www .msnbc.com, July 31.

24. 2006, Star Alliance, http://www.staralliance.com/en/travellers/index .html.

25. K. Iatrou & N. Skourias, 2005, An attempt to measure the traffic impact of airline alliances, *Journal of Air Transportation*, 10(3): 73–99.

26. C. Jones, 2006, JetBlue seeks international partnerships, *Deseret News*, Salt Lake City, March 16.

27. D. Rosato, 2006, How to score a cheap airline ticket, *CNNMoney*, http://www.cnnmoney.com, October 27.

28. 2007, US Airways withdraws offer for Delta Air Lines, press release, http://www.usairways.com, January 31.

29. C. Palmeri, D. Frost, & L. Woellert, 2006, Doug Parker wants to fly Delta, *BusinessWeek*, http://www.businessweek.com, November 16.

30. 2006, Southwest Airlines Co. Annual Report.

31. W. Zellner, 2005, Southwest: Dressed to kill . . . competitors, *BusinessWeek*, February 21.

32. R. E. Hoskisson, M. A. Hitt, & R. D. Ireland, 2003, *Competing for Advantage*, Mason, OH: South-Western, 24.

33. D. Reed, 2006, At 35, Southwest's strategy gets more complicated, *USA Today*, July 11.

34. 2006, Hoover's Company Reports: In-depth records, AMR Corporation, November 28.

35. 2006, AMR Corp Annual Report.

36. 2006, Hoover's Company Reports: In-depth records, UAL Corporation, November 28.

37. Ibid.

38. R. M. Schneiderman, 2006, Report: UAL looking to merge, *Forbes*, December 1.

39. C. Palmeri, D. Frost, & L. Woellert, 2006, Doug Parker wants to fly Delta.

40. 2006, USAirways Group, Inc. Annual Report.

41. 2006, Airline Domestic Market Share: September 2005–August 2006, *Bureau of Transportation Statistics—The Intermodal Transportation Database*, http://www.transtats.bts.gov/, December 6.

42. 2006, Hoover's Company Reports: In-depth records, Continental Airlines Inc., November 28.

43. R. Fozard, 2006, Continental's surprising ascent, *BusinessWeek*, July 31.

44. R. M. Schneiderman, 2006, Continental packs 'em in, *Forbes*, October 19.

45. 2006, Congressional testimony, *Congressional Quarterly, Inc.*, February 8.

46. Ibid.

47. Ibid.

48. E. Roston, 2005, Hedging their costs: Whether oil prices go up or down, smart airline companies are covered, *Time*, July 27.

49. 2005, Oil prices will prune revenue gains but Southwest, JetBlue look good, *Airline Business Report*, July 4, 23(12).

50. 2007, FAA aerospace forecast fiscal years 2007–2020, http://www .faa.gov/data_statistics/.

51. 2006, JetBlue Airways Corporation Form 10-K, Fiscal year ending December 31, 21.

52. C. Jones, 2006, JetBlue founder pushes for alternative fuel, http:// www.timesdispatch.com, November 15.

53. K. Johnson, 2005, Fuel hedging gets tricky, *Wall Street Journal*, May 19.

54. 2005, JetBlue Airways Corporation Form 10-K, Fiscal year ending December 31, 4.

55. Ibid, 9.

56. 2006, *Wall Street Journal* (Eastern edition), November 22.

57. 2005, JetBlue Airways Corporation Form 10-K, Fiscal year ending December 31, 2.

58. 2000, http://www.house.gov/transportation/aviation/hearing/ 12-05-00/12-05-00memo.html.

59. D. Bond, 2006, The FAA's demand-management plans for LaGuardia call for bigger aircraft, market-based slot turnover, *Aviation Week & Space Technology*, September 4.

60. 2005, JetBlue Airways Corporation Form 10-K, Fiscal year ending December 31, 69.

61. S. Overby, 2002, JetBlue skies ahead.

62. S. Lott, 2006, IAM fails in first attempt to organize JetBlue ramp staff, *Aviation Daily*, July 20.

63. 2006, Significant safety events since 2000 for JetBlue Airlines, AirSafe.com, LLC, http://www.airsafe.com, May 6.

64. J. Scott, 2005, http://www.aerospaceweb.org/question/planes/ q0245a.shtml, October 2.

65. R. Singal, 2003, Army admits using JetBlue data, Wired News, http:// www.wired.com, September 23.

66. 2002, United States District Court Eastern District of New York, Memorandum & Order, JetBlue Airways Corp: Privacy Litigation: 04-MD-1587 (CBA), http://www.epic.org/privacy/airtravel/jetblue/ decision_0705.pdf.

67. 2005, JetBlue Airways Corporation Form 10-K, Fiscal year ending December 31, 2.

68. 2006, JetBlue Announces 6.6 Percent Operating Margin for Third Quarter 2006, JetBlue Airways Corporation press release, October 24.

69. J. Miner, 2006, http://luxuryresorttravel.suite101.com/article/cfm./ jetblue_airways_pros_and_cons, November 13.

70. S. Salter, 2004, And now the hard part, *Fast Company*, http://www .fastcompany.com, May, 82: 67.

71. Ibid.

72. Ibid.

73. B. Harrell, 2005, http://www.yaleeconomicreview.com/issues/ fall2005/davidneeleman.

74. 2005, JetBlue Airways Corporation Form 10-K, Fiscal year ending December 31, 3.

75. S. Overby, JetBlue skies ahead.

76. Ibid.

77. R. Valdes, How VoIP works, http://electronics.howstuffworks.com/ ip-telephony.htm.

78. S. Salter, 2004, Calling JetBlue, *Fast Company*, http://www .fastcompany.com, May, 82.

79. 2005, JetBlue soars with Omniture Research Center, Omniture, Inc., http://www.omniture.com, December 2.

80. D. Sacks, 2006, Rehab: An advertising love story, *Fast Company*, http://www.fastcompany.com, June, 106.

81. Ibid.

82. B. Harrell, http://www.yaleeconomicreview.com/issues/fall2005/ davidneeleman.

83. 2005, JetBlue Airways Corporation Form 10-K, Fiscal year ending December 31, 3.

84. D. Sacks, Rehab: An advertising love story.

85. 2006, XS Lighting & sound lights JetBlue interactive kiosks, *Prism Business Media*, http://www.livedesignonline.com, June 7.

86. K. Prentice, Your client's ad, taking it to the streets, *Media Life Magazine*, Http://www.medialifemagazine.com, May 15.

87. Ibid.

88. 2005, JetBlue announces first quarter results, JetBlue Airways Corporation press release, April 1.

89. 2006, JetBlue announces 6.6 percent operating margin for third quarter, JetBlue Airways Corporation press release, October 24.

90. 2005, JetBlue Airways Corporation Form 10-K, Fiscal year ending December 31, 10.

91. Ibid.

92. R. M. Schneiderman, 2006, JetBlue courts Corporate America, *Forbes*, August 11.

93. D. Neeleman, 2006, http://www.jetblue.com/about/ourcompany/flightlog, December 14.

94. 2005, Introducing JetBlue getaways, JetBlue Airways Corporation press release, November 3.

95. 2005, JetBlue Airways Corporation Form 10-K, Fiscal year ending December 31, 1.

96. 2006, JetBlue Airways Corporation Form 10-K, Fiscal year ending December 31, 19.

97. Financial Accounting Module 3.

98. 2005, JetBlue Airways Corporation Form 10-K, Fiscal year ending December 31, 17.

99. 2006, Industry data from www.moneycentral.msn.com.

100. 2006, Yahoo! Finance, http://finance.yahoo.com/q/hp?s=JBLU&a=03&b=18&c=2001&d=10&e=30&f=2006&g=m.

101. K. Prentice, 2006, After backing away, some airlines turning to fuel hedging again, Associated Press State & Local Wire, September 4.

102. S. Salter, On the runway, *Fast Company*, http://www.fastcompany.com, May (82).

103. S. Salter, And now the hard part, 67.

104. D. Reed, 2006, Loss shifts JetBlue's focus to climbing back into black, http://www.usatoday.com, Feb 22.

105. Ibid.

106. M. Bobelian, 2003, JetBlue lands expansion plans, *Forbes*, http://www.forbes.com, June 10.

107. T. Reed, 2006, TheStreet.com, http://www.thestreet.com/stocks/transportation/10260392.html, January 6.

108. 2006, *Aircraft Technology, Engineering & Maintenance*, October/November, 99.

109. 2005, McGraw-Hill Companies *Overhaul & Maintenance*, Magazine for MRO Management, October 2.

110. Ibid, 5.

111. 2006, JetBlue Airways Corporation, Form 10-Q, October 24.

112. *Aircraft Technology Engineering & Maintenance*, 101.

113. 2006, JetBlue Airways Corporation Form 10-K, Fiscal year ending December 31, 41.

114. T. Reed, http://www.thestreet.com.

Case 14

Lufthansa: Going Global, but How to Manage Complexity?

Simon Tywuschik, Ulrich Steger

International Institute for Management Development

In the glamorous, but financially not so glorious, airline industry, Lufthansa is one of the three companies world-wide whose debt is rated as investment-grade. For most of the other companies, if they are not already in bankruptcy procedures or being bailed out by the government, the financial situation is simply a nightmare. Since World War II the industry has never earned its cost of capital over the business cycle. Especially after the de-regulation (beginning in 1978 in the United States), which increasingly replaced the government-organized IATA cartel,[1] the situation got worse. By 2005, the cumulative losses of airlines since 2001 amounted to about US$40.7 billion.[2] As mergers are still legally prevented across many country borders, the airlines' response to globalization was to form alliances (refer to Exhibit 1 for an overview).

Lufthansa is the leading, probably pivotal, member of the largest alliance, the Star Alliance. If globalization means increasing complexity (refer to Exhibits 2 and 3 for the characteristics of globalization and how it relates to complexity), alliances are even more complex to manage than individual companies because they lack the hierarchical conflict resolution mechanisms that individual companies can employ.

But despite their pride in mastering the turmoil of the past, some nagging questions remain for Lufthansa's management as the globalization of the airline industry moves full speed ahead.

- Is the current strategy sufficient to maintain Lufthansa's position as one of the few profitable airline companies, given the uncertainties and dynamics in the highly competitive but cyclical market?
- Has Lufthansa done enough to reduce complexity in the right places and to survive the competition, especially against the background of customer satisfaction and high value added?
- Are all employees in the corporation embraced culturally?
- Is Lufthansa prepared for the sustainability challenges—in particular global warming—which create new uncertainties?

Exhibit 1 Key Facts for the Main Airline Alliances

Key Features	Star Alliance	One World	Sky Team
Year of formation	1997	1999	2000
Members	18	8	10
Passengers (in millions)	425	258	373
Destinations	842	605	728
Fleet Size	2800	2161	2151
Market Share (Rev.)	28.4%	15.8%	23.9%
Headquarters	Frankfurt (Ger)	Vancouver (Can)	None
Organization type	Formalized organization	Governing Board	Committee

Sources: Web sites of the alliances, 2006; PATA, 2006. www.staralliance.com; www.oneworld.com; www.skyteam.com.

Research Associate Simon Tywuschik prepared this case under the supervision of Professor Ulrich Steger as a basis for class discussion rather than to illustrate either effective or ineffective handling of a business situation. This case has been compiled purely from public sources. Copyright © 2006 by IMD, International Institute for Management Development, Lausanne, Switzerland.

Exhibit 2 The Six Features of Globalization

Feature	Explanation
(1) Eroding Borders	Never before in history have so many boundaries in the social, political, and economic realm been weakened or abolished. However, boundaries fulfill two core functions: First, they contain effects (inside a certain entity); and second, they define the difference between "us" and others (identify creation). As a consequence of the erosion of boundaries, complexity increases (see also Exhibit 3).
(2) Mobility	The erosion of boundaries facilitates greater mobility of goods, capital, knowledge/technology, and people.
(3) Heterarchy	Organizations across all industries are not structured hierarchically (top down), but rather heterarchically (i.e., changing dependencies and interdependent influencing channels are common). Due to the interdependency between different organizational layers, the process of power exertion has become more costly.
(4) Erosion of Legitimacy	Because it is almost impossible to clearly identify one-way cause-and-effect relationships within complex systems, responsibilities (institutional as well as personal) are difficult to establish. This process leads to the erosion of legitimacy within many organizations, in particular of democratically elected governments. Although they can no longer provide for the welfare of nation states, they remain the only addressee of the voter, which therefore leads to disenchantment with politics.
(5) Variety of Options	In complex systems no foreseeable and stable structures are evident (from a person's choice of profession to a global player's determination of corporate strategy), but the number of options can (on a personal and institutional level) also lead to information overload and failure (anxiety).
(6) Asymmetry between Past and Future	Asymmetry between past and future: The future is not a smooth continuation of the past; rather abrupt breaks are characteristic of development of the economic, social, and political spheres.

Exhibit 3 Complexity and Consequences for Corporations

	Situation	Challenge	Approach
Definition and Key Concepts	In systems theory, complexity is defined by the number of different potential states of a system that depend on certain complexity drivers (see below for drivers).	Ashby's Law of Variety suggests that organizations can handle high external complexity only by a similar internal complexity. The internal implementation of such complexity would create problems particularly for multi-business line corporations. Hence, these corporations look for drivers that *decrease* complexity (see below).	The more open and globally spread out a system is, the greater the velocity of change. The main challenge of corporations is to manage complexity. A global company must be characterized by certain features in order to manage complexity and survive competition (see below).
Key Drivers and Features	• Difference and diversity of values, aims, interests, cultures, and types of behaviors. • Interdependence that provides for greater interaction. • Ambiguity of situations and of information in its meaning. • Fast flux: Through eroding borders, the number of actors and interdependencies increases. The different interests and information uncertainty increase the number and intensity of actions that influence a system. It means that adjustment processes occur continuously, which again cause interventions.	• A common business culture and values and one clearly formulated and focused business strategy should help to establish one clear direction. • Standardized processes decrease variations (and hence complexity) in the course of business and create more transparency. • Focus on certain activities (such as "core" competencies). • Decentralization of decision power reduces the need for coordination (and hence of interaction) and early warning systems allow for more time to adjust.	• Activities in several world regions provide for a certain homogeneity of demand on the one hand and advantages for corporations on the other hand, among others economies of scale. • One global strategy for the fulfillment of common aims. • Employees of different ethical and professional backgrounds. • Standardized norms and processes.

Surviving the Changes in the Airline Industry

In 1992 Lufthansa—similar to other airlines—was close to bankruptcy, as the first Iraq war reduced international air traffic. It became obvious that the massive European and global expansion strategy that Lufthansa had been pursuing since the early 1980s was not economically viable (refer to Exhibits 4 and 5 for an overview of passenger sales and growth rate).

The fixed costs were too high for a cyclical business. On the other hand, strong reasons supported the belief that the "network effect" and economies of scale were leading to a global airline industry, dominated by a handful of key players (similar to the car industry).

However, the deregulation process had not gone far enough to allow for major mergers (in the United States, foreigners can own only 25 percent of an airline; in the EU non-European ownership is limited to 49 percent; in most of Asia any acquisition of a major airline might not be illegal, but it is practically impossible). But deregulation and the erosion of the IATA cartel went far enough to allow for scores of new competitors. No-frills low-cost airlines spread from the United States to Europe and

Exhibit 4 Lufthansa's Passenger Transportation Turnover by Region, 1980, 1990, and 2000

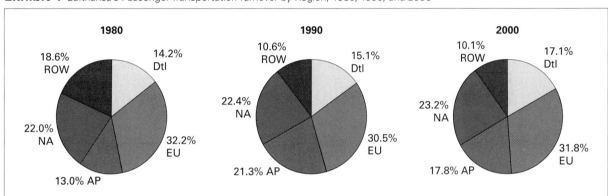

Note: Data for 1980 and 1990 also include cargo and mail services. Data for 2000 excludes CityLine.

Abbreviations: NA = North America; AP = Asia Pacific; ROW = Rest of the World; EU = Europe; Dtl = Germany

Sources: Lufthansa's annual reports; author's calculations.

Exhibit 5 Lufthansa's Annual Turnover Growth Rate in Passenger Transportation, 1981–2005

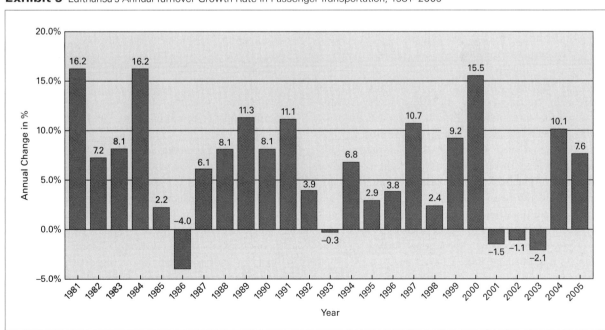

Note: From 1995, only passenger revenue is considered (excludes mail and cargo). Figures represent net sales.

Sources: Lufthansa's annual reports from 1981 to 2005; author's calculations.

then Asia, nurtured by the abundance of used aircraft and leasing opportunities (e.g., easyJet was started with less than £5 million). Unlike the "flag carriers," with their hubs, they offered point-to-point connections on high traffic density routes. Also business class passengers were targeted with new offerings (such as Virgin Airlines). Overcapacity and persisting government subsidies (especially in southern Europe, Asia, and Latin America) combined to create permanent price pressure: From the early 1990s, a minimum of 3 percent reduction in costs was needed every year, which was likely to continue.

Economic and political developments did not have a positive effect on the airline industry either. After recovering from the effects of the first Iraq war, air traffic was once again slowed down by the Asian financial crisis—starting in 1997—followed by similar events in Russia and Latin America. However, everything the airline industry had experienced so far was dwarfed when terrorists used airplanes as flying bombs on September 11, 2001.

The succeeding "War on Terror"—especially the second Iraq war—along with spreading tensions through the Middle East and the SARS scare delivered a three-year nightmare for the industry, which was in a cyclical business downturn anyway: Worldwide air passenger volumes fell by 3.3 percent and 2.4 percent in 2001 and 2003, respectively, and remained flat in 2002.[3] Lufthansa's traffic turnover even decreased between 2001 and 2003 by 4.6 percent.[4] Then, once passenger demand began to recover, oil prices escalated dramatically in 2005–2006. Currently, fuel costs are the second-highest cost category per seat kilometer, accounting for 26 percent of operating costs in Europe airlines (labor costs account for approximately 30 percent).[5]

Add in the issue above and the traffic jams and queues at major airports—which makes high-speed trains a more attractive alternative for journeys up to 500 kilometers—and a picture emerges. As such, the airline industry appears as a "high-growth–low-profit" industry. Everybody expects air traffic to grow—despite a highly volatile environment—but nobody expects a similar surge in profits. Because airline companies are now mostly privatized (Lufthansa since 1996, with about 40 percent held by diverse foreign owners), they have to fight for survival on their own. The bankruptcies of Swissair and Varig, for example, and the financial difficulties of Japan Airlines (JAL) indicate that the former flag carriers cannot bank on governments coming to their rescue. The fate of Pan Am—once the dominant international carrier and now defunct—is a sobering lesson for everyone.

Lufthansa: Continued Challenges

Since Lufthansa's turnaround in 1992–1993, in only one year have no new cost-cutting initiatives been launched, implemented, or (after 2001) even accelerated. In fact, a certain management routine on how to implement and control such cost-cutting initiatives has even been established. Compared to 1992, the cost base has been reduced by approximately 40 percent, despite rising wages, security and airport fees and the roller coaster of fuel prices.

Lufthansa needed to ensure cash flow (especially after 2001), and it needed to reduce costs (e.g., by hiring foreign crew members). Lufthansa transformed fixed costs into variable costs (by outsourcing), and rationalized every step in the value chain, especially via electronic processes which is very tricky when it comes to interfacing with the customer.

The "art" of the endeavor was to push the cost-cutting through, without losing consensus with the employees—who, like everywhere in the industry, are highly unionized[6]—and the strong work-councils, who had several levers to derail the whole process or at least slow it down considerably. With one exception of the strike in early summer 2001 by the pilots who have a separate union and felt "disrespected," the magic worked. But employers always face the risk of a "burn out" syndrome, when everybody asks: Will this ever stop?

However, sometimes Lufthansa executives think that cost-cutting is easier, relatively speaking, than managing the Star Alliance (refer to Exhibit 6 for an overview of its 18 members), now the biggest of the global airline alliances, with 28.4 percent market share and 842 destinations in 152 countries.[7] Many think of Lufthansa as the leader and integrator, because the biggest member, United Airlines, was preoccupied for more than three years with emerging from Chapter 11 bankruptcy procedures in the United States.[8] From the beginning, Lufthansa's strategy was to drive the Star Alliance from the revenue side by keeping more passengers in the network. This idea of "seamless" travel is implemented through "code-sharing," coordinated flight schedules, common lounges, baggage handling, and so forth, leading to a higher utilization of planes and infrastructure (lower cost per unit), and sometimes also to economies of scale in purchasing and sales.

A constant balancing act is necessary between the alliance members' independence (including the right to leave) and the need for common processes, especially in IT, and quality insurance. Another constant point of debate centers on the needs and expectations of global customers. Are they the same or do they differ by culture (e.g., in terms of greeting during the boarding process)? A crisis of individual members (especially Varig and United) could endanger the whole alliance, and Lufthansa was pushed to save Air Canada from bankruptcy in 1999, but could not prevent the Australian partner Anselt from going out of service (Varig and United still flew during the bankruptcy process and received only technical aid from Lufthansa). In any case, Lufthansa management

Exhibit 6 Global Airline Alliances and Their Members

STAR ALLIANCE THE AIRLINE NETWORK FOR EARTH.	oneworld	SKYTEAM
1. Air Canada	1. AerLingus	1. Aeroflot
2. Air New Zealand	2. American Airlines	2. Aeromexico
3. ANA	3. British Airways	3. Air France/ KLM
4. Asiana Airlines	4. Cathy Pacific	4. Alitalia
5. Austrian Airlines	5. Finnair	5. Continental
6. bmi	6. Iberia	6. Czech Airlines
7. LOT Polish Airlines	7. LAN	7. Delta
8. Lufthansa	8. Qantas	8. Korean Air
9. SAS Scandinavian Airlines		9. Northwest
10. Singapore Airlines		
11. South African Airways		
12. Spanair		
13. SWISS		
14. TAP Air Portugal		
15. Thai Airways International		
16. United		
17. US Airways		
18. Varig		
Market Share: 28.4%	**Market Share: 15.8%**	**Market Share: 23.9%**

Note: The membership structure of the alliances and market share undergo continuous changes.

Sources: Web sites of alliances, 2006; PATA, 2006. www.stralliance.com; www.oneworld.com; www.skyteam.com.

tries to avoid too much involvement in the affairs (and risks) of the other airline members and creates the perception that Lufthansa is seeking a role as a dominant force (e.g., looking for shareholdings in other airlines), a factor that contributed considerably to the downfall of SWISS in 2001. However, when its new incarnation, SWISS, was "up for grabs" in 2005, Lufthansa violated this principle and acquired the airline to prevent it falling into the hands of arch rival British Airways and the OneWorld Alliance. And more acquisitions may be in the cards: Lufthansa maintains 10 percent of its own shares (the legal maximum) for the purpose of a "reserve."

For Lufthansa—trained in the art of consensus more than others—it seems to be easier to accept only an 80 percent workable solution, if everybody is behind it and has bought into the compromise. Nevertheless, it was a learning process over several years; many compromises ran counter to a Lufthansa culture that takes pride in engineering excellence and maintaining standards, not only in back-office processes like IT, but also with customer interfaces (e.g., Lufthansa thought that the electronic check-in should be completed in half the time than the other alliance members found acceptable for their customers). Sometimes alliance initiatives run counter to the interests of Lufthansa divisions: The idea of creating a common Star Alliance IT infrastructure would rob the IT systems' divisions of most of their customers.

Despite the time-consuming negotiation and consensus-building processes in the Star Alliance management superstructure (refer to Exhibit 7) and despite the higher transaction costs, Lufthansa executives remained strong supporters of the alliance. The reason is quite simple: Because no alternatives (mostly M&As) are (legally) available, alliances are the only way to operate in a global network without increasing one's own investments in an economically unsustainable way (a lesson learned the hard way). It is estimated that for Lufthansa the net operating profit increase through the Star Alliance is about €500 million per year, which roughly corresponds to the profits for 2005. Hence, in the overall profitability equation for flag carriers, the regional business seems to fulfill a marketing activity for international routes rather than being a profit source of its own.

Exhibit 7 Organizational Structure of Star Alliance

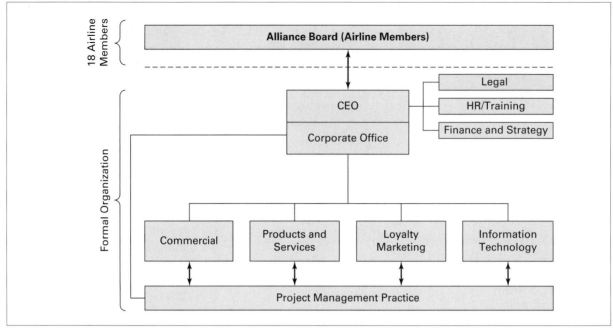

Source: Star Alliance, 2005. http://www.staralliance.com.

Exhibit 8 Structure of Lufthansa Holding and Lufthansa Regional

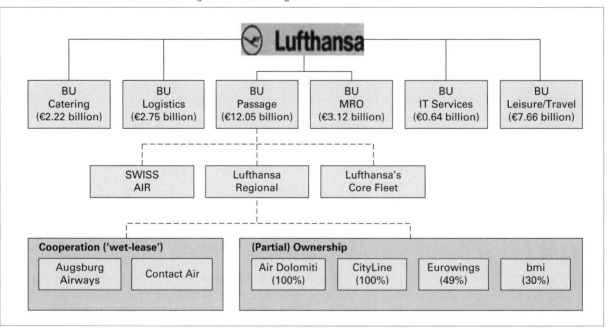

Note: Revenue figures refer to 2005.

Source: Company information, 2006. http://www.lufthansa.com.

Although the Star Alliance is great for intercontinental and business travel, it does not provide an answer to the onslaught of the low-cost carriers. Alongside some second-tier partnerships outside the Star Alliance, Lufthansa created "Lufthansa Regional" (refer to Exhibit 8 for the organizational structure), which carries out approximately 50 percent of the company's German and European flights. Within Lufthansa Regional, Eurowings and CityLine (partially) belong to the Lufthansa Group.[9] However, the planes from the other partners are operated via "wetleasing," whereby Lufthansa leases the aircraft complete with crew and maintenance contracts. In this case the planes are

181

Case 14 • Lufthansa: Going Global, but How to Manage Complexity?

integrated into Lufthansa's scheduling and the company carries the risk of the revenue side only.

Operating in a high-price competitive market, Lufthansa Regional needs a lower-cost structure than Lufthansa's core fleet. The cost savings at Lufthansa Regional come partly from the slightly lower wages, the smaller planes adjusted to the traffic density, a reduced service level, an operating base in second-tier airports, and point-to-point-service so that the time in the air is greater than for "network" airplanes. On the revenue side, Lufthansa gains through the "feeder function" to intercontinental flights (otherwise passengers might go via other big hubs) and the density of the connections: Only a few attractive routes can be developed by low-cost carriers without facing competition from the outset directly with Lufthansa (and its ability to cut prices when needed, a source of continuous controversy with the antitrust authorities).

However, as compelling as the business logic for Lufthansa Regional may appear to financial and industry analysts, the "two-class society" is a cause of friction and ongoing tension among the employees, as well as sometimes irritating to customers because of the different service standards, which are not matched in price differences. Another ongoing debate concerns in which category the newly acquired SwissAir belongs. Is it a low-cost provider or an equal partner in the Star Alliance? Often SWISS deliberately competes in its marketing efforts with the no-frill sector; on other occasions it refers to its tradition as a premium airline.

Can Organization Provide Stability?

Since 1996 Lufthansa has been organized as a holding with six business lines (refer to Exhibit 9 for a brief description), dissolving the once "integrated" corporation. Although "Passage" is dominant, with approximately two-thirds of the turnover, each division is fully responsible for its own financial results and any interactions with other group companies occur on market price terms. However, as in every decentralized organization, the holding company needs to unite its businesses under one "strategy

Exhibit 9 Evolution of the Organizational Structure of Lufthansa

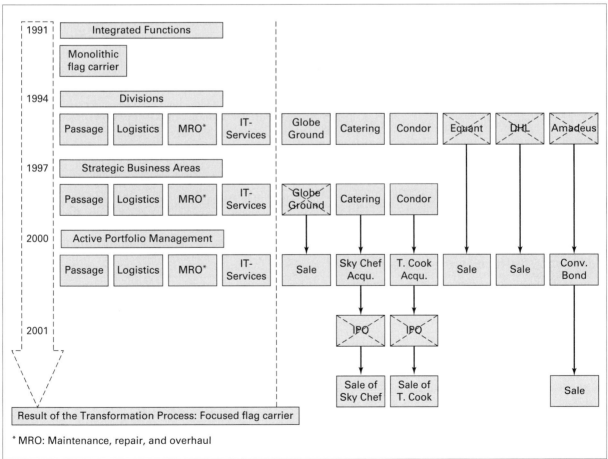

Sources: Company information; author's illustration, 2006.

182

Case 14 ▪ Lufthansa: Going Global, but How to Manage Complexity?

roof," avoiding "silos" and any duplication of functions. These goals might have been the drivers at Lufthansa for a more focused corporate strategy, the sale of Ground Globe (airport ground service) and several financial divestments (e.g., the shareholding in the reservation system Amadeus). Then, just at the very end of 2006, Lufthansa sold its 50 percent stake in Thomas Cook, the tourism company into which Lufthansa integrated its charter airline Condor, for €800 million to KarstadtQuelle.[10] And finally, even more might be for sale with LSG Sky Chefs (catering) when its turnaround is finalized (some parts of LSG Sky Chefs have been sold).

The permanent attempt to remove intermediaries is representative of the focus not only on cost cutting but also on streamlining the business model. In 2005 Lufthansa abolished any discount on its tickets for independent travel agencies (they now have to charge their customers for issuing tickets) and promotes direct booking via the Web or call centers or controlled distribution channels (e.g., LH City Centers, a franchise travel agency chain with 540 offices in 49 countries as of 2006).

Above All: Maintaining Financial Discipline

Every business cycle challenges the precious investment-grade rating that Lufthansa enjoys. In the crisis from 2001 to 2004, the gearing increased from 36 percent in 2000 to 85.4 percent in 2005, despite an increase in shareholder capital.[11] As a result, financial operating goals are dominant and Lufthansa has learned to focus its cost cutting on the cash flow impact. Depreciation of airplanes is higher than British Airways for example (12 vs. 20 years) to ensure a rapid capital recovery and reduce debt service as quickly as possible. Leasing part of the fleet allows for quicker adjustment of capacity (after 2001 approximately 20 percent of plane capacity was taken out of operation; now it is building up again).

Corporate Culture in Transition

Lufthansa was once known for its strong culture, based on pride in being a "Lufthanseat," the positive image of the company in Germany and its reputation for engineering excellence, underpinned by ongoing training and educational activities. Now approximately one-third of the workforce is non-German, and it has become more fragmented in its interests, perceptions, communication channels, and expectations. The pilots' strike in 2001, which put the pilots in confrontation with the ground personnel (who suffered the brunt of passenger anger), was not only about money. It was also about the pilots' feeling that they were no longer sufficiently appreciated, a lack of integration into the "normal" flow of communication and consensus building.

Management has tried to improve the situation; ongoing "town hall" meetings with members of the management board and the CEO are held, as well as an extensive written communication flow about the development of the company. Such initiatives are state-of-the-art in the industry today and Lufthansa has included them in the "leadership values" for its employees. As a result, every employee has individual targets and managers of all levels are evaluated on an annual basis (in a dialogue with his/her boss).

Continuous education and training is also high on the agenda, not only for employees but also for management. Among German-based companies, Lufthansa pioneered a "corporate university" in 1998. The "Lufthansa School of Business" is recognized worldwide as one of the best in the industry.

To increase employees' identification with the company and to help passengers "feel valued" (despite the high fuel consumption), Lufthansa is embarking on a wide range of social and environmental activities—from supporting children in need (via the "Help Alliance") to protecting endangered animals and recycling or introducing fuel efficiency initiatives (see http://konzern.lufthansa.com/en/html/ueber_uns/balance/index.html).

But Lufthansa management knows that past efforts are now being challenged by an issue of a completely new dimension—global warming. Although the airline industry claims that only 3 percent of global CO_2 emissions come from air traffic, the whole impact on global warming is approximately twice that factor (e.g., through NOx emissions at high altitude) and rapidly growing. Given current growth rates, the share of CO_2 emissions from air traffic might increase to approximately 20 percent by 2020.

Unlike many other energy sources in developed countries, fuel for airlines is not taxed—a point constantly raised in public criticism. So far the industry has avoided taxation because it would require some sort of international agreement, but the pressure is rapidly growing to price the "externalities" of air transport into travel costs. The industry is considering a kind of emission trading to avoid taxation, but even this approach would increase fuel prices considerably and may end the era of "cheap flights."

183

Case 14 • Lufthansa: Going Global, but How to Manage Complexity?

Notes

1. As of 2006, IATA (International Air Transport Association) represents 261 airlines comprising 94 percent of international scheduled air traffic.

2. IATA, 2006. The figure represents the sum of the net profits between 2001 and 2005 for all IATA member companies. These are (in US$ billion): −13.0 (2001), −11.3 (2002), −7.6 (2003), −5.6 (2004), −3.2 (2005). The estimated value for 2006 is US$ −1.7 billion.

3. Datamonitor, Airline Report, 2005; IATA Air Transport Statistics, 2001, 2002, and 2003.

4. Lufthansa's annual reports between 2000 and 2003. These figures represent the total passage revenue (including cargo and mail), which dropped from €12.55 billion for the year 2000 to €11.66 billion for the year 2003.

5. IATA, 2005, 2006. In the United States and Asia, the share of labor costs in operating costs is 38 percent and 20 percent, respectively.

6. Furthermore, in Lufthansa's case the chairman of the (Civil) Service and Transportation Union is the deputy chairman of the supervisory board due to the co-determination law.

7. Star Alliance; PATA, November 2006. PATA data are calculated on the basis of IACO data.

8. The formal bankruptcy procedure began on December 9, 2002, and closed on February 1, 2006.

9. The low-cost airline Germanwings is a 100% subsidiary of Eurowings.

10. Before this deal, KarstadtQuelle held the other 50% of Thomas Cook. Further, the deal that was announced in December 2006 makes Lufthansa a minority stakeholder in Condor.

11. Gearing is calculated as the ratio of a company's long-term funds with fixed interest to its total capital. A high gearing is generally considered speculative.

Case 15

Microsoft's Diversification Strategy

Ali F. Farhoomand, Samuel Tsang

University of Hong Kong

Since the early 2000s, a string of bad news had seriously undermined the future growth of Microsoft. The delay in rolling out the new version of the Windows operating system ("OS") announced in June 2005 further reinforced the prevailing impression that the software giant was in strategic disarray. In late 2005, Bill Gates finally announced a long-awaited corporate strategy to revamp the software giant. By formally recognizing the emerging business opportunities introduced by the new Internet era (Web 2.0),[1] Microsoft began to reinvent itself. It restructured key business units, streamlined decision-making processes, and realigned itself to become more nimble in producing software. The restructuring initiative was undertaken in tandem with the company's new diversification strategy of moving beyond the personal computer (PC) software business and into other devices such as mobile phones, television setup boxes, and game consoles.

In November 2005, Microsoft launched Xbox 360, its latest game console. It was an extraordinary event, not because of the glamorous business executives and journalists attending the event, the cool festival mood soaking Mojave Desert, or the graphic technologies dazzling the giant consoles surrounding the conference room. Rather, the air was filled with a mix of trepidation and excitement about the viability of the company's new strategy of moving beyond Windows-based PCs. Everybody in the room wondered whether Microsoft could regain its past glory by wading into new territories. What opportunities and challenges, they thought, awaited it in markets where it did not have proprietary advantage? What specific strategies would it adopt to capitalize on these opportunities and counter the challenges? How best could Microsoft execute its diversification strategy?

Brief History of Microsoft

In 1975, Bill Gates founded Microsoft in Albuquerque, New Mexico, after dropping out of Harvard. He partnered with Paul Allen to sell a version of BASIC, a programming language that the duo had written for Altair (the first commercial microcomputer) when Gates was still at Harvard. In 1979, Microsoft relocated to Seattle and began to develop software that helped users write their own programs. In 1980, IBM selected Microsoft to develop the operating system for its PCs. Subsequently, Microsoft bought QDOS, or "quick and dirty operating system," for US$50,000 from a Seattle programmer, and renamed it the Microsoft Disk Operating System (MS-DOS).

In 1983, Allen developed Hodgkin's disease and left the start-up. In the mid-1980s, Microsoft introduced Windows, a graphics-based version of MS-DOS that borrowed features from its rival Apple's Macintosh system. In 1986, Microsoft went public and Gates became the industry's first billionaire. In 1993, Microsoft introduced Windows NT to compete with UNIX, a popular operating system on minicomputers.

As Microsoft continued to dominate the desktop software market and expanded aggressively into other industry sectors, the U.S. Justice Department filed antitrust charges in 1998 against the software company, claiming that Microsoft had stifled Internet browser competition and limited consumer choice. The courts initially ruled in 2000 that Microsoft be split up into two companies. Subsequently, a tentative settlement was reached between the company and the U.S. Justice Department. The settlement left Microsoft intact, but imposed restrictions on the licensing policies for its operating systems. More specifically, Microsoft agreed to uniformly license its operating systems and allowed computer manufacturers

Samuel Tsang prepared this case under the supervision of Prof. Ali F. Farhoomand for class discussion. This case is not intended to show effective or ineffective handling of decision or business processes. © 2006 by The University of Hong Kong. This material is used by permission of The Asia Case Research Centre at The University of Hong Kong (http://www.acrc.org.hk). No part of this publication may be reproduced or transmitted in any form or by any means-electronic, mechanical, photocopying, recording, or otherwise (including the internet)—without the permission of The University of Hong Kong.

to include rivals' software with Windows. In addition, Microsoft also reached settlement agreements with major players (e.g., Netscape, Sun Microsystems, and IBM) in the market owing to the antitrust investigation. While Microsoft was settling the majority of its antitrust issues, an ongoing investigation was pending by the European Union (EU). In March 2004, the EU fined Microsoft and ordered it to offer European computer manufacturers a stripped down version of Windows by taking out its media player software. Microsoft announced plans to appeal the decision.[2]

With the growing importance of the networked economy, Microsoft was initially reluctant to adopt the Internet. Not until 1995 did it found Microsoft Network (MSN), a Web portal that offered a wide range of services. Like many other established IT companies, Microsoft experienced its toughest economic downturn due to the burst of the dot.com bubble. Although Microsoft recovered, its near-monopoly on PC operating systems and basic office software had been challenged by a string of start-ups. These new competitors were able to churn out popular programs such as e-mail, desktop search engines, and instant messaging over the Internet much faster than Microsoft. Such sluggishness in new product development was caused by Microsoft's inefficient approach. In particular, its flagship product, Windows, had been developed as a massive program that was stitched together into one gigantic computer program. The code base of Windows had become complex, and extremely

difficult to build and test. And in fact, the next generation of Windows (namely Vista) was two years behind its original schedule when it was rolled out in 2006. It would also mark the longest interval between two versions of Windows.[3]

In view of antitrust regulation in the United States and European Union, and increasing competition in the desktop software market, Microsoft was determined to move beyond the PC software industry. Its strategy was to extend its software products into Web-based services for businesses and consumers. By transforming itself from a traditional software provider to a broader technology services and media company, Microsoft aimed to position its operating systems, software, and services as a de facto standard for accessing, communicating, and doing business over the Internet.

Development Factors in the Emerging IT Industry

According to a study conducted by McKinsey & Co. in 2004 on IT spending trends, chief information officers (CIOs) from the *Fortune* 500 companies would spend money differently after the burst of the dot.com bubble. Although IT spending had increased since 2003 after three years of decline (see Exhibit 1), customers would expect to get more out of their technology investments. Companies had been more concerned about the value of IT and enforced stringent rules and guidelines for IT spending. For instance, procurement departments became more involved in the IT purchasing process, and in particular, for the commodity products such as PCs and desktop software. Many had applied formal bidding mechanisms that required vendors to go through a competitive process in finalizing the complex deals. In addition, chief executive officers (CEOs) became more demanding of the return on investment (ROI) on new technology spending. As a result, CIOs were required to develop stronger business cases to support their investments, and tie the overall performance of IT to their personal performance measures. Subsequently, the growth of overall IT spending was expected to be more modest (amount 4 percent to 6 percent) from 2003 onwards. This would be far below the double-digit figures of the heydays in the 1990s.[4]

The IT industry was considered to be in the midst of an eight-year period of "technology digestion." Hence, senior managers had become reluctant to make major technology investments. Forrester Research Inc., a technology and market research firm, explained "technology digestion" as follows: Investment in IT had continued to increase since 1956. In the United States, the ratio of IT investment to gross domestic product (GDP)

Exhibit 1 Aggregate Capital Expenditure of U.S. Companies on IT (US$ billion)

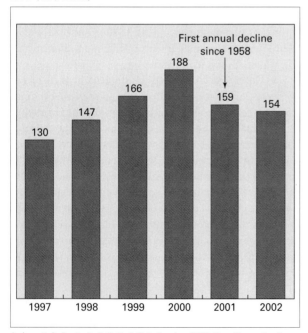

Source: K. B. Davis, A. S. Rath, & B. L. Scanlon, 2004, How IT spending is changing, *McKinsey Quarterly*.

Exhibit 2 Stages of Technology Innovation and Digestion

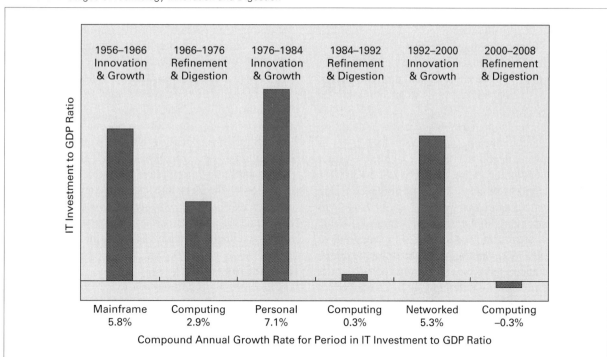

Source: Adapted from A. Bartels, 2004, IT spending outlook: 2004 to 2008 and beyond, Forrester Research Inc., Cambridge, MA.

increased from 1 percent in the mid-twentieth century to more than 4 percent at the beginning of the twenty-first century. However, such growth was not always constant. In fact, it was characterised by periods (8–10 years) of fast growth followed by equally long periods of slow or negative growth. Based on previous historical data, three growth periods were identified in the IT industry corresponding to the introduction of the new technologies (see Exhibit 2). The first period was the introduction of mainframe computing between the mid-1950s and mid-1960s. The second period was the introduction of personal computing from the mid-1970s to the mid-1980s. The third period was the introduction of network computing between the early 1990s and the early 2000s. In these periods, companies often invested in new technologies on faith and without strong links to ROI measurements. Subsequently, companies went many years before fully exploiting the technologies. During these digestion periods, companies often focused on changing the relevant business processes as well as the corresponding organizational structures, often leading to lower spending on new technologies. These spending lags were also noted by researchers from MIT's Center for eBusiness. Based on large-scale statistical results, they cited that companies often implemented new technologies years ahead of time before they could get value from them. This delay in value realization was particularly true in terms of infrastructural investments.[5]

Toward the Next Big Thing

Although the IT industry looked rather gloomy in 2006, analysts predicted, based on previous cycles, that the industry would take off again in 2007 or 2008. In particular, a number of emerging factors would drive the next growth cycle for the technology industry.[6] Some foresaw that software spending would reach US$325 billion by 2008, and the growth rate of the market was expected to be in the range of 3 percent to 7 percent annually.[7]

Service-Oriented Architecture and Web Services

Customers frequently looked for ways to modify and upgrade their enterprise applications to meet their changing business needs. However, many of them found that their IT infrastructure was unable to keep up with such rapid changes. In particular, their IT infrastructure was often confined to specific technologies, often proprietary, that were used by the functional applications. The IT department's infrastructural support was too limited to support the changes in business processes across the enterprises. To address such issues, companies began redesigning their IT infrastructures around business processes rather than functional applications. By leveraging the concept of service-oriented architecture (SOA), companies were able to capture business processes and represent them in a common digital form, (i.e., Web services). In this way, organizations could eliminate those silos of functional applications across business processes that were created by previously incompatible technologies.

More specifically, SOA was a conceptual framework that developed and integrated applications and emphasized code reuse and business modeling. It was also an evolution of distributed computing based on the loosely coupled design paradigm. With this architecture (i.e., its specification), developers would be able to package business logic and functions as Web services that could be used in different environments. All Web services would then be connected with each other through the Internet (the common communication backbone). Subsequently, developers could build applications by composing one or more of these services together without having to know the underlying implementation details of the services. For instance, a service could be implemented in Microsoft's .NET or in Sun Microsystems' Java, the lingua franca on the Internet, and the applications consuming the same service could be on different platforms (e.g., legacy mainframes or PCs).[8]

Applications as Services

Most Web sites were full of static information; executable functions (e.g., buy, search, and cancel) were rarely evoked to execute tasks that were not on the individual PCs but which were, rather, on the servers of the host Web sites. As new Web services technologies continued to take hold, players were able to develop and centrally maintain a variety of executable programs, or applications as services, which could be downloaded to the individual PCs and could then be used to carry out tasks locally. For instance, the search, desktop, toolbar, and map programs created by Google were prime examples of such executable programs. These programs would not only improve the productivity of desktop computing, but also bridge the divide between desktop computing and the Internet. Moreover, as many of these programs were available for free to customers (in the case of Google, these programs were funded by advertising and syndication), they would spread extremely fast on the Internet. Sooner or later, companies would have to incorporate these executables into their existing systems to stay relevant to their customers. In addition, because these free programs were as powerful as the paid desktop programs but far more flexible to use and cost effective, they would not only replace static Web pages on the Internet, but also standard desktop software, mostly created by Microsoft. Besides desktop applications, many had foreseen that enterprise applications such as enterprise resource planning (ERP), supply chain management (SCM), and customer relationship management (CRM) software would be increasingly developed and distributed under the application-as-services model, and perhaps enterprise applications would one day be given away freely.

Extended Internet

Businesses typically require various devices and systems to be connected beyond the virtual world, for which the Internet was extended. It connects computers in the digital world with various machines in the physical world (e.g., automobile and electronic appliances with built-in wireless connections, tracking devices with embedded radio frequency identification (RFID) technology, and biometric devices with remote sensing capability). In addition, the extended Internet can collect richer data gathered through these network-enabled devices. Subsequently, the information analyses will improve and the value of business intelligence deduced from these analyses will increase. Furthermore, with the extended Internet, organizations can tighten control over their assets, and improve the flow of goods and customers.

Social Computing

IT had reached deep into most households in developed economies. As social computing technologies such as storage devices, wireless networks, instant messaging, and others had become ubiquitous, having a tremendous influence on how people access the relevant information sources. In the case of the United States, broadband Internet access was expected to grow from 0.6 million households in 1998 to more than 63 million households in 2008.[9] Some analysts expected that home computer networks would connect PCs and other devices in more than 40 million households by 2008. Such an explosion in home computer networks would foster a convergence of IT with television and cable broadcast, entertainment, consumer electronics, and gaming industries. Social computing technologies would empower individuals through many activities such as searching, downloading, streaming, consumer-to-consumer commerce, blogging, podcasting, and instant messaging, and would change individual behaviors in communications, marketing, media, and commerce.

Microsoft's Strategic Repositioning

As the desktop software market matured, Microsoft continued to diversify and hoped to make headway into the non-PC markets. The company expanded its product lines into enterprise software, consumer products, and services markets. Facing fierce competition on all fronts, Microsoft was driven to reinvent itself. In September 2005, Microsoft announced a major restructuring exercise, which reorganized the company into three business units. The new diversification strategy was to group products and services that had high synergies, streamline decision making, and further realign the company to become nimbler in producing software. The first unit was the Platform Products and Services Division, which oversaw the Windows Client, Server and Tools, and MSN groups and aimed to leverage MSN's success in the development of Windows-based products. The second unit was the Business Division, which oversaw the Information Worker (Microsoft Office-related products) and Microsoft Business Solutions (enterprise application software products) groups. The third group was the Entertainment and Devices Division, which oversaw the Home and Entertainment group (Xbox videogame) and the Mobile and Embedded Devices group, and aimed to compete with players such as Apple and Sony. Ray Ozzie, the highly regarded guru from Groove Networks, would assist the three units in adopting a network-based development approach.[10]

Platform Products and Services Division

Microsoft had ventured into the services market through MSN in order to generate new revenue. MSN was a Web portal that offered a wide range of online services including: news, information search (which was once based on Google's technology before Microsoft developed its own search capability), e-mail (Hotmail was acquired by Microsoft in 1997), instant messaging, online shopping and games, chat rooms, and message boards. In addition, MSN also operated various fee-based services including a dial-up Internet service, MSN TV (interactive television based on WebTV Networks, a company purchased by Microsoft in 1997), Hotmail Plus (upgraded e-mail service), Radio Plus (commercial-free online music radio), MSN Music (online music business), and an online travel service that was offered in partnership with Expedia.

Based on its success in MSN, Microsoft had hoped to leverage its experience to transform its Windows-based platform products into Web-based services for consumers and enterprises. In late 2004, in view of this strategic move, Microsoft adopted the modular or Lego-like development approach that was adopted by MSN and favored by Google and other players. By first developing a core for Windows, the engineers of Microsoft could gradually add new features to the program. Through this new approach, Microsoft could more easily plug in and pull out new features without disrupting the entire Windows program. Moreover, Microsoft also leveraged MSN to generate revenue through traditional advertising on its Web site, and also sold text-based advertisements to compete with Google's AdWords and AdSense, and Yahoo! Search Marketing.

In 2005, the company acquired Groove Networks (founded by Lotus Notes developer Ray Ozzie), a collaboration software maker; Sybari Software, an antivirus security provider; and FrontBridge Technologies, an e-mail security developer. These technologies were critical to Microsoft's existing platform product lines.

Subsequently, Microsoft extended its Windows operating system as an online service (namely Windows Live). In addition, to complement its platform products and Internet services, Microsoft further strengthened itself in the Web services technology market by leveraging its .NET technology, which was originally developed to compete with the Java technology created by Sun Microsystems. Moreover, Microsoft had developed a number of essential tools that would help customers build the key elements in SOA platforms, and develop specific Web service-based modules and solutions.

Business Division

Traditionally, the Office application family within the Information Worker Group had been the second most money-generating division for Microsoft. However, in view of the pressing threats from Google and other players that provided similar software as free online services, Microsoft announced that it would provide its Office application product family as an online service, namely, Office Live. Although it was basically a repackaging of existing products, and they were not yet available as free software like the e-mail program provided by Google, the action demonstrated the seriousness of the matter in Microsoft's eyes.

In the enterprise software market, Microsoft deliberately chose not to compete with leading enterprise applications providers such as SAP and Oracle for large multinational companies. Instead, the software giant aggressively pursued opportunities with small and midsized enterprises. In 2001, after acquiring Great Plains Software, a long-time partner and a specialist in accounting applications for small and midsized businesses, for US$1.1 billion, Microsoft Business Solutions was formed. The new division combined the expertise of Great Plains with its existing small business software operations, including the bCentral small business services unit. The division grew substantially in 2002, when Microsoft acquired Navision, a Denmark-based enterprise software maker for about US$1.5 billion. Microsoft Business Solutions offered a wide range of software applications including accounting, customer relationship management, supply chain management, analytics and reporting, e-commerce, business portals and online business services, human resources, manufacturing and retail management, field services management, and project management.

Entertainment and Devices Division

In terms of the consumer market, one of Microsoft's most important moves was its entry into the video gaming business in 2001. Since the first launch of the video game console, Xbox, the software giant had sold 22 million units worldwide. According to Forrester Researcher

Inc., a technology and market research firm, this move put Microsoft in the distant second place behind Sony's Playstation 2 (92 million units sold) and slightly ahead of Nintendo's GameCube (19 million units sold). The gaming business was cyclical. Generally, every five to six years, a new generation of game consoles would be created. With the new Xbox 360, Microsoft was determined to capture the top spot in the latest cycle of the gaming business, and to challenge Sony's dominant position. First, the software giant's Xbox 360 was launched several months ahead of its rivals' products: Sony's Playstation 3 was expected to appear in the market in spring 2006; and Nintendo's Revolution would be launched in late 2006. Some believed that the success of Sony's Playstation 2 had been partly due to its advantage in reaching the market earlier than its rivals. Hence, Microsoft copied this marketing trick by becoming the first game console in the new business cycle. Second, learning from the flop of the original Xbox in Japan, this time Microsoft worked closely with the producers of the Japanese games in the hope of neutralizing the traditional advantages of its two main rivals. Third, Microsoft abandoned its previous approach of using off-the-shelf parts provided by Intel and Nvidia. Although efficient, that approach lacked the flexibility that Microsoft's rivals enjoyed in reducing the consoles' costs and increasing the profit margins during their lifetime. For instance, Sony had gradually reduced the number of chips required by its Playstation 2 without sacrificing its performance. So Microsoft adopted a new design for Xbox 360, hoping to achieve a new degree of flexibility that could help integrate various components and profitability in the future. In addition to producing and selling game consoles, Microsoft's Xbox Live had been a leader of online gaming. The system provided classic arcade games, game trailers, and upgrade packs that were downloadable.

In addition to gaming, Microsoft ventured into the mobile communications market. For years, the software giant was denied entry into the market by mobile handset manufacturers. In fact, these manufacturers even deliberately formed a consortium (called Symbian) to prevent Microsoft from developing smartphone software. In order to address this disadvantage, Microsoft went to the mobile operators. During this time, many mobile operators, particularly in Europe, started to leverage original design manufacturers (ODM), mostly in Taiwan, to produce handsets that would bear their own brand names in order to create market differentiators. Microsoft spotted this opportunity and persuaded the operators and handset manufacturers to develop phones based on its Windows Mobile operating system. In 2002, Orange launched the first Windows-based smartphone developed by High Tech Computer Corporation (HTC), a leading ODM in Taiwan. Other operators followed suit,

particularly owing to the large volume of data-driven, revenue-generating smartphones. In 2003, Motorola left Symbian and licensed the Windows Mobile software for some of its smartphones. Others would be based on Symbian software and Linux (the open-source operating system). In addition to the opportunity of partnering with the ODMs and operators, the convergence of mobile phone and handheld computers had played to Microsoft's strengths. In late 2005, Palm (Microsoft's rival in handheld devices) decided to adopt the Windows Mobile software and replace its Palm OS with its Treo smartphone. This move further signaled Microsoft's success in penetrating the mobile and handheld market segments. Although Microsoft had made huge progress in the mobile industry, it remained an outsider in many respects. Nonetheless, as mobile phones had become evermore like handheld PCs, particularly with the success of inexpensive PDA phones, Microsoft would have the opportunity to further establish itself in the market.

The cable television market was one in which Microsoft had struggled for many years. In particular, Microsoft had been deliberately kept out of the market by cable operators' refusal to adopt its software in their cable boxes. Cable operators were concerned that once Microsoft entered the market it would repeat its monopolistic practices of the PC business in the cable industry. In view of this situation, Microsoft had formed strategic partnerships, hoping to improve its position in the cable market. For instance, the software giant formed a partnership with NBC Universal Cable to provide MSNBC Interactive News and MSNBC Cable services. In 1999 Microsoft agreed to invest US$5 billion for a minority stake in AT&T as part of that company's move to acquire cable operator MediaOne. The overall results from these moves, though, were less than satisfactory. Microsoft saw a new opportunity, however, as telecom operators began to compete with cable operators by offering television service on top of their broadband data service. Television services delivered on the broadband networks was based on a technology called Internet protocol TV (IPTV), which could also support various kinds of interactivity such as video-on-demand services. Although the technology held great potential, telecom operators were reluctant to invest and build the entire system by themselves. Seeing this particular issue, Microsoft partnered with Alcatel, a French telecom technology provider, for it to provide the required hardware. In this way, Microsoft established itself as a leading IPTV technology provider. Through this arrangement, a number of leading telecom operators, including Deutche Telekom, SBC (acquired AT&T and BellSouth), Bell Canada, British Telecom (BT), and Telecom Italia, adopted Microsoft's software for their IPTV services.

Key Competitors

With the arrival of the new Internet era (Web 2.0) and the ongoing convergence of IT, telecommunications, and media, many players were eyeing the same markets. Hence, Microsoft was expected to face many more competitors as it moved beyond the PC business. The following section highlights Microsoft's key competitors (for performance details, see Exhibit 3).

Red Hat

Red Hat dominated the market for Linux, the open-source computer operating system, and the main rival to Microsoft's Windows-based products. Besides Enterprise Linux OS, Red Hat also provided other products such as database, content, collaboration management applications, and software development tools. The company also offered various services such as consulting, custom software development, support, and training.

Red Hat compiled and distributed the significantly improved version of Linux, first through CD-ROMs and later through the Internet. Because Linux itself was free, Red Hat's revenue came from manuals, technical support, and other value-added services that were challenged by the software's ever-changing source code. Until 1997, Linux and Red Hat's package was only known to a small group of programmers who were looking for an alternative to Microsoft's Windows. Only after Intel, Netscape, Compaq, IBM, Novell, Oracle, and SAP made investments in the company in the subsequent two years did Red Hat become famous. Subsequently, the company went public in 2000.

In 2001, Red Hat expanded its software products and included database applications and an e-commerce software suite designed for midsized businesses. In late 2003, Red Hat acquired Sistina Software of Minneapolis, a supplier of data storage infrastructure software for Linux operating systems. Sistina was founded in 1997 and had about 20 employees. Red Hat paid about US$31 million in stock to acquire Sistina. SAP Ventures, the venture capital arm of SAP, had invested in Sistina earlier in 2003. With Linux's popularity on the rise, Red Hat turned its focus to corporate customers. In particular, the company decided to end its routine maintenance of the Red Hat Linux line

Exhibit 3 Microsoft's Income Statement, 2003–2005 (US$ million)

Income Statement	June 2005	June 2004	June 2003
Revenue	$39,788	$36,835	$32,187
Cost of Goods Sold	5,345	5,530	4,247
Gross Profit	34,443	31,305	27,940
Gross Profit Margin	86.60%	85.00%	86.80%
SG&A Expense	19,027	21,085	13,284
Depreciation & Amortization	855	1,186	1,439
Operating Income	14,561	9,034	13,217
Operating Margin	36.60%	24.50%	41.10%
Nonoperating Income	2,067	3,162	1,509
Nonoperating Expenses	0	0	0
Income Before Taxes	16,628	12,196	14,726
Income Taxes	4,374	4,028	4,733
Net Income After Taxes	12,254	8,168	9,993
Continuing Operations	12,254	8,168	9,993
Discontinued Operations	0	0	0
Total Operations	12,254	8,168	9,993
Total Net Income	12,254	8,168	9,993
Net Profit Margin	30.80%	22.20%	31.00%
Diluted EPS from Continuing Operations ($)	1.12	0.75	0.92
Diluted EPS from Discontinued Operations ($)	0	0	0
Diluted EPS from Total Operations ($)	1.12	0.75	0.92
Diluted EPS from Total Net Income ($)	1.12	0.75	0.92
Dividends per Share	3.40	0.16	0.08

Source: Adapted from J. Lower, 2006, Microsoft Corporation, *Hoover's Company Information,* Austin, TX: Hoover's Inc.

in 2004 in order to focus on enhancing and supporting its Enterprise Linux products. Red Hat established the Fedora Project, an open-source software effort relying on the work of volunteer programmers, for support of its original Linux distribution. In 2005, Red Hat began to focus on the government sector and to establish a dedicated unit to look after that business (see Exhibit 4).

Google

Google had been revered as the most successful online search engine company in the world. The company operated one of the most popular search engines by offering search results from more than 8 billion Web pages. It was also about to become one of the most innovative software makers that stood to change the face of the software industry. Throughout the years, Google had rolled out a series of powerful programs (e.g., Toolbar, Desktop Search, Gmail, and Froogle—a comparison shopping service) that aimed to seamlessly bridge customers' desktops and the Internet. Many customers downloaded these free software products and used them extensively in their homes and offices. Moreover, Google changed the funding model for product development by using the income

earned from its advertisements and syndication to cover the costs of developing these innovative products. With the success of this subsidizing approach, some predicted that the software industry would one day be funded by advertising; whether it was for the consumer's desktop or for enterprise application software such as sales automation or supply chain software.

Since its beginning in 1998, Google upheld its unique company philosophy by first releasing new products and then perfecting them on the fly. It developed business plans based on the feedback it gathered from customers. Google went public in 2004 and successfully raised US$1.6 billion in a highly anticipated initial public offering (IPO). Besides developing innovative products and making them available for free in the market, Google had invested effort in digitizing books and other materials collected in the various university and public libraries, including those at Stanford, Harvard, and Oxford, as well works in the New York Public Library collection.

Although Google seemed to be ahead of the pack, it had been competing fiercely with Yahoo! and MSN in the search-driven advertising sector. Both these rivals launched their own search technology and targeted

Exhibit 4 Red Hat's Income Statement, 2003–2005 (US$ million)

Income Statement	Feb. 2005	Feb. 2004	Feb. 2003
Revenue	$196.50	$126.10	$90.90
Cost of Goods Sold	25.60	27.80	26.00
Gross Profit	170.90	98.30	64.90
Gross Profit Margin	87.00%	78.00%	71.40%
SG&A Expense	130.10	87.90	74.10
Depreciation & Amortization	13.90	7.30	6.50
Operating Income	26.90	3.10	−15.70
Operating Margin	13.70%	2.50%	—
Nonoperating Income	24.40	10.80	10.80
Nonoperating Expenses	6.40	0	0
Income Before Taxes	44.90	13.90	−6.40
Income Taxes	−0.50	0	0
Net Income After Taxes	45.40	13.90	−6.40
Continuing Operations	45.40	14	−6.30
Discontinued Operations	0	0	0
Total Operations	45.40	14	−6.30
Total Net Income	45.40	14	−6.60
Net Profit Margin	23.10%	11.10%	—
Diluted EPS from Continuing Operations ($)	0.24	0.08	−0.04
Diluted EPS from Discontinued Operations ($)	0	0	0
Diluted EPS from Total Operations ($)	0.24	0.08	−0.04
Diluted EPS from Total Net Income ($)	0.24	0.08	−0.04
Dividends per Share	0	0	0

Source: Adapted from J. Lower, 2006, Red Hat, Inc., *Hoover's Company Information*, Austin, TX: Hoover's Inc.

advertising programs. To further capture market share, Google continued to launch additional online services. Following its acquisition of Picasa in 2004, Google made the photo-sharing software freely available. Subsequently, the search company acquired Keyhole in the same year and released a free version of that company's 3-D satellite imaging software as the latest component of its localized content offerings. In 2005, Google introduced an instant messaging client, Google Talk. It also acquired Urchin Software, a maker of Web analytics tools.

Besides creating its own desktop programs, Google released data on its online information services, such as Google Maps, to encourage "mashing" (combining data and capabilities of various Web sites to produce hybrid sites). This prime example shows how Google leveraged open standards propagated by the Internet in generating innovations outside its four walls. In addition, the building of the mash-up sites let Google tap into the creativity of software developers around the globe, and further its advertising channels[11] (see Exhibit 5).

Yahoo!

As a pioneer in Internet search and navigation, Yahoo! had been one of the best-known online brands. It was the largest Web portal and the second most popular Internet search engine after Google. The company drew more than 345 million people to its sites (published in 15 languages in 20 countries) with a mix of news, entertainment, and a range of online services.

Afer the dot.com crash and the recession thereafter, Yahoo! had diversified its revenue streams with a mix of paid content and services. Besides offering registered users free personalized Web pages, e-mail, and message boards, Yahoo! earned revenue from sales of advertisements and subscriptions for premium paid services such as online gaming and music downloading. Moreover, Yahoo! provided fee-based online marketing and other commercial services. For instance, Yahoo! sold search results and targeted advertising through Yahoo! Search Marketing, and job listing services through Yahoo! HotJobs. In addition, it offered Web hosting and

Exhibit 5 Google's Income Statement, 2003–2005 (US$ million)

Income Statement	Dec. 2005	Dec. 2004	Dec. 2003
Revenue	$6,138.60	$3,189.20	$1,465.90
Cost of Goods Sold	2,277.70	1,309.20	570.80
Gross Profit	3,860.90	1,880.00	895.10
Gross Profit Margin	62.90%	58.90%	61.10%
SG&A Expense	1,459.80	890.30	497.60
Depreciation & Amortization	293.80	148.50	55
Operating Income	2,107.30	841.20	342.50
Operating Margin	34.30%	26.40%	23.40%
Nonoperating Income	124.40	10	4.20
Nonoperating Expenses	0	0	0
Income Before Taxes	2,141.70	650.20	346.70
Income Taxes	676.30	251.10	241.00
Net Income After Taxes	1,465.40	399.10	105.70
Continuing Operations	1,465.40	399.10	105.60
Discontinued Operations	0	0	0
Total Operations	1,465.40	399.10	105.60
Total Net Income	1,465.40	399.10	105.60
Net Profit Margin	23.90%	12.50%	7.20%
Diluted EPS from Continuing Operations ($)	5.02	1.46	0.41
Diluted EPS from Discontinued Operations ($)	0	0	0
Diluted EPS from Total Operations ($)	5.02	1.46	0.41
Diluted EPS from Total Net Income ($)	5.02	1.46	0.41
Dividends per Share	0	0	0

Source: Adapted from J. Bramhall, 2006, Google Inc., *Hoover's Company Information*, Austin, TX: Hoover's Inc.

merchant services to small businesses. Besides online services, Yahoo! provided branded Internet access through partnerships with telecommunications companies, including SBC Communications and Verizon i n the United States; BT Group in the United Kingdom; and Rogers Communications in Canada.

As online advertising continued to grow, Yahoo! faced challenges from Google and Microsoft's MSN. In particular, Google had significantly captured the search market by building a range of free Web services to attract customers. Although it lagged far behind both Yahoo! and Google, MSN had launched its own search-driven advertising program. In response to the threats, Yahoo! lured the former head of programming at ABC television, Lloyd Braun, to create original content and to form content partnerships with major studios. In addition, Yahoo! had improved its search technology by acquiring Inktomi in 2003. In the same year, its purchase of Overture, an online marketing firm, had

given Yahoo! a significant boost in advertising revenue. The company continued to strengthen its Web services portfolio through acquisitions. For instance, Yahoo! purchased Flickr, a photo sharing Web site; Dialpad Communications, an Internet telephony business; and Musicmatch, an online music downloading service to compete with Apple Computer's iTunes service and Napster.

Yahoo! expanded its international presence, which accounts for about a quarter of its revenue. In particular, the company acquired Kelkoo (a European comparison shopping service) and Yisou.com (a Chinese search site). In mid-2005, Yahoo! acquired a 40 percent stake in Alibaba.com, the leading e-commerce company in China, for US$1billion. Under the new partnership, Alibaba.com would take over operations of Yahoo! China. In addition, the company also announced plans to buy out the remaining shares of Yahoo! Europe and Yahoo! Korea from its partner SoftBank[12] (see Exhibit 6).

Exhibit 6 Yahoo!'s Income Statement, 2003–2005 (US$ million)

Income Statement	Dec. 2005	Dec. 2004	Dec. 2003
Revenue	$5,257.70	$3,574.50	$1,625.10
Cost of Goods Sold	1,808.30	1,133.20	252.8
Gross Profit	3,449.40	2,441.30	1,372.30
Gross Profit Margin	65.60%	68.30%	84.40%
SG&A Expense	1,944.50	1,441.70	917
Depreciation & Amortization	397.10	311.00	159.70
Operating Income	1,107.80	688.60	295.60
Operating Margin	21.10%	19.30%	18.20%
Nonoperating Income	1,226.10	591.40	95.20
Nonoperating Expenses	0	0	0
Income Before Taxes	2,671.90	1,280.00	390.80
Income Taxes	767.80	438.00	147.00
Net Income After Taxes	1,904.10	842.00	243.80
Continuing Operations	1,896.20	839.60	237.90
Discontinued Operations	0	0	0
Total Operations	1,896.20	839.60	237.90
Total Net Income	1,896.20	839.60	237.90
Net Profit Margin	36.10%	23.50%	14.60%
Diluted EPS from Continuing Operations ($)	1.28	0.58	0.19
Diluted EPS from Discontinued Operations ($)	0	0	0
Diluted EPS from Total Operations ($)	1.28	0.58	0.19
Diluted EPS from Total Net Income ($)	1.28	0.58	0.19
Dividends per Share	0	0	0

Source: Adapted from J. Bramhall, 2006, Yahoo! Inc., *Hoover's Company Information*, Austin, TX: Hoover's Inc.

Oracle

In 2003, Oracle launched a hostile takeover bid for PeopleSoft, which had just disclosed its own plans to acquire a mid-market rival, JD Edwards. Initially, the board of PeopleSoft rejected the offer of US$5.1 billion in cash: They considered the bid inadequate and were troubled by associated antitrust issues. After many rounds of negotiations and offers, Oracle finally reached an agreement to acquire PeopleSoft for US$10.3 billion in December 2004. Subsequently, Oracle cut the newly combined workforce by 9 percent. Although the layoff mostly affected PeopleSoft's employees, Oracle retained the majority of PeopleSoft's development and support teams.

In 2004, Oracle continued to pursue its acquisition-driven growth in order to strengthen its presence in the market. When SAP announced its plan to acquire Retek, a retail software developer, for about US$500 million, Oracle immediately acquired 10 percent of Retek and offered to buy the remaining shares. After a short bidding battle, Oracle purchased Retek for $670 million and formed a new business unit called Oracle Retail Global. In addition, Oracle acquired Oblix, a software developer for identity management; TimesTen, a software developer for data management; and ProfitLogic, a software developer for retail inventory management. In September 2005, nine months after acquiring PeopleSoft, Oracle announced its purchase of Siebel Systems Inc., the leading CRM software maker in the world, for US$5.8 billion. The deal was expected to close in early 2006.

In order to solidify its position in the enterprise software market after its strategic acquisitions, Oracle announced Project Fusion in early 2005. This new strategic initiative aimed to create a comprehensive platform of its next-generation enterprise technologies, applications, and services. The move sought to unite Oracle's full range of software products (from enterprise applications to database software) with the best functionality from the product lines of PeopleSoft, JD Edwards, Retek, Siebel, and other newly acquired companies through the Web services technologies. Through this strategic initiative, Oracle emphasized that it would create the most integrated and complete enterprise solution in the market to operate business processes for its customers. Oracle also promised to ensure continuity of the existing Siebel, PeopleSoft, and JD Edwards' product lines; provide customers options of staying with their existing technology platforms created by rivals (e.g., IBM's DB2 database management products, BEA's middleware products); offer customers more flexibility in creating their own upgrade schedules; and reduce the total cost of ownership of the enterprise software.[13]

Besides building the most comprehensive development and integration platform for large customers, Oracle continued to equip itself to be a provider of enterprise-software-as-a-service by hosting and running the enterprise applications at Oracle's premise. The service catered to small and medium-sized customers that did not have the resources or capabilities to deal with the complexities and costs of an on-site implementation of their enterprise application software[14] (see Exhibit 7).

SAP

In 2001, SAP conducted one of the most daring corporate campaigns in its 33-year-history—it opened up its proprietary software through its new technology, NetWeaver. SAP was determined to counter the increasingly heterogeneous nature of the computing environment by providing free access to its software. After putting in more than US$1 billion in research and development, SAP introduced NetWeaver—an open platform that allows applications to be developed and accessed as Web services. This new technology was designed to link up various applications (packaged as Web services) running on different systems, from legacy mainframes to Internet-enabled devices to enterprise applications. By leveraging NetWeaver, SAP was able to break up its software products into open and modular pieces. Customers were then able to pick and choose the specific SAP Web services modules that met their needs. Moreover, customers could add in modules developed by other companies as long as these products met the specification of the NetWeaver framework. As a result of SAP's move, customers could speed up the creation and modification of their own applications, improve the overall fit of the applications, and eventually reduce the associated development costs that it would normally have incurred.

Because the software products were broken up into smaller chunks, SAP changed the delivery mode of features and functions for its products. Rather than making customers wait for massive releases to take place periodically (minor releases can take months and major releases can take years), the Web services approach allows improvements of the software products to be made immediately. SAP found that with this new engineering approach, it solicited tremendous customer support. In 2003, SAP released the early version of NetWeaver as free bundled software, which was aimed at bridging SAP and non-SAP software programs by reducing the need for building customized links. The full version of the software launched in 2007. Since mid-2005, more than 1,300 customers had tested NetWeaver and some of them were highly satisfied with it and would welcome the opportunity to refer it to future buyers.

By leveraging a universally accepted platform, thousands of individual developers were able to develop specialized modules that would serve highly targeted industry segments, which were traditionally too fragmented to be

Exhibit 7 Oracle's Income Statement, 2003–2005 (US$ million)

Income Statement	May 2005	May 2004	May 2003
Revenue	$11,799	$10,156	$9,475
Cost of Goods Sold	2,445	2,083	2,015
Gross Profit	9,354	8,073	7,460
Gross Profit Margin	79.30%	79.50%	78.70%
SG&A Expense	4,552	3,975	3,693
Depreciation & Amortization	425	234	327
Operating Income	4,377	3,864	3,440
Operating Margin	37.10%	38.00%	36.30%
Nonoperating Income	164	102	1
Nonoperating Expenses	135	21	16
Income Before Taxes	4,051	3,945	3,425
Income Taxes	1,165	1,264	1,118
Net Income After Taxes	2,886	2,681	2,307
Continuing Operations	2,886	2,681	2,307
Discontinued Operations	0	0	0
Total Operations	2,886	2,681	2,307
Total Net Income	2,886	2,681	2,307
Net Profit Margin	24.50%	26.40%	24.30%
Diluted EPS from Continuing Operations ($)	0.55	0.5	0.43
Diluted EPS from Discontinued Operations ($)	0	0	0
Diluted EPS from Total Operations ($)	0.55	0.5	0.43
Diluted EPS from Total Net Income ($)	0.55	0.5	0.43
Dividends per Share	0	0	0

Source: Adapted from J. Lower, 2006, Oracle Corporation, *Hoover's Company Information*, Austin, TX: Hoover's Inc.

addressed by using the old one-size-fits-all approach. This factor was particularly important for SAP in capturing the millions of new small and midsized enterprise customers around the world. So, to realize this strategy based on NetWeaver, SAP fostered a new ecosystem. In the past, SAP mainly relied on its internal programmers (mostly residing in Walldorf, Germany) to develop its products. With the new NetWeaver platform, the software company needed to change from being an industry introvert that focused on its supreme engineering capabilities to an extrovert that attracted tens of thousands of individual developers in joining the virtual development network (see Exhibit 8).

IBM

Because software was a key component of its new corporate strategy, On Demand Strategy, IBM acquired a number of companies to strengthen its software capability. As a leader in the software industry, IBM Software Group offered a wide range of products, particularly in the areas of database management, systems management, and

application integration and development. The division was also a leader in collaboration and communication applications through its Lotus product line. In addition, the division's Tivoli product lines were well established in the storage and security software markets. The global strength of IBM's massive hardware and services businesses continued to sustain the growth of its software products, which accounted for 17 percent of IBM's total sales.

In order to streamline its diverse product lines, IBM Software Group consolidated its disparate software products into five major subgroups: information management software (DB2); collaboration software (Lotus); systems development software (Rational); systems management software (Tivoli); and application server and integration software (WebSphere).

WebSphere, in particular, was the centerpiece of IBM's software development and integration strategies, and was the answer to their rivals' competitive products, including SAP's NetWeaver. WebSphere was a platform for building a basic but robust Web services environment.

Exhibit 8 SAP's Income Statement, 2003–2005 (US$ million)

Income Statement	Dec. 2005	Dec. 2004	Dec. 2003
Revenue	$10,074.50	$10,179.10	$8,831.30
Cost of Goods Sold	3,212.40	3,221.40	2,913.70
Gross Profit	6,862.10	6,957.70	5,917.60
Gross Profit Margin	68.10%	68.40%	67.00%
SG&A Expense	3,870.10	3,942.00	3,479.30
Depreciation & Amortization	240.90	284.00	270.90
Operating Income	2,751.10	2,731.70	2,167.40
Operating Margin	27.30%	26.80%	24.50%
Nonoperating Income	9.70	96.40	71.20
Nonoperating Expenses	4.60	11.00	5.00
Income Before Taxes	2,741.30	2,807.60	2,233.60
Income Taxes	967	1,025.80	870.80
Net Income After Taxes	1,774.30	1,781.80	1,362.80
Continuing Operations	1,771.00	1,775.20	1,354.10
Discontinued Operations	0	0	0
Total Operations	1,771.00	1,775.20	1,354.10
Total Net Income	1,771.00	1,775.20	1,354.10
Net Profit Margin	17.60%	17.40%	15.30%
Diluted EPS from Continuing Operations ($)	1.43	1.42	1.09
Diluted EPS from Discontinued Operations ($)	0	0	0
Diluted EPS from Total Operations ($)	1.43	1.42	1.09
Diluted EPS from Total Net Income ($)	1.43	1.42	1.09
Dividends per Share	0.28	0	0.13

Source: Adapted from J. Lower, 2006, SAP Aktiengesellschaft, *Hoover's Company Information*, Austin, TX: Hoover's Inc.

Although Microsoft and others offered similar products, WebSphere contained most of the basic components and tools required, and a number of extensions that helped customers: integrate systems and applications with Web services applications; present data on various devices; deploy applications; secure and manage Web services application environments.

To further strengthen its WebSphere product line, IBM made a number of strategic acquisitions in 2005. They included Gluecode Software (an open-source application server developer), PureEdge Solutions (an electronic forms developer), and Ascential Software (a leading provider of data integration software for US$1.1 billion)[15] (see Exhibit 9).

Apple

Since the success of its digital music player iPod in 2002, Apple Computer has become a consumer electronics powerhouse rather than a computer vendor. After its initial launch, Apple provided regular updates to its iPod line, including color displays with video playing capability and flash memory-based models. In 2003, Apple launched its iTunes Music Store in the United States, an online music service. The site included songs from the five largest record labels in the world, allowing users to download songs for 99 cents, thereby further boosting sales of iPods. Subsequently the company created international versions of iTunes that served Canada, and European and Asian countries. Given the popularity of the online music service, Apple, Motorola, and Cingular Wireless launched the first iTunes-enabled mobile phone in the world in late 2005. Besides its vastly popular iPod products and iTunes services, Apple's desktop and laptop computers, including iMac, iBook, Power Mac and PowerBook, continued to capture small but significant shares of the consumer, education, and high-end design and publishing professional markets. Additionally, Apple offered servers (Xserve), wireless networking equipment (Airport), publishing and multimedia software, and database software through its FileMaker subsidiary.

Exhibit 9 IBM's Income Statement, 2003–2005 (US$ million)

Income Statement	Dec. 2005	Dec. 2004	Dec. 2003
Revenue	$91,134	$96,293	$89,131
Cost of Goods Sold	49,414	55,346	51,412
Gross Profit	41,720	40,947	37,719
Gross Profit Margin	45.80%	42.50%	42.30%
SG&A Expense	27,156	25,057	22,929
Depreciation & Amortization	5,188	4,915	4,701
Operating Income	9,376	10,975	10,089
Operating Margin	10.30%	11.40%	11.30%
Nonoperating Income	3,070	1,192	930
Nonoperating Expenses	220	139	145
Income Before Taxes	12,226	12,028	10,874
Income Taxes	4,232	3,580	3,261
Net Income After Taxes	7,994	8,448	7,613
Continuing Operations	7,994	8,448	7,613
Discontinued Operations	−24	−18	−30
Total Operations	7,970	8,430	7,583
Total Net Income	7,934	8,430	7,583
Net Profit Margin	8.70%	8.80%	8.50%
Diluted EPS from Continuing Operations ($)	4.91	4.94	4.34
Diluted EPS from Discontinued Operations ($)	−0.01	−0.01	−0.02
Diluted EPS from Total Operations ($)	4.9	4.93	4.32
Diluted EPS from Total Net Income ($)	4.88	4.93	4.32
Dividends per Share	0.78	0.7	0.63

Source: Adapted from J. Lower, 2006, International Business Machines Corporation, *Hoover's Company Information*, Austin, TX: Hoover's Inc.

Although it was no longer the top seller in the PC market, which had been dominated by Microsoft Windows software and Intel processors, Apple continued to attract and maintain a group of loyalists who were fond of the Macintosh's aesthetic sense and its user-friendliness. Moreover, this group of customers was willing to pay premium prices and tolerate any potential interoperability issues with Windows (which had largely been addressed through the years). In addition to its proprietary operating system, the basis of its unique interface and design, another differentiator for Apple's machines was its use of IBM's PowerPC processors. Nonetheless, in 2005, Apple decided to use Intel chips for its PC products starting in 2006, with complete transition by the end of 2007.

Although computer companies were increasingly interested in selling their machines only through the online channel, Apple made a significant effort to appeal to consumers via hundreds of retail stores in the United States, Canada, Japan, and the United Kingdom. In 2005, Apple generated 17 percent of its sales through its retail channel. In order to counter the sluggishness in the global PC sales, Apple cut prices on many of its products and continued to roll out unique offerings. For instance, Apple introduced Mac mini, its cheapest machine with a base price of US$499. Additionally, the company increasingly looked to software development to drive sales. Many of the company's multimedia applications such as iTunes, iMovie, and iPhoto were available for free, but the company charged for bundled versions of its software.

With its massive marketing campaign that urged Windows users to switch to Macs, Apple further complicated its relationship with Microsoft. Although it was an alternative to Microsoft's Windows operating system, Apple's relative size and market share had not been a real threat to the software giant. In fact, both Microsoft and Apple had long maintained a working relationship; the Mac-compatible version of Microsoft's popular Office suite was a key software title for Apple, and Apple had scored crossover hits with Windows-friendly editions of iPod and iTunes. Soon after Apple released its Safari Web

Exhibit 10 Apple's Income Statement, 2003–2005 (US$ million)

Income Statement	Sept. 2005	Sept. 2004	Sept. 2003
Revenue	$13,931	$8,279	$6,207
Cost of Goods Sold	9,709	5,870	4,386
Gross Profit	4,222	2,409	1,821
Gross Profit Margin	30.30%	29.10%	29.30%
SG&A Expense	2,393	1,910	1,683
Depreciation & Amortization	179	150	113
Operating Income	1,650	349	25
Operating Margin	11.80%	4.20%	0.40%
Nonoperating Income	165	57	93
Nonoperating Expenses	0	0	0
Income Before Taxes	1,815	383	92
Income Taxes	480	107	24
Net Income After Taxes	1,335	276	68
Continuing Operations	1,335	276	68
Discontinued Operations	0	0	0
Total Operations	1,335	276	68
Total Net Income	1,335	276	69
Net Profit Margin	9.60%	3.30%	1.10%
Diluted EPS from Continuing Operations ($)	1.56	0.36	0.1
Diluted EPS from Discontinued Operations ($)	0	0	0
Diluted EPS from Total Operations ($)	1.56	0.36	0.1
Diluted EPS from Total Net Income ($)	1.56	0.36	0.1
Dividends per Share	0	0	0

Source: Adapted from J. Lower, 2006, Apple Computer, Inc., *Hoover's Company Information*, Austin, TX: Hoover's Inc.

browser, however, Microsoft announced it would cease development of the Mac version of its Internet Explorer (see Exhibit 10).

Sony

Sony's PlayStation 2 had captured 70 percent of the game console market, whereas Nintendo's GameCube and Microsoft's Xbox had only about 15 percent each. Sony was one of the leading consumer electronics companies (e.g., digital cameras, Walkman stereos), and PC and semiconductor companies in the world. These products accounted for more than 60 percent of its sales. Sony's entertainment assets included recorded music and video (Epic and Columbia), motion pictures (Sony Pictures Entertainment, Sony Pictures Classics), DVDs (Sony Pictures Home Entertainment), and TV programming (Columbia TriStar). Sony had also partnered with Ericsson to develop and sell mobile phones. Moreover, Sony also owned an 8 percent stake in music club Columbia House.

Although the PlayStation product lines had dominated the video game market, its sales of other electronics (DVD recorders, TVs, and computers) and music products had dropped. Weak consumer demand, price wars, and increased competition from Apple Computer's iPod had undermined sales of Sony's CD and mini-disk Walkman, and TV products. These challenges, as well as costs incurred in streamlining operations, had significantly decreased its market value. To rectify the situation, Sony began to emphasise high-definition products for consumers and broadcasters, integrated mobile video, music, and gaming products, and semiconductors (aimed at achieving performance improvements of products, by reducing the total number of chips required by PlayStation).

In 2005, Sony brought in Sir Howard Stringer to replace Nobuyuki Idei as chair and CEO, the first non-Japanese chief of the company. Prior to this post, Stringer was the head of the company's U.S. and electronics divisions. Since taking over the top post, Stringer announced

Project Nippon, a corporate restructuring plan aimed at revamping the electronics business and fostering better collaboration between the company's divisions. Stringer also announced that he planned to implement a concrete research and development scheme with greater emphasis on consumer demands and to reestablish Sony's leading presence in Japan.

The new reorganization plan was to continue Sony's "Transformation 60," the restructuring exercise started in 2004 that aimed to reduce the company's headcount by 20,000, combine operating divisions, and shift component sourcing to low-cost markets such as China. Stringer's new plan aimed to cut 10,000 jobs, shut down 11 manufacturing plants, and reduce the company's electronics product lines by 20 percent. Moreover, Stringer had abolished Sony's "Network Companies" structure in favor of five product-focused business groups (i.e., TV, video, digital imaging, audio, and VAIO). In addition, Sony had streamlined its operations from R&D to distribution and marketing. The two new product development groups and two business units would focus on semiconductors and electronic components. The company spun off Sony Communication Network, the subsidiary that operated So-Net Internet service (which had nearly 3 million subscribers) in an IPO in December 2005.

Sony's PlayStation 3 was released in the spring of 2006, several months after Microsoft's Xbox 360. Similar to Xbox 360, PlayStation 3 was designed to be a multimedia entertainment hub. Its computing power allows users to play video games, chat online, listen to music, and view high-quality animations similar to those projected by the cinematic digital projector. The machine is also backward-compatible with games designed for previous PlayStations. In addition to the video game console, Sony's PSP (PlayStation Portable), a Walkman-like device with DVD-quality video was launched in Japan in late 2004. The marketing hype surrounding the device's U.S. launch led to long lines at Sony stores when it was released in early 2005. The PSP generated US$150 million in sales for Sony the first week it hit the stores. Lastly, PSX, an electronics and game technology, was released in Japan in late 2003 and in the United States in 2005. It also rolled out a "portable broadband TV" in 2004—the device plays television shows and videos and allows users to connect to the Internet.

To compete with its competitors, Sony was expected to invest US$1.67 billion to build a leading semiconductor plant in Japan. The company hoped that in 2006 it would be able to sell home servers for broadband and high-definition TV systems powered by its new Cell computer chip, jointly developed with IBM and Toshiba. This powerful chip would also power the new PlayStation 3. Sony also joined Matsushita and Samsung, plus a few other companies, to jointly develop the Blu-Ray Disc. The alliance, formed in 2004, aimed to establish the new DVD format for optical storage media. In late 2004, Disney agreed to use the Blu-ray format. Games designed for PlayStation 3 would be the first mass utilization of the Blu-ray format. In May 2004 the company launched Sony Connect (formerly known as Net Music Download), an online music service available to users of Sony's electronics and mobile devices. The service would eventually expand to include video downloads. This site was managed by a newly formed subsidiary of Sony Corporation of America. At the same time, Sony launched VAIO Pocket, a portable music player designed to compete with Apple's iPod. VAIO Pocket debuted in the United States in late 2004. Sony also introduced a similar product, Network Walkman—its first Walkman with a hard drive. In October 2004, the company launched a music download system in Japan dubbed MusicDrop. The system utilized Microsoft's Windows Media Player.

In the entertainment industry, Sony merged its music division with BMG and formed Sony BMG Music Entertainment. The company also led a consortium of companies, including Comcast (a cable company) and a number of investment firms, to acquire the movie studio MGM in early 2005. Such a move allowed Sony to license and distribute MGM's sizable film library. In addition, the deal enabled Sony to participate in film co-productions, cable channels, and video demand services that would likely generate additional revenue for the company through Comcast-Sony Networks, a joint venue between the cable and the electronics and media companies (see Exhibit 11).

Looking Ahead

By pursuing its diversification strategy, Microsoft continued to move beyond its comfort zone, the highly monopolized desktop and server software industry. Hence, one of the major challenges Microsoft would face was many new competitors in new segments.

As Microsoft's Windows-based products continued to hold the near-monopoly in the operating system market, the only product that could challenge Microsoft's dominant position would be Linux, the operating system created in the public domain and distributed by players such as Red Hat. Besides the Windows-based products, the MSN services were another critical component in its diversification strategy. The key competitors, Google and Yahoo!, had adopted the application-as-services model coupled with a new advertising-driven funding approach, which enabled them to develop open-source and free software products for the general public.

Exhibit 11 Sony's Income Statement, 2003–2005 (US$ million)

Income Statement	Mar. 2005	Mar. 2004	Mar. 2003
Revenue	$66,912	$72,081	$63,264
Cost of Goods Sold	40,673	42,175	40,672
Gross Profit	26,239	29,906	22,592
Gross Profit Margin	39.20%	41.50%	35.70%
SG&A Expense	18,856	22,152	15,402
Depreciation & Amortization	6,057	6,462	5,621
Operating Income	1,326	1,292	1,569
Operating Margin	2.00%	1.80%	2.50%
Nonoperating Income	644	377	379
Nonoperating Expenses	230	268	231
Income Before Taxes	1,740	1,401	1,717
Income Taxes	150	507	684
Net Income After Taxes	1,590	894	1,033
Continuing Operations	1,575	871	978
Discontinued Operations	0	0	0
Total Operations	1,575	871	978
Total Net Income	1,531	851	978
Net Profit Margin	2.30%	1.20%	1.50%
Diluted EPS from Continuing Operations ($)	1.52	0.89	1
Diluted EPS from Discontinued Operations ($)	0	0	0
Diluted EPS from Total Operations ($)	1.52	0.89	1
Diluted EPS from Total Net Income ($)	1.48	0.87	1
Dividends per Share	0.23	0.21	0.2

Source: Adapted from M. Drapes, 2006, Sony Corporation, *Hoover's Company Information*, Austin, TX: Hoover's Inc.

Bill Gates knows how to compete with anyone who charges money for products . . . but his head explodes whenever he has to go up against anyone who gives away products for free.

—***George Colony***

CHAIRMAN AND CEO, FORRESTER RESEARCH[16]

In addition, with the growth of online service businesses, Microsoft, Google, and Yahoo! had been fighting fiercely to become the primary gateway to the Internet or the leading Web portal. These players had provided Internet users a range of services from search to e-mail and discussion blogs to news. In particular, Google and Yahoo! had formed partnerships with various telecommunication or cable service providers in order to position their respective portals as the default entrance to the Internet. Google had struck a deal with Comcast, the largest cable provider in the United States and a partner of Sony's. Yahoo! had been working with SBC (AT&T) and Verizon, the top three telecommunication operators in the United States. Furthermore, Google had tied

the knot with AOL by acquiring 5 percent of the shares of the troubled online service pioneer owned by Time Warner. Although it was considered one of the smallest portals in the market, AOL was rich in content (thanks to its media parent) and still owned a sizable subscription base (through its dial-up access) in the U.S. market. Hence, such a partnership with AOL would help Google enrich its content and be on par with Yahoo! With these new arrangements, MSN was put in a highly unfavorable position against its competitors in the portal business.[17]

With the major mergers and acquisitions orchestrated by Oracle in 2004 and 2005 (the purchase of PeopleSoft and Siebel in particular), it seemed that the consolidation in the enterprise application segment would come to an end, because not many large players would be left in the market. SAP, Oracle, and IBM had emerged as dominant players in this segment. Traditionally, Oracle and SAP had been fierce rivals while Microsoft, IBM, and SAP were partners. For instance, SAP and Microsoft had been in partnership to jointly develop a product that would link Microsoft Office Applications to SAP products. IBM had been a SAP partner in implementation, middleware, and database software. As these software vendors began to develop their own unique SOA and Web services platforms, friction was expected to arise: As competition became fierce, long-term partnerships would likely be jeopardized.[18]

In the entertainment and consumer markets, with the Xbox game console and the ventures in mobiles and IPTV, Microsoft would be competing with players such as Apple and Sony. These players were much more consumer-oriented and media savvy than Microsoft. On one hand, Apple's iMac and iPod products, and iTunes services were designed to cater to the high-end media-centric consumers. On the other hand, although it had been in strategic disarray, particularly in the consumer electronics segment, Sony's video games and entertainment business remained one of the strongest in the industry.

With its new diversification strategy, Microsoft had entered various new markets in which it had no proprietary advantages. Facing many new challenges in such a fast-changing competitive landscape, Microsoft could not conquer these markets alone. It had to significantly leverage existing and new partnerships, particularly with established players in the newly targeted industries. Microsoft needed to constantly monitor the dynamic changes in the relevant ecosystems, and adjust its alliance strategies to capture opportunities in these markets.

Notes

1. With a range of Internet-enabled innovations introduced to the market, many had come to believe a new era of the Internet (Web 2.0) had arrived.

2. J. Lower, 2005, Microsoft Corporation, *Hoover's Company Information,* Austin TX: Hoover's Inc.

3. R. Guth, 2005, Microsoft Sets Big Restructuring Plan, *Wall Street Journal,* September 21; R. Guth, 2005, Microsoft Changes How it Builds Software, *Wall Street Journal (Europe),* September 27.

4. K.B. Davis, A.S. Rath, & B.L. Scanlon, 2004, How IT Spending is changing, *McKinsey Quarterly,* 2004 Special Edition; IT Spending growth to slow, *Red Herring,* August 1, 2005; D. Nystedt, IDC Lowers 2005 Global IT Spending growth forecasts, *Computerworld,* May 4, 2005; A. Bartels, 2004, IT spending outlook: 2004 to 2008 and beyond, Forrester Research Inc., Cambridge, MA.

5. E. Brynjolfsson and L. Hitt, 1998, Beyond the productivity paradox, center for e-business, Massachusetts Institute of Technology, Cambridge, MA.

6. C. Mines, 2005, The seeds of the next big thing, Forrester Research Inc., Cambridge, MA; G. Colony, 2005, My view: The Google future, Forrester Research Inc., Cambridge, MA.

7. Davis, Rath, and Scanlon, 2004, op. cit.; Bartels, 2004, op. cit.; Business's digital black cloud, *The Economist,* July 16, 2005; Software: Expect the giants to stay sluggish, *BusinessWeek,* January 10, 2005.

8. R. Heffner, 2005, Digital business architecture: Harnessing IT for business flexibility, Forrester Research Inc., Cambridge, MA.

9. Mines, 2005, op. cit.

10. R. Guth, 2005, Microsoft sets big restructuring plan, *Wall Street Journal,* September 21; R. Guth, 2005, Microsoft changes how it builds software, *Wall Street Journal Europe,* September 27; Spot the dinosaur, *The Economist,* April 1, 2006.

11. 2005, Mashing the Web, *The Economist,* September 17; G. Colony, My view: The Google future, forrester research inc., Cambridge, MA; J. Bramhall, 2005, Google Inc., *Hoover's Company Information,* Austin TX: Hoover's Inc.

12. J. Bramhall, 2005 Yahoo! Inc., *Hoover's Company Information,* Austin TX: Hoover's Inc.

13. J. Lower, 2005, Oracle Corporation, *Hoover's Company Information,* Austin TX: Hoover's Inc.; Reinhardt, 2005, op. cit.; J. Mirani and A. Ozzimo, 2005, Oracle applications: Committed to your success, Oracle's white paper, Redwood: Oracle Corporation.

14. B. Perez, 2005, Oracle unveils on-demand future, *South China Morning Post,* September 27.

15. J. Lower, 2005, International Business Machine Corporation, *Hoover's Company Information,* Austin, TX: Hoover's Inc.

16. *The Economist,* 2006, op. cit.

17. 2005, The battle of the portals, *The Economist,* October 20; S. Hansell and R. Siklos, 2005, Time Warner to sell 5% AOL stake to Google for $1 billion, *New York Times,* December 17.

18. Heng, 2005, op. cit.; A. Reinhardt, 2005, SAP: A sea change in software, *BusinessWeek,* July 11: J. Evers, and J. Blau, 2005, Microsoft and SAP to link Office with ERP, *Computerworld,* April 26.

Case 16

Nestlé: Sustaining Growth in Mature Markets

Dr. Sebastian Raisch, Flora Ferlic

University of St. Gallen

When Peter Brabeck-Letmathe took over as CEO of Nestlé in June 1997, he inherited a company that enjoyed the leading position in the global food industry. His predecessor Helmut Maucher, the CEO between 1982 and 1997, had divested the firm's unattractive activities, while establishing its position in higher-margin segments such as pet food and water. Maucher had transformed Nestlé from a manufacturer with a strong European base focused on milk and coffee, into a truly diversified global food company. During his 16-year reign, sales had more than doubled, profits had tripled, and the total return to shareholders was an excellent 17 percent annually.[1] (See Appendices 1 and 2.)

Despite Nestlé's success, one fundamental challenge would have to be dealt with in the coming years: revitalizing the group's organic growth in a maturing market. Maucher had heavily relied on acquisitions to develop Nestlé. He had invested more than CHF33.1 billion in a string of takeovers, including those of Carnation in 1985, Buitoni and Rowntree in 1988, and Perrier in 1992.[2] This expansion strategy had helped the firm reduce its dependence on coffee sales, while gaining sufficient scale and market reach in its new business segments. By 1997, however, the limits of the external growth strategy had been reached with Nestlé ranked first in nearly all the product segments in which it operated.[3] Brabeck was well aware of the need for strategic reorientation:

Our first priority is to achieve real internal growth. Internal growth reflects the company's performance and competitiveness better, even more so than acquiring another company's turnover. Acquisitive growth requires three people: a manager, a lawyer, and a banker. You need to activate 250,000 people for organic growth—the entire organization. However, it is a far more sustainable path to growth.[4]

One of Brabeck's first actions as CEO was to move Nestlé's goal of 4 percent real internal growth to the top of the company's strategic agenda.[5] Compared to an average market growth of just 2 percent in the mature global food industry, this goal was rather challenging.[6] To reach this target, Nestlé had to grow at twice its competitors' rate.

Nestlé first achieved its 4 percent internal growth target in 2000 and consistently repeated this performance in the subsequent years. Since 2000, the company has significantly outperformed the food sector and realized higher organic growth than any of its major competitors.[7] Nestlé's success can be related to Brabeck's unique campaign for profitable growth. In this case study, we return to the initial situation in 1997 and retrace the company's development over the following decade. The objective is to outline Brabeck's most important strategic and organizational initiatives that enabled the company to achieve a rate of profitable internal growth that was far above its competitors.

Nestlé in 1997

In 1997, Brabeck took control of one of the oldest and most truly global companies in the food industry, with international activities dating back to its beginnings in 1866. Over the previous 130 years, Nestlé had acquired profound knowledge of markets all over the world, and enjoyed great success in adapting its products to local tastes. The company operated factories in 77 countries and sold its products on all six continents. Offering thousands of local products, Nestlé is often referred to as a role model company that thinks globally but acts locally.

In 1996, the year before Brabeck took control, Nestlé had generated sales of CHF 60 billion and a net income of CHF 3.4 billion.[8] At the time, its product portfolio comprised 19 categories from coffee, milk, and confectionary to pet foods, clinical nutrition, and mineral water. The company was either the market leader or held a strong second position in most of its product segments. Businesses in which Nestlé had failed to reach a dominant position had largely been divested under Maucher's reign. Its core food and beverage businesses contributed to more than 95 percent of the company's 1996 sales. Its top five product categories (coffee, milk products, confectionary, ophthalmics, and dehydrated cooking aids) accounted for 60 percent of group sales and more than 75 percent of operating profits.[9]

Despite Nestlé's leading position, Brabeck was faced with considerable challenges that stood in the way of his objective of 4 percent real internal growth. The most important of these challenges was that the company generated more than 70 percent of its sales in mature markets with a limited potential for organic growth.[10] The leading countries in terms of market size, such as the United States, Russia, and Japan, were also the ones yielding the lowest growth rates. Besides the challenging market conditions, Nestlé was increasingly facing fierce competition as many food-producing rivals had achieved significant improvements in their operating efficiency. Although the number of truly global competitors was limited—the most notable being Kraft, Masterfoods, and Unilever—Nestlé was also facing strong competition at the national and regional level.[11]

The growing competitive pressure was exacerbated by Nestlé's relatively weak profitability, whose root causes could be traced to Nestlé's various acquisitions. Although strategically important, the acquisitions had required massive investments and their integration had negatively affected operational efficiency. The EBIT margin in the core business was roughly 12 percent, but the acquired businesses' margin had sunk to 6 percent.[12] Furthermore, Nestlé's portfolio included several low-margin product segments that negatively affected profitability. In 1997, the company ranked eighth among the world's top 12 packaged food companies in terms of returns on capital. Its net margin was only half that of its major rival Unilever.[13]

Earning the Right to Grow

Brabeck had to identify new growth opportunities to realize his goal of 4 percent internal growth. Organic growth in mature markets could only be reached by strengthening Nestlé's innovative capacity. This approach required significant investments in the group's R&D and marketing capabilities. Because Nestlé has always been a model of rock-solid accounting, Brabeck intended to generate the massive cash flows required for a large-scale growth offensive by improving the company's capital efficiency. His strategy was to force the businesses to become more

efficient by cutting back on their investment budgets: "The investment budget is declining. Our efforts must switch to maximizing existing assets, maximizing capacity utilization and maximizing distribution logistics."[14] Paradoxically, the first task on the road toward achieving the internal growth target was thus to strengthen the company's operational efficiency. Lars Olofsson, the former head of Nestlé Europe, explains: "The real objective is to generate growth. To reach this objective, however, costs have to be reduced so that we can have more resources that can be used to strengthen the brands, spur innovation and thus allow us to remain competitive."[15]

Initially, Brabeck launched a manufacturing efficiency program called MH97. The objective was to reduce raw material costs and to optimize production processes. Between 1997 and 2002, 165 factories were closed, which generated savings in excess of CHF 4 billion.[16] MH97 was followed by a program called Target 2004+ that focused on improving operating performance by creating a regional manufacturing network. The project relied strongly on benchmarking and best practice transfer. By refocusing on a small number of high-performing factories, the program generated savings of more than CHF 3 billion between 2002 and 2004.[17] Target 2004+ was succeeded by a program called Operation Excellence 2007 that redeploys many of the prior projects' concepts. This program's key objectives are to improve supply chain productivity, optimize planning, eliminate overheads, and reduce product complexity.

In addition to the manufacturing-related efficiency programs, Nestlé initiated the FitNes initiative to drive efficiency in the group's administrative processes. FitNes was launched in 2002, and it is predicted to incur savings in excess of CHF 1 billion.[18] Wolfgang Reichenberger, former CFO of Nestlé, comments on FitNes: "It's an area that the group has not addressed in the past, it's uncharted territory, and it's fascinating."[19]

The most important business transformation initiative in Nestlé's 140-year history is, however, the Global Business Excellence (GLOBE) initiative, launched in 2000. Although it covers a broad range of strategic objectives, the program is also designed to improve operational efficiency by integrating the company's businesses on a global scale. The project's major objectives are to establish best practices in business processes, to align data standards, and to install common information systems. Due to Nestlé's highly decentralized structure and its large number of acquisitions, it runs multiple versions of accounting, planning, and inventory software. Sharing information between markets and operating units is thus difficult. The project's impacts range from the way raw materials are bought, to production, marketing, and sales. "We're now transitioning to become a genuinely global food company, to behave as one," says the former CFO

Reichenberger. He describes the program's main benefits as follows: "When GLOBE has been introduced in the most relevant markets, all inter-market systems will communicate much better with each other than they do now. Through these aligned systems we should achieve substantial improvements over the years to come."[20] By the end of 2005, GLOBE had been rolled out to 30 percent of the businesses.[21] It is projected that GLOBE will enable total savings of CHF 3 billion.[22]

Besides these programs directed toward increasing Nestlé's operational performance, Brabeck also worked on reducing marketing expenditures by better exploiting the synergies between brands. Brand strategies were centralized as far as possible to drive synergies and increase control. The most important strategic initiative was to allocate as many of the company's 127,000 products as possible to six strategic brands: Nestlé, Buitoni, Maggi, Nescafé, Nestea, and Purina. By 2005, more than 70 percent of the company's portfolio belonged to one of these six brands.[23] These strategic brands deliver higher margins, occupy more shelf space, and help retailers generate top-line growth. Nescafé, for example, has a brand value of nearly CHF 15 billion, a name recognition of almost 100 percent in the world's leading markets, and margins of about 18 percent.[24] The remaining local brands have been complemented with the Nestlé logo, a bird's nest with a parent bird and two hatchlings, to strengthen product identity and to communicate product characteristics such as quality, taste, and safety.[25] (See Appendices 3, 4, and 5.)

The efficiency initiatives' combined outcome has been impressive. Nestlé's net margin rose from 5.7 percent in 1997 to 8.7 percent in 2005. The various cost initiatives incurred total savings of CHF 12 billion. Net income soared from CHF 4 billion in 1997 to CHF 8 billion in 2005, while the free cash flow nearly doubled.[26]

The Nutrition and Wellness Initiative

Nestlé's efficiency improvements were the basis for further strong investments in internal growth. Brabeck's primary task shifted toward generating new sources of growth for the company's future expansion. "It was clear that with tomato paste, oil, and dry pasta, we were not going to create value in the long term," Brabeck said, referring to the low-growth products that Nestle had largely divested in the past decade, "We had to identify areas from which new growth could come."[27]

Early on, Brabeck sensed that the growing demand for wellness and nutritional products could provide an excellent opportunity for sustained growth in Nestlé's mature markets. "Brabeck was on a nutrition kick long before it was fashionable," says John McMillan, analyst

at Prudential.[28] One of Brabeck's first official acts as CEO was the creation of a dedicated unit engaged in nutrition related to performance, infants, and diet. The rationale behind the new unit was to develop an innovative product segment with a strong potential for future growth and considerably higher margins than traditional products in the food industry. Building on this first initiative, Brabeck announced his vision of transforming Nestlé from a food company into a food, nutrition, health, and wellness company in 2000. An entire package of measures, which included strategic initiatives and organizational changes, was implemented to integrate nutritional thinking into the group as a whole. In pursuit of a strong internal growth potential, Brabeck aimed at two main strategic goals. The first objective was to develop nutrition and wellness as a value-added feature in the mainstream food and beverage business. The second objective was to reinforce the company's leading position regarding specialized nutritional products. The creation of two dedicated business units, the Corporate Wellness Unit and the Nestlé Nutrition Unit, reflected these twin objectives.

The creation of the Corporate Wellness Unit was directed at fulfilling the first strategic objective, namely spreading Nestlé's nutrition and wellness orientation throughout the group and across all product categories. Matt Hall, head of the strategic unit "Generating Demand," describes the strategy: "Nestlé remains within its traditional products and categories, but starts leveraging these products. We increase their value by adding health and nutritional elements."[29] Aspects of health, wellness, and nutrition are incorporated into a vast array of product categories, ranging from ice cream, frozen foods, and confectionaries to pet food. The elements added to the existing products promote digestive health, improve the immune system and skin's defenses, positively affect weight management as well as physical and mental performance, and contribute to healthy aging. To date, Nestlé has modified more than 700 products by adding nutritional functionalities.[30] An example of such a nutritional value added is Prebio, a supplement that promotes intestinal health and is added to infant nutritional products. Other examples are Calci-N, which promotes bone health, and ActiCol, which lowers plasma cholesterol. The company refers to these add-ins as "branded active benefits" (BABs). The first products enriched with BABs were introduced as long ago as 1998.

The Nestlé Nutrition unit is focused on the core nutrition business. The Nutrition unit provides products for those consumers whose primary purchasing motivation is the products' nutritional value, while taste is simply a value added. The product portfolio encompasses infant formulas, hospital nutrition, baby cereals, and sports nutrition. These products operate in a medical environment and require strong scientific support and long-term research and development. Nestlé devotes about one-fifth of its overall R&D budget to nutrition research. Three-quarters of the current projects at the central Nestlé Research Center (NRC) in Lausanne focus on health and well-being.[31]

Besides these two dedicated units, Nestlé established a number of ventures for growth into new areas related to wellness and nutrition. In cooperation with L'Oreal, one of the world's largest beauty and cosmetics companies, Nestlé moved into the area of nutricosmetics. Under the brand name Inneov, a joint venture by Nestlé and L'Oreal, a range of products has been developed that combines Nestlé's knowledge of nutrition with L'Oreal's expertise in beauty products. The products are aimed at improving the quality of skin, hair, and nails by supplying nutrients that are essential to their care. Inneov quickly gained a leading position in this high-growth segment. By 2005, Inneov had already achieved an 11 percent market share in Europe.[32]

Nestlé's nutrition business contributed significantly to the company's success. Sales generated by products with added nutritional benefits grew from CHF 200 million in 1998 to CHF 3 billion in 2005. Furthermore, these products' profit margins are twice as high as those of traditional food products, and thus contribute strongly to Nestlé's margin improvements.[33]

Strengthening Innovation

Nestlé is considered the innovation leader in the global food and nutrition sector. The driving force behind the innovation is the company's extensive research and development (R&D) network. More than 3,500 scientists work on improving existing products and creating tomorrow's nourishments.[34] Strengthening the company's R&D success was a key objective in Brabeck's quest for internal growth. Three strategic measures contributed to this objective.

First, Brabeck set the company's R&D activities a challenging target: one-fifth of the entire product portfolio has to be innovated or renovated every year. *Innovation* refers to moving the group into promising new product segments, whereas *renovation* relates to improvements to existing products, such as changes in the packaging, shape, taste, or quality. The distinction is an important one for Nestlé, as explained by Herbert Oberhaensli, Head of Economics and International Relations, "You always need to renovate your existing offer in order to keep the products alive. However, renovation and innovation do not contradict each other. Improving our products is a process of many small steps and a few big leaps. We

have to do both if we want to be successful."[35] Especially in mature markets where Nestlé generates the bulk of its sales, the continuous upgrading of existing products is an important source of internal growth. As Brabeck puts it, "There are no 'mature markets,' only mature managers."[36] Two-thirds of the company's R&D activities are dedicated to renovating existing products, while the remaining third is reserved for more radical product innovations.[37] (See Appendix 6.)

Second, a strong budgetary increase as well as improvement in its operating efficiency enabled the R&D to achieve these challenging targets. Nestlé's R&D expenditures nearly doubled, increasing from CHF 770 million in 1997 to CHF 1.5 billion in 2005.[38] At the same time, the R&D efficiency increased through improvements on the operational level. Rupert Gasser, who was in charge of Nestlé's R&D activities when Brabeck took over, said, "We eliminated a number of R&D units that were dealing with issues with resources that were below a critical minimum required to do an efficient job. We then redeployed their resources to established centers that had all the technical and scientific know-how needed to support the renovation and innovation process in a given business area."[39]

Third, a number of organizational changes were made to improve the R&D's connection with the markets in which Nestlé operates. The most relevant of these organizational measures were the creation of Product Technology Centers, Local Application Centers, and Clusters.

The Product Technology Centers' (PTC) objective is to transform research concepts provided by Nestlé's fundamental research centers into consumer products. These centers are closely linked to the company's strategic business units and are located in key consumer markets. The PTCs allow ground-breaking innovations to be transformed into marketable products more swiftly. Currently, there are nine PTCs located in France, Germany, Great Britain, Switzerland, and the United States.[40]

Local Application Centers work inside the most relevant regional markets and are concerned with adapting global products to local tastes and requirements. Local tastes in respect of culinary products, such as prepared dishes, cereals, or confectionary, vary widely. For a global company like Nestlé, market success depends heavily on the ability to adapt its products to local needs. Apart from adaptations in taste, color, and shape, the form and/or packaging of products are also frequently changed. There are, for example, more than 100 local variations of Nescafé offered around the world. As Jean-Daniel Luthi, senior vice president and group controller, explains, "You have to know the consumer in different places of the world; you need the capabilities to make your products in one place and sell them many thousands of kilometers away."[41]

Clusters are cross-divisional project structures designed to improve the communication and knowledge sharing between the R&D and the rest of the company. Clusters unite researchers with the heads of business and regional units that face similar market environments. The objective is to jointly launch R&D initiatives with respect to new product development. Cooperation in clusters results in synergies, shared investments, and faster product roll-outs. Products developed within these clusters are either implemented as global solutions, or as "cluster solutions" in the participating regions. If necessary, the company's local application centers adapt the provided solutions to the specific market requirements.[42]

Nestlé's seven strategic business units are the driving forces behind the clusters and, more generally, behind product development and consumer-oriented renovation and innovation. Contrary to geographical zones that are operationally responsible for their businesses, and have clearly set annual profit targets, strategic business units are free from such short-term targets and thus free to fully concentrate on sustainable long-term development. They develop global business strategies for their respective categories in which they describe how the product segments should evolve over the next three to five years, what innovations are required, and how much of the portfolio should be renovated. In close cooperation with the markets and R&D, the strategic business units lead Nestlé's innovation process and ensure cooperation and communication between the company's disparate units.[43]

External Growth as a Platform for Organic Growth

Despite his dedication to internal growth, Brabeck did not entirely turn away from acquisitions, but used external growth as a means to spur and enable Nestlé's internal growth. Luis Cantarell, executive vice president of Nestlé Europe, clarifies: "You cannot establish a company on external growth; however, you can use external growth to support internal growth."[44] Similarly, Brabeck understands acquisitions as first and foremost a platform for further organic growth: "The emphasis is clearly on organic growth, with acquisitions being used to accelerate it."[45]

One motivation behind Brabeck's acquisitions was to gain a critical mass in terms of market share in businesses in which scale is vital for success. As in many other industries, size provides considerable economies of scale in the food industry. Brabeck had always asserted that he wanted Nestlé to be the market leader, or at least hold a strong second position in all product categories. Although the company had indeed reached a critical mass with the majority of its businesses, some segments still had a poor geographical reach. Consequently, the acquisition of Dreyer's, for example, helped Nestlé to become market leader in the U.S. ice cream business.[46] The Ralston Purina acquisition in 2002 made the company the global leader in pet care. Most recently, the acquisition of Jenny Craig, a weight management company, reinforced Nestlé Nutrition's presence in the United States, the world's largest nutrition and weight management market.[47]

Besides the objective of reaching a critical mass in terms of market share, Brabeck used external growth to gain expert knowledge for further expansion into new product segments. Nestlé introduced two venture funds to gain access to new expertise, thus giving the research and development additional impetus. The company founded the Life Ventures fund (capitalized with CHF 235 million) in 2002, and the Nestlé Growth Fund (of CHF 790 million) in 2005. Both funds use acquisitions, as well as minority investments, licensing, and joint ventures to give Nestlé access to new technology and know-how. They both invest on a global scale and focus on long-term capital growth.[48]

The rationale behind the creation of the Life Ventures fund was to accelerate Nestlé's innovation process. By investing in start-ups in the area of nutrition and food science, Nestlé gains access to leading-edge know-how and may incorporate these ideas into its own R&D network. In 2003, for example, the fund invested in eight businesses in the fields of naturally derived bioactives, phytonutraceuticals, and health care nutrition.[49]

The Nestlé Growth Fund invests in companies on the verge of entering the market with their products. "This fund will contribute significantly to fostering and accelerating the group's expansion into health, wellness and nutrition, as it will be investing in companies with products or processes in the final testing stage or about to enter the market. The idea is to accelerate Nestlé's strategic repositioning as a health, nutrition and wellness company," said Francois-Xavier Perroud, a group spokesperson.[50] The idea is to grow these companies until they are large enough to integrate their products into Nestlé's mainstream business.

It should be noted that Nestlé is one of the most successful companies regarding the effective integration of acquisitions. Its secret recipe is its patience. There are, for instance, no rules whatsoever limiting the amount of time invested in integrating an acquired company. This slowness provides ample time to identify synergies and select the most appropriate integration approach. Additionally, great importance is accorded to retaining as many of the acquired company's employees as possible. Besides patience and the willingness to accept the acquired company's distinct culture, Nestlé's readiness to promote managers from the acquired company to its head office is regarded as a main success factor.[51] The CEO of Rowntree, a company that Nestlé bought in 1988, was, for example, appointed to its head office and became the general manager of its chocolate and confectionary business. As Tom Coley, head of Nestlé's dairy SBU, puts it: "You obtain additional sales and, what is a lot more important, you obtain additional competencies if you acquire a business."[52]

Besides acquisitions, divestitures played an important role in aligning the group's product portfolio to the objective of sustainable organic growth. Between 1997 and 2005, Brabeck divested numerous activities that either yielded low margins, or offered only limited growth opportunities. The divestitures were related to canned foods, cheese and meat, and parts of the frozen food and the confectionary businesses. In addition, Brabeck moved Nestlé from commodity food processes, such as raw material conversion, toward the consumer and added-value areas of the food industry's value chain by divesting manufacturing assets and processes. The proceeds of these divestures were reinvested in acquisitions and product development in areas promising higher growth and returns.[53] (See Appendices 7 and 8.)

Nestlé Today

Currently, Nestlé commands a product portfolio comprising food for every eating occasion, for every age, and for every evolutionary stage within a country. In 2005, the group posted sales of CHF 91 billion and record profits of CHF 8 billion.[54] Under Brabeck's tenure, the 140-year-old food giant has been revitalized and well-prepared for future challenges. Brabeck will hand over the company's reins in 2008. His successor faces the task of maintaining the successful company's momentum. Further efforts will be required to boost the health and nutrition sales in the face of tough competition. Relentless renovation and innovation are essential to retaining and improving the firm's position. (See Appendix 9.) In the words of Luis Cantarell, executive vice president of Nestlé Europe,

I think that the main challenge is a question of ambition. It is about people not accepting that our job is done. I think it is also a question of mind-set. We need to make sure that Nestlé's people are thinking about how we could be delivering better growth, because growth is the basis of everything we do.[55]

Notes

1. For more detailed information about Nestlé's development under its former CEO Helmut Maucher, please refer to E. Ashcroft and R. A. Goldberg, 1996, *Nestlé and the Twenty-First Century*, Harvard Business School Cases.

2. W. Hall, 1997, Maucher steps aside at Nestlé, *Financial Times*, May 7.

3. G. von Pilar, 1996, Nestlé erwartet Nachfragebelebung. *Lebensmittel Zeitung*, November 22.

4. Personal interview with Peter Brabeck (November 19, 2004; Vevey, Switzerland). For related quotes, please also see Brabeck's interview with S. Wetlaufer, 2001, The business case against revolution, *Harvard Business Review* 79: 112–119.

5. Real internal growth equals sales growth less impact from acquisitions, divestitures, price changes, and foreign currency exchange rates. At Nestlé, real internal growth of 4% equals an organic growth of roughly 6%.

6. For more details about the food industry's specific characteristics, please refer to M. O'Bornick, 2004, *The top 10 global leaders in food*, Business Insights Ltd.

7. Transcript of a presentation on *Strategic Demand Generation* held by Ed Marra at the Nestlé Investor Seminar 2005.

8. Nestlé Annual Report, 1996.

9. K. Mahon and A. Smith, 1998, *Nestlé'* Schroders Broker Report.

10. E. Ashcroft and R. A. Goldberg, 1996; op. cit.

11. M. O'Bornick, 2004; op. cit.

12. K. Mahon and A. Smith, 1998; op. cit.

13. Data taken from the *Thomson One Banker* database.

14. K. Mahon and A. Smith, 1998; op. cit.

15. G. von Pilar, 2004, Effizienz ist Treibstoff für Dynamik. *Lebensmittel Zeitung*, October 29.

16. N. A., 2004, Nestlé's future, *The Economist*, August 7.

17. http://www.ir.nestle.com.

18. Ibid.

19. B. McLannahan, 2003, Nestlé's crunch, *CFOEurope.com*, February.

20. B. McLannahan, 2003; op. cit.

21. W. Ackerman, A. Smith, S. Peterson, and J. Stent, 2006, *Nestlé SA*, Citigroup Broker Report.

22. N. A., 2002, Financing the future at Nestlé, *Corporate Finance*, November 1.

23. Personal interview with Matt Hall (September 21, 2005; Vevey, Switzerland).

24. R. A. Goldberg and H. F. Hogan, 2002, *Nestlé S.A.*, Harvard Business School Cases.

25. Personal interview with Luis Cantarell (January 16, 2006; Vevey, Switzerland).

26. We calculated these figures based on data published in Nestlé's annual reports.

27. D. Ball, 2004, With food sales flat, Nestle stakes future on healthier fare, *Wall Street Journal*, March 18.

28. J. Caplan, 2005, Nutritious Nestle, *Time Magazine*, April 11.

29. Personal interview with Matt Hall (September 21, 2005; Vevey, Switzerland).

30. M. Kowalsky and E. Nolmans, 2005, Peter Brabeck: Der Prophet des Wachstums, *Bilanz*, March.

31. D. Ball, 2004; op. cit.

32. Nestlé Annual Report, 2005.
33. W. Ackerman et al, 2006; op. cit.
34. N. A., 2002, Forschung ist die Grundlage des Erfolges, *Die Presse*, May 13.
35. Personal interview with Herbert Oberhaensli (October 12, 2005; Vevey, Switzerland).
36. Personal interview with Peter Brabeck (November 19, 2004; Vevey, Switzerland).
37. Personal interview with Matt Hall (September 21, 2005; Vevey, Switzerland).
38. Data taken from the *Thomson One Banker* database.
39. R. A. Goldberg and H. F. Hogan, 2002; op. cit.
40. Personal interview with Herbert Oberhaensli (September 12, 2006; Vevey, Switzerland).
41. Personal interview with Jean-Daniel Luthi (September 21, 2005; Vevey, Switzerland).
42. Personal interview with Tom Coley (October 17, 2005; Vevey, Switzerland).
43. Personal interview with Tom Coley (October 17, 2005; Vevey, Switzerland).
44. Personal interview with Luis Cantarell (January 16, 2006; Vevey, Switzerland).
45. M. Gelnar, 2006, Nestle will continue to look for acquisitions, *Dow Jones International News*, April 6.
46. N. A., 2003, Nestlé: Behörde gegen Fusion mit Dreyer's, *Lebensmittel Zeitung*, März 5.
47. Datamonitor Company Profiles, 2004, *Nestle S.A.—SWOT Analysis*, Datamonitor PLC.
48. Nestlé Annual Reports (2003; 2005).
49. Personal interview with Luis Cantarell (January 16, 2006; Vevey, Switzerland).
50. T. Wright, 2005, Nestle surprises with new finance chief and a fund, *International Herald Tribune*, September 27.
51. A. J. Parsons, 1996, Nestlé: The visions of local managers, *McKinsey Quarterly*, February.
52. Personal interview with Tom Coley (October 17, 2005; Vevey, Switzerland).
53. R. A. Goldberg and H. F. Hogan, 2002; op. cit.
54. Nestlé Annual Report, 2005.
55. Personal interview with Luis Cantarell (January 16, 2006; Vevey, Switzerland).

Appendix 1 Nestlé's Sales and Net Income Development

Total Sales 1997–2005 (in CHF millions)

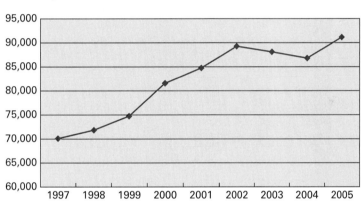

Source: Worldscope.

Net Income 1997–2005 (in CHF millions)

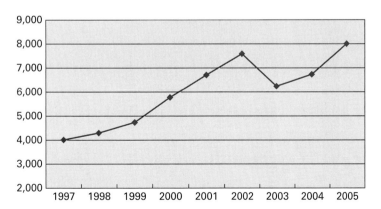

Source: Worldscope.

Appendix 2 Nestlé Financial Information, 1997–2005

In CHF millions	1997	1998	1999	2000	2001	2002	2003	2004	2005	CAGR
Sales	69,998	71,747	74,660	81,422	84,698	89,160	87,979	86,769	91,075	3.34%
Total Operating Expenses	62,758	64,423	66,344	71,924	75,622	80,530	79,108	78,082	79,706	3.03%
Costs of Goods Sold	33,127	33,354	33,223	35,205	35,025	35,790	34,920	33,362	35,218	0.77%
Research and Development Expenses	777	807	893	1,038	1,162	1,208	1,205	1,413	1,499	8.56%
EBIT	7,245	7,787	8,331	9,701	9,647	10,778	9,214	8,769	11,055	5.42%
Net Income	4,005	4,291	4,724	5,763	6,681	7,564	6,213	6,717	7,995	9.03%
Total Assets	53,727	54,401	56,646	62,955	91,868	85,833	88,163	85,648	101,700	8.30%
Current Assets	25,586	26,562	27,080	30,662	39,008	35,342	36,233	35,285	41,765	6.32%
Total Liabilities	28,396	30,805	31,568	32,442	57,639	50,201	50,340	45,372	50,265	7.40%
Current Liabilities	20,985	22,591	22,182	23,174	41,492	33,737	30,365	29,117	35,818	6.91%
Cash Flow	6,999	7,201	7,797	9,093	9,906	11,733	10,447	11,100	10,723	5.48%
ROE	16.41%	18.64%	19.32%	19.27%	19.85%	21.72%	16.85%	17.13%	16.04%	—
ROA	9.89%	10.03%	10.47%	11.76%	11.97%	9.25%	8.16%	8.43%	10.24%	—
Number of Personnel	225,808	231,881	230,929	224,541	229,765	254,199	253,000	247,000	250,000	1.28%

Source: Worldscope.

Appendix 3 Nestlé's Sales per Region and Product Segment, 2005

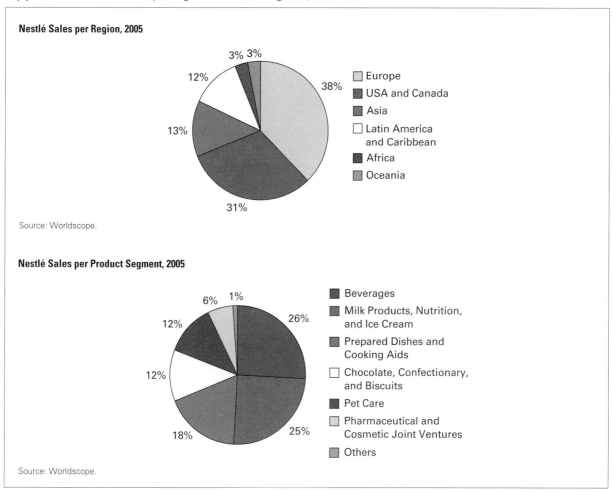

Nestlé Sales per Region, 2005

- Europe — 38%
- USA and Canada — 31%
- Asia — 13%
- Latin America and Caribbean — 12%
- Africa — 3%
- Oceania — 3%

Source: Worldscope.

Nestlé Sales per Product Segment, 2005

- Beverages — 26%
- Milk Products, Nutrition, and Ice Cream — 25%
- Prepared Dishes and Cooking Aids — 18%
- Chocolate, Confectionary, and Biscuits — 12%
- Pet Care — 12%
- Pharmaceutical and Cosmetic Joint Ventures — 6%
- Others — 1%

Source: Worldscope.

Appendix 4 Nestlé EBITA Margins per Region and Product Segment, 2005

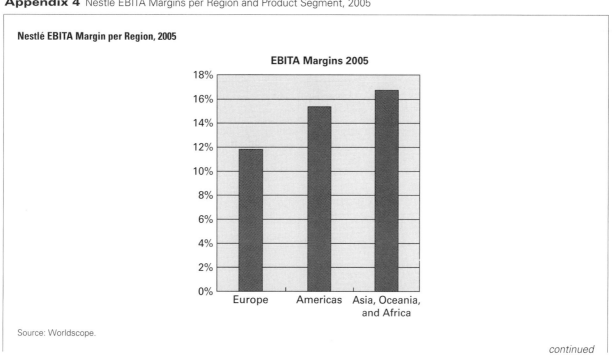

Nestlé EBITA Margin per Region, 2005

EBITA Margins 2005

Source: Worldscope.

continued

Nestlé EBTIA Margin per Product Segment, 2005

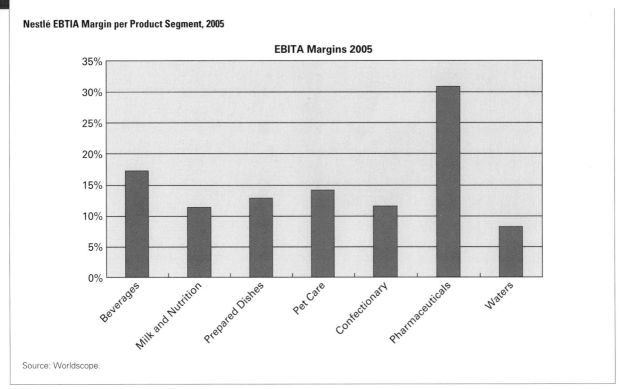

Source: Worldscope.

Appendix 5 Nestlé's Corporate Sign and the Six Strategic Brands

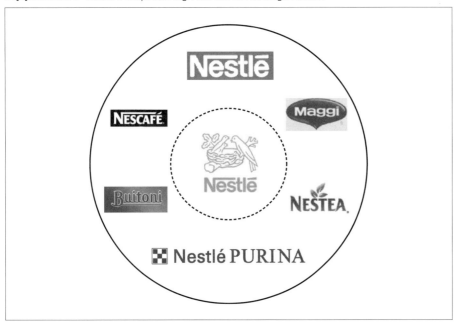

Appendix 6 Nestlé's Worldwide Research and Development Network

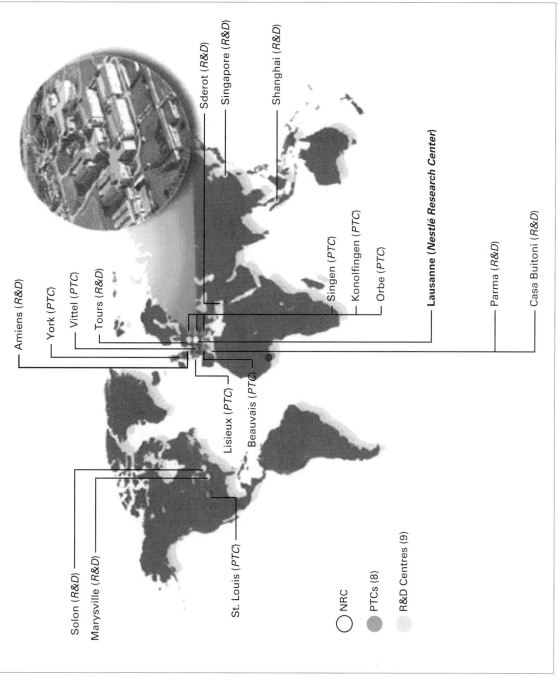

NRC

PTCs (8)

R&D Centres (9)

Amiens (*R&D*)

York (*PTC*)

Vittel (*PTC*)

Tours (*R&D*)

Lisieux (*PTC*)

Beauvais (*PTC*)

Sderot (*R&D*)

Singapore (*R&D*)

Shanghai (*R&D*)

Singen (*PTC*)

Konolfingen (*PTC*)

Orbe (*PTC*)

Lausanne (*Nestlé Research Center*)

Parma (*R&D*)

Casa Buitoni (*R&D*)

Solon (*R&D*)

Marysville (*R&D*)

St. Louis (*PTC*)

Appendix 7 Total Shareholder Return (TSR) Development in Health, Wellness, and Food & Beverages Markets, 1995–2005

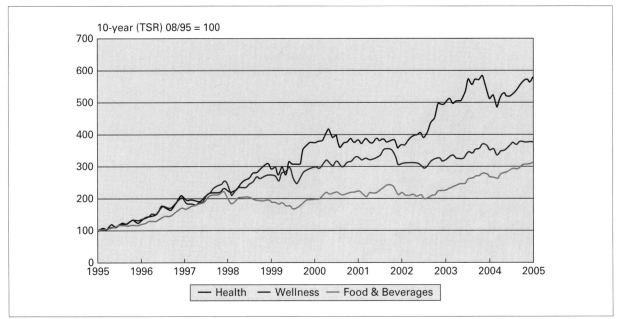

Source: http://www.ir.nestle.com/News_Events/Presentations/Group_Presentations/Group_General/.

Appendix 8 Total Shareholder Return of Nestlé and Its Main Competitors

Food	1 Year	3 Years	5 Years	10 Years
Hershey	1%	73%	88%	306%
Nestlé	**35**	**44**	**15**	**267**
Danone	32	46	20	248
Procter & Gamble	7	43	64	235
Unilever	22	10	0	190
Cadbury Schweppes	16	56	37	177
General Mills	2	13	26	127
Heinz	−11	13	−6	57
Campbell	2	36	−2	31
Coca Cola	3	−2	−27	26
Kraft	−19	−22	N/A	N/A

Source: http://www.ir.nestle.com/News_Events/Presentations/Group_Presentations/Group_General/.

Appendix 9 Timeline of Nestlé's Major Strategic and Organizational Changes on the Road to Sustaining Growth in Mature Markets

1997	1998	2000	2002	2004	2005
Announcement of 4% RIG target		Brabeck beats target of 4% RIG			Creation of clusters to spur innovation
Launch of first manufacturing efficiency program *MH97*		Launch of GLOBE initiative	Foundation of Life Ventures Fund		Foundation of Nestlé Growth Fund
Creation of a dedicated unit engaged in performance, infant, and clinical nutrition	Introduction of first products enriched with BABs	Announcement of transforming Nestlé into a food, nutrition, health, and wellness company	Launch of efficiency programs Target 2004+ and FitNes	Foundation of Nestlé Nutrition and the Corporate Wellness Unit	

Case 17

An Entrepreneur Seeks the Holy Grail of Retailing

Lauranne Buchanan

Thunderbird, The Garvin School of International Management

For an entrepreneur, Wal-Mart *is* the Holy Grail of retailers. With 5,300 outlets worldwide and 138 million customers per week,[1] a run in Wal-Mart can transform a niche product into a household name.

But landing a spot on Wal-Mart's shelves isn't easy. First, consider the competition—more than 10,000 suppliers vie for the opportunity to present to a Wal-Mart buyer each year. Then comes the interview: a mere 30 minutes to convince a seasoned—and skeptical—buyer for the world's most powerful retailer to give the product a chance. Finally, during the test period is the opportunity to prove that an unknown and underfunded product can hold its own against the biggest brand names in the industry.

If the process isn't discouraging, the statistics should be: Only 2 percent of vendors will be given a trial run; of those, only three quarters will make it past the test period. Even then, they won't move to permanent locations without proven sales figures.[2] Nonetheless, entrepreneurs everywhere dream of having the chance to supply Wal-Mart. On a rainy day in Bentonville last November, Colin Roche and Bobby Ronsse, the creators of PenAgain, had that chance.

The PenAgain is an ergonomically designed, writing instrument with a unique, wishbone shape. The idea for the pen came to Colin Roche while he was in Saturday detention at Palo Alto High School in 1987. "I was always that guy that was daydreaming of building something, making something," says Mr. Roche.[3] He attended California Polytechnic State University, San Luis Obispo, where he and a fraternity brother, Bobby Ronsse, ran a pet-sitting business employing other students. The two went different ways after college. But after the dot-com bubble burst, Mr. Roche returned to his idea. He phoned Mr. Ronsse, a mechanical engineer, and said he wanted to talk about the "pen, again"—hence the brand name. The two joined forces, putting in $5,000 each to form Pacific Writing Instruments. By December 2001, they had filed a patent approval, launched a Web site (www.penagain.com), and set up production in the Bay area.

PenAgain's design allows the writer to slip the index finger through the wishbone to guide the pen, while resting the shaft of the pen comfortably on the hand. "It makes writing fun," says Mr. Roche, who has suffered from writer's cramp since childhood. "It uses the natural weight of your hand and eliminates the need to grip tightly or push down hard."[4] In addition, the design lessens wrist strain—attractive benefits to aging Baby Boomers as they face the prospect of carpal-tunnel syndrome and arthritis. Despite the growing need for an easier-to-use pen, established competitors in the $4.8 billion writing instruments category have shown little imagination in addressing the problem. BIC and PaperMate, for example, have tinkered with the pen's length and width and the cushion grips at the tip, but they haven't altered the basic stick design of the pen.

Roche and Ronsse were therefore understandably nervous and excited as they arrived to present to the Wal-Mart buyer—an opportunity for which they had paid $10,000. But almost before they sat down, the buyer dismissed the product with, "I've seen this design before and passed."[5]

Come Prepared

But the two entrepreneurs were prepared for the buyer's skepticism. Before approaching Wal-Mart they had spent four years developing a track record with other retailers, building a broad product mix, and expanding their production capability.

To develop a market for their product, the entrepreneurs began by pounding the pavement, approaching

Don Hammond/Design Pics/Corbis

smaller retailers such as Edwards Luggage in San Francisco. Fred Ebert, the owner, later commented that the pen "was gimmicky, but it looked good." He took a chance on the newfangled pen and placed an order. Today, he sells about 700 pens a year at $12.95, making PenAgain his top-selling brand.

The two entrepreneurs also attended trade shows, once staying up all night to glue 300 pen samples in their hotel since the manufacturer hadn't heat-welded the pieces in time. These shows provided contacts with more buyers and distributors. But their big break came from their most unconventional channel—doctors' offices. The pen's unique design provides a natural benefit to those who suffer from arthritis and Parkinson's, and what better place to reach these people than through their doctor. So the team made a concerted effort to contact as many doctors as they could, many of whom started using the pen themselves and recommending it to their patients. As important as the sales were, the channel provided the entrepreneurs with something even more valuable: testimonials for the product and additional exposure. Scott Koerner, senior vice president of merchandising for Office Depot, saw the PenAgain in his optometrist's office and noticed on a return visit, that it had sold out. "We sell to a lot of small business, and this doctor happened to be a small business and that caught my attention," Mr. Koerner said.[6] That was enough for Office Depot to place an order for all 1,049 of its stores.

To maintain interest in the product, Roche and Ronsse knew they needed to be more than a one-product shop. So they began expanding the product line to include other writing instruments and tools. Over time, they introduced a pencil, highlighter, white-board marker, and children's pens, then a hobby knife—all based on the wishbone design. In addition, they expanded each product line with a wide array of colors and textures.

Sales grew. By 2004, PenAgain had $2 million in revenues across a wide range of retailers, including 5,000 independent stationery and office-supply stores, 200 Staples in Canada, and other chain outlets such as Fred Meyer and Hobby Lobby. In addition, the company picked up orders of 1.2 million units in Europe from promotional-products companies. And Internet sales have also been steady—providing revenues of approximately $5,000 each month. Among office supply products sold on Amazon.com, PenAgain has been the number one or two seller.[7]

But to break into the big league, the entrepreneurs knew they needed a lower price point and high-volume manufacturing capabilities—which meant moving production overseas. With funds from four outside investors, they went to China in search of manufacturers. Having located the right partners, they invested in having multiple molds produced, costing $10,000 each (roughly half of what they would pay in the United States). The additional molds meant that when a big order came in, PenAgain could ramp up quickly. "It allows us to push hard on expanding the distribution channels without fear of being unable to deliver," Mr. Roche says.[8] It also helped them reduce the price to $3.99 on one model—which would be critical to winning over Wal-Mart.

The Order

To the Wal-Mart buyer's outright dismissal of the product, Mr. Roche responded: "The difference is that we are building a brand. Rather than going to you first, we've got a base of independent retailers and distributors worldwide who have already picked us up."[9] He kept talking, showing her the testimonials, media write-ups, and product extensions. And she continued to take notes.

Their patience in approaching the super-retailer would make a difference: Before Wal-Mart takes on a new product, it wants to know that product will sell. "We like companies to have a sales history and to be sold somewhere else first, even if it's just a downtown boutique," says Excell La Fayette Jr., Wal-Mart's director of supplier development. Furthermore, Wal-Mart doesn't like to account for more than 30 percent of a supplier's total business.

Finally, the buyer closed her notebook and said, "OK, we will give you a trial period." The parameters of the trial: 500 stores would carry the product for six weeks, with the expectation that PenAgain would sell 85 percent of the product.[10] If they were unable to meet the goal, they would be out.

Even though many would consider this trial a win, the seasoned entrepreneurs knew the game had just begun.

The Trial

42 days. 500 stores. 85% product sell-through. Succeed, and one day PenAgain might be a household name like BIC. Fail, and the 34-year-old entrepreneurs would be blowing the biggest break of their five-year-old product.

From the time the buyer says "OK" to approval as an official Wal-Mart vendor takes some eight to ten months. Much of this time is spent completing the intensive paperwork. Until approval is granted, there are no guarantees. Even so, the entrepreneur cannot afford to wait to start production; upon receiving approval, they will have a narrow window in which to deliver product to the store. To ensure that they could meet Wal-Mart's deadlines, production had to be ramped up in advance.

By the time the PenAgain team received the official document on April 12, 2005, they had produced some 53,000 pens—the 48,000 Wal-Mart ordered, plus 5,000 as backup.

Every detail must be considered when working for Wal-Mart. Orders have to conform to Wal-Mart's rigid packaging and shipping requirements, or they won't be accepted. Packaging has to be printed with shipping labels that include purchase-order numbers and distribution-center details. And because the order of PenAgain was hurried out of China, all of this information had to be added to the boxes after they got to the United States. Store displays are just as critical. Any detail—from the thickness of the cardboard used in display cartons to the red stripe around the outside that says "stationery" —can delay getting the product on the floor. "We didn't sleep during that three weeks," said Mr. Roche.[11] Their sleepless nights paid off—the pens were delivered to and accepted by Wal-Mart's distribution center on time.

The mistake many hopeful vendors make, at this point, is to assume that being in Wal-Mart means the product will sell itself—or that Wal-Mart will sell it. Neither of which is true. "A lot of times, what will hurt suppliers more than anything is that they may not monitor the product very well. . . . They are busy still trying to sell the [Wal-Mart] buyer on that item. You've sold them. Now, just make sure that the information is out there, and drive customers to the product," says Mr. La Fayette of Wal-Mart. The PenAgain partners couldn't afford traditional advertising, so they reached out virally to anyone they felt would support the brand—from their national fraternity headquarters to the doctors, patients, and medical organizations who had already shown interest in the product.

Even more important, the entrepreneurs monitored store sales. And in doing so, they quickly learned that delivering the product didn't mean that it would get to the shelf right away or that it would get to the assigned spot. Some pens sat in stockrooms; others were placed near pet food or potato chips rather than on the assigned end-of-aisle displays. "The lesson is, 'Oh my God, there are these big companies with heavy back-end systems that can track everything. But if human beings are involved, problems are going to happen,'" says Mr. Roche.[12] They hired a third-party merchant service organization to send reps into stores to check out display placement and consumer traffic. They themselves visited 50 stores to check on displays. Without this type of monitoring, they wouldn't have known that by the end of the first month pens hadn't even shown up in 38 of the 500 test stores.[13]

Tracking sales every day from every store via Wal-Mart's Retail Link software system allowed Mr. Ronsse to demonstrate PenAgain's performance. He sorted sales data using Microsoft Excel to pinpoint exactly where the pen was selling and where it wasn't. "In some places, we were selling per day what we should do in a week," said Mr. Ronsse.[14] According to Wal-Mart's Mr. La Fayette, leaving this type of monitoring to Wal-Mart is another common mistake made by rookie suppliers. "When you have a buyer with 10 to 20 different categories, they cannot monitor everyone's pieces, and they depend on the supplier to inform them of what is going on."[15]

Again, the extra effort paid off for the entrepreneurs. By making sure the Wal-Mart buyer was aware of the most accurate sales figures when evaluating the results of the test market, the team won a limited reorder from the mass merchant—even though its 75 percent sell-through rate fell short of the target.

Balancing the Mix

Price—or more precisely, Wal-Mart's price—is a concern for other retailers. Wal-Mart sells the PenAgain for $3.76, compared to an almost identical version selling for $6.49 on Amazon and $12 elsewhere. By slashing the price for Wal-Mart, the PenAgain team risked angering their bread-and-butter base of 5,000 retailers, many of them being small stationery shops.

To appease this group, PenAgain founders created exclusive offerings for small stores, including an ergonomic sample set for $15 to $20 and a brushed metal pen for $20 to $30. Their smaller retailers welcome the effort: Fred Ebert, owner of Edwards Luggage, Inc., sells the same model as Wal-Mart at a higher price. He says Wal-Mart "worries" him and at some point, he will probably stop ordering PenAgain until it comes out with a higher-end model. "I don't want to be way out of line on pricing anything because it sends a bad message," he explained.[16]

In addition, PenAgain founders are assembling an advisory group of independent store owners to case the small retailers' concerns. One of the group's first assignments is to give the company feedback on the merchandisers. "If a Staples or a Wal-Mart sells a less-expensive product and then the manufacturer comes out with a nicer version, that can really build up the sales," says Bob Norins, store manager for Arthur Brown International Pen Shop in Manhattan.

The added exposure from Wal-Mart could double sales for PenAgain to $4 million to $5 million this year. But the loyalty of small retailers cannot be taken for granted. "That's our goal: to try and prove that we will live in both worlds," explains Mr. Roche.[17]

1. G. Bounds, 2005, The long road to Wal-Mart: What does it take for enterpreneurs to break into the nation's largest retailer? *Wall Street Journal*, Septemer 19, R1.
2. G. Bounds, 2005, One month to make it, *Wall Street Journal*, May 30, B1.
3. L. Thomas, 2004, Handy tool, http://www.sfgate.com, June 30.
4. Ibid.
5. Bounds, The long road to Wal-Mart.
6. Bounds, One month to make it.
7. Bounds, The long road to Wal-Mart.
8. Ibid.
9. Ibid.
10. Ibid.
11. Bounds, One month to make it.
12. G. Bounds, 2006, Pen maker's trial by Wal-Mart, Part III, *Wall Street Journal*, July 18, B1.
13. Ibid.
14. Ibid.
15. Bounds, One month to make it.
16. Ibid.
17. Ibid.

PSA Peugeot Citroën: Strategic Alliances for Competitive Advantage?

Sachin Govind, S. Sam George

ICFAI Center for Management Research

I don't want to boast, but I can say that we are probably the champions in the sphere of the joint projects.[1]

—**Jean-Martin Folz,**
President, Board of Directors, PSA Peugeot Citroën, in 2003

Introduction

In February 2005, PSA Peugeot Citroën (PSA) entered into an agreement with Mitsubishi Motor Corp.,[2] the ailing Japanese car maker. According to the terms of the deal, Mitsubishi agreed to supply 30,000 units of a new sports utility vehicle (SUV) every year to PSA, which would then be sold under the Peugeot and Citroën marques. The deal enabled Mitsubishi to utilize its idle production capacity, and PSA to fill a major gap in its product range.

The deal with Mitsubishi was typical of PSA's strategy of entering into alliances with other major automobile makers. Over the years, PSA has entered into long-term relationships with Renault S.A,[3] Fiat Auto SpA,[4] Ford Motor Co.,[5] Toyota Motor Corp.,[6] and BMW AG.[7] Such alliances have helped PSA share costs, risks, and investment. At the same time, PSA was also pursuing R&D independently to sharpen its competitive edge.

In January 2006, PSA announced that its profits for the year 2005 would be less than previously estimated. This profit warning—the second in three months—reflected the poor sales performance of the company's cars in Europe. The competition in the automobile market in Europe remained intense, which contributed to lower margins. PSA launched several new models in 2005. Even so, worldwide sales of Peugeot branded cars in 2005 fell by 1.5 percent. However, Citroën car sales were 3.5 percent higher in the same period.

The Peugeot arm of PSA expected to sell 2 million cars in 2006. The company hoped to sell, by the end of 2007, half a million units of its new model, the 207, a compact car launched in January 2006.

Background Note

About Peugeot

The history of PSA dates back to the nineteenth century. In 1810, Jean-Frederic Peugeot, together with his brother Jean-Pierre Peugeot, transformed their textile mill in Alsace, France, into a foundry. The brothers invented a new process of making sprung steel. Using this new technology, they started making saws, watch springs, and other products. In 1858, Peugeot adopted the now familiar lion logo as its symbol (refer to Exhibit 1 A for

Exhibit 1 Company Logos

Source: http://www.psa-peugeot-citroen.com.

the logo). In the 1880s, Peugeot was managed by Armand Peugeot, Jean-Pierre's grandson. In 1885, Peugeot started producing bicycles. In 1889, Peugeot unveiled its first automobile—a steam-powered three-wheeler. However, almost immediately, the steam engine was dropped in favor of the petrol engine patented by Gottlieb Daimler. The first "customer" car was delivered in 1891. In 1892, Peugeot made 29 cars and by 1899, production had increased to 300 cars a year.

Peugeot established a presence in several rallies and competitions in the 1890s. The first appearance of a Peugeot in a race was in the 1894 Paris-Rouen Trial (which is widely considered the world's first motor race). Peugeot tasted its first success in the 1895 Paris-Bordeaux-Paris race.

In 1896, Peugeot started making its own engines. The same year, Societe Anonyme des Automobiles Peugeot, a separate automobile company, was set up by Peugeot. In 1900, the company's first small car christened Bebe was launched. In 1902, the company opened a new factory in Lille. Soon, the factory started making motorbikes as well. With the success of its products, yet another factory was opened in 1910 in Sochaux. All this time, the company's cars continued to do well at motor races.

After World War I, the company began to concentrate on making diesel-powered cars. In 1922, Peugeot Quadrilette, a diesel car, replaced the Bebe. The Quadrilette was a huge success. In subsequent years, Peugeot acquired several companies including the Bellanger Car Company in Neuilly, and De Dion Bouton factory in Puteaux. In 1929, Peugeot launched the 201 model. The 1930s saw the launch of the 202 and 402 models, which went on to become bestsellers.

No new model launches occurred during World War II. In 1947, the 203 model was launched. During this period were made new acquisitions such as Chenard-Walcker and Hotchkiss. In 1955, the company launched the 403, which sold 1.2 million units in a decade.

About Citroën

In 1912, André Citroën paid a visit to Ford's plant in the United States and learned the operational details of mass producing cars. In 1913, André established the Société des Engrenages Citroën headquartered at Quai de Grenelle in Paris. Soon he made preparations to transform an armaments plant into an automobile factory. In 1919, the company launched its first car, the Type A, the first mass-produced model in Europe. Around this time, the chevron[8] shape of its gear teeth was adopted as the company logo (refer to Exhibit 1 B for the logo). In 1921, a second model—the B2—was launched, replacing the Type A. In 1922, a Citroën achieved the unique distinction of being the first car to cross the Sahara desert.

In 1924, a new company, Société Anonyme André Citroën, was created. The same year, sales subsidiaries were opened at Brussels, Cologne, Milan, Amsterdam, and other important cities in Europe. In 1924–1925, Citroën became popular for a motor expedition referred to as the black cruise.[9] In 1927, the C4 was launched. In 1931–1932, Citroën organized yet another motor expedition called the yellow cruise.[10] In 1934, the company launched the 7A, which incorporated several innovative features including front wheel drive, torsion bar suspension, aerodynamic body, hydraulic brakes, and so on. However, during this period the company faced financial problems. In 1934–1935, Michelin, the French tire maker, acquired a major stake in Citroën and started a restructuring exercise that included layoffs. Michelin was able to wipe off Citroën's debts and improve its efficiency. In 1935, André passed away.

During World War II, the Citroën factory was bombed, which led to a drastic fall in production. However, the company soon rebuilt the plant. In 1948, the 2CV van was launched. In 1953, the company entered into an agreement with Panhard, an armored vehicle maker, to partially merge the two companies' sales networks. In 1958, the company set up a new plant at Vigo, Spain, to manufacture its 2CV vans. In 1965, Citroën acquired Panhard. In 1967, the company acquired a majority stake in Berliet, another automobile company. In 1968, a parent company—Citroën SA, which owned Citroën, Panhard, and Berliet—was formed. In 1974, Peugeot acquired a 38.2 percent stake in Citroën SA.

PSA Peugeot Citroën

In May 1976, Peugeot took complete control of Citroën SA, and PSA Peugeot Citroën was formed. PSA, the holding company, was the full owner of both the companies (Automobiles Peugeot S.A and Automobiles Citroën S.A). In the same year, the 10 millionth Peugeot car rolled out of the factory premises (refer to Exhibit 2 for new model launches during 1977–2005). In 1977, Société Mécanique Automobile de l'Est (SMAE) was established to manufacture gear boxes and engines. In the same year, SAMM, an aeronautics component manufacturer, was also acquired by the group. In 1978, the European arm of Chrysler[11] (Chrysler France, Chrysler UK, and Chrysler Spain) was acquired by PSA. PSA sold the models of the former Chrysler's European subsidiaries, including Simca[12] and Sunbeam[13] under the Talbot marque. In 1980, Peugeot and Talbot merged and a single dealership for both marques was established. The marketing for both product ranges was handled by Peugeot.

In 1982, Citroën shifted its headquarters to Neuilly, France. In the same year, a new plant to manufacture gear boxes was inaugurated at Valenciennes. In 1986, the Talbot models were discontinued. In 1990, Peugeot celebrated its 100th year as an automaker. In 1991, Peugeot

Exhibit 2 New Model Launches, 1977–2005

Year	Models	Year	Models	Year	Models
1977	Peugeot 305	1986	205 convertible, 309 GTI, Citroën AX	1998	206, Partner Electric, Xsara Coupe, Xsara Estate, Berlingo Electric
1978	Citroën Visa, Simca Horizon	1987	405	1999	206 S16
1979	505, 604 turbo diesel	1989	605, Citroën XM	2000	Xsara Picasso, 607, 206 CC
1980	305 Station Wagon, 505 turbo, Talbot Solara	1991	106, Citroën ZX	2001	307, C5
1981	Peugeot J5, Samba, Tagora, Visa II, C25	1993	306, Citroën Xantia	2002	206 SW, 307 SW, 307 Estate, 807, C3, C8
1982	Citroën BX, 505	1994	806, 306 Convertible, Citroën Synergie, Relay	2003	307 CC, Citroën C2, C3 Pluriel
1983	205	1995	406, 106 electric, Peugeot Expert, Citroën Xantia Activa, AX Electric, Jumpy	2004	407
1984	205 GTI	1996	Citron Saxo, Berlingo, Saxo Electric, Peugeot Partner, 406 Estate	2005	107, C1, 1007, 407 Coupe
1985	309, BX Estate	1997	306 Estate, 406 Coupe, Xantia LPG, Berlingo Multispace, Xsara		

Source: http://www.psa-peugeot-citroen.com.

established its subsidiary, Peugeot do Brasil. In 1992, the group entered China and Egypt through partnership agreements.

In 1994, Citroën celebrated its 75th anniversary. In 1998, the group unveiled its new high-pressure direct injection (HDi) engine, which was incorporated in all its models. In 2001, the group received ISO 14001 certification for several of its facilities. In the same year, the group entered into an agreement with two French technology research institutions—Scientific Research Center (CNRS) and Atomic Energy Commission (CEA)—for joint research on fuel cells. In 2005, the group sold Panhard.

In 2005, PSA worldwide sales reached 3,389,900 units, with sales of the Peugeot marque totaling 1,995,450 units and the Citroën marque another 1,394,450 (refer Exhibit 3 for region-wide sales of PSA). As of 2006, the group was selling more than 22 models (refer to Exhibit 4 for a list of models of Peugeot and Citroën as of 2006).

Forging Alliances

PSA could be considered the pioneer of strategic alliances in the automobile industry. Its first alliance with Renault started in 1966. Over the years, the company benefited considerably from its strategic alliances with several automobile and auto component companies. Subsequently,

Exhibit 3 Regional Sales* for PSA, 2005

Region	Sales (in units)
France	777,000
Other Western European countries	1,583,400
Central Europe and Turkey	209,700
Africa	83,600
The Americas	194,500
Asia-Pacific	511,900
Other	29,800
TOTAL	**3,389,900**

*Sales include passenger cars and light commercial vehicles.
Source: http://www.psa-peugeot-citroen.com.

Exhibit 4 List of Models, February 2006

Peugeot	107, 206, 206cc, 207, 307, 307cc, 407, 607, 807, 1007, Partner Combi
Citroën	C1, C2, C3, C3 Pluriel, C4, C5, C6, C8, Berlingo, Xsara Picasso

Source: http://www.peugeot.com and www.citroen.com.

Exhibit 5 Some Strategic Alliances in the Automobile Industry

No	Companies	Year	Remarks
1	Fiat Auto and Tata Motors	2006	Tata Motors was to manage distribution and after-sales service for Fiat in India. Fiat, in turn, would provide access for Tata Motors to world markets.
2	Fiat Auto and Suzuki	2005	Fiat Motors and Suzuki co-developed an SUV. Suzuki was to use Fiat's 1.9 l diesel engines for its version of the SUV.
3	Nissan and Mitsubishi Motors	2000	Integration of forklift business of both companies—from product development to marketing.
4	Fiat Auto and General Motors	2000	Share engines as well as platforms and pool purchase and finance operations in Europe and Latin America.
5	Toyota and General Motors	1999	Joint research on fuel cell technology, joint operation of auto manufacturing plant in California.
6	Suzuki and General Motors	1987	Joint establishment and management of a company in Ingersoll, Canada. The objective of the alliance for Suzuki was to gain entry into the North American market, while GM attempted to gain insights into Japanese manufacturing methods and management.

Compiled from various sources.

other automobile companies took the cue from PSA and entered into alliances and partnerships with their competitors (refer to Exhibit 5 for alliances in the auto industry).

PSA and Renault S.A

PSA and Renault had a series of agreements that involved several joint industrial and technological projects. As noted above, Peugeot and Renault first collaborated in 1966 when the two companies entered into a cooperation agreement for the joint production of mechanical subassemblies. In 1969, the two companies further strengthened their partnership by establishing a joint venture—La Française de Mécanique (LFM)—to produce long-series components and engines that were to be used in Peugeot and Renault cars. The 50:50 joint venture was located in Douvrin, in northern France. In the same year a limited company called Société de Transmissions Automatiques (STA), owned 80 percent by Renault and 20 percent by Peugeot, was founded. STA was established primarily to produce automatic transmissions for Renault and rear-axle assemblies for Peugeot. The STA plant was located in Ruitz in northern France.

In 1971, Peugeot, Renault, and Volvo[14] came together to design a V6 engine.[15] The three automobile makers formed an equally owned company called Peugeot Renault Volvo (PRV). The engines were manufactured by LFM and by 1974, they were being used in the Peugeot 504 and 604, and the Renault 30. However, in 1989, Volvo pulled out from PRV. As a result, Peugeot and Renault became 50 percent partners in the company.

In 1992, PSA entered into a fresh technological and industrial agreement with Renault to develop a new series of automatic transmissions. Meanwhile, LFM continued

to develop improved versions of the V6 engines. In 1996, LFM introduced the new V6 ES 9 engine for mid-range and high-end Renault cars, the Peugeot 406, and the Citroën Xantia and XM models. Again in 1997, the self-acting automatic transmission—BVA—was jointly developed by PSA and Renault, with each company bearing FRF 2.8 billion as development costs. The transmission was manufactured at the STA plant in Ruitz and Peugeot's plant in Valenciennes.

In 2000, PSA and Renault launched an improved three-liter version of the V6 ES 9 engine. The new engine was installed in mid-range and high-end Renault, Peugeot, and Citroën cars and multipurpose vehicles. The LFM plant manufactured about 27,000 V6 ES 9 engines in 2000.

Fiat Auto SpA

PSA's strategic relationship with Fiat started in 1978 when the two companies signed their first cooperation agreement to design and manufacture a light commercial vehicle. A joint venture, Société Européenne de Véhicules Légers (Sevel SpA), owned 50 percent by Fiat, 25 percent by Automobiles Peugeot, and 25 percent by Automobiles Citroën, was established for this purpose. The production of the vehicles (Fiat Ducato, Peugeot J5, and Citroën C25) began at Val di Sangro facility, near Pescara, Italy, in 1981. In 1988, the scope of the joint venture with Fiat was expanded to include the design and production of multipurpose vehicles (MPVs).

In 1993, the Val di Sangro plant started the production of the Peugeot Boxer, and the Citroën Dispatch, both light commercial vehicles. The plant continued to manufacture Fiat Ducatos as well. In 1994, a new plant at Sevelnord, Valenciennes, France, began operations for the production of the Peugeot 806, the Citroën Synergie, and the Fiat Ulysses and Lancia Z (Zeta). The agreement between PSA and Fiat required the partners to manage the plants located in their country of origin (i.e., the Val di Sangro plant was managed by Fiat and the Sevelnord plant was managed by PSA). PSA and Fiat owned 50 percent in each plant and shared the production capacity equally. In 1995, the Sevelnord plant started production of the Peugeot Expert, the Citroën Relay, and the Fiat Scudo light commercial vehicles.

In 2002, PSA declared that its collaboration with Fiat in the development of light commercial vehicles would be extended through 2017 making it one of the most enduring alliances in the automobile industry. PSA and Fiat signed a major framework agreement that outlined various aspects of the collaboration. PSA and Fiat were to invest around €1.7 billion to manufacture two lines of light commercial vehicles.

In 2005, Tofas, a Turkey-based automobile manufacturer, entered into an agreement with PSA and Fiat, making it a three-way collaboration. The agreement involved the development and production of small, entry-level light commercial vehicles. The new models were to expand the product ranges of Peugeot, Citroën, and Fiat. They were to be manufactured at Tofas's plant in Bursa, Turkey, and were to be launched in 2008.

As of 2005, the PSA-Fiat partnership had jointly produced, since 1978, a total of 3.3 million light commercial vehicles and 400,000 multipurpose vehicles.

Ford Motor Co.

PSA's cooperation with Ford began in September 1998. The two automakers announced a large-scale agreement to jointly develop four families of small diesel engines incorporating the latest technologies, including Common Rail Direct injection (CRDi).[16] The initial announcement put the development time for the new engines at two and a half years. In 1999, the initial agreement was expanded to include an extended range of small aluminum direct injection diesel engines for cars and light commercial vehicles. The new agreement also included technological upgrades of a midsized second generation engine and a range of

V-diesel engines for the luxury vehicles of both companies. PSA and Ford shared the total cost of the project equally. The partnership with Ford developed in four phases.

In 2001, in the first phase, PSA and Ford unveiled the first direct injection diesel engine developed under the cooperation agreements, which replaced the TUD[17] range of engines. The 1,398 cc engines were sold as HDi 1.4 by PSA and Duratorq TDCi 1.4 by Ford. The engines were mounted on the Peugeot 206 and 307, the Citroën C2 and C3, and the Ford Fiesta and Fusion. Both companies identified 23 applications for the new engine family. The production of the engines at the Douvrin plant saw high productivity levels with daily production reaching 6,000 engines. As part of the first phase, a new 1.6-liter (1,590 cc) common rail diesel engine was also launched.

In early 2003, PSA and Ford introduced a 2-liter CRDi diesel engine (1,988 cc) developed in the second phase of their cooperative venture. These engines were manufactured at PSA's Trémery plant. The high-performance and low-noise engines were reportedly more fuel-efficient and cleaner than those available in the market. The aggregate investment for the development of the engines came to nearly €1 billion.

The first two phases of the cooperation were carried out under the leadership of PSA; the third and fourth phases were led by Ford. In June 2003, as part of the third phase, a new 2.7-liter V6 24-valve engine was unveiled. Production of the engine began in the following months. The engine was first mounted on the Jaguar S-Type. Subsequently, it was used in the Peugeot 607, the Land Rover Discovery, the Range Rover Sport, the Jaguar XJ, the Peugeot 407 Coupe, and the Citroën C6.

In October 2005, under the fourth phase of their cooperation, PSA and Ford started the production of a new series of 2.2-liter CRDi diesel engines for light and medium commercial vehicles. In addition, they introduced a new 2.2-liter HDi/TDCi diesel engine that was eventually mounted on several Peugeot, Citroën, and Ford upper/medium and executive passenger car platforms. The engines were produced at the Trémery plant. The HDi/TDCi engine showcased the companies' ability to work together in developing high-performance diesel engines (see Table 1).

Table 1 A Comparison of Different Manufacturers' Diesel Engines

Manufacturer	Engine	Max. Power (PS)	Max. Torque (Nm)	Vehicles
PSA/Ford	2.7-L V6	207@4000 rpm	440@1900 rpm	Jaguar S-Type, Peugeot 607
Isuzu	3.0-L V6	180@4000 rpm	370@1900 rpm	Saab: 9; Renault: Vel Satis; Opel: Vectra & Signum
Volkswagen	2.5-L V6	180@6200 rpm	370@1500 rpm	Audi A6
DaimlerChrysler	3.2-L I6	204@4200 rpm	500@1800 rpm	Mercedes E- and S-class

Source: http://www.autoreport.com.

In all, PSA and Ford jointly produced four families of CRDi diesel engines, namely 1.4-liter/1.6-liter engines, a second-generation 2-liter engine, a 2.7-liter V6 engine, and a new family of engines for light commercial vehicles. The cooperation made PSA-Ford the world's leading diesel engine manufacturer. By 2005, they were jointly manufacturing more than 9,000 engines a day.

Toyota Motor Corp.

In July 2001, PSA and Toyota signed a cooperation agreement in Brussels, Belgium, to establish a joint venture company. Toyota Peugeot Citroën Automobile (TPCA) Czech was established for the joint development and production of small cars designed mainly for the European market. The companies also announced that the small cars developed by the joint venture would be priced below the entry-level cars of the two partners, which meant that the factory for the production of these cars had to be established in a low-cost country and meet stringent requirements. After an extensive search, Kolin in the Czech Republic was identified as the location for the plant. The plant started production of Toyota, Peugeot, and Citroën branded cars in 2005. The capacity of the plant was 300,000 vehicles per year, with 100,000 cars for each of the brands—Peugeot, Citroën, and Toyota.

Toyota was in charge of development and production, while PSA was responsible for purchasing and logistics. The total investment, primarily for R&D and industrial expenditure, of about €1.5 billion, was shared between the two automakers.

BMW AG

In 2002, PSA entered into a cooperation agreement with BMW to jointly develop and produce an all-new family of small 4-cylinder petrol engines incorporating the latest technologies. In June 2005, PSA and BMW presented the industrial plan for production of the engines. The engines were later used in Peugeot and Citroën cars and by Mini[18] (wholly owned by BMW). While the main engine was manufactured solely at PSA's Douvrin plant in Northern France, the engine assembly was done at Douvrin for PSA and Hams Hall in the United Kingdom for the Mini. PSA and BMW implemented a coordinated process to enable complete transparency between the two engine plants in order to deal effectively with any quality issues. PSA's Charleville and Mulhouse Metallurgy Division plants were assimilated into the industrial plan as suppliers of raw castings.

The design and development of the engine was done largely by BMW. PSA provided the logistics support for production of the engines. A complete production module was brought on line in late 2005 at the Francaise de Mecanique plant in Douvrin. The module was based on the development of a highly integrated, independent production unit that could easily be replicated on other sites. The plant was designed to produce 2,500 units a day. The first module, with an investment of €330 million, produced an engine every 26 seconds. At its maximum production capacity, overall annual production was expected to reach 1 million units. At full capacity, the module employed 1,120 employees, working in four shifts.

The cooperation resulted in a number of innovations.[19] The engines set new standards in performance, driving comfort, fuel economy, and CO_2 emissions.

Mitsubishi Motor Corporation

In February 2005, PSA and Mitsubishi announced a cooperation agreement for a new SUV, with 30,000 vehicles to be produced every year in Japan and to be sold under the Peugeot and Citroën marques. The SUV model, which was expected to roll out by 2007, was to be styled differently for the Peugeot and the Citroën versions. However, the two versions were to be equipped with the latest HDi diesel engines. Initially, the SUVs were to be marketed only in Europe. However, the two companies were expected to enter other markets in the future.

The Rationale Behind the Alliances

In the 1990s and 2000s, intense competition in the auto industry led to a wave of consolidation. Several auto companies bought stakes in their competitors. For example, DaimlerChrysler bought a 37 percent stake in Mitsubishi, Ford bought a 33 percent stake in Mazda, GM held a 20 percent stake in Fiat Auto, and Renault acquired a 44 percent stake in Nissan. PSA did not make any effort to buy or acquire stakes in other auto companies. "We can definitely get by on our own,"[20] Folz said. PSA, however, concentrated on entering into strategic alliances to counter the challenges posed by its competitors. A major advantage of such strategic alliances over a merger or acquisition was that PSA did not have to look for massive debt financing and experience years of inefficiencies due to duplications in manufacturing. PSA entered joint ventures mostly with strong players: Ford, Renault, Toyota, and BMW. And the purpose of these alliances was to share costs and investments and create synergies.

PSA believed that an important factor for success was the ability to bring out a variety of models with minimum costs. Folz said, "The key to succeeding in this car market is to rapidly produce cars as varied and attractive as possible and to do that at a competitive cost."[21] PSA's alliances with Toyota and Fiat helped it to expand its product range. At the same time, by sharing the costs and risks, it was able to provide more choice to its customers with minimum investment.

PSA's strategic alliances were also meant to achieve economies of scale, which in turn helped lower per unit costs and risks. The company brought out several models of cars based on a single platform using its superior styling and design skills to differentiate the models. Folz said, "The key to survival in the car industry today is not to produce three, four, or five million cars. The real challenge is one's ability to produce a maximum number of cars on a limited number of platforms. That's what we're trying to do."[22] The alliances with Toyota for small cars and with Fiat for light commercial vehicles served to create new platforms, which would be used to launch several future models.

PSA's alliances with Renault, Ford, and BMW helped it develop engines with the latest technology, something that it might have found it difficult to manage alone. The alliances were successful in creating synergies between PSA and its partners. Owing to its alliances with the major players, PSA managed to remain at the forefront of engine technology.

The shared costs and risks helped PSA not only to price its cars competitively but also enjoy higher margins. Even though Volkswagen, the market leader and PSA's rival in the European market, had a profit margin of less than 1 percent[23] in 2004, PSA enjoyed a margin as high as 4 percent in the same period.

Apart from sharing costs, risks, and investments, strategic alliances also helped PSA to acquire and develop new technologies. In the joint venture with Toyota, though the production was controlled by Toyota, 10 managers from PSA were stationed at the plant, providing them with the opportunity to learn about the world-renowned production system followed by Toyota. This experience was expected to improve the production system at PSA in the future.

PSA also seemed to be reaping unexpected rewards from its joint ventures. A case in point was again its

Table 2 2005 J.D. Power & Associates Customer Satisfaction Index

Rank	Brand	Score
1	Lexus	84.8
4	Toyota	83.5
Industry Average		78.6
26	Citroën	76.6
30	Peugeot	74.6

Source: http://www.motor.org.uk.

joint venture with Toyota for the Peugeot 107, Citroën C1, and Toyota Ayga city cars. Toyota was known the world over for the superior quality and dependability of its cars. The high quality was the direct result of the famed Toyota Production System (TPS). On the other hand, PSA cars didn't figure very high on dependability, as evidenced by their poor customer satisfaction scores and low resale values. (See Table 2 for the 2005 J.D. Power and Associates' customer satisfaction index.) Analysts however expected the 107 and C1 cars to have higher resale values owing to Toyota's involvement in their production.

The success of any alliance depends to a large degree on the partners having similar goals and common interests (refer Exhibit 6 for a short note on making alliances work). In the case of PSA's joint ventures, the alliances were as beneficial to the other partner as to PSA. For example, the former president of Toyota Motor Europe, Shuhei Toyoda, who was part of the negotiations with PSA, said, "We needed a partner to get the right volume for costs."[24] And the volumes were achieved by entering into a joint venture with PSA.

Exhibit 6 Making Alliances Work

The success of an alliance depends on three main factors: partner selection, alliance structure, and the way in which the alliance is managed.

Partner Selection: The choice of partner can make or break the alliance. In other words, the strength and success of the alliance depends to a large extent on the partner's characteristics. A good partner helps an organization achieve its strategic goals, which could be to share costs, risks, and investment concerning new product development or to gain access to technology. Additionally, a good partner would have similar expectations for the alliance. And finally, a good partner would not exploit the alliance unfairly.

Alliance Structure: The structure of the alliance also has a bearing on the success and duration of the alliance. Issues such as percentage of ownership, mix of financing, technology, and machinery to be contributed by each partner figure prominently. The alliance should be designed in such a way that it is difficult to transfer technology that was not part of the agreement. Contractual safeguards should be included in the alliance to guard against risk of opportunism by a partner.

Managing the Alliance: The management of the alliance should be based on mutual trust. Such trust can be achieved by building interpersonal relationships between the managers/workforce of the partners. A major determinant of success of an alliance is the ability of partners to learn from each other. In most cases, learning takes place at the lower levels of the organizations. Therefore, the lower-level employees must be informed about the partner's strengths and weaknesses and taught the importance of learning particular skills from the partner so as to improve the competitiveness of the organization.

Source: Adapted from *Introduction to Business Strategy*, ICMR.

Going It Alone

PSA was well aware that in an increasingly competitive market, it could sell more only if its vehicles were superior, distinct and offered unique advantages. Therefore, in spite of its many alliances, PSA was investing in excess of €2 billion in exclusive research & development facilities and projects. Pascal Henault, vice president (Innovation and Quality) said, "Innovation is a way to differentiate our cars in terms of concepts, styling and features that deliver perceptible customer benefits at affordable cost."[25] At its R&D centers at Belchamp La Garenne-Colombes and Velizy, hundreds of engineers and scientists were working toward new and innovative solutions, with the result that PSA filed more than 300 patents every year. In October 2004, PSA unveiled a new design center named Automobile Design Network near Paris to give a further thrust to its research initiatives.

PSA's research and development efforts were based on a "Research and Innovation Plan" that was an integrated and comprehensive system of research projects covering every area of automobile development. For example, PSA engaged scientists to improve the ergonomics, architecture, production process, and other aspects of its vehicles.

At a strategic level, PSA adopted a product policy wherein it focused its research efforts particularly on three critical areas: safety, fuel economy, and comfort. To improve the safety of its vehicles, the company conducted research on driver-support, anti-skid, and emergency braking systems. It was also working on energy-absorbing deformable mechanical structures. Fuel economy was another area on which the company focused its research efforts. Diesel and petrol engines with improved mileage, fuel cell technology, and hydrogen storage systems[26] were some of the research projects in which PSA was engaged. Driver-vehicle interface ergonomics was another area of focused research for PSA. The objective was to enhance driving pleasure and comfort.

Challenges

Volkswagen was the undisputed leader (in terms of the number of cars sold) in the European car market in 2005. Even though PSA continued to retain its second position in Europe, the gap with Volkswagen was widening. Volkswagen managed to increase its market share from 18.6 percent in 2004 to 19.3 percent in 2005, while PSA's share fell from 13.8 percent to 13.5 percent. Though Toyota was a distant eighth in the rankings, it had improved its sales in a shrinking market.[27] Moving toward its goal of capturing 15 percent of the world automobile market by 2010, Toyota was intensifying its efforts in Europe—an important market for the carmaker.

PSA's strength was in compact cars, which were hugely popular in most countries in Europe, its traditional market. However, the Japanese players (especially Toyota and Honda) were increasingly targeting the same segment. Even DaimlerChrysler and BMW were expanding their product ranges to include small cars.

PSA received a mere 15 percent of its revenues from outside Western Europe. In other markets where PSA had a presence, the company was not doing too well. In China, GM and Volkswagen were ruling the roost.[28] PSA's market share in China was stuck at about 5 percent over several years. And in India the company was not even present. However, its sales in Russia and Brazil were picking up (refer to Exhibit 7 for PSA's international presence).

Though PSA collaborated with its competitors, it was also sometimes critical of them. For example, PSA criticized some technologies introduced by Toyota. PSA was of the opinion that the Prius gasoline-electric hybrid car introduced by Toyota in the early 2000s was high-priced. The high price resulted in low sales, which it felt didn't do much to help the environment. "When you are not satisfying the mass market you are simply not doing

Exhibit 7 PSA's Worldwide Production Sites

Country	Production Site	Output (2004)
Brazil	Rio de Janeiro	50,000
Argentina	Buenos Aires	70,000
United Kingdom	Ryton	180,000
France	Rennes	292,000
	Sevelnord	162,300
	Mulhouse	379,100
	Sochaux	430,000
	Poissy	302,400
	Aulnay	418,380
Portugal	Mangualde	53,450
Spain	Madrid	138,100
	Vigo	458,550
Italy	Val di Sangro	183,195
China	Wuhan	141,000#
Iran^	Tehran	293,000
Morocco^	Casablanca	8,000
Indonesia^	Jakarta	500
Turkey^	Bursa	n.a
Nigeria^	Kaduna	n.a
Egypt^	Cairo	n.a
Czech Republic	Kolin	105,000+
Slovakia*	Trnava	n.a

Notes: ^ = assembly plant; * = will start operations in 2006; # = 2005 figure; n.a = not available.

Source: http://www.psa-peugeot-citroen.com.

the job," said Marc Boquet, a spokesman for PSA. "At PSA we produce advanced technology for everyone."[29]

Though PSA was considered a champion of alliances, analysts felt that competition from its partners in the future might affect its relationship with them. However, other analysts felt that the purpose of alliances was to lower costs and risks, and PSA was certainly reaping these benefits. Carlos Ghosn, chief executive for Renault talking about his company's alliances once said, "It [entering into alliances] doesn't mean that people will be complacent of each other. We're still competitors, and competing heavily. But at the same time we are business people. That means when an agreement makes sense it has to be done."[30]

In October 2005, PSA announced that its operating profits for the year 2005 would be less than 4 percent of sales (PSA traditionally enjoyed operating profits of close to 4.4 percent of sales). In January 2006, the company announced a second profit warning that put the operating profits at 3.4 percent of sales (refer to Exhibit 8 for PSA's financials). PSA saw its sales in the European market slide by 2.7 percent in 2005 (refer to Exhibit 9 for PSA's worldwide sales and production).

Exhibit 8 Financial Data of PSA Peugeot Citroën
Consolidated Sales and Revenue (in millions)

	2004	2005
Automobile Division	45,239	45,071
Banque PSA Finance (car finance company)	1,601	1,656
Gefco (transportation and supply chain management company)	2,894	3,000
Faurecia (automotive equipment company)	10,719	10,978
Other Businesses	899	709
Intersegment Eliminations	(5,247)	(5,147)
Total	56,105	56,267
Consolidated Financial Highlights	**2004**	**2005**
Operating margin	2,481	1,940
Profit before tax and share in net earnings of companies at equity	2,439	1,530
Consolidated profit	1,680	990
Profit attributable to equity holders of the parent	1,646	1,029
Financial Position	**2004**	**2005**
Working capital	4,561	4,133
Gross capital expenditure	2,804	2,873
Equity	13,703	14,406
Net financial position of the manufacturing and sales companies	1,347	381
Number of employees	207,600	208,500

Source: http://www.psa-peugeot-citroen.com.

Exhibit 9 Worldwide Sales and Production of PSA

	2004	2005
Worldwide unit sales	3,375,300	3,389,900
Worldwide production	3,405,100	3,375,500

Source: http://www.psa-peugeot-citroen.com.

Exhibit 10 Europe Automobile Market Shares, 2005

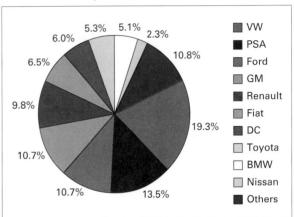

Compiled from various sources, and based on volume.

Exhibit 11 World Automobile Market, 2005

Region	Sales In 2005 (in million units)	Growth (% over previous year)
United States	7.60	1.4
Canada	0.84	3
Europe	15.22	−0.7
China	2.85	26.5

Source: Compiled from various sources.

Note: In 2005, the worldwide automobile market grew by 3.2 percent to 68.2 million passenger cars and light commercial vehicles. However, there was a marked difference in sales growth rates among different regions of the world. Owing to sluggish economic growth in several countries, the European automobile market shrank by about 3 percent. In the Central and East European market, after peaking in early 2004, a sharp decline occurred in 2005. Registrations in Poland slid 23.5 percent, and sales in Hungary slipped by 4.2 percent. The U.S. market showed growth with annual sales reaching 16.9 million units. The Canadian market grew by 3 percent to reach 1.58 million units. In Asia, the market expanded by 6.4 percent. The Latin American market rebounded with Brazil registering a healthy 9.5 percent. Argentina recorded a growth rate of 35.2 percent.

The 2005 full-year report, which was released in February 2006, showed a 37 percent drop in net profits compared to 2004. Intense competition (refer to Exhibit 10 for estimated market shares in 2005, and Exhibits 11 and 12 for general information on the world automobile market), a gloomy European economy, rising prices of gasoline, and an unfavorable product range were cited as reasons.

Exhibit 12 Estimated European Passenger Vehicle Sales by Company

Manufacturer	2005 Sales (in million units)	2004 Sales (in million units)
Volkswagen	2.944	2.853
PSA	2.061	2.122
Ford	1.628	1.686
GM	1.625	1.637
Renault	1.487	1.569
Fiat	0.988	1.129
DaimlerChrysler	0.914	0.922
Toyota	0.818	0.787
BMW	0.779	0.710
Nissan	0.357	0.381
Hyundai	0.317	0.313
Honda	0.259	0.236
Kia	0.242	0.173
Suzuki	0.234	0.204
Mazda	0.233	0.255
Mitsubishi	0.133	0.123
Others	0.195	0.225
Total	**15.222**	**15.332**

Compiled from various sources.

Outlook

The Peugeot 207 (refer to Exhibit 13 for a photograph of the Peugeot 207) was unveiled in early 2006, and was a successor to Peugeot 206—the company's most popular car ever. In 2005, PSA launched several models including the Peugeot 407 (saloon), the 407 coupe, the 1007 (a small car with electric sliding doors), the 107, the Citroën C1 city car, and the Citroën C6 luxury limousine.

In January 2006, PSA launched a new fuel cell called Genepac. Genepac was considered a major step in fuel cell technology because it could power a car for a distance of up to 500 kilometers, which was much more than all other fuel cells available in the market. However, it suffered from most other drawbacks that made fuel cells unviable. The 80 KW cell was the size of a large suitcase which made it difficult to use in ordinary passenger cars.

Exhibit 13 The Peugeot 207

Source: http://www.peugeot.com.

Moreover, the cost of manufacturing the cells was too high. PSA was conscious of the problems but felt that the technology had potential. Folz stated in a news conference, "This technology is still at its early stages but offers a real answer for the future."[31] The company promised that it would try and halve the price of the cells by 2010. It would also make efforts to make the cell more compact.

PSA's explicitly stated policy of cooperation and collaboration with independent auto companies was seen by the company as the best way to counter the challenges posed by globalization and its larger competitors. At the same time, the company was making sure that it secured competitive advantages by going solo on several vital research projects. This dual strategy demonstrated obvious advantages. At one level, PSA reaped benefits such as higher margins, lower development costs and less time to market new models. In Folz's words, "These 'win-win' agreements allow us to share development and production costs without renouncing our independence, and to pool skills and expertise. They also generate the economies of scale we need to be competitive, by speeding our development and increasing production capacity. In addition, such cooperations offer many opportunities to learn about each other's culture and processes."[32] At another level, the strategy allowed PSA maintain its lead in technology and thus enhance its competitiveness.

Notes

1. 2003, Different brands, common strategy, http://www.zr.ru, April.
2. Mitsubishi Motor Co. launched its first passenger cars in 1917. Until 1970, the company was part of Mitsubishi Heavy Industries (MHI), which was founded by Tsukomo Shokai in 1870. In the 2000s, Germany-based DaimlerChrysler acquired a 37 percent share in the company.
3. Renault, the French automobile maker, was founded by Louis Renault in 1898. As of September 2005, the Renault group revenues touched €30.8 billion (nine-month period).
4. FIAT or Fabbrica Italiana Automobili Torino, the Italian automaker, was founded in July 1899 by a group of investors. In the 2000s,

231

Case 18 • PSA Peugeot Citroën: Strategic Alliances for Competitive Advantage?

the company faced a severe financial crisis with losses touching $1.2 billion, which necessitated a major restructuring exercise.

5. Ford was founded in 1903 by Henry Ford and a group of investors. In 2004, the company reported a loss of $155 million in its automotive business.

6. Toyota, the Japanese automaker, was established in 1937. The company has grown to become the second largest auto manufacturer in the world with net income crossing ¥1,171 billion in 2004–2005.

7. BMW or Bayerische Motoren Werke was founded in 1913 as Rapp Motoren Werke by an engineer Karl Friedrich Rapp. In 1917, the name was changed to BMW. The company caters to the premium segment and in 2004, its net profit had reached £2.2 billion.

8. The general shape of the "V" character, or a triangular shape pointing upwards/downwards, is referred as chevron.

9. The black cruise, described as "a great route to a great isle," was a 28,000-kilometer trip undertaken by Georges-Marie Haardt and his team. The expedition, which started at Colomb-Bechar in Algeria, passed through Niger, Chad, Oubangui-Chari (Central African Republic), and the Belgian Congo (Democratic Republic of Congo). At Kampala, the team split into four groups and reached Tananarive in Madagascar, each taking a different route (Mombasa, Dar-es-salam, Mozambique, and the Cape).

10. The yellow cruise was meant to open up the old "Silk Route" (an ancient trade route that connected China, Persia, Arabia, and Europe) to cars. The 30,000-kilometer trip started in Beirut, Lebanon, and passed through the Pamir region (Central Asia). Another group, which started in Tien Tsin (Tianjin, China), joined the Pamir group at Aksu (Xinjiang Uygur, China) and together proceeded to Peking (Beijing).

11. Chrysler Motor Corporation was established in 1925 by Walter P. Chrysler. The company merged with Daimler Benz in 1998 to form DaimlerChrysler. In 2004, DaimlerChrysler's revenues exceeded US$ 192 billion.

12. Societe Industrielle de Mecanique et Carrosserie Automobile or SIMCA was founded by Henri Pigozzi in Nanterre, France, in 1934. Initially, the company produced FIAT models under a license agreement. Subsequently, with the success of its Aronde models, the company's dependence on FIAT decreased. In the 1950s, the company acquired automobile companies such as Unic, Automobiles Talbot, and the French arm of Ford. In 1963, Chrysler bought a majority stake in Simca.

13. Sunbeam Motorcar Company Ltd. was established in 1905 by John Marston. In 1920, it merged with Darracq, a French automobile company. Darracq had earlier acquired Clement-Talbot Ltd, a London-based automobile company. STD Motors Ltd (where STD stood for Sunbeam-Talbot-Darracq) was created as the holding company. In 1935, due to financial problems, Clement-Talbot Ltd was sold to the Rootes Group. Soon, Rootes also purchased Sunbeam. In 1967, Chrysler took complete control of the Rootes Group.

14. Until 1998, Volvo Cars was part of AG Volvo. AG Volvo was founded in August 1926 in Gothenburg, Sweden. Volvo Cars was acquired by Ford in 1998.

15. V6 engine is a V engine with six cylinders. A V engine is a common configuration for an internal combustion engine wherein the pistons are aligned so that they appear to be in a V when viewed along the line of the crankshaft. (Source: http://www.wikipedia.org.)

16. CRDi is a modern variant of direct fuel injection system for diesel engines. It features a high-pressure (1000+bar) fuel rail feeding individual solenoid valves as opposed to mechanical valves.

17. The PSA TU engines were a family of small four cylinder engines used in Peugeot and Citroen cars. The first TU engine was introduced in 1987. They came in petrol and diesel variants. The diesel variant was referred as TUD.

18. Mini is a wholly owned subsidiary of BMW since 2001. It manufactures the MINI, a small car, which is a retro redesign of the classic Mini—a car made by British Motor Corporation from 1959 to 2000.

19. The innovations that came out of the alliance included the lost foam process for cylinder heads, pressurized aluminium casings with cast-iron jackets inserted into the casting, steel crankshafts with unmachined counterweights, connecting rods forged using the double impression method, and so on.

20. Radu Boghici, 1999, France's Peugeot on look-out for joint ventures, http://www.vectorbd.com, April 15.

21. C. Tierney, 2000, Can Peugeot go it alone? http://www.businessweek.com, April 17.

22. R. Boghici, 1999, France's Peugeot on look-out for joint ventures, http://www.vectorbd.com, April 15.

23. 2005, Volkswagen brakes for epic change, http://www.businessweek.com, July 25.

24. 2005, Revved up for battle, http://www.businessweek.com, January 10.

25. Strategy, 2004 Annual Report, http://www.psa-peugeot-citroen.com.

26. As part of its research on fuel cell technology, PSA designed two demonstrators powered by fuel cells—the TaxiPAC and H_2O. The TaxiPAC system uses hydrogen stored on board the vehicle. This system requires further refinement, and PSA was conducting research on making the hydrogen storage system safer and more efficient.

27. According to ACEA, the total light vehicle registrations in Europe (26 countries) in 2004 were 1.11 million. In 2005, the registrations dropped to 1.07 million.

28. In the first half of 2005, with 10.9 percent and 9.25 percent market shares, GM and Volkswagen (through their joint ventures) were the market leaders (in terms of sales) in the Chinese automobile industry.

29. J. Kanter, 2005, Toyota leads Asia drive in Europe, http://www.iht.com, July 23.

30. J. Madslien 2002, French car maker takes on the world, http://www.bbc.co.uk, October 9.

31. 2006, PSA Peugeot Citroën unveils small fuel cell, http://www.fuelcelltoday.com, January 10.

32. 2005, Citroën: Strength through cooperation, http://www.citroen.com, July 11.

Additional Readings and Reference

1. 2006, PSA Peugeot Citroen to sell diesel hybrids in 2010, http://www.planetark.com, February 1.

2. 2006, PSA Peugeot Citroen "cautiously optimistic" about 2006, http://www.just-auto.com, January 18.

3. 2006, Peugeot launches new 207 small car line, http://www.greencarcongress.com, January 12.

4. J. Marsden, 2006, Poor car sales lead PSA to cut outlook, http://www.icbirmingham.co.uk, January 12.

5. 2006, PSA Peugeot Citroen unveils small fuel cell, http://www.fuelcelltoday.com, January 10.

6. J. Kanter, 2005, Toyota leads Asia drive in Europe, http://www.iht.com, July 23.

7. 2005, Ford and PSA Peugeot Citroen strengthen diesel cooperation, http://www.media.ford.com, October 5.

8. 2005, Peugeot deal boosts Mitsubishi, http://www.bbc.co.uk, February 4.

9. 2005, Revved up for battle, http://www.businessweek.com, January 10.

10. D. Huq, 2004, Toyota and PSA Peugeot Citroën unveil jointly developed cars, http://www.jcnnetwork.com, December 2.

11. 2003, Different brands, common strategy.

12. 2002, BMW and PSA form joint engine project, http://www.all4engineers.com, October 18.

13. J. Madslien, 2002, French car maker takes on the world, http://www.bbc.co.uk, October 9.

14. 2002, PSA Peugeot Citroën and Toyota announce the name of new joint-venture company, http://www.toyota.com, January 10.

15. 2000, PSA Peugeot Citroen and Ford Motor Company announce cooperation in telematics in Europe, http://www.ford.com, September 27.

16. C. Tierney, 2007, Can Peugeot go it alone? http://www.businessweek.com, April 17.

17. 1999, PSA aims to form joint venture with Japan's Koyo Seiko, http://www.bloomberg.com, November 25.

18. 1999, J.-M. Lamy, Renault, Puegeot-Citroën, Michelin: Three flagships of the French motor industry, April.

19. 1998, PSA launches mega depot joint venture, http://www.worldcargonews.com, July.

20. Mergers, takeovers and product differentiation, http://www.bized.ac.uk.

21. Engines: Peugeot (PSA Peugeot Citroën), http://www.grandprix.com.

22. http://www.psa-peugeot-citroen.com.

23. http://www.all4engineers.com.

24. http://www.media.ford.com.

Case 19

Sun Microsystems

Scott Jacobs, Prescott C. Ensign

The University of Western Ontario

Press Release

The fourth quarter ended June 30, 2005. On July 26, 2005, Sun Microsystems unveiled fiscal year (FY) 2005 results: Q4 revenues were US$2.98 billion (2004 Q4 revenues were US$3.11 billion, but had included income of US$1.6 billion from a legal settlement with Microsoft); for the full fiscal year 2005, Sun Microsystems reported revenues of US$11.07 billion (FY2004 revenues were US$11.19 billion).

Sun Microsystems' chief financial officer (CFO), Steve McGowan, commented, "We achieved impressive operational improvements in fiscal 2005 . . . our 16th consecutive year of generating positive cash flow from operations." Sun Microsystems employees, investors, and analysts recognized that Bill Gates had helped out last year. But what explained this year? Perhaps Sun was righting itself?

"Putting our cash to work, we've expanded our product portfolio and announced plans to acquire companies that deepen and broaden our systems strategy. We've maintained our R&D commitment and delivered crown jewels like Solaris 10 to the market," said Scott McNealy, chair and chief executive officer (CEO) of Sun Microsystems. "Big-time progress in FY05. The company is now in a position to take advantage of the investments we have made over the past few years and we believe there is more to come in FY06."

McNealy continued, "Our demand indicators for Q4 were positive. We have great partners, lots of cash, and a strong team across the board. FY05 was a year of stabilized revenue and earnings. Our opportunity for FY06 is sustained growth and profitability."

"Profitability?" was the incredulous reaction of many who had followed Sun's struggle.

A Strategic Crisis

At the beginning of 2004, Sun Microsystems found itself at a serious inflection point (see Exhibits 1, 2, and 3, on pages 234, 235, and 236, respectively). It had lost money in eight of the last 10 quarters. As its market share slipped, again, this time from 12.1 percent in 2002 to 10.3 percent in 2003, Sun announced its largest product offering update in company history. The products were intended to stop the bleeding that had caused the company's share price to plummet to only one-tenth of its high value in 2000, a decline that in 2003 raised speculation of a takeover. Scott McNealy, cofounder CEO & chair of the board of directors originally named the company Stanford Unified Networks in 1982.

Since developing the vision that had endured throughout the company's history, "The Network is the Computer," McNealy had come under great scrutiny as many industry analysts relentlessly questioned Sun's business-level strategy. Specifically, many doubted the effectiveness and competitiveness of the products that the company offered during its recent decline in profitability.

On December 8, 2004, Scott McNealy delivered a keynote address at an industry show in San Francisco, California. He relayed some statistics about Sun's Java platform: 579 million Java-enabled phones by the end of the year, almost 1 billion Java smart cards, and nearly 900 companies were now contributing to Java. He spoke of how the world had envisioned the computer 50 years prior and remarked, "It's hard to imagine where we'll be 50 years from now." Some in the audience members were scratching their heads wondering where Sun was headed in the near future.

Exhibit 1 Sun Microsystems Income Statement (US$ millions)

	1996	1997	1998	1999	2000	2001	2002	2003	2004	2005
Revenue	$7,094.8	$8,598.4	$9,790.8	$11,726.3	$15,721.0	$18,250.0	$12,496.0	$11,434.0	$11,185.0	$11,070.0
COGS	3,972.0	4,320.5	4,693.3	5,648.4	7,549.0	10,041.0	7,580.0	6,492.0	6,669.0	6,481.0
Gross Profit	**3,122.7**	**4,277.9**	**5,097.5**	**6,077.9**	**8,172.0**	**8,209.0**	**4,916.0**	**4,942.0**	**4,516.0**	**4,589.0**
Operating Expenses										
Selling, General, and Administrative	1,732.7	2,402.4	2,777.3	3,173.0	4,137.0	4,544.0	3,812.0	3,329.0	3,317.0	2,919.0
Research and Development	657.1	826.0	1,190.2	1,383.2	1,642.0	2,093.0	1,835.0	1,841.0	1,996.0	1,785.0
Other	57.9	23.0	—	—	—	261.0	517.0	2,496.0	393.0	262.0
Operating Income	**675.0**	**1,026.5**	**1,130.1**	**1,521.8**	**2,393.0**	**1,311.0**	**(1,248.0)**	**(2,724.0)**	**(1,190.0)**	**(377.0)**
Other Income and Expenses										
Net Interest Income and Other	33.9	94.7	46.1	83.9	378.0	273.0	200.0	71.0	1,627.0	193.0
Earnings Before Taxes	**708.9**	**1,121.2**	**1,176.2**	**1,605.7**	**2,771.0**	**1,584.0**	**(1,048.0)**	**(2,653.0)**	**437.0**	**(184.0)**
Income Taxes	232.5	358.8	413.3	574.4	917.0	603.0	(461.0)	776.0	825.0	(77.0)
Earnings After Taxes	**476.4**	**762.4**	**762.9**	**1,031.3**	**1,854.0**	**981.0**	**(587.0)**	**(3,429.0)**	**(388.0)**	**(107.0)**
Accounting Changes						(54.0)				
Net Income	**476.4**	**762.4**	**762.9**	**1,031.3**	**1,854.0**	**927.0**	**(587.0)**	**(3,429.0)**	**(388.0)**	**(107.0)**
Diluted EPS Continuing Ops	0.2	0.3	0.2	0.3	0.6	0.3	(0.2)	(1.1)	(0.1)	(0.0)
Diluted EPS	0.2	0.3	0.2	0.3	0.6	0.3	(0.2)	(1.1)	(0.1)	(0.0)
Shares	3,147.0	3,111.0	3,154.0	3,256.0	3,378.0	3,417.0	3,242.0	3,190.0	3,277.0	3,368.0

Source: Company files.

Boom to Bust

In 1997, Thailand could no longer back its currency, the baht. High levels of debt and years of trade deficits had resulted in a spectacular crash in the value of the baht. The ensuing economic crisis engulfed most of Asia and spread throughout the entire world, slowing down economies from east to west. Most importantly for Sun, the crisis adversely impacted Japan, its largest single source of foreign revenue, at 9 percent.

The global economic collapse continued in January of 1999 when Brazil's currency, the real, was devalued. The devaluation dashed any immediate growth plans and delayed future growth there indefinitely. Brazil had been one of the countries on which Sun had been counting to lead information technology (IT) spending in South America.

The Brazilian and Asian financial crises provided compelling evidence that, even though Sun's diverse portfolio appeared to protect it from individual blips in economic stability, its product sales were highly sensitive to macroeconomic conditions. In 1998, the company reported that more than 45 percent of its revenues were generated outside of the United States. By 2003, Sun's

reliance on foreign revenue had increased to more than 50 percent, and the economic crises had unfolded into a worldwide economic slowdown—with some analysts using the label "recession."

However, economic conditions alone did not lead to Sun's fall from profitability. Rather, the economic macro environment was a catalyst for change toward affordable enterprise computing. In addition, technological advancements led to performance improvements in the x86 platform.[1] Making use of these advances and using various sources of leverage to lower cost structures, many firms were able to offer products similar to Sun's, but at a fraction of the price.

Sun's expensive high-margin products lagged in demand while the company continued to present its same value proposition. To compound the adverse effect of developments in the x86 hardware space, Sun was also feeling competitive pressure from an inexpensive, and very controversial x86-based software product named Linux. This singular platform would change Sun's competitive environment drastically. Open source software on inexpensive standard hardware began to unravel Sun's offering: a product that bundled software, hardware, and service.

Exhibit 2 Sun Microsystems Cash Flows (US$ millions)

	1996	1997	1998	1999	2000	2001	2002	2003	2004	2005
Cash from Operating Activities										
Net Income	$476.4	$762.4	$762.9	$1,031.3	$1,854.0	$927.0	$(587.0)	$(3,429.0)	$(388.0)	$(107.0)
Depreciation/Amortization	284.1	341.7	439.9	627.0	776.0	1,229.0	1,092.0	918.0	730.0	671.0
Deferred Taxes	—	—	—	—	—	—	(673.0)	706.0	620.0	(315.0)
Other	(72.2)	0.9	323.7	858.6	1,124.0	(67.0)	1,048.0	2,842.0	1,264.0	120.0
Cash from Operations	**688.3**	**1,105.1**	**1,526.5**	**2,516.9**	**3,754.0**	**2,089.0**	**880.0**	**1,037.0**	**2,226.0**	**369.0**
Cash from Investing Activities										
Capital Expenditures	(295.6)	(554.0)	(830.1)	(738.7)	(982.0)	(1,292.0)	(559.0)	(373.0)	(249.0)	(257.0)
Purchase of Business	—	(23.0)	(244.0)	(130.3)	(89.0)	(18.0)	(49.0)	(30.0)	(201.0)	(95.0)
Other	170.9	33.3	(94.8)	(1,227.1)	(3,154.0)	(244.0)	647.0	(125.0)	(1,861.0)	(73.0)
Cash from Investing	**(124.7)**	**(543.7)**	**(1,169.0)**	**(2,096.1)**	**(4,225.0)**	**(1,554.0)**	**39.0**	**(528.0)**	**(2,311.0)**	**(425.0)**
Cash from Financing Activities										
Net Issuance of Stock	(467.5)	(374.8)	(190.8)	(242.7)	(285.0)	(899.0)	(354.0)	(317.0)	239.0	218.0
Net Issuance of Debt	—	—	—	—	1,500.0	—	(13.0)	(201.0)	(28.0)	(252.0)
Dividends	—	—	—	—	—	—	—	—	—	—
Other	18.9	(55.3)	(4.6)	88.7	4.0	(13.0)	—	—	—	—
Cash from Financing	**(448.6)**	**(430.1)**	**(195.5)**	**(154.0)**	**1,219.0**	**(912.0)**	**(367.0)**	**(518.0)**	**211.0**	**(34.0)**
Currency Adjustments	—	—	—	—	—	—	—	—	—	—
Change in Cash	115.0	131.3	162.1	266.7	748.0	(377.0)	552.0	(9.0)	126.0	(90.0)
Free Cash Flow										
Cash from Operations	688.3	1,105.1	1,526.5	2,516.9	3,754.0	2,089.0	880.0	1,037.0	2,226.0	369.0
Capital Expenditures	(295.6)	(554.0)	(830.1)	(738.7)	(982.0)	(1,292.0)	(559.0)	(373.0)	(249.0)	(257.0)
Free Cash Flow	**392.7**	**551.1**	**696.4**	**1,778.2**	**2,772.0**	**797.0**	**321.0**	**664.0**	**1,977.0**	**112.0**

Source: Company files.

Billion-Dollar Bets

In 2000, shares of Sun Microsystems hovered near US$60 per share. About that same time, Scott McNealy, CEO, put Masood Jabbar in charge of managing Sun's worldwide sales. McNealy was counting on Jabbar to formulate the right plan and strategy to capitalize on Sun's momentum and reputation for innovation. McNealy needed Jabbar to grow the business and build shareholder wealth.

In response, Jabbar developed a strategy that focused on five countries that were each potential billion-dollar-a-year markets for Sun's server business. They were Brazil, Spain, China, India, and Italy. Shareholders were optimistic about Sun's potential for growth.

Although shareholders responded positively to Sun's future, managers of the U.S. business at Sun's Palo Alto, California, headquarters were getting tense. It seemed as though a meeting could not take place without attention being diverted from the U.S. business toward conversations about foreign interest rates, political regimes, and foreign legal language. U.S. business managers simply could not have discussions on policy and strategy

without some "foreign distractions." Many of the U.S. managers involved began to feel that those managers representing Mexico, South America, and Canada were muddying the waters with talk about fluctuating currency exchange rates and political instability. In fact, those territories accounted for less than a few percent of Sun's business at the time. The United States had nearly always accounted for roughly half of Sun's multibillion-dollar annual sales.

However, Jabbar's "billion-dollar bets" required that these emerging areas get attention in order to shift the distribution of sales. And yet, international managers felt they were getting little cooperation and support to expand business in their emerging markets. Jabbar also knew that under the current structure, U.S. managers could not focus on their own strategy and planning, which meant that a considerable portion of Sun's revenue could be threatened. The current organizational structure was just not working. Something at Sun had to change.

Jabbar approached Bob MacRitchie, who was managing the South American, Mexican, and Canadian lines of business under the umbrella of the U.S. organizational

Exhibit 3 Sun Microsystems Balance Sheet (US$ millions)

	1996	1997	1998	1999	2000	2001	2002	2003	2004	2005
Assets										
Cash and Equivalent	$528.9	$660.2	$822.3	$1,089.0	$1,849.0	$1,472.0	$2,024.0	$2,015.0	$2,141.0	$2,051.0
Short-Term Investments	460.7	452.6	476.2	1,576.1	626.0	387.0	861.0	1,047.0	1,460.0	1,345.0
Account Receivable	1,206.6	1,666.5	1,845.8	2,286.9	2,690.0	2,955.0	2,745.0	2,381.0	2,339.0	2,231.0
Inventory	460.9	438.0	346.5	307.9	557.0	1,049.0	591.0	416.0	464.0	431.0
Other Current Assets	376.6	511.2	656.8	856.5	1,155.0	2,071.0	1,556.0	920.0	899.0	1,133.0
Total Current Assets	**3,033.7**	**3,728.5**	**4,147.5**	**6,116.4**	**6,877.0**	**7,934.0**	**7,777.0**	**6,779.0**	**7,303.0**	**7,191.0**
Net Property, Plant, and Equipment	533.9	799.9	1,300.6	1,608.9	2,095.0	2,697.0	2,453.0	2,267.0	1,996.0	1,769.0
Intangibles						2,041.0	2,286.0	417.0	533.0	554.0
Other Long-Term Assets	233.3	168.9	262.9	695.1	5,180.0	5,509.0	4,006.0	3,522.0	4,671.0	4,676.0
Total Assets	**3,800.9**	**4,697.3**	**5,711.1**	**8,420.4**	**14,152.0**	**18,181.0**	**16,522.0**	**12,985.0**	**14,503.0**	**14,190.0**
Liabilities and Stockholders' Equity										
Accounts Payable	325.1	468.9	495.6	753.8	924.0	1,050.0	1,044.0	903.0	1,057.0	1,167.0
Short-Term Debt	87.6	100.9	47.2	1.7	7.0	3.0	205.0	—	257.0	—
Taxes Payable	134.9	118.6	188.6	402.8	422.0	90.0				
Accrued Liabilities	801.6	963.0	1,126.5	1,646.6	2,117.0	1,862.0	1,739.0	1,506.0	1,930.0	1,727.0
Other Short-Term Liabilities	140.2	197.6	265.0	422.1	1,289.0	2,141.0	2,069.0	1,720.0	1,869.0	1,872.0
Total Current Liabilities	**1,489.3**	**1,849.0**	**2,122.9**	**3,227.0**	**4,759.0**	**5,146.0**	**5,057.0**	**4,129.0**	**5,113.0**	**4,766.0**
Long-Term Debt	60.2	106.3			1,720.0	1,705.0	1,449.0	1,531.0	1,175.0	1,123.0
Other Long-Term Liabilities			74.6	381.6	364.0	744.0	215.0	834.0	1,777.0	1,627.0
Total Liabilities	**1,549.4**	**1,955.3**	**2,197.4**	**3,608.6**	**6,843.0**	**7,595.0**	**6,721.0**	**6,494.0**	**8,065.0**	**7,516.0**
Total Equity	**2,251.5**	**2,741.9**	**3,513.6**	**4,811.8**	**7,309.0**	**10,586.0**	**9,801.0**	**6,491.0**	**6,438.0**	**6,674.0**
Total Liabilities and Equity	**3,800.9**	**4,697.3**	**5,711.1**	**8,420.4**	**14,152.0**	**18,181.0**	**16,522.0**	**12,985.0**	**14,503.0**	**14,190.0**

Source: Company files.

division. The infrastructure was already in place. What remained was an official transition that emphasized Sun's commitment to pursuing its billion-dollar bets.

However, the transition itself was not easy. The same U.S. business managers who previously decried the waste of precious resources on those underperforming emerging markets felt a sense of loss they had not anticipated—a loss of power. "Egos were involved here," Jabbar explained. "It was hard to get those guys to give up the control."

Apart from being a functional decision, it was symbolic of the attention and commitment Sun would give to these emerging areas. Sun's strategy was to develop these billion-dollar bets in the midst of a booming economy that increasingly demanded enterprise computing products. Sun did not have to chase customers. The sales, it seemed, were coming to them. However, neither Sun nor any other company could contend with the competitive pressure created by the volatile nature of the new global economy.

Attack of the Giant Penguin—Linux

John Gantz, International Data Corporation's (IDC) chief research officer predicted that "Linux [would] eat Unix,"[2] in 2003. The irony was subtle—the Linux mascot was an innocuous penguin. Linux, an operating system named after its creator Linus Torvalds, took the enterprise computing industry by storm. Its open source, community approach to application creation was not only revolutionary in theory, but in practice as well.

Linux is open source, inexpensive, and scalable. Adoption of Linux products spread rapidly, especially internationally. In fact, countries outside the United States found Linux to be a viable alternative to Microsoft's Windows operating system, which many critics felt was unsecure and not readily scalable. In 2003, Brazil's government urged its federal agencies to adopt Linux in an effort to cut costs. Brazil represented no small piece of the pie; it imported more than US$1 billion more in software than it exported in 2001. Brazil was not alone.

China, Japan, and South Korea also switched to Linux to get IT spending under control.

Sun had resisted Linux for a long time because Sun designed its own operating system, Solaris. In addition, Sun's past success was due in large part to its strategy of integrating proprietary software (Solaris), hardware, and its own SPARC Unix microprocessor.[3] By developing not only its own microprocessors, but also its own operating system, the company could have complete control of the integration of the system hardware and software. This strategy ensured optimization and control over the entire design process. In effect, Sun created a lot of value for its customers through this integration. However, Sun's strategic focus on its operating system, Solaris, and its SPARC microprocessors prevented it from seeing the threat that Linux presented. Eventually, an x86 or Unix server running Linux offered customers a close substitute to Sun's products.

In February 2002, after years of denial, Sun Microsystems could no longer fend off the waves of criticism—it gave in to Linux. To demonstrate its commitment to Linux, Scott McNealy gave his keynote speech (in a penguin suit) at a Sun trade show to announce the company's new Linux products. Typically, Sun attacked other platforms by suggesting that they were not as reliable or did not offer the features of its own Unix servers. However, with the advent of Linux, users found a new, reliable, inexpensive choice to expensive Sun products.

The problem was serious. If Sun refused to offer Linux products, it would be cutting itself out of a considerable portion of the server market. Linux was dominating the inexpensive x86 server space. Yet, if Sun were to produce its own x86 products, it would have to purchase microprocessors from a third party for a new line of x86 hardware. Because essentially only one company was developing highly respected enterprise-level x86 microprocessors, Sun had few choices. Entering the x86 market would mean teaming up with a tried and true competitor—Intel.

For Sun, doing business with Intel would not only mean accepting the rise of Linux, but also the commoditization of enterprise computing, at least at the low end. Moreover, Sun's value proposition became increasingly diminished as the company lost control of the integration process. By using Intel chips, Sun would no longer offer value to customers through engineering and innovation as it had previously, but rather via an assembly of outsourced components. Although similar to some of Sun's competitors, that value proposition was a substantial departure from its original model. To counteract this change, Sun developed its own middleware, the Java Enterprise System, that would operate in Unix or Linux and offered a unique pricing model that made scalable enterprise computing more affordable.

In 2003, the People's Republic of China and Sun announced a deal. The arrangement was for 500,000 to 1 million copies per year of Sun's Java Enterprise System. Most industry observers believed the blockbuster result of this deal would not be the revenue, but rather the market share. Indeed the revenue would likely not be significant and would even take quite a while to capture, given the extended time frame of the agreement. With Java Enterprise System, Sun was trying to inject value into its offerings through research and development, one of Sun's competitive advantages.

Continuing to partner with Intel, however, remained a strategic disadvantage. After years of competition, joining forces and integrating development initiatives with Intel seemed unrealistic. Sun's future in the x86 space continued to look uncertain until November 2003, when Sun announced a newly formed strategic alliance with an emerging x86 microprocessor developer—AMD.

A New Entrant, Old Competitors, and Big Threats

In 2003, Advanced Micro Devices, also known as AMD, agreed to collaborate with Sun in a new strategic venture. By providing its x86-based Opteron chips for use in Sun's low-end servers, AMD stood to combat years of dominance by its rival Intel. AMD's new Opteron technology took its x86 technology to 64 bits,[4] a feat Intel had yet to master. In doing so, AMD became an industry leader. Along with that status came new friends. Sun was not the only firm to form an alliance with AMD—HP and IBM both struck similar deals, although seemingly less integrated than Sun's alliance.

Intel leveraged its technology, manufacturing capabilities, and market share in the PC space to produce chips able to compete in the enterprise computing domain, at least in the low-end segment. And it certainly did not suffer from diminishing relations with Sun. Dell capitalized in the low-end space by selling a large volume of servers running Linux on Intel. Finding operating efficiencies allowed Dell, the fourth largest server maker behind Sun, to turn the low-end server market into a battlefield by steadily dropping prices.[5]

Sun attempted to compete on the basis of price, but found it difficult to outprice companies such as Dell and even IBM, who reduced costs through sources of leverage, such as unit volume and consulting services, respectively. As a result, Sun was losing the low-end battle against Dell, IBM, and HP, and there continued to be little demand in the high-end for its expensive Unix servers. As if this situation were not bad enough, another competitor was posing a significant threat to Sun.

Japan's Fujitsu, ranked as the fifth largest server maker, licensed Sun's proprietary UltraSPARC chip designs to power its own SPARC64 chips found in its line of Unix servers. Fujitsu had great success in taking Sun's SPARC chips and turning them into more powerful SPARC64 Fujitsu chips—and winning Sun customers in the process. Fujitsu was much quicker to market than Sun, which was reliant on Texas Instruments to churn out its chips. The situation presented a difficult decision for Sun. Should it discontinue its relationship with Fujitsu or get in even tighter with the Japanese giant?

Sun Microsystems desperately needed the revenue from the licensing agreement, so it was extremely reluctant to cease the licensing contracts. To complicate matters further, Fujitsu was not only licensing Sun's chipset designs, it was also a leading reseller of Sun products. Fujitsu was more than a manufacturer; it served also as a reseller or channel partner. In fact, Fujitsu's role was significant. Sales to Fujitsu accounted for a large portion of Sun sales in Japan, Sun's leading foreign market in revenue terms.

Rumors surfaced in 2003 about a possible alliance or even merger with the Japanese firm. However, for Sun, forming a tighter alliance with Fujitsu might cause more problems than it would address. For instance, if Sun were to begin using the SPARC64 chips, it might mean spurning its long-standing chipproducing partner, Texas Instruments. Given a large installed base, such bridges were not to be burned hastily. Moreover, despite the fact that Sun and Fujitsu used the same instruction set for the microprocessors, Sun and Fujitsu products could not be used together without some reprogramming. Adopting the SPARC64 chips would mean massive reconstruction of its current products and the products it had in the pipeline, which suggested that Fujitsu would remain a competitor in the future.

Executive Exodus

A month-long executive exodus culminated with the chief operating officer (COO) and president Ed Zander resigning. He and four other high-level officers—all with at least 15 years each at Sun—departed effective July 1, 2002. The naysayers on Wall Street were having a field day: "The Captain goes down with the ship." McNealy was going to do it alone; he named no successor for the president and COO's position. Sun also now had vacancies for the vice president, two executive VPs, and the CFO. On July 18, 2002, it was announced that Masood Jabbar would retire from Sun after 16 years of service. The stock was at a 52-week low, hovering at about US$7 per share.

And things did get worse, at least according to the stock market. The share price slowly but steadily, in the coming years, fell to a mark below US$3. It would be almost two years before a president and COO was named, when the 38-year-old Jonathan Schwartz received the nod from McNealy in April 2004. Schwartz had come to Sun in 1996 when it acquired Lighthouse Design, Ltd.—the firm for which Schwartz was then CEO.

All Bets Are Off

Growth in the server industry was not flat by any means. IDC expected tech spending would increase in 2005 and beyond, regaining some of its lost momentum from the bubble burst of 2000.

Scott McNealy's vision of everything and everyone connected to the network was probably not that far from the eventual truth (see Exhibit 4). Yet, Sun's ability to determine the long-term direction of computing was more refined than its value-added strategy.

Exhibit 4 Sun Microsystems' Strategic Direction

A singular vision—The Network Is the Computer—guides Sun in the development of technologies that power the world's most important markets. Sun's philosophy of sharing innovation and building communities is at the forefront of the next wave of computing: the Participation Age.

VISION: Everyone and everything connected to the network.

Eventually every man, woman, and child on the planet will be connected to the network. So will virtually everything with a digital or electrical heartbeat—from mobile phones to automobiles, thermostats to razor blades with RFID tags on them. The resulting network traffic will require highly scalable, reliable systems from Sun.

MISSION: Solve complex network computing problems for governments, enterprises, and service providers.

At Sun, we are tackling complexity through system design. Through virtualization and automation. Through open standards and platform-independent Java technologies. In fact, we are taking a holistic approach to network computing in which new systems, software, and services are all released on a regular, quarterly basis. All of it integrated and pretested to create what we call the Network Computer.

Source: 2006 http://www.sun.com, February 11.

Most of Sun's billion-dollar bets that were developed by Masood Jabbar failed to materialize. In fact, Sun Microsystems was now desperate, fighting for revenue each quarter. In retrospect, Sun might have put the cart before the horse. Instead of focusing on the evolution of its competitive environment, it was distracted by the economic euphoria that reigned in the late 1990s. McNealy admitted, "Looking back, we probably hired too many people and signed too many leases, but we had a very natural and understandable desire to fill all the orders we could."

The network was still the computer, but recent product offerings and industry conferences suggested Sun Microsystems and especially McNealy had succumbed to some inevitable truths about the competitive environment of the industry. One was that the x86 platform was not going away as McNealy had once envisioned. It became clear that Sun's future strategy would include x86- and Linux-based products, as well as more compelling and competitive high-end Unix servers.

To sell Sun products, McNealy was banking on a healthy return on research and development. He asserted, "Sun is doing things that Intel isn't doing or AMD isn't doing." Innovation, however, was costly. Sun's R&D budget had been about US$2 billion annually for the last few years, dwarfing its competitors. Innovation was a key component of Sun's current strategy, but the results were not yet readily quantifiable. Still, McNealy claimed, "[Over the decade,] we're going to spend $20 billion to $30 billion minimum on R&D." Clearly, Sun was intent on continuing to add value through innovation rather than being relegated to a game of economies of scale and efficiencies.

Charles Cooper, editor of CNETNEWS.com, remarked, "[Sun's] strategy—if you can call it that—has been to throw a lot of stuff against the wall and wait to see what sticks." It was still hard to tell what the firm and specifically Scott McNealy were learning from the devolution of Sun's business. The well-known CEO admitted to strategic missteps but quipped, "I try to make a mistake only once. If your strategy isn't controversial, you have zero chance of making money. You have to have a wildly different strategy and you have to be right. It's that second part that gets tricky." McNealy recognized, "There's lots more to do." Now was the time to do it.

Notes

1. x86 hardware stands for x86 central processing units (CPUs) developed by Intel. This CPU forms the base of PCs. History of the chip: 286, 386, 486, 586 (dubbed Pentium), Pentium Pro, Pentium II, Celeron, Pentium III, Pentium IV, etc. Other manufacturers, such as Advanced Micro Devices (AMD) and Cyrix, have used the same CPU machine code with their own architecture to create equivalent chips, but with a lower price-to-performance ratio.

2. Unix software is an abbreviation for UNiplexed Information and Computing System, originally spelled "Unics." It is an interactive time-sharing operating system developed at Bell Labs in 1969. In the 1990s, Unix was the most widely used, multi-use, general-purpose operating system in the world. Unix is presently offered by many manufacturers and is the subject of international standardization efforts.

3. SPARC is an abbreviation for Scalable Processor ARchitecture, designed by Sun Microsystems in 1985. SPARC is not a chip per se, but a specification. The first standard product based on SPARC was produced by Sun and Fujitsu in 1986. In 1989, Sun transferred ownership of the SPARC specifications to an independent, nonprofit organization, SPARC International.

4. 64 bit is a computer architecture term, which refers to the bandwidth of the arithmetic logic unit, registers high-speed memory locations in the CPU and data bus (connections between and within the CPU, memory, and peripherals).

5. HP was the server market leader, followed by IBM.

Case 20

Teleflex Canada: A Culture of Innovation

Andrew C. Inkpen

Thunderbird, The Garvin School of International Management

Teleflex Canada, a division of Teleflex Inc., manufactured a range of products, including marine hydraulic steering systems, trim components for marine propulsion, heating equipment for both the truck and bus industries, a range of proprietary fluid controls, and field cookstoves for the U.S. Army. Over the past 30 years, Teleflex Canada grew from sales of a few million dollars to more than $160 million in 2004. The company has a reputation as a world leader in the design and manufacture of hydraulic and thermal technology products. Within Teleflex Canada was a consensus that continual innovation in product design, manufacturing, and marketing was critical to the success of the organization.

In 2005, Teleflex Canada executives were faced with various questions: Would size inhibit the ability to innovate? Would increased corporate centralization at Teleflex Inc. impact Teleflex Canada's ability to respond quickly to new market opportunities? At the Teleflex Inc. corporate level, different questions were being asked: Could the culture of innovation in Teleflex Canada be transferred to other parts of the company? What was the appropriate level of corporate support and control necessary to foster innovation and high performance at Teleflex Canada and at other Teleflex business units?

Teleflex Inc.

Teleflex Inc., a diversified manufacturing company was headquartered in Limerick, Pennsylvania, just outside Philadelphia. The company had three principal business segments: Commercial, Medical, and Aerospace.

Commercial

The Commercial segment manufactured various products for automotive, marine, and industrial markets, including manual and automatic gearshift systems; transmission guide controls; mechanical and hydraulic steering systems; vehicle pedal systems; heavy-duty cables; hoisting and rigging equipment for oil drilling and other industrial markets; mobile auxiliary power units used for heating and climate control in heavy-duty trucks, industrial vehicles, and locomotives; and fluid management products for automobiles and pleasure boats.

Medical

The Medical segment manufactured health care supply and surgical devices including anesthesiology devices, sutures, ligation solutions, chest drainage systems, and high-quality surgical and orthopedic instruments.

Aerospace

The Aerospace segment manufactured products for the commercial and military aerospace, power generation, and industrial turbine machinery markets. Aerospace businesses provided repair products and services for flight and ground-based turbine engines; manufactured precision-machined components and cargo-handling systems; and provided advanced engine surface treatments.

Products in the Commercial segment were generally produced in higher unit volumes than that of the company's other two segments. In the fiscal year ended December 31, 2004, Teleflex's consolidated sales were $2.49 billion, with 48 percent coming from the Commercial segment, while Medical and Aerospace represented 30 percent and 22 percent, respectively. With approximately 21,000 employees and major operations in more than 70 locations worldwide, Teleflex Inc. operations were highly decentralized, with dozens of small profit centers and a corporate office consisting of a few senior executives and support staff. A few years ago, a major effort was begun to redefine Teleflex as a unified operating company that shared people, products, and processes across divisions and business units. The objective of the reorganization was to establish some common operational standards to improve productivity. Not surprisingly in a company where autonomy had always been the hallmark of business unit activity, increased efforts at standardization, consolidation, and sharing of resources were met with some managerial resistance at the business unit level.

Teleflex Canada

Teleflex Canada, based in Richmond, British Columbia, in the metropolitan Vancouver area, had been one of the best performing business units within Teleflex for several decades. Through internal development, licensing, and acquisition, its growth rate averaged 20 percent per year for 25 years. As previously noted, total sales in 2004 were about $160 million. Teleflex Canada designed and produced a variety of products utilizing hydraulic and thermal technologies.

Marine and Industrial Hydraulic Systems

Teleflex Canada was created in 1974 when Teleflex Inc. purchased part of Capilano Engineering, a small machine shop in Vancouver that was developing hydraulic steering systems for boats. At that time, another Teleflex unit was producing marine steering systems with mechanical cable steering. Teleflex management knew that as marine engines got larger and more powerful, mechanical steering would become obsolete because it could no longer provide the necessary comfort and safety.

Teleflex Canada's hydraulic steering systems—SeaStar, SeaStar Pro, and BayStar—were designed to enable more comfortable control of pleasure boats. These products fundamentally changed the marine steering industry. In 2004 Teleflex Canada sold more than 100,000 SeaStar systems, an increase of more than 30 percent over the previous year (retail prices for the higher-end products ranged $1,200–$1,500 per system, while lower-end systems were about $250). The company had an estimated 95 percent market share in North America and 50 percent share in markets outside the continent. Teleflex Canada's steering products were usually among the highest-priced products available in the marketplace.

The marine steering industry had two main market segments. One segment included stern drive engine companies such as Volvo Penta, which would purchase a private label steering system and integrate it with its own engine to provide a complete steering and controls package to boat builders. A second segment was the marine distribution and dealer network that sold Teleflex-branded products to boat companies and individual boat owners. Sales of marine products were split almost equally between original equipment manufacturers (OEMs) such as Volvo Penta and aftermarket dealers.

In addition to steering systems, Teleflex Canada also produced components for marine engine companies, including Bombardier and Volvo Penta. These products were referred to as industrial actuation systems.

Energy

Teleflex Canada was successful in applying its boat-based technology to the needs of other markets. In 1985 Teleflex Canada began licensing an engine governor technology for large diesel trucks. In 1990 an auxiliary heater business for large trucks and buses was purchased from Cummins, which led to the development of the ProHeat vehicle heater product line. The heater technology was adapted in 1997 to create cookstoves, called modern burner units (MBUs), for use in army field kitchens. A major contract was signed with the U.S. military for the production of MBUs. By 1999 Teleflex was producing 10,000 MBUs per year for military purposes.

Innovation, Technology, and Product Development

Teleflex Canada's innovation focused on product and market development that solved customers' problems or created new markets. Much of Teleflex Canada's success has come about because demand was identified for new products in niche markets that were ready for a change in technology. As explained by a Teleflex Canada executive:

Our fundamental belief is that we don't use any technology that is not proven. We call ourselves product developers. We will not develop any technology that cannot be robust and highly reliable with a low repair requirement. We take existing technology and tweak it to make a better. . . . We usually don't invent anything radically new (although sometimes new technology had to be invented to solve a customer's problem). We are a company that has been innovative in applications engineering. We focus on products we know we can sell because we are close to the market and know the customers. . . . Innovation at Teleflex Canada involves three questions:

1. *How do we exploit existing technology?*
2. *How do we develop reliable and robust products from that technology?*
3. *How do we penetrate and dominate some market niche with that product?*

For example, we are looking for new areas where we can use electro-hydraulic applications. There are other markets where this technology could work, such as dental chairs and hospital beds or suspension systems for lawn and garden equipment. These are markets that will pay a premium for a customer-built system using hydraulics.

SeaStar Development

When Teleflex Inc. acquired Capilano Engineering, the intent was to expand into new markets. At that time, the company was producing a heavy-duty commercial hydraulic steering system. In 1978 Teleflex Canada introduced Syten, the world's first low-cost hydraulic system for the mass pleasure boat market. Cost was a big factor because Syten competed against low-priced mechanical steering systems. Unfortunately, Syten's plastic parts deteriorated when used beyond their mechanical capability, leading to unsatisfied customers and a risk that Teleflex Canada would lose its position in hydraulic steering. At that time, Teleflex Canada had about 10 percent of the hydraulic steering market (the largest competitor had a share of about 80 percent).

Teleflex Canada developed a new hydraulic steering system called SeaStar, which was introduced in 1984. SeaStar became the leading product on the market. In 1989 the new SeaStar was introduced. The mandate for the development team was to develop a smaller size to expand the potential market, lower cost, and better performance. Using some patented technology (a floating spigot), the new SeaStar was 30 percent cheaper to produce, 18 percent more efficient, and sold at the same price as the older model. In 1993 SeaStar Pro was introduced and was successful in the bass boat market where performance was the primary purchase criterion. BayStar, introduced in 2002 for the lower-end market, was also successful (although it cannibalized sales of a mechanical steering system produced by another Teleflex division).

Again, a Teleflex Canada executive explains:

To regain our reputation in the marketplace, we had to come out with an overkill approach with the product. We developed a much more sophisticated and rugged all-metal system, which became SeaStar. This decision involved heated internal debates because the development costs were substantial. This required a lot of trust from Bim Black (Teleflex Inc. chairperson and former CEO). He was willing to take some risk in the investment. There were a lot of skeptics. But the hydraulics technology was well-proven and used in automotive systems. We were applying existing technology to a customized marketplace. From a technology perspective, the risk was not high. From a market point of view, we knew that our current line of cables (from another Teleflex Inc. business unit) was not going to satisfy customers as boat engines got bigger and more difficult to steer.

We have 35 patents but the technology was not earth-shattering. The marketplace wanted higher horsepower and more comfort, and we were able convince people to change to hydraulics.... Harold (Copping, Teleflex Canada president at the time) kept a nice fence between corporate and Teleflex Canada. And we were small enough to fall under the radar screen at corporate. For example, we were able to order some tooling without approval.

When the development of SeaStar was done, the marine industry was going through a downturn. Our competitors were laying off engineers and trying to survive. We kept our engineers developing products. When we came out of the downturn, we had new products that allowed us to grow.

There are two keys to the success of SeaStar over the years. One we always kept innovating. Our competitors would copy our designs and in about six months we would have a better product on the market. Since our products were 30–40 percent better than the competition we could keep our margins up. As time went on, the performance gap narrowed. But, because we built scale economies through our size and innovated in manufacturing, we have the lowest cost. So, we have the lowest cost and the best-performing product. Two, a lot of our success is through innovation on the shop floor to ensure that we had a cost-effective product. The corporation pushed us to use more advanced machine tools and to be more analytical. SeaStar involved innovation in technology, product development, marketing, and manufacturing processes that were developed at the shop floor level. The product designs were enhanced because of the manufacturing processes, some of which must be kept in-house because they are proprietary.

Also, having a good product is only part of the story. You also need to sell the product. To me, selling is like being a farmer. You go out and spread some seeds, water them daily, and eventually they come to fruition. I always fought corporate—they kept telling me to close the deal. I was very patient. I was very generous with our product. I would give away our product and let them try it. I am out there constantly talking with customers, looking at the competition.

Our competitors are getting better, but our market share makes it difficult for other companies to compete on cost. We continue to focus on being the best and never giving any customers an excuse to go looking elsewhere. . . . One day, all boats will steer as comfortably as cars. That has been my mission. To make that happen. I have never deviated from it.

Energy Product Development

ProHeat, an auxiliary power and climate control system for trucks and buses, was introduced in 1992.

To get into heaters we bought a product line from Cummins Engine. Cummins was not successful with the product so we bought the remaining inventory. This got our foot in the door, and it is much easier to start a business when you have something to sell. When we did the deal with Cummins, we had already concluded that the product [the truck heater] was not any good. We did the deal anyway because it got us into a new market that we thought we could serve better with new products.

We never actually produced any of the Cummins products, but we learned a lot about the market. There was a clear demand for a product that could be used to heat trucks and was more fuel-efficient than leaving the engine idling. We were able to figure out the type of product innovation that was necessary and spent about two years bringing the product to market. The first truck heater was ProHeat in 1992. Once we had some success in the Canadian market to we looked to the U.S. market. We needed a different product because of air conditioning. Teleflex usually doesn't like to start from scratch so we looked around for a possible acquisition. We bought a small company in Ontario that had a product that allowed us to get into the market.

We then took the truck heater to the transit bus market. We started talking to different city bus companies and were able to adapt our technology for the bus market. These were not huge leaps, and to us they seemed very obvious. We never say build it and they will come. We try to get the order first and then build the product. We start by selling concepts along with our credibility in the market.

The development of the truck heater, along with several other products, including a heater for tents used by the military, provided Teleflex Canada with a solid base of experience in combustion technology. This expertise led to the development of the military cookstove called the MBU. The MBU used the same combustion technology as the truck heater and could be used as a block heater, passenger heat source, barbeque, or oven.

The MBU project started with an inventor who had built a prototype stove. The inventor was able to convince the U.S. Army to put the project out for bid based on the specifications he had developed in his prototype. Harold Copping described how the military cookstove project got started:

We understood the military market. When we did our licensing deal for the tent heater, we had an understanding that we would not develop a cookstove. Eventually, we agreed to license the technology for the cookstove. I visited the military and made sure the funding was in place. I knew the U.S. Army liked the design, and I saw a huge opportunity for Teleflex. I saw this as a chance to back a winner and take a gamble. We put together a team of some of our best people to develop a working prototype. It was not a big risk because I knew that we had very good burner technology and I knew the Army liked the people and the design. We were in their good books because we had had great success with previous projects for them. We spent $500,000 and it worked out well. Our people improved the inventor's design and made it manufacturable and safer.

Another Teleflex executive added the following comments about product development:

To make these programs work, it started at the very top of Teleflex Inc. There were skunk works going on, but they

were tolerated. When we were trying to diversify the business, Harold protected us from the operations mentality. For each of the key projects, we put a dedicated team together whose priority was not operations. For several programs we moved engineers out of the building to off-site locations. We wanted these engineers to worry about the development project, not the stuff that was in production. We wanted their full attention on the product development. There has to be a wall between development and existing operations. The next challenge is how to reintegrate the new business into operations and try to avoid the us-and-them attitude. Operations people like stability, and design engineers like change.

You need a focused team that says our mission is to capture this market. In other groups in Teleflex, there is not the same acceptance about product development teams that may take years to bring a product to market. They ask: how can you justify that over the next quarter?

Teleflex Canada Culture

Harold Copping describes some of the characteristics of the Teleflex Canada culture:

I joined the company two years after the acquisition [by Teleflex Inc.]. My strength was an ability to recognize the strengths of other people. I cared a lot about people enjoying their work and doing interesting jobs. We had one person who was a mechanical genius but very difficult to work with. He was a great source of innovation in improved manufacturing methods and quality. He had a very temperamental personality, and in the early days there were fisticuffs on the shop floor and all kinds of things that should not happen. I protected him because I recognized how much he could do. We had another engineer who was brilliant and could think out of the box. He was off the wall and I had to protect him on two occasions against his bosses. I believed something good was going to come out of this guy [he is still at Teleflex Canada].

Right from the beginning, there was a nucleus of very good people in Teleflex Canada in terms of inventive creativity and willingness to solve problems and make things happen. There was some adversity that forced us to work together, such as vast quantities of products being returned by customers [the first innovative hydraulic steering system]. This helped me understand who contributed to solutions and who didn't. It also allowed me to play on the theme that if we did not do this right, the corporation will take it away from us. This was our chance to show them that we could manufacture in Vancouver.

We had discipline but we also had freedoms. We allowed a pretty free rein on innovation, and at the same time were adding systems and standardization. I tried to build the organization around a spirit of independence and risk-taking with a passionate group of people. I wanted the organization to work around the innovative people even if they were eccentric and hard to work with. Enthusiasm and passion are variables that are not measurable. I maintain that one degree of passion is worth 10 degrees of efficiency. All of our customers could sense the enthusiasm. People really cared at Teleflex Canada.

We had a culture of admiration for people with innovative engineering talent. We were also strongly motivated never to be second-class. There were drivers in the marketplace that pushed us to excel, and there was a constant focus on continuous improvement.

You have to create an identity and differentiation that is different from the rest of the corporation. If you lose the identity, you become an employee. You don't have the nice feeling of being part of a cause and a culture that you understand. Therefore, there has to be some symbolism around the identity and also some competition with other divisions of Teleflex. We tried to identify threats so that people would be scared and there would never be complacency. We used threats to draw people together. Some of our greatest successes came about when there was a lot of adversity because of customer problems or breakdowns.

Other managers echoed Harold Copping's views:

Harold was able to maintain a chemistry between individuals who had to make it happen. That is easier when you are a small company. Harold surrounded himself with people who were passionate about what they believed in. If there was a common denominator, it was passion to be the best and the most successful. If you did not believe in this, you were gone. We were almost competing with each other but still working together as a team. The chemistry was as good as it could have been.

Everybody can question anyone about technical details. We have always had a culture that allows people to question everything. Everyone realizes that they are in a position where they could be questioned. We all have egos, but people have to check them at the door at Teleflex Canada. Harold knew that if you put people on too high a pedestal, it can cost you money. . . . Harold was the president, but he did not have his own parking space. People related to that. He did not try to be better than anyone.

We had some people who were unorthodox but were real technical geniuses. We also had some managers who were eternal optimists. If you have a negative attitude, it will kill entrepreneurial thinking.

Managerial commitment to Teleflex Canada was another key element in the company culture, as indicated by the following statement:

After the reorganization in May 2004, we realized there were a few businesses that were in serious trouble. The first company I was asked to visit was in Ontario. Within the first few hours of discussion, I discovered that the fundamental issue was the uncontrolled financial expense relative to a declining market. I was asked to run the company as general manager for the next 3 to 4 months. This was not the best time from a personal perspective: I was in the middle of building a new house (acting as general contractor) and had a number of personal issues involving the sale of my current house and dealing with the planned move of my family.

I spoke to my wife and family the next day, and we both agreed that the need for me to work in Ontario was greater than the need for me to continue as general contractor for the house. She rearranged her work schedule, and my parents stepped in to help get the kids to their various activities. On May 30, 2004, I took the red-eye from Vancouver and went straight into work on arrival in Toronto. For the next 8 months I flew out every Sunday night, spent long hours at work from Monday to Thursday, and flew back for the weekend. Even the weekend we moved into our new house, I flew back on Friday, moved into the house, and flew out on Sunday. I appreciated the opportunity Teleflex Canada had provided me over the past few years, and this was my way of showing them how dedicated I was to the company's success.

Teleflex Inc. and Teleflex Canada

Harold Copping described the relationship between Teleflex Canada and Teleflex Inc.:

I was running a remote subsidiary in a decentralized company. That was a huge advantage. From the very outset, I had a feeling of positive support from corporate and a feeling that I was controlling my own destiny. I tried to help the staff understand that it was really up to us, and I tried to create a culture where we controlled our own destiny.

The relationship was not "control by corporate." It was "help being available from corporate." We had people available from corporate to help teach us about quality and engineering. I always felt that I could choose to use the corporate resources that were available to me. If I could use local resources cost effectively, I did so. I pushed back when someone tried to force corporate resources on me. . . . Access to the corporation definitely played a role in our progress. [Chairperson] Bim [Black] fostered a climate of cross-pollination between divisional and general managers by holding interesting meetings, although as the company got bigger there were fewer meetings. These meetings were very good in helping us know where to go and who to call. I used to find an excuse to visit other Teleflex facilities.

There was enough interaction and influence from corporate to allow people to create successful business relationships [with other parts of Teleflex Inc.]. Since they were not forced by corporate, only the viable relationships occurred. If we could help each other, we did. The attitude was based on open markets. . . . There were many benefits to being part of a large corporation. It was a nice environment to be in. As we got bigger, we were increasingly under the microscope.

We did not know the term core competence at the time. By the early 1980s we began to think that we were not really limited to the marine market. We were small enough and far enough away from corporate that nobody really cared what we did. We could explore new opportunities without being unduly restrained. As long as we were making money and growing, we had a lot of latitude. Nobody restricted me—freedom was a big factor.

Pull-Through Strategy

Rather than designing products and then looking for channels through which to sell them, Teleflex Canada focused on end users. Executives described this strategy as a pull-through strategy:

Our strategy in the truck business is pull-through. The reason why the truck companies [OEM manufacturers] put our ProHeat product on the truck is because the customer [the truck fleet operators] wanted it. The same thing happens with SeaStar. The boat builders buy it from us but the customer [the boat buyer] demands it.

A pull-through strategy is pragmatic. I can call on OEMs all day long but if no end users are asking for the product, we won't sell anything. We still have to negotiate with OEMs, but they don't get to make the call. It is the fleet customer who says we want ProHeat. We are trying to keep our products from becoming commodities, where the OEMs only care about price. They never ask for better—they only ask for cheaper. A lot of companies are confused about who their customers really are. The OEM is not the customer; the OEM is the channel. The customer is the person who will actually use the products.

The SeaStar technology was developed for a market that was prepared to pay a premium for higher comfort. People have asked, "Why don't you leverage this technology into high volume sectors like automotive?" The problem with those markets is that the pricing pressures are intense and the volumes are much higher. We build about a half-million steering systems per year. Plus, we see automotive as more of a commodity market. Marine customers are using surplus funds to buy their products. Nobody has to own a boat. Boats are not a commodity, and we can demand a higher premium in the marine market. We have never entered another steering market.

We want to move boats closer to car steering comfort levels. Our next level of product innovation is to take comfort to a new level through power steering. We thought we would sell 2,000 power steering systems this year and it

looks like we will sell 20,000. The boat builders initially resisted the shift to power steering. We gave the boat builders the new systems to try. Our philosophy is not to sell to the boat builders; we want them to buy it from us.

It does not matter what the technology is. The market will decide. Everybody is willing to pay a fair price for fair value. . . . We always try to be a few steps ahead of our customers. For example, we have an expensive power steering system for 60- to 100-foot luxury yachts. It is a very technical product and there are varying levels of expertise within the boat building companies. We believe that if we want to capture a bigger share of the market, we will have to simplify the technology and make it "bubba-proof." That is what we strive for: How do we make our product better and easier for our customers to use? Since our competitors are followers they cannot think like this.

The Future

As Teleflex Canada executives looked toward the future, they faced various issues, such as the degree of vertical integration, the relationship with Teleflex Inc., managing the size of the organization, and the future for new product development.

Vertical Integration

Teleflex Canada had always been vertically integrated. The consensus was that, in the future, the company would be less vertically integrated.

All our customers want us to be as cost-effective as possible. In the past we were incredibly vertically integrated. For example, when we started with ProHeat, we needed various parts, like a flame sensor, a compressor, a blower, and a water pump. Nobody built any of these parts to our specs, so we developed them ourselves from scratch. What are we doing developing a flame sensor? There are companies out there who should be able to do these things better than us. We spent a lot of money doing a lot of things, and we would have been better served if we had had the option to look outside. We developed some stuff that we had no business developing. As a generalization, we will buy technology rather than develop technology. We will develop new products. That is not the way we got here, but it is the way we need to go.

We have developed a strategic plan that involves core and noncore capabilities. We went through all our manufacturing processes and asked what is really core, from process and intellectual property points of view. We have to protect intellectual property. We identified about 80 percent of our manufacturing processes as noncore.

We are going to try to shift from a manufacturer to an integrator and a tester. We will only fabricate what is considered absolutely core for protecting our manufacturing *and quality processes and our intellectual property. Everything else is up for grabs. If we cannot be competitive here, the work will go elsewhere. We are going through a rapid change. We want to focus on marketing, sales, product development and engineering, prototyping, final assembly, and testing. Fabrication and subassembly may go elsewhere. We want to be an OEM or a tier 1 player.*

Not everyone was in complete agreement that the shift from manufacturer to integrator and tester was the basis for a unique strategy. According to one manager:

Every company in the world is trying to be an early adopter with low-cost manufacturing and outsourcing of noncore activities. That is not a strategy—that is good business practice. If you lose the ability to innovate on the production floor, you lose some of the ability to lower costs. That is my fear with off-shore production. Also, how are we going to protect key product designs and innovation when we spread work out to partners?

Relationships with Teleflex Inc.

Within all of Teleflex Inc., an ongoing debate argued the merits and drawbacks of centralization and unified operating processes. Within Teleflex Canada, this debate was particularly relevant given the history of the subsidiary (i.e., 3,000 miles from headquarters) and its successful innovations:

The bigger area of conflict from a corporate unified perspective involves market and product development, who owns it, and how do we keep the innovation happening. With more centralization going on, how do you make sure you don't kill the entrepreneurialism? Everybody knows that if you go completely centralized, you totally lose the innovation. What we have agreed on is that product development has to stay close to the market. There has to be some consolidation at a group level but not at a corporate level. We are creating centers of excellence such as hydraulics and power generation.

I understand the need for centralization. I also understand that the centralization pendulum usually swings too far. As far as the centralization of patent attorneys, this will take away from our ability to get prompt intellectual property. We will get it, but it will be slower. It is critical to understand your intellectual property before you spend too much time in development. Centralization of HR may also affect us. For example, corporate edicts about raises may make it hard to keep engineers, since Vancouver is such a hot tech area.

If you take away all of the divisional autonomy, you cripple the divisions. Before, purchases for $25,000 or less could be approved at the division. Now everything has to go to corporate. Unless you are yelling or screaming, it can be a two- or three-month process to get approval. Because

of Sarbanes-Oxley, things have to be done in a specific way. Too many rules will take away someone's incentive to stick their neck out and try something different. The old environment is gone, but we will make it happen somehow.

Managing Size

Teleflex Canada had grown rapidly over the past three decades. Size brings its own variety of challenges, as the following comments demonstrate:

We went from $4.5 million when I started to $160 million today. Every time we made a big jump in revenue, there were benefits and downsides. Getting big can be a problem, which is one reason Harold split the company into three divisions—he saw that we were getting too big.

The problem with growth is that as you get bigger, it gets more difficult to manage and control. Then you get to a point where the corporation becomes huge and the latest flavor of the month comes in, like "go to China for your raw materials." Now the buzz word is "cut costs, cut costs." If all we focus on is cutting costs, we will stifle the entrepreneurialism and that is the beginning of the end. Once you stifle entrepreneurialism, passion, and creativity, you become like any other corporation. Margins will drop because you cannot be fast and innovative. You slowly start losing. We are on the edge.

As we get bigger we have to follow more processes, sign more forms; and by the time you get done, it is too late. It is not how big you are that makes you successful—it is how fast you are to market. In efforts to consolidate, we are risking our fast response time. When we were smaller, I could get things done in 24 hours. Now it takes forever.

We have always been known as a company that solved customer problems. We were very good at getting to the root cause of the problem. When a customer calls us, we take care of them. This got us a lot of respect and market share, and this was not the way our competitors did it. As we get bigger we may not be able to react quickly enough.

To keep our edge, we need to keep up with the technology, move fast, and make sure quality does not suffer as we experiment with offshore sourcing. Basically, we need to continue to deliver what we promise. Do not take cost-cutting to the point where it affects what you have promised your customers.

One way we are trying to deal with size is with the Virtual Development Center. We are leaving too many opportunities on the table. This Center will be a small group that acts as an interface between the customers and the divisions. The Center will have two main objectives: (1) to make sure the customers get proper focus from the people best qualified to deal with their problems; and (2) to make sure the development project goes to the appropriate division. . . . Our goal is to provide a customer with a conceptual design in 7 days and a prototype within 30 days. In a way, we are trying to break free of the shackles of size by responding quickly to customers. Once we have a customer, we will put the product into the appropriate division to develop it, make it manufacturable, optimize it, etc.

There is a limit to how big the firm can get and still be innovative and entrepreneurial. It is easier with smaller groups. Once an organization gets over 150 people, it should be subdivided. You need to strike the right balance between operational efficiency, serving the customer well, and maintaining a spirit of identity. . . . Balancing operational efficiency with subdividing the organization is more of a challenge because there are trade-offs. When people work together in subunits and depend on each other for overall success, politics is minimized. The challenges are to work with people and stay connected with people at every single level. If people believe that they succeed together and make things happen together, they will have some job security and will reap some rewards. It is much easier to excite people about a portion of the business rather than the whole business.

Forward Thinking: New Product Development and New Technologies

New product development was central to the success of Teleflex Canada and central to continued growth. Executives were generally confident that the organization would continue to develop and exploit existing technologies. Some comments about the marine area follow:

I don't see an issue with product development. The bigger challenge is dealing with new technologies. The risk is that our existing products get replaced by new technologies in which we have no expertise. Take steering systems. We know that hydraulics will go away eventually, and the market will demand more comfort at lower prices. The boat builders may integrate steering into their outboards. Most stern drive engine steering uses a cable with a power steering system.

We will have to reduce costs and develop more robust designs for larger outboard engines. There will be new technologies that replace hydraulic steering. Electro over

hydraulic with programmable tension and torque levels is the next generation and will come out soon. The next shift will be to electromechanical actuation or steer-by-wire, which is disruptive technology. We believe we can bring this to market, and we had the foresight to realize that we were going to become an electronics company. Five years ago we engaged a local university professor—an expert in fault tolerant systems—to work with us privately on steer-by-wire. Corporate and other engineers did not know we were doing this. We scavenged the money where we could and eventually bought an equity stake in an offshoot company owned by the university and the professor. When corporate found out what we were doing, they saw that it made sense and gave us steer-by-wire responsibility for the corporation. We are going to be ready with a steer-by-wire product when the world is ready for the technology.

We are also trying to develop new products for boats. We know that we will lose market share when hydraulic steering goes away. We also know that the engine companies want to integrate steering with their engines. We need to be forward-looking and help our customers sell their products. We need to make sure we are the company that the engine manufacturer wants as the integrator. Our plan is to develop new business with Yamaha, Bombardier, and other engine companies.

Conclusion

Teleflex Canada provided a high margin contribution to the Teleflex corporation for many years. Would success breed complacency and stagnation? Or would Teleflex Canada continue to grow, innovate, and develop new products? According to one executive:

We can't get fat and lazy, because that will be the beginning of the end. We have to continue to solve our customers' problems and make their lives easier. As long as we do what we promise and don't get arrogant, we will be fine. If we start acting like an 800-pound gorilla, customers will find a way to deal with us. We need to work with our customers and make their lives easier. It is a fine line and you need to know where the line is. Most of our boat builders are entrepreneurs; there are no barriers to entry in the boat business. This helps keep the automotive mentality out of this industry.

Case 21

Tyco International: A Case of Corporate Malfeasance

Michael J. Merenda, Alison Volk, Allen Kaufman

MICHAEL J. MERENDA
UNIVERSITY OF NEW HAMPSHIRE

ALISON VOLK
UNIVERSITY OF WISCONSIN

ALLEN KAUFMAN
UNIVERSITY OF NEW HAMPSHIRE

On June 17, 2005, Tyco's former chief executive, Dennis Kozlowski, and its former chief financial officer, Mark Swartz, were convicted of grand larceny, conspiracy, and fraud. In September 2005 Kozlowski and Swartz received 8- to 25-year sentences at Mid-State Correctional Facility near Utica, New York. State Supreme Court Justice Michael Obus ordered Kozlowski and Swartz to pay a total of $134 million in restitution; in addition, Kozlowski was fined $70 million, Swartz $35 million. The sentences end a case that exposed the executives' extravagant lifestyle after they pilfered some $600 million from the company including a $2 million toga birthday party for Kozlowski's wife on a Mediterranean island and an $18 million Manhattan apartment with a $6,000 shower curtain.[1]

Kozlowski and Swartz were just two of the more celebrated corporate malfeasance cases decided in the first half of this decade. John Regas, former CEO of Adelphia Communications, was sentenced to 15 years (it would have been longer but he was 80 and in poor health at the time of his sentencing) and his son Timothy, its chief financial officer got 20 years. They were found guilty of stealing $100 million and hiding $2 billion in corporate debt, thus looting and defrauding shareholders. Other notable sentences were Andrew Fastow of Enron (10 years), Sam Wakal of ImClone Systems (7 years), Jamie Olis of Dynergy (24 years), and Bernie Ebbers of WorldCom (25 years). What is significant about these cases is the severity of the sentences. Traditionally, corporate malfeasance cases resulted in convictions that amounted to a mere slap on the hand. These individuals

received longer prison terms that are similar to sentences received by hardened criminals. Hubris cost these executives dearly in terms of retribution payments, personal freedom, and integrity.

These instances of corporate malfeasance ushered in a new era in corporate governance. They dramatically changed the relationship between corporate executives and company boards of directors and their shareholders. Increasingly shareholders' are voting against the recommendations of managers, particularly on the method by which members of the boards of directors are elected and the basis for keeping their seats on the board. One particular hot issue being fought by radical shareholders is their ability to vote out the chairperson of the board's compensation committee at any firm they think overpays managers.[2]

It is also evident that Tyco's board of directors did not exercise its fiduciary duties to the shareholders. Questions arise as to where and why it failed and whether the directors receive prison sentences because of their irresponsible and unethical behaviors. Finally, people are reluctant to question success, and they tend to give those responsible for "successful undertakings" too much leeway. These factors, coupled with the ethical and moral values of Kozlowski and the voodoo accounting of Swartz, resulted in the outcomes described in this case.

This case traces the events and decisions that led to Kozlowski's and Swartz's demise at Tyco and their public disgrace in the court room. It looks at management actions that not only violate public trust, but undermine the fabric of a democratic society. It is clear in the case that the principal characters not only behaved unethically and were socially irresponsible, but also broke the law and misappropriated monies that should have been distributed to shareholders.

Three issues need to be addressed: (1) What things led to Tyco's present state? (2) What can be done in the organization to prevent these situations from arising in the future? and (3) What resources does Tyco's new management team have at its disposal to enhance the reputation of the firm and turn it around? See Exhibits 1, 4 (on page 258), and 5 (on page 259) for financial highlights and financial ratios and indicators.

Tyco: The Pendulum Swings

Arthur Rosenberg, Tyco's Founder

Tyco, Inc., began in 1960 as an investment and holding firm in Waltham, Massachusetts. At that time, Tyco had two principal holdings, Tyco Semiconductor and the Materials Research Laboratory, which conducted industrial research and development in solid-state sciences and energy conversion. When Tyco merged these two divisions in 1962, its major customer remained to be the U.S. government.[3] However, Arthur Rosenberg, Tyco's founder, saw commercial opportunities. Over the next two years, Tyco became an industrial products manufacturer, going public in 1964. Tyco grew steadily over the next few years, adding 16 companies by 1968. Five years later, Tyco generated $40 million in sales.

Joseph Gaziano: Growth through Acquisitions

In 1973, Joseph Gaziano, an engineer trained at MIT, took over for Rosenberg as president and CEO. Under his leadership, Tyco pursued a path of aggressive and often hostile acquisitions. He wanted to turn Tyco into a $1 billion company by 1985, using any means necessary.

Gaziano died of cancer in 1982. The company he left behind, however, was large and diverse. It had a net worth of $140 million and was bringing in more than $500 million in sales. The conglomerate housed manufacturers of products as varied as undersea fiber optic cables, fire sprinkler systems, polyethylene film, and packaging materials.

John Fort: Performance over Growth

John Fort, an aeronautical engineer who held degrees from Princeton and MIT, became Tyco's third CEO in 1982. As Tyco's new CEO, Fort decided to set a different tone. He veered away from the acquisition-centered growth strategy of his predecessor and immediately trimmed the tremendous debt that Gaziano had accumulated and focused instead on cutting costs wherever possible. Fort told investors, "The reason we were put on earth, was to increase earnings per share."[4] He was thrifty and unglamorous, preferring to gain Wall Street's respect through his own economic restraint. Under Fort's leadership, Tyco became a company without frills. When it came time to find a location for the company's headquarters, for example, Fort had builders clear land in Exeter, New Hampshire. The facility that they consequently constructed consisted of three unpretentious, low-rise office buildings, without even a cafeteria on site.[5] He drastically cut costs and discarded a number of businesses that were not directly related to Tyco's operations. He separated the company's

Exhibit 1 Tyco International: Historical Stock Price, 1990–2002

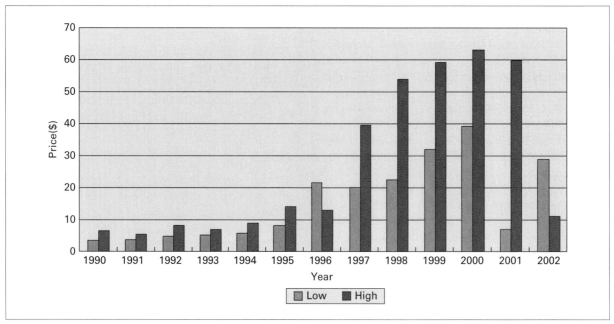

various businesses into three parts: Fire Protection, Electronics, and Packaging. This consolidation, however, did not signal an end to Tyco's acquisition strategy. Tyco simply became more selective about the companies that it pursued. Fort's main focus was on profits rather than growth. The stock price rose from $1.55 in January 1982 to $29.56 in July 1990. Sales grew to $3 billion in 1991. Fort retired in 1992 after serving 10 years as CEO. Dennis Kozlowski, Tyco's then chief operating officer, replaced him and further refined Tyco's art of acquisition.

Dennis Kozlowski: The Early Years

Kozlowski's Background

Dennis Kozlowski was the product of a working class family from Newark, New Jersey. His father was an investigator with Public Service Transport (which would later become New Jersey Transit) and his mother was a school crossing guard. He went to Seton Hall University in South Orange and majored in accounting. He lived at home to help save money and he worked at a variety of different jobs.

Kozlowski graduated from Seton Hall in 1968 and landed his first job as an auditor for SCM Corporation. In 1974, he was hired at Nashua Corporation, an office equipment manufacturer in New Hampshire, as the director of auditing. William Conway, Nashua's former CEO, described Kozlowski as "a smart young guy who could really help a business. Any problem that came up in the company—in administration, selling, manufacturing—he always had suggestions about how to fix it."[6]

Kozlowski stayed at Nashua for a year and was then approached by a headhunter to work at Tyco as the assistant comptroller and head of auditing. Shortly after he began, Gaziano purchased Grinnell Fire Protection from I.T.T. Kozlowski was promoted to vice president. At the time Grinnell was the largest of Tyco's divisions, but it was barely scraping by. In six months, Kozlowski cut costs and Grinnell showed $1 million in profit. Over the next seven years, Grinnell increased profits to $212 million. In 1983, Kozlowski became president of the division. In the next four years he managed to raise the division's profits to $700 million. His performance earned him an invitation to serve on Tyco's board in 1987, followed by a promotion to president and COO in 1989. In fact, Kozlowski engineered the acquisitions that generated the enormous revenue growth (from $1 billion in 1988 to $3 billion in 1991) under Fort's watch. Three years later, he took over the reigns from John Fort as CEO.

Kozlowski: The Great Conglomerator

I never started out with a game plan to be a $76 billion company. But I always envisioned one that had to grow every year in order to be successful.[7]

During Kozlowski's 10-year reign at Tyco, the same word kept popping up to describe him—*aggressive*. One Tyco board member said, "Dennis has only one gear—forward at 300 miles an hour. There is no reverse." He pursued acquisitions with a vigor that Tyco had not seen since the days of Gaziano. His style, however, was markedly different. He told the *Boston Globe* that he always followed two rules for acquisitions: Never do a hostile deal and immediately cut costs at the new facility.[8] He had learned from watching Gaziano that unfriendly takeovers often lead to failed business ventures. Kozlowski preferred that deals be made quickly and on good terms.

When Kozlowski took over as CEO, Tyco was a $1.3 billion (net revenue) company divided into four divisions: fire protection; valves, pipes and "flow control products"; electrical and electronic components; and packaging materials. Fire protection generated 53 percent of Tyco's revenues, flow control 23 percent, electronics 13 percent, and packaging 11 percent.[9] Even though Tyco operated in many industries, the majority of its divisions sold products to the construction industry, which accounted for 80 percent of Tyco's income.[10]

Changing the Product Mix

Kozlowski wanted to decrease Tyco's reliance on the construction business, which is infamously unpredictable, and transition into manufacturing products for more reliable consumers. This sentiment led the new CEO to suggest buying Kendall International in 1994, a producer of medical supplies, for $1 billion. Tyco's board balked, considering that Kendall had filed Chapter 11 two years earlier and their revenues were only increasing by 3 to 4 percent per year. Kozlowski, however, was determined to repair the company and the board agreed to the acquisition.

In the long run, Kozlowski's gamble paid off. After one year, the acquisition helped Tyco's earnings grow to $214 million. Kendall became the center of Tyco Healthcare, which, in turn, became a major producer of medical supplies, second in the country only to Johnson & Johnson.[11] By 1998, Tyco had six divisions: fire protection, flow control, disposable medical products, Simplex Technologies, packaging materials, and specialty products.

Between 1992 and 1998, Kozlowski perfected Tyco's acquisition strategy. In many respects, it resembled the conglomerate strategy developed during the 1960s and then abandoned by the 1980s. Originally, conglomerates assembled businesses in unrelated fields to counter business cycle movements. When one business was strained during the downside of a business cycle, another division would be performing well. This portfolio approach was to assure the corporate holding company a steady stream of cash. The central office functioned as a bank, using the firm's operating cash to weather economic storms, to acquire new cash-generating companies and to divest those firms that no longer fit the conglomerate portfolio. As long as cash streams steadily grew, the conglomerate's stock price rose, allowing the company's stock to be takeover currency.

Bring on the Hungry Young Talent

Tyco's central office functioned much like a conglomerate holding company, acquiring and divesting parts. However, Tyco did not seek out unrelated acquisitions to beat the business cycle. Instead, Kozlowski hunted after targets that fit into Tyco's broadly defined business divisions. Targets had to be the sort that investment bankers had favored for takeovers during the 1980s: "underperforming firms that were fat, dumb and happy."[12]

He would then replace highly paid executives with young, energetic middle managers, preferably ones who were "smart, poor and who wanted to be rich," which is how Kozlowski saw himself when he was younger. These ambitious individuals would strive for productive efficiency by closing facilities and dislocating workers. For example, in consolidating the firms that it acquired in 2001, Tyco closed approximately 300 plants and eliminated approximately 3,000 jobs.[13]

In this loosely held empire, the central office set stringent budgets and financial controls to oversee performance. By focusing on its financials, Tyco imitated the conglomerates that preceded it. But, to ensure that Tyco had synergy Kozlowski would annually ask investment bankers to map out a break-up strategy. If it beat Tyco's current value, then Kozlowski promised that he would undo the company.[14] Until 2002, Tyco outperformed break-up scenarios and Kozlowski did not have to make good on his promise.

In 1999, *BusinessWeek* reported that Kozlowski was scouting anywhere from 30 to 40 different business opportunities at a time. Tyco's biggest acquisitions during this period included Earth Technology Corporation (1995), builders and operators of wastewater and water treatment facilities; Carlisle (1996), makers of packaging materials and clothing hangers; and AMP (1999), manufacturer of electrical, electronic, and fiber-optic wireless devices.[15]

The merger with Bermuda-based ADT in 1997 was one of Tyco's most notable additions during this time period. The $5 billion plus deal added the world's largest producer of home security systems to Tyco's portfolio. The merger also allowed Kozlowski to transfer Tyco's headquarters from New Hampshire to Bermuda. The move saved Tyco $400 million in taxes in just one year.[16]

Under Kozlowski, Tyco had become larger and more diversified than ever, with subsidiaries that manufactured everything from medical syringes to undersea fiberoptic cables. Between 1997 and 2002, Tyco purchased more than 1,000 companies and spent $60 billion on acquisitions.[17] This growth enabled Tyco's stock to climb from just over $5 per share in 1992 to a high of $62 in 2001.[18] Between 1996 and 2001, revenues increased by 48.7 percent per year.[19] *BusinessWeek* named Tyco one of the 50 best companies in 1997.

Tyco's board members seemed to be relatively pleased with Kozlowski's performance. He was given a lot of freedom in running the company. In 1997 the board voted to allow the CEO to spend up to $50 million on an acquisition without getting their approval first. That number was increased to $100 million in 1999 and then $200 million in 2000. Tyco's steady stock climb allowed Kozlowski to borrow heavily to fund his purchasing spree. At its peak, Tyco's debt reached $28 billion, a figure that exceeded shareholder equity.

Management Incentives and Compensation

Running the Company

Kozlowski preferred Tyco to be a decentralized organization. The divisions acted almost entirely independent of one another. Managers from different operating segments rarely spoke to each other. Some thought that this kept Tyco from experiencing restraints on its growth potential. One top lieutenant said, "There is no limit to how big the company could get because of the way we manage it."[20] It seemed that Kozlowski had a deep disdain for bureaucratic hierarchies or managerial organization. He forbade memos and kept meetings short. He preferred communicating briefly with others, either over the phone or through e-mail. Kozlowski wanted his employees to be accountable for their own work and compensated or penalized accordingly.

Compensation Packages

To get the most out of his executives, Kozlowski liked the idea of a compensation package with a low base salary but weighted heavily with incentives. Tyco's managers would not get a bonus unless their division had achieved 15 percent of earnings for the year. If the division hit 15 percent, then the executives would receive compensation that would be, at a minimum, equal to their salary. If the division surpassed 15 percent, then "the sky was the limit."[21]

For senior executives, Tyco, like other large oldline companies, used stock options for incentive pay.

This preference arose from the Reform Tax Act of 1993, which disallowed firms to pay executive salaries that exceeded $1 million for tax purposes. During the 1992 presidential contest between George Bush and Bill Clinton, CEO pay became a contentious issue. Although wages for average workers remained stagnant during the Bush administration, CEO pay had increased steadily. Once in the White House, Clinton pursued tax policies designed to curb excess CEO salaries, hence the Tax Reform Act's deduction limit on executive salaries. The Tax Act, however, still allowed companies to continue to write off incentive-based pay. Congress believed that performance-based pay was compensation well deserved.

Stock Options and Other Incentives

Among the various sorts of incentive pay, corporate board compensation committees found stock options to be the most attractive. Although the federal government allowed these bonuses to be tax deductible, accounting rules did not require firms to report options as an expense. Thus, from a tax vantage point, options reduced the firm's tax burden. From an accounting standpoint, they were costless compensation. Shareholders were enamored by these plans for they allegedly aligned managers to shareholders' interests. Tyco's board did not differ from its *Fortune* 500 peers. Driven by tax and accounting incentives, Tyco's board loaded executive compensation packages with stock options. For example, in 2002, Kozlowski owned 3 million Tyco shares and held option on another 10 million.[22] Tyco's executives now had powerful incentives to push up shareholder value by any means possible. Tyco's compensation structure illustrates this change. In 1999, Kozlowski's first year as CEO and chairperson, he earned $1.2 million while Tyco's second highest executive received $950,000. By 2000, Kozlowski earned more than twice the second highest paid executive (CFO Mark Schwartz).

The Fame Game

In the late 1990s, Tyco's board brought in an image-consultant from New York City to help bolster Kozlowski and Tyco's reputation. Tyco modeled this campaign after GE's celebrity CEO, Jack Welch. As institutional investors came to dominate the stock market, money market managers increasingly relied on a CEO's reputation when evaluating investment opportunities. If a CEO had charisma, the markets reacted favorably. CEO charisma requires a publicity campaign that gives the CEO a larger-than-life appearance—a perception that is generally achieved with large offices, fancy suits, corporate jets, and expensive tastes.[23]

At Tyco, Kozlowski gave openly to charity, spoke at well-publicized events, and joined the boards of for- and not-for-profit organizations. Kozlowski's presence was felt especially in southern Maine and New Hampshire, where a number of local agencies benefited from his philanthropy. The Berwick Academy in South Berwick, Maine, was able to build a multimillion-dollar athletic center in 1997 after receiving a $1.7 million contribution from Tyco. The University of New Hampshire, Franklin Pierce College, St. Anselm's College, and the United Way of the Greater Seacoast also received a number of large donations from the company at the CEO's request. UNH in particular was able to set up a Tyco scholarship in the College of Engineering and Physical Science after the company presented a $5 million gift to the UNH Foundation Office. Kathy Gallant, owner of Blue Moon Market and Green Earth Café in Exeter, described Kozlowski as "the most engaging, generous human being."[24]

CEO/Senior Executive Entitlement

At the same time that he was giving openly to not-for-profit agencies, Kozlowski started buying lavish homes in New York and Boca Raton and filling them with exquisite furnishings and decorations. He used Tyco's cash to bankroll these investments. He also used Tyco's resources to benefit other members of his inner executive circle. These decisions seemed to make good business sense. For example, once Tyco decided to move corporate headquarters to New York, the Board's compensation committee approved Kozlowski's relocation expenses under the firm's New York City Corporate Headquarters Relocation Loan Program. It awarded relocated executives interest-free home loans, with some restrictions. In May 2000, Kozlowski received more than $7 million as a loan to relocate to 610 Park Avenue.

Kozlowski soon left this address and took up residence in a co-op at 950 Fifth Avenue that better suited Tyco's business needs than the Park Avenue address. Stephen Schwartz, a well-known investment banker and president of the prestigious Blackstone Group, owned the co-op, which had only seven units. Like other Fifth Avenue co-ops, Kozlowski had to gain the co-op board's approval. He interviewed with two co-op owners: Jonathan Tisch, CEO of Loews Hotels and member of the Tisch family, which controlled Loews Corporation; and Robert Hurst, a vice chairman at Goldman, Sachs, the investment banking firm with which Tyco had dealings. This move cost Tyco $16 million. Still, Kozlowski's name appeared on the title because the co-op prohibited corporate ownership.

TME Corporation and Tyco's Board of Directors

However, not every transaction that benefited Kozlowski or senior executives had board approval. Although Tyco under Kozlowski grew into a global company with more than 2,000 subsidiaries and 270,000 employees, corporate headquarters consisted of a staff of fewer than 400. These employees received their pay from another subsidiary, TME Management Corporation, which constituted Tyco's headquarters' company and employed about 40 senior executives.[25]

As a publicly traded corporation, Tyco's board of directors had final authority over the enterprise and its executives. To carry out its responsibilities, Tyco's board established a number of committees, including a board nominating and governance committee, an audit committee, and a compensation committee. Legally, TME Management answered to the board and its committees. Yet, as Tyco expanded rapidly and as Tyco's market value continued to grow, TME gained *de facto* discretionary powers in a variety of corporate functions. These divested responsibilities could easily be acquired because TME had separate treasury, tax, finance, investor relations, human resources, and internal audit units. Within TME, Kozlowski, as Tyco's CEO and board chair, exerted considerable influence. For example, TME's internal audit committee reported to him rather than directly to the board's audit committee. (See Exhibit 2 for a listing of Tyco's directors, officers, and key management.)

Mark Swartz and KELP

Tyco's chief financial officer, Mark Swartz also had considerable powers within TME. Appointed CFO in 1997, he joined Tyco's board in 2001. Within TME, Swartz controlled fund transfers, accounting entries, and those parts of human resources that oversaw various executive compensation, bonus, and loan programs.[26] Employees had few incentives to question Swartz's authority and powerful incentives to comply. For example, Patricia Prue, head of human resources, earned $15.1 million between 1999 and 2001.[27]

One policy—the Key Employee Loan Program (KELP)—became particularly useful for TME executives. Originally established in 1983, this program offered executives, who had been awarded stock as part of their compensation, loans to pay off state and federal taxes once the stock vested. Yet, Kozlowski used this program in 1997 and 1998 to borrow more than $18 million for personal properties in Connecticut, New Hampshire, Nantucket, and Boca Raton—monies that were never reported in the Director and Officer Questionnaire. Swartz, along with several other senior executives, benefited from this program as well. Control over the accounting books also allowed loan forgiveness. For example, in 1999, Kozlowski

Exhibit 2 Tyco International Directors, Officers, and Key Management

Directors	Officers
L. Dennis Kozlowski Chairman of the Board and Chief Executive Officer	L. Dennis Kozlowski President Chief Executive Officer
Lord Ashcroft KCMG Chairman Carlisle Holdings Limited	Mark A. Belnick Executive Vice President Chief Corporate Council
Joshua M. Berman	Michael J. Jones Secretary
Richard S. Bodman Managing General Partner Venture Management Services Group	Mark H. Swartz Executive Vice President Chief Financial Officer
John F. Fort	**Business Segment Presidents**
Stephen W. Foss Chairman and Chief Executive Officer Foss Manufacturing Company, Inc.	Jerry R. Boggess President Tyco Fire and Security Systems
Wendy E. Lane Chairman Lane Holdings, Inc.	Albert R. Gamper, Jr. President Tyco Capital
James S. Pasman, Jr.	
W. Peter Slusser President Slusser Associates, Inc.	Jurgen W. Gamper President Tyco Electronics
Mark H. Swartz Executive Vice President and Chief Financial Officer	Richard J. Meelia President Tyco Healthcare
Frank E. Walsh, Jr. Chairman Sandy Hill Foundation	
Joseph W. Welch Chairman and Chief Executive Officer The Bachman Company	

Source: *Tyco International Annual Report 2002*, 90.

and Swartz were able to make accounting entries that reduced Kozlowski's KELP debt by $25 million and Swartz's by $12.5 million.

Kozlowski viewed this KELP financing of senior executives' homes and other private purchases as sound business decisions. Kozlowski reasoned that senior executives would have to sell off large amounts of their vested stock and stock options in order to buy large ticket items such as real estate and yachts. These sales would have surely spooked big investors, pushing down Tyco's stock value and hurting the average shareholder. Even though Kozlowski and other senior executives exercised KELP in dealings for which it was not designed, Kozlowski found these actions were true to KELP's spirit.[28]

The "Art" of the Deal

In 2001, Kozlowski used KELP to purchase artwork worth nearly $12 million for his New York City residence. Again, Kozlowski judged these purchases as Tyco investments. His well-provisioned Fifth Avenue co-op substituted as an office where he negotiated acquisition deals with investment bankers under the pretense of shared collector enthusiasm. Through this ruse, Kozlowski hid his acquisition deal-making from the business press. Conventional wisdom informed Kozlowski and other Tyco executives that had these negotiations become public, the news would have adversely affected Tyco's purchase price, as investors bid up target company stock.

Finally, without board approval, TME dispersed bonuses to select executives. For example, after Tyco's successful public offering of TyCom's shares and the lucrative divestment of ADT's (a Tyco subsidiary) automobile auction division, Tyco's top executives received handsome bonuses. In the TyCom issue, Tyco executives garnered $76.5 million, with $33 million going directly to Kozlowski. Tyco senior executives did not fare as well after the ADT divestiture. They earned $56 million in bonuses, with Kozlowski pocketing nearly half.

Although these sums may seem large, they were only a small portion of the profits that these transactions put into Tyco's coffer. The ADT division sold for more than $300 million over the price for which Tyco purchased it three years earlier. The TyCom issue yielded a one-time profit of $1.76 billion after executive bonuses were deducted. Surely such lucrative deals warranted rewards for the executives involved, even though TME did not report these bonuses to Tyco's board or to shareholders.[29] In fact, TME withheld or modified accounting figures reported to the board, all to sustain the steady rise of Tyco's stock price.

By all outward appearances, however, Kozlowski was running a tidy, reliable business, portraying a lot of the same no-frills qualities of his predecessor. He landed on the cover of *Barron's* in April 1999 under the heading: "Tyco's Titan: How Dennis Kozlowski Is Creating a Lean, Profitable Giant." The article reported that Tyco's offices were practically bare, claiming that Kozlowski clearly "hasn't forgotten where he came from."[30] *Time* magazine called the conglomerate "lean." *BusinessWeek* extended that description to "ultra-lean" and put Tyco high on their list of 50 top-performing companies.

The Beginning of the End: Denouement

David Tice

Despite the positive press, in October 1999, rumors began to circulate around Wall Street that Tyco's accounting practices might not be completely legitimate. David Tice, an analyst and mutual fund operator, wrote in his newsletter "Behind the Numbers" that Tyco was overstating its earnings and inflating its profits through unorthodox bookkeeping. He wrote, "Tyco's game plan is to buy bloated businesses, strip them of excess personnel and facilities, and treat the costs as nonrecurring in the company's income statement."[31] Even though the newsletter only reaches a couple hundred money managers, it garners a fair amount of respect. The newsletter has been credited with issuing warnings about Sunbeam, Mercury Finance, and Southland, long before anybody else predicted their failure.[32] A week after Tice issued his report, Tyco's stock dropped by 20 percent.[33]

At the same time, the *New York Times* reported that two of Tyco's acquisitions, U.S. Surgical (USSC) and AMP had taken big write-offs immediately before they were acquired. Before the USSC deal closed October 1, 1998, the company reported that it had earned $69 million in the nine months preceding its June 30, 1998 quarterly report. However, in an 8-K form filed with the SEC on December 10, 1998, Tyco recorded that USSC had lost $212 million dollars for the year ending September 30, 1998, and USSC had taken a $190 million write off just before Tyco closed the deal. Similar discrepancies occurred in the AMP acquisition. In its final 10-K report covering the fiscal year ending December 31, 1998, AMP reported a $376 million write-off from plant closures, plant consolidations, and employee discharges.[34] But Tyco did not divulge these write-offs to investors.[35] These write-offs enabled Tyco's profits to rise because it did have to depreciate charges. And Kozlowski made much of Tyco's gains from the acquisitions in a July press release, helping to push up Tyco stock.

Just after the release, Kozlowski, Swartz, and several other Tyco executives sold Tyco shares. Kozlowski sold more than 3 million shares for a tidy $160 million. A Tyco director, Michael Ashcroft, joined these executives in unloading 413,700 of Tyco shares for nearly $21 million. Kozlowski and Ashcroft sold their shares in range from $45.25 to $50.39 per share. On October 1, 1998, Tyco shares opened at $26.93.[36]

In December of 1999 the SEC began a "nonpublic informal inquiry" into Tyco's accounting practices. Tyco assured investors that nothing was wrong, but people began to grow wary of the company's operations. The stock price fell to $22.50, the lowest it had been in over a year.

Seven months later, in July 2000, the SEC relented that they had not uncovered anything illegal or suspicious about Tyco's activities. Although the company itself may have been reassured by the clean bill of health, Tice's allegations continued to worry investors. Tyco desperately needed to regain Wall Street's respect if it wanted to continue to grow.

By the end of 2001, Tyco's share price was roughly equivalent to what it had been at the beginning of the year. The stock seemed stable but dormant, which worried shareholders, particularly Tyco senior executive shareholders. Their fortunes rode on Tyco stock. In 2001, Kozlowski received stock grants priced at $50 per share. If he cashed in, taxes would surely eat up half of his returns. If the stock dropped down into the $20 dollar range he would have to take an after-tax loss. Moreover, Tyco's board had decided to put their interests in line with shareholders by taking their $75,000 annual fee in Tyco stock options. If it wasn't about the money, then, it was about Kozlowski's (and the board's) reputation. Tyco had been a growth star. Even in 2000 when the NASDAQ dropped by 17 percent, Tyco stock stayed the upward course.

Shifting the Business Model: Acquisition to Operating Company

Then, investment bankers from Goldman Sachs presented Kozlowski a scenario by which to increase Tyco's value. The bankers argued that Tyco's acquisition strategy for creating shareholder value had come to an end. Tyco was simply too large to gain significant growth from the sort of acquisitions in which the firm excelled. Having reached this limit, Tyco had to shift its business model from an acquisition to an operating model. To do so, Tyco had two options. It could either consolidate its holdings, converting its central office into a hands-on strategic unit. Or, the board could approve a company breakup. Goldman Sachs favored the spin-off strategy, arguing that shareholders could net up to $75 per share, more than a $20 increase of what the shares were selling. (Of course, Goldman Sachs stood to gain as well through $240 million in fees if the breakup went forward.) In January 2002, Kozlowski, after gaining board approval, announced the plan to separate Tyco into four publicly traded units, claiming that the parts were worth more than the whole.

Although the stock started to rally, it soon sloped under Enron's weight. Investors believed that such a drastic strategic change suggested deceitful accounting practices. Soon after, a number of claims began to surface concerning questionable activities on the part of Kozlowski and his CFO Mark Swartz. First, reports revealed that Kozlowski and Swartz had unloaded $500 million worth of their company shares since 1999. Additionally, Tyco admitted to making 700 acquisitions and spending close to $8 billion in the previous three years without alerting shareholders.[37] Finally, Kozlowski admitted publicly that he had approved paying Tyco director Frank Walsh a $20 million finder's fee for the eventual acquisition of CIT, a New York–based financial services firm.

When Josh Berman, a lawyer and Tyco director, was notified of the fee, he became outraged. He called the payment "a blatant conflict of interest" and demanded that Walsh return the money.[38] Walsh, a former chairperson of Wesley Capital, a prominent leveraged buyout firm, simply refused. After all, the acquisition was a $9 billion deal, rendering his fee immaterial. When the board met in January 2002, the directors unanimously voted for Walsh to reimburse Tyco. Walsh stood up and left the room.

Public Outcry

Public reaction to all of these events was heated. Tyco seemed to be in an uproar, and, in the wake of the Enron scandals, eyebrows began to rise. By February, Tyco's stock fell to $25, half of what it had been at the start of the year.[39] The stock price continued to fall throughout March and the beginning of April. The company's market value fell from $120 billion in December 2001 to $40 billion.[40] In an effort to calm the market's reaction, Kozlowski called off the break-up plan on April 25, hoping the public would read the announcement as a sign of Tyco's stability. Instead, the change of plans made Kozlowski seem erratic and unsure about the direction of the company.

On May 31, 2002, Kozlowski learned that he would be indicted for sales tax evasion. It became transparent that since August 2001 he had been buying art and shipping boxes to New Hampshire to avoid paying more than $1 million in sales tax. Apparently the boxes had been empty and the actual paintings were delivered directly to his Manhattan home.[41] When the Tyco directors learned about the legal proceedings they immediately called for Kozlowski's resignation.

The End of the Kozlowski Years

On June 3, 2002, Dennis Kozlowski stepped down from his role as CEO, and John Fort, a current director, took over as interim chair and CEO. He had held these positions for 10 years immediately proceeding Kozlowski's term. Tyco announced that the move was temporary and that same day they were planning to search for a replacement. In light of the questions surrounding Tyco's accounting procedures and the company's future, the resignation did not help investor confidence. That same morning, Tyco's stock fell 19 percent to $18. John Maack, a money manager at Crabbe Huson in Manhattan said, "This is just one more piece of uncertainty and the share price is telling you what shareholders think. What we needed here were signs of stability and that things were going to be OK. Not this."

On June 4, 2002, Dennis Kozlowski was led into a New York City courtroom, head hanging, shoulders slumped. It was a startling image and one that not many had seen before. This man was the CEO who had helped Tyco's stock climb to more than $63 per share. Over 10 years he built the company into a diversified, international presence (see Exhibit 3 for an overview of Tyco's divisions and products as of 2002). He had been lauded on the covers of *Barron's* and *Forbes*. He had watched as Tyco was named on *BusinessWeek's* list of 50 top-performing companies (see Appendix A). Brimming with self-confidence, he once seemed like the model of the modern American executive. Now, the CEO of this once thriving company was being indicted for tax evasion. His career was finished. The company he left behind was in disarray.

For Fort, this scandal must have proved particularly troubling. All the misreporting and executive compensation concealment had occurred while he was a board member. How could he and Tyco's other directors confidently say that they had acted as corporate fiduciaries? How could they tell investors that they had acted with a duty of care? Fort had little time to sort out these and other issues facing the company. In July 2002, Edward Breen took over as CEO. Prior to joining Tyco, Breen was president and chief operating officer of Motorola from January 2002 to July 2002; executive vice president and president of Motorola's Networks Sector from January 2001 to January 2002; executive vice president and president of Motorola's Broadband Communications Sector from January 2000 to January 2001.[42]

Breen's immediate task was to find ways to regain investor confidence, boost Tyco's image, and dissociate himself and Tyco's board from the lying, cheating, and stealing that suddenly seemed to be overtaking Tyco and corporate America. With Tyco's severe liquidity crisis many were wondering whether the conglomerate would even survive.[43] (See Exhibits 1, 4, and 5 for pertinent financial information.)

Exhibit 3 Tyco's Divisions and Products

Electronics: Worldwide supplier of active and passive electronic components. Products can be found in computers, telecommunications equipment, industrial machinery, aerospace and defense applications, automobiles, household appliances, and consumer electronics.

Engineered Products and Services: Consists of four global businesses: flow control, fire and building products, electrical and metal products, and infrastructure services. Valve and control products are used to transport, control, and sample liquids, powders, and gasses in oil and gas, chemical, petrochemical, power generation, waste and waste water, pharmaceutical, pulp and paper, food and beverage, commercial construction, and other industries.

Healthcare and Specialty Products: Worldwide manufacturer, distributor, and service provider of medical devices, including disposable medical supplies, monitoring equipment, medical instruments, and bulk analgesic pharmaceuticals and chemicals. Business segments include medical, surgical, respiratory, imaging, pharmaceutical, and retail products.

Plastics and Adhesives: Maker of products used in packaging, including polyethylene films, laminated and coated products, tapes, adhesives, plastic garment hangers, bags and sheeting, disposable dinnerware products, and tapes for industrial applications. This division was comprised of A&E products, Ludlow Coated Products, Tyco Plastics and Tyco Adhesives.

Fire and Security Services: Worldwide leader in fire protection and electronic security. It designs, manufactures, installs, and services electronic security systems, fire protection, detection and suppression systems, fire sprinklers, and extinguishers. It consists of more than 60 brands that are represented in more than 100 countries. It also makes electronic security systems and monitoring for consumers and business, including aviation, marine, transportation, and government security systems. Anti-theft systems for large and small retailers as well as video surveillance and life safety systems are also among its products.

Exhibit 4 Tyco International's Financial Highlights, 1998–2002

	Year Ended September 30,				
	2002	2001	2000	1999	1998
	(in millions, except per-share data)				
Consolidated Statements of Operations Data:					
Net revenues	$35,643.7	$34,036.6	$28,931.9	$22,496.5	$19,061.7
(Loss) income from continuing operations	(3,070.4)	4,401.5	4,519.9	1,067.7	1,168.6
Cumulative effect of accounting changes, net of tax	—	(683.4)	—	—	—
Net (loss) income	(9,411.7)	3,970.6	4,519.9	1,022.0	1,166.2
Basic (loss) earnings per common share:					
(Loss) income from continuing operations	(1.54)	2.44	2.68	0.65	0.74
Cumulative effect of accounting changes, net of tax	—	(0.38)	—	—	—
Net (loss) income	(4.73)	2.20	2.68	0.62	0.74
Diluted (loss) earnings per common share:					
(Loss) income from continuing operations	(1.54)	2.40	2.64	0.64	0.72
Cumulative effect of accounting changes, net of tax	—	(0.37)	—	—	—
Net (loss) income	(4.73)	2.17	2.64	0.61	0.72
Cash dividends per common share					
Consolidated Balance Sheet Data (End of Period):					
Total assets	$66,414.4	$71,022.6	$40,404.3	$32,344.3	$23,440.7
Long-term debt	16,486.8	19,596.0	9,461.8	9,109.4	5,424.7
Shareholders' equity	24,790.6	31,737.4	17,033.2	12,369.3	9,901.8

	Year Ended September 30, 1998	Nine Months Ended September 30, 1997	Year Ended December 31,		
			1996	1995	1994
	(in millions, except per-share amounts)				
Consolidated Statements of Operations Data:					
Net sales	$ 12,311.3	$ 7,588.2	$8,103.7	$6,915.6	$6,240.9
Operating income (loss)	1,923.7	(476.5)	(18.8)	649.6	653.6
Income (loss) before extraordinary items	1,177.1	(776.8)	(296.7)	267.5	304.8
Income (loss) before extraordinary items per common share:					
Basic	2.07	(1.50)	(.62)	.58	.65
Diluted	2.02	(1.50)	(.62)	.57	.63
Cash dividends per common share	.10				
Consolidated Balance Sheet Data:					
Total assets	$16,526.6	$10,447.0	$8,471.3	$7,357.8	$7,053.2
Long-term debt	4,652.6	2,480.6	1,878.4	1,760.7	1,755.3
Shareholders' equity	6,136.9	3,429.4	3,288.6	3,342.7	3,030.0

Source: 2007, Hoovers' 10-K report, January.

Exhibit 5 Tyco International's Financial Ratios and Indicators, 1997–2002

Profitability Ratios	9/30/2002	9/30/2001	9/30/2000	9/30/1999	9/30/1998[1]	9/30/1997[2]
Return on Equity (%)	−12.39	14.72	26.54	8.36	11.8	−22.65
Return on Assets (%)	−4.66	4.29	11.22	3.12	4.85	−7.44
Return on Investment	−47.83	17.67	74.4	22.79	34.93	−19.73
Gross Margin	0.035	0.042	0.038	0.036	0.033	0.033
EBITDA of Revenue (%)	1.82	24.66	18.92	9.5	16.25	−6.28
Operating Margin (%)	−4.43	17.04	18.92	9.5	10.22	−6.28
Pre-Tax Margin	−7.89	17.04	22.34	7.34	8.93	−7.77
Net Profit Margin (%)	−26.4	14.67	15.62	4.38	6.12	−11.01
Effective Tax Rate (%)	−9.17	23.86	29.79	37.56	31.37	−31.71
Liquidity Indicators						
Quick Ratio	0.62	1.23	0.62	0.82	0.82	0.61
Current Ratio	1.01	1.38	1.1	1.29	1.37	1.03
Working Capital/Total Assets	0	0.12	0.03	0.08	0.11	0.01
Debt Management						
Current Liabilities/Equity	0.79	1.06	0.69	0.74	0.71	1.16
Total Debt to Equity	0.67	1.2	0.56	0.74	0.55	0.72
Long Term Debt to Assets	0.25	0.35	0.23	0.28	0.23	0.24
Asset Management						
Revenues/Total Assets	0.54	0.33	0.72	0.68	0.79	0.73
Revenues/Working Capital	269.01	2.84	25.45	8.51	7.38	64.86
Interest Coverage	−1.61	—	8.65	4.02	6.53	−3.29

[1]As reported in the 1999 Annual Report; Certain prior year amounts have been reclassified to conform with current year presentation.
[2]For 9 months due to fiscal year end change.
Source: 2007, Mergent Online, January.

Notes

1. 2005, *Associated Press,* September 20.
2. 2006, The shareholders' revolt, *The Economist,* June 17, 71; 2005, A bad week to be bad, *The Economist,* June 23.
3. http://tycoint.com/tyco/history.asp.
4. A. Bianco, W. Symonds, & N. Byrnes with D. Polek, 2002, The rise and fall of Dennis Kozlowski. *BusinessWeek Online,* December 23.
5. J. B. Stewart, 2003, Spend! Spend! Spend! Where did Tyco's money go? *The New Yorker,* February 17.
6. Bianco, Symonds, & Byrnes, The rise and fall of Dennis Kozlowski.
7. S. Syre & C. Stein, 1999, The quiet giant: Tyco International takes unglamorous road to riches, *Boston Globe,* June 30.
8. Ibid.
9. Bianco, Symonds, & Byrnes, The rise and fall of Dennis Kozlowski.
10. Ibid.
11. Ibid.
12. J. Thottam, 2004, Can this man save Tyco? *Time,* February 9, 48.
13 2001, Tyco planning 11,000 job cuts, *Financial Times,* August 14.
14. D. J. Collis & C. A. Montgomery, 1998, Creating corporate advantage, *Harvard Business Review,* May–June, 71–83.
15. http://tycoint.com/tyco/history.asp.
16. A. Berenson, 2002, Ex-Tyco chief, a big risk taker, now confronts the legal system, *New York Times,* June 10, C1.
17. Reuters, 2003, Ex-Tyco chief had broad acquisition authority, *New York Times,* October 15; R. M. Cook, 2004, Tyco decline leaves void

in jobs, donations, *Daily Democrat,* March 28; S. Tully, 2004, Mr. Cleanup: Ed Breen has scrubbed the scandal out of Tyco. Now can he make it another GE? *Fortune,* http://www.fortune.com/fortune/ceo/articles/0,15114,735903,00.html, November 1.
18. http://timesonline.co.uk.
19. Bianco, Symonds, & Byrnes, The rise and fall of Dennis Kozlowski.
20. S. Finkelstein, 2003, Why smart executives fail: Seven habits of spectacularly unsuccessful people, *Business Strategy Review,* Winter.
21. W. C. Symonds, 2001, The most aggressive CEO, *BusinessWeek Online,* May 28.
22. J. B. Stewart, Spend! Spend! Spend! Where did Tyco's money go?
23. R. Khurana, 2002, The curse of the superstar CEO, *Harvard Business Review,* 80(9), September, 60.
24. R. M. Cook, 2004, Tyco decline leaves void in jobs, donations.
25. Supreme Court of the State of New York, The People of the State of New York against L. Dennis Kozlowski and Mark H. Swartz, Indictment No. 5259/02.
26. Ibid.
27. Mark Maremont, 2004, Kozlowski's defense strategy: Big spending was no secret, *Wall Street Journal,* February 9, 1.
28. J. B. Stewart, "Spend! Spend! Spend! Where did Tyco's money go?
29. Ibid.
30. J. Laing, 1999, Tyco's titan: How Dennis Kozlowski is creating a lean profitable giant, *Barron's,* April.

31. H. Weber, 2002, Decade of meteoric growth over for Tyco as company struggles to break itself apart, *Portsmouth Herald,* March 3.

32. http://www.thestreet.com/funds/funds/795362.html.

33. S. Woolley, 2000, The conglomerator wants a little respect, *Forbes,* October 16.

34. *Re Tyco International, Ltd., Securities Litigation,* U.S. District Court for the District of New Hampshire, 185 F. Supp. 2d 102, February 22, 2002.

35. F. Norris, 1999, Tyco shares plunge after company discloses SEC inquiry, *New York Times,* October 29.

36. *Re Tyco International, Ltd.*

37. J. Thottam, Can this man save Tyco?

38. J. B. Stewart, Spend! Spend! Spend! Where did Tyco's money go?

39. Ibid.

40. C. Ayres, 2002, The Tyco juggernaut grinds to a halt, http://www.timesonline.co.uk, June 5.

41. J. B. Stewart, Spend! Spend! Spend! Where did Tyco's money go?

42. A. Weinberg, 2002, Breen cleans Tyco's house, *Forbes Online,* August 2.

43. W. Symonds, 2004, Tyco: Lazarus with a ticker symbol, *BusinessWeek* Online, May 5.

Appendix A Tyco Timeline

1960	Arthur Rosenburg founds Tyco
1962	Becomes incorporated as Tyco Labs
1964	Goes public
1965	Makes first acquisition: Mule Battery Products
1968	Has acquired 16 companies by this time
1973	Joseph Gaziano becomes CEO
1974	Acquires Simplex Technology, undersea fiber optics telecommunications cable manufacturer
1975	Dennis Kozlowski starts at Tyco as assistant comptroller and head of auditing
1976	Acquires Grinnell Fire Protection Systems, fire sprinkler systems manufacturer
1979	Acquires Armin Plastics, polyethylene film products manufacturer
1981	Acquires Ludlow Corporation, packaging products manufacturer
1982	John Fort becomes CEO, organizes Tyco subsidiaries into 3 business segments: Fire Protection, Electronics, and Packaging
1983	Kozlowski becomes director of Fire Protection Division
1986	Acquires Grinnell Corporation
1987	Kozlowski joins Tyco board
1987	Acquires Allied Tube & Conduit, brings Tyco into Steel Tube Market
1989	Acquires Mueller Company, manufacturers of water and glass flow control products
1991	Acquires Wormald International Ltd., fire protections systems and products
1992	Kozlowski becomes CEO
1993	Company changes name to Tyco International
1995	Opens New York City office on Fifth Avenue
1997	Becomes incorporated in Bermuda by way of ADT Security Systems acquisition
1997	*BusinessWeek* names Tyco one of top 50 companies
1998	Acquires AMP Inc., biggest maker of electronic conductors
1999	New York District Attorney's office performs brief investigation to determine whether a Tyco director illegally sold his $2.5 million Florida home to the company's general counsel; investigations are inconclusive
Apr. 1999	Kozlowski is on the cover of *Barron's* "Tyco's Titan: How Dennis Kozlowski Is Creating a Lean, Profitable Giant"
Aug. 1999	Tyco pays $38.5 million in allegedly unauthorized bonuses to top executives
Oct. 1999	David Tice, analyst and money manager, newsletter "Behind the Numbers" accuses Tyco of inflating reported profits
Oct. 1999	*New York Times* article reports two of Tyco's acquisitions had taken big write-offs just before they were acquired; article accuses Tyco of not disclosing the write-offs to the SEC in November–December 1999; SEC begins "nonpublic informal inquiry"
July 2000	SEC ends investigations, reporting that Tyco's accounting practices look clean; Tice maintains his criticisms
Aug. 2000	Tyco pays $18 million for Fifth Avenue duplex for Kozlowski
Sept. 2000	Tyco pays $96 million in unauthorized bonuses to 50 employees
Oct. 2000	Kozlowski is on the cover of *Forbes,* "The Conglomerator Wants a Little Respect"
June 2001	Tyco buys CIT, a financial services firm, for $10 million
June 2001	Tyco pays for half of Kozlowski's wife's $2.1 million birthday party in Sardinia
Aug. 2001	Kozlowski begins buying art for his Manhattan apartment and having empty boxes shipped to New Hampshire
2001	Tyco cuts 11,000 jobs and closes/consolidates 300 plants in attempts to reduce costs
Jan. 2002	Kozlowski makes public plan to split Tyco up into four publicly traded units; met with strong resistance from shareholders

Jan. 2002	Investors learn of $20 million finder's fee paid to Tyco director Frank Walsh for acquisition of CIT without board's approval
Jan. 2002	Manhattan district attorney begins looking into tax evasion/money laundering scheme involving Kozlowski and Manhattan-based art dealer
April 2002	Kozlowski calls off Tyco break-up plan
June 2002	Kozlowski resigns
June 2002	Fort names interim CEO
July 2002	Edward Breen takes over as CEO (Prior to joining Tyco, Mr. Breen held executive positions with Motorola.)
June 2005	Kozlowski and Mark Swartz convicted of grand larceny, conspiracy and fraud
Sept. 2005	Kozlowski and Swartz received 8- to 25-year sentences at Mid-State Correctional Facility near Utica, New York, and ordered to pay a total of $134 million in restitution along with fines of $70 million for Kozlowski and $35 million for Swartz

Case 22

Vodafone: Out of Many, One[1]

Johannes Banzhaf, Ashok Som

ESSEC Business School

Abstract

In 2006, Vodafone Group PLC was the world's largest cell phone provider by revenue. Since 1999, Vodafone had invested US$270 billion (€225 billion) mostly in stock, building an empire spanning 26 countries. It controlled cell phone operations in 16 countries and had minority stakes in companies in 10 other countries. This case traces the history of Vodafone's growth and its capability to transform and adapt itself to the dramatically changing market environment in the dynamic telecommunication sector. The case analyzes Vodafone's growth through acquisitions and the subsequent integration of acquired units with a key focus on how it manages to coordinate its businesses on a global scale.

Arun Sarin reclined in his seat in a first-class compartment en route to London. The CEO of Vodafone, the world's largest mobile telephone operator, began reflecting on the events of the last few days, in particular Vodafone's decision to exit the Japanese market by selling Vodafone's stake in Japan Telecom to Tokyo-based Softbank in a deal valued at $15.4 billion, confirming that after the sale the company would return $10.5 billion to its shareholders. Vodafone had trailed behind NTT DoCoMo and KDDI since its entry into Japan in 2001, thanks to fickle consumers, the lack of a low-end tier in the segment, and the challenge of coordinating terminals and technologies across borders. The time had come to make a hard decision, and Sarin had made it.

It was not the first time he had been faced with such a decision. Two years earlier Vodafone had made headlines in the financial press with its failed attempt to take over the U.S. mobile operator, AT&T Wireless. After a long takeover battle, Vodafone's American rival Cingular Wireless had offered $41 billion in cash for AT&T Wireless.[2] At the time, Sarin had not been sure whether to regret the failed takeover. He could have easily financed a larger sum for the bid, but major shareholders had been explicit that anything beyond an offer of $38 billion would be detrimental to their interests.[3] Vodafone's offer had forced Cingular to increase its bid from $30 billion to $41 billion, meaning that it might take Cingular many years to digest the merger (refer to Exhibit 1 for share prices of Vodafone since 1989). More promising and cheaper ways to enhance its presence in the world's largest economy with a huge growth potential might also come Vodafone's way.

Sarin knew he could not afford to alienate Vodafone's shareholders by pursuing growth at all costs. However, Vodafone's current hold in the U.S. market (the noncontrolling stake in Verizon Wireless but the only one in the United States) was not comforting either. The relationship with the other main shareholder, Verizon, was quite strained, management had refused to adopt the single Vodafone brand, and had insisted on using the outdated American CDMA network standard instead of the groupwide GSM/UMTS standard.[4]

Being the CEO was definitely not an easy job, with so many things to consider and the shadow of his larger-than-life predecessor Sir Chris Gent looming over him. But these reasons were exactly why he was being paid £1.2 million a year as base salary.[5]

Company Overview: Vodafone Group Plc

In 2005, Vodafone was the leading mobile phone operator in the world. It had more than 150 million customers worldwide in 26 different countries.[6] Vodafone employed approximately 67,000 people around the world and had its headquarters in Newbury, England. Being listed on the stock exchanges of New York (ticker: VOD), London, and Frankfurt, it boasted a market capitalization

Exhibit 1 Vodafone Share Price Since 2001 (in pence)

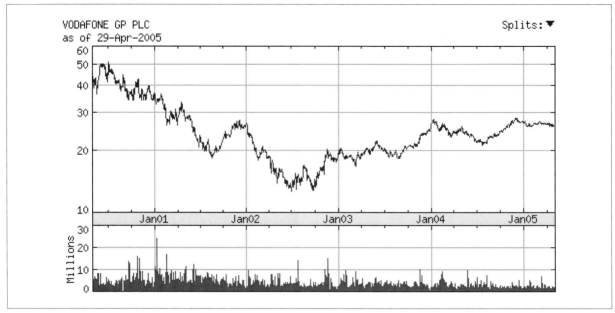

Source: http://finance.yahoo.com.

of US$165.7 billion[7] making it the eleventh most valuable company in the world. In FY2003 it suffered a loss of US$15.5 billion (on revenues of approximately US$48 billion). This figure was the result of large write-downs on the goodwill of acquired companies and huge amortization charges related to the acquisition of other mobile operators like Mannesmann D2. These charges amounted to US$18.8 billion.[8] In fact, if one excluded these extraordinary noncash charges, Vodafone was profitable, as indicated by its gross margins and its capacity to generate huge positive cash flows: The cash flow from operating activities (before capital expenditure and other outflows) amounted to £12.3 billion (approximately US$22.7 billion) in financial year 2004, while free cash flow exceeded an unbelievable £8 billion (US$15.7 billion—refer to Exhibit 2 for an overview of Vodafone Group's financials).[9] Vodafone had been consistently paying dividends and had recently announced a £3 billion share repurchase program.[10]

History of Vodafone[11]

The company was formed as Racal Telecom Limited in 1984 as a subsidiary of Racal Electronics Plc., a British electronics manufacturing company. It successfully bid for a private sector U.K. cellular license in 1982 and hosted the first-ever mobile phone call in the United Kingdom in 1985. The customer base stood at 19,000 on December 31, 1985.

In October 1988, Racal Telecom Ltd. went public by offering approximately 20 percent of the company's stock to the public. Three years later, it was fully de-merged

from Racal Electronics and became an independent company, with a different name—Vodafone Group Plc—which was listed on the London and New York stock exchanges. Corporate legend has it that the "founders had the foresight to realize that people would do more than talk over their phones and so created a future-proof name that would embrace both VOice and DAta mobile communication: Vodafone."[12] Due to its early start, it managed the largest mobile network in the world by 1987.

In 1992, Vodafone pioneered again when it signed the world's first international "roaming" agreement with Telecom Finland, allowing Vodafone's customers to use their phone on a different network while still being billed in their home country. Four years later, Vodafone became the first operator in the United Kingdom to offer so-called prepaid packages that do not require the customers to sign a long-term contract.

Christopher Gent succeeded Sir Gerald Whent at the helm of the company on January 1, 1997. Gent was responsible for shifting Vodafone's growth strategy from organic to aggressive external, orchestrating its move toward globalization. In the same year, Vodafone's 100th roaming agreement was signed.

In early 1999, Vodafone signed up its 10 millionth customer, 5 million of them in the United Kingdom. Vodafone's growth reached the next level when it successfully merged with AirTouch Communications Inc. of the United States—a $61 billion deal. Vodafone renamed itself briefly into Vodafone AirTouch and more than doubled its customer base to 31 million customers worldwide (September 1999), having operations in

Exhibit 2 Vodafone Key Financials, 1995–2004

For the Financial Year Ended March 31	Turnover (in £m)	Profit (loss) for the Financial Year (after taxation, in £m)	Net Cash Inflow From Operating Activities (in £m)	Dividends per Share (pence)	Registered Proportionate Customers (in thousands)
1995	1,153	238	386	3.34p	2,073
1996	1,402	311	615	4.01p	3,035
1997	1,749	364	644	4.81p	4,016
1998	2,408	419	886	5.53p	5,844
1999	336	637	1,045	3.77p	10,445
2000	7,873	487	2,510	1.34p	39,139
2001	15,004	(9,763)	4,587	1.40p	82,997
2002	22,845	(16,155)	8,102	1.47p	101,136
2003	30,375*	(9,819)	11,142	1.70p	119,709
2004	33,559	(9,015)	12,317	2.03p	133,421

*See following chart for group turnover by geographic region.

Source: Company annual reports.

(in £ million)	2003	2002
Mobile Telecommunications		
Northern Europe	6,057	
Central Europe	4,775	
Southern Europe	8,051	
Americas	5	
Asia Pacific	8,364	
Middle East and Africa	290	
= **Total mobile operations**	**27,542**	**20,742**
Other Operations		
Europe	854	
Asia Pacific	1,979	
= **Total Group Turnover**	**30,375**	**22,845**

Note: "Other operations" mainly include the results of the group's interests in fixed line telecommunications businesses in Germany (Arcor), France (Cegetel), and Japan (Japan Telecom). The turnover figure for the Americas does not include the 45% stake in Verizon Wireless (U.S.).

Source: Adapted from company annual report, 2003.

24 countries across five continents.[13] In the late 1990s and the early new millenium, stock markets were steering toward a bubble, with "mobile" being the latest hype and insane sums being paid for mobile operators and the licenses to operate mobile networks. At the end of November 1999, the company had a market capitalization of approximately £90 billion. Vodafone's North American branch was integrated into a new entity branded Verizon Wireless together with Bell Atlantic's mobile business, with Vodafone retaining a 45 percent stake in the new venture. Verizon Wireless was the largest mobile phone operator in 2003 in a fragmented North American market (36 million customers, 24% market share as of September 30, 2003).[14]

In a move that sent shockwaves through corporate Germany in 1999, Vodafone launched a €100 billion takeover bid for Mannesmann in order to get hold of its D2 mobile phone business, the private market leader in Germany. A bitter struggle for Mannesmann's independence ensued, but finally the board of Mannesmann gave in and the deal was closed in 2000: €190 billion paid in stocks made it Germany's largest takeover ever.[15] The customer base was once again doubled and Vodafone found itself among the 10 largest companies in the world in terms of market capitalization. The mobile telephony boom reached its peak and former national providers (such as Deutsche Telekom, France Télécom, Telefonica) embarked on a buying binge that brought them on the verge of bankruptcy, when the bubble finally burst (Deutsche Telekom shares fell from more than €100 to €15).

The year 2001 saw a consolidation and restructuring within Vodafone, which reported 82.9 million customers for the financial year ending March 31, 2001. It grew at a somewhat slower pace than in previous years, about half of it generated by internal growth and the other half by acquisitions (e.g., acquiring Ireland's Eircell and increasing its stake in Spanish AirTel Movil to 91.7%). However, slower growth still meant that Vodafone had added approximately 20 million customers by the end of the year 2002. At that time, the company board announced that the Indian-born American Arun Sarin would take over the CEO position on July 30, 2003.

No large scale acquisitions took place in 2002 and 2003, but instead a host of smaller deals and partnership agreements were made. In February 2004, Vodafone's bid for AT&T Wireless in the United States failed against a higher offer by Cingular, clearly indicating that Vodafone had all but renounced its growth ambitions.

Growth at Vodafone

Traditionally growth at Vodafone was by acquisitions rather than organic. It had a track record in takeovers and their subsequent successful integration, Germany's Mannesmann being the most prominent example. Branded as "Vodafone Germany," Mannesmann was the group's most profitable venture (in terms of EBIT, which surpassed £2 billion in 2003) and its largest subsidiary. On the mobile telephony acquisition strategy, Alan Harper, Group Strategy and Business Integration Director, commented,

In the past 10 years there had been a sea of change in the evolution of the telecommunication industry. The rule in this industry has been "Hunt or Be Hunted." The strategy of the global players had been mobile-centric, multi-market strategies. Most of the companies like Hutchison, Mannesmann, Airtouch started much smaller, like a start-up, did not have any history as an operator and the parent company was usually a trading company. Vodafone acquired Mannesmann, Airtouch and the rest of the small players. FT acquired Orange. Docomo was restructured back into NTT.

Unlike many of its competitors, Vodafone used shares for its acquisitions. This practice might be one of the reasons why Vodafone emerged from the telecom crisis relatively early and could concentrate on growth again, while virtually all of its competitors were still occupied in trying to reduce their debt burden (Deutsche Telekom, France Télécom, MMO2, KPN, etc.).[16] However, Vodafone's shares had shown only lackluster performance in prior months, which meant that Vodafone increasingly had to use hard cash to increase its holdings in subsidiaries or for new acquisitions. Because Vodafone did not want to compromise its good credit ratings (by industry standards) under any circumstances, it slowed down on acquisitions and focused on internal growth for the preceding two years (refer to Exhibit 3 for Vodafone's strategic intent).

Vodafone had acquired other businesses along with the mobile phone business as in the case of Japan Telecom and Mannesmann, where it got ownership of fixed line operations. Vodafone had been always explicit in its concentration on its core business of mobile telecommunications. Usually it started looking for potential buyers for the other business. In the words of Alan Harper, Group Strategy and Business Integration Director,

We had been always mobile focused. In 1995, when I joined Vodafone, it was mobile focused. It has a turnover of £8 billion, it was the third largest mobile operator in the UK and had 80% business in the UK. Today, in 2005, we are still mobile focused, with a turnover of £100 billion, biggest in the world and only 10% in the UK.

Exhibit 3 Strategic Intent of Vodafone

The Company had maintained a strategy of focusing on global mobile telecommunications and providing network coverage to allow its customers to communicate using mobile products and services. The Company's strategy was increasingly focused on revenue growth and margin improvement from providing enhanced services to its customer base. This growth strategy had three principal components:

- to grow voice and data revenues through an increased marketing focus on our established high-quality customer base;
- to extend our operational leadership of the industry through maximizing the benefits of scale and scope, through the use of partner network agreements, by increasing equity interests in businesses where the Group had existing shareholdings and by promoting the Vodafone brand; and
- to extend service differentiation, investing in delivering Vodafone branded, easy to use, customer propositions for mobile voice and data.

Where appropriate, and if circumstances allow, the Company may also make further acquisitions or disposals of businesses.

Source: http://www.vodafone.com.

Vodafone balanced its investment options by taking its time to ensure a good investment and disinvestment option. For example, it sold Japan Telecom's fixed line operations in 2003 for ¥261.3 billion (£1.4 billion)[17] while it reinforced its long-term commitment to Japan in 2005 by making a further investment of up to £2.6 billion. Arun Sarin pointed out,

Our transactions in Japan will simplify the structure, confirm our commitment to the Japanese marketplace, and enable us to deliver on the changes needed to improve our position.

Arcor was not divested and was still part of Vodafone Germany as of 2005. Arcor might even serve as a strategic weapon to cannibalize on incumbent Deutsche Telekom's profitable fixed line business.[18]

Since mid-2001, Vodafone had entered into arrangements with other network operators in countries where it did not hold any equity stake. Under the terms of so-called Partner Network Agreements, Vodafone cooperated with its counterparts in the development and marketing of global services under dual brand logos. By 2003, Vodafone had extended its reach into 11 other countries, thus establishing a first foothold in these markets.[19] Such an agreement was a classic win-win situation: Vodafone not only gained new market insight with little risk, but at the same time was able to assess the quality of the partner in order to identify possible takeover targets, while the partner benefited from Vodafone's unique marketing and technological capabilities.

Vodafone's acquisition strategy always followed a similar pattern: First, the number one or two player within a national market was identified, while it carefully avoided acquiring the incumbent mobile operator that was linked to the state-owned telecom monopoly (like T-Mobile, which was the mobile division of Deutsche Telekom, or Orange, a business unit of France Télécom). It seems that Vodafone feared a bureaucratic inertia of these organizations, and would rather focus on more flexible, entrepreneurially minded challengers (with Mannesmann's D2 once again being a good example, or France's SFR) that would challenge the incumbents in different local markets. Referring to this strategy Alan Harper explained,

Our vision has been to leverage scale and scope benefits, reduce response time in the market, and ensure effective delivery to customers. This we have achieved by collecting or acquiring national (operational) companies and gave them a mission of a "challenger company" in each of the national markets. For example, Vodafone with SFR is a challenger to France Telecom in France, Vodafone UK is a challenger to British Telecom in the UK, and Vodafone Germany a challenger to Deutsch Telekom in Germany. Together with this challenger mind-set, we nurture and

instill an entrepreneurial spirit inside Vodafone Group companies, and in this respect we do not behave as a traditional telephone company. Since we differ from being a traditional company, the cultural alignment of people working for Vodafone is a key issue in sustaining this challenger and entrepreneurial mind-set. To focus on this cultural alignment, we give autonomy to the local entity and reiterate that the local entity did not join a global company like IBM or HP. The local entity has to work in a matrix structure and keep alive the "challenger mind-set" on fixed line telephony and other incumbents, challenge the status quo every day, and evolve by being local entrepreneurs.

Branding, Identity, and Pricing

After a successful bid for a takeover target, Vodafone followed a diverse strategy in terms of branding, creating its identity and its own pricing models. Alan Harper explained,

We play different models of creating Vodafone's identity in the market. Which way we adapt depends on a number of factors and considerations, such as the strength of the local brand, the prevalent company culture and the general fit between Vodafone's processes and the acquired business' processes. But frankly, at the end of the day, it comes down to a question of management judgment. For example, in New Zealand when we acquired Bellsouth, we changed Bellsouth almost overnight to Vodafone New Zealand. Similarly in Portugal, we undertook an overnight integration of Telecel to Vodafone Portugal. Telecel transformed into Vodafone Portugal and became challenger to the traditional PTT. Whereas in Italy, when we acquired Omnitel, it took us 2.5 years to change Omnitel to Omnitel Vodafone. Onmitel colours were Green and White and we could not change it to Vodafone Red immediately. It was because Omnitel had a strong brand image, very well known and we had to be very cautious during the transition. The market would never have accepted it. The same was the case with DT in Germany.

The management judgment of fast or slow rebranding turned on the customer and organizational response of the acquired market and acquired company. Usually the national brand was kept alive for some time until the dust of the takeover battle had settled. Vodafone then carefully launched its phased rebranding campaign to bring the new subsidiary under the "Vodafone" umbrella. Usually, they added "Vodafone" to the original corporate brand. To better coordinate these branding efforts, Vodafone appointed David Haines, a former Coca-Cola manager, as global brand director.[20] Davin Haines explained,

For example "D2" became "D2 Vodafone." Within a year, Vodafone modified the logo to its typical red color and changed the order of company name, for example "D2 Vodafone" to "Vodafone D2." During the last phase, the original "national" name was eliminated completely and only the global brand and logo remained. This process could take more than two years and usually passed almost unnoticed by the customers, who got accustomed to the new logo due to the extensive branding campaigns, often in conjunction with the launch of a new global product (like Vodafone's Mobile Connect Card, enabling e-mailing and Internet access via a laptop and the mobile network) or service (e.g., Vodafone live! mobile Internet portal). Following this pattern, Vodafone Omnitel in Italy and J-Phone Vodafone in Japan became a single brand in May 2003 and October 2003, respectively.[21]

Vodafone launched its first truly global communications campaign in the beginning of August 2001 to reinforce its brand awareness and a global brand identity. Arun Sarin reiterated,

Throughout the past few years, Vodafone has done a terrific job of building brand awareness as we have moved toward a single global brand. Beyond brand awareness, we want people to understand that the Vodafone name represents great service, great value and great innovation. When our name becomes synonymous with these attributes we will achieve brand preference and expect to see our market share climb as a result.

Across all media, a homogenous corporate brand and identity was communicated including the slogan "How are you?" and introduced the inverted comma as logo. To keep in sync with Vodafone's global aspirations, the group selected two globally recognized brands: It sponsored the Manchester United Football Club and the Ferrari Formula 1 team to improve awareness and perception of the brand. In addition, it supported its brand by individual sponsorship contracts and other marketing communication programs at the local level. According to a Vodafone statement,

An audit of the first year of sponsorship of Scuderia Ferrari reveals that the sponsorship had outperformed all of the annual targets set internally by Vodafone and helped establish exceptional global brand awareness.[22]

Being number one or number two in most markets[23] it had entered, Vodafone never used "low prices" to attract new customers. Instead, it focused on creating and marketing new value-added services that enticed customers to sign up with Vodafone, even if it implied paying not the lowest rates available. According to Arun Sarin,

We have rededicated ourselves to delighting our customers because we believe this is the foundation for our continued success. We recognise that every customer interaction provides another opportunity to win loyalty and that's why we continue to raise standards on the quality of customer care in our call centres and our stores and the quality of our networks. Key to delighting our customers is our ability to deliver superior voice and data services according to differing customer needs.

Vodafone was not immune to the pricing policies of its competitors, which meant that it lowered its tariffs whenever the price differential became too great and the new subscriber market share dropped below a critical level. Given its size and healthy finances, it could usually weather price wars and simply waited until the aggressive player lost its thrust. Appendix I explores in some detail the role of fixed costs and their impact on pricing in the mobile telecommunication market.

Integrating to One Vodafone

Vodafone realized that real business integration extends far beyond having a single brand. Critics had pointed out that establishing a global brand and logo is among the easier tasks of managing a multinational corporation. Alan Harper stressed,

The careful re-branding policy not only targeted customers, but also tried to address the needs and concerns of the employees. The employees had to adjust to the fact that though they were "national challengers with an instilled entrepreneurial spirit," they were also part of the family of the global Vodafone Corporation based in Newbury, England. It was perceived that most employees were proud of having contributed to the success of challenging the incumbent operator and were reluctant to be incorporated into a larger corporation that they perceived as "distant."

After the heady days of Chris Gent and the acquisitions by the dozen, Arun Sarin had to find innovative ways to integrate "a disparate group of national operations" into one company. Arun Sarin recognized that winning over the hearts of the employees and achieving cultural alignment was perhaps the "biggest challenge of all." An analyst of Merrill Lynch praised Arun Sarin as "smart" and "strategically as good as it gets."[24] Sarin seemed to be a good fit for this extraordinary task ahead, as he was described as "an operating man rather than a dealmaker" and "the archetypal international executive."[25] The portrait of Sarin went on like this:

Born and brought up in India, but now an American citizen, Mr Sarin's background was an asset. There might seem to be a certain irony in putting an Indian-American in charge of the world's biggest mobile-phone operator, each of these countries had made a mess of introducing wireless telecoms. But Vodafone was a British company that aspired to be a true multinational. It had large operations in Germany, where it bought Mannesmann in 2000, in Italy and in Japan. To put another Brit into the top job might have bred resentment. [. . .] The son of a well-to-do Indian military officer, he went to a military boarding-school, but his mother encouraged him not to follow his father's career. Instead, he took an engineering degree at the Indian Institute of Technology, the country's equivalent of MIT. From there he went to the University of California at Berkeley on a scholarship, to earn a further degree in engineering and a MBA. He had lived in America ever since. The main remnants of his origins were an Indian wife (whom he met at Berkeley), a touch of an accent and a passion for cricket, which he shares with Sir Chris [Gent, his predecessor].[26]

Sarin, however, was not the only director on Vodafone's board with a distinct international background. As a result of Vodafone's past acquisitions and their pragmatic integration into the group, many skilled foreign (non-British) managers had been retained and had since joined the board, including two Germans, one Italian, one South African, and one Swede (see Exhibit 4(a) and (b)).

At the annual general meeting in July 2003, Sarin emphasized the need to benefit from economies of scale and scope. In June 2004, Arun Sarin redefined,

At Vodafone, everything we do furthers our desire to create mobile connections for individuals, businesses and communities. Our Vision is to be the world's mobile communications leader and we're delighted by the prospects for the future of our industry. Our commitment to this industry is underlined by our company values, which state that everything we do is driven by our passion for customers, our people, results and the world around us. . . . Operating in 26 markets (together with Partner Networks in a further 14 countries, with approximately 151.8 million registered customers, and approximately 398.5 million total venture customers) puts us in an enviable position to leverage our global scale and scope. . . . Another competitive advantage is our leadership position on cost and time to market. From network services to sales, and marketing to customer care and billing, we have many varied systems in use across the business. With strong cooperation between our various operating companies we can achieve further savings.

To coordinate, restructure, and integrate its various systems across 26 countries, Vodafone launched its "One Vodafone" initiative that aimed to boost annual pretax

Exhibit 4(a) Vodafone's Executive and Nonexecutive Directors

As of July 30, 2005, Vodafone had six executive directors and eight nonexecutive directors, including the chairperson, Lord MacLaurin.

- **Lord MacLaurin of Knebworth,** *Chairperson*
- **Paul Hazen,** *Deputy Chairperson and Senior Independent Director*
- **Arun Sarin,** *Chief Executive* (Indian-born and raised, graduated from the Indian Institute of Technology, but now American citizen. Former chief executive officer for the United States and Asia Pacific region until April 15, 2000, when he became a nonexecutive director. Former director of AirTouch from July 1995 and president and chief operating officer from February 1997 to June 1999. Appointed chief executive on 30 July 2003.)
- **Peter R. Bamford,** *Chief Marketing Officer*
- **Thomas Geitner,** *Chief Technology Officer*
- **Julian M. Horn-Smith,** *Group Chief Operating Officer*
- **Kenneth J. Hydon,** *Financial Director*
- **Sir John Bond**
- **Dr. Michael J. Boskin**
- **Professor Sir Alec Broers**
- **Dr. John Buchanan**
- **Penelope L. Hughes**
- **Sir David Scholey, CBE**
- **Professor Jürgen Schrempp**
- **Luc Vandevelde**

Exhibit 4(b) Vodafone's Executive and Nonexecutive Directors

- **Arun Sarin,** Chief Executive
- **Sir Julian Horn-Smith,** Deputy Chief Executive
- **Ken Hydon,** Financial Director
- **Peter Bamford,** Chief Marketing Officer
- **Thomas Geitner,** Chief Technology Officer
- **Jürgen von Kuczkowski,** Chief Executive Germany
- **Pietro Guindani,** Chief Executive Italy
- **Bill Morrow,** Chief Executive United Kingdom
- **Paul Donovan,** Regional Chief Executive
- **Brian Clark,** Chief Executive Asia Pacific and Group Human Resources Director Designate
- **Shiro Tsuda,** Chief Executive Japan
- **Alan Harper,** Group Strategy and Business Integration Director
- **Phil Williams,** Group Human Resources Director
- **Stephen Scott,** Group General Counsel and Company Secretary
- **Simon Lewis,** Group Corporate Affairs Director

Source: http://www.vodafone.com.

operating profit by £2.5 billion by FY2008.[27] Alan Harper explained in detail:

We are in a period when we are integrating our company. With acquisitions all over the world, one of our challenges is to integrate seamlessly not only technology (which by the way is more or less similar across the world) but people. And this is a key part of the Branding Evolution that we had witnessed. The challenge of this restructuring program is to balance the need of coordination and synergies while encouraging local initiatives.

The One Vodafone program is a business integration activity and we are in the process of "gradual integration of our business architecture." For example, we are running down a real-time billing system to an integrated system for 28mn customers. It is a very difficult task if one tries to understand the billing system of mobile telephones. Under the One Vodafone, there are currently 8 programs, Networks (design and supply procurement, coordination, and consolidation initiatives), IT (design, back office, billings, ERP/HR, operations—data centre processes), Service platforms, Roaming (mapping footprints), Customer (next practice services), Handset portfolio, MNC accounts, Retailing (one won't believe, we are the eighth largest retailer in the world taking together our stores that are owned or franchised). . . . We are trying to integrate national operating units across footprints and trying to leverage scale and scope while trying to retain the local autonomy and responsiveness of our challenger national units.

Alan Harper agreed that implementation of "One Vodafone" is a challenge. He explained,

To implement One Vodafone, we have undertaken a change in organizational structure of the Group [refer to Exhibit 5]. We still operate in a matrix format. What One Vodafone tries to achieve is to simplify the integration issues in terms of brand strength and integrating local culture and processes. We centralize all our marketing efforts, branding and product development. Technology is standardized. Network design (switching, radio) are coordinated. Best practices are benchmarked by Advance Services such as service platforms and portals (Vodafone Live!). Knowledge is shared via the HQ, HR, strategy, and Marketing departments, through lateral processes, including our governance processes. We keep and encourage local initiatives such as customer services, sales, network billing, and IT systems. We are trying to incorporate the best of all the cultures to the maximum extent possible and in this way we tried to transform Vodafone UK into a new Vodafone.

One Vodafone was clearly communicated across the company via the Internet, intranet, different training programs as well as a monthly employee magazine called "Vodafone life! The global magazine for all Vodafone people." The HR department prepared special "initiation" training programs to acquaint new employees to the Vodafone way, labeled the "Vodafone footstep," which included its vision and values (see Exhibit 6) and the "Ten Business Principles."[28] On translating the vision and values alongside changes in structure and systems, Vodafone witnessed revamping of people processes within the organization. Commenting on employees, Arun Sarin explained,

As the business expands and the environment around us evolves, it is crucial for us to develop, recruit and retain the

Exhibit 5 Board Changes and New Organizational Structure as of January 2005

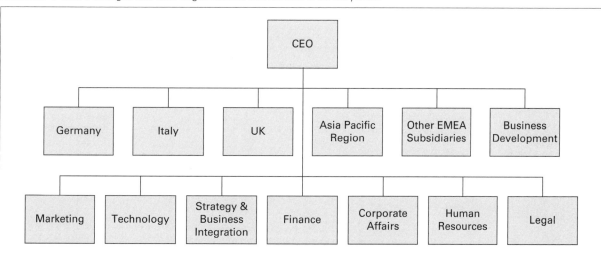

Vodafone Group Plc ("Vodafone") announces Board changes and a new organisational structure which will enable continued improvement in the delivery of the Group's strategic goals. This structure will become effective as of 1 January 2005.

The new organization is designed to:

- Focus more attention on customers in Vodafone's local markets;
- Enhance Vodafone's ability to deliver seamless services to corporations;
- Facilitate coordinated delivery of 3G across all markets;
- Function as an integrated company, delivering on One Vodafone; and
- Simplify decision-making, accountabilities and governance structures to speed up execution.

Vodafone will simplify its existing regional structure with major countries and business areas reporting to the Chief Executive. All first-line management functions in the Operating Companies will have a dual reporting line to the respective functions at Group level.

Arun Sarin, Chief Executive said: "We are creating an organisation that is better positioned to respond to the high expectations of our customers. Faster execution will enable us to extend our lead within the mobile industry and deliver the benefits to our customers, our employees and our shareholders."

Main Board Appointments

Sir Julian Horn-Smith will be appointed Deputy Chief Executive with effect from 1 January 2005. Vodafone separately announces that Andy Halford has been appointed Financial Director Designate. Andy will succeed Ken Hydon when he retires on 26 July 2005.

Operating Company Structure

Vodafone's operating company structure will be streamlined to ensure effective and fast decision making, enabling improved time to market across a number of business initiatives. Consequently, the following operating companies and business areas will report directly into the Chief Executive:

- European Affiliates (Belgium, France, Poland, Romania and Switzerland) and Non-European Affiliates (China, Fiji, Kenya, South Africa and United States), led by Sir Julian Horn-Smith;
- Germany, led by Jürgen von Kuczkowski;
- Italy, led by Pietro Guindani;
- United Kingdom, led by Bill Morrow;
- Other EMEA Subsidiaries (Albania, Egypt, Greece, Hungary, Ireland, Malta, Netherlands, Portugal, Spain and Sweden), led by Paul Donovan;
- Asia Pacific (Australia, Japan and New Zealand), led by Brian Clark who will also be appointed Group Human Resources Director Designate.

Vodafone's Group functions will be strengthened to support the delivery of seamless global propositions and Vodafone's continued integration. The following functions will also report directly to the Chief Executive:

- Marketing, led by Peter Bamford, the Chief Marketing Officer. This function will be reinforced by a newly created Multi National Corporate unit which will assume full accountability for serving Vodafone's global corporate customers. Group Marketing will also manage the global handset portfolio and procurement;
- Technology, led by Thomas Geitner, the Chief Technology Officer. In addition to standardized network design and global supply chain management, this function will introduce the concept of shared service operation for IT and service delivery;

continued

- Business Development, a new function led by Sir Julian Horn-Smith. Sir Julian will be responsible for driving Vodafone's product and services portfolio into Vodafone's affiliates and the Partner Networks. In addition, this function will assume responsibility for expanding and consolidating Vodafone's footprint through the Partner Network programme and any Corporate Finance activities.

New Governance Structure

Vodafone also announces changes to its governance process. The Group will have two management committees which will oversee the execution of the Main Board's strategy and policy.

- The Executive Committee

  Chaired by Arun Sarin, this committee will focus on the Group's strategy, financial structure and planning, succession planning, organizational development and group-wide policies.

- The Integration and Operations Committee

  Chaired by Arun Sarin, this committee will be responsible for setting operational plans, budgets and forecasts, product and service development, customer segmentation, managing delivery of multi-market propositions and managing shared resources.

Source: http://www.vodafone.com.

Exhibit 6 Vodafone's Vision and Values

We have one vision and a set of values that underpins everything we do. Both our vision and our values were shared throughout the global organization.

Our Vision

To be the world's mobile communications leader—enriching customers' lives, helping individuals, businesses and communities be more connected in a mobile world.

- Our customers use mobile communications to make their lives richer, more fulfilled, more connected. They will prefer Vodafone because the experience of using Vodafone will be the best they can find.
- We will lead in making the mobile the primary means of personal communications for every individual around the world.
- Through our leadership, our scale, our scope, and our partnerships, we will bring online mobile services to the world.

Our Values
Passion for customers

Our customers have chosen to trust us. In return, we must strive to anticipate and understand their needs and delight them with our service.

- We value our customers above everything else and aspire to make their lives richer, more fulfilled and more connected.
- We must always listen and respond to each of our customers.
- We will strive to delight our customers, anticipating their needs and delivering greater quality and more value, faster than anyone else.

Passion for our people

Outstanding people working together make Vodafone exceptionally successful.

- We seek to attract, develop, reward, and retain outstanding individuals.
- We believe in empowerment and personal accountability.
- We enjoy what we do.
- We believe in the power of our teams.

Passion for results

We are action-oriented and driven by a desire to be the best.

- We are committed to be the best in all we do.
- We all play our part in delivering results.
- We seek speed, flexibility, and efficiency in all we do.

Passion for the world around us

We will help people of the world to have fuller lives—both through the services we provide and through the impact we have on the world around us.

- We recognize the responsibilities that accompany the growth we have achieved.
- We will be a force for good in the world.
- A spirit of partnership and mutual respect is critical in all our activities.

Source: http://www.vodafone.com.

people that will lead us into this new world. We are working hard to make sure our employees have the right skills and knowledge to anticipate our customers' needs. We are identifying new ways to share the best of what we do on a global basis. We continue to reap the benefits of a motivated team with a strong customer service culture, which will help earn a reputation for Vodafone that is second to none.

The HR Department had set up a fast-track career path (the Global Leadership Programme, GLP) for high-potential managers, rotating them across business functions and countries and equipping them with crucial multicultural skills.

Despite the integration and standardization efforts, the corporate headquarters had to ensure a certain level of independence for individual country subsidiaries to take into account differing business models and customer expectations. For example, 48 percent of Vodafone's customers in Germany had a contract, while this kind of long-term commitment to an operator was almost unheard of in Italy (92 percent were prepaid customers).[29]

To orchestrate the move toward greater coordination as well as to identify and disseminate best practices, the group created two new central functions, Group Marketing (to drive revenue growth), and Group Technology and Business Integration (to drive cost and scale benefits).[30] Communicating Vodafone's new focus on integrating the bits and pieces resulting from past acquisitions was clearly a top management task. The Integration and Operations Committee was instituted, staffed with members of the executive board and chaired by Arun Sarin himself. This committee was responsible for "setting operational plans, budgets and forecasts, product and service development, customer segmentation, managing delivery of multi-market propositions and managing shared resources" across geographies.[31] Alan Harper, who had been heading the group strategy department at Vodafone since 2000, saw his job title changed to Group Strategy and Business Integration Director. Simultaneously, Vodafone restructured itself at the corporate level to include the two new functions, which directly reported to the group's COO, Julian Horn-Smith.

Thomas Geitner was appointed head of the new unit Group Technology & Business Integration as chief technology officer.

The purpose of Group Technology will be to lead the implementation of a standardized architecture for business processes, information technology and network systems. This will support the next generation of products and services and the critical role of introducing and operating 3G capacity.[32]

A key focus of the Group Technology activities were the management and control of group-wide projects in relation to the ongoing rollout of "third generation" (3G) networks, the enhancement of Vodafone live! and the development of the Group's business offerings. This work included the continued development of technical specifications, creation and management of global contracts with suppliers as well as testing of terminals.[33]

It was committed to provide underlying terminal and platform technologies on a global basis. Within the mobile phone industry, a shift of power away from handset makers (Nokia, Siemens, Ericsson, etc.) could be observed. Global operators such as Vodafone had increasingly succeeded in forcing the producers to offer specially designed and branded products: the thriving Vodafone live! multimedia service was launched on Sharp GX-10 handsets, exclusively manufactured and branded for Vodafone.[34] If this trend persisted, Vodafone would be the first to benefit from its huge purchasing power and could even force Nokia (which had an almost 40 percent world market share) to cater more toward Vodafone's needs.[35] Vodafone could also use its unrivalled clout when negotiating with network equipment suppliers (such as Alcatel, Nokia, Siemens, etc.) to squeeze their margins.

Peter Bamford was appointed chief marketing officer and head of the Group Marketing department, which was in charge of

"providing leadership and coordination across the full range of marketing and commercial activities including brand, product development, content management, partner networks and global accounts."[36]

For Vodafone, the question was how customers could derive a benefit from Vodafone's increasingly global reach, ultimately driving top-line growth. Alan Harper explains,

We are a technology and sales & distribution group focused on local companies winning market share against incumbents in respective countries. We do not develop technology but we are users of technology. Technology is developed by companies such as Nokia, Ericksson, Nortel. We buy their technology—and technology evolution in our sector is more or less standard, it evolves, grows without major differentiations and after a period of time it is standardized. Now the challenge is how best we can leverage using and integrating the technology across our companies. . . . With the evolution and growth of our company we are today more of a company that prides itself in the differentiation of services that we bring to our customers. We are still 100 percent sales driven but we are much more customer centric and customer service oriented and take pride in understanding customer needs as we graduate to offering our customers the next best service and focusing on customer delight (e.g., Amazon). We now execute much better and it is because of the reason of the shift in our competencies.

Vodafone started creating service offerings and product packages directly leveraging Vodafone's network and delivering tangible value to customers. For example, it created a tariff option that enabled customers to seamlessly roam the globe, on a special per minute rate, on the same network, without having to worry about high interconnection fees or differing technical standards. A new unit within Group Marketing was created to develop and market services specifically tailored to the needs of global coordination, such as seamless wireless access to corporate IT systems and special rates for international calls on the network. Such a global service offering could clearly serve as a differentiating factor to competitors that could not match Vodafone's global footprint.

Woes in the United States and France

There were still two nagging issues for Arun Sarin: Vodafone's 45 percent stake in Verizon Wireless and the unresolved issues about control in France's SFR, for which Vodafone had been at loggerheads with Vivendi for several years now. Vodafone was far from happy about these minority stakes, because it did not fit with its single-brand, "One Vodafone" strategy.

In the United States, Vodafone customers still could not use their cell phones on the Verizon Wireless network, because it operated under a different standard. It was indicated that this situation was likely to continue well into the era of 3G, because Verizon planned to adopt an incompatible standard.[37] Without a single technological platform and a uniform brand, Vodafone could extract little value from its American venture (except the cash dividend of $1 billion a year it received from it).[38] After the failed bid for AT&T Wireless, Vodafone had several options at its disposal, all of them with their own pros and cons.

Probably the most obvious option would be to take over Verizon (the parent company of Verizon Wireless) completely, including its fixed line business, in order to force them to adopt Vodafone standards. It was deemed likely that such a bid could escalate to a US$150 billion hostile takeover battle, a figure that might be too large even for juggernaut Vodafone.[39] Verizon's management clearly was not willing to cede the wireless operations to Vodafone, but dreamed of becoming the single owner of Verizon Wireless itself.

Alternatively, Vodafone could buy another operator outright. But regulatory constraints would require it to sell its stake in Verizon Wireless first, because it was prohibited from owning more than a 20 percent stake in two competing operators at once. Under the current agreement with Verizon, Vodafone held a put option, which allowed it to sell some of the shareholding each year at a fixed price to Verizon. If Vodafone decided to exercise this option, it had to do so by July 2006 in order to realize a maximum value of US$20 billion. Verizon could choose to pay Vodafone either in cash or stock, although Vodafone had a right on a minimum cash sum of US$7.5 billion.[40]

Some observers questioned the idea of selling Verizon and buying another operator, because Verizon Wireless was the most successful and profitable one—why swap "a minority stake in a very good operator for a controlling stake in a less good one?"[41]

In France, Vodafone was in an equally uncomfortable position. It shared ownership of Cegetel, the parent company of France's number two mobile phone business SFR (35 percent market share with 13.3 million customers), with Vivendi having the majority stake in the venture. On March 31, 2003, Vodafone's ownership interest in SFR was approximately 43.9 percent, comprising a direct holding of 20 percent in SFR and an indirect holding through its stake in Cegetel.[42] Commenting on Vodafone's struggle with Vivendi about SFR, an analyst at Global Equities SA joked: "We have a saying: small minority shareholdings for little idiots; big minority shareholdings for big idiots."[43]

Even though Vodafone managers had a certain say about the operations and strategy of SFR (SFR launched the co-branded multimedia services of Vodafone live!), Vivendi continued to refuse to sell SFR to Vodafone. Several talks between Sarin and Fourtou, the CEO of Vivendi, had not yielded any results, and Vivendi's true strategic intentions with SFR remained unclear.[44] The remaining 56 percent stake in SFR was valued at roughly £8 billion ($13 billion).[45] After Vivendi declined Vodafone's offer for SFR in 2002, Vodafone issued a statement claiming that it was "a long-term investor in Cegetel and SFR" and that it "looks forward to continuing its successful partnership with Vivendi."[46]

"France is a very simple market for us," noted Alan Harper in April 2005. *"We know the market, we know the business model and we know the management of SFR, which takes part in routine Vodafone management meetings."* Pugnaciously, he added, *"The natural home of SFR is Vodafone. We are a very patient company."*

It remains to be seen whether Vivendi wants to keep its cash cow or if it was simply trying to push the price in this cat-and-mouse game.

Challenges Ahead

Arun Sarin knew that his job would not become uninteresting anytime soon, as many challenges lay ahead! Certainly, Vodafone was the largest player in the industry, but being active in 26 countries out of 200 in the world left a lot of room to grow. As he closed his eyes and thought of Vodafone's global footprint, instantly he was reminded that Vodafone was not present in Latin America and in many African countries. Then there was the Middle East. Vast untapped markets lay ahead with today's mobile penetration of about 1.7 billion, of which Vodafone has about 3.5 million. In five years it shall be 2.5 billion, only half of world's population! And there was his native country, India, where he invested US$1.5 billion to buy a 10 percent stake in Bharti Tele-Ventures, the largest mobile operator in the country. Countries of Eastern Europe, many of which had recently entered the European Union (EU), should definitely become Vodafone's home turf: Vodafone had just announced that it would be willing to invest up to US$18 billion on acquisitions in Russia and other Eastern European countries.[47] The 2005 acquisition of the mobile operators MobiFon (Romania) and Oskar (Czech Republic) was certainly just the first step in enlarging Vodafone's footprint.[48] Not to mention China. The sheer size of the market was awe-inspiring. Vodafone's strategic partner, China Mobile, alone had more than 150 million customers, but Vodafone only had a minuscule 3.27 percent stake in the company.[49] For Vodafone, according to Alan Harper, this stake served as a:

strategic foothold in a very important market with a relatively small scale investment. China Mobile is the fastest growing mobile company in the world today, connecting about 2–3 million customers a month. It has 70% of the Chinese market share. Vodafone clearly understands that China Mobile can never become Vodafone China. That is a reality due to investment options and quasi-political situation of Chinese mobile telephony market. Knowing all this we still invested in China mobile because we feel that we learn everyday from China Mobile and our intention is to have regular knowledge flow between Vodafone and China Mobile. This is because our strategy is to make the technology standardized so that the learning between us is much faster. . . . Our investment in China mobile is through China Mobile HK. We have a clear exit strategy with liquid assets, if our investment does not do well in the future. If it does well, we might think of increasing our foothold but not to a sizeable extent. We are happy to have a foothold in one of the largest and fastest growing markets of the world, with our investment we have an insider position, we have a position of influence with the operator, with the Chinese government, we have seat on the board, we have regular dialogue and our interest is to make China use the same technology as ours so that we can benefit from the scale and scope.

At the same, significant business risks lurked in all markets and Arun Sarin was well aware of them. In 2006, the merger of AT&T with Bellsouth Corp. put pressure on Verizon Wireless to buy off Vodafone and force it to exit the U.S. market. The introduction of 3G, which had

a very promising start in Germany with good sales of mobile connect cards, might shift the focus of the whole industry away from networks to content. Revenue from voice traffic was flat or even declining due to competing technologies such as Internet calling that was fundamentally changing the telecom industry. Sarin knew that most of the growth would have to come from new data services. Competitors had also begun to get their feet on the ground again, with rumors about a merger between MMO2's German operations (O2 Germany) and KPN's E-Plus.

Nokia had just presented its first WiFi-powered phone that did not need the traditional mobile network but a wireless LAN hotspot. If this technology should ever become popular, it would undermine Vodafone's current business model and could turn billions of fixed assets into worthless electronic scrap.[50]

At the beginning of 2006, Arun Sarin made some tough decisions. He faced up to slowing growth in his core market by unveiling an impairment charge of £23 billion to £28 billion ($40 billion to $49 billion) and exited the Japanese market by selling its stake to Tokyo-based Softbank in a deal valued at $15.4 billion and confirmed that after the sale it would return $10.5 billion to its shareholders. Vodafone had trailed behind NTT DoCoMo and KDDI since its entry in 2001 in Japan, due to fickle consumers, the lack of a low-end tier in the segment, and the challenge of coordinating terminals and technologies across borders. He managed to tighten his grip on the company and put down a boardroom revolt that had questioned his leadership. He not only won a public expression of support from Lord Ian MacLaurin, the company's board chair, but he also forced out Sir Christopher Gent, the honorary life president and former chief executive.

Arun Sarin thought Vodafone could have the best of two worlds. Now was the time to combine Vodafone's superior skills in acquiring companies with best-of-breed business integration and operational capabilities. He could ensure Vodafone's exceptional profitability for many years to come by keeping Vodafone a wireless company to the core and also use innovations such as broadband wireless technology known as WiMAX, to offer new services. It was now up to him to shape Vodafone's future.

Appendix I
The Economics of the Mobile Phone Market: The Role of Fixed Costs

The mobile phone market was characterized by extremely high fixed costs. The setting up of a nationwide network could require significant investments running into billions of euros.[51] Usually, an operator did not have the choice to offer network coverage limited to metropolitan areas (which would dramatically reduce the scale of initial investment required), either because of regulations prohibiting such a selective offer, or simply because national coverage was a key success factor for literally "mobile" customers.

In some countries, the licenses to operate using a certain bandwidth cost as much as €8 billion (the record price each operator in Germany paid for its UMTS license to the government), adding huge financing charges to the already existing fixed costs.[52] However, once capacity is installed, the cost of an additional customer using the network is virtually zero, and every euro of revenue adds to the companies' bottom line. An installed and running network provides a foundation for reaching very high operating margins. Vodafone, for example, estimates that once the initial investments had been made, less than 10 percent of revenues were needed to maintain the network.[53] Even the marketing campaigns benefited from the economies of scale: The larger an operator's customer base, the lower its per-user cost of such advertising efforts.

Much of the costs described here were not only fixed, but also sunk, further aggravating the problem of price pressure. The investment into network could hardly be sold to anybody else (because of differing technological standards) and hence the initial cost was "sunk." Companies realized that they could not undo their decision to invest, because the infrastructure was already there. Therefore, it is rational for companies to act as if their initial investment was zero.

The existence of high fixed costs explained the periodic price wars that had driven prices down ever since mobile telecommunications started. Some operators had begun offering free calls or flat rates during the weekend (when capacity utilization was at the lowest). Usually, it was the smaller operators and the new market entrants who offered lower prices to reach as quickly as possible a critical mass. In Germany, one of the largest markets for mobile telephony with more than 60 million customers and a high population density, the threshold for an acceptable return on investment was estimated to be about 20 percent of the total market share, which had neither been attained by O2 (a subsidiary of MMO2) nor by E-Plus (KPN).

The economics of the market necessitated no more than three or four operators in a country (refer to Exhibit 7). In Germany, Mobilcom and Quam never reached the critical size and had to exit the market in 2003 and 2002, respectively, writing off their individual investments of €8 billion each in 3G licenses.[54]

Growth for a mobile phone company had so far mainly come from increased penetration, which stood

Exhibit 7 Customers by Country, June 30, 2003

Country	Customers
United Kingdom	13,313
Ireland	1,765
Germany	23,261
Hungary	952
Netherlands	3,312
Sweden	1,331
Italy	15,044
Albania	364
Greece	2,373
Malta	126
Portugal	3,129
Spain	9,184
United States	15,332
Japan	10,035
Australia	2,593
New Zealand	1,349
Egypt	1,609
Others	17,614
Group Total	122,686

Source: Adapted from Interim Report November 2003.

at about 80 percent (e.g., Germany: 74%) in most mature markets. With new customers becoming increasingly rare (refer to Exhibit 8 for customers by country of Vodafone), operators were constantly searching for new sources of revenues and had introduced text messaging and other basic value-added services, such as downloadable ringtones and logos.[55] The standard measure in the industry to gauge the quality of the customer base was the average revenue per user (ARPU).[56]

As the new 3G networks (third generation, enabling high-speed data transmission) go online, available capacity will take another quantum leap with unpredictable consequences for pricing. There seems to be promising opportunities to concentrate on the huge market for fixed line telephony. Not surprisingly, there was a clear relation between the per minute price of a call and the average amount of cell phone usage. Conversely, there was no relation between the ARPU and the average price per minute charged, which indicated that customers substituted their fixed line minutes with cell phone minutes whenever a price drop occurred. In other words, the increased quantity usually compensated the operator for the lower revenue per minute (refer to Exhibit 9).

Another key performance indicator that had attracted management attention in recent years was the

Exhibit 8 Vodafone's Subsidiaries, Partners, and Investments around the Globe

Country	Service Name	Ownership (%)	Subsidiary (S), Associate (A), or Partner (P)	Proportionate Customers (1000s)	Number of Competitors
Europe					
Albania	Vodafone Albania	83.0	S	472 (31 Dec 2003)	1
Austria	A1	n/a	P	n/a	n/a
Belgium	Proximus	25.0	A	1,067 (31 Mar 2003)	2
Croatia	VIP	n/a	P	n/a	n/a
Cyprus	Cytamobile	n/a	P	n/a	n/a
Denmark	TDC Mobil	n/a	P	n/a	n/a
Estonia	Radiolinja	n/a	P	n/a	n/a
Finland	Radiolinja	n/a	P	n/a	n/a
France	SFR	43.9	A	5,931 (30 Jun 2003)	2
Germany	Vodafone Germany	100.0	S	24,668 (31 Dec 2003)	3
Greece	Vodafone Greece	98.2	S	2,373 (30 Jun 2003)	2
Hungary	Vodafone Hungary	87.9	S	1,170 (31 Dec 2003)	2
Iceland	Og Vodafone	n/a	P	n/a	n/a
Ireland	Vodafone Ireland	100	S	1,871 (31 Dec 2003)	2
Italy	Vodafone Italy	76.8	S	15,852 (31 Dec 2003)	3
Lithuania	Bite GSM	n/a	P	n/a	n/a
Luxembourg	LUXGSM	n/a	P	n/a	n/a
Malta	Vodafone Malta	100.0	S	162 (31 Dec 2003)	1
Netherlands	Vodafone Netherlands	99.8	S	3,400 (31 Dec 2003)	4
Poland	Plus GSM	19. Jun	A	949 (31 Mar 2003)	2
Portugal	Vodafone Portugal	100.0	S	3,332 (31 Dec 2003)	2
Romania	Connex	20. Jan	A	537 (31 Mar 2003)	3
Slovenia	Si.mobil	n/a	P	n/a	n/a
Spain	Vodafone Spain	100.0	S	9,685 (31 Dec 2003)	2
Sweden	Vodafone Sweden	99.1	S	1,409 (31 Dec 2003)	3
Switzerland	Swisscom Mobile	25.0	A	3,635 (31 Mar 2003)	3
United Kingdom	Vodafone Group	n/a	n/a	n/a	n/a
United Kingdom	Vodafone UK	100.0	S	13,947 (31 Dec 2003)	4
Americas					
United States	Verizon Wireless	44.3	A	16,638 (31 Dec 2003)	Various
Africa and Middle East					
Bahrain	MTC-Vodafone Bahrain	n/a	P	n/a	n/a
Egypt	Vodafone Egypt	67.0	S	1,838 (31 Dec 2003)	1
Kenya	Safaricom	35.0	A	303 (31 Mar 2003)	1
Kuwait	MTC-Vodafone	n/a	P	n/a	n/a
South Africa	Vodacom	35.0	A	2,756 (31 Mar 2003)	2
Asia Pacific					
Australia	Vodafone Australia	100.0	S	2,676 (31 Dec 2003)	4
China	China Mobile (Hong Kong) Ltd	3.3	Investment	4,048 (31 Mar 2003)	2
Fiji	Vodafone Fiji	49.0	A	44 (31 Mar 2003)	None
Japan	Vodafone K.K. (Japan)	69.7	S	10,268 (31 Dec 2003)	3
New Zealand	Vodafone New Zealand	100.0	S	1,527 (31 Dec 2003)	1
Singapore	M1	n/a	P	n/a	n/a

Source: Adapted from http://www.vodafone.com.

Exhibit 9 Relationships between Per-Minute Prices and ARPU in European Countries

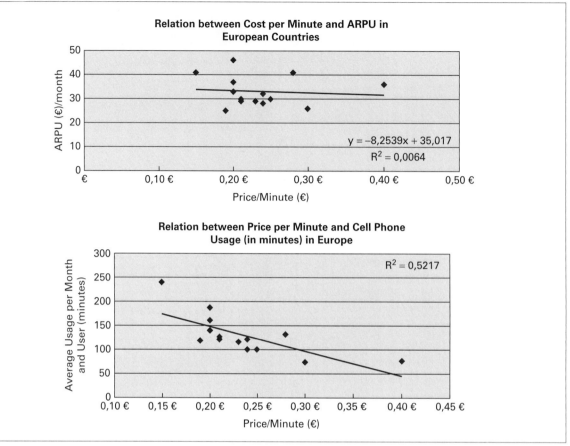

Note: Countries included in this sample are Belgium, Germany, Netherlands, Spain, Greece, Austria, Sweden, Italy, Denmark, France, Ireland, United Kingdom, Portugal, and Finland.

Source: Author's analysis based on data by Merrill Lynch, Diamond Cluster; published in the *Frankfurter Allgemeine Zeitung,* Octobre 27, 2003, 21.

so-called "churn rate," a percentage of the customer base being lost to competitors each year. In competitive markets with high handset subsidies, churn rates of operators could be anywhere between 19 percent (Germany) and 30 percent (UK).[57] In other words, on average after three to five years, an operator had churned its entire customer base! These churn rates carried high costs for the operators, because they had to spend heavily mainly on marketing and handset subsidies to attract new customers and to retain the old ones. Customer acquisition costs easily exceeded €100 per new customer or made up to 12.4 percent of service revenue (figure for Vodafone Germany).[58] If an operator added low-value customers (i.e., those with a low monthly ARPU), it could take many months until the operator could break even on a customer.

Notes

1. Out of many, One comes from Latin *E Pluribus Unum,* signifying the harnessing of global scale and scope synergies of OneVodafone.

2. The scenario described herein was fictional. However, all data relating to the AT&T Wireless deal was factual. *Financial Times Deutschland,* February 17, 2004, http://www.ftd.de

3. *Financial Times Deutschland,* February 12, 2004, http://www.ftd.de

4. *Financial Times Deutschland,* February 17, 2004, http://www.ftd.de

5. Equal to Christopher Gent's compensation as reported in the Company Annual Report 2003. This figure does not include stock options and performance-based pay.

6. Source: Corporate website http://www.vodafone.com/, data current as of December 31, 2003.

7. Source: Yahoo! Finance, http://finance.yahoo.com, March 13, 2004.

8. Annual Report 2003, available at http://www.vodafone.com.

9. Interim Results for the Six Months to 30 September 2003, published November 18, 2003; available at http://www.vodafone.com.

10. Company Annual Report 2004.

11. Source: This historic overview follows information provided at http://www.vodafone.com/, accessed on March 5, 2004.

12. http://www.vodafone.com.

13. Reportedly, Sir Gent closed the deal with AirTouch via his cell phone from Australia, where he was watching a game of cricket. *The Independent* (London), January 17, 1999: "Vodafone's boss realises longheld ambition with the acquisition of AirTouch."

14. *Financial Times Deutschland*, February 17, 2004, http://www.ftd.de

15. A chronology of the takeover battle was provided at http://www.managermagazin.de/unternehmen/artikel/ 0,2828,242161-2,00.html.

16. A New Voice at Vodafone, *The Economist;* August 2, 2003, Vol. 368.

17. Interim Results for the Six Months to 30 September 2003, published November 18, 2003; available at http://www.vodafone.com

18. Vodafone Starts Wireline Attack, First in Germany, *Dow Jones International* News; March 10, 2005.

19. Ibid.

20. Keeping pole position, *Total Telecom Magazine*, August 2003.

21. Ibid.

22. www.vodafone.com.

23. With Australia and Japan being notable exceptions.

24. Quoted in "Vodafone dominance tipped to keep rolling," *Utility Week*, January 31, 2003.

25. A new Voice at Vodafone, *The Economist;* August 2, 2003, Vol. 368.

26. Ibid.

27. Presentation to analysts and investors on September 27, 2004, available at http://www.vodafone.com.

28. http://www.vodafone.de and http://www.vodafone.com.

29. Ibid, p. 8.

30. Press release on June 23, 2003, available at http://www.vodafone.com.

31. http://www.vodafone.com.

32. Ibid.

33. Interim Results for the Six Months to 30 September 2003, p. 16.

34. According to the "Key Performance Indicators" for the quarter ended December 31, 2003; released on January 28, 2004; available at www.vodafone.com, Vodafone live! had over 4.5 million customers in 15 countries as of November 13, 2003.

35. Keeping pole position, *Total Telecom Magazine*, August 2003.

36. Ibid.

37. A new Voice at Vodafone, *The Economist;* August 2, 2003, Vol. 368.

38. Where Does Vodafone Turn Now? *Business Week Online;* February 18, 2004. Keeping pole position, *Total Telecom Magazine*, August 2003, quotes £564 million as cash dividend in financial year

39. Where Does Vodafone Turn Now? *Business Week Online;* February 18, 2004

40. Keeping pole position, *Total Telecom Magazine*, August 2003.

41. Bob House of Adventis, a consultancy, quoted in: Vodafone's dilemma, *The Economist*, Feb 12, 2004.

42. Annual Report 2003.

43. Laurent Balcon quoted in: Keeping pole position, *Total Telecom Magazine*, August 2003.

44. Clear as mud: Vodafone versus Vivendi, *The Economist;* December 7, 2002.

45. *Euromoney,* Nov 2003, Vol. 34 Issue 415.

46. Clear as mud: Vodafone versus Vivendi, *The Economist;* December 7, 2002.

47. www.Vwd.de Vereinigte Wirtschaftsdienste GmbH, February 26, 2004.

48. According to a Vodafone press release on March 15, 2005, the Group paid approximately US$3.5bn in cash for the transaction and thus could add 6.7 m customers.

49. Annual Report 2004, p. 8.

50. Nokia takes leap into Wi-Fi Phones, *Wall Street Journal Europe*, February 23, 2004.

51. Vodafone for example had £24.1 bn as gross fixed assets in its balance sheet, 83% of which were accounted for by network infrastructure. Annual Report 2003, p. 90.

52. Vodafone prescht im Rennen um UMTS-Einführung vor, Handelsblatt, February 13/14, 2004.

53. Annual Report 2003, p. 94.

54. Vodafone prescht im Rennen um UMTS-Einführung vor, Handelsblatt, February 13/14, 2004.

55. In some instances, these new services already generate up to 20% of revenues. Ibid.

56. For example, Vodafone's ARPU in the UK was £297 and 312€ in Germany for the year, according to the Interim Results for the Six Months Ended September 30, 2003; available at http://www.vodafone.com.

57. Data for Vodafone, which can be considered as representative for the industry. Ibid.

58. Ibid.

Case 23

Wal-Mart Stores, Inc. (WMT)

Francine Barley, David Bragg, Misty Dawson, Hammad Shah, Brian Sillanpaa, Nathan Sleeper

Arizona State University

Lee Scott ignored his fear of public speaking as he prepared to step in front of 20,000 people at the Bud Walton Arena in Fayetteville, Arkansas, on June 1, 2007.[1] For his seventh year as Wal-Mart CEO, Scott addressed his company's shareholders at its annual meeting.

Outside the building, the local "Against the Wal" protesters were back for the fourth year in a row, clutching a list of seven demands: "living wage," "affordable health care," "end discrimination," "zero tolerance on child labor," "respect communities," "respect the environment," and "stop union busting."[2]

Inside the arena, shareholders had their own concerns, with declining share prices and 11 shareholder proposals—all opposed by the company.[3] Since Scott became CEO in 2000, Wal-Mart's stock price has dipped about 27 percent, from $64.50 to the $47 range.[4] In the same timeframe, competitor Costco's stock price has appreciated roughly 20 percent, and Target's has climbed more than 70 percent[5] (see Exhibit 1). Analysts are saying Wal-Mart's "glory days are over" and its stock is "dead money."[6] Some observers are speculating that Scott's days as CEO may be numbered if he is unable to get the company back on track soon.

It is a big company to change. From its humble origins 45 years ago as a single shop in the Ozarks, Wal-Mart has grown to 1.8 million employees supporting more than 6,700 stores in 14 countries, serving 175 million customers per week and pulling in an average of $6.6 billion in weekly sales.[7] Over the past decade, Wal-Mart doubled its store count, tripled its revenue, and nearly quadrupled its net income[8] (see Exhibits 2 and 3). Wal-Mart earned more in its first quarter of fiscal 2007 ($78.8 billion)

Exhibit 1 Changes in Stock Price: Wal-Mart, Target, and Costco, January 3, 2000, through May 14, 2007

Source: 2007, Yahoo! Finance, http://finance.yahoo.com/charts#chart6:symbol=wmt;range=20000103,20070518;compare=cost+tgt;indicator=volume;charttype=line;crosshair=on;logscale=on;source=undefined, May 17.

Exhibit 2 Wal-Mart Retail Units and Sales, 1997–2007

	2007	2006	2005	2004	2003	2002	2001	2000	1999	1998	1997
Number of retail units											
Wal-Mart Stores	1,074	1,209	1,353	1,478	1,568	1,647	1,736	1,801	1,869	1,921	1,960
Supercenters	2,257	1,980	1,713	1,471	1,258	1,066	888	721	564	441	344
Neighborhood Markets	112	100	85	64	49	31	19	7	4	0	0
SAM'S Clubs	579	567	551	538	525	500	475	463	451	443	436
US Stores Total	4,022	3,856	3,702	3,551	3,400	3,244	3,118	2,992	2,888	2,805	2,740
International Stores	2,760	2,181	1,480	1,248	1,163	1,050	955	892	605	568	314
Total Stores	**6,782**	**6,037**	**5,182**	**4,799**	**4,563**	**4,294**	**4,073**	**3,884**	**3,493**	**3,373**	**3,054**
Percentage of total retail units											
Wal-Mart Stores	26.7%	31.4%	36.5%	41.6%	46.1%	50.8%	55.7%	60.2%	64.7%	68.5%	71.5%
Supercenters	56.1%	51.3%	46.3%	41.4%	37.0%	32.9%	28.5%	24.1%	19.5%	15.7%	12.6%
Neighborhood Markets	2.8%	2.6%	2.3%	1.8%	1.4%	1.0%	0.6%	0.2%	0.1%	0.0%	0.0%
SAM'S Clubs	14.4%	14.7%	14.9%	15.2%	15.4%	15.4%	15.2%	15.5%	15.6%	15.8%	15.9%
International	40.7%	36.1%	28.6%	26.0%	25.5%	24.5%	23.4%	23.0%	17.3%	16.8%	10.3%
Sales by segment											
Wal-Mart	$226,294	$209,910	$191,826	$174,220	$157,120	$139,131	$121,889	$108,721	$95,395	$83,820	$74,840
SAM'S Clubs	$41,582	$39,798	$37,119	$34,537	$31,702	$29,395	$26,798	$24,801	$22,881	$20,668	$19,785
International	$77,116	$59,237	$52,543	$47,572	$40,794	$35,485	$32,100	$22,728	$12,247	$7,517	$5,002
Total	**$344,992**	**$308,945**	**$281,488**	**$256,329**	**$229,616**	**$204,011**	**$180,787**	**$156,250**	**$130,523**	**$112,005**	**$99,627**
Percentage of sales by segment											
Wal-Mart	65.6%	67.9%	68.1%	68.0%	68.4%	68.2%	67.4%	69.6%	73.1%	74.8%	75.1%
SAM'S Clubs	12.1%	12.9%	13.2%	13.5%	13.8%	14.4%	14.8%	15.9%	17.5%	18.5%	19.9%
International	22.4%	19.2%	18.7%	18.6%	17.8%	17.4%	17.8%	14.5%	9.4%	6.7%	5.0%
Percentage of sales											
Domestic	77.6%	80.8%	81.3%	81.4%	82.2%	82.6%	82.2%	85.5%	90.6%	93.3%	95.0%
International	22.4%	19.2%	18.7%	18.6%	17.8%	17.4%	17.8%	14.5%	9.4%	6.7%	5.0%
Percentage change in sales											
Domestic	7.3%	9.1%	9.7%	10.6%	12.0%	13.3%	11.4%	12.9%	13.2%	10.4%	2.0%
International	30.2%	12.7%	10.4%	16.6%	15.0%	10.5%	41.2%	85.6%	62.9%	50.3%	25.9%
Percentage sales change											
Domestic	50.4%	75.6%	80.2%	74.6%	79.3%	85.4%	61.8%	59.3%	74.5%	79.7%	
International	49.6%	24.4%	19.8%	25.4%	20.7%	14.6%	38.2%	40.7%	25.5%	20.3%	

Source: 2007, 2002, Wal-Mart Annual Reports.

Exhibit 3 Wal-Mart Income, 1997–2007

	Income Statement (figures in $ millions; fiscal year ends 1/31)										
	2007	2006	2005	2004	2003	2002	2001	2000	1999	1998	1997
Total Operating Revenue	$348,650	$312,101	$284,310	$252,791	$226,479	$201,166	$178,028	$153,345	$129,161	$112,005	$99,627
Cost of Sales	$264,152	$237,649	$216,832	$195,922	$175,769	$156,807	$138,438	$119,526	$101,456	$88,163	$78,897
Gross Operating Profit	**$ 84,498**	**$ 74,452**	**$ 67,478**	**$ 56,869**	**$ 50,710**	**$ 44,359**	**$ 39,590**	**$ 33,819**	**$ 27,705**	**$ 23,842**	**$20,730**
Gross Margins	24.2%	23.9%	23.7%	22.5%	22.4%	22.1%	22.2%	22.1%	21.4%	21.3%	20.8%
Operating, Selling, G&A Exp.	$ 64,001	$ 55,739	$ 50,178	$ 43,877	$ 39,178	$ 34,275	$ 29,942	$ 25,182	$ 21,469	$ 18,831	$16,437
Operating Income	**$ 20,497**	**$ 18,713**	**$ 17,300**	**$ 12,992**	**$ 11,532**	**$ 10,084**	**$ 9,648**	**$ 8,637**	**$ 6,236**	**$ 5,011**	**$ 4,293**
Net Interest Expense	$ 1,529	$ 1,178	$ 980	$ 825	$ 930	$ 1,183	$ 1,194	$ 837	$ 595	$ 716	$ 807
Income Before Taxes	$ 18,968	$ 17,535	$ 16,320	$ 12,167	$ 10,602	$ 8,901	$ 8,454	$ 7,800	$ 5,641	$ 4,295	$ 3,486
Taxes	$ 6,365	$ 5,803	$ 5,589	$ 3,071	$ 2,662	$ 2,183	$ 2,008	$ 2,218	$ 1,432	$ 871	$ 508
Effective Tax Rate	33.6%	33.1%	34.2%	25.2%	25.1%	24.5%	23.8%	28.4%	25.4%	20.3%	14.6%
Net Income from Operations	$ 12,603	$ 11,732	$ 10,731	$ 9,096	$ 7,940	$ 6,718	$ 6,446	$ 5,582	$ 4,209	$ 3,424	$ 2,978
Other Items	$ (894)	$ (177)	$ (215)	$ (42)	$ 15	$ (126)	$ (211)	$ (258)	$188	$ 80	$ 64
Net Income	$ 11,709	$ 11,555	$ 10,516	$ 9,054	$ 7,955	$ 6,592	$ 6,235	$ 5,324	$ 4,397	$ 3,504	$ 3,042
Shareholder Income											
EPS (diluted) ($dollars)	$ 2.71	$ 2.68	$ 2.41	$ 2.07	$ 1.79	$ 1.50	$ 1.44	$ 1.25	$ 0.94	$ 0.76	$ 0.65
Dividend ($dollars)	$ 0.67	$ 0.60	$ 0.52	$ 0.36	$ 0.30	$ 0.28	$ 0.24	$ 0.20	$ 0.16	$ 0.14	$ 0.11

Source: 2007, 2002, Wal-Mart Annual Reports.

283

than Target made all year ($59.5 billion).[9] Wal-Mart's revenue gave it the No. 1 spot on *Fortune's* April 2007 list of America's largest corporations.[10] By contrast, its profit as a percentage of revenue came in at 3.2 percent, and its total return to investors was 0.1 percent, earning Wal-Mart sub-par ranks by those measures (no. 354 and no. 355, respectively).[11]

Over the past several years, Wal-Mart has stumbled upon a variety of compounding difficulties. Opposition has been mounting against not only Wal-Mart's practices, but also its very presence, due to multiple relationship issues with employees, communities, and governments.[12] It is increasingly challenging for the company to expand at its current rate, both in the United States and abroad. Meanwhile, key competitors have been "growing two to five times faster than Wal-Mart" in same-store sales.[13]

As a result, the company has gradually been losing some of its luster, even in the eyes of its former admirers. In 2004, Wal-Mart had been number one on *Fortune* magazine's list of "America's Most Admired Companies" for the second year running, notwithstanding "a year of bad press and lagging stock price."[14] In 2007, by contrast, Wal-Mart was tied for number 19, behind Costco (no. 18) and Target (no. 13).[15]

What had worked in the past was no longer sustainable in the current competitive environment. Scott wondered whether the change efforts he had started over the past few years would begin to have a positive effect or whether he should somehow adjust Wal-Mart's course.

Company History

Origins

Before founding Wal-Mart, Sam Walton accumulated experience in variety store retailing as a JCPenney management trainee and a franchisee of Ben Franklin stores.[16] Anticipating discount market growth, Walton opened his first Wal-Mart store in Rogers, Arkansas, in 1962, the same year Kmart and Target were founded.[17] Wal-Mart opened 24 more stores by 1967.[18] This start was slow compared with Kmart, which had already opened 162 stores by 1966.[19] Wal-Mart went public in 1970, giving it access to the financial resources needed to begin a decades-long expansion campaign that led to the opening of 3,800 stores by 2005.[20] Wal-Mart opened its first Sam's Club warehouse in 1983 and its first international store in 1991, and the company's national and international multiplatform expansion continues[21] (see Exhibit 4).

Recent History

Wal-Mart's growth soared in recent years, with the company adding nearly one new store every day (since 2006).[22] The company's rapid expansion brought its total retail store presence to 6,782 units worldwide as of February 8, 2007.[23] Wal-Mart spread with a missionary zeal, to "save people money so they can live better."[24] As Wal-Mart's presence continued to grow, so did its sales, to a record $345 billion in the fiscal year ended January 31, 2007 (hereafter referred to as 2007).

The company's massive growth brought with it massive controversies, however. Wal-Mart faced multiple accusations, charges, and lawsuits, many resulting in fines, including environmental violations, child labor law violations, use of illegal immigrants by subcontractors, and allegedly poor working conditions for associates.[25] Side effects of these issues include communities rejecting expansion of Wal-Mart stores into their neighborhoods.[26] Anti-Wal-Mart press is also on the rise, with books such as *How Wal-Mart Is Destroying America and the World: And What You Can Do About It* by Bill Quinn, and Robert Greenwald's film, *Wal-Mart: The High Cost of Low Price*. By one estimate, Wal-Mart's reputation issues have cost it $16 billion in market capitalization and an unknown amount of lost business in each store category or business segment.[27]

Business Segments

Wal-Mart's three business segments are Wal-Mart Stores, Sam's Club, and Wal-Mart International.[28] The Wal-Mart Stores segment includes walmart.com and three retail store formats in all 50 of the United States, including 2,257 Supercenters, 1,074 Discount Stores, and 112 Neighborhood Markets.[29] The Neighborhood Markets have the smallest format, with an average size of 42,000 square feet, and a primary focus on grocery products.[30] Wal-Mart's Discount Stores "offer a wide assortment of general merchandise and a limited variety of food products" within 107,000 square feet of selling space.[31] Supercenters average 187,000 square feet and add a full line of food products to Discount Stores' typical selection.[32] Wal-Mart converted 147 Discount Stores into Supercenters in 2007.[33] Overall, Wal-Mart Stores opened 303 new units in 2007 (276 Supercenters, 15 Discount Stores, and 12 Neighborhood Markets).[34]

Membership-based Sam's Club operates in a retail warehouse format, as well as online at samsclub.com. The segment's 579 clubs average 132,000 square feet, and provide "exceptional value on brand-name merchandise at 'members only' prices for both business and personal use."[35] Sam's Club opened 15 new units in 2007.[36]

Wal-Mart International added 576 (net) new stores in 2006—on its way to doubling its total retail unit count over the past few years.[37] Wal-Mart now operates 2,760 stores outside the United States in various formats, under diverse brand names, in 13 foreign countries and territories.[38] Wal-Mart International includes "wholly owned operations in Argentina, Brazil, Canada, Puerto

Exhibit 4 Wal-Mart Key Events, 1962–2004

1960s

1962:	Company founded with opening of first Wal-Mart in Rogers, Arkansas.
1967:	Wal-Mart's 24 stores total $12.6 million in sales.
1968:	Wal-Mart moves outside Arkansas with stores in Missouri and Oklahoma.
1969:	Company incorporated as Wal-Mart Stores, Inc., on October 31.

1970s

1970:	Wal-Mart opens first distribution center and home office in Bentonville, Arkansas. Wal-Mart stock first traded over the counter as a publicly held company. 38 stores now in operation with sales at $44.2 million. Total number of associates is 1,500.
1971:	Wal-Mart is now in five states: Arkansas, Kansas, Louisiana, Missouri, and Oklahoma.
1972:	Wal-Mart approved and listed on the New York Stock Exchange.
1973:	Wal-Mart enters Tennessee.
1974:	Wal-Mart stores now in Kentucky and Mississippi.
1975:	125 stores in operation with sales of $340.3 million and 7,500 associates. Wal-Mart enters ninth state: Texas.
1977:	Wal-Mart enters its 10th state: Illinois.
1979:	Wal-Mart is the first company to reach $1 billion in sales in such a short period of time: $1.248 billion. Wal-Mart now has 276 stores, 21,000 associates and is in its 11th state: Alabama.

1980s

1981:	Wal-Mart enters Georgia and South Carolina.
1982:	Wal-Mart enters Florida and Nebraska.
1983:	First Sam's Club opened in April in Midwest City, Oklahoma. Wal-Mart enters Indiana, Iowa, New Mexico, and North Carolina. For eighth year straight Forbes magazine ranks Wal-Mart No. 1 among general retailers.
1984:	Wal-Mart enters Virginia.
1985:	Wal-Mart has 882 stores with sales of $8.4 billion and 104,000 associates. Company adds stores in Wisconsin and Colorado.
1986:	Wal-Mart enters Minnesota.
1987:	Wal-Mart's 25th anniversary: 1,198 stores with sales of $15.9 billion and 200,000 associates.
1988:	First Supercenter opened in Washington, Missouri.
1989:	Wal-Mart is now in 26 states with the addition of Michigan, West Virginia, and Wyoming.

1990s

1990:	Wal-Mart enters California, Nevada, North Dakota, Pennsylvania, South Dakota, and Utah.
1991:	Wal-Mart enters Connecticut, Delaware, Maine, Maryland, Massachusetts, New Hampshire, New Jersey, and New York. International market entered for first time with the opening of two units in Mexico City. Wal-Mart has entered 45 states with the addition of Idaho, Montana, and Oregon. Wal-Mart enters Puerto Rico.
1993:	Wal-Mart enters Alaska, Hawaii, Rhode Island, and Washington.
1994:	Three value clubs open in Hong Kong. Canada has 123 stores and Mexico has 96.
1995:	Wal-Mart Stores, Inc., has 1,995 Wal-Mart stores, 239 Supercenters, 433 Sam's Clubs, and 276 International stores with sales at $93.6 billion and 675,000 associates. Wal-Mart enters its 50th state, Vermont, and builds three units in Argentina and five in Brazil.
1996:	Wal-Mart enters China through a joint-venture agreement.
1997:	Wal-Mart replaces Woolworth on the Dow Jones Industrial Average.
1998:	Wal-Mart enters Korea through a joint venture agreement.
1999:	Wal-Mart has 1,140,000 associates, making the company the largest private employer in the world.

2000s

2000:	Wal-Mart ranked 5th by Fortune magazine in its Global Most Admired All-Stars list.
2001:	Wal-Mart named by Fortune magazine as the third most admired company in America.
2002:	Wal-Mart ranked #1 on the Fortune 500 listing.
2002:	Wal-Mart has the biggest single day sales in history: $1.43 billion on the day after Thanksgiving.
2003:	Wal-Mart named by Fortune magazine as the most admired company in America.
2004:	Fortune magazine placed Wal-Mart in the top spot on its "Most Admired Companies" list for the second year in a row.

Source: 2007, The Wal-Mart Timeline, Wal-Mart Facts, http://www.walmartfacts.com/content/default.aspx?id=3, April 1.

Rico, and the United Kingdom; the operation of joint ventures in China; and the operations of majority-owned subsidiaries in Central America, Japan, and Mexico."[39] In 2006, Wal-Mart divested its operations in Germany and Korea.[40] Mike Duke, vice chairperson of Wal-Mart Stores and head of the International Division, commented that it had "'become increasingly clear that in Germany's [and South Korea's] business environment it would be difficult to obtain the scale and results we desire.' Wal-Mart seeks markets where it feels that there is potential for it to become a top three retailer, an opportunity that did not exist for it in Germany [or South Korea]."[41] Wal-Mart International's U.K.-based Asda subsidiary brings in the largest share of the company's international revenue, at

Exhibit 5 International Wal-Mart Retail Units and Banners, 2007

2,760 total units

Country	Retail Units	Date of Entry
Mexico	889	November 1991
Puerto Rico	54	August 1992
Canada	289	November 1994
Argentina	13	November 1995
Brazil	302	May 1995
China	73	August 1996
United Kingdom	335	July 1999
Japan	392	March 2002
Costa Rica	137	September 2005
El Salvador	63	September 2005
Guatemala	132	September 2005
Honduras	41	September 2005
Nicaragua	40	September 2005

Sources: 2007, International Data Sheet, Wal-Mart Stores, http://walmartstores.com/Files/Intl_operations.pdf, February 8; 2007, Wal-Mart Annual Report, 24.

37.4 percent.[42] Wal-Mart de Mexico provides the next largest share, at 23.6 percent of Wal-Mart International sales[43] (see Exhibit 5).

One of the challenges for each of Wal-Mart's segments is determining the appropriate product offerings for each location.

Product/Service Diversification

Wal-Mart continues to build on the discount general-store concept that reflects founder Sam Walton's ideals: "a wide assortment of good quality merchandise; the lowest possible prices; guaranteed satisfaction with what you buy; friendly, knowledgeable service; convenient hours; free parking; [and] a pleasant shopping experience."[44] The company's Neighborhood Market locations provide an average of 29,000 items per store; its Discount Stores offer 120,000 items in each store; and its Supercenters stock more than 142,000 different items. Walmart.com offers customers 1 million SKUs (stock keeping units or items in stock), multiple times the number offered in Wal-Mart's retail stores.[45] Sam's Club features appliances, electronics, furniture, jewelry, and office products, plus healthcare, business, personal and financial services.[46] Interestingly, Wal-Mart "caters heavily to customers with little or no access to banking services, often described as the 'unbanked.'"[47] This category fits 20 percent of Wal-Mart's customer base and, as such, Wal-Mart provides substantial financial services for this customer segment by providing services such as check cashing. It has 170 money centers in its approximately 4,000 U.S. stores.

Product and service offerings are just one of the many complex decisions that Wal-Mart's strategic leaders have to make.

Strategic Leaders

Ultimate leadership control has remained in the Walton family, with chairmanship changing hands only once, from father to son. Successors to the highest executive positions at Wal-Mart have always come from within the company. After eight years as CFO and executive vice president, David Glass succeeded Sam Walton as president and later as CEO.[48] H. Lee Scott joined Wal-Mart in 1979 and was named CEO by David Glass in 2000[49] (see Exhibit 6).

Decision Makers

Twenty-five senior Wal-Mart officers meet via weekly videoconferences "to review the Company's ongoing performance, focus on initiatives to drive sales and customer service, and address broader issues"[50] (see Exhibit 7). Eight of these senior officers currently have the most critical roles.

The most powerful among them is S. Robson (Rob) Walton, first son of Sam Walton and chair of the board of directors since 1992.[51] Rob Walton was initiated into the fledgling family business one night in the early 1960s after he earned his driver's license when Sam recruited him to truck goods from a garage in Bentonville to a Wal-Mart store.[52] Rob officially joined the company in 1969, shortly after graduating from law school, worked

Exhibit 6 History of Leadership Succession at Wal-Mart

History of Leadership Succession at Wal-Mart			
Year	President	CEO	Chairman
1962	Sam Walton	Sam Walton	Sam Walton
1984	David Glass	Sam Walton	Sam Walton
1988	David Glass	David Glass	Sam Walton
1992	David Glass	David Glass	Rob Walton
2000	H. Lee Scott	H. Lee Scott	Rob Walton

Sources: 2007, The Wal-Mart Timeline, Wal-Mart Facts, http://www.walmartfacts.com/content/default.aspx?id=3, April 1; D. Longo, 1998, Wal-Mart hands CEO crown to David Glass, *Discount Store News*, February 15.

his way up to the vice chair position, and became board chair in 1992 after his father died.[53] "We lead when we embrace my dad's vision," according to Rob, "to improve the lives of everyday people by making everyday things more affordable."[54] Rob now lives in Colorado, where he races bicycles and sports cars in his spare time, and flies the company jet to his Bentonville office.[55] He continues to serve as the primary conduit for Walton family input related to company proceedings.[56]

CEO Lee Scott "rose through the ranks by excelling at the mechanical aspects of retailing, playing an indispensable part in Wal-Mart's technology-induced rebound in the latter half of the 1990s."[57] The son of a gas station owner and a music teacher in small-town Kansas, Scott worked factory night shifts to pay for college, while he, his wife, and their baby lived in a mobile home.[58] He put his business degree to use in logistics, first as a dispatcher for Yellow Freight, then as a "headstrong," "aggressive, even abrasive" Wal-Mart transportation manager.[59] His skill in reducing costs helped him ascend to senior logistics jobs, then into the top merchandising post, where he cut billions in excess inventory in the late 1990s.[60] Next Scott ran the 2,300-unit Wal-Mart Stores Division for a year before becoming Wal-Mart's chief operating officer and vice chairperson in 1999.[61] He became CEO in January 2000.[62]

Mike Duke, an industrial engineer who had 23 years of experience with Federated and May Department Stores, followed Scott's path, climbing the distribution and logistics ladder to the leadership of Wal-Mart Stores Division.[63] Now he oversees international operations as vice chairperson.[64]

John Menzer, who joined Wal-Mart in 1995 after 10 years with Ben Franklin Retail Stores, served as Wal-Mart's chief financial officer before becoming CEO of Wal-Mart International in 1999.[65] He led the acquisitions of Seiyu (a majority-owned subsidiary in Japan) and Asda.[66] Now as vice chairperson, Menzer is responsible for Wal-Mart Stores and various corporate functions, including strategic planning.[67]

A native of Ecuador, Eduardo Castro-Wright leads the Wal-Mart Stores Division in the United States after leading Wal-Mart de Mexico from 2001 to 2005, following a distinguished career with Nabisco in the Latin America and Asia-Pacific regions.[68]

Doug McMillon became president and CEO of Sam's Club after a 15-year career with Wal-Mart, first as a buyer, then as a merchandising manager and leader.[69]

Nineteen-year Target veteran John Fleming ascended through Walmart.com in the early 2000s to become Wal-Mart Stores' chief marketing officer, prior to his January 2007 induction as chief merchandising officer for Wal-Mart Stores.[70]

Exhibit 7 Wal-Mart Senior Officers, May 2007

Eduardo Castro-Wright
Executive Vice President and President and Chief Executive Officer, Wal-Mart Stores Division

M. Susan Chambers
Executive Vice President of People Division

Patricia A. Curran
Executive Vice President, Store Operations, Wal-Mart Stores Division

Leslie A. Dach
Executive Vice President, Corporate Affairs and Government Relations

Linda M. Dillman
Executive Vice President, Risk Management and Benefits Administration

Michael T. Duke
Vice Chairman, Responsible for International

Johnnie C. Dobbs
Executive Vice President, Logistics and Supply Chain

John E. Fleming
Executive Vice President and Chief Merchandising Officer, Wal-Mart Stores Division

Rollin L. Ford
Executive Vice President, Chief Information Officer

Craig R. Herkert
Executive Vice President and President and Chief Executive Officer, The Americas, International

Charles M. Holley, Jr.
Executive Vice President, Finance and Treasurer

Thomas D. Hyde
Executive Vice President and Corporate Secretary

Gregory L. Johnston
Executive Vice President, Club Operations, SAM'S CLUB

Thomas A. Mars
Executive Vice President and General Counsel

C. Douglas McMillon
Executive Vice President and President and Chief Executive Officer, SAM'S CLUB

John B. Menzer
Vice Chairman, Responsible for U.S.

Stephen Quinn
Executive Vice President and Chief Marketing Officer, Wal-Mart Stores, Inc.

Thomas M. Schoewe
Executive Vice President and Chief Financial Officer

H. Lee Scott, Jr.
President and Chief Executive Officer

William S. Simon
Executive Vice President and Chief Operating Officer, Professional Services and New Business Development

Gregory E. Spragg
Executive Vice President, Merchandising and Replenishment, SAM'S CLUB

S. Robson Walton
Chairman of the Board of Directors of Wal-Mart Stores, Inc.

Claire A. Watts
Executive Vice President, Merchandising, Wal-Mart Stores Division-US

Steven P. Whaley
Senior Vice President, Controller, Wal-Mart Stores Inc.

Eric S. Zorn
Executive Vice President and President, Wal-Mart Realty

Source: 2007, Senior Officers, WalMartStores.com, http://walmartstores.com/GlobalWMStoresWeb/navigate.do?catg=540, May 25.

After 13 years in marketing roles with PepsiCo, Stephen Quinn joined Wal-Mart as senior vice president of marketing in 2005, and then in January 2007 took over Fleming's former position as chief marketing officer for Wal-Mart Stores.[71]

These eight leaders are supported and monitored by the board of directors.

Board of Directors

Wal-Mart has an active, high-caliber, 14-member board of directors that may soon get even more powerful. "The Board has been instrumental in encouraging the company to more quickly address critical issues, and I am extremely pleased that they are not reticent about sharing their opinions," Rob Walton recently wrote, adding: "Today's Board is the furthest thing from a rubber stamp."[72] Two out of three board members have held

CEO positions and/or chaired the boards of various companies. Retail turnaround guru Allen Questrom, who overhauled JCPenney, joined the board in June 2007.[73] Questrom recently told *Women's Wear Daily*: "[Wal-Mart is] never going to be a leader in fashion apparel. That's not their calling. But can they improve on that, sure they can."[74] The most famous former board member is New York Senator and Democratic presidential candidate Hillary Rodham Clinton, who served on the Wal-Mart board from 1986 to 1992 as a "loyalist reformer"[75] (see Exhibit 8).

Several board members are among the largest shareholders in the company.

Shareholders

Of the 4.1 billion Wal-Mart shares outstanding, insiders and beneficial owners hold 42 percent, while institutional investors and mutual funds hold 37 percent.[76]

Exhibit 8 Wal-Mart Board of Directors, May 2007

Aida M. Alvarez, 57
Former Administrator of the U.S. Small Business Administration; joined board in 2006

James W. Breyer, 45
Managing Partner of Accel Partners; joined board in 2001

M. Michele Burns, 49
Chairman and CEO of Mercer Human Resources Consulting; joined board in 2003

James Cash, Jr., Ph.D., 59
Retired Professor of Business Administration at Harvard Business School; joined board in 2006

Roger C. Corbett, 64
Retired CEO and Group Managing Director of Woolworths Limited; joined board in 2006

Douglas N. Daft, 64
Retired Chairman of the Board and CEO of The Coca-Cola Company; joined board in 2005

David D. Glass, 71
Former President and CEO of Wal-Mart Stores, Inc.; joined board in 1977

Roland A. Hernandez, 49
Retired Chairman and CEO of Telemundo Group, Inc.; joined board in 1998

Allen I. Questrom, 67
Former Chairman and CEO of JCPenney Company; Barneys New York, Inc.; The Neiman Marcus Group, Inc.; and Federated Department Stores, Inc.; standing for election in June 2007

H. Lee Scott, Jr., 58
President and Chief Executive Officer of Wal-Mart Stores, Inc.; joined board in 1999

Jack C. Shewmaker, 69
Retired Vice Chairman of Wal-Mart Stores, Inc.; joined board in 1977

Jim C. Walton, 58
Chairman of the Board and CEO of Arvest Bank Group, Inc.; joined board in 2005

S. Robson Walton, 62
Chairman of the Board of Directors of Wal-Mart Stores, Inc.; joined board in 1978

Christopher J. Williams, 49
Chairman and CEO of The Williams Capital Group, L.P.; joined board in 2004

Linda S. Wolf, 59
Former Chairman of the Board and CEO of Leo Burnett Worldwide, Inc.; joined board in 2005

Sources: 2007, Board of Directors, WalMartStores.com, http://walmartstores.com/GlobalWMStoresWeb/navigate.do?catg=502, May 25; 2007, Wal-Mart Stores, Inc., Form DEF 14A, Proxy Statement, Notice of 2007 Annual Shareholders' Meeting, U.S. SEC, April 19.

The Walton family owns almost 1.7 billion shares through its holding company, Walton Enterprises, LLC, whose directors were five of America's ten wealthiest individuals in 2005: Sam's three sons, Rob Walton, director Jim C. Walton, and John T. Walton (d. 2005); daughter Alice L. Walton; and widow Helen R. Walton (d. 2007).[77]

Top non-Walton inside shareholders include CEO Lee Scott (1.2 million shares), director David D. Glass (1.2 million shares), director Jack C. Shewmaker (557,674 shares), Mike Duke (413,213 shares), and John Menzer (401,883 shares).[78]

Some 1,127 institutions own Wal-Mart stock.[79] Nearly 536 million Wal-Mart shares are owned by 785 mutual funds.[80]

In total, as many as 312,423 shareholders held common stock in Wal-Mart on March 16, 2007, when the company finalized its annual report for fiscal 2007.[81]

Financial Results

Fiscal 2007 and Recent Years[82]
Over the past 10 years, Wal-Mart's net income has nearly quadrupled, from $3 billion in 1997 to $11.7 billion in 2007. Revenues have more than tripled, from $100 billion to $345 billion. Meanwhile, operating, selling, and general administration expenses have quadrupled, outstripping the increase in revenue and net income, averaging 14.6 percent of sales. Despite the increase in expenses, steadily higher gross margins have boosted operating income (refer to Exhibit 3).

Wal-Mart had assets totaling $151 billion in 2007, up from $39 billion in 1997. Concurrent with the increase in assets, liabilities have grown 319 percent over the same period, from $21.4 billion to $89.6 billion. Shareholder return on equity measured 22 percent in 2007, close to its 10-year average. Total shareholder equity rose from $17.2 billion in 1997 to $61.8 billion in 2007 (see Exhibit 9).

Wal-Mart has improved its profitability over the last several years. Compared with an average operating profit margin of 5.1 percent in the prior three-year period, Wal-Mart has averaged 6.0 percent in the past three years. In 1997, Wal-Mart's operating profit margin was 4.3 percent. From a debt perspective, Wal-Mart has fluctuated up and down, with a debt ratio between 55.1 percent and 61.5 percent over the last 10 years. As of 2007, it measured 59.3 percent, 150 basis points over its 10-year median (see Exhibit 10).

Comparative Revenue[83]
Sales by Region. Of nearly $345 billion in total sales in 2007 (not including Sam's Club fees), domestic U.S. revenues totaled nearly $268 billion, or 77.6 percent of sales, while international revenues were $77 billion, or 22.4 percent of sales. International operations are becoming increasingly important to the company. Driving

Exhibit 9 Wal-Mart Balance Sheet, 1997–2007

Balance Sheet
(all figures in $millions; fiscal year ends 1/31)

	2007	2006	2005	2004	2003	2002	2001	2000	1999	1998	1997
Assets											
Inventories	$ 33,685	$ 31,910	29,419	26,263	24,098	21,793	20,710	18,961	16,058	16,005	15,556
Other Current Assets	$ 12,903	$ 11,915	$ 8,494	7,285	$ 4,769	$ 4,122	$ 4,086	$ 4,021	$ 3,445	$ 2,584	$ 1,829
Total Current Assets	$ 46,588	$ 43,825	$ 37,913	$ 33,548	$28,867	$25,915	$24,796	$22,982	$19,503	$18,589	$17,385
Net Property, Equipment & Leases	$ 88,440	$ 77,865	$ 66,549	$ 57,591	$50,053	$44,172	$39,439	$34,570	$24,824	$23,237	$19,935
Goodwill & Other Long-term Assets	$ 16,165	$ 13,934	$ 12,677	$ 11,316	$11,309	$ 9,214	$10,082	$ 9,738	$ 2,739	$ 2,395	$ 1,251
Total Assets	**$151,193**	**$135,624**	**$117,139**	**$102,455**	**$90,229**	**$79,301**	**$74,317**	**$67,290**	**$47,066**	**$44,221**	**$38,571**
Return on Assets	8.8%	9.3%	9.8%	9.7%	9.6%	9.0%	9.3%	10.1%	9.6%	8.5%	8.0%
Liabilities & Shareholder Equity											
Current Liabilities	$ 51,754	$ 48,348	$ 42,609	$ 37,308	$31,752	$26,309	$28,096	$25,058	$13,930	$15,848	$10,432
Long-Term Debt	$ 27,222	$ 26,429	$ 20,087	$ 17,088	$16,545	$15,632	$12,453	$13,650	$ 6,875	$ 7,169	$ 7,685
Long-Term Leases	$ 3,513	$ 3,667	$ 3,073	$ 2,888	$ 2,903	$ 2,956	$ 3,054	$ 2,852	$ 2,697	$ 2,480	$ 2,304
Other Liabilities	$ 7,131	$ 4,009	$ 1,974	$ 1,548	$ (432)	$ (788)	$ (693)	$ (148)	$ 505	$ 2,123	$ 999
(minority interest, discontinued ops, deferred taxes)											
Total Liabilities	**$ 89,620**	**$ 82,453**	**$ 67,743**	**$ 58,832**	**$50,768**	**$44,109**	**$42,910**	**$41,412**	**$25,925**	**$25,702**	**$21,420**
Shareholder Equity	**$ 61,573**	**$ 53,171**	**$ 49,396**	**$ 43,623**	**$39,461**	**$35,192**	**$31,407**	**$25,878**	**$21,141**	**$18,519**	**$17,151**
Return on Equity	22.0%	22.9%	23.1%	22.4%	21.8%	20.7%	23.0%	24.5%	22.0%	19.6%	18.8%

Source: 2007, 2002, Wal-Mart Annual Reports.

Exhibit 10 Wal-Mart Financial Ratios, 1997–2007

	2007	2006	2005	2004	2003	2002	2001	2000	1999	1998	1997
Stability											
Debt Ratio	59.3%	60.8%	57.8%	57.4%	56.3%	55.6%	57.7%	61.5%	55.1%	58.1%	55.5%
Stockholders Equity to Assets	40.7%	39.2%	42.2%	42.6%	43.7%	44.4%	42.3%	38.5%	44.9%	41.9%	44.5%
Leverage	2.50	2.46	2.36	2.32	2.27	2.31	2.47	2.43	2.30	2.32	n/a
Debt to Equity Ratio	1.46	1.55	1.37	1.35	1.29	1.25	1.37	1.60	1.23	1.39	1.25
Debt to Capitalization Ratio	0.38	0.39	0.34	0.33	0.33	0.34	0.32	0.39	0.32	0.39	0.39
Liquidity											
Current Ratio	0.90	0.91	0.89	0.90	0.91	0.99	0.88	0.92	1.23	1.33	1.67
Quick Ratio	0.25	0.25	0.20	0.20	0.15	0.16	0.15	0.16	0.22	0.19	0.18
Profitability											
Operating Profit Margin	5.9%	6.0%	6.1%	5.1%	5.1%	5.0%	5.4%	5.6%	4.8%	4.5%	4.3%
Operating Ratio	18.4%	17.9%	17.6%	17.4%	17.3%	17.0%	16.8%	16.4%	16.6%	16.8%	16.5%
Net Profit Margin	3.3%	3.6%	3.6%	3.6%	3.5%	3.3%	3.5%	3.5%	3.4%	3.1%	3.1%
Total Asset Turnover	2.4	2.5	2.6	2.6	2.7	2.6	2.5	2.7	2.8	2.7	n/a

Source: 2007, 2002, Wal-Mart Annual Reports.

Wal-Mart's overall growth, international sales growth has averaged 33.6 percent over the past 10 years, whereas domestic sales have grown an average of only 11.0 percent in the same period. In the last three years, domestic sales growth has averaged 8.7 percent versus average international growth of 17.8 percent (refer to Exhibit 2).

Wal-Mart has experienced varying rates of growth in international markets. Nonetheless, international revenue has been a constant source of sales growth for Wal-Mart, outpacing the revenue contribution from the Sam's Club segment since 2001.

Sales by Segment. Wal-Mart Stores brought in 65.6 percent of all sales in 2007, down from 75.1 percent of sales in 1997. Wal-Mart International was responsible for 22.4 percent of sales, up from 5.0 percent a decade earlier, while Sam's Club accounted for 12.1 percent of sales in 2007, down from 19.9 percent in 1997 (refer to Exhibit 2).

Sam's Club has suffered against rival Costco for years, losing the battle for comparable-store sales in "64 of the past 73 months," according to one researcher, as well as the battle for membership renewals.[84] Average annual sales per warehouse were $73 million for Sam's Club versus $135 million for Costco in fiscal 2006.[85]

Wal-Mart's online business has not been a significant source of revenue, bringing in an estimated $135 million in sales in 2002, the same year JCPenney.com had sales of $324 million and Amazon.com reached sales greater than $3 billion.[86]

Wal-Mart Supercenters drove 56.1 percent of the company's sales, reflecting the company's competitive strength in traditional nonmembership discount formats.

Results Relative to Competitors

Market Leadership. Wal-Mart is the number one retailer in 77 of the 100 largest general merchandise markets in America, squaring up against Target or Costco in all but 11 of these markets.[87] Either Wal-Mart, Costco, or Target holds the top position in 91 of the top 100 largest general merchandise markets in the United States.[88] Geographically, Wal-Mart is the dominant retailer in the South and throughout midsized and small-town markets, while Costco is the leader in California and Washington.[89] According to ACNielsen, (the world's leading marketing information company), in the United States, Wal-Mart "controls 20 percent of dry grocery, 29 percent of non-food grocery, 30 percent of health and beauty aids, and 45 percent of general merchandise sales."[90] It also controls 45 percent of the retail toy segment.[91] However, Target, Kroger, and Family Dollar Stores are all growing revenue faster than Wal-Mart, threatening its dominance (see Exhibit 11).

Financial Ratios. From a competitive profitability perspective, Wal-Mart's 5.87 percent operating margin and 3.23 percent net margin put it in the middle of the pack relative to its key competitors (refer to Exhibit 11). Target enjoys higher margins, closer to those of JCPenney, while Costco has lower margins, closer to those of Dollar General and Kroger. Wal-Mart's

Exhibit 11 Comparison of Financial Ratios

	Financial Ratios of Select Retailers (sorted by revenue growth, as of May 26, 2007)					
	Quarterly Growth (yoy)		Profitability (ttm)		Management Effectiveness (ttm)	
	Revenue Growth	Earnings Growth	Net Profit Margin	Operating Margin	Return on Assets	Return on Equity
Amazon.com, Inc.	32.30%	117.60%	2.18%	3.74%	10.37%	73.86%
Target Corporation	16.30%	19.20%	4.69%	8.52%	8.93%	18.68%
Kroger Co.	14.50%	36.50%	1.69%	3.47%	7.10%	23.95%
Family Dollar Stores, Inc.	12.20%	66.00%	3.49%	5.70%	9.44%	17.68%
Wal-Mart Stores, Inc.	9.60%	8.10%	3.23%	5.87%	8.81%	21.80%
Costco Wholesale Corp.	7.50%	−15.80%	1.73%	2.55%	6.25%	12.07%
J.C. Penney Corporation	3.10%	13.30%	5.90%	9.73%	9.57%	26.43%
Dollar General Corp.	3.00%	−65.50%	1.50%	2.67%	5.24%	7.96%
Sears Holdings Corporation	1.30%	26.50%	2.81%	4.59%	5.06%	12.25%

Sources: 2007, Key Statistics, Capital IQ, A Division of Standard & Poor's, Yahoo! Finance, http://finance.yahoo.com/q/ks?s=WMT, http://finance.yahoo.com/q/ks?s=TGT, http://finance.yahoo.com/q/ks?s=COST, http://finance.yahoo.com/q/ks?s=KR, http://finance.yahoo.com/q/ks?s=DG, http://finance.yahoo.com/q/ks?s=FDO, http://finance.yahoo.com/q/ks?s=SHLD, http://finance.yahoo.com/q/ks?s=JCP, http://finance.yahoo.com/q/ks?s=AMZN, May 26.

margins are nearest those of Family Dollar Stores and Sears Holdings (Kmart and Sears). Wal-Mart's profit margin may be held down somewhat by its presence in the lower margin grocery business, especially in its Neighborhood Markets format.[92] In Supercenters, groceries serve a larger role of driving store traffic and drawing customers toward higher margin products. From a management effectiveness standpoint, Wal-Mart is creating a return on equity that is higher than Target's and much higher than Costco's and a return on assets that is nearly identical to Target's and higher than Costco's.

First Quarter, Fiscal 2008 (Quarter Ending April 30, 2007)

Wal-Mart had a difficult first quarter. Revenue and earnings "were not where we would have expected [them] to be, nor where we believe they should be," according to CEO Scott.[93] "Quite honestly, we're not satisfied with our overall performance."[94] Wal-Mart increased company sales (not including Sam's Club fees) by 8.3 percent in the first quarter to $85.3 billion.[95] Overall operating income increased 7.9 percent year-over-year, with nearly 53.1 percent of the change coming from Wal-Mart's international operations[96] (see Exhibit 12).

Closing out the first quarter on a down note, Wal-Mart's April same-store sales decrease was the worst ever recorded in 28 years of tracking: an overall U.S. comparable-store sales slide of 3.5 percent for the month, with a 4.6 percent drop at Wal-Mart Stores offset by a 2.5 percent increase at Sam's Clubs.[97] Much of the April decline was blamed on the apparel business, which

constitutes 10 percent of Wal-Mart's sales.[98] Recent failed forays into fashion appear to have dragged down overall same-stores sales.[99] Wal-Mart wasn't the only retailer to have a bad April. The International Council of Shopping Centers reported an average 2.3 percent drop in same-store sales across 51 chains.[100] Against the trend, Costco posted a 6 percent same-store sales gain in April (see Exhibit 13).

The financial situation might be better considered with an understanding of the competitive situation in Wal-Mart's industry.

Competitive Situation

We face strong sales competition from other discount, department, drug, variety and specialty stores and supermarkets, many of which are national, regional or international chains, as well as internet-based retailers and catalog businesses. Additionally, we compete with a number of companies for prime retail site locations, as well as in attracting and retaining quality employees ("associates"). We, along with other retail companies, are influenced by a number of factors . . . cost of goods, consumer debt levels and buying patterns, economic conditions, interest rates, customer preferences, unemployment, labor costs, inflation, currency exchange fluctuations, fuel prices, weather patterns, catastrophic events, competitive pressures and insurance costs. Our Sam's Club segment faces strong sales competition from other wholesale club operators, catalogs businesses, internet-based and other retailers."

—*2007 WAL-MART ANNUAL REPORT, 28–29*

Exhibit 12 Wal-Mart Fiscal 2008 First Quarter Results versus Target

Wall-Mart Stores, Inc. Fiscal 2008 First Quarter Results Quarters Ending 4/30, all figures in $millions			
Income	Q1 2008	Q1 2007	YoY% Chng
Total Operating Revenue	$86,410	$79,676	8.5%
Cost of Sales	$65,311	$60,237	8.4%
Gross Operating Profit	**$21,099**	**$19,439**	8.5%
Gross Margins	24.4%	24.4%	
Operating, Selling, G&A Exp.	$16,249	$14,944	8.7%
Operating Income	**$ 4,850**	**$ 4,495**	7.9%
Net Interest Expense	$ 392	$ 368	6.5%
Income Before Taxes	$ 4,458	$ 4,127	8.0%
Provision for Taxes	$ 1,532	$ 1,388	10.4%
Effective Tax Rate	34.4%	33.6%	2.2%
Net Income from Operations	$ 2,926	$ 2,739	6.8%
Other Items	$ (100)	$ (124)	
Net Income	**$ 2,826**	**$ 2,615**	8.1%
Shareholder Income (*$dollars*)			
EPS (diluted)	$ 0.68	$ 0.63	7.9%
Dividend	$ 0.67	$ 0.60	
Comparable-Store Sales Growth	**0.6%**	**3.8%**	
Wal-Mart Stores	−0.1%	3.8%	
Sam's Club (excl. fuel)	4.7%	4.3%	
Segment Breakdown			
Revenue by Segment			
Wal-Mart Stores	$55,437	$52,499	5.6%
Sam's Club	$10,323	$ 9,775	5.6%
International	$19,627	$16,561	18.5%
Total (excludes other income)	$85,387	$78,835	8.3%
Operating Income by Segment			
Wal-Mart Stores	$ 3,927	$ 3,858	1.8%
Sam's Club	$ 363	$ 303	19.8%
International	$ 903	$ 757	19.3%
Total (excludes other income)	$ 5,193	$ 4,918	5.6%
Operating Margins by Segment			
Wal-Mart Stores	7.1%	7.3%	−3.6%
Sam's Club	3.5%	3.1%	13.4%
International	4.6%	4.6%	0.7%
Total (excludes other income)	6.1%	6.2%	−2.5%
Cash Flows			
Net Income	$ 2,826	$ 2,615	
Change in Inventories	$ (1,280)	$ 259	
Accounts Payable	$ (1,115)	$ (442)	
Accounts Receivable	$ 62	$ 219	
Cash Flows from Operating Activities	**$ 493**	**$ 2,651**	

Target Corporation Fiscal 2008 First Quarter Results Quarters Ending 5/5/07 and 4/29/06, all figures in $millions			
Income	Q1 2008	Q1 2007	YoY%Chng
Total Operating Revenue*	$14,041	$12,863	9.2%
Cost of Sales	$ 9,186	$ 8,473	8.4%
Gross Operating Profit	**$ 4,855**	**$ 4,390**	10.6%
Gross Margins	34.6%	34.1%	
Operating, Selling, G&A Exp.**	$ 3,655	$ 3,373	8.4%
Operating Income	**$ 1,200**	**$ 1,017**	18.0%
Net Interest Expense	$ 136	$ 131	3.6%
Income Before Taxes	$ 1,064	$ 886	20.2%
Provision for Taxes	$ 413	$ 332	24.5%
Effective Tax Rate	38.8%	37.5%	3.6%
Net Income from Operations	$ 651	$ 554	17.6%
Other Items	$ –	$ –	
Net Income	**$ 651**	**$ 554**	17.5%
Shareholder Income (*$dollars*)			
EPS (diluted)	$ 0.75	$ 0.63	19.6%

*includes sales and net credit card revenues
**includes SG&A, credit card expenses, depreciation and amortization

Comparable-Store Sales Growth	**4.3%**	**5.1%**	

Sources: 2007, Wal-Mart Stores, Inc., Form 8-K, U.S. SEC, May 15; and 2007, Target Corporation, Form 8-K, U.S. SEC, May 23.

Exhibit 13 April 2007 Same-Store Sales Growth

April 2007 Same-Store Sales Growth	
Discounters	
Wal-Mart	–3.5%
Costco	+6.0%
Target	–6.1%
Dollar General	–2.4%
Department Stores	
Federated	–2.2%
JCPenney	–4.7%
Nordstrom	+3.1%
Dillard's	–14.0%
Neiman Marcus	+1.0%
Saks	+11.7%
Apparel	
TJX	–1.0%
Kohl's	–10.5%
Gap	–16.0%
Limited	–1.0%
AnnTaylor	–12.8%
Teen Apparel	
Abercrombie & Fitch	–15.0%
American Eagle Outfitters	–10.0%

Source: J. Covert, 2007, Retail-sales slide fuels concern: Decline of 2.3% in April among worst on record; even Wal-Mart slipped, *Wall Street Journal*, May 11, A3.

Competitors

Target. Target Corporation operates 1,318 general merchandise stores and 182 SuperTarget stores in 47 states, in addition to its online business, target.com.[101] Target describes itself as "an upscale discounter that provides high-quality, on-trend merchandise at attractive prices in clean, spacious and guest-friendly stores."[102] Target has grown

revenue from $33 billion in 2001 to more than $59 billion in 2006, a compound annual growth rate of 12.5 percent.[103] Profits have risen as well, as earnings from continuing operations averaged an annual growth rate of 20.4 percent over the same period[104] (see Exhibit 14).

Costco. Costco Wholesale Corporation runs 510 warehouses, averaging 140,000 square feet, in 38 states, six foreign countries (Canada, Mexico, the United Kingdom, Taiwan, Korea, and Japan), and Puerto Rico.[105] Costco offers three kinds of membership and roughly 4,000 products, 10 to 15 times fewer than many competitors, according to the company.[106] Costco benefits from a limited number of products sold in high volumes, high inventory turnover, low costs via purchasing discounts and a no-frills approach, and favorable real estate locations. Gross margins have averaged about 10.6 percent over the past five years, and operating income has increased an average of 10.5 percent over the same period[107] (see Exhibit 15).

Kroger. The Kroger Co. is "one of the nation's largest retailers, operating 2,468 supermarket and multi-department stores under two dozen banners including Kroger, Ralphs, Fred Meyer, Food 4 Less, King Soopers, Smith's, Fry's, Fry's Marketplace, Dillons, QFC, and City Market."[108] Kroger's operating income fell 13.1 percent between 2002 and 2006, from $2.8 billion to $2.2 billion, despite an increase in revenue of 27.7 percent.[109] Operating margins have averaged 24.8 percent over the last three years, up from 15.7 percent in the three years prior[110] (see Exhibit 16).

Other General Discount Competitors. Sears Holdings (Kmart and Sears) offer some additional U.S. competition in general merchandise, while Tesco of Britain and Carrefour of France compete with Wal-Mart internationally. Carrefour is the second-largest retailer in the world

Exhibit 14 Target Performance, 2001–2006

Target	2001	2002	2003	2004	2005	2006
Revenue	$33,021	$ 37,410	$42,025	$46,839	$52,620	$59,940
COGS	$23,030	$25,948	$28,389	$31,445	$34,927	$39,399
Gross Margin	$ 9,991	$11,462	$13,636	$15,394	$ 17,693	$20,541
Gross Margin %	30.3%	30.6%	32.4%	32.9%	33.6%	34.3%
Operating Income/EBIT	$ 2,246	2,811	3,159	3,601	4,323	5,069
		25.2%	12.4%	14.0%	20.0%	17.3%
Net Income	$ 1,101	$ 1,376	$ 1,619	$ 1,885	$ 2,408	$ 2,787
Net Income % chg		25.0%	17.7%	16.4%	27.7%	15.7%

Note: $ in millions

Source: 2006, Target Corporation Annual Report.

Exhibit 15 Costco Performance, 2001–2006

Costco	2001	2002	2003	2004	2005	2006
Revenue	$34,137,021	$37,994,608	$41,694,561	$ 47,148,627	$51,879,070	$58,963,180
COGS	$30,598,140	$33,983,121	$ 37,235,383	$ 42,092,016	$46,346,961	$52,745,497
Gross Margin	$ 3,538,881	$ 4,011,487	$ 4,459,178	$ 5,056,611	$ 5,532,109	$ 6,217,683
Gross Margin %	10.4%	10.6%	10.7%	10.7%	10.7%	10.5%
Operating Income/EBIT	$ 992,267	1,131,535	1,156,628	1,385,648	1,474,303	1,625,632
		14.0%	2.2%	19.8%	6.4%	10.3%
Net Income	$ 602,089	$ 699,983	$ 721,000	$ 882,393	$ 1,063,092	$ 1,103,215
Net Income % chg		16.3%	3.0%	22.4%	20.5%	3.8%

Note: $ in thousands

Source: 2006, Costco Wholesale Corp. Annual Report.

Exhibit 16 Kroger Performance, 2001–2006

Kroger	2001	2002	2003	2004	2005	2006
Revenue	$49,000	$51,760	$53,791	$56,434	$60,553	$ 66,111
COGS	$36,398	$ 37,810	$39,637	$42,140	$45,565	$ 50,115
Gross Margin	$12,602	$13,950	$14,154	$14,294	$14,988	$15,996
Gross Margin %	25.7%	10.6%	10.7%	25.3%	24.8%	24.2%
Operating Income/EBIT	$ 2,359	$ 2,573	$ 1,374	$ 843	$ 2,035	$ 2,236
		9.1%	−46.6%	−38.6%	141.4%	9.9%
Net Income	$ 877	$ 1,202	$ 285	$ (104)	$ 958	$ 1,115
Net Income % chg		37.1%	−76.3%	−136.5%	$ 1021.2%	$ 16.4%

Note: $ in millions

Source: 2006 The Kroger Co. Annual Report.

(after Wal-Mart) and is probably its closest international competitor from a strategy perspective, as it focuses on hypermarkets (similar to Supercenters), in addition to a variety of other formats.[111] Tesco emphasizes convenience and competes primarily in groceries, but also in general merchandise against Wal-Mart's U.K. subsidiary Asda.[112] Tesco is looking to expand to the West Coast of the United States in 2007.[113] Amazon.com adds another level of global competition for Wal-Mart due to its high number of SKUs and its convenience.

Niche Competitors. Other retailers compete with Wal-Mart at the department level, including Safeway, Best Buy, Circuit City, Home Depot, Ace Hardware, Lowe's, Kohl's, Mervyn's California, Barnes & Noble, and Borders, among others. In order to provide lower prices than its competitors, Wal-Mart has developed a unique relationship with its suppliers.

Suppliers

Wal-Mart's 1,600-member Global Procurement Services team, based in 23 countries, buys merchandise from suppliers in more than 70 countries, including 61,000 suppliers in the United States.[114] Leveraging its size, "Wal-Mart not only dictates delivery schedules and inventory levels but also heavily influences product specifications. In the end, many suppliers have to choose between designing goods their way or the Wal-Mart way."[115] In return, companies with a streamlined product and supply chain can benefit greatly. "If you are good with data, are sophisticated, and have scale, Wal-Mart should be one of your most profitable customers," says a retired consumer-products executive.[116] "Wal-Mart controls a large and rapidly increasing share of the business done by most every major U.S. consumer products company," about 28 percent of the total sales of Dial and almost a quarter of the sales of Del Monte Foods, Clorox, and Revlon.[117]

Customers

Wal-Mart attracts 175 million people to its stores each week.[118] According to ACNielsen (the world's leading marketing information company), the typical Wal-Mart shopper has an annual household income of $10,000 to $50,000.[119] These shoppers account for 54 percent of Wal-Mart's sales.[120] Wal-Mart also attracts an affluent segment (with household incomes of at least $75,000) that accounts for 26 percent of its customer base.[121] The affluent segment cross-shops the most with Costco (27 percent) and Target (28 percent).[122] These upscale shoppers likely have lower price elasticity, a relatively lower switching cost, but a higher sensitivity to brand reputation.

Even though Wal-Mart recently hired some well-known public relations experts and ended its relationship with its Ad Agency of 32 years in hopes of creating a more positive image, according to a 2004 study, "2 to 8 percent of Wal-Mart consumers surveyed have ceased shopping at the chain because of 'negative press.'"[123] Shoppers interviewed by the authors of this case have strong opinions about Wal-Mart (see Exhibits 17 and 18).

Wal-Mart's recent struggles with bad press and lawsuits have created urgency to find a way to protect its market share from potential entrants or substitutes.

Other Sources of Competition

Customers have many alternatives for each of the products and services that Wal-Mart provides, but few alternatives exist for the large-scale discount superstore or warehouse shopping experience. The same products can be purchased at different types of retailers, but it is difficult to replicate the convenience, price, and diversity of merchandise found at a Wal-Mart. Also, new potential market entrants with similar scale would have difficulty competing in any substantial volume on price across a wide array of merchandise. Other large incumbents such as Target and Costco have also built economies of scale that would be difficult for a start-up to replicate. Supply chains must be extensive and very efficient. Product differentiation is usually minor in discount store merchandise. However, switching retailers would be easy for customers in well-served areas.

Beyond these retail industry forces, more general external trends also influence Wal-Mart's competitive situation.

External Trends

Government. Wal-Mart has become a "poster company" on political issues related to trade, health care, the environment, discrimination, worker pay, and general

Exhibit 17 Wal-Mart Shopper Profile

Income

	% of sales
<$50,000	54%
$50–$75000	20%
$75,000 +	26%

Education

	% of sales
Less than a High School Diploma	20%
High School Diploma (incl. some college)	57%
Bachelor Degree and above	23%

Leisure Pursuits—Typical Customer

	% of customers
Tend Their Garden	43%
Listen to Country Music	30%
Like Auto Racing	17%
Go Fishing	17%
Go Camping	19%

Leisure Pursuits—Affluent Customer

	% of customers
Listen to Talk Radio	34%
Go to a Theme Park	32%
Listen to Contemporary Music	25%
Go to the Museum	21%
Go to the Zoo	18%

Source: S. Kapinus, 2006, Rollback sushi and discount organics: What Wal-Mart's push to upscale consumers means to you, *ACNielsen Consumer Insight Magazine*, http://us.acnielsen.com/pubs/2006_q2_ci_rollback.shtml, Q2.

anticorporate sentiment. Many activists even contend that Wal-Mart is breaking antitrust laws by using its "power to micromanage the market, carefully coordinating the actions of thousands of firms from a position above the market."[124] Concerns about Wal-Mart's handling of hazardous waste have prompted local, state, and federal officials in the southwestern United States to initiate official actions. In addition to activists and union groups, U.S. political figures are lashing out against Wal-Mart. Democratic presidential candidates are "denouncing Wal-Mart for what they say are substandard wages and health care benefits."[125] Wal-Mart's political action committee's contributions to candidates (even to a former board member) are being returned as a sign of protest.[126] This sentiment is not only surfacing nationally, but locally as well. Governments in Inglewood, California, Cedar Mill, Oregon, and Vancouver, Canada, have rejected Wal-Mart expansion plans.[127]

Exhibit 18 Interviewee Perspectives on Wal-Mart, 2007

The environment steps are baby steps at the moment. We hope they will take substantive and [significant] action around the critical issues of the environment. Sadly, in the past, much of their efforts have been about publicity and positive spin, not about substance. We will wait to see what level of real commitment they will make around the environment.

— **ROBERT GREENWALD, PRODUCER/DIRECTOR,**

WAL-MART: THE HIGH COST OF LOW PRICE *(2007, E-MAIL INTERVIEW, MAY 22)*

[Wal-Mart has] a problem with blight. They leave behind in some cases blight by opening a new Supercenter and leaving their old stores empty. They need to have a plan for communities and not leave those huge buildings empty. In Hood River, the community didn't want Wal-Mart to open a Supercenter because they would leave the old store vacant, and Wal-Mart listened. They didn't open the Supercenter.

— **FRED G.,**

55, SUBURBAN WAL-MART SHOPPER *(2007, PERSONAL INTERVIEW, MAY 21)*

[B]eing the low-cost provider loses some of the service, the pleasure of going shopping. Target has wider aisles, and less product on the shelf. In contrast, Wal-Mart bombards you with tons of products.

— **OLIVER DAVIS,**

TARGET SHOPPER *(2007, PERSONAL INTERVIEW, MAY 21)*

There was a long time I didn't shop at Wal-Mart, and that had to do with the store's image of ruthlessness when it came to destroying the competition. To be honest, I feel a certain amount of shame at shopping there. As a mother, though, I'm afraid budget and convenience rule. In other words, I've sold out.

— **LILI N.,**

34, AFFLUENT SHOPPER *(2007, E-MAIL INTERVIEW, MAY 19)*

I shop at Wal-Mart for convenience-type items, but if the item I need is over $100 or is something that I need of quality, I will shop elsewhere. . . . I do not believe that Wal-Mart is capable of becoming related to quality items in the near future like Target and I do not believe that they will be successful at both discount and high quality.

— **ANDRE S.,**

26, BUDGET-CONSCIOUS SHOPPER *(2007, PERSONAL INTERVIEW, MAY 20)*

The [Wal-Mart] store itself is a little overwhelming—too many people, parking is usually tight, and the lines at the check-out are long. Also, there are so many [unfamiliar] employees working in a single Wal-Mart, that my shopping experience has no personal touch. I enjoy going to my neighborhood HEB [grocery store] because I see familiar faces— both at the check-out and in the aisles. If Wal-Mart would be willing to downsize a bit and have more of a neighborhood feel to it, I might consider stopping in more often.

— **ANGIE R.,**

29, AFFLUENT SHOPPER *(2007, E-MAIL INTERVIEW, MAY 20)*

Wal-Mart . . . lets you stay in their parking lot overnight. Friends stay at the "Wally-World" when we go windsurfing in Hood River. You can use their facilities and treat the parking lot like a campground. I like to shop there because of that corporate policy.

— **FRED G.,**

55, SUBURBAN WAL-MART SHOPPER *(2007, PERSONAL INTERVIEW, MAY 21)*

I shop at Wal-Mart very infrequently because I find it hard to find things, [and the store is] often not very clean. There doesn't seem to be well-laid-out aisles like Target; it is more of a jumbled maze. However, one plus is the live fish they have. Kids love to go by and see them! And they usually have better prices. If I am looking for a particular item, like a kids' outdoor toy/sandbox, that is what usually gets me there, because you can find it cheaper.

— **CRYSTAL B.,**

35, AFFLUENT SHOPPER *(2007, E-MAIL INTERVIEW, MAY 21)*

Wal-Mart neighborhood grocery is OK if you just need staples—it'll be cheap. I won't go into the 24-hour Supercenter down here. I think that was the store that had a stabbing over a Black Thursday laptop deal or something like that. SuperTarget is almost as bad during midday Sunday, but at least the store is cleaner and the meat looks a little better.

— **MICHAEL C.,**

35, WAL-MART SHOPPER *(2007, E-MAIL INTERVIEW, MAY 21)*

(continued)

Exhibit 18 Interviewee Perspectives on Wal-Mart, 2007 *(Continued)*

When I was an Operations Manager for a Fortune 500 company, we were having a yearly employee appreciation picnic . . . [so] my secretary and I hopped into a company van, shot down to Sam's Club, loaded up four shopping carts of hamburgers, hotdogs, beverages, and all the fixings, got to the checkout, pulled out my Visa, and then found out that Sam's club didn't accept Visa. After a few minutes of arguing with an unhelpful and unsympathetic manager, I left all four carts at the checkout and have never been back since.

—Brian S.,

former Sam's Club member (2007, discussion-board posting, May 22)

Wal-Mart has been such a negative experience that it would be hard for me to go back. I have been hesitant to go to a neighborhood Wal-Mart because of my poor shopping experiences around the country at different big-box Wal-Marts. The Wal-Mart I am closer to is a lower socioeconomic neighborhood, and I drive past it to go to Target because I perceive it as being safer and I feel that I am getting a higher quality product.

—Oliver Davis,

Target shopper (2007, personal interview, May 21)

[Wal-Mart] will continue to grow, and will make many changes in that time. Some are for the better and some are not. Unfortunately, sometimes plans that are not well [thought-out] are implemented and mandated, which only causes frustration/irritation. Other times workers are stuck in [their] ways and don't want to change.

—Anonymous

Wal-Mart manager (2007, e-mail interview, May 21)

[Wal-Mart needs better] price marking, more UPC scanners in the store. I see something and the price is ambiguous. They don't mark the prices. They can also make checkout faster. Why is it so slow? I don't go to Kmart anymore because a lot of times the UPC of something doesn't ring up at the cash register. It isn't in their system. If it is on the shelf, the UPC should be in the computer. Wal-Mart is also getting worse at this.

—Fred G.,

55, suburban Wal-Mart shopper (2007, personal interview, May 21)

[Wal-Mart] does offer a big variety [of benefits for associates], some much better than other companies and some not so good in my opinion. Some examples of good discounts are 10% discount on most items (excludes grocery, clearance, and a few other items—biggest complaint on this is that tax in most areas eats up most of the discount), vacation (depends on variety of factors, but generally 2 weeks for full time and 1 week for [part-time] 1st year, and increases thereafter), personnel days (day off with pay—earned up to a certain # each year (average 2)), sick days, holiday pay, etc. On the other side of the coin, [I] think much more needs to be done to provide better health care for its workers, and a goal should be done to improve this every year. Many co-workers I know have dropped [their] coverage or rely on state assistance programs. Wal-Mart also did away with some of its [benefits], such as Christmas bonuses, unless you are grandfathered in (must have been hired before the change was made).

—Anonymous

Wal-Mart manager (2007, e-mail interview, May 21)

We have an Associates Fund that everyone chips into in case someone is in critical need. For example, if a cashier were to, heaven forbid, have their house burn down, the fund would immediately come to help out by supplying a place to stay, warm clothes, and food, pretty much everything that the associate would need to get back on her feet, up to and including a replacement house, if that's what it takes. . . . A happy associate is more productive.

Sergio Jimenez,

Wal-Mart store co-manager (2007, personal interview, May 20)

Wal-Mart takes care of their people in dire situations. When my friend's wife died, they brought them groceries and really took care of them.

—Wendy S.,

46, friend of Wal-Mart associate (2007, personal interview, May 20)

One thing the company does . . . every year is [to] hold [grassroots] meetings for associates to come and vent about things they don't like, in the hope that something will change. Sadly, most associates (workers) feel that they are allowed to vent, but not without [retaliation] any more, or at best [their] input will not change anything. I think the company

(continued)

should not just write down the input they are being given, but act on it when possible. If they would do so it would boost morale, and more effort would be given, [causing] customer satisfaction to go up and sales to boost as well.

> —ANONYMOUS
> WAL-MART MANAGER (2007, E-MAIL INTERVIEW, MAY 21)

If I [were] to change Wal-Mart, I would reduce product on the shelves and change the lighting, and widen the aisles. [T]he bouncing ball for Wal-Mart gives it a cartoon-ish edge, whereas Target does an ad that goes coast to coast, with a heavy CGI aspect that it isn't cartoon-y. It has a big-city feel whereas Wal-Mart has a small-town middle America feel. I am partial to bigger cities. . . . Smaller towns that have limited options [make] me feel constrained, which is one of the reasons I like Target, which has hip trends, whereas Wal-Mart just has the bouncy smiley face. [T]he smiley face reduces [Wal-Mart's] seriousness. I would go to more subtle references to being the low-cost provider, and pitch one-stop shopping, but push the option to have your own personal brand, and reduce the number of SKUs on the walls so you don't feel overwhelmed by the experience there.

> —OLIVER DAVIS,
> TARGET SHOPPER (2007, PERSONAL INTERVIEW, MAY 21)

I would LOVE a coupon for a certain amount off any item the store. Sort of what Michael's has (40% off any item) or Bed Bath and Beyond has (20% off). I also find Target's returns the most convenient I've ever experienced: they can locate the item you purchased by sliding your credit card through the reader so you don't have to go searching for your receipt. I appreciate that kind of convenience.

> —LILI N.,
> 34, AFFLUENT SHOPPER (2007, E-MAIL INTERVIEW, MAY 19)

Legal. Class-action lawsuits against Wal-Mart have become commonplace. In *Savaglio v. Wal-Mart Stores, Inc.*, the "plaintiffs allege that they were not provided meal and rest breaks in accordance with California law, and seek monetary damages and injunctive relief."[128] A jury ruled in favor of those plaintiffs and awarded them a total of $198 million.[129] In *Dukes v. Wal-Mart Stores, Inc.*, currently pending on behalf of all present and past female employees in all of Wal-Mart's retail stores and warehouse clubs, Wal-Mart is alleged to have "engaged in a pattern and practice of discriminating against women in promotions, pay, training, and job assignments."[130] These lawsuits are providing ample fodder for Wal-Mart opponents to inflict ongoing reputation damage.

Global. The globalization trend that began in the 1990s persists. As trade barriers continue to come down around the world and as technology enables greater access to information, the world is becoming one mega-market of labor, capital, goods, and services. Bilateral and multilateral free trade agreements are continuing to shape markets.

Technology. The development of radio frequency identification (RFID) is expected to play a major part in the next evolution of supply chain management in the retail industry. This technology may better enable retailers to track inventory locations, store shelving status, packages en-route to and from suppliers, warehouses, shelves, and even shoplifting.[131] Recent developments in the technology include a movement toward "common standards and practices that could make RFID as ubiquitous as bar codes," and a push to lower the cost per RFID tag from the current 10-cent mark to the Wal-Mart target of 5-cents.[132] RFID chips are increasingly "able to hold much more information and fit into different shapes and sizes—woven inside clothing, slipped into a paper-thin tag or molded inside a key chain."[133]

Another technology development impacting the retail industry is the unabated growth of electronic commerce, and the increasing pervasiveness of broadband Internet access in most developed countries. As consumers at various socioeconomic levels come to rely more on the Web for information, entertainment, and shopping, retailers are discovering the need to use their online presence not just to spur online sales, but to drive traditional-format sales as well.

Demographics. Americans, like those in many developed nations, are getting older. The Census Bureau estimates the number of those aged 65 and up will rise from approximately 35 million in 2000 to 86.7 million by 2050. The age 65 and up cohort made up 12.4 percent of the total U.S. population in 2000; by 2050, it will make up 20.7 percent of a projected population of nearly 420 million.[134]

The country is also becoming more diverse.[135] Ethnic and gender diversity in the U.S. workforce is on the rise. In 1995, whites/non-Hispanics made up 76 percent of the workforce, but this is projected to decrease to 68 percent in 2020. According to the U.S. Department of Labor, women comprised 46 percent of the labor force in 2006.[136] The percentage of women over the age of 16 in the labor force has risen 23 percent in 44 years to 59 percent in 2004.[137]

The distance in America between the "haves" and the "have-nots" is growing. Increasing returns to education have created a bifurcation in income distribution.[138] The bottom quintile has seen its mean income increase 34.5 percent in real terms from 1967 to 2005, whereas the top income quintile had an increase in mean income of 80.8 percent over the same time period.[139] Average income growth for the bottom three quintiles was only 30.4 percent. The typical Wal-Mart customer is in the middle-income quintiles.

As Wal-Mart's competitive landscape continues to evolve, the company is taking its strategic cues from Sam Walton's words of wisdom: "Everything around you is always changing. To succeed, stay out in front of that change."[140]

Current Strategies

To manage its competitive environment, Wal-Mart is currently deploying a variety of strategies, most of which stem from its relentless core generic strategy of cost leadership, but some of which represent beyond-cost approaches. "Our everyday low price position is the basis for our business," wrote Rob Walton in Wal-Mart's 2006 annual report.[141] He added, "While this core principle is critical to our growth and business strategy, by itself it is not enough anymore."[142] According to Scott in this year's shareholder letter, Wal-Mart is confronting "a period of perhaps the most rapid and profound change in our Company's history. With our transformation plan, we are committed to staying 'Out in Front' of the changes around us."[143] The corporate plan, encompassing previous change initiatives as well as newer ones, rests on "five pillars": "broadening our appeal to our customers, making Wal-Mart an even better place to work, improving operations and efficiencies, driving global growth, and contributing to our communities.[144]

Strategies to Deal with External and Reputational Challenges. Wal-Mart is pursuing two key strategies that will help them overcome external issues affecting the company, including environmental and community-impact issues, among others. These strategies include sustainability efforts and localized charitable giving to help portray it as being a responsible corporate citizen and a good neighbor. Wal-Mart launched its global environmental sustainability initiative in 2004 and has since taken action toward several sustainability goals: sell 100 million compact fluorescent bulbs by 2008; reduce packaging by five percent by 2013; buy fish from certified fisheries; sell "more organic and environmentally friendly products"; and make company facilities and trucks more energy-efficient.[145] The Wal-Mart Foundation in 2006 gave "more than $415 million in cash and in-kind merchandise to 100,000 organizations worldwide," making it the "largest corporate cash contributor in America."[146] The Foundation "gave most of the money at the local level where [it] can have the greatest impact."[147]

Wal-Mart has beefed up pro-community, pro-sustainability, pro-health care information on its Web site, on its television ads, and in its annual report. The company recently launched *In Front with Wal-Mart*, a 30-minute television show airing on the Lifetime and USA networks that "gives [Wal-Mart] a chance to showcase [its] incredible associates and the variety of ways they give back to their communities, bettering the lives of America's working families" and "sheds light . . . on some of [Wal-Mart's] eco-friendly practices."[148] Wal-Mart created an interactive Web site on sustainability, dedicated a page of its 2007 annual report to sustainability, and will soon publish a separate Sustainability Report.[149]

In its public outreach, Wal-Mart also stresses its benefits to suppliers and communities, as well as its commitment to providing affordable health care and competitive wages for its associates.[150] These efforts tie into its supply-chain innovation and people strategies.

Supply-Chain Innovation and People Strategies

As previously mentioned, Wal-Mart creates value for customers with a highly efficient and innovative supply-chain management operation. This operation combines tough, low-cost procurement tactics, leading-edge information systems and "rocket-science" logistics.[151]

There's not much negotiation at all. The manufacturer walks into the room. I've been in these little cubicles, I've seen it happen. The buyer says, "Look, we want you to sell it to us for 5 percent on a dollar—at cost—lower this year than you did last year." They know every fact and figure that these manufacturers have. They know their books. They know their costs. They know their business practices—everything, you know? So what's a manufacturer left to do? They sit naked in front of Wal-Mart. You know, Wal-Mart calls the shots. "If you want to do business with us, if you want to stay in business, then you're going to do it our way." And it's all about driving down the cost of goods.

—**FORMER WAL-MART STORE MANAGER JON LEHMAN ON FRONTLINE IN 2004**[152]

All Wal-Mart suppliers must participate in Retail Link, a computerized system in which they "plan, execute, and analyze their businesses."[153] Along with electronic data interchange, suppliers receive purchase order information and supply invoices electronically, thereby lowering expenses and increasing productivity. Suppliers must meet Wal-Mart's strict lead-time and shipping requirements by using the technology and complying with operating procedures. The Wal-Mart logistics team uses an Internet-based Transportation Link system that complements a Backhaul Betty telephone voice-response system to help them move goods. In one year, Wal-Mart estimated nearly 1 million loads of general merchandise moved to Distribution Centers throughout the country.[154] Store-bound shipments travel by the company's 7,000 trucks, one of the largest fleets in the world.[155] The company relentlessly strives to develop its supply-chain process. For example, "[t]o ensure greater supply chain visibility, satellite-based tracking technology is being installed in the Company's entire fleet of over-the-road trailers. The data generated . . . increases productivity, reduces costs and enhances security."[156]

In the stores, Wal-Mart's legendary inventory management capability is driven by its advanced Texlon barcode system. In addition to tracking the sales price, inventory levels of each product, and a history of quantities sold, Texlon can record trends and predict future needs. Quantities sold can be traced to specific weeks, days, or even hours of each day. Seasonal projections can be documented, and shopping habits are noted. Information is sent daily at midnight to the warehouses, so depleted products are restocked the following night. Reliance on this kind of technology to drive the supply chain enables Wal-Mart's suppliers to use "pull production" instead of "push production." The barcode system will eventually be replaced by an RFID-based system, technology Wal-Mart is driving.

Wal-Mart's technological supply-chain sophistication is intended to provide "value for customers, associates, and shareholders."[157] The system depends on Wal-Mart's 1.8 million associates to provide the final link in the value chain to customers. Wal-Mart's people strategy involves "[g]iving our associates the tools and opportunities they need to be as productive as possible," which has enabled "workforce productivity gains in every quarter of the last

two years."[158] Associates who feel overworked may create a weak link in the value chain.

I would say that some customers are happy, but most are not. . . . [M]any workers feel they are being overworked due to mainly understaffing issues, which causes workers to treat the customers worse, then causing customers to become upset. Many customers have at one time been [Wal-Mart] associates and understand how things are handled at each store level and can relate. Personally, [I] believe that overall morale a few years ago was much higher with workers, and that attitude was passed along to the customers. Today many customers feel that [Wal-Mart] only wants them for [their] money, and does not care about them."

—**ANONYMOUS WAL-MART MANAGER (2007, E-MAIL INTERVIEW, MAY 21)**

Reassuring its "valued long-term associates" that the company "is listening to them," Wal-Mart "again increased [its] average full-time hourly wage in the United States."[159] The company is against unionization of its associates.

Wal-Mart's operational effectiveness goals of improving return on investment, comparable-store sales, and working capital productivity are setting the agenda for its business-segment strategies.[160]

Wal-Mart Stores Segment Strategies

The Wal-Mart Stores segment is in its second year of a three-year strategic plan to improve ROI, people development, and customer relevancy.[161] Customers have become the prime focus since January 2007, when Wal-Mart Stores elevated its new marketing and merchandising chiefs and completed its management reshuffle.

In 2006, Wal-Mart Stores rolled out a $4 generic prescription program, a clear opening-price-point approach. Merchandising has been characterized by the product-focused "opening price point" strategy, which relied on attractive low prices on entry-level items in every category to set the stage for higher-margin prices on more desirable items.[162] This single strategy has served to focus each of the two dozen departments at a typical Wal-Mart Supercenter (see Exhibit 19). Wal-Mart stores often offer retail space to other vendors that provide services, such as nail salons, hair salons, coffee shops, food and beverage vendors (e.g., McDonald's and Subway), full-service banks, and even employment agencies in some locations.

Recently, Wal-Mart Stores "realigned [its] merchandising . . . around five key power categories—entertainment, grocery, health and wellness, apparel, and home."[163] Global Procurement meanwhile is "establishing groups

Exhibit 19 List of Departments in Wal-Mart

Wal-Mart Departments	
Grocery	Pharmacy
Bakery	Health & Beauty
Produce	Vision Center
Deli	Jewelry
Frozen Foods	Lawn & Garden
Apparel	Portrait Studio
Housewares	Photo Lab
Entertainment	Hardware
Electronics	Furniture
Tire & Lube Express	Sporting Goods
Automotive	Toys & Games
School Supplies	Office Products & School Supplies

Source: http://www.walmart.com.

of technical experts—specialists that focus on the many important dynamics of a particular category purchase."[164]

The Wal-Mart Stores customer segmentation and merchandising strategies have been in flux over the past few years, with three different strategies in play to move Wal-Mart Stores toward a more customer-focused position.

The first customer-focused strategy—mimicking Target's upscale, fashion-forward appeal—flopped. "In working to broaden our appeal to our customers, we moved too quickly in the rollout of some of our fashion-forward apparel in the United States," according to Scott.[165] Wal-Mart Stores has at least partially retreated from this strategy.

The second customer-focused strategy—localizing selections based on store-neighborhood demographics—continues to drive various store changes, though it may be waning. In 2006, Wal-Mart "launched six different types of customized stores to attract different demographics, from inner-city residents, to affluent suburbanites, to rural shoppers."[166] With these stores, Wal-Mart attempted to target African-Americans, Hispanics, empty-nesters, suburbanites, rural residents, and the affluent. Wal-Mart expanded and empowered regional marketing teams, moving many executives away from headquarters into regions to better understand Wal-Mart's wide customer base.[167] These changes were inspired by localized merchandizing selection in Wal-Mart de Mexico stores aimed at different mixes of inventory for different income levels.[168] For example, the localization strategy expanded the mix of hip-hop, gospel, and R&B music in a store outside Chicago and led to plans for larger pharmacy sections and fewer children's clothes at a store geared toward empty-nesters.[169] In his March letter to shareholders, Scott wrote, "We continue to strive to make sure every Wal-Mart store is a 'Store of the Community'—one that reflects the individual needs of each neighborhood we serve."[170]

The third customer-focused strategy—appealing to the three universal types of low-price-seeking customers who currently shop at Wal-Mart—now guides merchandising and marketing decisions. According to Fleming and Quinn, the three types are "'brand aspirationals' (people with low incomes who are obsessed with names like Kitchen Aid), 'price-sensitive affluents' (wealthier shoppers who love deals), and 'value-price shoppers' (who like low prices and cannot afford much more)."[171] For these types, the Wal-Mart Stores segment is concentrating on developing unique, innovative products and providing distinguished brands (such as the recently added Dell desktop computers) to better appeal to its core customers as the low-price leader on well-known brands.[172]

This is a much better strategy for Wal-Mart than the store segmentation strategy path . . . they were going down before . . . because it aligns with their basic brand proposition (EDLP) and basic consumer rather than trying to attract a new consumer by adding high-end fashion and complicated assortments. For the same reason, it aligns better with Wal-Mart's supply chain strength. It's far easier to roll out a national brand in stores nationally than it is to ship different assortments to different stores within a region without disrupting the cost efficient supply chain that is Wal-Mart's core competitive advantage. I'm not sure what took them so long but it looks like Wal-Mart is back to a strategy that is sustainable and executable for them.

—FORRESTER RESEARCH SENIOR ANALYST LISA BRADNER[173]

Sam's Club Segment Strategies

Sam's Club, meanwhile, is focused on three areas: "reinvigorating the brand" by broadening products and services; improving inventory management and other performance measures; and optimizing the "in-club experience."[174] Sam's Club stores offer members products such as frozen and dry food goods in bulk, electronics, computer equipment, clothing, books, electronic entertainment, and general merchandise. Sam's Club recently restructured its management layers to give stores additional flexibility and to boost service.[175] Rumors have circulated that Sam's Club may spin off from Wal-Mart, in part to set its own direction in attracting and retaining members and associates, two key groups who are generally less loyal to Sam's Club than to its rival Costco.[176]

Wal-Mart International Segment Strategies

Wal-Mart International's strategy is to prioritize "where the greatest growth and greatest returns exist," what the segment calls "majoring in the majors."[177] The majors appear to include the Americas primarily, followed by the United Kingdom and Japan, as well as China and India over the long term.[178] Wal-Mart International is labeling this strategy "focused portfolio execution."[179] Its second strategy is global leverage, or "taking full advantage of our worldwide assets, including formats, information systems, purchasing organizations, category expertise, and shared best practices."[180] In the past year, it has concentrated on turning around Asda in the United Kingdom through "improved execution in all phases of customer service, differentiation with competitors, and development of new channels and formats."[181] To better compete against U.K. leader Tesco, second-largest Asda reportedly may be considering acquiring the third-largest U.K. retailer, the J. Sainsbury chain of grocery and convenience stores.[182] Wal-Mart's international stores are varied in their mix of products and services, and they stick to the motto of "offering working families the things they need at the prices they can afford."[183]

Just as the business segments are looking to focus on the right challenges for their short- and long-term success in the marketplace, the company must ensure it is applying its greatest resources against its greatest strategic challenges across the enterprise.

Strategic Challenges

The challenges Wal-Mart faces today are actually not much different from what they have been for the past several years. These following quotes come from an article in April 2003: "Even though it is the nation's largest apparel retailer with more than 12 percent of the market, Wal-Mart could be doing better in this category"; "It would like to be a fashion retailer and take on Target with good quality at a low price-point, but it hasn't convinced the American consumer it should be a destination for casual fashion"; "Wal-Mart is . . . looking abroad for future sales growth"; "Wal-Mart will need to struggle against the urge to centralize operations and eliminate decision making from the frontlines where managers have face-to-face contact with customers"; and "The only area in which Wal-Mart has not been able to pummel its competition is against Costco."[184] One of the company's challenges may be to stop proliferating nearly identical sets of challenges each year.

Like the stock price, the challenges appear to be stuck in a holding pattern.

One key new challenge is the sluggishness of same-store sales relative to Wal-Mart's competitors. According to *BusinessWeek,* Wal-Mart faces "the diciest conundrum in retailing today . . . can it seduce . . . middle-income shoppers into stepping up their purchases in a major way without alienating its low-income legions in the process?"[185]

Another growing challenge is the difficulty of expanding in the domestic market, whether because of community opposition or geographic saturation (see Exhibits 20 and 21).

These and other strategic challenges are weighing on the minds of Wal-Mart's shareholders, especially on the two with the most responsibility for the company's fate.

Questions Wal-Mart Leaders Must Address

CEO Lee Scott and Chairman Rob Walton are grappling with some vexing questions as they head into the 2007 Wal-Mart Annual Shareholders' Meeting:

- How can Wal-Mart Stores and Sam's Club increase same-store sales?
- How should the company capture share of middle- and upper-income wallets?
- Should Wal-Mart Stores fully retreat from fashion-forward merchandising and marketing? Will its neighborhood-store-localization strategy increase sales enough to offset the associated costs? What should it do to make its new three-types-of-customers segmentation strategy work?
- Should the company spin off Sam's Club? If not, what should it do to compete more effectively against Costco?
- Is Wal-Mart expanding the right kind of new stores at the right pace and in the right places? How and where should the company continue to grow internationally? Should Asda buy J. Sainsbury?
- What will it take to restore the company's reputation in America?
- Should Lee Scott change Wal-Mart's course? If so, how?
- Should Rob Walton replace Lee Scott? If so, when and with whom?

Exhibit 20 Spread of Wal-Mart Stores, 1970–1995

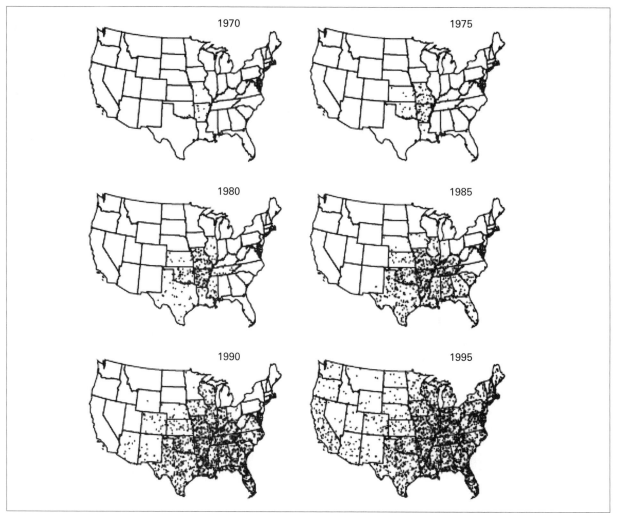

Source: E. Basker, 2004, Job creation or destruction? Labor-market effects of Wal-Mart expansion, University of Missouri, January, Figure 1, 28.

Exhibit 21 Number of Counties Having a Wal-Mart Store, 1963–2006

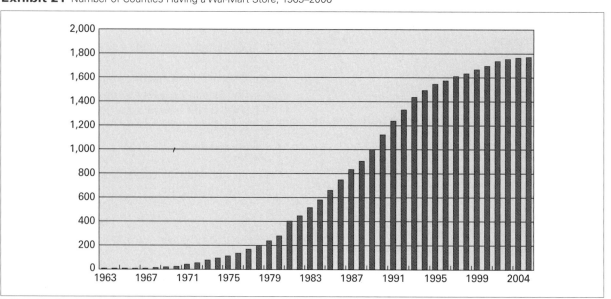

Source: 2005, The economic impact of Wal-Mart, Global Insight, Business Planning Solutions, Global Insight Advisory Services, November 2, Figure 4, 33.

1. A. Bianco, 2006, *The Bully of Bentonville: The High Cost of Wal-Mart's Everyday Low Prices*, New York: Doubleday Publishing, 1.
2. 2007, 7 demands for change, Against * The * Wal, http://www.againstthewal.net/7demands.html, May 18.
3. 2007, Notice of 2007 Annual Shareholders' Meeting, DEF 14A, Proxy Statement, Wal-Mart Stores, Inc., U.S. SEC, April 19, 52–68.
4. A. Bianco, 2006, *The Bully of Bentonville: The High Cost of Wal-Mart's Everyday Low Prices*, 267; 2007, Yahoo! Finance, http://finance.yahoo.com/charts#chart6:symbol=wmt;range=20000103,20070518;compare=cost+tgt;indicator=volume;charttype=line;crosshair=on;logscale=on;source=undefined, May 17.
5. 2007, Yahoo! Finance, http://finance.yahoo.com/charts#chart6:symbol=wmt;range=20000103,20070518;compare=cost+tgt;indicator=volume;charttype=line;crosshair=on;logscale=on;source=undefined, May 17.
6. A. Bianco, 2007, Wal-Mart's midlife crisis, *BusinessWeek*, April 30, 46–52.
7. 2007, Wal-Mart Data Sheet, http://walmartstores.com/Files/US_operations.pdf, February 8.
8. 2007, Wal-Mart Annual Report.
9. 2007, Wal-Mart Stores, Inc., Form 8-K, U.S. SEC, May 15; and 2007, Company Overview, Target.com, http://investors.target.com/phoenix.zhtml?c=65828&p=irol-homeProfile, May 25.
10. L. Michael Cacace & K. Tucksmith, 2007, *Fortune* 500 largest U.S. corporations, *Fortune*, April 30, F2.
11. Ibid.
12. A. Bianco, 2007, Wal-Mart's midlife crisis, 49–52.
13. A. Bianco, 2007, Wal-Mart's midlife crisis, 46.
14. 2004, Wal-Mart Tops *Fortune*'s List of America's Most Admired Companies, *Fortune*, http://www.timeinc.net/fortune/information/presscenter/fortune/press_releases/02232004AMAC.html, February 23.
15. 2007, America's Most Admired Companies 2007, *Fortune*, CNNMoney.com, http://money.cnn.com/magazines/fortune/mostadmired/2007/top20/, May 18.
16. W. Zellner, 2004, Sam Walton: King of the discounters, *BusinessWeek*, August 9.
17. Ibid.
18. Ibid.
19. A. A. Thompson & A. J. Strickland, *Strategic Management, Concepts & Cases*, 10th ed., New York: Irwin/McGraw-Hill.
20. 2007, The Wal-Mart Timeline, Wal-Mart Facts, http://www.walmartfacts.com/content/default.aspx?id=3, April 1; D. Longo, 1998, Wal-Mart hands CEO crown to David Glass, *Discount Store News*, February 15, 1988.
21. 2007, Wal-Mart Annual Report, 19; 2007, The Wal-Mart Timeline, Wal-Mart Facts, http://www.walmartfacts.com/content/default.aspx?id=3, April 1.
22. A. Bianco, 2007, Wal-Mart's midlife crisis, 46–54.
23. 2007, Data Sheet, Wal-Mart Stores, http://walmartstores.com/Files/US_operations.pdf, February 8, May 25; and 2007, International Data Sheet, Wal-Mart Stores, http://walmartstores.com/Files/Intl_operations.pdf, February 8, May 25.
24. 2007, Wal-Mart Annual Report, 1.
25. A. Biesada, 2007, Wal-Mart Company Overview, Hoovers Online, http://premium.hoovers.com, May.
26. Ibid.
27. P. Engardio, 2007, Beyond the green corporation, imagine a world in which eco-friendly and socially responsible practices actually help a company's bottom line. It's closer than you think, *BusinessWeek Online*, January 29.
28. 2007, Wal-Mart Annual Report, 18-19.
29. 2007, Wal-Mart Annual Report, 31.
30. 2007, Wal-Mart Annual Report , 28.
31. Ibid.
32. Ibid.
33. 2007, Wal-Mart Annual Report, 31.
34. Ibid.
35. 2007, Wal-Mart Annual Report, 28.
36. 2007, Wal-Mart Annual Report, 36.
37. 2007, Wal-Mart Annual Report, 32.
38. 2007, International Data Sheet, Wal-Mart Stores, http://walmartstores.com/Files/Intl_operations.pdf, February 8.
39. 2007, Wal-Mart Annual Report, 32.
40. 2007, Wal-Mart Annual Report, 51-52.
41. 2006, IGD looks at Wal-Mart's decision to pull out of Germany, http://www.igd.com/CIR, March 8.
42. 2007, Wal-Mart Annual Report, 32.
43. 2007, Informe Annual 2006, Wal-Mart de Mexico, http://library.corporate-ir.net/library/19/194/194702/items/231792/AR06.pdf, May 21; and 2007, *CIA World Fact Book*, Mexico, https://www.cia.gov/library/publications/the-world-factbook/geos/mx.html#Econ, May 21.
44. 2007, Wal-Mart Facts: The Wal-Mart Story, http://www.walmartfacts.com/content/default.aspx?id=1, April 1.
45. 2006, CNBC Interview with Carter Cast, http://www.hoovers.com/global/co/interviews/player.xhtml, November 7.
46. 2007, About Sam's Club, Samsclub.com, http://pressroom.samsclub.com/content/?id=3&atg=524, March 1.
47. K. Hundson, 2007, Wal-Mart Pushes Financial-Services Menu, *Wall Street Journal*, June 6, A3.
48. 2007, The Wal-Mart Timeline, Wal-Mart Facts, http://www.walmartfacts.com/content/default.aspx?id=3, April 1; D. Longo, 1998, Wal-Mart hands CEO crown to David Glass, *Discount Store News*, February 15.
49. 2007, The Wal-Mart Timeline, Wal-Mart Facts, http://www.walmartfacts.com/content/default.aspx?id=3, April 1.
50. 2007, Wal-Mart Annual Report, 14; 2007, Senior Officers, Wal-Mart Stores, http://walmartstores.com/GlobalWMStoresWeb/navigate.do?catg=540, May 6.
51. 2007, S. Robson Walton, Wal-Mart Stores, http://walmartstores.com/GlobalWMStoresWeb/navigate.do?catg=540&contId=15, May 6; 2005, Forbes: America's richest 400, MSN Money, http://moneycentral.msn.com/content/invest/forbes/P129955.asp, September 23.
52. A. Bianco, 2006, *The Bully of Bentonville: The High Cost of Wal-Mart's Everyday Low Prices*, 61.
53. 2007, S. Robson Walton, Wal-Mart Stores.
54. 2007, Wal-Mart Annual Report, 13.
55. A. Bianco, *The Bully of Bentonville: The High Cost of Wal-Mart's Everyday Low Prices*, 104.
56. Ibid.
57. A. Bianco, *The Bully of Bentonville: The High Cost of Wal-Mart's Everyday Low Prices*, 79.
58. Ibid.
59. A. Bianco, *The Bully of Bentonville: The High Cost of Wal-Mart's Everyday Low Prices*, 80.
60. A. Bianco, *The Bully of Bentonville: The High Cost of Wal-Mart's Everyday Low Prices*, 81.
61. 2007, H. Lee Scott, Jr., Senior Officers, WalMartStores.com, http://walmartstores.com/GlobalWMStoresWeb/navigate.do?catg=540&contId=17, May 25.
62. Ibid.
63. 2007, Michael T. Duke, Senior Officers, WalMartStores.com, http://walmartstores.com/GlobalWMStoresWeb/navigate.do?catg=540&contId=22, May 25.
64. Ibid.
65. 2007, John B. Menzer, Senior Officers, WalMartStores.com, http://walmartstores.com/GlobalWMStoresWeb/navigate.do?catg=540&contId=19, May 25.
66. Ibid.
67. Ibid.

68. 2007, Eduardo Castro-Wright, Senior Officers, WalMartStores.com, http://walmartstores.com/GlobalWMStoresWeb/navigate .do?catg=540&contId=41, May 25.

69. 2007, C. Douglas McMillon, Senior Officers, WalMartStores.com, http://walmartstores.com/GlobalWMStoresWeb/navigate .do?catg=540&contId=33, May 25.

70. 2007, John E. Fleming, Senior Officers, WalMartStores.com, http://walmartstores.com/GlobalWMStoresWeb/navigate .do?catg=540&contId=42, May 25.

71. 2007, Stephen Quinn, Senior Officers, WalMartStores.com, http://walmartstores.com/GlobalWMStoresWeb/navigate .do?catg=540&contId=6396, May 25.

72. 2007, Wal-Mart Board of Directors, Walmart.com, June 28.

73. M. Halkias, 2007, Questrom nominated to Wal-Mart board, *Dallas Morning News*, http://www.dallasnews.com/sharedcontent/dws/bus/ industries/retail/stories/042507dnbusquestrom.36b21ad.html, April 24.

74. Ibid.

75. S. Braun, 2007, At Wal-Mart, Clinton didn't upset any carts, *Los Angeles Times*, http://www.latimes.com/news/nationworld/nation/ la-na-hillary19may19,0,5168474.story?coll=la-home-center, May 19.

76. 2007, Morningstar, Wal-Mart Stores (WMT), http://quicktake .morningstar.com/StockNet/powerbrokers.aspx?Country=USA&S ymbol=WMT&stocktab=owner, May 6; 2007, Wal-Mart Stores Inc. (WMT), Major Holders, Yahoo! Finance, http://finance.yahoo.com/q/ mh?s=WMT, May 6.

77. 2007, Wal-Mart Stores Inc. (WMT), Major Holders, Yahoo! Finance, http://finance.yahoo.com/q/mh?s=WMT; May 6; and 2005, Forbes: America's richest 400, MSN Money, http://moneycentral.msn.com/ content/invest/forbes/P129955.asp, September 23; 2002, Proxy, Wal-Mart Stores, http://www.walmartstores.com/Files/proxy_2002/proxy_ pg05.htm; M. Weil and M. Barbaro, 2005, John T. Walton, 58; Heir to Wal-Mart Fortune, *The Washington Post*, http://www.washingtonpost .com/wp-dyn/content/article/2005/06/27/AR2005062701471.html, June 28; 2007, Associated Press, *Washington Post*, Helen R. Walton; Philanthropic wife of Wal-Mart chief, http://www.washingtonpost .com/wp-dyn/content/article/2007/04/20/AR2007042002060.html, April 21.

78. 2007, Wal-Mart Stores Inc. (WMT), Insider Roster, Yahoo! Finance, http://finance.yahoo.com/q/ir?s=WMT, May 6.

79. 2007, Wal-Mart Stores Inc. (WMT), Major Holders, Yahoo! Finance, http://finance.yahoo.com/q/mh?s=WMT, May 6.

80. 2007, Morningstar, Wal-Mart Stores (WMT), http://quicktake .morningstar.com/StockNet/powerbrokers.aspx?Country=USA&Symb ol=WMT&stocktab=owner, May 6.

81. 2007, Wal-Mart Annual Report, 64.

82. 2007, 2002 Wal-Mart Annual Reports.

83. Ibid.

84. 2007, Sam's Club vs. Costco: Battle of the brands, *BloggingStocks*, AOL Money & Finance, http://www.bloggingstocks.com/2007/04/12/ sams-club-vs-costco-battle-of-the-brands/, April 12.

85. T. Otte, 2007, Spinoff in Bentonville revisited, Value Investing, MotleyFool.com, http://www.fool.com/investing/value/2007/05/07/ spinoff-in-bentonville-revisited.aspx, May 7.

86. M. Wagner, 2003, Where's Wal-Mart: Wal-Mart's web revenue hardly registers on its ledger, *Internet Retailer*, http://www.internetretailer .com/internet/marketing-conference/70624-wheres-wal-mart.html, April.

87. D. Pinto, 2005, Mass market retailers, http://www .massmarketretailers.com/articles/Every_winner.html, May 16.

88. Ibid.

89. Ibid.

90. A. Bianco, 2007, Wal-Mart's, midlife crisis, 48.

91. D. Pinto, Mass market retailers.

92. M. Holz-Clause & M. Geisler, 2006, Grocery Industry, Grocery Retailing Profile, AgMRC, http://www.agmrc.org/agmrc/markets/ Food/groceryindustry.htm, September.

93. 2007, Wal-Mart F1Q08 (Qtr End 4/30/07) Earnings Call Transcript, SeekingAlpha.com, http://retail.seekingalpha.com/article/35633, May 15.

94. Ibid.

95. 2007, Wal-Mart 1st Quarter 2008 Earnings Release, May 10.

96. Ibid.

97. 2007, Wal-Mart April Sales News Release, May 10.

98. R. Dodes & G. McWilliams, 2007, Fashion faux pas hurts Wal-Mart, *Wall Street Journal*, May 21, A8.

99. G. McWilliams, 2007, Wal-Mart net rises as weakness persists, *Wall Street Journal*, May 16, C6.

100. J. Covert, 2007, Retail-sales slide fuels concern: Decline of 2.3% in April among worst on record; even Wal-Mart slipped, *Wall Street Journal*, May 11, A3.

101. 2007, Target Corporation, Form 8-K, U.S. SEC, May 23; 2007, Company Overview, Target.com, http://investors.target.com/phoenix .zhtml?c=65828&p=irol-homeProfile, May 25.

102. Ibid.

103. 2006, Target Annual Report, 2.

104. Ibid.

105. 2007, Company Profile, Costco Wholesale Investor Relations, http:// phx.corporate-ir.net/phoenix.zhtml?c=83830&p=irol-homeprofile, May 5.

106. 2006, Costco Annual Report, 9.

107. 2006, 2002 Costco Annual Report.

108. 2007, The Kroger Co., Form 10-K, U.S. SEC, April 4.

109. Ibid.

110. Ibid.

111. 2007, Carrefour profile, Hoovers, Lexis/Nexis Academic, May 8.

112. 2007, Tesco profile, Hoovers, Lexis/Nexis Academic, May 8.

113. Ibid.

114. 2007, Global Procurement, WalMartStores.com, http://walmartstores .com/GlobalWMStoresWeb/navigate.do?catg=337, May 26.

115. A. Bianco & W. Zellner, 2003, Is Wal-Mart too powerful? *BusinessWeek*, http://www.businessweek.com/magazine/ content/03_40/b3852001_mz001.htm, October 6.

116. Ibid.

117. Ibid.

118. 2007, Wal-Mart Facts, http://www.walmartfacts.com/ FactSheets/3142007_Corporate_Facts.pdf, March 14.

119. S. Kapinus, 2006, Rollback sushi and discount organics, *ACNielsen Consumer Insight*, http://us.acnielsen.com/pubs/2006_q2_ci_rollback .shtml, Q2.

120. Ibid.

121. Ibid.

122. Ibid.

123. Barney Gimbel, 2006, Attack of the Wal-Martyrs, http://money.cnn .com/magazines/fortune/fortune_archive/2006/12/11/8395445/index .htm, November 28.

124. B. C. Lynn, 2006, It's time to enforce antitrust law and break up Wal-Mart, *Harper's Magazine*, July.

125. A. Nagourney & M. Barbaro, 2006, Eye on election, Democrats run as Wal-Mart foe, *New York Times*, August 17.

126. Ibid.

127. 2006, Beaverton council rejects Cedar Mill Wal-Mart plan, *Beaverton Valley Times*, August 8; 2005, No Wal-Mart for Vancouver, *CBC News*, June 29; 2004, Inglewood Wal-Mart proposal defeated, http:// www.laane.org/pressroom/stories/walmart/040407CityNewsService .html, April 6.

128. 2007, Wal-Mart Annual Report, 56.

129. Ibid.

130. Ibid.

131. C. Harrison, 2003, Commitment from Wal-Mart may boost tracking technology, *Dallas Morning News*, July 15.

132. Ibid.

133. Ibid.

134. 2004, U.S. Census Bureau, Interim Projections Consistent with 2000 Census, http://www.census.gov/population/www/projections/ popproj.html, March.

135. Ibid.

136. 2007, U.S. Department of Labor, Women's Bureau: Statistics & Data, http://www.dol.gov/wb/stats/main.htm, May 14.

137. E. L. Chao & K. P. Utgoff, Women in the labor force: A databook, U.S. Bureau of Labor Statistics, May 2005, 1.

138. G. Becker & K. Murphy, 2007, The upside of income inequality, *The American*, May/June, 24–28.

139. 2007, U.S. Census Bureau, Historical Income Inequality Tables, http://www.census.gov/hhes/www/income/histinc/ineqtoc.html, May 21.

140. 2007, Wal-Mart "Out in Front," Fact Sheets, WalMartFacts.com, http://www.walmartfacts.com/FactSheets/4112007_Wal-Mart__Out_in_Front_.pdf, April 11.

141. R. Walton, 2006, Wal-Mart Annual Report, inside cover.

142. Ibid.

143. H. L. Scott, 2007, Wal-Mart Annual Report, 10.

144. 2007, Wal-Mart "Out in Front."

145. 2007 Wal-Mart Annual Report, 5, 12; and Wal-Mart Stores Overview, http://walmartstores.com/GlobalWMStoresWeb/navigate.do?catg=345, May 25.

146. 2007 Wal-Mart Annual Report, 8, 12.

147. Ibid.

148. 2007, In Front with Wal-Mart, Wal-Mart Stores, Inc., http://www.infrontwithwalmart.com/about.aspx, May 20.

149. 2007, Wal-Mart Annual Report, 5.

150. 2007, Wal-Mart Annual Report, 11.

151. 2003, Knowledge@Wharton, The Wal-Mart Empire: A Simple Formula and Unstoppable Growth, Research at Penn, http://www.upenn.edu/researchatpenn/article.php?631&bus, April 9.

152. 2004, FRONTLINE co-production with Hedrick Smith Productions, Inc., WGBH Educational Foundation, http://www.pbs.org/wgbh/pages/frontline/shows/walmart/etc/script.html.

153. 2007, Wal-Mart supplier requirements and processes, http://walmartstores.com/GlobalWMStoresWeb/navigate.do?catg=331, May 19.

154. Ibid.

155. 2007, Wal-Mart Sustainability, http://walmartstores.com/microsite/walmart_sustainability.html, May 19.

156. 2007, Wal-Mart Annual Report, 16.

157. Ibid.

158. 2007, Wal-Mart Annual Report, 11.

159. Ibid.

160. 2007, Wal-Mart Annual Report, 21.

161. 2007, Wal-Mart Annual Report, 18.

162. S. Hornblower, 2004, Always low prices: Is Wal-Mart good for America? *Frontline*, http://www.pbs.org/wgbh/pages/frontline/shows/walmart/secrets/pricing.html, November 23.

163. 2007, Wal-Mart Annual Report, 18.

164. 2007, Wal-Mart Annual Report, 17.

165. H. L. Scott, 2007, Wal-Mart Annual Report, 11.

166. B. Helm & D. Kiley, 2006, Wal-Mart leaves draft out in the cold, *BusinessWeek*, http://www.businessweek.com/bwdaily/dnflash/content/dec2006/db20061207_540888.htm?campaign_id=rss_innovate, December 7.

167. A. Zimmerman, 2006, To boost sales, Wal-Mart drops one-size-fits-all approach, *Wall Street Journal*, http://online.wsj.com/article/SB115758956826955863.html?mod=hps_us_pageone, September 7.

168. Ibid.

169. Ibid.

170. H. L. Scott, 2007, Wal-Mart Annual Report, 11.

171. M. Barbaro, 2007, It's not only about price at Wal-Mart, *New York Times*, http://www.nytimes.com/2007/03/02/business/02walmart.html?ex=1330491600&en=5a72ddc69030ce62&ei=5088&partner=rssnyt&emc=rss&pagewanted=print, March 2

172. 2007 Wal-Mart Annual Report, 17; P. Svensson, 2007, Dell to sell computers at Wal-Mart, Associated Press, Yahoo! Finance, http://biz.yahoo.com/ap/070524/dell_wal_mart.html?.v=11, May 24.

173. T. Ryan, 2007, From RetailWire: Wal-Mart classifies customers for growth, *Supply Chain Digest*, http://www.scdigest.com/assets/newsViews/07-03-27-2.php?cid=977, March 27.

174. 2007, Wal-Mart Annual Report, 19.

175. 2007, Wal-Mart cutting managers at Sam's Club, Reuters, http://www.reuters.com/article/businessNews/idUSN2628417520070426?feedType=RSS, April 26.

176. T. Otte, 2007, Spinoff in Bentonville revisited, value investing, MotleyFool.com, http://www.fool.com/investing/value/2007/05/07/spinoff-in-bentonville-revisited.aspx, May 7.

177. 2007, Wal-Mart Annual Report, 19.

178. Ibid.

179. Ibid.

180. Ibid.

181. 2007, Wal-Mart F1Q08 (Qtr End 4/30/07) Earnings call transcript, retail stocks, *SeekingAlpha*, http://retail.seekingalpha.com/article/35633, May 15.

182. 2007, Wal-Mart evaluating options in possible bid for the UK's J. Sainsbury chain, *Supply Chain Digest*, http://www.scdigest.com/assets/newsViews/07-03-27-3.php?cid=978, March 27.

183. 2007, Wal-Mart Retail Divisions, http://www.walmartfacts.com/articles/2502.aspx, April 4.

184. 2003, The Wal-Mart Empire: A simple formula and unstoppable growth, *Knowledge@Wharton*, http://www.upenn.edu/researchatpenn/article.php?631&bus, April 9.

185. A. Bianco, 2007, Wal-Mart's midlife crisis, 56.

Case 24

WD-40 Company: The Squeak, Smell, and Dirt Business (A)

Gerry Yemen, Marcia Conner, James G. Clawson

University of Virginia

In the fall of 1999 Garry Ridge, the newly appointed CEO of WD-40 Company, was plowing through his homework. In addition to running the company, Ridge had enrolled in the first class at the University of San Diego's two-year graduate program in executive leadership. The class of 27 included students from Cymer, Kyocera America, Amor Ministries, and the U.S. Marine Corps, working nights and weekends on their master's degrees in leadership. Ridge enrolled in the program in hopes it would help him usher in change to the highly successful but now somewhat static WD-40 Company. He wanted to find ways of rejuvenating the company and stimulating its employees to look beyond the firm's relatively narrow focus of the last 43 years. The nature of WD-40 Company's success in capturing the market had created its own limited growth opportunities.

The Blue and Yellow Can

Norm Larsen and three investors founded Rocket Chemical Company in 1952 to supply rust inhibitors to various customers including aircraft and missile manufacturers. The one-room operation had a three-person staff. Larsen, the lead chemist at the firm, was searching under contract for a formula that could be used to prevent corrosion on airplanes and Atlas missile skins and remove moisture from electrical circuits. After forty tries, Larsen came up with a water displacement (WD) formulation that seemed to work, so he called it WD-40. Although the product seemed to meet the needs of the immediate contracts, over time, engineers at the firm discovered that the creation was equally useful for other difficulties they encountered. They began sneaking it out of the plant to unstick locks and fix sticky doors at home. By 1958, the company had started producing the material in small blue and yellow aerosol cans and marketing it to retail outlets. Sales representatives sold the product directly out of their cars to sporting goods and hardware stores. Rocket Chemical Company grew to include seven employees with sales of about 45 cases a day.

By the mid-1960s, the firm had stopped production of its other products (rust resistors and removers for metal parts and tools) and focused on its most popular product, WD-40. In 1968, sales had reached $1 million, and the firm changed its name to WD-40 Incorporated. The business went public in 1973 (see financial data in Exhibit 1) and was so successful in its market niche that it had no competitors.

Worldwide alternative uses for WD-40 had grown far beyond what Larsen and his cofounders imagined. Letters poured into the company explaining the various and ingenious uses for WD-40. The Denver fire department reported using the product to extract a nude burglar from a café vent. A physician extracted a child's arm from an elevator door. And a python snake was removed from the undercarriage of a city bus in Asia. A veterinarian used WD-40 to remove Cookie, the parakeet, from a sticky mousetrap tray in Vista, California. And although the American Medical Association did not approve WD-40 as a cure, it did have an article that recommended the use of the product for a toe stuck in the bathtub faucet or a finger stuck in a soda bottle (see Exhibit 2 for a list of 50 most novel uses). Dave Barry, a humor columnist at *The Miami Herald*, once advanced the theory that Roman civilization collapsed because it didn't have any WD-40! By 1999, 83 percent of households in the United States owned at least one can. Ridge noted that Americans were more likely to use WD-40 than dental floss. Yet the company's success created an interesting business problem. Because the market was saturated, sales growth was difficult to obtain and the stock price became stagnant.

© Don Hammond/Design Pics/Corbis

Exhibit 1 Selected Financial Data

Income Statement

(dollar amounts in millions except per share amounts)	Aug 99	Aug 98	Aug 97
Revenue	$146.3	$144.4	$137.9
Cost of Goods Sold	63.7	62.2	58.4
Gross Profit	82.6	82.2	79.5
Gross Profit Margin	56.5%	56.9%	57.7%
SG&A Expense	46.4	45.9	42.6
Depreciation & Amortization	2.4	2.2	2.2
Operating Income	33.8	34.1	34.7
Operating Margin	23.1%	23.6%	25.2%
Nonoperating Income	0.2	0.1	(1.2)
Nonoperating Expenses	0.0	0.0	0.0
Income Before Taxes	34.0	34.2	33.5
Income Taxes	12.1	12.4	12.0
Net Income After Taxes	21.9	21.8	21.5
Continuing Operations	22.1	21.9	21.4
Discontinued Operations	0.0	0.0	0.0
Total Operations	22.1	21.9	21.4
Total Net Income	22.1	21.9	21.4
Net Profit Margin	15.1%	15.2%	15.5%
Diluted EPS from Continuing Operations ($)	$ 1.41	$ 1.40	$ 1.37
Diluted EPS from Discontinued Operations ($)	0.00	0.00	0.00
Diluted EPS from Total Operations ($)	1.41	1.40	1.37
Diluted EPS from Total Net Income ($)	1.41	1.40	1.37
Dividends per Share	1.28	1.28	1.25

Balance Sheet	Aug 99	Aug 98	Aug 97
Cash	$ 9.7	$ 8.6	$ 10.9
Net Receivables	28.6	27.0	22.6
Inventories	8.0	3.7	5.5
Other Current Assets	5.8	10.4	3.4
Total Current Assets	52.1	49.8	42.4
Net Fixed Assets	3.9	3.6	4.2
Other Noncurrent Assets	35.9	17.6	18.9
Total Assets	92.0	70.9	65.4
Accounts Payable	11.3	6.9	6.7
Short-Term Debt	2.5	0.8	0.8
Other Current Liabilities	6.6	6.2	3.9
Total Current Liabilities	20.4	13.9	11.4
Long-Term Debt	14.1	0.9	1.7
Other Noncurrent Liabilities	1.4	1.1	1.0
Total Liabilities	35.9	15.9	14.1
Preferred Stock Equity	0.0	0.0	0.0
Common Stock Equity	56.2	55.0	51.3
Total Equity	56.2	55.0	51.3
Shares Outstanding (mil.)	15.6	15.6	15.6

(continued)

Exhibit 1 Selected Financial Data (*Continued*)

Cash Flow Statement	Aug 99	Aug 98	Aug 97
Net Operating Cash Flow	$25.8	$23.7	$ 23.3
Net Investing Cash Flow	(18.6)	(6.7)	(1.1)
Net Financing Cash Flow	(6.0)	(19.4)	(18.2)
Net Change in Cash	1.2	(2.3)	4.1
Depreciation & Amortization	2.4	2.2	2.2
Capital Expenditures	(24.6)	(1.3)	(1.5)
Cash Dividends Paid	(20.0)	(20.0)	(19.4)

Source: 2002, Hoover's Company Information, http://hoovers.com, August 2.

Exhibit 2 Fifty Most Novel Uses for WD-40

Spray on trees to prevent beavers from chewing on them

Removes tar, sap, and splattered bugs from vehicles

Cleans surfaces of adhesives, label, tape, and stickers

Removes dirt and grime in kitchens and bathrooms

Extracts nude burglar from a café vent

Lubricates dirty or stuck locks and latches

Cleans and protects tools

Extracts a child's arm from an elevator door

Cleans and lubricates bicycle chains

Extracts a python snake from city bus undercarriage

Attracts fish when sprayed on bait

Cures dog mange

Prevents squirrels from climbing into birdhouses when sprayed on metal pole

Sprayed on hips and knees to keep joints limber

Removes toe stuck in bathtub faucet

Removes finger stuck in soda bottle

Silences noisy bedsprings

Removes crayon from clothes dryer (make sure to unplug dryer first)

Lubricates hydraulic rams on slide out of 5th wheel

Shines leaves of artificial houseplants

Keeps snow from sticking to shovel

Cleans ashtrays

Cleans old muffin tins

Cleans doggie doo from tennis shoes

Removes gunk when replacing old faucets

Removes berry stains from patio furniture

Removes gum stuck to concrete

Cleans heavy dirt from shovels

Cleans dog hair from sliding door rollers

Removes lipstick from fabric

Cleans peanut butter from shoestrings

Shines wheelbarrow tires

Spray on trash can lids to keep messes from sticking

Unkinks gold chains

Helps reclaim rusted plumbing snake

Lubricates table leafs

Removes makeup from carpet

Lubricates pulley on sump pump

Frees stuck Lego blocks

Lubricates mouse trap machinery

Shines mailboxes

Lubricates cigarette case hinges

Stops squeaks on Tonka trucks

Cleans rust off Santa's sleigh runners

Cleans pigeon droppings from cars

Removes dog slobber from dash and seats in vehicle

Cleans magazines for an AK-47

Cleans bed pans

Eases removal of solidified spitballs

Spray WD-40 on plant holders to stop squeaks during wind

In an attempt to fight the stagnation, WD-40 Company acquired Reckitt and Colman's "3-in-One" oil business during 1995. This purchase provided the firm with an existing network of distribution in 17 countries that included several new markets for WD-40.[1] In 1996, WD-40 Company launched a new product, T.A.L. 5, a synthetic lubricant.[2] Management developed a new corporate logo to reflect the integration of the two new products. In 1999, WD-40 bought the Lava brand of heavy-duty hand cleaners from the Block Drug Company. This one-product business and brand consisted of two sizes of soap bar and one size of liquid soap. Management decided to add the Lava Towel, a waterless hand cleaner, and two new sizes of Liquid Lava. Once more, the reason for buying the brand was to increase access to consumers, the brand had high awareness and a common user base to the WD-40 brand, yet it had gaps in its distribution that the WD-40 Company business model could close, expanding distribution channels.

After adding new products, the organization continued to focus on international growth. WD-40 Company opened new manufacturing and sales operations in San Diego, California (near corporate headquarters), and London, and sales offices in Australia, Canada, France, Germany, Italy, Malaysia, and Spain.

Investors bought shares because the company was known to provide high dividends. For almost two decades, WD-40 Company's low cash needs meant it paid out close to 100 percent of earnings to stockholders.[3] Many investors were most comfortable with the company because it delivered a reliable yield that substantially exceeded market averages. Stock was traded at $20.75 in 1998 and paid annual dividends of $1.28 (see Exhibit 3 for average stock prices). Investors were satisfied with yields of 5.2 percent, more than three times that of the S&P 500.

One year after WD-40 Company turned 45 years old in 1999, there were 177 employees around the world: 106 in the U.S. parent corporation, of which six were based in the Malaysian sales office; 10 in the Canadian subsidiary; 52 in the United Kingdom subsidiary, of which nine were in Germany, eight in France, and six in Spain; six in the Australian subsidiary; and three in the company's manufacturing subsidiary (see Exhibit 4 for worldwide sales information). The majority of WD-40 Company employees were engaged in sales and/or marketing activities. With the consolidation of companies in the retail industry, increased portions of WD-40s sales were made to fewer, but larger, clients with greater purchasing power. Despite the firm's new product strategy and steady stock prices, sales remained sluggish, and Garry Ridge, previously traveling salesperson, was called on to lead the company to new growth.

Garry Ridge: The Maniacal Shark

Ridge had first encountered WD-40 Company in Australia as the managing director of a WD-40 licensee. In his role, he developed good relationships with WD-40 Company

Exhibit 3 WD-40 Company Stock Price, 1991–1999

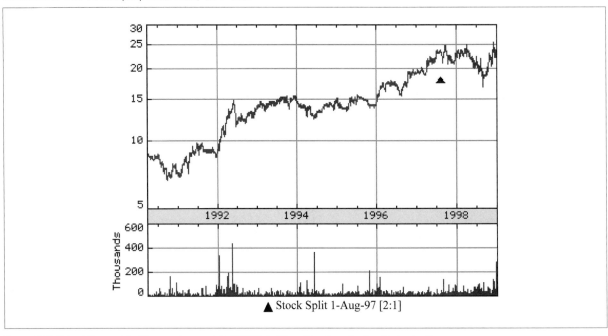

Source: 2000, Yahoo! Finance, http://finance.yahoo.com/q?s=WDFC&d=c&t=my&l=on&z=m&q=l, on September 3.

Exhibit 4 Sales for WD-40's Three Trading Blocs, 1997–1999

	(dollar amounts in millions)					
	August 1999		**August 1998**		**August 1997**	
Americas	$ 96.90	66%	$ 98.6	68%	$ 93.4	68%
Europe	37.3	26	34.9	24	32.2	23
Asia/Pacific	12.1	8	10.9	8	12.3	9
Total	$146.30	100%	$144.40	100%	$137.90	100%

Source: 1999, Form 10-K, WD-40 Company, Securities and Exchange Commission, http://web.lexisnexis.com/universe/document?_m=89e5d23a9b3e6cdc 8565be08ff036524&_d, August 31.

management, so that when WD-40 Company terminated the license and planned to open a wholly owned subsidiary in Australia to explore the Asian market, Ridge was invited to join the new organization. He recalled:

I loved the brand. My dad was an engineer, and he worked for one company for 50 years, and I went to him for his blessing. I told him, "They've made me an offer to work for WD-40 Company." And he said, "You can't get along without that product, son." I thought, "Well, this is a great opportunity to work for an American company, and start an Australian operation from scratch."

After five years of building the Australian and Asian markets, Ridge began to get bored. He called the vice president of the company and said, "I could have the best job in the world here. I get to play golf and socialize, and have developed a marketing distribution model in Asia. But I'm bored." The VP revealed that WD-40 Company wanted to turn up the volume on their international operations, and he asked Ridge to move to San Diego and

take over as vice president of International Operations. Ridge accepted. A little more than three years later the president of the company retired, Ridge threw his hat into the candidacy ring, and got the job.

Ridge felt he was chosen because he knew both the old WD-40 Company and had a desire to create a bridge to a "new" company. He recalled, "We had to change everything from the backroom to the boardroom, and I think I knew enough about what the brand was not to do anything stupid to hurt it. But at the same time, I knew we had to go somewhere else and was willing to run that race."

Now What?

As the new CEO, Ridge was concerned about the flat growth that WD-40 had encountered worldwide. He saw around him people with long tenure in the company who were devoted to the WD-40 brand, yet they seemed to lack a sense of direction or energy. Ridge wondered what he could do to revitalize the company.

Notes

1. 1999, Form 10-K, WD-40 Company, Securities and Exchange Commission, Washington, DC 20549, http://web.lexis-nexis.com/ universe/document?_m=89e5d23a9b3e6cdc8565be08ff036524&_d August 31. (Accessed on August 5, 2002).

2. Shortly after the Lava purchase in 1999, the company decided to discontinue marketing the T.A.L. 5 lubricant. The product did not produce the revenues management and investors expected.

3. J. Palmer, 2001, The Cult of WD-40: Customers love the product; should investors love the stock? *Dow Jones Capital Market Report,* November 30, http://ptg.djnr.com/ccroot/asp/publib/story_clean_spy .asp?articles=CM0133400172DJFIN.

Case Title	Manu-facturing	Service	Consumer Goods	Food/Retail	High Tech-nology	Transportation/Communication	International Perspective	Social/Ethical Issues	Industry Perspective
3M Cultivating Core Comp.	●		●		●		●		
A-1 Lanes	●						●		●
AMD vs Intel	●				●				●
Boeing	●						●		●
Carrefour in Asia				●			●		
Dell	●		●		●				●
Ford	●		●						●
GE Welch & Immelt	●	●			●			●	
Home Depot		●		●			●		
China's Home Improvement				●			●		
Huawei	●				●		●		
ING Direct		●		●					
JetBlue		●				●	●		●
Lufthansa		●				●	●		
Microsoft		●			●				
Nestlé	●		●	●				●	
PenAgain	●		●						
PSA Peugeot Citroën	●		●				●		
Sun Microsystems		●			●		●		
Teleflex Canada	●				●				
Tyco International	●							●	
Vodafone		●			●	●	●		
Wal-Mart Stores				●			●	●	
WD-40	●		●				●		

Case Title	Chapter 1	2	3	4	5	6	7	8	9	10	11	12	13
3M Cultivating Core Comp.			●				●						●
A-1 Lanes								●					●
AMD vs Intel					●								●
Boeing				●	●			●	●				
Carrefour in Asia		●						●					
Dell		●		●		●							
Ford				●	●							●	
GE Welch & Immelt							●					●	●
Home Depot				●	●							●	
China's Home Improvement	●				●			●					
Huawei					●			●					
ING Direct				●								●	●
JetBlue		●		●	●								
Lufthansa								●	●		●		
Microsoft					●	●							
Nestlé	●							●			●		●
PenAgain									●				●
PSA Peugeot Citroën			●						●				
Sun Microsystems	●			●				●					
Teleflex Canada						●						●	●
Tyco International						●				●	●	●	
Vodafone	●		●				●	●					
Wal-Mart Stores	●	●	●	●									
WD-40			●	●				●					●

Name Index

A

Abbott, A., 239n
Abe, N., 30n
Acedo, F. J., 28n, 30n
Adams, M., 270n
Adams, R. B., 304n
Adjaoud, F., 363n
Adler, P. S., 364n, 365n
Adner, R., 29n
Afuah, A., 67n, 120n
Agami, A. M., 205n
Agarwal, R., 120n, 388n
Aggarwal, R. K., 176n
Agins, T., 268n
Agle, B. R., 30n, 176n
Aguilera, R., 301n, 303n, 305n
Ahlstrom, D., 65n, 66n, 94n, 241n, 243n, 269n, 335n
Ahmadjian, C. L., 305n
Ahuja, G., 29n, 93n, 206n, 364n, 387n
Aiello, R. J., 208n
Ajinkya, B., 303n
Alcacer, J., 94n, 238n
Alexander, M., 176n
Allaire, Paul, 81
Allen, I. E., 389n
Allison, K., 149n
Almeida, P., 241n, 270n
Almond, P., 239n
Alred, B. B., 239n
Alvarez, S. A., 364n, 386n, 387n, 388n
Amason, A. C., 30n, 176n, 388n
Ambos, B., 238n, 242n, 334n, 388n
Ambrose, M. L., 364n
Amburgey, T. L., 334n
Amit, R., 30n, 93n, 94n, 303n, 389n
Ammann, M., 175n
Anand, J., 204n, 206n, 208n, 268n, 271n, 304n, 365n
Andal-Ancion, A., 65n
Andaleeb, S., 363n
Andersen, P. H., 337n

Andersen, T. J., 334n, 335n
Anderson, N., 64n
Anderson, P., 93n, 206n
Anderson, R. C., 179n, 301n, 302n, 303n
Andrews, T. G., 243n
Anglada, L. M., 269n
Anhalt, K. N., 337n
Anthony, S. D., 365n
Antia, K. D., 241n
Antoine, A., 242n
Aoyama, Y., 239n
Apesteguia, J., 270n
Argenti, P. A., 30n, 336n
Argyres, N., 66n
Arikan, A. M., 364n
Arikan, A. T., 335n
Arino, A., 268n, 269n
Armstrong, Lance, 261
Armstrong, R. W., 151n
Arnaud, A., 365n
Arndt, M., 93n, 120n, 302n, 364n
Arnott, R., 305n
Arora, A., 240n
Arregle, J.-L., 241n, 270n, 389n
Arrunada, B., 94n
Artz, K. W., 67n
Asaba, S., 29n, 67n, 149n
Asakawa K., 29n, 238n, 242n
Ashton, J. E., 387n
Aston, A., 93n
Audia, P. G., 93n
Audretsch, D. B., 386n
Autio, E., 237n, 387n, 388n
Avolio, B. J., 363n

B

Babakus, E., 240n
Babüroglu, O. N., 28n, 119n
Baden-Fuller, C., 337n
Bailey, M. N., 240n
Bailey, W., 243n
Baiman, S., 336n
Baker, G. P., 302n
Baker, L. T., 150n
Baljko, J., 151n

Ballinger, G. A., 363n
Bamford, J., 241n
Banerji, K., 239n
Bannert, V., 206n
Bansal, P., 30n, 150n
Bao, Y., 362n
Baraldi, E., 362n
Barbaro, M., 363n
Barber, B. N., 207n
Barger, P. B., 150n
Barkema, H., 65n, 206n, 334n, 362n, 387n
Barker, R. G., 239n
Barner-Rasmussen, W., 239n, 243n
Barnes, S. F., 335n
Barnett, M. L., 30n, 151n
Barney, J. B., 27n, 28n, 30n, 92n, 94n, 149n, 151n, 176n, 207n, 335n, 336n, 364n, 386n, 388n
Baron, R. A., 387n
Bartol, K.M. 362n
Barr, P. S., 243n
Barrett, A., 150n
Barringer, B. R., 119n, 270n, 386n
Barroso, C., 28n, 30n
Barsade, S., 363n
Barthelemy, J., 270n
Bartiromo, M., 119n
Bartlett, C. A., 66n, 239n, 240n, 336n, 365n
Bassi, L., 362n
Bates, K. A., 93n
Bates, T. W., 28n, 179n, 302n
Battelle, J., 387n
Baum, J. A. C., 334n
Baum, J. R., 30n, 336n
Baumol, W. J., 386n, 389n
Baur, A., 150n
Bayazit, O., 151n
Baysinger, B. D., 303n
Bayus, B. L., 92n, 271n
Beal, B. B., 121n
Beal, B. D., 64n, 66n, 67n, 239n

Beamish, P. W., 239n, 242n, 243n, 270n
Bebchuk, L. A., 304n
Becerra, M., 363n
Beck, K. A., 30n, 336n
Beck, T. E., 150n
Becker, B. E., 364n, 365n
Becker, W. M., 92n
Beechler, S., 92n, 240n
Beer, M., 362n
Begley, T. M., 92n, 238n, 336n, 387n
Belderbos, R., 28n, 120n, 241n
Bell, G. G., 271n, 337n
Bellman, E., 207n, 208n
Belson, K., 363n
Benner, M. J., 94n, 150n
Bercovitz, J., 150n
Berfield, S., 270n
Bergen, M., 28n, 92n, 176n
Bergh, D. D., 149n, 176n, 177n, 208n, 304n, 386n
Berle, A., 303n
Berman, D. K., 205n
Berman, S., 93n, 268n
Bernardo, A. E., 178n, 270n
Berner, R., 363n
Berns, S., 241n
Berry, H., 238n
Berry, L. L., 150n
Berry, T. K., 302n
Berthon, P., 93n, 149n
Best, A., 207n
Bethel, J. E., 208n
Bettis, J. C., 304n
Bettis, R. A., 28n
Bhatnagar, P., 121n
Bhojraj, S., 303n
Bianco, A., 150n, 363n
Biemans, W. G., 271n
Bierly, P. E., III, 268n
Bierman, L., 65n, 121n, 151n, 207n, 239n, 242n, 364n, 387n, 389n
Biggs, T. W., 304n
Bigley, G. A., 92n, 243n, 335n

Biller, S., 151n
Birkinshaw, J., 336n, 365n
Bish, E. K., 151n
Bitar, J., 93n
Biziak, J. M., 304n, 179n, 302n
Bjorkman, I., 239n, 241n, 243n
Black, S. S., 268n
Blake, Frank, 288–289
Blasberg, J., 93n
Blavatnik, Len, 263
Bliss, R., 178n
Blomqvist, K., 268n
Blumentritt, T. P., 243n
Blyler, M., 30n
Boateng, A., 208n
Bogner, W. C., 150n
Bolton, L. E., 150n
Bonardi, J.-P., 64n, 65n
Bonazzi, L., 303n
Boneparth, Peter, 339
Bonifazi, C., 94n
Boone, A. L., 304n
Borener, S., 362n
Borgatti, S. P., 337n
Borrelli, L., 388n
Borus, A., 302n
Borza, A., 241n, 270n, 389n
Bosma, N., 387n
Bossidy, L., 362n
Bou, J. C., 120n
Boulding, W., 121n
Bouquet, C., 241n
Bourdeau, B. L., 269n
Bowen, H. P., 242n
Bower, J. L., 177n, 336n
Bowman, E. H., 29n
Boyacigiller, N. A., 92n
Boyce, Gregory H., 74
Boyd, B. K., 178n, 302n, 305n
Boyd, D. P., 92n, 238n, 336n, 387n
Boyd, G., 363n
Boyd, N. G., 30n
Boyer, K. K., 121n
Boynton, A., 388n
Braam, G. J. M., 335n
Bradbury, H., 268n
Bradely, Todd, 97
Bradley, F., 242n
Brady, D., 30n, 302n, 363n
Bragger, D. 364n
Bragger, J. D., 364n
Brandenburger, A., 67n
Brannen, L., 304n
Brannen, N. Y., 240n
Brant, J., 363n
Brauer, M., 207n, 208n, 209n
Breen, B., 151n
Bremner, B., 305n
Brennan, R., 362n
Brennen, David, 190
Brett, J., 31n
Brews, P. J., 334n
Bricker, R., 301n
Briggs, T. W., 303n

Brin, W. D., 177n
Bris, A., 301n
Britt, R., 178n
Bromiley, P., 176n, 302n
Brousseau, K. R., 240n
Brouthers, K. D., 66n, 240n, 241n
Brouthers, L. E., 66n, 240n, 241n
Brown, C. J., 302n
Brown, J. A., 301n
Brown, J. S., 388n
Brown, S. W., 151n
Brown, T. E., 365n
Browne, John, 13
Bruce, A., 151n
Brush, C. G., 29n, 92n
Brush, T. H., 176n, 302n
Bruton, G. D., 28n, 65n, 66n, 208n, 209n, 243n, 387n
Bryan-Low, C., 178n, 205n, 206n, 269n
Bryce, D. J., 28n, 178n
Bucerius, M., 205n, 206n
Buchholtz, A. K., 301n, 302n, 335n, 363n
Buchholz, T. G., 362n
Buckley, C., 241n
Buckley, George, 69–70
Buckley, P. J., 65n, 238n
Buffet, Warren, 197
Bunderson, J., 362n, 364n
Burgelman, R. A., 362n, 364n, 365n, 386n, 388n
Burke, L. M., 363n
Burns, T., 334n
Burritt, C., 150n
Burton, R. M., 336n
Busenitz, L. W., 93n, 206n, 208n, 209n, 269n, 362n, 386n
Bush, J., 271n
Bushman, R., 302n
Butler, J. E., 30n, 365n
Buysse, K., 64n
Byrne, J. A., 30n, 31n, 150n
Byrnes, N., 93n, 336n
Byron, E., 176n

C

Cabous, C., 301n
Cabrera, R. Valle, 302n
Cala, A., 305n
Calantone, R., 64n, 93n, 121n
Caldwell, C., 30n, 305n, 365n
Callaway, S. K., 29n
Camerer, C. F., 206n
Cameron, A.-F., 271n
Cameron, D., 150n
Camp, S. M., 28n, 65n, 93n, 149n, 206n, 269n, 271n, 385n, 386n, 387n, 388n, 389n
Campbell, A., 176n, 336n
Canina, L., 66n
Cannella, A. A., Jr., 119n, 149n, 178n, 208n, 242n, 301n, 304n, 336n, 363n
Cantwell, J., 238n

Capaldo, A., 29n, 337n, 388n
Capron, L., 176n, 178n, 179n, 204n, 205n, 206n
Carbone, L. P., 150n
Carbonell, P., 121n
Cardinal, L. B., 176n, 178n, 206n, 385n
Cardon, M. S., 386n
Carey, D. C., 301n
Carini, G., 66n
Carleton, J. R., 206n
Carlson, L. R., 303n
Carney, M., 301n, 302n, 305n
Carpenter, M. A., 66n, 178n, 239n, 303n, 304n, 305n, 363n
Carr, N. C., 337n
Carrera, A., 387n
Carroll, G. R., 121n
Carroll, J., 268n
Carson, S. J., 93n
Carter, A., 120n
Carter, B., 270n
Carter, M. E., 304n
Carter, R., 177n
Cartwright, P. A., 65n
Case, B. M., 149n
Cashen, L. H., 120n, 176n, 178n, 302n
Castanias, R., 362n
Castillo, J., 178n
Castrogiovanni, G. J., 208n
Cattani, K., 65n
Cavusgil, S. T., 66n, 240n, 336n
Cawood, S., 364n
Celuch, K., 29n
Certo, T., 302n
Chacar, A., 242n
Chaharbaghi, K., 92n, 335n
Chakrabarti, A., 177n, 179n
Chakraborty, A., 305n
Chakravarthy, B., 29n, 92n
Challagalla, G., 177n
Champion, Charles, 339
Champlin, D. P., 177n
Chan, C. M., 243n
Chance, D., 304n
Chandar, N., 301n
Chandler, A., 309, 311, 313, 315, 335n, 336n
Chandra, A., 177n
Chandy, R. K., 207n
Chang, S.-J., 28n, 177n, 205n, 242n, 243n, 303n
Chan-Olmsted, S. M., 242n
Charan, R., 301n
Charavarthy, B., 364n
Chari, M. D. R., 238n
Charitou, C. D., 387n
Charkham, J. P., 305n
Charns, M. P., 271n
Chatman, J. A., 65n
Chatterjee, S., 176n, 177n, 178n, 207n, 269n, 304n
Chattopadhyay, P., 64n, 205n

Chen, C. C., 269n, 302n
Chen, H., 242n
Chen, J.-S., 238n
Chen, M.-J., 119n, 120n, 121n
Chen, Q., 302n
Chen, S.-F. S., 205n
Chen, W., 65n, 334n
Cheng, H. F., 240n
Cheng, J. L. C., 120n, 238n
Chesbrough, H. W., 29n, 388n
Chhaochharia, V., 302n
Chidley, J., 303n
Child, J., 149n, 239n, 241n, 242n
Chiu, W. K. C., 238n
Chiu, Y.-H., 242n
Chmielewski, D. A., 92n, 121n
Cho, H.-J., 365n
Choi, C. J., 305n
Chompusri, N., 243n
Chowdhry, B., 178n, 270n
Chrisman, J. L., 386n
Christen, M., 121n
Christensen, C. M., 29n, 92n, 365n, 388n
Christensen, Clayton, 73
Christensen, P. R., 337n
Christophe, S. E., 242n, 336n
Christy, J., 176n
Chui, Y., 240n
Chung, L., 242n
Chung, W., 66n, 121n, 238n, 240n
Chvyrkov, O., 387n
Cimilluca, D., 205n
Clark, D. 27n, 177n
Clark, I., 239n
Clark, K. D., 29n, 64n, 93n, 386n
Clegg, J., 65n
Clegg, L. J., 238n
Cleverly, Bruce, 153–154
Clissold, T., 205n
Clohessy, G. R., 386n
Coakley, L., 178n
Cochran, P. L., 30n, 365n
Coff, D. C., 149n, 268n
Coff, R. W., 30n, 93n, 149n, 177n, 178n, 205n, 206n, 268n, 302n, 304n
Coffee, J. C., 178n
Cohen, S. K.,. 151n, 387n
Cohen, S. S., 363n
Colella, 364n
Coleman, J. J., Jr., 337n
Coles, J., 303n, 363n
Coles, Michael, 140
Collella, A., 362n
Colling, T., 239n
Collins, C. J., 29n, 31n, 64n, 93n, 386n
Collins, J. D., 121n, 365n
Collins, Jim, 275–276, 348
Collis, D., 176n, 177n, 335n
Colquitt, J. A., 364n, 388n
Colvin, G., 94n, 205n, 364n

Combs, J. G., 93n, 178n, 270n, 363n, 364n
Comes-Casseres, B., 337n
Comino, S., 269n
Conant, Doug, 342, 343
Conger, J. A., 301n, 303n, 362n
Conkey, C., 302n
Conlin, M., 362n
Connell, J., 271n
Connelly, B., 65n, 94n, 238n, 239n, 242n, 335n, 337n
Connor, J. M., 270n
Contractor, F. J., 243n
Cook, F. X., Jr., 387n
Cool, K., 150n, 205n, 207n
Coombes, S., 386n
Coombs, J. E., 304n, 386n
Coombs, J. G., 268n
Cooper, A. C., 178n, 271n, 388n
Cooper, Fredrick, 124
Cooper, S. M., 362n
Cordeiro, J. J., 178n
Cornett, M. M., 303n
Costa, A. C., 365n
Costa, L. A., 28n
Cotterill, R. W., 205n
Cottrell, T., 120n
Cousins, P. D., 271n
Covin, J. G., 92n, 208n, 269n, 334n, 365n, 388n
Cox, Christopher, 282
Cox, R., 176n
Craft, S. H., 150n
Cramer, R. D., 65n
Crane, A., 67n
Cresswell, J., 304n
Criado, J. R., 271n
Crittenden, V., 64n
Crittenden, W. F., 301n, 365n
Crockett, R. O., 66n, 150n
Cronin, M. A., 388n
Cronink, J. J., Jr., 269n
Cropanzano, R., 364n
Crosby, L. B., 121n
Crosby, P. B., 121n
Croson, D. C., 302n
Cross, A. R., 238n
Crossan, M. M., 362n, 386n
Crossland, C., 242n, 301n, 305n
Croyle, R., 178n
Cui, A. S., 66n, 240n
Cullinan, G., 205n, 207n, 208n
Cummings, J. L., 30n
Cunningham, S. W., 65n
Currie, A., 176n
Czipura, C., 269n

D

d'Aspremont, C., 270n
D'aunno, T., 243n
D'Aveni, R. A., 28n, 29n
D'Innocenzio, A., 150n
D'Ovidio, R., 67n
Da Silva, N., 94n
Dabic, M., 66n, 240n

Dacin, M. T., 64n, 66n, 94n, 241n, 243n, 269n, 270n, 389n
Dacin, T., 334n
Daellenbach, U., 363n
Dahan, E., 65n
Dahlsten, F., 64n
Daily, C. M., 208n, 301n, 302n, 303n, 363n
Daizadeh, I., 335n
Dalsace, F., 94n
Dalton, C. M., 303n
Dalton, D. R., 208n, 301n, 302n, 303n, 363n
Dalziel, T., 302n, 303n
Daneshkhu, S., 205n
Danneels, E., 92n, 388n
Darby, M. R., 268n
Darr, A., 177n
Das, S., 94n
Das, T. K., 241n, 268n, 269n, 271n, 337n
Datta, D. K., 206n, 362n, 363n
Davenport, T. H., 28n, 94n
David, P., 238n, 303n
David, R. J., 151n
David, S., 119n
Davidson, W. N., 302n, 303n
Davidsson, P., 28n, 30n, 364n, 365n, 386n
Davies, H., 242n
Davis, C., 386n
Davis, G. E., 301n
Davis, J. H., 30n, 271n, 363n
Dawson, C., 337n
Day, G. S., 119n
Day, J. D., 335n
de Brentani, U., 271n
De Carolis, D. M., 30n, 66n, 93n
de Cock, C., 177n
de la Fuente Sabate, J. M., 66n
de la Torre, C., 303n
de Luque, M. S., 242n
de Miguel, A., 303n
De Rond, M., 92n
Debaise, C., 65n
DeCastro, J., 93n
Decker, C., 177n
Deeds, D. L., 94n, 269n, 388n, 389n
Deephouse, D. L., 66n, 93n
Delaney, K. J., 67n
Delios, A., 177n, 205n, 241n, 242n, 304n
Dell, Michael, 97, 98, 312
Delmar, F., 28n
Delmas, M., 64n
Delong, G., 176n
DeMarie, S. M., 28n, 64n
DeMiguel, 303n
Deming, W. E., 121n
Demise, N., 305n
Deng, F. J., 365n
Deng, P., 241n
DeNisi, A. S., 29n, 94n, 239n, 337n, 362n, 364n

DePass, D., 92n
Desai, A., 302n
Deshpande, R., 239n
DeSouze, K. C., 94n
Dess, G. G., 28n, 149n, 150n, 151n, 207n, 365n
DeTienne, D. R., 385n
Deutsch, C. H., 120n
Deutsch, Y., 92n, 304n
Devaraj, S., 238n
Devers, C. E., 28n, 121n, 269n, 304n
DeVito, R., 121n
Dewett, T., 119n
DeYoung, R., 209n
Dhanaraj, C., 270n, 388n
Dhar, R., 149n
Di Gregorio, D., 387n
Di Gregorio, R. M., 207n
Dial, J., 208n, 209n, 362n
Diamantopoulos, A., 178n
Dickson, P. H., 270n
Diedrich, F. J., 335n
Dienhart, J. W., 305n
Dinc, I. S., 305n
Dino, R. H., 363n
Dipboye, R. L., 65n
DiPietro, R. B., 270n
Disney, Roy, 114
Disney, Walt, 114
Dobbs, R., 204n, 207n
Dobni, C. B., 149n, 334n
Dobrev, S. D., 121n
Doh, J. P., 30n, 65n, 242n
Dokko, G., 270n
Dollinger, M., 207n
Domoto, H., 337n
Donaldson, G., 30n
Donaldson, L., 334n, 363n
Done, K., 305n
Dong, L., 270n
Donoher, W. J., 335n
Dorfman, P. W., 242n, 364n
Dou, W., 240n
Dougherty, D., 388n
Douglas, A. V., 302n
Douglas, T. J., 30n, 119n, 149n
Doukas, J. A., 205n, 242n
Douma, S., 305n
Dous, M., 28n
Dow, S., 301n
Dowell, G., 150n
Dowling, G. R., 121n
Down, J., 93n, 268n
Doz, Y. L., 29n, 31n, 337n, 362n, 365n, 387n
Dranikoff, L., 208n
Driscoll, C., 365n
Driver, M. J., 240n
Droge, C., 64n, 93n
Droge, D., 121n
Drucker, P. F., 315, 336n, 370, 386n
Drummond, A., 64n
Drzik, J., 149n

Du, J., 242n
Duarte, C. L., 271n
Dubin, J. A., 93n
Duffy, D., 386n
Dufwenberg, M., 270n
Duhaime, I. M., 29n
Dukes, A., 205n
Duncan, C., 207n
Duncan, W. J., 30n
Dunfee, T. W., 301n
Dunning, J., 238n
Dussauge, P., 176n, 270n, 337n
Duta, S., 66n
Dutra, A., 150n
Dutta, D. K., 386n
Dutta, S., 92n, 93n 176n, 364n
Dutton, J., 30n
Duysters, G., 206n, 268n, 270n
Dvir, T., 363n
Dyer, J. H., 28n, 151n, 241n, 268n, 270n, 271n, 337n, 364n
Dysters, G., 207n, 242n

E

Easterby-Smith, M., 239n
Easterwood, J., 208n
Eastvold, R., 149n, 268n
Ebenkamp, B., 240n
Echamabadi, R., 388n
Echambadi, R., 120n, 337n
Edelman, L. F., 268n
Eden L., 240n
Eden, D., 363n
Eden, L. E., 64n, 121n, 238n, 241n, 242n, 270n, 337n
Edmondson, G., 121n, 335n, 365n
Edwards, J., 305n
Edwards, P., 150n
Edwards, T., 239n
Eesley, C., 31n, 64n
Egelhoff, W. G., 336n
Ehrenfeld, J. R., 31n
Einhorn, B., 150n, 239n
Eisenbeliss, S. A., 362n
Eisenberg, M. A., 301n
Eisenhardt, K. M., 29n, 64n, 92n, 175n, 177n, 206n, 269n, 336n
Eisenmann, T. R., 336n
Eisenstat, R., 177n, 362n
Eisner, Michael, 265
Elango, B., 239n
Elango, D., 241n
Elbanna, S., 149n
Eldomiaty, T. I., 305n
Elenkov, D. S., 94n, 178n, 205n, 242n, 302n, 365n, 385n
Ellis, P. D., 150n
Ellison, Larry, 185
Elms, H., 66n, 149n
Emden, Z., 66n
Engardio, P., 93n, 119n
Engel, E., 302n, 305n

Ennis, N., 65n
Enrich, D., 207n, 208n
Enright, M. J., 238n
Entin, E. E., 335n
Enz, C. A., 66n
Eppinger, S. D., 335n
Epstein, M. J., 31n
Ernst, D., 241n
Eroglu, S., 270n
Espejo, C. A.-D., 302n
Ethiraj, S. K., 93n, 151n, 334n, 335n, 364n, 388n
Ethirau, S. K., 29n
Ettenson, R., 179n
Evans, B., 335n
Evans, G., 151n
Evans, P., 31n, 388n

F

Fahey, L., 64n, 66n
Fairbank, J. F., 205n
Faleye, O., 305n
Fama, E. F., 179n, 301n, 302n
Fan, J. P. H., 205n
Fang, E., 205n, 207n
Fang, Y., 242n
Faraci, R., 208n
Faria, A., 151n
Farrell, D., 387n
Farzad, R., 242n
Fassbender, H., 387n
Fealey, T., 177n
Fee, C. E., 205n
Feldman, L. F., 29n
Felin, T., 94n
Felo, A., 305n
Felps, W., 92n
Fenn, P., 151n
Fennell, T., 65n
Ferguson, G., 29n
Fern, M. J., 176n, 206n, 385n
Fernandez, N., 120n
Fernández-Aráoz, C., 301n, 303n, 363n
Ferner, A., 239n
Ferrary, M., 271n
Ferreira, D., 304n
Ferreira, R. D. S., 270n
Ferrier, W. J., 28n, 119n, 120n, 121n, 206n, 365n
Fich, E. M., 303n
Fiegenbaum, A., 269n
Field, L. C., 304n
Fiet, J. O., 386n
Filatotchev, I., 65n, 238n, 240n, 269n, 304n
Filer, L., 119n
Finegold, D. L., 301n, 303n
Fink, G., 28n
Fink, L. S., 93n
Fink, R. C., 268n
Finkelstein, S., 31n, 93n, 178n, 302n, 304n, 363n
Fiol, C. M., 93n, 364n

Fiorina, Carly, 340
Firstbrook, C., 205n
Fischer, B., 388n
Fischer, E., 93n
Fischer, H. M., 304n
Fischer, S., 305n
Fisher, A., 364n
Fisk, N., 150n
Fiss, P. C., 305n
Fitch, 240n
Fladmoe-Lindquist, K., 28n, 239n, 241n
Flanagan, D. J., 209n
Fleming, L., 387n
Fleming, T., 65n
Flood, P., 362n
Florida, Richard, 70, 92n
Florin, J., 364n
Folta, T. B., 268n, 270n, 365n
Fong, M., 65n
Foote, N., 177n
Forbes, D. P., 92n, 120n, 121n, 151n, 303n
Ford, Henry, 19
Forest, S. A., 177n
Forsyth, M., 208n
Forza, C., 66n
Fosfuri, A., 120n, 240n
Foss, N. J., 92n
Foust, D., 150n
Fowler, C. L., 206n
Fowler, G. A., 305n
Fowler, S. W., 150n, 239n, 388n
Fox, M., 305n
Fram, E. H., 303n
Frank, C. B., 242n
Franklin, Martin, 167
Franko, L. G., 386n
Frary, J., 150n
Fraser, J. A., 387n
Frazier, G., 177n
Fredrickson, J. W., 66n, 239n, 301n, 334n
Freeman, R. E., 29n, 30n, 65n, 119n, 176n, 177n, 334n, 364n, 365n
Freeman, V. M., 92n
Fridman, Mikhail, 263
Fried, J. M., 304n
Friedman, T., 28n
Frooman, J., 30n
Frost, T. S., 387n
Fubini, D., G., 241n
Fuentelsaz, L., 176n, 269n
Furner, J., 268n

G

Gaba, V., 242n
Gadiesh, O., 31n
Galan, J. L., 28n, 30n
Gallagher, S., 268n
Gal-Or, E., 205n
Galpin, T., 335n

Galunic, D. C., 177n, 364n
Galvin, T., 119n
Gammelgaard, J., 206n
Ganapathi, J., 305n
Ganesan, S., 149n
Ganguli, N., 151n
Gani, L., 336n
Gannon, M. J., 121n, 242n
Garcia, T., 362n
Garcia-Canal, E., 271n
Garcia-Pont, C., 66n
Gardner, T. M., 30n, 121n
Garg, V. K., 64n
Garrett, K. A., 239n
Garrette, B., 270n, 337n
Gartner, W. B., 28n
Garud, R., 389n
Gary, M. S., 176n
Gates, Bill, 59
Gatignon, H., 206n
Gavetti, G., 93n, 149n
Gavusgil, S. T., 66n
Gebauer, H., 120n
Gedajlovic, E., 302n, 305n
Geiger, S. W., 120n, 176n, 178n, 302n
Geletkanycz, M. A., 178n, 268n, 302n
George, G., 149n, 237n, 387n
Geppert, M., 239n
Gerard-Varet, L.-A., 270n
Gerchak, Y., 205n
Gerety, M., 304n
Geringer, J. M., 239n
Gerwin, D., 121n, 268n
Ghemawat, P., 151n, 238n, 239n, 270n, 334n
Ghosh, A., 302n, 304n
Ghoshal, S., 29n, 66n, 239n, 240n, 302n, 336n, 365n
Ghosn, Carlos, 255
Giarrantana, M. S., 120n
Gibbert, M., 64n, 94n
Gibson, C. B., 65n, 239n
Gibson, R., 207n, 336n
Gietzmann, M., 303n
Gilbert, B. A., 386n
Gilbert, C., 29n
Gilbert, J. L., 31n
Gilley, K. M., 304n
Gilson, R., 178n
Gimeno, J., 64n, 66n, 67n, 119n, 120n, 121n, 177n, 239n, 303n
Girod, S., 240n
Gittel, J. H., 365n
Givray, H. S., 362n
Glaister, K. W., 270n
Glazer, Malcolm, 181
Glazer, R., 148n
Gleason, K. C., 303n
Glick, W. H., 64n, 205n, 363n
Globerman, S., 243n
Gloor, P.A., 362n

Glunk, U., 362n
Glynn, M. A., 243n
Gnyawali, D. R., 120n
Goerzen, A., 270n, 337n
Goes, J., 28n, 119n
Gold, D. L. 305n
Golden, B. R., 270n, 301n, 363n
Golden, Michael F., 164
Goldenberg, J., 387n
Goldman, E. F., 362n
Goldstein, D., 304n
Goleman, D., 362n
Goll, I., 64n, 362n
Gomes, L., 304n
Gomez, J., 176n, 269n
Gomez-Mejia, L. R., 301n, 302n, 304n, 388n
Gong, David, 142
Gong, Y., 241n
Gonzalez, I. S., 66n
Goold, M., 176n, 177n, 335n, 336n
Goteman, I., 151n
Gottfredson, M., 29n
Gottschalg, O., 92n
Gove, S., 362n
Govindarajan, V., 28n, 365n
Goyal, V. K., 205n
Grandry A. A., 150n
Grant, D., 30n, 268n
Grant, J., 303n
Grant, R. M., 28n, 64n, 241n
Gratton, L., 29n, 92n
Gray, S. R., 178n
Greckhamer, T., 66n, 149n
Greco, J., 336n
Greenaway, D., 269n
Greene, J., 66n
Greene, P. G., 92n
Greenwood, R., 386n
Griesser, D., 362n
Griffin, D. A., 177n
Griffith, D. A., 66n, 239n, 240n
Grimm, C. M., 64n, 119n, 120n, 121n
Grinstein, Gerald, 49
Grinstein, Y., 302n
Grohmann, B., 270n
Grosse, R., 243n
Grossman, W., 178n, 301n, 303n, 386n
Grove, A. S., 362n
Grundei, J., 29n, 121n
Grunwald, R., 270n
Guay, T. R., 65n
Gudridge, K., 177n
Guerrera, F., 177n, 206n, 303n
Gulati, R., 149n, 151n, 177n, 269n, 388n
Gunkel, J. D., 365n
Gupta, A. K., 28n, 151n, 237n, 238n, 365n
Gupta, D., 205n
Guth, R. A., 67n

Guthrie, J. P., 363n
Gutierrez, Carlos, 280
Gutierrez, I., 269n, 302n
Gutierrez, M., 240n
Gutierrez-Cillan, J., 119n
Gwynne, P., 208n

H

Haahti, A., 240n
Haas, M. R., 92n
Habbershon, T. G., 302n
Hafeez, K., 94n
Hafsi, T., 93n
Hagedoorn, J., 207n, 242n, 270n
Hagel, J., III, 388n
Haiken, M., 269n
Hair, J. F., Jr., 150n
Haleblian, J., 178n, 204n, 207n
Hall, B. J., 302n
Hall, D. T., 387n
Hall, K., 238n
Hall, R. H., 336n
Hambrick, D. C., 30n, 31n, 93n,
    119n, 121n, 207n, 241n,
    242n, 301n, 302n, 304n,
    305n, 334n, 362n, 363n
Hamburg, C., 205n
Hamel, G., 29n, 94n, 337n, 388n
Hamm, S., 121n, 388n
Hammer, M., 334n
Hammonds, K. H., 29n
Hamner, S., 150n
Handfield, R. B., 238n
Hanig, T. R., 31n
Hansen, M. T., 92n, 364n
Hantula, D. A., 364n
Hanvanich, S., 64n, 93n, 121n
Harder, J., 94n
Harding, D., 207n, 208n
Harding, R., 387n
Hardy, C., 30n, 268n, 269n
Harford, J. 304n
Harper, N. W. C., 178n
Harrigan, K. R., 29n, 177n
Harris, R., 208n
Harrison, D. A., 30n, 362n, 365n
Harrison, J. S., 29n, 30n, 65n,
    66n, 119n, 176n, 177n, 178n,
    204n, 205n, 206n, 207n,
    208n, 241n, 268n, 269n,
    270n, 304n, 334n, 337n,
    364n, 365n, 389n
Harrison, S., 337n
Harstad, B., 336n
Hart, M. M., 92n
Hart, S. L., 238n
Hartzell, J. C., 304n
Harvey, M. G., 239n, 364n
Harzing, A.-W., 241n, 269n
Haslam, S. A., 363n
Haspeslagh, P., 205n
Hass, M. R., 364n
Hassan, S. S., 150n
Hastings, Reed, 14–15, 105

Hatch, N. W., 151n, 364n
Hatten, K. J., 268n
Haveman, H. A., 119n
Hawawini, G., 30n, 66n, 92n
Hayashi, Y., 305n
Hayes, C., 206n
Hayes, L. A., 365n
Hayes, R. M., 305n
Hayward, M. L. A., 151n, 179n,
    206n, 207n, 362n
Healey, T. J., 302n, 305n
Heath, C., 365n
Heath, D., 365n
Hebert, L., 241n
Heeley, M. B., 334n
Hegarty, W. H., 207n, 243n, 269n
Hehner, S. P., 150n
Heijitjes, M. G., 362n
Heimeriks, K. H., 268n
Heine, K., 93n, 151n
Heine, L., 388n
Heineman, B. W., Jr., 31n
Hekman, D. R., 31n
Helfat, C. E., 29n, 175n, 206n,
    336n, 362n, 385n
Helm, B., 364n
Henderson, A., 301n
Henderson, R., 29n
Hendricks, R., 387n
Hendrickx, M., 176n, 302n
Hendry, K., 301n
Henisz, W. J., 242n, 243n
Hennart, 151n
Henriques, I., 30n, 305n
Henry, N., 120n, 337n
Herrick, T., 303n
Herrmann, P., 242n
Hesen, G., 270n
Hesterly, W. S., 94n, 337n, 363n
Higgins, M. C., 388n
Higgs, Derek, 297
Hill, C. W. L., 29n, 65n, 93n,
    150n, 151n, 177n, 206n,
    207n, 208n, 268n, 334n,
    336n 365n, 389n
Hillebrand, B., 271n
Hiller, N. J., 93n, 362n
Hillman, A. J., 30n, 65n, 301n,
    302n, 303n, 304n, 305n
Hilpirt, R., 335n
Hilton, B., 305n
Himelstein, L., 205n
Hitt, M. A., 27n, 28n, 29n, 30n,
    64n, 65n, 66n, 67n, 92n,
    93n, 94n, 119n, 120n, 121n,
    149n, 150n, 151n, 176n,
    177n, 178n, 204n, 205n,
    206n, 207n, 208n, 209n,
    239n, 242n, 243n, 268n,
    269n, 270n, 271n, 301n,
    303n, 304n, 305n, 334n,
    335n, 336n, 337n, 362n,
    363n, 364n, 365n, 385n,
    386n, 387n, 388n, 389n

Hoang, H., 268n
Hodgson, G. M., 177n
Hoegl, M., 94n, 365n
Hof, R. D., 334n
Hoffmann, W. H., 364n
Hoi, C., 304n
Hoiweg, M., 121n
Holbrook, M. B., 93n
Holburn, G. I. F., 64n
Holcomb, T. R., 67n, 92n, 208n,
    242n, 268n, 362n, 386n
Holcombe, R. G., 386n
Holden, N., 28n
Hollenbeck, G. P., 364n
Holmes, R. M., Jr., 66n, 304n
Holmes, S., 66n, 93n, 120n
Holt, D. B., 93n
Holt, D. T., 386n
Homburg, C., 206n
Homqvist, M., 240n
Hong, J. F. L., 239n, 334n
Honig, B., 364n
Hood, N., 365n
Hopkins, H. D., 119n, 239n
Hornsby, J. S., 64n, 335n, 365n
Horowitz, R., 387n
Hoshi, T., 305n
Hoskisson, R. E., 29n, 30n, 64n,
    65n, 66n, 67n, 93n, 121n,
    177n, 178n, 179n, 206n,
    207n, 208n, 209n, 238n,
    239n, 240n, 241n, 242n,
    243n, 268n, 269n, 270n,
    271n, 301n, 302n, 303n,
    304n, 305n, 334n, 335n,
    336n, 362n, 363n, 365n,
    386n, 387n, 388n, 389n
Hough, J. R., 64n, 92n, 149n,
    175n
Houghton, K. A., 240n
House, R. J., 242n, 363n
Howell, J. M., 388n
Howell, L. J., 242n
Howell, R. A., 30n, 336n
Hoy, F., 270n, 337n
Hribar, P., 302n
Hsieh, L.-F., 206n
Hsu, C. C., 243n
Hsu, J. C., 242n
Huafang, X., 363n
Hubbard, T. N., 207n
Huber, G. P., 64n, 205n
Huff, A., 30n, 66n
Huff, L., 241n
Hughes, Catherine Elizabeth,
    349
Hughes, J., 305n, 389n
Hughes, J. P., 207n
Hughes, M., 269n
Hulbert, J. M., 93n
Hulland, J., 178n
Hult, G. T. M., 29n, 64n, 94n,
    334n, 335n, 336n, 364n
Humphreys, J., 30n

Hunt, M. S., 66n
Hurd, Mark, 340
Hurlbert, M., 363n
Huselid, M. A., 364n, 365n
Hutchings, K., 65n
Hutt, M. D., 388n
Hutzler, C., 65n
Huy, Q. N., 208n
Huyghebaert, N., 121n
Hymowitz, C., 301n

I

Iannotta, G., 303n
Ibrayeva, E. S., 386n
Icahn, Carl, 297
Ihlwan, M., 335n
Immelt, Jeffrey, 307, 308, 311,
    348, 350
Indejikian, R. J., 177n
Inderst, R., 336n
Inkpen, A. C., 29n, 269n, 270n
Insinga, R. C., 94n
Iravani, S. M., 151n
Ireland, R. D., 27n, 28n, 29n, 30n,
    64n, 65n, 67n, 92n, 93n,
    94n, 119n, 121n, 149n, 178n,
    204n, 205n, 206n, 207n,
    208n, 239n, 240n, 241n,
    268n, 269n, 270n, 271n,
    334n, 335n, 337n, 362n,
    364n, 365n, 385n, 386n,
    387n, 388n, 389n
Irwin, R. D., 334n
Isaac, S., 151n
Isaak, R., 240n
Isagawa, N., 305n
Islam, S. M. N., 303n
Ito, K., 238n
Ivancevich, J. M., 65n
Iverson, R. D., 92n, 209n
Izushi, H., 239n

J

Jackson, E. M., 304n, 305n
Jackson, G., 301n
Jackson, S. E., 29n, 94n, 362n,
    364n
Jacobides, M. G., 93n, 302n
Jacoby, S. M., 303n, 305n
Jacque, L. L., 243n
Jaffe, E. D., 66n
Jagersma, P. K., 241n
Jain, S., 389n
James, C. R., 364n
James, E. H., 363n
Janne, O. E. M., 238n, 242n
Janney, J. J., 28n, 149n, 178n
Jardins, J. D., 389n
Jargon, J., 178n, 305n
Javenpaa, S., 94n
Javidan, M., 238n, 242n, 387n
Jawahar, I. M., 64n
Jayachandran, S., 119n, 120n
Jayne, M. E. A., 65n

Name Index

Jay-Z, 97
Jenkins, M., 120n, 337n
Jensen, M. C., 178n, 205n, 207n, 301n, 302n, 363n
Jensen, R. J., 64n
Jeong, E., 208n, 364n
Jermias, J., 336n
Jespersen, F. F., 150n
Jiang, C. X., 387n
Jiang, F., 238n
Jianguo, Y., 363n
Jiraporn, P., 302n, 303n
Jobe, L. A., 65n, 150n, 176n, 177n, 205n, 269n, 388n
Jobs, Steve, 10, 265
Johnson, J. H., 270n
Johnson, J. L., 270n
Johnson, J. P., 241n
Johnson, L. K., 150n
Johnson, M., 240n
Johnson, M. E., 177n
Johnson, Magic, 261
Johnson, R. A., 177n, 179n, 206n, 207n, 208n, 242n, 301n, 303n, 304n, 335n, 363n, 365n, 386n, 387n, 389n
Jolly, D. R., 269n
Jonacas, H., 269n
Jones, A., 65n
Jones, C., 337n
Jones, G., 239n
Jones, T. M., 30n, 92n
Jordan, Michael, 261
Joshi, M. P., 334n
Judge, W., 242n, 365n
Julian, S. D., 335n
Jung, Andrea, 326, 349
Jung, J., 242n
Junttila, M. A., 93n

K

Kaeufer, K., 268n
Kager, P., 178n
Kahai, S. S., 363n
Kahan, M., 178n
Kale, P., 29n, 93n, 241n, 268n, 270n, 271n, 364n
Kalnins, A., 66n, 121n
Kan, O. B., 242n
Kandemir, D., 271n
Kane, Y. I., 178n
Kang, E., 302n
Kang, J.-K., 208n
Kang, S. C., 92n
Kang, S.-H., 302n
Kant, S., 334n
Kaplan, D., 92n
Kaplan, R. S., 121n, 365n
Karandikar, H., 336n
Karim, S., 206n, 335n
Karnari, A., 121n
Karnik, K., 386n
Karp, J., 94n
Karpak, B., 121n

Karpoff, J. M., 304n
Karri, R., 30n, 305n
Ka-shing, Li, 157
Kashyap, A. K., 305n
Kates, S. M., 149n
Kathuria, R., 334n
Katila, R., 93n, 206n, 364n, 386n
Kato, Y., 365n
Katz, G., 92n
Katz, J. A., 335n
Katz, M., 94n
Katzenberg, F., 150n
Kaufman, R., 30n
Kaufmann, P. J., 270n
Kawaura A., 305n
Kay, N. M., 178n
Kayes, D. C., 92n, 365n
Keats, B. W., 28n, 64n, 334n, 335n, 336n, 364n
Keels, J. K., 209n
Keenan, F., 66n, 205n
Keil, M., 94n, 388n
Keil, T., 92n, 304n, 337n, 386n
Keim, G. D., 30n, 65n, 305n
Kelleher, Herb, 110
Keller, S. B., 150n
Kelley, L., 241n
Kellogg, W. K., 348
Kelly, L. M., 301n
Kelly, M. J., 269n
Kenis, P., 271n, 337n
Kenney, M., 207n
Kerwin, K., 151n
Kesner, I. F., 120n
Ketchen, D. A., Jr., 364n
Ketchen, D. J., Jr., 29n, 31n, 64n, 93n, 94n, 149n, 270n, 268n, 364n, 386n
Keuslein, W., 178n
Khan, M. A. A., 303n
Khanna, T., 28n, 177n, 238n, 243n
Khermouch, G., 150n
Kidd, D., 301n, 303n, 363n
Kiechel, W., III, 208n
Kiel, G. C., 301n, 363n
Kieser, A., 270n
Kiley, D., 30n, 94n
Kim, E., 149n
Kim, H., 29n, 238n, 242n, 271n, 301n, 305n, 334n, 363n, 389n
Kim, J., 207n, 303n, 336n, 240n, 243n
Kim, J.-M., 208n
Kim, J.-Y., 178n, 204n, 271n
Kim, K., 269n
Kim, S. H., 242n
Kim, W. C., 387n
Kim, Y. J., 240n
Kim, Y. Sang, 302n
Kim, Y.-H., 178n
King, A. W., 92n, 94n, 150n, 388n
King, D. R., 269n

King, Karen, 352
Kini, O., 304n
Kirkland, R., 28n
Kirkman, B. L., 65n
Kirkpatrick, S. A., 30n
Kirnan, J., 364n
Kisfalvi, W., 179n
Klausner, M., 304n
Kleiman, D., 268n
Klein, K. E., 386n
Klein, S., 305n
Kleinschmidt, E. J., 271n
Kline, D., 240n
Kline, J. P., 177n
Kline, M. J., 301n
Kling, K., 151n
Klossek, A., 240n
Kneip, T., 387n
Kneller, R., 269n
Knight, D., 362n
Knight, G. A., 241n
Knoedler, J. T., 177n
Knott, A. M., 66n, 92n, 119n, 178n
Knowles, J., 179n
Ko, S., 365n
Kochhar, R., 178n, 207n, 364n, 386n, 387n, 388n, 389n
Kola-Nystrom, S., 387n
Koller, T., 208n
Konopaske, R., 65n
Koors, J. L., 304n
Kopczak, L. R., 177n
Kor, Y. Y., 65n, 120n, 302n
Korsgaard, M. A., 241n
Kosnik, R., 304n, 305n
Kosonen, M., 31n, 362n
Kostova, T., 238n, 336n
Kotabe, M., 151n, 337n
Kotha, S., 28n, 65n, 121n, 150n, 238n
Kothandaraman, P., 177n
Kotter, J. P., 362n
Koudsi, S., 28n
Kozlowski, Dennis, 298
Kracaw, W., 304n
Kranhold, K., 28n, 177n
Krapfel, R., 64n
Krasoff, J., 208n
Kriesel, S., 387n
Kripalani, M., 208n
Krishnan, H. A., 206n, 207n, 208n, 209n, 242n, 271n
Krishnan, M. S., 29n, 93n, 364n
Krishnan, R., 268n
Krivogorsky, V., 303n
Kroc, Roy, 342
Kroll, M., 30n, 178n, 205n, 302n
Krug, J. A., 207n
Kuemmerle, W., 238n, 386n
Kuenzi, M., 365n
Kulkarni, M., 150n
Kumar, M. V. Shyam, 270n

Kumar, P., 302n
Kumar, R., 269n, 271n, 304n
Kumar, S., 334n
Kumar, V., 150n
Kumaraswamy, A., 389n
Kumaresh, T. V., 151n
Kundu, S. K., 243n
Kuratko, D. F., 64n, 335n, 365n, 386n, 388n
Kutcher, E., 364n
Kwak, M., 175n
Kwok, C. C., 238n, 243n
Kwon, S.-W., 364n, 365n
Kwong, R., 177n

L

Laamanen, T., 92n, 304n
Labaye, E., 387n
Lado, A., 30n, 205n, 302n
Lafley, A. G., 311
Lafontaine, F., 270n
Lages, C. R., 240n
Lages, L. F., 240n
Lagrotteria, B., 269n
Lai, M.-F., 365n
Lakshman, N., 388n
Lamb, C. W., Jr., 150n
Lampert, C. M., 29n
Lampert, M., 387n
Landstrom, H., 240n
Lane, P. J., 178n, 241n, 271n, 388n
Lang, L. H. P., 205n, 207n, 242n
Langley, M., 208n
Langowitz, N., 389n
Lankau, M. J. 30n, 176n
Lanzolla, G., 120n, 268n, 386n
Larcker, D. F., 336n
Larimo, J., 238n
Larraza-Kintana, M., 304n
Larsen, K., 388n
Larson, M., 364n
Larsson, R., 240n
Laseter, T. M., 121n
Lash, J., 269n
Lattman, P., 64n
Lau, C. M., 238n, 243n, 387n
Lavelle, L., 302n
Lavie, D., 31n, 65n, 150n, 271n
Lawler, E. E., III, 301n, 303n
Lawler, E. E., Jr., 364n
Lawrence, P. R., 177n, 269n, 334n, 335n, 388n
Lawrence, R. Z., 240n
Lawrence, T. B., 30n, 239n, 268n, 269n
Lawson, B., 271n
Lawson, E., 335n
Lawton, C., 176n
Lazzarini, S. G., 67n, 241n, 269n, 337n
Le Breton-Miller, I., 31n, 301n, 302n, 363n
Le Nadant, A.-L., 209n
Le Roux, J.-M., 205n, 207n, 208n

Le, Q. V., 303n
Leask, G., 120n
Leavitt, H. J., 334n
Leavitt, T., 31n
Lechner, C., 271n
Lee, C., 337n, 388n
Lee, G. K., 238n, 271n
Lee, G.-G., 365n
Lee, H., 64n, 93n, 119n, 120n,
    242n, 302n, 305n, 336n,
    364n, 388n, 389n
Lee, H.-U., 208n
Lee, J., 66n
Lee, J. H., 305n
Lee, J-R., 238n
Lee, K., 66n, 302n, 337n, 388n
Lee, L., 120n
Lee, M., 30n
Lee, P. M., 93n, 209n, 302n, 305n,
    363n, 387n
Lee, R. P.-W., 270n
Lee, S. K., 303n
Lee, S.-H., 238n, 386n
Lee, Y.-H., 64n
Lehrer, M., 29n, 238n, 242n
Lei, D., 27n, 149n
Leiblein, M. J., 94n
Leleux, B., 120n
Lemire, C., V208n
Lemmon, M. L., 179n, 302n,
    304n
Lenox, M. J., 31n, 64n
Lenway, S. A., 238n
Leonard, G. K., 270n
Leonard-Barton, 94n
Lepak, D. P., 92n
Lepine, J. A., 66n, 149n
Leslie, K., 335n
Levav, A., 387n
Levicki, C., 335n
Levin, I. M., 364n
Levine, J., 241n
Levinthal, D. A., 93n, 149n, 334n,
    335n
Levitas, E., 30n, 66n, 94n, 241n,
    243n, 269n, 270n, 389n
Levy, O., 92n
Lewin, A. Y., 238n, 239n
Lewis, M., 335n
Lewis, P., 67n
Ley, B., 365n
Li, 302n
Li, D., 121n, 241n, 270n, 337n
Li, J., 241n
Li, L., 239n, 242n, 243n, 335n
Li, M., 302n
Li, S., 66n, 237n, 242n, 243n
Li, Y., 335n
Lichtenstein, B. B., 268n, 386n
Lichtenstein, Warren, 297
Lie, J. R., 121n
Lieberman, M. B., 29n, 67n,
    120n, 149n
Liebeskind, J., 208n

Lien, Y.-C., 238n
Liesch, P. W., 241n
Lifsher, M., 269n
Linder, J. C., 94n
Lineberry, C. S., 206n
Litan, R. E., 386n, 389n
Liu, R. C., 268n
Liu, W.-L., 208n
Liu, X., 238n
Liu, Y., 93n, 335n, 364n
Ljungquist, U., 92n
Llaneza, A. V., 271n
Locke, E. A., 30n, 93n, 362n
Locke, R., 94n
Lodish, L. M., 93n
Lodorfos, G., 208n
Loeb, M., 31n
Lohr, S., 94n, 205n, 335n
Lombard, Didier, 256
London, T., 238n
Long, T., 304n
Long, W. F., 209n
Longenecker, C. O., 93n
Lopez, E. J., 178n
López-Sánchez, J. I., 176n
Lorenzoni, G., 337n
Lorsch, J. W., 30n, 178n, 303n,
    334n, 335n, 388n
Lounsbury, M., 386n
Love, L. G., 120n, 334n, 336n
Lowe, J., 177n
Lowe, K. B., 65n
Lowenstein, L., 178n
Lu, C.-C., 204n
Lu, J. W., 242n
Lu, Y., 243n
Lubatkin, M., 66n, 120n, 150n,
    176n, 177n, 178n, 205n,
    271n, 363n, 364n
Luce, R. A., 66n, 67n, 305n
Lucier, C., 389n
Ludema, R. D., 240n
Luffman, G., 149n, 334n
Lumpkin, G. T., 150n, 151n,
    336n, 365n, 386n
Lundin, M., 271n
Lunsford, J. L., 177n, 302n, 206n,
    269n
Luo, Y., 28n, 64n, 66n, 206n,
    238n, 239n, 240n, 241n,
    242n, 268n, 270n, 336n,
    337n
Luthans, F., 364n, 386n
Lyles, M. A., 151n, 241n, 270n,
    271n
Lynall, M. D., 301n
Lynch, D. F., 150n
Lynch, L. J., 304n

M

Ma, H., 270n
Macintosh, G., 121n
Mackay, David, 348
Mackey, A., 30n

Mackey, T. B., 30n, 149n
MacKinnon, Don, 371
MacMillan, I. C., 120n, 239n,
    365n, 387n
Madan, M., 238n
Madhavan, R., 120n
Madhok, A., 93n, 241n
Madsen, T. L., 66n
Madupu, V., 240n
Magnusson, P., 29n
Mahajan, A., 240n
Mahate, A. A., 205n, 301n
Maheshwari, S. K., 335n
Mahmood, I. P., 65n, 177n, 179n,
    238n
Mahoney, J. M., 305n
Mahoney, J. T., 28n, 65n, 120n,
    239n, 305n
Mainkar, A. V., 66n,
    150n, 205n
Mair, J., 208n
Maitlis, S., 30n
Makadok, R., 66n
Makhija, M. V., 30n, 92n, 335n
Makino, S., 243n
Makri, M., 388n
Malak, N., 94n
Mallette, P., 206n
Malnight, T. W., 335n
Malter, A. J., 149n
Mandel, M., 336n
Manev, I. M., 94n, 270n, 385n
Mangelsdorf, M. E., 92n
Mani, S., 241n
Mankins, M. C., 149n
Mannix, E. A., 334n
Manolova, T., 29n
Mansi, S. A., 175n
Mapes, T., 243n
March, J. G., 336n
Marcus, A. J., 303n
Maremont, M., 304n, 336n
Mariel, P., 269n
Marin, P. L., 120n
Marino, A. M., 205n
Marino, L., 271n
Markham, S. K., 388n
Markides, C. C., 175n, 207n,
    208n, 336n, 387n
Markoczy, L., 208n, 362n
Marks, M. L., 176n, 208n
Marquez, P., 301n
Marquis, C., 386n
Marr, M., 65n, 177n, 364n
Marsh, S. J., 388n
Marshall, F., 150n
Marshall, J., 304n
Marshall, John, 140
Martin, D., 335n
Martin, R., 93n, 362n
Martin, X., 268n, 271n, 337n
Massimilian, D., 362n
Massini, S., 239n
Masulis, R. W., 304n

Matheren, B. P., 386n
Mathews, J. A., 66n, 337n
Mathis, J., 243n
Mathur, I., 303n
Mathur, S., 29n
Matta, E., 304n
Matten, D., 239n
Mattern, F., 151n
Matthyssens, P., 94n
Mauborgne, R., 387n
Maula, M. V. J., 386n
May, D. L., 178n
May, R. C., 28n
Mayer, D., 93n, 207n
Mayer, K. J., 92n
Mayer, Marissa, 367
Mayer, R. C., 271n
Maynard, M., 207n, 363n
Mazursky, D., 387n
McBride, S., 29n, 66n
McCabe, K., 94n
McCall, M. W., Jr., 364n
McCarthy, A., 363n
McCarthy, D. J., 28n
McCarthy, I., 149n
McCarthy, M. J., 65n
McCartney, Paul, 371
McCary, J., 304n
McComb, William, 195–196
McDaniel, C., 150n
McDonald, Mackey J., 167
McDougall, P. P., 208n, 386n,
    387n
McEvily, B., 271n
McEvily, S. K., 29n, 92n, 94n,
    364n
McGahan, A. M., 28n, 29n, 66n,
    205n
McGee, J. E., 150n, 151n, 362n
McGee, S., 205n
McGrath, R. G., 93n, 239n, 365n,
    387n
McGrath, R. S., 120n
McGree, J., 93n
McGuire, J., 301n, 304n
McIntyre, T., 207n
McKee, A., 362n
McKee, M., 365n
McKendrick, D. G., 239n
McKenna, T. M., 64n
McKeown, A., 65n
McKinley, W., 208n
McKinnon, J. D., 302n
McLaughlin, G. L., 64n
McMahan, G. C., 150n
McMullen, J. S., 334n, 386n
McMurrer, D., 362n
McNamara, G., 28n, 66n, 67n,
    121n
McNerney, W. James, Jr.,
    69, 291
McNulty, T., 303n
McVea, J., 30n
McWilliams, A., 30n, 242n

McWilliams, G., 121n
McWilliams, V., 303n, 363n
Means, G., 303n
Meckling, W., 302n
Megicks, P., 149n
Mehri, D., 150n
Mela, C. F., 93n
Melcher, B. A., 121n
Mellewigt, M., 177n
Mendelow, A. L., 365n
Mendez, A., 364n
Menguc, B., 30n
Menipaz, E., 207n
Menn, J., 67n
Merchant, H., 177n
Mesquita, L., 387n
Mester, 207n
Meulbroek, L. K., 304n
Meyer, K. E., 29n, 66n, 208n, 239n, 240n
Mezias, J. M., 93n, 149n, 337n
Mian, S., 304n
Miao, C. F., 205n, 207n
Michael, S. C., 270n
Michaels, D., 30n, 269n
Michailova, S., 65n
Miles, G., 337n
Miles, M. P., 92n
Miles, R. E., 334n, 337n
Millar, C., 305n
Miller, C. C., 38n, 92n, 149n, 178n, 362n, 363n
Miller, D., 31n, 121n, 176n, 177n, 301n, 302n, 335n, 363n
Miller, D. J., 176n, 206n, 385n, 386n
Miller, J. S., 304n
Miller, K. D., 334n, 335n, 364n
Miller, S. R., 64n, 240n, 270n
Miller, S., 238n
Miller, T., 65n, 66n, 238n, 242n, 335n
Milliken, F. J., 303n
Millman, J., 65n
Mills, P. K., 335n
Milton, L., 303n
Min, S., 120n
Miner, A. S., 271n
Minguela-Rata, B., 176n
Minniti, M., 386n, 389n
Minow, N., 275, 301n
Mirabal, N., 209n
Mirvis, P. H., 176n, 208n
Misangyi, V. F., 66n, 149n
Mische, M. A., 365n
Mishina, Y., 94n
Mitchell, R. K., 30n
Mitchell, W., 29n, 64n, 150n, 176n, 179n, 205n, 206n, 268n, 270n, 271n, 335n, 337n
Mobley, W. H., 364n
Moeller, T., 301n
Moensted, M., 271n

Moesel, D. D., 206n, 207n, 301n, 303n, 304n, 335n, 389n
Moffett, S., 64n
Mok, V., 121n
Mol, M. J., 94n
Molleman, E., 362n
Mollenkamp, C., 208n
Mollenkopf, D. A., 121n
Moller, K., 337n
Monaghan, Craig, 339
Monks, R. A. G., 301n
Montes-Sancho, M. J., 64n
Montgomery, C. A., 175n
Montgomery, D. B., 67n, 120n
Montoya-Weiss, M. M., 64n, 388n
Moon, D., 207n, 302n
Mooney, A. C., 31n, 302n, 304n
Moore, M. C., 67n
Moran, P., 302n
Morgan, R. E., 269n
Morris, M. H., 386n, 387n
Morris, S. S., 92n
Morrow, J. L., Jr., 67n, 92n, 208n, 268n, 362n, 386n
Morse, E. A., 239n
Mosakowski, E., 28n
Moschieri, C., 208n
Moss, N. J., 175n
Mossberg, W., 150n
Mtar, M., 207n
Mudambi, R., 206n, 387n
Mudd, S., 243n
Mulally, Alan, 348
Mulcahy, Anne, 349
Muller, H. M., 336n
Muncir, K., 388n
Murata, H., 242n
Muriel, A., 151n
Murphy, G. B., 29n
Murphy, P. E., 365n
Murray, A., 303n
Murray, J. Y., 151n
Murtaugh, Philip, 211
Murtha, T. P., 120n, 238n
Muth, M., 305n
Myer, K. E., 242n

N

Nachum, L., 239n, 305n
Nadkarni, S., 29n, 66n, 335n
Naik, N., 304n
Naiker, V., 302n
Nair, A., 28n, 119n
Nalebuff, B., 67n
Nam, D., 149n
Nambisan, S., 92n, 94n
Narasimhan, O., 66n, 93n, 364n
Narayanan, V. G., 337n
Narayanan, V. K., 29n, 64n, 66n, 335n
Nardelli, Robert, 287, 288, 292
Narula, R., 270n
Nasser, Jacques, 37
Nault, B. R., 120n

Naveen, L., 302n
Navissi, F., 302n
Nazario, Ronaldo, 261
Ncube, L. B., 365n
Ndofor, H. A., 30n, 119n, 120n, 121n
Nebenzahl, I. D., 66n
Nederegger, G., 150n
Nee, V., 65n
Needleman, S. E., 302n
Neff, J. J., 92n
Nelson, S., 269n
Nerer, A., 120n
Nerkar, A., 29n
Neubert, M. J., 93n
Neville, B. A., 30n
Newbert, S. L., 30n, 121n
Ng, W., 177n
Nibler, M., 305n
Nicholas, S., 269n
Nichols-Nixon, C. L., 29n, 65n
Nicholson, G. J., 301n, 363n
Nidamarthi, S., 336n
Nielsen, B. B., 337n
Nielsen, T. M., 92n, 365n
Nielsen, U., 240n
Nigh, D., 243n
Nijssen, E. J., 335n
Nippa, M., 240n
Nishiguchi, T., 337n
Nixon, R. D., 66n, 208n, 364n, 386n, 388n, 389n
Nobeoka, K., 337n
Nocera, G., 303n
Noe, R. A., 364n
Noe, T. H., 207n
Nohria, N., 66n
Nonnemaker, L., 119n
Noorderhaven, N., 206n, 268n, 271n
Nooyi, Indra K., 79
Norburn, D., 305n
Nord, W. R., 30n
Norman, P. M., 67n, 271n
Norton, D. P., 121n, 365n
Nosella, A., 271n
Novicevic, M. M., 364n
Numagami, T., 239n
Nummela, N., 387n
Nunez-Nickel, 302n
Nutt, P. C., 28n, 93n
Nyaw, M.-K., 206n, 241n, 270n

O

O'Connell, V., 240n
O'Connor, E. J., 93n
O'Connor, G. C., 387n
O'Connor, J. P., 304n
O'Donnell, S., 304n
O'Neill, H. M., 305n, 334n, 335n, 336n, 387n
O'Neill, J., 208n
O'Reilly, C. A., 301n
O'Shaughnessy, K. C., 209n

O'Sullivan, A., 388n
O'Sullivan, N., 205n
O'Toole, J., 364n
Obel, B., 336n
Ocasio, W., 120n
Ofek, E., 304n
Oh, C. H., 66n, 240n
Ohlsson, A.-V., 206n
Oldroyd, J. B., 149n
Olhager, J., 271n
Olian, J. D., 362n
Oliver, C., 29n, 64n
Olk, P., 269n
Olsen, D. M., 239n
Olson, B. J., 362n
Olson, E. M., 334n, 335n, 336n
Opper, S., 65n
Ordonez, J., 65n
Ordonez, L., 365n
Oum, T. H., 269n
Overdorf, M., 388n
Oviatt, B. M., 387n
Oxley, J. E., 270n
Ozment, J., 150n

P

Pacheco-de-Almeida, G., 28n
Paez, B. L., 178n
Pagano, 207n
Paik, Y., 242n
Paladino, A., 92n, 121n
Palepu, K. G., 28n, 177n
Palich, L. E., 178n
Palmatier, R. W., 205n
Palmer, D., 207n
Palmer, J., 206n
Palmer, T. B., 29n, 64n
Palmeri, C., 120n, 205n
Pan, Y., 239n, 241n, 242n
Panagiotou, G., 64n
Pangarkar, N., 121n
Panjwani, A., 150n
Pantzalis, C., 240n
Pappas, J. M., 64n
Parayitam, S., 362n
Parente, R., 151n
Park, C., 176n, 178n, 206n
Park, D., 66n, 207n, 208n, 209n, 242n
Park, J.-H., 269n
Park, N., 149n
Park, S. H., 64n, 66n, 120n
Park, S., 28n, 243n
Parker, D., 120n
Parkhe, A., 270n, 388n
Parmigiani, A., 205n
Parvinen, P., 206n, 335n
Pasariello, C., 93n
Pascale, R. T., 31n
Patel, P. R., 29n
Patsalos-Fox, M., 301n
Patsuris, P., 208n
Pattnaik, C., 239n
Patton, K. M., 64n

Paulson, Henry, 282
Pauwels, P., 94n
Pearce, C. L., 362n
Pearce, J. A., 30n
Pearce, J. A., II, 305n
Pearson, J. M., 121n
Pedersen, T., 303n
Pegels, C. C., 270n, 362n
Pehrsson, A., 175n
Pelled, L. H., 362n
Penalva, A. D. F., 301n
Peng, M. W., 65n, 66n, 177n,
    205n, 238n, 240n, 241n,
    302n, 386n
Penner-Hahn, J., 238n, 242n
Pennings, J. M., 337n, 388n
Perdreau, F., 209n
Pereira, J., 150n
Perez, Antonio, 247
Perez, E., 94n, 150n
Perrone, V., 271n
Perry, M. L., 64n
Perry-Smith, J. E., 387n
Peteraf, M. A., 66n, 92n
Peters, J. W., 121n
Petersen, B., 240n
Petersen, K. J., 238n
Peterson, J., 363n
Petitt, B. S. P., 302n
Petkova, A. P., 121n
Petra, S. T., 303n
Petrick, J. A., 362n
Petroni, G., 271n
Pett, T. L., 240n
Pettigrew, A., 239n, 301n
Pettit, R. R., 205n
Phan, P. H., 208n
Philips, S., 29n
Phillips, N., 269n
Picou, A., 303n, 304n
Pierce, Charlie, 154
Pierson, D., 151n
Piesse, J., 238n
Pil, F. K., 121n, 151n, 387n
Pinch, S., 120n, 337n
Pindado, J., 303n
Ping, E. J., 238n
Pisano, G., 28n
Pisano, V., 28n, 205n, 241n, 304n
Pistre, N., 176n, 205n
Pitcher, P., 179n
Pitre, N., 204n
Pitt, L. F., 149n
Plowman, D. Ashmos, 150n
Ployhart, R. E., 364n
Pollock, T. G., 94n, 151n, 269n,
    301n, 304n, 362n
Polo, Y., 269n
Porac, J. F., 94n, 120n, 269n
Porrini, P., 208n, 241n
Porter, M. E., 28n, 29n, 66n, 67n,
    94n, 131, 149n, 150n, 151n,
    175n, 176n, 177n, 218, 239n
Porter, A. L., 65n

Porth, S. J., 334n
Posen, H. E., 119n, 178n
Post, J. E., 362n
Pouder, R. W., 335n
Powell, T. C., 28n, 119n
Power, M. J., 94n
Pozen, R. C., 303n
Prabhu, J. C., 207n
Prahalad, C. K., 94n
Prasad, S., 238n
Prescott, J. E., 92n
Pressler, Paul, 339–340
Preston, L. E., 362n
Price, G. K., 270n
Price, R., 386n
Priem, R. L., 30n, 64n, 92n, 120n,
    149n, 304n, 334n, 336n, 362n
Priestland, A., 31n
Prince, C. J., 301n
Prince, Charles, 199
Prince, E. T., 30n, 364n
Probst, G., 28n, 365n
Prospero, M. A., 28n
Provan, K. G., 271n, 337n
Pucik, V., 365n
Puckett, John, 140
Puffer, S. M., 28n
Puranam, P., 151n, 176n, 177n,
    206n, 269n, 271n, 363n,
    389n
Puryear, R., 29n
Putin, Vladimir, 234
Puumalainen, K., 387n
Pyoria, P., 365n

Q

Quah, P., 205n
Quang, T., 176n
Quelch, J. A., 239n
Quin, J., 305n
Quinn, J. B., 93n
Quinn, J. F., 362n
Quintens, L., 94n
Quittner, J., 92n

R

Rabinovich, E., 121n
Racanelli, V. J., 66n
Raes, A. M. L., 362n
Ragatz, G. L., 238n
Ragozzino, R., 208n
Raheja, C. G., 304n
Raisch, S., 28n, 92n
Rajadhyaksha, U., 30n
Rajagopalan, N., 178n, 204n,
    207n, 362n, 363n
Rajala, A., 337n
Rajan, M, V., 336n
Rajan, R., 302n
Rajand, M., 208n
Rajgopal, S., 302n
Rajiv, S., 66n, 93n, 364n
Ram, M., 150n
Raman, A. P., 93n, 337n

Ramaswamy, K., 119n, 205n,
    302n, 304n
Ramirez, G. G., 363n
Rangan, S., 64n, 240n
Rappaport, A., 205n, 207n
Rasheed, A. M., 64n, 362n
Raven, P. V., 270n
Ravenscraft, D, J., 177n, 209n
Raymond, M. A., 240n
Raynor, M. E., 150n, 177n
Ready, D. A., 362n
Reardon, K. K., 93n, 362n
Rebeiz, K., 303n
Rebello, M. J., 207n
Redding, G., 365n
Reeb, D. M., 175n, 238n, 301n,
    303n
Reed, A., II, 150n
Reed, R., 335n
Regan, Judith, 349
Reger, R. K., 66n
Rehbein, K., 65n, 304n
Reibstein, D. J., 119n
Reilly, D., 302n
Reinartz, W., 150n
Reinert, U., 243n
Reinhardt, A., 66n
Reuber, R., 93n
Reuer, J. J., 94n, 205n, 207n,
    208n, 240n, 241n, 268n,
    269n, 270n, 389n
Reynolds, S. J., 31n
Rho, S., 66n
Ricart, J. E., 66n, 238n
Rice, M. P., 387n
Rico, R., 362n
Rigby, D., 238n, 240n
Rindfleisch, A., 241n
Rindova, V. P., 121n, 151n, 362n
Ring, P. S., 243n
Rishi, M., 303n
Rivkin, J. W., 149n, 335n
Robbins, G. E., 305n
Roberson, Q., 364n, 388n
Roberts, D., 93n, 362n
Roberts, E., 242n
Roberts, J., 303n
Roberts, K. H., 335n
Roberts, P. W., 120n, 121n
Robertson, C. J., 365n
Robertson, P. L., 29n
Robie, C., 65n
Robin, A., 304n
Robins, J. A., 241n, 336n
Robinson, R. B., Jr., 305n
Robinson, W. T., 120n
Roche, Gerard R., 288
Rock, E. B., 178n
Rodan, S., 364n
Rodriguez, A. I., 121n
Rodriguez, Eddie, 41
Rodriguez, G. C., 302n
Rodriguez-Duarte, A., 176n
Rodriguez-Escudero, A. I., 119n

Rodriguez-Pinto, J., 119n
Rodriquez, P., 242n
Roe, R. A., 362n
Roengpitya, R., 302n
Roller, L. H., 120n
Romis, M., 94n
Rooke, D., 31n
Rose, E. L., 238n
Rose, J., 208n
Rose-Ackerman, S., 178n
Rosen, R., 178n, 207n
Rosenkopf, L., 29n, 270n
Rosenzweig, P. M., 205n, 242n
Ross, D., 177n
Ross, J., 269n
Ross, Steven J., 23
Roth, K., 304n, 336n
Rothaemel, F. T., 29n, 65n, 150n,
    176n 177n, 205n, 206n,
    238n, 268n, 269n, 271n,
    388n, 389n
Rouse, T., 207n, 208n, 243n
Rovit, S., 208n
Rowe, W. G., 179n, 336n, 365n
Rowels, C. M., 335n
Rowley, C., 176n
Roy, J.-P., 64n
Rubach, M. J., 303n, 304n
Rubineau, B., 335n
Rudberg, M., 271n
Ruefli, T. W., 92n
Rufin, C., 65n, 238n
Rugman, A. M., 66n, 240n
Ruhe, J. A., 30n
Rumelt, R. P., 150n, 176n, 177n,
    178n, 336n
Rupp, D. E., 305n
Russo, M. V., 64n
Rust, K. G., 208n
Rutherford, M. A., 301n, 302n,
    363n
Rutherford, M. W., 386n
Ryan, H. E., Jr., 302n
Ryan, M. K., 363n
Ryman, J. A., 30n, 119n, 149n

S

Saarenketo, S., 387n
Sachs, S., 362n
Sahay, A., 119n
Saini, A., 270n
Salk, J. E., 151n, 241n, 271n
Salmador, M. P., 66n
Salomo, S., 271n
Salomon, R. M., 30n, 92n, 93n
Salter, A., 388n
Salvador, F., 66n
Sambharya, R., 362n
Sampson, R. C., 65n, 270n, 334n,
    388n
Samwick, A. A., 176n
Sanchez, C. M., 208n
Sanchez, R., 121n, 151n
Sanchez-Manzanares, 362n

Sandberg, J., 364n
Sanders, L., 178n
Sanders, P., 31n
Sanders, W. G., 178n, 304n, 305n
Sandonis, J., 269n
Sandulli, F. D., 176n
Sandvig, J. C., 178n
Sanna-Randaccio, F., 64n
Santala, M., 335n
Santiago-Castro, M., 302n
Santini, L. 305n
Santos, J., 29n, 387n
Santos, V., 362n
Saparito, P. A., 269n, 302n, 386n
Sapienza, H. J., 30n, 237n, 241n,
    269n, 271n, 386n, 387n,
    388n
Sappington, D. E. M., 205n
Sarasvathy, S. D., 386n
Sarkar, M. B., 120n, 337n, 388n
Satorra, A., 120n
Satpathy, A., 151n
Saunders, A., 303n
Sawhney, M., 94n
Sawyer, K., 271n
Saxton, T., 207n
Sayles, L. R., 386n
Schaan, J.-L., 269n
Schlegelmilch, B. B., 388n
Scheitzer, M. E., 365n
Schelfhaudt, K., 64n
Schendel, D. E., 150n, 177n, 336n
Scherer, R. M., 177n
Schick, A. G., 208n
Schildt, H. A., 386n
Schilling, M. A., 334n
Schindehutte, M., 386n
Schine, E., 121n
Schlegelmilch, B. B., 242n, 334n
Schlosser, J., 240n
Schmidt, G., 65n
Schmidt, J. A., 205n, 206n
Schminke, M., 365n
Schmitz, P., 387n
Schneider, A., 208n
Schneider, M., 363n
Schoch, H., 387n
Schoemaker, P. J. H., 30n, 93n
Schoenberg, R., 177n
Schoenecker, T., 363n
Scholes, M., 178n
Scholnick, B., 363n
Schonwalder, S., 151n
Schoorman, F. D., 271n, 363n
Schorr, I., 66n
Schrage, M., 119n
Schramm, C. J., 386n, 389n
Schroeder, R. G., 93n
Schuler, D. A., 65n
Schultz, F. C., 31n
Schultz, H. D., 387n
Schultz, Howard, 371
Schulze, W. S., 66n, 150n, 205n,
    364n

Schumpeter, J., 120n, 121n, 386n
Schwartz, M. S., 301n
Scifres, E. L., 209n, 335n
Scott, Lee, 33–34
Scrempp, Jurgen, 199
Scullion, H., 66n, 243n
Searcey, D., 28n
Sebenius, J. K., 205n
Sechler, B., 208n
Segars, A. H., 335n
Selden, L., 205n
Selsky, J. W., 28n, 119n
Selton, R., 270n
Semadeni, M., 120n, 150n, 204n,
    206n, 207n
Sen, B., 388n
Sen, N., 303n, 363n
Sender, H., 238n
Senge, P. M., 268n
Sengupta, P., 303n
Sengupta, S., 64n
Seph, T. W., 388n
Seppanen, R., 268n
Servaes, H., 302n
Seth, A., 29n, 205n, 208n
Severt, D., 270n
Seward, J. K., 179n
Sexton, D. L., 28n, 65n, 93n,
    149n, 206n, 240n, 269n,
    271n, 385n, 386n, 387n,
    388n, 389n
Sexton, P., 387n
Shachmurove, Y., 240n
Shaffer, M. A., 120n, 334n
Shah, B., 29n
Shahrokhi, M., 240n
Shahrur, H., 204n
Shalley, C. E., 387n
Shamir, B., 363n
Shamsie, J., 29n, 66n, 92n, 119n,
    121n
Shane, S., 386n
Shank, M., 121n
Shankar, V., 92n, 271n
Shanley, M., 66n
Shannon, V., 239n, 243n
Shao, A. T., 240n
Shapiro, D. M., 243n, 305n
Sharma, A., 302n
Sharma, P., 386n
Sharma, S., 30n, 305n
Shaver, J. M., 178n, 238n, 242n
Shaw, J. D., 207n
Shedlarz, David, 315
Sheehan, N. T., 92n
Shen, W., 178n, 304n, 363n
Shenkar, O., 206n, 239n, 240n,
    241n, 270n
Shepherd, D. A., 334n, 335n,
    385n, 386n
Shervani, T. A., 177n
Shevlin, T., 302n
Shi, Y., 94n
Shields, M. D., 365n

Shimizu, K, 29n, 65n, 149n, 151n,
    178n, 205n, 207n, 209n,
    239n, 241n, 242n, 304n,
    364n, 387n, 389n
Shimizutani, S., 30n
Shipilov, A. V., 151n, 270n, 388n
Shirouzu, N., 28n
Shivdasani, A., 303n
Shleifer, A., 177n
Shook, C. L., 362n
Short, J. C., 29n, 64n
Shortell, S. M., 151n, 271n
Shrivastava, P., 28n, 30n
Shropshire, C., 304n, 305n
Shuen, A., 28n
Shvyrkov, O., 362n
Siebert, Muriel, 349
Siegel, D. S., 30n, 208n
Siggelkow, N., 335n
Siklos, R., 270n
Silverstein, M. J., 150n
Simmering, M. J., 364n
Simon, B., 28n, 29n
Simon, D., 67n, 119n, 120n
Simon, H. A., 335n
Simons, T., 364n
Sims, H. P., 362n
Sims, K. T., 151n
Sims, R. R., 365n
Simsek, Z., 120n, 271n, 363n
Sinatra, A., 335n
Singer, J., 177n
Singh, H., 151n, 177n, 206n,
    208n, 241n, 268n, 270n,
    271n, 335n, 389n
Singh, J. V., 29n, 93n,
    176n, 364n
Singh, K., 177n, 179n, 268n
Singh, M., 302n, 303n
Sinha, J., 28n, 177n
Sinha, R., 205n, 304n
Sirmon, D. G., 27n, 28n, 92n,
    93n, 149n, 178n, 208n, 268n,
    362n, 365n, 386n, 389n
Sironi, A., 303n
Sirower, M. L., 205n, 207n
Skill, M. S., 178n, 363n
Slangen, A. H. L., 241n
Slater, S. F., 334n, 335n, 336n,
    364n
Sleuwaegen, L., 28n, 120n
Slevin, D. P., 334n
Slocum, J. W., 27n, 149n
Slywotzky, A. J., 149n
Smallwood, N., 363n
Smart, D. L., 150n, 207n
Smith, A. D., 121n, 302n
Smith, C. G., 178n
Smith, G., 177n
Smith, H. J., 93n
Smith, K. A., 362n
Smith, K. G., 29n, 64n, 92n, 93n,
    119n, 120n, 121n, 362n,
    386n, 387n

Smith, M. P., 303n
Smith, R. D., 178n
Smith, W., 206n
Snell, R. S., 239n
Snell, S. A., 92n
Snow, C. C., 31n, 149n, 334n,
    337n
Snyder, W. M., 388n
Sohi, R. S., 94n
Somaya, D., 386n
Somech, A., 388n
Song, J., 149n, 240n, 241n
Song, K. P., 205n
Song, M., 64n, 93n, 121n, 388n
Song, Y. I., 270n, 362n
Sonnenfeld, J. A., 30n, 176n,
    363n
Sorcher, M., 363n
Sorenson, O., 387n
Sorenson, T. L., 119n, 268n
Sorescu, A. B., 207n
Sosa, M. E., 335n
Soule, E., 365n
Soupata, L., 94n
Spataro, S. E., 65n
Spencer, J., 120n, 176n, 238n,
    364n
Spicer, A., 243n
Spinosa, C., 334n
Spulber, D. F., 119n, 150n
Srikanth, K., 176n, 206n, 271n,
    389n
Srinivasan, M., 177n
Srivastava, A., 120n, 362n
Stadler, C., 93n
Stahl, G. K., 241n
Stalk, G., Jr., 176n
Stalker, G. M., 334n
Stanley, B., 241n
Staples, C. L., 304n
Starbuck, W. H., 93n
Starks, L. T., 304n
Steele, R., 149n
Steensma, H. K., 30n, 65n, 205n,
    238n, 270n, 271n, 334n,
    365n
Steers, R., 238n, 387n
Stein, W., 151n
Steinberg, B., 177n, 240n, 302n
Steindel, C., 178n
Steptoe, S., 30n
Sternin, J., 31n
Stevens, J. M., 30n, 365n
Stewart, J. B., 205n, 208n
Stewart, T. A., 93n, 337n
Stieglitz, N., 93n, 151n, 388n
Stiles, P., 301n, 303n
Stimpert, J. L., 29n, 149n
Stinebaker, K., 94n
Stirling, D., 92n, 365n
Strang, S., 151n
Strange, R., 238n
Strebel, P., 206n
Street, C. T., 271n

Street, V. L., 31n, 149n
Stringer, Howard, 349
Stroh, L. K., 31n
Su, K.-H., 120n
Suarez, F. F., 120n, 268n, 386n
Subramani, M. R., 268n
Subramaniam, M., 28n, 386n, 388n
Subramanian, V., 30n, 66n, 92n
Sudarsanam, S., 205n, 301n
Suddaby, R., 386n
Suh, T., 240n
Sull, D. N., 334n
Sundaramurthy, C., 305n, 335n
Sundqvist, S., 268n
Sutcliffe, K. M., 64n, 121n, 364n
Sutton, R. I., 387n
Svahn, S., 337n
Svobodina, L., 66n, 94n, 241n, 243n, 269n
Swaminathan, A., 179n, 205n
Swan, K. S., 239n
Swarts, W., 28n
Szuchman, P., 151n
Szulanski, G., 64n

T

Tadesse, S., 243n
Tagliabue, J., 121n
Tahir, R., 238n
Takeishi, A., 388n
Talaulicar, T., 29n, 121n
Tallman, S., 28n, 120n, 239n, 241n, 337n, 239n
Talmud, I., 177n
Tam, P.-W., 94n
Tan H. H., 65n, 271n
Tan, C. M., 240n
Tan, D., 149n, 239n
Tan, J., 64n, 66n, 149n
Tan, W.-L., 387n
Tandon, K., 302n
Tanriverdi, H., 176n
Tapley, M., 304n
Tata, J., 238n
Tata, Jamsetji Nusserwanji, 201
Taylor, A., 238n
Taylor, E., 177n
Taylor, M. Susan, 92n
Taylor, P., 28n, 177n
Taylor, S., 92n
Taylor, Tom, 339
Teece, D. J., 28n, 150n, 177n, 336n
Tehranian, H., 303n
Tempel, A., 239n, 334n
Teng, B.-S., 30n, 120n, 241n, 268n, 269n, 337n, 388n
Terranova, C., 208n
Tesfatsion, L., 269n
Tetrick, L. E., 94n
Thang, L. C., 176n
Thietart, R. A., 92n

Thomas, C., 301n, 303n, 363n
Thomas, H., 29n, 93n, 120n
Thomas, J. S., 150n
Thomas, S., 205n
Thomas-Solansky, S., 150n
Thompson, Kevin, 23
Thompson, T. A., 301n
Thomsen, S., 303n
Thornhill, S., 151n, 386n
Thornton, E., 205n, 207n
Thurm, S., 94n, 304n, 303n
Thursby, M., 269n
Tierney, C., 151n
Tihanyi, L., 65n, 179n, 208n, 238n, 242n, 243n, 269n, 270n, 303n, 334n, 335n, 363n, 387n
Tikkanen, H., 206n
Tippins, M. J., 94n
Tiwana, A., 94n, 388n
Todd, R., 304n
Toffler, D. G., 365n
Tolbert, W. R., 31n
Tomas, G., 334n, 336n
Tompson, G. H., 67n
Toms, S., 209n, 304n
Tong, T. W., 66n, 240n, 269n
Tongll, L., 238n
Tooker, R. N., 151n
Torikka, J., 270n
Tortorici, V., 204n
Tosi, H. L., 301n
Townsend, J. D., 336n
Trachtenberg, J. A., 240n
Travis, D. V., 150n
Trevino, L. K., 31n, 365n
Tsai, W., 120n, 387n
Tsai, Y.-T., 206n
Tsang, E. W. K., 29n, 241n, 269n
Tschang, C.-C., 362n
Tschirky, H., 206n
Tse, D. K., 241n
Tsui, A. S., 241n, 362n
Tucci, C. L., 334n, 362n
Tuch, C., 205n
Tully, S., 178n
Tung, R. L., 238n
Tunisini, A., 362n
Turk, T., 178n, 302n
Turner, J., 363n
Turner, K. L., 335n
Tuschke, A., 305n
Tushman, M. L., 94n, 206n
Tuunanen, M., 270n, 337n
Tyler, B. B., 66n

U

Ucbasaran, D., 93n, 240n
Uhlenbruck, K., 29n, 65n, 120n, 151n, 204n, 206n, 207n, 239n, 242n, 269n, 387n, 389n
Ulrich, D., 363n, 365n

Underwood, R., 387n
Ungson, G. R., 242n, 335n
Urbany, J. E., 67n
Useem, M., 31n, 94n, 305n

V

Vaaler, P. M., 28n, 121n, 243n
Vaara, E., 241n
Vaidyanath, D., 93n, 205n, 241n, 268n, 270n, 304n, 364n, 389n
Välikangas, L., 64n, 94n
van de Gucht, L. M., 121n
Van de Laar, M., 205n, 207n
Van de Ven, A. H., 271n
Van der Vegt, G. S., 362n
Van Fleet, D. D., 242n
Van Ness, B., 205n, 302n
Van Oijen, A., 176n
van Oyen, M. P., 151n
van Putten, A. B., 120n, 239n
Van, A., 241n
Van, Y., 239n, 241n
Vanden Bergh, R. G., 64n
Vanhaverbeke, W., 206n
Vara, V., 178n
Varadarajan, P. R., 119n, 120n
Vassolo, R., 268n, 365n, 387n
Vazquez, X. H., 94n
Veiga, J. F., 120n, 363n
Vekeselberg, Viktor, 263
Veliyath, R., 178n, 302n, 304n
Venkataraman, N., 28n
Venkataraman, S., 386n
Venkatraman, N., 176n, 268n, 388n
Vera, D., 362n
Verbeke, A., 64n, 240n
Verdin, P., 30n, 66n, 92n
Verhofen, M., 175n
Vermeulen, F., 65n, 179n, 206n, 207n
Vernon, Raymond, 213, 238n
Vester, J., 206n
Vestring, T., 243n
Veugelers, R., 64n
Victor, B., 388n
Viguerie, S. P., 178n
Vilanova, L., 30n
Villalonga, B., 205n, 303n
Vincenzo, P., 304n
Virmani, A., 28n
Vishny, R. W., 177n
Vishwanath, V., 93n
Vissa, B., 242n
Voelpel, S. C., 28n
Vogelstien, F., 67n
von Krog, G., 92n
von Krogh, G., 335n
Voola, R., 271n
Voorhees, C. M., 269n
Voss, H., 238n
Vranica, S., 121n
Vuocolo, J., 178n, 305n

W

Wade, J. B., 269n, 301n, 304n
Wade, M., 242n
Wadhwa, A., 150n
Wailgum, T., 268n
Waldman, D. A., 363n
Walenbach, P., 239n, 334n
Walker, G., 66n
Walker, L., 149n
Wall, E. A., 150n
Wally, S., 336n, 363n
Walsh, J. P., 30n, 179n, 208n, 304n, 305n
Walters, B. A., 64n
Wan, J. C., 66n
Wan, W. P., 29n, 64n, 65n, 67n, 121n, 177n, 179n, 237n, 239n, 242n, 243n, 271n, 305n, 365n
Wang, C., 304n
Wang, D. Y. L., 238n
Wang, F., 120n
Wang, H., 176n, 237n, 362n
Wang, L., 335n
Wang, Vera, 97
Wang, X., 305n
Wang, Y., 269n
Ward, A. J., 30n, 176n, 363n, 387n
Warner, A. G., 205n
Warner, M., 176n
Warner, Thomas, 263
Warneryd, K., 336n
Warren, S., 150n
Wasburn, M. H., 365n
Wasserman, N., 179n, 386n
Watanabe, K., 121n
Waters, R., 149n
Watkins, M. D., 208n
Watts, Claire, 348
Weaver, G. R., 31n, 365n
Weaver, K. M., 270n, 271n
Webb, A., 238n
Webb, E., 305n
Webb, J. W., 29n, 92n, 119n, 271n, 334n, 337n, 365n, 385n, 386n, 387n
Webber, A. M., 93n
Webber, B., 120n
Weber, J., 302n, 363n
Weber, K., 64n
Weber, R. A., 206n
Weber, Y., 206n
Webster, F. E., Jr., 149n
Weddigen, R.-M., 205n, 207n, 208n
Wei, C.-P., 64n
Weibel, A., 365n
Weick, K. E., 121n
Weinberg, H. S., 150n
Weingart, L. R., 388n
Weintraub, A., 150n, 336n
Weiser, J., 64n, 389n
Weitzel, U., 241n

Welbourne, T. M., 304n
Welch, D., 94n, 151n, 240n
Welch, J., 69, 82, 307, 336n, 348, 350, 364n, 365n
Welch, L. S., 240n
Welch, S., 336n, 364n, 365n
Wellington, F., 269n
Welsh, D. H. B., 270n
Wen, Xie, 339
Wenger, E. C., 388n
Werder, A. V., 29n, 121n
Werdigier, J., 363n
Werle, M. J., 94n
Wernefelt, B., 121n
Werner, S., 66n, 240n
Wernerfelt, B., 176n, 178n
Werther, W. B., 363n
West, Catherine, 339
West, G. P., III, 93n
Westbrook, R. A., 31n
Westhead, P., 93n, 240n
Westney, D. E., 240n
Westphal, J. D., 151n, 179n, 303n, 305n, 363n
Wexner, Leslie, 88
Whalen, J., 176n, 205n, 206n
White, 242n
White, B., 206n
White, E., 303n
White, M. A., 64n, 92n
White, R. E., 151n, 179n, 208n, 238n, 335n
Whitehead, Kim, 140
Whitman, Meg, 221, 235, 349
Whitney, J. O., 335n
Wicks, A. C., 30n
Wiebel, A., 335n
Wiersema, M. F., 179n, 208n, 242n, 336n
Wiggins, R. A., III, 302n
Wiggins, R. R., 92n
Wiklund, J., 149n, 365n
Wilkerson, D. B., 178n
Willem, A., 177n
Williams, C., 64n, 305n, 335n, 364n
Williams, G., 121n

Williams, J. R., 121n, 178n, 269n
Williams, K., 239n
Williams, R., 121n
Williamson, O. E., 177n, 207n, 302n, 336n
Williamson, P., 28n, 29n, 175n, 336n, 387n
Wilson, D. T., 177n
Wingfield, N., 65n
Winklhofer, H., 240n
Winter, S. G., 93n
Wise, R., 150n
Wiseman, R. M., 269n, 301n, 304n
Witkin, C., 335n
Witt, M. A., 238n
Witt, P., 305n
Wolf, B., 31n, 388n
Wolf, J., 336n
Wolf, M., 305n
Wolff, J. A., 240n
Wolff, M. F., 336n
Wolfson, M., 178n
Womack, J. P., 150n
Wong, M., 121n
Wong, S., 65n
Woo, C. Y., 29n, 65n, 120n, 177n
Wood, D. J., 30n
Woods, Tiger, 261
Woodward, J., 334n
Wooldridge, B., 64n
Wright, G., 305n
Wright, M., 65n, 93n, 208n, 209n, 238n, 240n, 269n, 362n
Wright, P., 30n, 150n, 178n, 205n, 242n, 302n, 336n, 365n
Wright, R. P., 301n
Wright, T., 205n
Wrigley, L., 176n
Wu, J. B., 362n
Wu, T., 93n
Wu, W.-P., 238n

Wu, X., 301n
Wujin, C., 271n

X
Xie, 304n
Xie, F., 304n
Xin, K., 241n, 362n
Xu, D., 239n, 240n
Xu, K., 240n

Y
Yago, G., 207n
Yan, A., 387n
Yang, B., 362n
Yang, J., 270n
Yang, Q., 387n
Yao, J., 243n
Yaprak, A., 66n, 239n
Yavas, U., 240n
Yeniyurt, S., 336n
Yermack, D., 304n
Yeung, G., 121n
Yeung, V. W. S., 151n
Yi, S., 208n
Yin, X., 335n
Yip, G. S., 65n
Yip, P., 64n
Yiu, D., 29n, 177n, 243n, 301n, 305n, 363n, 365n, 387n
Yli-Renko, H., 388n
Youndt, M. A., 386n
Young, D., 176n, 177n, 335n
Young, G. J., 119n, 120n, 121n, 271n
Young, S., 205n
Young-kyoon, Kwak, 297
Yu, C., 269n
Yu, L., 29n, 238n, 388n
Yu, T., 119n, 149n, 242n, 336n
Yucel, E., 305n, 364n, 389n
Yung, K., 150n

Z
Zábojnik, J., 205n
Zaheer, A., 66n, 240n, 241n, 271n, 337n

Zaheer, S., 28n, 30n, 66n, 149n, 206n, 209n, 237n, 238n, 240n, 241n, 269n, 303n, 365n, 386n, 387n
Zajac, E. J., 302n, 303n, 305n, 335n, 363n
Zalewski, D. A., 177n
Zamiska, N., 240n
Zamora, V., 302n
Zander, Ed, 374
Zatzick, C. D., 92n, 209n
Zaun, T., 363n
Zbaracki, M. J., 28n, 92n, 176n
Zeghal, D., 363n
Zeiner, B. A., 243n
Zeithaml, C. P., 94n, 150n
Zelleke, A. S., 178n, 303n
Zellmer-Braun, M., 239n
Zellweger, T., 301n
Zemsky, P., 28n
Zeng, M., 28n, 205n
Zetsche, Dieter, 194, 199
Zhang, M. J., 29n
Zhang, Y. B., 94n, 363n
Zhang, Z.-X., 362n
Zhao, H., 240n
Zhao, J. H., 208n, 242n
Zhao, Z., 271n
Zheng, P., 238n
Zhou, D., 120n, 336n
Zhou, L., 238n
Zhu, G., 387n
Zietsma, C., 386n
Zimmerman, M., 242n
Zingales, L., 302n
Zolkiewski, J., 362n
Zolli, R., 30n
Zollo, M., 92n, 206n, 207n, 241n, 270n, 389n
Zook, C., 31n, 238n, 240n, 335n
Zott, C., 30n, 94n, 150n
Zucker, L. G., 268n
Zuniga-Vicente, J. A., 66n
Zweig, P. L., 177n

Company Index

A

Abbey National, 181
Abercrombie & Fitch, 12
Accenture, 57
Ace Hardware, 260
Acer, 47, 101
Adidas, 78
Advanced Micro Devices, 259
Air Canada, 331
Air China, 252
Air France, 62, 252
Airbus, 3–4, 22, 24, 52, 53, 58, 106, 230, 294, 339
AirTran Airways (ATA), 49
Albany Nanotech, 380
Alcan, 182
Alcas Corporation, 39
Alcoa, 182
Alhambra's Kitchen, 142
All Nippon Airlines, 62
Allegro Coffee Company, 381
Altria Group, 226
Amazon, 7
Amazon.com, 14, 38, 126–127, 169
AMD, 380
American Airlines, 62, 131, 252, 256
American Chinese Restaurant Association, 142
American Express, 197
American Standard Companies, 200
Amrion, 381
Anheuser-Busch Cos., 102
Anne Fontaine, 143
AOL, 169
Apple Computer, 7, 10, 11, 14–15, 81, 137, 140, 376
Arby's, 44
ArcelorMittal, 251
Arctic National Wildlife Refuge, 140–141
Arkansas Best, 101
Artemis Pet Food Co., 70, 81–82
Association of American Publishers, 46

AstraZeneca, 190–191, 382
AT&T, 46, 47, 49
Authors Guild, 46
Autostrade SpA, 181
Avon Products, Inc., 326–327, 349

B

BAA, 181
Baidu.com, 368
Ball Canning Jars, 167
Banco Santander, 181
Bank One, 37
Barnes & Noble (barnesandnoble.com), 126
Barneys New York, 339
BASF, 165, 219
Bavarian Motor Works (BMW), 56, 111, 199, 309
Bell Helicopter, 323
Benetton, 12, 144
Beretta, 164
Berkshire Hathaway, 197
Best Buy, 33, 36, 53, 97, 107, 309, 310, 312, 353
Bharti Enterprises, 34
Bic Camera Inc., 98
Bicycle Playing Cards, 167
Big Lots Inc., 133
BJ's Wholesale Club, 107
Black & Decker, 164
Blockbuster, 7, 14, 104, 105
Blue Coral Seafood & Spirits, 320
Boeing, 3–4, 5, 22, 52, 53, 58, 106, 230, 247, 291
Bonefish Grill, 320
Bose, 137
Boston Consulting Group, 11, 370
Botoratin Cinentos SA, 182
Boundary Waters Canoe Area, 141
Bread & Circus, 381
Bread of Life, 381
British Airways, 62, 252, 256
British Petroleum (BP), 13, 263

BT Group PLC, 254
Bucyrus-Erie, 226
Buick, 211
Burger King, 102
Burlington Northern Santa Fe, 197

C

Cadbury Schweppes, 156
Callaway, 137
CalPERS, 284, 286, 292
Cambridge Antibody Technology, 191
Campbell Soup Co., 156, 342, 343
Canon, 248
Caremark, 162, 185, 186
Caribou Coffee Company, Inc., 139, 140–141
Carrabba's Italian Grill, 320
Carrefour, 103, 107
Carrier Corporation, 189
Casketfurniture.com, 142
Caterpillar Inc., 80, 103, 104, 137, 226
Cathay Pacific, 62
CBS, 259
Cementos Argos SA, 182
CEMEX SA, 126, 182, 187, 221–222
Center for Science and Environment (CSE), 79
Cerberus Capital Management LP, 198, 199
Cessna Aircraft, 323
Chanel, 76
Chaparral Steel, 80
Cheeseburger in Paradise, 320
Chevy, 109
Chili's, 44
China Resources Enterprises, Limited (CRE), 326
China Southern Airlines, 62
Choice Hotels, 382
Chrysler Corporation (see also DaimlerChrysler), 111, 199

Chrysler, 9, 183, 184, 194, 198, 199–200, 348
Chrysler Financial Services, 199
Chubb PLC, 189
Cia Siderurgica Nacional, 193
Cigna Insurance Corporation, 102
CinemaNow, 14
Cisco Systems, 57, 189, 196, 246, 255, 262, 332, 382
Citibank, 163, 193
Citigroup Inc., 163, 170, 196, 200, 202, 249
Clairol, 311
Clear Channel Communications, 56
Coca-Cola, 50, 79, 84, 98, 140, 164, 197, 215, 325, 371
Coleman Camping Goods, 167
Colgate-Palmolive (Colgate), 153–154, 167, 320
Commerzbank, 294
Compagnie Financiere Richemont AG, 249
Compaq, 112, 340
Concord Music Group, 371
Confederate Motor Co., 143
ConocoPhillips, 256
Consumer Finance, 307
Continental Airlines, 62, 98, 101, 130, 131
Continental Lite, 130
Conway Inc., 101
Corrections Corp. of America, 249
Corus Group PLC, 182, 193, 201, 203
Costco Wholesale, 33, 36, 53, 107, 110, 134, 135
Crate & Barrel, 80
Credit Suisse First Boston, 193
Crock-Pot Cookers, 167
CSI TV, 41
CSN, 193
CultureRX, 310

Cummins Engine, 226
Cutco Cutlery, 39
CVS, 33, 36, 53, 162, 185–186

D

Daimler, 184, 194, 198, 199–200
DaimlerBenz, 111, 184, 199
DaimlerChrysler, 183, 184, 194r, 199–200
Darden Restaurants, Inc., 103
Dell Inc., 11, 54, 88, 97–98, 99, 101, 112, 115, 125–126, 162, 249, 252, 262, 312, 340
Dell Linux, 252
Delta Air Lines, 49, 62, 98, 252
Delta's Song, 130
Deutsche Bank, 294
DHL, 161
Dimension Films, 163
Disney Co., 14, 19, 339, 353
Disney Stores, 114
Disney.com, 18
Disneyland Paris, 223
DoubleClick, 46, 186, 367
Dow Chemical Co., 88
Dow Jones Industrial Index, 307
Dragonair, 252
DreamWorks Animation, 44
DreamWorks SKG, 44
Dresdner Bank, 294
DuPont, 315

E

EADS, 3, 294
Eastman Kodak Company.
    See Kodak
Easyjet, 62
eBay, 169, 221, 234–235, 349
Eddie Bauer, 145
EDS, 57
EDS Agility Alliance, 332
Electronic Data Systems (EDS), 88
Elevation Partners, 112
Ellen Tracy, 128
Elpida Memory, 171
EMC, 332
Emirates, 62
Enron, 276, 282, 285, 298
Ericsson, 196, 261
Express Scripts, 162

F

FAW China, 229
Federal Trade Commission, 187
FedEx, 85, 102–103, 161, 192, 228
FedEx Freight, 101
Ferrobial, 181
Fiat, 194, 195
FileNet, 58
Fleming's Prime Steakhouse & Wine Bar, 320
Flextronics, 162
Food Avenue, 145

Food For Thought, 381
Ford Motor Company, 9, 19, 37, 89, 162, 194, 199, 217, 255–256, 348
France Telecom, 254, 256
Freescale, 380
Fresh & Wild, 381
Fresh Fields, 381
Frito Lay, 129, 116, 164, 352
Frontier Airlines, 140
Fuji, 248
Fuji Heavy Industries, 195
Fujitsu, 259
Future Shop, 310
Fuze Beverages, 371

G

Gallaher Group PLC, 181
Galvin Manufacturing Corporation, 374
Gap Inc., 12, 127, 143,144, 339–340
Gateway, 11, 112
Gazprom, 264
GE Capital, 200
General Electric (GE), 7, 8–9, 19, 25, 69, 82, 157, 165, 190, 253, 288, 291, 307–308, 311, 348, 350–351
General Mills, 116, 140, 257, 280
General Motors (GM), 9, 73, 162, 195, 199, 211, 212, 216, 217, 220, 226–227, 229, 230, 231, 233, 235, 262, 315, 348
Geo Group Inc., 250
Gerber Products, 161, 184
Gilead Sciences, 188, 189
Gillette Co., 153–154, 159, 167, 168, 171, 172, 187, 311
Gloria Vanderbilt, 339
GMAC, 199–200
Godiva, 343
Goldman Sachs Group, 170
Gome Appliances, 250
Good Technology, 375
Google Inc., 46–47, 48, 51, 53, 59–60, 186, 259, 367–368, 371
Goya Foods, 141
Great Wall Motor Company, 110
Green Oil, 256–257
Greif & Company, 141
Greyhound Lines Inc., 132
Grupo Cementos de Chihuahua SA, 182
Guangzhou Automotive Group, 229
Guess Inc., 106

H

H&M, 144
Hamilton Sundstrand, 189
Harley-Davidson Financial Services, 319

Harley-Davidson, Inc., 51, 78, 143, 164, 319–320
Harley-Davidson MotorClothes, 78
Harrah's Entertainment, 126
Harry's Farmers Market, 381
HealthSouth, 298
Heineken, 102
Heinz, 137
Henkel KGaA, 167
Hermes, 76
Hershey, 116, 156
Hewlett-Packard (HP), 14, 54, 56, 57, 97–98, 101, 112, 115, 125–126, 160, 245, 246, 248, 249, 262, 340
Hilton, 45, 226, 260
Hindalco Industries Ltd., 182
Hitachi, 54, 259
Hoechst, 219
Holcim Ltd., 182, 187, 221
Hollywood Pictures, 163
Home Depot, 58, 107, 287, 288–289, 292, 339
Honda, 51, 109, 160, 217
Hong Leong Group, 47
Hugo Boss, 80
Hutchison, 157
Hynix Semiconductors, 171
Hyperion Solutions, 185
Hyundai Motor, 75, 199

I

Ian Schrager Company, 25
IBM (International Business Machines), 7, 23, 46, 56, 57–58, 112, 186, 187, 235, 247, 259, 262, 245–246, 379–380
IKEA, 141–142, 143, 214
Illinois Tool Works (ITW), 166, 167
Inditex SA, 144
Infineon AG, 171
Infosys Technologies Ltd., 182
Innovative Brands, 167
Intel, 11, 162
International Harvester, 226
Internet Security Systems, 245
Intuit, 370
IronPort Systems Inc., 189
Iscar, 197
Ispat International, 47

J

J.C. Penney, 107, 339
J.D. Edwards, 185
J.D. Powers, 229
Jamba Juice, 106
Japan Airlines Int'l, 62
Japan Tobacco Inc., 181
Jarden Corporation, 167
Jason's Deli, 128
Jay-Z, 97

JetBlue, 49, 98, 101, 131
Johnson & Johnson, 157
Jones Apparel Group, 339

K

Keebler Co., 280
Kellogg Co., 116, 257, 280, 348
Kemps, 140
Keurig, Inc., 140
Kia Motors, 71
Kidde PLC, 189
Kimberly-Clark, 124
Kleenex, 137, 139
KLM, 62
Kodak, 108–109, 156, 247, 248
Kohl's, 107, 110
Komatsu Ltd., 80, 103, 104, 226
Konica Minolta, 253
Kraft Foods Inc., 116, 156
Kroger, 33, 36, 53
KT&G, 297

L

L'Oreal, 78
Lafarge SA, 182, 187, 221
Land's End, Inc., 223
Lee Roy Selmon's, 320
Lehman Brothers Holdings Inc., 88
Lenore Bags and Totes, 381
Lenovo, 7, 101, 112, 246
LexisNexis, 11
Lexus, 75, 136–137, 111
Li & Fung, 47
Lifetime Fitness, 140
Limited Brands, 88, 348
Li-Ning, 78
Liz Claiborne Inc., 195–196
LNP, 19
Lockheed Martin, 247
Long John Silver's, 44
Lord & Taylor, 380, 381
Louis Vuitton, 76, 137
Lowe's, 58, 107
Luby Cafeterias, 72
Lucent, 196
Lufthansa, 60, 62, 252, 331
LUKOIL, 256
Luxottica, 163, 164

M

Mail Boxes Etc., 192
Mall of America, 140
Manchester United, 181, 261
Marks & Spencer, 45
Marriott International Inc., 25, 226, 258
Matsushita, 54
Maxent, 99
Maxwell Shoe Company, 339
May Department Stores, 348
McDonald's Corporation, 18, 19, 45, 102, 260, 331, 342, 352
McKinsey & Co., 80, 81, 137

Medco Health, 162, 185
MedImmune Inc., 191
Men's Wearhouse, 41
Mercedes-Benz, 56, 111
Merchant of Vino, 381
Merck & Company, 156
MetroJet, 130
MG Rover Group, 228
Michael Graves, 145
Micron Technology, 171
Microsoft, 7, 11, 46, 47, 51,
    59–60, 80, 185, 186, 252,
    254, 256, 332
Microsoft/Novell, 252
Miller Brewing, 326
Miller Genuine Draft, 326
Miller Global Properties,
    258–259
Mitsubishi, 54
Mitsubishi Electric, 259
Mitsubishi Motors Corp., 199
Moody's, 193
Mossimo, 145, 250, 261, 373,
    374–375, 377
Movielink, LLC, 14
MRO Software, 58
Mrs. Fields Cookies, 260
Mrs. Gooch's, 381
MSN, 60
MSN Autos, 127
MSNBC, 7
MTV, 367
Mustang Engineering, 83
Myogen, Inc., 188

N

Nabisco, 116
Nanjing Automobile, 199
Natural Balance, 82
Nature's Heartland, 381
NBC Universal, 7, 259, 307
NEC, 54, 259
Nestlé SA, 161, 184
Netflix, 7, 13, 14–15, 104, 105
Netscape, 59
New York Stock Exchange, 285
News Corporation, 259
News Corporation's Fox
    Interactive Media, 367
Nickelodeon, 258–259
Nike, 78, 261
Nikko Cordial Corporation,
    249
Nippon Steel Corporation, 251
Nissan (see also Renault and
    Renault-Nissan), 109, 255,
    258, 266
Nokia, 45, 261, 377
Nordstrom Inc., 80, 185
Norrell Corporation, 80
Nortel, 196
Northwest Airlines, 62
Novartis AG, 161, 184
Novelis Inc., 182

Novell, 252
Nucor, 251
NutraSweet, 52

O

Oakley, Inc., 164
Olive Garden, 103
Oneworld, 252
Oracle, 185–186, 190, 312, 332
Organization for Economic Co-
    operation and Development
    (OECD), 183
Otis Elevator Co., 80, 189
Outback Steakhouse, 320

P

PacifiCorp, 197
Palm Inc., 112
Peabody Energy Corp., 74
PeopleSoft, 185
Pepperidge Farm, 116
Pepsi Co., 50, 78, 79, 80, 84, 98,
    129, 215, 351–352
Perfigo Inc., 189
Peroni Nastro Azzurro, 326
Perry Ellis International, 185
Pet Foot, 123
PETCO, 123
PetSmart, 70, 123–124
PetSmart Charities, 123
Petters Group, 37
Peugeot Citroen, 71
Pfizer, Inc., 315
Philip Morris International, 226
Phillips Electronics, 199
Pilsner Urquell, 326
Pixar, 264–265
Polaroid Corp., 37, 73–74
Polo Ralph Lauren Corp., 80, 249
Polo Ralph Lauren Watch and
    Jewelry Co., 249
Porsche, 75, 358
Post, 257
Pratt & Whitney, 189
Prestige Brands Holding,
    Inc., 167
Procter & Gamble (P&G), 8, 78,
    80, 153–154, 156–157, 159,
    167, 168, 171, 172, 187, 311,
    328, 342
ProfitLogic, 185
Protego Networks Inc., 189
Prudential Insurance, 102

Q

Quaker Foods, 129, 257, 351–352
Quaker Oats, 351

R

Radisson, 45
Rainforest Alliance, 141
Raketu, 7
Ralph Lauren, 137
Renault, 255, 258, 266

Renault-Nissan, 253, 255
Rentokil Initial PLC, 189
Residential Capital Corp, 200
Retek Inc., 185
Reuters Group, 170
Riverhead Networks Inc., 189
Robert Talbott, 136, 137, 139
Rosneft, 264
Rover, 199, 211
Roy's Restaurant, 320
Russell, 197
Ryanair, 62, 83

S

S&P 500, 278
SABMiller, 325–326
Safeway, 33, 36, 53
Sam's Clubs, 135, 316
Samsung Electronics Co., 54, 157,
    171, 261, 309, 374
SanDisk, 12
Sanyo Electric, 170
SAP, 185, 186, 190, 245,
    312, 332
Sara Lee Corporation, 292
Sargento Foods, 113
SAS, 331
SAS Institute, 129
Sears, Roebuck and Co.,
    223, 339
Select Fish, 381
Sesame Street Workshop, The,
    226
Shanghai Airlines, 252
Shanghai Automotive Industry
    Corporation (SAIC),
    211–212, 216, 217, 219–220,
    226–227, 228
Shanghai General Motors, 216
Sheraton, 226
Shinhan Financial Group, 297
Sikorsky, 189
Singapore Airlines, 62
SIRIUS, 12, 56, 58
Six Flags Corporation, 139
SK Corporation, 298
SkyTeam, 252
Smith & Wesson Holding Co.,
    161, 163, 164
Solectron Corp., 162
Song, 130
Sonia Kashuk, 145
Sony Corporation, 11, 80, 223,
    248, 261, 349, 380
Sony Ericsson, 261
South African Breweries, 326
Southwest Airlines, 49, 62, 83, 98,
    101, 110, 130–131
Sprint, 253
SSangyong, 211
St. Regis, 226
Standard & Poor's, 193
Stanley Works, 164
STAR Alliance, 60, 252, 331

Starbucks, 44, 139, 140, 262, 371
Starwood Hotels and Resorts
    Worldwide, 25, 226
Steel Partners, LLC, 297
Strategic Vision, 75
Subway, 260
Sun Microsystems, 56, 57–58,
    245, 246, 259, 332, 367
Suning, 250
SunPower Corp., 263
SuperTarget, 145
SUSE Linux Enterprise
    Server, 252
Symbol Technologies, Inc., 374

T

TAG, 167
Target, 33, 36, 37, 53, 107, 110,
    143, 145, 226
Tata Group, 182, 201
Tata Steel, 193, 201, 203
Tata-Corus, 193
Telefonica, 181
Ten United, 167
Terayon, 375
Textron Finance, 323
Textron Inc., 157, 323
Textron Industrial, 323
Thai, 331
Thales SA, 230
Thermo Electron, 160
Thompson/Center Arms
    Company, 164
Thomson Consumer Electronics,
    80
Thomson Corp., 170
3M, 69–70, 291
360Commerce, 185
TIAA-CREF, 284, 292
Time Warner, 23, 169
Tiny Trapeze, 381
TNK-BP, 263–264, 265
Toshiba, 259, 380
Touchstone Pictures, 163
Toyota Motor Company, 9, 45,
    75, 89–90, 109, 136–137,
    199, 212, 216, 217, 223, 229,
    230, 231, 233, 235, 262,
    330–331
Trane, 200–201
Tropicana, 129
Tyco, 298
Tyson Foods, 256

U

U.S. Steel, 251
UBS, 163, 170
Unilever, 167, 221
United Airlines, 60, 62, 98, 130,
    252, 256, 331
United Parcel Service (UPS),
    83, 102–103, 156, 161, 192,
    228, 230
United Shuttle, 130

United Technologies Corp. (UTC), 157, 165–166, 189, 194
US Airways, 62, 130
USA Today, 140

V

Vans Inc., 129
Vector Marketing, 39
Vera Wang, 97
Verizon Wireless, 353
VF Corporation, 167
Viacom, 46, 47, 258, 259
Virgin Group Ltd., 160
Volkswagen (VW), 56, 71, 75, 194, 211, 212, 217, 229, 230, 231, 233
Volvo, 194

W

Wabco, 201
Walgreens, 33, 36, 53, 162, 186
Wal-Mart Stores Inc., 8–9, 11, 12, 14, 23, 33–34, 36, 37, 45, 53, 80, 99, 103, 104, 106, 107, 110, 123, 133–134, 135, 167, 185, 197, 316–317, 348
Walt Disney Co., 114, 139, 163, 223, 264–265
Wandering WiFi, 140
Warner Brothers, 14
Washington Post Company, The, 197
Webify Solutions, 58

Wella, 311
Wells Fargo, 197
Wellspring Grocery, 381
Wendy's International, 382
Westin, 226
Westinghouse, 99
Whampoa Limited (HWL), 157
Whole Foods, 380, 381
WholePeople.com, 381
Wild Oats, 381
Wilderness Society, 140
Williams-Sonoma, Inc., 382
Witt Gas Technology, 80
Wm. Wrigley Jr., Company, 155–156
World Retail Congress, 144

WorldCom, 282, 285, 298
Worthington Foods Inc., 280

X

Xerox Corporation, 81, 247, 248, 325, 332, 349
XM, 12, 56, 58

Y

Yahoo! Inc., 12, 59–60, 221, 339
YouTube, 46, 47, 259, 367
YRC Worldwide, 101

Z

Zara, 144, 145
Zuka Juice, 106

Subject Index

A

Ability, 100, 104
Above-average returns, 4, 73, 124, 142, 145, 342
  defined, 5
  I/O model of, 13–16
  resource-based model of, 16–18
Acquisition strategies, 182, 183–184
Acquisitions, 173, 225, 227–228, 230, 380
  attributes of, 198
  cross-border, 181–182, 183, 187–188, 227
  defined, 184
  effective, 196–198
  failed, 199
  horizontal, 160, 185–186
  innovation through, 382
  pharmaceutical industry activity in, 188–189
  problems in, 191–196
    debt, 193
    diversification, 194–195
    firm size, 196
    focus, 195–196
    integration, 192
    synergy, 193–194
    target evaluation, 192–193
  reasons for, 184–191
    capabilities, 190–191
    competitive scope, 190
    diversification, 189–190
    entry barriers, 187–188
    increased speed to market, 188–189
    lower risk, 189
    market power, 184
    new product development, 188–189
  related, 187
  vertical, 185–186
  See also Mergers
Actions
  competitive, 106, 112
  drivers of, 103–104

of strategic leadership, 350–358
  strategic, 106
  tactical, 106, 107
Activist foreign shareholders, 296
Activist hedge funds, 275, 297
Activist shareholders, 275, 286, 288–289
Activities
  primary, 84, 86, 125, 137, 142, 159
  sharing, 159, 160, 163
  support, 84, 86, 125, 137, 142, 159, 352
  value-creating in cost leadership strategy, 134
  value-creating in differentiation strategy, 138
Actor's reputation, 112
Adaptability in acquisition, 197
Advanced information technologies, 245–246
Aerospace industry, 189, 230
Affiliation dimension of relationships, 126–128
African American workers, 43
Age structure in demographic segment, 40
Agency costs, 281–282
  defined, 281
Agency relationships, 279–280
  defined, 279
  problem in, 280–281
Aggressive pricing, 107
Air cargo industry, 228–230
Air carriers, 331
Air transportation industry, 247
Airline industry, 3–4, 52
  activity maps, 131
  capital market stakeholders, 22
  costly to imitate capabilities, 83
  retaliation, 51
  strategic alliances in, 250, 252
Alliance network types, 263
Alliances, 380
  equity-based, 227
  See also Strategic alliances

American steel industry, 251
Animal health business, 127
Antitrust regulation, 168–169
Antitrust laws, 46, 51
Artificial boundaries, 72
Asia
  boundary-less retailing, 8
  building conglomerates in, 201
  communitarianism, 45
  competitive possibilities for Polaroid, 37
  international expansion into, 235
  Internet auction markets, 234–235
Asia Pacific countries, dragon multinationals, 47
Asian American workers, 43
Assessing, 37, 39
  business-level cooperative strategies, 257–258
  corporate-level cooperative strategies, 260–261
Assets
  direct investment in, 212
  managerial decisions involving, 73–76
  production, 77–78
  restructuring of, 166
  return on, 312
Attack, likelihood of, 106–111
  first-mover incentives, 107–109
  organizational size, 109–110
  quality, 110–111
Automobile industry, 54, 75, 211–212
  complementary resources and capabilities in global, 255–256
  failed merger in, 199–200
  global industry sales leader, 216
  horizontal complementary strategic alliance, 253
  mergers in, 184

overdiversification in, 194
  product quality, 111
Automobile manufacturers, 217, 233, 348, 358
  acquisition of, 228
  world's largest, 229, 230
Autonomous strategic behavior, 376
Autonomy, 354, 355
Average returns, defined, 6
Awareness, 100, 103

B

Baby Boom generation, 128
Baby foods market, 161
  acquisitions in, 184
Balanced scorecard, 357–358
  defined, 357
Banking industry, 294
Bankruptcy, 199
Bargaining power of buyers, 52
  in cost leadership strategy, 133–134
  in differentiation strategy, 137
Bargaining power of suppliers, 52
  in cost leadership strategy, 135
  in differentiation strategy, 138–139
Barriers to entry, 49–51
  overcoming by acquisitions, 187–188
Best of ITS Award for Research and Innovation (2006), 374
Biotechnology firms, pharmaceutical firms acquisition of, 189, 190–191
Blackmail, 60
Blogging, 367
Bluetooth, 254
Board of directors, 277, 284–287, 346, 359
  classifications of members, 285
  defined, 286
  enhancing the effectiveness of, 286–287
Boundaries, artificial, 72

Boundary-less retailing, 8
Boundary-spanning positions, 37–38
Brand loyalty, 137
Brand name, 78
  food items, 137
  tarnished, 79
Brazil
  acquisition strategies in, 183
  baby foods market, 161
  debt in acquisitions, 193
  foreign market production, 9
Breakfast cereal, 280, 348
British auto producer, 228
British Office of Fair Trading, 256
Broad target of competitive scope, 132
Browser, 10
Bureaucratic controls, 196
Bus service, cost leadership strategy, 132
Business market, globalization of, 45
Business-level cooperative strategy, 252–258
  assessment of, 257–258
  competition response strategy, 253–256
  competition-reducing strategy, 256
  complementary strategic alliances, 252–253
  defined, 252
  implementing of, 330–331
  uncertainty-reducing strategy, 256
Business-level financial offerings, 200
Business-level international strategy, 217
Business-level strategies, 25, 73, 124–125, 154, 311, 357
  customers' relationship with, 125–129
  defined, 124
  functional structure, 314, 315–318
  international, 218–220
  purpose of, 129–131
  simple structure, 314
  types of, 131–147
Buyers
  bargaining power of, 52
    in cost leadership strategy, 133–134
    in differentiation strategy, 137
    particular group of, 141

C

California's Silicon Valley, 262
Canada
  age structure in demographic segment, 40

boundary-less retailing, 8
contingency workers, 43
international expansion into, 235
Capabilities, 76, 80
  acquisitions gain new, 190–191
  costly-to-imitate, 82
  managerial decisions involving, 73–76
  nonsubstitutable, 82, 83–84
  of competitor, 58, 59
  rare, 82
  valuable, 82
Capability, defined, 16
Capital, 165
  financial, 351
  intellectual, 341
  See also Human capital; Social capital
Capital market
  external, 165
  internal 165–166
  stakeholders, 20–22
Capital requirements, 50
Capital structure change, 293
Car radios, 374
Cash flows, uncertain future, 170
Causally ambiguous, 83
Cell chips, 380
Cell phones, 18, 374
  global market, 377
Celler-Kefauver Antimerger Act (1950), 168
Cement companies, 182, 187, 221–222
Centralization, 315, 320
CEO, 22, 287, 359
  and top management team power, 346–347
  corporate governance effect on, 275–276
  duality, 346
  family or outside, 278
  hiring a new, 346
  role of, 285–286
  selecting of, 347–349
  short lives of, 339–340
  strategic leader, 19
  succession, 349
  tenure, 339–340, 346–347
CES Mark of Excellence Award (2006), 374
Chewing gum company, low levels of diversification in, 156
Chief operating officer (COO), 75
China
  acquisition strategies in, 183
  admission into the WTO, 45, 161, 212, 217
  age structure in demographic segment, 40
  air cargo market, 228–230
  auto manufacturing industry, 217, 228, 230, 233

baby foods' market, 161
collectivism and social relations, 44
competitor analyses, 57
emerging markets in, 214
environmental pressures on Wal-Mart, 34
global economy and, 8
global strategy and local markets in, 221
global trade, 42
guanxi (personal relationships or good connections), 47
inhwa (harmony), 45–47
international beers, 326
international expansion into, 235
Internet auction markets, 235
manufacturing companies, 219–220
mobile phone market, 250
population size in demographic segment, 40
trends toward improved governance, 297
Chinese food restaurants, 142
Client-specific capabilities, 80
Coal industry, 74
Code of conduct, Toyota, 89
Collaborative advantage, 247
Collaborative relationship, 261
Collusive strategy, 246
Combination structure
  defined, 328
  transnational strategy, 328–329
Combined Code on Corporate Governance of the United Kingdom, 297
Commercial aircraft, global competitive battle, 3–4
Communitarianism, 45
Comparison shopping, 367
Competence misrepresentation, 264
Competencies, 88–90, 330
Competition
  between HP and Dell, 97–98
  five forces model of, 13, 48
  response strategy, 253–256
Competition-reducing strategy, 256, 258
Competitive action
  defined, 106
  drivers of, 103–104
  type of, 112
Competitive advantage, 70, 131, 142, 182, 218, 342, 382, 383
  defined, 5
  four criteria of sustainable, 81–84
  gradual erosion of a sustained, 114
  using innovation to maintain, 11

Competitive aggressiveness, 354, 355
Competitive agility, 351
Competitive and public policy intelligence, 59
Competitive battles between Netflix and Blockbuster, 105
Competitive behavior, defined, 98
Competitive dynamics, 143–147
  defined, 98
  from competitors to, 99
  in fast-cycle markets, 113
  in slow-cycle markets, 113
  in standard-cycle markets, 113
Competitive environment, Netflix, 14–15
Competitive Equality Banking Act of 1987 (CEBA), 169
Competitive form
  defined, 322
  of the multidivisional structure, 322–324
Competitive landscape, 6–13
  global economy, 7–8
  technology and technological changes, 10–13
Competitive possibilities, 37
Competitive response, defined, 106
Competitive risk
  of cost leadership strategy, 135–136
  of differentiation strategy, 139
  of focus strategies, 143
  of integrated cost leadership/ differentiation strategy, 146–147
  with cooperative strategies, 263–265
Competitive rivalry, 105–106, 154
  defined, 98
  model of, 99–100
  strategic and tactical actions, 106
Competitive scope, 131, 190
Competitive speed, 351
Competitive structure of an industry, 56
Competitor analysis, 36, 58–60, 100–103
  component, 59
  framework of, 103
  market commonality, 100
  resource similarity, 101
Competitor environments, 15, 35–37
Competitor intelligence, defined, 58
Competitor rivalry
  high exit barriers, 54–55
  high fixed costs or high storage costs, 54

high strategic stakes, 54
intensity of, 53–55
lack of differentiation or low
switching costs, 54
numerous or equally balanced
competitors, 53
slow industry growth, 53
Competitors
analyses of, 57–58, 59
defined, 98
future objectives of, 58, 59
Complementary strategic
alliances, 252–253
defined, 252
See also Strategic alliances
Complementors, defined, 60
Complexity, 74
Comprehensive decision-making
process, 76
Computer-animated features,
264
Conglomerate, 157, 167–168,
189, 194, 201
discount, 165
holding company, 197
Constraints, 37
Consumer electronics retailer,
310
Consumer foods' producers, 116
Consumer markets, 128
Consumer product companies,
167–168
Contingency workers, 43
Continuous learning, 13
Continuous product innovation,
317
Control, level of, 144
Cookies, 38
Cooperative form
defined, 318
of the multidivisional
structure, 318–320
Cooperative relationships, 248
Cooperative strategies, 25,
245–246, 251, 357, 380
competitive risks with,
263–265
defined, 246
innovation through, 379–380
managing of, 265–266
matches between network
structures and, 329–330
strategic alliances, 247–252
Copyright laws, violation of, 47
Copyrighted content, 46
Core competencies, 73, 76,
81, 182
availability of substitutes for, 71
building of, 81–87
costly to imitate capabilities,
82
defined, 17
exploiting and maintaining,
351–352

four criteria of sustainable
competitive advantage,
81–84
imitability of, 71
managerial decisions
involving, 73–76
nonsubstitutable capabilities,
82
rare capabilities, 82
rate of obsolescence, 71
transferring of, 160–161, 163
valuable capabilities, 82
value chain analysis, 84–87
Core ideology, 350
Core rigidities, 88
Corporate charter amendment, 293
Corporate control
managerial defense tactics,
292–293
market for, 290–293
Corporate entrepreneurship,
defined, 369
Corporate governance
CEOs and, 275–276
defined, 276
global, 297–298
in Germany, 294–295
in Japan, 295
Corporate Green Globe Award,
141
Corporate headquarters, 321
Corporate level strategies, 357
Corporate relatedness, 157, 159,
160–161, 163, 164
Corporate tax laws,
diversifications and, 169
Corporate-level cooperative
strategy, 245, 258–261
assessment of, 260–261
defined, 258
diversifying strategic alliance,
258–259
franchising, 259–260
implementing of, 331
synergistic strategic alliance,
259
Corporate-level core
competencies
defined, 160
transferring of, 159
Corporate-level international
strategy, 217
Corporate-level strategy, 25, 182
defined, 154
functional structure, 314
international, 220–222
matches between the
multidivisional structure
and, 318–324
Cost disadvantages independent
of scale, 51
Cost leadership strategy, 15, 126,
131, 132–136, 217
defined, 132

using the functional structure
to implement, 316–317
Cost minimization management
approach, 265
Cost-based synergy, 186
Costly to imitate resources, 18
Costly-to-imitate capabilities,
defined, 82
Counterfeiting, 139
Craig's List, 190
Cross-border acquisitions,
181–182, 187–188, 227
Cross-border M&As, 183
Cross-border strategic alliance,
defined, 261
Cross-functional product
development teams,
377–378
Cross-functional teams, 379
Cross-selling goods, 380
Cultural factors, limits to
international expansion, 235
Currency exchange rates, 225
Current strategy of competitor,
58, 59
Curvilinear relationship
between diversification and
performance, 170
Customer characteristics, 127
Customer demands, shifts in, 74
Customer perspective, 357
Customer relationship
management (CRM), 145
Customer segmentation, basis
for, 128
Customer-centric company, 127
Customers' relationship with
business-level strategies,
125–129
Customers, 69–70
as product market
stakeholders, 20, 22
bargaining power of, 133–134,
137
determining core competencies
necessary to satisfy, 129
determining which needs to
satisfy, 128–129
determining who to serve,
127–128
effectively managing
relationships with, 126
Customization, 50

D

Database management providers,
190
Database management software,
185
Debt, acquisition problem of, 193
Decentralized approach, 220
Demand conditions, Porter's
model, 219
Demographic factors, 127

Demographic segment, 35–36,
40–41
defined, 40
Dependence on the market, 113
Deregulation, 295
Derek Higgs report, 297
Determinants of national
advantage, 218
Determining strategic direction,
350–351
defined, 350
Diamond model, 219
Differentiation, lack of, 54
Differentiation strategy, 15, 131,
136–139, 217
defined, 136
using the functional structure
to implement, 317–318
Diffuse ownership, 283, 284
Digital fraud, 60
Digital technology, 143
Direct costs, 194
Direct investment
foreign, 181
in assets, 212
Directors (board members), 285
Discount chain, cost leadership
strategy, 133
Discussion groups, 367
Diseconomies of scope, 163
Disruptive technologies, 10–12
Distributed strategic networks,
331, 332
Distribution, 80
channels, 51
Diverse labor force, 43
Diversification
acquisition problem of too
much, 194–195
acquisitions increase, 189–190
curvilinear relationship
between performance
and, 170
firm performance and, 173
levels of, 156–157
low levels of, 155–156
moderate to high levels of,
156–157
of product lines, 283
reasons for, 157–158
resources and, 171–172
unrelated, 163–166
value-creating, 158–163
very high levels of, 156
Diversification strategy,
153–154, 167
related and unrelated, 189
value-creating, 159
Diversify, incentives to,
168–171
Diversifying strategic alliance,
258–259
defined, 258
See also Strategic alliances

Divestiture, 200
Division of the Budget (DOB), 247
Domestic market, 187, 372, 383
Domestic strategic alliances, 262
Domestic-only firms, 261
Dominant business diversification strategy, 156
Downscoping, 200–201, 202
Downsizing, 200, 202
Dragon (multinational firms from Asia Pacific countries), 47
DRAMs (Dynamic Random-Access Memory chips), 171
Drivers of competitive actions and responses, 103–104
Due diligence, 192–193, 197
Dynamic alliance networks, 263
Dynamics of mode of entry, 230–231

E

Eavesdropping, 60
E-commerce, 162
Economic environment, defined, 42
Economic risks, 233, 234–235
Economic segment, 35–36, 42
Economic trends, rapidly changing, 74
Economies of learning, 215–217, 372
Economies of scale, 49–50, 196, 215–217, 255, 372
Economies of scope, 163, 172, 255, 307, 372
defined, 158
Educational institutions, cooperative strategies, 250
Efficiency and innovation, managing the tension between, 69–70
Electronics market, 190
Electronic-security company, 189
Elements of general environment, 36
Emerging economies, 182, 183, 187, 230
Emerging markets, 214
Emotional barriers, 55
Employee buyouts (EBOs), 201
Employees as organizational stakeholders, 20, 22
Entertainment business, 163
partnerships in, 7
Entrepreneurial mind-set, 354
defined, 371
Entrepreneurial opportunities, 369–370
defined, 369
Entrepreneurial ventures, downsizing generated new, 202
Entrepreneurs, defined, 371

Entrepreneurship, 369–370
defined, 369
Environment
competitor, 35–37
general, 35–37
industry, 35–37
Environmental pressures on Wal-Mart, 33–34
Environmental trends, 222–224
liability of foreignness, 223
regionalization, 223–224
Envisioned future, 350
Equity strategic alliance, defined, 249
Equity-based alliances, 227
Ethical behavior, governance mechanisms and, 298–299
Ethical considerations, 60–61
Ethical practices, emphasizing, 355–356
Ethnic mix in demographic segment, 41
Europe
acquisition strategies in, 183
age structure in demographic segment, 40
boundary-less retailing, 8
building conglomerates in, 201
global economy and, 7
international expansion into western, 235
European Union (EU), 43, 224
Modernizing Company Law and Enhancing Corporate Governance, 298
Transparency Directive, 298
Everything matters exponentially (EM²), 229
Evolutionary patterns of strategy and organizational structure, 313–330
functional structure, 314
matches between business-level strategies and the functional structure, 315–318
matches between cooperative strategies and network structures, 329–330
matches between corporate-level strategies and the multidivisional structure, 318–324
matches between international strategies and worldwide structure, 324–329
multidivisional structure, 314–315
simple structure, 314
Executive compensation, 277, 287–290
defined, 287
effectiveness of, 289–290
excessive, 288–289

Exit barriers, 54–55
Explicit collusion, 256
Exporting, 225, 230
External capital market, 165
External environment, 34–35, 90, 124
External environmental analysis, 24, 37–39
assessing, 39
components of, 37
forecasting, 39
monitoring, 38–39
scanning, 38
External investors, 165
External managerial labor market, 348
defined, 347
External pressures, market power and, 46–47
External social capital, 354

F

Face-to-face meetings, 345
Factors of production, Porter's model, 218
Failed acquisition, 199
Failed merger, 199–200
Family CEO, 278
Family-controlled firms, 278
Fast-cycle markets, 100, 108, 113, 114–145, 250, 251–252
defined, 114
Fast-food companies, 128–129
Federal Communications Commission (FCC), 169
Federal Trade Commission (FTC), 38, 167
Financial Accounting Standards Board, 169
Financial capital, 351
Financial controls, 356
defined, 311
in balanced scorecard framework, 358
Financial economies, 158, 166
defined, 163
Financial Instruments and Exchange Law of Japan, 297
Financial perspective, 357
Financial resources, 77, 173
Financial services company, 196
Financial services groups, 249
Firm infrastructure, support activities, 86
Firm performance, 345–346
Firm size, 280
acquisition problem of, 196
Firm strategy, structure, and rivalry, Porter's model, 219
Firm-specific knowledge, 83

First-mover
defined, 107
incentives, 107–109
Five forces model of competition, 13, 48
Fixed costs, 54
of exit, 55
Flash memory business, 259
Flexibility, 145
effective acquisition strategies and, 197
Flexible manufacturing systems (FMS), 145
Focus strategies, 139–143
competitive risk of, 1437
defined, 141
simple structure, 314
Focused cost leadership strategy, 131, 141–142, 217
Focused differentiation strategy, 131, 142, 217
Food and Drug Administration (FDA), 114
Food industry, 343
Forecasting, 37, 39
Foreign direct investments, 181, 230
Foreign government economic policies, 261
Foreign institutional investors, 296
Formality, value of, 45
Formalization, 315, 320
Formulation, 24
For-profit organizations, 87, 250
Framework of competitor analysis, 103
Franchising, 259–260, 331
defined, 259
Fraudulent behavior, 282
Free cash flows, 168, 280
Free-market-based societies, 202
Functional structure
defined, 314
for cost leadership strategy, 316–317
for differentiation strategy, 317–318
for integrated cost leadership/differentiation strategy, 318
matches between business-level strategies and, 315–318
Furniture retailer, 141–142, 214

G

Garns-St. Germain Deposit Institutions Act of 1982 (GDIA), 169
Geek Squad, 310
General environment, 35–37
defined, 35
demographic segment of, 40–41

economic segment of, 42
elements of, 36
global segment of, 45–48
political/legal segment of, 42–43
segments of, 35–36, 39–48
sociocultural segment of, 43–44
technological segment of, 44–45
Generation X, 128
Generic, 125
Geographic distribution in demographic segment, 41
Geographic market, different, 141
Geographically clustered firms, 262
Germany
    corporate governance in, 294–295
    structures used to govern global companies, 277
Global economy, 7–8
    cross-border acquisitions and, 187–188
    defined, 7
Global labor market, 70
Global markets
    choice of entry, 225
    reaching for, 211–212
Global matrix design, 328
Global mind-set, defined, 71–72
Global phenomenon, 372
Global segment, 35–36, 45–48
    defined, 45
Global strategy, 218, 221–222, 326
    and worldwide product divisional structure, fit between, 328
    defined, 221
    using worldwide product divisional structure to implement, 326–327
Globalfocusing, 47
Globalization, 8, 379
    march of, 8–9
    of business markets, 45
Golden parachutes, 291, 292, 293
Google Labs, 367–368
Googling, 367
Governance mechanisms, 172
    agency costs and, 281–282
    ethical behavior and, 298–299
Governance systems, 294
Government and social restrictions, 55
Government antitrust policies, 168
Government policy, 51
Government regulators, executive compensation as a target for, 288–289

Green initiatives, 34
Greenfield ventures, 230
    defined, 228
Greenmail, 293
Grupos, 201
Guanxi (personal relationships or good connections), 47

H
Handgun manufacturer, 164
Health care costs, 40
Health care products, 153–154
Hedge funds, 290
Heterogeneous top management team, defined, 345
Hierarchical order, value of, 45
High-technology businesses, 166
High-velocity environments, 115
Hispanic market, 141
Hispanic workers, 43
Horizontal acquisitions, 160, 185–186
Horizontal complementary alliances, 257
Horizontal complementary strategic alliance, 253, 254
Horizontal integration, 168
Horizontal organizational structures, 378
Host communities as product market stakeholders, 20, 22
Hostile takeover, 197, 291, 292, 339
    defense strategies, 293
Hotel business, 258–259
Human capital, 82, 379, 383
    defined, 352
    developing, 352–354
    downsizing loss of, 202
    intensive, 228
Human resource management, 352
    support activities, 86
Human resources, 77, 80
Human-resource dependent, 166
Hybrid form of combination structure for implementing a transnational strategy, 328
Hybrid strategy, 147
Hybrid structure, 326
Hydrogen-fuel-cell business, 189
Hypercompetition, 7
Hyperlinks, 127

I
I/O model. See Industrial organization (I/O) model
IEEE-Standards Association Corporate Award (2006), 374
Image library, 367
Imitation, 135, 139
    defined, 370
Implementation, 24

Inbound logistics, 132
    primary activities, 86
Incarceration, outsourcing to private contractors, 249–250
Incentives, 166–172
    to use an international strategy, 213–217
Incentives to diversify, 168–171
    antitrust regulation and tax laws, 168–169
    low performance, 169–170
    synergy and firm risk reduction, 170–171
    uncertain future cash flows, 170
Income distribution in demographic segment, 41
Incremental innovation, 373–376
Independent frames of reference, 378
India
    acquisition strategies in, 183
    debt in acquisitions, 193
    emerging economies, 182
    emerging markets in, 201, 214
    environmental pressures on Wal-Mart, 34
    global economy and, 8
    growing high-tech sector, 41
    population size in demographic segment, 40
    soft drink industry, 79
Indirect costs, 194
Induced strategic behavior, 376–377
Industrial markets, 128
Industrial organization (I/O) model, 6
    of above-average returns, 13–16
Industry
    defined, 48
    growth, 53
    interpretation of analyses, 55
Industry environment, 35–37
    defined, 36
Industry environment analysis, 48–55
    bargaining power of buyers, 52
    bargaining power of suppliers, 52
    intensity of rivalry among competitors, 53–55
    threat of new entrants, 49–51
    threat of substitute products, 52–53
Information age, 12
Information networks, 145–146
Information technology (IT) industry, 252, 263
Information-rich relationships, 12
Infrastructure management services, 181

Inhwa (harmony), 47
Innovation, 81, 116, 307, 353, 354, 367–368, 370–371
    acquisition strategies and, 197
    at world-class levels, 379
    defined, 370
    efficiency and, 69–70
    facilitating, 378
    incremental and radical, 373–376
    internal, 373–377
    R&D and, 374–375
    resources, 77
    through acquisitions, 382
    through cooperative strategies, 379–380
    to create technology trends and maintain competitive advantage, 11
    Whole Foods and, 381
Innovation-related abilities, 69–70
Innovative Freedom vs. Six Sigma Control, 70
Innovativeness, 354, 355
Insiders, 285–286
Instant messaging, 367
Institutional factors, limits to international expansion, 235
Institutional investors, 287, 292
Institutional owners
    defined, 283
    growing influence of, 283–284
Intangible resources, 77, 78
    defined, 76
Integrated cost leadership/ differentiation strategy, 130, 131, 143–147, 217
    competitive risks of, 146–147
    defined, 143
    using the functional structure to implement, 318
Integrated strategy, 145
Integrating both sides of the coin, 144
Integrating mechanisms, 327
Integration, 24
    difficulties, 192
    facilitating, 378
Intellectual capital, 341
Intentional proactive management strategy, 200
Interactive maps, 367
Internal analysis
    components of, 72
    context of, 71–72
Internal business processes perspective, 357
Internal capital market, 165
    allocation, 165–166
Internal corporate venturing, 375, 377, 382
    model of, 375
Internal gatekeeper role, 367

Internal governance
    mechanisms, 291
Internal innovation, 373–377,
    380
    autonomous strategic
        behavior, 376
    creating value from,
        378–379
    cross-functional product
        development teams,
        377–378
    facilitating integration and
        innovation, 378
    implementing, 377–379
    incremental and radical
        innovation, 373–376
    induced strategic behavior,
        376–377
Internal managerial labor
    market, 348
    defined, 347
Internal organization
    analyzing of, 24, 71–76
    challenge of analyzing, 73–76
    context of internal analysis,
        71–72
    creating value, 72–73
International beers, 326
International business-level
    strategy, 218–220
International cooperative
    strategy, 261–262
    implementing of, 331–332
International corporate
    governance, 293–298
International corporate-level
    strategy, 220–222
    global strategy, 221–222
    multidomestic strategy,
        220–221
    transnational strategy, 222
International diversification, 213
    defined, 231
    innovation and, 232
    returns and, 231
International entrepreneurship,
    372–373
    defined, 372
International entry mode
    acquisitions, 227–228
    choice of, 224–231
    dynamics of, 230–231
    exporting, 225
    licensing, 225–226
    new wholly owned subsidiary,
        228–230
    strategic alliances, 226–227
International environment, risks
    in, 233–235
International expansion, limits
    to, 235
International markets, 45, 383
    overcoming barriers to enter,
        187

probability of entering, 372
    survival depends on, 216
International negotiations for
    acquisitions, 227
International opportunities
    economies of scale and
        learning, 215–217
    identifying of, 213–217
    increased market size,
        214–215
    location advantages, 217
    return on investment, 215
International strategic alliances,
    227
International strategies, 212,
    217–222, 357
    business-level strategy,
        218–220
    corporate-level strategy,
        220–222
    defined, 213
    matches between worldwide
        structure and, 324–329
    of the largest automaker in the
        world, 229
    opportunities and outcomes
        of, 213
Internet, 12, 38
    exporting and, 225
    prominent applications of in
        the value chain, 87
    search engine, 367
Internet-based venture, 126
Interstrategic group competition,
    56
Interunit conflict, 378
Intraorganizational conflicts, 74
Intrastrategic group competition,
    56
Invention, defined, 370
Investment
    bankers, 193
    banking, 141, 163
    return on, 215, 312
iPhone, 11, 137, 376
iPod, 10, 11, 18, 137, 140, 376
Italy, international beers, 326
iTunes, 11, 14, 140, 376

J

J.D. Power's Initial Quality
    Study, 75
Japan
    age structure in demographic
        segment, 40
    automobile manufacturers,
        54, 230
    contingency workers, 43
    corporate governance in, 295
    Financial Instruments and
        Exchange Law, 297
    financial services groups, 249
    global strategy and local
        markets in, 221

inhwa (harmony), 45–47
    international beers, 326
    Internet auction markets, 235
    overseas takeovers by, 181
    soft drink industry market, 215
    steel manufacturer, 251
    structures used to govern
        global companies, 277
    wa (group harmony and social
        cohesion), 47
Job autonomy, 310
Joint venture, 245, 249, 261, 380
    defined, 247
Judgment, 74
Junk bonds, 193
Just-in-time manufacturing
    system, 144

K

Keiretsu, 262, 295
Knowledge, increasing intensity
    of, 12–13
Knowledge-intensive industries,
    371
Korea
    cigarette maker, 297
    herbal products, 297

L

Laptop computers, 249
Large-block shareholders,
    defined, 283
Late mover, defined, 109
Latin America
    building conglomerates in, 201
    contingency workers, 43
    countries, environmental
        pressures on Wal-Mart,
        34
    firms buying U.S. firms, 182
    Spanish banks in, 181
Lean production system, 331
Learning
    and growth perspective, 357
    economies of, 215–217, 372
Levels of diversification, 156–157
Leverage, 72, 78
Leveraged buyout (LBO),
    201–202
Leveraging a firm's knowledge,
    353
Liability of foreignness, 223
Licensing, 225–226, 230
Limited domestic growth
    opportunities, 261
Litigation, 293
Location advantages,
    international opportunities,
    217
Low levels of diversification,
    155–156
Low performance as an incentive
    to diversify, 169–170
Loyalty to a brand, 137

M

Management buyouts (MBOs),
    201
Management information
    systems, 80
Management problems, limits to
    international expansion, 235
Management services, merging
    train and airport, 181
Management structure,
    cooperative relationship,
    259
Manager and shareholder risk
    and diversification, 281
Managerial control and
    ownership, separation of,
    278–282
Managerial defense tactics,
    292–293
Managerial discretion, factors
    affecting, 344
Managerial employment risk, 280
Managerial labor market, internal
    and external, 347–349
Managerial motives to diversify,
    172–174
Managerial opportunism,
    defined, 279
Managerial revolution, 278
Managerial succession, 347–349
Managers, 233
    compensation of top-level, 287
    overly focused on acquisitions,
        195–196
    role of top-level, 343–347
    strategic decisions of, 73–76
Manufacturing, 80
Market commonality, 100,
    101–102, 104
    defined, 102
Market firms, 201
Market for corporate control,
    290–293
    defined, 290
    managerial defense tactics,
        292–293
Market or geographic
    diversification,
    multidivisional structure,
    314
Market power, 161–162
    acquisitions increase, 184
    defined, 161
    enhanced, 196
    external pressures and, 46–47
Market segmentation, defined,
    127
Market size, international
    opportunities for increased,
    214–215
Marketing, 80
    and sales, primary activities, 86
Market-leading services platform,
    332

Markets
acquisitions and increased
speed to, 188
dependence on, 113
no-growth or slow growth, 53
of one, 50
Matrix organization, 320
Means of differentiation, 139
Media, executive compensation
is a target for, 288–289
Merger strategies, 183–184
Mergers, 173
antitrust laws prohibiting, 168
cross-border, 183
defined, 184
failed, 199–200
See also Acquisitions
Mexico
boundary-less retailing, 8
foreign market production, 9
international expansion into,
235
Micropolitan areas, 44
Middle-market consumers, 129
Military equipment firms, 230
Mission, 19–20
defined, 19
Mobile phone market, 250, 261
Mode of entry, dynamics of,
230–231
Model of competitive rivalry, 100
Moderate to high levels of
diversification, 156–157
Modernizing Company Law
and Enhancing Corporate
Governance of the European
Union, 298
Mom and pop culture, 83
Monitoring, 37, 38–39
Motivation, 100, 104
Motorcycle industry, 143
market retaliation, 51
Movie rental business, 13, 14–15
Multidivisional structure
(M-form), 314–315
and corporate-level strategies,
matches between, 318–324
defined, 315
three variations of, 319
Multidomestic strategy, 218,
220–221, 325
defined, 220
fit between worldwide
geographic area structure
and, 328
using the worldwide
geographic area structure
to implement, 324–326
Multimarket competition,
defined, 98
Multimedia, 18
Multinational companies, 372
Multinational corporations
(MNCs), 8, 261

seeking to enter emerging
economies, 187
Multinational firms
competitive rivalry and, 231
complexity of managing,
232–233
Multipoint competition, defined,
161
Music market, 371
Mutual forbearance, 257
Mutually interdependent, 100

N

Nano 50th Award for Nano
Emissive Display
Technology, 374
Nanotechnology, 311
Narrow customers' perceptions
of value, 139
Narrow target of competitive
scope, 132
National advantage,
determinants of, 218
National Medal of Technology
(2004), 373, 374
Natural food retailer, 381
Network cooperative strategy,
262–263
alliance network types, 263
defined, 262
Network structures and
cooperative strategies,
matches between, 329–330
Network-based VoIP solutions,
253
New wholly owned subsidiary,
225, 228–230
Next-generation services, 375
No-growth markets, 53
Noncyclical businesses, 189
Nonequity strategic alliance,
defined, 249
Nonsubstitutable capabilities, 82,
83–84
defined, 83
Nonsubstitutable resources, 18
North America, age structure in
demographic segment, 40
North American Free Trade
Agreement (NAFTA), 224,
225
Not-for-profit agencies, 87

O

Office of the State Comptroller
(OSC), 247
Offshore outsourcing, 231
Oil and gas, 264
Oil tycoons, 263–264
Online advertising, 223
Online businesses, vertical
acquisitions of, 186
Online movie rental business, 135
Online video, 18, 259

Operational relatedness, 157,
159–160, 163, 164
Operations, primary activities, 86
Opportunities and outcomes of
international strategy, 213
Opportunity
defined, 37
maximization management
approach, 265
Organic food, 381
Organic light emitting diodes
(OLED), 253
Organization, analyzing the
internal, 71–76
Organization of American States
(OAS), 224
Organizational controls, 308,
311–312
balanced scorecard, 357–358
defined, 311
establishing balanced, 356–358
Organizational culture, 82, 368
defined, 23, 354
entrepreneurial mind-set, 354
restructuring and changing
the, 355
sustaining an effective,
354–355
Organizational ethics, 25
Organizational politics, 378
Organizational resources, 77
Organizational size, 109–110
Organizational stakeholders,
20–22
Organizational structure, 73, 308,
309–311
defined, 309
evolutionary patterns of
strategy and, 313–330
Outbound logistics, 132
primary activities, 86
Outcomes from combinations
of criteria for sustainable
competitive advantage, 84
Outside CEO, 278
Outsiders, 285–286
Outsourcing, 45, 85, 87–88, 249
defined, 87
Overdiversification, 194
Ownership and managerial
control, separation of,
278–282
Ownership concentration, 277,
283–284
defined, 283
Ownership percentages, 283
cooperative relationship, 259

P

Parcel delivery service, 83,
102–103
integration difficulties, 192
overnight and ground
shipping, 161

Partnering for success, 248
Patent laws, 114
Patents, 370, 373
PDAs, 10
PE ratio, 166
Pension funds, 275, 291
Performance
curvilinear relationship between
diversification and, 170
summary model of
relationship between
diversification and, 173
Perpetual innovation, 10
Personal computers (PCs), 97
business, 245–246, 340
global market for, 101
market, 125–126, 112, 115
Pet care industry, 123–124
Pharmaceutical companies, 162
foreign direct investment into
China, 214
Pharmaceutical industry,
acquisition activity in,
188–189, 190–191
Pharmacy-benefits manager
(PBM), 185–186
Photo sharing, 367
Photographic equipment using
digital technology, 37
Photographic film products, 248
Physical capital-intensive plants,
228
Physical resources, 77
Poison pill, 292, 293
Political risks, 233, 234
Political trends, rapidly changing,
74
Political/legal segment, 35–36,
42–43
defined, 42
Pooling of interests method of
accounting, 169
Population size in demographic
segment, 40
POS (positively outrageous
service), 23
Potential entrants
in cost leadership strategy, 135
in differentiation strategy, 139
Price coordination, 256
Price differential, 139
Price-centric pitches, 110
Primary activities, 86, 125, 137,
142, 159
defined, 84
Private equity firms, 201, 275,
291
Private equity investors, 199
Private synergy, 194
Privatization of industries and
economies, 251
Proactiveness, 354, 355
Procurement, support activities,
86

Product champion, 376
Product development,
    acquisitions and cost of
    new, 188–189
Product differentiation, 50
Product diversification, 155
    as an example of an agency
        problem, 280–281
    multidivisional structure, 314
    strategies, 182
Product line, different segment
    of, 141
Product market stakeholders,
    20–22
Product quality dimensions, 111
Product substitutes
    in cost leadership strategy, 135
    in differentiation strategy, 139
Production assets, 77–78
Products, threat of substitute,
    52–53
Profit maximization, 19
Profit pools, defined, 24
Public policy agendas, 372
Publicly held firms, 172
Publicly traded firms in Japan,
    296
Pure strategies, 147

Q

Quality, 110–111
    defined, 110
    Hyundai cars and, 75
Quality dimensions of goods and
    services, 111

R

R&D and innovation, 374–375
Race to learn, 330
Radical innovation, 373–376
Radio format, 56
Ralph Lauren Watch and Jewelry
    Company, 249
Rare capabilities, 82
    defined, 82
Rare resources, 18
Rate of technology, 115
Reach dimension of
    relationships, 126–128
Ready-to-eat segment of U.S.
    cereal market, 257
Real estate business, 166
Reciprocal relationship, 15
Regional focus on markets, 223
Regionalization, 223–224
Regulatory requirements, 114
Related acquisitions, 187
Related and supporting industries,
    Porter's model, 219
Related constrained diversification
    strategy, 156, 159
    characteristics of the structures
        necessary to implement,
        323

Related constrained
    diversification, 158–163
Related constrained strategy, 155
    using cooperative form of the
        multidivisional structure
        to implement, 318–320
Related diversification, 155
    strategies, 189
Related linked diversification,
    158–163
Related linked diversification
    strategy, 156, 157
    characteristics of the structures
        necessary to implement,
        323
Related linked strategy, 155
    using the strategic business
        unit form of the
        multidivisional structure
        to implement, 320–321
Related outsiders, 285
Relational advantage, 247
Relationship-capitalism, 296
Relationships between strategy
    and structure, 312–313
Reputation, 78
Reputational resources, 77
Renewable energy, 311
Research and development
    (R&D), 69–70, 80, 370, 373
Residual returns, 278
Resource dissimilarity, 104
Resource intangibility, 160
Resource portfolio
    developing human capital and
        social capital, 352–354
    effectively managing the
        firm's, 351–354
    exploiting and maintaining core
        competencies, 351–352
Resource similarity, 100, 101,
    102–103
    defined, 102
Resource-based model, 6
    of above-average returns,
        16–18
Resources, 76–78, 166–172
    costly to imitate, 18
    defined, 16
    diversification and, 171–172
    financial, 77
    human, 77, 80
    innovation, 77
    intangible, 76, 77, 78
    managerial decisions
        involving, 73–76
    nonsubstitutable, 18
    organizational, 77
    physical, 77
    rare, 18
    reputational, 77
    tangible, 76, 77–78
    technological, 77
    valuable, 18

Response
    competitive, 106
    drivers of competitive,
        103–104
    likelihood of, 111–113
    strategic, 106
    tactical, 106
Restructuring, 198–203
    and changing the
        organizational culture, 355
    defined, 198
    downscoping, 200–201
    downsizing, 200
    leveraged buyouts, 201–202
    of assets, 166
    outcomes, 202–203
Retailing, boundary-less, 8
Retaliation, 49, 51
Retirement planning, 43
Return on assets (ROA), 312
Return on invested capital
    (ROIC), 323
Return on investment (ROI),
    195, 312
    international opportunities,
        215
Revenue-based synergy, 186
Reverse engineering, 115
Richness dimension of
    relationships, 126–128
Risk reduction as an incentive to
    diversify, 170–171
Risk strategy, 146
Risk taking, 354, 355
Risks
    acquisitions lower, 189
    defined, 5
    in an international
        environment, 233–235
    in global markets, 47
    new wholly owned subsidiary
        and, 228
Rivalry
    among competitors, 53–55
    competitive, 105–106
    model of competitive, 99–100
Rivalry with existing competitors
    in cost leadership strategy, 133
    in differentiation strategy, 137
ROWE (results-only work
    environment) program, 309,
    310, 312
Russia
    collectivism and social
        relations, 44
    oil and gas, 264
    political risks in, 234

S

Sarbanes-Oxley (SOX) Act, 42,
    275, 282, 285–286, 297, 312
SBU divisions, 321
Scale economies, 215–217,
    255, 372

Scanning, 37, 38
Scope, diseconomies of, 163
Scope economies, 158, 163, 172,
    255, 307, 372
Scope of the firm, 153
Second mover, defined, 138
Securities and Exchange
    Commission (SEC), 275,
    288, 291, 312
Security software for networks,
    189
Segments of general
    environment, 35–36, 39–48
Self-control, value of, 45
Service
    primary activities, 86
    quality dimensions, 111
Shareholder and manager risk
    and diversification, 281
Shareholder value, 278
Shareholders as capital market
    stakeholders, 20
Sharing activities, 159, 163
Simple structure, defined, 314
Singapore's Silicon Island, 262
Single business diversification
    strategy, 155, 156
Six Sigma Control vs. Innovative
    Freedom, 70
Six Sigma program 69–70
Slack, 108
Slow-cycle markets, 110, 113–
    114, 250, 251, 251
    defined, 113
Slow-growth markets, 53
Smart growth, 70
Social capital, 266, 379, 383
    defined, 353
    developing, 352–354
    external, 354
Social complexity, 83
Societal values, transformations
    in, 74
Sociocultural segment, 35–36,
    43–44
    defined, 43
Soft drink industry, 79, 129, 215,
    351–352, 371
Soft infrastructure, 166
Software providers, 187
South America, boundary–less
    retailing, 8
South Korea, sociocultural and
    institutional attributes, 45
Specialization, 315
Specialized assets, 55
Specialty clothing company, 144
Specialty coffee company,
    140–141
Spin-off, 200
Sports drinks industry, 351–352
Sportswear apparel, 195–196
Stable alliance network, 263
Stakeholder capitalism, 296–297

Stakeholders, 20–22, 69–70, 359
  capital market, 20–22
  classifications of, 20–22
  defined, 20
  organizational, 20–22
  product market, 20–22
Standard-cycle companies, 116
Standard-cycle markets, 100, 113,
  115–117, 250, 251, 252
  defined, 115
Standardization, cooperative
  structure, 320
Standstill agreement, 293
Start-ups, 369
Steel manufacturer, 251
Stewardship theory, 346
Stock, 278
  option-based compensation
    plans, 290
Storage costs, 54
Strategic action or a strategic
  response, defined, 106
Strategic alliances, 225, 226–227,
  230, 245, 380, 382
  as a primary type of cooperative
    strategy, 247–252
  defined, 247
  reasons firm develop, 250–252
  reasons for, 251
  three types of, 247–250
  See also Complementary
    strategic alliances
Strategic and tactical actions, 106
Strategic business unit (SBU)
  form, 321
  defined, 320
  of the multidivisional
    structure, 320–321
Strategic center firm, 262, 329
Strategic change, 345–346
Strategic competitive outcomes,
  231–233
  complexity of managing
    multinational firms,
    232–233
  international diversification
    and returns, 231
  international diversification
    and innovation, 232
Strategic competitiveness, 124,
  125, 298
  defined, 4
Strategic controls, 356
  defined, 311
  in a balanced scorecard
    framework, 358
Strategic decisions, 88–90
  predicting outcomes of, 24
Strategic entrepreneurship, 383
  creating value through, 382
  defined, 368
Strategic flexibility, defined, 12
Strategic group, 55–58
  defined, 55

Strategic interrelationships, 55
Strategic leader, 22–24, 356, 357
  CEO, 19
  defined, 22
  work of effective, 23–24
Strategic leadership
  defined, 340
  determining strategic
    direction, 350–351
  effectively managing the firm's
    resource portfolio, 351–354
  emphasizing ethical practices,
    355–356
  establishing balanced
    organizational controls,
    356–358
  exercise of effective, 350
  in the future, 359
  key actions of, 350–358
  providing effective, 343
  strategic management process
    and, 341
  style and, 340–342
  sustaining an effective
    organizational culture,
    354–355
Strategic management process, 5,
  24–25, 183
  defined, 6
  strategic leadership and, 341
Strategic network, 329
Strategic outsourcing, 330
Strategic priority, 79
Strategic stakes, 54
Strategy, 124
  and organizational structure,
    evolutionary patterns of,
    313–330
  defined, 4
  effects of CEO succession and
    top management team
    composition on, 349
  relationships between
    structure and, 312–313
  structural changes for GE and,
    307–308
  structure growth pattern and,
    313
Strengths, 88–90
Structural approach to increased
  performance and job
  satisfaction, 310
Structural flexibility, 309
Structural stability, 309
Structure, relationships between
  strategy and, 312–313
Suppliers, 69–70
  as capital market stakeholders,
    20
  bargaining power of, 52
  in cost leadership strategy,
    135
  in differentiation strategy,
    138–139

as product market
    stakeholders, 20, 22
Supply chain management, 12
Support activities, 86, 125, 137,
  142, 159, 352
  defined, 84
Sustained advantage, developing
  temporary advantages to
  create, 116
Swing generations, 127
Switching costs, 50, 54
Synergistic strategic alliance,
  defined, 259
Synergy, 153
  acquisition problem of
    inability to achieve,
    193–194
  as an incentive to diversify,
    170–171
  defined, 171

T

Tacit collusion, 257
Tacit knowledge, 247
Tactical action or a tactical
  response
  aggressive pricing as, 107
  defined, 106
Takeover, defined, 184
Tangible resources, 77–78, 171,
  173
  defined, 76
Tax laws, 168–169
Tax Reform Act (1986), 168–169
Technological development, 86
Technological resources, 77
Technological segment, 35–36,
  44–45
  defined, 44
Technology, 330
  and services company, 325
  and technological
    changes, 10–13
  diffusion, 10–12
  disruptive, 10–12
  increasing knowledge
    intensity, 12–13
  information age, 12
  new proprietary, 74
  rate of, 115
  trends, 11
Technology-based service, 332
Telecom industry and business,
  256
Telecommunication firms and
  banks, merging of, 181
Tension between innovation and
  efficiency, managing of,
  69–70
Textile industry, 45
Threat
  defined, 37
  of new entrants, 49–51
  of substitute products, 52–53

Top management team, 344–347
  composition of, 349
  defined, 345
Top-level managers, role of,
  343–347
Top-level strategic leaders, short
  lives of, 339–340
Total quality management
  (TQM), defined, 146
Trade agreements, 224
Trademark infringements, 46
Trade-offs, 20, 145
  decisions, 21
Transaction costs, 194
Transformational leadership, 342
Transformational technology,
  253
Transnational strategy, 218, 328
  defined, 22
  using the combination
    structure to implement,
    328–329
Transparency Directive of the
  European Union, 298
Transportation fuel, 256
Transportation industry, 101
Trespassing, 60
Trust, cooperative strategies, 266
Trust-based working
  relationships, 83
Twenty-first-century competitive
  landscape, 373, 379, 382

U

U.S. Census Bureau, 44, 129
U.S. Department of Justice, 256
U. S. firms, downscoping in, 201
Uncertain future cash flows as an
  incentive to diversify, 170
Uncertainty, 74
Uncertainty-reducing strategy,
  256
Uniform Commercial Code, 60
Unions as product market
  stakeholders, 20, 22
Unique historical conditions, 82
United Kingdom
  Combined Code on Corporate
    Governance, 297
  debt in acquisitions, 193
  environmental pressures on
    Wal-Mart, 34
  open borders and open
    markets, 181–182
  structures used to govern
    global companies, 277
United States
  age structure in demographic
    segment, 40
  baby foods' market, 161
  contingency workers, 43
  foreign market production, 9
  structures used to govern
    global companies, 277

Unrelated diversification, 163–166
  efficient internal capital market allocation, 165–166
  restructuring of assets, 166
Unrelated diversification strategy, 156, 157, 166, 189
  characteristics of the structures necessary to implement, 323
  using competitive form of the multidivisional structure to implement, 322–324
Unrelated strategy, revival of, 167–168

V

Valuable capabilities, 82
  defined, 82
Valuable resources, 18
Value, defined, 72
Value chain, 125, 137
  analysis, 84–87
  basic, 85
  prominent applications of the Internet in, 87
Value-creating, 72–73
  activities with cost leadership strategy, 134

activities with differentiation strategy, 138
from internal innovation, 378–379
reasons, 172
strategy, 70
through strategic entrepreneurship, 382–383
Value-creating diversification, 157, 158–163
  corporate relatedness, 160–161
  market power, 161–162
  operational relatedness, 159–160
  simultaneous operational relatedness and corporate relatedness, 163
  strategies, 159
Value-neutral diversification, 157, 158, 166–172
Value-neutral reasons, 172
Value-reducing diversification, 157, 158, 172–174
Vertical acquisitions, 185–186
Vertical complementary strategic alliance, 252–253, 254, 331
Vertical integration, 162, 168
  defined, 162
Very high levels of diversification, 156

Video on demand (VOD), 7, 13, 14–15
Virtual integration, 162
Vision, 18–19
  defined, 18
Voice over the Internet protocol (VoIP), 7

W

Wa (group harmony and social cohesion), 47
Weaknesses, 88–90
Web technology, 126
Webmail, 367
Western Europe, contingency workers, 43
White knight, 348
Whole-firm buyouts, 201
  LBOs, 203
Wireless communication technology, 44–45
Wireless Fidelity (WiFi) technology, 10, 139, 254
Women's clothing market, 143
Word-of-mouth advertising, 223
World Trade Organization (WTO), 42, 45, 161, 212, 217, 219

Worldwide geographic area structure
  at Xerox, 325
  defined, 324
  fit between multidomestic strategy and, 328
  using to implement the multidomestic strategy, 324–326
Worldwide product divisional structure
  defined, 326
  fit between global strategy and, 328
  using to implement the global strategy, 326–327
Worldwide structure and international strategies, matches between, 324–329

X

Xerography, 81

Z

Zizhu pinpai (self-owned brand), 211